FARM POLICIES OF THE UNITED STATES, 1790-1950

A Study of Their Origins and Development

FARM POLICIES OF THE UNITED STATES 1790-1950

A STUDY OF THEIR ORIGINS AND DEVELOPMENT

By Murray R. Benedict

1966

OCTAGON BOOKS, INC.

New York

Reprinted 1966
by special arrangement with The Twentieth Century Fund

OCTAGON BOOKS, INC.
175 FIFTH AVENUE
NEW YORK, N.Y. 10010

LIBRARY OF CONGRESS CATALOG CARD NUMBER: 66-28382

Printed in U.S.A. by
NOBLE OFFSET PRINTERS, INC.
NEW YORK 3, N. Y.

FOREWORD

FOR THE BETTER PART of a century after the founding of the Republic, agriculture was by far the most important industry in the United States from every point of view—economic, political, social, even psychological. It represented the largest amount of capital and the largest working force; government policies were largely oriented to an agricultural economy; the small independent farmer and his family set the basic pattern of our social life; and the rugged, individualistic, freedom-loving traits of the American people—their dominant characteristics—had their roots in the conquest and cultivation of the land.

With the coming of the industrial revolution and the growing domination of the factory and the machine, the primacy of agriculture in the American economy in terms of size obviously declined; but the economic and political problems generated have proportionately increased. As these problems have grown, the government has increasingly intervened in this area of our economy. During recent years it has exercised far-reaching controls over agricultural production and prices and is putting more federal funds and effort into this field than any other except those relating to defense and war.

As the urban population has increased, however, the majority of Americans have come to be completely divorced from the land and, as a result, the general public understanding of agriculture and its problems has declined. Even American farmers themselves, driven by the daily necessities of making both ends meet and bewildered by the growing complexities of their individual lives, have found it increasingly difficult to comprehend and deal with the collective problems of American agriculture—both as farmers and as citizens. Because of the problems themselves and also the lack of understanding of them, agriculture has now become one of the most controversial areas of our economic and political life.

The swelling flood of books—often partisan—about various aspects of American agriculture has reflected our growing concern with its problems. Strangely, however, no adequate attempt seems to have been made to give the general public an impartial, over-all picture of the vast governmental operations in the field of agriculture and of their causes and effects. In the belief that a study of this kind would meet a pressing need, the Twentieth Century Fund undertook, late in 1951, to fill it.

Under the direction of Murray R. Benedict, Professor of Agricultural Economics, Giannini Foundation of Agricultural Economics, University of California, and with Oscar C. Stine, formerly Assistant Chief, Bureau of Agricultural Economics, U.S. Department of Agriculture, as associate, a special staff is preparing a thorough description and assessment of government programs in behalf of, or relating to, the American farmer. The study, to be published in 1954, will seek to give Americans some idea both of their gains and their losses from the farm programs of the past twenty years—years that have included depression, war and postwar prosperity. Included with the study will be a series of proposals for constructive action to deal with agricultural problems developed by a special committee of distinguished citizens associated with the project.

Before he undertook the directorship of the Fund study, Dr. Benedict had been working for some years on a comprehensive history of United States farm policies from 1790 to 1950. It was obvious that such a volume would be an almost essential complement to the new Fund study of the more recent governmental activities in the field of agriculture. Only through a knowledge of their historical roots can come a thorough understanding of present policies and programs.

The Fund, therefore, commissioned Dr. Benedict to finish the historical study under the Fund's auspices. The present volume is the result. The Fund hopes that a completely objective and thoroughgoing review of the past such as this—especially in conjunction with the forthcoming companion study—will make a genuine contribution to a better understanding of one of the most crucial and complex areas of our economic life and to more effective action in dealing with the difficult problems it presents.

EVANS CLARK
Executive Director
The Twentieth Century Fund

330 West 42d Street
New York City
February 13, 1953

ACKNOWLEDGMENTS

It is a pleasure as well as a duty to acknowledge the generous assistance of the many associates who have helped in bringing this study to completion.

I am especially indebted to Dr. Elizabeth Kelley Bauer for her generous, untiring and scholarly cooperation in searching through the hundreds of books, pamphlets and other source materials that tell the story of more than a century and a half of policy development relating to or affecting American agriculture. Her wide acquaintance with historical source materials and her high standards of accuracy, completeness and balance were an invaluable aid in carrying out the study. Her contribution is especially significant in respect to the period 1790 to 1930, which was written between the fall of 1946 and the summer of 1949 when she was associated with me as research assistant. She has given valuable assistance later in a recheck of references and footnotes for the volume as a whole and in preparing the index.

My thanks are due also to Mrs. Grace Larson, who assisted me in the early stages of the study, to Mr. Boyd Huff, who worked with me from the fall of 1949 to the spring of 1951 in bringing together the materials relating to the period 1930 to 1950, and to my wife, who has not only given continuous encouragement as the work progressed, but has been most helpful in reviewing the manuscript in its final stages. Miss Orpha Cummings and Miss Patricia Golton of the Giannini Foundation library have likewise contributed greatly through their generous aid in locating source materials on numerous phases of the study.

I am deeply indebted to Mr. George Soule who, as editor for the Twentieth Century Fund, contributed many helpful suggestions, particularly as to reorganization of the earlier chapters. Mr. Orville Poland has assisted most generously in the final checking of the manuscript. The interest and cooperation shown by the several members of the stenographic staffs who have assisted in the preparation of the manuscript at various stages are also much appreciated.

The study was made possible through the excellent facilities afforded by the University of California, and especially by the cordial cooperation of Dean C. B. Hutchison of the University of California College of Agriculture, and Director H. R. Wellman of the Giannini Foundation of Agricultural Economics. Their interest and encouragement were essential in freeing time for the long period of research required.

Lastly, my thanks are due to Mr. Evans Clark and Dr. J. Frederic Dewhurst, Director and Economist, respectively, of the Twentieth Century Fund, and to the Trustees and staff of the Fund, for their wholehearted cooperation in the arrangements for publication.

One further group, far too numerous for individual mention, warrants comment in this acknowledgment. It has been my privilege for a period of more than thirty years to be associated in some degree with scores of farmers and agricultural leaders, and at times to participate in their deliberations and programs. My interest in the problem has grown out of these intimate and numerous contacts. For whatever understanding of their problems and ways of thinking is reflected in this study I owe them a deep debt of gratitude. They may not agree with the interpretations made, but their wisdom and firsthand contact with the problems as they see them have nevertheless contributed greatly in this effort to present a comprehensive picture of the way our present farm policy has come into being and the reasons for it. It is my hope that such a review of past actions will prove rewarding to them both in the satisfactions to be derived from choices well made and in a clearer recognition of mistakes which should be avoided in the future.

MURRAY R. BENEDICT

CONTENTS

INTRODUCTION xi

1. FORMATION OF AMERICAN LAND POLICY, 1785-1900 3
2. FARMER INTEREST IN THE MONEY SYSTEM 23
3. TARIFF POLICY: ORIGINS AND DEVELOPMENT 44
4. ROADS, CANALS AND RAILROADS 61
5. THE CHANGING BACKGROUND OF FARM POLICIES 76
6. FARMER ORGANIZATIONS AND THEIR POLICIES, 1870-1900 . . . 94
7. AMERICAN AGRICULTURE COMES OF AGE 112
8. THE WILSON ADMINISTRATION: REFORM AND WAR . . . 138
9. ORGANIZATION FOR ACTION 173
10. "EQUALITY FOR AGRICULTURE" 207
11. THE HOOVER PERIOD 239
12. FROM DEFENSE TO ATTACK 276
13. THE LONGER-TERM PROGRAM 316
14. NEW TACTICS, REVISED STRATEGY 349
15. PROGRAM OF THE LATE 1930'S 375
16. WAR CHANGES THE EMPHASIS 402
17. FOOD PROGRAM OF THE WAR YEARS 431
18. POSTWAR BOOM AND NEW LEGISLATION 460
19. CHANGES IN LONG-TERM POLICY 491
20. U.S. FARM POLICIES IN PERSPECTIVE 507
INDEX 523

INTRODUCTION

AMERICAN FARM POLICY has been a major political and economic issue during the past three decades. It has been widely discussed, both as an aid to recovery and a contributor to inflation; and the effectiveness of the various farm programs in bettering the condition of agriculture itself still is controversial. These are matters of concern both to farmers and to the public at large.

The activities most vigorously debated in recent years do not, however, constitute the whole of American farm policy, nor can they be well understood without knowledge of their antecedents, and of the framework that has grown up over the years since the nation was founded. The policies which now reflect the national attitude toward agriculture, and the aspirations of the farm groups, have been taking shape throughout the nation's history. They have emerged by a process of evolution, and are still heavily influenced by our long period of pioneer development. This pioneer background has contributed both constructively and destructively to the policies we now have.

During recent decades we have been making strenuous efforts to adapt our farm policies to the changed conditions of a twentieth century environment. The process is still going on, but it is one of grafting onto a deeply rooted basic structure, rather than something wholly new. Throughout our history farmers have been affected by, and have helped to shape, the national policies adopted. During the early years policy was largely made by and for farmers, since the great majority of the population lived on farms and gained its livelihood therefrom. In recent decades agriculture has ceased to occupy this dominant position in American affairs. Farmers are now a minority group, though still a large one. The economic environment in which they operate has undergone very significant changes. As yet the adjustment to these new conditions is incomplete and not well thought out.

Government, labor, business and agriculture all have developed comprehensive organization, concentration of control and mechanisms for making controls effective. But the ends to be sought in using this newly won power are far from clear, and an orderly and constructive balance among these power groups has not been achieved. It is not our purpose here to seek to resolve this vast and complex array of problems. It is rather to trace the development of policies relating to agriculture and the people on farms, and to bring into clearer perspective the ways in which farm people and the national economy have been affected.

Policies and the Policy-Making Process

Few people know what our farm policy is or how it came about. Some features of it are as old as the country itself. Others have come into being much more recently. Farm policies, like other policies, seldom emerge and get accepted quickly. Nations are ponderous things, and the impatient reformer, bent on bringing about quick and drastic change, is likely to find life a frustrating experience. Reform movements, if they are to achieve significant results, must have vigorous and continuing support, sometimes for a generation or more. In fact, most of our major policies are the result of long-continued pressures. For example, it took more than half a century for our pioneer forebears to achieve the kind of land policy they wanted, though there was little organized opposition to the solutions they proposed. They themselves came only slowly to full realization of the kind of land policy best suited to their needs. The farmer efforts to bring about changes in the money system persisted for nearly forty years, and even then were not successful. The various laws which brought railroad rates under effective control also were the product of thirty years or more of continuing agitation. Even the farm program of the 1930's, though seemingly a hastily devised attack on emergency problems, was in fact an outgrowth of more than a decade of intense political pressure by highly organized farm groups. It is important, therefore, that the nature of the policy-making process be more clearly understood, especially by those who wish to take some part in it.

National agricultural policies, as reflected in laws and administrative action, are an outgrowth of differences and conflicts in the attitudes and purposes of diverse agricultural and nonagricultural groups, and, in some cases, of viewpoints expressed through administrative action. In short, nearly all national policies with respect to agriculture are compromises—compromises between the divergent views of different groups in agriculture, compromises between the groups and blocs in Congress and compromises between the apparent intent of the law and the personal philosophies and interests of the administrators.

Often a policy or a program is rationalized after it has been undertaken. The real motivation at the time it is initiated may be expediency in dealing with some acute, temporary political or social problem or court decision. Once taken, the action must usually be defended by the group or administrator that sponsored it. A body of reasoning, argument and data will be built up around it that may be quite different from the considerations that actually brought it into being. Or a function or agency whose first purpose has been fulfilled may be continued on the basis of reasoning and argument unlike those advanced when it was first proposed. Thus the very agencies created to implement policies may become powerful factors in causing them to be retained long after they would have been abandoned if not fostered by those having a vested interest in their continuance.

Perhaps more important, however, is the failure to adopt clear, effective policies to meet needs long recognized but for which no provision is made. The evils of an unregulated transportation system, and the growth of monopoly power, were widely recognized long before the passage of the Interstate Commerce Commission Act and the Sherman Antitrust Law. Conservation of woodlands, and of petroleum, were not built into national policy as early as widespread public support for them became evident. The inadequacies of the American land tenure system, especially in respect to rented lands, have been pointed out repeatedly in recent decades, but as yet no fundamental approach to the problem has been devised and accepted. Likewise the difficulties growing out of the relationships between farm employers and farm wage workers thus far have not been approached on anything but a short-run basis, and the complex problem of extensive underemployment in the farm labor force has hardly been touched.

It is important also to distinguish between the objectives of given policies and the programs designed to achieve them. Often there are several proposals for attaining what is essentially the same end. In the decades following 1920 the supporters of the McNary-Haugen plan, the administrators of the Federal Farm Board and the officials in charge of the Agricultural Adjustment Administration, all had essentially the same policy objective, namely, to raise the prices of farm products. The programs or mechanisms proposed or used were quite different.

Sharp differences often arise as to methods when there is little significant disagreement about the basic objective itself. Partisans may in fact become strong supporters of a given method, and lose sight of the similarities between their objectives and those of their opponents. Such positions may, of course, rest on conscientious differences in judgment as to the effectiveness or collateral effects of this or that plan. In other cases they merely reflect pride of authorship, or considerations of personal advantage.

Long-Term as Well as Short-Run Policies Needed

Policy making should not confine itself merely to meeting recurring emergencies. It should be purposeful in a well-considered way, and realistically related to long-term, fundamental trends that are powerful enough to override the plans of men. This means some degree of conscious planning, but not the often-erected straw man of economic planning in the totalitarian sense. We can plan for more reliance on private initiative or more freedom of action, as well as less, if we are willing to pay the price of that freedom, and if we are not running counter to a tide so strong that man-made plans are swept before it.

The choice at times lies between an active policy that will bring material advantage to a group at the cost of some loss in freedom of action, and a passive policy that protects intangible values, but inhibits action designed to correct widely recognized evils. The American tenancy system, for example, contributes to soil depletion, insecurity of tenure and bad social conditions. It could undoubtedly be changed to overcome some of these defects, but only by surrendering highly regarded types of freedom of action on the part of the owners of rented lands.

The drift of recent years has been toward rapid expansion of active policies, but this should be recognized as in part a result of an extremely dynamic period in which changes were so violent, and so sudden, that the slower processes of automatic adjustment seemed wholly inadequate. Though such types of positive action may at times be necessary, it is important to distinguish between short-run policies designed to meet emergencies and those which relate to longer-term values.

Policy makers often are plagued by the difficult choice between a search for stability, essentially a maintenance of an existing situation (or a return to some earlier one), and a quicker and more orderly adjustment to a basically changed environment. Should we, for example, strive to maintain or regain the self-sufficiency of pioneer agriculture, or strike out boldly to adjust our thinking and policies to the highly commercialized agriculture of recent times?

New Problems Constantly Arising

Policies cannot be static in a changing world. Problems exist now that were undreamed of half a century ago. Other difficulties which were reasonably solvable then by individual action can now be dealt with only through large organizations, strongly financed, or through government action. Our institutions and attitudes are rooted deeply in the past, and seldom are abreast of the real problems and conditions of the time. For that reason, if no other, it is imperative that we gain perspective and seek to understand whether we are trying to restore a world that existed a century ago, or to adapt ourselves realistically to the one that exists today.

We find agriculture increasingly mechanized, increasingly commercialized and increasingly dependent on conditions in other industries and other lands. It is faced with larger bargaining units in labor, industry and commerce; its own structure, the conditions of its tenure and the mores of its people are changing. Group consciousness, possibly even class-consciousness, has grown apace. There is a lack of clear understanding of the longer-term and wider implications of some of the policies advocated. For example, is the growth of governmental intervention a long step in the direction of a regimented and governmentally planned economy; or is it, as some contend, the only means of saving a modified form of capitalism and free enterprise? Whether we can answer these questions to the satisfaction of ourselves and our readers, we can at least undertake to map the roads we have traveled, see where they have led us and consider the routes available to us as we make the history of tomorrow.

Readers to Whom the Study Is Addressed

The people for whom this study is intended will obviously have varied interests and reasons for perusal of its pages. Those who are directly concerned in the making of farm policy, such as farm organization leaders, legislators and influential farmers may seek more perspective in the formulation of plans. Many, no doubt, will wish specific information on particular incidents or legislation, and should find the book useful as a reference.

Administrators, farm advisers and other educators and researchers will, it is hoped, find in it both useful background material, and a coordinated body of factual information that may contribute to their work and save much time in seeking out specific information. Other groups less intimately acquainted with agricultural activities, such as businessmen, labor leaders, historians, educators and publicists, will find it a means of easy access to information about the policies adopted and the ways in which they came about. It is to be hoped, of course, that many general readers will find in it the means to a better understanding of one of the major public issues of our time, one which affects them both as consumers and as taxpayers, and one which touches intimately many facets of the general problem of the relation of government to society.

The study is particularly intended as a means of making available to college students a more adequate foundation for their study of current farm problems. Many of them, especially those in the agricultural colleges, will shortly be taking a hand in policy formation, or carrying on research and educational work in regard to it. Few of them have adequate knowledge of what has gone before and what things have become rather settled policy, or of the lessons to be learned from past activities in this realm. Very few, indeed, have a grasp of how policies come into being.

The leadership in agriculture is drifting more and more into the hands of college-trained men and women. The policy makers of a decade or two hence are mostly now in the colleges and universities. It is here that the best opportunity exists for gaining a broader and deeper foundation than was possessed by their predecessors.

For graduate students, such material as that here presented should, of course, be followed by more detailed, analytical treatment of current farm policy problems. This, however, if unsupported by broad and solid knowledge of the roots and antecedents of the problems dealt with, is likely to prove insubstantial and unrealistic. Farm policy must be built on solid foundations if it is to contribute soundly to the welfare of society and of farm people.

FARM POLICIES OF THE UNITED STATES, 1790-1950

A Study of Their Origins and Development

CHAPTER I

FORMATION OF AMERICAN LAND
POLICY, 1785–1900

EMERGENCE OF THE PROBLEM

THE FIRST CONGRESS of the United States (under the new Constitution) assembled in New York during March and April of 1789. George Washington took the oath of office on April 30. Under the Congress of the Confederation the young nation had already laid the groundwork of a land policy which was to be unique in world history—one which would affect profoundly the economic pattern and social outlook of the new nation.

The Constitution, a masterpiece in long-range planning, had provided the broad framework within which policies could be formulated and carried out, but most of the great questions which were to concern farmers over the coming years were uncrystallized, or had not yet emerged. Nevertheless, decisions taken during this early period were to affect generations of farmers down to the present day, and in times still to come.

Was the new nation to follow patterns deeply rooted in the cultural heritage derived from its European forebears, or to strike out boldly into paths peculiarly its own? Would it continue or expand an aristocracy of owners of manorial estates on the English pattern? Would it become wholly a master-and-slave economy? Or would it turn toward a semiequalitarian program based on strongly rooted property rights in land, and a rugged, deeply democratic society of shirt-sleeved farmers?

To many, even in the legislative halls of the young republic, the desires and demands of the land-hungry settlers seemed radical. But the underlying motivation was conservative by present-day standards. The landless had no thought of state-owned farms, social control of the means of production, or limited titles to land. Each wanted to be a landowner, a capitalist in his own right, and to hold land in complete freedom from all controls, either state or personal.

The attitudes then prevalent have persisted to our own times, and have contributed both constructively and destructively to the character of our later development. The pioneer philosophy still pervades much of our thinking on agricultural problems—at its best providing the foundations of a sturdy, productive citizenry; at its worst defending doggedly the right of the individual to wreck the soils entrusted to him, and to rearrange land patterns and tenure in ways that create social problems of first magnitude.

Aside from purely organizational matters, the dominating policy problems of the new government were largely agricultural. Ninety per cent or more of the population lived on farms or in small villages, and had farming as a major source of income. There were small but active and growing industrial, commercial and banking groups, but many of the problems they were concerned about were almost equally important to those engaged in agriculture. The nation lacked an organized and effective government; its money system was in confusion; and there was great need for a more adequate system of highways and canals.

While it is true that in the struggles between Alexander Hamilton and Thomas Jefferson, which began almost immediately, it is generally assumed that Hamilton represented the commercial and banking interests and Jefferson the agricultural interests, the basic controversy between them was more fundamental than mere difference in group interest. Hamilton wanted a balanced economy.

3

He recognized the weakness of the money system and the shortage of manufactured goods of all kinds. To overcome these defects he stressed the need for a strong banking system and the stimulation of industry and trade. Jefferson, on the other hand, visualized a nation of small farmers. He was willing to forgo some of the material advantages of trade and industry for moral values and elements of stability which he assumed to be inherent in the agricultural way of life.

The Jeffersonian type of agricultural fundamentalism has persisted throughout the ensuing century and a half, and is still frequently pressed with great vigor, particularly by writers whose idealism outweighs their realism and knowledge of economics. Yet to question the soundness of Jefferson's doctrines on national and agricultural policy as applied to present-day conditions is to do him less than justice. He was thinking and writing in a time when the land systems of the western world were predominantly aristocracies, built on privilege, and shockingly unjust and inefficient. The mass of misery that was France was seething with unrest and revolution. What are now Germany, Poland, Austria and Hungary were still largely feudal in their agricultural structure. England, though beginning to emerge into a more liberal atmosphere, was still strongly dominated by a hereditary, landowning aristocracy.

It was natural, therefore, and a demonstration of the clarity of his vision, that Jefferson, seeing about him a numerous rural population desirous of owning farms, and a vast national domain of unsettled lands, should strive to bring the two together on a basis likely to strengthen the new democracy to which his life had long been dedicated.

Organization of the Government

As the new government took up the reins so loosely held by the Confederation, its first task was obviously to establish more orderly and efficient executive and judicial branches. Jefferson was named Secretary of State; Hamilton, Secretary of the Treasury; and Henry Knox, Secretary of War. Edmund Randolph became Attorney General. Steps were taken to create an adequate federal judiciary system as authorized by the Constitution.

Bringing order to the financial affairs of the new government was naturally a "must" of the first order, and immediately became a primary concern of Alexander Hamilton, who was directed by the Congress to prepare a plan for the support of the public credit. We need not be concerned here with his brilliant performance in carrying out this task, since much of it lies outside the complex of problems under discussion. Nevertheless Hamilton's views on various problems affecting agriculture will merit further consideration.

The young nation was desperately poor. Its credit was almost nil. Its ability to levy taxes for its support had not yet been demonstrated. By far the largest asset under its direct control was the huge public domain, larger even then than the entire settled area of the original thirteen states. It would be inconceivable that such an asset would not immediately command the interest of a hard-pressed Secretary of the Treasury seeking to establish the nation's credit and make good on its bonds; hence the early clash of opinions about how these lands should be transferred into private ownership and settled.

Origin of the Public Domain

The public domain originated over the period from 1781 to 1803. The seven states which had claims to western lands surrendered them to the national government largely as a result of pressure from the six states that had no western claims. Maryland spearheaded the demand that western lands "wrested from the common enemy by blood and treasure of the Thirteen States should be considered as common property," and in fact refused to sign the Articles of Confederation unless these demands were met. There were other reasons as well, however. In some cases the claims of the different states overlapped, and were a potential source of interstate friction. Much of the land was unexplored and was considered of little value. Control over it implied obligation to defend it against attack from Indians, a task better suited to a central government than to that of a state.

Later the public domain was greatly enlarged, through the Louisiana Purchase (1803), acquisition of the Floridas from Spain (1819), negotiations with England for the Oregon Territory (1846), cession of lands by Mexico (1848), purchase of lands claimed by Texas (1850) [1] and the Gadsden purchase from Mexico (1853). Pre-existing private claims to lands in these domains were numerous and caused almost endless litigation. In general, however, the United States followed a liberal policy in honoring valid claims acquired under other governments prior to the acquisition of the land by the United States.

Possibly never in the world's history has a new government, representing so few people, had so free a hand in deciding what kind of an agricultural economy it wanted to develop on so large an area of rich and reasonably accessible lands. Much of the area was unexplored; there were no roads worthy of the name; and settlements already made consisted in the main of a few hardy adventurers, many of them more interested in hunting and exploring than in farming.

Hamilton Versus Jefferson on Land Policy

There were many reasons why the Congress was soon under pressure to establish a policy. The lands were of little value until occupied; soldiers and officers wanted lands promised them for war service; and land-seekers were pressing westward. Furthermore, rapid settlement of the public domain by loyal citizens would serve as a defense against Indians and would tend to hold in check the power of Spain and England in the western areas. This latter consideration was important since the fast growing territories of the West were held to the Union only by the most tenuous of ties.

All of the leaders in the government

1. Texas, when it joined the Union, retained possession of its public domain.

wanted early settlement of the public domain, but there were differences as to how this should be brought about. Hamilton and his followers, in search of funds for an empty treasury, wanted to sell the lands to the best financial advantage of the federal government. This meant restricting entry to less than the amounts of land desired by settlers, in order that scarcity might create higher values. They were not much concerned with the form of the social structure that would result. It was purely a business matter. If sale in large units to speculative subdividers, or to those who might eventually create manorial estates, would yield more revenue to the treasury, there was no prejudice against this.

Jefferson, with a different philosophy and a closer touch with the pioneer land-seekers, wanted easy access to the land, small units and a nation of farmers who personally worked their own lands. He opposed sales in large units to speculators. Hamilton, who wanted a strong, centralized government, would perhaps have been sympathetic even to a new-world monarchy, independent of the British Crown. Large landholdings, and possibly even an extensive landed aristocracy, were in no way distasteful to him, though these were not his specific objectives. His thinking envisioned the nineteenth-century type of free enterprise, American style — that is, unregulated industrial development behind tariff walls. His philosophy included elements of the dying mercantilist doctrine of the eighteenth century and also elements of the coming age of laissez faire. Jefferson sought a semiequalitarian society based on widely distributed ownership of land and a minimum of authority in the central government.

EARLIER LAND SYSTEMS

Land systems that lay within their field of observation were of three general types: the township system of New England; the "hybrid" pattern of the middle colonies — New York, New Jersey, Pennsylvania, Delaware and Maryland; and the scattered, irregularly shaped holdings of the South, interspersed with manorial estates patterned after the English system.[2] The main elements of the plans adopted are to be found in one or another of these earlier land systems. A brief review of them will therefore aid in understanding the controversies of the period.

The New England Plan of Settlement

The New England colonies had established during the seventeenth century a township system, usually on the basis of setting up a community as a unit. The most common practice was for a group known as "the proprietors" to secure from the colonial legislature a "Plantation Right." Under this "Right," a community would be established, and, if successful, request would be made after two years for a "Town Right." The Town Right, if granted, entitled the community to one representative in the colonial legislative body. The town itself continued under the control of the proprietors and their heirs, acting either as a whole or through a town council.

Townships were surveyed in advance of settlement, and presumably were settled in accordance with an agreed plan. The lands were assigned to settlers, usually by the proprietors, and tracts were customarily reserved for the church and for general village purposes. Common lands for pasturage and wood, and in some cases for tillage, were retained by the proprietors either in the form of "commons" available only to the proprietors, or of "town commons" available to all residents. To insure that the lands would continue to be held by proper persons, there was customarily a provision, in the early period, that lands might not be sold except by permission of the town officials. This provision was designed to check undue concentration of holdings and to prevent sales to "strangers" unacceptable to the community.

The amounts of land granted to individual settlers were apportioned roughly in accordance with their prospective contributions to the community. The size of the family was the criterion most commonly used, but special grants were made to ministers of the gospel, teachers and others considered desirable additions to the group. No charge was made for the lands, but settlers were required to pay taxes for support of local institutions. There were some class distinctions, for example those between "Proprietors" and "Freemen." The former had the right to vote in town meetings and were kept together by joint ownership of the unassigned lands. The freemen, though able to own property, usually were not granted the franchise.

County governments were later established, particularly for maintenance of courts and laying out of highways, but the township long remained the most significant unit of local government. Out of this structure grew the democratic procedure and outlook which have long been recognized as a characteristic feature of New England life.[3]

The pattern described above is based on the English manorial system but without a manorial head. With minor modifications it was the characteristic plan of settlement throughout the New England colonies. It began to break down in the early part of the eighteenth century, largely as a result of pressure for speculative development of lands which became general in all the colonies. By that time the New England legislatures had begun to lay out townships beyond the frontiers of settlement and to make grants to veterans of the colonial wars. Such outlying lands were often bought up by moneyed individuals interested primarily in speculation. These persons were commonly known as proprietors, though they did not assume the same functions as the "Proprietors" mentioned above.

2. Primogeniture and entailing of lands had already been outlawed, for the Northwest Territory by the Confederation Ordinance of 1787, and elsewhere by colonial or state law, but, through the use of other devices, their forms persisted in some of the states.

3. Percy W. Bidwell and John I. Falconer present an excellent description of this system and its effects in Chapter 5, *History of Agriculture in the Northern United States, 1620-1860*, Peter Smith, New York, 1941.

Land Systems of the Middle Colonies

The middle states — New York, Pennsylvania, New Jersey, Maryland and Delaware — developed their land systems out of a different background from that of New England. These, under British rule, were proprietary colonies, that is, grants made to individuals — Lord Baltimore, William Penn and the Duke of York (New York and New Jersey later became royal provinces on the accession of the Duke to the throne). New York had a brief prior development under the Dutch, and retained some remnants of the Dutch influence long after the conquest of the colony by the British in 1664. In Delaware, and in Pennsylvania as well, there were non-English groups that long retained elements of their European cultural heritages, notably their traditional languages and systems of farming. Among these were the German communities of western Pennsylvania (Pennsylvania Dutch) and the Swedish and Finnish settlements of the lower Delaware country.[4]

New Netherland, with headquarters at New Amsterdam, had been established by the Dutch West India Company, a private, corporate trading venture. The emphasis was on trade in furs and other items rather than on colonization and the development of agriculture, though these were elements in the plan. Agricultural development was desired by the Company, but the methods chosen were poorly suited to accomplish it. To stimulate migration to the colony, extensive grants were made to several of the stockholders. The plan contemplated a number of huge estates along the Hudson. The grantee, or "patroon," as he was called, was to have practically the authority of a feudal lord. He could require payments of produce from his tenants — sometimes a tenth of the product, sometimes as much as a half. He was given authority to organize the courts and had jurisdiction over the property and even the lives of the tenants. Sale of the lands to the operating farmers was not contemplated. Fines were prescribed for alienation of title by the owner. Inheritance was presumed to be perpetual, and the laws of primogeniture were generally accepted.

The Company thus sought to establish in America, the most unpromising of locations, the medieval institutions that were already dying out in Europe.[5] Men saw no reason to accept a life of feudal vassalage in a land where fertile lands could be had in neighboring colonies almost for the asking. Only a few of the patroonships, notably Rensselaerswyck, Pavonia and Swaanendael, were actually developed under the West India Company Plan. The largest and most significant of these was Rensselaerswyck which included more than seven hundred thousand acres.

The plan was foredoomed to failure, and most of the huge, vaguely defined grants were almost deserted as early as the end of the seventeenth century. Thus, while the manorial system was of Dutch origin, it made little headway until after the British conquest. With the capture of New Amsterdam by the British, the entire colony of New Netherland was made a proprietary grant to the Duke of York, younger brother of the King.[6] Some effects of the early tenure forms persisted since the English proprietor, under the terms of the capitulation, confirmed most of the Dutch grants and made no immediate change in the land law of the province.

4. Swedish settlements were made on the Delaware as early as 1624, and Germans were allowed to settle there after 1633. The Dutch took over again in 1655, only nine years before the transfer of the whole area to English control in 1664.

5. These provisions were somewhat liberalized by the issue of a new Charter of Freedoms and Exemptions in 1640. This provided formal deeding of lands to settlers, and smaller grants to private persons, but specified fine and forfeiture if they failed to occupy and cultivate the lands. After a term of years a quitrent of one tenth of the produce plus the increase in livestock was to be paid. Thus there was retained a mild form of feudal arrangement. See Clarence White Rife, "Land Tenure in New Netherland," *Essays in Colonial History, Presented to Charles McLean Andrews by His Students,* Yale University Press, New Haven, 1931, p. 47.

6. The original grant to the Duke of York included Pennsylvania and Delaware as well as New York. In 1680, Pennsylvania was leased by the Duke to William Penn for a period of 10,000 years. Delaware was assumed by Penn to have been included in this lease, and though under partially separate government after 1691, Delaware did not become wholly independent of Pennsylvania until it achieved statehood in 1776.

Confirmation of these pre-existing privileges, and later grants made by the Duke, caused the rise of the only fully developed manorial system in the colonies. In some areas settled by emigrants from New England the characteristic New England town system appeared, but this was not general. In 1683 ten county governments were set up. These took over the functions exercised by the village and the patroon courts under the Dutch, and became the dominant local units of government.

The inability of small farmers to gain free and unrestricted title to lands discouraged settlement throughout the colonial period. The English quitrent system, which the Duke's agents sought to develop, was unpopular and poorly enforced. These payments, though nominal in value, were, on principle, a source of irritation to settlers. They had originated in medieval England as substitution of a payment in kind, or in money, for the tenant's obligation to do a specified amount of work in the lord's own fields and holdings. In parts of New York and New Jersey the controversies between settlers and the nominal owners over rentals and quitrents persisted until near the middle of the nineteenth century, sometimes taking violent form.

Pennsylvania and Delaware Land Systems

The proprietary grants of Pennsylvania and Delaware had many of the characteristics of the New York situation, though with less influence from the brief period of Dutch control. Pennsylvania provided the easiest terms that had yet been afforded to immigrants in North America.

From the beginning, lands were sold to settlers, and in the early years the prices charged were very moderate. (Later, Penn's heirs raised prices, and many settlers went west seeking cheaper lands.) Penn also offered easy terms to tenants. Two hundred acres could be cultivated at an annual fee or quitrent of one penny per acre. Five-thousand-acre estates together with a city lot could be bought for £100. In each one hundred

thousand acres granted, the proprietor retained 10,000 acres as a proprietary reserve. These reserves, in some cases, became manorial estates. No manorial courts were provided, though Penn had authority to establish them had he desired to do so. As in many of the other colonies, fines were provided for alienation of title to a third party, and when transfers were made from the original grantee, quitrents payable to Penn were retained.[7]

The headright system that prevailed in many of the colonies was also used in Pennsylvania. That is, a settler was entitled to a free grant of land for each person brought into the colony, normally the members of his family and his indentured servants.[8] In the southern colonies the headright, when applied to slaves as well as members of the family, sometimes resulted in building up very large plantations.

From New York south, the township system of government was of little significance. County governments were established for levying taxes, organizing militia and administering justice. In New Jersey some towns were established by emigrants from New England, but as proprietary authority came to be asserted county governments became

7. The quitrent system appears to have been specified largely as a means of providing revenue to the proprietor, but in most of the colonies the provision was laxly administered and the revenue received was small. There seems also to have been a desire to retain some semblance of feudal control over the land. Note, for example, the leasing of Pennsylvania to Penn and his heirs for 10,000 years instead of granting title in perpetuity. The fine for alienation of title, so general in colonial law, should likewise theoretically have discouraged land speculation and engrossment without tillage. Except in the earliest period of settlement, particularly in New England, neither provision seems to have been sufficiently well enforced to be effective in providing revenue, maintaining feudal prerogatives or preventing speculation. See Lewis C. Gray, *History of Agriculture in the Southern United States to 1860*, Carnegie Institution, Washington, 1933, Vol. I, pp. 384–85.

8. In Pennsylvania every freeman who would transport himself before January 1665, and provide himself with a musket, ammunition and six months' provisions, would receive 150 acres of land. In addition, 150 acres would be allotted for each able-bodied manservant similarly equipped. Lesser allotments were authorized for later immigrants. Land was held in free and common socage but subject to a yearly quitrent of one-half penny per acre. Bidwell and Falconer, *History of Agriculture in the Northern United States*, p. 60.

more important. New York, Pennsylvania, New Jersey, Delaware and Maryland developed similar characteristics though modified in each case by differences in the provisions of the original grants. All included some provision for large holdings and manorial estates as well as grants, sales and leases to small farmers. In Maryland and farther south, manors proved impractical, for the most part, until there were large numbers of slaves. White servants could become landholders so they would not stay on the manors to work them. In all of the middle colonies fines were legally assessable for the alienation of lands to third parties, but Maryland was the only colony in which this provision was enforced.

Land Systems of the Southern Colonies

The land pattern of Virginia and the colonies to the south took still other forms, in part as a result of the adaptability of slavery to the kinds of farming engaged in. Most original grants were in small units, usually with quitrents reserved. There were few large manors until the advent of slavery. Proprietary reserves were generally retained in each county and leased to tenants. Sharecropping was a common method of rental.

In some cases groups of settlers were allowed to establish virtually autonomous communities known as "hundreds." Most of the land, both in large and small holdings, was taken up under indiscriminate location without prior survey; hence the confused pattern of farm boundaries which still prevails in many of the states of that region.

As tobacco and cotton came to be more widely produced, and slaves more available, large units became profitable and many of the small isolated holdings were merged into plantations resembling manors, but worked by slaves. Once established, the large manors of Virginia tended to be kept intact by laws providing primogeniture and entail. These provisions were eliminated at about the time of the Revolution, but their effects tended to be perpetuated through bequest.

Throughout the South, the county was the primary governmental unit, but in the Caro-

linas and Georgia even the county system was little developed until shortly before the Revolution. Early land units were designated as corporations, hundreds, cities and boroughs. In North Carolina, "counties" were provided for in the Fundamental Constitution of the province but apparently with the idea of establishing something comparable to the European "palatinate" under the control of a margrave or other titled official.[9] The proprietors later referred to them as "colonies." Here and in Maryland, as the English Church gained favor, there was a tendency to use the parish as the smallest unit of local government.

Georgia, originally a trusteeship set up for humanitarian purposes, later became a royal colony, but with peculiarities resulting from its original purpose of providing a haven for destitute emigrants from England. The original plan provided for settlement in the form of small holdings. Fifty acres were granted to each charity colonist, and five hundred acres to any self-supporting settler who brought in a family of six. In the beginning, slavery was forbidden but this restriction, together with that on size of holding, was later removed as a result of dissatisfaction on the part of the settlers.[10]

Retained Features of Colonial Systems

The colonial forms of land tenure and local government afford an interesting picture of transplanted cultures and legal practices, and also of the diverse forms the plans of men may take when they seek to create a so-

9. This constitution, drawn up by John Locke, is a fantastic instrument and runs counter to the democratic principles expressed in many of his other writings.

10. Gray states that "The lack of profitable commercial agriculture, the impracticable system of land tenure, and the restrictions on slaves were insuperable obstacles to progress. The motley rabble was demoralized by years of public support and bounties on silk and provision crops. A large number of the landholdings remained unimproved. The Colony seemed incapable of self-support. The colonists fell deeper in debt to the Trustees, and public sentiment in favor of repudiation developed. Finally, when the Trustees closed the public store in 1739, a large percentage of the colonists abandoned the enterprise. The discontent of the Georgia colonists was carefully fostered by South Carolina planters eager to build up plantations in Georgia." *History of Agriculture in the Southern United States,* Vol. I, p. 99.

ciety in keeping with their ideals. But the flooding tide of self-reliant settlers was brushing aside the restrictions laid upon them by the planners. Flushed with the heady wine of newly won independence, the pioneering settlers were soon to demand full freedom to settle the vast lands of the new nation, and the urge to create new farms and homes without reference to warmly debated policies had become well-nigh irresistible.

None of the plans escaped modification as the New West took shape. The stern, orderly, democratic New England system was perhaps retained more fully than the others, but in a vastly freer atmosphere. The feudalism of New York's system and the idealistic plans of Penn were thrust aside with equal disdain, but the South continued more generally in the direction already established in a relatively planless rural economy. Yet some elements of nearly all these patterns of settlement were carried over into the new lands that were now becoming available. The rectangular survey and township system of New England were prominent in the new territories, and still are potent influences in the shapes and sizes of farms. Penn's thoughtful provision for "great roads from city to city not to contain less than forty foot in breadth," and for the reservation of proprietary tenths, appears in modified form in the later provisions for highways and reserved sections for schools; likewise some features of his views on freedom to prospect for minerals. The new states of the South were to draw heavily on the traditions and customs of Virginia and the Carolinas. Of all the types, probably the forms developed in New York by the Dutch and English were to prove least acceptable to the turbulent hordes moving westward to settle the public lands.

Policies Established by the Confederation

Building on the foundations laid during the colonial period, the Confederation had already taken steps of prime importance in setting up a land policy. A congressional resolution passed on October 10, 1780 provided that unappropriated lands ceded by the states were to be disposed of for the common benefit of the United States, and were to be formed into states which were expected to become members of the Union. The Congress was to regulate the granting and settling of the lands.

With this policy as a basis, various proposals were made for putting it into effect. Pelatiah Webster, a Philadelphia merchant, advanced a plan in 1781. A New Englander, trained in theology at Yale, Webster was familiar with the New England township system. He proposed that the land be surveyed in townships of six, eight or ten miles square. The townships were to be laid out in tiers and sold in that fashion. Only when one tier was settled was the next to be put on sale. Intruders should be removed and punished. Salt licks, coal and mineral lands should be reserved for public use. The land was to be sold at auction to the highest bidder, but with a minimum price of one Spanish dollar per acre. Purchasers were to settle on and improve the land in two to three years or forfeit it.

The Army came forward with a plan in 1783. By the terms of this proposal the bounty offers of the Congress were to be satisfied out of public domain lands. This was similar in principle to the military grants of the colonial period. All surplus lands were to become common property of the states to be created. There was to be no national government ownership of land within a state. Total exclusion of slavery was proposed. The land would be laid out in townships six miles square. The grants would be free to ex-soldiers, but if not settled on and cultivated within a specified time they would be forfeited. The common lands of the state were to be disposed of for establishing schools and academies, and possibly also for support of the ministry. This plan failed in Congress even though supported by Washington.

A so-called "Financiers' Plan" was also proposed in 1783, by Bland of Virginia. Under this plan the lands were to be used for satisfying military bounties and other forms of arrearage. They would be laid off in districts not exceeding 2 degrees latitude and 3 degrees longitude and in townships of sizes to be specified. Grants were to be made without charge to ex-soldiers. These would be free of taxes and quitrents for a period of seven years after passage of the ordinance. Ten thousand acres out of each 100,000 were to be reserved for "founding seminaries of learning," any surplus to be used for building and equipping a navy. Exterior lines were to be run by surveyors appointed and paid by the United States. This proposal was not acted upon after being referred to committee.

During 1784 two committee reports relating to the western territory were presented. Both committees were headed by Jefferson. One considered the organization of government for the trans-Appalachian country; the other, the method of disposing of public domain lands. The committee on form of government proposed that the public domain be divided into states by two parallels of latitude and by meridians;[11] that hundreds, of ten geographical miles square, and lots, of one geographical mile square, be established;[12] and that county and township organizations be provided for electing members of the territorial legislatures. States could not interfere with the primary disposal of lands by the United States or with ordinances of the Congress securing title. No tax was to be imposed on lands owned by the United States. No nonresident taxpayer was to be taxed at a higher rate than a resident. This report was passed, after elimination of a provision barring slavery, but was not put into effect.[13]

The report on methods of disposing of

lands recommended that surveys precede sales, and that the proceeds of land sales be applied solely to the sinking fund. Lands would be sold for warrants which could be purchased with specie, loan-office certificates, certificates of the liquidated debt, or with military warrants. Prospective settlers would purchase warrants for a "lot" or "hundred" and then would locate it. No provision was made for educational or religious reserves. Consideration of this report was postponed by the Congress, but sections from it were later incorporated in the Ordinance of 1785. It reflects presumably the thinking of Jefferson and others at this stage, though his views were considerably modified in succeeding decades.

Ordinance of 1785—Rectangular Survey

Out of the proposals described above there emerged the first effective action by the Confederation on disposal of lands in the new public domain. It provided that surveyors should divide them into townships six statute miles square, with lines running due north and south and east and west. There was to be progressive numbering of the ranges and sections, the latter numbered from 1 to 36.[14] In every township sections 8, 11, 26 and 29 were reserved for future sale by the United States; also one third of the gold, silver, lead and copper mines found on the land. The formation of states was not a prerequisite to the sale of the lands. Half of the townships were to be sold entire, the other half in sections of 640 acres each.

The mechanism prescribed for disposing of land was as follows: Commissioners of the loan offices of the several states were to sell at public auction alternate townships in whole. Those between were to be sold in sections. The Secretary of War was directed to take by lot such number of townships as would equal one seventh of the land, these to be reserved for veterans of the late Continen-

11. The report recommended that ten states be established in the territory between the Ohio and Mississippi rivers, and proposed names for them, such as Polypotamia, Assenisipia, Metropotamia and Cherronesus.

12. The geographical mile contained 6,086.4 feet instead of the 5,280 feet of the statute mile later adopted. The geographical square mile would have contained 850.4 acres instead of the 640 acres contained in the sections established by the laws which were later enacted.

13. It is often assumed that the report on political organization became the basis of the Ordinance of 1787, but this is disputed by Nathan Dane, one of the drafters of that ordinance. See his *General Abridgment and Digest of American Law, with Occasional Notes and Comments,* Cummings, Hilliard, Boston, 1829, Vol. IX, Appendix, Note A, pp. 74-76.

14. The term "section" was first used as a designation for these units in the Act of 1796. Previously they were referred to as "lots." The term "section" is used here as likely to be more familiar to the reader.

tal Army. Purchasers secured deeds to specific tracts, not warrants permitting future location. Seven ranges were to be surveyed before the land could be sold. A surveyor from each state was to be appointed by the Congress or by a committee of the states. The minimum price was one dollar per acre in specie, or its equivalent in loan-office certificates or certificates of liquidated debt of the United States. Purchasers must pay for the land at the time it was sold. Otherwise it would be resold.

Section 16 in every township was retained for the maintenance of local public schools. The proposal that a section be reserved in each township for the support of religious training was stricken out. This was due mainly to the way in which the vote was taken, as apparently the requisite majority desired such a reservation to be made.[15]

As early as 1787, the Act of 1785 began to be modified, and here for the first time the element of credit was introduced. The amendments of 1787 abolished the system of sales in the states and provided that these should be at the seat of Congress. (Later amendments permitted sales at New York, Philadelphia or elsewhere as directed by the Board of the Treasury.) Two military reserves were set aside to satisfy claims of holders of military bounty warrants.

These first credit arrangements were extremely limited. One third of the purchase money was to be paid immediately, the balance in three months. Failure to pay the balance at that time called for forfeiture of the first payment. As will appear later, the credit feature was to be greatly liberalized in later years, particularly in the irrigation projects of the West. The gradual liberalizing of credit arrangements that occurred over the

15. An amendment was proposed striking out the reservation of a section in each township for the support of religion. The question was put, "Shall the words [of the original proposal] stand?" Five states favored retention, two were opposed, two were divided, and three were not sufficiently represented to cast a vote. As seven states did not support the motion it was lost and the words stricken out, although seventeen of the members present favored, and only six opposed. Payson Jackson Treat, *The National Land System, 1785-1820,* E. B. Treat, New York, 1910, p. 36.

years brought with it a train of perplexing problems.

Ordinance of 1787—Form of Government

The second major action relating to public lands, the Ordinance of 1787, was primarily to establish a form of government. Counties and townships were to be laid out as soon as Indian titles were extinguished. Territorial governments were authorized, and when a given area came to have 60,000 or more inhabitants it might have a constitutional convention and establish itself as a state.[16] Slavery was prohibited in the then-existing public domain (namely, the Northwest Territory consisting of what is now Ohio, Illinois, Indiana, Wisconsin and Michigan). It was directed that schools and religious training be encouraged. The Ordinance also contained lengthy provisions concerning the division of estates of persons dying intestate and other related matters. Equal parts were to go to all descendants. (This meant the prohibition of primogeniture.) Certain exceptions to the provisions of the Ordinance were made as to citizens of Virginia, who were to be governed by the laws of Virginia.

PROPOSALS AND LEGISLATION, 1789-1820

By 1789 the main features of the coming struggle over land policies began to appear. In the first Congress, Scott of Pennsylvania led the opposition to sales of million-acre tracts to companies, and to the high cost of surveys. He proposed that land be sold in small units, the purchasers to pay for the surveys. Land offices should be opened near the public lands, and only certificates of indebtedness should be received. He considered the township system unnecessary. More important, he brought up an issue which was later to be of major significance, namely, the proposal that pre-emptors — that is, illegal settlers or squatters on lands not yet opened for settlement — should be allowed to buy the lands occupied by them. He held that it was

16. This was not a general authorization for the creation of new states. It applied only to the lands of the Northwest Territory.

useless to try to drive settlers off the land once they were on it.

Hamilton's Proposals

In 1790 Hamilton presented his "Report of a Uniform System for the Disposition of the Lands, the Property of the United States." His plan ignored the Ordinance of 1785, and approached the problem as though no land system existed. Recommendation was made that three land offices be established, one at the seat of government for large sales, one in the Northwest and one in the Southwest. He advocated a modified form of indiscriminate location and preferred private sales to auctions.

The plan called for three tracts — one to be available to subscribers to the government loan then under consideration, one for actual settlers and one for sale in townships ten miles square. In the first, the units were to be of five hundred acres or more; in the second, to be limited to one hundred acres per holding; and in the third, to be very large and designed for subdivision. The price was to be 30 cents per acre, no credit to be given on purchases of less than a one-hundred-square-mile tract. On these tracts one fourth of the price was to be paid at time of purchase and some security besides the land to be given for the balance. No credit was to run for more than two years. Government surveys were to be run at the expense of the purchaser, but survey prior to sale would not be required. The whole program would be under the control of a board of three commissioners.

By this time the issues had become clearer than they had been in the time of the Confederation. The principal ones were the following: should land be sold in small parcels to actual settlers or perhaps given away, or should individuals or companies be allowed to come between the government and the settler, buying up large areas for speculative gain? If sold, was the price to be all the traffic would bear or a mere nominal payment? Was credit to be extended? Should land be sold to aliens? What arrangements were to be made for delivery of title?

The Act of 1796

The first serious attempt of the new government to settle the land problem was made in the Land Act of 1796. This related to the Northwest Territory, defined as the lands west of Pennsylvania and north of the Ohio River as far west as the Kentucky River. It retained many features of the Ordinance of 1785 but not all of them. Lands were to be divided into townships six miles square. Half the townships were to be divided into sections of 640 acres each. The government of the United States reserved salt springs and four sections at the center of each township.

No reserves for schools and colleges were provided. Surveys were to be made at the expense of the government, and the act authorized that a receiver of monies be appointed by the President. There was also provision for the sale of townships surveyed under the Ordinance of 1785. These were to be put up in units of one fourth of a township. Sales were to be by public auction, sections to be sold at Cincinnati and Pittsburgh, quarter townships at the seat of government.

The credit of the government had now improved, and with a less insistent demand for revenue, minimum prices were increased to $2 per acre. (Hamilton in his report of January 14, 1790, had recommended payment of the public debt partly in land at 20 cents per acre.) Patents would be issued on completion of payments. Failure to complete payment meant forfeiture of the land and the deposit. Fees were charged for the certificates of patent.

The provision of credit was virtually nil. A deposit of one twentieth of the price was required, payment of the remainder of the first half in thirty days, and the balance within one year. A 10 per cent discount for cash was provided. These were onerous terms for frontiersmen who perhaps did not see as much as $5 in cash in a year.[17] Even a hun-

17. In the western areas nearly all trade was carried on by barter. Bank bills were unknown. Spanish dollars

dred years later, with a much more developed economy, it was not uncommon for a farm family to struggle along for years in paying off a mortgage of a few hundred dollars. The plan agreed on meant, therefore, either sales to men of some wealth, or resort to moneylenders and payment of excessive rates of interest.

The act by no means satisfied the land-hungry settlers. Agitation for easier terms, sales in smaller parcels and the elimination of land speculation grew in volume during the succeeding administration. But the government was still in conservative hands. John Adams, a New Englander, was busy with other problems of more interest to him than the tribulations of a disorderly horde of frontiersmen. Jefferson had become the leading spokesman for the western settlers, but the relations between him and Adams had become strained, and there was little effort on the part of the Congress or the administration to deal with the problems of the frontier areas until near the end of Adams' term of office.

The Harrison Land Act of 1800

William Henry Harrison became the first representative in Congress from the new territorial assembly of Ohio. Long afterward, when aged and feeble, he was to become the nation's ninth President. At this time he was the principal spokesman for the western pioneers, and pressed with vigor the views and wishes of his constituents. He was instrumental in getting passed the act known as the Harrison Land Act of 1800. But it was far short of the desires of the settlers and soon ended in failure. It provided for sale of some lands in sections and half sections (only those west of the Muskingum). Congressional reserves at the centers of townships were retained, but might be leased for periods up to seven years.

The auction plan was continued, but after

lands had been exposed for sale for three weeks they might be sold privately. Buyers were to pay surveying expenses of $6 per section. The minimum price of $2 per acre was retained. Pre-emption rights — that is, rights to purchase at the minimum price — were allowed to those who had settled before an area was legally open for settlement if they had built mills and had gone in before passage of the act. Credit arrangements were liberalized slightly, one fourth of the price to be paid in forty days, and the balance in three annual payments at 6 per cent interest. Failure to pay on schedule authorized the government to sell the land at auction for recovery of the arrears or to have it revert to the United States if bids were less than the amount owed.

This still was an impossible plan for most new settlers. Wooded farms that would take years to clear and bring under tillage could not yield income for such payments in the short term of three years. The real need was for more credit to speed development rather than a quick payment of obligations assumed in the purchase of raw land. Again the settlers were barred from land purchase or made easy prey for rapacious moneylenders.

The Ohio Enabling Act

The need for better highways to the West had long been in the minds of emigrants and statesmen. Even the young Washington, surveying the vast holdings of Lord Fairfax fifty years earlier, had seen the need for highways to open up this vast domain and had retained an interest in such projects throughout his life. But how such highways were to be financed and built was to become later a full-fledged issue. A first step in dealing with the problem was taken in the Ohio Enabling Act of 1802. Under this act, the people of that territory were authorized to form a state government and seek admission to the Union. Section 7 of the act contained a provision under which the first great national highway was to be constructed. One twentieth of the net proceeds from lands sold by the federal government, within the borders of Ohio, was

---

were often cut into halves or quarters, and corporations, tradesmen and even churches issued bits of cardboard or slips of paper to be used as fractional currency. Wealth was measured in such things as lands, cattle, slaves and whiskey rather than in gold or silver dollars.

to be used for laying out and constructing public roads leading from the navigable waters of the coastal area "to the Ohio, to the said state, and through the same, such roads to be laid out under the authority of Congress, with the consent of the several states through which the roads shall pass."

An act of March 3, 1803, provided further that three fifths of the fund thus established should be assigned to the state for building roads within its borders, thus leaving the other two fifths to the national government for building a road from navigable waters leading into the Atlantic to a place on the Ohio River contiguous to the state of Ohio. Under the terms of these acts the road from Cumberland, Maryland, to Wheeling, Virginia (now West Virginia), was begun in 1806.[18]

The legislation relating to the admission of Ohio to the Union contained other new features, among them the provisions that one section out of each township should be granted to the state, the proceeds to be used for schools, and that the state was to exempt all lands sold by the United States from state, county and township taxes for a period of five years from the date of sale. The Ohio Act became a model for similar agreements entered into with the later public-land states.

The arrangement in regard to taxation was largely one of mutual convenience to avoid conflicts in title. The period of credit had by now been increased to five years. Since federal title would not pass to the purchaser until final payment was made, any attempt by the state to enforce tax collections in the meantime would bring the two jurisdictions into conflict. On the other hand, if the state could not take title in the event of failure to pay taxes assessed by it, or its local units, confusion would result.

18. By December 1805, the national government's portion of this fund amounted to $12,652. This was used in the preliminary work of locating and clearing the right of way. Substantial federal appropriations were made from time to time as construction progressed. These amounted in all to $1,645,679.20 by 1823. The highway to Wheeling (130 miles) was opened to traffic in 1818, though it was not entirely complete.

Act of 1803, Mississippi Territory

By this time another area of settlement, the Mississippi Territory, began to assume importance, and was provided for in a special act (March 3, 1803). This legislation was similar in many respects to that of the Northwest Territory, but the region still included large areas to which title was vaguely held by the Indians. The act provided that wherever the Indian titles had been extinguished the land should be surveyed in half sections. These parcels, except school reserves, were to be sold on the same basis as the lands north of the Ohio. A section (640 acres) was granted to any who had settled in the territory before the evacuation of the Spanish troops in 1797. Pre-emption rights were recognized for those who had settled in the territory by the time the act was passed.

Gallatin's Plan

In 1804 Albert Gallatin, the able Secretary of the Treasury under Jefferson, wrote a letter to the Congress recommending changes in the land laws which would bring them more into harmony with his own and Jefferson's views, and also with the wishes of the settlers. He recommended a reduction in the size of units to be offered for sale, down to quarter sections of 160 acres each, and also suggested a price of $1.25 per acre for whole and half sections and $1.50 for quarter sections. He felt it to be doubtful policy to withhold from sale the lands reserved to the national government, and suggested that the conditions south of Tennessee were such as to make inexpedient the use of the same system there and in the Northwest Territory. He also maintained that the recognition of pre-emption rights was irreconcilable with plans for drawing revenue from the sale of lands. Here, and in his recommendation that credit beyond forty days be abolished, he was going counter to the wishes of the pioneering farmers, but was on sound ground from the standpoint of efficiency and ease of administration.

In the Indiana Territory Act of 1804 significant steps in the direction of Gallatin's recommendations were taken. All public lands north or south of the Ohio were to be sold in quarter sections. Congressional reserves under the acts of 1785, 1796 and 1800 were to be sold. Interest was not to be charged until payments were due. All fees were abolished. The sixteenth section in every township was to be reserved for schools.

Thus over a period of twenty years there emerged the main outlines of a plan for transferring lands from the public domain into the hands of farmers that has had much to do with the agricultural pattern of the North Central and some of the Lower Mississippi Valley states, including the bulk of the great general farming area of the United States. Here the customary farm unit is a quarter section or a multiple or subdivision of it. Roads quite generally follow section lines, and the whole appearance of the countryside has characteristics that are seen in few other rural areas of the world. The farms developed under this plan are predominantly family farms on which the labor is performed mainly by the farmer and his family.

The size and type of farm that appeared as a result of this method of selling and granting lands was apparently well suited to the cropping systems, attitudes and resources of the farmers who settled there. Had this not been so, the pattern would not have survived over the succeeding century and a half. Had large estates or tiny peasant holdings been better suited to the conditions and more economical to operate than the units thus laid out, other types and sizes of farms would have appeared and might by now be dominant.

Though the pioneering farmers had thus achieved some of the ends they sought, they were by no means satisfied. The troubles of the national government in disposing of its lands were not at an end.

Land Policy for the Louisiana Territory

In the Louisiana Territory other problems had to be considered. Here some beginning had been made in granting lands under the laws of Spain, and later under those of France. The southern portion of the area was suitable for growing cotton and hence for a slave economy. Since settlers tended to move westward rather than from north to south or vice versa, there was a tendency to reproduce in each new area the customs, institutions and economic structure common to the parent area to the east of it. The cultural heritage of the Southwest was largely, therefore, that of the Carolinas, Georgia and Virginia but, at the same time, that of the small man rather than the wealthy planter.

For many of these settlers, particularly in the hill sections, the road led downward. They became economic competitors with the slave labor of the larger plantations, and eventually (after the War Between the States) many of their descendants became white croppers, economically little better off than the ex-slaves competing with them. Others remained on small, isolated, self-sufficient farms in the hill areas which were not suited for cotton production. High birth rates and poor economic opportunity have kept these areas in the problem class economically, educationally and culturally.

The Congress recognized some differences between the Louisiana Territory and that of the Northwest, but sought to establish roughly comparable land policies for the two. In 1804–1805 the Louisiana Territory was set up as two territories. The system of rectangular surveys was extended over the area, replacing the systems of Spain and France. Because of reports of improper actions by Spanish officials and American adventurers the laws in regard to settlement were more severe than in the Northwest. Settlement on lands ceded to the United States was prohibited until permitted by law, and penalties of fine and imprisonment for violation were provided. These provisions were not enforced after 1814. No donations of land were to be made, and pre-emption rights were not recognized, but were eventually granted under later legislation.

Settlers' Relief Acts, 1800–1820

As might be expected, many settlers found themselves unable to meet their payments for land as these fell due. This was notably true after the passage of Jefferson's Embargo Act of December 22, 1807. The period of easy money and active speculation had now come to an end for the time being. Depression continued until the War of 1812 brought on a new period of inflation and speculative activity. The West, like the rest of the nation, suffered a severe money shortage, and petitions for relief came into Washington in ever-increasing numbers and urgency. Jeremiah Morrow, chairman of the House Committee on Public Lands, recommended in 1809 an extension of credit because of the bad financial conditions. He also proposed, however, that the granting of new credit be abolished and the price of lands reduced.

As so often happens, the Congress chose the palliative rather than the remedy. The Senate bill, providing only for extending the time in which payments could be made, was adopted. Once started on this road of palliative treatment of a basic problem, it was difficult to halt, or to retrace steps. Session after session passed acts for credit relief — twelve in all between 1809 and 1820. Thus was established a pattern of action which has continued into recent times in the handling of similar problems in many of the federal irrigation projects — a practice which lends itself to unwarranted efforts to exploit the government, as well as to demands based on genuine need for relief.

The Land Law of 1820

As a result of the difficulties encountered under the earlier acts a new one was passed in 1820. Though it did not grant pre-emptions and donations to settlers as desired by the western pioneers, it marked a step forward in the establishment of policy. It was made applicable to all public lands of the United States, thus providing a uniform method for disposing of them regardless of location. They were to be sold at public auction in half and quarter sections. Private sale also was permitted. Some pre-emption rights were recognized for settlers who paid in part for their lands and gave up part. At private sale, purchasers might buy as much as a section, or as little as eighty acres. The minimum price was set at $1.25 per acre. No credit was allowed. Hence this act marked a reversion to straight cash sales.

GROWING DEMAND FOR EASY ACCESS TO LAND

Settlers continued to push westward ahead of surveys and to take up lands not yet legally open for settlement. Rugged, self-reliant and widely scattered, they were impatient of restraint and not easily brought within any orderly framework of land settlement.[19] Yet the government had a powerful hold on them in its control over titles to the land. As the western regions developed and their population increased, their voice in national legislative halls grew in strength and belligerence, gradually drowning out the more conservative counsels of older sections such as New England. With popular and vigorous spokesmen, such as Andrew Jackson and others of his party, they came presently to a dominating position in the national government.

By 1828, when Jackson was elected President, the national income from tariffs had become so large that emphasis on the public lands as a source of national revenue was on the wane. Such lands were looked upon more as providing an opportunity for settlement and growth than as a source of revenue. Relief acts of various kinds were common during this period. Pre-emption was more and more generally recognized and permitted, and the drift both in legislation and administration was in the direction desired by the settlers.

19. The strong feeling about government sales of pre-empted lands led in many instances to the formation of claims clubs to protect pre-emptors on unsurveyed lands. At auction sales, the selling of improved lands was often prevented by violence or social ostracism of the purchasers. Wherever efforts have been made to dispossess farmers on any large scale, violence has resulted. Such was the result in England at the time of the so-called "farthing" sales. It appeared in Massachusetts at the time of Shays's Rebellion; in New York during the tenancy wars; and again in the Midwest in the 1930's.

Sectional Differences in Attitude

It became increasingly clear, however, that no one plan of administering the public domain would satisfy everyone. The North and East complained about the drawing off of their young people and the newly arrived immigrants. They desired revenue and slower settlement which would be less disturbing to their labor supplies. The South was interested in limiting the power of the national government and in maintaining a political balance with the North. It was willing to support the West in its demand for a low price, or none at all, on lands of the public domain, in the belief that low prices would favor westward migration. Furthermore, many of its own people were interested in settling lands in the states west of them.

Thomas Hart Benton of Missouri urged cession of unsold lands to the states and donation to settlers of lands not readily sold at the regular price. He contended that the farmer was a public benefactor and entitled to a reward. He also championed, in many sessions of the Congress, a downward graduation in price for the poorer, unsold lands. Both the West and the South favored these proposals. The East, on the other hand, clung to the idea of more restricted sales and distribution of the proceeds to all the states.[20]

Land Speculation in the 1830's

The heavy migrations of the 1830's brought to view some of the defects of the Land Act

20. When Henry Clay evolved a scheme for distributing the income from land sales in this way, Jackson opposed it as favoring the eastern states when most of the revenue came from the West. Nevertheless, an act was finally pushed through Congress in 1836 which provided for distribution among the states of some $28 million of surplus federal revenue. The major cause of the treasury surplus was the tariff, but there was reluctance to tamper with the compromise tariff of 1833. Though Jackson had repeatedly urged distribution of the surplus, he signed the Act of 1836 with repugnance, and only at the solicitation of Van Buren. He often afterwards expressed publicly his regret that he had approved it. The majorities for it, both in House and Senate, were well over the two thirds needed to override had he chosen to veto the bill. The form of the grant was that of a loan to the states, but no one expected it to be repaid, and it never was. As the financial panic of 1837 developed, it became necessary to halt the distribution.

of 1820. During the earlier period land sales were in modest volume. Treasury receipts from them averaged from a million to a million and a half dollars a year. But in the seven years 1830–1837 more than 57 million acres were sold. Well over half of this acreage (36 million) was sold in 1836 and 1837, reflecting the enormous speculative activity of that period. The general land office could not keep surveys ahead of settlement. Poorer people, and those who were impatient for surveys, "squatted" or "pre-empted" the unappropriated lands, thus creating an ever-growing problem in the administration of land sales. The time was ripe for general legislation that would establish more orderly procedures and meet more fully the demands of the settlers.

Pre-emption and Graduation Acts

Freer and more orderly access to the unsettled lands was provided in the Pre-emption Act of 1841. Any settler, citizen or alien, who had improved land, and who owned no more than 320 acres elsewhere, could obtain title to 160 acres so improved by paying the minimum price, $1.25 per acre, and could do so without competition from other bidders. Pre-emption was allowed ahead of survey in six of the new states, but could not apply on the lands reserved for schools. Grants of land were made to the states for internal improvements. A more adequate system of government land offices was established, with power to settle arguments over prior rights though the right of appeal to the Secretary of the Treasury was retained.

With the exception of the Graduation Act of 1854,[21] the Act of 1841 marks the end of the early period in establishing the general pattern of land settlement in the United States and the policies which were to govern it. Full fruition of this policy was yet to come, however, in the Homestead Act, but this was

21. The Graduation Act provided for the sale of certain lands at less than the generally prescribed minimum. Land on the market for ten years could be sold at $1 per acre; that unsold for fifteen years, at 75 cents; twenty years at 50 cents; twenty-five years at 25 cents; and thirty years or more at 12½ cents.

blocked for the time being by growing opposition from the southern states.

THE HOMESTEAD ACT AND SETTLEMENT OF THE WEST

The Homestead Act of 1862 was the logical culmination of the long struggle for freer access to the public domain by pioneer farmers. It was merely a short step further along the road clearly indicated in the Pre-emption Act. The main battle for free, or nearly free, lands had been won in the earlier years. From about 1850 on, free-homestead bills were presented from time to time, but were consistently opposed by the southern representatives in Congress. They realized that legislation of this kind would stimulate settlement in the Northwest and would tend to upset the balance between the free and slave states. Lincoln, a western pioneer, naturally was favorable to further liberalization of the land laws, and a free-land plank was included in the Republican platform of 1860. With a widening gap between the North and the South, the states of the Northeast were more anxious to placate the West and bind it into the Union. Consequently, when the southern representatives withdrew from Congress, there was little opposition to redeeming the party's campaign pledge, and taking the final step in establishing a policy that looked to rapid settlement of the public domain by working farmers on family-size farms.

The act provided for the grant of full title for 160 acres, to the actual settler, after five years of residence. The underlying principle was good, but the act was loosely drawn and badly administered. Immense acreages of the best timber and mining lands passed into the hands of large corporations, either through dummy homesteaders and employees, or by purchase under the commutation privilege which permitted homesteaders to obtain title six months after filing, by paying $1.25 to $2.50 per acre. These abuses crept in mainly after 1880. Up to that time, most homesteaders obtained their lands by actual residence.[22]

22. The entries perfected under the Homestead Act varied only within rather narrow ranges during the

In part this misuse of the homestead procedure was due to the opening for settlement of lands that should have been retained in public ownership or handled in a different way. Long afterward, when the bulk of the nation's best timberlands had passed into private hands for destructive exploitation and the creation of huge fortunes, steps were taken to conserve those remaining in public ownership. These, however, were mainly in remote areas or were too poor to be attractive to private operators.[23] The best lands had been disposed of, but not in accordance with any plan that would result in either stable forest production or the creation of productive farms.

Homesteading in the Semiarid Areas

While one aspect of the homestead procedure led to overgenerous granting of good lands to private companies and individuals,

latter part of the nineteenth century, usually running from 2 to 3 million acres annually. The largest alienation through these procedures, nearly 39 million acres, occurred between 1916 and 1920. Entries dropped off sharply after 1925: 11 million in 1926–1930, 6.2 million in 1931–1935, 6.8 million in 1936–1940, and only 764,000 in 1941–1945. *Statistical Abstract, 1935*, p. 129, and *1949*, p. 161. Purchases of government land fluctuated much more widely, reaching a level of nearly 8 million acres in 1888, and dropping to only 417,000 in 1895. See Benjamin H. Hibbard, *History of the Public Land Policies*, Peter Smith, New York, 1939, p. 114. Hibbard gives, on p. 570, a pie chart showing the amounts of public land alienated up to 1924 under the various acts. The Homestead, Timber Culture, Desert Land and Reclamation Acts accounted for 256 million acres; sales amounted to 220 million acres; forest reserves and parks to 170 million acres; and railroad, wagon road and canal grants to 137 million acres. It will be noted that these figures are not consistent with some shown in other sources. They do, however, show in a general way the relative importance of each of the major categories. See also Roy M. Robbins, *Our Landed Heritage, The Public Domain 1776–1936*, Princeton University Press, Princeton, 1942, chart on p. 344.

23. There was little good land remaining available for homesteading after about 1890. This period is often referred to as marking the end of the frontier. The filling in of areas already settled was to go on for decades, and, in a small way, is still occurring, but the turn of the century marks approximately the time when American agriculture entered a new era — one of more developed farming, increasing land values and more complex social relationships. Thereafter, the landless young farmer had, for the most part, to take the slow route to ownership through the hired hand and tenant stages, or turn to urban employment. The opportunity to take up good land free had become a thing of the past in American agriculture.

another phase resulted in the settlement of lands unsuited for either farming or forestry. Though the better farm lands had mostly passed into private ownership by the latter part of the nineteenth century, there still were many landless farmers and others who sought independence or profit through homesteading. They continued to press farther and farther into the semiarid areas, settling on lands that were unsuited for crop farming or that could be farmed successfully only in large units. Many found themselves involved in a bitter struggle for survival in which all the odds were with the forces of nature.

Many such settlers were unequipped by training or experience to achieve what little success was possible under the conditions of a semiarid grazing country. The result was the gradual wastage of their small savings and ultimate abandonment of the land, either to the state for nonpayment of taxes or by sale for a pittance to ranchers able to combine it with larger holdings for use in livestock production. Few, if any, of the states had adequate arrangements for administering tax-delinquent lands.

Much of the later homesteading resulted from the insistent demand for wheat that accompanied World War I. It brought into crop production millions of acres better suited for grass and for livestock production. Much of this land was capable of producing crops only in periods of relatively good rainfall. When the drought years of the 1930's made deserts of such areas the result was the "Dust Bowl" so frequently described in recent literature. Enormous damage had been done to millions of acres of good grassland, much of which will be restored to its earlier productivity, if at all, only after years of rejuvenation.

Other millions of acres were left in public ownership but open to homesteading. Like the tax-delinquent lands, they were used and abused by ranchers who grazed them without title, lease or payment of compensation. The result over vast areas was serious overgrazing and progressive deterioration of the range, since the grass belonged to him who could first get his livestock on it. The stockmen, unable to be sure of reaping the benefits, had little incentive for constructive range management. Only after the establishment of the Grazing Service in 1934 was such land withdrawn from entry and placed under management.

The homestead procedure was an unplanned development wholly in keeping with the spirit of the times. Conservation of natural resources was as yet almost unthought of. The resources were so boundless that they seemed inexhaustible. Private exploitation was the only method known. The government itself, then as in the earlier periods, had no adequate organization for implementing a more conservative policy. Not until the time of Theodore Roosevelt and Gifford Pinchot was there to be an aroused public consciousness with respect to the wastage of forest resources, and, still later, a public interest in the conservation of soils. An adolescent, fastgrowing nation was claiming a glorious heritage and giving little thought to the future.

Land Dispersal Through Other Channels

The taking up of land was not confined to homestead entries. The railroad companies were selling off huge acreages. Much land was still being bought at auction and under the Pre-emption Act of 1841, which remained in effect until 1891. The alienation of public lands was given a new impetus under the Desert Land Act of 1877. This permitted settlers, in the eleven states and territories specified, to purchase 640 acres instead of 160, on condition of "reclaiming" the land by "conducting water upon it." Large acreages, especially of lands having water (which would give control of much grazing land unsupplied with water), were entered, but few were ever proved up. Much of the land so taken was sold speculatively, and huge acreages were obtained fraudulently, in part because the law itself was poorly suited to the fostering of orderly settlement under the conditions prevailing.[24]

24. Two other land acts of this period should be mentioned though neither was important agriculturally:

Homestead Policy Impractical in West

There was a tendency for the Congress to adhere to concepts and patterns of action which had evolved as a means of settling the humid areas farther east. The conditions of the West, especially that part of it lying west of the 100th meridian, were so different as to present an entirely new set of problems. Here the rainfall was too light and too uncertain for crop farming in the pattern of the East and Middle West. Much of the land was excellent for grazing and many of the riverbottom lands were capable of supplying supplemental feed, along with the water which was so essential for livestock production. But successful operation of such lands required large acreages and special patterns of organization closely related to the availability of water.

Since the small farmer could not operate successfully on 160 acres, or even on 640 acres, the land tended either to be left as public domain or to fall into some vague status of partially completed entry or tax delinquency. The large livestock ranchers took over and used lands of this kind without much regard to ownership, and without compensation to the government or other nominal owners.

Where small farmers sought to settle (perhaps unwisely but in accordance with law) in areas predominantly organized for grazing, bitter conflicts resulted. Violence was common not only between ranchers and small farmers but between cattlemen and sheepmen. Sheep growers and cattlemen seldom operate harmoniously on a common range. The methods of competition were ruthless, especially where the close-grazing

namely, the Timber Culture Act of 1873 and the Timber and Stone Act of 1878. Under the first of these, farmers could obtain title to an additional 160 acres by planting trees on 40 acres of it (later reduced to 10 acres), and caring for them for a specified length of time. The Timber and Stone Act was passed ostensibly to permit purchase of timberland to be used in homemaking. Actually it was used mainly by purchasers serving the interests of large lumber companies. Its effect was to transfer into private hands large acreages of good timberlands, usually at the minimum price of $2.50 per acre. While this act had little effect on farming, it was important in alienating from the public domain some of the best remaining forest lands.

sheep tended to spoil the range for cattle. Land titles remained chaotic even well into the present century, and law enforcement agencies were little developed. Hence the strong operators tended to grow stronger, and the weak ones to be eliminated.

But the drive for more intensive agriculture is powerful and persistent. Small farmers continued to press farther west on any lands suited to their use, despite the opposition of the cattlemen. Where they sought to farm on lands unsuited for cropping, the problem tended to be solved automatically since they were unable to make a living and presently were forced out. But this process was not fast enough to suit the ranchers and often they assisted nature in its process of eliminating unsuitable types of agriculture.

Logic and economic law often were on the side of the rancher while man-made law was on the side of the small farmer. Unsuccessful farming ventures which resulted in plowing up lands best suited for grazing were likely to make them virtually useless for grazing long after the would-be farmer had departed from the scene. In later periods rancher interests were also adversely affected by the fact that scattering settlements of small farmers tended to cause much surrounding land to be valued, for assumed potential farming use, at prices above those it could support as a grazing resource. This brought all the problems of higher taxes, and demands for schools, roads and other institutions that go with closer settlement. It also brought the problems and expense of fencing, and of interference with the movement and management of herds and flocks. Possibly more serious was the fact that some of the lands could be farmed successfully, but usually only in the limited areas needed by the ranchers for producing winter feed and for protecting their water supplies.

The result of the unrealistic policy adopted by the Congress was to leave millions of acres of public domain, and interspersed private and state lands, virtually unorganized except for the semifeudal forms established by the cattle barons and sheepmen. While grazing lands remained plentiful this did not result in serious deterioration of the resource, but as competition became keener the problems associated with overgrazing began to appear. The quality and carrying power of vast areas were seriously affected, and erosion became more of a problem. It has now become evident that the allocation of lands in the grazing regions in accordance with the rectangular survey, and in standardized units, is unworkable and undesirable. Here the operating units, to be efficient, must consist of appropriate water supplies and sources of winter feed combined with open grazing lands.

Pioneer Stage Near Its Close

The Desert Land Act, the Timber Culture Act and the Timber and Stone Act constituted the closing stages of legislation in the pioneer pattern. A new approach was in the making, but was not to gain significant public attention until after 1900.

During this first century of policy development in respect to the lands of the United States the emphasis had been on rapid settlement. It was generally assumed that virtually all of the nation's land resources would eventually pass into private hands, and be owned and operated by individuals and corporations, without restraint or guidance by government. The principal controversies were over the methods of making the transfer to private ownership. That problem was settled, though only by a slow and gradual process.

The result was a land system well suited to the humid areas, where the principal emphasis was on crop production, and to a pioneer country in which rapid settlement was undoubtedly in the national interest. The procedure developed was less suitable for dealing with forest lands and grazing areas. Here, other patterns of organization and policies clearly were needed, and were shortly to come under consideration. However, the basic pattern of American agriculture had come to be well established by 1900, and the main features of present-day land tenure and policies had come to be rather universally accepted. New emphases were to appear in the more developed economy of the twentieth century, but mainly as modifications, not as major changes. The pioneer period had shaped a pattern of American agriculture that is not likely to be changed radically in the foreseeable future.

FARMER INTEREST IN THE MONEY SYSTEM

CONTROVERSIES AND PROBLEMS, 1790–1860

IN THE EARLY YEARS of the Republic, the land problem naturally took precedence over most others. The money problem was equally urgent but was harder to grasp, and the frontier farmers did not see so clearly what they wanted the government to do. Sectional and group interests began to appear even before the Constitution was adopted. In most farming areas, the Constitution itself was not warmly received.[1] Farmers, particularly the frontiersmen, looked upon government mainly as a policeman to keep order and handle such minimum of foreign affairs as might be inescapable. They did not feel the need for any strong central government. Yet, it was only through positive action by a strong government that the chaotic money system of the time could be put in order and some start made in providing more adequate credit.

Hamilton's Plan

One of the first actions taken by the new government was a plan designed to establish the nation's credit and create an effective banking system. Hamilton, as Secretary of the Treasury, presented to the Congress, in his Reports on the Public Credit (January and December 1790), a vigorous and forthright plan. This included the levying of im-

1. The Constitution had been sponsored mainly by the shipping interests, who desired a navigation law; by creditors, who would benefit from the contract clause; by holders of public securities, who hoped a new government would pay off the nation's debts; by some of the slaveholders, who saw advantages in a central government in the event of a slave insurrection; and by owners of western lands who hoped for an increase in the value of their holdings under a strong central government. The manufacturing interests, though not large, also favored the Constitution as a means of providing protective tariffs.

port and excise taxes to provide income, the assumption by the federal government of the war debts incurred by the states during the Revolution, and the funding of the foreign and domestic debts at par. Included in the First Report was a proposal for a sinking fund to stabilize the prices of government securities and prepare for repayment of principal. The Second recommended the creation of a Bank of the United States modeled after the Bank of England. In accordance with this recommendation, the first Bank of the United States was chartered in 1791 with a capital of $10 million, the charter to run for twenty years.

As a means of establishing the nation's credit, Hamilton's plan was an immediate success. By August 1791, United States 6 per cent bonds had gone above par in London and Amsterdam, and the new government's credit was better than that of many of the nations of Europe. But his bold solution of the financial problem also carried within it the seeds of dissension.

Like most major monetary adjustments, the arrangement gave some groups unearned profits and laid burdens on others. Most of the bonds representing the public debt had come into the hands of men of means in Philadelphia, New York and Boston. Some of them had been bought for as low as fifteen cents on the dollar. Now the nation was to be taxed to pay them at par. Massachusetts, with the largest war debt, profited most by the assumption of state debts. Other features of Hamilton's program were popular in New England. Her foreign trade was favored by the generally low-level tariffs, and her shipyards gained from the tonnage duties favoring American-built vessels. Thus, to many people of New England, and likewise those of New York and Philadelphia, the plan seemed statesmanlike and sound.

But in Virginia and among the farmers of the South and West the reaction was quite different. The Virginia planter and the frontier farmer knew little about business and finance. The idea of establishing a strong credit rating did not seem important to them. They felt that the bonds should have been bought up at market value. Payment at par was an unwarranted and unconstitutional gift to avaricious city financiers. They saw little reason for being taxed to pay the debts of other states. Understanding little of the complexity of the problems requiring solution they soon became suspicious of the motives and methods of the Federalist group for which Hamilton was the spearhead.

Farmers Oppose Bank of United States

When the first Bank of the United States was proposed in 1791, the reaction of the farmers of the West and the planters of the South was one of distrust and antipathy. The House vote on it was sectional. Of thirty-five members from the states north of the Mason and Dixon Line, only one voted against it. From south of the Line there were twenty-four members, of whom only five voted for the measure. Washington, at first favorable to it, was thrown into doubt by the vigorous arguments of Jefferson and Randolph, but finally signed the bill after holding it almost to the legal time limit.[2]

To understand the fierce and ignorant opposition to the Bank in the South and West it is necessary to consider the complete lack of experience with banks over most of the country. Few people had ever seen a bank note. In the western regions the customary mediums of exchange were military warrants and guard certificates, horses, cows, oxen, cowbells and acres of land. In western Pennsylvania whiskey was so used. In the South the

2. Somewhat in doubt as to the constitutionality of the bill, Washington asked Hamilton, Jefferson and Randolph to prepare written opinions on that point. Hamilton's argument, one of the best of his state papers, convinced Washington, and the bill was signed.

custom was for planters to keep such money as they had in strongboxes in their homes. Only four banks existed in the entire country, these being at Philadelphia, Boston, New York and Baltimore. Thus, in the eyes of the planter and farmer, banks were moneyed monopolies — aristocratic institutions which encouraged usury, took coin out of circulation, set up false credits and unsettled trade. It was the duty of government to destroy monopolies, not to create them.

The Assumption Act and the funding operations gave little ground for continuing agitation. Once accomplished, they were past history, but their effect, together with that of the Revenue Act, was to launch the country on a period of prosperity.

The Bank, in spite of its inauspicious start, quickly became an important factor in establishing the nation's credit and bringing order into banking activities. Large advances were made to the government, and cordial and helpful working relations were soon established with the private banks then in existence. Nevertheless, its career was to be a stormy one, and its continuance a political issue of major import for nearly half a century.

Dissolution of the Bank

The southerners continued to be antagonistic and, with the triumph of the Jeffersonian party in 1800, it became evident that the Bank would not have easy sailing when its charter came up for renewal. A memorial for renewal was presented to the House as early as March 1808, but was not acted upon. During the recession that followed enactment of the Embargo and Nonintercourse Acts, the bank contracted its loans. Other banks took similar action. This caused distress among businessmen, particularly in Philadelphia, and led to charges that the Bank was exerting political pressure to obtain renewal of its charter. The stockholders submitted a second memorial for renewal in December 1810, only three months before the charter was to expire.

The state banks, even though their note issues and discounts had been kept in check by the Bank of the United States, generally favored renewal of the charter. So also did many of the trade organizations of the country. The rural areas of the North and West, and practically all groups in the South, opposed the new charter, basing their opposition largely on the issues of constitutionality and expediency. Though the Bank had the support of such powerful figures as President Madison, Albert Gallatin and Senator Crawford, it was finally defeated on the closest possible margin of votes after vigorous and strongly partisan debate. The vote in the House was 65 to 64, and in the Senate, 17 to 17. Vice President Clinton, an enemy of both Madison and Gallatin, cast the deciding vote against the renewal. Thus were foreshadowed the bitter struggles which were later to rage over continuance of the second Bank of the United States and which were to pave the way for almost a hundred years of badly organized and inadequate banking facilities.

Consequences of the Bank's Dissolution

The bad effects of the dissolution did not appear at once, nor were they so disastrous as the Bank's proponents had predicted. By this time the state banks had gained in strength and experience, and were able to take over much of the load. Nevertheless, the dissolution did result in transmitting abroad some $7 million in foreign capital which was still much needed in this country. By 1815, 120 new state banks had been chartered, and some $30 million in banking capital had been added to that previously available. Though much of this was needed to supply the rapidly growing nation, the size of the increase was undoubtedly more than was required. Without the restraining influence of the Bank of the United States, there was little check on excessive expansion of note issues. Bank note circulation rose from about $45 million in 1812 to about $100 million in 1817.[3] The state

bank notes circulated usually at a considerable discount and were not generally acceptable outside the localities in which they were issued. There were no means for transferring either private or public funds from one part of the country to another.

The War of 1812 together with the lack of a unified system of banking and currency brought about a spectacular rise in prices, which was followed by an equally spectacular and much more painful collapse. The Congress was reluctant to vote adequate taxes for financing the war, and its usual source of loans, the Bank of the United States, was no longer in existence. Loans had to be obtained from private banks. Currency conditions were so chaotic by 1816 that the Republican administration, which had bitterly opposed the first Bank of the United States, took the lead in establishing the second Bank.

There was more or less general agreement that a United States Bank was needed, but disagreement as to how it should be organized and financed, and what powers it should have. A bill setting up a bank in which the government was not to participate was vetoed by Madison. It was evident, however, that steps must be taken to settle the currency, which was in great disorder, and to resume specie payments. Secretary of the Treasury Dallas contended that the state banks could not be used successfully to provide a uniform national currency, and President Madison, in his seventh annual message (December 5, 1815), stated that, if the operation of the state banks could not provide such a currency, "the probable operation of a national bank will merit consideration." The outcome was the passage in 1816 of an act establishing a Bank similar to the first one, but now with a capital of $35 million instead of $10 million. The United States was to participate in the same

---

3. Davis R. Dewey, *Financial History of the United States,* 12th edition, Longmans, Green, New York, 1934, p. 144. This figure is at variance with estimates made by Gallatin at the time. Gallatin put the note issues at

$28.1 million in 1811 and estimated that they had expanded to $45.5 million by 1813, and to $68 million by 1816. In the meantime specie had increased only from $15.4 million to $19 million. Thus, there was a much more than proportional increase in notes as compared to specie. The paucity of financial data for the period makes difficult any dependable estimate even in later years. It is probable, however, that Gallatin's estimate was low, and that Dewey's is nearer the true figure.

proportion as in the first bank, namely, to the extent of one fifth of the capital.

Money Troubles of the Jackson Era

The election of Jefferson in 1800 has sometimes been called the "second American revolution"; that of Jackson in 1828, the "third revolution." In the election of 1800 the agrarian interests gained ascendancy over the commercial, but leadership rested in the hands of men from the slave states of the Old South, not those of the New West. It was still a leadership composed of men of culture and learning. "Aristocrat" dominance in the national government continued until the election of Jackson. This latter shift in leadership put the frontiersmen in the saddle. Whatever their virtues in other respects, their rise to power boded ill for continued progress in the development of a sound monetary and banking system.

Jackson had a strong bias against banks in general.[4] The Bank of the United States, though well managed from 1819 on, under the able leadership of Nicholas Biddle, was not popular in the frontier states. It was a specie-paying bank and therefore tended to restrain note issues by state banks to amounts that could be supported by the hard money then in the country. Since the notes of the state banks were called for redemption in specie as soon as they came into the hands of the Bank of the United States, the state banks were forced to confine their note issues to amounts they could support with specie in

their interregional clearings. There was, of course, some tendency for the arrangement to draw specie away from the frontier areas and thus some deflationary influence was exerted. The state banks could not maintain so large a volume of note circulation as they would have done if not required to redeem their notes with specie.

In his first message, Jackson questioned both the constitutionality and expediency of the Bank. Nevertheless, both the House and the Senate reported favorably on it. But Clay, soon to be the 1832 presidential candidate of the National Republican party, in opposition to Jackson, thought the Bank would make a campaign issue favorable to him. He induced Biddle to apply for renewal of the charter in 1832, four years before expiration of the charter then held. The bill was passed, but Jackson vetoed it. Thus the Bank became a major campaign issue.

From this time on Jackson became increasingly suspicious of Biddle, and more determined that the Bank should be abolished. Many personal and political elements were involved in the controversy. Biddle, as well as Jackson, was arrogant and determined. It is by no means clear that Jackson's charges about his use of the Bank to build up political forces antagonistic to Jackson were unfounded. Prominent defenders of the Bank were among Jackson's bitterest political enemies, notably Clay and Webster. Webster served both as a director and attorney for the Bank, and at the same time was borrowing heavily from it.

In the ensuing controversy the economic significance of the Bank itself was not the main consideration. The issue was fought out on personal lines, with Jackson in the most strategic position. Not only was he able to prevent rechartering of the Bank, but, even before its dissolution, he was able to weaken it materially by placing the government deposits in various private or "pet" banks about the country.[5] This caused many of them to

4. His opposition to the Bank of the United States, as to banks in general, was evident even before he became President. He was dissuaded from making any unfavorable comments in his Inaugural Address, but early expressed his opposition. In a letter to Nicholas Biddle, written in November 1829, he said, "I do not dislike your Bank any more than all banks. But ever since I read the history of the South Sea bubble I have been afraid of banks." C. J. Ingersoll affirmed this attitude, writing to Biddle on February 2, 1832, "I understand from Dickins . . . that General Jackson's antipathy is not to the Bank of the United States in particular, but to all banks whatever. He considers all the State Banks unconstitutional and impolitic and thinks that there should be no Currency but coin, that the Constitution designed to expel paper altogether as any part of our monetary system." Quoted from the Biddle Papers (ms), by Ralph C. H. Catterall, *The Second Bank of the United States*, University of Chicago Press, Chicago, 1903, pp. 184–85, footnote.

5. The Bank's charter was terminated in 1836, through Jackson's veto of the bill granting it continuance. A later effort to re-establish it was vetoed by Tyler, on constitutional grounds, in August 1841.

overexpand their note issues. Furthermore, it was looked upon as favoritism, if not worse, by the banks that did not participate in the favors.

Though Jackson was at heart a hard-money man and sought to restore the use of metallic money, conditions were already shaping up for a major inflation.

Speculative Excesses

Speculation was rife, particularly in the West. Lands were being bought and resold on a prodigious scale, largely with money borrowed from the local banks. The state legislatures, inexperienced in monetary matters, were lending the credit of the states to all sorts of hazardous internal improvement undertakings and were borrowing both at home and abroad for canal and railroad development. To make matters worse, a crop failure in 1835 resulted in the balance of trade turning against the United States, thus causing specie to be drawn out of the country for settlement of foreign balances.

At this most inopportune time (July 11, 1836), Jackson issued his "Specie Circular," which required payment for public lands to be in specie.[6] There was little specie in the western areas, and much of the land purchase was made either with bank credit or bank notes, which amounted to the same thing. Naturally these notes, varying widely in value and now unusable in payment for government lands, quickly fell into disrepute. At about the same time various domestic and foreign business houses failed. The English demand for American cotton fell off. By the end of May 1837, every bank in the country had suspended specie payment. Bank note circulation shrank from $149 million in 1837 to $58 million in 1843. This was a larger decrease proportionately than even the disastrous shrinkage in bank credit which occurred between 1930 and 1935.[7] Thus the country entered the worst depression it had encountered up to that time. Public land sales fell off from $20 million in 1836 to $1 million in 1841. The severity of the depression led to the passage of a special bankruptcy law in 1841 under which some 39,000 persons canceled $441 million in debts.[8]

Excess Revenue Distributed

In 1837 the Treasury disbursed to the states $28 million of excess revenue. Though the actual distribution occurred after Jackson left office, the action authorizing it was taken during his administration. Both Jackson and the Congress looked upon this merely as money unneeded by the federal government and therefore properly to be distributed to the states. They would have distributed it as readily to accentuate a boom as to alleviate a depression. There was no suitable plan for its distribution, this being left to the states individually, and the amount was not large enough to counteract the tremendous shrinkage that was occurring in the nation's purchasing power. Consequently it had little significance as an antideflation measure.

Private Bank Policies

Private banks, then as in 1930, were moved by every consideration of self-interest to contract loans and gain liquidity if possible, before the alternative of closed doors and bankruptcy was forced upon them. The reaction following the orgy of speculation was sharp, convulsive and disastrous to bankers, farmers, businessmen and planters alike. Specie was virtually out of circulation, and the country was in the throes of a major depression that was to last for several years — one that probably could not have been avoided but that could have been kept to smaller proportions by wiser handling of monetary issues and retention of the Bank of the United States.

6. This action was taken with a view to checking the speculative excesses then so much in evidence, but was an unsuitable way of accomplishing that end as well as being badly timed.

7. The decline in bank loans and discounts between 1930 and 1935 was from $40.5 billion to $20.4 billion, approximately 50 per cent. *Statistical Abstract, 1946*, p.

389. The shrinkage in bank note circulation between 1837 and 1843 was approximately 61 per cent.

8. Harold U. Faulkner, *American Economic History*, 6th edition, Harper and Brothers, New York, 1949, p. 168.

Inadequate monetary and banking policies, some of them initiated in this period, were to plague the country for most of the succeeding century. There was to be no paper money sanctioned by the federal government until 1863, and no adequate central banking system until 1914. There was little effective supervision of banking operations, especially in the rural areas. The banks were very vulnerable to depressions and to sudden losses of confidence on the part of depositors. Thus farmers and businessmen alike suffered from the lack of stable and adequate sources of credit. Interest rates were high, and loans were subject to call on short notice. These difficulties were to become more evident as industry and commerce grew, and as farmers came to use more credit. As yet, however, agriculture was relatively self-sufficient. Widespread farmer interest in money and credit problems did not arise until after the Civil War.

If a more centralized and orderly banking system had been retained or developed in this period, it is probable that many of the money and credit troubles of later decades would have been eased or avoided. However that may be, the action taken by Jackson in destroying the second Bank of the United States set a pattern that was to last throughout the century. In large part he was expressing the views and carrying out the wishes of the frontier farmers, as well as his own. The opposition to a more centralized banking system became so firmly established that, even as late as 1914, farmer sentiment was against central bank control. The federal reserve system was to be accepted somewhat reluctantly by the organized farmers of that later period, and only after modification of the degree of centralization originally proposed.

Van Buren's Administration

As often happens, Jackson's political heir and successor suffered most of the ill effects of his monetary policies. Van Buren, elected by the supporters of Jackson, took office in 1837. Faced with a country struggling in the quagmire of depression, and with little of the personal appeal that Jackson had, his influence was small and his administration uneventful. One further step in the evolution of monetary and banking policy should be noted, however, in connection with Van Buren's administration. Recognizing the weakness of the government's position in respect to the "pet banks," he proposed establishment of an independent treasury with subtreasuries. Through these the government would make its own collections and disbursements, using its own officials. By this plan it was hoped not only to divorce the government from the business of banking, but, by paying out specie, to promote the use of hard money in place of bank notes.

The Independent Treasury was finally established in 1840, but only after much opposition from the Democrats, and naturally with little support from the Whigs. It was abolished by the Whigs in 1841 but re-established by the Democrats in 1846. Thereafter, the plan continued in operation as a relatively satisfactory mechanism until abolished in 1921 under an act of 1920. The Whigs sought to re-establish a central bank but failed. There was no further federal legislation in this realm until the passage of the National Bank Act of 1863.

Experiments With State-Owned Banks

Between 1830 and 1840, many of the states were learning about banking the hard way. State banks were set up in several of the southern states, usually for the purpose of aiding agriculture. South Carolina, Mississippi, Alabama, Louisiana, Georgia and Arkansas undertook banking ventures of this kind. While more soundly conceived than were the land banks of the colonial period, these later ventures likewise were uniformly unsuccessful. Their troubles resulted both from incompetent and dishonest management and from the mistake of connecting commercial banking with lending on real estate. Long-term real-estate loans could not provide liquid securities such as are needed by a commercial bank issuing circulating currency. The device of selling long-term bonds to supply funds for farm loans was not yet known in this country, though already well established in Germany. The bank officials were rather generally subject to the legislatures. Politically selected, they tended to enter into corrupt deals with favorites, to overvalue lands and to make excessive note issues.

As a consequence of these practices most of the banks could not pay the bonds issued by or for them when they came due. Since the bonds had been guaranteed by the states, the bondholders naturally turned to the states for reimbursement. The state legislatures not only had not expected to pay the bonds but had anticipated net revenue to the states from the banking operations. The result was eventual repudiation of these obligations by several of the states, and the closing of an unsavory chapter in the history of American agricultural credit operations.

Declining Interest in Monetary Policy

In the years following the depression of the 1830's farmer interest in the bank problem receded. The hated Bank of the United States had passed out of the picture and no new agency had come into being to serve as a focus for farmer resentment and opposition. Banking facilities were by no means adequate or stabilized, but the system was decentralized. The standing of each bank rested heavily on the personal reputation of the banker in charge, usually a local man and a principal stockholder. The money system was chaotic, and few bank notes of western banks had anything like general circulation. Both business and agriculture were severely handicapped by the lack of a universally accepted national currency.

Nevertheless, the country learned to live without a strong and stable banking system. The pace of development was swift. The business, farm and banking units that went under were small, and the opportunities for making a new start were plentiful. Farmers could weather the periodic bank panics and money stringencies unless heavily in debt. The country worked out gradually from the financial chaos that followed the dissolution of the second Bank. State banking laws became more adequate, especially in New York and New England, and the larger New York banks came gradually to fill in some measure the gap resulting from the lack of any official central banking system. Thus, at the beginning of the Civil War period the banking system was wholly private, almost entirely decentralized, and very vulnerable to panics and severe depressions.

Up to this time farmer interest centered on banking and credit problems rather than on monetary issues. Some of the financial arrangements made during the Civil War reversed this emphasis and brought into focus an issue that was to be prominent in farm-state politics for more than a quarter of a century, namely, the proposition that prices be maintained or raised by means of a regulated volume of fiat currency or through wider use of silver.

MONETARY POLICIES IN THE CIVIL WAR PERIOD

During the first four years of the Civil War, the Treasury was under the leadership of Salmon P. Chase of Ohio. Chase lacked the vision of Hamilton, and was in no way capable of drawing up any such vigorous, comprehensive plan of finance as that which Hamilton had presented to the first Congress for meeting its difficulties. Under Chase, makeshift devices of one kind and another were the rule. Loans, special taxes, increased tariffs and the national bank plan all were used, and a very modest income tax was levied. It must be admitted, however, that a large part of the difficulty lay in the lack of confidence, both here and in Europe, in the ultimate triumph of the Union cause. This militated against any plan for sale of bonds to the general public in the North and hampered efforts to sell bonds to foreign buyers.

At the beginning of the war there was no national paper currency. The money in use, aside from specie, consisted of notes issued by some sixteen hundred banks chartered by the states. These notes circulated at varying rates of discount depending upon confidence in the issuing bank and the distance from it. There were about seven thousand different kinds of legitimate notes, and possibly as many as four thousand others that were spurious. Such a confusing array of legitimate notes obviously made counterfeiting easy, and few persons could be expert enough to risk acceptance of any but locally issued money.

The monetary system was in great confusion. As a result of the cessation of specie payments by the banks early in the war, gold — the normal international money of the time — went out of circulation. Silver was of negligible significance. It had been undervalued in the 16 to 1 ratio adopted in 1834 and hence had practically disappeared from circulation, since it was more valuable as bullion than as coin. The upsurge in gold production in the 1850's had further increased the disparity. The gold-versus-silver controversy was not an issue, however, until later in the century when silver became much cheaper in terms of gold.[9]

The Legal-Tender Acts

To meet part of the cost of prosecuting the war, the Congress passed in 1862 the first of a series of acts authorizing the issue of legal-tender United States notes, commonly known as "greenbacks." These were simply negotiable, noninterest-bearing promises to pay, and at the time had no specific specie backing. They were made legal tender for payment of debts both public and private, except customs duties and interest on the public debt which were payable in coin.[10] They were also made convertible into 6 per cent, five- to twenty-year bonds, and were receivable the

same as coin for loans to the government. When received by the Treasury they might be reissued. Provision was likewise made for the issue of $500 million in bonds to fund the notes, these to be sold at market value for coin or Treasury notes — that is, at less than their face value. Coin from customs revenues was pledged for payment of interest on the public debt and for a sinking fund to back the greenbacks. Certain other financial provisions were also made in the Act of 1862, but these need not concern us here.

Few of the men charged with responsibility at the time believed that the legal-tender acts were constitutional. When these acts were passed they were considered warranted only by extreme necessity, as a temporary measure to save the Union and hence the Constitution itself.[11] If the banks had been able to maintain specie payment, and if the banks and the people had been willing to accept the demand notes at full value, the legal-tender provision would have been unnecessary. The provision meant then that the government sought to force people to accept this kind of money at more than its market value.

The divergence between greenback dollars and gold dollars increased as the war progressed. By November 1864, the greenback dollar was worth only 43 cents in gold. In a sense this reflects the degree of monetary inflation resulting from the financing policies followed during the war. It also reflects some lack of confidence in the ultimate success of the war effort. Nevertheless, it meant to the debtor class a significant easing of the burden of debt payment. Had the western farmers been compelled to pay their debts in gold or its equivalent, and thus to accept the much lower prices their products would have brought in a currency interchangeable at par with gold, their situation would have been much more difficult. As it was, the ease of

9. During the war, fractional currency went out of circulation because of the premium on the precious metals. In July 1862, Congress authorized the use of postage stamps and other stamps as small change, and in March 1863 authorized issuance of fractional paper currency in denominations as low as three cents, the money which afterward came to be known as "shinplasters." These were not legal tender but could be used for minor transactions. They were issued at first in the form of postage stamps engraved on the notes. Subsequently other forms were used. In all, the authorizations for noninterest currency of this kind amounted to $50 million.

10. Later acts provided that interest on some types of bonds might be paid either in coin or in "lawful money."

11. This view is challenged by some writers. See, for example, Don C. Barrett, The Greenbacks and Resumption of Specie Payments, 1862–1879, Harvard University Press, Cambridge, 1931, pp. 53–57. A minority group in the Ways and Means Committee took a similar view at that time.

repaying old debts, then as in 1919, encouraged the contraction of new debts. In spite of the superb opportunities afforded by war-inflated prices, farmers have seldom come out of a war period with smaller debts than when they went into it. The experience in World War II is a notable exception to the general rule.

Creation of the National Banks

Though greenbacks constituted a form of national currency, they were not issued for that purpose. They were, in fact, intended only as a temporary means of financing the war, and were in the nature of a forced loan without interest. It was expected that they would be retired as soon as possible after the emergency was over. A further step was taken, however, which looked more definitely to the establishment of a uniform national currency. This action — the Sherman Act of 1863 — created a system of banks chartered by the national government. It was partly for the purpose of creating a uniform currency and partly to afford an outlet for government bonds at low rates of interest. While primarily designed for the purposes mentioned above, a collateral benefit was to be that of bringing many of the nation's banks under more adequate supervision. Though the new system was an improvement over that immediately preceding it, it did not provide an elastic national currency suited to the expanding and contracting needs of the country.

The act provided for granting national charters to groups of not less than five stockholders. These banks could buy government bonds, deposit them with the Treasurer of the United States, and in return receive national bank notes amounting to 90 per cent of the current market value of the bonds.[12]

Thus the banks could have the use of this 90 per cent of the money invested, and at the same time receive interest on the bonds deposited with the Treasury. The amount of money so issued was not related to the currency needs of the nation but rather to the amounts the banks found it profitable to acquire in this way and to the available issues of bonds. Banks were likely to have little money to invest in bonds when currency was scarce. In particular, there was a natural reluctance to expand national bank note issues to care for the high seasonal needs that came with the marketing of crops in the fall. This defect was to be met later by the more flexible arrangements provided in the Federal Reserve Act of 1914, but over the intervening years the currency supplies were much too rigid — a fact that caused frequent difficulties for farmers and businessmen as well.

The new banking system got under way only slowly. The first banks were organized in Ohio, Indiana and Illinois. These were farm states in which the need for more currency was apparent. A new law — passed in June 1864 — recast the original act, correcting many of its defects and added some features that made it more acceptable to the bankers. Provision was made for redemption of notes of all the national banks at agencies in certain of the principal cities, thus providing a clearing-house system. The amount of capital required for establishing a national bank was increased, and stricter provisions were made for paying in capital. The banks were given a status somewhat more independent of the Treasury than was at first contemplated. The Independent Treasury Act was modified to give the Secretary power to select banks as depositories of public money (except receipts from customs) on deposit of United States bonds as security.

A further step, embodied in the Act of March 3, 1865, placed a 10 per cent tax on notes issued by state banks, beginning with July 1, 1866. (It was extended to individuals as well as banks by an amendment of July

12. The amount of stock required for chartering a national bank was graduated for cities of different sizes. Many small banks, especially in the rural areas, did not, and still do not, have sufficient capital to make them eligible for national bank charters. Hence many banks have continued under state charter, despite the fact that the major part of the nation's banking has now come to be handled through national banks. Some banks large enough to qualify for national bank charters have chosen to continue as state banks for other reasons. Among these are the less rigorous restrictions on amounts

and kinds of loans that can be made, and freedom from certain requirements placed upon the national banks.

13, 1866.) This forced state and private bank notes out of circulation and made national bank notes and greenbacks the only forms of currency in general use. These steps resulted in a more orderly system of banking and currency, but one which was too loosely integrated and too rigid to meet fully the needs of a rapidly growing country in which currency needs varied considerably both seasonally and sectionally.

Kinds and Amounts of Currency in Use

During the war, provision had been made for $450 million in greenbacks, of which $428 million were issued. As of October 1865, the national currency included in addition $185 million in national bank notes, $65 million in state bank notes and $26 million in fractional currency.[13] Thus the greenbacks in use amounted to somewhat more than half the total currency in circulation. Specie was of course out of circulation entirely, but gold was bought and sold for settlement of international balances much as any other commodity. The value of the gold dollar was roughly double that of the paper dollar. Through the war period the value of the greenback fluctuated as a result of speculation and varying estimates about the outcome of the war.

Efforts to estimate what the effect on prices would have been had the government refrained from printing fiat money are somewhat fruitless.[14] Various other currency changes were occurring simultaneously, and an increased use of bank credit as a medium of exchange cannot be ignored. Most students agree that prices in wartime could be held close to peacetime levels if people were willing to tax themselves heavily enough and to apply rigorous controls over prices and distribution. But these are modern devices not then well understood, and for which there was neither adequate government and pri-

vate organization nor available data. Small wars could be financed without much deficit spending or inflation (the Mexican War, for example), but not large ones.

During the war, the South tended to keep taxes low, and turned to much more inflationary policies. With half the population of the North and a third of its wealth, the Confederate government issued about a billion dollars in fiat currency. In addition, the various southern states issued their own notes, and even counties, cities, banks, railroads and finally individuals issued notes and tickets that passed as money. The result, as might be expected, was a rapid deterioration in the value of such money — in other words, an enormous increase in prices. As the ultimate outcome of the war became more evident, such currency, like that of the Continental Congress during the Revolution, became virtually worthless. The long record of "printing-press money" in the French Revolution, in the Russia of World War I, in Italy, in Germany, and more recently in China, has been one of inadequate restraint and ultimate disaster. In light of the experience of other nations in this realm, the Civil War history of paper money inflation does not seem an uncreditable one.

Be that as it may, the legislators of the postwar period were faced with a major policy problem. The nation was off the gold standard, but it had important interests in international trade where gold was the standard medium of exchange. Much irredeemable currency was in circulation, and prices were high. How should it regain its international standing, check speculation in its currency, and yet avoid intensifying the price deflation that was bound to follow the cessation of war?

THE RISE OF THE GREENBACK ISSUE

The eastern bankers, and most political leaders, took it for granted that the greenbacks would be retired and that the currency would again be made redeemable at face value in gold. That action, however, would inevitably reduce the amount of money in

13. There were also numerous short-term treasury notes that passed almost as money.

14. Dewey says that "The total effect of paper issues in increasing the cost of the war has been estimated at between $528 million and $600 million." *Financial History of the United States*, p. 293.

circulation and depress prices. The effect was bound to be especially severe in view of the fact that war demand was falling off, and state bank notes were being taxed out of existence. Nevertheless, there was not, at first, any strong opposition to retirement of the greenbacks. Many doubted that they constituted a proper and legal form of money, and felt that their purpose had largely been accomplished now that the war was over.

The farmers of the western states soon came to have other views. Their prices were falling. Money had never been plentiful in the farm areas and farmers feared that the action proposed would make it still more scarce, and would contribute to further and more disastrous reductions in farm prices. Many of them were debtors. Lower prices and scarcity of money would make it harder to meet their obligations, and could be of benefit only to the moneylenders of the East and to city consumers. Soon they were to be opposing the retirement of greenbacks with all the organized might at their disposal. They had initiated a struggle over monetary policy that was to continue during most of the succeeding thirty years.

The Congress was concerned not merely with the economic problems arising from having an inflated and inconvertible currency. The old issue of constitutional limitations on its powers was involved. Had it the power, under the Constitution, to issue legal-tender paper currency? If not, the issues already made were illegal, and presumably should be retired as soon as practicable. Even if the actions providing for issue of greenbacks were found legal, the economic problems still were troublesome. Should the greenback issues be enlarged or contracted? Should specie payment be resumed? If so, how and when?

Contraction of Greenbacks

Hugh McCulloch, as Secretary of the Treasury, took the initiative in the attempt to solve the problem. In his review of finances (December 1865) he contended that the legal-tender acts should be regarded as war measures and that the statute making the notes legal tender for all debts, public and private, was, under ordinary circumstances, not within the scope of the powers of Congress. He did not recommend repeal of the legal-tender provisions but thought they should not remain in force longer than would be necessary to enable the people to return to the use of constitutional currency.

On December 18, 1865, the House passed a resolution expressing concurrence in the view that the currency must be contracted and that specie payments should be resumed as soon as practicable. The resolution further stated that "we hereby pledge cooperative action to this end as speedily as possible." This was in accordance with orthodox banking views, and the fact that only six votes were cast against it indicates that sentiment against the policy had not yet crystallized. It will be recalled, however, that the former Confederate states were not at this time represented in the Congress. The banking structure of the South had been ruined during the war. Since the Confederate notes now had no value, there was desperate need for currency and for banking facilities throughout that area. The southern states, however, were in no position to exert a significant influence.

A funding act of April 12, 1866 gave the Treasury power to convert temporary and short-term interest-bearing securities into long-term bonds. Authority was also granted to retire $10 million in greenbacks during the next six months, and not more than $4 million in any one month thereafter. The question of resumption of specie payments was left unsettled, and the country remained in uncertainty as to when this would occur.

Opposition to retirement of the greenbacks developed rapidly. By February 1868, it was strong enough to bring about passage of an act suspending further contraction of the currency. From then on the pressure for retention of the greenbacks then in circulation was strong enough to prevent further reduction, but the issue came up repeatedly in Congress for more than a decade thereafter.

McCulloch had withdrawn about $77 million in greenbacks, thereby reducing the volume to about $356 million.[15] In succeeding administrations some reissues by Secretaries Boutwell and Richardson brought the amount to $382 million at which level it was eventually fixed by Congress (as a maximum) in the Act of 1874. The Resumption Act of 1875 provided for reducing the maximum issue to $300 million, but in 1878 the Greenbackers again were able to push through legislation which suspended further contraction. This act provided that the amount then outstanding, $346,681,016, was not to be reduced. It has not been changed, and the authorized quantity of greenbacks has remained at that level.

Greenbacks and Politics

The struggle over the greenback issue was marked by confused thinking, bitter political rivalries and meager knowledge of the fundamentals of the problem. When the legal tender acts were passed, the Democrats had opposed them, contending they were unconstitutional, but they now shifted ground and became champions of the greenback cause. The Republican Congress, which as late as December 1865 had pledged cooperative action with respect to McCulloch's program, soon yielded to the pressure. In February 1868, it passed the act suspending further contraction of greenbacks. The aroused feeling in the West and South had by then reached such a pitch that neither party could ignore it. Crop failures, speculation and business failures added strength to the movement.

The same kind of dilemma as that which faced Hamilton and the first Congress came into the argument. Many bondholders had bought bonds with depreciated currency. If these were now paid off in gold, the bondholders would receive large unearned bonuses. So also would the holders of mortgages and other private debts, if the greenbacks were retired and the currency reestablished on a gold basis. The more extreme advocates of paper money urged

paying off the entire public debt with non-interest-bearing paper currency. A more moderate group favored "the Ohio plan," which called for paying off in paper money all bonds that did not specifically call for payment in gold. The more conservative groups continued, of course, to press not only for repayment of bonds in gold or its equivalent, but for retirement of the greenbacks and speedy resumption of convertibility between paper money and gold.

The question of bond payment had been met in the first Congress by the decision to pay the bonds at par, thus giving first importance to placing the government's credit on a sound basis, but at the cost of serious inequities as between bondholders and taxpayers. Now, there was less reason to be concerned over the nation's credit standing. Other considerations bulked larger in the arguments over the greenback issue and the resumption of gold.

The anti-resumptionists wanted basically an increase in prices, or at least a check to price decreases. Many feared that depression would result from further contraction of the currency, and that not only would agriculture and business suffer but the government itself would experience a serious decrease in its revenues. It was held that contraction would lower the rate of foreign exchange, and thus diminish exports and imports. The resumptionists, on the other hand, contended that further use of irredeemable paper money would raise prices, which would decrease exports and increase imports, with a resulting drain of gold out of the country. Few on either side had any clear view of the causes of the difficulties facing them, or of the real needs of the country in respect to banking structure and currency policies.

The Republican party, already leaning toward the conservative business interests of the Northeast, and oriented toward the policies earlier espoused by Hamilton, came out for "hard money" and the strengthening of the national credit, for "radicalism"[16] in Re-

15. Faulkner, *American Economic History*, p. 547.

16. Radicalism is used here in a special sense. It does not imply "left-wing" economic policies. The radical Re-

construction and conservatism in economic matters. Selecting as its nominee the popular war hero, Ulysses S. Grant, it won the election in 1868, and the greenback movement suffered a major setback. The Democrats, badly divided as a result of the war, drew up a platform advocating the Ohio Plan, but nominated Seymour of New York, a weak candidate and a hard-money man. The election was bitterly contested. While Grant carried the electoral votes of all but eight states, his popular vote was not impressive. His majority of 300,000 rested heavily upon the votes of 700,000 Negroes.

But the monetary issue was by no means settled. The agitation of the Greenbackers continued and took more definite form in the Greenback party of the 1870's. The party put up a presidential candidate, Peter Cooper, in 1876, and in 1878 polled more than a million votes in the Congressional elections. It was this showing of strength that resulted in the Act of 1878, which prohibited further contraction of greenbacks. The Greenbackers ran candidates in the presidential elections of 1880 and 1884, but their efforts for a more inflated paper currency were gradually merged into the free-silver and Populist movements. Farmer interest in monetary inflation was to continue strong throughout the century. It appeared again sectionally in the 1930's, in the effort of Congressman Lemke of North Dakota to pay off the debts of farmers by a $3 billion issue of paper currency.

Greenbacks and the Monetary Problem

The farmers lost in this first major struggle over national policy. Only loosely organized, and as yet able to express themselves only through their representatives in the national Congress, they found themselves battling a complex enemy which they only vaguely understood, namely, the disastrous decline in the prices of their products, and the increasing burden of their debts. While they had gained a minor victory in checking the retirement of the greenbacks, the tide was against them. Hard times continued and even grew more acute. The Republicans lost control of Congress in the elections of 1874, but before going out of office passed the Resumption Act of 1875. This provided for retirement of the fractional currency and its replacement with subsidiary silver coin, and for the redemption of greenbacks in coin after January 1, 1879. Thus the stage was set for return to the gold standard and the establishment of "sound money." But the opposition still was significant. Not one Democrat voted for the measure. In the Senate the vote was 32 to 14, but 27 senators did not vote. In the House it was 136 to 98, but 54 members refrained from voting.

To form any conclusion as to the merits of the farmer attitudes of the period, it is necessary to consider: first, whether the objective sought was a reasonable one; second, whether the cause of the distress in agriculture had been correctly interpreted; and, third, whether the measures proposed would have accomplished the ends sought.

First, what did the farm groups want to accomplish?[17] They wanted their prices maintained at wartime levels, in other words, the continuance of a cheap dollar. Their prices had risen more during the war than had wages and nonfarm prices. Therefore, if they could retain their wartime price levels, they were in a more favorable position than in the prewar years, except for such debts as they had incurred during the war.

---

constructionists ignored what had been accomplished under the lenient Lincoln and Johnson plans, and began again on "Reconstruction" at the bottom. They succeeded in re-establishing military control over the South, two years after Appomattox. Stringent restrictions were placed on the franchise, which had the effect of permitting only "scalawags" (Southerners who favored the North) and Negroes to vote. Reconstruction also has two meanings: one, the broad sense, relating to the economic rebuilding of the South; the other, the bringing of the "rebel" states back into participation in the national government.

17. For simplicity, the western farmer position and that of the "Greenbacker" are taken as synonymous. That, of course, is an oversimplification. There were nonfarm groups in various parts of the country which espoused the greenback cause, and there were people in the farm areas who opposed it. However, since there were no direct spokesmen for organized farmers as an occupational group, this is the nearest we can come to a recognizable farmer attitude. In this period as in the following decades, the centers of inflationary sentiment were in the rural areas of the West.

Price Changes in the Civil War Period

Statistics relating to the Civil War period are crude and inadequate, and do not provide a clear comparison as to farm and nonfarm prices. However, such illustrative data as are available seem to bear out the conclusion stated above. Money wages rose 53 per cent between 1860 and 1865. They continued to rise after the close of the war, reaching a peak in 1871 which was 83 per cent above the level of 1860. Thereafter they declined until 1879 when they stood at about 40 per cent above the levels of 1860. Because of a decline in the cost of living, real wages continued to rise until 1897, except for major recessions during the years 1872 and 1877 and a less severe one in the years 1880-1882.[18]

Wholesale prices of all commodities, including the products of agriculture, rose from 92 in 1860 (1909-1914=100) to 200 in 1865, and dropped off rapidly thereafter, to 176 in 1866, 159 in 1867, and 148 in 1868. By 1879 they had reached a low of 89.[19] Thereafter they recovered until 1883 when the downward trend was resumed. The rapid decrease in prices of farm products was, of course, an important factor in reducing the all-commodities index. Wheat, which had brought about $1.40 per bushel (at New York City) in the five years before the war, rose to $2.63 in July 1864 and stood at $2.55 in January 1865. The close of the war brought an abrupt drop, to $1.48 in July 1865, but the price was back to $2.30 by October of that year. It remained high throughout 1866 and reached a peak of $3.17 in April 1867.

By present-day standards wheat was still high as late as 1874, having ranged, for the most part, between $1.25 and $1.65 during the intervening years.[20] The price increase (for wheat) during the war had been in the order of 80 per cent as compared to a 53 per

cent rise in wage rates. Wheat prices during all of this period showed extreme variations within the year, providing thereby opportunities for large speculative gains. Such gains went mainly to the traders. Farmers were not in a position to profit much from postseason price increases under the poorly developed storage and trading conditions of the time.

Corn showed a less spectacular rise except for the single month of January 1865, when it stood at $1.87 as compared to a little over 70 cents in the prewar period. Its price fluctuated widely during the war, but tended to remain near prewar levels, except in 1864 and 1865. During the first years of the war it was even below the levels of earlier years, in part because the South had been an important market for northern corn. From 1865 through 1870, the price remained relatively high, and dropped only moderately below the levels prevailing before the war. It held up well even in the severe depression of the 1870's.

Wool prices were approximately doubled during the war, and dropped back to near prewar levels after its close. Butter and cheese showed a somewhat similar pattern but remained well above prewar levels through 1874, for the most part some 50 per cent above. Hog prices were approximately doubled, and remained high through 1866 but dropped back thereafter to about prewar levels or a little below.

All in all, it would appear that farmers did not fare badly in view of the vast and fertile areas that were then being opened up. Their price declines were much less severe than those which followed World War I. From 1861 to 1865 their incomes were definitely more favorable than were those of wageworkers. But after the close of the war this advantage was reversed, since wages continued to increase and showed less tendency to decline after the peak had been reached. In the war years the general level of wholesale prices advanced slightly more than the prices of most farm products, and considerably more than wages. It was a time of high profits and great speculative activity, but both farmers

18. From Alvin H. Hansen, "Factors Affecting the Trend of Real Wages," *American Economic Review,* March 1925, p. 32. Warren's data, drawn largely from the Aldrich report (S.Rep. 1394, 52nd Cong., 2nd sess., 1893), show an increase in money wages of 51.5 per cent between 1860 and 1865.

19. G. F. Warren, *Prices of Farm Products in the United States,* USDA Bulletin No. 999, 1921, p. 2.

20. *Ibid.,* p. 30.

and wageworkers were inadequately organized to exploit fully their opportunities for gain. Undoubtedly the employers, handlers and speculators profited more than did either farmers or workers.

It is not easy, perhaps not possible, to appraise accurately the significance of greenbacks in the period here under discussion. It seems clear that the Greenbackers were right in their feeling that the nation's money supply was being contracted too violently. It is less clear that the solution proposed by them was a sound one.

Money in Circulation

Money in circulation in 1800 amounted to only $4.99 per capita. The trend had been upward at a rather gradual rate until 1860 when it stood at $13.85. By 1865 it had more than doubled (to $31.18). Thus the increase in the five years of the war had been twice that of the sixty years preceding the war. The amount dropped back by 1870 to $20.10, slightly above the level of the trend established in the prewar years.[21] By 1865 the issues of national bank notes had more than compensated for the withdrawal of greenbacks, but not enough to offset, in addition, the withdrawal of state bank notes. These stood at $207 million in 1860, were down to $143 million by 1865, and had practically disappeared by 1870. Bank deposits grew only slowly from 1865 to 1870, but much more rapidly thereafter. They afforded an alternative medium of exchange, and one that soon became more important than the volume of money in circulation, especially as the better supervision of national banks, as compared to state banks, came to make banking facilities more widely used.

The figures on volume of actual money in circulation do not tell the whole story. Demand notes issued by the government had also been used as bank reserves. These had been converted into bonds under the Act of April 12, 1866. The legal-tender backing of bank deposits had therefore been contracted

21. *Statistical Abstract, 1946*, p. 388.

more than is shown by unqualified figures on money in circulation.

It seems clear that there was not enough money per capita in circulation to meet the needs of a rapidly growing and increasingly commercialized economy, in view of the limited use of bank deposits and checks that was then customary. It is also evident that enlarging the amount of fiat currency, with no specific criterion to govern the amounts issued, was not a good way to meet the difficulty.

Because of the general use of gold in international transactions, it was important that the United States dollar be brought into a definite and stable relationship to gold. In the absence of such a relationship, the dollar was subject to speculation, and the basis for international trading was confused and uncertain. During 1864 the value of the gold dollar, in United States paper currency, varied from $1.55 to $2.58. Speculative influences played an important part in these fluctuations and became virtually a public scandal. Obviously, under such conditions international transactions could be carried on only at great risk and high cost. Since the United States already had a considerable export trade, it was important that the dollar be re-established on a gold basis, not necessarily at the old gold value.

Gold Resumption a Deflationary Influence

Through the Resumption Act of 1875, and its eventual implementation in 1879, the dollar was again made convertible into gold, undoubtedly a boon to trade and a blow to speculation, but at the same time a measure that tended to reduce prices. Much of this deflationary effect could have been avoided by resuming gold on the basis of a smaller gold dollar. That is a logical procedure, and one well suited to gold resumption in a situation where prices, wages and other economic relationships have become adjusted to an inflated paper currency. In effect, it recognizes current prices and wage levels and seeks to relate them to a new gold value, rather than to attempt the slow, inequitable and painful process of forcing them back to some pre-existing relationship. Revaluing a currency in terms of gold, as here suggested, looks to stabilization rather than to either deflation or further inflation. In more recent times that device has been used successfully in various countries, but at the time here under discussion it was not well understood, and apparently was not considered.[22]

Greenbacks and Deficit Financing

The mere printing of additional money would not necessarily have meant more money in circulation. The greenback issues of the war period were deficit financing — that is, a part of the process in which the government spent more than it collected. Part of such deficit spending came about through issuance of long-term bonds. These, if actually bought with income that would otherwise have been spent for goods and services, took out of the flow of purchasing power an amount equivalent to that put into it. Greenbacks and negotiable short-term bonds, on the other hand, were inflationary, since they involved government spending without a corresponding mop-up of purchasing power in the economy.

If, on the other hand, government expenditures shrank to no more than government receipts, money printed in excess of that needed for the country's money transactions and bank reserves would merely accumulate in the Treasury, and would have no significant effect on the economy. Where the government is collecting more than it spends, and is paying off bonds, the process is deflationary regardless of how much currency may be printed.

22. In considering the implication of this comment it should be recognized that the situation in the post-Civil War period was different from that of 1933 when the gold value of the dollar was reduced. With a limited supply of gold, the decision to keep down or reduce paper money to an amount at which exchangeability with gold could be resumed was definitely deflationary, since it meant keeping in circulation a smaller volume of currency than would otherwise exist. It does not follow that reducing the gold value of the dollar at a time when there is abundant currency in circulation, and adequate provision for reserves to support bank credit, would cause a rise in prices. This latter action is discussed in a later chapter.

Government Receipts and Expenditures

Between 1861 and 1865, government expenditures averaged about $684 million annually. Ordinary receipts were only about $523 million. For the period immediately following (1866-1870), annual expenditures were about $378 million; annual income about $447 million. Thus the budget was more than balanced, and the general effect of the government fiscal arrangements was somewhat on the deflationary side, a situation that was favorable to the government's credit standing and regarded as a proper policy by conservatively minded people. This amount of deflationary influence probably would not have been very significant had bank loans, and the issue of national bank notes, been increasing as fast as the needs of the economy called for. As it was, such increases in purchasing media other than money were moderate, and the over-all effect of the positive balance of government receipts over expenditures was deflationary. In a rapidly growing economy such as that of the United States, the need was for an expanding volume of money and credit, once the inevitable readjustment following the war had been made.

The government continued to have a positive balance of receipts over expenditures until 1890, though not a large one. From that date to 1910 the balance was generally on the deficit side except for the period 1901-1905. The amounts in either direction were small, however, and, in view of the low level of government collections and expenditures then prevailing, not very significant in their effect on the economy. From 1870 on, bank credit increased rapidly, and bank checks came more and more to take the place formerly held by currency. The heavy exports of the period added substantially to the gold reserves of both the government and the banks, and afforded, in terms of the banking mores and laws of the time, a sound monetary system.

Greenbackers Oppose National Banks

The Greenbackers, while advocating larger issues of United States notes (greenbacks), were rather generally opposed to the national bank system, largely because it permitted the national banks to make what they regarded as unwarranted profits, through the use of their funds both as purchase money for bonds and as national bank notes. A rather typical attitude is that expressed by the Illinois Farmers Association:

Resolved, That we favor the repeal of our National Banking Law, and believe that the Government should supply a legal tender currency directly from the Treasury, interchangeable, at the option of holder, with Government bonds bearing the lowest possible rate of interest.[23]

The Dollar Reaches Par in Gold—1879

While there was little enthusiasm for the Resumption Act at the time it was passed, and much doubt that it would actually be carried out, the operation was entirely successful from the standpoint of establishing the standing of the American dollar. The Treasury accumulated $133 million in gold to meet possible demands on it. The revived credit of the government was demonstrated by the fact that only $125,000 worth of paper was presented for gold on the first day after resumption, and $400,000 in gold was turned in for paper. Greenbacks were quoted at par with gold for some time before the date set for resumption.[24]

THE CAMPAIGN FOR "FREE SILVER"

The greenback issue had virtually been settled by the Republican victories of 1868 and 1872, and the passage of the Resumption Act of 1875. Nevertheless, there were many who continued to believe that the greatest need of the times was for more money in circulation. The continuing downward trend of farm prices, and the rigidity of the monetary and credit system, kept attention focused on this phase of the national economy. The need for actual money was becoming more seasonal. The prairie and plains states that were being so rapidly brought under cultivation were mainly producers of wheat, corn and hogs. By far the heaviest movement of these products was during the fall months, a fact which made necessary heavy transfers of cash from the eastern money centers to "move the crops" in the West. The pioneer farmers, many of them first-generation immigrants, were not accustomed to the use of checks. Hence much of the business was carried on with paper money and coin.

Since the lawmakers had definitely turned thumbs down on the expansion of unsupported paper currency, the proponents of a bigger supply of money turned their attention

---

23. As quoted by Jonathan Periam in *The Groundswell, A History of the Origin, Aims and Progress of the Farmers' Movement,* E. Hannaford Company, Cincinnati, 1874, p. 565. Some writers were much more violent in their denunciation of the system. See, for example, R. W. Jones, *Money Is Power,* Davis and Freegard, St. Louis, 1878, pp. 44–46: "The Bankers draw coin interest on these bonds from the Government and pay no taxes upon them. The Government allows them to issue about ninety per cent of the amount of their bonds in notes, thus without any cost to the banks except the tax on their issues increasing their interest-bearing capital ninety per cent . . . Thus the people pay from thirteen to eighteen per cent interest to the national banks on every dollar of 'Blackbacks' in circulation. . . .

"It defies the inventive genius of man to find out a financial system more variable in its effects, . . . more pernicious to society, and more disastrous to the peace of nations . . . than that of bank issues based on coin. During half the last sixty years both England and the United States have groaned and writhed under excruciating tortures caused by this vicious banking system and kindred principles."

24. The constitutionality of the greenbacks had in the meantime been threshed out in the courts. The result was an adverse decision in *Hepburn* v. *Griswold,* 8 Wallace 603 (1870), with three justices dissenting. In the decision, the acts passed during the war were declared invalid so far as they applied to pre-existing debts. Chase, the Chief Justice, who had been Secretary of the Treasury when the greenbacks were issued, seems to have taken this means of expressing the disapproval he had felt all along.

Meanwhile, Congress had authorized increasing the number of justices from seven to nine, and Grant had sent to the Senate the nominations of two new justices on the day the decision in *Hepburn* v. *Griswold* was announced. Historians still disagree as to whether the appointments were made with the express purpose of obtaining a reversal of the Court's decision. Apparently such was not the case. Be that as it may, the enlarged Court did reverse the previous decision in part, in *Knox* v. *Lee,* 12 Wallace 457 (1871) (*Legal Tender Cases*). It upheld the power of the government to make paper money legal tender as applied to contracts made both before and after the passing of the legislation. Strong gave the opinion of the Court, with Bradley concurring but presenting an extensive opinion of his own. Chase, Clifford and Field dissented vigorously. Later, in *Juillard* v. *Greenman,* 110 U.S. 421 (1884) the Court asserted the constitutional power to make treasury notes legal tender in times of peace as well as war. The power was especially associated with the power to borrow money and to provide a national currency

to the increased coinage of silver, though this transition did not occur at once.

The "silver issue" came into prominence in a somewhat indirect way. Silver had been underpriced in the ratio to gold which was adopted in 1834. By the 1850's the silver dollar was not being used commercially, and, in the Coinage Act of February 12, 1873, it was dropped from the coinage list without significant protest from anyone. This was the action that later came to be known as "The Crime of '73."

Around this time, however, several things happened to bring about a rapid cheapening of silver in relation to gold. The Comstock Lode in Nevada, and other western mines, added greatly to the world's supply of silver. At about the same time, a number of European nations went on the gold standard, and thus in some cases became, for the time being, sellers instead of buyers of silver.[25] Gold, on the other hand, was tending to appreciate in value.[26] The result was that the trend of silver prices was sharply downward for a quarter of a century, and the ratio between the prices of the two metals became more and more favorable to gold which, by now, had become the generally accepted medium

of exchange in international transactions throughout the western world.[27]

The Bland Bill—1876

Little realizing that he was launching a campaign that would last for twenty years, and would outrank the one on the greenback issue, Representative Bland of Missouri introduced, in 1876, a bill "to utilize the product of gold and silver mines and for other purposes." Bland was chairman of the Committee on Mines and Mining. His bill provided that the owners of either gold or silver might deposit it at the mints or assay offices and receive in exchange "coin notes" which were to be full legal tender, and would be redeemable in coin made from the bullion deposited. The rates of payment were to be, for gold, 23.22 fine grains per dollar — its lawful coinage value — and for silver, 371.52 grains, a ratio of 16 to 1.

No limit was to be placed on the transactions. Consequently, in accordance with Gresham's Law, silver, the cheaper metal, would drive gold, the dearer one, out of circulation; just as gold had replaced silver under the earlier ratio which overpriced it in relation to silver.

The legislation was proposed as a measure for the protection of an important industry, and at this stage was not put forward as a solution for the nation's economic troubles. But the resumption of specie payments still was three years away, and in the troubled conditions of the time many were doubting the justice and practicability of carrying out the resumption program. Since the increasing value of the greenbacks coincided with a declining value of silver, it was natural that public interest should turn to silver as a possible medium for redemption of the greenbacks.

The silver miners, who sought the legislation as a means of enhancing the price of their product, were soon joined by the debtor farmers of the Middle West, who had no in-

25. Germany in particular bought gold and sold silver on a huge scale following her monetary reform of 1872. See R. G. Hawtrey, *The Gold Standard in Theory and Practice,* 3rd edition, Longmans, Green, London, 1933, pp. 68 ff.

26. The real value of gold when used as money is not its value in dollars (or other monetary units) but its value in commodities. Hence a high value for gold means low prices for commodities, if the money in customary use is freely exchangeable for gold as was the case in most of the western countries in this period. The demand for gold, as a result of the general shift to the gold standard, far outran the production of new gold, and resulted in bidding up the price of gold (in terms of commodities) almost all through the world. This meant a progressive decline in prices, especially for those products entering into international trade. Under these conditions there was logic in the argument for the inclusion of silver with gold as a metallic base for the world's currencies, provided it could be done practically. Had all the nations, or a substantial portion of them, been willing to adopt the bimetallic standard, the pressure for acquisition of gold would have been eased, and prices might have risen substantially throughout the world. But the trend of the times was strongly in the opposite direction; and the prestige of the British pound, now firmly based on gold, was so great that no country wanted to disrupt its international trading arrangements by shifting to silver, and no one country could establish the bimetallic standard without being immediately drained of its gold.

27. Up to 1870, the world prices of the two metals continued fairly stable at about 15½ to 1. By 1903 this ratio had dropped to about 43 to 1.

terest in the price of silver as a product but supported the movement in the belief that it would mean a cheaper dollar. It was not difficult for the Greenbackers to shift their arguments so as to support the silver program. Consequently, the campaign for increased use of silver got off to a favorable start with much of the old Greenbacker support, plus that of the silver states of the West.

Passage of the Bland bill, which was reintroduced in 1877, would obviously have meant putting the United States on the silver standard along with India and China. The result would have been a United States dollar that fluctuated in value, in terms of gold standard currencies, as the price of silver bullion changed in relation to that of gold bullion. With silver prices declining in relation to those of gold, this would have been, in effect, a progressive depreciation of the United States dollar, a factor favorable for United States exports but unfavorable to other nations desiring to export to the United States.

Foreign Trade and the Silver Issue

From 1870 to 1875, United States imports and exports were about in balance, but by 1876 exports began to exceed imports by substantial amounts, even with the United States on the gold standard, and continued to do so throughout the remainder of the century.[28] In fact, this unbalance has persisted during the first half of the twentieth century. In general, the exchange was of American raw products for manufactured goods, principally from the United Kingdom, and, in the latter part of the century, from Germany. The general effect of a depreciated American dollar would have been, therefore, to grant added protection to American manufacturers, already profiting from a high level of tariffs and a vast unsaturated market for their products.

But the implications of such a policy were by no means clear to the American farmer of the time, nor, in fact, to the advocates of the gold standard. The proponents of the gold standard were mainly conservative businessmen, interested in a stable value for the dollar in relation to foreign currencies, and strongly imbued with the preference for gold that had been established by long tradition.

The silver interests, then as in all the decades since, were little concerned with the effects of their policies upon the national economy, and wanted merely some provision that would increase the demand for and price of silver. Their arguments about the desirability of more coinage of silver are, in the main, rationalizations built up to help in attaining that objective, and cannot, for the most part, be granted the merit either of sincerity or of sound economic analysis. The "Silver Senators" have, however, frequently held a balance of power that enabled them to blackmail later Congresses and Presidents into support of silver purchases that were uneconomic, wasteful and undesired by the great majority of the nation's citizens.

Silver Act Passed

In 1878, the Bland bill was amended in the Senate in accordance with suggestions made by Senator W. B. Allison of Iowa, and passed. President Hayes vetoed the bill, but it was passed over his veto. The new legislation, which came to be known as the Bland-Allison Act, directed the Secretary of the Treasury to purchase at the market price from two to four million dollars worth of silver each month, and to coin it into silver dollars at the ratio of 16 to 1. Provision was also made for the issue of silver certificates in denominations of not less than $10, against silver dollars deposited in the Treasury.[29] This meant limited coinage of silver, not free coinage as the sponsors of the measure desired.

Various difficulties not anticipated by the proponents of the measure resulted from the operations in silver. Secretary Sherman and his successors sought to limit these by purchasing only the minimum amounts required under the law. There were coined in all, under this act, some 378,166,000 silver dollars.

---

28. Except for minor reversals in 1888, 1889 and 1893.

29. $1.00, $2.00, and $5.00 silver certificates were authorized in a later act (1886).

Since the Treasury maintained a policy of exchanging gold dollars for silver dollars, though not required to do so by law, this amounted to much the same thing as though the government had, over this period (to 1890), doubled the amount of greenbacks in circulation. The effect was the same, but the maintenance of a huge unused stock of silver for this purpose was, of course, a very expensive way to provide additional money.[30]

The silver purchase operations did not bring about the hoped-for cheapening of the dollar, for the very simple reason that, in so far as the dollars and silver certificates got into use, they merely replaced other money that would have been used had they not been available. It was difficult to keep the silver money in circulation. Secretary Sherman stated in 1880 that only about 35 per cent of the dollars coined could be kept in use. When received they were taken to the banks, and thence transferred to the Treasury via the reserve city banks. The Treasury managed to offset this to some extent by hoarding the smaller legal-tender notes (greenbacks), thus creating a demand for the silver certificates. The banks continued, however, to resist the use of silver certificates even in the face of legislation which sought to force more general acceptance of them.

The Sherman Silver Purchase Act of 1890

When the Fifty-first Congress convened in 1889, its main business was to pass a new tariff act, but the silver issue was very promptly injected into the discussions. The western representatives were unwilling to support the proposed tariff adjustments unless something was done for silver. Various proposals in regard to silver had been made during the years following passage of the Bland-Allison Act, but none had achieved acceptance. Among them was one for agreement among the nations on an international bi-

metallic system in which the mints of the leading nations of the world would be open to the free coinage of both metals. This would have overcome a major objection to the larger use of silver, but found little support in the European countries, none of which was an important producer of silver.

Secretary Windom recommended the issue of Treasury notes against silver bullion, at the market price of silver when deposited, the notes to be redeemable in either gold or silver at the current market price. This plan, which would have avoided the otherwise inescapable pressure on Treasury gold reserves, was not acceptable to the silver advocates and was dropped.

The price of silver continued to fall during the 1880's and by 1890 was down to a ratio of 20 to 1. Farm prices had also continued to decline. It was clear, therefore, that the Bland-Allison program had neither stopped the decline in the price of silver nor cheapened the dollar. Nevertheless the drive for free coinage of silver continued, and was only partially blocked by a second compromise measure, the Sherman Act of 1890. This required the Treasury to buy 4.5 million ounces of silver a month or 54 million ounces per year, the estimated annual output of all the silver mines in the United States. The silver was not to be coined but was to be paid for in Treasury notes redeemable in gold or silver. This placed a heavy drain on the Treasury gold reserves, if the country was to remain on the gold standard which was the policy chosen by the Treasury.

Repeal of the Sherman Act

The decline in the Treasury's gold reserve, which began in 1890, threatened the standing of the American dollar among the gold standard countries, and in 1893 forced Cleveland to make a humiliating personal appeal to the New York banking interests for support of the nation's credit. He felt that failure to maintain the gold standard would be a breach of public faith, and chose to risk the success of his tariff reform and other programs to preserve it. He called the Congress into spe-

30. The coins minted amounted to some $70 million more than the cost of the silver. This was looked upon by some as a profit, but actually it was not. $378 million in paper currency would have served precisely the same purpose, and would, of course, have cost an infinitesimal fraction of the $308 million spent in buying the silver.

cial session and proposed repeal of the Sherman Act. Through a combination of eastern Republicans and eastern Democrats, the act was repealed on October 30, 1893, but at the cost of an alienated West and South.

Political Effects

Neither the farmers nor the silver representatives had any desire to "save the gold standard." Great numbers of farmers believed, whether rightly or wrongly, that continuance of the gold standard meant continuance of low prices for their products. No doubt their basic conception was correct, but there is little evidence to support the view that a mere shift to a silver standard, or, as they interpreted it, to a bimetallic standard, would have solved their problems. The basic need was for an improved banking system, and aggressive action by the government to revive business and improve purchasing power. But such measures were not in the minds even of the economists of the time, and would have been considered highly unorthodox had they been suggested.

The net result of the monetary measures taken, the depression and the defection of the South and West was to set the stage for the "Populist revolt" and the free-silver campaign of 1896. Since the Democrats, stampeded by the eloquent William Jennings Bryan, seemed drifting toward the free-silver view, the Republicans committed their party to the gold standard, and won out in a bitterly fought contest, electing conservative William B. McKinley, author of the McKinley Tariff of 1890.

Rising wheat prices, due largely to short crops abroad, helped not only to carry the election for the Republicans, but proved to be a forerunner to a gradually improving economic condition. World production of gold began to increase shortly thereafter and contributed to a gradual rise in prices throughout the world. Popular interest in silver as a solution for the farmer's problem became less general, and the issue tended to disappear in the relatively prosperous first decade of the present century. Free silver was again made an issue in the campaign of 1900, and Bryan was again the standard-bearer, but McKinley won, and conservative money policies seemed firmly established in the American tradition. They were not again to be seriously challenged until the regime of Franklin D. Roosevelt, though various reforms in keeping with conservative tradition were to come in the liberal administration of Woodrow Wilson.

CHAPTER 3

TARIFF POLICY: ORIGINS
AND DEVELOPMENT

TARIFF POLICY TO 1860

FARMERS HAVE EVINCED strong interest in tariff policy almost all through our history. Attitudes have varied from region to region, and the nature of the problem has changed as the nation developed. The South took an early stand in favor of low tariffs or virtually free trade. As heavy exporters of cotton and tobacco, and buyers of most kinds of manufactured goods, this position appeared logical to them. It presently became their settled policy. The farmers of the middle and far western states were likewise heavy exporters of farm products, but their policy has been less clearly defined. On the whole they have tended to favor protective tariffs rather than free trade. The cattle and sheepmen of the range areas have long been strongly and consistently protectionist.

In recent years the South has shown more interest in protective tariffs, while some other agricultural regions have become less strongly protectionist than in earlier years. The world situation has changed greatly from what it was in the nineteenth century, and a new outlook on world trade is taking shape. The nature of this change and the problems growing out of it will be clearer if considered in the light of past experience with tariffs and the conditions to which earlier tariff policies were related.

Beginnings of Tariff Policy

The tariff issue came under consideration very soon after the first Congress came into being. The Constitution itself had grown out of a conference called to adjust conflicts between the states over the raising of interstate barriers to trade. Now that the power to levy import duties had been made an exclusive function of the federal government, there was need for it to establish a policy on tariffs. There was urgent need for revenue and few sources from which it could be drawn. The levying of import duties was undoubtedly the simplest and easiest way of providing it. It was natural, too, that a new nation so recently at war with the mother country should wish to develop its own industries and work itself out from under the economic domination of British manufacturers and commercial interests.

Nevertheless, sentiment for protective and revenue tariffs was by no means unanimous. Only a few years earlier the colonies had been opposing violently the efforts of Britain to raise revenues in similar ways. Sectional differences in viewpoint appeared almost immediately. The South wanted unrestricted commerce that would promote a market for its agricultural products and permit purchase abroad of manufactured goods needed by its predominantly rural population. The New England and middle states wanted protection against foreign manufactures, primarily those of England. The differences were not so great, however, that regional differences could not be reconciled.

The compromise arrived at was presented by Madison and adopted on July 4, 1789, only two months after Washington's inauguration. Revenue was the principal objective. The level of duties provided suggests expectation of continuing imports rather than an effort to shut them out and build up American industries. A 5 per cent duty was laid on all goods not otherwise enumerated. There were higher ad valorem rates on articles of luxury. Carriages were highest, with a duty of 15 per cent. There were specific duties on some selected articles — hemp, cordage, nails, manufactures of iron and glass, sugar, cheese, cotton goods, beer, tobacco, indigo and wool cards. Wool and cotton were on the free list. The intent, in addition to raising revenue, was to stimulate domestic production, but the rates were moderate. The average is estimated at 8½ per cent.

Several important principles were established in this first tariff act — specific and ad valorem rates, the granting of drawbacks on exports of goods imported, and discrimination against goods imported in foreign-owned vessels. An amendment passed in 1790 made a few minor changes. Among the items added were tariffs on some agricultural products, for example, plums, prunes, oranges and lemons. Some rates were raised, and there was a change in the provision relating to goods imported in foreign vessels. These were now to take a rate 10 per cent higher than that specified by the act,[1] whereas in the earlier act goods imported in American vessels took a rate 10 per cent below the listed rate. The Act of 1790 remained in force until 1797.

Development of Tariff Policy to 1816

For more than two decades after the passage of the Act of 1789 the tariff did not become a major party issue. The general drift of the rate of duty was slightly upward, partly in keeping with the protective policy recommended by Hamilton, but more as a result of Treasury needs. Minor changes were made in 1792, 1794, 1797, 1800, 1804 and 1812. In all, twenty-five tariff acts were passed. In only one category were the duties decreased or abandoned. The Act of 1794 repealed the tariffs on horses, cattle, sheep, swine and other animals imported for breeding purposes. An act passed in 1812 doubled all duties as a means of raising revenue for the prosecution of the war. It was to expire automatically one year after the peace.

1. This change, while retaining the 10 per cent discrimination against goods imported in foreign vessels, had the effect of increasing duties by 10 per cent.

The Tariff Act of 1816

The year 1816 brought the first vigorously protective tariff. By this time both America and Europe were feeling the aftereffects of the Napoleonic wars, and of the ending of hostilities between the United States and Britain. The first effect of the war's cessation was a wild spree of buying. Whole fleets of British ships came in loaded with goods that had been unavailable during the war. Buyers bid against each other in the auctions where most of the goods were sold and forced prices to fantastic levels, returning to the British exporter sometimes as much as $16 for each British pound invested. British manufacturers, unable to go into European and South American markets, emptied their warehouses on the United States, and Americans bought with avidity the silks, satins, muslins, hardware, tea and other household goods that they had been unable to get during the war years.

By the fall of 1815 this flood of goods had prostrated the American woolen and cotton industries, and was threatening others. Petitions for protection from foreign goods flowed in upon the Congress from nearly all sections of the country. Many of the new domestic industries had experienced almost every kind of stimulus in the period preceding 1815: the Nonimportation Act, the Orders in Council, the French decrees and the war demands, as well as bounties and exemptions from taxation. Thus the revival of trade with England seemed likely to deal a death blow to many of them.

By 1816 the depression had become so severe and the demand for protection so general that the opposition to protective duties virtually disappeared. In the action on the bill there was little evidence of sectional differences.[2] The votes both for and against were

2. Even the Virginia group appears not to have been opposed to substantial tariff protection at this time. There was formed at Philadelphia in 1817 "An American Society for the Encouragement of American Manufactures." It was launched by New York capitalists for the purpose of influencing Congress and creating sentiment favorable to protection. Vice President Tompkins was chosen president of this group, and Adams, Jefferson, Madison and Monroe were elected members. Only Monroe, of the above group, refused

well distributed. Principal opposition was from the coastal areas of New England, where commercial shipping interests feared the effects on their trade. Even so, the bill was backed by Webster of Massachusetts, as well as by Clay of Kentucky and Calhoun of South Carolina; in fact, by almost all of the leading men except John Randolph of Virginia.

The new act provided specific duties on beer, almonds, cheese, cotton, currants, figs, hemp, indigo, spices, plums, prunes, raisins, ochre, sugar and manufactured tobaccos. Plants, trees and animals imported for breeding purposes were on the free list. Drawbacks were permitted in some cases. The highest permanent rate of duty was 20 per cent. On enumerated articles, including most agricultural products, the rate was 15 per cent. For goods imported in foreign vessels the 10 per cent higher duty was retained, but with provision that it should not apply where in conflict with other acts of Congress or with treaties.

The general price level in the United States had dropped from 235 in 1814 to 185 in 1815 and to 157 in 1816.[3] The war period had been marked by a sharp increase in prices, from around 160 to the 235 peak mentioned above. Thus the immediate readjustment was to about the level preceding the war. While this deflation in prices undoubtedly stimulated interest in higher tariffs, the added protection afforded by the Act of 1816 did not check the downward trend. The decline in prices after 1816 was due in considerable measure to rapidly increasing production in the United States, and to gradual stabilization of the money system, partly through the influence of the second Bank of the United States.[4]

Growing Sentiment for Protection

Agitation for higher protective tariffs gained strength in the years following 1816. In 1820 a new bill, more protective than the Act of 1816, was introduced by Baldwin of Pennsylvania, and lost by only one vote in the Senate. It was reintroduced in 1821 and 1822, but not strongly pressed. Principal backing for this measure was in the middle states, New York, New Jersey and Pennsylvania, and in the western states, Ohio and Kentucky. In New England there was a split between the shipping interests and the manufacturing interests, but the dominant attitude was against increasing protective duties. The South was by now more actively opposed to protection.

The Act of 1824 embodied the first and most direct results of the growing protective sentiment. By this time the financial condition of the government was such that revenue considerations were minor. The vote on the measure followed sectional lines — the middle and western states supported it; the South was in opposition; and New England was divided, Rhode Island and Connecticut being for, and Massachusetts and the other states against the bill. Adams, Clay, Crawford and Jackson all gave support. The attempt to introduce the "principle of the minimum" on woolens failed because of southern opposition.[5] Duties were provided, however, on raw and manufactured wool, and the "minimum" on cotton was raised.

In 1827 the Harrisburg Convention, consisting largely of manufacturers and politicians, took a strong position in favor of higher duties on agricultural products. Its major concern, however, was to help the woolen industry.

The Tariff of Abominations — 1828

The Act of 1828, commonly known as "The Tariff of Abominations," was the re-

election; all the others expressed sympathy with the objects of the society.

3. G. F. Warren, *Prices of Farm Products in the United States*, USDA Bulletin No. 999, 1921, p. 2. The Warren index is based on 1909–1914 as 100.

4. Prices continued to fall, reaching an index of 117 by 1820 and as low as 100 by 1830. From then until 1860 they tended to level off though maintaining a general downward trend except for the period of speculation and wild banking which lasted from 1836 to 1839. Warren, *loc. cit.*

5. The "principle of the minimum" was that imported goods would be assumed to have cost certain minimum amounts even though they had been bought for less. It was considered especially applicable in respect to cotton goods imported from India where wages were very low.

sult of a political maneuver that misfired. Jackson believed that he had been tricked out of the presidency in 1824 by a corrupt deal between Clay and Adams whereby Clay was to lend his support to Adams in return for appointment as Secretary of State.[6] The merits of this controversy need not concern us here. Suffice it to say that Jackson's antipathy for Adams and Clay caused him to lend himself to this effort at manipulation.

Protectionist sentiment was strong in the middle and western states. The South felt, no doubt justifiably, that the rates already in effect were too high. The struggle which resulted in the Missouri Compromise of 1820 had already brought it face to face with the fact that there was a relationship between the growth of manufactures and the slavery issue. The slave economy was not adapted to the development of manufactures. Hence the South would continue to be an importer of manufactured goods, either from abroad or from the North. Thus the higher level of duties, if translated into higher prices, meant higher costs to the South while at the same time it tended to build up a rival regional economy already well known to be antagonistic to slavery.

The Jackson men were determined, however, to elect their candidate to the presidency in 1828. Underestimating his popularity, they assumed that he would need support in the North to win the election. It was decided, therefore, to support a generally high level of duties, with rates especially high on raw materials and thus sure to be obnoxious to New England. The Jackson men, both the protectionists from the North and the free traders from the South, were to unite in preventing any amendments, and thus present a bill so objectionable that Adams and the New England group would have to vote against it. The southern representatives who had opposed all amendments would also vote against it on the final vote. Thus the bill would be defeated, but Jackson would not have to bear the onus of failure to sympathize with the needs of domestic industry, while the stigma of having defeated the bill would fall upon Adams and his followers.

To the surprise of its authors, the bill was passed, partly through the influence of Daniel Webster who voted for it and carried some New England senators with him. Thus was placed on the books a tariff act that was unsatisfactory both to the free-traders of the South and the protectionists of the North. The act was so obviously drawn for purposes of political manipulation that extended discussion of its economic implications will not be useful. "The whole scheme," as Taussig points out, "was a characteristic product of the politicians who were then becoming prominent as the leaders of the Democracy, men of a type very different from the statesmen of the preceding generation."[7]

When Jackson became President, Calhoun, then Vice President, hoped he would insist on a reduction of tariffs, but Jackson showed little interest in the issue. Nevertheless, the tariff problem continued to be discussed. In September and October of 1831 a Free Trade Convention was held in Philadelphia, consisting of representatives from fifteen of the twenty-four states. Berrien of Georgia and Gallatin of New York participated in the drafting of its memorial to Congress. They opposed protective tariffs and urged that duties be reduced recommending that, after the public debt was paid off, only those amounts of tariff needed to provide revenue for the government be retained. They wanted a uniform ad valorem duty, and suggested 20 per cent as a proper level. They held that 25 per cent should be a maximum.

By 1832 the protectionists themselves took

6. There were four candidates, Adams, Clay, Crawford and Jackson — all nominally Republicans. Jackson received 99 electoral votes, Adams 84, so neither had a majority. As a consequence the election went to the House. Clay asked his supporters to vote for Adams, and thus carried the election for him. Randolph of Roanoke characterized the arrangement as "the coalition of Blifil and Black George" (the combination of the puritan and the blackleg). Adams appointed Clay as Secretary of State, thus intensifying the suspicions of the Jacksonians, and increasing the unpopularity of his administration.

7. F. W. Taussig, *Tariff History of the United States*, 8th edition, G. P. Putnam's Sons, New York, 1931, p. 95.

steps to do away with the "abominations" of the Act of 1828, and returned most of the rates to the levels of 1824. Wool, one of the few exceptions, was left at 4 cents a pound plus 40 per cent, but even here the most objectionable feature was removed by admitting, duty-free, wool valued at less than 3 cents a pound. The minimum system was abolished, as it had worked badly under the Act of 1828.

The Compromise Tariff of 1833

Though the Act of 1832 corrected many of the worst features of the Act of 1828, it was by no means satisfactory to the South. In fact, the tariff revision of 1832 even increased the South's antagonism to the protective principle. It had regarded the Act of 1828 as only a temporary makeshift, whereas the Act of 1832 seemed to be establishing a permanent high-tariff policy.[8] When Jackson not only failed to take the lead in correcting the inequities of the Act of 1828, but signed the Act of 1832 consolidating the high levels of duty, the South felt the time had come to assert itself. The result was the attempt by South Carolina to nullify a federal act and forbid the collection of duties in her ports. Jackson took prompt and vigorous steps to assert the superior authority of the national government over that of the states, but the pressure for tariff reduction continued and eventually took form in the Compromise Tariff of 1833.

The Compromise Act provided for retaining a considerable amount of protection, but for gradual reduction until 1840 and a more rapid reduction thereafter to bring the level to a uniform 20 per cent rate in 1842. On all duties of more than 20 per cent, reductions amounting to one tenth of such excess were to be made in 1834, 1836, 1838 and 1840. One

8. A more subtle influence was at work to increase this feeling of inequity. Already the relatively poor soils of the coastal states of the South were declining in fertility under the heavy drains of their cash-crop agriculture. In most regions population was growing at a phenomenal rate, but here the westward migration absorbed most of the increase. Thus, with population growth virtually at a standstill, and with their prosperity declining, these seaboard states of the South found it easy to attribute to the tariff more sinister effects than were its due.

half of the remaining excess was to be done away with on January 1, 1842 and the other half on July 1, 1842. As a political measure the act was commendable, but the drafting was bad from the economic and financial points of view. No provision was made for reducing specific duties, yet it was apparent that the Congress intended that these should be reduced as well as the ad valorem rates.

The Secretary of the Treasury, consequently, had to take it upon himself to frame rules as to the manner of ascertaining the ad valorem equivalents of specific duties, and to make the reductions called for by the act. Some duties in the Act of 1832 were very high; for example, that on rolled bar iron stood at around 95 per cent. Here the application of the formula called for a reduction from 65 per cent to 20 per cent between January 1 and July 1, 1842. The flat 20 per cent rate provided presumably as the permanent level was a crude, undiscriminating formula agreed to at the insistence of the South. It did not provide sufficient revenue to meet the needs of the government.[9]

The Tariff Act of 1842

The new 20 per cent level of duties had been in effect only two months when it was replaced by the act of August 30, 1842. This was entitled "An Act to provide revenue." While the provision of more adequate revenue was part of the reason for its adoption, its main purpose was protective, and it was the first of a long series of tariff measures sponsored and designed largely by the particular producers desiring protection. There was no such popular feeling behind it as had marked the tariffs of 1816 and 1824. In the farming states enthusiasm for the home market idea had cooled. This was largely a manufacturers' tariff. It was passed by the Whigs as a party measure, sponsored in the House by Fillmore. Tyler was opposed to protection, but his veto message on a temporary measure of June 1842 indicated that he did not wish

9. Some minor changes in the tariff had been made by an act passed in 1841, but they are not important in the longer view of the problem.

to take a strong stand either way. Furthermore, he wanted to avoid combining the tariff issue with that of land distribution, as provided in Clay's "American system."

The scale of duties in the Act of 1842 was similar to that of 1832, though there were many differences in detail, some items being higher and some lower. Wool was lower, but none of it free. The minimum on cotton was restored. The list of specific duties was increased, and there were more minute classifications. It was considered necessary to provide an average duty of 30 per cent on the gross amount of importation in order to assure the revenues needed. In general the rates were made higher on manufactured goods and lower on raw materials and noncompeting items. On all unenumerated articles the rate was to be 20 per cent ad valorem.

The nation prospered under the Act of 1842, but the reasons for the increased prosperity are still a matter of debate. The country was developing rapidly, and people were able to buy more goods both domestic and foreign. But the wages of labor did not increase. In some cases they declined.[10] It was a period of free enterprise in its freest sense. Industrial units were small and labor almost unorganized. Thus competition tended to cause the decreases in cost that were resulting from technological improvement to be reflected in lower prices. Extensive monopolization by manufacturers was not yet possible, and the workers were not yet sufficiently organized to demand that these gains go to labor in the form of higher wages. But labor, together with all other consuming groups, achieved somewhat higher buying power through the downward drift in prices. The price index stood at 107 in 1841 (1909–14 = 100) and moved downward gradually to 91 by 1849.[11]

Prosperity can result from lowered prices and larger consumption, as well as from higher wages, provided the price reductions are due to lower costs. With lower prices the benefits are more widely distributed than with higher wages. It may be doubted that the tariff had any very large effect on either prices or wages in this period. The country was undergoing rapid development both industrially and agriculturally, and was not heavily dependent on foreign trade, either as an outlet for farm products or as a source of supply for industrial goods, except for certain critical materials for railroads and factories. The Mexican War of 1846–1848 apparently did not disturb the economy greatly. The price level rose moderately, some three or four points, and the general downward drift of prices was interrupted during these years, but the main current of national development continued with little interruption.

Walker's Report of 1845

A basic document in the history of the free-trade argument was presented by Robert J. Walker, Secretary of the Treasury, in 1845.[12] Walker had been a senator from Mississippi and was a consistent advocate of free trade before coming into the Cabinet. The Walker document was in a sense a crystallization of liberal views rather than an argument in favor of free trade. He argued that no more money should be collected than was needed to run the government economically, and that no duty should be imposed on any article higher than that which would yield the greatest revenue. This was assumed to be 20 per cent, though with no real analysis to support it since obviously such a rate would vary from commodity to commodity. He was merely accepting the 20 per cent level previously popularized in the South. Where the rate was less than 20 per cent discriminations might be made, or articles might be put on the free list, provided there were imperative reasons for doing so. All "minimums" and specific duties were to be abolished. Duties should be assessed on market values and

10. See R. J. Walker, "Report from the Secretary of the Treasury" for 1845, in F. W. Taussig, *State Papers and Speeches on the Tariff*, Harvard University, Cambridge, 1892, pp. 214–51.
11. Warren, *Prices of Farm Products*, p. 2.

12. See analysis in Edward Stanwood, *American Tariff Controversies in the Nineteenth Century*, Houghton Mifflin, Boston, 1903, Vol. II, pp. 44–69. The text of the report is given in Taussig, *State Papers and Speeches on the Tariff*, pp. 214–51.

should operate equally throughout the Union, being neither for nor against any class or section. Highest duties should be on luxuries, because all taxation, direct and indirect, should be in proportion to property.

The Tariff Act of 1846

The Tariff Act of July 30, 1846, carried out essentially the recommendations made in Walker's report. It remained in effect for eleven years, the longest period any tariff act has been in operation without change. The bill, though presented as a free-trade measure, was actually a modified form of protection, but with all duties in ad valorem form. It was passed by the Democrats on a vote that followed party lines.

Some of the rates thus established were by no means low, but in the main these high rates were on products that were either luxury goods or of little significance in international trade. In the early years following passage of the act there was some demand for a return to more rigorous protection, but after a time agitation for changes in the tariff died out almost entirely. Interest in the rapid westward expansion of the time was dominant, domestic industry was expanding, and birth rates and rates of immigration were high, thus contributing to an abundant and cheap supply of labor. The period 1846 to 1857 was, on the whole, one of great prosperity. The act was successful as a revenue measure and, in fact, produced more revenue than was needed. Imports were stimulated and there was an increased demand abroad for American farm products, because of famine in Europe at a time when the United States had good crops.

Reciprocity With Canada

An important modification of American tariff policy appeared in the Canadian Reciprocity Treaty of March 6, 1854. The negotiations were handled by Webster up to 1852, and thereafter by Marcy, Secretary of State under President Pierce. Numerous articles were put on the free list by both countries, among them grain, flour, animals, meats, cotton, wool, seeds, vegetables, fruits, poultry, eggs, butter, cheese, tallow, unmanufactured tobacco and fish.

Canada was eager for such an arrangement following repeal of the corn laws in England and the ending of colonial preference (1846). In the United States the fishing interests and the South favored the plan. The act proved generally beneficial, especially to the lumbering and fishing interests. United States citizens could navigate the St. Lawrence and the Canadian canals subject only to the same duties as the Canadians paid. The rise of protectionist sentiment in Canada was the main factor in causing the treaty not to be renewed when it expired at the end of the ten-year period for which it was originally negotiated.

The Tariff Act of 1857

Under the Act of 1846 revenues became larger than the needs of government. With the independent treasury system then in effect, this resulted in excessive accumulations of specie in the Treasury and consequent failure of the funds to flow back into the ordinary channels of business. President Pierce assumed that the principle of levying tariffs for revenue and not for protection had become "the settled policy of the country." Therefore an excess of revenue called for a lowering of tariffs. These views were expressed in his various messages on the subject, and the Act of 1857 was passed to implement them. Practically everyone agreed that a reduction in revenues was called for. In neither house was there anything more than scattered opposition.

The Act of 1857 was the first tariff act since that of 1816 in which politics was not involved. The Congress acted with soberness and impartiality, seeking to correct in the national interest a situation that was tending to concentrate specie in the national treasury and thus to undermine the money and credit structure of the country. The act retained the framework established in 1846. New rates for classes A and B were 30 per cent instead of 100 per cent; C, 24 per cent instead of 30 per cent (this was the main protective category); D, 19 per cent instead of 25 per cent; E, 15 per cent instead of 20 per cent; F, 12 per cent instead of 15 per cent; G, 8 per cent instead of 10 per cent; and H, 4 per cent instead of 5 per cent. Unenumerated articles took a rate of 15 per cent, and the free list was enlarged, mainly by exempting more raw materials. Some items were transferred to different schedules.

The Morrill Act of 1861

One further change was made in the pre-Civil War period, the Morrill Act of March 2, 1861. Though the southern Democrats had already withdrawn from the Congress, the Morrill Act forms no part of the financial legislation of the war. The new Republican party had gained control of the House in 1858, mainly on the slavery issue and not on pre-existing party lines. Many northern Democrats had joined with the Republicans, and Lincoln had been elected in the fall of 1860. Morrill and others wanted to attract support to the Republican party from some of the groups that had suffered severely in the panic of 1857, particularly the iron interests of Pennsylvania and the woolgrowers of Ohio. Most of the manufacturing interests remained aloof from the movement for higher tariffs. By this time the doctrines of Adam Smith had a wide following in England and the United States, and the earlier mercantilist doctrines were less generally accepted.

The framers of the act intended to restore approximately the rates of 1846. Many duties were changed from ad valorem to specific, and most were raised, particularly those on iron and wool. The new act had been in effect only a few months when the exigencies of war made new rates necessary.

CHANGES IN TARIFF POLICY AFTER 1860

The numerous tariff acts passed during the war were largely for the purpose of financing the war rather than for protection of American industries. National policy did, however, take a strong turn toward protectionism at this time — a tendency that was to be dominant during most of the time from then un-

til 1913. The southern states were, of course, not represented in the Congress during the war, nor, in any effective way, for some time after its close. Such opposition to tariff increases as appeared came mainly from the western Republicans, and they were not strong enough to carry their point.

The Act of August 5, 1861, designed to provide revenue, levied duties on tea and coffee and increased the duties on sugar, molasses, spices, salt, fruits, drugs, hemp, etc. The average level was about 19 per cent. All of the Democrats voted against the measure, but it was passed as soon as proposed. The need for revenue was obvious. As the war progressed, many internal taxes were levied, and a tariff act of July 14, 1862 was intended largely as an offset to these taxes. Those in charge of the legislation had protectionist leanings, but the act stated that it was "increasing temporarily the duties on imports." The average rate applied was about 36 per cent, and the free list was reduced. The protection given was in some cases more than adequate to compensate for internal taxes, but there seems to have been little opposition to the legislation.

An act passed on June 30, 1864 was of the same general nature. It left in effect the provisions of the acts of 1861 and 1862 but changed rates so generally that it was virtually a new general law. Rates were raised all along the line, bringing the average level up to about 47 per cent. The free list was curtailed again so that hardly anything was exempt except a few crude raw materials used by manufacturers. Practically all opposition to tariffs disappeared, not only during the war but for several years thereafter. Protectionist sentiment became so strong that even after the war almost any rate a manufacturer asked was readily granted.

Reform Measure Rejected

In 1867, after the failure of a reform measure prepared by David A. Wells, Special Commissioner of the Revenue, and supported by the Secretary of the Treasury, a special act was passed granting extreme protection to wool and woolen goods. The Wells measure was protectionist, and Wells himself leaned to this view. However, there was little sentiment in the Congress for freer trade, and the failure of the simple reform measure proposed by Wells gave more confidence to the extreme protectionists. In the special act the tariff on the type of wool most commonly grown in the United States was doubled, but this increase was concealed under a change in classification. The compensating-duty principle was used on woolens. The rate was increased from 24 cents per pound of woolen cloth (Act of 1864) to 50 cents, and a 35 per cent ad valorem duty was added. This was even higher protection than the wool manufacturers had asked for.

Wells had come into office a protectionist, but in the course of time changed to a vigorous opponent of high tariffs. Though northern protectionists regarded him as a traitor and distrusted his motives, his reports made him a leader of the tariff reform movement. By 1870 he was advancing orthodox arguments for freer trade in raw materials. He became an important influence on thinking relative to tariffs during the years immediately following passage of the wool tariff, but the forces of protection were still dominant. Small reductions were made in the Act of July 14, 1870, but they were in the main downward revisions of the revenue tariffs enacted during the war and not significant as a change in protectionist policy.

At the time most of these duties were laid, internal excises were so high that many manufacturers would have been crushed if additional protection had not been provided. The internal taxes were reduced after the close of the war, but the tariffs remained at high levels for twenty years. Thus manufacturers came to have an inordinately high protective tariff. While this was clearly to the disadvantage of the farmers of the West, and an added stimulus to the roaring progress of industrial development, the significance of the change was not recognized by the farmers, and no important resistance developed. Freer entry of foreign goods after the war would

have made them available to farmers at low prices, and would have placed some check o the excessive profits of domestic manufactu ers who were reaping a harvest by selling i an undersupplied market.[13]

The Export Situation

Exports of foodstuffs were gaining rapidl particularly after 1870, so there was no si nificant gain to farmers in maintaining high level of tariffs. Imports of manufacture goods fell off sharply from 1876 to 1880 an hardly more than recovered to the levels o 1871–1875 even during the 1880's, in spite o the rapid growth of the country and the fa that exports of foodstuffs had nearly quad rupled between the late 1860's and the earl 1880's.

In these years American exports, about ha of them foodstuffs, exceeded imports by abo $150 million a year. The United States wa not then a capital-exporting country an would have been little inclined to build u balances abroad. A reduction of exports t what could have been paid for by impor would have been a severe blow to the whea cotton and tobacco growers as well as to th producers of hogs and cattle. These produc made up then, as now, a very substantial pa of the gross farm income which in that perio ranged between $2 and $3 billion. The d pendence on export outlets for these majo products was such that a weakening of price abroad would, of course, have lowered price in this country, thus reducing the prices o products consumed in this country as well a of those sent abroad.

This dilemma was avoided by the circum stances of the time. The United States was user of large amounts of foreign capital, pa ticularly in building its railroads and fa

13. Many farmers of the Northwest retained the allegiance to the Republican party, less on econom grounds than on emotion and tradition. The Democra were regarded as the "secessionist" party. The antip thy of the North to slavery and secession had bee built up to an intense degree during the war, and th farmers of the West were not disposed to join force with the party considered mainly responsible for brin ing on the war, even though a more sober view mig have revealed a considerable parallelism in their interes and those of the South.

tories. The creditors were, in the main, the United Kingdom, France, Germany and the Netherlands. Much of the balance of exports over imports could, therefore, be used for payment of interest, and retirement of principal, on international capital transfers of this kind.

For the most part, the products of American farms were highly acceptable to the more industrialized countries of Europe. In a sense it may be said, therefore, that American farmers, from the standpoint of market outlets for their products, escaped the full impact of the unbalanced foreign trade which resulted in part from a high level of tariffs. On the buying side they were at the mercy of American manufacturers in a market that was peculiarly favorable to the manufacturers.

Re-emergence of the Tariff Problem

During the first half of the decade of the 1860's, the struggle for preservation of the Union overshadowed all other issues, and farmers as well as other groups gave little thought to the tariff problem. After the close of the war, they were far more interested in acquiring new lands, in getting railroads built and in reaching quick solutions to their problems via the greenback route than in arguing about tariffs. Industrialists had little to complain about. In these years demand was good and business was expanding. The tariff had not, in fact, been a dominant issue since the early 1830's. American industry was fast becoming more adequate as a supplier of home needs, and the growing volume of farm product exports gave little excuse for farmers to look to protective tariffs as a solution for the kinds of problems that concerned them. Antiprotectionist sentiment began to appear in the latter part of the 1860's but did not become strong enough to have much influence on legislation.

After 1870 the sentiment for tariff reform grew rapidly, especially in the West. An act had been passed in 1870 that made a few minor reductions, chiefly on revenue items such as coffee and tea, but no real attempt was made to meet the demands of the groups advocating reductions in the high wartime tariffs.

The Republican party, continuously in power from 1861 to 1875, showed little interest in tariff reform or, in fact, in constructive reforms of any kind. The election of Grant in 1868 brought into power the most corrupt government in the nation's history. By 1872 the opposition to the President was so widespread that a Liberal Republican organization came into being. It joined with the Democrats and the two together might have unseated Grant had they been able to agree on a suitable and able candidate. As it turned out, they accepted Horace Greeley, a candidate for whom neither group had any marked enthusiasm. The abler and better qualified candidates had been eliminated one by one as a result of internal conflicts in the heterogeneous group which was in agreement on only one thing, its opposition to Grant. Grant carried all but six states, but with a popular plurality of only about 200,000. Even this small margin was heavily dependent upon the Negro vote, plus widespread disfranchisement of southern whites.

Temporary Tariff Reduction: 1872 to 1875

By 1872, an election year, the tariff revolt in the western states had grown to an extent that the party in power was forced to take account of it. This resulted in the introduction of a bill in the House of Representatives, the stated purpose of which was "to divest some industries of the superabundant protection which smells of monopoly and which it was never intended they should enjoy after the war."[14] The Dawes bill, the one finally passed, provided a 10 per cent blanket reduction in tariffs.[15] Even this modest adjustment was opposed by the protected interests, but

14. Introduced by Representative Burchard of Illinois.
15. For a more intimate account of the way in which the blanket reduction came to be substituted for the more carefully drawn bill previously under consideration, see George F. Hoar, *Autobiography of Seventy Years,* Charles Scribner's Sons, New York, 1903, Vol. I, pp. 202–03; Edward Stanwood, *American Tariff Controversies in the Nineteenth Century,* pp. 178 ff.; and Taussig, *Tariff History of the United States,* pp. 182 ff.

when it became apparent that the alternative might be a more drastic reduction even John L. Hayes, Secretary of the Wool Manufacturers' Association, supported the 10 per cent reduction.

The duties were removed entirely from coffee and tea, these being purely revenue tariffs; and hides and jute were added to the free list. The 10 per cent horizontal reduction was primarily on manufactured goods. Both free traders and protectionists considered the act a victory for their respective groups. As later events showed, the protectionists were right. The 10 per cent reduction was repealed in the Act of 1875, thus nullifying in a very simple and easy way the change made in 1872. At the same time a 25 per cent increase was made in the duties on molasses and sugar. This restored the duties that had been in effect before 1872.

The repeal of 1875 did not attract widespread attention, but was vigorously opposed in both the House and the Senate. The final vote in the House was 123 to 114 and in the Senate 30 to 29. Except for very skillful political maneuvering the bill would have been lost in both houses. Some writers undertake, not too convincingly, to make a case for the protectionist position, but it seems evident in retrospect that the Act of 1872 was in the main a political maneuver designed to get the party safely past a critical election.[16]

The repeal act was entitled "An Act to further protect the sinking fund and to provide for the exigencies of government." Actually, it was a protective measure, not a revenue measure. Tariffs for revenue are relatively low, and designed to permit importation, thus providing customs income to the government. Protective tariffs are relatively high, and are designed to check or prevent imports. Hence they do not ordinarily provide much revenue even though rates are substantially higher than are the so-called "revenue tariff" rates. The fact that tariffs were not reimposed on coffee and tea, which

are natural sources of income from duties on imports, affords clear evidence that the purpose was not mainly the increase of revenue though the argument was presented in those terms. Treasury receipts were unquestionably below expectations, but the act passed was in no way likely to solve the problem, especially in a period of depression when imports were already tending to drop below their normal trend of increase.

Tariff Issue Less Prominent After 1875

For some years after 1875 the tariff did not occupy a prominent place in public discussions. Farmers saw little advantage to themselves from higher tariffs on the products they used. Their interest was strongly centered on the reduction of freight and passenger rates and on monetary issues. By 1876 the scandals and ineptitude of the Grant administration had become so notorious that there seemed little prospect of a Republican victory at the polls. The public reaction to this situation and the bitterness of the campaign tended to minimize discussion of specific issues such as the tariff. The country was groping its way out of one of the most serious depressions in its history. Exports were still rising, but not at so fast a rate as in the previous decade. Imports had fallen off from $642 million in 1873 to $437 million in 1878. This, except for the war years, was the only period up to then in which either exports or imports had failed to show an increase.

The Democrats, especially those from the South, still favored lower tariffs. They came close to gaining control, but lost out by the narrowest of margins. In the election of 1870, even more than in that of 1872, the Republicans seemed certain to be defeated. Scandal after scandal in official circles had come to public attention. The Congress had voted itself a 50 per cent increase in salaries, and then had made the increase retroactive for two years. It had doubled the salary of the President, in spite of an ever-increasing array of evidence of corruption, ineptitude and fraud in government circles. The Republicans

16. For an opposite view see that presented in Stanwood's *American Tariff Controversies in the Nineteenth Century,* Vol. II, pp. 184-85.

nominated Rutherford B. Hayes of Ohio, while the Democrats chose a reformer, Samuel J. Tilden of New York.

In a very confused election Tilden obtained a popular majority of 250,000 votes and appeared to have been elected, but the results in South Carolina, Florida, Louisiana and Oregon were in doubt, thus leaving Tilden one electoral vote short of the number necessary for election. Two sets of returns were sent in from each of these states, and the decision went to a bipartisan commission of fifteen senators, representatives and Supreme Court justices. On strictly party votes of 8 to 7 the commission awarded all four states to Hayes and he was declared elected. Thus the Republicans managed to retain a precarious hold on the executive branch of the government.

The Tariff in the Election of 1880

In the election of 1880 three Civil War generals were nominated—James A. Garfield of Ohio by the Republicans, Winfield Scott Hancock of Pennsylvania by the Democrats, and James B. Weaver of Iowa by the Greenbackers. There was little public interest in the tariff at the beginning of the campaign. Hancock dismissed it as "a local affair," a remark that caused general amusement but was not far from the truth. The nation had no clear policy on tariff matters. The individual items and rates were in the main a result of the demands of specific local groups.

The Democratic platform, written by Colonel Henry Watterson of Kentucky, called for a "tariff for revenue only," but there is doubt whether the party seriously intended to take action looking in that direction. The stand adopted did, however, arouse the Republicans to vigorous support of the protective system. The Republican platform, in terms similar to those used in 1876, stated that "the duties levied for the purpose of revenue should so discriminate as to favor American labor." This new note of protection to American labor had not been prominent in the earlier discussions of the tariff. The America of the early 1800's was traditionally short of labor. Now, almost for the first time, industrial unemployment had become an important problem, and the labor vote was a thing to be reckoned with. The protectionists argued that a reduction of tariffs would add to unemployment and reduce wages. These arguments became a powerful weapon in the hands of the protectionists and, as in later decades, tended to hold the support of labor groups for relatively high tariffs.

The election left the Republicans in control of the presidency and they managed to secure control of the Congress, though both the Senate and the House were almost evenly divided.[17] The responsibility for leadership of the tariff issue rested, therefore with the Republican administration. Little was done about it except to set up a Tariff Commission composed of persons who were not members of the Congress. Nevertheless opposition to the unreasonably high rates was gaining strength. David A. Wells began, in 1875, the publication of a series of articles in the *Atlantic Monthly* in which he advocated lower tariffs. William Graham Sumner, a Yale professor, began to preach the doctrine of "the forgotten man" (the ordinary citizen whose pockets are picked by the tariff) and Frank W. Taussig of Harvard soon rivaled Sumner as an expounder of this point of view.

Attempts to Revise Tariffs, 1880's

By 1882 the national revenue had again become redundant and the need for revision of the tariff was rather generally accepted.[18] The government was collecting about $100 million per year more than the Congress could find ways to spend. Much of this revenue came from tariffs. President Arthur after attempting to induce more suitable men to serve, finally appointed to the newly created Tariff Commission John L. Hayes, Secretary of the National Association of Wool

17. The popular vote of the two leading candidates was so close as to be almost a tie. Garfield's plurality over Hancock was only about 9,000 in an election in which more than 9,000,000 votes were cast.
18. Revenues had also been in excess of needs in 1870–1872.

Manufacturers, as chairman, and eight others, all avowed protectionists. Hicks states that four of the nine members had a direct financial interest in protection.[19] Even though constituted in this way, the Commission brought in a report recommending reductions in tariff that would have brought down the general levels by about 20 per cent.

Neither party had a clear policy. Both contained advocates of extreme protection and likewise advocates of tariff reform. The Republican-controlled Congress, now to be replaced by one consisting of a Democratic House and a Republican Senate, sought to push through in the short session an act reducing the general level of tariffs. Both houses worked on it concurrently. The act finally passed has been referred to by Ida M. Tarbell as the "Mongrel Tariff" (1883). Actually it made little reduction in the prevailing levels of duties.[20] At the same time, however, substantial reductions were made in internal taxes so the net effect was, in many cases, an increase in the protection afforded to manufacturers.

The rates finally accepted were considerably higher than those in the bill previously passed by the Senate, and in some cases higher than those that had been accepted by the House before the two bills went to conference. Final passage in the Senate was on a strict party vote of 32 to 31. Senator Sherman stated that the action of the conference committee "restored nearly all the inequalities and incongruities of the old tariff, and yielded to local demands and local interests to an extent that destroyed all symmetry and harmony." Lobbyists representing the leading tariff-protected industries had been extremely active in Washington while the bill was under consideration. This together with a considerable amount of log-rolling was the principal reason for the failure to make constructive changes. The stated purpose of adjusting tariffs in terms of their effects on government

finances had very little to do with the final outcome.[21]

In 1884 a bill was introduced by Morrison of Illinois which called for a general horizontal reduction of 20 per cent in tariff rates. This, however, was lost in the House, with 41 Democrats joining the Republicans in voting against it. Had it reached the Senate it would have been killed there.

Cleveland Urges Reduction of Tariff

In the campaign of 1884, Cleveland versus Blaine, the tariff was not a major issue.[22] It was evident that the Democrats were drifting more and more toward a low-tariff position and the Republicans toward a consistent advocacy of high tariffs. The issue was not clearly drawn as a party issue, however, until Cleveland brought it sharply into focus by devoting his third annual message to Congress (December 6, 1887) exclusively to this problem. Cleveland knew that he could not get legislation to lower the level of duties then in effect. He wanted, however, to put his party definitely on record in favor of lower tariffs, partly as preparation for the elections of 1888. His action may have had the effect of strengthening protectionist sentiment in the Republican party. It is thought by Taussig to have been a major influence in bringing about passage of the McKinley Tariff of 1890.[23]

In 1888 the Democratic House passed the Mills bill reducing the general level of tariffs from about 47 per cent to about 40 per cent (Hicks), and the Republican Senate passed the Allison bill maintaining a generally high level of duties. Neither house was willing

19. For fuller discussion, see John D. Hicks, *The American Nation*, Houghton Mifflin, Boston, 1941, pp. 197-200.

20. Taussig, *Tariff History of the United States*, p. 250.

21. For fuller discussion of the controversies and events relating to the Act of 1883 see Hicks, *The American Nation*, pp. 198-200, and Taussig, *Tariff History of the United States*, Chapter 4.

22. The campaign of 1884 is interestingly described in Hicks, *The American Nation*, pp. 200-05. The election was marked by an important defection of progressive Republicans from the party's standard-bearer. These men, including such personalities as Carl Schurz, George William Curtis, Henry Ward Beecher, Charles W. Eliot, Theodore Roosevelt, and Henry Cabot Lodge, accepted the nickname "Mugwumps" and virtually forced the nomination of Cleveland whom they then supported wholeheartedly.

23. Taussig, *Tariff History of the United States*, p. 256.

to accept the other's bill and no compromise was acceptable, so neither bill was passed.

Both parties appeared to have an eye on the coming election. The House committee framed its bill in secret, to avoid pressure from lobbyists, while the Senate committee held open hearings to which all lobbyists were invited. The victory of Harrison over Cleveland in 1888 was considered a mandate from the people to proceed with a strongly protective policy. Actually, the results did not bear out this claim. Cleveland had a popular majority of some 100,000 votes, though Harrison's electoral vote was larger. The Republicans had discovered, however, that the tariff issue made an excellent means of prying large campaign contributions out of protected industries. They collected and expended money in the campaign in amounts and in ways that became an open scandal and gave impetus to demands for election reform. Both houses became Republican but only by a slender margin.

The McKinley Tariff of 1890

With definite control of the executive and both houses of the Congress for the first time since 1875, the Republicans proceeded to push through a new and major tariff act, the McKinley Tariff of 1890. This provided the highest protection yet afforded by any tariff established by the United States (general level about 49.5 per cent). It also brought back the minimum valuation feature of the Act of 1828. Highest duties were on manufactured goods, and some even gave protection to non-existent industries such as tin plate, if responsible persons could demonstrate that they intended to begin manufacture of these products. Nevertheless, the act was entitled "An Act to reduce the revenue, to equalize duties on imports, and for other purposes." Revenues still were redundant, and Cleveland had already pointed out, in 1887, that there were serious dangers in the government's continuing to take more money out of circulation than it put back in, thus appreciating the dollar and forcing prices down. Under the new act some of the duties were intentionally placed so high as to be prohibitive, thus automatically contracting customs receipts.

Provisions of the Act of 1890

The Act of 1890 represented a new departure in several respects. Politically it was consciously designed to bring the farmers of the West into a closer tie with the Republican party. In this it was largely successful. Many of the western farmers were shortly to part company with the Republicans on monetary issues, but the support of protective tariffs was to become a settled policy with them — one in which few major changes occurred for some forty years thereafter. The new act, for the first time, provided a complete schedule of protective duties on farm products. The rates on meats were doubled; the tariff on barley was raised from 10 cents to 30 cents, largely as a protection against Canadian barley; wheat was raised from 20 cents to 25 cents; eggs were removed from the free list and given a tariff of 5 cents a dozen; corn was raised from 10 cents to 15 cents; potatoes from 15 cents to 25 cents; and butter from 4 cents to 6 cents. Many other changes of similar kind were made.

Here for the first time appears a faint hint of the principle which was later developed in the bargaining provisions of the Trade Agreements Act of 1934. The President was given authority to impose by proclamation certain duties on sugar (one half cent per pound), molasses (4 cents per gallon), tea (10 cents per pound), coffee (3 cents per pound) and hides (1½ cents per pound) if he considered that any country exporting these commodities to the United States "imposes duties or other exactions on the agricultural or other products of the United States, which, in view of the free introduction of sugar, molasses, tea, coffee and hides into the United States, he may deem to be unjust or unreasonable."

Also the act provided a forerunner to the principle of the Jones-Costigan Act of 1934 in providing a bounty of 2 cents per pound to domestic sugar producers as an offset for the admission of raw sugar duty-free.[24] To protect American sugar refiners, a duty of one half cent per pound on refined sugar was levied.

The increased duties on farm products did not and could not have much effect on their prices, except perhaps in a minor way for those near the Canadian border. However, as a political measure the act accomplished its purpose. The farmers were taken into the partnership and became as staunch advocates of protection as the eastern industrialists who were the real beneficiaries. Not until the 1920's did the farmers of the Middle West become generally aware of the fact that protective tariffs were of little value to them. They then undertook a program looking to "making the tariff effective for agriculture" rather than one of reducing tariffs on manufactured goods.

Political Effects of the McKinley Tariff

The McKinley Act did reduce revenue — a fact that was to prove embarrassing shortly after its passage. This came about through the fact that the high duties discouraged imports, but more especially through placing raw sugar, a natural revenue producer, on the free list, and providing bounties from the federal treasury.

The act was unpopular almost from the beginning. Large Democratic majorities were returned in the election of November 1890, thus bringing in a Democratic House though the Senate remained Republican. The working of the law was satisfactory, however, to those who were instrumental in passing it, except that it proved inadequate as a revenue measure. By 1893 the troublesome surplus had become a $70 million deficit.

In the election of 1892 the tariff was a decisive factor. The Democrats exploited the situation skillfully, and put on an "educational campaign." They advocated "free" wool to attract the wage earners, "free" cot-

ton ties to appeal to the South, "free" binder twine to appeal to the grain-growing states and "free" tin plate to appeal to the fruit-growing areas. The Democrats carried the election and returned Grover Cleveland to the presidency. For the first time since 1861 the Democrats controlled the executive branch and both houses of Congress.

The advantage of this victory was largely destroyed in respect to tariff reform by circumstances over which Cleveland had no control. Not only had the McKinley tariff resulted in a reduction of approximately $100 million in revenue, but the bounties to sugar producers had added a heavy drain on the Treasury. Still more serious was the cost of the extravagant pension measures passed during the Harrison administration and the burden on gold reserves resulting from the operation of the Sherman Silver Purchase Act. Silver could be exchanged for gold, and, since it was constantly being presented at the Treasury, the Treasury's gold reserves dwindled rapidly.

To meet the crisis in respect to the gold reserve, Cleveland was forced to break with the "Silver Senators" and congressmen of the West. The result was a serious split in the Democratic party which rendered the President impotent to push through a genuine tariff reform despite the fact that this had been the party's major campaign pledge.

The Wilson Act of 1894

William L. Wilson of West Virginia, as chairman of the Ways and Means Committee, introduced a measure, patterned after the Mills bill of 1888, which was substantially in accord with the Cleveland policy. It placed many of the raw materials on the free list, reduced the tariffs on manufactured goods and abolished the sugar bounties. It also provided a 2 per cent tax on incomes in excess of $4,000.

The bill was wrecked, mainly in the Senate, through the connivance of various Democrats, particularly the "sugar" senators from Louisiana and Senator Gorman of Maryland,

24. Only about one eighth of the United States sugar consumption was being produced domestically at that time. The bounty was intended to save these growers from ruin.

co-sponsor of the bill.[25] The Republicans, with the aid of these dissident Democrats, succeeded in attaching 633 amendments to the bill. It was a typical product of the log-rolling tactics which had become standard practice in tariff making. The schedule of duties set up, though somewhat lower than that of the McKinley tariff, was about at the level of the Act of 1888. The House reluctantly accepted the Senate amendments, but Cleveland refused to sign, letting the act become law without his signature. In a letter to Wilson he referred to it as "an act of party perfidy." The act went into effect in the worst stage of the depression, and thus came to be associated with the depression in the minds of many people. The Democrats were badly defeated in 1894.

The Dingley Tariff of 1897

In the elections of 1896 the Republicans again came into full control of the government. The bitterly contested campaign was fought out mainly on the monetary issue, with William Jennings Bryan giving eloquent leadership to the free-silver advocates, and William McKinley serving as standard-bearer for the ultraconservative industrial and banking groups which were fighting to retain the gold standard.

It was natural, however, that the new Republican administration headed by the principal author of the tariff act of 1890 should undertake immediately a revision of the tariff. The result was the Dingley tariff, passed in July 1897, less than five months after the new administration took over. This was the last tariff act of the nineteenth century and remained in effect until 1909. In it the general level of duties was raised to 57 per cent (Faulkner), a level higher than that of any previous tariff in the nation's history. Since the western "Silver Senators" held the balance of power, various concessions to them were made. They were wool senators as well as silver senators and some of them represented states that were interested in the pro-

duction of sugar beets, though that industry as a whole was still small.

Duties were reimposed on imports of wool and hides, which had been on the free list (wool: 11 cents a pound on clothing wool and 12 cents on combing wool as in the Act of 1890; 15 per cent on hides, as desired by the western representatives). Compensating duties on woolen cloth were provided.

Among other features the act included the reciprocity provisions of the Act of 1890. On all tariff-bearing articles the President might negotiate treaties with foreign nations to scale down the American rates as much as 20 per cent. Under this authority eleven treaties were negotiated, but all were rejected by the Senate.[26] The act also included some rates that could be lowered by presidential proclamation. This was done in a few instances, mainly with respect to products of the soil.

Effects of the Dingley Tariff

The specific effects of tariff changes are difficult to determine in any accurate way. Many other influences are at work as well as those stemming from the tariff. It seems clear, however, that many of the rates provided in the Dingley tariff were so high as to discourage imports. During the first year that the new rates were in effect the total revenue collected from tariffs fell off by some $25 million despite the fact that recovery from the depths of depression was well under way by that time. Though nearly all historians and economists agree that the act was bad, and written in the interest mainly of the powerful business interests that were then so influential in legislative affairs, it did not arouse widespread popular opposition. The public interest of the time centered successively upon the silver issue, the Spanish-American War and the growing imperialism. The country

---

25. The Senate opposition was led by Gorman and by Brice of Ohio, both Democrats.

26. This principle, commonly attributed to the Franklin D. Roosevelt administration, as a result of the Trade Agreements Act of 1934, was really a feature of the two major tariff acts passed under administrations that were among the most strongly protectionist in sentiment of any in the nation's history. What the Act of 1934 did was to make possible the negotiation of such agreements without the necessity for Senate confirmation. Thus it became possible to use the mechanism in actual tariff bargaining with other nations.

was recovering from the worst stages of the depression and entering a long period of relative prosperity and rising prices. The tariff did not again become a major issue until 1909.

Farmers' Role in Tariff Struggles

Farmers were active and keenly interested participants in nearly all of the tariff controversies of the nineteenth century, but seldom were they united either in support of or opposition to protective tariffs. The positions taken reflected sectional differences in attitude and economic interest rather than a division between farm and nonfarm groups.

Almost from the first the agricultural South took a strong stand on the tariff issue. It opposed protective duties in every period except that which followed the War of 1812. Except for the defense of slavery and of states rights, this opposition to tariffs became the most persistent and vigorous feature of the policy of the southern states. It was mainly a policy of and for the agricultural groups, which were the dominant ones in that section of the country.

The South's advantages over almost every competing region of the world in the production of cotton and tobacco gave it every incentive to become both a monoculture and a heavy exporter. Thus its economic interest lay in fostering international trade, not in stifling it. Furthermore, its growing antagonism to the North over the slavery issue caused it to become more and more opposed to the protective tariffs desired by the industrial groups of the North and Northeast.

The southern states did not achieve sufficient political strength to force adoption of their views on tariffs. However, they did exert a significant moderating influence, especially between 1790 and 1860. It was the agricultural South and the tariff issue that brought the first major threat to the Union, and that checked the drift toward autarchic trade policies in the early part of the nineteenth century.

As the West developed, its farmers took a different view of tariffs and, in the early years, tended to favor a protectionist and nationalistic policy. Their exports were small, and the prices of goods bought by them were affected far more by high costs of transportation than by tariffs. Later, as the West became a heavy exporter of farm products the farmers of that area became more critical of high, protective duties on manufactured goods, but did not become active advocates of freer trade. Other issues bulked larger in their thinking and became the principal features of their political programs. By then, too, the industrial interests which were the chief beneficiaries of protective tariffs had become too strongly entrenched to be easily dislodged from their dominant position.

The flow of foreign capital to the United States and the rapid industrialization of Europe enabled farmers to continue their heavy exports without suffering serious handicap from the lack of balance between exports and imports. As a consequence, effective farmer agitation for lower tariffs did not appear.

The latter part of the century brought a crystallization of sentiment in favor of protective tariffs in which the western farmers joined forces with the industrialists. Wheat, hogs, cotton, tobacco and many other farm products still were being exported in large quantities, and the time had not come when any important segment of agriculture could benefit from protective tariffs. Nevertheless, the belief that the welfare of farmers and that of the country depended on such protection had been skillfully fostered, and there was little organized farmer opposition to it except in the South.

As the new century developed, farmers became even more strongly protectionist and, in fact, became the leading exponents of protectionist policy. The livestock and dairy groups and some of the organizations representing the growers of specialty crops have continued to hold these views. Some writers contend that they now constitute the hard core of protectionist sentiment in the United States. Farmer interest in the tariff issue has grown as some of the older issues, such as railroad rate regulation and the greenback and free-silver controversies, have receded into the background.

CHAPTER 4

ROADS, CANALS AND RAILROADS

THE RISE AND DECLINE OF FEDERAL PARTICIPATION

WHILE THE NATION'S money system was being put in order and the initial policy on tariffs adopted, another issue even closer to the hearts of the frontier farmers was taking shape. This was the question of internal improvements, that is, of highways for moving farm products to the eastern seaboard.

The need for interstate highways was evident, but the means of providing them was less clear. The possible ways of developing roads and waterways were through private investment, state action or federal undertakings. The heavy investments needed, and the long periods necessary for recouping the expenditures through tolls, did not make large-scale ventures in this realm attractive to investors. There were, however, many lesser toll roads and a good many toll bridges.

The Question of Constitutionality

Most of the states lacked revenues for extensive highway development. They could not build coordinated interstate roads except through cumbersome agreements with each other which most of them found unattractive. The federal government lacked clear constitutional authority to undertake highway building, and many of the states, already jealous of the growing power of the federal government, were opposed to federal control of highways within their jurisdictions. Furthermore, funds were by no means plentiful in the federal treasury.

Madison proposed, apparently in 1796, that a surplus of post office revenues be used for building post roads. Jefferson wrote Madison, in March of 1796, that he did not favor the idea, that in his opinion it would be "a source of boundless patronage to the executive, jobbing to members of Congress and

their friends, and a bottomless abyss of public money." He also raised the question whether the constitutional power to "establish" post roads was specific enough. A constitutional amendment might be necessary. Hamilton, in a memorandum to Representative Drayton, expressed the view that an amendment to the Constitution would be necessary to authorize the general government to open canals through the territory of two or more states. He also said, however, that such an amendment would be advisable, partly because the making of these improvements by the federal government would be "a useful source of influence."[1]

The Ohio Act of 1802

Gallatin wrote in 1802 to Giles, a member of Congress, recommending that one tenth of the net proceeds of lands sold in Ohio be used in laying out turnpikes or other roads. These were to run first from the navigable waters emptying into the Atlantic to the Ohio, and then on through the new state. Such roads were to be laid out under the authority of Congress with the consent of the states through which they would pass. Gallatin's ideas were adopted in the act admitting Ohio, except that the amounts assigned for road building were set at one twentieth of the receipts rather than one tenth.

This was the first act of major significance in the federal government's program of internal improvements.[2] In accordance with this plan an act of March 29, 1806, au-

1. This memorandum, found in Van Buren's papers, is undated and may or may not be authentic.
2. The federal government had earlier participated in a minor way in what came to be known as internal improvements. In 1796 a grant of land was made to Ebenezer Zane to aid in the construction of a road from Wheeling, Virginia, to Maysville, Kentucky. See William MacDonald, *Jacksonian Democracy, 1829–1837,* American Nation Series, Vol. XV, Harper and Brothers, New York, 1906, p. 134.

thorized survey of the Cumberland Road from Cumberland, Maryland, to the Ohio. The road was to be four rods wide, a standard later used in laying out the majority of section-line highways over the country. Consent of the states traversed was to be obtained before starting construction.

The Gallatin and Jefferson Plan

Gallatin, with the collaboration of Jefferson, put forward in 1808 the first comprehensive plan for a national system of highways and canals — a plan that was extremely ambitious for its time. This proposed four major developments: (1) a canal system paralleling the seacoast together with a great turnpike road from Maine to Georgia; (2) improvement of the rivers flowing eastward or westward, with four roads across the Appalachians to connect them; (3) highways to run north and northwest connecting the Hudson River with Lake Champlain and Lake Ontario, including a canal around Niagara Falls; and (4) the improvement of local highways related to these. Thus the plan was designed to combine and satisfy nearly all parts of the country.

When Jefferson mentioned this idea favorably in his message of 1806, it had been in preparation for a year or more. It was thought the plan could be carried out in ten years by appropriations of $2 million a year and that by selling to private parties the stock thus created the fund could be made into a permanent resource for further improvements. At the time it was first proposed there was expectation of a $5 million-a-year surplus of federal funds. However, by the time the plan appeared in developed form the clouds of war had gathered on the horizon, the embargo and nonintercourse acts had reduced federal revenues and the climate was not favorable for large new undertakings of this kind.

The Erie Canal and the Cumberland Road

The year 1811 is significant because of two major efforts to connect the western states with the eastern seaboard. In that year the

Cumberland Road was begun. Permission for its construction had been given by Maryland in 1806 (on condition that it touch Washington), and by Pennsylvania in 1807 (on condition that it touch Uniontown). In 1824, Ohio expressed approval of its westward extension.

Also in 1811, New York began to agitate for a canal connecting the Great Lakes with the Hudson River. A commission headed by Gouverneur Morris, and with DeWitt Clinton as one of its members, sought federal aid for the project. Madison, in a letter to Congress dated December 24, 1811, pointed out the national significance of the canal, called attention to the signal advantages to the United States from a general system of internal "communication and conveyance," and stated that it would "have an intimate connexion with arrangements for the general security . . ." However, in the troubled times of that period no action was taken by the Congress, and New York shortly undertook the building of the canal as a state project, completing it in 1825. Through its influence New York City became shortly the nation's leading port and commercial center.

The Cumberland Road was completed to Wheeling, Virginia, in 1818 and mail coaches were running between Washington and Wheeling by the end of that year. There was a flood of traffic over the new highway almost as soon as it was completed, and the problem of upkeep soon presented itself, thus raising a question which was to be widely discussed for many years. The Cumberland Road, with its later westward extension known as the National Road, was the only major highway directly constructed by the federal government.

Other Proposals for Internal Improvements

During 1816 and 1817 the matter of internal improvements again came under active discussion. Calhoun proposed that the bonus derived from the second Bank of the United States and the annual proceeds from the government-owned stock in the Bank be set aside as a permanent fund for internal improvements. Clay, as Speaker of the House, supported Calhoun's proposals, and in the debates came forward with this as a part of his "American system," a coordinated plan consisting of internal improvements, a high protective tariff, a national bank and a more satisfactory system for disposal of the public lands. John Randolph also supported the plan, on condition that the southern states would get their share. In general, however, the South opposed it as likely to lead to excessive exercise of power by the federal government. New England disliked it as another "western scheme." The West very naturally supported it.

The bill passed on March 1, 1817, but was reluctantly vetoed by Madison on March 3, a day before his retirement from office. Though favorable to internal improvements, Madison wrote, "I am constrained by the insuperable difficulty I feel in reconciling the bill with the Constitution of the United States . . ." The power to take such action was not one of those enumerated in the Constitution, and Madison, as a strict constructionist, could not bring himself to sign the bill despite the fact that during the two years preceding this time he had been recommending that the Congress consider the problem. His suggestions had not been acted upon because of lack of funds.

In Monroe's first annual message, December 2, 1817, he stated definitely that he did not believe the Congress had the right to establish a system of improvements (roads and canals). He therefore recommended a constitutional amendment to give it the necessary authority. In the debates which followed, a House resolution was presented declaring that the Congress had the power to appropriate money for the construction of military and other roads, for the building of canals, and for the improvement of water courses.

Debate turned on the word "establish" in the Constitution as against the word "construct," which did not appear. The proponents, feeling they did not have a large enough vote to override a veto, and unwilling to hazard the rights they claimed to possess by appealing to the states for a constitutional amendment, were at an impasse. Eventually, the House decided against the federal government's power to construct post roads and military roads, against the power to construct roads and canals necessary to commerce, and against the power to construct canals for military purposes. A basic issue was, of course, the implication of federal authority over property lying within a state.

Growing Interest in Internal Improvements

Sentiment for federal action on internal improvements grew by leaps and bounds as the need for highways became more acute. This was the issue that lay closest to the hearts of the western settlers, and they were aggressively reaching for the seats of power. Clay, a vigorous advocate of internal improvements, was already well entrenched as Speaker of the House, and the era of Jackson was just around the corner.

Calhoun presented a report in 1819 outlining a comprehensive system of roads and canals. He was then Secretary of War, and based his argument mainly on the authority of the government under its military powers. He maintained, however, that if roads and canals were constructed for commerce and transport of mails, they would at the same time serve for the most efficient defense of the United States. In this way he hoped to get around the constitutional issue.

In May 1820, an act was passed to provide $10,000 for laying out a road from Wheeling to the Mississippi, but action was delayed because of a depleted treasury. In 1822 a bill was passed to provide for repairs on the Cumberland Road. It envisioned toll gates and provided fines for violation of the laws of the road, a feature which meant active projection of federal administration into the states concerned. Monroe vetoed the act on the ground of constitutionality, but hinted that the federal government might promote internal improvements by appropriating funds without assuming jurisdiction over the highways when built. Clay believed the power to execute a complete highway system already existed, and there were implications of this view in some of Marshall's decisions. The Congress took the hint dropped by Monroe, and passed in February 1823 an act which appropriated funds for repairs to the Cumberland Road.[3]

Two years of pondering, some recognition of federal participation in internal improvements as an accomplished fact and the vigor of the drive for internal improvements brought Monroe to a point where he finally was willing to approve the Survey Act of 1824. This authorized the War Department to undertake a large-scale program of surveys for such roads and canals as the President deemed of national importance. The evident intention was to prepare for a program of appropriations and for subscription by the government to the stock of companies engaged in these enterprises.

Clay tried to commit Congress to the exercise of the power to construct interstate highways and canals which could not be undertaken by the states, but John Randolph opposed it, saying, "If the Congress can do that, it can emancipate the slaves." Van Buren, already functioning as the "fixer" in difficult situations, offered a resolution denying the Congress power to build roads and canals within the respective states and proposing a constitutional amendment granting the power with limitations. The Senate, however, declined to act on it. Nevertheless, an appropriation of $150,000 in 1825 made possible a start on a westward extension of the Cumberland Road to Zanesville, Ohio.

Adams' Plan for a System of Highways

John Quincy Adams took over the reins of

government in 1825 with visions of constructing a great system of roads and canals irrespective of local interests. These were to be for the nation as a whole. He hoped that the increased prices of federal lands resulting from the improvements would furnish a large and steadily increasing fund for turnpikes and canals. He shared Clay's views on the "American system," and expressed them in successive annual messages.

By the middle of Adams' administration the popularity of the internal improvements program was so great that the movement seemed irresistible, though the South was still opposed. But the American people were not anxious for a considered and nationally oriented system either for internal improvements or for the disposition of public lands. The pork barrel had been rolled out and every section was eager to be at it. Appropriations for internal improvements during Adams' administration were more than double all previous ones combined. Subscriptions to stock in improvement companies by the United States between 1825 and 1828 included the Chesapeake and Delaware Canal Company (1825), the Louisville and Portland Canal Company (1826), the Dismal Swamp Canal Company (1826) and the Chesapeake and Ohio Canal Company (1828). In addition, there were grants to Illinois and Ohio for canals, and of land to Alabama to aid in improving navigation of the Tennessee River.[4]

In the rivalry between the followers of Jackson and Adams for western support each

---

3. By March 1823 sentiment for internal improvements had so far progressed that the first of the long procession of "pork-barrel" bills could be passed—an act appropriating money to improve navigation on the Ohio and Mississippi rivers. Clay, at the height of his power, made his classic speech on the "American system" on March 30, 1824. Here he advocated the protective tariff and the home market. Later he connected the tariff with internal improvements. He asked both the East and the West to support his program. The West was back of it, the East growing more friendly, but the South remained adamant against the protective tariff, and made the Clay program a failure as a political solution.

4. According to a letter from the Secretary of the Treasury, dated December 20, 1830 (H.Doc. 11, 21st Cong., 2nd sess.), the total disbursements for internal improvements between 1789 and 1830 amounted to $5,310,930.11. The money had been apportioned as follows:

Old North (including Maryland and Delaware)	$ 567,543.65
Old South	37,434.68
Old Northwest and Michigan Territory	671,056.37
New South (including Arkansas and Missouri)	224,704.40
Florida	102,955.16
Cumberland Road	2,443,420.20
Federal subscriptions to canals	1,083,500.00
Improving Mississippi and Ohio rivers	180,315.65

See Edward Channing, *A History of the United States,* Macmillan, New York, 1921, Vol. V, p. 417, footnote.

group presented its own bill donating lands for the canals of Ohio. Both bills were passed. Thus Ohio got double the amount of land originally asked for. Indiana, Illinois and other western states immediately memorialized Congress for aid with their plans for canals. Local interests and the pressure of corporations eager to receive federal subscriptions to their stock broke down the unity of Adams' system. Districts combined with one another for local favors. Rival political parties bid against each other for the support of states which asked federal aid for their roads and canals. Thus came into full flowering the logrolling practices so characteristic of the decades to follow, and thus ended the period of high statesmanship which made the early years of this nation a landmark in the political history of the world.

Jackson and Internal Improvements

Andrew Jackson's accession to the presidency in 1829 constituted a sharp change in the kind of leadership afforded by the White House. Now for the first time the pioneer West was in a dominant position and able to exert a major influence on national policy, but as yet it was not too sure what it wanted.

As a senator from Tennessee, Jackson had voted for internal improvements, in common with his frontier colleagues, but he had not yet thought through the national implications of such measures. Between 1824 and 1829, he veered toward the strict-construction view, possibly in part because of his antipathy for Adams and Clay, who were ardent supporters of internal improvements constructed at federal expense. In his first message (1829) he suggested that, since internal improvements were questioned on constitutional grounds, there might be an apportionment of surplus federal revenue among the states in accordance with their representation in the Congress.[5] If such distribution were regarded

5. This proposal was somewhat similar to the plan now used, though the funds currently assigned to this purpose can scarcely be called "surplus." Present-day provisions relate the payments to highway mileage and density of traffic, and also require establishment of satisfactory arrangements within the states for administering the funds.

as unwarranted, he proposed that a constitutional amendment be considered.

By 1830, Jackson had come to have more settled views on the matter. A bill had been passed authorizing subscription by the government of $150,000 in stock of the Maysville, Washington, Paris and Lexington Turnpike Road Co., incorporated by the legislature of Kentucky. Both Polk and Tyler opposed the bill vigorously, possibly on partisan grounds, since obviously it was a project of special interest to Clay. Jackson vetoed the bill, basing his veto partly on the ground that it was unconstitutional, but mainly on the contention that the Maysville Road was a work of local, not national, character. He favored reducing taxes and paying off the national debt before engaging in undertakings of this kind. He stated further that there should be a constitutional amendment if the people wanted the federal government to do such work.

Whatever one's view as to the merits of the bill itself, there can be little question that the veto message expresses a considered, reasonable and courageous judgment of the matter as Jackson saw it. It is neither a politician's undiscriminating acceptance of the views and wishes of his own frontier following nor undue appeasement of opposing interests. It shows Jackson still favorable to internal improvements, but feeling that where doubts exist about the constitutionality of a major policy these should be cleared up by specific decision of the people themselves, through acceptance or rejection of a constitutional amendment. It was a position that was hard for any reasonable person to quarrel with, and at the same time one that showed good political judgment. Even Calhoun had to admit the propriety of the proposal for a constitutional amendment. Clay thought the veto would strengthen the opposition, and even suggested to Webster an amendment restricting the veto power. But here, as on other occasions, history shows Jackson's judgment to have been both sounder politically and based on more fundamental concepts than Clay's.

Effects of the Maysville Road Veto

The veto of the Maysville Road project put a stop, for the time, to the development at federal expense of interstate communications by means of roads and canals.[6] It did not, however, touch the larger field of river and harbor development which has long been a prolific source of extravagance and pork-barrel politics. Its date, coinciding almost precisely with the opening of the nation's first railroad, the Baltimore and Ohio, marks the beginning of nearly a century's development of major interstate communication by private corporations in the form of railways. Not until the advent of the automobile, after 1900, does the question of federal participation in highway construction again become prominent.

Some writers of our time undoubtedly would contend that the turn taken in this period was the wrong one, and that the federal government should have proceeded to absorb the whole field of interstate communication, including the development of railroads. While it can well be argued that such a procedure could, if ideally handled, have resulted in a better system of communication than we now have, realistic appraisal of the situation raises much doubt that this would have been the outcome. Such a program would have been an open invitation to every local community to demand its pound of flesh. With the inadequate control of expenditures then existing, extravagance and corruption would have been inevitable, and it is very probable that the later development of railways would not have been so aggressive or effective as it was under private ownership.

Widespread corruption did, of course, occur in the private developments. This was later to give rise to a major problem of governmental policy. But in Jackson's time, and for many decades thereafter, mechanisms for preventing fraud and corruption were far from adequate either in government or private business. Adams' conception of an orderly and comprehensive program of improvements laid out in the national interest had been quickly tossed aside in favor of numerous undertakings of local and personal interest. This tendency would undoubtedly have grown by leaps and bounds had the federal government overcome its doubts about constitutionality and embarked wholeheartedly on an extensive program of federal development of interstate communications.

Railroad construction was often undertaken in ill-advised locations and at inappropriate times. But under political leadership the amount of useless mileage constructed might have been greater; or, with an overcautious Congress, development might have been slow and inadequate. Almost certainly the prodigious rate of progress that resulted from the growth of the railway network would not have been attained.

For realms other than transportation, private enterprise was almost universally accepted as the natural form of economic activity. The world was only a few decades removed from the time when many of the colonial governments of the world were in the hands of private corporations. Thus, to project backward to this period conclusions based on recent studies of public utility economics is to inject into Jackson's time thinking and knowledge that did not then exist. As will appear later, however, the enormous growth of monopoly power, which resulted from private development of the American railway system, was to be a matter of grave concern to farmers of later periods, and full solution of the problems resulting has not yet been achieved.

One further step in the evolution of internal improvements policy under Jackson requires mention — the Appropriation Act of June 24, 1834, providing funds for continuing

6. Though federal aid for highway and canal construction thus was virtually ended for the time being, many of the states were plunging forward in an orgy of borrowing, spending and granting of lands which was to be halted only by the increasingly serious financial involvement of the states concerned and by the growing popularity of the railroads as an alternative means of providing for internal communication. The effort to obtain federal aid was not entirely dead, however. During Tyler's and Polk's administrations measures of this kind gained sufficient support to pass the Congress, but were lost after being vetoed.

the Cumberland Road and for repairs. Under the terms of this act the states accepted sections of the road surrendered to them, and the highways thus transferred were not to be a source of further federal expense for upkeep. This policy, which had been emerging since 1825 or earlier, superseded the earlier plan of federal construction and jurisdiction. It thus became the settled national policy in respect to highway construction and maintenance.

THE GROWTH OF FARMER INTEREST IN RAILWAY TRANSPORTATION

Railroads were beginning to come into their own as a more efficient and economical means of transporting freight and passengers. Farmer interest soon was turning irrevocably to the wider possibilities of a railway network. Some construction of canals did continue even into the 1840's, but, except for a few connecting links between natural water routes, it was too expensive, the movement too slow and the possibilities for reaching various parts of the territory too meager for it to survive in competition with the rails.

This new type of transportation became an attractive field for private investment, thus lessening the need for public aid. Furthermore, the enthusiasm for commitment of public funds for business ventures was on the wane. Most of the states had borrowed heavily for road and canal construction and in some cases for the establishment of banks. Strict interpretation of the Constitution had limited federal aid mostly to grants of land, but the states plunged ahead with little discretion or knowledge of finance. State debts, which amounted to only $12,790,728 in 1820, had increased by 1835 to $66,482,186, and by 1838 to more than $170 million. Even in the depression years they continued to rise, and by 1840 amounted to more than $200 million.[7] The panic of 1837, partly brought on by this intemperate splurge of construction

and debt creation, brought much of the work to a halt. Many of the states found themselves unable to meet their obligations and several of them — Mississippi, Louisiana, Maryland, Pennsylvania, Indiana and Michigan — repudiated their debts.

Many of the projects were sold to private companies, and a number of the new state constitutions forbade the use of public credit for such purposes. Thus the responsibility for transportation development was shifted to private corporations, a policy that was to hold for the remainder of the century and still dominates our transportation activities.

Enthusiasm for Railroads

Once the practicability of railways had been demonstrated, enthusiasm for them grew and "when the railroad comes through here" came to be a prime consideration in many a farmer's plans. Construction got under way slowly. By 1850 only 9,000 miles of line had been laid down, but in the succeeding ten years more than 20,000 miles were added. The rail lines reached Chicago around 1850, and, in the succeeding decade, opened outlets for the products of the fertile soils of Illinois, Wisconsin and Iowa. As yet the lines were merely joinings of numerous short sections owned by different companies. Movement both of goods and people was slow, expensive and inconvenient, but so vastly better than the old methods that farmers welcomed the railroads with open arms, granting rights of way, purchasing stock and facilitating legislation.

Though many farmers were eager participants in these highly speculative ventures, they were not important as a source of funds for railway construction. Their capital resources were far too meager for them to make any important contribution toward the huge sums needed. Much of the capital, aside from that supplied by the federal and state governments, came from abroad or from the states of the Northeast where investment capital was becoming more abundant.

It was an age of speculative, get-rich-quick promotion, and many a farmer's dollar, often

7. Harold U. Faulkner, *American Economic History,* 6th edition, Harper and Brothers, New York, 1949, p. 282.

a borrowed one, was swallowed up, never to return. But for the most part, at this stage, the railroads were still in the hands of actual builders. The more vicious forms of fraud and manipulation were to come later. In the early stages troubles came largely from over-optimistic building with inadequate capital. Traffic could develop only after the roads were built, and in many cases the companies formed were not strong enough financially to wait out the period required for attaining a profitable volume of business.

Investing farmers often found their money gone, the company bankrupt and the property eventually sold into new hands and capitalized on a basis that made profits possible. Nevertheless, though he may have lost on the direct investment, the over-all effect was a tremendous growth in the movement of products of the land and a rapid increase in land values. Abuses in the way of stock manipulation, rate agreements, discriminatory charges and political activity were not yet general enough to dampen seriously the popular enthusiasm for railway building.

The First Transcontinental Railroad

The political and economic importance of a rail connection to the West Coast was widely recognized within a few years after the acquisition of California.[8] As early as 1853 the Congress authorized surveys to determine the most practical route. Few questioned the need for contact with the West, but there was much disagreement as to its location. The southern representatives wanted a southern route. The North naturally sought a northern route. So vigorous was the controversy that no action was taken until the withdrawal of the southern members of Congress gave the northern members a free hand. The result was the Pacific Railway Act of 1862 (amended in 1864), which authorized construction of a transcontinental line by the central route from Omaha to Sacramento and

made substantial grants for its building. The line was completed through the historic joining of the Union Pacific and the Central Pacific at Promontory Point, Utah, in May 1869.

The fascinating story of courage, ingenuity, perseverance, cupidity and corruption which brought this great project to completion lies outside the scope of our present study. Our main concern here is with the nature and significance of the governmental policies adopted and their relation to agricultural development. The view that the purchase of stock in such corporations by the government was in conflict with the Constitution was widely accepted. But the western railroad had to be built, and private capital alone was inadequate for such an undertaking. Hence alternative means were explored. Their merit is dubious, but through them the road was constructed, though at inflated cost and with an aftermath of problems that still persists in some areas.

Methods of Financing

No doubt the simplest and cheapest procedure would have been direct federal financing and construction; but this was contrary to the spirit of the times and politically impossible, and the federal treasury had no funds to spare. Here again, as in the earlier periods of canal and railroad building, it seemed logical to turn to the nation's one great resource, the public domain. The new roads ran through lands that were mostly in territorial status. Hence the problem of state-federal relationships was not a prominent factor. The solution arrived at was to grant to the companies huge acreages of the public domain, and to loan government credit in amounts varying from $16,000 per mile on the level plains to $48,000 per mile in the mountainous sections.

The credit operation was accomplished by giving to the companies government bonds secured by second mortgages on the railroad properties. More than $27 million was thus supplied to the Union Pacific and Central Pacific. In addition, the companies raised vast sums through the sale of bonds to private in-

8. There had been some earlier agitation for a transcontinental rail line to provide easier access to the Orient via the West Coast, but it had not gained sufficient strength to have serious consideration in Congress.

vestors, many of them British or German, or residents of other European countries. Common stocks normally were given away as a bonus for the purchase of bonds, and represented merely a hope of future earnings in excess of the amounts needed to service the bonds. This heavy reliance on bonds for financing, resulting as it did in high fixed charges, was to prove an embarrassment and a cause of frequent financial disaster in the years to come. The high level of bonded debt in proportion to stock capital has long been a source of financial instability of the railroads of the United States.

The other form of aid in railroad building, namely, the granting of huge acreages of the public domain, proved unwise and relatively ineffective. The need of the companies was for ready cash with which to pay workers and buy supplies. The lands granted had potential value but no current salability. They represented in the main a bonus, like the common stock, which presumably would eventually come to have value as settlement progressed and traffic developed. No doubt they made purchase of bonds more attractive, as did the gifts of common stock, but it was an expensive way to encourage bond purchase. In principle, the reasoning was that the construction of the railroads would give value to the lands and hence that the promoting companies should reap part of the profits.

To accomplish this the companies were given alternate sections of land, in a checkerboard pattern, to a distance of twenty miles on each side of the line.[9] With a view to speeding settlement and preventing speculation, the law provided that lands not sold within three years after the completion of the railroad should be subject to pre-emption and should be sold to the pre-emptors by the railroad at $1.25 per acre. Under these acts the Union Pacific obtained some twelve million acres of the public domain and the Central Pacific about ten million. Later grants to the northern and southern lines were even more extravagant.

Defects of the Plan

The federal government had no adequate machinery for supervising these or other public lands, and shady practices were common. Lands were obtained in behalf of railroads not built. The indemnity clauses gave the railroads rights to first choice on lands many miles from their lines, thus giving them great advantages over the settlers. Railway officials, by grants of special favors, were enabled to build huge fortunes through speculation in lands and townsites, and through private construction companies taking contracts from the railroad companies, of which they were officers.

Settler opposition grew in volume and bitterness, and the making of new grants was terminated in 1871. The controversies continued, however, and have resulted in repeated appeals to, and action by, the Congress and the courts virtually up to the present time. Where lands remaining in public ownership are checkerboarded with those still held by the railroads, no adequate administration of them, either public or private, is possible.

The railroads, on the other hand, had signed a blank check which was to cause them many worries in later years. In return for the aid given them by the federal government, they agreed to transport military personnel at special rates for an indefinite period. With the vast troop movements of recent years, such as no one even imagined at the time the agreements were made, they find themselves continuing to pay for long-dead horses, horses that in all too many cases were stolen and used by past officials of the railroads and hence made little contribution to the incomes of the companies then, and none now.[10]

The mistaken principles adopted in this connection contributed to a long period of

---

9. The alternate sections retained by the government were to be sold at $2.50 per acre—twice the normal rate—in order to counteract the argument that huge gifts were being given to the railroad companies.

10. For a fuller discussion of the controversies relating to the land-grant railroads, see B. H. Hibbard, *History of the Public Land Policies*, Peter Smith, New York, 1939, pp. 243–67.

speculative manipulation, and large-scale graft and corruption in officialdom, in which the railroad corporations were major offenders. Among the lessons to be learned from the experience are the inadvisability of turning over to private corporations vast equities which cannot provide current funds for accomplishing the immediate objectives of the grant, and the desirability of making both the aid given and the *quid pro quo* definite and specific. A direct grant of either government funds or credit would undoubtedly have been far cheaper in the long run and less of a temptation to sharp practices and outright corruption. That this lesson has not yet been fully learned is evident in the vagueness still existing in many of the provisions relating to the benefits to be derived from vast federal expenditures on irrigation projects, flood control and other undertakings of the government.

Impact of Railroads on Farming

The construction of the Union Pacific-Central Pacific link with the West Coast was followed by a long period of railway construction, which reached its peak in the 1880's. The rate of railway development in the United States between 1880 and 1890 exceeded that for any similar area in the world either before or since. Even in the decade 1870–1880, more than 40,000 miles of new railway mileage were laid down. In the succeeding ten years the new trackage reached the stupendous total of 70,000 miles, the equivalent of nearly three times around the world.

Though slacking off to a somewhat more moderate pace, railway construction continued in tremendous volume through the 1890's (30,000 miles) and the first decade of this century (47,000 miles). From then on it fell off sharply and by 1930 railway mileage was actually decreasing though the capacities of many of the trunk lines were being increased through double tracking, heavier rails and stronger engines.

This enormous expansion of rail facilities made possible the commercial production of farm products on millions of acres of land which previously had no outlet to markets. The new construction was, however, so much more rapid than the development of the lands to be served that many of the western roads were for years unable to get enough traffic to make them profitable. A very large portion of the investment in a railroad is for trackage, fills, cuts, tunnels, bridges, stations and water supplies. With heavy traffic the annual costs assignable to this investment can be spread over many tons of freight. But if only one or two trains a day are operated, all of this huge expense must be borne by that small volume of traffic, or written off as loss.

Under these conditions freight rates were high, service was poor and farmer antagonism to the railroads widespread. Farmer resentment was in no way mitigated by the fact that the shipper was completely at the mercy of the carrier whose officers were remote and unknown to him, and whose requirements seemed to him arbitrary in the extreme.

Widespread Discrimination and Corruption

Faced with the necessity to earn money in every possible way, the railroad companies charged exorbitant rates wherever other lines were unable to compete, and, on the other hand, unfairly low rates at points where competition was keen. The result was a rate system of intolerable discriminations. Where competition existed it led to the grossest kinds of favoritism to large shippers. Secret rebates, special favors in supplying cars, the monopolization of sites for grain elevators, and many other abuses of the most flagrant kind were prevalent. Sometimes the western local rate would be four times as great as that charged for the same commodity and the same distance in the East. Wheat could actually be sent from Chicago to Liverpool for less than the cost of shipping from certain points in Dakota to the Twin Cities.

Secret rate understandings between the railroads and elevator companies were hard to prove, but were known to exist. Often farmers were required to ship through existing elevators, many of which were owned by line companies whose managements were interrelated with those of the railroads. Cars would not be furnished to individual shippers if they did not have elevators, and in some cases sites or switches were denied even where the farmers were willing to build such elevators.[11]

There were many other abuses in the railroad situation. One which created endless animosity was the bad manners of railway employees. A prominent writer of that period describes the condition in the following colorful language:

Taken as a class, the manners of the employees of the Western railroad system are probably the worst and most offensive to be found in the civilized world. It is difficult to see why the official should regard the traveller or the person having dealings with the railroad as his natural enemy; but it is apparent that he does. If it were an ordinary manifestation of the American fondness for asserting equality on all occasions it would be endurable; it commonly, however, partakes of a more aggressive and hostile character. A ticket is sold, and the purchaser is at the same time made to feel that a favor has been conferred upon him, — that he is on no account to ask any questions, — and, indeed, had best speedily remove himself out of the way. The gruffness of the baggage-master is, as a rule, only excelled by his violence to the baggage. Indeed, it would sometimes seem as though it must be a prominent rule laid down by the companies for the guidance of their servants, that they are to show the least possible degree of respect or consideration to any person having business with the company; and so thoroughly is this principle applied, that — always excepting Mr. Pullman's cars, in which an excellent discipline is maintained — the railroads of the West are the single institution anywhere to be found from whose servants money will not at times buy civility even of the commonest kind.[12]

Intensifying the public indignation was the open and widespread political corruption associated with the railroads. They dominated the political situation in nearly every western state. They controlled nominating conventions, used passes to gain favor from governors, judges, editors, lawyers and public men generally, and bought or intimidated legislators.

With the best of management the situation would have been difficult. Few of the western railroads could be expected to attain quickly a volume of traffic adequate to yield profitable returns on the huge investments required. But railway management in this period was notoriously dishonest and irresponsible, especially in the promotional and financing parts of the business. There are few records anywhere of such widespread and flagrant business corruption as existed in the American railroad practices of this period. There was no public control over the issuance of securities, and no official regulation of the levels and equitableness of rates charged or the quality of service performed.

Fraudulent Charges for Construction

Some of the worst abuses grew out of the practice on the part of railroad company directors of awarding construction contracts to separately organized companies owned and operated by themselves. Thus, instead of guarding the interests of the railroad stockholders whom they were supposed to represent, they exploited them, and built up huge personal fortunes for themselves. For example, the Union Pacific, using the Crédit Mobilier which was organized to construct the road, issued some $111 million in securities to raise $74 million of cash for constructing a railroad that actually cost about $60 million. Capitalization exceeded actual cost by about 2 to 1.[13] As a result, the Union Pacific hovered on the verge of bankruptcy while the Crédit Mobilier paid dividends of 348 per cent in a single year. To protect themselves against the repercussions likely to result from

11. Cf. U. S. Congress, Senate, *Testimony Taken by Interstate Commerce Commission, Oct. 15–Nov. 23, 1906, in Matter of Relations of Common Carriers to the Grain Trade*, S.Doc. 278, 59th Cong., 2nd sess., 1907. See especially pp. 6, 21–22, 24, 43–44, 160, 497–502, 515–16, 647–48.

12. Charles Francis Adams, Jr., "The Granger Movement," *North American Review*, April 1875, pp. 402–03. Also reprinted separately by the University Press, 1875.

13. William Z. Ripley, *Railroads: Finance and Organization*, Longmans, Green, New York, 1915, p. 35.

exposure of these manipulations the company sought to bribe even the United States Congress itself. Blocks of Crédit Mobilier stock were placed with congressmen and senators where they supposedly "would do the most good." Exposure of this scheme brought disgrace to a number of the recipients of such favors, especially Oakes Ames of Massachusetts, James Brooks of New York, Senator Patterson of New Hampshire, and even the Vice President of the United States, Schuyler Colfax. Doubts were raised as to the integrity of various others including even Garfield of Ohio.[14]

While the Union Pacific scandal was perhaps the one most widely publicized, there were innumerable cases where similar practices were indulged in. For the Central Pacific, from Sacramento to Ogden, the work was done under "Crocker contracts." These were executed by a contract and finance company of which the sole owners were Crocker, Hopkins, Huntington and Stanford. The cost to the Central Pacific Company was about $100,000 per mile whereas the actual cost of construction was about half that amount. For one section the cost of the road and equipment was about $3.5 million whereas the four directors voted themselves $8.3 million in railroad securities in payment. Precise information on many parts of the line cannot be had, as the books were purposely destroyed. The bonds alone, at par, exceeded the cost of construction. The stock represented no investment whatever.[15]

According to the report of the Industrial Commission, the Southern Pacific cost $6.5 million. However, $15 million was paid to a construction company, and the bankers' syndicate which financed the road received $40 million in securities, or an average of $6 in bonds and stock for each dollar of actual cost.[16]

Stock Manipulation and Rates

In addition to scandals relating to construction costs the period was marked by innumerable frauds and sharp practices in the manipulation of stocks and bonds of railroads already constructed. While these malpractices, when exposed, added fuel to the flame of farmer resentment, their actual impact was in the main upon the purchasers of railroad stocks and bonds rather than on the shippers. In the absence of any public control over railroad rates and service the carriers could be expected to charge whatever the traffic would bear. Hence excessive bond and stock issues would not necessarily increase the rates charged to shippers, but would instead reduce the returns on common stock and possibly depreciate the values of the bonds. A desperate struggle to carry on with an overloaded capital structure did undoubtedly tend to retard investment in improved equipment and facilities, and no doubt had some effect on rates paid for railway labor.

In general, however, the concern of farmers with overcapitalization and "watered stock" came later when rates had been brought under public control and the amount of investment was taken into account in arriving at the charges permitted for service. This issue, which became prominent in the early 1900's, resulted in an elaborate physical inventory of railway properties between 1913 and 1934.[17] When the results were in, it was found, however (to the surprise of those who sponsored the legislation), that the plowing in of railroad earnings over the years had brought the physical assets of most of the companies up to or above the par value of their outstanding stocks and bonds. As of 1930 the Interstate Commerce Commission's valuation of railroad properties stood at $23,-734,000,000. The par value of stocks and

---

14. See Samuel Eliot Morison and Henry Steele Commager, *The Growth of the American Republic*, 3rd edition, Oxford University Press, New York, 1942, Vol. II, p. 72.

15. Ripley, *Railroads: Finance and Organization*, pp. 35–36.

16. Emory R. Johnson and Thurman W. Van Metre,

Principles of Railroad Transportation, D. Appleton, New York, 1916, p. 118.

17. Senator Robert M. La Follette, in 1910, estimated the cost of such an inventory at $2.4 million. The Interstate Commerce Commission estimate was $3 million. By 1932 the government had spent $45 million on the undertaking, the railroad companies had likewise spent huge sums, and the further expense to the government was then estimated to be $3 million.

bonds outstanding at that time was $19,006,-276,000. Thus, despite the excesses and scandals of the earlier period, the railroads had by 1930 built up actual investments that were in excess of the securities held against them.[18]

Reasons for Farmer Opposition

As of the time here under discussion, farmer grievances against the railroads may be summarized briefly as follows:

(1) High rates.
(2) Local rates much higher proportionally than rates for longer hauls.
(3) Flagrant discrimination between shipping points and between different shippers from the same points. (Extremely high rates where no competition existed, low rates for similar hauls where competition did exist, rebates to large shippers, much discrimination in the supplying of cars, monopolization of loading facilities, sites, etc.)
(4) Control and corruption of public officials and interference in legislative matters.
(5) Combinations to prevent or minimize competition (rate agreements, agreements not to compete in certain areas, and the pooling of earnings). Many of these devices of the railroads grew out of the fact, then little recognized, that prices cannot be established effectively by competition in activities that consist in the main of natural monopolies, which the railroads were at that time.
(6) Bad public relations of the railroads, arrogance of railway employees, and general disregard of the convenience and wishes of the public.
(7) "Stock watering" and dishonest manipulation of railroad finances.
(8) Affiliation between railroads and elevator companies.
(9) "Theft" of public lands.

The last of these bulked large in the minds of the pioneer western farmers. Its significance was no doubt exaggerated as a result of the fact that it became a campaign issue in the elections of 1884 when the Democrats

stressed it as an example of the extravagance and corruption of the Republican party. As a part of this campaign the Democrats issued a broadside carrying a map which some writers contend greatly exaggerated the amounts of land granted to the railroads. The grants made were unquestionably huge, but probably not so large as they are often assumed to have been.

The total acreage which was patented to the railroads directly by the federal government was 131,350,534, out of a total land area in the states concerned of 1,389,805,440, or about 9.5 per cent. Largest percentages were in North Dakota (23.7 per cent), Washington (22 per cent), and Minnesota (18.5 per cent).[19] In addition the states granted to the railroads about 49 million acres. Most of these state grants, except the ones made by Texas, may be regarded as indirect federal grants. Part of the confusion in respect to the amounts of land granted arises from the fact that some 35 million acres originally granted were later forfeited for failure to construct lines as contemplated, and about 8 million acres were released to the government under the Transportation Act of 1940.

Possibly even more adverse to the interests of the settlers than the size of the grants actually made was the practice of prohibiting settlement in large areas near the railroads until titles to "in lieu" lands awarded to the railroad companies as replacement for lands not open for assignment to them could be settled.

Offsetting Gains to the Government

As against the well-warranted criticism of these huge grants of public lands, it is only fair to point out that vast acreages contained in the grants were of little value. Some in fact have not proved salable even up to the present time. Furthermore, the requirement that the carriers transport government freight, troops and mail at rates substantially below the regular tariffs (50 per cent for gov-

18. See Harold G. Moulton and Associates, *The American Transportation Problem,* The Brookings Institution, Washington, 1933, p. 418. There are, of course, many controversial aspects to the valuation problem. The bases used are discussed in D. Philip Locklin, *Railroad Regulation Since 1920,* A. W. Shaw, Chicago, 1928, Chapter 10.

19. Robert S. Henry, "The Railroad Land-Grant Legend in American History Texts," *Mississippi Valley Historical Review,* September 1945, pp. 174–94.

ernment freight and troops, and 80 per cent for mail) resulted in huge later returns to the government which probably more than offset the values of the original grants.

A congressional committee estimated in 1945 that the value of these concessions had amounted in total to about $500 million on the part of the land-grant railroads by June 30, 1945, and that the railroads were contributing an additional sum of $20 million each month in the period following. The government had received additional concessions amounting to some $400 million from the carriers that did not receive land grants, these concessions being made for the purpose of meeting the government rates applicable on the land-grant roads. Critics of the claims made by the carriers contend that this latter amount is not properly considered as an offset to the value of the lands assigned to the land-grant roads. It would appear, however, that these concessions would not have been made, at least not on so large a scale, if the agreements with the land-grant railroads had not been in existence.[20]

Colonel Robert S. Henry, in an able article presenting the railroad point of view, contends that the government had recaptured by 1945, as a result of these concessions, some $900 million and that this is about twice the amount the railroads have received for lands sold plus the estimated value of such lands still owned by them.[21]

Some writers take exception to the conclusions drawn by Henry, and contend that the gains to the carriers were much larger than his figures imply, and the disadvantage to the settlers greater.[22] A satisfactory analysis of the problem has not yet appeared, and more settled conclusions must await further historical study. It seems apparent that the writers of many of the history textbooks, keenly aware of the unsavory record of railroad financial management in this period, have tended to overstate somewhat the magnitude of the railroad land grants. There is no doubt, however, that the grants made were enormous, and that this was not a wise or equitable procedure for constructing the transcontinental railroads. Their need was for immediate funds with which to build the lines, not for unsalable assets of later and uncertain value. Both the railroad companies and the government were entering into an arrangement in which the values granted and received could not be quantified at the time, and in which the future interests of neither party could be adequately safeguarded.

There can be no doubt, however, that the national interest was furthered immeasurably by construction of the transcontinental lines. Though the mechanism used was not a wise one, it was almost certainly a better solution of the problem than to have delayed the development for want of means to carry it through. Nevertheless, the granting to private interests of assets of such uncertain, but potentially huge, value as a means of speeding up development is of dubious merit. It is a device that is likely to be inefficient for the ends sought at the time, and unexpectedly expensive or profitable to the government or the private interests concerned as the future brings forth events and conditions that cannot be foreseen.

However that may be, the land-grant railroad controversy seems to be nearing its close, except as a subject of debate by historians. The Transportation Act of 1940 eliminated most of the special concessions to the government, except the 50 per cent reduction in rates for transporting military and naval personnel and property.[23] Such of the lands ac-

20. For an excellent and informative treatment of the rate concessions made by the land-grant carriers and others see David Maldwyn Ellis, "Railroad Land-Grant Rates, 1850–1945," *Journal of Land and Public Utility Economics,* August 1945, pp. 207–22.

21. "The Railroad Land-Grant Legend in American History Texts," p. 189, quoting from the congressional committee report.

22. See, for example, the series of "Comments" on Henry's article in *Mississippi Valley Historical Review,* March 1946, pp. 557–76. Also William S. Greever, "A Comparison of Railroad Land-Grant Policies," *Agricultural History,* April 1951, pp. 83–90.

23. As a condition of canceling part of the concession on rates, the carriers were required to release any claims they had for land under the grants. Later legislation, passed in 1945, canceled the special rates for military and naval personnel and property (effective October 1, 1946). For further details see U.S. Congress, House,

quired under the land-grant acts as are still held by the carriers are, for the most part, poorly located and of little value. The record so far as the carriers are concerned is not a creditable one, and huge private fortunes were derived from the construction and later handling of the land-grant railroads. These, however, have long since been drawn out of the corporate structures of the companies now operating the roads, and the land-grant roads are now on essentially the same basis financially and otherwise as other carriers.

Control of Rates Becomes Major Issue

From 1870 onward the control of railroad rates and practices became a major objective of the farm groups of the West and Middle

West. They were then becoming organized in such a way that they could make their influence felt both in state legislatures and in the national Congress. Since this movement centered mainly in the militant farmer movement of the period, further discussion of it is deferred to Chapter 6. Out of it was to come the framework of a different and broadly inclusive national policy relating to the position of public utilities in the national economy — one which also had important implications in respect to other types of monopoly which were to come under scrutiny at a later date.

Aside from these developments, which looked in the direction of regulation of private enterprise rather than direct government participation, there was to be little further change in national policy in respect to internal improvements until the initiation of federal aid for highway construction in 1916. Government expenditure for river and harbor development continued, but largely along lines already laid down, and not in a form that gave rise to major concern on the part of farmers.

Discontinuance of Land-Grant Rates for Transportation of Government Traffic, H.Rep. 393 to accompany H.R. 694, 79th Cong., 1st sess., March 26, 1945, p. 4, and the various articles and reports cited by Ellis, "Railroad Land-Grant Rates, 1850–1945," *loc. cit.*

For a brief history of land-grant legislation see U.S. Congress, House, *Repeal of Land-Grant Reduced Rates on Railroad Transportation of Government Traffic,* H.Rep. 1910, to accompany H.R. 6156, 77th Cong., 2nd sess., which includes this interesting point: "Winding up the land-grant problems, on February 2, 1941, it was declared that the United States was closing its books on the 'greatest real estate deal since the Louisiana Purchase.' " p. 3.

CHAPTER 5

THE CHANGING BACKGROUND
OF FARM POLICIES

NINETEENTH CENTURY AMERICA was undergoing change and growth at a rate seldom equaled in the world's history. Inevitably this gave rise to new interests and new grievances on the part of farmers. Whereas in the early years their attention centered on the land problem, money matters, the tariff and internal improvements, most of these were gradually overshadowed by concern over the slavery issue, the monopoly problem and the desire to achieve better organization of marketing and buying activities. Monetary disputes continued to be prominent in their thinking, and gained new impetus through the greenback and free-silver campaigns. But in most other matters the changing character of the economy was bringing into the foreground new issues and interests.

OLD INSTITUTIONS IN A NEW SETTING

During the early years of the century the economic institutions and governmental structure of an older civilization were transferred quickly to a quite different setting. In the main the pattern was that of Britain, but with important modifications growing out of a different combination of resources and a more heterogeneous population. Britain herself, at the beginning of the century, was in the midst of an industrial revolution. Her labor supply was considered more than adequate and her agriculture static. Malthus, Ricardo and other economists of the time were painting gloomy pictures of the dangers of overpopulation and inadequate food supply. Manufactured goods, however, were being turned out at a rate which was already stimulating the search for new markets.

In America this situation was almost reversed. Land was abundant and cheap. Labor was scarce, and the market for industrial goods was undersupplied. Population was growing at a faster rate than in Britain, but there was no evidence of population pressure on resources. The adjustment to these conditions took various forms. In the South the effort to solve the labor shortage was largely through increasing and perpetuating the use of slave labor. In the North the shortage was overcome by immigration and the rapid invention and adoption of laborsaving machinery.

As the century progressed, the industrialists came to have an almost ideal setting for large profits and quick growth. An ample and growing market was at hand, natural resources were abundant and cheap immigrant labor was available. As a further stimulus, protective tariffs were provided in order to keep down the competition from foreign goods. Almost the only adverse feature was a poorly developed banking system which gave rise to frequent and disastrous banking crises.

The facilities for transporting farm products grew at a pace never equaled anywhere, and by the latter part of the century were in fact overdeveloped. New methods and sudden access to some of the world's richest agricultural lands were bringing into the foreground the problem of farm surpluses which was to dominate farmer thinking for seventy-five years or more. These changes did not, of course, affect all farmers alike, and there was seldom any universal farmer attitude on national policy. The tendency was rather for sectional interests and attitudes to appear. Even had farmer interests in the various regions been similar the lack of nationwide contact would have been sufficient to prevent unified effort in the field of farm policy.

Opening of West No Boon to East

The opening of the Northwest was in some respects a real disadvantage to the farmers of New England and New York. This was particularly true after improved transportation enabled products from the fertile prairie states to come into competition with those of the thin-soiled, rocky farms of the Northeast. It was natural, therefore, that farmers in the transmountain areas should demand and encourage rapid development of cheaper transport, while those of the seaboard states would be less keen for such development, and might actually oppose it.

In the older sections, except along the Erie Canal and in the areas served by the new railroads, land prices tended to decline as products from the rich, new farming areas of the West became more available. The returns from farming in New England and New York showed a downward tendency not only through lower prices for their products, but as a result of decreasing fertility as well. The eastern counties of New York, for example, were showing evidence of soil exhaustion by 1840 or earlier. Other factors were in part responsible for the decreased yields, among them insects and diseases such as the wheat midge, the Hessian fly and wheat rust. Many farms were abandoned as the younger members of farm families moved west to take up better lands, or went to the cities.

Thus the completion of the Erie Canal in 1825 and the spread of the railroad network in the succeeding decades, while the greatest of boons to the prairie farmers, were a menace to the prosperity of the farmers of the East and Northeast. The impact was eased, however, by the rapid growth of manufactures in the East and the farming opportunities still available on the western frontier. Many of the young men were drained off, either to urban pursuits or to the new lands of the West. The old stayed on.

Advantages of the Older Areas

The advantages were not all on one side. New England was a developed, going concern. It had schools, churches, roads and other amenities not afforded by the pioneer West. Direct individual incomes might be smaller, but there was a large intangible income — the result of past investments in community assets and of the growth of social organization.[1] All this the western pioneer had to forgo. Crude surroundings, isolation, poor roads and limited educational facilities were part of the price he was paying for a growing equity in his land and for the income received from sale of his low-cost products. But many of these early pioneers were descendants of old New England families — people who had a tradition of good living, of education and of refined social intercourse. They soon undertook to establish in the new states a social pattern similar to that which they had left, and the imprint of the New England culture is strong in the newer states, especially those of the eastern part of what are now the North Central states.

Farther west, and at a later date, the raw, new lands drew hordes of land-hungry immigrants, particularly those from Germany and the Scandinavian countries. For the most part they placed a lower value on education and social organization than did the descendants of the older American stock. Since many of them had been landless farm workers in the countries from which they came, the possibility of becoming landowners loomed large in their calculations. But the desire for schools and roads soon became general, among foreign-born as well as American-born settlers. Lacking accumulated wealth and improved highways, and the endowed schools of the East, they early developed a strong interest in publicly supported education, in improved highways and in better though often flamboyant houses. New England, on the other hand, continued more generally to depend upon privately supported

1. New York had similar advantages but for various reasons did not attain the levels of cultural and educational advancement enjoyed by New England.

institutions of higher learning, and to frown upon liberal federal grants to the emerging western economies.

FARMER DIFFERENCES ON SLAVERY ISSUE

Other clashes of interest and policy were to appear in the years to come: the cattle baron against the sheepman and small farmer; the western irrigator versus the farmer of the humid East; the feed-buying farmers of the coastal areas and the feed-selling farmers of the Corn Belt. But none was so deep and specific as the schism between the cotton and slave economy of the South and the free-labor, diversified-farming economy of the North.

The issue here was more than economic. It struck deep into the basic philosophies and ways of life of the populations resident in the two areas. In the South, the slaveowners had imposed their philosophy, not alone on their own class but on non-slaveowners as well, and had built up a society that included slavery together with the mores and customs associated with it. There were, to be sure, very important contrasts in the material interests of the two major sections of the country, but conflicts in economic interest alone cannot account for the widely divergent attitudes of the farmers of the North and the planters of the South. Humanitarian interests and differences in social philosophy had much to do with their growing antagonisms, so evident in the years before the Civil War.

Origin of the Problem

Negro slavery crept into the colonial South only gradually and without definite plan. Much of the labor supply during the early colonial period consisted of indentured white servants. There was little free labor available for hire since men eligible to take up land preferred to do so, and thus became independent farmers. In the northern colonies, where farms were small, the agriculture diversified and the climate healthful, the usual practice was for most of the farm work to be done by members of the owner's family.

In the South, where cash crops were more general, where holdings tended to be larger and where white labor found the climate oppressive and unhealthful, there was a continual shortage of labor up to the time when Negro slaves came to be generally used.

The practice of bringing over indentured servants, particularly young boys and girls, was established early in the colonial period. Since the number offering themselves for indenture seldom equaled the demand, the methods of recruitment often included forceful abduction, especially from the streets of London. The indentured servant had, however, a definite term of service and a recognized status on completion of his term. The indenture procedure was tolerated in part because of the desperate poverty and unemployment existing in England at the time. The enclosure movement had been gaining headway over much of the preceding century. Because of the use of former cropland for sheep raising, wheat was scarce and high. Wages were at starvation levels. Many displaced tenants and small holders were driven to vagabondage, and actual starvation was common.

Under these conditions it was considered an act of benevolence to bring to America people who had no prospects in England. Despite the many and terrible abuses under this system, it did not involve permanent ownership of the person of the indentured servant. Furthermore, having the status of an apprentice, the servant could sue in court, and had other legal rights though he could not vote or hold office or bear arms.

The first Negroes brought in were regarded technically as servants, but this status was gradually changed to one of outright slavery in which the owner had full power to buy and sell the person of the victim and to do with it almost as he pleased.

In the period following the Revolutionary War there was a considerable philosophic revulsion against the institution of slavery, especially among the Virginia planters, but except in individual instances it did not get beyond the talk stage. George Washington wrote to a friend in 1794: "Were it not, then, that I am principled against selling Negroes as you would do cattle in the market, I would not, in twelve months, . . . be possessed of a single one, as a slave. I shall be happily mistaken if they are not found to be a very troublesome species of property ere many years pass over our heads . . ."[2] Patrick Henry admitted that slavery was wrong in principle, but confessed that he was unwilling to do without the ease of life that resulted from it.[3]

Slavery and Cotton

As cotton production grew and became more profitable, slavery became more and more firmly fastened upon the rural economy of the South. After the invention of the cotton gin in 1793 made the growing of short-staple, upland cotton profitable, the philosophic objections of the more educated planters were brushed aside, and the institution of slavery came to be widely accepted as an established part of the social structure. Cotton culture was peculiarly suited to slave labor. It could use labor of all ages and both sexes.

2. Washington to Alexander Spotswood, November 23, 1794, in *The Writings of George Washington from the Original Manuscript Sources, 1745–1799*, John C. Fitzpatrick (ed.), Government Printing Office, Washington, 1940, Vol. XXXIV, pp. 47–48.

3. Many prominent Virginians expressed strong disapproval of slavery, among them Jefferson, Madison and Monroe; and among the western leaders Clay and Benton took a like stand. As early as 1786 Washington in a letter to John Mercer said, "I never mean, unless some particular circumstances should compel me to it, to possess another slave by purchase, it being among my *first wishes* to see some plan adopted by which slavery in this country may be abolished by law." Jefferson recorded himself repeatedly as opposed to the system and wrote into the first draft of the Declaration of Independence a condemnation of the traffic. Monroe in a speech in the Virginia Convention recognized that slavery was to be deplored on even broader grounds than those of humanitarian feelings: ". . . we have found that this evil has preyed upon the vitals of the Union, and has been prejudicial to all the States, in which it has existed." John Randolph of Roanoke freed all of his slaves at his death and expressed in his will his regret that legal obstacles prevented him from doing so during his lifetime. For fuller treatment of these views see Hinton Rowan Helper, *The Impending Crisis of the South: How to Meet It*, Burdick Brothers, New York, 1857, Chapter 3.

Northerners in particular are not aware that anti-slavery societies appeared first in the South, and were more numerous there than in the North until the rise of the militant abolitionist movement around 1830.

As then carried on, it was nearly an all-year-round business — planting in the spring, hoeing and chopping in the summer, harvesting in the fall, and ginning and baling in the winter.

Only simple skills and little judgment were needed. The labor could be worked in gangs under overseers who would decide what to do and when to do it, and would see that it was done. Eli Whitney's cotton gin reduced costs, and the insistent demand for cotton in the various countries of the world made the industry increasingly profitable. The price of able-bodied slaves rose from around $300 in 1776 to $800 in 1830, and by 1860 had reached a price of $2,000, a figure probably higher than the industry could really afford.

Slave Labor Unsuited to the North

In the North both conditions and sentiment were from early times unfavorable to slavery. Most of the farm land had been laid out in small units. Farms were diversified and required a wide range of skills as well as much self-direction on the part of those who worked them. Most of the northern farmers had only modest cash incomes from the sale of crops since much of the family living was produced on the farms. Thus they had little money to pay out for slaves even if they had wanted them. Furthermore, their own philosophies were not congenial to slavery. Most of them had started with little but their bare hands. Hence they had no tradition of an aristocracy living in idleness. Many were immigrants who had fled Europe to escape the exactions of an overlord class, and asked only the right to create a modest home on a modest farm which they themselves would work with pride and satisfaction.

The factories and hand trades of the North were calling for skills not generally possessed by Negro slaves; and in the robust, hard-working spirit of the time, with wage rates low, the northern whites were undoubtedly lower-cost producers than Negro slaves, even if the latter could have done the work at all. European immigration came in generally by way of New York and found its opportunity either in the northern factories or on the farms of the Northwest. Landless and without capital, these people found little to attract them into competition with Negro slave labor.

Thus the North grew rapidly in population, and in an atmosphere such that new inventions and aggressive new industrial enterprises flowed forth in an ever-growing stream. There was little objection to a ban on slavery in the Northwest Territory when it was opened up, but within a few decades thereafter the slaveholding aristocracy of the South was to be fighting a defensive battle for its very existence, and would resist every effort to place restrictions on the spread of the slave system.

Militancy of Slave-Owning South

As is usual in such cases, the social group under attack organized to defend itself. This has happened again and again in farming, in industry, in banking and in commerce. Once the battle lines are drawn it is seldom that the power of self-regulation or objective analysis is retained. Moral obligations and philosophic abstractions are brushed aside as irrelevant "star gazing." Yet in most cases the ultimate outcome is a concession which, if accepted earlier and in a more reasonable spirit, would have been milder than the one eventually forced upon the recalcitrant group. The cattle barons of the West resisted with arrogance and violence the influx of the farmer and the sheepman, but the settlers forced their way in. The railroads scorned the idea of self-regulation, but were eventually brought under rigid control. The banks, the trusts, the meat packers, the security-changes and the drug industry organized to fight regulation rather than to correct evils in time to prevent drastic measures imposed by the public.

That the slave-based cotton and tobacco economies of the South were inefficient is testified by the rapid deterioration of soils that characterized their westward march. Though few of the contemporary accounts can be regarded as unbiased, they do afford a mass of evidence of the evil effects which accompanied this type of agriculture. The soils of the older sections were being rapidly depleted and in many cases abandoned. On the other hand, in the newer, more fertile areas, the system gave rise to social changes that tended to destroy the small independent farmer. A comment by Frederick Law Olmsted in his *Journey in the Back Country* (1860) emphasizes this type of change:

The cotton-growing portion of the valley of the Mississippi, the very garden of the Union, is year by year being wrested from the hands of the small farmer and delivered over to the great capitalists . . .

All the great cotton lands were first opened up by industrious settlers, with small means and much energy. No sooner is their clearing made, and their homestead growing in comfort, than the great planter comes up from the East, with his black horde, settles down on the district, and absorbs and overruns everything. This is precisely the process which is going on, day by day, over the greater portion of Louisiana and Mississippi. The small farmers, that is to say, the mass of the white population, are fast disappearing. The rich bottom lands of that glorious valley are being concentrated in the hands of the large planters, with one hundred to one thousand negroes.[4]

Certainly the small farmer who did not own slaves had different interests from those of the man on the big plantation. He was looked upon with condescension by the planter, while the blacks often regarded him with contempt as a white man who worked with his hands. Gradually he was pushed back to the poorer hill lands, there to beget a race of underprivileged, self-sufficient, poorly educated "hillbillies." Yet in the struggles then beginning he was not to raise his voice in behalf of his own real interests. Instead he gave his support to the slave-owning minority who had had most to do with bringing him to his unenviable position. Loyalty to state was to outweigh loyalty to the nation, and emotional prejudices were to be stronger

4. Quoted by Frederick Law Olmsted, *A Journey in the Back Country*, Mason Brothers, New York, 1860, pp. 329–30, from an unnamed country newspaper in the South.

han economic self-interest, though in some
ew sections antislavery sentiment persisted,
notably in the mountain regions of Kentucky
and Tennessee, and also in North Carolina
and western Virginia.

Though difficult to understand now, such
attitudes are customary rather than exceptional. Prestige, wealth and political leadership were the trump cards of the plantation
aristocracy. Many a small farmer hoped
vaguely that he would eventually become a
plantation aristocrat himself. Not many of
the ruling class of the South belonged to the
old colonial aristocracy. Most were self-made
men who had come up rapidly in the social
scale as a result of shrewdness, energy, luck
and conformity to local customs. Many of the
planters lacked education themselves, but
usually they provided good educations for
their children. In proportion to their numbers, they had more students in colleges than
did the North, and sons were generally sent
to the military schools of the time. Education was, however, rather generally limited
to the upper classes. The children of the
small farmer had far less opportunity for education than did comparable groups in the
North, and the Negro slave had none.[5]

Contrasts Between North and South

There was little in the nature of the southern economy to stimulate mechanical ingenuity, versatility and an advancing general level
of education. Cotton, rice, sugar and tobacco,
the main staples of the South, were especially
well suited to slave labor. There were almost
no mechanical devices for reducing hand
labor, except the cotton gin. In fact, a significant trend toward agricultural mechanization did not occur until well into the
twentieth century. The demand for cotton
was such that huge profits could be made

on the rich new lands without any important
improvement in methods.

Cotton production stood at about 160 million pounds in 1820 and was already the
chief source of income for the South. By 1850
it had grown to 2 billion pounds and by 1860
to 2.3 billion. This enormous increase in production, without sharp declines in price, was
made possible by the accelerating tempo of
the industrial revolution in England, and the
rapid growth of the textile industry of New
England. It resulted from continuing westward development, much of it on lands naturally more fertile than those previously in
use, rather than from improved methods. The
system of farming used depleted the soils and
left in its wake, as it moved westward, an
ever-increasing area of worn-out lands supporting a poor and ignorant population.

In sharp contrast was the conservative
farming of the "Pennsylvania Dutch" of
western Pennsylvania. These thrifty German
farmers, bringing with them the soil-conserving traditions of their native land, have maintained the fertility of their soils and built
upon them an enduring prosperity. In general, however, the pioneer farmer of the
Northwest was little more concerned over
soil maintenance than his southern contemporary, and his record on the wheatlands of
the Middle West is little better than that of
the cotton grower. Nevertheless, the types of
farming common to the northern states were
more diversified than those of the South, and
tended to maintain soils better, even without
a conscious effort in that direction. When
the centers of wheat production moved westward, livestock farming became more general
and the speed of soil depletion was checked.

The markedly different traditions and interests of the farmers of the North and those
of the South led to an ever-widening gap
between them, a clash that was first to strike
fire in the border warfare over the status of
Kansas. The war itself is not our concern
here. Nevertheless, the aftermath of the war
was to bring into prominence major problems of agricultural policy for both the North
and the South — the North in its readjust-

5. In many of the states there were stringent laws
against giving any education at all to Negro slaves. In
several instances slaveowners were prosecuted even for
undertaking to teach certain of their slaves to read and
write. See the trial of Mrs. Douglass for teaching colored children to read, Norfolk, Virginia, 1854, in John
D. Lawson (ed.), *American State Trials*, F. H. Thomas
Book Company, St. Louis, 1917, Vol. VII, pp. 56 ff.

ment to lower prices and expanding production, the South in the complex and continuing problem of adjusting racial relationships and reorganizing its agriculture.

Educational and Social Activities

While this deepest division ever to separate the farmers of the nation was looming ever more menacingly, beginnings were being made on other policies that were eventually to form common bonds among farm people in all parts of the nation, though here too the southern farmers gradually lagged behind those of other sections.

Most of the nation's early leaders were agriculturists, and deeply interested in the improvement of farming methods.[6] Agricultural societies began to be formed before 1800 and became much more numerous during the early part of the nineteenth century. The first of these, founded at Philadelphia in 1785, included both Washington and Franklin in its membership. Agricultural fairs became common after 1807. Somewhat later a number of farm journals began publication—the *American Farmer* in 1819, the *Cultivator* in 1834, the *Prairie Farmer* in 1840, and many others less well known. These developments stimulated a new interest and pride in agricultural pursuits.

There was little attempt as yet to induce farmers to think or act in unison as an occupational group, but the beginnings of an occupational consciousness were taking shape. The interest at this stage was largely in improving intellectual, cultural and social opportunities — a bent which appeared strongly at a later date in the basic tenets of the Patrons of Husbandry.

6. For example, both Washington and Jefferson took a keen interest in agricultural experiments and the improvement of crops and livestock. Washington, the greatest agriculturist of his period, turned from tobacco raising to other enterprises. He established the mule-raising industry in the United States, using some of the best jacks of France and Spain. These had been sent to him as presents from Lafayette and the King of Spain. Experiments with improved breeds of sheep and other animals likewise engaged his attention. Jefferson was in frequent correspondence with leading agriculturists of England, such as Arthur Young, and sought to introduce new types of farming in his own operations and those of his neighbors.

In the older areas, it was an age of high achievement among the intellectuals, a vigorous self-taught group who did not confine their researches to libraries and drawing rooms. There was much interest in botanical matters and wild life. Dozens of naturalists and explorer-historians such as John James Audubon and Francis Parkman were traveling through the western areas painting and describing the things they saw. But most rural communities still had very limited opportunities for education and social contact, and for expressing their views on national problems.

FIRST STEPS IN THE TECHNOLOGICAL REVOLUTION

While the cleavage over slavery versus free labor was becoming ever more dominant as a policy problem, two developments that were to be of very great significance in the agriculture of later periods were occurring, with farmers in general scarcely aware of their importance. These were the rapid improvement of agricultural implements and the beginning of the agricultural college system. The mechanical improvements were not the result of any conscious policy. They grew out of the ingenuities of individuals, though the general shortage of labor in the fast-developing nation no doubt afforded a major stimulus. The development was mostly in the North. The differences in the character of work to be done had something to do with the dissimilarities. Yet the new inventions looked mainly to performing by machinery precisely those tasks that were tedious and repetitive, and those which required hard labor — tasks that might well have been considered suitable for slaves.

Rapid Development of New Machines

It is interesting to speculate on the reasons for the great upsurge in mechanical invention which swept the western world from the eighteenth century on, after centuries of relatively static methods, but substantiation of any given explanation is far from easy. In part the invention of certain basic contrivances, such as the steam engine, was a necessary prerequisite. But many of the inventions which were to affect American farming so profoundly did not depend upon steam or water power, except in the construction of the machines themselves. Probably the contact of a sparse population with vast agricultural resources, but without slave labor, had much to do with it. In addition the increasing commercialization of agriculture, made possible by the railroad and steamship, provided money income with which new machines could be bought and, at the same time, an outlet for the larger quantities that could be produced. Higher prices, too, were a stimulus. Not only the improvements in transportation but the repeal of the English corn laws in 1846 had opened up new opportunities for the American farmer, and he was not slow to take advantage of them.

The steel moldboard plow appeared in 1833 and soon came into general use. In 1845 there were seventy-three plow factories in Massachusetts alone, with an output of more than 61,000 plows.[7] The first patent for a mowing machine was granted to John Manning in 1831. Obed Hussey and Cyrus McCormick secured patents on the reaper in 1833 and 1834. The threshing machine appeared in 1850. Already the horse-drawn rake, which saved the work of eight or ten men, had come into use (from about 1820 on). Seed drills for sowing grain were introduced in the 1840's, and shortly thereafter came the corn planter and corn cultivator. While these improvements were to become more significant as the great prairie areas were brought into use, they were already reducing farming costs, often by as much as half. These machines and their successors were soon to make the American farmer pre-eminent in the world for economy of manpower in agricultural production.

In the main, the mechanical revolution in farming was a laborsaving change. Its purpose was not the conservation of soils or better farming. Nevertheless, such improvements as those made in the plow did lead to better farming, and in recent years power machinery is by no means a negligible element in the drive for terracing, ditching and other soil conservation measures.

Beginnings in Agricultural Education

The major developments in agricultural research and education were to come in later periods, but certain small beginnings deserve mention here — beginnings which were the forerunners of a far-reaching influence on agriculture, on agricultural organization and on agricultural policy.

Education up to this time, aside from the "three R's," had been mainly classical. Neither the sciences nor the applied arts, such as agriculture, had any significant place in the curricula of institutions of higher learning. There was as yet little general demand among farmers for scientific research or for "book learning" applied to agriculture. But the matter was being discussed in farmers' clubs and in farm journals. Some few pioneering spirits, worthy successors of Washington and Jefferson in this realm, were beginning to agitate for formal instruction in agriculture in collegiate institutions. To some extent the idea, later more definitely implemented, had been incorporated in early land laws relating to the Northwest Territory.

Michigan included in her constitution specific authorization for the establishment of a college of agriculture. Such a college was established, and opened its doors in 1857 to become the first state agricultural college in the United States. Maryland and Pennsylvania followed this lead in 1859, and in 1862 the land-grant college system, which was to grow to such large proportions, was made more general through passage of the Morrill Act.[8]

7. Harold U. Faulkner, *American Economic History,* 6th edition, Harper and Brothers, New York, 1949, p. 220.

8. Justin H. Morrill of Vermont first introduced, in 1857, a bill for the establishment of an agricultural and mechanical college in each state. The bill finally passed both houses, but was vetoed by President Buchanan in 1859. Morrill reintroduced the bill late in 1861. It passed both houses and was signed by Lincoln in 1862. The act provided for a grant of thirty thousand acres of land, or its equivalent in scrip, to the several states for

A second step in the creation of a nation-wide system of agricultural education and research agencies was taken in the passage of the Hatch Act of 1887. This provided an annual grant of $15,000 to each state for carrying on research in the agricultural sciences. It initiated the system of state agricultural experiment stations which are in most states associated with the state colleges of agriculture. The federal support for state agricultural experiment stations was enlarged in 1906 through passage of the Adams Act, which provided an additional $15,000 per year to each of the states for research on agricultural problems. Additional and larger grants have been made in the 1920's, 1930's and 1940's.

The Aftermath of Civil War

The close of the Civil War brought hardship to farmers. They had experienced great prosperity during the war, but now were faced with reduced demands for their products at the very time when their production was sharply on the increase. As in other major war periods (except World War II), many of them had incurred heavy debts. The frontier areas were at all times short of capital. Since their populations consisted mainly of farmers, there was a strong tendency throughout the nineteenth century for pioneering farmers to have a debtor outlook on national problems. Hence monetary issues were central in their thinking.

Prices increased markedly during the war, showing much the same pattern as that of the War of 1812. The peak reached was not so high as in 1814, but the advance started

from a lower level. The index of prices rose from 160 in 1811 to 235 in 1814 (1909-1914 = 100), an advance of 75 points. In the pre-Civil War period prices were strong during the early 1850's — 104 as compared to about 95 during the 1840's — but dropped back to around 93 during the panic of 1857 and the years immediately before the war. From this level the rise was to 200 in 1865. Thus the price increase during the Civil War was larger than that of the War of 1812, and the dislocations resulting from a longer war in a more developed economy were naturally more severe.

With the close of the war there began a long, irregular downward drift of prices which was not to reach its nadir until 1896. The declines in the first postwar years were not extreme but seemed so to farmers who at that time had little knowledge of the usual pattern of prices following major wars. Prices dropped to 176 in 1866, to 159 in 1867, to 148 in 1868, and reached 131 by 1870.[9]

During the war the rapid growth of western agriculture had been checked. Young men were drawn off into the armies, and the wave of railroad building had spent itself for the time being. The war brought with it an insistent demand for foodstuffs and fibers which, in the loosely organized economy of the time, forced prices up with no check except that afforded by the supplies reaching the market. Not only were large quantities needed for feeding the armies: the nation's population was growing rapidly; levels of employment were high; and the number of industrial workers was increasing. In addition, there was strong demand from Europe during most of the war period. England had poor harvests in 1860, 1861 and 1862. Having to choose between northern wheat and southern cotton, she could make only one choice, namely, to retain her access to the food resources of the North.[10]

---

each representative and senator in Congress, the proceeds to be used for the endowment, support and maintenance of at least one college in each state. These were to be schools of science rather than classical colleges, but were to be of essentially the same level as classical colleges, not trade schools of lower grade.

In the years since their establishment the land-grant colleges have become the focal points of scientific research, collegiate training and adult education in agriculture in the various states. It seems probable that such institutions would have been developed by state action even if there had been no Morrill Act. Such development would, however, have been slower, less uniform and less universal. The action of the federal government gave funds, stimulus and some degree of leadership in the movement.

9. 1909-1914=100. G. F. Warren, *Prices of Farm Products in the United States*, USDA Bulletin No. 999 1921, p. 2.

10. This choice was an obvious one, particularly in view of the fact that the excellent cotton crops of the immediate prewar years had resulted in large accumulations of cotton in England. Her stocks did not become

The close of the war released thousands of young men interested in establishing themselves as farmers under the favorable terms of the newly enacted homestead law. The expansion of the time was largely to the fertile, easily broken prairie lands, and production, especially that of wheat, surged upward. In 1866, 15.5 million acres were producing 169 million bushels of wheat. A million and a quarter more acres brought the production of 1867 to 210 million bushels; and another 2.4 million acres raised it to 246 million bushels in 1868. Thus in the short space of two years production of this main cash crop of the Northwest was increased by half. The upward trend was to continue almost unbroken for more than two decades. The production of cattle and hogs was likewise expanding at a rapid rate.

RAPID DEVELOPMENT AFTER 1870

The Census of 1870 showed 2,659,985 farms in the United States. By 1900 this number had grown to 5,737,372, an increase of 114 per cent. The acreage in farms grew from 407,735,041 to 838,591,774. Though the Department of Agriculture's index of over-all agricultural production goes back only to 1909, the data on production of certain basic crops are indicative of the enormous outpouring of farm products that occurred between 1870 and the end of the century.[11] Wheat production rose from 236 million bushels in 1870 to 522 million bushels in 1900; corn from 1,094 million bushels to 2,105 million

bushels; cotton from 1,451 million pounds to 4,757 million pounds.[12]

Western Europe a Growing Market

Not only was American agriculture providing for our own rapidly growing population a food supply seldom equaled for abundance and cheapness in the whole history of man; it had also become the major overseas food producer for the peoples of western Europe. That area was now turning to industrial production at a prodigious rate, and was building up population far in excess of the ability of its own agriculture to supply it with food. United States exports of wheat and flour rose from about $68 million in 1870 to more than $200 million in the banner year 1898 even though prices by then were little more than half those of the earlier period.[13] During these same years the exports of meat and meat products rose from $21 million to more than $175 million, an increase of more than 700 per cent.

Production increases of such magnitude would have been completely disastrous in their price effects had it not been for the huge and growing market in western Europe. That market, so far as the American farmer was concerned, was made possible by a number of circumstances. American foodstuffs were cheap, and hence attractive to the European nations which were shifting rapidly to major reliance on industry. The United States was still short of industrial goods and was absorbing a large volume of imports from western Europe. Furthermore, there was a substantial flow of European investment capital into the United States; and, in addition, the annual interest payments on foreign capital already invested in the United States helped make it feasible for our exports to be larger than our imports without creating a shortage of dollars with which to buy the excess.[14] Thus it was a particularly fa-

---

seriously short until about 1863. In addition, considerable amounts of cotton were smuggled through the blockade, especially during the early years of the war. See Faulkner, *American Economic History*, p. 352.

11. Frederick Strauss and Louis H. Bean present a general index of total farm production going back to 1869, in *Gross Farm Income and Indices of Farm Production and Prices in the United States, 1869–1937*, USDA Technical Bulletin No. 703, 1940, p. 125. This appears to be the only one currently available that covers the period here under review. The two computations use different base periods and are not closely comparable. The official series, with a 1935–1939 base period, is shown in *Agricultural Statistics, 1946*, p. 560. The Strauss and Bean index (arithmetic, 1910–1914 base) rose from 37.6 in 1870 to 89.3 in 1900 (p. 124); dairy products from 24.9 to 82.3 (p. 132); fruits from 24.1 to 128.7 (p. 133); cattle, sheep and hogs for slaughter and export from 57.0 to 91.1 (p. 135); and textile raw materials from 25.4 to 72.4 (p. 139).

12. U.S. Industrial Commission, *Final Report of the Industrial Commission*, 1902, Vol. XIX, p. 48.

13. The year 1898 was, to be sure, one of exceptionally high production, but even in 1900, a relatively poor year, wheat exports amounted to more than $140 million.

14. Nathaniel T. Bacon estimated in 1900 that for-

vorable combination of circumstances both domestic and foreign that made possible the enormously rapid development of American agriculture during this period.

Increased Application of Horsepower

The huge expansion of acreage in American farms was not, of course, the only reason for their enormous increase in output. Of major importance in the transformation of American agriculture during this period was the rapid increase in the use of animal power to replace human labor. In this respect American farmers outstripped those of all other nations of the world. This too was in part a result of special circumstances. The United States had lands especially well suited to mechanized types of farming. These lands were available in such quantity that each farmer could secure a sizable acreage. The prairie lands of the Middle West were especially suited to rapid development by means of horsepower and almost unmanageable without it. Furthermore, the major crops grown, especially the small grains and corn, lent themselves readily to mechanized farming, and the rural areas, like the cities, were chronically short of labor.

The significance of this shift to horsepower can best be shown by an oversimplification in which we consider men and horses merely as motors, ignoring for the moment the powers of judgment, flexibility and skill. As a motor, a human being when operating continuously for a working day of eight hours can generate about 1/10 of a horsepower, as this is rated technically. A horse can generate

continuously about eight times this amount of power.

Thus, from the standpoint of power, the introduction of a machine that could use two horses effectively was equivalent to adding 16 men for the time the machine was in use. To be sure, the change was not from complete use of manpower to complete use of horsepower, and all of the gains made were not net gains. Nevertheless, the increase in effectiveness of manpower as applied to American agricultural lands during this period was enormous.

Data on hours required per unit of product are scattered and can at best be only very rough approximations. They do, however, provide a general view of the significance of machine production as compared to hand labor. In 1830 the production of a 20-bushel crop of wheat required 57.7 man-hours of labor per acre. One hundred years later this work could be done on the most highly mechanized farms with 3.3 hours of labor.[1] A 40-bushel corn crop in 1855 required 33.6 hours of man-labor. At the present time an 80-bushel crop can be produced under the most favorable conditions with about 6 hours of man-labor.[16]

15. The data given in this section are, in the main from an unpublished manuscript by Professor H. B Walker, head of the Division of Agricultural Engineering, University of California College of Agriculture. The figures given reflect, of course, the enormous reduction in manpower requirements that came with the tractor the combine and other recently developed machines. The reductions made by the latter part of the nineteenth century were less sensational, but nevertheless of great significance.

16. The most careful analyses available on the reduction in manpower required for producing wheat between the early part of the nineteenth century and the latter part of that century are those contained in Dr Leo Rogin's study, The Introduction of Farm Machinery in Its Relation to the Productivity of Labor in the Agriculture of the United States During the Nineteenth Century, University of California Publications in Economics, Vol. IX, University of California Press, Berkeley, 1931 Rogin presents scattered historical records for the period 1790 to 1830. These in general range from 60 to 80 hours of man-labor per acre of wheat produced. Comparable figures for such states as Nebraska, Kansas and Illinois in the 1890's, where the use of the grain binder but not the combine had become general, show hours per acre required ranging from about 10 to 14. See pp. 218, 219, 234 and 235. Thus by the 1890's, hours of man-labor per acre required in wheat production had been reduced to one fourth or less of what they were in the first decades of that century.

eign investments in the United States amounted to $3,330 million, of which $2,500 million were held in Britain. Holland ranked second with $240 million and Germany third with $200 million. "American International Indebtedness," Yale Review, November 1900, p. 276. The United States continued to be a major outlet for British investment abroad through 1913, though after 1900 it did not absorb so large a volume of such investment as did Canada. See C. K. Hobson, "British Oversea Investments, Their Growth and Importance," Annals of the American Academy of Political and Social Science, November 1916, pp. 23–35. See also America's Experience as a Creditor Nation, by John T. Madden, Marcus Nadler and Harry C. Sauvain, Prentice-Hall, New York, 1937, Chapter 2.

These, however, are the crops in which mechanization could make rapid strides. Many agricultural operations have shown no such striking reductions in manpower required. Dairying, for example, along with most other livestock enterprises, has continued to require much labor. Tobacco, cotton, fruits and truck crops are still to a large extent on a hand-work basis. Furthermore, it must be evident to the most casual observer that such changes consist in part of transfers of work from farm to city. Machines, though used on farms, are built in cities. The process consists in part of supplementing farm labor with city labor.

Proportion of Farmers Declines

One important effect of the mechanical revolution in agriculture was to reduce greatly the proportion of the nation's population required in producing its food and fiber crops. At the time of the first census in 1790 more than 94 per cent of the population was classed as rural. This percentage has declined in every census since then. In the 1870's the number of people gainfully employed in agriculture dropped below the number in other occupations for the first time in the nation's history. This meant that each farm family produced at least enough foods and other farm products to supply itself and one nonfarm family, plus such amounts as might be exported. This trend has continued. By 1930 only 20.7 per cent of the nation's gainfully employed were in agriculture. Today there are, on the average, six or seven nonfarm families dependent on the production from each average farm.

This means commercial agriculture, not self-sufficient agriculture. The tide had already turned strongly in that direction by 1880. From that time on, the farmers, though still in a dominant position politically, were a minority group.

Immigration and a Changing Environment

The great influx of immigrants during the closing decades of the nineteenth century and before had a marked influence on the rate of agricultural development, the social customs, the outlook of the farm groups and also on the character of the agriculture. Strong as this influence was, however, it was, in general, the English tradition that eventually won out and set the pattern for the rural areas of the middle and western states.

Immigration was on a very modest scale during the first decades of the century, but the rate stepped up rapidly after 1830. Until the time of the Civil War this stream of immigrants consisted mainly of Irish, German and English families. Irish immigration reached its peak shortly after the great famine of 1846, while the peak of the prewar German influx came after the political struggles of 1830 and 1848.

The Irish tended to remain in the cities of the North Atlantic Coast states. They lacked both the capital and inclination for pioneering in the new lands of the West. Moreover, their desire to live in strongly Catholic communities and among their own kind undoubtedly exerted considerable influence. The German and English immigrants more generally went into the western states, though by no means all of them went to the land. Cincinnati and St. Louis had large German colonies, and Milwaukee became virtually a German city, with German customs and religion. It even retained, to a considerable extent, the German language. There was extensive settlement of farm lands in Wisconsin and Minnesota by German immigrants, and their cultural influence was still strong at least up to the time of World War I.

Up to 1860 the dominant settlement of western lands was not by immigrants from Europe but by the younger members of families already long established on the farms of the eastern states. In general the institutions, methods of farming and political outlook were in the New England tradition rather than that of any foreign country. The Germans, except in urban concentrations such as those of Milwaukee and other typically German cities, soon adopted American ways and developed higher standards of living. They also sought more generally the educational opportunities of the public schools rather than those of the Lutheran and Catholic parochial schools.

Shift of Immigrant Origins

Even during the decade of the 1860's immigration amounted to more than 2.3 million people, almost all of them from northern and western Europe. Between 1870 and 1900 the influx was heavy, especially in the 1880's. Nearly twelve million immigrants came into the United States during these three decades.[17] After 1880 there began an important shift in immigrant origin, from northern and western Europe to southern and eastern Europe, with more than half the total coming from the latter area after 1890. This tendency became even more marked after 1900.

These later immigrants, mainly Italians, Russians, Austrians, Poles and Jews, tended to congregate in the cities. Most were too poor to buy the livestock and machinery necessary for settlement on the land, and, with different languages, religions and customs, they found life in the foreign colonies of the great cities easier and more congenial than in the open country. But the north Europeans, particularly the Scandinavians, continued to go to the land, and presently came to constitute a large part of the rural populations of such states as Minnesota, Illinois, Iowa, the Dakotas and Nebraska.

Farther west, in the Plains and Mountain states and on the Pacific coast, the population, except for non-Caucasians engaged in manual labor, was derived predominantly from older American stock, mainly of English descent.

The result of this combination of circumstances was that the farming areas of the United States, except in the South, were mostly settled on a basis of family-type farms operated by working farmers. The stock wa almost exclusively north European, and the political outlook intensely democratic. The political climate did not lend itself to bossism as in the great cities, though it afforded a happy hunting ground for the demagogic political orator. On the other hand the farm population was sufficiently independent economically to assert itself individually and collectively. It became a major political force in American life, and has continued to hold an important balance of power in political affairs long after ceasing to have a majority vote in national elections. While diverse in make-up its political, educational and social outlook is that of sturdy individualism drawn largely from the traditions of the rural sections of northeastern United States.

The Decline of New England Agriculture

While the western lands were being populated and were coming into production at a rate unparalleled in the whole history of agriculture, other farming areas were finding themselves in a far different situation. America's surplus production brought about a drastic reduction in the prices of farm products in Europe, especially of those in Britain. Germany and some other countries sought to ease this impact by the imposition of tariffs. Britain, on the other hand, retained its free-trade policy through the latter half of the century. Some parts of the United States were also affected in much the same way as those of western Europe and almost as severely. This was particularly true of New England and New York.

During the last thirty years of the nineteenth century the competition of the West was felt most keenly in wheat. Wheat production in Vermont fell by 92 per cent between 1869 and 1899. Maine's corresponding decline was 58 per cent, while that of New Hampshire was 98 per cent.[18]

As a result of the depressed conditions in New England agriculture, many young peo-

---

17. Immigration was fostered vigorously by the western railroads with lands to sell. Advertisements prepared by the railroad companies were posted far and wide in the European countries likely to furnish new settlers. These painted the opportunities open to settlers in the West in the most glowing terms. The advertisements frequently were followed up by personal solicitation in the countries of origin, and whole trainloads of immigrants were taken west at company expense. See John D. Hicks, *The Populist Revolt,* University of Minnesota Press, Minneapolis, 1931, pp. 14-15.

18. Harold Fisher Wilson, *The Hill Country of Northern New England, Its Social and Economic History, 1790–1930,* Columbia University Press, New York, 1936, p. 98.

ple moved to other areas and other occupations, and many farms were abandoned. Farm lands fell sharply in value, and by 1890 many were listed at $3.00 to $10.00 per acre, including buildings which often had cost more than the current value of the farm.

This decline in values was in large measure an inevitable adjustment to changed conditions. Much of the New England land was poor and rocky. Its only advantage in the earlier period was that of location. The railroads and canals had now destroyed that advantage. Such a process of new development and shifting comparative advantage is constantly going on, but usually in less acute form. It has an important bearing on the farm policies of the regions that are losing out competitively, since the very natural and human tendency is for the farmers of those areas to fight a long, losing battle to retain the industry in the face of insurmountable odds.

The adjustment could often be made more easily by quicker acceptance of the inevitable and by more positive efforts to shift to other kinds of production. In New England the logical shift was toward fluid milk production, poultry husbandry, and fruit and truck crops, but this shift came only after long efforts to retain types of farming that could no longer compete with similar types in the newer areas. The experience in New York and some of the other eastern states was similar though less acute, since most of them had soils that were more productive than those of New England.

Conditions in the South

In the early years following the Civil War the farmers of the South were desperately poor and many of them disfranchised. Hence they were in no position to make constructive contributions in national or even regional policy. Slavery had been abolished, but the problems of the South were by no means solved. It still had its one-crop agriculture, its soils were continuing to deteriorate and it still had its acute social problem stemming from the differences in backgrounds and traditions of the two races that made up its population. Manufacturing was little developed, and it lacked both capital and leadership for new ventures. There were almost no banks. Land formerly worth $100 an acre would not bring $5. In Mississippi alone almost six million acres were sold for nonpayment of taxes.

The South had also suffered vastly greater physical devastation than the North. In many of the areas over which the troops had swept, houses, barns, cattle, hogs, sheep and horses were gone. Bridges had been destroyed, roads were almost impassable and fences had disappeared. To add to the confusion and despair, the long struggle over Reconstruction, in which the "radicals" of Congress held the upper hand, kept the former Confederate states unorganized, many of their former leaders disfranchised, and, in some areas, unable even to maintain law and order or reestablish such simple services as those of the schools and post offices.

Not until the withdrawal of federal troops in 1878 did the South begin rebuilding, under its own leadership, its shattered social and economic structure. For decades it was to be immersed in the poverty and disorganization that are the usual heritage of a defeated realm. Wiser and more constructive policies on the part of the Congress could have greatly speeded the recovery, but war-born animosities overrode considerations of future welfare.

Out of the prewar pattern of southern agriculture and the ill-considered policies adopted by the postwar Congress, there emerged a southern agricultural problem that has persisted to the present time. Little effort was to be made to solve it, however, until after 1900. The Negro slave became overnight a "free" man, but with little or no preparation for that status. He was uneducated, without money or property, or even a home, and had no experience in fending for himself.

Gradually he returned to a relationship not greatly different from that which he had occupied before. He was a cropper or hired hand but did much the same kinds of work.

He had legally more freedom to change jobs or localities, but little practical opportunity for doing so. Cotton growing continued to be the dominant agricultural enterprise. Soils continued to deteriorate. Over most of the South educational opportunities for both whites and blacks were poor and inadequate. Birth rates remained high among the blacks and the poorer classes of whites. With its paucity of industrial outlets the South continued to suffer from overpopulation, underemployment, poor methods of farming and inadequate capital.

The "Cropper" System in the South

Throughout the latter part of the nineteenth century this one-crop system, based on a cropper type of tenure, became more and more firmly fixed on the agriculture of the South.[19] A principal means of implementing and perpetuating it was the country store. This institution came to be the cropper's main source of credit for subsistence while making the crop, and his outlet for the crop when it was sold, since it was usually pledged far in advance of the harvest. The country store was likewise the post office, the place of contact and, to some extent, the mechanism through which instructions were given and management functions carried out. On the larger plantations it was usually owned and managed by the plantation operator. Where smaller holdings prevailed, it was generally the commercial and financial center for the farming community.[20]

The retention of a semifeudal agriculture in the South was to some extent a result of nostalgic sentiment for the old life which had been swept away by the war. Many southerners, whose attitude was typified by that

of Jefferson Davis, idealized the old way of life and sought in every way possible to re-establish as near an approximation to it as they could. Others, such as Robert E. Lee, put the past behind them and turned their efforts in the direction of building a new South, more efficient, more industrialized and better oriented to the modern world.[21] This latter attitude marks the South of today, but it is, in the main, a recent development.

Until the end of the nineteenth century, the southern farmer was in general falling behind his northern contemporary, retaining hand methods while the other adopted more and more machines, standing firm on a one-crop agriculture while the other diversified, and clinging to timeworn institutions that had never found a place in the agriculture of the North. These differences in economic interest, in outlook and in institutional surroundings naturally had their effect upon attitudes toward national problems whether in foreign trade, in credit, in education or in marketing. In this period (1865–1900), the initiative in agricultural policy was in the hands of the farmers of the new West, not those of the South or of New England.

THE GROWTH OF CORPORATE POWER

Before the Civil War, American industry consisted for the most part of small plants, individually owned, and in many cases oriented to a local market. This situation still was characteristic until around 1880. At about that time there began a rapid expansion in the use of corporate forms of organization and in large-scale production. With them came increasingly the delegation of management, indirect ownership and, of course, limited liability. Important new inventions were appearing in nearly all lines, and the now extensive network of railroads made possible much wider markets than had been practicably available theretofore.

In the industrial world the period of the 1880's was one of rapid growth and ruthless

---

19. One writer summarizes the situation as follows: "Staple crops meant routine in production, in distribution, in exchange and in consumption of wealth. The credit system hung upon repetition of crops, and all else hung upon the credit system." Broadus Mitchell, "Growth of Manufactures in the South," *Annals of the American Academy of Political and Social Science,* January 1931, p. 23.

20. The nature and place of the country store in southern rural life are described in a most interesting way in Thomas D. Clark's *Pills, Petticoats and Plows,* Bobbs-Merrill, Indianapolis, 1944.

21. See the discussion of this divergence in William B. Hesseltine, *The South in American History,* Prentice-Hall, New York, 1943, pp. 540 ff.

competition. The doctrine of free enterprise was in its heyday. Stock promotion was rampant, and, with almost no legal protection to the buyer, the doctrine of *caveat emptor* prevailed generally. The railroads could and did charge what the traffic would bear. Modern methods of supervision were as yet almost unknown. There were few restraints on corporate combinations and understandings, and about the only hindrance to monopolistic practices was the difficulty of making them work.

At the same time business conditions were inexorably forcing resort to devices designed to restrict competition. As local factories and industries grew in size and sought wider markets, they inevitably came into bitter conflict with rival firms in other areas. Cutthroat competition developed on a large scale. So destructive were the results in many cases that competitors found themselves faced with the alternative of reaching some understanding among themselves or ruining each other through disastrous price wars. Naturally, in the absence of legal provisions against it, they chose the former alternative.

Once an understanding had been reached or perhaps the actual monopolization of an industry achieved, the tendency was, of course, to exploit the advantage to the fullest extent possible. The result in most cases was not merely to eliminate cutthroat competition, but rather to maintain a monopoly price well above that justified by the costs of production. In this way, the foundations were laid for some of the huge fortunes of the period.

Railroads and the Monopoly Problem

In the effort to avoid the destructive effects of unrestrained competition, the railroads early took the lead. Because of their heavy sunken investments and high fixed costs in relation to variable costs, competition could not serve effectively to establish rates so long as most of the carriers were not using their facilities to full capacity. As a result, they were subject to recurring rate wars so destructive to railroad revenues that neither the public nor the carriers could countenance their continuance.

This situation is illustrated by the violent rate wars of the 1890's. The U.S. Industrial Commission, in its report of 1902, states that in 1893 a bitter war over transcontinental business broke out. During this conflict freight was carried from New York to San Francisco for as little as 30 cents per 100 pounds. The following year (1894) witnessed entire demoralization in freight rates throughout the southern states. Every carrier in that section was involved. During June and July rates were cut in some instances as much as two thirds. Thus, the rate from New York to Atlanta on first-class freight was reduced from $1.14 to 40 cents.[22] Similar problems arose in the competitive relations between industrial concerns though not in such exaggerated form. They, too, having found excessive competition unprofitable and often ruinous, turned to price agreements, divisions of territory, corporate or trust combinations and so on.

In many cases the competition between the various railroad companies fostered the growth of monopolies. The intense rivalry of the carriers for the larger aggregates of freight business led them to grant rebates and to enter into secret agreements of other kinds with the bigger shippers. This gave advantages to the shippers thus favored, and enabled them to crowd out many of their smaller competitors.

The Standard Oil Company, for example, not only received rebates on its own shipments over certain lines, but in some instances was paid a certain percentage on all shipments of oil over the line, including those of its rivals. In return for these favors, the oil company not only gave to the friendly carriers a large volume of business but provided special facilities for them, and to some extent adjusted shipments so as to facilitate the pooling arrangements entered into by the carriers.[23]

22. *Final Report of the Industrial Commission,* Vol. XIX, pp. 352–53.
23. *Ibid.,* p. 597.

Other Types of Monopoly

Many other business combinations of one kind or another came into prominence during this period. Contracts operating as restraints of trade were unenforceable under English and American common law, but there was no specific prohibition of them.[24]

The principal devices used in effectuating monopoly arrangements were the *pool*, the *trust* and the *holding corporation*. The oldest of these, the pool, took various forms, but was usually a secret agreement to fix and maintain prices, to abstain from competing in specified and assigned territories, to buy over and control the entire output or a large part of it, and so on. Some were, and still are, very informal, amounting in substance to little more than an understanding or "gentleman's agreement." Others, such as the patent pool, might be highly monopolistic and capable of gouging from the public huge unwarranted profits. Generally, however, the pool was difficult to maintain since its leaders could not resort to the courts to punish recalcitrant members or producers who chose to remain outside the group. The pools usually broke down if attempts were made to raise prices sharply above competitive levels, and often it was impossible to hold them together even where the agreement was designed mainly to steady prices with benefit to the industry and no serious harm to the public.

As a result of these weaknesses in the pool type of organization, there was developed a legal mechanism known as a *trust*. Under this plan all of the capital stock of the constituent companies was assigned to a board of trustees who thereafter determined policies with respect to amount and distribution of the products. Following dissolution of the trusts as a result of the Antitrust Act of 1890

and the judicial interpretations that grew out of it a third device, known as the *holding corporation*, came into extensive use.

This consisted of an arrangement whereby stocks of various subsidiary corporations were held by a holding company which might or might not have any operating or other duties except that of holding the stocks of the subsidiary companies and determining general policies.[25] Many holding companies aided in the financing of subsidiaries and facilitated coordination among them, especially where their activities were complementary to each other as when an automobile company obtained its engines, bodies, wheels, etc., from other companies under the same general control.

The holding company device did not as a rule lend itself to monopolization of a whole industry but did exert a powerful influence in the direction of larger aggregations of industry operating under a single general policy-making directorate. It made possible such complex organizations as United States Steel, General Motors and Transamerica. There are merits as well as demerits in this form of organization, but it lends itself to the concentration of economic power and may be used in monopolistic ways. Ripley states that until about 1890 "the weight of legal authority had been adverse to the holding of the stock of one corporation by another." Railroads, however, had for a generation been allowed by special provision of law to control subsidiary companies in this way.[26]

Farmer Opposition to Big Business

The lush growth of these various "trusts" and "monopolies" gave rise to intense farmer antagonism, an opposition that was sometimes well justified and in other cases based upon vastly inflated misconceptions. The dislike of private monopoly is deep-seated and

24. Such legislation came into being in the Sherman Antitrust Act of 1890, but in such brief form that it marked the beginning of a long period of judicial interpretation which is, in large measure, the present body of law pertaining to monopolies and trusts. For an excellent discussion of this background see William Z. Ripley, *Trusts, Pools and Corporations*, revised edition, Ginn and Company, Boston, 1916, especially Chapter 14 and following.

25. The major development of the holding company mechanism came after the period here under discussion, especially from 1900 on. See William H. Anderson, "Public Utility Holding Companies: The Death Sentence and the Future," *Journal of Land and Public Utility Economics*, August 1947, pp. 244–54.

26. Ripley, *Trusts, Pools and Corporations*, p. xix.

lmost universal. It was easy therefore for he cartoonist to picture the trusts as huge at millionaires in top hats and loaded with liamonds, and for political orators to rake hem with the most lurid kinds of campaign ratory.

Certainly their sins were legion. There can e little doubt, however, that the glare of ublicity focused on these picturesque and ometimes imaginary monsters blinded the arm groups to other causes of their difficul- ies, and led them to ignore solutions that night have helped to better their condition. Low grain prices resulting from production beyond the reasonable requirements of the market were often attributed to manipula- ions of the "grain trust"; low hog prices were the fault of the "packing trust" and so on. True, these operators often were taking exorbitant profits, and not infrequently were engaged in manipulations that would not bear the light of day, but the tribute they ex- tracted was hardly sufficient to make the dif- ference between prosperity and depression in agriculture.

The things which make political issues are not necessarily the true causes of the voters' troubles, but rather the things they think are the causes. The monopoly problem came to be a very lively policy issue in the last dec- ades of the nineteenth century. The concen- tration of business control is more prevalent now, but it is not, at present, prominent in farmer interest and attitudes.

CHAPTER 6

FARMER ORGANIZATIONS AND THEIR
POLICIES, 1870–1900

BEFORE THE CIVIL WAR, farmers were virtually unorganized as an occupational group. Since they constituted the major part of the population, the leaders chosen in national elections did, of course, tend to represent farmer viewpoint, and many of them were themselves farmers. In the early decades of the nation's history, sectional interests, heavily dominated by the farm groups, became important in the establishment of national policy as, for example, in the administrations of Jefferson and Jackson. In New England the commercial, shipping and industrial interests were dominant, while in the South and West the small urban communities tended to think and vote like the farmers. The Middle Atlantic states reflected a mixture of rural and urban interests that did not, for the most part, bring into focus major national issues. During the decades in which the tariff and slavery held the center of the stage, the major divisions tended still to be on sectional lines rather than rural versus urban.

Most of the early presidents—Washington, John Adams, Jefferson and Jackson — and later, Lincoln, had strong ties with agriculture. The same was true for a good portion of the congressmen and senators. This situation changed in the latter part of the century when politics came to be dominated by industrialists, railroad companies, big-city bosses and lawyers.[1] Farmers came to feel

that they must band together to fight for their interests, and to oppose the malevolent influences of the corporations, the railroads and the city politicians.[2]

There had been some slight effort to create a common front of agriculture and labor in New England in 1830 through organization of the New England Farmers and Mechanics Union. This, however, was a labor movement rather than a farmer movement. It gained little farmer support, and its policies were determined by the laborers, not the farmers, in its membership. Farmers of that time had hardly enough in common to warrant organizing among themselves, let alone combining with groups in other occupations.[3]

---

1. "The Forty-third Congress of the United States, in session from 1873 to 1875, will furnish an example of this lack of representation in the councils of the nation, of which the farmers complained. Sixty-one per cent of the members of this Congress were lawyers, sixteen per cent were engaged in commercial or manufacturing pursuits, and only seven per cent professed the occupation of farming. Yet the census of 1870 shows that forty-seven per cent of the working population of the country was still engaged in farming while commerce and manufacturing could claim only thirty-one per cent. That this

situation was not confined to national politics can be seen from the statistics of the legislature of Illinois in 1874. This included but eight farmers among fifty-one senators and forty farmers among the one hundred fifty-three members of the lower house, in spite of the fact that over half of the population of the state was agricultural. . . . Similarly, a constitutional convention in Ohio in 1873 contained sixty-two lawyers and sixteen farmers out of a total of one hundred and two members." Solon J. Buck, *The Granger Movement, 1870–1880*, Harvard University Press, Cambridge, 1913, p. 35 and footnote.

2. Jonathan Periam, writing in 1874, describes the farmer's view of the situation as follows: "A large proportion of the heroes of the Revolution left the plow for the battle-field, and when the war was over returned again to their peaceful art.

"Those, indeed, were days that may never again return. Then there was no swindling, no stock jobbing, no Crédit Mobilier, no open buying and selling of votes, no fine art of lobbying, no overshadowing monopolies. The offer of a bribe was scorned, and the tempter held up to public indignation." *The Groundswell, A History of the Origin, Aims, and Progress of the Farmers' Movement*, E. Hannaford, Cincinnati, 1874, p. 62.

3. There were, of course, numerous local farmers' clubs and organizations. Most of them were educational and social in character, though some turned more specifically to political and economic objectives. See, for example, Periam, *The Groundswell*, Chapters 8 and 9, and Edward Wiest, *Agricultural Organization in the United States*, University of Kentucky, Lexington, 1923, Chapter 15.

The Rise and Decline of the Patrons of Husbandry

The first important national organization of farmers was started in 1867. It was not a spontaneous farmer movement but very soon took on the character of one. The idea grew out of proposals made by Oliver Hudson Kelley, a temporary employee of the United States Department of Agriculture. Kelley, a Minnesota farmer, ran into difficulties as a result of the droughts of 1862 and 1863. As a means of improving his situation he obtained, in the winter of 1864, a clerkship in the Department of Agriculture, but returned to Minnesota in the spring of 1865. He was later recalled to Washington, and in January 1866 was instructed to travel through the southern states with a view to re-establishing sources of statistical and other information pertaining to that region. In the course of his travels he became deeply impressed with the poverty, ignorance and lack of social life in many of the farm communities. He also met and talked with a number of people who were similarly concerned.

Out of these conferences, and others held later, he evolved the idea of a national fraternal organization of farmers. Its main purpose was to be the improvement of farming, the provision of wholesome recreation and the broadening of knowledge and acquaintance among farmers. Since Kelley and several of those interested in the plan were Masons, they drew on the Masonic ritual for many of their ideas in developing a formal plan of organization. There was difference of opinion about the merit of making the organization a secret society, but as it was eventually drawn up, the plan included this feature. A ritual was developed and provision was made for a series of degrees. After much preliminary work, the Order was launched in 1867 as the National Order of the Patrons of Husbandry, commonly known as the Grange.[4]

Kelley and his associates had great ambitions for a huge membership blanketing the rural areas of the nation. But the early progress of the organization was by no means in keeping with these expectations. Kelley wrote of the situation in the summer of 1868, "If all great enterprises, to be permanent, must necessarily start from small beginnings, our Order is all right. Its foundation was laid on *solid nothing* — the rock of poverty — and there is no harder material. Riches take wings and fly away, but poverty is not inclined to be migratory."[5]

But the time was ripe for farmers to become organized and militant. The prices of farm products had fallen off still further after the precipitous decline that marked the close of the Civil War. There was growing unrest in the farm areas; increasing antagonism to the railroads, corporations and banking interests; and a new class consciousness on the part of farmers that made them receptive to any medium that would make possible organized expression of their views. In such a setting the aggressive efforts of the promoters of the Grange began to bear lusty fruit. The farm communities, with their dearth of organized recreation and their lack of recognized local leadership, accepted the Grange as filling a long-felt need. Kelley states that in the month of February 1874, he and his associates organized 2,234 Subordinate Granges — "a work unparalleled in the history of organizations."[6] By 1873 there were Granges in all states except Nevada, Connecticut, Rhode Island and Delaware.

Economic Activities of the Grange

The interests which drew farm people into the Grange were different from those its founders had envisioned. Their conception was of an organization devoted to cultural interests and self-improvement, not one concerned with political and economic issues. In a letter outlining the plan, written in Septem-

---

4. The early history of the Patrons of Husbandry is described in great detail in O. H. Kelley's *Origin and Progress of the Order of the Patrons of Husbandry in the United States: A History from 1866 to 1873*, J. A. Wagenseller, Philadelphia, 1875.

5. *Ibid.*, p. 117.
6. *Ibid.*, p. 239. In the table on p. 422, the number is given as 2,239. In January, February and March of that year the number of Subordinate Granges organized exceeded 2,000.

ber 1867, Kelley said, "Among the objectives in view may be mentioned a cordial and social fraternity of the farmers all over the country. Encourage them to read and think; to plant fruits and flowers, — beautify their homes; elevate them; make them progressive."[7]

But farmers do not long remain satisfied with mild objectives when faced with pressing economic and political problems. As in a later period when the "Farm Bureaus" were established for educational purposes, the farmer members quickly took the bit in their teeth, and plunged into discussions and actions that seemed to them more important. Though many of the local Granges continued to serve in greater or less degree the social and cultural purposes the founders had in mind, the main interest, in the period of the Grange's greatest power, was in economic issues.

As early as 1871 the Grange members began to undertake, through their organizations, activities of a more directly economic character. In that year they began buying household and farm supplies cooperatively. This led shortly to purchase and sale through agents appointed by the Granges, and presently to efforts to make special agreements for the manufacture of machinery. It was but a step from this to the purchase and operation of manufacturing plants. This latter venture, as might be expected, was almost a complete failure. The Grange members had little experience with business activities, and their organization, designed for a very different purpose, was poorly suited to operate as a buying, selling or manufacturing agency.

The troubles of the Grangers stemmed in the main from overenthusiasm, misconception of the causes of their low selling prices and high buying prices, and a lack of understanding that the successful operation of business-type functions requires capital, skill and special kinds of organization, plus time in which to get the business established. Sensational results were expected long before they

could possibly be achieved, and the resulting disillusionment reacted strongly against the popularity of the organization. Coupled with this was the difficulty every new and fast-growing organization faces, namely, that many people join with no realistic understanding of the purposes of the organization, the obligations it involves and what can reasonably be expected of it. Farmer organizations usually experience heavy mortality of membership in their early years. Gradually they shake down to memberships consisting of people really interested in their programs, willing to take some part in making them successful and prepared to keep up their dues.

In addition, the farmers of that period lacked knowledge of the methods and organization necessary for successful cooperative businesses, and did not have the legal authorizations needed for setting them up. They were compelled either to adopt the regular corporate form of organization, with voting rights and dividend payments related to stock-ownership, or, as many of them did, proceed without formal organization, thus exposing themselves to the risks involved in unincorporated, underfinanced business operations.

Certain kinds of economic activity on the part of the Granges were more successful. Among them were the cooperative stores, the cooperative shipping associations (especially those shipping wheat from California) and the cooperative fire insurance companies. There was precedent for the cooperative stores in the Rochdale societies of England, which had been started in the 1840's. The shipping associations required only simple business operations and little capital. Cooperative fire insurance associations were well suited to local management in rural communities and did not need to be capitalized. Some of the Grange stores still survive, mainly in the East and South, and not a few of the farmers' elevators now in existence owe their origin to the Grange, though mostly in a later period than that here under discussion. Over the years the tendency has

7. *Ibid.*, p. 22.

been to separate the business organizations from those more concerned with social, political and educational purposes.[8]

On broader economic problems the Granges were much more influential. They favored monetary reform, and were generally against a single gold standard and redeemable greenbacks. They tended to oppose high protection but were by no means unanimous in that attitude. They wanted the railroads controlled, and, later, were strong supporters of the Sherman antitrust bill.

Political Objectives

In politics the "Grangers" came to exert a very significant influence, and in some states were able to control the elections. The organization was intended by its founders to be nonpolitical, but this proved a hard line to hold. Political meetings often were held by the same group in the same hall after the Grange ritual had been completed, and in several states the Grange groups, during the 1870's, were influential in passing specific legislation. Finally, in 1883, the National Grange itself came out for greater attention to politico-economic questions and advocated wide discussion of them in the local Granges.

"Granger" Legislation in Illinois

As a result of the upsurge in farmer organization and discontent, there came into being a general movement now commonly referred to as the "Granger Movement." Out of it came both significant legislation and the establishment of some basic national policies. This campaign was by no means confined to the organized Granges.[9] It was rather a broad, general farmer movement in which prominent Grangers took a leading part. Most of the other farm organizations, which by now were springing up on every side, held similar views and supported the legislative program of the Grangers. In a sense the political movement seized upon the order of the Patrons of Husbandry as "an efficient means of organization and a convenient rallying point."[10]

Most important of the aims of the Grangers was the public control of railroad rates. In espousing this cause they were bucking a philosophy that had become deeply ingrained in American thinking, namely, the *laissez-faire* doctrine popularized by Adam Smith's *Wealth of Nations* which was published in England in 1776, and came to be widely read and accepted in this country after 1800. This doctrine, at least as then understood, held that the national interest would be best served by relatively complete freedom for the entrepreneur to seek his own best interest — in other words, that the sum of the maximized individual self-interests would add up to maximum national well-being.

Ignoring the fact that Smith's treatise was in large measure a protest against the excessive controls that existed in England at the time it was written, the business groups of England and the United States seized upon it as a complete and irrefutable argument for avoiding all controls. Firmly fixed in this view both by self-interest and sincere belief, they were prepared to oppose every measure that would restrict in any way their exploitation of the farmer, the investor or their labor.

The farmers themselves were by no means anxious to have extensive interference by gov-

---

8. There appears to be in recent years some reversal of this trend in that some of the general farm organizations, particularly the Farm Bureau Federations, have entered rather extensively into the insurance and petroleum products fields. It is perhaps too early to form an opinion as to whether or not these arrangements will persist.

9. Frank M. Drew, writing in 1891, summarized the relation of the Grange to the "Granger" legislation as follows: "Grangerism has come to be an established term in politics, yet the Grange as such had nothing to do with the war waged against railways in Illinois and other Western states in the seventies. The present constitution of Illinois was adopted in 1870, the drastic anti-railway laws were enacted in 1871, while the state

Grange was not organized until 1872. Nor had the Grange any official connection with the famous Granger Cases of the United States Supreme Court. In Illinois at least, the railroad war was carried on by 'farmers clubs,' — open and avowedly political organizations, like the present Farmers' League. . . ." Drew, "The Present Farmers' Movement," *Political Science Quarterly*, June 1891, p. 282.

This appears to be an understatement of Grange influence. Drew centered his attention on the "Alliance" and dismissed the Grange with the briefest of comment. Buck's later studies developed more fully the part played by the "Grangers" in the events of this period.

10. Buck, *The Granger Movement*. Preface, p. v.

ernment in economic affairs. Extreme individualism and impatience with legal restraints had long characterized the frontier populations, but, like most people, farmers were not averse to having others controlled so long as their own freedom of action was not disturbed. Nevertheless, though they understood little of the economics of the situation, they had come to realize that railroad and other monopolies, and the money system, could hurt them, and that these types of business were in some way different from farming.

In buying monopolized commodities or services, the customer could not turn to some other supplier if he was dissatisfied with quality or price, and the forces of competition could not be depended upon to correct maladjustments. As this feeling grew and became crystallized, the farm groups initiated the long series of legislative acts designed to bring under control, in the public interest, those types of business which by their nature are not self-regulatory.

First Granger Laws Unworkable

The first efforts of the Grangers were clumsy and unworkable, but it should be recognized that they were blazing a new trail and undertaking to carry public regulation into a realm where it had not previously been used.[11] Illinois, a predominantly agricultural state, took the lead. Its constitution of 1870 states (in Article XI, Section 12) that

Railways . . . are hereby declared public highways, and shall be free to all persons for the

11. There had been some earlier efforts to regulate the railways, but these were of the mild or "weak" form. New Hampshire established a railroad commission in 1844, and three other New England states had mild forms of regulation by the time of the Civil War. Massachusetts, in 1869, established a more adequate commission but one that was still of the "weak" or advisory type.

The right of legislative bodies to determine what is reasonable compensation for services in which the public has an important interest had long been accepted in English common law. But it had not become a part of the written law of the United States, nor had workable procedures been developed for continuous exercise of this function. Furthermore, the railroads were a recent development. They were generally assumed to be strictly private property and the idea of their being subject to regulation was not accepted readily.

transportation of their persons and property thereon, under such regulations as may be prescribed by law. And the General Assembly shall, from time to time, pass laws establishing reasonable maximum rates of charges for the transportation of passengers and freight on the different railroads of this state.

Section 15 of the same article was designed to meet a second main criticism by the farm groups, that of discrimination. It provided that

The General Assembly shall pass laws to correct abuses and to prevent unjust discrimination and extortion in rates of freight and passenger tariffs on the different railroads in this state, and enforce such laws by adequate penalties, to the extent, if necessary for that purpose, of forfeiture of their property and franchise.

A third provision, also in Article XI, defined public warehouses and required railroad companies to weigh or measure grain at point of shipment, to receipt for it and to deliver to the consignee provided his warehouse was connected with the tracks of the railroad company. All railroad companies were to permit such connections to be made by any warehouseman.

These provisions represented advanced thinking for their time. They struck directly at the things on which farmer complaints were loudest. The method itself was not workable for the reason that railroad rates and problems of discrimination, even then, were too complex and varied to be handled adequately by direct legislative action and enforced by the ordinary agencies of government. But the technical commission was as yet little known or developed in American government, and there was to be a long period of struggle, and of trial and error, before the principle and the mechanism could become established, and accepted as lying within the powers granted by the federal Constitution.[12]

12. The general setting of this problem and an analysis of the early state actions looking to the development of such controls are well discussed in Robert E. Cushman's *The Independent Regulatory Commissions*, Oxford University Press, New York, 1941, Chapters 1 and 2.

Development of Control in Illinois

Although other states were taking up the fight along similar lines, and at about the same time, it will be simplest to consider in sequence the legislation and court decisions in Illinois since these, to a considerable extent, set the pattern which later became established national policy. The General Assembly passed legislation in 1871 designed to implement the constitutional directives already mentioned. Provision was made for dividing railroads into classes based on their gross earnings per mile. Variable maxima of charges for passengers ranging from 2½ cents to 5½ cents per mile were specified. On freight, it was provided that no railroad should charge as much for a given haul as for a longer haul upon the same road. This was the forerunner of the long-and-short-haul controversy which received much public consideration at a later date.

Freight rates were to be further controlled through a formula establishing normal or maximum rates for any date, which should be no higher than those for the corresponding day of the year 1870. This was obviously a makeshift, and particularly bad in view of the fact that there had been unusually great fluctuations in rates in 1870. Furthermore, it was merely a device for preventing rates from going higher rather than one for determining what rates would be reasonable. In a fast-developing area with considerable competition among carriers, rates should show a downward trend even if no restrictions were established. Thus the provisions against discrimination were probably more significant than the provisions relating to the level of freight rates.

The legislation also provided regulation of warehouses with maximum charges for storage put at 2 cents per bushel for the first thirty days and ½ cent for each 15 days thereafter. In addition, all warehousemen were required to publish their rates for each year during the first week in January, and were prohibited from increasing them thereafter. There was to be no discrimination between customers. A further act regulated the receiving, transportation and delivery of grain by railroad corporations, and forbade discrimination between shippers and warehouses in the handling of grain.

The General Assembly also passed legislation that looked in the direction of modern regulatory methods, but did not undertake to delegate legislative power, an issue that was to be much discussed in legislative halls and the courts during the 1890's and later. This legislation provided for the establishment of a board of railroad and warehouse commissioners, and required that every railroad company doing business in the state make an annual report to the board. These reports were to show capital stock, assets, liabilities, debt, amount of business, monthly earnings, expenses of operation and so on. The board could, at its discretion, add other inquiries to the list. Warehousemen were also required to make such statements as the board might require.

As compared to the freedom of action existing previously, these were long steps in the direction of aggressive regulation of public utilities. The utilities were, of course, unwilling to accept them without a vigorous fight. Besides, they constituted a change in the functions of government which many people sincerely regarded as unconstitutional and undesirable, even if permissible under the Constitution.

Regulatory Laws Challenged in the Courts

Many of the carriers and warehousemen refused to conform to the new laws, and the board lacked clear authority and mechanisms for enforcing compliance. Some farmers took the law into their own hands, attempting to ride for the legal fares and giving trainmen the alternative of accepting the lower fares or throwing them off bodily.[13] Bitterness grew, and was intensified by an adverse decision handed down by Chief Justice Law-

13.. Solon J. Buck, *The Agrarian Crusade, A Chronicle of the Farmer in Politics*, Yale University Press, New Haven, 1920, p. 52.

rence of the State Supreme Court.[14] Several suits had been brought in the state courts which involved parts of the new legislation. Judge Lawrence held that the legislature had power to prohibit *unjust* discrimination but not every type of discrimination. The reasoning here was somewhat similar to that which took form a few decades later in the United States Supreme Court's doctrine of the "rule of reason" in respect to the proposed dissolution of the Standard Oil Company.[15] Judge Lawrence also contended that the state constitution was violated through failure to allow the companies to explain the reasons for the discriminations shown.

A case was also brought by the board of railroad and warehouse commissioners against Munn and Scott in order to test the validity of the warehouse law. The state won in the lower courts, and the case was appealed to the United States Supreme Court under the name *Munn* v. *Illinois*.[16] Final de-

cision for the state was rendered in 1876, and this became one of the foundation decisions establishing the right of government to regulate public utilities. It was the first of the celebrated "Granger Cases."

The adverse action of the courts on the legislation of 1871 brought vigorous criticism from the farmers and resulted in the formation of the Independent Reform Party which defeated Lawrence for re-election. Though possibly unjust and dangerous in its implications, the campaign against Lawrence was a very natural outcome, and quite in keeping with the usual farmer preference for direct and positive action without much concern for legal niceties.[17]

Legislation Revised and Clarified, 1873

Lawrence's decision, while unpopular at the time, and adverse to his own interests, proved a constructive factor in the evolution of legislation relating to public utilities. It brought about passage of the more carefully drawn "Railroad Act of 1873" on unjust discrimination and extortion. This act has remained the basis for railroad control in Illinois, and has served as a model for legislation in other states. It declared that any railroad company charging more than a fair or reasonable rate should be deemed guilty

14. *Chicago and Alton Railroad Co.* v. *The People ex rel. Gustavus Koerner et al.*, Comrs., 67 Ill. 11 (1873).
15. *Standard Oil Co. of New Jersey et al.* v. *U.S.*, 221 U.S. 1 (1911).
16. The substance of *Munn* v. *Illinois*, 94 U.S. 113 (1876) was as follows: The plaintiffs sued on the ground that
   a. Warehousing is not a public calling and the business is therefore not within the regulatory power of the state.
   b. The fixing of rates deprives the owners of the power to establish higher rates and thus deprives them of their property without due process of law, contrary to the Fourteenth Amendment to the United States Constitution.
   c. If the courts decide that warehousing is a public calling it is the work of the judiciary and not the legislature to determine a fair charge.
Chief Justice Waite held, however, that "Property does become clothed with a public interest when used in a manner to make it of public consequence, and affect the community at large. When, therefore, one devotes his property to a use in which the public has an interest, he, in effect, grants to the public an interest in that use, and must submit to be controlled by the public for the common good to the extent of the interest he has thus created." (94 U.S. 113 at 126.) "We must," he said, "look . . . to the common law, from whence came the right which the constitution protects . . ." He further held that the fixing of rates was a legislative and not a judicial matter, asserting that "it has been customary from time immemorial for the legislature to declare what shall be a reasonable compensation under such circumstances, or, perhaps more properly speaking, to fix a maximum beyond which any charge made would be unreasonable." (94 U.S. 113 at 133–34.)
   In this decision the guiding principle with respect to regulation of public utilities generally was established,

but the achievement of adequate methods for carrying the principle into effect was still far in the future.
17. The explanations of this action differ somewhat, according to the biases of those writing them. Periam, in *The Groundswell*, pp. 312–13, says, "The farmers felt themselves slighted in not being consulted on the renomination of Lawrence . . . and resolved to hold a meeting on the subject, not with any intention of supplanting Judge Lawrence (whom the originators of the Convention intended to nominate), but with the object of showing that the people were determined to be consulted on questions affecting their interests. Unfortunately, between the calling and the meeting of the Convention, Judge Lawrence, in accepting the nomination, expressed himself in contemptuous terms about the power of the people. This put the farmers on their mettle. They considered themselves as much entitled to be represented as any other class, and determined to run a candidate of their own."
   The fact remains, however, that the resolutions adopted by the Convention undertook to specify what interpretation should be made of the pertinent sections of the constitution, and recommended that the anti-monopolists "nominate such candidates for Supreme and Circuit Judges as are pledged to sustain the Constitution and laws of this State in accordance therewith." *Ibid.*, p. 314.

of violating the act. Section 3 defined discrimination as the making of a difference in the charge as between persons and places for the same service *in the same direction*. The Act of 1871 did not distinguish between movements in one direction, which might consist almost wholly of loaded cars, and that in the opposite direction, where the trains might consist largely of empties for which any kind of a load, even at low rates, would be an advantage to the carrier and socially desirable.

Sections 4 and 5 provided means of enforcement by actions in the name of the state to recover fines ranging from $1,000 to $5,000 for first offenses up to $25,000 for the fourth and subsequent offenses. Section 6 provided that the aggrieved party might recover three times the amount of the damages sustained, plus costs and attorneys' fees. The act also made it the duty of the railroad commission "to personally investigate and ascertain whether the provisions of this act are violated" and to "cause suits to be commenced and prosecuted against any railroad corporation which may violate the provisions of this act."

Section 8 marked a further step in the direction of modern procedures. It directed the commission to prepare schedules of maximum rates for the transportation of passengers, freight and cars upon each railroad. After January 15, 1874, rates so established were to be taken as *prima facie* evidence of reasonableness in all suits involving charges of railroad companies. This meant placing decisions on maximum rates in the hands of a specialized administrative agency, instead of trying to establish them through the uninformed and usually prejudiced voting of legislators in a general assembly. It also established the principle of delegating legislative powers, a principle that was to come under heavy fire in the national government at a later date.

The constitutionality of the act was finally confirmed by the State Supreme Court in June 1880. It upheld the right of the state to prevent unjust discrimination and extortion, even when the charter of the railroad company expressly conferred upon it the right to fix charges. There was little further difficulty in enforcing the law, and by 1880 the frantic demands for lower rates had almost entirely subsided, in part no doubt because of the gradual increase in prosperity, and also because of the general tendency for rates to decline during the decade immediately following the decision. After 1880 there was relatively little friction between the commission and the railroad companies. The commission prevented any serious abuses, but did not interfere much with the business of the companies.

Railroad Legislation in Adjoining States

While this battle was being fought out in Illinois similar struggles were being joined in nearly all the states of the Middle West, particularly in Minnesota, Iowa, Wisconsin and Missouri. The acts passed were less effective, however, than those of Illinois. The laws, for the most part, were not well thought out and were less carefully drawn. Some were too arbitrary and restrictive.

In Minnesota the railroads denied the validity of the new laws and, though the legislation was finally upheld in the courts, the legislature had in the meantime virtually given up the effort to enforce it. In Iowa more reliance was placed on the effort to fix rates directly by legislative action. While this was more successful than in some other states it resulted in a less flexible and scientific procedure than that which had been achieved in Illinois.

In Wisconsin controversy centered largely around the Potter Law of 1874. This was an extreme measure, but similar in character to the earlier legislation of Illinois and Iowa. The Potter Law and a companion measure, the Anti-pass Act of 1874, constitute the main body of the Granger legislation in Wisconsin.

After several trials of strength in which neither the antiregulation group nor the radical Grangers proved strong enough to force its own measures through, various compromises were arrived at. As a result of these, the Vance Act of 1876 virtually surrendered the principle of effective control, and repealed most of the preceding legislation including the anti-pass law. Missouri followed more closely the lead of Illinois, while in Kansas and Nebraska railroad legislation was delayed until the 1880's, because of the fear of discouraging further new construction.

Meanwhile the issue was prominent in California and various other states. California passed, in 1876, the O'Connor Law designed to curb the Central Pacific. This act, however, did not provide any specific rate control, and was too general to be of value. The state's constitutional convention of 1878 was a turbulent one considerably dominated by a militant minority of "Kearneyites" or labor delegates, joined on some issues by the unorganized farmer delegates. They wrote into the new constitution railroad provisions that Buck characterizes as "the most radical . . . ever embodied in a state constitution."[18] All railroad and other transportation companies were declared to be common carriers and subject to legislative control. The constitutional provisions were embodied in an act passed in 1880, but the agitation that had produced them had died down, and the elective commission provided does not seem to have subjected the railroads to any serious restrictions.[19]

Significance of the Granger Laws

The Granger movement was an important factor in achieving and shaping legislation of this kind both nationally and in a large number of the states. Its indirect influence can be traced in practically all of the public utility legislation of these years and since. The principal features of railroad legislation that are primarily of Granger origin are:

(1) The fixing of maximum rates by direct legislation. For freight rates this was usually followed by the setting up of commissions with power to establish schedules of maximum rates.

(2) Provision that such maximum rates are *prima facie* evidence of reasonableness before the courts.

(3) Laws designed to prevent discrimination between places by means of "long-and-short-haul" clauses.

(4) The attempt to preserve competition by forbidding consolidation of parallel lines.

(5) Laws prohibiting the granting of free passes to public officials.[20]

Thus was laid the groundwork for a new outlook on an extensive array of public problems — one that was to be greatly enlarged in later periods. The proposition was established legally that a state may, under its police powers, regulate, to the extent of fixing maximum charges, any business which is public in nature or has been "clothed with a public interest." It also settled the issue that, although a railroad charter is a contract, it is subject to the general laws under which it is obtained, and the state is not inhibited from regulating charges made by the carrier unless the charter contains a direct stipulation to that effect. Two other propositions set up were later lost through adverse action by the higher courts: (1) that a state may, at least until Congress acts on the matter, regulate interstate commerce so far as its citizens are affected; and (2) that the power of the state to regulate rates is not subject to restraint by the courts.[21] This latter proposition was to be the subject of lengthy controversy between the Interstate Commerce Commission and the courts even after the federal government itself undertook the regulation of rates.

Agitation for Federal Control

Paralleling the efforts at state control, there

18. Buck, *The Granger Movement*, p. 198. The manipulations by which this result was accomplished are described in detail in Carl Brent Swisher, *Motivation and Political Technique in the California Constitutional Convention, 1878–79*, Pomona College, Claremont, California, 1930.

19. The activities and point of view of the Grange in California just prior to this period are well described in Ezra S. Carr, *The Patrons of Husbandry on the Pacific Coast*, A. L. Bancroft and Company, San Francisco, 1875.

20. Buck, *The Granger Movement*, p. 205.

21. The power of the courts to review such legislatively established rates was upheld in the Minnesota rate case — *Chicago, Milwaukee and St. Paul Railway Company* v. *Minnesota*, 134 U.S. 418 (1890) — in which the Supreme Court took the stand that the reasonableness of rates is ultimately a judicial question. This position was eventually modified by subsequent legislation and court decisions. See Cushman, *Independent Regulatory Commissions*, p. 469.

was a long period of agitation for federal legislation to control the railroads. This began in the Fortieth Congress (1867–1868). Later the Grange and other farm organizations took a prominent part in the controversy. After about 1880 the demand for regulation became more general. In the early period the main drive was for cheaper transportation, with emphasis on the view that the problem was to be solved through competition, either by constructing publicly owned water and rail facilities to compete with the privately owned carriers[22] or by bringing about more active competition between them.

This view was stressed by the Windom Committee in its report, April 24, 1874.[23] That committee had been appointed in 1873, at the height of the Granger movement, with Senator Windom of Minnesota as chairman. The report also proposed various restrictions on the carriers, requirement for complete publicity of rates, prohibition of increases without due notice, prevention of consolidation of competing lines, prohibition of certain types of discrimination, and so forth. Here also appears the proposal to establish a bureau of commerce to collect information on rates and fares, rebates and discrimination, receipts and expenditures, bonds and stocks, and so on.

No action was taken on the Windom report. Competition was beginning to force rates down on long-distance traffic and the general level of rates was lowered substantially over the succeeding ten years. Freight rates were declining generally during the 1880's, thus easing the pressure for official action with respect to them. Rates on carload lots from California to the East were reduced nearly 50 per cent between 1880 and 1889 and those from California to New York more than 50 per cent.[24]

Rates were not reduced correspondingly on shipments from stations served by only one railroad. In consequence, there were gross discriminations between different towns and cities. This resulted in a changed emphasis, main consideration being given to discrimination rather than to the general level of rates. Various bills embodying these ideas were introduced, among them the Reagan bill of 1878. Reagan, a Texan, was a member of the Patrons of Husbandry, and his bill may be assumed to represent the Grange view of that time. Its main emphasis was on preventing discrimination. Though presented several times, it failed of enactment.[25] This period marked approximately the close of Granger leadership in railroad legislation. The Grange was by now being supplanted by other farm organizations which were more interested in other issues.

Interstate Commerce Act of 1887

After 1880, nonfarm groups became more active in fostering railroad legislation. The Cullom Committee (headed by Senator Cullom of Illinois) reported in 1886, and Cullom brought in a bill which became the Interstate Commerce Act of 1887. Congress was deadlocked for a time on the proposal, but the Wabash decision of 1886 brought about its passage. That decision denied the states the right to regulate interstate traffic, and thus made it evident that if such rates (which covered the bulk of the movement) were to be regulated, control would have to be exercised by the federal government.[26]

Though far from perfect, the new act established the system under which the great

22. A similar line of thinking appears later in the federal legislation of 1924 which created government-owned barge lines on the Mississippi and Missouri rivers; and, in Canada, in the building of the Canadian National line paralleling the Canadian Pacific.

23. U.S. Congress, Senate, *Report of the Select Committee on Transportation Routes to the Seaboard*, S.Rep. 307, 43rd Cong., 1st sess., 1874.

24. Annual address of William H. Mills, *Transactions*

of the Califorina State Agricultural Society . . . , September 1890, p. 192.

25. The Reagan bill was much discussed. Various substitutes were proposed. The House Committee, in the session of 1884–1885 substituted a much less stringent bill. The House reversed the committee action, and passed the Reagan bill. The Senate presented a more moderate bill of its own. Agreement was not reached and neither bill was passed. See Arthur T. Hadley, *Railroad Transportation, Its History and Its Laws*, G. P. Putnam's Sons, New York, 1900, pp. 140–41. See also Davis R. Dewey, *National Problems, 1885–1897*, Harper and Brothers, New York, 1907, pp. 96–98.

26. *Wabash, St. Louis and Pacific Railway Company*, v. *Illinois*, 118 U.S. 557 (1886). For fuller discussion of the

majority of freight and passenger rates are controlled. It was in large measure an outgrowth of the first great organized movement of farmers in the United States. Before it could attain the effectiveness and prestige it now has, many important court decisions became necessary and additional legislation had to be passed. But the later legislation was, in the main, in keeping with the purposes and provisions of the original act and designed to make it more effective.

The Decline of Grange Influence

By 1875 the Grange had reached its peak membership of 858,000.[27] It has been estimated, however, that twice that number participated in its activities. As has been noted, its growth had been sensational, but many mistakes had been made, and the organization lacked the close integration, settled policies and continuing appeal to maintain its huge and diverse membership. The greatest losses were in the upper Mississippi Valley where members had been most numerous. This also was the area in which antimonopoly sentiment had been most radical and where there had been the heaviest involvement in business ventures, most of which were not successful.

There are dangers to any general farm organization in centering the interest of its members too exclusively on one or two issues. If the objectives are achieved, the reason for the organization ceases to be. If their achievement is long delayed, it is difficult to maintain interest in what seems to be a futile struggle. A more diverse program with strong social as well as economic objectives and a modest but continuous record of achievement appear to be more conducive to long life in farm organizations, except where they have a specific continuing economic function.

From Michigan eastward to New England the Granges gave more stress to social and educational activities, and became less involved in sensational but often impractical business ventures and political undertakings. Here the Grange has shown great power of survival, and has maintained its position as a stable local institution. For the country as a whole membership fell off rapidly after 1875 and was down to 124,000 by 1880, little more than one seventh the number it had five years earlier. Thereafter Grange membership remained at a very modest level until after the turn of the century, when it experienced a new and more stable growth. The period of lowest membership was from 1884 to 1889 when it ranged between 110,000 and 120,000. By 1900 it was again approaching 200,000.[28]

Accomplishments of the Grange

The influence of the Grange movement was, however, by no means so limited as its later modest membership would indicate. Grange ideas and Grange ideals are discernible in almost all of the farm organizations that succeeded it, and the Grange itself had a sizable record of accomplishment during the decades here under discussion. It had grown too fast, it had attempted too much, and the methods of organization used were better suited to rousing enthusiasm than to maintaining it. Nevertheless, its less widely publicized activities were important.

Their influence was mainly on farm people and their communities rather than upon national policies. Hence they do not appear in the general histories of the period and are less well known. The organization took steps to safeguard and assure proper use of lands and funds assigned to the state colleges of agriculture. The fraternal features of the Order, and the contacts established, did much to allay the bitterness between farmers of the North and those of the South. Appropriations were ob-

---

case and its background, see Cushman, *The Independent Regulatory Commissions*, p. 38.

27. Thomas Clark Atkeson, *Semi-Centennial History of the Patrons of Husbandry*, Orange Judd, New York, 1916, p. 350.

28. Atkeson, *Semi-Centennial History of the Patrons of Husbandry*, p. 350. Though originally conceived as a means of bettering rural conditions in the South, the Grange did not find in that region the most fertile soil for its growth. Its main strength in the 1870's was in the North Central states and, later, in New York and New England.

tained for the dissemination of agricultural literature, and many local agricultural fairs were established.

Largely through Grange influence the Department of Agriculture was raised to Cabinet status. Farmers' institutes were encouraged, and agitation was begun in 1880 for the teaching of agriculture in the public schools. The Grange was active in getting the agricultural experiment stations established (1887), and in obtaining rural mail delivery and, later, the parcel post system. The organization opposed, almost from the beginning, fraud and adulteration in food processing. It fought monopoly, and worked against bribery and corruption among public officials.

It called for preservation of the forests, favored woman's suffrage, fostered crop reporting, advocated ballot reform, and opposed the extension of patent privileges. In many of these proposals are the germs of ideas that later became full-fledged national policies. Where it became well established the social activity fostered by the Grange was a very real contribution to the quality of living in rural areas isolated by poor roads, slow transportation and inadequate contact.

The early history of the Grange and the organizations that followed or were contemporary with it provides many lessons both in its successes and in its mistakes. The organization wisely refrained from direct political action in its own name. Nevertheless it made political action possible by establishing contact and mutual confidence among farmers within communities and among those of different areas. If many of the business ventures undertaken proved ill-advised, it should be recalled that there was little precedent to draw on, and much to learn. Many a more recent organization has made the same mistakes, with far less excuse for doing so.

The movement's surprising feature is not the errors made but rather the clarity of vision it showed in recognizing so many of the fundamental problems of the time, and the initiation of so many lines of thought that ultimately matured into accepted national policies. The fraternal and secret features of the Order seem overemphasized in the light of present-day attitudes, but they were clearly in keeping with the spirit of the times and probably helped to strengthen the organization. It was a time when fraternal societies flourished throughout the land both among urban and rural people.

CONTEMPORARY AND SUCCESSOR ORGANIZATIONS OF FARMERS

Farmers' clubs, organized locally and without state or national affiliation, had long been a feature of American rural life. In the period 1872–1875, as class consciousness developed in the farming areas, these groups quite generally organized into state associations for mutual stimulation, and especially to pursue political and economic objectives. They marked the first definite entrance of farmers as a class into politics. The Grange movement did not satisfy all farmers. Many objected to its secrecy and nonpartisanship. The farmers' clubs of this period, especially in the West, were nonsecret and avowedly political. They multiplied much as the Granges did and for the same reasons. Much of the so-called Granger power resulted from common objectives on the part of the Granges and the farmers' clubs.

In the South, the farmers' club movement was revived around 1871. This led to the First National Agricultural Congress in 1872. Here the desire was mainly to advance agriculture and its kindred interests after the destruction that had occurred during the war years. The initiative stemmed more from business and professional men than from farmers. Partisan politics was to be ignored, though the agricultural groups wanted adequate representation of farmers in state and national councils. Subjects having even a remote bearing on politics were considered not proper for discussion.

The Agricultural Wheel

The Agricultural Wheel was a purely agricultural organization originally known as the Wattensas Farmers Club. It spread through parts of the Southwest, becoming strongest in

Arkansas. Starting in 1882, as a secret society with seven members, it set up a state organization in 1883, at which time its membership numbered five hundred. By 1887, the Agricultural Wheel had 500,000 members and was able to establish a national organization, with separate divisions for white and colored farmers.

The Wheel condemned the mortgaging of livestock and growing crops. It was against "soulless" corporations. It put forward the idea of reducing acreages of crops so as to reduce production and raise prices. It also proposed graduated income taxes and the limiting of tariffs to luxury products. It opposed the national banks. Among other things it wanted more farmers in legislative bodies and direct election of all officers of the national government.

The National Farmers' Alliance

The name Farmers' Alliance was a popular one and was used in one form or another by many of the organizations of the period. The main developments under this name were in the Southwest, whereas the Grange had its principal strength in the northern Mississippi Valley states. The Alliance movement began around 1872 and was a part of the broad general struggle that grew out of the discontent in the farm areas that characterized these decades. At first these organizations were known as Settlers' Protective Associations, Settlers' Leagues or Settlers' Alliances.

Their principal purposes were to resist the encroachment by the railroads on pre-empted lands, particularly in the Osage area of Kansas. They were primarily trade associations. One of their accomplishments was to obtain passage of an enabling act permitting action to be brought in the name of the United States to set aside patents on Osage lands which had been issued to railroad companies. A decision by the United States Supreme Court, in 1875, authorized pre-emptions in these areas.

A somewhat similar movement appeared in Texas, in 1874 and 1875, under the name Texas Farmers' Alliance. The original purpose was to oppose the "land sharks." Other activities included development of brand registration, formulation of plans for purchasing supplies and support of the greenback proposals. This latter objective brought involvement in politics, and the Alliance was crushed by the dominant party of the state. It did, however, adopt a declaration of principles which became the basis for that of the larger organization later established under the same name. Moreover, its disastrous experience with politics served as a warning to its successor.

Efforts to Draw in Labor Groups

As a result of the consolidation, in 1887, of the Texas Farmers' Alliance and the Farmers' Union of Louisiana, the National Farmers' Alliance and Cooperative Union of America was formed, with a federal charter. In 1888 the Agricultural Wheel joined with this group, the joint organization then taking the name Farmers' and Laborers' Union of America. The name was again changed, in 1889, to National Farmers' Alliance and Industrial Union, at which time the Farmers' and Laborers' Union of Kansas became a part of the organization. In that year also an agreement was made with the Knights of Labor with a view to encouraging joint action by farmers and industrial workers on national problems.[29]

This heterogeneous group of organizations

29. The Knights of Labor was a general and comparatively radical organization which started in Philadelphia around 1873. It grew rapidly and by 1885 had a membership of more than half a million. The Knights believed that "all laborers—skilled and unskilled, men, women, whites, and blacks—should band together in one mighty organization without distinction of trade and craft." They did not favor or attempt collective bargaining, and by 1886 were following a line directly opposed to that of the newly formed American Federation of Labor which sought primarily advantages for skilled labor, whereas the Knights were willing, if necessary, to "level down" the skilled workers in order to benefit the unskilled. They engaged rather successfully in a violent struggle with the Gould system of railways in 1885, introducing the tactic now known as "sabotage." They were active and influential until the 1890's, but disappeared during that decade. Their activities are well described in Mary R. Beard's *A Short History of the American Labor Movement,* George H. Doran, New York, 1925, pp. 116–26.

is commonly referred to as the "Southern" or "Southwestern" Alliance. It was the first large-scale attempt to combine the farm and labor groups in a common front. As in all similar attempts since that time, the tie proved a difficult one to maintain. The interests of farmers and of industrial labor, while superficially similar, have always thus far shown considerable divergence when specific programs were considered. The farmer is an entrepreneur, and, even when not actually an employer, he tends to think more like an employer than like an employee. Generally speaking he will uphold, in principle, the right of labor to organize, but tends to look coldly upon labor's demands for shorter hours, its restrictions on output and even its wage demands, which to him have usually seemed excessive.

In these realms farmers and industrial workers are likely to have interests that are not only seemingly but actually in conflict. On the other hand, their true interests may very well be in harmony on broader issues which affect the prosperity of the country as a whole, as for instance fiscal and monetary issues. Be that as it may, the efforts to combine farmers and industrial workers in a single organization with a common platform have not been notably successful. There appears to be much more promise in organizations that are more specifically oriented, each adopting its own program but joining with others on issues in which their interests coincide. The Alliance was no exception to the general rule in this respect. It had a turbulent and relatively brief history.

Eight of the state Alliances were granted, in 1888, almost complete local autonomy. They were expected to deal with local conditions as they saw fit. The parent organization had relatively little authority in determining policies. At that time there were 10,-000 sub-Alliances and about 400,000 individual members. By 1890 the organization had a foothold in 35 states and numbered somewhere between one million and three million members.

The Alliance of the Southwest virtually

disappeared in the election of 1892. It was torn asunder and destroyed by the third party issue. The smaller faction joined with the Populists; the larger one supported the Democratic party.

Other Farm Organizations

Several other organizations sprang up temporarily during the 1880's, and eventually were absorbed either directly or indirectly by the Alliance. "The Brothers of Freedom" was formed in 1882 as a secret organization centering principally in Arkansas. The name derived from the Revolutionary group known as "The Sons of Freedom." It was formed "to enable farmers to obtain a just reward for their hard labor, and to incite proper rivalry among merchants and dealers." When the organization was absorbed by the Agricultural Wheel, in 1885, it had 643 subordinate units.

The Farmers' Cooperative Union, another localized organization, grew up in Louisiana, mainly from 1885 on. It was a revival of a farmers' club group dating from about 1880, and was nonsecret. It sought more equitable taxation, equal rights in transportation, lower rates of interest and cheaper administration of the laws. It also advocated more farmer representation in legislative bodies. In its later form the organization adopted a ritual derived from a defunct Grange, but with one degree instead of seven. It eventually was merged with the Texas Alliance.

Alliance of Colored Farmers

There was also formed during these years an Alliance of Colored Farmers of Texas (in December 1886). This began in Houston County and spread rapidly through Texas. It was nonpartisan and was designed to promote agriculture, suppress prejudice, and improve colored farmers as workers and as members of the community. A ritual was adopted. The officials were colored, but the general superintendent, who was white, handled the work of organization.

By 1888 the Texas plan had spread into several other states and as a result the Colored Farmers' National Alliance and Cooperative Union was formed in December of that year. It was chartered as a trade union under the laws of the United States but retained its agricultural character. By 1891 subordinate state organizations were operating under state charter in 10 states, and as many as 10 other states had some arm of the organization. Membership had grown to 1,200,000 (750,000 men, 300,000 women and 150,000 youths under twenty-one). The "colored" Alliance, like the "white" one, disappeared in the turbulent political struggles that marked the first part of the 1890's.[30]

Though the Alliance movement had its greatest strength in the Southwest, there were similar developments in a number of the northern states at about the same time, though with somewhat different objectives because of the different problems facing the farmers of those areas. In the Southwest much attention was given to problems affecting the cattle industry. Alliance brands were developed, and steps were taken looking to protection against cattle and horse stealing and to the return of livestock that had strayed.

The clarification of land titles and resistance to the land claims of the railroads were prominent in the thinking of settlers. The Alliance was also strongly opposed to "the exactions of the money-lenders." However, as they became organized the farmers of both North and South gave attention to more general problems though they never achieved the unity of purpose that marked the western segment of the Grange group.

Later Policies of the Alliance

By 1890 the Alliance was asking for financial reforms of inflationary character, though not necessarily free silver. It protested against the ownership of land by aliens and excessive landholdings of railroads, and expressed concern over the disappearance of the public lands. By this time it was demanding that the government take over and operate all means of transportation and communication. Other demands were for lower interest rates, less stringent laws for the protection of mortgage-holders and the abolition of national banks.[31]

Political action was contemplated, but the plan was to work within existing parties. Over the period as a whole, Alliance men exerted political influence in the middle western states, but the laws enacted at their insistence, especially those affecting railroads, proved abortive, partly because the farmers found themselves unable to get reliable representatives into the state legislatures.

While the political aspects of the Alliance program have received most attention, these were not, at the time, considered its main objectives. The national organization was loosely formed and had little authority. It was a delegate body designed to link together the various state and local units, each of which was left free to work out its own problems in its own way. The objectives were stated as, first, social; second, educational; third, financial; and fourth, political. Circulating libraries were formed in the locals, and, like the Grange before it, the Alliance became a great "National University." The

30. See "History of the Colored Farmers' National Alliance and Co-operative Union," by General R. M. Humphrey, Superintendent, in N. A. Dunning (ed.), *The Farmers' Alliance History and Agricultural Digest,* Alliance Publishing Company, Washington, 1891, pp. 288–92.

At about this same time there was formed in Texas a Negro farmers' association known as The Farmers' Improvement Society of Texas, which was more permanent. It was reported to have in 1907, 415 branches in Texas and Oklahoma and 10,000 members. Principal objectives were to fight the credit or mortgage system which was characterized as "the Negro's second slavery," to improve farming methods, and to cooperate in buying and selling, See W. E. Burghardt Du Bois (ed.), *Economic Cooperation among Negro Americans,* Atlanta University Press, Atlanta, 1907, pp. 172–73.

31. The violence of the growing opposition to the national banks is illustrated by a statement from the *Journal of Agriculture,* official organ of the Farmers' and Laborers' Union of Missouri, the Missouri branch of the Southern Alliance, issue of August 14, 1890:

"These [national] banks were conceived in infamy and were organized for no other purpose but to rob the many for the benefit of the few. The establishment of national banks was of the same character of vicious legislation that demonetized silver and changed the terms for the payment of our national bonds. The infamous scoundrels who perpetrated these frauds, if they had lived in any other country under the sun, would have been hung without judge or jury or sent to the penitentiary for the rest of their natural lives, either of which would have been no more than they deserved." Quoted in Drew, "The Present Farmers' Movement," p. 295.

numbers and circulation of farm papers increased enormously. A National Reform Press Association consisting of pro-Alliance newspapers was formed.[32] These papers carried on a vigorous campaign in behalf of the Alliance program.

Attempt to Unite Alliances

An attempt was finally made, in 1889, to unite the Northern and Southern Alliances in a single national organization. The gathering revealed willingness of the two groups to work together for common objectives and to accept whatever assistance they could get from organized labor. As a move for outright consolidation, however, it failed completely, largely because the third party idea had by then come under discussion. Union of the two groups was likely to prove embarrassing both to those who favored and to those who did not favor the creation of a third party.[33]

The Alliance produced an "intellectual ferment," and, as Hicks states, its main strength lay in its awakening of a thoroughgoing class-consciousness.[34] Drew, viewing the movement in 1891, described it in the following terms:

There is a phenomenon known to quarrymen as "creeping," — that is, the expansion of deep-bedded rock-strata when relieved of the pressure of the overlying mass, which may be used as a figure of the farmers' movement. For a time the rock moves with irresistible force; but when the mass has become adjusted to its natural level, the motion ceases. If we are to believe the farmers, all they ask for is to be freed from the burdens of others, and given a chance to take their natural position. There are cheering signs in the agitation. A new body of men is taking upon itself political responsibilities. These men are orthodox in religion, earnest, honest, hard-working, — the very class whose active participation in civil affairs is desirable. If they go wrong it will be the fault of their heads, not of their hearts; and no one will be more to blame than he who, knowing how to instruct, does nothing but sneer or find fault.[35]

The People's Party (Populists)

The Alliance movement, though avowedly nonpartisan, and with stated objectives that minimized political activity, had nevertheless been moving inexorably toward an independent venture in the political field. Such a movement began to take shape as early as 1887 in the formation of the Union Labor Party at Cincinnati. This was an attempt to organize and make effective the widely prevalent discontent of the farm and labor groups.

A national ticket was put up in 1888, and an appreciable number of votes polled in Kansas, Missouri, Iowa, Wisconsin, Illinois, Texas and Arkansas. The effort failed as a nationwide movement for reform. Its name carried the implication that it was an outgrowth of the radical union labor movement of the middle 1880's. However, in most of the states mentioned it furnished a convenient means for the expression of dissatisfaction with the older parties. There was apparently at the time a better prospect of survival for state parties, based on local issues, than for a single new national party.

On June 12, 1890, there was called at Topeka, Kansas, a convention which was attended by 41 Alliance men, 28 representatives of the Knights of Labor, 10 from the Farmers' Mutual Benefit Association, 7 Grangers and 4 singletaxers. It nominated a third party state ticket. Similar conventions

32. This was an effort to counteract the "numerous falsehoods" published by the non-Alliance press. Drew says, "The editors composing this association are obliged to sustain the St. Louis platform in every particular. Failure so to do subjects them to suspension from the Alliance by the national president. All this indicates narrowness, and yet one can find excuse for the feelings shown, after reading a few of the columns of mingled abuse, misrepresentation and ridicule, which so many papers published in 1890, under the heading 'Alliance News.'" Drew, "The Present Farmers' Movement," p. 310.

33. The organizations discussed in the preceding pages were, in the main, those of the West and Southwest, and in nearly all cases were more or less involved in politics. In the Northeast and in the East North Central states other organizations of a less militant and political type were organized during these years, among them the Farmers' League, Massachusetts (1889), The Patrons of Industry of North America, Michigan (1889), and the Ancient Order of Gleaners, Michigan (1894). These, in general, were more conservative and similar in type to the Granges of the northeastern states, though only the Gleaners was secret and fraternal. They did not exert any important national influence.

34. John D. Hicks, *The Populist Revolt*, University of Minnesota Press, Minneapolis, 1931, p. 104.

35. Drew, "The Present Farmers' Movement," p. 310.

were held in Nebraska and the Dakotas, and eventually third party tickets were nominated in all of the Middle Border states where the Alliance was strong. In the South the effort was centered on getting control of the machinery of the Democratic party rather than on creating a new party. The Southern Alliance had turned to politics when its business cooperatives failed.

The so-called "sub-Treasury" plan, which had been put forward by the Southern Alliance, was again brought up at the Topeka convention. It had aroused tremendous opposition at the St. Louis meeting of 1889 and came near to splitting the ranks of the reformers. Under this plan it was proposed that the system of using certain banks as United States depositories be abolished, and that instead there be established in each agricultural county a sub-Treasury office, together with elevators and warehouses. Agricultural products were to be accepted for storage, and 80 per cent of the local value was to be advanced in legal-tender paper money at an interest charge of one per cent per year on condition that the product be sold within one year (or auctioned off at the end of the year).[36] The plan continued to draw fire from its opponents, and soon dropped into oblivion.

The election results of 1890 were gratifying to third party advocates in the North and to reformers in the South. Third party candidates held the balance of power, though not outright control, in Kansas, Nebraska, South Dakota and Minnesota. Reform governors were elected in South Carolina, North Carolina and Georgia, and Alliance forces had control of the legislatures of eight states. They also elected two United States senators and several sympathetic congressmen.

The results in the way of legislation were not satisfying to the reform groups. Newly elected legislators are seldom effective as against more experienced ones. Furthermore, the new parties had not had time to work out

specific and detailed legislation or to become expert in shepherding legislation through law-making bodies and governors' offices. In most cases they did not have sufficient strength to push their measures through against skilled opposition. Moreover, many of the things they wanted required national legislation. All signs pointed, therefore, to the need for a national third party to supplement the state parties, if their ends were to be attained.

The Cincinnati Convention of 1891

Through the initiative of the Northern Alliance, plus a few southerners, a third party convention was assembled at Cincinnati in May 1891. It drew representation from all leading organizations and from some that few people had ever heard of. The name People's party, which had originated in Kansas, was chosen for the national organization. The primary source of membership was the New West and the New South.

This meeting was followed by a convention held at St. Louis in February 1892 and by an official nominating convention held at Omaha in July of that year. James B. Weaver of Iowa was nominated for the presidency, and James G. Field of Virginia for the vice-presidency. The platform committee endorsed government ownership of railroads and of telephone and telegraph lines. The sub-Treasury plan was approved, though interest in it had declined. The party's platform also demanded return to the government of lands granted to railroads and other corporations except such as were actually needed by them. Alien ownership of lands was condemned.

The issue of free coinage of silver was included as were also the graduated income tax, savings banks and shorter hours for labor. Among other reforms sought were the introduction of the Australian ballot, direct election of United States senators, a single term for president and vice president, and the initiative and referendum.[37]

36. For a fuller description see Hicks, *The Populist Revolt*, p. 188. Note similarity to some features of the farm storage and loan program adopted in 1938.

37. For text of the platform see Hicks, *The Populist Revolt*, pp. 433–34. The demands listed are not identical in the various formulations of the platform, and

The "Populists" hoped to present a united farmer-labor front, but, of the labor groups, only the Knights of Labor were willing to cooperate. The American Federation of Labor, following a policy that became traditional with it, refused to be drawn into party affiliation. It also contended that farmers were employers, and hence could not have a common interest with labor. The election of 1892 revealed strength in the movement but by no means sufficient strength to threaten either of the major parties. Weaver polled 1,027,329 votes as against 5,554,414 for Cleveland and 5,190,802 for Harrison.

Decline of Populist Influence

After 1892, the silver issue came more and more into prominence. At first it cut across party lines, but in 1896 the Republicans came out for the gold standard. The Democrats, largely as a result of Bryan's famous "Cross of Gold" speech at the Chicago convention, appropriated the free-silver issue, a main feature of the Populist program. Bryan was selected as the standard-bearer for the Democrats. The Populists had little choice but to make him their nominee as well, and, by that action, virtually passed out of existence as a political factor, though they did put up tickets in 1900 and 1904.

The Alliance movement, having by now lost itself in the People's party, went down with it, and left surprisingly little in the way of continuing organization or activity. Though no great leaders were produced, the movement was based on real grievances, and its delegates were expressing honestly the sentiments of the communities from which they came. Its silver proposal was a panacea rather than a program and the party's pre-

some appear in the "resolutions" rather than in the platform itself.

occupation with that issue left it with little basis for popular appeal after "free silver" had been taken up by the Democrats. Nevertheless, the Populists achieved a great deal of strength in the West. Supported by Democrats, "silver" Republicans and Populists, the silver advocates captured the party organizations in many of the western states. The advantage was short-lived, however, since the silver program required national legislation.

The election of McKinley in 1896 sounded the death knell to free silver as a national issue, though Bryan's personal popularity enabled him to run a close second to McKinley in the election of 1900. By that time, however, reviving prosperity had lessened the pressure for monetary reform. Agricultural conditions were becoming more stable, and farmers were soon to find their interests shifting away from the issues that had seemed most important in the decades just past.

Nevertheless, many of the proposals put forward in this period were to come up again in later years, and not a few of them have become parts of our national policy. Already the antimonopoly agitation, which had been spearheaded by the farm groups, had culminated in the Sherman Antitrust Act of 1890. The Department of Agriculture had been given Cabinet status in 1889, and the Hatch Act for aid to agricultural experiment stations had been passed in 1887. Rural free delivery of mail had been achieved in 1896, and South Dakota had taken the lead in adopting the initiative and referendum in 1898. These measures were to achieve greater importance after the turn of the century, but they represented, even at this time, lasting additions to national policy which had grown out of the efforts of the farm groups to redress their grievances and achieve fuller participation in national affairs.

CHAPTER 7

AMERICAN AGRICULTURE COMES
OF AGE

THE OPENING of the twentieth century began a new era in American agriculture—one of new problems, new interests, and new outlook. The era of pioneer farming was nearing its close. Most of the nation's good farm lands had come under private ownership leaving only those of poorer quality or in remote areas available for homesteading.[1] Free land no longer afforded a "safety valve" outlet for excess urban workers, surplus young people from the farms or newly arrived immigrants.

The number of workers engaged in agriculture was to reach its peak within the first decade of the new century, and thereafter would be static or declining. Thus the problems facing agriculture were those of a relatively mature economy rather than of one based on rapid development and exploitation of virgin resources. The problems of credit, of market organization and of price relationships in a highly commercialized economy were coming to assume larger proportions.

The lack of good lands for homesteading had become evident as early as 1889. In that year the Territory of Oklahoma was made available for settlement. The lands composing the new territory were purchased by the government from the Five Civilized Tribes and were opened to homesteaders with the firing of a gun at noon on April 22. The Kansas border was lined with shouting, cursing, would-be settlers and land speculators held in check by soldier guards. On the stroke of twelve they surged over into the new territory on horseback, in wagons, on bicycles and with every other type of conveyance imaginable. Guthrie and Oklahoma City became towns almost overnight, and by November of that year, 60,000 people had settled in the new territory. In ten years its population grew to 800,000.[2]

Land values in the settled areas were increasing rapidly. Farmers' equities and net worth were likewise growing at a rapid pace. If heavy borrowing could be avoided, the increasing value of land brought an annual accretion in value which, in the newer areas, was often as much as 5 to 10 per cent of the current value of the farm.[3] But farm mortgage debt was increasing also. Since equities were growing and the credit rating of agriculture had improved, there was little pressure for repayment of mortgage loans.

The tendency was rather to continue, even to increase, indebtedness, and use current income and the proceeds from new loans to

1. Though homesteads were still available in the West, the skilled young farmer usually preferred to buy or rent land in the more productive and better located areas. Nevertheless, homesteading did continue on a considerable scale even after 1900, much of it by inexperienced people unable to cope with the adverse farming conditions of these semiarid regions. Between 1900 and 1910 more than 38 million acres were so acquired, chiefly in the West, and 74 million between 1910 and 1920. This increase was due mainly to a series of acts that permitted homesteading on easier terms, or in larger tracts, in the arid regions—the Kinkaid Act (1904), the Forest Homestead Act (1906), the Enlarged Homestead Act (1909), the Three-Year Homestead Act (1912) and the Stock-Raising Homestead Act of 1916. Under this latter act entries continued in considerable volume into the 1920's, partly as a result of the demand for lands on the part of returning soldiers. For fuller details see Benjamin H. Hibbard, *A History of the Public Land Policies,* Peter Smith, New York, 1939, pp. 391–402.

2. The turbulence of the rush to secure homesteads in this last large area of good farm lands is vividly described in Edna Ferber's *Cimmaron,* Doubleday, Doran, Garden City, 1930, pp. 23–25. A land rush of such character and scale probably has not been seen in this or any other country before or since.

3. In Minnesota, for example, the value of farm lands about doubled between 1900 and 1910, though the acreage of improved land increased by little more than 5 per cent. In South Dakota the valuation in 1910 was more than four times that of 1900. Iowa's land values more than doubled, and the national value was up 100 per cent. *Statistical Abstract, 1914,* pp. 116–21.

improve buildings, herds and equipment. Furthermore, the transfer of farms to new owners, or to sons and sons-in-law, usually involved the assumption of larger amounts of mortgage debt. Thus agricultural credit was to be more prominent in farm policy discussions than in previous decades. The interest in agricultural education and technological improvement was likewise growing and there was much discussion of the problem of keeping young people on the farm. At the same time some of the problems that had bulked large in farmer interest during the preceding century had now to some extent been solved or had dropped into the background.

THE AGRICULTURAL SITUATION AT THE BEGINNING OF THE CENTURY

In the 110 years that had passed since the adoption of the Constitution, the new nation had settled a number of fundamental policies relating to agriculture. Some of them were later to be modified, and undoubtedly these and others will experience further changes as time goes on. Nevertheless, certain broad principles had become so well established that major changes in them are not to be expected in the foreseeable future.

Land policy had been firmly established on the basis of private ownership, full and rapid settlement of lands suited to crops and, in general, the family-size farm granted in fee simple, either without charge or at a nominal price. The policy contained no element of restriction on regrouping into larger units, and this had occurred extensively in some areas, notably in the Old South and in parts of the West. Neither legislation nor custom had as yet placed much restraint on destructive exploitation of farm lands, forests or mineral resources. A new attitude with respect to the conservation of natural resources was beginning to take shape, but it had made little effective headway up to 1900.

Slavery had been abolished, but the forces tending to maintain the one-crop, commercial pattern of agriculture that developed along with it were still strong. The new century was to bring vigorous efforts to alter that pattern, but this movement had not as yet become evident or progressed very far. One-crop agriculture was in its heyday in the South and in the Plains states, but was dying out in the Corn Belt and in the eastern and northeastern states.

In principle at least, railroads and other public utilities had been brought under public control. There was much still to be done in establishing workable mechanisms for exercising such control, and farmer interest in transportation problems was by no means at an end, but it was to take other forms in the new century now at hand.

Monopoly, Tariff and Money Issues

A beginning had been made in the effort to control monopolies, but so weak and inadequate a beginning that it can hardly be called more than a declaration of principle. The problem has grown in the meantime, and even now its true significance, and appropriate measures for dealing with it, are little understood by farmers or the public at large. Nevertheless, the first decade of the twentieth century was to see significant efforts to establish policy in this realm.

The tariff had been vigorously discussed almost all through the nineteenth century, and, for the time being, a strongly protectionist position had apparently become the settled policy of most farm groups, except in the South, and likewise of most of the important labor and industrial organizations. The balance of power on tariff matters has long been a precarious one, however, and the tariff is still an active political issue, with attitudes tending to become more local and specialized as interests change.

The monetary issue, in its earlier form, had been fought out, with the farm groups of the West defeated in their efforts to achieve inflation through fiat money, silver or a bimetallic standard. By 1900 the nation had, in general, taken the most conservative position possible on monetary matters. It still lacked an adequate banking system, but neither farmers nor others had gained a clear appreciation of the nature of the difficulty. Farmer opposition to the national bank system was, for the most part, ill-advised. The need was not for abolition of the national banks but for strengthening and unifying the banking system through greater participation by the government, a conclusion that even conservative bankers were soon to accept.

A significant but little noticed start had been made in putting agricultural experimentation and education on a new footing with strong subsidization by the government. Up to the end of the century only the groundwork had been laid, but results were to become far more noticeable and influential in succeeding decades.

Farmer organizations were at a low ebb, but were not again to be as inconsequential as they had been during the first seventy-five years of the nation's history. They had demonstrated that organized farmers could exert a significant influence on national policies. Much had been learned about tactics in the attainment of given ends, and the dangers of direct political affiliation with specific parties. Among other things, farmers and their leaders were coming to be more aware of the fact that some of the less sensational activities of their associations may be more enduring than those which raise great expectations and create much popular enthusiasm. Of all the great array of farmer organizations that had sprung up during the three previous decades, only the Grange, with its modest program of social and educational activity, had survived on a significant scale. Farmers had also become more aware of the fact that successful business activity by farmer groups requires specialized business-type agencies, capital and competent management.

Improved Rural Living

The last half of the nineteenth century was marked by wretched housing and poor living throughout most of the frontier areas. Temporary shelters had been thrown up, often of logs or even prairie sod. Roads were poor and frequently impassable in wet weather. Schools were primitive, and the facilities for social life inadequate. Clothing and furniture were of the roughest kind.

Gradually, however, these conditions changed. The great forests of the Lake states were denuded to provide lumber for better houses and barns, and for building up the towns. Roads were graded and kept moderately passable. Bridges were constructed New schools and better churches appeared Lodge halls were built, and finally, around the end of the century, rural free mail delivery, farmers' institutes and chautauquas began to bring the western farmers into touch with the outer world. Grand Rapids furniture and store clothes, supplied in part through the far-flung selling organizations of the mail-order houses Montgomery Ward and Sears, Roebuck, were adding to and replacing the home-produced consumer goods of earlier periods.

The older states of the Northeast and the East had, of course, long possessed good farm houses and a vastly better cultural life. But these advantages had been insufficient to hold the younger generation against the lure of the West. Those areas continued to decline in agricultural importance and to be peopled by older, more conservative farmers. The South was still, until near the end of the century, too poorly financed and too unprosperous to make much progress in the improvement of farm living. Even the old mansions already built were in decay, and such new building as was done was, for the most part of the poorest kind. Education lagged, social life was at a low ebb and material comfort at a minimum.

Rapid Improvement in Prices and Incomes

The first decade of the new century brought substantial advances all along the line. Prices of farm products moved strongly upward. In 1900 they stood at 69.0 (1909 1913 = 100). An almost uninterrupted rise brought them up to 105.0 in 1910.[4] This was

4. Frederick Strauss and Louis H. Bean, *Gross Farm Income and Indices of Farm Production and Prices the United States, 1869-1937*, USDA Technical Bulletin No. 703, 1940. Figures used are for the arithme

a gain of 52 per cent in ten years, a rate of increase that has seldom been duplicated in peacetime since the nation began.[5]

It was the closing years of this prosperous era (the years 1910–1914) which later came to be known as the "parity" period. Since every group tends to feel that its portion of the national income is less than it should be, it was natural for farmers in later and less prosperous times to look upon the relation between farm and nonfarm prices in these years as the normal or "proper" one. While a case can be made for the proposition that farmers have generally throughout history received less than a fair share of the national income, it should also be recognized that the period chosen as representing "parity" or normal relationships was one of the best, from the farmer's standpoint, that had occurred up to that time. In other words, what the farmers have been seeking in their quest for "parity" is the re-establishment of the relationships that existed in what has sometimes been called "the golden age of agriculture."[6]

There is, of course, more warrant for the adoption of 1910–1914 as a base period than

this brief comment implies. It was a time of peace and relative prosperity throughout most of the western world. The rapid development of virgin farm lands had virtually come to an end. The population was relatively mobile, and entrance into almost any occupation was reasonably possible for most young workers. In other words, the argument that interoccupational relationships were fairly well in balance has much to support it. On the other hand, the competitive bidding which was rapidly forcing upward the prices of farm lands indicated that many were willing to pay a substantial part of this improved income for the privilege of farming the lands, thus giving support to the view that real incomes in agriculture were high relative to those in other occupations. Excess farm income used in bidding up the prices of farm lands does not contribute effectively to better living on farms and is in large measure a social waste.

Land Improvements and Increased Debt

By no means all of the increase in farm land values was mere unearned increment. Many of the farms, by now, had been substantially improved. Forest lands were cleared, prairie sods were broken, wells were dug, fences built, and improved barns and houses constructed. Stones had been removed from rocky soils, and considerable investments had gone into community facilities such as roads, schools and churches. The pioneer farmer, generally, plowed into the business the full value of his labor, and that of his family, over and above what was required for a meager living. He accumulated his savings in the increasing value of the farm.[7]

In addition many farmers were borrowing large amounts for new buildings and other equipment as well as for the purchase of land. The more stable conditions in agricul-

---

index, p. 140. For the years here discussed the movements of the price index were as follows:

1900—69.0   1904—75.1   1908— 87.3   1912— 97.2
1901—75.0   1905—78.1   1909— 98.2   1913—105.5
1902—75.7   1906—77.7   1910—105.0   1914—100.4
1903—77.1   1907—87.0   1911— 94.9   1915—103.2

5. Prices increased generally throughout the world during this period. The development of new gold fields in Alaska and South Africa increased the rate of production substantially. Gold production in the United States (including Alaska) was at a rate more than double that of the period 1860–1895. Probably more important in the falling value of gold was the fact that most of the western nations had by then completed their shift to the gold standard. Hence the abnormal demand which marked the last part of the nineteenth century had virtually come to an end. With gold transfers and use unrestricted, as they were at that time, gold movement into or out of the banks operated to increase or decrease bank loans and deposits, and thus could affect rather directly the amount of money and credit in use. Under these conditions, the value of gold had an important bearing on the general level of prices. With the demand for gold declining in relation to the amounts produced, that influence was heavily in the direction of higher prices. See R. G. Hawtrey, *The Gold Standard in Theory and Practice*, 3rd edition, Longmans, Green, London, 1933, Chapter 3.

6. For fuller development of this view, see Joseph S. Davis, "An Evaluation of the Present Economic Position of Agriculture by Regions and in General," *Journal of Farm Economics*, April 1933, pp. 247–54.

7. This tendency was to be a cause of serious difficulty for farm owners in the 1920's and 1930's, since it had become customary to price lands on the expectation that part of the income would be in the form of increased land values. When land prices finally turned downward, this became a minus income rather than a plus one, often a minus income of substantial size.

ture made farm loans a better risk than formerly, capital for the making of loans was accumulating and the facilities for lending were becoming better organized. Reliable estimates of the amount of farm mortgage debt are not available before 1910, but by that date it had reached $3,207,863,000, and a further increase brought it to $4,990,785,000 by 1915.[8] In the same period (1900–1910) the estimated value of all land in farms in the United States rose from $13,058 million to $28,476 million.[9] It is apparent therefore that there had been a very substantial increase in the value of the equities held by farm owners.

Nevertheless, two aspects of the situation were beginning to cause uneasiness in some quarters. One was the increase in the proportion of farms operated by tenants, the other the growing amount of mortgage debt. Tenure data were first taken in the Census of 1880. At that time about 25 per cent of the farm operators were listed as tenants. By 1900 this percentage had grown to 35.3, and in 1910 it stood at 37.0.[10] Between 1880 and 1900 farm operators' equities in the land are thought to have been declining at a rate of about 4 per cent per decade, though dependable data are not available. This tendency had probably been checked or reversed between 1900 and 1915 as a result of the increasing value of the equities held by farmers, and the increasing prosperity of agriculture.

But uneasiness based on the tendencies apparent in the long preceding period of depressed farm prices continued to exist. Another cause of concern was the movement of young people from farms to the cities and the declining percentage which farmers constituted of the total population. This was to be

a dominant note in both farm and city attitudes through much of the decade under review.

Both the increasing percentage of tenancy and the larger volume of mortgage debt were natural concomitants of the disappearance of available homestead lands and increasing land values, but this was not widely recognized at the time. Whether natural consequences or not they did bring with them increasing social problems and a growing feeling of insecurity among farm operators. With wholly inadequate laws relating to tenancy, the tenant farmer in particular had very insecure tenure, and tended to fall into an unsatisfactory status both socially and in quality of farming, except where he was closely related to the owner of the farm.

Technological Problems Increase

As the farm lands came to be more closely settled, and transfers of animals and crops more common, both plant and animal diseases became more serious. Foot and mouth disease was first reported in the United States in 1870. The cotton boll weevil crossed the Rio Grande into the United States between 1895 and 1900, and began to spread north and east. These and various other pests and diseases constituted serious threats to considerable segments of American agriculture and stimulated interest in the researches being undertaken in the Department of Agriculture and in the state experiment stations.

Grasshopper plagues, which were very serious in the West between 1872 and 1876, had led to the establishment of the United States Entomological Commission in 1877. Bordeaux mixture for the control of fungus diseases in fruit trees was brought out in 1882 and in that same year Koch discovered the tubercle bacillus. The carrier of tick fever was identified in 1889 and also in that year an improved method of anthrax innoculation was developed. Methods were found for the eradication of pleuropneumonia in 1892.

While these new problems, and the earlier scientific advances relating to them, appeared before 1900, they did not become matters of

8. Donald C. Horton, Harald C. Larsen and Norman J. Wall, *Farm Mortgage Credit Facilities in the United States,* USDA Miscellaneous Publication No. 478, 1942, p. 1.

9. *Statistical Abstract, 1914,* p. 121.

10. Joseph Ackerman and Marshall Harris (eds.), *Family Farm Policy,* University of Chicago Press, Chicago, 1947, p. 92. The number of tenants is a somewhat vague figure because of the Census practice of including as tenants approximately half a million croppers whose status is regarded by many students as more that of a laborer paid in kind than a true tenancy relationship.

general farmer interest until the agricultural colleges and experiment stations, and the United States Department of Agriculture, came to play a larger role in the affairs of agriculture. That did not occur until after the turn of the century. The agricultural experiment stations, which had been established under the Hatch Act of 1887, were by now attracting more trained men, and were getting to a point where they could begin to show results. New and improved varieties of crops were being brought out and disseminated. Work was being done on the control of hog cholera, on methods of eradicating tuberculosis in animals and on the problem of contagious abortion in cattle. Considerable attention was given to the conservation of fertilizing elements in animal manures.

In the mechanical field, the period was marked more by the wider adoption and improvement of machines already developed than by distinctly new departures. The dairy industry, however, was greatly changed by the Babcock test and the hand-operated cream separator. The first of these was developed to a stage of practical usefulness around 1890 through the work of S. M. Babcock of the Wisconsin Agricultural Experiment Station.[11] The hand-operated cream separator came later in that decade. These put the dairy industry on a new basis, and led gradually to the abandonment of farm buttermaking in the major dairy regions.

11. Like most inventions, the Babcock test was not based on a new idea. The general principle had been developed earlier, especially by DeLaval in Sweden. Babcock succeeded in devising a simple and practical machine for measuring accurately the fat content of milk. This was an essential step in the evolution of dairying as a large-scale, commercial industry. Instead of patenting the process for private gain, which would have made him a fortune, Babcock gave his invention to the world without charge, holding that it was the product of work paid for by the people of his state. The cream separator had been developed earlier, largely through the work of DeLaval, but the hand-operated separator, introduced in 1894, came into general use around 1900, and brought about considerable change in the organization of the dairy industry. See Edward Wiest, *The Butter Industry in the United States,* Columbia University Press, New York, 1916, pp. 25–30. Also T. R. Pirtle, *History of the Dairy Industry,* Mojonnier Brothers, Chicago, 1926, pp. 83–84.

Regional Differences

Dairy farming grew in scale and became a main commercial industry rather than a sideline. It helped to turn the Lake states and New York away from the exploitative agriculture of the preceding century and into new lines on which a prosperous and permanent agriculture could be built. These states, with their thin soils, were unsuited for a continuing wheat economy and were rapidly losing out in their competitive struggle with the rich prairie lands farther west and south.

Their forest resources were far gone. Their farms were small. Many of them were stony and cluttered with stumps; and soils had been worn down by erosion and repeated cropping to wheat, oats and barley. Dairy farming provided a use for the excess labor on such farms and enabled them to rebuild their soils. Thus, it was a type of agriculture especially well suited to the small units into which the land had been divided. New England and New York turned more and more toward fluid milk production to supply the fast-growing city populations of that region, while in New Jersey and the states to the south, truck crops came into prominence.

Farther west, wheat production was being undertaken on a broader scale with improved and larger machinery. In the Plains area the fencing of the ranges was going on, and the break-up of the huge, vaguely defined cattle and sheep spreads was at hand. Barbed wire had been invented about 1873, and for the first time had made practical the fencing of large holdings on the treeless plains.[12] As this occurred, land ownerships tended to become more clearly defined, and the rights of smaller operators could be better protected.

While these changes were occurring in the North and the West, the South was lagging behind. Its experiment stations and agricultural colleges did not get under way as soon

12. See Walter Prescott Webb, *The Great Plains,* Ginn and Company, Boston, 1931, pp. 295–318, for an interesting account of the invention of barbed wire, its growth as an industry and its sociological effect on the agricultural life of the Plains.

or as vigorously as those in the North. Its one-crop cotton and tobacco economy did not lend itself so readily to technological improvement as did the agriculture of the North, and the heavy reliance on uneducated Negro labor placed emphasis on purely mechanical operations suited to traditional methods of supervision. Soils had been seriously depleted by long cropping in cotton and tobacco and by erosion. A new approach to the problem of the Negro farmer was in the offing, through the work of such men as Booker T. Washington and George Washington Carver and in the various state Negro colleges. As yet, however, the effort along these lines was on a modest scale and not widely recognized.[13] The problems of southern agriculture as a whole were not to be attacked vigorously until the 1930's and after.

The Far West, particularly California, was rapidly becoming more important agriculturally. In the 1870's, 1880's and 1890's it had passed through stages of predominant emphasis on cattle and sheep raising and on the production of wheat. The improvements in transportation, especially during the 1880's, the growth of irrigation and the beginnings made in market organization appropriate to areas far distant from the consuming centers were setting the stage for a phenomenal development along new lines. In the Pacific Northwest there was still a heavy emphasis on wheat growing, but the apple industry and some other fruits were responding to forces similar to those at work in California.

The Intermountain states were changing least of all. Natural conditions limited their agriculture mainly to range livestock production. In a few areas intensive agriculture was gaining a foothold. This was limited almost wholly to the small areas that could be irrigated, such as those growing sugar beets in Colorado, potatoes in Idaho and more general crops in Utah. Fencing of the ranges was

not common in these states, so even the methods of livestock production continued little changed from those of earlier periods.

Department Influence Grows

In the first decade of the new century the United States Department of Agriculture began to exert a more positive influence on agriculture and to attract more attention from farmers. Established as a separate agency with bureau status in 1862, it had been made a regular department with a Secretary of Cabinet rank in 1889. The early growth was slow, but a good beginning had been made in scientific research. Much of the money appropriated for the Department in these early years went for the collection of statistical information and for the free distribution of seeds. The collection of data was important, and had been one of the original reasons for setting up an agriculture section in the Patent Office, which was created in 1836. Henry L. Ellsworth, the first Patent Commissioner, as early as 1838 began to ask Congress to appropriate money for collecting and distributing, free of charge, various kinds of seeds, and for gathering agricultural statistics.[14]

An appropriation of $1,000 was made in 1839 and the Agriculture Division of the Patent Office was established to carry on these activities. The work remained in that agency until May 15, 1862, when President Lincoln signed the act creating what is now the United States Department of Agriculture, with bureau status and with a Commissioner of Agriculture at its head.

The distribution of free seeds became popular with congressmen since the seeds were sent out under their names, and constituted a convenient and (to them) costless method of currying favor with their constituents. The practice was much criticized by farmers, and all of the Secretaries of Agriculture recom-

13. Booker T. Washington began his pioneer work at Tuskegee in 1881. After his speech before the National Education Association at Madison, Wisconsin, in 1884, he came to be in demand as a public speaker on Negro education and race relations. He was, however, an advocate of slow advance and modest goals.

14. Ellsworth had already started distributing seeds in 1836 and 1837, at his own expense and without congressional authorization. He was a lawyer and a son of Oliver Ellsworth, third Chief Justice of the United States Supreme Court, but included among his other activities the operation of a farm in Connecticut and membership in the Hartford County Agricultural Society.

mended its discontinuance. It was not abandoned, however, until 1923, and even then only as a result of pressure on the part of farmer representatives. Up to the latter part of the nineteenth century only very modest beginnings had been made on other types of work. Gradually, however, the foundation was being laid for the important developments that were to come around the beginning of the following century.

New Leadership

The appointment of James F. Wilson of Iowa as Secretary of Agriculture, in 1897, began a new era in the work of the Department. Wilson was a native of Scotland. He had become a prominent farmer and agricultural leader in Iowa, and had served in the state legislature. He had also had three terms in the United States Congress. Thereafter he was made Professor of Agriculture and head of the experiment station at Iowa State College, which was then just getting started. At the suggestion of Henry Wallace, father of Henry C. Wallace and grandfather of Henry A. Wallace, McKinley appointed Wilson to the agriculture secretaryship. He remained in that position for sixteen years, through the administrations of McKinley, Theodore Roosevelt and William Howard Taft, the longest tenure of any Cabinet officer in the nation's history.

Shortly before Wilson took office most of the employees of the Department were brought under civil service. The new Secretary reorganized the Department, brought in a distinguished group of scientists and, in a few years, built up an outstanding research organization. He also began the collection of foreign seeds and plants, and gave new impetus to the distribution of scientific information acquired by the Department so that both the Department and its contributions became much more widely known.

Among the scientists brought into the Department were Seaman A. Knapp and Gifford Pinchot, as well as other men of stature. Dr. Harvey Wiley, who was later to become a leader in the pure food controversy, was already there. Knapp originated the idea of demonstration farms and adult education in the rural communities. This work was stimulated by the rapid spread of the cotton boll weevil and the insistent demands of farmers for help on that problem. The magnificent work done by Knapp and his associates made a great impression, and led ultimately to the creation of the agricultural extension service.[15]

Wiley, as Chief of the Bureau of Chemistry, became a prime factor in bringing about passage of the Food and Drug Law of 1906. As a result the Bureau of Chemistry was charged with its enforcement, and thus the Department entered more significantly into the field of regulatory activity which has since come to be one of its very important functions.[16]

Gifford Pinchot, a man of wealth, who was deeply interested in the conservation of forests, was brought into the Department in 1901 to head the newly created United States Forest Service. He did an outstanding job, not only in establishing policies and procedures for handling the national forests, but in arousing the public to the need for conservation of its natural resources.

Growth of Scientific Skills

By 1903 the Department was serving as a postgraduate institution for the training of young scientists, and thus was helping to provide more competent personnel not only for the Department itself but for the state agri-

15. The fascinating story of Knapp's pioneer work in the South is well presented in Joseph Cannon Bailey's *Seaman A. Knapp, Schoolmaster of American Agriculture,* Columbia University Press, New York, 1945. After a number of years of successful teaching and leadership at Ames, Iowa, Knapp became associated with Jabez B. Watkins in the development and colonization of a huge tract of swampland in Louisiana. It was here that he began his demonstration work which was presently to attract nationwide attention and to lead to his later association with the United States Department of Agriculture.

16. Some small beginnings in regulatory work had been made earlier. The first legislation of this kind was that establishing the Bureau of Animal Industry, in 1884, for the purpose of inspecting animals exported. There was, however, no such general interest in the Department's previous regulatory activities as that which came with the establishment of standards for foods and drugs.

cultural experiment stations as well. Farm management work was started in the Bureau of Plant Industry in 1908, and in that same year the Department took an active part in the work of the President's Country Life Commission.

These varied and, for the most part, progressive and appropriate activities helped to introduce into the nation's agriculture a more enlightened and scientific attitude. The agricultural colleges likewise were becoming more active and better known. Associated with them was a system of short courses and farmers' institutes that brought to thousands of farmers the findings of the research agencies. In most of the rural areas the attitude during the early 1900's was one of optimism, accompanied by a marked desire for scientific progress. Interest centered chiefly on technological problems, improved breeds of livestock and better homes.

The efforts of the Department of Agriculture and the agricultural colleges were ably supported by a large and growing group of farm magazines, many of them well edited, cheerful in tone and attractive in format. Many of them were of good literary quality and carried a pronounced note of idealism.[17] Economic questions were little discussed and little studied. Farm products were in good demand, and most farmers were more concerned with how to achieve better yields and improved quality than with how to influence prices.

It would be incorrect, of course, to imply that farmers were unconcerned with economic problems. There was a growing interest in cooperative selling, and considerable complaint about the credit facilities available to agriculture. Nevertheless, this was not a period of general unrest among farmers. Incomes were modest but reasonably adequate, and no marked changes in levels of prices

had occurred in the recent past or were expected in the future. Droughts, grasshoppers, frosts and animal diseases were the things farmers worried about. They complained about the bankers, the livestock buyers, the packers and the grain trade, but did not expect to do much about them. Their club meetings and other gatherings were for the most part social affairs or educational activities rather than meetings for politics or protest.

Production and Exports

The output from American farms continued to increase after 1900 but not at so rapid a pace as in the three preceding decades. Total farm production rose from 87.3 in 1900 to 95.4 in 1910, and by 1915 had reached a level of 107.8 (1910–1914 = 100).[18] The high 1915 figure was due largely to the record-breaking wheat crop of that year rather than to the establishment of a new and higher norm. Except for 1915, the general level remained around 100 until 1918 and thereafter.[19]

With a slower rate of increase in agricultural production and a fast-growing population, the United States was becoming less dependent upon foreign markets as an outlet for its farm products, though such items still constituted the bulk of its exports. The total value of agricultural exports continued to increase, though they were becoming a smaller percentage of all exports (an average of 53.8 per cent for the years 1907 to 1911 as compared to 65.8 per cent for the years 1897 to 1901). During the 1880's, United States exports of agricultural products averaged about $570 million per year. For the 1890's this average had risen to about $730 million, even though prices were at low levels. From 1900 to 1910 it stood at about $900 mil-

---

17. This characteristic was particularly noticeable in such widely read farm magazines as the *Breeders' Gazette*, the *Farm Journal*, the *Country Gentleman*, *Hoard's Dairyman* and many others; also in the breezy and cheerful articles of such free-lance writers as Joseph E. Wing who stressed the building up of soils through increased use of leguminous hay crops.

18. As computed by Strauss and Bean, *Gross Farm Income*, USDA Technical Bulletin No. 703, p. 125.

19. The computed indexes seem to take account of the large wheat crop of 1915 though the amount produced is much understated in the table on page 129. *Ibid.* Wheat production is shown there as 780.1 million bushels for 1915 whereas *Agricultural Statistics* gives 1,008,637,000 bushels for that year. *Agricultural Statistics, 1937*, p. 10.

lion, though the physical volume of exports had fallen off moderately. In the succeeding decade, because of war needs and some unusually large crops, together with high prices, a level far above any previously experienced was reached.[20]

While the over-all value of farm exports was increasing as indicated, the kinds of products exported were changing. Wheat exports (including flour), which had been running above the 200 million bushel mark around 1900, fell off to less than 100 million bushels by 1909, and seemed likely to remain around that level. The demands of the war years, however, brought them back to and above any previous levels. In the interwar years, they again fell off sharply.

Corn exports likewise declined after 1900, also those of oats and flaxseed. By 1910 the United States was on a deficit basis with respect to flaxseed. As to rice, it was approaching self-sufficiency, and by the 1920's was to become an important exporter. Cotton exports had reached a high level of more than seven million bales just before 1900, and held approximately at that volume, or even higher, until 1915. Except for the 1920's more cotton was exported in the first decade of the century than in any other in the nation's history.

Tobacco exports also remained high during this period and were destined to go much higher in the two decades immediately thereafter. Exports of hog products were large from 1900 to 1906, but fell off sharply from that time until the demands resulting from World War I brought them up again.

The Foreign Exchange Situation

No serious difficulty in maintaining foreign buying power for American products had as yet appeared though this problem had begun to be considered. The excess of exports over imports was still running close to a half billion dollars per year, but invisible imports tended to offset a good portion of it and exchange unbalances did not reach levels too great to be dealt with through the usual types of gold transfer.

20. For data see *Statistical Abstract, 1946,* p. 631.

There were still heavy foreign investments in the United States on which we were paying interest. European travel on the part of Americans was supplying to the European countries more tourist money than was flowing in the opposite direction, and there was a sizable transfer of remittances from immigrants in the United States who still had close relatives living in the countries from which they came. There were other transfers to cover invisible imports, such as premium payments to foreign insurance companies operating in the United States and payments for services performed by foreign-owned vessels.

The situation was not one that created great interest in tariff matters over most of the country. The South, for the most part, clung to its traditional free-trade or low-tariff views. The labor groups and a good portion of the farmers of the Middle West had become strongly imbued with the belief that tariffs were an important factor in maintaining the high standards of living they enjoyed as compared to most foreign laborers and farmers. At the same time, the rising prices of farm products left little ground for farmers themselves to seek higher levels of tariff as a means of affording relief to their industry.

There arose, however, a movement among the farmers of the Middle West, which came to be known as the "Iowa Idea." This called for a lowering of duties, particularly on manufactured products. It started about 1902, and marked the beginning of a clearer recognition of the true economic interests of the agrarian groups. Proponents of the Iowa Idea contended that high duties on manufactured articles increased the prices of things they had to buy, and that the limiting of imports tended to depress the foreign markets for agricultural products. They pointed out that most of the major farm commodities were produced in excess of the needs of the domestic market. Hence, the levying of duties on them would not raise United States farm prices above those of the world markets. While not attaining the significance of the tariff revolt of the 1870's, this agitation became active enough to compel some recognition of the tariff problem in the platforms of both the major parties in the campaign of 1908.

The Roosevelt Policies, 1901–1909

The troubled conditions of Cleveland's second term, and the bitter struggle over the silver issue, had brought into power the conservative Republican group, represented by William McKinley. Its political philosophy was dominant from 1897 to 1901. McKinley was re-elected in 1900, but his assassination in September 1901, only a few months after beginning his second term, brought into the White House a man of very different temperament and outlook. Theodore Roosevelt, the youngest president ever to assume office, took up the reins with the announced purpose of carrying on the McKinley policies — a stand he felt obligated to take since it was McKinley who had been elected to the presidency, not himself. Nevertheless, his own exuberance and progressive attitude soon caused him to strike out on new lines which certainly were more his own than those of McKinley.

The McKinley election of 1896 had been won largely by virtue of the skillful but rough-shod leadership of Mark Hanna. Hanna was a wealthy Ohio industrialist, new to the political arena, but no less cynical and ruthless than the "Old Guard" of the Republican party that had managed its affairs over the preceding decades. Money was used lavishly both in the nominating convention and in the election that followed.

Roosevelt's nomination as vice-president in 1900 had been both a slap at Hanna by the Republican "Old Guard" and an attempt to shunt Roosevelt onto a sidetrack where it was hoped he might remain or at least become relatively innocuous. Hanna regarded him as a "madman" and a troublemaker of the most dangerous sort. Nevertheless, Roosevelt's progressive leadership in the Civil Service Commission, the Navy Department, the New York police commission and the gov-

ernorship of New York had caught the popular imagination. Aided by a colorful personality and high "news value," he was soon to turn both the Republican party and the nation into new paths which bore little resemblance to those laid out by Hanna and McKinley.

The main features of the new trend were a pronounced emphasis on the conservation of natural resources, a more aggressive foreign policy, a campaign against "trusts" and monopolies, further reform of the civil service and the curbing of abuses such as those in the food and drug industries. Though none of these was specifically agricultural in objective or origin, Roosevelt's popularity in the farming regions and the nature of the issues themselves were such that farmers, particularly those of the Middle West, gave his program vigorous support. Some of the measures, such as the conservation and Panama Canal projects, had important implications for agriculture, but, generally speaking, the policies were broadly social rather than agricultural.

The Conservation Program

When the nation was established, rich forests extended from New York westward through all the states bordering on the Great Lakes. They covered much of the Old South, and in the Pacific Northwest and California timber stands of unparalleled magnificence were still untouched. By 1900 the best of the forests of the Lake states had been cut over. For lumber supplies the East and the Middle West were being forced to rely more and more on the timber resources of the Pacific Northwest and the South. This meant higher freight costs and consequent higher prices for lumber. Furthermore, it began to be apparent that the shortage was likely to become more serious as time went on since timber cutting was outrunning new growth.

Gifford Pinchot, who was a close friend of the new President and an ardent proponent of forest conservation, had been brought in to head the new Forest Service. He was familiar with the much more stable and permaent forest programs of the older European countries, and proceeded vigorously to popularize the forest conservation movement. With Roosevelt's wholehearted cooperation, he was able to make the nation more forest-conscious than it had ever been.

A Forest Reserve Act had been passed in 1891. This provided that the President could withdraw from entry forest lands owned by the government, and designate them as permanent forest reserves.[21] Presidents Harrison, Cleveland and McKinley had set aside, under his act, 46,828,429 acres. These actions, particularly that of Cleveland in setting up thirteen new forest reserves just before retiring from office, brought vigorous criticism from the western states and served in some measure to crystallize anticonservation sentiment in the West.[22]

The attempts to nullify the Cleveland forest orders and to repeal the Act of 1891 did, however, serve to increase public discussion of the problem and in some measure paved the way for the program initiated under Roosevelt. During McKinley's term, the conservationists had been on the defensive. The vigorous leadership and encouragement supplied by his successor provided the spark needed to give the movement new life and an influence it had not previously attained.

Under the stimulus of Pinchot's enthusiasm and his own keen interest in life in the open, Roosevelt proceeded vigorously in sequestering forest and mineral lands remaining under government ownership. By the time he left office he had set aside more than 125 million additional acres. Much of this land, and of the reserves established earlier, was, to be sure, forest land little desired by the lumber interests, as it was too remote or too thinly covered. In the Pacific Northwest, however, prompt action on Roosevelt's part blocked a plan to transfer to private parties the bulk of the remaining good timberlands.

Western opposition to the conservation measures taken by Roosevelt between 1901 and 1906 had become so strong that the western representatives were able to push through a rider to an appropriation bill whereby the Forest Reserve Act of 1891 was repealed. The rider made various other changes in the laws relating to public lands. Roosevelt decided to sign the bill, but before doing so issued an order, on March 6, 1907, setting up twenty-one new forest reserves in the six northwestern states. Thus the main purpose of the anticonservationists in passing the bill was defeated.[23]

The National Conservation Conference

Once launched on the program of conserving natural resources, Roosevelt proceeded to popularize the idea in his own spectacular way. He arranged, in March 1908, a notable meeting of prominent people in many fields. The group included state governors, Supreme Court justices, Cabinet members, congressmen, businessmen and numerous technical experts. The meeting, held at the White House, lasted three days. It focused attention on the subject and received wide publicity. It brought influential support for a number of Roosevelt's favorite conservation policies — the protection of navigable waters in streams, the control of forest fires, government regulation of the cutting of timber, the retention by the government of underground mineral rights in lands granted to private interests and so on.

21. Before 1891, the Land Office had for some years been recommending the setting aside of forest reservations, but had gained little support for its views. The American Forestry Association and the American Association for the Advancement of Science were responsible for enlisting the interest of President Harrison and bringing these proposals under congressional consideration. The West, almost solidly opposed to conservation measures, contended that they would hamper development of the West, work hardships on the settlers and favor the large timber operators. The westerners particularly wanted mineral resources left open for exploitation.

22. A compromise was finally arrived at under which Cleveland's executive orders establishing the new forest reserves were set aside until March 1, 1898, after which they were again to become effective. Concessions to the western representatives were made, particularly in regard to the exclusion of mineral lands. On June 4, 1897, President McKinley signed the bill which included these compromises.

23. These controversies and the legislative and administrative actions relating to them are well described in Roy M. Robbins, *Our Landed Heritage, The Public Domain, 1776–1936*, Princeton University Press, Princeton, 1942, Chapters 19 and 20.

After the conference the President appointed, on his own initiative and without congressional sanction or appropriation, a National Conservation Commission of forty-nine members. This Commission brought out a comprehensive three-volume report which contained much information and helped markedly in the campaign to stimulate interest in the conservation movement.[24] As a result of the increased interest in these problems forty-one of the states set up state conservation commissions which helped to spread information and propaganda in regard to the problem. Magazines, newspapers and private agencies joined in. Among other results of the President's interest in the matter was an order, from him to the Secretary of the Interior, to withdraw from entry, in addition to the forest lands already set aside, "some eighty million acres of coal lands, a million and a half acres of land adjacent to water-power sites and nearly five million acres of phosphate lands."[25]

Naturally these actions and the philosophy back of them did not go unchallenged. They constituted a definite and abrupt change from the national policies that had characterized the latter part of the nineteenth century. The large lumber interests, the hydroelectric power corporations and the mining groups opposed the conservation measures vigorously, and deprecated any attempt to hamper "free enterprise" in its search for profits, regardless of the destruction of longer-term values that often accompanied its exploitation of natural resources. The West, generally, remained unsympathetic to the program, except in respect to irrigation enterprises, feeling that it would tend to hamper development in these newer parts of the country.

Roosevelt was far more successful in rousing public support, and in doing the things that already lay within his legal powers, than in getting new legislation to implement his policies. Hicks characterizes his attitude as follows:

No lawyer, Roosevelt was unimpressed by the traditional allocation of separate powers to the executive, the legislature, and the judiciary.

The President, as the head of the government, was, in his judgment, meant to lead. If laws were needed to accomplish a purpose that the President deemed useful, then it was his duty to see that the laws were passed.[26]

Not blessed with an acquiescent Congress, as was the later Roosevelt who held similar views, "Teddy" soon found himself in bitter conflict with the legislative bodies. His challenge to individualism both in matters of conservation and in the management of large corporations marked the beginning of a new national policy in these realms, but one that was to take shape only slowly. The issue is still active, and attitudes with regard to it are confused and vague.

In the realm of conservation Roosevelt was much more influential than in the control of "trusts" and monopolies. The emphasis, however, was on forests, water power, coal, oil and minerals rather than on soils. The latter concern was to come into focus much later, in the administration of the second Roosevelt. Nevertheless, the beginning of the conservation movement as a significant phase of national policy dates from the administration of Theodore Roosevelt. Educational forces were then set in motion that were to spread and to grow in influence over the years.

Arid Land Reclamation

The early land legislation which culminated in the Homestead Act of 1862 related almost wholly to land watered naturally by rainfall. When the arid regions farther west began to be taken up by farmers it soon became evident that the settlement plans designed for the humid areas were poorly suited to the lands of the Plains and Mountain states and to those of the Pacific Coast. Where irrigation was not to be undertaken the quarter sections provided under the regu-

24. U.S. Congress, Senate, *Report of the National Conservation Commission,* S. Doc. 676, 60th Cong., 2nd sess., 1909.

25. See John D. Hicks, *The American Nation,* Houghton Mifflin, Boston, 1941, p. 398. In Chapter 18 of this volume Hicks gives probably the best concise account of this phase of the Theodore Roosevelt administration.

26. Hicks, *The American Nation,* p. 380.

lar homestead act were far too small to support families. Where the land was to be irrigated, through large-scale projects, a 160-acre farm was likely to impose an outlay larger than the settler could undertake, and, if used for intensive agriculture, to require more manpower than the farmer and his family could supply. Furthermore, farms laid out in terms of the rectangular survey are not well adapted to the range country where organization for grazing tends more generally to be oriented to natural boundaries, the location of water holes and the possibilities of growing winter feed than to artificial lines such as those resulting from surveys. Thus the traditional 160-acre homestead plan was poorly adapted for either dry-land farming or irrigated agriculture.

As this problem became more evident various laws were passed to alleviate it.[27] These did not meet the situation adequately though they afforded some relief. By an act passed in 1866 (amended in 1870) the federal government relinquished any control it might have over the waters of nonnavigable streams in the West, and acknowledged water rights established under local customs and laws.[28] This was to give rise to important policy controversies in a later period, but was a logical course when the act was passed.

The Desert Land Act of 1877 did little to correct the situation, though a good deal of land was taken up under its provisions.[29] A

more considered effort to meet the problems of the arid West took shape in the Carey Act of August 18, 1894. This was designed to meet recognized defects in the Desert Land Act and the Act of October 2, 1888. The Act of 1888 included provision for surveys by the Geological Survey to determine which lands in the arid regions could be reclaimed by means of irrigation. It also directed that lands designated as suitable for reservoirs, ditches and canals should be held as the property of the United States and not subject "to entry, settlement or occupation until further provided by law."[30]

The Carey Act granted one million acres to each state containing arid lands, on condition that the state provide for the necessary reclamation. The states were to determine the procedure to be used. The usual plan was for them to contract with construction companies to reclaim specified areas and to sell "water rights" as a means of recovering their investments. The land was sold by the states at nominal prices, but only to those who had contracted for the purchase of water rights.

The results were far from satisfactory. The construction companies sold bonds which many investors thought were in some way guaranteed by the federal and state govern-

Ray P. Teele, *The Economics of Land Reclamation in the United States*, A. W. Shaw, Chicago, 1927, p. 64.

27. For a fuller discussion of this problem and the laws pertaining to it, see E. Louise Peffer, *The Closing of the Public Domain, Disposal and Reservation Policies, 1900–50*, Stanford University Press, Stanford, California, 1951, Chapter 8, "Homesteading the Arid West." In addition, her statistical appendix, which brings the figures up to 1945, gives later data than those used in this section which are taken from Teele's study (see n. 29).

28. There had been some earlier legislation relating to classified lands, namely, the acts turning over to various states swamplands of specified types. These acts (1849, 1850 and 1860) were designed to facilitate the reclamation of lands subject to overflow. Title was transferred to the states in fee simple, with provision that proceeds from sale of the lands should be used for reclaiming them by means of levees, drains, etc. In all, more than 64 million acres of public lands were transferred to the states in this way.

29. Original claims under the act (to June 30, 1925) amounted to 32,573,970 acres, and proofs of compliance had been filed on 8,579,664 acres as of that date.

30. Much controversy arose over the interpretation of this act. "The Department of the Interior and the Acting Attorney-General interpreted the language to mean that 'entries should not be permitted therefor upon any part of the arid regions which might possibly come within the operation of the Act.'" (*Ibid.*, pp. 65–66.) The reaction in the West to this interpretation, which meant virtually the withdrawal from entry of all public lands in the arid regions, was so vigorous that the provision was repealed in 1890. In the congressional debates it was claimed that the act constituted a "system of national irrigation." They thus foreshadowed the controversies over reclamation policies in California which developed in the 1940's. The Department of the Interior already was laying claim to broader powers than the farmers of the West were willing to concede to it. Teele concludes (p. 66) that "Congress in providing for these surveys did not intend to establish a system of national irrigation, and that the advocates of such a system in the Department of the Interior defeated their purpose by enlarging the scope of the reservation provided for far beyond the intent of Congress. This destroyed what might have grown into a nationally controlled development of the arid lands of the West and restored or reinstated the policy of leaving unobstructed the course of private development."

ments. It was also widely believed that the bonds constituted a lien on the lands. Neither of these assumptions was correct, though the Congress intended that such costs should become a lien on the land. As a result of these misconceptions, bonds were more salable than they otherwise would have been, and many unsound projects were undertaken. Since the act applied only to public lands, the scope for operation under it has been continually decreasing owing to the alienation of such lands under other legislative provisions.[31]

The Newlands Reclamation Act of 1902

The time was ripe for a change of policy in respect to irrigation development. When settlement of the arid regions was first begun, small irrigation systems were developed by individual farmers who took water from streams adjoining or running through their properties. Even before that, modest developments had been made by the mission fathers in California, and, at an early date, group efforts had been undertaken by the Mormons in what is now the state of Utah. Individual farm-irrigating systems were also common in the Black Hills of South Dakota and in the valleys of California and Colorado. Numerous water systems were also developed by the miners in California after the gold discoveries of the middle of the century, and much of the custom and law relating to water rights in California grows out of their use in mining rather than agriculture.

The amount of land that could be irrigated through these rudimentary arrangements was limited, indeed, and in no sense adequate to meet the growing demand. With the passage of enabling acts in the various states and the activities initiated under the Carey Act, group projects for the building of dams and canals and the distribution of water became common. Most of these were organized as irrigation districts with many of the powers and characteristics of minor civil divisions

of government. Some were corporate ventures privately owned.

By the turn of the century most of the better irrigable areas, especially those that could be developed at modest expense, had been brought under irrigation in these various ways. There were lands that still could be irrigated, some of them very good lands, but the structures required called for huge investments suited only to government undertakings rather than to the resources of private corporations or small groups of farmers. The West was eager for settlement and development, and, with its disproportionate representation in the Senate, it was coming to have a powerful influence in legislative matters. Furthermore, the growing interest in conservation, coupled with a new if somewhat unwarranted fear that we were approaching a situation of chronic underproduction of foods, gave impetus to federal action in creating more farms. The interest of the President was easily enlisted in a project of this kind.

The result was a new law, the Reclamation Act of 1902, which marked a significant change in American land policy.[32] First, it

32. This new approach to the land problems of the arid West had been implied in the work of Major John Wesley Powell, which began at a much earlier date. Powell, a veteran of the Civil War, explored the Grand Canyon of the Colorado in 1869. His reports led presently to a survey under the auspices of the Smithsonian Institution. As a result of Powell's pioneer work and the publication, in 1878, of his *Report on the Lands of the Arid Region of the United States*, H. Exec. Doc. 73, 45th Cong., 2nd sess., he became Director of the United States Geological Survey in 1880. A Public Lands Commission had been authorized in 1879, with orders to submit to the Congress, within one year, a codification of the laws relating to the survey and disposition of the public domain. It was also to provide a system and standards for classifying public lands as arable, irrigable, timber, mineral, etc., and was to include the recommendations of the Commission for disposal of the remaining part of the public domain. The voluminous and carefully prepared report, of which Powell was one of the authors, included recommendations for the classification of public lands and the repeal of the pre-emption laws and the Timber and Stone Act of 1878. See *Report of the Public Lands Commission*, H. Exec. Doc. 46, 46th Cong., 2nd sess., 1880. Both Powell's work and the report of the Commission were in advance of the thinking of the time and gave rise to considerable opposition. Powell's retirement as Director of the Geological Survey in 1894 was in part a result of antagonism to his policies though it was also due in part to ill health. His views and his contribution to knowledge

31. As of June 30, 1925, 3,843,290 acres had been segregated under the act. 1,158,926 had been patented, and 264,850 were still segregated but not patented. *Ibid.*, p. 68.

was an attempt to set up, for irrigable lands in the West, a policy that was specifically designed for that area. Secondly, it provided funds, without interest, for the development of such lands. Thirdly, it implied more paternalism on the part of the government than had characterized any previous land legislation. In addition, it brought up the question of government versus private production of hydroelectric power. Roosevelt had already expressed himself strongly on this latter issue by vetoing a bill which would have authorized private development of power at Muscle Shoals, Alabama.[33] More and more the public was coming to regard water power as an asset to be developed as a public resource rather than to be turned over to private corporations for their profit.

Result of the Reclamation Act

The Reclamation Act created a revolving reclamation fund derived from the sale of public lands. This was to be used in constructing great storage and power dams, and for the canal systems required for irrigation. Settlers were to receive their lands free in much the same way as under the Homestead Act, *but* were to repay in ten years, without interest, the cost of the structures built by the government. The period of repayment was later increased, as the ten-year period was found unsatisfactory and impractical.

By 1915 some twenty-five projects had been initiated under the Reclamation Act, and the federal government had invested more than $80 million in them.[34] The Salt River project in Arizona, served by the great Roosevelt Dam, was the first of the huge installations of this kind built by the government. Since

that time even larger developments have been undertaken, among them the Hoover Dam project, the Grand Coulee and Bonneville Dams in the Northwest, and the Shasta and Friant Dams in California. The policy adopted meant much subsidization by the government over and above the contribution of the land itself. This was a new departure, though the general principle had been to some extent implied in various acts relating to federal leadership in protecting lands of the lower Mississippi Valley from floods.[35]

In arid country the development of irrigation provides benefits to railroads, merchants, industries and others as well as to the farmers living on the irrigated lands. It also tends to stabilize the economy, making it less dependent on a limited range of products and less vulnerable to droughts affecting the feed supplies for livestock. Because of these more general benefits, the allocation of costs, as between users of irrigation water and hydroelectric power and other beneficiaries, has continued to be highly controversial. The new act was a departure from earlier legislation in its attempt to recoup from the farmers benefited a part of the cost, while making a public contribution toward the less tangible benefits derived. Neither the basic philosophy nor a rational method of measuring and allocating costs and benefits has as yet been worked out. Thus far decisions in regard to federal reclamation have been heavily tinged

about the West were, however, to be increasingly recognized as the interest in land policy grew.

33. This site was later used for the huge Muscle Shoals project built by the government during World War I, which later became the center of the long struggle over government versus private operation that led to the creation of the Tennessee Valley Authority.

34. The background of the Federal Reclamation Act is sketched briefly in Dorothy Lampen's *Economic and Social Aspects of Federal Reclamation,* Johns Hopkins Press, Baltimore, 1930, Chapter 1. Chapter 2, "Progress under the Federal Reclamation Law," gives in some detail the amounts expended, location of projects and policies adopted up to 1929.

35. The Congress began consideration of methods for controlling flood damage along the lower Mississippi as early as 1849. All of the acts up to 1880 provided only for surveys and plans made by engineers in the employ of the federal government. They did not contemplate actual federal construction of the works needed. In 1881, the Mississippi River Commission (created in 1879) received a federal grant of one million dollars for river improvement. From this beginning the flood control activities have grown over the years and now involve large expenditures. While the projects are ostensibly designed as aids to navigation, the collateral benefits to farm lands subject to inundation are by no means inconsequential. The flood control program has not, however, included provision for repayment of costs by the lands benefited. The gradual development of policy relating to flood control is concisely sketched in War Department, Corps of Engineers, U.S. Mississippi River Commission, *The Improvement of the Lower Mississippi River for Flood Control and Navigation,* U.S. Waterways Experiment Station, Vicksburg, Mississippi, 1932 Vol. I, pp. 8–21.

with political considerations, and there has been relatively little careful and competent economic analysis of the program.

Other Policies Affecting Farmers

The reclamation and forest conservation programs touched most closely the farm groups, but even these measures were not initiated or vigorously pushed by farmers as a class. The forestry issue was one in which urban as well as rural groups took an interest, but much the same kind of an interest as that which they had in other general national policies. The reclamation program was almost wholly an outgrowth of western pressure. Even in the West the active proponents were more generally chambers of commerce and politicians than farmers. People already established as farmers were not greatly concerned about bringing in new lands, and those who were to occupy the reclaimed lands were, of course, not yet a part of the farm populations of the areas concerned.

There was comparatively little in the way of "national" organization among farmers, and the few general farmer organizations then in existence gave little attention to national policy problems. Nevertheless, the relatively unorganized farmers all through the country, like their urban counterparts, were keenly interested in the "dragons" T. R. was presumably in the process of slaying. These, mostly in the realm of "Big Business," were commonly and loosely referred to as the "Beef Trust," the "Grain Trust," the "Oil and Steel Trusts," and so forth. They were larger aggregations of business than had been customary in earlier times, before the economic life of the country had become so complex.

Small country flour mills were dying out, and the big mills and elevators of Minneapolis, Chicago and Buffalo were taking their place. Grain prices were being made in the central grain exchanges by forces little understood by the farmers. Likewise, the local slaughterhouse was giving way to large-scale packing establishments around the major livestock markets. The manufacturers of farm machinery were now fewer and larger, and therefore more prominent as targets for public criticism. In the financial realm, the large city banks had come to play a more dominant role — one that was regarded with distrust by farmers, and even by many of the country bankers.

As such businesses became larger and less well understood, it was natural for farmers to attribute to them controls over prices that they did not possess, though their operations were by no means free of antisocial practices. Gains, some of them unquestionably real ones, which resulted from increased size and more complex organization, were generally overlooked, or were assumed to accrue wholly to the industrialists. Except for railways the idea of control and supervision of "Big Business" had not gained much headway. Nor were farmers thinking much about large-scale cooperative agencies owned by themselves. The drive was rather to break up trusts, monopolies and holding companies, thus restoring competition along lines implied by the Sherman Act of 1890.

Roosevelt and Big Business

Roosevelt took the lead, at least in the newspapers, in the campaign against these business giants, and came to be known popularly as the "trust-buster" with the "big stick." Robert Marion La Follette, then Governor of Wisconsin, outdid Roosevelt in denunciation of the "trusts," and farmers rather generally applauded these efforts. Other lesser lights among the political leaders of the time and a number of magazine writers, the "muckrakers," took up the battle. These efforts resulted in some reforms but not many. The attention-getting qualities of the campaign were far more significant than its powers to increase understanding.

The first test in Roosevelt's effort to resuscitate and make effective the Sherman Act came in the Northern Securities case. The Attorney General, at the President's order, instituted suit against the Northern Securities Company, formed in 1901 for the purpose of merging three northwestern railroads.[36] The government sought dissolution of the company. In a five-to-four decision, handed down in 1904, the Supreme Court upheld the government's position and the company was ordered dissolved. This verdict was taken by Roosevelt as a vindication of his policy and a go-ahead sign for further prosecutions. Some twenty-five suits were brought during his administration, but only a few of them were decided in favor of the government. Among these was the decision requiring dissolution of the "Beef Trust." Some 60 per cent of the dealers in fresh meats had agreements whereby they avoided bidding against one another for their meat supplies.

On the whole the attempts to restore competition were not highly successful. Some writers have compared them to efforts to unscramble an egg. The regulation of such businesses seemed to offer more promise, but Roosevelt, like his successor, Taft, was unable to get from a hostile Congress legislation looking to that end. The President eventually turned to the attitude known as the "rule of reason." This doctrine was that the mere fact of combination was not in itself illegal unless it resulted in *unreasonable* interference with interstate commerce. It eventually came to be accepted by the Supreme Court and was given expression in the Standard Oil case of 1911. The gist of the "rule of reason" approach had been formulated in a minority opinion by Justice Edward D. White as early as 1892 (in the Trans-Missouri Freight Association case). Roosevelt, in his own colorful way, chose to rephrase it and sought to make a distinction between "good trusts," which showed a proper concern for the welfare of the consumer, and "bad trusts," which sought only selfish ends.[37]

President Taft continued even more vigorously the campaign for the control of corporations and the dissolution of trusts and monopolies. He, like Roosevelt, sought a law to provide incorporation of interstate businesses by the national government, but was not able to persuade Congress to enact it. Two important cases were won, but not so fully as the government desired. These were the Standard Oil case, in which the "rule of reason" doctrine was enunciated in the majority opinion, and the tobacco trust cases.[38] The monopoly problem had not been solved, however, and was to continue to engage the attention of Presidents, legislators and the Department of Justice in succeeding decades.

Railroad Regulation

In railway regulation the first decade and a half of the twentieth century are marked mainly by a consolidation of the position established through passage of the Interstate Commerce Act of 1887. The Commission had been hampered by adverse court decisions, and had proved unable to cope with the growing concentration of power in the big railroad systems. The Elkins Law (1903) corrected one weakness by outlawing rebates and requiring railroads to charge the published rates. This was acceptable to the carriers, since, with increasingly full use of their facilities, they were under far less pressure to grant rebates than in earlier periods when their lines were much overbuilt in relation to the traffic available.

The Hepburn bill (1906) roused far more opposition. It would have granted the Commission full authority to *regulate* railroad rates without obtaining judicial approval of its decisions. Though passed by a heavy majority in the House, a compromise was required to get it through the Senate. As finally passed, the legislation gave the Commission power to regulate rates, though the carriers could appeal to the courts for invalidation of its decisions.

The change made was important, how-

36. The Northern Securities Company was engineered by James J. Hill and largely financed by J. P. Morgan. It was organized under the laws of New Jersey as a holding company and capitalized at $400 million. Presumably the new company would have eliminated competition, but it also contained possibilities for improving the organization of the railways of the Northwest.

37. Hicks, *The American Nation*, p. 388.

38. These cases are well and briefly discussed in Carl Brent Swisher, *American Constitutional Development*, Houghton Mifflin, Boston, 1943, pp. 542–43.

ever. The Commission was no longer compelled to go to court to enforce its orders.
The carriers either had to accept the rates
set by the Commission or themselves make
the appeal to the courts. The law also
brought other common carriers, such as express companies, pipe lines, sleeping-car companies, bridges and ferries, under the jurisdiction of the Commission, and forbade the
granting of free passes. In addition, the Commission was empowered to prescribe a uniform system of bookkeeping. Its membership
was raised from five to seven.

With this strengthening of the basic law,
and of its personnel, the Commission was
able to bring about substantial reductions in
rates in the course of a few years. Through
able and judicious handling of the situation it
gained the respect of the public, the courts
and of the carriers themselves. Thus after a
struggle lasting thirty-five years, most of the
Granger objectives in the realm of railroad
legislation had been achieved. Farmer concern over railroad problems was to come up
in later times, but not in the same form. The
basic pattern of railway regulation had been
established.

Monetary and Credit Problems

Farmers had complained about banks and
credit arrangements for more than a hundred
years. Their demands had taken various
forms. In the Jackson period, and after the
Civil War, they opposed contraction of paper
currency and convertibility as between paper
and specie. Later they opposed the national
banks and generally espoused "free silver."
The bitter struggle which resulted in the
abolition of the second Bank of the United
States had virtually closed the door to any
serious consideration of a central bank. But
more and more the need for an improved
banking system was becoming evident. The
country was dotted with thousands of small
banks, many of them chartered under state
laws and subjected, in most states, only to
nominal supervision. The larger ones generally were chartered as national banks and
were better supervised, through the office of

the Comptroller of the Currency. But even
they were too unrelated to pool their resources effectively when faced by serious financial crises.

The result was a banking system that was
exceedingly unstable. Any sudden loss of
confidence could start a run on an individual
bank and force it to close its doors. Such
runs tended to spread to other banks, and
banking panics were easily generated and
disastrous in their effects. Not only was the
credit formerly supplied by the closed banks
wiped out, but the banks still open naturally
sought to contract loans outstanding and refrained from extending new loans. This situation created a tendency for the banking
system itself to accentuate booms and depressions, expanding credit too much when
times looked good, and contracting too much
when times were bad. Since bank checks
based on deposits and bank loans had come
to constitute a large part of the customary
monetary medium, these fluctuations had a
marked effect on the health of the economy
both urban and rural.

In an effort to meet these defects, unofficial
groupings of bank resources became common. Most small banks associated themselves
in some degree with strong banks in the
larger cities. These larger "correspondent"
banks would usually, within limits, come to
the aid of the associated smaller banks in the
event of runs on them. Often, however, such
help as they were willing to give was too
little and too late. The system gave considerable joint strength to the banks that were
banded together in this way, but lacked com-
prehensiveness and flexibility. Even the large
banks could not create new currency, on the
basis of productive loans, to meet seasonal
and cyclical needs. If a large bank had to
close its doors, the result was likely to be a
spreading panic that would throw the whole
economy into a tailspin. Furthermore, the
system resulted in relatively high rates of interest to borrowers from the small country
banks. The latter, especially in the capital
deficit areas, usually charged a substantial
margin for their services, over and above the

rates charged them by the city correspondent banks, to whom they transferred loans they could not carry with their own resources.

A short sharp panic in 1903, known as the "Rich Man's Panic," and a more serious one in 1907, which was touched off by failure of the Knickerbocker Trust Company of New York, served to focus attention on the inadequacy of the banking system. The Congress passed, in 1908, the Aldrich-Vreeland Act, which permitted the national banks, for a period of six years, to issue emergency currency in times of stringency. This was only a temporary arrangement. The important step taken was the creation of a National Monetary Commission to shape plans for a comprehensive reform of the banking system.[39] This took shape under the administrations of Roosevelt and Taft, but was not to be enacted into law until after they had gone out of office.

Farm Mortgage Inadequacies

Farmer interest centered more directly on the inadequacies of farm mortgage credit. The growing amount of indebtedness and the chronic deficit of loan funds in the newer areas made farmers more and more conscious of this problem. They objected both to the high rates of interest and to the terms under which loans were made. Bankers and mortgage companies seldom made such loans for as long as five years. Often they were for three years, and frequently for as short a term as one year. Clearly the loans could not be paid in these short periods, and neither the borrower nor the lender expected they would be. The farmer-borrower was, however, placed in a very insecure position, since renewal of his loan was subject to denial at frequent intervals, and such denial might mean the loss of his farm if his mortgage fell due in a period when money was tight and conditions bad. The frequent renewals also involved heavy expense for loan commissions, title search, and so on.

These defects in the credit system gave rise to vigorous demands for longer-term mortgages and more orderly methods of repayment, demands which the commercial banks were ill-equipped to meet even had they desired to do so. Though there was general acceptance of the need for a better farm credit system, and most people recognized that the commercial banks were poorly equipped for making farm mortgage loans, specific action looking to the improvement of agricultural credit facilities was not to be undertaken until the latter part of the Taft administration, and the beginning of Woodrow Wilson's.

Tariff Changes: The Payne-Aldrich Act

In the years immediately following the Republican victories of 1896 and 1900 the tariff issue was not prominent in farmer thinking.[40] The anti-high-tariff movement in the Middle West, known as the "Iowa Idea," did, however, gain sufficient headway in the early 1900's to force both parties to take cognizance of it in their 1908 platforms. The Democrats declared unequivocally for a reduction of tariffs. The Republicans were far from unequivocal. They cautiously settled on a plank that called for duties that would "equal the difference between the cost of production at home and abroad, together with a reasonable profit to American industry."[41] Taft carried the East, Middle West and West while Bryan carried the solid South plus Nebraska, Colorado and Nevada. A moderate progressive, Taft was personally favorable to a lowering of duties, but handled the issue ineptly in his public utterances relating to it, and drew

39. These events and their setting are more fully described in Hicks, *The American Nation*, pp. 414–15.

40. Roosevelt, early in his administration, adopted an aggressive foreign policy, especially with respect to the Monroe Doctrine, Panama Canal development and so on. It did not, in the main, have tariff implications. The nearest approach to that was the so-called "open door" policy enunciated by his Secretary of State, John Hay. This was in some respects a philosophical forerunner of the freer trade program pursued so vigorously by Cordell Hull in the administration of Franklin D. Roosevelt. Hay, like Hull, advocated uniform treatment of the nationals of all countries, but sought to apply this doctrine only to China, which was the area of chief interest at the time. The Hull policies looked to freeing international trade from hampering restrictions throughout the world.

41. Hicks, *The American Nation*, p. 422.

criticism from both the protectionists and the advocates of lower duties.

The Congress was controlled by staunch protectionists and proceeded to pass a strongly protective measure, the Payne-Aldrich Tariff of 1909. The President, wishing to avoid a party split, signed the bill, and thereby became still more unpopular in the Midwest farming areas.

The new act did not depart importantly from the general philosophy of the McKinley and Dingley tariffs; the average rate on dutiable goods was raised about one per cent. Reductions were made on a good many inconsequential items, but not on those of major importance. Farmers generally disliked the act, and it was widely criticized and lampooned by the liberal press as the work of Aldrich and his Rhode Island manufacturers. Hundreds of amendments had been added in Aldrich's committee in the Senate, most of them providing increases in duties.

The act contained a few innovations. One was the introduction of the European system of maximum-minimum rates which permitted the President to apply higher rates against countries that discriminated against the United States. Another provided for a bipartisan tariff board to study relative costs of production in the United States and abroad.[42]

An important group of progressives from the middle western states broke party lines and voted against the bill. Ably led by Norris of Nebraska and La Follette of Wisconsin they were soon to bring about, through cooperation with the Democrats, significant changes in congressional procedure, and were able to break the power of the ultraconservative Speaker, Joseph G. Cannon of Illinois. While, as a whole, the Payne-Aldrich Act made little change in the tariff system, its repercussions were important. It helped to bring about in the farm areas a dissatisfaction with the leadership of the "regular" Republicans which led to the Bull Moose movement of 1912, and thus indirectly aided in the election of Wilson, a liberal Democrat. The disapproval of Taft's tariff views in the farm areas was still further increased by his effort to establish reciprocity with Canada by removing duties on a number of farm products.[43] His bill designed for this purpose was finally passed by the House and Senate, but the plan was rejected by Canada.[44]

The Food and Drug Law

One of the major accomplishments of the Roosevelt administration, in the way of preventing abuses in business, was the passage, in 1906, of the Food and Drug Act. This prohibited the manufacture, sale or transportation in interstate commerce of adulterated, misbranded, poisonous or deleterious foods, drugs, medicines or liquors. Penalties and policing arrangements were provided for the enforcement of the act.

The new law struck directly and, in the main, effectively, at widespread abuses in the food and drug trades, a realm in which the individual consumer is peculiarly helpless since the detection of adulterants, undesirable preservatives and misleading brands is usually possible only through careful chemical analyses.[45]

The new act became effective on January 1, 1907, and in April of that year the Secretary of Agriculture set up the Board of Food and Drugs Inspection to consider all questions arising in its enforcement. The analytical work was assigned to the Bureau of Chemistry. Food inspection laboratories were established at various places throughout the

42. This illogical and useless approach to the tariff problem remained prominent in Republican doctrine for some twenty years thereafter.

43. Another serious blow to the Taft prestige came with the so-called "Ballinger scandal." Ballinger, Taft's Secretary of the Interior, chose to institute a moderate reversal of the conservation policy established under Roosevelt. He released certain water-power sites for private exploitation, and some coal lands in Alaska. These actions brought widely accepted charges of corruption, and, among other things, resulted in the dismissal of Gifford Pinchot and Louis R. Glavis, an Interior Department official, for corresponding directly with Congress on the matter.

44. Hicks, *The American Nation*, pp. 422–39.

45. The passage of the act was the result of a long campaign vigorously led by Dr. Harvey Wiley, Chief of the Bureau of Chemistry in the United States Department of Agriculture. Investigations of food adulterants and their effects had been going on under Dr. Wiley's direction for many years. He became Chief of the Division (later Bureau) in 1883.

country, and inspectors traveled about collecting samples for analysis. Many controversies arose as to whether certain substances such as boric acid, salicylic acid, benzoate of soda and so on were or were not harmful to consumers. Dr. Wiley and his associates tended to take somewhat extreme views on the dangers from substances of this kind, but on the whole did a conscientious and constructive job. Their work gained the respect and backing of the public including the farm groups.[46]

Broader Provision for Meat Inspection

Another bill passed on the same day as the Food and Drug Act (June 30, 1906) enlarged still further the functions of the Department of Agriculture in protecting the interests of the consumer. This was a broadening of the meat inspection work which had been started in 1884. The earlier legislation was brought about by the serious losses on American livestock exported to Britain. The British placed embargoes on the importation of live animals from the United States, alleging that animal diseases had thereby been introduced into Britain. Difficulties had also arisen through transfers of animal disease in the opposite direction.

The Act of 1884 directed the Commissioner of Agriculture to organize a Bureau of Animal Industry and to appoint a competent veterinarian as its chief. Not only was this bureau to conduct researches relating to the control of animal diseases; it was given regulatory powers with respect to exportation of livestock and poultry, and for prevention of the spread of animal diseases from one state to another.

These earlier measures clearly were designed to serve the interests of producers. That has been the principal orientation of the Department of Agriculture throughout its history. Measures such as the Food and Drug Act and the Meat Inspection Act of 1906 marked an important deviation from

this preoccupation with producer problems.

Upton Sinclair's book, *The Jungle,* appeared early in 1906. It dramatized the lack of sanitary precautions in the packing industry, and created wide interest in the problem. Public clamor for correction of this situation resulted in an act which was really the Beveridge Amendment to the Agricultural Appropriation Act. It made mandatory the post-mortem examination of the carcasses of all cattle, sheep, swine and goats prepared for human consumption and for transportation in interstate commerce.[47]

While primarily designed for consumer protection, the act was, for the most part, acceptable to farmers as well. They did not at the time, however, foresee its longer-term ramifications. It was to become a powerful stimulus for the eradication of certain widely prevalent animal diseases, particularly tuberculosis. The question of the appropriate orientation of the efforts of the Department of Agriculture, whether towards the interests of the producer or toward the more general public interest, had not thereby been resolved — nor has it been since. Nevertheless, it is clear that from this time on the Department was to have mixed loyalties which would at times prove embarrassing to it. The protection of the health and welfare of the consumer had become definitely an accepted part of the over-all function of government.

FARMER MOVEMENTS DURING THE FIRST PART OF THE TWENTIETH CENTURY

Most of the general national and regional farm organizations of the late 1800's had passed out of existence by the end of the century. Of the more important, only the Grange remained. Its emphasis on local social and educational activities, and its forward-looking but conservative program for agricultural legislation enabled it to retain the interest of a modest membership, especially in New

46. For a fuller account of these developments, see Gustavus A. Weber, *The Food, Drug, and Insecticide Administration, Its History, Activities and Organization,* Service Monograph of the United States Government No. 50, Johns Hopkins Press, Baltimore, 1928.

47. A fuller account of these developments is presented in John M. Gaus and Leon O. Wolcott, *Public Administration and the United States Department of Agriculture,* Committee on Public Administration of the Social Science Research Council, Chicago, 1940, especially pp. 160–90.

York and New England. After 1900 the organization experienced an unsensational but stable growth. In 1910, it had a national membership of 425,033, which by 1915 had increased to 540,085.[48] Dr. T. C. Atkeson had begun his long career as lobbyist for Grange measures in Washington, and was doing an effective job, mostly, however, on matters that did not make headlines or arouse vigorous opposition.

The Farmers Union

A new organization, the Farmers Educational and Cooperative Union of America, was started in Texas in 1902. The original society was formed by Newton Gresham, formerly an organizer for the Alliance. He was deeply impressed by the poverty of the cotton growers, burdened as they were by an oppressive credit and mortgage system. The organization was secret, but had little ritual and no degrees. It soon spread to other southern states and attempted to improve the price of cotton. This was undertaken, in Texas, through the formation of a cotton exchange to fix prices. For a time, around 1906, it seemed to be having some success with that procedure.

In 1905 a national organization was formed with representatives from Texas, Arkansas, Oklahoma, Alabama, Georgia, Mississippi and Louisiana, and, in 1906, the Farmers' Relief Association (organized in 1900) merged with the Union. The Union was still further expanded in 1907 when the remnants of one of the older organizations came in (the Farmers' Mutual Benefit Association) as did the Farmers Social and Economical Union of Illinois, which had been founded in 1900.

The movement reached its peak for this period in 1907. At that time it was organized in about twenty states, principally in the South, and had approximately a million members. It was limited to farmers (whites and Indians), though it accepted country mechanics, teachers, clergy and so on, but no bankers, lawyers or speculators in farm products. These provisions were similar to those of the Alliance. The main emphasis was on cooperation. Boards of trade, cotton exchanges and other forms of speculation were condemned. The organization was also interested in tenancy problems and farm credit, and expressed friendship for labor.

The Union sought to control prices directly by refusing to sell for less than specified amounts. It attempted to limit output in order to make price control feasible, and in 1907 engaged in a campaign for plowing up 10 per cent of the cotton crop and holding part of it for higher prices. Efforts were made to finance farmers in order that they might carry out the price-raising program, and some warehouses were built for this purpose. Many of the Unions sought to sell independently of the local dealers and the cotton exchanges. Improved methods of grading and sampling cotton were advocated, and some educational activities were undertaken. Political activities were prohibited, but the effort to keep them out was not entirely successful.

The Union did not have any important effect on national policies or legislation. Its impractical efforts to force prices up by holding supplies off the market and by destruction of crops were continued in some measure even into the 1920's. Thereafter, under new leadership and with broader policies, the organization began to exert more influence.

The American Society of Equity

At about the same time the American Society of Equity, founded in Illinois in 1902, experienced a similar growth in the North Central states. Its chief organizer was J. A. Everitt, editor of a newspaper and author of The Third Power. The organization claimed at one time a membership of a million, but probably had about one seventh that many.[49]

48. Thomas Clark Atkeson, *Semi-Centennial History of the Patrons of Husbandry*, Orange Judd, New York, 1916, p. 350. Grange membership increased in most of the years between 1900 and 1915, but tended to level off from 1913 on. It stood at 187,482 in 1900.
For a later history of the Grange, see Charles M. Gardner, *The Grange—Friend of the Farmer—1867-1947*, The National Grange, Washington, 1949.

49. Benjamin H. Hibbard, *Marketing Agricultural Products*, D. Appleton, New York, 1921, pp. 231-32.

Its main strength was in the wheat regions of Minnesota and the Dakotas, but in 1906 there were state organizations in Indiana, Illinois, Kentucky, Michigan, Wisconsin, Minnesota, North and South Dakota, Nebraska, Kansas, Oklahoma, Arkansas and New York.

The Equity, like the Union, sought to raise prices by holding farm products off the market. Its founders recommended that farmers cease to look for aid through legislation and try to do their own marketing in a more efficient way. The organization encouraged the building of elevators and tried to give help in financing them. It campaigned for dollar wheat and tried to establish a grain exchange in St. Paul. Somewhat similar organizations formed in the tobacco areas, particularly those of Kentucky, apparently had some success in raising the price of Burley tobacco but lost control of the market in 1909.[50] Their members continued, however, to market their crop more effectively than before the movement was started.

The Society of Equity was split by internal dissension in 1907. A faction led by M. Wes. Tubbs, the secretary of the organization, won control from the group led by J. A. Everitt, the president. The Tubbs faction objected to the crop-holding plan and wanted to substitute a cooperative marketing program. The Everitt faction held a rump convention and eventually formed a separate organization, the Farmers' Society of Equity, which survived for some ten years though it did not achieve much success.

The Tubbs group sought the cooperation of several labor organizations, and, in 1907, chartered, in New Jersey, an organization to supervise the local cooperative exchanges and guarantee their financial responsibility. This group also encountered difficulties and was only regional in scope. An attempt to merge it with the Farmers Union, in 1910, was not successful. However, the efforts to combine the two resulted in the formation of a third organization, the Farmers' Equity Union, chartered in Illinois. The Equity Union gave principal attention to organizing cooperative elevators and creameries. As late as 1923 it had about 65,000 members.

The Society of Equity continued to exist for some years. It entered politics, but much of its political thunder was taken over by the Nonpartisan League. Some remnants of its cooperative ventures were eventually merged with the Farmers Union.[51]

Development of Farmer Cooperatives

Before 1900, and for some years thereafter, the farmer efforts to engage in business were, in the main, attempts to handle business as a phase of the activities of the general farm organizations. The Grange efforts along these lines generally were failures. The same was true of the Alliance and other general farm organizations. After 1900 the American Society of Equity and the Farmers Educational and Cooperative Union undertook business activities of similar kinds and with much the same results.

After the beginning of the century, and to some extent even before, another type of farm organization became important. This

50. The American Tobacco Company had a virtual monopoly of Burley tobacco. The idea was therefore to develop a single seller to meet a single buyer. The Burley Society, an association patterned on the Planters' Protective Association of Virginia, Kentucky and Tennessee (organized in 1904), was formed at Winchester, Kentucky, in 1907. This group agreed to sell only through a single agent, and managed to hold its 1907 crop off the market when the American Tobacco Company refused to buy at its price. When the Burley Society pledged itself to grow no tobacco in 1908 (as 100 million pounds of the 1907 crop were still on hand), it encountered the troubles arising out of nonmember production, chiefly that of the "hillbillies" who were looked upon in much the same light as "scabs" in labor circles. "Night-rider" groups, similar to those of the Ku Klux Klan proceeded to "educate" the "hillbillies" by burning their barns, whipping them, and, if need be, killing them.

It has been estimated that property losses amounting to more than a million dollars were inflicted by these lawless bands. They did succeed for a time in obtaining better prices though with a reduction in output that makes questionable any significant gain in income. The movement obviously could not be established on a lasting basis by such methods, and soon died down. For a fuller account, see Anna Youngman, "The Tobacco Pools of Kentucky and Tennessee," *Journal of Political Economy*, January 1910, pp. 34–49, and contemporary periodical articles.

51. See Robert H. Bahmer, "The American Society of Equity," *Agricultural History*, January 1940, pp. 33–63.

was the specialized business cooperative, organized usually on a local basis. By this time state laws were coming into existence which made specific provision for cooperative business organizations.[52] Most of these were set up on the general lines of the Rochdale stores of England. Many of the articles of incorporation included the Rochdale principles of one vote per man, limited return on capital and distribution of surplus income in accordance with the amount of business done with the association. Some followed these practices informally without specific provisions in their articles and bylaws. Others were organized as straight farmer-owned stock corporations with profits distributed in accordance with amounts of stock owned.

Though the Rochdale plan was designed to meet the needs of buyers rather than sellers, it proved reasonably suitable for the small-scale producers' cooperatives, which were the principal ones of that period. Local cooperative grain elevators constituted the bulk of the early group of business cooperatives. They were soon followed, in the dairy regions, by cooperative creameries and cheese factories, and, more generally, by mutual fire insurance companies. Some cooperative shipping of livestock also began to appear. Except for the abortive efforts of the general farm organizations which have already been mentioned, there was little attempt as yet to enter the terminal markets. Such thinking as there was about market agencies in the large centers looked in the direction of regulatory legislation rather than direct business participation.

Beginnings were being made, however, on a cooperative "big business" approach to the farmers' marketing problems, particularly in the special crop areas distant from markets.

The most notable and successful one was the California Fruit Growers Exchange. This was organized in 1895 as an outgrowth of a number of previous unsuccessful attempts dating back as far as 1885.[53] G. Harold Powell became manager of the Exchange in 1912, a post he held until his death in 1922. Powell, an outstanding leader in cooperative matters, laid a foundation that enabled the Exchange to become one of the giants among farmers' cooperatives, and paved the way for farmers to challenge "big business" on its own ground, by seeking to handle their own affairs on a large-scale and efficient basis.

This approach, in contrast to that of looking to legislative aid for the farmer, is one that has since become deeply rooted in the thinking of many farm groups, particularly those whose policy influence is now exerted through the National Council of Farmers' Cooperatives. Other organizations of similar type were founded during this period, especially on the West Coast. Among them were the Walnut Growers and Almond Growers Exchanges in California. Most of them, however, did not achieve great importance until after World War I.

Agriculture's Gains, 1900–1915

The period from 1900 to 1915 was one of marked progress on policies of great importance to farmers, but not one in which they themselves took the lead. Yet the farm organizations of the latter part of the nineteenth century had initiated discussion of many of these matters, and had made the first proposals for their solution. The public regulation of railroads had now emerged from the stage of an accepted principle to a fully implemented program. Conservation of natural resources, only hinted at by the farm groups in the earlier period, had become a widely discussed issue, and to a considerable extent an established policy. The monopoly

52. The emergence during this period of special laws governing the organization of farmers' cooperatives is described in E. G. Nourse, *The Legal Status of Agricultural Co-operation*, Macmillan, New York, 1927, Chapter 2. The largest growth in numbers of cooperative associations was to come between 1916 and 1920. There was a rapid increase, however, in grain, dairy, fruit and nut, livestock, cotton and purchasing cooperatives between 1906 and 1915. See R. H. Ellsworth and Grace Wanstall, *Farmers' Marketing and Purchasing Cooperatives, 1863-1939*, Farm Credit Administration, Miscellaneous Report No. 40, 1941, p. 7.

53. These earlier attempts at cooperative selling of citrus fruits are briefly described in Rahno Mabel MacCurdy's *The History of the California Fruit Growers Exchange*, Los Angeles, 1925. See also Kelsey B. Gardner and A. W. McKay, *The California Fruit Growers Exchange System*, Farm Credit Administration, Circ. C-135, May 1950.

problem, though by no means solved, had become a major public issue and was under active study.

Agricultural experimentation and education, urged and sponsored by the earlier farm organizations, had made great strides. Credit reform for agriculture and banking reform in the general field had been initiated though their major development was to come later. Little significant progress had been made in tariff matters, but farmer sentiment in regard to tariffs was not clearly crystallized in this or earlier periods. Important regulatory activities in food and drugs and meat inspection had come into being though largely as a protection to consumers rather than as an aid to farmers.

Among the little-noticed occurrences of the period was the beginning made in the study of the economic problems of the farmer. Work in farm management had been started in the Bureau of Plant Industry, and the Bureau of Markets was established in the Department of Agriculture in 1913. Perhaps even more important in its long-time effects was the fact that a notable group of educators had started studying farmers' economic problems and training graduate students for work in that field. Chief among them were H. C. Taylor at the University of Wisconsin, G. F. Warren at Cornell, Hayes and Boss at Minnesota, Thomas Nixon Carver at Harvard and W. J. Spillman in the United States Department of Agriculture. These teachers were laying a groundwork that was to give rise to intense farmer interest in the 1920's, and to become an important factor in the national agricultural policies adopted during the 1930's.

CHAPTER 8

THE WILSON ADMINISTRATION:
REFORM AND WAR

WHEN THEODORE ROOSEVELT stepped out of office in March 1909, and the mild, easy-going
Taft took over, the nation entered a time of
settled conditions and quiet progress that has
since come to be known as the "parity" period. The first years of the new century were,
in a way, the Indian summer of the Victo-
rian Era that had come to a close in 1901.
The general setting changed little during the
time Taft was in office, but the tempo was
slower. Roosevelt's colorful leadership was
gone, and the crusading reformers of his period were growing older. American business
was digesting the changes brought about by
them, and had in some measure accommo-
dated itself to a more liberal economic philosophy.

The major shock of the nineteenth century revolution in transportation had been
absorbed both in the United States and in
Europe. The western world was becoming
adjusted to a changed pattern of production
and consumption. The leading European nations, except Russia, had shifted heavily in
the direction of industrial production and dependence upon foreign sources of food, particularly those of North America. At the
same time the rapid growth of urban population in the United States had helped to
overcome the unbalance in agricultural production that occurred during the last part of
the nineteenth century, through rapid settlement of new lands and growth of the railroad network.

Agriculture was prosperous, land values
were rising, and farm people reflected the
general feeling of confidence and stability
that prevailed. Since 1900, political sentiment
had been generally favorable to evolutionary

reform and clean government. Though
widely publicized, the changes brought about
under the leadership of Roosevelt, La Follette,
Cummins, Beveridge and others were not
radical or sensational, but, rather, were in
keeping with the more "respectable" traditions in American government. Nevertheless,
the bubbling enthusiasm of the Theodore
Roosevelt era had subsided in the less colorful and milder liberalism of the Taft administration.

Taft's political ineptitude, together with
the launching of the Bull Moose party by
Roosevelt, split the Republican ranks, and resulted in the election of Woodrow Wilson in
1912. Backed by a Democratic Congress, Wilson proceeded to carry forward the reform
program. Though not so adept in catching
the popular fancy as Roosevelt, Wilson was a
far more profound student of government.
In the main his proposals were the result of
careful study, and related to significant, fundamental issues. Though progressive and
forward-looking, they constituted no important break with tradition. The objectives, so
far as domestic policy was concerned, did not
differ greatly from those of the preceding
Roosevelt and Taft administrations.

In the realm of international relations the
differences were more marked. Roosevelt had
personified a "new nationalism" bordering
on, if not actually constituting, imperialism as
that term is understood today. Wilson's
views, on the other hand, tended toward internationalism and emphasized a "new freedom" for the individual. In economic affairs
he carried further the leaning toward freer
international trade which had begun to take
shape in the Taft administration.

Legislative Program of Wilson's First Term

The Wilson program included steps designed to lower tariff barriers, to curtail the power of corporations and monopolies, to strengthen and reorganize the banking system, to provide better credit facilities for agriculture, to improve the scientific and educational facilities available to farm people and to halt the wasteful use of natural resources. The early part of his first term is characterized by almost unprecedented accomplishment in solid, evolutionary progress which, however, was cut short by his growing preoccupation with the problems relating to the war in Europe. Many of the reforms that came to fruition at this time had, to be sure, been initiated in the two previous administrations, notably those in banking and rural credits, and the antitrust measures. Nevertheless, all of them showed the effects of Wilson's modifying influence, and some undoubtedly would have failed of enactment under a less skillful and vigorous President. Roosevelt had been particularly well qualified to initiate and popularize reform measures. Wilson was better suited for the more prosaic task of refining them, and carrying them through to completion.

Legislation Sought by Agriculture

During this period the farm groups were not highly organized. They interested themselves in many of the issues of the time such as meat inspection, control of the food and drug industries, direct election of senators, the elimination of monopolies and trusts, and in some more specifically agricultural objectives, such as parcel post, the retention of the tax on oleomargarine and the repeal of the Canadian Reciprocity Act. On many of the general issues they tended to react in much the same way as their urban counterparts, rather than as a special interest group.

The Grange considered itself the major general spokesman for farmers, though it was not organized on a nationwide scale and did not have continuous representation in Washington.[1] It depended instead upon stimulating its members to write their congressmen on matters which the national and state Granges considered crucial.

The national organization had formulated, by the latter part of the Taft administration, a rather definite program of legislation to be advocated. While this contained some of the measures that were to be under active consideration in the following years, there is no specific mention of several of the more important ones, such as farm credits and federal supervision of warehouses, which might have been expected to bulk large in the minds of farmers. In the issue of November 1911 (p. 10), *The National Grange Monthly* stated its policy on legislation as follows:

The Grange favors:
1. Federal aid for road improvement
2. A Parcels Post law
3. Conservation of natural resources
4. Direct election of United States senators
5. A non-partisan Tariff Commission
6. A national income tax
7. Effective railroad regulation
8. Peace and universal arbitration

It is opposed to:
1. Ship subsidies
2. A Central United States Bank
3. Amendment of the oleomargarine law in the interests of imitation butter

The Grange also favored agricultural education and extension services (with emphasis

1. The Grange had some 540,000 members on its rolls in 1915. However, since Grange memberships were individual and not by families, this probably represented no more than 150,000 families. The American Society of Equity had declined to a position of small importance, and the Farmers Union, chiefly active in the Southwest, was not a significant factor in national politics. Edward Wiest puts the average membership of the Farmers Union at 121,826 for the years 1908 through 1910 and at 140,066 for 1917–1919. *Agricultural Organization in the United States,* University of Kentucky, Lexington, 1923, p. 476.

In addition to the organizations mentioned above, the Farmers' National Congress achieved some prominence as a crystallizer of sentiment relative to farm problems. It was a loosely organized forum without significant local organization or much genuine farmer membership. Meetings were held annually in widely scattered cities over the period 1880 to 1920. During part of the time a legislative representative was maintained in Washington. For a fuller description of its activities, see Farmers' National Congress, *Official Proceedings,* especially those of 1912 through 1916.

on agricultural education in the secondary schools); increased study of home economics; discontinuance of the distribution of free seeds; and amendment of the antitrust laws to define more clearly what acts on the part of corporations would be considered detrimental to public welfare.[2]

The regulation of railroads had been achieved. Direct election of United States senators and the federal income tax were on their way, largely through more general backing, though the Grange claimed credit for their initiation and ultimate passage.[3] Thus no major agricultural issue was claiming the attention of American farmers and stimulating agitation on their part. The new President proceeded, however, to put forward, in broad outline, a farm program that showed understanding and vision, though it had no great popular appeal in the rural areas.

Wilson's Program for Agriculture

In his Inaugural Address, Wilson made specific references to the legislative needs of agriculture.

We have [he said] a body of agricultural activities never yet given the efficiency of great business undertakings or served as it should be through the instrumentality of science taken directly to the farm, or afforded the facilities of credit best suited to its practical needs; watercourses undeveloped, waste places unreclaimed, forests untended fast disappearing without plan or prospect of renewal, unregarded waste heaps at every mine. We have studied as perhaps no other nation has the most effective means of

2. During this period the Farmers Union gave its main attention to local and self-help programs rather than to national legislation. For a description of its activities, see R. L. Hunt, *A History of Farmer Movements in the Southwest, 1873–1925*, privately published, no place, no date; and A. C. Davis, *The Farmers' Educational and Co-Operative Union of America, What It Is and What It Is Doing*, Four States Press, Texarkana, 1913; and *Supplement A to What It Is and What It Is Doing*, Four States Press, Texarkana, 1917[?]. See also Commodore B. Fisher, *The Farmers Union*, Vol. I, No. 2, Publications of the University of Kentucky, Lexington, 1920.

3. The Sixteenth Amendment authorizing the levying of graduated income taxes was declared ratified on February 25, 1913; and the Seventeenth Amendment providing for the direct election of United States senators was declared ratified on May 31, 1913. A Parcels Post Act had already been passed, in 1912.

production, but we have not studied cost or economy as we should either as organizers of industry, as statesmen, or as individuals.[4]

It was not, however, the agricultural program that was to receive first attention in the new administration. Other problems, many of them important to agriculture, were to take precedence, particularly the tariff and the reform of the banking structure. These issues had been even more sharply high-lighted in the Inaugural Address, and obviously were of broader national interest than the agricultural program.[5]

4. Woodrow Wilson, *The New Democracy, Presidential Messages, Addresses and Other Papers, 1913–1917*, ed. by Ray Stannard Baker and William E. Dodd, Harper and Brothers, New York, 1926, Vol. I, p. 4.

5. The main features of this more general program were briefly outlined as follows: "We have itemized with some degree of particularity the things that ought to be altered and here are some of the chief items: A tariff which cuts us off from our proper part in the commerce of the world, violates the just principles of taxation, and makes the Government a facile instrument in the hands of private interests; a banking and currency system based upon the necessity of the Government to sell its bonds fifty years ago and perfectly adapted to concentrating cash and restricting credits; an industrial system which, take it on all its sides, financial as well as administrative, holds capital in leading strings, restricts the liberties and limits the opportunities of labor, and exploits without renewing or conserving, the natural resources of the country. . . . [Here follows the section on agriculture quoted in the text above.]

"Nor have we studied and perfected the means by which government may be put at the service of humanity, in safeguarding the health of the Nation, the health of its men and its women and its children, as well as their rights in the struggle for existence. This is no sentimental duty. The firm basis of government is justice, not pity. These are matters of justice. There can be no equality or [sic] opportunity, the first essential of justice in the body politic, if men and women and children be not shielded in their lives, their very vitality, from the consequences of great industrial and social processes which they can not alter, control, or singly cope with. Society must see to it that it does not itself crush or weaken or damage its constituent parts. The first duty of law is to keep sound the society it serves. Sanitary laws, pure food laws, and laws determining conditions of labor which individuals are powerless to determine for themselves are intimate parts of the very business of justice and legal efficiency.

"These are some of the things we ought to do, and not leave the others undone, the old-fashioned, never-to-be-neglected, fundamental safeguarding of property and of individual right. This is the high enterprise of the new day: To lift everything that concerns our life as a Nation to the light that shines from the hearthfire of every man's conscience and vision of the right. It is inconceivable that we should do this as partisans; it is inconceivable we should do it in ignorance of the facts as they are or in blind haste. We shall restore, not destroy. We shall deal with our economic system as it is and as it may be modified, not as it might be if we had a clean sheet of paper to write upon; and step by

Proposals for Tariff Reform

Within a month after his inauguration Wilson called the Congress into session to consider revision of the tariff. He was among the first to recognize clearly the changes that were occurring in our domestic and international environment, and set forth his views in concise, clear language in outlining to the Congress the reasons for calling the special session:

While the whole face and method of our industrial and commercial life were being changed beyond recognition the tariff schedules have remained what they were before the change began, or have moved in the direction they were given when no large circumstance of our industrial development was what it is to-day. Our task is to square them with the actual facts. The sooner that is done the sooner we shall escape from suffering from the facts and the sooner our men of business will be free to thrive by the law of nature — the nature of free business — instead of by the law of legislation and artificial arrangement.
. . . We long ago passed beyond the modest notion of "protecting" the industries of the country and moved boldly forward to the idea that they were entitled to the direct patronage of the Government . . . Consciously or unconsciously, we have built up a set of privileges and exemptions from competition behind which it was easy by any, even the crudest, forms of combination to organize monopoly; until at last nothing is normal, nothing is obliged to stand the tests of efficiency and economy in our world of big business, but everything thrives by concerted arrangement. Only new principles of action will save us from a final hard crystallization of monopoly and a complete loss of the influences that quicken enterprise and keep independent energy alive.
. . . We must abolish everything that bears even the semblance of privilege or of any kind of artificial advantage, and put our business men and producers under the stimulation of a constant necessity to be efficient, economical, and enterprising, masters of competitive supremacy, better workers and merchants than any in the world. . . . [The] object of the tariff duties

henceforth laid must be effective competition, the whetting of American wits by contest with the wits of the rest of the world.
It would be unwise to move toward this end headlong, with reckless haste, or with strokes that cut at the very roots of what has grown up amongst us by long process and at our own invitation. It does not alter a thing to upset it and break it and deprive it of a chance to change. It destroys it. We must make changes in our fiscal laws, in our fiscal system, whose object is development, a more free and wholesome development, not revolution or upset or confusion . . . We must build up industry as well, and must adopt freedom in the place of artificial stimulation only so far as it will build, not pull down.[6]

But such a change in tariff policy was not to be achieved by mere rhetoric and good intentions. Washington was flooded with special-interest propaganda and overrun by lobbyists; so much so that Wilson, an astute tactician, appealed directly to the people over the heads of the lobbyists and of the members of Congress as well.[7] He resorted also to the party caucus as a means of keeping members of his own party in line, and did not hesitate to use patronage and other methods of persuasion to achieve his ends.[8]

The Republicans, in 1908 and 1909, had made much of the doctrine of equalizing the cost of production at home and abroad, which came to be spoken of as the "true principle."[9] This notion was first given expression

6. *Ibid.*, Vol. I, pp. 32–34. First special address in Congress asking immediate revision of the Payne-Aldrich Tariff, April 8, 1913.
7. See *ibid.*, Vol. I, p. 36, for statement issued to the press, May 26, 1913, on the "Influence of the Lobbyist in Washington."
8. Thus in the hands of the most highly trained student of government ever to occupy the White House the presidency regained the leadership that had been lost under the easy-going Taft. At this time it probably reached as great an influence as was achieved in any administration prior to that of the second Roosevelt.
The relation of the executive to the legislative branch of government is significant in the study of policy, especially in recent decades, since it has bearing on the way in which policies and legislation come to be adopted. In this first term of the Wilson administration we can observe the results of strong executive leadership, skillfully handled, in bringing into effect a clearly defined, well-considered program.
9. See Republican platform of 1908. "In all tariff legislation the true principle of protection is best maintained by the imposition of such duties as will equal the difference between the cost of production at home and abroad, together with a reasonable profit to American industries." Republican National Committee, *Re-*

step we shall make it what it should be, in the spirit of those who question their own wisdom and seek counsel and knowledge, not shallow self-satisfaction or the excitement of excursions whither they can not tell. Justice, and only justice, shall always be our motto." Baker and Dodd (eds.), *The New Democracy*, Vol. I, pp. 3–5.

in the Republican platform of 1904. The logic
of the proposition is dubious in the extreme,
though it has had a strong appeal, and has
proved a popular political slogan throughout
the years following its promulgation. If all
countries adopted the principle of equalizing
costs of production on all products (assuming that the necessary data could actually be
obtained), the result would obviously be that
no trade would occur, except perhaps in minerals that are absolutely nonexistent in certain countries. Even coffee, bananas and co-
coa could be grown in the United States,
though possibly at a cost of ten, twenty or
thirty times what it would cost to import
them.

The most extreme exponents of autarchy
did not, of course, propose to carry their
principle to such absurd extremes. They
did, however, advocate canceling out by
means of tariffs substantially all of the advantages of trade between nations, thus com-
pelling each to produce, at no matter how
high a cost, virtually everything it used.
Though never implemented in this extreme
form, the principle was, however, to be written into the Republican tariff of 1922, and
some efforts were made to carry it into effect.

The Underwood-Simmons Tariff

The Democrats were modifying their earlier position of advocating "a tariff for revenue only," and had adopted in substance the
idea that tariffs should be "competitive,"
though that expression does not appear in
their platform until 1928.[10] The precise mean-

ing of the "competitive" principle is none too
clear, but it presumably meant that tariffs
would not be so high as to forestall active
competition between foreign and domestic
suppliers. Special emphasis was given to this
concept because of the growing antagonism
to "monopolies," many of which were
thought to be fostered by the high tariffs that
had been in effect all through the period in
which such combinations had been coming
into prominence.

As the new tariff bill began to take shape
under the leadership of Congressman Underwood of Alabama and Senator Simmons
of North Carolina, farm groups became concerned over the proposals to transfer numerous agricultural products to the free list.[11]
The Grange became active in opposing this
policy.[12] It had criticized vigorously the
Payne-Aldrich Act of 1909 as "unjust and unfair to farmers," and demanded a "genuine
revision of the tariff, based on careful investigation by a non-partisan commission."[13]
It claimed the defeat or retirement of more
than fifty senators and representatives responsible for the Payne-Aldrich Act. On the
other hand, the Grange opposed the legislation for reciprocity with Canada on the
grounds that it would deprive agriculture of
protection comparable to that on manufactured goods. During these years the Grange
was not strongly protectionist, but rather took
the position of demanding equality of treatment for agriculture in any tariff legislation
enacted.[14]

publican Campaign Textbook, 1908, Dunlap Publishing
Company, Philadelphia, 1908, p. 462.

10. Senator Simmons, in his memoirs, states that he
and Oscar Underwood had worked out by 1913 the
principle that later came to be known as "the competitive idea," and that it had a prominent place in their
thinking in shaping the act of that year. As he states it,
"The Republicans find out what the manufacturers want
and give it to them. I would find out what they need—
not by letting them tell me what they need, but
through careful investigation of experts. I would grant
them the privilege of enjoying the benefit of the market, but not the privilege of exploiting it." *F. M. Simmons, Statesman of the New South, Memoirs and Addresses,* compiled and edited by J. Fred Rippy, Duke
University Press, Durham, 1936, p. 57. For another
account of the legislative history and points of view in
regard to the tariff of 1913 see Oscar W. Underwood,

Drifting Sands of Party Politics, Century Company,
New York, 1928, Chapters 16–20.

11. The Democrats, having gained control of the
House in 1910 and now assured of presidential support,
had started work on a new tariff act even before Wilson
took office.

12. The Farmers Union does not appear to have
exhibited much interest in the tariff problem at this
time. The American Society of Equity likewise seems
to have given the matter relatively little attention. Editorial comment in the (Wisconsin) *Equity News,* in so
far as the subject was touched upon, was mildly favorable to the reductions provided in the new act. See, for
example, "The New Tariff Bill," *Equity News,* October
10, 1913, p. 164.

13. Editorial, *National Grange Monthly,* January
1911, p. 8.

14. A policy statement transmitted to the Congress by
the Grange legislative committee in 1913 read in part as
follows: "There is no misunderstanding the position of

Though unsatisfactory to the Grange and other farm organizations, the Underwood-Simmons bill became law, through approval by the President, on October 3, 1913. It was not a free-trade measure nor did it actually provide a generally low schedule of tariffs, though a good many products were transferred to the free list and significant reductions were made on some others. It could more properly be characterized as a recession from the extremely high levels marked by the McKinley, Dingley and Payne-Aldrich tariffs.[15]

Products placed on the free list were iron, agricultural implements, raw sugar (the reduction to go into effect gradually), coal, lumber, live cattle, meats, eggs, milk, cream, wheat, flour, corn, flax, tea, hemp, leather boots and shoes, gunpowder, wood pulp, wool and print paper. Of the agricultural products probably the one most significant from the standpoint of the groups directly concerned was wool. This had borne a rate equivalent to about 44 per cent. Hence its transfer to the free list was a very large reduction. Nearly all woolen fabrics were reduced to 35 per cent, the level established in 1867. The tariff schedules on wool and woolens had long been criticized in the public press. The rates established in the famous Schedule K (wool schedule) under the Act of 1909 had drawn particularly vigorous criticism because of Senator Aldrich's dominant influence in the framing of the act. Hides, which had been one of the most controversial items in the Act of 1909, were left on the free list where they had finally been placed at the strong insistence of President Taft.

While these transfers to the free list appeared to be a relative setback for agriculture most of them were actually of little significance at the time. There were no large imports of cattle, meats, eggs, milk, cream, wheat or corn. Wool and flaxseed were imported in substantial quantities, but do not seem to have experienced any major price disturbance. The farm price of wool stood at 20.5 cents in 1910, but dropped to 15.6 cents in 1911. It recovered to 18.1 cents in 1912, stood at 16.4 cents in 1913, and rose to 17.7 cents in 1914. Thereafter it rose continuously through 1918, as a result of war demands.[16] Flaxseed prices at the farm stood at 127.8 cents in September 1913. They fell off to 118.7 cents in November of that year, but by February 1914 had recovered to the October level. In November 1914 the price again stood at 118.7.[17]

It is, of course, impossible to state with assurance that the price was not held up in 1914 by the war influence. It seems unlikely, however, that this influence was significant at that time since the war did not start until August, and did not appear to have very marked effects on commodity prices in the United States until considerably later.[18]

Attempts to appraise the effects that would have resulted from the Act of 1913 had the war not occurred are futile, since trade came to be dominated by war restrictions so shortly after its passage. These distortions in trade conditions were to continue until after the resumption of a high tariff policy in 1921.

the National Grange upon the tariff question. The Grange has not undertaken to say whether protection, tariff for revenue, or free trade is the best policy for this government, and being a non-partisan organization, its members belong to all political parties and of course have different views upon economic questions, but there is practically unanimous agreement that whatever the policy of the government may be, that [*sic*] the farmers should receive a horizontal rate of protection with the manufacturer or, in other words, 'tariff for all or tariff for none.'" *Ibid.,* July 1913, p. 5.

15. For a good account of the contrast in circumstances surrounding the enactment of the Payne-Aldrich and Underwood tariffs see F. W. Taussig, *The Tariff History of the United States,* 8th edition, G. P. Putnam's Sons, New York, 1931, Chapters 8 and 9. Also note Rippy, *F. M. Simmons;* and Underwood, *Drifting Sands of Party Politics.*

16. USDA, *Agriculture Yearbook, 1925,* p. 1173. Imports of wool did, however, increase substantially in the first year following passage of the new act, from 195,-293,000 pounds in 1913 to 247,649,000 in 1914. The higher average price for 1914 was apparently due in part to the outbreak of war, though this influence was slight. The price had stood at 15.7 cents in January 1914, but rose to 18.4 cents by June of that year, despite the heavy imports of the preceding year, and before there was reason to expect a war demand. (Price data from USDA, *Yearbook, 1922,* p. 886 and imports from *ibid., 1916,* p. 725.)

17. USDA, *Yearbook, 1922,* p. 652.

18. Except for cotton on which prices declined sharply.

Banking Reform

The panic of 1907, though of only short duration, came in the midst of a period of general prosperity, and focused attention on the defects of the banking system. Nearly all informed groups were agreed that banking reform was needed. A National Monetary Commission was set up in 1908 to study the problem. This Commission, headed by conservative ex-Senator Nelson W. Aldrich of Rhode Island, submitted its report and recommendations in January 1912, by which time the Democrats had come into control of the House. The plan proposed was for a single central bank in the general tradition of the first and second Banks of the United States and the Bank of England.

While Republicans and Democrats alike recognized that something must be done about the banking and currency situation they were by no means agreed as to methods. Wilson had expressed opposition to control of the money system by "small groups of capitalists," and in fact had contended, while still Governor of New Jersey, that a combination of banks in New York was exercising all the powers of a central bank, except the power of issue, without being subject to the public responsibility that would be imposed upon a central bank chartered by the federal government.

Though opposing the new Aldrich plan, he was hesitant to propose an alternative "No man," he said, "can in a moment put great policies together and reconstruct a whole order of life." This cautious attitude, though reflecting the qualities of a trained mind and responsible statesmanship, was far from popular among the politicians of his own party. Bryan in particular demanded to know whether he was for "Wall Street" or the "exploited West."[19] An alternative and less carefully considered plan was presented by the House Committee on Banking and Currency, headed by A. P. Pujo.[20]

19. Ray Stannard Baker, *Woodrow Wilson, Life and Letters*, Doubleday, Doran, Garden City, 1931, Vol. IV, pp. 135-37.
20. U.S. Congress, House, Committee on Banking and

Creation of the Federal Reserve System

With the aid of Representative Carter Glass, Wilson developed the legislation that finally took shape as the Federal Reserve Act of December 23, 1913.[21] It abandoned the idea of a single central bank and provided instead for twelve regional reserve banks coordinated and supervised by a Board appointed by the President and subject to confirmation by the Senate. The regional reserve banks are bankers' banks owned by the member banks in their respective districts, but three of the nine directors of each reserve bank are appointed by the Federal Reserve Board and three of the elected members must be individuals actively engaged in commerce, agriculture or industry. Of the three directors appointed by the Board of Governors, one is designated as Chairman and also serves as Federal Reserve Agent.[22]

The framework for a coordinated banking system had thus been created for the first time since the abolition of the second Bank of the United States in 1836. The solution arrived at was a compromise, both as between a fully centralized system and a decentralized one, and as between complete government control and complete private control. The new system introduced flexibility in the supply of money, permitting the issuance or withdrawal of currency as business needs might dictate. It also provided for pooling the resources of the member banks in such a way that banks with sound assets were far less vulnerable to panicky withdrawals of cash than they had been previously.

Thus the dangers of currency shortages and

Currency, *Report of the Committee Appointed Pursuant to House Resolutions 429 and 504 to Investigate the Concentration of Control of Money and Credit*, February 28, 1913. See pp. 166-73 for suggested legislation.
21. There has been considerable controversy about the authorship of the act, though no one denies the significant influence of Wilson in determining its final form. Glass's account of the events relating to the legislation is well presented in his *Adventure in Constructive Finance*, Doubleday, Page, Garden City, 1927.
22. Some changes in the administrative arrangements were made by the Banking Act of 1935. For a fuller statement of these organizational changes, see W. Randolph Burgess, *The Reserve Banks and the Money Market*, revised edition, Harper and Brothers, New York, 1946, Chapter 13.

money panics were substantially lessened. The new system did not, however, include all banks. All national banks were required to become members of it. State-chartered banks were permitted to become members if they could meet specified standards, but were not required to do so. The majority of them, either through choice or inability to qualify, did not become members. This incompleteness of coverage constituted a weakness from the standpoint of full coordination of the banking system and protection against serious breakdowns in credit facilities, particularly in the rural areas. This weakness was to become strikingly evident in the 1920's, but was not widely recognized in the period here under discussion.

The new banking system was set up in 1914. It was scarcely in full working order when the abnormal conditions of the war period turned its efforts in the direction of war financing rather than those for which it was designed. Lacking precedent and settled policy, it was soon to encounter vigorous farmer criticism.

Growing Interest in Agricultural Credit

While the tariff and the banking system were to receive first consideration, the Congress and the President soon turned their attention to a major phase of the farm problem—rural credits. The mortgage credit facilities available to farmers had been a sore subject with them for many decades. The fast-growing western farm areas were, from the beginning, short of loan funds. Interest rates were high, loans were limited to short periods, and many abuses existed, such as excessive charges for renewal of loans, repetitious title searches, and avaricious foreclosure in times of credit stringency. The older sections of the Northeast had become surplus areas for loan funds, but there was little in the way of orderly machinery for safe transfer of these funds to the deficit areas of the West.

Farm mortgage corporations for buying and selling mortgages came into being, but they were loosely supervised and often inadequately capitalized or irresponsible in their methods of operation. Their charges were high, and their frequent failures and refusals to accept responsibility for delinquent loans made them a far from satisfactory channel for the investment of funds in the hands of estates, and of widows and elderly people, in the capital surplus areas. Many commercial banks likewise bought and sold farm mortgages, but their activities were subject to many of the same defects as those of the farm mortgage corporations.

Farmers, seeing interest rates as high as 10, 12 or even 15 per cent in the more remote and newer areas as compared to 5 and 6 per cent or even lower in the older areas, became increasingly critical. The rapid rise in land values, together with the lack of good homestead lands for settlement led more and more farmers to seek loans, thus adding to the number who were concerned about the availability and cost of mortgage credit. Public interest in the problem was further stimulated by the emphasis placed on the growing proportion of tenancy and by the "back-to-the-land" movement which was widely publicized during the administration of Theodore Roosevelt.

The problem was brought out specifically by the Country Life Commission, appointed in 1908, which listed among the causes contributing to the deficiencies of country life "a lack of any adequate system of agricultural credit whereby the farmer may readily secure loans on fair terms." Suggestion was made that a system of cooperative credit would prove of great service. This idea was given further support through a favorable account of the German "landschaften" which was included in the report of the National Monetary Commission.

The American Bankers' Association and the Southern Commercial Congress became interested in the problem and undertook a study of various European cooperative credit systems, particularly that of Germany. In the spring of 1912 President Taft had become sufficiently impressed with the need for improvement in the credit facilities for agriculture that he instructed the American embassies and legations in western Europe to gather information on the forms and effectiveness of the various rural credit systems then existing in Europe. These reports were assembled and written up under the direction of Myron T. Herrick, American Ambassador at Paris, and were released in published form by the Department of State on October 11, 1912.[23] The report was sent to the governors of the states with a personal letter from President Taft approving its recommendations and inviting the governors to a special conference relating to it. This conference was held at the White House on December 7, 1912.

The American and U.S. Commissions

Earlier in that year, the Southern Commercial Congress, meeting at Nashville, Tennessee, had taken preliminary steps with a view to sending to Europe a commission to study agricultural credit and cooperation in the European countries.[24] During the summer of 1912, all of the major parties — Republican, Democratic and Bull Moose — adopted planks in their platforms advocating action by the government in the field of agricultural credit.

By the spring of 1913, interest in the subject was sufficiently developed for President Wilson to appoint, with congressional approval and on his first day in office, an official "United States Commission" to accompany the "American Commission" sponsored by the Southern Commercial Congress. This "Joint Commission" left New York on April 26, 1913 and returned on July 25. The results of its studies were presented in a joint report,

Agricultural Cooperation and Rural Credit in Europe (S. Doc. 214, 63rd Cong., 1st sess., 1913). Shortly thereafter, the two commissions submitted separate reports embodying their conclusions and recommendations.[25]

The American Commission submitted both a majority and a minority report. The majority favored a federal law similar to the National Bank Act of 1863. This would provide for chartering land banks either as joint stock banks or as cooperative banks, but without government aid. The minority opposed venturing into cooperative credit, and suggested instead the formation of small associations to cooperate with local banks and possibly eventually to form a central association which could issue bonds.

The United States Commission recommendations were substantially in line with those of the majority report of the American Commission in proposing that associations be authorized either as profit-making institutions or as cooperative bodies. These recommendations were embodied in the Moss-Fletcher bill, introduced on January 29, 1914. The Moss-Fletcher bill was vigorously opposed by the groups favoring a cooperative system similar to those widely used in Europe. Still other groups, including many of the farm organizations, urged direct loans by the government through an agency set up in the United States Treasury.[26] As a result of the ensuing deadlock, a second plan was worked out and introduced as the Hollis-Bulkley bill. This provided for the establishment of co-

23. U.S. Congress, Senate, *Preliminary Report on Land and Agricultural Credit in Europe, Including the letter of President William H. Taft to the Governors of States and the Recommendations of Ambassador Myron T. Herrick in connection with the proposal of President Taft to introduce Cooperative Credit in the United States,* S.Doc. 967, 62nd Cong., 3rd sess., 1912. See also the account of the background of this report in Col. T. Bentley Mott, *Myron T. Herrick, Friend of France,* Doubleday, Doran, Garden City, 1930.

24. This action by the Southern Commercial Congress resulted from a conference on the subject of rural credits, directed by David Lubin, American delegate to the International Institute of Agriculture. See Olivia Rossetti Agresti, *David Lubin, A Study in Practical Idealism,* 2nd edition, University of California Press, Berkeley, 1944, pp. 274 ff.

25. *Agricultural Cooperation and Rural Credit in Europe, Report of the American Commission,* S. Doc. 261, Part 1, 63rd Cong., 2nd sess., 1914; and *Agricultural Credit, Land-Mortgage or Long-term Credit, Report of the United States Commission,* S. Doc. 280, 63rd Cong., 2nd sess., 1914.

26. A typical expression of the farm organization viewpoint is the following from *The National Grange Monthly,* July 1913, p. 12:

"Repeated emphasis has been placed in these columns upon the fact that the whole question of farm credits and money for agricultural loans will be settled, and without any more expensive investigations or junkets to foreign lands, by simply making provision by law so that the millions now being drawn into deposit by the Postal Savings Banks can be loaned out direct to farmers, instead of first passing through the banking channels which today are reaping exorbitant profits upon the people's savings."

erative credit associations and for twelve
federal land banks which were to be owned
eventually by the associations. A portion of
the initial capital was, however, to be pro-
ded by the federal government. This bill in
turn drew vigorous criticism from those who
.d favored the Moss-Fletcher bill. Others
who felt the Hollis-Bulkley bill did not go far
ough in providing government aid threw
eir support to a third plan known as the
athrick bill.[27]

federal Land Bank System Established

The controversy continued for many
onths, and was finally resolved only by
compromise that took substantially the
rm of the Hollis-Bulkley bill. It was not
until July 17, 1916, nearly two and one half
ears after the introduction of the initial bill,
at favorable action was finally obtained,
ough the general idea of legislating in this
alm had apparently had, from the begin-
ing, the advantage of bipartisan support in
the Congress and administration approval.[28]
The legislation finally enacted authorized
oth a cooperative system of twelve federal
nd banks and a system of joint stock land
anks to be organized with private capital
d for private profit. Whichever form was
sed, the amortization plan of repayment was
equired and the rate of interest that might
e charged was limited. A Federal Farm
oan Board was substituted for the commis-
oner plan proposed by the United States
ommission, and the full joint liability cus-
mary in many of the European cooperative
anks was modified to a joint liability equal
nly to twice the value of the capital stock

owned by the borrower. Both the land banks
and the joint stock land banks were placed
under the supervision of the Federal Farm
Loan Board.

Thus the first units of the extensive federal
farm credit system now in existence came
into being. Their progress in the first few
years was slow. The high incomes received
during this period made farmers less debt-
conscious than they had been previously, and
the plan of organization for the cooperative
credit system was sufficiently novel to require
a considerable period of education and popu-
larization. The development of the system
was additionally handicapped by a challenge
to the constitutionality of the act, initiated by
the farm mortgage bankers, which checked
bond sales from the fall of 1919 until the act
was upheld by the United States Supreme
Court on February 28, 1921.[29]

Even after conclusion of the litigation over
the constitutionality of the act, farmers proved
reluctant to enter into the cooperative arrangements provided in the federal land bank
system, and proponents of the cooperative
banks feared for a time that the joint stock
land banks, with their simpler, more orthodox procedure and more liberal arrangements,
might eventually come to overshadow them.[30]
Though experiencing a rapid rate of growth
in the early 1920's, the joint stock banks soon
ran into difficulties and began to decline in
numbers as early as 1924. Their volume of
loans continued upward, however, until 1930.
Their financial condition became steadily
worse during the late 1920's, and after the
general reorganization of the farm credit
agencies in 1933 all of the remaining ones
were liquidated.

The cooperative land bank system experienced a modest but steady growth through
the 1920's but was not to achieve full acceptance and wide use until the great depression
of the 1930's dried up private sources of credit
and increased the need for farm loans. Con-

27. The Bathrick bill was given active support by
he American Society of Equity. See, for example, *The
(Wisconsin) Equity News, April 10, 1914, p. 360.
28. For a somewhat fuller summary of these develop-
ents, see Carl Herbert Schwartz, Jr., *Financial Study
*f the Joint Stock Land Banks, A Chapter in Farm
ortgage Banking, Washington College Press, Wash-
gton, D.C., 1938, pp. 9 ff.
The above account is presented in some detail since
provides a good illustration of the processes whereby
ifficient interest and backing are built up to achieve
nactment of a major piece of legislation, and the diffi-
ulties that beset the backers of such legislation, even
ter rather general support appears to have been
chieved.

29. *Smith* v. *Kansas City Title Co., et al.,* 255 U.S.
180.
30. This had been predicted by some legislators even
before the act was passed. Cf. Schwartz, *Financial Study
of the Joint Stock Land Banks,* pp. 13–14.

siderable changes were eventually made in the system of federally sponsored rural credit, but the legislation of 1916 marks a major development in national policy for agriculture.

Control of Monopolies

Farmers had early become aware of monopolistic practices on the part of the railroads and of grain elevators and warehouses, but their grievances against other forms of "big business" were less tangible. They resented what seemed to them the arbitrary and non-competitive making of prices for both the things farmers sold and the things they bought. They were not able, however, to distinguish between businesses that were highly competitive though large and those in which considerable elements of monopoly existed.

Their approach to the problem could only be along some one or more of three lines: one, to organize cooperatively and carry on the business themselves; two, to aid in bringing about through government action the dissolution of large-scale businesses considered to be monopolistic; and three, to advocate government regulation of prices charged. Public ownership was little discussed or considered, except in the northern wheat belt where the Nonpartisan League was advocating a thoroughgoing program of state ownership and operation of mills, elevators, banks and similar enterprises.

The principle of regulating railroads and other natural monopolies through public utility commissions had become well established and was generally approved. Cooperative ownership was being more and more discussed, but as yet was limited mainly to local enterprises. The larger businesses such as meat packing, farm machinery manufacture and grain milling were recognized as too complex and too highly capitalized for successful operation by cooperatives. Interest turned therefore toward some type of government control or the breaking down of large businesses through action on the part of the government.

But powerful economic forces were driving the economy inexorably in the direction of larger aggregations of business, some based on real economies, others on stock manipulation and monopoly practices. Roosevelt's "trust-busting" efforts had not proved effective. Wilson, who was strongly opposed to the concentration of great economic power in few hands, also was seeking a method of lessening the abuses and limiting the power of big business. In his campaign speeches he had stated that the Sherman Act was not definite enough, and that there was need for a more careful statement of what constituted unlawful practices so that legitimate business could know when it was within the law and when in conflict with it.

The Clayton and FTC Acts

The Congress undertook to implement these ideas by means of two major acts passed within a few days of each other, the Clayton Antitrust Act and the Federal Trade Commission Act. The Clayton Act prohibited discriminations in price between purchasers when such discrimination lessened competition or tended to create monopoly. It also made it unlawful for a manufacturer to sell goods to a dealer under a proviso requiring the dealer not to handle the products of competitors. This was an attempt to break down the so-called "tying" agreements. The act prohibited the acquisition of the stock of one corporation by another if the effect was to lessen competition substantially. The holding of such stocks solely for investment purposes was permitted.

Interlocking directorates were prohibited where capital, surplus and undivided profits amounted to more than one million dollars, if the firms involved were engaged in interstate commerce and if they were competitors. It was also made unlawful for a director of a bank to serve as a director of another bank if either of the institutions had deposits, capital, surplus and undivided profits of more than $5 million. Labor unions and farmers' organizations were specifically declared not to be conspiracies in restraint of trade.[31]

31. The farm and labor organizations thus gained what they regarded as an important victory by having

The basic philosophy of the Clayton Act was similar to that of the Sherman Act and in line with the general positions taken by Theodore Roosevelt, Robert La Follette and other "trust-busters" of the preceding decade. The idea was to prevent large aggregations of power in closely related businesses. That effective implementation of such a policy would be extremely difficult was evident then, and has been amply demonstrated since.

The means of control were supposedly provided through creation of the Federal Trade Commission (September 26, 1914). It was the business of this agency to investigate persons or corporations (other than interstate carriers and banks) which were subject to the antitrust laws, and to make reports on their activities. The Commission also had power to issue orders requiring such businesses to cease illegal practices. If these were not obeyed the Commission might apply to the federal court of the district in which the violation occurred for enforcement of its order. This was in a sense an enlargement of the functions of the old Bureau of Corporations, which was taken over by the Commission. The framers of the act assumed that it would function in respect to corporations much as the Interstate Commerce Commission did with respect to railroads. Actually, however, it never achieved this status, and has continued to be an investigating body rather than an administrative agency.

The Commission proved less effective than its sponsors expected it to be, in part because of public reluctance to approve procedures that did not involve resort to the courts. Its record during the first years following its creation was one of substantial though unsensa-

tional accomplishment. Since the Commission was designed primarily as a fact-finding agency its main function was to investigate and publicize situations involving practices considered to be in violation of law. If, after such investigation, improper practices were continued, relief was to be sought through prosecution by the Department of Justice under the antitrust laws.[32]

Under McReynolds and Gregory, Wilson's first Attorneys General, the practice initiated in previous administrations of entering into "consent decrees" with offending corporations was continued. Under this procedure the Department of Justice would agree not to prosecute provided the corporation concerned would agree to correct the abuses complained of. A number of important cases had already been settled by this process, notably those against the International Harvester Company and the American Corn Products Company. More and more vigorous judicial and public criticism of the practice developed, however. It was felt that offenders were being allowed to go unpunished when they should be punished, and, furthermore, that in the hands of unscrupulous public officials such a procedure might be used to force corporations to agree to settlements that amounted virtually to blackmail. Thus, despite its obvious advantages, this method of dealing with monopoly problems gradually fell into disuse.[33] It was to be used, however, as late as 1920 in a major case, that of the meat packers, which is discussed in the next section.

FTC Meat and Grain Probes

Prominent among the early investigations of the Commission were those of the food industries initiated in 1917 by specific instruction from President Wilson. The first of these, relating to monopoly in the meat pack-

their organizations virtually exempted from prosecution under the antitrust laws. This provision was referred to by Samuel Gompers as "the industrial Magna Charta upon which the working people will rear their structure of industrial freedom." It was unquestionably more significant for labor than for agriculture. A similar provision had been vetoed by Taft, but Wilson, who was more friendly to labor, accepted it.
The significance of the Clayton Act, and related legislation, in the development of national policy in regard to labor and agriculture is well and briefly discussed in Harry L. Purdy, Martin L. Lindahl and William A. Carter, *Corporate Concentration and Public Policy*, Prentice-Hall, New York, 1946, pp. 314–21.

32. For a good study of the workings of the Commission, see Gerard C. Henderson, *The Federal Trade Commission, A Study in Administrative Law and Procedure*, Yale University Press, New Haven, 1925.
33. An excellent brief summary of the antitrust activities of the first part of the Wilson administration is given in Carl Brent Swisher, *American Constitutional Development*, Houghton Mifflin, Boston, 1943, pp. 573-77.

ing industry, led to a preliminary report in July 1918 and to a voluminous full report published in 1919.[34] The Commission contended, on the basis of its study, that the five major packing companies were so extensively interconnected as to constitute a monopolistic combination which controlled about 80 per cent of the total interstate slaughter of cattle and calves, 86 per cent of the sheep and lambs, and more than 60 per cent of the hogs. Principal recommendations of the Commission were that all rolling stock used for the transportation of livestock be acquired by the government; that the principal stockyards be likewise taken over; that the government purchase all privately owned refrigerator cars; and that certain of the branch houses, cold storage plants and warehouses be acquired with a view to facilitating competition.[35]

As a result of the Commission's investigation the Department of Justice took steps, in 1919, to prosecute the packers under the antitrust laws. This in turn led to negotiations with the industry and an agreement under which proceedings were suspended and a consent decree was entered on February 27, 1920. By the terms of this decree the five major packers, Armour & Co., Swift & Co., Wilson & Co., Morris & Co. and the Cudahy Packing Co. were enjoined from entering into any contract, combination or conspiracy in restraint of trade; and were required to

(1) dispose of their holdings in public stockyards;
(2) dispose of their interest in stockyard railroads and terminals;
(3) dispose of their interest in market newspapers;

(4) dispose of their interest in public coldstorage warehouses except where these were necessary for storage of their own meat products;
(5) dissociate themselves from the retail meat business;
(6) discontinue using their facilities for purchase, sale and handling of certain wholesale grocery lines stated to be unrelated to the meat-packing industry;
(7) dissociate themselves from manufacturing, selling, jobbing or distributing such unrelated commodities; and
(8) cease to own as individual companies 50 per cent or more of the voting stock of any corporation or firm engaged in manufacturing, jobbing, selling or distributing certain enumerated unrelated commodities.[36]

A similar extensive investigation of the grain trade resulted in a series of volumes, the first of which appeared in September 1920, though the study as a whole was not completed and published until the middle of 1926.[37] The grain trade investigation did not reveal a tightly knit combination such as had

34. *Food Investigation, Report of the Federal Trade Commission on the Meat-Packing Industry,* Summary and Part I [no title]; Part II, *Evidence of Combination Among Packers;* Part III, *Methods of the Five Packers in Controlling the Meat-Packing Industry;* Part IV, *The Five Larger Packers in Produce and Grocery Foods;* Part V, *Profits of the Packers;* and Part VI, *Cost of Growing Beef Animals, Cost of Fattening Cattle, Cost of Marketing Livestock,* Washington, 1919–1920.

35. In appraising the seemingly radical nature of these proposals it should be recognized that the railroads were at this time in government hands. Hence, if the control of railway equipment was to be taken from the packers it would as a matter of course be taken over by the government.

36. For details of the consent decree, see *Packer Consent Decree Letter from the Chairman of the Federal Trade Commission,* transmitting in response to a Senate Resolution of December 8, 1924, a Report Concerning the Present Status of the Consent Decree in the Case of *United States* v. *Swift and Co., et al.,* entered in the Supreme Court of the District of Columbia, February 27, 1920, S. Doc. 219, 68th Cong., 2nd sess., 1925.

Items (6), (7) and (8) resulted from pressure by the wholesale grocers, and undoubtedly were designed more to ease competition with the wholesale grocers than to benefit the public. Considerable evidence was presented to show that handling these sidelines resulted in economies for the packers and benefits to the consumers. The grocers contended, however, that it constituted unfair competition. Their position has dubious merit. If the principle were applied generally, many businesses that engage in sidelines to stabilize their work loads and make fuller use of their facilities would be affected. See also the comments of Commissioner Gaskill, *Commission's Letter on the Packer Consent Decree,* Doc. 219 (as cited), pp. 34–37.

37. *Report of the Federal Trade Commission on the Grain Trade:* Vol. I, *Country Grain Marketing* (September 15, 1920); Vol. II, *Terminal Grain Markets and Exchanges* (September 15, 1920); Vol. III, *Terminal Grain Marketing* (December 21, 1921); Vol. IV, *Middlemen's Profits and Margins* (September 26, 1923); Vol. V, *Future Trading Operations in Grain* (September 15, 1920); Vol. VI, *Prices of Grain and Grain Futures* (September 10, 1924); and Vol. VII, *Effects of Future Trading* (June 25, 1926).

The Commission also made a study of the grain export business which appeared separately as *Report of the Federal Trade Commission, on Methods and Operations of Grain Exporters;* Vol. I, *Interrelations and Profits* (May 16, 1922); and Vol. II, *Speculation, Competition and Prices* (June 18, 1923).

een shown in the meat-packing industry. The Commission, in fact, tended to emphasize the keenness of the competition in this phase of agricultural marketing. Attention centered chiefly on the economic significance of the dealings in grain futures, a phase little understood by farmers and one of which they had long been suspicious. Generally speaking, the investigation of the grain trade did not lead to clear-cut conclusions and recommendations as had been the case in the investigation of the meat packers. The Commission did make some suggestions for change but none of very striking significance.[38]

The two major Federal Trade Commission studies in the food field helped to pave the way for action on legislation sought by the farm groups in the immediately succeeding years. The handling of livestock was shortly to be regulated through the Packers and Stockyards Act, and an attempt would be made to correct certain abuses in the grain trade through passage of the Grain Futures Act. These are discussed in the following chapter.

New Leadership in the Department

Under the long tenure of James Wilson the Department of Agriculture had made much progress, and had become one of the large and important agencies of the government. Though Wilson was generally popular with farmers, the press and the Congress, he was reaching advanced age, and his contribution had been made. During the last year of his tenure as Secretary, he was vigorously attacked by the Grange because of his action in bringing about the resignation of Dr. Harvey Wiley, Chief of the Bureau of Chemistry, and also because of his alleged friendliness to the liquor industry.

Objection to the Secretary's action in forcing the retirement of Dr. Wiley was undoubtedly the major cause for the critical attitude that developed toward his administration of the Department.[39] The Bureau of Chemistry was the agency charged with enforcement of the Food and Drug Act. Wiley had been its Chief for twenty-nine years and had been a principal factor in pushing through the Food and Drug Act of 1906. An aggressive reformer and an able publicizer of his views, his name had become a household byword throughout the country.

The press, the farm groups and also the general public were back of him. But in scientific circles, in the food industry and within his own bureau he was not highly regarded. There was strong feeling that the scientific work of the Bureau was on a low level, that propaganda and vituperation were being substituted for constructive, scientific research on the qualities of foods and that objectivity was often sacrificed to sensationalism in the administration of the Food and Drug Act.[40]

To fill the position vacated by Wiley, a brilliant young biochemist, Dr. Carl Alsberg of Harvard University, was brought in to head the work in this field. Under his able administration, the scientific quality of the Bureau was built up to a high level, its standing in industry and in scientific circles was enhanced, and the more sensational aspects of its work gradually dropped into the background.

Houston New Secretary of Agriculture

The time was ripe, however, for the introduction of new blood and new ideas into the Department as a whole. These were to come under the new Secretary, David F. Houston,

38. See, for example, the suggestions listed in Vol. III, *Terminal Grain Marketing*, p. xiii.

39. For a fuller account of this controversy see *Harvey W. Wiley, An Autobiography*, Bobbs-Merrill, Indianapolis, 1930, Chapter 19; and Earley Vernon Wilcox, *Tama Jim*, The Stratford Company, Boston, 1930, Chapter 14.

40. The stir over Wiley's resignation gave rise to more general criticism of Departmental administration. From 1907 on, the Department had been under investigation by the House Committee on Expenditures in the Department of Agriculture. The report on the so-called "Wiley Investigation," conducted under the chairmanship of Ralph W. Moss of Indiana, was published as H.Rep. 249, 62nd Cong., 2nd sess., January 22, 1913. Commenting on this report, the *National Grange Monthly* urged strongly the retirement of Secretary Wilson, reorganization of the Department and the adoption of new methods. See especially the issue of March 1912.

and a succeeding Secretary, Henry C. Wallace, who came in under Harding. Houston was, at the time of his appointment, Chancellor of Washington University at St. Louis, and had been president of the Texas College of Agriculture and Mechanic Arts.[41] He was a native of South Carolina, and had been educated there and at Harvard. He brought to the Department a good background of administrative experience, a high conception of public responsibility and a well-trained mind. His outlook and temperament, however, were those of the educator and scientist rather than of the farmer. He lacked the common touch that had characterized his predecessor. The Grange greeted his appointment with no marked enthusiasm but in the spirit that any change would be an improvement. It remarked (in *The National Grange Monthly* of March 1913, p. 10),

> That he will put into force in his department a policy different than has prevailed under the Wilson regime is certain, a fact to which the farmers of the country will give instant approval — even without inquiry into what the details of that policy will be. The very fact that a change has come is of supreme importance and there can be nothing but hopeful anticipation of the work ahead.

Mr. Houston himself commented in one of his first interviews with the press: "I feel that agriculture is peculiarly the educational and developmental department of the government. Of course I realize that all of them have that aspect, but the agricultural depart-

ment is peculiar." This view was soon to be given practical implementation in ways that would affect enormously the pattern of agricultural work over succeeding decades.

Knapp's Program in the South

The agricultural demonstration work conducted by Dr. Seaman A. Knapp in the South was coming to be widely recognized as a new and significant departure in agricultural education.[42] The essence of the Knapp philosophy was to show farmers what could be done rather than to try to convince them through lectures and sales talks. He contended that, "What a man hears, he may doubt. What he sees, he may possibly doubt. But what he does himself, he can not doubt." He also told his men, "Keep things simple: Do not go before people with an elaborate program. The average man, like the crow, can not count more than three. Do not confuse people."[43]

As the Knapp philosophy took root and grew, private as well as public funds began to flow in for the expansion of his program. The General Education Board, with money contributed by Rockefeller, gave its support. Contributions were made by local businessmen and later by the grain exchanges, the railroads and the mail-order houses, particu-

41. Walter H. Page apparently was the one who first suggested Houston for this post. Wilson had been casting about for a suitable man to head this important department but had come to no conclusion. At his request, Page wrote him on November 27, 1912, suggesting Houston. Colonel E. M. House furthered the recommendation by arranging for Wilson and Houston to meet at a dinner, given by House in New York on December 7. The arrangements were made entirely through Colonel House, and Houston states in his memoirs that he never was asked personally by the President to become a member of his Cabinet. These events are described in an interesting way in Burton J. Hendrick, *The Life and Letters of Walter H. Page*, Doubleday, Page, Garden City, 1926, Vol. I, pp. 114–15; Charles Seymour, *The Intimate Papers of Colonel House*, Houghton Mifflin, Boston, 1926, Vol. I, Chapter 8; and David F. Houston, *Eight Years with Wilson's Cabinet, 1913 to 1920*, Doubleday, Page, Garden City, 1936, Vol. I, Chapter 2.

42. Knapp, like his friend "Uncle Henry" Wallace, had in his earlier life combined the occupations of farming, preaching and teaching. In this process, he had learned much about practical agriculture and about the processes of instructing and leading farm people. Knapp and Wallace, together with James Wilson, had been close friends and collaborators in efforts to improve the agriculture of Iowa. Through experimentation on their own farms and in years of private and public discussions, they had crystallized their views on the need for more realistic teaching, more "outdoor" research and more direct contact with farmers. All of them made their principal contributions late in life. Wallace, at the age of fifty-seven, founded *Wallaces' Farmer;* Knapp did some of his most notable work after he was seventy; and Wilson spent nearly the whole of his later life (from 62 to 78) as Secretary of Agriculture.

43. As quoted by Russell Lord in *The Agrarian Revival, A Study of Agricultural Extension,* American Association for Adult Education, New York, 1939, pp. 62 and 67. Lord's very readable and detailed account of this early period in agricultural extension work will pay rich dividends to the reader interested in obtaining a clear picture of the personalities and conditions responsible for the initiation of the program. See especially pp 29–99. See also Joseph Cannon Bailey, *Seaman A. Knapp Schoolmaster of American Agriculture,* Columbia University Press, New York, 1945.

larly Sears, Roebuck and Company.[44] Among the supporters drawn into the Knapp camp during these early years was the young president of Texas A. and M. College, David F. Houston, who was later to be charged with the task of launching a nationwide agricultural extension service under public sponsorship.

For the most part, however, the early extension work was not closely related to that of the state colleges and experiment stations. Their relations were marked rather by a mutual disdain. Knapp is said to have commented to one of his aides, "These idiots still think that A. and M. College means 'Academic and Military'" rather than Agricultural and Mechanical, and referred to their information as not extending "beyond the three-mile limit."[45]

The extension idea took hold more rapidly and more widely in the South than in the North. Northern farmers tended to look upon it with skepticism. Many of them ridiculed the notion that "book farmers" could be useful to them, or were actually hostile to the innovation.[46]

Smith-Lever Agricultural Extension Act

Gradually, however, the plan gained a foothold in scattered counties, usually under auspices other than those of working farmers. Nevertheless, sentiment for a nationwide system of publicly supported agricultural extension was growing. A bill drawn by Kenyon L. Butterfield, then president of Rhode Island State College, with the aid of John Hamilton

of the Office of Experiment Stations, was introduced in the House as early as 1909.[47] Other bills followed, but support was by no means unanimous even from the agricultural colleges. They wanted the money but were fearful of federal domination.

Finally, with the backing of the administration, the bill took shape after numerous revisions and redraftings. It was sponsored in the House by Asbury F. Lever of South Carolina, and in the Senate by Hoke Smith of Georgia. But the controversy over the measure was long and bitter. Farm representatives both in and out of Congress looked upon it as an effort to increase production — whereas they contended that what the farmer needed was better markets. Others charged that it was socialistic or that it was class legislation. Bitter conflict arose over the inclusion or exclusion of Negro farmers in the program, a conflict eventually resolved only by setting up two separate branches, an Office of Extension Work, North and West and an Office of Extension Work, South.[48]

The bill finally became law on May 8, 1914. It provided an annual base allotment of $10,000 to each state plus an initial federal input of $600,000 to be allocated in proportion to the amount of rural population. There was to be an annual step-up of $500,000 for seven years bringing the total, aside from the flat $10,000 per state, to $4,100,000. This $3,500,000 increment over the first year's appropriation was to be matched by funds from the states or other sources.

Thus there came into being, fifty-two years

44. These "tainted" funds, though helpful at the time, were to prove seriously embarrassing to many a later county farm adviser faced with the task of winning the support and cooperation of a suspicious or even hostile farm constituency.

45. As quoted by Lord, *The Agrarian Revival*, pp. 70 and 71.

46. The following comment by T. C. Atkeson in *The National Grange Monthly* is characteristic of the views expressed by many northern farmers when the proposed legislation was brought under discussion: "Just why the taxpayers should pay the salaries and expenses of 'expert farm demonstrators' is not very clear, and the question might be asked, why the taxpayers should not with equal propriety be expected to pay the salary and expenses of expert coal-mining demonstrators or experts in any other department of human endeavor." (October 1913, p. 3.)

47. By Representative J. C. McLaughlin of Michigan. Lord, *The Agrarian Revival*, p. 88.

48. These Offices were set up, in 1915, as part of the new States Relations Service which included also the Office of Home Economics and the Office of Experiment Stations. In 1923 these agencies were reorganized into separate units, the Bureau of Home Economics, the Office of Experiment Stations and the Extension Service. The Office of Extension Work South and the Office of Extension Work North and West had been combined in 1921 following the retirement of Dr. Knapp as chief of the work in the South. See John M. Gaus and Leon O. Wolcott, *Public Administration and the United States Department of Agriculture*, Committee on Public Administration of the Social Science Research Council, Chicago, 1940, pp. 40, 44 and 216; also Alfred Charles True, *A History of Agricultural Extension Work in the United States, 1785–1923*, USDA Miscellaneous Publications No. 15, 1928, pp. 116, 171–74.

after the original founding of the agricultural colleges, the third major phase of their work. Out of it has grown not only a vast educational mechanism but a related organization of farmers that has had much to do with the course of agricultural policy in the decades since 1920.

The Smith-Hughes Act

Closer to the hearts of farm people was a proposal for more specific instruction in agriculture in the secondary and elementary schools. Farmers had long felt that the tendency of the public school system was to educate young people away from the farm. For years the Grange, the Alliance and other farm organizations had urged "practical" vocational agricultural instruction in the school system. In some cases they had undertaken to foster education of this kind through their own local units.

By 1904 interest in agricultural education was sufficiently evident to cause the Director of the Office of Experiment Stations to initiate study of the vocational work being done in the various states. The American Association of Agricultural Colleges and Experiment Stations and the National Education Association began official study of the problem in 1905 and 1906. The movement was given further impetus by the Roosevelt "Back-to-the-Land" movement and the reports of the Country Life Commission.

By 1915 there was considerable demand from the states for aid in developing secondary education in agriculture, and the Grange and other farm organizations had come out definitely for federal aid and leadership in this field.[49] So general was the support for such work that the Congress passed with little opposition, on February 23, 1917, the Smith-Hughes Act, which provided for federal aid to schools offering vocational education and

established the Federal Board for Vocational Education.[50] Under this program agricultural and other vocational courses have been established widely over the country.

The Federal Warehouse Act

In harmony with the general program for putting the credit resources available to farmers in more orderly form, the Congress passed in August 1916 a measure known as the United States Warehouse Act. This action corrected a long-standing defect in the marketing and financing mechanisms available for handling agricultural products. At the same time it avoided putting the government directly into the warehousing business.

The act provided that the Department of Agriculture would issue licenses to warehouse operators, if they had suitable facilities for storing the designated products, could show adequate financial responsibility, would agree to abide by the regulations and would operate as public warehouses open to all users on equal terms. Against products so stored federal warehouse receipts would be issued. These could be used, and were generally acceptable, as collateral for bank loans.

Thus in addition to the Federal Reserve system, which now provided a flexible currency capable of adjusting to the varying needs of the economy, and a federal land bank system designed to mobilize and make more usable the farm credit resources based on land, the farmer had at long last a warehouse system that could make possible full use of his credit in the form of stored, nonperishable crops. Orderly marketing under appropriate financial arrangements was at

49. For the background of the developmental work preceding passage of the Smith-Hughes Act see Rufus W. Stimson and Frank W. Lathrop (compilers), *History of Agricultural Education of Less than College Grade in the United States,* Vocational Division Bulletin No. 217, Agriculture Series No. 55, Federal Security Agency, U.S. Office of Education, 1942, pp. 570-73.

50. 39 Stat. 929; 20 U.S. Code 11-28. The act authorized continuing appropriations to be expended under state plans for the promotion of vocational education. The work was later expanded under the George-Reed Act, the George-Ellzey Act, and the George-Deen Act. The George-Deen Act was amended in 1946 (60 Stat. 775; 20 U.S. Code 15h). The functions of the Federal Board for Vocational Education had been transferred in 1933 by executive order to the Commissioner of Education in the Department of the Interior. All functions of the U.S. Office of Education were transferred to the Federal Security Agency on July 1, 1939, in accordance with the President's reorganization plan No. 1. The Federal Board was discontinued on July 16, 1946, under the President's reorganization plan.

least mechanically feasible. Thus was put into workable form an idea first put forward in the subtreasury plan of the Farmers' Alliance in 1889. The new plan could, of course, get under way only slowly. A vast array of grade-standards, regulations and other details had yet to be worked out, and the act had to be popularized with warehousemen, banks and farm organizations, especially with farmers' cooperative associations. Its true significance was not to become apparent until the 1920's. It did, however, mark a sound and well-considered forward step in the process of making possible the orderly handling of many agricultural commodities.[51]

Wilson and the Liberal Trend

It is evident that the unusual record of basic, forward-looking legislation that characterized the first years of the Wilson administration was made possible by the vast amount of agitation and study that had occurred in the preceding years. Few of the new measures had their origin in the period here under discussion. Banking reform and agricultural credit had been under study at least since 1908; a federal income tax and the direct election of United States senators had long been a part of the programs of the Grange and other agencies; tariff reform had been constantly advocated since the latter part of the Roosevelt administration; extension education and federal aid for vocational education in high schools were by no means new proposals.

The particular significance of President Wilson's leadership was in selecting well-considered and fundamental issues to push through to completion, and providing the skilled tactical leadership needed for accomplishing that end. In most cases the hand of the President can also be seen in the specific forms taken by the various pieces of legislation prior to their passage.

Other parts of the legislative program, less

specifically formulated and with lower priorities, were lost in the growing preoccupation with war. Among these were the proposals with respect to conservation of forests and soils, advocated by the Grange and favorably considered by Wilson. The Bureau of Reclamation had run out of funds for further expansion of federal irrigation projects. Hence this phase of conservation was in abeyance.

A federal approach to the highway problem had long been taking shape and some progress was made on it during these years. Direct federal aid had been undertaken experimentally in 1913 through a $500,000 fund assigned to the Post Office Department. These beginnings emerged more definitely in the Federal Aid Road Act of 1916. In keeping with the precedents of the early nineteenth century, first emphasis was to be placed on through trunk highways. As the federal program got under way, however, the farm groups came to insist more and more strongly on a shift in emphasis in the direction of "farm-to-market" roads.

Taken as a whole, the period from 1901 to 1916 was one of solid progress along moderate-liberal evolutionary lines. There was no sharp break with the past, and, as yet, there was a marked reluctance to inject government directly into economic affairs. The Federal Reserve system, the Federal Land Bank system, the federal warehousing program and others, all were set up with main reliance on private initiative rather than direct government action. Government was to sponsor and guide, but not to dominate. Except for a minor movement, taking shape under the aegis of the newly formed Nonpartisan League, there was little agitation for government ownership and operation of economic enterprises. So deep-seated was this attitude that, even in the 1920's when faced with disastrously low prices and mounting debts, farmers were slow to accept the idea of direct government intervention in price-maintenance and marketing activities.

In the field of labor legislation the Wilson administration likewise took a mildly liberal position. A separate Department of Labor

---

51. For a brief but fuller discussion of the act and its significance, see John H. Frederick, *Public Warehousing, Its Organization, Economic Services and Legal Aspects*, Ronald Press, New York, 1940, pp. 228–37.

was created in 1913, by splitting it off from the Department of Commerce and Labor which had been set up in 1903. Labor thus gained a more recognized and influential status in governmental affairs. Labor organizations were still, however, strongly dominated by the relatively conservative philosophy of Samuel Gompers which discouraged direct political activity by labor unions.

They were, nevertheless, gaining political power and prestige. Farmers gave support to the provision of the Clayton Antitrust Act which exempted labor unions and farmers' cooperatives from the provisions of that act. As of that time farmers concerned themselves little with the problems of organized labor. In so far as they did the attitude was one of benevolent tolerance toward the struggles of another working group that was trying to better its condition. In later years it became evident that labor unions were far more able to exercise monopolistic powers than were farm organizations, and that some of these practices could have a very direct bearing on the welfare of farmers.

Food and Agricultural Policies of the War Years

The war broke suddenly and unexpectedly in August 1914. The man-on-the-street had smiled tolerantly at the saber-rattling antics of the German Kaiser, but had not expected a resort to arms. Such organizations as the Grange had long advocated the peaceful adjustment of international differences by judicial means, and many felt that the foundations for such a procedure had been laid at the Hague Conferences of 1899 and 1907, and in the establishment of the Permanent Court of Arbitration.[52]

The Situation When War Came

American agriculture was approaching the end of its golden age. No longer were the plains of the West pouring out new accre-

tions of foodstuffs at a rate far in excess of domestic needs. The railway net was virtually completed. Significant homesteading had slacked off, and the situation had stabilized. Europe was providing a good market for the exportable surpluses of cotton, wheat, pork and other products, and had in large measure become adjusted to the new balance between agriculture and industry that had resulted from the rapid development of Western Hemisphere agriculture in the latter part of the nineteenth century. American farm prices were relatively high and comparatively stable, and land prices were rising. At the same time industrial activity was at a level that facilitated the transfer out of agriculture of the normal surplus of young people growing up on the farms.

It is little wonder, therefore, that farmers were to look back upon this period as a suitable goal to strive for in price and other relationships.[53] In that respect it had much to recommend it. Conditions had been sufficiently stable for a long enough time that something approximating a natural balance may be said to have been achieved. Shifts from one line of endeavor to another were relatively easy. Industrial occupations were not yet highly unionized. Hours of work were long both in country and city, but probably more onerous in many urban industries than on the farms. As yet the heavier and more disagreeable tasks were largely performed by recent immigrants. Education, even in the rural areas (except in the South), was reaching a level such that migrating native-born rural youth tended to move into

52. While the United States had not adhered to the Court officially, it maintained observers at the Hague, and, from the beginning, an American sat as a member of the panel of judges.

53. It should not be concluded from the above statement that farmers of that period felt satisfied with the prices received by them. There was considerable talk about "the high cost of living" even among farmers, and much feeling that their portion of the consumer's dollar was less than it should be. Urban people were, of course, more actively and justifiably concerned with the rising cost of food. It was not until around 1924 that farmers began to realize the favorableness of the 1910–1914 period. At first the data pertaining to those years were used merely to show relationships in the latest peacetime period. More and more, however, the price relationships of this "base period" came to be regarded as the "normal" or desirable ones. They presently became an accepted goal in farm policy that has persisted to the present time.

the better paid, more attractive lines of work such as railroading, merchandizing, banking, manufacturing and so on, leaving to the poorly organized and exploited immigrants the less attractive tasks.

In terms of complete mobility and equality of opportunity the balance would seem to have been in favor of agriculture since entry to other industries was easier than into agriculture.[54] Already the prices of farm land had reached a level such that entry into the business required significant amounts of capital, except as the would-be farmer was willing to accept wage worker or tenant status. For the wage worker, urban or rural, and for the tenant, there was little protection against exploitation. The farm owner-operator was moving toward preferred status through the normal operation of inheritance customs and the increasingly capitalistic nature of agriculture. Thus the young farmer who was not in a position to take over the home farm, and who did not have capital, tended to find opportunities more attractive in urban occupations where his labor could be associated with larger amounts of capital, provided from sources other than his own savings.

The fact that prospective buyers were bidding higher and higher for the privilege of owning and operating farms and that substantial increments in value were accruing to those who already owned lands would indicate that farm owner-operator status was somewhat more attractive than alternative economic opportunities. The attempt of recent years to measure statistically the equality or inequality of returns in major segments of the economy is at best a very rough process highly charged with subjective and emotional considerations. It seems fair to say, however, that the so-called "parity" period was a relatively favorable one for agriculture, and that the attempt of later years to maintain the

price relationships characteristic of that period has been an attempt to retain for agriculture the relationships prevailing in the most favorable period it has known except in wartime.[55]

This may or may not be justifiable as a goal in national policy. Conclusions with respect to it are bound to reflect individual or group judgments based upon attitudes relating to the significance of agricultural prosperity as a national goal.[56] It is evident, however, that the social gains which may be assumed to flow from maintaining agriculture at levels of income (tangible and intangible) that are higher than those in other occupations are dependent on the translation of such higher earnings into higher levels of living. To the extent that they are dissipated in higher payments for land, neither society nor agriculture benefits.[57]

Defects of Farm Life Minimized

Whatever the conclusion with respect to the relative positions of agricultural and nonagricultural workers there were many opportunities for improving the conditions on farms — improvements which would have constituted a better use of the higher farm incomes than that of continually bidding up the investment in farm lands. Many farmers, however, disliked having the defects of rural

54. Real wages in industry had apparently been declining slightly between 1909 and 1914, partly through a decrease in real earnings per hour and partly through a somewhat smaller number of hours worked per week. See Paul H. Douglas, *Real Wages in the United States, 1890–1926*, Houghton Mifflin, Boston, 1930, pp. 205, 207 and 208.

55. See, for example, Joseph S. Davis, "An Evaluation of the Present Economic Position of Agriculture by Regions and in General," *Journal of Farm Economics*, April 1933, pp. 247–54, in which he challenges the assumption that 1909–1915 can be regarded as a period of normal relationships between farm and nonfarm prices.

56. For an excellent discussion of doctrinaire attitudes concerning the importance of agriculture in the national economy, see also by Davis, "Agricultural Fundamentalism," in *On Agricultural Policy, 1926–1938*, Food Research Institute, Stanford University, 1939, pp. 24–43. For a somewhat different point of view, see John D. Black, *Agricultural Reform in the United States*, McGraw-Hill, New York, 1929, pp. 40–61.

57. The drift of young people away from the land was often cited as evidence of the decadence and unfavorable position of agriculture. However, since the agricultural population was continually producing more than enough young people to offset deaths and retirements in that group, the retention of all or most of them on the farms could only have resulted in overpopulation of the rural areas and lowered standards of living. This was particularly true in view of the increasing mechanization of agricultural operations.

life pointed out specifically. They were just emerging from a period in which the dominant note in farm magazines and public meetings had been one of optimism and of glorification of the farmer's way of life. Farmers were inclined to complain about the hardships of their vocation but they did not want nonfarmers to talk about them. Secretary Houston early encountered this attitude. *The National Grange Monthly* of December 1913 expressed disapproval of one of the first of the new Secretary's public addresses. Houston had sought to bring to the attention of farm leaders some of the defects of the prevailing conditions on American farms, and in doing so had said:

The story that comes from every section is substantially the same: — It is a story of increasing tenancy and absolute ownership; of inadequate business methods; of chaotic marketing and distribution; of inferior roads; of lack of supervision of public health and sanitation; of isolated and ill-organized social activities and of inferior intellectual provision.[58]

In editorializing on the address, *The National Grange Monthly* challenged both the accuracy of the picture presented and the wisdom of the policies implied.

As an academic literary paper, Secretary Houston's address at Manchester, every word of which was read from manuscript, was an elaborate production of great merit. As a statement of the present agricultural conditions of this country, it was pessimistic to the extreme; as a forecast of what the government intends to do for its farms and its farmers it was absolutely disappointing. No better idea of the general tone of the address can be given than by the simple statement that though it was delivered to an audience of 1500 representative farm people of the country, most of the address was received in

complete silence and that scarcely a single sentence called forth any evidences of enthusiasm. Mr. Houston himself must have been impressed with the way his address was received and could not have misunderstood the reason why.

The National Grange Monthly does not propose to analyze the address, nor even to criticize it, except to say that the picture of rural life in this country which Mr. Houston drew and which he emphasized throughout his entire address as absolutely correct, is not the one which the Grange has been working half a century to create nor the one which is represented by thousands of farms and farm homes in 30 states that are owned and occupied by Grange members. To accept Mr. Houston's delineation of rural life would be to declare that 50 years of Grange effort for rural improvement had been a flat failure, and that The National Grange Monthly declines to do. Nor does it believe that Mr. Houston himself, undoubtedly sincere in his present view of rural conditions, will repeat his Manchester address two years from now, after he has become actually familiar with some of the rural conditions of the country.[59]

War Period to Spring of 1917

The outbreak of war found most of the nations poorly prepared. Few plans had been laid for carrying through a long period of fighting. The German strategy looked to a quick decision through the capture of Paris and the conquest of France, a goal that was very nearly attained in the first months of the war. The Germans hoped that Britain would remain aloof, and there was confident expectation, both in Germany and the United States, that the United States would not be drawn into the struggle.

As a consequence the early part of the war was marked by hastily contrived emergency measures. Britain, poorly equipped for land fighting, immediately made use of its assumed naval supremacy to blockade the Central Powers.[60] Financial arrangements were handled, in the early period, through liquida-

58. Houston, a southerner and one whose main contacts had been in the South, was, of course, more familiar with conditions there than in the North and West. The South still reflected widely the impoverished conditions that followed the War Between the States. Its educational standards were low, roads poor and its soils impoverished. Relatively little progress had been made in raising the level of education or the working conditions of its huge Negro population. Hence the comments made in the preceding pages, with respect to the relative prosperity of agriculture, are inapplicable to most of the South, especially to its rural Negro population that still was uneducated, poorly paid, poorly housed and living at a bare minimum of subsistence.

59. *The National Grange Monthly*, December 1913, p. 17.
60. Though its naval establishment was larger than that of Germany, Britain had a vastly more extensive area to cover, and its naval supremacy was not fully established until the Battle of Jutland on May 31, 1916 and the ultimate victory over the German submarines through combined British, American and French effort.

tion of foreign assets and transfers of gold. Both Britain and France were in strong position, and not likely to be seriously embarrassed except in a long drawn-out struggle. Their industrial resources, though not so fully mobilized, were comparable to if not greater than those of Germany. The supplying of Britain and France with foodstuffs, especially wheat, early assumed large importance in the plans of the Western Allies. Britain had become heavily dependent on outside sources of food, and France, a heavy user of breadstuffs, had lost control of much of the area that normally supplied its grains.

The United States increased its wheat acreage from 53.5 million in 1914 to 60.5 million in 1915. As a result of this and the highest yield per acre in its history (16.7 bushels) it produced a record-breaking billion-bushel crop.[61] This huge output was part of a record-breaking world crop. Hence prices remained relatively low and United States agriculture did not immediately feel a strong impact from the war.[62] Acreage was back to 50 million in 1916. With only a 636-million-bushel outturn, and a short world crop, the wheat problem began presently to take on a different aspect, one that was further emphasized by the poor crop of some 600 million bushels in 1917. As a result, the price of wheat at Chicago, which stood at about $1.06 in June 1916, had gone to $3.40 by May 1917.[63] This spectacular rise emphasized the importance of wheat in the war program, and also gave rise to vigorous demands that the government take steps to check speculation in this basic food.

Relief Activities Under Herbert Hoover

The sudden onset of war in Europe had caught many American tourists in situations from which they could not readily extricate themselves. At the request of Walter Hines Page, American ambassador to Britain, Herbert Hoover, a mining engineer with large international experience, undertook arrangements for the aid of these stranded groups. As a result of his brilliant performance in this connection, Hoover's fame as an organizer and administrator spread rapidly.

In the meantime, contrary to German expectations, American public sentiment swung strongly toward the side of the Western Allies. This came about in part through American reaction to Germany's violation of its treaty with Belgium, and in part from cleverly handled public relations work on the part of the British. American sympathy for war-devastated Belgium became a potent force. In October 1914 a Commission for the Relief of Belgium was organized and Hoover became its chairman. This was a buying and shipping organization for handling all relief supplies to the occupied regions of Belgium and northern France. It entered into agreements with the belligerent governments, and, until the United States came into the war officially, was responsible for executing these agreements.[64]

The tight British blockade was relatively effective in stopping the flow of German

61. Production had been 763 million bushels in 1913 and, in 1914, 892 million bushels.

62. One of the major crops, cotton, was in fact sharply depressed as a result of the outbreak of war. Its price dropped from 12.4 cents in June, July and August 1914 to 8.7 cents in September, reaching a low of 6.3 cents in November. The price remained low through 1915, and did not get up to 12 cents again until June 1916. Thereafter it rose steadily to a high of 37.7 cents in May 1920. The first effect of the war, for the cotton country, was to bring on a serious financial crisis that persisted through 1915. This was due in part, however, to the record crop of 1914. Production fell in the following year from 16,135,000 bales to 11,192,000, which was some 3 to 4 million less than the amounts produced from 1911 through 1913. Acreage was also reduced, from 36,832,000 in 1914 to 31,420,000 in 1915. Data from USDA, Yearbook, 1920, pp. 637, 640.

63. For No. 1 Northern Spring, USDA, Yearbook, 1917, p. 621. In part the spectacular rise of May 1917 was due to the frantic efforts of futures dealers to cover on short sales made earlier.

64. When the United States became an active belligerent, this task was delegated to a neutral Spanish-Dutch committee, but Hoover continued as its chairman, and arranged for financing, purchase and transport of most of the food supplies. The Commission remained in operation until August 31, 1919, when the Belgian and French governments took over the care of their people. The postwar phases of the relief program and a brief account of this earlier program are presented, together with voluminous data on the operations, in Frank M. Surface and Raymond L. Bland, American Food in the World War and Reconstruction Period, Operations of the Organizations Under the Direction of Herbert Hoover, 1914 to 1924, Stanford University Press, Stanford University, California, 1931.

and neutral shipping to the Central Powers. As a countermeasure, the Central Powers launched, and built up to a high degree of effectiveness, a counterblockade along unorthodox lines. This consisted of submarine warfare directed at Allied and neutral shipping. The submarine campaign, by its very nature, did not lend itself to compliance with the accepted rules of warfare. The United States and Germany soon found themselves in bitter conflict over the sinking of "neutral" American merchant and passenger vessels. Finally, in April 1917, the United States, as a result of a series of "incidents," came into the war on the side of the Western Powers.[65]

Food Policy: April to August 1917

Aside from its own military preparations, which took shape rapidly after April 1917, United States policy centered heavily upon supplying foodstuffs, producing the ships to carry them, and making loans that would enable the nations associated with her to continue purchasing in this country. The short wheat crop of 1916 and the rapid rise in wheat prices in the spring of 1917 threw emphasis upon the problems of increasing food production and conserving such amounts as were produced.

Hoover returned to the United States on May 19, 1917, and, at the request of the President, immediately began preparatory work which led to the establishment of the United States Food Administration. The government of the United States, long accustomed to peacetime objectives, had little knowledge of how to go about preparing for war. Its record in administering war activities had, in fact, been bad in every war it had ever engaged in. Fraud and incompetence in supplying military requirements during the Civil and Spanish-American wars had been

particularly notorious. With the vastly more complex requirements of modern warfare the need to build more adequate civilian organization was of prime importance. The steps taken marked great progress over those of previous war periods, but look crude and sketchy in light of the comprehensive organization required in more recent years.

War Powers Used

Until August 1917 the President lacked specific legislation for setting up a war food administration. He therefore used his war powers to authorize Hoover to take such steps as were possible in organizing for the voluntary conservation of food.[66] Under a newly organized Council of National Defense and the Exports Administrative Board, predecessor of the War Trade Board, it was possible to exercise considerable control over the export movement of foodstuffs, and to channel the available supplies to the Allied countries.

On April 24, 1917 the Congress authorized the Treasury to extend credits to the Allied governments in the amount of $3 billion.

65. These difficulties were, of course, aggravated by various activities of the German government within the United States, notably the sabotaging of American munitions industries, highlighted by the Black Tom explosion in New Jersey. While officially neutral, it is clear that as a result of the British blockade and the preponderant anti-German sentiment in the United States, this country was in effect an unofficial ally of the Western Powers long before it entered the war officially.

66. The civilian organization for prosecution of the war as eventually set up under various congressional authorizations included six powerful agencies — the Shipping Board, the Food Administration, the Fuel Administration, the Railroad Administration, the War Trade Board and the War Industries Board. These agencies were responsible directly to the President and their heads met with him weekly as a sort of war Cabinet. They exercised powers that went much beyond those available to the President in peacetime, such in fact as to give rise to congressional criticism of the "dictatorial" authority assumed by the President. His powers were eventually formalized, however, through passage of the Overman Act of May 20, 1919, which was designed to promote efficiency and facilitate coordination. This act gave the President authority, until six months after the close of the war, "to utilize, coordinate, or consolidate any executive or administrative commissions, bureaus, agencies, offices, or officers" at will. He could create new agencies and abolish old ones, and could utilize funds for any purpose that he deemed appropriate for attaining the ends sought. For a fuller summary of the organization for war see John D. Hicks, The American Nation, Houghton Mifflin, Boston, 1941, pp. 508–16. The events relating to passage of the Overman Act are more fully discussed in Frederic L. Paxson, America at War, 1917–1918, Houghton Mifflin, Boston, 1939, pp. 224 ff.
The activities and policies of the Food Administration as a whole are described in considerable detail in William Clinton Mullendore, History of the United States Food Administration, 1917–1919, Stanford University Press, Stanford University, California, 1941.

Both Britain and France were feeling the strain of war, and the darkest hours of the submarine campaign, as well as of the military drive in France, were yet to come. Prior to this time both nations had depended for dollar purchasing power upon the sale of foreign assets, transfers of gold and the floating of loans through private banking institutions, notably that of J. P. Morgan and Company.[67] From here on the loans made were to be mainly on a government-to-government basis, a fact that was to bring the settlement of loans prominently into discussions of national policy in the decade following the war.

To avoid demoralizing American markets, the act provided that purchases made under the funds provided should be only with permission from the United States Treasury. Nevertheless, agents of the various countries tended to bid against each other for scarce supplies. As a result the Treasury appointed, in August 1917, a Purchasing Commission the function of which was to coordinate all Allied purchasing. Thus was begun the policy of wartime centralization of buying which was to be carried much further in World War II. It strengthened enormously the bargaining position of the government as against the more numerous sellers of commodities.

Efforts to Increase Food Production

Until passage of the basic Food Control Act, all efforts to increase food supplies were on a voluntary basis, except for such administrative actions as could be taken by the various government agencies under existing laws. Among the steps taken were the following:[68]

1. By the Department of the Interior:

   a. The Bureau of Reclamation undertook a drive to increase production on reclaimed lands.
   b. The Commissioner of Education urged the schools to aid in a food-growing campaign.
   c. Employees of all kinds were urged to grow food on lands controlled by the government or by private corporations.
   d. Enlarged homesteads were permitted — 320 acres instead of 160 on certain lands.
   e. On June 2, 1917, announcement was made that 240 million acres of unallotted public land were awaiting the farmer and herdsman. Patriotic Americans were urged to homestead them to increase food supplies in order to avert world famine.

2. By the Department of Commerce:

   a. Periodic reports on new types of edible fish were initiated by the Bureau of Fisheries (an article almost every week).
   b. Recommendation was made that whale meat be used. It was pointed out that the whale is a mammal. Therefore its meat was supposed to be somewhat like beef.
   c. Permission was given to use Fisheries Bureau facilities for production of food, after regular hours. Also, employees could catch and use fish for domestic purposes.

3. By the Department of Labor:

   a. Of special interest to western agriculture was an order issued on May 24, 1917, waiving restrictions on immigration from below the Rio Grande.[69]
   b. Cooperation was given to the Department of Agriculture in sending city workers to the farms. A College Men and Boys' Working Reserve had been organized (on paper at least) in 40 states by the first of June.

4. By the Department of Agriculture:

   a. The most important step taken was that of extending the network of county

67. Williams estimates total United States exports during the four years of war at $22,974 million. Of this, $11,166 million was paid for by imports. The excess of exports ($11,808 million) was financed as follows: through shipment of gold, $1,029 million; through return of securities from Europe, $2,000 million; through private foreign bond issues, mostly in the early years of the war, $1,520 million; and through advances by the United States government under credits established in favor of the Allied governments, $7,319.5 million. John H. Williams, "The Foreign Trade Balance of the United States Since the Armistice," *American Economic Review*, March 1921, Proceedings Supplement, pp. 22–39.

68. *Official Bulletin*, published by the Committee on Public Information, May-July 1917, *passim*.

69. Under this provision some 29,000 Mexican laborers were recruited between the spring of 1917 and June 30, 1919 for work on the farms of the western and southwestern states, thus setting a pattern that was to be repeated in World War II and a policy that was to be frequently urged by western farmers in later years. For data, see *Annual Report of the Commissioner General of Immigration to the Secretary of Labor*, 1919, p. 25.

farm advisers throughout the nation. This work, begun informally around 1904, and formalized through the Smith-Lever Act of 1914, had made but slow progress up to 1917. Many states had no more than three or four such workers and some had none at all. As a war measure, the plan was widely accepted by farmers, though often with reluctance. Once established it took root, and the county farm agents came to be the key contacts between the government and the farmers in guiding and stimulating food production.[70]

Until the Food Administration was created, the main drive to conserve available food was through the Department of Agriculture. Even after that, much of the propaganda relating to food conservation was disseminated through Department of Agriculture personnel since most of its field agents were appointed as representatives of the Food Administration.

The food conservation program was an intensive one, and undoubtedly accomplished much of what the food-rationing program sought to accomplish through other means in World War II. This is not to say that such a program would have been adequate in the latter period. The conditions surrounding the two programs differed greatly. Emotional appeals to patriotism were apparently much more effective, and much more widely used, in World War I than in World War II. At that time the nation had not been engaged in a major conflict for more than fifty years. The glamor of war outweighed in the public mind its drabness, suffering and horror. It took on the character of a crusade. Here was a war to end war. The disillusionment that was to follow the failure of the League of Nations and the outbreak of World War II was not then a factor to be reckoned with. Under these conditions educational and emotional programs were widely effective. Public opinion reacted powerfully on noncooperators. In addition the publicity programs were both comprehensive and very intensive.[71]

The Food and Fuel Control Act

After long delay, occasioned by a congressional deadlock, the new Food and Fuel Control Act was passed on August 10, 1917. The very nature of the delay indicated the unpreparedness of the nation for war. The administration bill called for a single chairman, who would obviously be Herbert Hoover. It did not provide for Senate approval of the appointee. Senators who disliked Hoover amended the bill, which the House had passed, to provide for a three-man board to head the organization.[72] A prohibition amendment was inserted, and long moralizing debates followed. Debate on the minimum price of wheat took much time. In addition the Senate had added a rider calling for a joint committee on military expenditures. This was the final point to be discussed and discarded.[73] The act was finally passed, and Hoover was immediately named Administrator under it.

Provisions of the Act

The major provisions of the new act were as follows:

1. The President was to have power to license industries in connection with the importation, manufacture, storage, mining or distribution of any necessaries. If storage charges, commissions, profits, or practices of licensees were found unjust they must be corrected or punishment was prescribed.

70. The number of county farm advisers increased from 542 in the summer of 1917 to 1,133 in the summer of 1918. In important agricultural states the coverage was nearly complete by 1920. By that time Ohio, for example, had county farm advisers in all but two of its 88 counties. See Lord, *The Agrarian Revival*, pp. 103 and 109.

71. It should also be recognized that World War I was a short war so far as direct participation by the United States was concerned. Whether this high pitch of patriotic cooperation could have been maintained through a longer period is a matter on which we can only speculate.

72. Later changed again to provide for a single administrator.

73. Wilson, like Lincoln, was essentially a man of peace, and the reorientation to war leadership was as difficult for him as for his famous predecessor, and likewise for the Congress and people he led. Coupled with this was the friction engendered by the bitterly fought campaign of 1916, and the feeling among many leading Republicans that Wilson's election slogan "He kept us out of war" had been a subterfuge quickly disregarded after his re-election.

2. The President was authorized to requisition foods, feeds, fuels and other supplies necessary to the support of the Army and Navy. Compensation was to be provided.

3. The President was authorized to purchase, store and sell for cash at reasonable prices, wheat, flour, meal, beans and potatoes.

4. Provision was made for control of the practices of exchanges and boards of trade.

5. The President could, when necessary to stimulate production, guarantee the price of wheat.

6. He also had power to control farm implements and fertilizers, these being considered "necessaries" in the production of foods.

7. After 30 days from the approval of the act no food materials were to be used in the production of distilled spirits for beverage purposes. The President could regulate the use of food materials in malt or vinous liquors. He could also commandeer any or all distilled spirits in bond or in stock for redistribution as munition, military or hospital supplies.

8. An appropriation of $150 million was made for use by the Food Administration.[74]

9. Under the fuel provisions the President could fix the prices of coal and coke.

10. No person could, in government capacity, pass on contracts in which he had a financial interest.

11. Destruction of necessities to enhance the price was made unlawful; also hoarding, except by producers including farmers' cooperative associations.

On the same day that the Food and Fuel Control Act was passed the Congress approved an act providing for a food survey. This was for the purpose of gathering information on the demand for food, and data pertaining to its production, distribution and utilization.

Methods Used by the Food Administration

The controls exercised by the Food Administration rested chiefly on (1) the power to enter into voluntary agreements; (2) the power to license and to prescribe regulations

for licensees; and (3) the power to buy and sell foodstuffs.

The first of these made possible agreements which, if entered into otherwise, would have been in violation of the antitrust laws. In some cases where there were not too many diverse elements in the trade it was possible to get unanimous or nearly unanimous consent of the industry to follow certain practices, thus broadening considerably the powers specifically granted. For example, speculative activity could to some extent be controlled in this way, though such control was not clearly authorized. Agreement by the entire industry was not essential. A case in point is that of the milling industry. In 1917–1918 only 3,143 of the 9,000 millers actually signed the agreement. These 3,143, however, represented 95 per cent of the production, and made possible enforcement of the accepted regulations. Nonagreement firms could be brought into conformity by issuing licenses and prescribing regulations for licensees. In a number of cases agreements were reached with foreign buyers as to prices they would pay in fairness to American farmers. With respect to hogs the Food Administration entered into agreements with the organized producers. In return for their promise to increase output the Food Administration agreed to use its influence to maintain prices of hogs at Chicago at levels above those that would be established by the free play of market forces. These arrangements were followed by agreements with Allied buyers.

The principal classes of license regulations used were the following:

1. Those limiting margins and profits.
2. Those eliminating unnecessary distribution functions.
3. Those preventing waste.
4. Those designed to assure equitable distribution and the prevention of hoarding.

Retailers having gross sales of less than $100,000 per annum, and also producers, were, under the act, exempted from control through licensing. Because of this, regulation by the Food Administration was concerned

---

74. This was inadequate to make more than a start on the fund required shortly thereafter for the Grain Corporation. It was necessary to raise $385 million of private capital in addition.

almost entirely with control of the spread between producer and retailer, not with the over-all price.

It was Hoover's policy to depend as much as possible on voluntary cooperation worked out through conferences with the trade groups, and to avoid resort to the penalty provisions of the act. Actual arrests made for violations were negligible. However, in some cases violators of license regulations were given a choice between official punitive action and a voluntary contribution to the Red Cross, a choice which was invariably accepted. As a whole these informal procedures worked surprisingly well.

Hoover discouraged rigid departmentalization and formal organization charts. He preferred freedom of action, and a policy of choosing for each problem as it arose the most capable man available, giving him a relatively free hand, and then discontinuing the division when its purpose had been served. Even the more permanent divisions were constantly changing form or expanding or contracting their responsibilities as the tasks before them changed. In the field the program was largely managed by state administrators operating under regulations and directives from Washington. This was in contrast to the characteristic structure in World War II, in which most functions were organized on a regional basis. Assisting the state administrators were county and district administrators who served without pay. Because of the heavy reliance on voluntary cooperation and compliance the functions of these officials were much more largely education and propaganda than actual administration.

The Critical Foodstuffs

Fats. The food products mainly sought by the European Allies were bread grains, fats and sugar. Pork products constituted the chief and almost the only available source of fats in the United States. Both the Food Administration and the United States Department of Agriculture did their utmost to stimulate pork production. As a result pork and lard

exports from the United States were stepped up from an average of 941 million pounds (1909-1913) to 2,279 million pounds in 1918, and to 2,681 million pounds in 1919.[75]

Sugar. Before 1914 Germany, Austria-Hungary and the Netherlands had been heavy suppliers of beet sugar in the European markets. These sources were, of course, cut off by the war. The United States, on the other hand, had long drawn heavily on Cuba for its supplies of sugar. To meet the deficit caused by the loss of Central European sugar, an International Sugar Committee was formed. This, however, proved unable to cope with the situation. A Sugar Equalization Board was therefore incorporated under the laws of Delaware (July 11, 1918). This board, with a capitalization of $5 million, purchased all of the Cuban crop, and pooled it with the United States domestic crop.[76] Both the United States and the Allies were rationed on the basis of this supply. As a result the people of the United States got less than they were accustomed to (2 pounds per month per capita), and the Allied nationals were limited to much lower quotas. Nevertheless, the limited supplies were distributed in an orderly, though rather informal, way, and no major

75. The details of the hog program are given in Frank M. Surface, *American Pork Production in the World War*, A. W. Shaw, Chicago, 1926.

The ratio of hog prices to corn prices had fallen to about 9 to 1 during the fall of 1917, despite the fact that hog numbers were down to about 60 million as compared to 65 million in the preceding year. There was grave fear that farmers would reduce hog production still further at a time when large supplies of pork would be needed. The average ratio was said to be about 12 to 1. With a view to stimulating hog production, the Food Administration announced that it would endeavor to maintain a hog-corn ratio of 13 to 1 for the hogs farrowed in 1918. Considerable difficulty was experienced in controlling both prices and rates of marketing, and much farmer criticism developed. For a fuller account of the episode, see Walter T. Borg, "Food Administration Experience with Hogs, 1917-19," *Journal of Farm Economics*, May 1943, pp. 444-57.

76. Under this plan basic prices paid per cwt. for raw sugar were as follows: Cuban, $5.50; Hawaiian, $7.28; Puerto Rican, $7.28; Louisianan, $7.28; and for U.S.-grown beet sugar (refined), $9.00. The supplies from all sources were pooled and sold on a common price basis that was above that which would have resulted from using as a basis the costs of the cane sugars and lower than that which would have resulted from resale of the beet sugars without loss. See Joshua Bernhardt, *Government Control of the Sugar Industry in the United States*, Macmillan, New York, 1920, Chapters 1-4.

difficulties or criticism developed. Estimates made by Bernhardt place the saving in United States sugar consumption for 1918 at about 1,300 million pounds, around 17 per cent of the amount customarily used, thus freeing this amount for use by the Allies.[77] The British portion of the raw sugar from Cuba was refined in the United States, for the Royal Commission on Sugar Supplies, thus relieving the labor situation in Britain.

Wheat. Major interest with respect to food-stuffs centered around grains, particularly wheat. Bread is a basic diet of the people of Western Europe. All of Europe (except Russia, Rumania, Austria-Hungary and Bulgaria) depended heavily on imported grains before the war. In addition grain production had been greatly reduced in France, Italy and Belgium. In these countries and the United Kingdom, wheat production in 1917 amounted to only 344 million bushels, an outturn which was less than 60 per cent of that of the pre-war years.[78] To supply the Allied nations with bread rations equal to those to which they had been accustomed would have meant importing from overseas nearly 600 million bushels of wheat. None of this could be obtained from Russia or the Balkan countries, which had previously supplied about one fourth of the imports of these countries. Thus the European Allies were needing about twice the non-European imports they had previously required.

At the same time the growing intensity of Germany's submarine warfare was reducing shipping to a point where vessels could not be spared for the long hauls from Australia, India and Argentina. Australia and India produced good crops in 1917, but the Argentine crop was poor. The burden of supplying the Allies therefore rested mainly on North America. The United States carry-over from the small 1916 crop was practically at a minimum, since the small crop of that year (636 million bushels) was barely enough to cover normal United States requirements. Thus it was necessary to reduce consumption in the United States if the Allies were to be supplied. This work was handled by the Conservation Division of the Food Administration. The United States managed to export to the Allies and the American Expeditionary Force, for the 1917–1918 crop year, about 138 million bushels of wheat. This represented a saving by the American people of about 110 million bushels.[79]

Canada, with a somewhat better than average crop, supplied about 150 million bushels. Thus the United States and Canada together supplied nearly half of the 600 million bushels needed, and more than 100 million bushels in excess of their average prewar exports. Their contribution amounted to 66 per cent of the imports of Great Britain, France and Italy as compared to 30 per cent before the war. It is evident that, under these circumstances, and with consumer incomes reaching new highs, prices would have skyrocketed had there been no controls. There had been in fact, as a result of competitive bidding by neutrals and Allies, a major speculative rise in mid-1917 after more than 90 per cent of the crop had left the farmers' hands. In May 1917 the wholesale price of flour reached $17.80 per barrel as compared to $9.10 in the preceding December.[80]

Mechanisms of Control

An Allied Wheat Executive was organized on November 29, 1916. Its American representative was the Wheat Export Company, Inc., which was organized in the same month. This was purely a buying organization and had no important function except that of handling the buying of wheat in a more or-

77. *Ibid.*, pp. 3, 125.
78. Frank M. Surface, *The Grain Trade During the World War*, Macmillan, New York, 1928, p. 19.

79. It is of interest to note that there was in this case an actual reduction in the amounts of food consumed whereas, in World War II, despite rationing, there was a substantial increase in the United States per capita consumption of food. Total United States civilian food consumption per capita, in 1941, stood at 108 per cent of the 1935–1939 average. By 1945 this index had risen to 114, and in 1946 stood at 118. The use of flour and grain products also increased (from 100 in 1941 to 107 in 1945). The use of meats, poultry and fish increased even more strikingly (from 111 in 1941 to 120 in 1945). BAE, *The National Food Situation*, October-December 1947, p. 32.
80. USDA, *Yearbook, 1917*, p. 622.

derly way than that of allowing each purchasing mission to operate independently.

In order to check speculation and bring wheat supplies and prices under control, the Food Administration Grain Corporation was created by Executive Order on August 14, 1917, and incorporated under the laws of Delaware.[81] Directors of the company were Herbert Hoover, Julius H. Barnes, Gates W. McGarrah, Frank G. Crowell, Curtis H. Lindley, Edgar Rickard and Mark L. Requa. Julius Barnes, a prominent grain operator of Duluth, Minnesota, was made president of the new corporation. It was capitalized at $50 million out of the $150 million appropriated to the Food Administration. All officers were required to divorce themselves entirely from the grain trade and to sign sworn statements that they had no pecuniary interest in this trade in any form. All of them served without compensation. Because of delay in passing the Food Administration Act the corporation was unable to begin operation until September 4, some two months after the new crop had begun to move.

The basic plan of operation was to establish definite government buying prices at each terminal market and then, by cooperation with the trade, to insure that farmers would receive a fair reflection of this price at their local selling stations. When adequate supplies had been accumulated the corporation stood ready either to sell or buy wheat at the established price, thus effectively stabilizing the price at that level.[82] The "fair price" was determined by an independent committee of twelve men not connected with the Food Administration nor with the Grain Corporation.

The President announced, on August 30, 1917, a "fair price" of $2.20 for No. 1 Northern Spring at Chicago for the 1917 crop, and thereafter the Grain Corporation agencies stood ready to buy any wheat offered at that price. This was slightly below the price prevailing in the market just previously ($2.30). The crop movement during July and August had been smaller than normal owing to a hope on the part of growers that the government would set a price higher than the prevailing market price. The wheat market was in a somewhat chaotic state since trading in wheat futures on boards of trade had been discontinued on August 25.

In June 1918 the railroads were granted a flat percentage increase in rates of 25 per cent in view of their increased operating costs.[83] This tended to reduce prices in the areas of origin as compared to those at the terminal markets. To offset this, the guaranteed price for the 1918 crop was raised to $2.26, effective July 1, 1918. On September 2 of that year President Wilson issued a proclamation extending the price guarantee to cover the 1919 crop up to June 1, 1920. On March 4, 1919, the Congress amplified the powers of the President in controlling the marketing and distribution of wheat and appropriated one billion dollars for maintenance of the guaranteed price on the 1919 crop.

On May 14, 1919, an executive order discontinued the Food Administration Grain Corporation as of June 30, 1919, and created its successor, the United States Grain Corporation, which functioned until May 31, 1920. Trading in futures on the Chicago Board of Trade was resumed on July 15, 1920.[84]

---

81. A primary purpose of the Grain Corporation was, of course, to provide a method of putting into effect the congressional guarantee of the price of wheat to the producer.

82. The Grain Corporation also undertook to see that wheat supplies were equitably distributed to American mills, and to control the prices at which flour and other products were sold by the mills to the consumer. It also controlled cereal supplies for export to Allied and neutral governments. This control was handled through the War Trade Board, which would not issue export licenses unless these were approved by the War Food Administration and by the Treasury, which had a committee to coordinate all Allied buying in the United States. The Grain Corporation sold its cereals and cereal products (for export) to the Wheat Export Company in New York, which was a part of the Allied Wheat Executive established by the Allied governments in London.

83. This rate increase was considerably less in percentage than the increase in wage rates and other costs. The general effect of the rate levels maintained during the war was to keep transportation relatively cheap and thus to favor outlying areas as compared to those near the central markets. This preference was to be sharply reversed through the major freight rate increases of August 1920.

84. The course of wheat acreage, production, prices

Changes During the War Years

The policies adopted by the government, including those of the Food Administration, were more effective in bringing about conservation and effective distribution of the supplies available than in positive stimulation of increased production. This result was due in part to the shortness of the period covered by official United States participation in the war, and in part to a series of relatively poor crop years. The drives for home gardens, home canning and similar activities were useful in stimulating interest in the food problem but not highly significant as a contribution to over-all food supplies. Sizable increases could come only from major adjustments in commercial production, a type of change that could get under way only slowly.

The rapid expansion in numbers of county farm advisers and similar agencies was intended as a means of expanding production. Actually, however, most of these agents did not get their work started until the summer of 1918, and even then they were hampered by lack of experience, farmer resistance, shortages of labor, and adverse weather and supply conditions. The corn crop, a major element in the food program, was seriously affected by an unprecedented shortage of viable seed in the spring of 1918. Many fields had

to be replanted; considerable acreages had poor stands; and some land was shifted to other crops. As a result, acreage fell off from 111 million in 1917 to 102 million in 1918; yields were down about 9 per cent, and production was only slightly above that from the poor crop of 1916.[85]

Wheat acreage was up in 1918 from the very low level of 1917, and slightly above that of the record 1915 crop, but yields were about average resulting in a crop of about 900 million bushels. Sugar production in 1917 and 1918 was below that of 1915 and 1916, and cotton production was off substantially from that of the years 1911 through 1914. Among the adverse factors was a desperate shortage of farm labor in many areas which farmers were unable to offset, as was done in World War II, through fuller use of machinery. Few of the major laborsaving devices that became so important in later years were perfected or available.

Hog numbers, resulting from high prices, reached a record level of 61,200,000 head as of January 1, 1918, but were not to show the full effect of the price stimulus until 1919.[86] Beef cattle numbers were on the upgrade, but this represented in the main an increase in inventories rather than an addition to available supplies of meat. The over-all volume of agricultural production was only moderately above that of the preceding years, and was not to reach its peak until 1920.[87]

With this very moderate increase in production and an enormously increased demand, prices of foodstuffs rose rapidly and continuously throughout the remainder of the war period. Employment and wage rates were stepped up sharply, and the policies followed in financing the war tended to increase greatly the available purchasing power. Consequently, there was little in the way of checks

and exports during this period is shown below (by production years, numbers in thousands).

Harvest Year	(a) Acres Planted	(b) Bushels Produced	(c) Bushels Exported	(d) Farm Price
1909–13 average	50,829	690,108	100,787	0.869
1914	54,691	891,017	147,955	0.971
1915	61,592	1,025,801	335,702	0.956
1916	56,852	636,318	246,221	1.43
1917	56,191	636,655	205,962	2.04
1918	65,177	921,438	132,579	2.05
1919	76,683	967,979	287,402	2.16
1920	65,988	833,027	222,030	1.82

Sources:

(a) and (b): Surface, *Grain Trade During the World War*, p. 150. For a recent revision of the production figures, see BAE, *Wheat — Production, Farm Disposition, and Value, by States, 1909–44*, March 1948, p. 2. The older figures are used in order that the relationships between acres planted and bushels produced may be shown.

(c) BAE, *Foreign Trade of the United States, Annual, 1790–1929: Wheat and Wheat Products . . .*, Report F.S. 46, by Caroline G. Gries, February 8, 1930, p. 41.

(d) BAE, *Wheat — Production*, p. 2.

85. *Agricultural Statistics, 1937*, p. 39.
86. *Ibid.*, p. 257.
87. The USDA indexes of volume of agricultural production for sale and home consumption during these years are as follows (1935–1939 = 100):

1912	85	1915	86	1918	90
1913	81	1916	83	1919	91
1914	86	1917	86	1920	92

Agricultural Statistics, 1945, p. 437.

on the inflationary upswing in prices. Government war bonds were sold widely and aggressively, but banks were permitted to make loans for their purchase, taking the bonds as security. Bank credit therefore increased rapidly and enormously in volume.[88] The price effects of the government's financial program thus were similar to those of the Civil War period though the mechanism was different. There was little to choose between the Civil War practice of issuing fiat currency directly from the Treasury and the World War I practice of letting much of the new government debt take the form of Federal Reserve notes and bank credit based on government obligations.

The index of wholesale prices for all commodities rose from 99 in 1914 (1910–1914 = 100) to 102 in 1915; 125 in 1916; 172 in 1917; 192 in 1918; 202 in 1919; and 225 in 1920. The prices of farm products rose even faster but reached their peak about a year earlier. Starting at 100 in 1914, they remained stable in 1915; reached 118 in 1916; 181 in 1917; 208 in 1918; and 221 in 1919. The sharp decline in farm prices which occurred in the fall of 1920 brought a drop to 211 for the index of that year; this was followed by a disastrous slump to 124 in 1921.[89] Gross farm income rose from a general level of about $7.5 billion in the period 1910–1914 to $16.2 billion in 1918 and $17.7 billion in 1919.[90] This increase was almost wholly a result of inflation rather than of increased production.

Agriculture in the First Postwar Years

These years of temporary prosperity were not to result in real progress for the agricultural areas. During the war the opportunities for buying new equipment, improving farm homes and raising the general level of farm living were limited. Farmers accumulated substantial amounts in the form of Liberty Bonds, but rather generally did not hold them as a backlog of savings for future use. The

high earnings of farm lands soon generated a major land boom, which began to get under way as early as 1916 but did not take on sensational proportions until 1919 and the early part of 1920. For the United States as a whole the index of land prices rose from 129 in 1918 (1912–1914 = 100) to 170 in 1920.[91] The advance was not uniform but was much more marked in the Corn Belt and the South Atlantic states where the index reached well over 200. The valuation placed on all farm lands and buildings rose from $35 billion in 1910 to $66 billion in 1920.[92] The bulk of this increase was sheer inflation, an added dead weight of investment to be carried by American agriculture; a valuation supported by the input of large amounts of wartime savings and a greatly increased farm mortgage debt.

Whereas, in 1914, farmers owed about $4.7 billion on real estate mortgages, such loans had grown by 1920 to $10.2 billion and were to go still higher in the depressed period of the early 1920's. Thus after enjoying a long period of unprecedented prosperity during which they took in some $18 billion more in net income than if prices and costs had remained at the levels of 1914, farmers were poorer, their lands and buildings more run down, and their debts larger than they had been in 1914.[93] An opportunity which might for the first time in its history have put American agriculture in a strong financial position was recklessly squandered.

Not all of the dissipation of wartime savings occurred through land speculation. There was a similar, though less expensive, boom in purebred livestock. Fantastic prices were paid for breeding animals, $50,000 and $60,000 being not uncommon. A climax was reached in the purchase of the Holstein-Friesian bull, Rag Apple the Great, late in May 1919 for $125,000 at the dispersal sale of Oliver Cabana at Elma, New York. Farmer savings in the form of Liberty Bonds were further dissi-

---

88. Loans and discounts of all active banks increased from $15,759 million in 1915 to $30,650 million in 1920. *Statistical Abstract, 1946,* p. 389.

89. *Agricultural Statistics, 1937,* p. 403.

90. *Statistical Abstract, 1946,* p. 623.

91. *Agricultural Statistics, 1937,* p. 406.

92. *Statistical Abstract, 1946,* p. 573.

93. For the basis of these estimates see M. R. Benedict, *Farm Finance: Dangers and Opportunities in Wartime,* California Agricultural Extension Service, Circ. 126, 1942, p. 3.

pated through investment in speculative or worthless stocks. Stock salesmen were active, and very ready to accept Liberty Bonds and farmers' notes, many of which were to prove seriously embarrassing when the boom receded.[94]

Reasons for Overoptimism

Why was the situation so badly misjudged? A number of reasons, then obscure but more readily seen now, contributed to the overoptimism that prevailed. Farmers, generally, expected a quick decline in prices after the Armistice in November 1918. There was in fact a slight slacking off at that time. Shortly, however, demand picked up and prices moved to even higher levels. Farmers, though all too well acquainted with depressions, had had little experience with inflation. They quickly came to believe that a new, permanent and higher level of prices had been established, and that there would be no return to the levels prevailing before the war. On this assumption lands were actually worth more, and the prospects appeared bright enough to permit laxities in financial management that would not have been considered in the frugal, conservative prewar days.

The reasons for the unexpected continuance of wartime prosperity in the first postwar years were obscure and little understood. The European nations that had been associated with the United States during the war were desperately in need of continuing outside help. Though unable to buy in normal ways they were permitted to use for purchases in the United States some of the unexpended credits set up for prosecution of the war.[95]

Domestic buying power was still high, and many urgent demands were unsatisfied. The policies adopted by the Federal Reserve Board likewise tended to prolong and intensify the inflationary forces. The credit extended by the reserve banks was getting near to the limits legally permitted in relation to their gold reserves. Sound banking policy called for an increase in discount rates and a contraction of credits. The Treasury, however, wished to float its fifth and last major loan in an easy money market and at the lowest possible rate of interest. The Treasury view prevailed, and the Federal Reserve Board, with little peacetime precedent or experience to guide its decisions, was to defer the unavoidable contraction of credit until the following year when much of the damage had been done. It was in the immediate postwar boom that the wildest speculative excesses occurred and that the basis was laid for the major troubles of farmers in the years to follow.

Changed Position in International Trade

Two other factors, both little recognized by farm people at the time, were shaping up in a way to cause trouble later. Until 1914 the United States had been, on balance, a debtor nation particularly with respect to Britain, France, Holland and Germany. Under these circumstances it could export more than it imported without disturbing international exchange relations. Now the United States had suddenly become the world's greatest creditor nation.[96] If it was to continue exporting on a prewar scale, it needed to take more imports or extend more loans. It did not wish to do either. Consequently, the discontinuance of wartime credits to the Allied countries in June 1919 helped to bring on a sudden and catastrophic drop in foreign demand for the products of American agriculture which by now had come to be overexpanded.

This decrease in demand, operating as it did in a relatively free market, did not appear mainly as a reduction in the amounts exported but rather in the prices paid for them. Once produced the products had to move.

94. To farmers, unfamiliar with investment funds and accustomed to borrowing at much higher rates of interest, the returns on government bonds seemed ridiculously low. Hence their receptiveness to glowingly described investment opportunities that they were told would yield much higher returns.

95. These credits were discontinued in June 1919. Thereafter the dollar value of foreign currencies declined rapidly, reaching a low in February 1920. See Williams, "The Foreign Trade Balance of the United States," p. 24.

96. A net outward payment of about $160 million a year had been changed to a net inward payment of about $525 million, if the European nations were to make full payment on their commitments. *Ibid.*, p. 23.

and the value of those moving into export was determined in the main by the amounts the importing countries were willing and able to pay. In dire need but desperately impoverished, these countries could pay prices in no way comparable to those that had prevailed during the war. Wheat prices dropped to less than half, corn to a third, and hogs to less than half. Wool became almost unsalable. Most other farm products reacted accordingly. The situation was made more difficult by the sharp drop in employment that followed the war, and some reduction in wage rates. However, these readjustments were less fundamental, so far as farm products were concerned, than the abrupt change in the status of the United States in respect to world trade.

The Freight Rate Increase of 1920

The second factor, also little appreciated, was that railroad earnings and replacement had been held far below comparability with wage rates and the cost of service. So evident was the need for higher rates and rehabilitation of the carriers that the Congress passed and the President signed, on February 28, 1920, the Esch-Cummins Transportation Act. This act directed the Interstate Commerce Commission to establish rates such that the carriers as a whole would earn a fair return on the aggregate values of their properties. Such fair return was specified, for the two years beginning March 1, 1920, as 5½ per cent on the value of the properties. The Commission was authorized, at its discretion, to increase this by one half of one per cent to provide funds for needed capital improvements.[97]

In an effort to comply with this directive the Commission authorized, as of August 26, 1920, blanket percentage increases in rates ranging from 35 to 40 per cent in various sections of the country. By chance this rate increase coincided closely with the beginning of the disastrous decline in the prices of farm products, which occurred in the fall of that year and in 1921. As a result, farmer attention was focused sharply on freight rates as a major cause of the distress in agriculture. Though not the main cause of the farmers' troubles, and less significant than farmers thought them to be, these increases in freight costs were nevertheless a painful setback added to an already serious situation. The result was to make transportation problems an important phase of farm policy in the years immediately following.

Farm Policy Not Crystallized During War

The war period brought into being a set of conditions that was to affect profoundly both agriculture and the policy attitudes of farmers. The war years themselves, however, did not produce any important crystallization of farm policy. This is, of course, a natural consequence of the conditions surrounding agriculture at the time. It was experiencing an unexampled period of prosperity. Farmers, like others, were preoccupied with prosecution of the war, and there was neither time for nor practical purpose in discussing long-term objectives such as the highway and credit programs, rural education, tariffs and similar problems.

The war program itself had not emphasized positive planning with respect to the civilian economy. Though efforts were made to guide production by means of propaganda, and to some extent through price manipulation, main reliance was placed on the normal functioning of the price system. Comparatively little effort was made to protect the consumer by price controls or rationing. Price controls were instituted on a few products, mainly those bought by the government.[98] Wheat and sugar were the principal ones of direct concern to farmers. For wheat the effect of the program was to hold prices substantially below what they otherwise would have been.

---

97. For a comprehensive review of the provisions of the act and the various proposals before Congress at the time, see Rogers MacVeagh, *The Transportation Act, 1920*, Henry Holt, New York, 1923.

98. For a fuller discussion of the price policies followed, see F. W. Taussig, "Price-Fixing as Seen by a Price-Fixer," *Quarterly Journal of Economics*, February 1919, pp. 205–41.

For sugar a high-priced domestic supply was pooled with a lower-priced Cuban supply, both being sold to the consumer at a uniform price lower than would otherwise have prevailed. The hog program affected prices, but it is not clear that its result was to restrain them. There is, in fact, some basis for the contention that this program acted as a positive impetus for an upward spiral in both hog and corn prices which resulted in some embarrassment to the government and unwarranted hardship to the consumers.

Encouragement of the importation of Mexican farm labor introduced a new element into the labor policy of western farmers — one that was to continue prominent in their thinking and was to become a part of the agricultural program in World War II. The mechanical revolution, based on internal combustion motors rather than horsepower, was not yet in full swing. The tractor, the combine-harvester and the mechanical corn-picker were only beginning to appear. Their period of rapid increase was to come in the 1920's.

Organized farmers were not a significant factor in the making of policy during the war years. Except for the Farmers Union, which concerned itself mostly with local problems, the Grange was about the only large, general farm organization, and even its representation was sectional rather than comprehensive. With little reason for dissatisfaction, it tended in general to support and facilitate the over-all national program rather than to initiate one of its own. One group, the Nonpartisan League, had developed a radical program centering in the spring wheat region. This gained temporary adherence from thousands of farmers in Minnesota and South Dakota, but did not achieve national status or lasting strength except in North Dakota.[99]

The functions of the United States Department of Agriculture grew enormously during the war years. Of particular importance was the expansion of its extension program. By 1918 county farm advisers were employed in more than 2,400 of the 3,000 agricultural counties of the United States, and the groundwork for the great postwar program in agricultural extension had been laid. This, in ways not contemplated by its founders, was to become the framework for a new major farm organization, the American Farm Bureau Federation, which was shortly to become an important influence in the formulation of agricultural policy in the United States.

Postwar Slump in Farm Prices

By the fall of 1920 the short postwar boom in farm commodity and land prices had passed its peak, and the prices of farm products were skidding downward at a rate that was even faster than the spectacular rate of increase in 1916, 1917 and 1918. Agricultural prices reached their highest level in July 1919 (at 246 per cent of the 1913 base), approximately a year before the highest point of the all-commodity index was reached (272 in May 1920).[100] Food prices to the consumer continued to climb for some time after prices at the farm had begun to fall. Their maximum, like that for all commodities, was reached in May 1920 at an index of 287.

99. In South Dakota its strength was undermined through shrewd adoption of parts of its program by the incumbent Republican governor, Peter Norbeck. In Minnesota the movement died down though, in cooperation with labor, it succeeded in retaining for many years a Farmer-Labor senator and some House members in the United States Congress. In North Dakota the League achieved control, and launched an extensive socialistic program, including a state-owned bank, state-owned mills and elevators, and a state home-building program. An ironical twist of the situation was that the unorthodox Bank of North Dakota, unable to borrow freely during the boom years, did not make large volumes of loans in that period and hence came into the depression with a rather moderate volume of bad farm mortgage loans. The South Dakota Rural Credits System, planned along more orthodox lines, was able to borrow more than $40 million, most of which was loaned on dubious security. Thus it entered the depression years burdened with a staggering load of delinquent loans and unsound paper. Both systems were badly managed. The North Dakota program shortly became involved in numerous scandals which tended to discredit it. Its influence was to be felt in the state, however, for many years. For fuller discussion of the League and its program see Paul R. Fossum, *The Agrarian Movement in North Dakota*, Johns Hopkins Press, Baltimore, 1925, especially Chapter 4.

100. U.S. Congress, House, *The Agricultural Crisis and Its Causes, Report of the Joint Commission of Agricultural Inquiry*, H.Rep. 408, 67th Cong., 1st sess., 1921. Part I, p. 29.

Cloths and clothing reached their peak in February and March 1920 (at 356), and house furnishings in September and October (at 371). Lumber and metals, which had remained at lower levels during the war years, moved up rapidly, lumber reaching a top of 341 in April and May 1920, and metals a high point of 195 in April.[101]

Thus, by the spring of 1921, American agriculture found itself in a more unfavorable position than it had experienced at any time in the memory of men then living, or possibly at any time since the nation's beginning. The purchasing power of farm products in terms of nonagricultural products was down to 63 per cent as compared to prewar.[102] Many farms were carrying large debts contracted in purchasing land during the speculative boom of the two preceding years; costs were high; and the rural banks were heavily loaded with farmers' notes that could not be quickly liquidated. Foreign markets for farm products were weak, and the tighter policy now being adopted by the Federal Reserve system was adding to the difficulty of financing agricultural operations and purchases. The outlying, surplus-producing areas in particular were hard hit.

By the winter of 1921 farmers in the Dakotas and Nebraska were burning corn for fuel, and trading wool for needed socks and shirts. The clamor for relief took on new forms and greater intensity. It was in this setting that the newly formed American Farm Bureau Federation began its campaign for farm legislation. The Grange and Farmers Union took on new life, and various radical farm organizations gained strength. As a result, the succeeding decade was to see a marked change in the legislative activities of farm organizations and in farmer attitude concerning the role of government in agricultural affairs. These new and aggressive farmer movements are described in the two succeeding chapters.

101. *Loc. cit.*
102. *Ibid.*, p. 27.

CHAPTER 9

ORGANIZATION FOR ACTION

THE SHOCK OF THE POSTWAR break in farm prices was intensified by its unexpectedness. There had been widespread acceptance of the view that a new and higher level of prices had come to stay. Farmers expected fluctuations in their prices, since all their previous experience suggested that, but it was felt that these now would be ups and downs within a higher range. The earnings of city workers and the prices of things farmers must buy were well above those of the prewar period.[1] It seemed reasonable therefore to expect that farm prices would likewise remain high.

Secretary Houston and some others saw the situation more clearly, but their views did not penetrate the farm areas, or, if they did, were not taken seriously by the majority of farm people. In his memoirs, Houston summarized his interpretation of the situation at war's end in these words:

Exports from the United States will decline, prices will fall, especially prices of agricultural products. Europe will first try to produce her own foodstuffs, and she will turn in part to other countries where she can get them at lower rates. . . . That this would occur, I warned the farmers in the fall of 1918 and throughout 1919. I predicted before and just after the Armistice that, on the return of peace, there would probably be a period of optimism and of feverish trading, that there would then begin a decline, especially of agricultural prices, and this would start an agrarian movement, and that the farmers, in ignorance of underlying causes, would see a conspiracy on the part of the bankers to ruin them. I felt that the farmers would not be able to control their production quickly and that, because of the lessened demand from Europe, for the reasons I have indicated, and for the further reason that we had stopped lending Europe money, prices might go very low. And yet, business men were urging that farmers produce and produce. I protested against this in the Industrial Conference in Washington in the late fall of 1918, saying that farmers should not be urged to produce as much as they had or more, unless business men were prepared to protect them against a drop in price. This, I knew, could not be done. I warned the Conference that a drop in general prices would come and that, if they were prudent, they would arrange to weather the storm. I advised farmers to return to a balanced agriculture and to pursue practices best suited to their own needs and to those of their community. I urged this in official statements and in addresses in the latter part of 1918, and, especially, in 1919 and 1920.[2]

Whether Houston's foresight was as clear and detailed as his memoirs imply, his ex post facto analysis is accurate and penetrating. Europe did increase quickly her own production of foodstuffs and did turn to countries other than the United States for a larger portion of her imports. Farm prices in the United States fell sharply in the fall of 1920 and continued to decline until the late summer of 1921. In the meantime the period of optimism he had predicted had made its appearance and had subsided.

DECLINING LAND VALUES AND OVEREXPANDED CREDIT

The inflated farm incomes of the war years had led to markedly freer spending in the rural areas. This tendency was especially pronounced in the first postwar years, particularly through 1919 and the first half of 1920.

1. Average weekly earnings of wage workers reached a level of 235 in 1920 (1914 = 100). They dropped to 188 in 1921, but by 1922 were already starting up again. In 1923 they were back to 212 and by 1928 had reached 218. Farm prices, on the other hand, fell from 231 in 1919 to 124 in 1921, and recovered only slowly thereafter. *Statistical Abstract, 1929*, p. 350 and U.S. Department of Agriculture, *Agriculture Yearbook, 1923*, p. 1192.

2. David F. Houston, *Eight Years with Wilson's Cabinet*, Doubleday, Page, Garden City, 1926, Vol. II, pp. 63–64.

Large outlays went into the purchase of automobiles and tractors which were then coming
into more general use. These in turn led to
more interest in highway improvement, and,
as a result, to higher public expenditure for
roads.[3] Farm lands were in great demand and
active speculation carried their prices in some
areas even beyond values predicated upon
wartime levels of earnings. This speculative
upsurge in the price of farm land was accompanied by a heavy increase in the amount
of mortgage debt. The similar inflation in
the prices of purebred livestock absorbed
other large amounts of free capital and led
to the assumption of unwise debts.

Except in old regions like New England,
farmers had had little experience with savings
for investment outside agriculture. They
tended to apply their enlarged buying power
to the things they knew best — land and livestock — things which in all their experience
had proved good investments with a generally
rising trend of prices. Now, almost for the
first time, they found that the price of farm
land could go down as well as up. The
change in land values, which for a quarter of
a century had constituted a noncash supplement to whatever income they could make
from farming, was suddenly reversed to become a much larger deduction from income.

Costs of operation were still high, and many
farmers were soon to find themselves unable
to cover even the cash outlays required to
carry on their farm operations. The increased
requirements for taxes, interest and debt retirement added still further to their difficulties. Hence, they were in dire need of additional credit to weather the depression. But
the rural banks were in no mood to extend
such credit. Most of them were already overexpanded and under pressure from their correspondent banks and the Federal Reserve
system to reduce borrowing.

3. Expenditures for rural highways (by states, counties, townships and districts) had totaled $240 million in
1914, and were only $389 million in 1919. By 1921,
such expenditures had passed the billion dollar mark
and, except for a slight recession in 1923, continued upward throughout the 1920's. See *Statistical Abstract,
1929*, p. 381.

Federal Reserve Policy

The Federal Reserve system had maintained an artificially low discount rate
throughout the war, and, in the interest of
facilitating the financing of the war, had not
exercised its expected function of keeping in
check the amounts of credit supplied by the
banks. This easy credit policy was continued
into 1920 and was an important factor in the
postwar boom that carried prices well above
their wartime peaks. In retrospect it appears
that it should have been reversed in September 1919. Strong action was not taken until
the early summer of 1920 when rediscount
rates were raised sharply, from about 4¾ per
cent in late 1919 to as high as 6 and 7 per
cent in the summer of 1920. This sharp advance increased the pressure on member
banks to reduce their volumes of loans.[4]

Opinions differed as to the mechanics of
the deflationary policy of the reserve banks.
Anna Youngman, writing in the *American
Economic Review* for September 1921, stated
categorically: ". . . it is not believed that
the changes in discount rates were the directly
effective weapons of credit control. Down-
right refusal to expand certain classes of
loans and pressure for repayment of others
were the potent factors in credit contraction.
. . ."[5] Whether through increased discount
rates or more forceful measures, it seems clear
that the reserve banks could not avoid taking
steps to check the increase in borrowings
which was rapidly getting out of hand.[6]

The reserve banks denied vigorously that
their policies had singled out the farmer for
discriminatory credit contraction.[7] Secretary
Houston also challenged the view that the

4. See A. C. Miller, "Federal Reserve Policy," *American Economic Review*, June 1921, pp. 177-206.
5. "The Efficacy of Changes in the Discount Rates
of the Federal Reserve Banks," *American Economic Review*, September 1921, p. 476.
6. See analysis by O. M. W. Sprague, "The Discount
Policy of the Federal Reserve Banks," *American Economic Review*, March 1921, p. 23; and H. G. Moulton,
"Banking Policy and the Price Situation," *ibid.*, March
1920, Proceedings Supplement, pp. 156-75.
7. See, for example, Federal Reserve Bank of Minneapolis, *The Federal Reserve Bank and the Farmer and
Stockman*, 2nd edition, Minneapolis, April 2, 1921, pp.
6 and 14.

farmers were being "deflated." Writing later, in his memoirs, he commented:

The ignorant part of the community, including many demagogues, in and out of public life, unable or unwilling to see the facts, resorted to the easy and usual practice of attributing the financial ills to the banking machinery of the country, even going so far as to charge that there was a deliberate conspiracy on the part of the Reserve Board and of many bankers to crush the farmers. Their usual way of putting it was that the Federal Reserve Board was deflating the farmers. It was obvious that they did not know what they really meant. They did not really understand what is meant by deflation. They knew that there was a fall in the prices of certain commodities, and they called that deflation. They were unaware that by deflation is meant a lessening of the money or credit of the nation, and that a decrease of the volume of credit in itself would affect all prices equally. If there was real deflation and it alone was operating, there would not be at the same time, because of it, a tremendous drop in farm prices, a smaller decline in prices of many industrial products, and an increase in the prices of others. Their easy explanation also did not account for the great fall of prices of farm products in the other countries of the world. The truth is that, while some prices, particularly those of farm products, greatly declined, there was no real deflation. There was no decline in the volume of credit during 1920, when prices of agricultural products dropped so sharply. There was, as a matter of fact, an enormous increase. Between the date of the Armistice and October 1, 1920, the loans and investments of all banks increased more than $7,000,000,000 and the Federal Reserve notes more than $740,-000,000. In the period from January 23, 1920, to the end of September, by which time the drop in agricultural products had occurred, the loans and investments of all the banks expanded a billion dollars or more, and the Federal Reserve note circulation $460,000,000. What is more important is the fact that accommodations extended to agriculture, industry, and commerce, increased in the same period between $3,000,000,000 and $4,000,000,000. From the beginning of the crop-moving season in July, to October 16th, the bills discounted and purchased by the Federal Reserve banks gained at an average rate of $22,-000,000 a week, and the Federal Reserve note circulation at the rate of $20,000,000. The peak of the credit expansion was not reached until the close of the year. When the declining loans appeared, in 1921, it was not primarily because of any action of the Federal Reserve System but because business had fallen off and the demand for loans had decreased.[8]

Despite these disclaimers there can be no doubt that the federal reserve banks were endeavoring to bring about a retreat from their overexpanded situation. However, the more insistent pressure on farmers resulted from the efforts of the country banks to reduce their loans and get into stronger position. Only a year or two earlier they had been encouraging, even urging, farmers to borrow. Now the farmer in need of more credit not only met with a cold negative but was asked to reduce the loans already made to him.

Farmers became highly critical of the Federal Reserve system and its policies. They demanded new and more dependable sources of credit for agricultural operations. They also developed an aggressive interest in the marketing system and launched a vigorous campaign for lower freight rates. Considerable numbers demanded action by the government to fix the prices of farm products at more equitable levels. This movement centered mainly in the regions producing export crops in locations far from central markets, since these were the areas hardest hit both by the weakened foreign demand and the freight rate increases of 1920. For the most part, however, farmers were not yet ready to seek direct intervention by the government. The traditional attitude of self-reliance and minimum dependence on government was still strong.

FARM ORGANIZATIONS GAIN NEW IMPETUS

For more than twenty years there had been little militant activity on the part of farmers as an organized group. Some of their major objectives had been achieved, notably the control of railroad rates and the passage of antitrust legislation. The collapse of the Populist movement had destroyed many of the more aggressive farm organizations, and no new major issues had arisen that were sufficiently vital to unite farmers generally. Of the many

8. Houston, *Eight Years with Wilson's Cabinet*, Vol. II, pp. 105–07.

organizations active in the last part of the nineteenth century, only the Grange had continued to have a following of any importance. During the intervening years, it espoused a forward-looking but relatively conservative program.

The Farmers Union had continued in existence but with less general coverage, less able leadership and less influence than the Grange. It had about 140,000 members at the close of the war.[9] The American Society of Equity made some headway in the North Central states, but did not achieve great importance as a national movement. At the end of the war it had about 40,000 members, mostly in Wisconsin. An offshoot, the Farmers Equity Union, had been formed in 1910, with emphasis almost wholly on the creation of cooperative buying and selling agencies. Central market units, each more or less independent of the others, had been established at Denver, Kansas City, Chicago, St. Paul and various other points. The handling of grain and supplies was a prominent feature, but a number of Equity Union creameries were also included, particularly in Nebraska.[10]

9. Commodore B. Fisher, *The Farmers Union,* Vol. I, No. 2, Publications of the University of Kentucky, Lexington, 1920, p. 15.

Gladys Talbott Edwards describes the situation during and immediately after the war as follows:

"During the war years no new states were chartered. The membership of the Unions then in existence fell away. Prices were high, and farmers had their eyes on the will-o'-the-wisp goal of quick riches. Money was easy to get. Farms were mortgaged to buy Liberty Bonds, to buy more land and machinery to raise more wheat to win the war. 'Food will win the war,' was the slogan on every lip, and 'whip the Kaiser' the thought in every mind. There seemed no need of a farm organization when prices were so high, no time to attend meetings when there was war work to do, and war prices to be had. . . . Locals died and were not even missed. As a social gathering they were replaced and crowded out by Red Cross and war work meetings. . . .

"By 1920 the Union membership had declined to its lowest point since 1903 . . .

"The convention report of 1921 shows an increase of twenty thousand members in the year. But the report of 1922 shows that the same number had been lost. Those who had joined had done so believing that quick relief would come through the Union, not realizing that the Union itself had lost its power through their neglect." *The Farmers Union Triangle,* revised edition, Farmers Union Education Service, Jamestown, North Dakota, 1941, pp. 30-32.

10. For a fuller description, see Edward Wiest, *Agri-*

With the emergence of new problems that affected farmers all over the nation the time was ripe for a sharp increase in farm organization activity. This could have occurred through revitalizing and expanding one or more of the older organizations. In the main it did not take that form. New organizations with new programs usually have more drawing power than older ones whose policies are more familiar and whose accomplishments can be more readily appraised. Usually, too, the new organizations have younger, more vigorous and more crusading leadership. The Grange, which would have been the logical organization to step into the gap, was somewhat handicapped by its ritualistic and secret features. The mood of American farmers had changed, and the secret society or lodge type of organization was losing its appeal.

Rise of the Farm Bureau

Inadvertently the administrators of the agricultural extension services had, in the meantime, set up a mechanism which was ideally suited for the creation and rapid expansion of a new type of general farm organization. In most of the states, county organizations, known as farm bureaus, were organized in connection with the agricultural extension program authorized under the Smith-Lever Act. The purpose of these groups was in part to provide a means of contact and guidance that would make the work of the county farm advisers more effective. In most counties the farm bureaus also had the responsibility of raising, through memberships and by representations made to county boards of supervisors, part of the funds needed for support of the county extension activities.[11] To accomplish these purposes, it was necessary to create a definite organization with a board of directors, general officers and a substantial membership.

As originally contemplated, the farm bu-

cultural Organization in the United States, University of Kentucky, Lexington, 1923, pp. 532-36.

11. In some states, for example in Illinois, such groups had been financing virtually all of the cost of maintaining farm advisers before federal, state and county funds became available.

aus were to concern themselves solely with
ducational and demonstration programs. It
as not expected that they would undertake
usiness activities, legislative programs and
milar functions normally performed by the
ore general farm organizations. It was natu-
l, however, for these groups of prominent
d progressive farmers, when they got to-
ether, to discuss the whole range of prob-
ms in which farmers were interested, and
was but a short step from there to proposals
do something about them.

In the meantime there had been a growing
ndency for the county farm bureaus to form
emselves into state federations for consid-
ation of mutual problems. Thus leading
rmers came to know each other and became
terested in finding ways for more effective
xpression of the views of farmers on county,
ate and national affairs. The county farm
lvisers, who were in close contact with
rmer thinking, tended to sympathize with
ese aspirations, but they were pressed by
eir state administrators to confine them-
lves to authorized programs and to eschew
tivities that lay outside their educational
nction, or that were likely to be "hot."

ederation of State Units

The farm advisers tended, however, to be
ore responsive to the wishes of their constitu-
ts than to those of extension administrators,
d frequently took matters into their own
nds. At a meeting of the National Associa-
n of County Agricultural Agents, held in
hicago in December 1918, resolutions were
opted declaring that the time was ripe for the
rmation of state and national federations of
rm bureaus which could serve the farmer
ore effectively. Speeches were made urging
e need for an aggressive farm organization
hich would not only advise the farmer in
s production operations, but which would
so serve him in his dealings with other in-
rests.[12]

On February 12, 1919, a conference, attended by representatives from a dozen states,
was held at Ithaca, New York, at the invitation of the New York State Farm Bureau
Federation. An organizing committee was appointed and a vigorous campaign to form
new state federations was undertaken. On
November 12 and 13 of that year a national
convention of farm bureaus was held at the
LaSalle Hotel in Chicago.[13] As the meeting
got under way, there was evidence of significant sectional differences in viewpoint concerning the appropriate functions of such an
organization. The East and South felt that
the primary purpose should be educational.
The Middle West, especially the representatives from Illinois, Iowa and Indiana, thought
that if a national organization was to be effective it must serve the business and economic
interests of the farmer as well as his need for
educational work on production problems.
This divergence of opinion was similar to
that which had beset the Grange in its forma-
tive years, and the outcome was much the
same. Those advocating the inclusion of economic and legislative activities won out.

The discussions at Chicago did not, however, fully settle the issue. A compromise was
arrived at, though one that did not wholly satisfy either group. A constitution was drawn
up. Plans were made for further meetings, and
a few resolutions of rather general nature were
passed. These included recommendations for
legislation regulating corporations, including
packers and other dealers in foodstuffs; opposition to government ownership of utilities;
and advocacy of prompt return of the railroads to private control. Economy in government expenditures and an increase in the
limit on federal land bank loans, from $10,000
to $25,000, were also urged.

A ratification convention was held at Chicago in March 1920, and the organization
was officially launched at that time. James R.

12. Editorial in *Wallaces' Farmer*, January 3, 1919,
4. See also Alice M. Christensen, *Agricultural Pres-
e and Government Response in the United States:
19-1929*, unpublished doctoral dissertation, University

of California, Berkeley, 1936, p. 23. (Paging follows
copy in Library of the Giannini Foundation.)
13. Orville Merton Kile, *The Farm Bureau Through
Three Decades*, The Waverly Press, Baltimore, 1948, pp.
47-55.

Howard of Iowa had been elected president at the preceding November meeting and John W. Coverdale, also of Iowa, had been selected as secretary. When the convention assembled, in March, eight of the state federations had already ratified the constitution. By December thirty-seven states had become affiliated, and by July 1921, forty-two state federations were in existence.

Success of the Federation

Had the organizers of the movement been endowed with the power to look into the future they could not have chosen a more favorable setting. The almost nationwide network of county farm bureaus was already in existence. The new organization had been launched with the specific purpose of furthering the farmer's economic and legislative objectives. Then came the catastrophic decline in farm prices which made farmers throughout the nation acutely aware of their need to unite for economic and legislative action. It was this combination of circumstances that accounted for the almost immediate emergence of the Farm Bureau Federation as a major spokesman for agriculture, with more comprehensive coverage than any farm organization had previously achieved.

The leaders chosen were able and aggressive. The Federation grew rapidly. By 1922, it had a paid-up national membership of some 450,000 families, with probably at least as many more who were affiliated in one way or another with the local farm bureaus, but for whom dues to the national had not been paid.[14] Thus the Federation had become the most strongly financed among the farm organizations, and slightly larger in membership than the Grange, which was its leading competitor. As yet, however, there was much vagueness and difference of opinion as to what farmers were paying for with their membership money. Part of it went for support of the work of the county farm advisers, a branch of the publicly supported educa-

tional system. Part went to the state and n[a]tional farm bureau federations. Some farme[rs] gave support mainly for the one purpos[e,] some for the other.

Since the educational program of the exte[n]sion services had appealed to the more e[n]lightened and progressive farmers of t[he] various communities, the Farm Bureau Fe[d]eration, on the whole, tended to inclu[de] mainly the more educated, commercial farm[m]ers rather than a cross section of all farme[rs.] The views of this group were consequent[ly] the ones which appeared most prominent[ly] in the program of the Federation. It sought [to] duplicate, in agriculture, a pattern similar [to] that which prevailed in American busines[s.] These farmers did not picture themselves [as] a down-trodden segment of the economy. I[n]stead they encouraged their organization [to] take its place as an equal partner with grou[ps] representing other industries. By this sam[e] token the Federation did not interpret i[ts] function as that of representing the unde[r]privileged groups in agriculture. It was e[s]sentially a middle class, mildly conservati[ve] movement following traditional lines [of] thinking.

Early Program of the Federation

The Federation opened offices in Chicag[o] and Washington, and selected Gray Silver [of] West Virginia as its full-time Washingto[n] representative. A professional publicity ma[n] was employed, and the movement quick[ly] began to attract public attention. Even in t[he] Sixty-sixth Congress, the first after the Armi[s]tice, its influence began to be felt. On t[he] insistence of the farm organization represe[n]tatives the daylight saving law was repeale[d] over President Wilson's veto. All far[m] groups, except the Farmers' National Cou[n]cil, urged return of the railroads to priva[te] control.[15] The Farm Bureau Federation lik[e]

14. See *ibid.,* chart, p. 368. Kile gives a very readable account of the early years of the Federation in Chapters 3 to 9 inclusive.

15. Virtually all business organizations, and ma[ny] others, were likewise advocating such action. These pr[es]sures, mainly from groups other than the farm organiz[a]tions, resulted in passage of the Esch-Cummins Act [of] 1920.

The Farmers' National Council, the only farm gro[up] in opposition to the Esch-Cummins bill, was made up [of] the Washington State Grange, the North Carolina Farm[...]

wise took an active interest in plans for use of the Muscle Shoals Dam, power plants and nitrate factories, though this issue was not to be finally threshed out for many years to come.

Pressure also began to be applied looking toward clearer definition of the legal status of cooperative associations, and control of the packers and stockyard companies. By the fall of 1920 farmers and congressional representatives from the farm districts were agitating for revival of the War Finance Corporation as an aid in strengthening the export market for farm products. They believed that Europe still afforded a strong market for their products if means could be found for providing credits to the importing countries. Such credit had been extended by the War Finance Corporation between March 3, 1919 and May 10, 1920. This was handled by making loans to exporters or to banks which in turn loaned to exporters.[16] Secretary of the Treasury Hous-

ton halted this practice on the ground that exports were being adequately financed by private interests, and that further lending by the War Finance Corporation would force it to withdraw funds from the Treasury or sell bonds to the public.[17] Farmer criticism of Houston's action was further emphasized by the growing resentment over the policies of the Federal Reserve Board.

Despite considerable pressure to reverse his stand, Houston continued to oppose revival of the War Finance Corporation. Nevertheless, a congressional joint resolution ordering reactivation of the Corporation was passed overwhelmingly in December 1920. It was vetoed by the President, on January 3, 1921, but was immediately and strongly passed over his veto. The revived War Finance Corporation did not play an important role as a financer of exports. Instead, its major contribution was the taking over, at a somewhat later date, of frozen assets of country banks, mainly in the spring wheat region, thereby enabling the banks aided to weather the storm, and allowing the farmer borrowers time in which to reduce their indebtedness.

This operation was brilliantly performed, though with little fanfare, under the direction of Eugene Meyer, Jr., who had again been made managing director after being reappointed to the Board in March 1921.[18] The

ers Union, the Gleaners, the Michigan Potato Growers' Exchange and a few others. Wiest, *Agricultural Organization*, p. 553. See also Christensen, *Agricultural Pressure and Government Response*, p. 11.

16. An Act of March 3, 1919 added Section 21 to the War Finance Corporation Act. Under this section the Corporation was authorized to extend credits to European buyers of American products for periods ranging up to five years. The amendment was designed to aid in preventing a sharp decline in American exports. The European nations still had a pressing need for imports, especially of foodstuffs, but were unable to export on a scale adequate to pay for them. Under the amendment, and other authorizations, the Treasury and the War Food Administration had continued to extend credit on a government-to-government basis. The discontinuance of such credits, in May 1920, thus tended to weaken the export demand for American farm products, though not so much as was commonly assumed at the time. Up to November 30, 1920, the War Finance Corporation made loans, under Section 21, of about $46 million. However, in 1919, exports exceeded in dollar value even hose of 1918, nearly $8 billion as against slightly over $6 billion in 1918, and continued at a high level during 1920. It is thus apparent that the War Finance Corporation credit to foreign purchasers constituted only an inconsequential portion of the total credit extended to them. Nevertheless, the availability of this lending power apparently had some stabilizing influence since it tended to strengthen confidence in the ability of the war-torn nations to carry on during the immediate postwar years. For fuller interpretation of this period see War Finance Corporation, *Third Annual Report*, S.Doc. 341, 66th Cong., 3rd sess., 1920.

Though it is true that the dollar value of United States exports rose substantially in 1919 as compared to 1918, and in 1920 as compared to 1919, the physical volume of exports began to decline in 1920, going from an index of 142 to 137 (1913 = 100). Thereafter it fell

off sharply, to 120 in 1921, and to 112 in 1922. Though recovering from 1923 on, it did not again reach the level of 1919 until 1926. *Statistical Abstract, 1929*, p. 464.

17. Houston had been shifted from the Agriculture secretaryship to that of the Treasury on February 20, 1920. He was succeeded, as Secretary of Agriculture, by E. T. Meredith, publisher of *Successful Farming*, an Iowa farm paper. Meredith's influence, in his short tenure of office, was not great. His principal effort was an attempt to publicize the work of the Department of Agriculture and make the public more aware of its accomplishments.

18. The Corporation was placed in liquidation on April 5, 1929. During its period of operation, after its revival in 1921, it made total loans on agricultural and livestock products of $296,987,962.47. Of these, $295,-146,759.15 were repaid. Through this means many banks with slow assets were enabled to carry their customers for longer periods, and some were enabled to make new loans that they could not otherwise have supplied. For a summary of the Corporation's activities, see *Liquidation of the War Finance Corporation*, Letter from the Acting Secretary of the Treasury . . . Transmitting the Final Report of the War Finance Corporation, January 21, 1943, especially p. 18.

A phase of the Corporation's activity which attracted much attention was the appointment, in November 1921,

success of the operation and the simplicity of the mechanism used led to the creation of the Reconstruction Finance Corporation along similar lines in 1932. The importance of this device and its flexibility resulted in its use by the Hoover administration and by that of Franklin Roosevelt as a means of financing under both depression and war conditions.

The 1920 Political Campaign

The campaign of 1920 had been marked by bitter denunciation of Wilson. His slighting of Republican leadership in negotiating the peace, and his championing of the League of Nations, had brought him into a struggle to the death with the small but powerful group of "irreconcilables" in the Senate. Broken in health and virtually unable to exercise any leadership during his last year in office, he was thrust into the background by the politicians who had long resented domination by "the White House." Both the House and the Senate had gone Republican in 1918, though the Republican control of the Senate was extremely precarious. The people as a whole were restive and anxious for a change from the emotional tension of the war years and there was little desire on the part of the politicians for resumption of the strong executive leadership which had characterized Wilson's first term.

The voters in 1920 wanted to "get back to normalcy," and this Warren Harding promised them.[19] Little did he or they realize that

instead of moving into a period of normalc they were entering one of major price disto tions, unstable prosperity, and wild specul tion that would lead to the most disastro depression on record.

Farm Problem Not Yet Apparent

The major trouble spot was in agricultur Business activity suffered a sharp decline b ginning near the end of 1920, but by the mi dle of 1921 it had turned the corner and w again on the upgrade. By the fall of 1922 was up to normal and heading into the p riod of high activity that was to last unt 1929, except for minor and brief recessior in 1924 and the latter part of 1927. Agricu ture, on the other hand, had sunk into a m jor depression that was to keep its buyin power low and its workers dissatisfied for number of years.

The severity and persistence of the break i agricultural prosperity were not yet apparer when the elections of 1920 were held. Conse quently the agricultural planks of the part platforms were drafted in terms of norm conditions rather than as measures to mee depression. Both parties pledged a law se ting forth clearly the rights of farmers' c operative marketing associations. Both prom ised to make scientific studies of domestic an foreign costs of producing farm product and to encourage the export of such product They also promised to make improvement in the federal farm loan system. In additior the Republican platform contained a promis to give farmers more representation on fec eral boards and commissions. It also pledge

of a Corn Belt Advisory Committee under the chairmanship of Governor Warren T. McCray of Indiana. This included President J. R. Howard of the Farm Bureau Federation, former Secretary of Agriculture E. T. Meredith, and other prominent farm leaders of the Middle West. It sought to bring about more effective effort on the part of the midwest bankers for meeting the critical situation that had resulted from the harvesting of two large corn crops in the face of a demoralized livestock situation. See *Fourth Annual Report of the War Finance Corporation,* H.Doc. 143, 67th Cong., 2nd sess., 1922, pp. 11–13.

19. Just prior to the election, Houston, in his diary, analyzed the situation as follows:

"What a drop there will be to either Cox or Harding. If Mr. Harding is elected, the contrast will be painful. It will be somewhat tragic to have a man of Mr. Wilson's intellect and high standards succeeded by a man of Mr. Harding's mediocre mind and ordinary standards of thinking and action. At this time, particularly, the nation needs a leader, and Mr. Harding will not be a

leader. He cannot be. He has never stood for any grea cause. He knows very little, has no vision, very littl sense of direction, and no independence. He was no nominated to lead. He was selected because he wa colourless and pliable. If he is elected, he will be th tool of such tried leaders as Lodge, Penrose, and other He will play the game of the Senate. The Senate wi be supreme. The old policies will be revived. Protectio will raise its head again and raise it higher than eve The revolt of the people against the Paine [sic]-Aldric Tariff Bill will be forgotten. This element of the Repul lican party which will be in the ascendant knows exactl where it is going. It will go back to where it was befor 1915. What a trial it will be to have to witness M Harding's efforts to think and his efforts to say what h thinks." Houston, *Eight Years with Wilson's Cabine* Vol. II, p. 93.

uthorization of associations for extending
ersonal credits, and promised to institute in-
uiry into the coordination of water, rail and
notor transportation. "Unnecessary price-fix-
ng" and "ill-considered" efforts to reduce the
rices of farm products were to be discontin-
ed. With a weak candidate and demoralized
arty leadership the Democrats were over-
vhelmed in the ensuing election, and a
veakly led Republican administration came
nto power.

Organization of the "Farm Bloc"

The increasing severity of the distress in
he farm areas soon brought the farm organi-
ations and the new Republican leaders to
rips with the farm problem. On April 11,
921, an almost unprecedented aggregation
f agricultural leaders came together in
Washington for some ten days of intensive
onsideration of legislative programs. It in-
luded the executive committee of the Ameri-
an Farm Bureau Federation, some state
Farm Bureau officers, the National Grange,
he National Board of Farm Organizations,
he National Milk Producers Federation, the
International Farm Congress and the Farm-
rs Union.

Among the government officials present
were Henry C. Wallace, the newly appointed
Secretary of Agriculture; Herbert Hoover,
he newly appointed Secretary of Commerce;
W. P. G. Harding, Governor of the Federal
Reserve Board; A. F. Lever of the Federal
Farm Loan Board; Chairman Edgar E. Clark
of the Interstate Commerce Commission and
others.

At the same time a separate conference was
held by the more radical organizations: the
People's Reconstruction League, including
some members of the Farmers' National
Council, the United Farmers of America, the
Nonpartisan League, the Gleaners and various representatives of organized labor. The
main show, however, was that of the more
conservative and orthodox-minded organizations.

Shortly after the close of this conference,
on May 9, 1921, Gray Silver and Senator Ken-

yon sponsored a meeting of senators in Silver's office to consider ways of effectuating
the legislative program desired by the agricultural organizations. This group consisted
of senators from the dominantly agricultural
states and from both parties. Those who attended were Kenyon of Iowa, Norris of Nebraska, Kendrick of Wyoming, Gooding of
Idaho, Capper of Kansas, Smith of South
Carolina, Fletcher of Florida, LaFollette of
Wisconsin, Sheppard of Texas, Ladd of
North Dakota, Ransdell of Louisiana and
Heflin of Alabama.[20] It was a widely representative, bipartisan group of experienced and
powerful senate leaders. Senator Kenyon was
elected chairman, and the loose organization
which quickly came to be known as the
"Farm Bloc" had come into being.[21] It was
to wield much power in the succeeding years,
and frequently caused serious embarrassment
to the conservative, Republican leadership of
the period.

Silver outlined to the meeting the things
the farmers felt they needed and wanted.
These were in the main measures which had
already been introduced — commodity financing, personal credits, a broader and more
tolerant definition of the status of cooperative associations and readjustment of freight
rates. He stated that they were also interested
in tariff legislation, taxation, regulation of
meat-packing companies, trading in grain futures, truth-in-fabric legislation, highways,

20. The meeting was also attended by A. F. Lever of
the Farm Loan Board, by three representatives of the
United States Department of Agriculture (H. C. Taylor,
Elmer E. Engelbert and Chester Morrill), John Lee
Coulter, Dean of the West Virginia College of Agriculture, and E. B. Reid who was handling public relations
for Silver in the Washington office of the Farm Bureau
Federation.
The account of these events is drawn largely from
Christensen, *Agricultural Pressure and Government Response*. Miss Christensen had access to the typewritten
records in the office of the Farm Bureau Federation.
21. The term "Farm Bloc" was not intended nor desired by the sponsors of the group. In fact it was somewhat embarrassing to them. The term was used facetiously by a newspaper man, and was quickly picked up
and continued in use throughout the country. Though
charged with implications that members of the group
were somewhat hesitant to accept, the idea proved
popular with farmers, and undoubtedly helped to rally
support for the Farm Bureau Federation, which was
recognized as an active leader in the movement.

fertilizer manufacture, cold storage, and in certain amendments to the Farm Loan Act and the Federal Reserve Act. On most of these measures the Federation's proposals had not yet taken specific form.

Study Committees Set Up

The members of the Bloc organized themselves somewhat formally for an unofficial group of this kind. They agreed to take up definite questions for study and discussion with a view to recommending legislation where needed. Reports were to be made at subsequent meetings. Senator Kenyon, as chairman, appointed subcommittees for these purposes, among them the following: a committee on amendments to the Federal Reserve Act; one on transportation; another on the Lever plan of commodity financing; and a fourth on miscellaneous bills.

A House group under the leadership of Congressman L. J. Dickinson of Iowa held a similar meeting a few days later. It also organized itself into subcommittees, on transportation, tariff, taxation and revenue, miscellaneous bills and finance.

The House group was much looser than that of the Senate, and its membership more indefinite. Some congressmen joined with it at times and remained aloof at others. It was said to consist at one time of about a hundred members, but the usual number participating in its activities was much smaller.[22]

The Senate and House blocs held frequent meetings during the summer of 1921. They worked out recommendations for additional farm credit legislation, and considered a bill introduced by Senator Norris which proposed a $100 million corporation to buy farm products in America for cash and sell them in foreign markets on time. Many other proposals came under discussion and the main outlines of a farm legislative program, largely worked out in cooperation with the American Farm Bureau Federation, began to emerge.[23]

Legislative Program of the Farm Bloc

Because of its size, its wide representation, its bipartisan make-up and its aggressive leadership, the Bloc quickly became important politically. It was soon to be a major headache for party leaders, particularly for the administration. Here was a group with large voting strength which was not amenable to the usual types of party discipline. Furthermore, it had set up, unofficially, a committee system for consideration of problems that were also before the official committees of the Congress. In the Senate, the Bloc included a majority of the members of the Committee on Agriculture. Thus, in the event of disagreement between the two, it was clear that the Bloc proposals rather than those of the majority party group in the official committee would prevail.[24]

In the summer of 1921 farm-group pressure proved strong enough to prevent early adjournment of the Senate, which was proposed as a means of concentrating on tariff legislation. An early adjournment would have meant sacrificing or postponing legislation

22. The original Senate group was shortly enlarged through inclusion of McNary (Oregon), Norbeck (South Dakota), Harreld (Georgia), Ashurst (Arizona), Harrison (Mississippi), Wesley Jones (Washington), Stanfield (Oregon), Kellogg (Minnesota) and Swanson (Virginia).

23. The hand of the Bloc was strengthened on several major legislative proposals through a device used by the Farm Bureau Federation wherein a referendum on the measures was circulated to the Farm Bureau locals (in May 1921). The resulting expressions of sentiment by the farmer members or their officers were played up as a "grass-roots" mandate for particular proposals. The plan had important educational possibilities, but in practice the referendum was so drafted as virtually to assure an overwhelming pro vote, as is usual when pressure groups query their members on matters which are already settled policy so far as their officers are concerned. The form of questionnaire used was privately much criticized by agencies like the United States Chamber of Commerce which had long used referenda in which the propositions were more fully and objectively analyzed. The Farm Bureau referendum presented little except arguments for the propositions being voted upon. The Federation and the Farm Bloc were, however, able to make effective use of the results by indicating to each congressman how his farm bureau constituents presumably wished him to vote.

24. This conflict between party leadership and Farm Bloc leadership continued nearly all through the period of active farm organization pressure which characterized the 1920's. After 1929, the more general distress tended to lessen the contrast between conditions in agriculture and those in the rest of the economy, and the efforts to provide relief for agriculture became part of a broader antideflation program.

desired by the Farm Bloc.[25] By agreement with the President and with party leaders in both houses, five of the measures advocated by the Bloc were passed and signed prior to the adjournment of the Senate. These were:

1. The Packers and Stockyards Act (approved August 15, 1921).[26]
2. The Future Trading Act (approved August 24, 1921).[27]
3. The Emergency Agricultural Credits Act (approved August 24, 1921).[28]

4. An amendment to the Farm Loan Act (August 13, 1921), raising the interest on farm loan bonds, to the investor, from 5 to 5½ per cent, without increasing the rate to the borrower.
5. Another amendment to the Farm Loan Act (July 1, 1921), increasing the capital of the federal land banks and authorizing an increase in the maximum size of loan.

Gray Silver also claimed Farm Bloc credit for the Emergency Quota Act limiting immigration, though the date of its passage (May 19, 1921) would appear to make this claim rather dubious.[29]

25. At that time, Harding asked Senator Lodge to adjourn the Senate until the House could complete the drafting of a new tariff. This meant tabling the agricultural measures when the session reconvened, presumably until after the tariff legislation could be disposed of. Gray Silver led the opposition to this move, and, by telegraphing 1,500 county farm bureaus, brought in a flood of telegrams opposing the adjournment. As a result, Lodge's motion was defeated 27 to 24. Harding is reported to have sent for Silver and asked him what the Farm Bureau wanted from the Congress at that time. A compromise was arrived at whereby it was agreed that if six out of about a dozen bills advocated by the farm leaders could be passed, they would not oppose adjournment of the Senate.

26. This was essentially the Haugen bill, a milder control than was provided by the Norris bill which the Farm Bloc favored. The act prohibited "unfair" practices, apportioning of supplies between packers, dividing of territory, and the creation of conditions tending toward monopoly. The stockyards were subjected to regulation of rates and practices as public service corporations. Enforcement was lodged with the Secretary of Agriculture rather than in the Federal Trade Commission as had been proposed in the Norris bill. Legislation looking to these ends had been before the Congress since 1918, but had not previously had strong backing.

27. The Future Trading Act grew out of a long period of agitation which was sharply intensified as a result of the collapse in grain prices in the fall of 1920. Many farmers believed that the price decline was in large part due to speculation on the boards of trade. The act as passed (the Capper-Tincher bill) placed a tax of 20 cents per bushel on all sales of grain for future delivery and also on certain questionable transactions known as "privileges," "bids," "offers" and "puts and calls." The major feature, the tax on future trading, was invalidated by the Supreme Court less than a year later (May 15, 1922) on the ground that it constituted an improper use of the taxing power. To get around this decision the Congress passed in September 1922 a new act known as the Grain Futures Act of 1922. This set up the Grain Futures Administration in the Department of Agriculture, limited the amounts of price fluctuation permitted in a given trading period and eliminated the tax feature. Its results have not been striking, but it has provided a general, official supervision of practices in the "contract markets."

28. The Farm Bloc originally supported the Norris bill setting up a government corporation to buy for cash and sell abroad on credit over a period of five years. Secretary Hoover opposed the plan, and Secretary Wallace did not give it support. While hearings on the Norris bill were in progress, President Harding sent a message to the Congress suggesting that the War Finance Corporation be authorized to take care of agricultural needs through enlarged capital for financing exports.

This resulted in substitution of the Kellogg amendment, virtually a new bill drafted by Secretary Hoover and Chairman Eugene Meyer, Jr., of the War Finance Corporation. This bill, which was the basis of the act as passed, increased to one billion dollars the credits the corporation might have outstanding at any one time, and gave it rather broad powers to aid agriculture in adjusting to the new conditions of domestic and foreign trade. It authorized advances not only to exporters and banks, as in the past, but to farmers' cooperative associations and foreign purchasers. Loans to banks and cooperative associations for breeding, raising, fattening and marketing livestock were also permitted, and, under some circumstances, the purchase from banks of paper secured by agricultural products. This latter provision was later to be of considerable importance in saving the banking structure of some of the more distressed agricultural areas. The Farm Bloc accepted reluctantly the Kellogg substitute for the Norris bill, but afterward claimed this legislation as a part of its accomplishment.

29. The immigration problem aroused considerable interest in farm as well as labor circles. *The Country Gentleman*, in a brochure issued in March 1921, entitled "The Wolves at Our Door," expressed the prevailing sentiment as follows: "This much is certain: Immigrants are coming in as fast as the steamships can carry them. After-the-war poverty abroad and exaggerated reports of American prosperity are bringing them over in armies. Most of them are poor. During Christmas week, for example, 8000 arrivals had only twenty dollars each, while 4000 hadn't a cent. They are bound for the cities — New York, Detroit, Pittsburgh, Philadelphia and Cleveland get most of them. Are they settling in the overpopulated slums because 'The Land of Liberty' has a melodious ring in their ears, or because reports place factory wages at figures that are fortunes when translated into the debased money of the homeland? Into the melting pot they go. Can we make efficient, productive Americans of them? Do they want to become Americans?"

In 1917 the Congress had passed, over the President's veto, an immigration act that ended the traditional American policy, and prohibited entry of many undesirable types of immigrants, including illiterates, but did not place limits on the numbers that might be admitted. The Act of 1921, a temporary measure, limited numbers admissible from any given country, for the year ending June 30, 1922, to 3 per cent of the number of foreign-born persons of that nationality present in the United States in 1910. In May 1922, the act was extended to June 30, 1924. On May 26, 1924, a new and more stringent, permanent act was passed. This reduced the percentage for each nationality from 3 to 2, and specified 1890 as the base period instead of 1910. These

Other Legislation Advocated

Though not limiting their activities to leg-islation, the farm groups continued to press for action along the lines agreed upon at the time the Bloc was established. After passage of the Packers and Stockyards and Future Trading acts, interest centered on repeal of the "guarantee" clause of the Esch-Cummins Transportation Act, specific authorization of cooperative marketing, and further legisla-tion on agricultural credits. The efforts to change the Esch-Cummins Act were not suc-cessful, but the continuing agitation for lower freight rates led eventually to passage of the vague and somewhat contradictory Hoch-Smith Resolution of 1925.[30]

Though they supported the restoration of higher tariffs, the farm groups did not look upon this as a significant farm relief measure. They recognized the difficulty of making tar-iffs effective on the agricultural commodities produced in surplus, but, generally speaking, held the view that agriculture and industry should be placed on an equal basis with re-spect to tariffs. They also talked, somewhat vaguely, of a flexible tariff which would be more "scientific." The fact of the matter is that they had not thought through the rela-tion of tariffs to agriculture, and were giving support to the strong sentiment for protec-tion in nonfarm segments of the economy without realizing that the over-all effect of the protectionist policy was adverse to their interests.

Cooperative Marketing Act Passed

"Orderly marketing" had come to be a popular slogan in farm circles. This interest was given further powerful impetus by the widely publicized "Sapiro" campaign for the organization of cooperative selling agencies on regional, national and commodity-wide bases, which was launched in the summer of 1920.[31] The elements of monopoly principle embodied in the Sapiro approach made it doubly important that the legal standing and limitations of cooperative associations be more clearly defined.

Though there was little concerted opposi-tion to such a measure a cooperative market-ing bill sponsored by Senator Capper and Congressman Volstead failed of enactment in the Sixty-sixth Congress. It was reintro-duced early in the Sixty-seventh Congress and, in light of the steadily worsening con-dition of agriculture and the growing interest in "orderly marketing," was passed over-whelmingly (295 to 49 in the House and 58 to 1 in the Senate). It became law on Febru-ary 18, 1922.

The new act went substantially beyond the authorization provided in the Clayton Act which was limited to nonstock, nonprofit as-sociations. The new definition was drawn to cover any association, corporate or otherwise, with or without capital stock, operating for the mutual benefit of its producer members and conforming to one or both of two re-quirements: (1) that no member be allowed more than one vote because of the amount of stock or membership capital owned by him, and (2) that the association not pay div-idends on stock or membership capital in ex-cess of 8 per cent. Such associations could, without losing their status under the act, deal in the products of nonmembers in an amount not exceeding the business handled for mem-bers. Jurisdiction with respect to their price-controlling activities was placed with the Sec-retary of Agriculture rather than with the Federal Trade Commission.[32]

The Intermediate Credits Act of 1923

The effort to create additional credit fa-cilities for agriculture involved much more difference of opinion. At least three ap-proaches were proposed. Senator Lenroot of Wisconsin introduced a bill calling for a

acts and others pertaining to immigration are well sum-marized in Henry Steele Commager, *Documents of American History,* 5th edition, Appleton-Century-Crofts, New York, 1949, Vol. II, pp. 315–17 and 372–74.

30. More fully discussed on pp. 191–94.
31. See pp. 194–98.

32. For a fuller discussion of the implications of the act, see E. G. Nourse, *Legal Status of Agricultural Co-operation,* Macmillan, New York, 1927, pp. 252–66. Also Lyman S. Hulbert, "Capper-Volstead Act . . . Co-op Magna Charta but no special privilege," *News for Farmer Cooperatives,* October 1948, pp. 6, 17 and 18.

separate personal credit system in each of the federal land banks, with segregated assets and liabilities, but operating under the same management and supervision as the land bank. These agencies were to make loans directly to cooperative associations whose members were producing and marketing agricultural products, including livestock.[33]

Senator Capper, with the support of Representative McFadden, chairman of the House Committee on Banking and Currency, introduced a plan to extend the powers of the federal reserve banks and to strengthen the existing country banks so as to give better service to agriculture. It also authorized the formation of private agricultural credit corporations for making loans to livestock growers. The Lenroot plan was the one favored by the agricultural organizations. In the Cabinet, Secretary Mellon favored the Capper bill, while Secretaries Wallace and Hoover preferred the Lenroot plan. The Senate passed both bills. At the same time the House Committee on Banking and Currency had been attempting to combine the major features of a number of bills, using the Capper bill as a basis. In the meantime the House had passed the Strong bill liberalizing the federal farm loan system by increasing the maximum loan authorized from $10,000 to $16,000. (In exceptional cases, with the approval of the Federal Farm Loan Board, loans might be made up to $25,000.)

A new bill that was virtually an amalgamation of the Capper, Lenroot and Strong bills was reported out by the House Committee on February 24. It was passed, and was approved on March 4, 1923. The act thus placed on the books was the second major step in creating a comprehensive, federally sponsored credit system for American agriculture.[34] It was regarded as one of the major achievements of the Farm Bloc. Actually, it was much less significant than its backers assumed it to be.

Farmers and farm organization leaders were strongly of the opinion that contraction of credit had been a major factor in the price debacle of 1920 and 1921 and that this could have been eased substantially by different policies on the part of the Federal Reserve Board and by a credit system in which loans to farmers would be for terms corresponding to the length of the production process.[35] In part they were right though their interpretation of the situation placed more emphasis on credit policies and credit mechanisms than seems warranted when the situation is viewed in retrospect. More important elements in the weakened position of agriculture were the 16 per cent decline in physical volume and 44 per cent decline in value of United States exports between 1919 and 1921,[36] the cessation of purchases by the government of the United States and the rapid liquidation of

33. Considerable interest in the possibilities of state action in the farm mortgage field had also developed, particularly in the West North Central states. South Dakota had established a state loan system in 1917, partly as a means of diverting support from the Non-partisan League. This agency was borrowing heavily on state credit and making many loans in the first postwar years, but ran into serious difficulties in the early 1920's as a result of bad management, malfeasance and too high a limit on loans (70 per cent of appraised value as compared to 50 per cent in the federal land bank system and in most private lending agencies). The Bank of North Dakota was likewise making farm mortgage loans, and, in 1923, Minnesota set up a Rural Credit Bureau along lines similar to those used in the South Dakota Rural Credits System. All three of these agencies experienced heavy losses and fell into disfavor within a few years after their initiation.

34. The act established a system of twelve intermediate credit banks associated with the twelve federal land banks and under the supervision of the Federal Farm Loan Board. The new banks were capitalized directly by the federal government, and were authorized to sell debentures, to make loans to cooperative associations, and to discount agricultural paper submitted by agricultural finance corporations, livestock loan companies and local banks. Such paper might be discounted for nine months, or, if based on maturing livestock, for periods up to three years. (In practice these loans were made for shorter periods, but with privilege of renewal.) Provision was also made for the organization of "national" agricultural credit corporations with minimum capital, privately supplied, of $250,000. The act also authorized more liberal credit terms for agriculture through the Federal Reserve system, and extended the life of the War Finance Corporation to February 29, 1924.

35. In the congressional discussions of this problem violent attacks were made on the Federal Reserve Board and its policies, particularly by the southern members of Congress. As an illustration of this point of view, see George W. Armstrong, *The Crime of '20: The Unpardonable Sin of "Frenzied Finance,"* Press of the Venney Company, Dallas, 1922; also Arthur S. Link, "The Federal Reserve Policy and the Agricultural Depression of 1920–21," *Agricultural History*, July 1946, pp. 166–75.

36. Based on data from *Statistical Abstract, 1929,* p. 464.

stocks held by the government. Once the break had started, the overextended position of the local banks, and their efforts to protect themselves, aggravated the situation and contributed to forced and panic selling of farm commodities.

The Role of Credit Overemphasized

In light of knowledge then available in banking and government circles, and the legal requirements of the Federal Reserve Act, the logical way to restore the banking system to health was to raise discount rates and encourage credit contraction. The gold reserves of the federal reserve banks as a whole had fallen nearly to the 40 per cent minimum required by law, and in some districts were well below it. Thus the banks were under both legal and moral pressure to reduce loans and put themselves in a sounder position.

Even so, reserve bank pressure on member banks was eased somewhat in 1921. The raising of rediscount rates and contraction of credit contributed to a chain of events already taking shape which reacted with particular severity on farmer borrowers.[37] Their borrowings were normally for rather long periods, whereas, in the customary types of commercial and industrial loans, for which the reserve system was primarily designed, borrowings were usually for short terms and geared to a rapid turnover.

But the trouble was not merely in the length of loan. More important was the fact that the disastrous drop in prices reduced farmers' incomes to such an extent that they were little more likely to be able to pay after

a longer period than at the time the note was due. Certainly the poor prospect for repayment was a strong factor in the reluctance of banks to make new loans, and this difficulty was not to be overcome merely by making it legally possible for them to lend for longer terms. Many farmers were to find their way out only by converting short-term obligations into long-term, land mortgage form. Others, who were already mortgaged too heavily, had to give up their farms and start again.

The new Intermediate Credit Act was intended also to make possible more orderly marketing of farm products. It was felt that if farmers had been able to borrow against their crops in storage the slump in prices could have been ameliorated or prevented. This view, though widely held, had little to support it.[38] The artificial, war-supported demand here and abroad had largely disappeared, especially that part of it which resulted from deficit financing on the part of the United States government. Under these conditions the mere ability to hold crops off the market for a longer period was not likely to help prices very much. Some fundamental readjustments were needed and their nature was as yet by no means clear.

Intermediate Credit Banks Little Used

The intermediate credit banks got off to a slow start.[39] Being new and untried they followed conservative lending policies. The co-

37. This does not mean that the federal reserve banks decreased the amounts of credit supplied by them to the agricultural areas. Agricultural paper rediscounted with the federal reserve banks increased from $729,266,000 in 1919 to $1,980,063,000 in 1920. See Link, "Federal Reserve Policy," p. 172.

That is not the whole story, however. The increase of reserve bank credit based on agricultural paper reflects the pressure on the banks in the rural areas. Faced with declining demand deposits and slow collections on their outstanding notes, they turned to the reserve banks for additional funds, while, at the same time,· they made every effort to bring about a reduction in the loans due them from farmers. Thus, while the reserve banks were increasing their lendings, the total loans of all national banks declined from $13,544 million in 1920 to $11,466 million in 1921. *Statistical Abstract, 1929*, p. 269.

38. In the fall of 1920, various organizations of farmers in Kansas, Oklahoma, Nebraska and the northwestern states advised farmers to hold their wheat for a price of $3.00 per bushel. The National Farmers Union, at its Kansas City convention in November of that year, went on record officially in support of this idea, and, in addition, recommended that if prices were not restored to "profit-making" levels, farmers devise steps to curtail future production. See *Wallaces' Farmer*, issue of November 5, 1920, pp. 2559 and 2566 and the issue of November 26, 1920, p. 2690. Many farmers, particularly in Kansas and Nebraska, undertook to carry out this recommendation, and, as a result, lost heavily when prices continued downward instead of recovering as was expected.

39. As late as the end of 1926, the twelve banks combined had only $53 million in direct loans outstanding and $40 million in rediscounts. They had called only $35 million of the $60 million capital authorized. *Tenth Annual Report of the Federal Farm Loan Board, 1927*, p. 26.

perative associations, which were supposed to be among their principal borrowers, found their procedures slow and cumbersome and did not use them extensively, especially since credit came to be more available through private banking channels. More important was the fact that the intermediate credit banks lacked a connecting link with the farmer for making production loans. They could not lend directly to farmers. Loans, except those to cooperative marketing associations, had to be made in the first instance through some local agency, such as a finance corporation, a livestock loan company or a bank. The farmers did not have finance corporations, nor the money to form them, and the prospects for profits were not such as to encourage private capital to enter this field.

The country banks showed little interest in rediscounting with the federal intermediate credit banks, where their profit margins were limited to 1½ per cent, whereas they could use their normal agencies, the federal reserve banks, without such limitation. As a result, the lending operations of the intermediate credit banks in their earlier years were largely limited to livestock loan companies, some few cooperative marketing associations and small finance corporations set up by banks as a means of getting rid of some of their frozen assets. The additional credit machinery set up by the new act could not, therefore, provide any fundamental solution to the farmer's problem. Some progress had been made, however, in building a more comprehensive credit system for agriculture. This was desirable as part of a long-term agricultural program, but of little significance as an emergency measure.

Federal Aid for Highway Construction

The experimental appropriation in 1912 for federal aid in road construction and the Federal-Aid Act of 1916 had opened the way for an expanding program of state-federal highway construction.[40] The Act of 1916 had pro-

vided $5 million for the year 1917, $10 million in 1918, $15 million in 1919, $20 million in 1920 and $25 million in 1921. These funds were to be apportioned by the Secretary of Agriculture as follows: one third in the ratio which the area of each state bears to the total area of all the states, one third in the ratio which the population of each state bears to the total population of all the states, and one third in the ratio which the mileage of rural delivery routes and star routes in each state bears to the total mileage of such routes in all the states.

By an amendment approved on February 28, 1919, the provisions of the act were broadened and certain restrictions were removed, thus making the program more acceptable to the states. The farm groups were favorable to federal aid for highways, but criticized the tendency to spend the major portion of the funds on through, trunk highways of major interest to tourists, as against inadequate provision for farm-to-market roads. As a new and larger appropriation for federal highway aid began to take shape in 1921 the farm organizations, spearheaded by the Farm Bureau, demanded specific provision for farm-to-market roads.[41] The Act of 1921, as passed, took account of this demand. It required that federal-aid highways be divided into two classes — primary or interstate roads and secondary or intercounty highways. Not more

40. This new approach to the touchy problem of state-federal relations in highway construction was for the federal government to make an appropriation to the state, this being contingent, however, upon establishment by the state of a technically competent highway commission satisfactory to the federal administrators of the fund, the appropriation by the state of a specified supplementary fund (in the early legislation twice the amount of the federal contribution), and construction in accordance with agreed patterns and standards of quality. This arrangement eliminated most of the stumbling blocks that had hampered federal participation in highway construction in the first decades of the nineteenth century. The portion of the cost which might be borne by the federal government was later raised to 50 per cent. This device, which came to be referred to as "dollar matching," was used not only in the construction of highways but likewise in financing agricultural extension work. Because of its use in this latter connection the whole idea of conditional federal appropriations was bitterly attacked by the Farmers Union and some other organizations.

41. The Grange had long been urging more emphasis on farm-to-market roads, but had not gained much legislative support for its position. This was in large measure due to the fact that a substantial start needed to be made on the major highway network before a practical farm-to-market program could be undertaken.

than 60 per cent of the federal aid allotted to any state might be spent on primary or inter-state highways.[42]

The Nonpartisan League

While the Farm Bureau Federation and the Farm Bloc took the spotlight in agricultural affairs during this period, and were unquestionably the most influential organizations, other groups were also seeking to better farm conditions. Some of these activities began to take shape during and even prior to the war.

The Nonpartisan League had been founded by Arthur C. Townley in 1915. Between 1915 and 1918 it swept over North Dakota and gained a following in Minnesota and South Dakota. The strength of the movement rested heavily on emotional considerations and high-pressure salesmanship. The devils to be exorcised were the terminal elevators, the flour mills and the big-city bankers.[43] This was to be accomplished by establishing state-owned mills, elevators and banks within the borders of the "producing" states.

The movement quickly drew the interest, and often the participation, of left-wing individuals from many parts of the United States. Its "socialism" did not, however, extend to farming. In a state almost wholly composed of farm people the idea was to socialize most other types of business and to run the state in the interests of the farmers.

The League soon gained virtually complete control of all political offices in North Dakota, and launched its program of state-owned banking, milling, housing and elevator operation. Because of lack of experience on the part of the administrators, and various scandals involving the handling of funds by state officials, the movement soon bogged down. Charges of disloyalty in the war period likewise injured it. Nevertheless, an entrenched group of League politicians managed to retain control of most of the state offices of North Dakota for a period of years.[44]

In Minnesota and South Dakota the movement soon receded and virtually disappeared. The aggressive membership campaigns, motivated heavily by the substantial take of the field organizers, afforded a poor foundation for continuing support. The organization lacked a well-considered philosophy, and did not have a program suited for expansion beyond a regional basis. In large part its strength lay in capitalizing on the widespread suspicion and dislike which the wheat farmer had for the milling, elevator and banking institutions of Minneapolis. Since its plan of action necessitated gaining full control of state governments in order to show tangible results, its power in any particular state was broken when it failed to achieve that goal.

42. A concise summary of these developments is given in Thomas R. Agg and John E. Brindley, *Highway Administration and Finance*, McGraw-Hill, New York, 1927, Chapter 7.

43. There were undoubted abuses in the operation of these agencies, but the criticisms heaped upon them by the League were gross distortions of the true situation.

44. The League had passed its peak of power in North Dakota by 1922, at which time it lost the governorship to an anti-League candidate. Parts of the League program remained popular, however, and the groups identified with the organization continued to exert influence in senatorial and congressional elections. But its state program in the milling, elevator, banking and housing fields ran into serious difficulties and was gradually abandoned.

Most of the studies pertaining to the League appeared at the beginning of the decade of the 1920's and hence lack perspective. Among those of principal interest are Andrew A. Bruce, *Non-Partisan League*, Macmillan, New York, 1921; Herbert E. Gaston, *The Nonpartisan League*, Harcourt, Brace and Howe, New York, 1920; and Charles Edward Russell, *The Story of the Nonpartisan League, A Chapter in American Evolution*, Harper and Brothers, New York, 1920. For a highly critical account, see also William Langer, *The Nonpartisan League, Its Birth, Activities and Leaders*, Morton County Farmers Press, Mandan, North Dakota, 1920. A relatively objective analysis is presented in Alvin S. Tostlebe, *The Bank of North Dakota: An Experiment in Agrarian Banking*, Columbia University Press, New York, 1924. For a more recent study in which the League is viewed in longer-term perspective, see Theodore Saloutos, "The Expansion and Decline of the Nonpartisan League in the Western Middle West, 1917–1921," *Agricultural History*, October 1946, pp. 235–52. Also Theodore Saloutos and John D. Hicks, *Agricultural Discontent in the Middle West, 1900–1939*, University of Wisconsin Press, Madison, 1951.

A movement that was somewhat similar, though less widely publicized, swept over Oklahoma in 1922 and resulted in the election of Jack C. Walton, the Farmer-Labor candidate, as Governor. The implementation of his program was halted at a relatively early stage by his impeachment, in November 1923. This movement is described in Gilbert C. Fite, "Oklahoma's Reconstruction League: An Experiment in Farmer-Labor Politics," *Journal of Southern History*, November 1947, pp. 535–55.

The Farmers' National War Council

There had been organized during the war
loosely federated group known as the
Farmers' National War Council. This included the American Society of Equity, the
Progressive State Granges," some of the
State Farmers Unions, the Gleaners and other
minor groups.[45] It maintained an office in
Washington staffed by George P. Hampton
of the Progressive State Grange Movement
and Benjamin C. Marsh.[46]

This group met in Washington after the
Armistice and drew up proposals for an agricultural program. Included were the advocacy of government ownership of natural
resources, the railways and the merchant marine; adoption of the Federal Trade Commission recommendations with respect to the
meat-packing industry (which also implied
considerable government ownership); the
main features of a single tax on land; and
government ownership of terminal elevators.
A sound and economic marketing system and
cheap credit for farmers also were advocated.

The name of the organization was changed
to Farmers' National Council, and Hampton
and Marsh were retained as the Washington
representatives. The Council's continued advocacy of government ownership of railroads
and its efforts to maintain cooperation with
labor organizations served to keep it sepa-
rated from the main group of more orthodox-
minded farm organizations. Its influence was
not large.

45. The Progressive State Grange Movement was
made up of the Colorado, Kentucky, Maine, Oregon,
Pennsylvania and Washington Granges that were dissatisfied with the conservative attitude of the National
Grange. It had been in existence since 1910, and had
maintained a Washington representative. After the close
of the war only the Washington State Grange continued
to give active support to the Farmers' National Council.
46. Marsh had long been identified with organizations
seeking to better the condition of underprivileged urban
groups, but had almost no background in agriculture.
He had served with the Philadelphia Society for Organizing Charity, with the Pennsylvania Society to Protect
Children from Cruelty and with the Committee on Congestion of Population in New York. His point of view
was that of the idealistic ultraliberal, and he found few
realistic points of contact with the leaders of the more
hard-boiled "practical" farm organizations.

The National Board of Farm Organizations

A more effective federation of farm
groups took shape under the leadership of
the National Farmers Union. Starting in
1917 as the Federal Board of Farm Organizations the group shortly thereafter changed
its name to National Board of Farm Organizations. Its membership consisted of the
Farmers Union, the Pennsylvania Rural
Progress Association, the Farmers' National
Congress, the National Dairy Union, the National Conference on Marketing and Farm
Credits, the National Milk Producers Federation, the Farmers Society of Equity, the
Pennsylvania State Grange, the Farmers
Equity Union and the American Society of
Equity.

The legislative program of the National
Board of Farm Organizations, though less
ambitious, was not notably different from
those of the Grange and the American Farm
Bureau Federation. This program, which was
drafted in 1918 and published in a pamphlet
entitled *Farmers Win the War,* was, however, one of the earliest statements of objectives that later came to be important items in
the general program demanded by the agricultural organizations. The program included
legislation in behalf of farmers' cooperative
marketing associations, farmer representation
on federal boards and commissions, government control of the packing industry and
government regulation of terminal grain markets.

The Board was active in legislative matters during the early 1920's, but not so much
in the spotlight as the Farm Bureau Federation with its aggressive leadership and strong
financing, or as the Farm Bloc with its strategic position in legislative matters. These
three groups tended, however, to cooperate
on major issues despite some jealousies and
bickering. Their legislative aims were similar.
Differences appeared more in the later claims
in regard to credit for accomplishments than
in the programs themselves.[47]

47. The National Board of Farm Organizations ceased
its activity in the late 1920's and its headquarters building in Washington was sold in 1931.

The Grange likewise became more active in the postwar period. It had appointed legislative committees annually from 1885 on, but had considered that the maintenance of a paid representative in Washington smacked too much of "lobbying." This policy was now changed and a Washington office was opened, in January 1919, with Dr. T. C. Atkeson in charge.[48] Atkeson's work was skillfully performed, though with less fanfare than that of the Farm Bureau Federation. The positions taken were, for the most part, relatively conservative, and created less uneasiness in legislative circles than did those of the Farm Bureau.

Criticism of the Farm Bureaus

Criticism of the Farm Bureau movement was growing, however, in the Grange and especially in the Farmers Union. Both organizations felt, with some justification, that a "Johnny-come-lately" farm organization was receiving unwarranted aid from publicly supported personnel in a way that operated to the disadvantage of the older organizations. Already, in 1921, some of the state Farmers Unions were making violent attacks on the state farm bureaus, charging them with being offshoots and protégés of "big business" and the agricultural colleges, and challenging their right to speak for the working farmers. The contention that they were dominated by big business rested on the fact that Sears, Roebuck and the railroads and the chambers of commerce had given financial and moral support to the county agent movement in its early stages.[49]

In some of the states these attacks proved seriously embarrassing to both the Farm Bureaus and the agricultural colleges. At times they took the form of so-called "petitions in boots"; that is, delegations of Union farmers descending on legislatures to oppose appropriations for the extension services, or to sabotage legislation advocated by the Farm Bureau groups.

Reasons for Attacks on Farm Bureau

The Farmers Union opposition was based in part on differences in objective, and in part on grievances growing out of the very real contribution of the county farm advisers to the success of drives for Farm Bureau membership.[50] The Union attitude was rather generally one of noncooperation not only with other farm organizations but with chambers of commerce, corporations and other urban agencies. Its program tended toward radical points of view, and, generally speaking, lacked the informational background that could have been supplied by the specialists from the agricultural colleges had not their services been so scornfully rejected.

The Farm Bureau, on the other hand, prided itself on its policy of cooperating on equal terms with urban groups. Its national officers in fact welcomed contacts in banking, railroad and industrial circles, and frequently joined them in conferences on problems of mutual interest. While this gave some ground for fear on the part of farmers that their leaders might be overpersuaded or unduly influenced by interests considered adverse to

---

48. Atkeson had long been active in Grange affairs. He was a farmer and lawyer, educated at the University of West Virginia and the University of Kentucky. He received an honorary Ph.D. from Barboursville College (W. Va.) in 1892. He had also served as a professor at the University of West Virginia and as president of Barboursville College. In addition to his other activities he edited the *West Virginia Farmer* (Charleston) from 1909 to 1915, and served as master of the West Virginia State Grange from 1896 to 1920. He was the Washington representative of the National Grange from 1919 to 1927, at which time he retired. He died in 1935.

49. As of this time the Farmers Union did not claim to represent the small farmer as against the large farmers, which it later charged were represented by the Farm Bureau Federation. Its criticism was leveled more at the supposed domination of Farm Bureau policy by business

interests inimical to those of working farmers. There is reason to think, however, that the antagonism stemmed largely from resentment over the rapid growth of a rival farm organization which the Union felt, quite justifiably, was receiving financial support and aid from public agencies supported by all the people, including members of the Union. The effort of the Union to serve as spokesman for the small farmer came, in the main, at a late date.

50. The criticism of the close tie between county farm advisers and the Farm Bureau Federations led to an extensive congressional investigation of the matter, and to threats by some congressmen that Smith-Lever funds for agricultural extension work would be discontinued. See U.S. Congress, House, *Farm Organizations,* Hearings before the Committee on Banking and Currency, 1921, especially the testimony of J. R. Howard and J. W. Coverdale on July 20, 1921, and that of C. H. Chilton on August 19.

theirs, the general attitude of the rank and file of Farm Bureau members was favorable to this policy. Certainly it tended to result in more sophisticated and better-informed handling of farmer representation than had ever existed in the past.[51] On the other hand, the inferiority complex so prevalent in the Farmers Union, with its concomitant tendency to isolation, led often to somewhat narrowly conceived policies based upon very inadequate information and technical counsel.

The Grange attitude toward the close interconnection between the Farm Bureau and the Extension Service was based more on vested interest considerations. As the oldest of the existing farm organizations, it felt itself disadvantaged and handicapped through having to compete with a new, aggressive farm organization aided substantially by publicly employed officials who were supported in part by the Grange members themselves. On major issues, the general philosophy of most of the Granges and of the farm bureaus did not differ importantly. Both advocated legislative programs that constituted no important break with tradition.[52]

51. Both the Farm Bureau and the Grange urged strongly the appointment of "farmer-minded" members on national boards and commissions. The administration took steps to meet this demand, but gave recognition almost exclusively to the Farm Bureau. E. H. Cunningham, Secretary of the Iowa Farm Bureau Federation, was appointed to the Federal Reserve Board, and its vice-president, C. W. Hunt, was made a member of the Federal Trade Commission. W. S. Hill, an ex-president of the South Dakota Farm Bureau, was appointed to the United States Shipping Board.

52. There were other similarities between the Grange and the Farm Bureau. At the local level, both fostered educational and social activities. In the local farm center meetings of the Farm Bureau, emphasis centered more on educational features, and more use was made of professional help from the extension services. The Grange relied more heavily on local talent, and, generally speaking, gave more attention to social activities.

The Grange legislative program, as of this period, included economy in government expenditures, opposition to the nationalization of key industries, consideration of the effect on agriculture when industrial controversies are settled by increasing wage rates or shortening hours and affirmation of the worker's right to work or not work as he sees fit. It also advocated legislation to encourage farm ownership and discourage absenteeism, opposed grants of water-power rights to private interests, favored control of corporations, opposed price-fixing and recommended cooperative buying on the part of its members. The legislative objectives paralleled closely those of the Farm Bureau Federation, but were more numerous, more diverse and less specific. For the full list, see National Grange of the Patrons of Husbandry, *National Legislative Recommendations, 1921* (pamphlet).

The feeling of the Grange that the Farm Bureau had fallen heir to an unfair advantage in the competitive struggle between organizations was understandable, and, in considerable measure, justified. Nevertheless, it may be doubted if either the Grange or the Farmers Union could have attained the comprehensive organization of the nation's farmers that the Farm Bureau achieved, or gained as strong a position in legislative bargaining as that brought about through the activities of the Farm Bureau Federation. The time was ripe for a new wave of farmer organization. There was a widespread feeling that agriculture was entitled to a more effective voice in national affairs, and the Farm Bureau was particularly well equipped to exploit that interest.

OTHER EFFORTS TO AID FARMERS
The Drive for Lower Freight Rates

Even before the Farm Bureau and Farm Bloc legislative program got into full swing the Federation leaders had initiated action on two other fronts. In the summer of 1920, before the price break occurred, steps had been taken looking toward organization of a nationwide system of cooperative marketing for the major agricultural products. (See pp. 194-98.) While this was still in the planning stage, the Interstate Commerce Commission acted favorably on the request of the carriers for substantial increases in freight rates, and, almost simultaneously, the prices of farm products broke disastrously. The effect of this coincidence of timing was to center attention immediately and intensively on the transportation problem rather than on longer-term programs like that of reorganizing the marketing system.

With respect to freight rates, the farmers were not, as in credit, tariff and other matters, dependent upon new legislation. There was already open to them a court of appeal, namely, the Interstate Commerce Commission. Since it had authorized, at the behest of the carriers, a heavy increase in freight charges it could presumably, if enough pressure was brought to bear, reverse that action and grant relief to the farmers who had been so adversely affected by the rate increase.

True, the Commission had acted in accordance with the terms of the Esch-Cummins Act which had had support from the more powerful farm organizations when it was passed only a few months earlier.[53] Nevertheless, the Commission had authority to modify rates both through general changes and individual adjustments. The blanket increases promulgated with a view to rehabilitating the railroads and bringing their earnings more into line with requirements were a crude device at best. Their impact was most severe on the outlying areas, which generally were also the areas heavily dependent upon export markets, and hence already hard hit by the decline in prices at the central markets.

The new pattern of rates had reversed sharply a trend that prevailed during the war period. Up to 1920 only one rather moderate increase was granted to the carriers (25 per cent in June 1918). In view of the rapid rise in prices this left freight charges relatively low, and served as a stimulus to the areas distant from terminal markets, as compared to those near at hand. The flat percentage increases granted in 1920, on the other hand, resulted in much larger additions to the cost of transport for long hauls than for short ones.[54]

This meant, especially in outlying areas, a heavy reduction in the price paid the farmer in addition to that which occurred in the terminal markets. It was especially disastrous to the areas that had already been made marginal or submarginal as a result of the general price decline. For example, the farm price of potatoes in Idaho fell from $1.51 in 1919 to $.31 in 1922, a drop of $1.20 per bushel. In Wisconsin, another important potato state but one which lies close to its market, the price fell from $1.40 to $.33 or $1.07 per bushel. Corn in Idaho dropped from $1.65 in 1919 to $.50 in 1921, a decline of $1.15, while Illinois corn fell from $1.30 to $.38, a decline of $.92.[55] In some areas the squeeze resulting from these forces brought prices at the local shipping stations so low that returns would scarcely cover freight charges alone. As a result, some products in some areas, especially the bulky, low-value crops, became virtually worthless at the farm.

The Freight Rate Hearings of 1921

The Farm Bureau Federation took the lead in seeking a downward adjustment in transportation costs. It asked the Interstate Commerce Commission for a general hearing on farm conditions and freight rates, and employed Clifford Thorne, an able and well-known rate attorney of Chicago, to organize the case and arrange for witnesses. The Commission granted the request and hearings were held before the full Commission, in Washington, during the summer of 1921.

In the huge, sweltering hearing room, farm witness after farm witness, most of them having their first experience at testifying before such a tribunal, set forth the desperate condition of agriculture, and the evil effects that would result if freight rate reductions were not granted. Such presentations in the past had mostly been made by professional rate experts and lawyers, but the Commission was now hearing, almost for the first time, a type of evidence and a kind of viewpoint that were to become more familiar to it over the succeeding years. No longer were rate controversies to be chiefly the concern of compet-

53. The Esch-Cummins Act, at the time of its passage, had been supported by most of the major farm organizations because of their desire to see the railroads returned to private control. They had not, however, taken full account of the implications of those provisions of the act which specified the principles to be used by the Interstate Commerce Commission in determining the levels of rates to be authorized.

54. The increases authorized, as of August 26, 1920, were as follows: On passenger fares and milk and cream carried in passenger trains, 20 per cent; freight rates in eastern territory (east of the Mississippi River), 40 per cent; in southern and Mountain-Pacific territory, 25 per cent; and in western territory, 35 per cent. On interregional traffic, which affected most of the longer hauls, the increase was 33⅓ per cent. Cf. D. Philip Locklin, *Railroad Regulation Since 1920*, A. W. Shaw, Chicago, 1928, p. 26. For complete text of the order see Interstate Commerce Commission *Reports*, 1921, Vol. 58, pp. 220-60, 302-03, Ex Parte 74.

55. *Agriculture Yearbook, 1923*, pp. 771, 675.

ing market centers or of large corporate shippers and the railroads. The small man had found a way to make his voice heard, and to exert an influence in a realm that formerly had been left to the professionals.

The Commission was faced with a serious dilemma. The Esch-Cummins Act had directed it to authorize rates that, for the first two years, would enable the carriers to earn between 5½ and 6 per cent on their investment.[56] They were not earning that much even at the new higher level of rates.[57] Yet the farmers were in obvious difficulties, and reductions in freight rates could give them some relief, though not as much as they thought.

The outcome was a compromise. The Commission ordered a general reduction averaging about 10 per cent, which went into effect on January 4, 1922.[58] While this saved farmers millions of dollars annually, it was by no means a solution for their major difficulties, which stemmed from other causes. Freight rate changes might make the difference between 80 cent and 90 cent wheat, but they could not make the difference between 90 cent and $2.25 wheat.

Agitation for lower freight rates continued over the following years, but the preparation of evidence and presentation of cases was gradually taken over, in the main, by the specialists of the state public utility boards, chambers of commerce and other agencies.

The Hoch-Smith Resolution

The continued agitation for lower freight rates had another result which, at the time, was considered a major victory for the farm groups. The Congress passed, in January 1925, a policy directive known as the Hoch-Smith Resolution.[59] This declared the "true policy" in rate making to be "that the conditions which at any time prevail in our several industries should be considered in so far as it is legally possible to do so, to the end that commodities may freely move."

The Commission was directed to make a comprehensive investigation of freight rates in order to remove unreasonable, unjustly discriminatory or preferential rates found to exist. The heart of the matter so far as agriculture was concerned was a section specifically directing the Commission, in view of the existing depression in agriculture

to effect with the least practicable delay such lawful changes in the rate structure of the country as will promote the freedom of movement by common carriers of the products of agriculture affected by that depression, including livestock, at the lowest possible lawful rates compatible with the maintenance of adequate transportation service.

The policies to be adopted by the Commission in carrying out the directive were far from clear. By implication at least, it assigned more weight to considerations of what the traffic would bear and less to those of cost of service. The first of these, if carried to extremes, could of course result in rates that would be confiscatory so far as the carriers were concerned. It might also create serious inequities between different classes of shippers. Furthermore, the farm groups had long opposed the principle of allowing carriers to charge "what the traffic would bear" where this meant relatively high rates. On the other

---

56. Thereafter rates were to be authorized on a basis that would give the carriers a return considered by the Commission to be "fair." The Commission was of the opinion that a return of 6 per cent was fair and reasonable, and would attract the necessary capital. This, however, was to include federal income taxes (which at that time absorbed about one-quarter of one per cent) whereas the 5½ to 6 per cent specified for the first two years was supposed to be on income after taxes. Cf. Locklin, *Railroad Regulation Since 1920*, p. 30.

57. The rate of return on investment for all roads during the early 1920's was as follows:

1921	3.07 per cent	1924	5.54 per cent
1922	3.83 per cent	1925	5.09 per cent
1923	4.66 per cent	1926	5.36 per cent

From Walker D. Hines, *War History of the American Railroads*, Yale University Press, New Haven, 1928, p. 228.

58. The western roads, at the instance of the Interstate Commerce Commission, had made reductions of 10 per cent late in 1921. The new order required all roads throughout the country, which had not made reductions of 10 per cent, to reduce their rates by that amount. *Loc. cit.* For details of the finding and order, see Interstate Commerce Commission *Reports*, 1922, 1923, Vol. 64, pp. 85–106, No. 12929; and Vol. 68, pp. 676–747, "Reduced Rates, 1922," No. 13293.

59. Public Resolution No. 46, 68th Cong., 2nd sess., 43 Stat., 801. For a good discussion of the substance, implications and significance of it, see Locklin, *Railroad Regulation Since 1920*, Chapter 5.

hand, cost of service could not be used practically as a single criterion. The practice of applying class rates, commodity rates, joint through rates and similar modifications had long been in use, and undoubtedly was in the public interest.[60] Furthermore, costs of service were not amenable to specific determination. Any attempt to arrive at them required innumerable arbitrary assumptions and selected methods of accounting.

The passage of the Hoch-Smith Resolution did, however, result in extensive investigations and hearings relative to the whole structure of agricultural rates, particularly in the West. The rate structure was heavily affected by historical factors — rate relationships that had been established in the early years of railroad operations, provisions that had been inserted at the behest of influential market centers and so on.

Under the able and high-minded leadership of Commissioner B. H. Meyer of the Interstate Commerce Commission a vast amount of information was gathered. This did not result in any large-scale, general reduction of rates. However, many minor inequities were ironed out, and some fairly substantial reductions were ordered. Probably the most important result was to lead the members of the Commission in the direction of applying more basic and objective principles in the establishment of rates. They now thought more in terms of distance scales, that is, rates related to length of haul, as against the earlier reliance on historical bases and comparisons with rates for similar hauls. There was likewise a tendency to avoid horizontal percentage increases or decreases. This practice, again revived after World War II, becomes necessary in the event of major changes in price level, but tends to cause great inequities as between areas and classes of shippers.

The heavy emphasis on railroad rate reductions did not provide the answer to the farm-

ers' problem. It brought about a thorough review of the freight rate structure, and, in the aggregate, especially in the rate reductions of 1922, saved the farmers many millions of dollars in freight payments. Nevertheless, as a basic approach to solution of the farm problem it was, like most of the legislation proposed in the early period, of second, third or fourth order of importance.[61]

The Sapiro Movement

Though the legislative program, and the efforts to better conditions through appeals to established government agencies such as the Interstate Commerce Commission, held the center of the stage these were not the only methods tried by the farm groups. As yet farm sentiment, as well as business sentiment, favored solutions that did not require direct government action and financing. Government was expected to facilitate action, but not to perform business functions itself.[62]

60. For a brief description of these types of rates see M. R. Benedict, *Freight Rates and the South Dakota Farmer*, South Dakota Agricultural Experiment Station Bulletin 269, Brookings, 1932, pp. 7–23.

61. A different approach to the railroad problem known as the Plumb Plan gained considerable support in the early part of the decade. Railroad labor had fared well during the period of centralized government control of the railroads, and would have preferred to see it continued. It was apparent, however, that the public did not want the wartime arrangement retained. A plan put forward by Glenn Edward Plumb of Chicago called for purchase of the railroads by the government, and their operation as a unit under a board of directors which would include representatives of the railroad operators, the public and the workers. The railroad unions gave support to this plan, and also the left-wing group of farm organizations which had joined forces in the Farmers' National Council. This latter group at one time received some financial support from the Plumb Plan League, an organization formed to push the plan and largely supported by railroad labor. (Cf. Christensen, *Agricultural Pressure and Government Response*, p. 11, footnote.) The spirit of the times was, however, markedly averse to socialistic approaches. The movement soon died out.

62. This view continued to be dominant in the more conservative groups through the early 1920's. As late as 1923 an attempt was made to deal with the wheat problem by improving efficiency of production, raising quality and making adjustments in output to bring production into better relation to demand. This undertaking grew out of a "National Wheat Conference" held in Chicago on June 19 and 20, 1923. It brought together some 500 farmers, millers, bakers, bankers, railroad representatives and others. The more conservative elements dominated and the conference passed a resolution setting up the Wheat Council of the United States, of which Congressman Sydney Anderson, former chairman of the Joint Commission of Agricultural Inquiry, was named chairman. (See pp. 199–201.) Its backing centered largely in the milling interests of Minneapolis and Chicago. Two reports were issued by it, *Make Wheat Growing Profitable*, Report of the Wheat

In the summer of 1920, the American Farm Bureau Federation launched an ambitious program for large-scale cooperative handling and selling of farm products. It issued a call for all farmers' cooperative associations interested in marketing grain and livestock to attend a conference held at Chicago on July 23 and 24. The seriousness of the agricultural depression then in the making had not yet become apparent. Consequently the group that met at Chicago was, in the main, concerned with long-term development of cooperative marketing rather than with emergency measures.

The Federation president, J. R. Howard, opened the meeting by introducing a young lawyer from California, Aaron Sapiro, who was at that time almost unknown in the Middle West. Sapiro had served as attorney for several of the California cooperatives, and was convinced that their practices, so far used in connection with localized, specialty crops, could be used for handling major national crops such as wheat and livestock.[63] He made a stirring address to the 400 delegates of the conference, and gave expression to a philosophy of cooperation which was new to most representatives of middle western cooperative associations. His dynamic personality and vigorous exposition won converts even against their more sober judgment, and led the conference to launch a program of cooperation that transcended anything previously undertaken in that realm.[64]

Methods Advocated by Sapiro

Sapiro stressed what he called "cooperation American style" as contrasted with the English Rochdale type, a consumers' cooperative form which had been adapted for the selling of grain, livestock and many other products throughout the Middle West. He advocated strongly centralized producer cooperatives, legally authorized to enter into binding contracts with their members, these contracts to assure delivery of the grower's product to the cooperative over a period of years. In the event of the member's failure to make delivery he was to be subject to heavy "liquidated damages" for nonperformance of contract. These contracts were then to be used as a basis for much more extensive and continuing credit than was available to the older type, loosely organized cooperatives of the Middle West.[65]

Instead of confining their activities to the local shipping point, these nationally or regionally organized cooperatives were to enter the terminal markets and take over the selling, warehousing and other functions customarily handled by the commission merchants, line elevator companies, centralized creameries and so on.[66]

Production Committee, Chicago, 1923; and *The European Situation as Affecting the Demand for Wheat*, by Alonzo E. Taylor, Chicago, 1923. This approach did not gain significant farmer backing and was soon dropped as an organized effort, though the gradual adjustment advocated by the group was, of course, continuing to work itself out through natural economic forces.

63. For a brief summary of Sapiro's earlier connection with the California Prune and Apricot Growers, Inc., see Herman Steen, *Coöperative Marketing, the Golden Rule in Agriculture*, Doubleday, Page, Garden City, 1923, Chapter 3. Steen also gives an interesting account, in Chapter 2, of the violent struggles which accompanied the efforts of the burley tobacco growers of Kentucky to bring about pooling of their product in 1906 and 1907.

64. The Sapiro speech, together with the question and answer dialogue that accompanied it, appears in a pamphlet published by the American Farm Bureau Federation, entitled *Co-operative Marketing*, Chicago, 1920. For a supplementary, and, in some respects, fuller discussion of the Sapiro point of view, see Aaron Sapiro,

Cooperative Marketing, North Carolina Agricultural Extension Service Circ. No. 110, Raleigh, 1921.

This conference, though ostensibly called to consider both grain and livestock marketing, centered its attention so exclusively on the marketing of grain that the Federation agreed to arrange a later conference at which the problems of livestock marketing would be given principal attention.

65. Few of the states had legal provisions which would permit cooperatives to operate along these lines. As the Sapiro idea gained popularity, legislature after legislature passed laws, either drawn by Sapiro or based on those drawn by him, which gave specific authorization for contract-type cooperatives, the assessment of liquidated damages, and so on. By 1926, some forty states had adopted laws embodying substantially the provisions of the so-called "Sapiro Act." See Nourse, *The Legal Status of Agricultural Cooperation*, pp. 100–14.

66. The Sapiro plan envisaged the use of numerous subsidiary corporations, usually set up under the laws of Delaware and known as "Delaware corporations." These were intended as the mechanism for raising capital and performing, on a contract basis, many of the selling, warehousing and processing functions. Assuming an assured volume of business, which was supposed to be provided through contracts between the parent organization and its farmer members, these activities could be carried on at a profit and with comparatively little risk. However, if the parent organization failed to retain the support of its members the whole structure fell apart.

By implication at least, the directing boards of the new organizations were to estimate what prices could be obtained for the quantities available, in view of the demand outlook, and to set prices which they considered appropriate for moving the crop. What he proposed was the use of what has since come to be called "administered pricing" whereas the normal procedure for major farm products consists of shipping them to large, competitive terminal markets, and accepting the prices arrived at through the interplay of supply and demand in those markets. Surpluses were not to be allowed to depress prices unduly. These would be determined, held off the domestic market, and sold at whatever price they would bring, presumably abroad.

Sapiro also stressed the necessity for highly skilled, highly paid management and legal talent, and insisted upon the necessity for the cooperative to gain control of substantially the entire crop; for practical purposes he indicated 90 per cent of it. This latter feature was essential if the organization was to have a degree of control that would make possible the monopoly-pricing technique he proposed.

U.S. Grain Growers, Inc.

The Sapiro speech aroused great enthusiasm and led directly to action by the conference. It authorized the establishment of a "Committee of Seventeen" to study and recommend a plan for a huge nationwide grain marketing cooperative. This committee worked through the winter of 1920–1921, and brought out, in the spring of 1921, a plan for a national grain marketing cooperative association to be known as U.S. Grain Growers, Inc.[67]

The plan proposed was a very ambitious one. The new organization was to include district sales offices, an export corporation, a terminal warehouse company, a finance corporation, service departments and other subsidiaries, thus supplying through one organization nearly all of the services commonly provided by several types of private agencies. The Committee's work and the resulting plan were given wide publicity, and a national ratification conference was called at Chicago, for April 6–8, 1921. This conference is said to have included official representatives from nearly every farmers' organization in the twenty-three grain states. Though the delegates were by no means unanimous in their approval of all parts of the plan, the conference accepted it and initiated steps designed to put it into effect. C. H. Gustafson, President of the Nebraska Farmers Union, was named president; J. M. Anderson of the Equity Cooperative Exchange in St. Paul, vice president; and W. G. Eckhardt, Director of the Grain Marketing Division of the Illinois Agricultural Association, treasurer. The other eighteen directors were prominent farm organization leaders relatively inexperienced in grain marketing, except George C. Jewett, who was general manager of the Northwest Wheat Growers' Association of Spokane, Washington.[68]

Internal dissension was rife in the organization almost from the beginning, and many of its undertakings were visionary and impractical. The grain exchanges did not, of course, remain aloof from a program designed to eliminate them. They fought it vigorously and with considerable success. The membership campaign bogged down, and by early

In a few cases, particularly in the tobacco cooperatives, scandals arose because of the contracting out of certain functions operated for private profit by officers of the parent association.

67. For a full description of the plan, see *Outlined Explanation of the proposed Grain Marketing Plan of the Farmers Grain Marketing Committee of Seventeen,* Chicago, March 1921.

68. Many of the officers and members of the state associations of farmers' elevators were unfriendly to the plan from the beginning. They represented altogether some four or five thousand local cooperative farmers' elevators, and would have seemed the natural leaders for such a movement if it was to be undertaken with reasonable prospect of success. Their ties, however, were with the organized grain trade at the terminal markets and they believed thoroughly in the method of terminal grain marketing that had grown up over the years.

Their opposition to the pooling feature of the new plan was sufficient to force a compromise which permitted farmer-members to make a choice between the pooling procedure and outright sale in accordance with traditional methods. This, of course, scuttled the idea of a closely controlled monopoly over supplies. The lukewarm or antagonistic attitude of many of the farmers' elevator men resulted in the selection of a board clearly inadequate, in terms of experience, to carry through such an ambitious and complicated program.

1922 it was evident that the venture was a failure.[69]

Livestock Marketing Plan Launched

As agreed in the July meeting, a conference on livestock marketing was called. Its first meeting was held at Chicago on October 8, 1920. A group known as the Committee of Fifteen was appointed and was charged with working out a comprehensive plan for a nationwide system of cooperative livestock marketing. The Committee brought out, after nearly a year of consultation, a plan for a series of producers' livestock commission associations, a National Livestock Producers Association, and for producers' stocker and feeder companies and a network of local cooperative livestock shipping associations.[70]

The livestock marketing plan was developed along lines similar to those of cooperative commission associations already in successful operation at South St. Paul and Sioux City. It bore little resemblance to the plans advocated by Sapiro, since these related chiefly to nonperishables. Livestock could not be stored. The plan therefore implied mainly more efficient handling of livestock, and a free flow to the markets in accordance with well-established practices. It was more realistic and less ambitious than the grain marketing plan. Out of it grew the National Livestock Producers Association and a number of related agencies which continued to operate through the 1920's, and were eventually absorbed by the National Livestock Marketing Association, set up in 1930 under the auspices of the Federal Farm Board.[71]

Collapse of the Sapiro Movement

In the meantime Sapiro had moved on to more fertile fields, helping to organize the cotton growers, the tobacco growers and others, and serving as attorney for the new organizations during and after their incorporation. This proved for the time being a very lucrative type of legal practice. The period of prosperity was short, however, and most of the Sapiro-type organizations were soon in difficulties.[72] They had been organized too fast, and with too much high-pressure salesmanship, and had given rise to unattainable expectations. One after another they collapsed, and the day of the highly centralized marketing organization came to an end so far as the major staple crops were concerned. It continued to be the pattern for some of the more localized specialty crops, especially in California.

Over most of the country the drift was to-

69. A year or two later, a second abortive attempt to organize a farmer-controlled national grain marketing organization was undertaken under the leadership of Gray Silver and J. W. Coverdale. This group launched, in 1924, the Grain Marketing Company, organized under the 1923 cooperative marketing law of Illinois.

It was to have one million shares of common or membership stock at $1 per share, and one million shares of preferred stock at $25 per share. It acquired options on four major grain handling firms — Armour Grain Company, Rosenbaum Brothers, Rosenbaum Grain Corporation of Chicago and Davis-Noland-Merrill Company of Kansas City. These firms owned or controlled more than 40 million bushels of elevator capacity, and agreed to continue to manage the firms for a period of five years after the new company took over. Gray Silver resigned as Washington representative of the Farm Bureau Federation to become president of the new company, and J. W. Coverdale resigned his position to become its secretary-treasurer. This ambitious plan did not achieve widespread farmer interest or support. After a year of unsuccessful operation, it passed out of existence. For a detailed description of the plan of organization, see *The Grain Marketing Company*, by Gray Silver, a pamphlet issued by the Company, Chicago, October 1924. See also Kile, *Farm Bureau Through Three Decades*, Chapter 9.

70. These plans are described in *Live Stock Marketing Plan of the Farmers' Live Stock Marketing Committee of Fifteen*, published by the Committee, Chicago, 1921.

71. The growth of the cooperative livestock marketing movement during the 1920's is well described in E. G. Nourse and J. G. Knapp, *The Cooperative Marketing of Livestock*, The Brookings Institution, Washington, 1931, Chapters 8 through 14. The merger of 1930, under Federal Farm Board auspices, together with a review of past accomplishments, is discussed in some detail in an article entitled "National Producers Merge in Larger Unit," *National Livestock Producer*, July 1930, pp. 3 and 16.

Other conferences of a similar type were called during the year, but did not attract so much attention as those mentioned above. Among them were those which led to the appointment of a Committee of Twenty-one to work out a national fruit marketing plan, a Committee of Eleven to work out a national dairy marketing plan, a Committee of Ten on vegetable marketing and a Committee of Twenty-five on wool marketing.

72. The kinds of difficulties encountered are well illustrated in the experience of the tobacco cooperatives. For a good account of these see Carl C. Taylor, "The Story and the Lesson of the Tri-State Tobacco Cooperative Association," *American Cooperation*, American Institute of Cooperation, Washington, 1933, Vol. II, pp. 489–519. A more general history of the efforts to organize the burley tobacco growers is given in Verna Elsinger, "The Burley Tobacco Growers Experiment," *ibid.*, 1928, Vol. II, pp. 499–621.

ward the federated type of organization seeking to function as an efficient selling agency rather than to gain monopoly control of the industry. The "Sapiro Movement" had virtually ended by about 1924.[73] It did, however, leave a residue in the form of new and stronger state legislation relating to farmers' cooperatives, and a more definite interest on the part of farmers in pushing cooperation beyond the local shipping point into the central markets. Farmer thinking had likewise been shifted to new ground in the matter of need for able, high-salaried management and legal personnel. The old idea that a good, honest farmer could take over and manage a complex business in which he had no experience had come to be questioned. The cooperative movement was passing out of its adolescent stage into maturity.[74] Much of the general philosophy of the Sapiro movement was to appear again in the activities undertaken by the Federal Farm Board in 1929 and 1930.[75]

73. Sapiro had become a controversial figure both in and out of the Farm Bureau Federation. He sought to gain control of the Cooperative Marketing Department of the Federation, then headed by Walton Peteet, and in the ensuing struggle was able, in December 1923, to force the resignation of J. W. Coverdale as secretary of the Federation. At the same time, he was aiding in the creation of a rival organization, the National Council of Farmers Cooperative Marketing Associations. At the annual convention held shortly after Coverdale's resignation, the Farm Bureau Federation turned strongly against Sapiro, replaced 9 of the 12 directors, and turned the organization toward more conservative policies with respect to the fostering of cooperative marketing. Coverdale was reinstated, and Sapiro's influence declined rapidly. See Kile, *Farm Bureau Through Three Decades*, pp. 114-19.

74. One factor in this was the American Institute of Cooperation established in 1925. Here, for almost the first time, there was a planned effort to bring together practical operators and directors of cooperatives, and the economists and other specialists from the state agricultural colleges and the United States Department of Agriculture. The result was to damp down extravagant claims and expectations, and to focus attention on the business problems of the cooperatives.

The movement for a more businesslike approach to the problems of cooperatives was given further impetus by the passage of the Cooperative Marketing Act of 1926, which established, in the Bureau of Agricultural Economics, a Division of Cooperative Marketing to undertake research on problems relating to farmer cooperatives and to provide advice and other types of service to aid in their development.

75. A third attempt to launch a wheat marketing cooperative was made in 1924. This took the form of a series of state wheat pools, abandoning the idea of direct sales which had never been acceptable to Sapiro. The

Price-Fixing Proposals

While these efforts on the part of the established farm organizations and the Farm Bloc were taking shape, other and more radical proposals were being put forward. Many farmers were not content with the relatively conservative programs principally under discussion. In the northern Plains states in particular, there were demands for outright government price-fixing. Of the various mechanisms suggested for this purpose, the one most publicized was that of W. H. Lyon, an attorney of Sioux Falls, South Dakota. His somewhat naïve plan proposed merely that the government establish a price for each major farm product, and buy up any surplus not sold at that price. The reasoning back of it was that the 3.8 per cent of American farm production that was sent abroad automatically fixed the price of the 96.2 per cent sold at home. Therefore why not take this small amount off the market and establish the domestic price at a higher level?

The idea was a plausible one since the government's Wheat Corporation had been doing just that, so far as wheat was concerned — doing it, however, in a market where demand was, for all practical purposes, unlimited. Mr. Lyon, native son of a wheat and corn state, did not trouble himself greatly about what to do with cotton, tobacco, raisins, prunes or pork products, for some of which the proportion exported ran up to 50 per cent or more of the United States production. Nevertheless his plan, ably presented by him, gained support in influential circles. Representative Knutson (Minnesota), Republican whip in the House, commented:

movement was rather closely related to the political ambitions of some of its sponsors, and did not gain general farmer or farm organization support. State wheat pools were formed in a number of states, however, and operated in a small way for a number of years under the general guidance of a National Wheat Growers Advisory Committee headed by ex-Governor Frank O. Lowden of Illinois. For a stimulating defense of the Sapiro viewpoint, which by then was being sharply criticized, see Sapiro's address entitled *Cooperative Wheat Marketing*, given before the Indiana Wheat Marketing Conference at Indianapolis on December 18, 1924, published by the National Wheat Growers' Advisory Committee, Chicago.

The stabilization plan is the only scientific method and must ultimately be adopted and in my opinion within a very short time. I am for it, heart and soul, and will do everything possible to put it over.[76]

Samuel Gompers spoke favorably of it. The Sioux Falls Clearing House Banks and other country banks supported it, and the South Dakota assembly voted unanimously in favor of it.[77]

The plan was introduced in Congress on July 12, 1921 as the Christopherson bill (H.R. 7735, 67th Cong., 1st sess.). The more conservative and realistic farm organizations were quick to point out its fallacies. With no developed organization to back it the plan quickly dropped out of sight in the struggle

76. As quoted in William H. Lyon, *Stabilization of Prices of Farm Products,* Sioux Falls, South Dakota, 1921.

77. The Lyon plan is of interest as providing, somewhat inadvertently, one of the first expressions of the idea of forward pricing so strongly publicized in recent years. While most supporters of the plan, and probably Mr. Lyon himself, assumed that prices would be set on the basis of cost-of-production plus a profit, his brochure of May 1921 puts the proposition in the following language, which comes close to stating the general idea of forward pricing:

". . . Our average annual net exports of corn and oats do not exceed 60 and 125 million bushels respectively. If the surplus of any crop should prove excessive, the stabilizing commission, fairly representing both producers and consumers, appointed by the President, would probably reduce the price for the following year and increase the price of other products in which a shortage might exist and thereby induce our farmers to increase production of flax, wool, and sugar which we now so largely import, at a cost of several hundred million dollars a year. Would it not be far better to do this and export less of the fertility of our soil in the form of wheat, oats, cotton and tobacco? . . .

"The elimination of speculation and resulting fluctuation in the price of corn and grain feeds will greatly lessen the risks of stock feeders and largely stabilize the cost of meat production. The cost of living, being thus largely stabilized, will also tend to stabilize wages which will be advantageous to every line of industry. What the business and industrial world requires above all things is stability. Even if the guaranteed minimum price were fixed at less than the actual cost of production, it would still be beneficial to every line of industry as the country would know when prices had reached bottom and that conditions could not possibly become worse. . . .

"The government, therefore, would have no surplus to absorb, but the guaranty to purchase the surplus, if any, would stabilize the price of the entire crop. The national government would, of course, take charge of the disposition of the surplus of other crops and either export or carry it over as a protection against a possible shortage, or furnish it to the starving and impoverished millions in foreign lands."

Ibid., pp. [4–5].

over more considered and strongly sponsored proposals. Nevertheless, it contained the germ both of the forward-pricing plan put forward in the 1940's and of the export-dumping plans that were soon to occupy the center of the stage.

Decline of the Farm Bloc

The Farm Bloc began to disintegrate after Senator Kenyon stepped out of the chairmanship. His successor, Senator Capper, worked somewhat more closely with the administration and followed a less aggressive policy. A number of the measures which were high on the priority list of the Farm Bloc had been passed, thus removing some of the incentive for joint action. It was difficult to hold together so diverse a group, and the administration continued to oppose it as inimical to party discipline. Apparently no effort was made to organize the Bloc formally in the Sixty-eighth Congress, which took office in 1923. There continued to be, however, a bipartisan group in both House and Senate which consistently supported agricultural legislation. As time went on, Gray Silver tended to work less and less with the Farm Bloc and more with smaller groups concerned with putting through specific pieces of legislation. Furthermore, the postwar unity of the major farm organizations, engendered by the initial severity of the depression, was becoming less evident.

GOVERNMENTAL REACTION TO THE FARM PROBLEM

By the spring of 1921 it was evident that American agriculture was in serious difficulties and that the Congress and the Administration would be expected to do something about it. There was, however, little understanding of what had happened, or why, and still less of what to do about it. Even the farm organizations, though pressing for some kind of action that would afford quick relief, still were proposing in the main, types of legislation that were of long-term character rather than measures to offset acute depression. The Congress proceeded cautiously, taking the view that more information was needed before an appropriate legislative program could be undertaken.

Joint Commission of Agricultural Inquiry

As a first step in developing a farm relief program, the Congress passed, on June 7, 1921, a concurrent resolution providing for a Joint Commission of Agricultural Inquiry. The Commission was directed to determine:

1. The causes of the present condition of agriculture.
2. The cause of the difference between the prices of agricultural products paid to the producer and the ultimate cost to the consumer.
3. The comparative condition of industries other than agriculture.
4. The relation of prices of commodities other than agricultural products to such products.
5. The banking and financial resources and credits of the country, especially as affecting agricultural credits.
6. The marketing and transportation facilities of the country.[78]

The resolution required the Commission to report within 90 days after its passage. The time was subsequently extended to the first Monday in January 1922. The Senate members of the Commission were appointed on June 10 and the House members on June 15.[79] The Commission proceeded as quickly as possible to hold hearings, and accumulated a huge amount of data and testimony, much of which consisted of reiteration of the desperate condition of agriculture but did little to indicate clearly things that might be done to improve the situation.

The Commission's voluminous but colorless analysis of the situation, though essentially correct, was far from satisfying to farm leaders demanding quick and sensational action, and to congressional leaders needing to make a show of activity in behalf of the farmers. The report was submitted in October 1921, in four parts — *The Agricultural Crisis and Its Causes; Credit; Transportation;* and *Marketing and Distribution*.[80] Its principal recommendations were the following:

1. That the federal government authorize more specifically cooperative combinations of farmers for marketing, grading, sorting, processing and distributing their products.
2. That provision be made, through the existing banking system, for credit to farmers for periods of six months to three years so as to correspond more closely to the periods of turnover in agricultural production and marketing.
3. That improvements be made in the provisions for federally licensed warehouses, and that the states be encouraged to pass uniform legislation regulating the liability and practices of warehousemen operating under state license.
4. That there be an immediate reduction in the freight rates on agricultural products.
5. That the collection of statistics by the Department of Agriculture be expanded.
6. That provision be made for agricultural attachés in the principal foreign countries producing and consuming agricultural products.
7. That trade associations, under state and federal sanction, develop more accurate, uniform and practical grades for agricultural products.
8. That adequate appropriations be made for better record keeping on the costs of production of farm products.
9. That an extended and coordinated program of research through state and national departments of agriculture and the agricultural colleges be undertaken with a view to reducing the hazards of weather conditions, plant and animal diseases and insect pests.
10. That more adequate wholesale terminal facilities be provided, especially for perishables.
11. That the roads from farms to markets be improved, and that joint facilities for con-

78. U.S. Congress, Joint Commission of Agricultural Inquiry, *The Agricultural Crisis and Its Causes,* Part I of the *Report of the Joint Commission of Agricultural Inquiry,* H.Rep. 408, 67th Cong., 1st sess., 1921, p. 9, quoting from Senate Concurrent Resolution No. 4.

79. Congressman Sydney Anderson of Minnesota was named chairman. The other House members were Ogden Mills of New York, Frank Funk of Illinois, Hatton Sumners of Texas and Peter Ten Eyck of New York. The Senate members were Lenroot of Wisconsin, Capper of Kansas, McNary of Oregon, Robinson of Arkansas and Harrison of Mississippi. It was a notably strong group, nearly all of its members later coming into greater prominence.

80. Though the full report was submitted in October 1921, the last three parts were not in print until early in 1922.

necting rail, water and motor transport be provided at the terminal markets.

12. That greater effort be directed to the improvement of community life.

It was further stated that

The renewal of conditions of confidence, and industrial as well as agricultural prosperity is dependent upon a readjustment of prices for commodities to the end that prices received for commodities will represent a fair division of the economic rewards of industry, risk, management, and investment of capital. These results can not be brought about by legislative formulas but must be the result for the most part of the interplay of economic forces. The Government and the States within their respective spheres should do by legislative and administrative action what it may be possible to do, based upon sound principles to facilitate this readjustment.[81]

Here, as in the major farm organizations, the emphasis was on the elements of a conservative long-term program of agricultural legislation, not upon measures to meet a major depression in agriculture or to deal with emergency situations. The Commission, in fact, missed the point of the whole inquiry. It interpreted the difficulties in terms of business cycle phenomena rather than of worldwide disorganization resulting from war. It remarked that "Business cycles of alternating great prosperity and succeeding great depression, such as that from which we are now emerging, have occurred in a more or less regular way among all modern highly organized nations."[82] It had not yet recognized that this was no ordinary business cycle nor that farmers would have little patience with proposals to let the situation be worked out through the slow and painful process of uncontrolled economic forces. The legislative proposals made were, however, in keeping with those of the major farm organizations, possibly in the main merely a reflection of the views then held by the leaders of those groups.

National Agricultural Conference of 1922

While the Congress was investigating agricultural conditions by way of the Joint Commission, the Administration was likewise seeking to convince farmers that it was aware of their problems and anxious to do something about them. Its effort, suggested by Secretary Wallace, took the form of a National Agricultural Conference called in January 1922. Representatives of the principal farm organizations, the livestock associations, the state agricultural colleges, the farm papers, the fertilizer and implement industries, the millers and the meat packers were invited to come to Washington for the purpose of discussing ways and means of alleviating the distress in agriculture. The Conference was in part an effort on the part of Wallace to induce the President to take a more favorable view of the aspirations of the farmers, and in part a countermove to offset the growing influence and power of the Farm Bloc.[83]

As in most conferences of its type, the recommendations were largely, if unobtrusively, guided by representatives of the Administration. Such a diverse group is seldom equipped with leadership, preparatory spadework, cohesiveness and unity of purpose to produce a significant program. The Conference recommended repeal of the "guarantee clause" of the Esch-Cummins Transportation Act, development of the Great Lakes-St. Lawrence Waterway and further federal aid in the construction of farm-to-market roads. It endorsed the pending legislation authorizing joint action by farmers through cooperative marketing associations and recommended standardization of containers, further regulation of federally licensed warehouses and the provision of credit based upon warehouse receipts. It also endorsed certain agricultural tariffs and recommended establishment of a

81. *Report of the Joint Commission of Agricultural Inquiry,* Part I, p. 11. For full summary of the Commission's findings see *ibid.,* pp. 9–25.
82. *Ibid.,* p. 11.

83. In opening the Conference, President Harding remarked that the problems of agriculture were of national importance and therefore not the concern of either a class or a section, and added, extemporaneously, "or a bloc." *New York Times,* January 24, 1922, as cited by Christensen, *Agricultural Pressure and Government Response,* p. 58, footnote. This interpolation does not appear in the printed proceedings of the conference.

tariff adjustment board, together with provision for flexible tariffs in some cases.[84]

The Conference was relatively inconclusive and did not have important influence. As is usual in such cases, it served in part to build administration fences through the lift given the egos of key leaders by being called into conference by the President of the United States. But stronger measures were needed to ease pressure from the Farm Bloc. As a means to that end, Senator Kenyon was appointed to a federal judgeship, in February 1922, thus taking from the Bloc its most effective leader. Senator Capper succeeded Kenyon as chairman, and the Bloc continued to have a powerful influence in Congress. From this time on, however, it tended to become less widely discussed and less closely knit.

The Return to Higher Levels of Tariff

The protectionist groups had long been uneasy about the lower tariffs provided in the Underwood Act of 1913.[85] Actually the conditions prevailing almost from the time of its enactment had been such as to prevent any important relationship between tariffs and the levels of international trade. The Underwood tariff had been in effect only ten months when the war began in Europe. From then on the supplying of war needs was the overriding influence in the trade between the western powers. Britain and France and the nations associated with them transferred gold, floated loans and obtained credits from the United States government, to meet their pressing need for dollar exchange, instead of depending upon normal trade arrangements. The facilities for normal trade did not exist during the war years. Shipping was scarce and subject to submarine attack, and the production resources of the European Allies were heavily involved in supplying war materials. After the Armistice, all of the belligerents were too disorganized to be able to resume usual peacetime trade practices quickly.[86]

Nevertheless, the return to power of the Republican party, and decline of the Wilson influence, cleared the way for re-establishing the traditional tariff policy of the Republicans. That it was wholly unsuited to the new creditor position of the United States in international affairs was little recognized, and scant consideration was given to the views of the few who saw more clearly the implications of this reversal in policy. An emergency tariff act was pushed through in the special session of the Sixty-seventh Congress, and was signed on June 27, 1921.[87] It provided sharp increases in the duties on wheat, corn, meat, wool and sugar.

Tariffs Could Not Solve Problem

None of these duties could possibly have much effect on domestic prices, except possibly that on sugar. All of the other commodities were in excess supply and seeking export outlets, and even sugar was entering a period of demoralized world markets which did not lend itself to effective control by so simple a device as the tariff. In the few short years between 1914 and 1921 the United States, which formerly had needed a balance of exports over imports of nearly half a billion dollars annually, to meet foreign obligations, had become the world's leading creditor nation. Some $2 billion in European-held securities issued by American corporations had been returned as payment for war materials and

---

84. For a full account of the Conference, see U.S. Congress, House, *Report of the National Agricultural Conference, January 23–27, 1922,* H.Doc. 195, 67th Cong., 2nd sess., 1922.

85. Even before Wilson's retirement, the Republican Sixty-sixth Congress passed an emergency tariff act designed to aid agriculture. This was vetoed by Wilson on March 3, 1921, his last day in office, and the House failed to override the veto.

86. United States loans, credits and gifts financed, in 1919, roughly $4 billion of United States exports out of a total of $9.5 billion. For 1920, total United States exports fell to $8.4 billion, of which only about $1.6 billion were financed by United States loans, gifts and credits. By 1921, total exports had fallen sharply, to $5.2 billion, of which only about $1.25 billion were financed by United States loans, gifts and credits. From Dun and Bradstreet, chart entitled "How U.S. Exports Have Been Financed, 1919–1947," New York, 1947.

87. The act was originally enacted for a six-months' period with a view to giving time for the passage of more permanent legislation. When it became evident that continuing legislation would not be ready at the expiration of the emergency act, that act was extended for an indefinite period.

other exports, together with more than a billion dollars in gold.[88]

In addition, the European Allies had floated about $5 billion in bonds in this country by 1917. Thereafter they borrowed heavily from the United States government. It is not clear, however, that the readjustment in foreign trade called for by this change of status would have been insurmountable had it not been for our insistence on early assumption by the debtor nations of responsibility for making payments of interest and principal on the war loans that had been made to them by the government of the United States.

Between 1896 and 1914, United States outpayments had averaged about $487 million consisting of $160 million in interest payments, $150 million in tourist expenditures and $150 million in immigrant remittances, plus certain minor items such as payments for ocean carriage in foreign vessels.[89] This permitted a substantial excess of exports over imports without creating financial strain. Now, however, the interest payment balance, if the European nations had been able to undertake such a burden, would have been changed from an outpayment of about $160 million to an inpayment of about $525 million.[90]

It is evident that if this abrupt change in international financial relations was to be surmounted without a disastrous break in the export markets, particularly for American farm products, further credits to the former European belligerents were needed, and early and effective steps to increase American imports of European goods.[91] But American business and farm sentiment had long been strongly protectionist. Farmers had been told, and many had believed, that tariffs on their products made for higher prices, and that the high American standard of living was a result of protective tariffs.[92] Labor groups likewise held tenaciously to this view. American industries were to be unable for nearly a decade to supply domestic demand at anything short of highly profitable prices, but, naturally, they wanted no undercutting in this favorable market by cheaper European manufactures. The action taken was one which could have no other effect than to slow up the essential readjustment, and its major impact was on foreign outlets for the products of American farms.

It would be nonsensical to suggest that merely refraining from the re-enactment of higher tariffs would have solved the farm problem of the early 1920's. Agriculture's position would have been difficult with or without the imposition of higher tariffs. The time had come, however, when the United States should have begun its transition from a net export trade balance to a net import balance, or a greatly enlarged volume of foreign investment, but such changes seldom occur quickly except in wartime. The new wave of protectionism merely delayed the making of a start toward realistic adjustment to the changed position of the United States in the world economy.

High Duties Retained in Act of 1922

Support for the new tariffs did not come from the Farm Bloc as such. Because of its bipartisan make-up, the Bloc obviously could not take a positive stand on an issue about which the two parties differed so sharply. Instead a tariff bloc of twenty-four Republican senators was formed, under the chairmanship of Senator Gooding of Idaho. This group had as its purpose the continuation of the high

88. See John H. Williams, "The Foreign Trade Balance of the United States Since the Armistice," *American Economic Review*, March 1921, Proceedings Supplement, pp. 22–39.

89. *Ibid.*, p. 22.

90. *Ibid.*, p. 23.

91. The United Kingdom had, in the previous century, followed a policy of exporting more than it imported, taking part of its payment in the form of increased foreign investments. This process of leaving as investments abroad part of the payment for its exports had, however, been a slow one which did not have serious repercussions. The emergence of the United States as a creditor nation occurred so suddenly that its people were totally unprepared in their thinking, as in their trade policies, for the adjustments needed in a situation that at best would have been extremely difficult.

92. In a more specific way, the dairy groups were concerned about the importation of cheap vegetable oils from the Pacific area, and the sugar producers objected to the preferential treatment allowed on sugar imported from Cuba.

duties of the emergency act in the permanent tariff then being drafted.

The revised schedule, known as the Fordney-McCumber Tariff, was finally adopted in September 1922. It provided rates that were higher than those of 1913, but not so high as in the Republican tariffs of 1883 to 1909.[93] The farm organization representatives, and even some Democratic members of the Congress, had, however, thrown away their bargaining power in their all-out support of the Emergency Act of 1921. With the Republicans overwhelmingly in the majority in Congress there was almost no restraining influence to hold rates down.

The tariff bill was held up in the Senate for more than a year, and in that body and in the conference committee, many of the rates were raised above those of the House bill. The western states had much influence in the Senate, and gave special emphasis to relatively meaningless increases in various agricultural tariffs. Wheat was put at 30 cents (25 cents in the Act of 1909) and rye at 15 cents (10 cents in 1909). Corn remained at 15 cents, beef was put at 3 cents a pound, and lamb at 4 cents, as compared to $1\frac{1}{2}$ cents in 1909. The rates on lemons, nuts and similar products were placed at near the 1909 levels, as a concession to California where protectionist sentiment was, to quote Taussig, "vehement."[94] As a further, though meaningless,

gesture to farmers, agricultural implements, including wagons, were put on the free list. These, however, had long been produced and sold more cheaply in the United States than elsewhere. Hence there was little reason to import them even without a tariff.

The rates on sugar and wool, on the other hand, were of importance both to producers and consumers. Here again the western influence, reflected by way of the Senate, was strong. Sugar was put at 2.206 cents per pound (Cuban sugar at 20 per cent less), and wool at 31 cents per pound of clean content. The 1909 rate on sugar had been $1\frac{1}{3}$ cents, that of 1913 — $1\frac{1}{4}$ cents. The new duty on wool provided a desirable technical change, the assessment being on the basis of clean content instead of on wool in the grease. It provided, however, a sizable increase over the 1909 rate of 12 cents in the grease, and the 15 cent rate applicable under the Act of 1921. The new schedule provided increases of 50 to 100 per cent in the duty on most types of clothing wool, as compared to the rates in the Payne-Aldrich Tariff of 1909.[95] The rate increase for "carpet wools," if used with other fibers in making low-grade clothing, was put at 12 cents per pound, thus making its use for such purpose prohibitively expensive.

High Duties on Manufactured Goods

As usual the concessions to the wool growers were much increased when it came to the manufacturers. Raw wool took a rate of 31 cents, but that same wool, if imported in the form of cloth, carried a compensating duty of 37 to 45 cents on the wool content, plus an ad valorem duty of 50 per cent. With regard to textiles as a whole, however, rates were left at about the levels of 1897 and 1909. They were sufficient in the main to make importation impractical.

Chinaware was raised to unprecedented levels, 60 per cent if white and 70 per cent if decorated. Cheap types of jewelry were put

93. There is no wholly satisfactory way of computing the average level of tariff rates, though this has often been attempted. It is clear that a simple average of all rates will yield a different result from one which is weighted in accordance with the amounts of the various products imported. Still other results would be obtained if account were taken of products not traded in because of prohibitively high tariffs. The level of prices likewise affects the percentage figures. Nevertheless, some very rough conclusions are possible. Allen T. Treadway of Massachusetts, an avowed protectionist, writing in May 1935, estimated the tariff level of the Act of 1913 at 27 per cent, that of 1922 at 38.5 per cent, and that of 1909 at 40.7 per cent. "History of the U.S. Tariff," Part III, *National Republic*, May 1935, p. 21. Comparable figures for other tariffs of recent decades, as computed by Treadway, are as follows: 1883 — 45 per cent; 1890 — 49 per cent; 1894 — 41 per cent; 1897 — 46 per cent; and 1930 (Smoot-Hawley) — 52.8 per cent. See table based on Treadway's article in American Farm Bureau Federation, *Official Letter*, December 6, 1938, p. 4.

94. F. W. Taussig, *The Tariff History of the United States*, 8th edition, G. P. Putnam's Sons, New York, 1931, p. 455. The tariffs on wheat, lemons and nuts had

some effect on prices, but, taken as a whole, the price increases brought about by the tariff were not important in relation to the agricultural problem as a whole.

95. For a detailed analysis see Taussig, *Tariff History*, p. 460.

at 80 per cent, and toys were placed at 70 per cent. Laces, window curtains and similar items were put at 60 to 90 per cent. Cotton gloves were "limited" to 75 per cent.[96] Pocket knives carried combined rates ranging from 80 to 170 per cent, while clippers, razors, guns, etc., took duties amounting in some cases to as much as 400 per cent. Cotton and hides remained free, though only after "long and acrimonious debate." Boots, shoes and leather also remained on the free list, at the insistence of the agricultural representatives. Scientific apparatus for laboratories was put at 40 per cent, and glassware for hospitals and educational institutions, formerly free, took a duty of 65 per cent.

The new act, generally speaking, not only worked against a satisfactory solution of the difficult international problem which faced the United States and its farmers, but represented a change of attitude so far as American farmers themselves were concerned. During the Taft administration the farm groups, and the progressive Republicans, had criticized sharply the rates provided in the Payne-Aldrich Tariff of 1909. The new act, with considerable farm support, pushed the rates up to levels close to those of 1909. In particular the rates were raised sharply on the very products which the European nations needed to send to the United States in order to increase their buying power, and which for the most part were in short supply and high in price in the United States. At best, however, the export market for American farm products would have been weak.[97]

96. The only previous ad valorem duty as high as the 90 per cent rate on lace was the 100 per cent duty on brandies and spirits in the Act of 1846. *Ibid.*, p. 470.

97. E. G. Nourse summarizes the situation as follows: "European production, though showing some increase under the stimulus of post-war inflation, had proved insufficient to provide the means of liquidating the import credits as they matured [after cessation of United States Government credits]; and at the same time, inflation and the failure to balance budgets had seriously disorganized the exchanges. The basis of European credit was therefore undermined and, in consequence, European merchants became but weak competitors in the markets where our agricultural products sought a profitable sale. Since, as has been shown above, these products continued to come forward in mighty volume, it was inevitable that prices should fall both fast and far." *American Agriculture and the European Market*, McGraw-Hill, New York, 1924, pp. 76–77.

The Bureau of Agricultural Economics

The United States Department of Agriculture had long collected crop and livestock data, and had established in later periods two additional agencies for economic research and service, the Office of Farm Management and Farm Economics, and the Bureau of Markets. There had been as yet no comprehensive attack on the host of economic relations affecting agriculture, and the available basic data needed by legislators and farm leaders were sketchy and inadequate as to quality. The need for more information of this kind had been painfully apparent during the war, and the intense concern with economic problems which followed the war gave strong impetus for further development of statistical work and economic research. But there were few trained workers, and much collecting of basic data still needed to be initiated.

Most of the teaching and research in the young field of agricultural economics pertained to the management of the individual farm. This was the main focus of pioneers like G. F. Warren at Cornell, Andrew Boss at Minnesota and W. F. Handschin at Illinois. Dr. Henry C. Taylor had begun the development of a more comprehensive approach at the University of Wisconsin shortly after the turn of the century, and had trained a group of outstanding graduate students during the years between 1910 and 1919. Secretary Houston, in 1919, drew Taylor into the Department of Agriculture as Chief of the Office of Farm Management and Farm Economics. There he began the development of a more general program of social science research. This was continued under Secretaries Meredith and Wallace, and in 1922 the Office of Farm Management, the Bureau of Crop and Livestock Estimates and the Bureau of Markets were combined to form the Bureau of Agricultural Economics, with Taylor as its head. He associated with him a number of his former graduate students, and rapidly advanced the new bureau to an outstanding place among the research agencies of the federal government.

The Taylor program was strongly supported by Secretary Wallace, and the data and findings coming out of the new Bureau came rapidly into use by farm leaders, legislators and others. The increasing availability of data together with the growing interest of farmers in economic problems gave a considerable stimulus to research in this field in the state experiment stations as well as in the Department at Washington. From this time on, farm organizations were to develop a more sophisticated and informed approach to economic and legislative problems, and were to seek and use the services of a rapidly growing corps of trained agricultural economists.

A New Approach to the Farm Problem

The thinking of both the farm leaders and the legislators during the early years of the depression was along traditional lines. For the most part the laws they sought and obtained were of kinds that had long been advocated by farmers' organizations. The exigencies of the depression gave them the necessary fillip to bring about their adoption. But it soon was apparent that these new laws, many of them commendable enough in themselves, would not cure the ills of agriculture in a desperate situation such as the one it then faced. More radical measures began to be talked of, and some of the reluctance to call for direct government intervention began to disappear. Agricultural production remained high, and foreign markets continued uncertain and depressed. To some it seemed logical, therefore, to seek some means of insulating the American farm markets from the depressing effects of those abroad. The prophets of a new approach were on the scene, and stepped forward with what was shortly to become widely known under the general term "Equality for Agriculture," and more specifically as the McNary-Haugen plan.

CHAPTER 10

"EQUALITY FOR AGRICULTURE"

THE NEW APPROACH to the farm problem known as the McNary-Haugen plan did not come into prominence at once. Several plans for raising the prices of farm products were put forward during the early years of the depression. Most of them broke too sharply with widely accepted views on the role of government in economic affairs, or were too sectional or too impractical to gain whole-hearted support even from the farm organizations. The prevailing sentiment both in and out of government still was conservative, and opposed to radical changes in economic organization or governmental policy.

But disillusionment was growing. Many were aware that prosperity was not to be restored merely by controlling grain exchanges and the packing industry, or by establishing new credit agencies, or even by a reduction in freight rates. It was recognized that the insatiable war demands had disappeared, and the position of American agriculture in world trade had been radically altered. Yet there was comparatively little discussion of fundamental adjustment to the new situation. Little thought was given to reducing output, or to increasing the food-buying power of America's own low-income groups, or to making possible larger imports so as to increase the buying power of still hungry foreign peoples. Instead the main emphasis was on artificial supports for a weak and wobbly foreign market.

LEGISLATIVE PROPOSALS OF THE EARLY 1920's

Various bills that looked in this direction were introduced. Among them were the Norris bill, the Christopherson bill, the Ladd-Sinclair bill, the Gooding bill and the Little bill.[1]

1. S. 1915, 67th Cong., 1st sess. (Norris); H.R. 7735,

The Norris bill[2] proposed establishing a $100 million government corporation to buy farm products in the United States for cash and sell them abroad on time. The foreign securities thus obtained were to be used as a basis for bonds to be sold to American investors. The new agency was to operate essentially in the same manner as the War Finance Corporation had done, but with the added power of being permitted to do business with foreign corporations, individuals and nations. This bill was supported by the National Board of Farm Organizations and the Farmers' National Council, and was favorably regarded by the Farm Bloc. It was set aside reluctantly, only because the Kellogg substitute amendment providing for revival of the War Finance Corporation apparently could be passed, whereas the Norris bill in its original form probably could not.[3]

The Christopherson bill, which sought to implement the Lyon plan for government price-fixing, was the subject of extensive hearings by the House Committee on Agriculture in 1922, but was not reported out until too late for consideration by the House as a whole.[4]

67th Cong., 1st sess. (Christopherson); S. 2964, 67th Cong., 2nd sess. (Ladd-Sinclair); S. 4478, 67th Cong., 4th sess. (Gooding); and H.R. 13352, 67th Cong., 4th sess. and H.R. 78, 68th Cong., 1st sess. (Little). S. 1915, the Norris bill, was reported favorably by the Senate Committee on Agriculture and Forestry in the 67th Congress. S.Rep. 192, 67th Cong., 1st sess., *Farmers' Export Financing Corporation Act, 1921*, June 30, 1921.

2. See Chapter 9, p. 183, footnote 28.

3. S. 1915 was passed, but it was the Kellogg substitute, not the original Norris bill.

4. Cf. Chapter 9, pp. 198–99 for summary of the Lyon plan. For the hearings, see U.S. Congress, House, Committee on Agriculture, *Stabilizing Prices of Farm Products*, Hearings . . . on H.R. 7735 and H.R. 9461, 67th Cong., 2nd sess., January and February 1922, Series O and four supplements, 1922. The bill was reported in H.Rep. 1672, 67th Cong., 4th sess., February 20, 1923. (Report includes text of bill.)

The Ladd-Sinclair bill directed the United States Grain Corporation to buy up sufficient quantities of certain specified commodities to make it possible for producers to sell at fixed minimum prices which were to cover production costs plus a reasonable profit. Products so purchased might be sold to domestic users at prices sufficient to cover costs to the Corporation, or to foreign buyers at such prices as the Corporation might deem advisable. An appropriation of one billion dollars was to be authorized, and the life of the Corporation was to be extended to July 1, 1927.

The Gooding bill proposed formation of a $300 million government corporation to buy wheat produced in 1923, 1924 and 1925. The corporation was to purchase the 1923 crop at a minimum price of $1.75 per bushel, for No. 1 Northern Spring, and to sell at such price as the corporation might deem best for the public welfare. It was to establish minimum prices for the crops of 1924 and 1925.[5]

The Little bill provided an appropriation of $30 million with which the Secretary of Agriculture was to buy and store wheat at a price of $1.40 to $1.50 per bushel, if the price fell below that level. When 25 million bushels had been thus stored, the Secretary of the Treasury was directed to issue additional Treasury certificates as the wheat accumulated. The Secretary of Agriculture was to sell wheat whenever the price reached $1.85 in New York and Chicago.

In the winter of 1923-1924 there was a revival of interest in the export-corporation idea previously embodied in the Norris bill, particularly on the part of the wheat states of the Northwest. This was now introduced as the Norris-Sinclair bill.[6]

Though these efforts were supported by the Farmers' National Council, they did not gain the backing of the two largest farm organi-

zations. During this period the American Farm Bureau Federation and the National Grange refrained from lending support to any of the export corporation and stabilization plans. The measures constituted, in the opinion of these organizations, a combination of price-fixing and government in business that was contrary to their basic principles. None of them, except the Norris-Sinclair bill, had any prospect of being passed by the Congress or accepted by the administration. Their significance lies in their emphasis on more direct action in regard to farm prices and more participation by government, an emphasis that was to gain much wider support in the succeeding years. These early plans were too crude, and too unworkable, to gain and hold widespread backing, even if the political climate had been more favorable for action along these lines.

The Peek-Johnson Plan

Outside the Congress a more elaborate scheme was beginning to take shape. This plan, advanced by George N. Peek and Hugh S. Johnson, both of the Moline Plow Company of Moline, Illinois, was soon to become the subject of the most bitterly fought legislative battle of the decade. Since the effort to put this law on the books was more highly organized than any previous one and occupied a larger place in congressional discussions, it is presented in some detail as a case study in pressure group techniques, and as the forerunner of national agricultural policies which were to assume larger importance in the 1930's.

The campaign for enactment of the plan illustrates, perhaps better than any other farmer movement in our history, the amount of organization and persistence required to bring about a major policy change of this kind. It also points up the futility of poorly organized, briefly pursued efforts to alter traditional attitudes. Major policy changes do not come quickly or easily. Even this effort, widely supported and ably led as it was, did not achieve its immediate objective. It did, however, bring into being a new major in-

5. The bill also called for an embargo on imports of wheat and wheat products until July 1, 1926.

6. This bill, introduced as S. 4050 and H.R. 12966 in the 4th session of the 67th Congress and as S. 1642 and H.R. 2659 in the 1st session of the 68th Congress, was substantially the same as the Norris bill mentioned above, but with more emphasis on physical handling of commodities.

uence in legislative affairs which succeeding Congresses could not ignore.

Peek and Johnson proposed privately, in the fall of 1921, a partly formulated plan for maintaining domestic prices of the export types of farm products at levels in keeping with those of nonfarm commodities, while selling the exportable surplus at world market prices. During the discussions a reporter remarked facetiously that what this plan needed was a good slogan. Seizing upon that idea Peek came up with the phrase, "Equality for Agriculture," a term that was soon to be in popular use from one end of the country to the other.

Peek was a delegate to the National Agricultural Conference of January 1922, and hoped to be able to present his plan at one of the general sessions. The program was so arranged, however, that he could not obtain a hearing. When the Conference resolved itself into committees, Peek was assigned to the subcommittee on Marketing Farm Products. In the subcommittee there was strong left-wing sentiment for straight-out, government price-fixing. This approach was led by John A. Simpson, President of the Oklahoma Farmers Union, who offered a resolution endorsing government price-fixing. Peek then offered and supported a substitute motion which was eventually carried. It read as follows:

Agriculture is necessary to the life of the Nation; and, whereas, the prices of agricultural products are far below the cost of production, so far below that relatively they are the lowest in the history of our country; therefore, it is the sense of this committee that the Congress and the President of the United States should take such steps as will immediately reestablish a fair exchange value for all farm products with that of all other commodities.[7]

7. Report of the *National Agricultural Conference,* H.Doc. 195, 67th Cong., 2nd sess., 1922, p. 171.
The above account is based on Alice M. Christensen, who drew it partly from published sources and partly from a personal conversation with Mr. Peek. See *Agricultural Pressure and Government Response in the United States: 1919–1929,* unpublished doctoral dissertation, University of California, Berkeley, 1936, Chapter 4. (Paging follows copy in Library of the Giannini Foundation, University of California, Berkeley.)

Shortly thereafter Peek and Johnson prepared, anonymously and for private circulation, a pamphlet entitled *Equality for Agriculture,* which outlined their views on the subject. The response to this pamphlet was sufficiently encouraging to lead them to bring out, later in the year and under their own names, a second edition which was widely read, and became the basis for what later came to be known as the McNary-Haugen plan. Peek and Johnson summarized the main features of their proposal as follows:

The doctrine of protection must be revised to insure agriculture equality of tariff protection and a fair exchange value with other commodities, on the domestic market, or the protective principle must perish.

It can be so revised only by some plan, in respect of surplus crops, to equalize supply with demand on the domestic market, at not to exceed fair exchange value with other commodities, to protect that value by a tariff, and to divert surplus to export and sell it at world price.[8]

Analysis Faulty, Conclusions Important

It is not important for our purpose to analyze in detail the confused, often contradictory, statements presented by the authors of the pamphlet. It was not the crude and faulty analysis by which they arrived at their conclusions, but the conclusions themselves which caught the public interest. They proposed that a certain "ample" portion of the crop be withheld, and fed into the domestic market only as required to supply the demand at fair exchange value. Amounts in excess of those required to supply the domestic demand at fair exchange value were to be sold abroad at world market prices. Whatever loss there would be as a result of selling surpluses at the lower world price "must be

8. George N. Peek and Hugh S. Johnson, *Equality for Agriculture,* 2nd edition, Moline Plow Company, Moline, Illinois, 1922, p. 3.
In brief, their supporting argument was that "Agricultural tariffs do not protect agriculture. World price fixes domestic price of every crop of which we export a surplus. Industrial tariffs can and do protect prices of articles for which crop is exchanged. The fair exchange value of the crop is thus reduced in proportion to the protection afforded industry. The protective principle is operated for the benefit of industry to the detriment of agriculture which can no longer afford to bear the burden." *Loc. cit.*

absorbed by the producers and spread evenly over the whole crop." It was held that this principle should apply since

. . . agriculture ought not to produce a surplus which cannot be sold above cost of production, and if it does so produce it must stand the loss. Every farmer who produces contributes to that loss and ought to stand his share of it. Any plan which would assess that loss against the nation would encourage increased surplus, and consequent dissipation of national wealth on foreign shores.[9]

Here then was a seemingly simple plan that would quickly right the wrongs by which the farmer was burdened. It could be carried out through the central markets without the need for dealing individually with the hundreds of thousands of farmer producers. It did not involve price-fixing, in its ordinary sense, and it seemed eminently fair. Its boldness, directness and simplicity were factors in its favor.

The central idea took hold and soon attracted much attention. For those who had been criticizing the emphasis on credit, it provided a direct and tangible approach to the price problem. For others who had opposed the cruder proposals for price-fixing and government buying, it provided a mechanism that did less violence to customary notions of the relation of government to business. Wartime legislation and the Webb-Pomerene and Edge laws, already on the books, afforded precedent for an approach along these or similar lines.

The Webb-Pomerene Act, sometimes referred to as the Webb Export Act, was passed on April 10, 1918. It exempted from the provisions of the Sherman Antitrust Act corporations set up "for the sole purpose of engaging in export trade and actually engaged solely in such export trade," provided they did not enter into conspiracies to control prices or restrain competition. The Edge Law, approved on December 24, 1919, authorized the formation of corporations to engage in international or foreign banking and related lines of business. These acts, while

not designed specifically for the purposes proposed by Peek and Johnson, did encourage formation of special corporations to foster the exportation of commodities produced in the United States, and offered them exemption from prosecution for practices not permissible in the domestic market.[10]

Growing Support for the Idea

Peek and Johnson did not attempt to lay out the details of a working plan, but centered their efforts on popularizing the general principle they had set forth. As a result of their persistent efforts in Washington, Secretary Wallace became sufficiently interested to call a conference of businessmen to hear a discussion of the plan.[11] The reaction of this group was unfavorable, but Wallace continued to think over the idea and shortly thereafter initiated a series of studies in the Bureau of Agricultural Economics with a view to testing the possibilities of the plan and devising a mechanism whereby it might be implemented.

By the fall of 1923 the results of these studies began to be available. Secretary Wallace became increasingly favorable, though he realized that it would be difficult to interest President Coolidge in so radical a departure from established procedure. Much of what he had accomplished in gaining the interest of President Harding in the problems of farmers had been lost when Coolidge succeeded to the presidency. On September 25, Wallace presented, in a Cabinet meeting, a report on the wheat situation.[12] In this he stated that he had little faith in the effectiveness of arbitrary government price-fixing with respect to any one crop, but said in conclusion that

Inasmuch as the first step looking toward increasing the domestic price requires the disposi-

9. Peek and Johnson, *Equality for Agriculture*, p. 15.

10. For full texts of the acts, see Public No. 126, 65th Cong., 2nd sess., and Public No. 106, 66th Cong., 2nd sess. (40 Stat. 516, and 41 Stat. 378).

11. Christensen, *Agricultural Pressure*, p. 81.

12. *Ibid.*, pp. 87 and 88. The report was subsequently published in pamphlet form as *The Wheat Situation, A Report to the President*, by Henry C. Wallace, Government Printing Office, Washington, 1923, and in the *Agriculture Yearbook, 1923*, pp. 95-150.

tion of the surplus over and above domestic needs, and inasmuch as the facts presented in the foregoing pages indicate that the world production of wheat will probably be overlarge for another year or so, the suggestion that the Government set up an export corporation to aid in the disposition of this surplus is worthy of the most careful consideration. Such a corporation necessarily would need rather broad powers. It would not be necessary that it should undertake to handle the entire crop, and it could probably carry on its activities in cooperation with existing private agencies. If it should be found necessary to arrange for the sale of the surplus exported at a price much lower than the domestic price, the loss so incurred would properly be distributed over the entire crop.[13]

Attention Focused on Wheat

In various speeches made during that fall, Wallace said that a plan for an agricultural export commission designed to restore farm purchasing power by withdrawing exportable surpluses from the domestic market was "receiving the very careful consideration of the Department of Agriculture." The problems of the wheat growers were the ones most in the public eye, and various factors and events served to focus attention on them. In the first place, wheat was the best-known crop. The relationships involved were more concrete and easily understood when applied to that crop than to any of the others. As a consequence, wheat was almost invariably the crop used for illustration in describing the Peek-Johnson plan.

The wheat growers were experiencing a third successive year of low prices. Returns were lower than in any year since 1913, and lower relative to the prices of nonfarm commodities than at any time since the depression years of the 1890's. Wheat acreage was being reduced, but production had remained close to the 1920 level, whereas domestic demand was falling off.[14] Interest in the wheat

problem was further high-lighted in a report made to President Coolidge by Eugene Meyer and Frank Mondell of the War Finance Corporation.[15] They had been asked by the President to make a tour of the wheat-growing states of the Northwest, and inform him in regard to conditions and sentiment in that area. They reported considerable interest in government purchase and exportation of "surplus" wheat.

Bankers and wheat growers in the Pacific Northwest, as an outgrowth of a meeting of bankers at which Meyer and Mondell were guests, organized the Export Cooperative League to press for the formation of an export corporation with government sanction. The Peek plan had already been endorsed by the Oregon Cooperative Grain Growers' Association. A Washington Export Commission League was also formed to foster legislation of this general type. This group later gave unanimous endorsement to the McNary-Haugen bill.[16]

At about the same time Secretary Wallace sent Dr. H. C. Taylor, Chief of the Bureau of Agricultural Economics, into the wheat regions to investigate conditions and report to him. Taylor also found much discussion of the problem of re-establishing prewar price ratios, and a generally favorable sentiment toward some form of export corporation as a means of making the tariff effective for agriculture.[17]

The First McNary-Haugen Bill (1924)

In the meantime, Wallace had invited Peek and Johnson to come to Washington to help in drafting legislation designed to implement their plan. They declined to take the lead in this task, suggesting that, instead, it be assigned to someone in the Department of Agriculture. A bill was eventually drawn up

13. Wallace, *Wheat Situation*, p. 74; *Agriculture Yearbook, 1923*, p. 150.
14. The European situation as of this time is well stated in an address given by Alonzo E. Taylor of the Food Research Institute, before the National Wheat Conference at Chicago, published under the title *The European Situation as Affecting the Demand for Wheat*, Wheat Council of the United States, Chicago, 1923.

15. Eugene Meyer, Jr. and Frank W. Mondell, *Report to the President on the Wheat Situation*, Government Printing Office, Washington, 1923.
16. Cf. Christensen, *Agricultural Pressure*, p. 95.
17. Taylor, like most economists, was not a proponent of high protective tariffs. He apparently felt, however, that if some action could be taken to make more evident the ineffectiveness of the tariffs on farm products a wholesome purpose would be served.

by Charles J. Brand, former Chief of the Bureau of Markets. After being worked into shape by the Senate drafting service it was introduced on January 16, 1924, by Senator McNary of Oregon and Representative Haugen of Iowa (S. 2012 and H.R. 5563). Thus was launched, in legislative form, the so-called McNary-Haugen plan, which was to be the central feature in the struggle over farm legislation during the second half of the decade.

The basic principle of all of the five McNary-Haugen bills that came under consideration through the years 1924 to 1928 was the same.[18] The proposed mechanism differed somewhat as the plan evolved. These changes, in the main, resulted from efforts to meet objections raised in Congress and in the veto messages of President Coolidge.

Main Features of the Plan

The central idea of the plan was relatively simple, but practical application of it would have been far more difficult than its proponents thought. The many kinds of crops, and the great variations in location, type and quality of products, would have made the operation more complex than it appeared in the simple formulations chiefly discussed. The proposal was that a government export corporation be set up. This was to be capitalized at $200 million. It would buy up the specified agricultural commodities on a scale sufficient to bring the domestic price up to the "ratio-price." The ratio-price was defined as the amount which would bear the same relation to the general price level as the price

18. In the long controversy over the McNary-Haugen legislation, the bill took numerous forms as a result of committee discussions, group pressures and presidential vetoes. In the account here presented, the versions are numbered consecutively by the sessions in which they were introduced, as follows:

    First   — 68th Cong., 1st sess., 1924
    Second — 68th Cong., 2nd sess., 1925
    Third — 69th Cong., 1st sess., 1926
    Fourth — 69th Cong., 2nd sess., 1927
    Fifth   — 70th Cong., 1st sess., 1928

Though modified in minor respects during each session, the major variations in form were those which occurred from session to session. Each of the bills designated as the First through the Fifth was introduced in each house, some of them more than once.

of the commodity supported had borne t the general price level in the period ju. prior to the war, a period regarded as one c normal and equitable relationships.

The prewar price of each commodity ei tering into the Bureau of Labor Statistic wholesale price index would be taken as 10 for purposes of comparison. Thus the al commodity index, so computed, would stan at 100 for the prewar period. As prices ros or fell after that period the weighted averag of their percentage changes would give th new all-commodity index for any given yea

By 1923 the all-commodity index stood a 156. This meant that prices as a whole wer 56 per cent higher than they had been in th prewar period. The prewar price of whea had been 98 cents a bushel. To be on a pa with the all-commodity index, wheat in 192 would have had to sell at 156 per cent of 9 cents or $1.53 per bushel. This would be th "ratio-price" for wheat. It would supposedl enable the farmer to exchange a given quan tity of wheat for the same quantity of othe commodities as he had been able to obtain fo that amount of wheat in the prewar years This price was, of course, the one which late (with slight modifications) came to b known as the "parity" price. The actual pric of wheat received by farmers in 1923 was 9 cents a bushel.

As a means of bringing the price of whea up to the ratio level the Corporation was t buy wheat whenever the domestic price fel below $1.53, and to sell it at that price to any domestic consumer who wished to buy. This would maintain the price, within the United States, at or very near the ratio-price figure in much the same way as the Food Administration Grain Corporation had maintained the price established by the government during the war years. The plan differed from that used by the Grain Corporation in that the price of wheat would not be a fixed amount but would increase or decrease as the general price level rose or fell. Thus if the all-commodity index rose to 170 the ratio-price of wheat would be $1.67 instead of $1.53. If it dropped to 125 the ratio-price of wheat would be $1.23. It was on this ground that the supporters of the plan contended that it was not a price-fixing scheme.

How Plan Was to Operate

To maintain prices at these levels on commodities produced in excess of domestic needs, the Corporation would have to buy more than could be sold in the domestic market. This excess would then be sold abroad at whatever price prevailed in the world markets. On the quantity exported the Corporation would take a loss of the difference between the domestic ratio-price, at which the wheat was purchased, and the world price at which it was sold. Tariffs would have to be at least equal to this difference. Otherwise wheat could be purchased outside the United States and imported at a profit.

To provide funds to offset the loss from selling wheat abroad at a lower price than that at which it was bought at home, the original bill provided what was known as the "scrip" plan. The Corporation would place on sale a special type of money referred to as scrip. Every first purchaser of wheat would be required to pay the wheat producer the full ratio-price, but in two forms of money. A specified portion, approximately the free, world-market price, would be paid in regular money. The remainder would be paid in scrip which the buyer of the grain would purchase at full face value, from the post office, the proceeds going into the Corporation treasury. The farmer could use the regular money portion in the usual ways. The scrip was presumably to be held by him until the end of the year.[19] At that time it would be redeemed by the Corporation at some fraction of its face value, the size of that fraction to be determined by the losses incurred through exporting the surplus.

The Plan as Applied to Wheat

Taking the year 1923 as an example, assume that the amount of wheat sold by farmers in the United States was 800 million bushels. For this they would have received in cash and in scrip $1.53 per bushel, or a total of $1,224 million, of which $736 million would have been in cash and $488 million (61 cents per bushel) in scrip. The price actually received by farmers in 1923 was approximately 92 cents per bushel. This presumably was the "world market" price, less freight and handling costs. It was 61 cents per bushel less than the ratio-price. Let us assume that 600 million bushels were resold in the domestic market. Two hundred million bushels would then have to be sold abroad. Since the world market would return only 92 cents per bushel on wheat sold in the United States for export, this would mean that the 200 million bushels exported would have to be sold at a loss of 61 cents on each bushel, or a total loss (ignoring administrative costs) of $122 million.

The Corporation would thus have remaining in its treasury, against the $488 million in face value of scrip issued, $366 million in cash.[20] This would enable it to redeem the scrip at the rate of 366/488 of face value, or 75 cents for each dollar of scrip issued. Thus the farmer would receive in all approximately $1.38 per bushel. Of this, 92 cents would be cash received at the time of sale. The remainder (46 cents, which is 75 per cent of the 61 cents paid in the form of scrip) would be received later in exchange for the scrip. Actually there would be administrative expenses and unavoidable losses which would further reduce the return to the farmer, perhaps by several cents per bushel. Even so, however, he would receive a price of possibly $1.34 to $1.36 as against the 92 cents he did receive for his 1923 crop.

This plan did not actually mean paying the

19. After the wheat had been bought by the first handler it would be bought and sold, in the domestic market, on the basis of the ratio-price. The handler would have invested in it, in cash, the full ratio-price, since he would have paid the farmer partly in cash and partly in scrip for which he had paid full face value in actual money.

20. It was assumed by proponents of the measure that the lower redemption value of the scrip that would result from large crops would tend to focus attention on the export surplus and cause growers to cut back on production.

farmer the full ratio-price. It merely lessened the disparity between the price received by him and the ratio-price. Furthermore, he would have to hold the scrip until after the close of the marketing year if he was to receive the full amount of its redemption value. Thus it would be in effect a bonus over and above what he would have received in an open, competitive world market.

Practical Difficulties

Opponents were quick to point out that the scrip would be of uncertain value until the redemption rate had been announced by the Corporation. Hence, in view of the fact that the scrip would be negotiable, there was every prospect that much of it would be sold to speculators by farmers too hard pressed for funds to wait for the redemption period.

It was apparent also that operations of this type in all the multitude of farm products would be impossibly complicated. Recognizing this difficulty the drafters of the bill limited its application to certain so-called "basic" agricultural commodities, namely, wheat, cotton, wool, cattle, sheep, swine and rice. It was argued that if the prices of these products were raised substantially the prices of other farm commodities would tend to move up with them, or at least would be under less competitive pressure as a result of farmers' efforts to shift out of the "basic" crops into the "nonbasic" ones.

Producers of the "nonbasic" crops and of some of those termed "basic" were dubious. They drew attention to the limitations of the plan with respect to their particular products. Growers of the "nonbasic" crops doubted the secondary effects claimed, and some, the more thoughtful of the dairymen, for example, saw in the plan a prospective increase in their feed costs without likelihood of a corresponding increase in their incomes. Wool, sheep and cattle were not heavily dependent on export markets and hence would not benefit directly. They were, in fact, likely to be affected adversely through increased costs for feed grains. The cotton growers pointed out that the large percentage of their crop exported would reduce returns to them under the plan to a level where the price increase would be of negligible importance. Furthermore, the southern cotton growers were traditionally free traders, whereas the new plan looked in the direction of building to even higher levels the American protective system.

Early Support Mainly in the Wheat States

The tendency to analyze the plan in terms of wheat gave it a plausibility and spurious simplicity that could not be carried over into analyses pertaining to most other crops. As a consequence, the scheme gained most of its early converts in the wheat regions. These, and other areas producing export products, were the ones most severely affected by the weakened foreign demand. Export leagues were formed in a number of the wheat states of the Northwest. Frank Murphy of Wheaton, Minnesota, a lawyer and large landowner, became associated with the movement, and, during the succeeding years, became one of the principal lobbyists for it. George C. Jewett, President of American Wheat Growers, Associated, a federation of state wheat growers associations centering in the Northwest, also became an early and vigorous supporter of and lobbyist for the plan.

The Corn Belt groups did not give significant backing to the movement in the early period. Individual officers of farm organizations in that area did, however, come out in support of it, among them A. Sykes, President of the National Livestock Producers Association; C. E. Hearst and C. W. Hunt, President and Secretary of the Iowa Farm Bureau Federation; and S. H. Thompson, President of the Illinois Farm Bureau Federation.

Farm Bureau Dubious

The American Farm Bureau Federation was lukewarm to the plan, and did not put itself on record in favor of it until January 1924 when its Executive Committee passed a resolution favoring "an amended McNary Haugen bill providing for an export corporation to dispose of agricultural surplus."[21] Gray Silver gave some support in the hearings, but suggested provision for eventually turning the corporation over to the cooperatives, and for an increase of 10 or 15 per cent in the ratio-price to allow for the increased indebtedness and larger interest payments of farmers, as compared with those of the pre-war period.

Silver was accused by McNary-Haugen supporters of being only halfhearted in his advocacy of the bill. It was contended that his interest was centered almost wholly on the Muscle Shoals project, and also that he tended to favor Hoover over Wallace in the then current feud between the two Secretaries. The Washington correspondent of the *Prairie Farmer* stated that even though the Federation had officially endorsed the measure, nearly every member of the executive committee doubted that it would work. *Wallaces' Farmer* also criticized the Federation sharply for failing to give more active support.[22]

The Muscle Shoals project had, by this time, become a major plank in the platform of the American Farm Bureau Federation. Proposals relating to the Muscle Shoals section of the Tennessee River had been before Congress in one form or another since the 1820's. The primary interest during the nineteenth century was in canal development, to permit navigation around the shoals. Shortly after 1900 the power possibilities of the site became a matter of interest both to private corporations and the Congress.

During World War I the government made large investments in the project as a means of producing nitrates from the air. After the close of the war, the farm groups became much interested in the continued operation of these plants as a source of cheap fertilizer, which was a prime need throughout the cotton and tobacco states and the eastern seaboard area. Gray Silver, a West Virginian and an orchardist, was particularly

responsive to these desires, whereas the farmers of the corn and wheat states, who made little use of commercial fertilizer, did not take a similarly keen interest in the Muscle Shoals project.[23]

The Norbeck-Burtness Proposal

While the individuals and groups mentioned above were focusing attention upon the McNary-Haugen plan, other individuals and groups were thinking of less radical measures. Since it was the wheat and corn areas that were most seriously affected, and that likewise had been most evidently thrown out of balance by the emphasis on wheat and pork production during the war years, it was proposed that these sections be given special aid in readjusting to the conditions facing them. This approach was particularly stressed with respect to the spring wheat region which had a notoriously unbalanced, one-crop economy.

The plan proposed was for a special grant of government credit to the farmers of that region, to aid them in shifting from their one-crop agriculture to a mixed grain and livestock economy that would provide more continuous work through the year, and would make their prosperity less dependent on the ups and downs of wheat prices and yields. Implementation of this policy was proposed in a bill introduced by Senator Peter Norbeck of South Dakota (S. 1597, 68th Cong., 1st sess., 1924) and Representative Burtness of North Dakota (H.R. 4159, also 1924), thereafter referred to as the Norbeck-Burtness bill. It proposed an appropriation of $50 million for loans to farmers of the Northwest Central states to aid them in

23. The Muscle Shoals issue was an active one throughout the period here under discussion and during Herbert Hoover's administration. It is discussed more fully in Chapter 13 in tracing the steps which led to the creation of the Tennessee Valley Authority. For a brief account of the controversy in this period, see Joseph Sirera Ransmeier, *The Tennessee Valley Authority, A Case Study in the Economics of Multiple Purpose Stream Planning*, Vanderbilt University Press, Nashville, 1942, pp. 34–53, and C. Herman Pritchett, *The Tennessee Valley Authority, A Study in Public Administration*, University of North Carolina Press, Chapel Hill, 1943, pp. 5–26.

21. *AFBF Weekly News Letter*, January 24, 1924, as quoted in Christensen, *Agricultural Pressure*, p. 98.
22. *Ibid.*, pp. 99–100.

purchasing livestock and securing equipment needed for a shift out of wheat and into diversified agriculture.

The basic idea was sound and probably workable, since it proposed to accelerate a type of adjustment that was tending to occur naturally in response to economic forces. Private lending agencies were sympathetic to such a plan, and were willing to give it both moral support and some financial aid, through the expansion of credit. It was also much more acceptable to the administration than was the McNary-Haugen plan. The Norbeck-Burtness approach received much favorable publicity, and at one time seemed to have good prospects of passage, though it was overshadowed by the more dramatic McNary-Haugen plan.

President Coolidge, faced with a growing demand for some type of farm legislation and with an election in the offing, came out in favor of the Norbeck-Burtness bill, in February 1924. In the preceding month, the Executive Committee of the American Farm Bureau Federation had likewise endorsed it, and the bill was reported favorably from the House committee on March 1, 1924. It failed of passage by five votes, Kile says, because of resentment on the part of southern congressmen over "Mr. Burtness' gratuitous slurs against Muscle Shoals a few days previously."[24]

Lacking the organized support that had by now taken shape behind the McNary-Haugen plan, and the vigorous leadership exercised by the proponents of that measure, the Norbeck-Burtness proposal quickly fell into the background, and was dropped from consideration. It had gained only sectional support, and even if broadened to a national plan, its effects were bound to be too modest and too slow to satisfy the groups that were demanding more direct and vigorous aid from the government.

The revived War Finance Corporation met, in part, the need for new credit in the spring wheat region, but was handled more

as a rescue operation than as an active promoter of change in the type of agriculture. The agriculture of the area did gradually become more diversified over the succeeding years, but not on a scale that could have any important effect on the price of wheat. Such a result could not reasonably have been expected even if the Norbeck-Burtness bill had been passed. It would, however, have been a helpful measure, not only as a means of providing credit but perhaps more importantly as a way of emphasizing the need for readjustment in the agriculture of the wheat regions.

CAMPAIGN FOR ADOPTION OF THE McNARY-HAUGEN PLAN

Meanwhile the effort to secure passage of the McNary-Haugen bill had continued unabated, but with only nominal support from the American Farm Bureau Federation, which was the most powerful of the general farm organizations. The Federation was plagued by the same difficulties that beset any national organization. Strong support of the McNary-Haugen plan might have alienated some of the southern states. These states, on the other hand, were keenly interested in gaining acceptance of the Henry Ford offer for the Muscle Shoals nitrate plant, in the hope that this would mean cheaper fertilizers for their farms. Though the farmers of the West and Middle West were not opposed to the Muscle Shoals project, they had no strong feeling in favor of it. Gray Silver undertook to get both sections to support both projects, but was not able to bring this about.

Defeat of the First McNary-Haugen Bill

The McNary-Haugen bill, formerly H.R. 5563, was introduced as H.R. 9033 on May 2, 1924.[25] It was immediately reported back

24. O. M. Kile, *The Farm Bureau Through Three Decades*, The Waverly Press, Baltimore, 1948, p. 130.

25. The Senate Committee had eliminated cotton from the list of crops designated. This action grew out of a unanimous caucus vote bv the Senate and House representatives from the cotton states. They pointed out that the ratio-price for cotton at that time would be 19 cents per pound whereas they were then getting 30 cents, and that, with 65 per cent of the cotton crop being exported, it would be impossible to fix a satisfactory ratio-price. They also contended that the plan would serve to

from the agriculture committee and referred to the Committee of the whole House. A resolution (H.Res. 317) declaring an emergency to exist in agricultural commodities was considered on May 20 and agreed to. The House then began debate on the McNary-Haugen bill. Opponents charged that the plan was "unconstitutional," "unworkable," "sectional," and that it was "price-fixing." They also contended that the plan would lead to retaliation by foreign governments. Debate continued until June 3, when a vote was taken and the bill was defeated 223 to 155. The vote was sectional with the South and the industrial East almost solidly arrayed against the bill.[26]

Regrouping for a Major Assault

Though defeated in their first battle the proponents of the McNary-Haugen plan were by no means ready to relinquish the struggle. On the contrary they took immediate and vigorous steps to broaden and strengthen their campaign.

It was evident from their experience with the first McNary-Haugen bill that they would have to gain interest and backing for it over a wider area. This they promptly set about doing with particular emphasis on the Corn Belt states. Since the national farm organizations were in some measure inhibited from espousing vigorously measures on which different regions held conflicting views, several temporary organizations designed specifically for support of this legislation were set up. Chief among these were the American Council of Agriculture, the Corn Belt Committee and the Committee of Twenty-two.

The American Council of Agriculture

The American Council of Agriculture grew out of a conference called by George C. Jewett at St. Paul on July 11 and 12, 1924. He had been elected chairman of the group working for the McNary-Haugen bill at the time of its defeat, and had announced, immediately after the vote, the determination of his group to continue the fight for legislation embodying these principles. The Council contemplated eventual inclusion of five representatives from each national farm organization and each major commodity association.

At the St. Paul meeting Peek, as the father of the movement, was elected president. Both Murphy and Jewett, who had been nominated, withdrew in his favor. The Executive Committee included prominent officers from nearly all the major farm organizations.[27] Headquarters were opened at Chicago, and plans were laid for a nationwide campaign in behalf of the McNary-Haugen idea.

One of the Council's first moves was to ask President Coolidge to direct the Secretary of Agriculture to appoint a special commission to study the basic needs of agriculture and recommend definite remedial legislation with a view to securing its enactment during the short session which was to convene in December. Peek's letter to the President, in which this request was made, included, of course, a strong plea for legislation that would establish agriculture on a par with industry and labor through extending to it the benefits of protection. He empha-

---

increase the prices of meats and other products bought by them. See Christensen, *Agricultural Pressure*, p. 106.

26. Christensen attributes the failure of the bill at this stage to the fact that the lobby supporting it had not yet become well organized, and to the general feeling that it was a narrowly sectional plan supported mainly by the wheat states of the Northwest. Because of the strong sectional opposition to the measure, national organizations like the Farm Bureau Federation could not take as definite a stand on it as those taken by Middle West state federations such as the ones in Iowa and Illinois. *Ibid.*, pp. 106–07.

27. Among them were O. E. Bradfute, President of the American Farm Bureau Federation; John G. Brown, President of the National Livestock Producers Association; William J. Brown, President of the American Wheat Growers, Associated; Charles E. Hearst, President of the Iowa Farm Bureau Federation; Charles H. Hyde, Vice President of the Oklahoma Farmers' Union; George C. Jewett, former President of the American Wheat Growers, Associated; George C. Lambert, President of the Equity Cooperative Exchange, St. Paul; John D. Miller, President of the National Cooperative Milk Producers' Federation; and Louis J. Taber, Master of the National Grange. See Christensen, *Agricultural Pressure*, p. 111, quoting the American Council of Agriculture, *Minutes of Organization Meeting*, p. 15.

sized the contention that this was an economic rather than a political question.[28]

McNary-Haugen Issue in 1924 Campaign

Efforts were made in the course of the
presidential and congressional campaigns of
1924 to obtain commitments in favor of the
McNary-Haugen plan on the part of congressional candidates, and of each of the
three major candidates for the presidency.
John W. Davis, the Democratic candidate,
pledged himself, if elected, to call a special
session of the Congress to consider the legislative needs of the country including those
of agriculture. Senator La Follette, the Progressive party candidate, promised not only
full support of such measures as the McNary-
Haugen and Norris-Sinclair bills but a long
list of other steps presumably desired by the
farmers. Among them were changes in the
legislative and administrative policies relating to the Federal Reserve system so as "to
render . . . impossible . . . a deflation policy such as was instituted in 1920 by the
Democratic administration and carried out
by the present Republican administration
throughout the country."[29]

La Follette also promised lower freight
rates, repeal of the Esch-Cummins Act, reduction of the high tariff rates of the Fordney-McCumber Act, appointment of "real"
farmers to various federal commissions and
all possible government assistance in the
transition from the speculative system of
marketing to a cooperative system of distribution for farm products.[30]

28. Christensen, *Agricultural Pressure*, pp. 111–12.
29. As quoted by Christensen, *ibid.*, pp. 112–13, from
a letter of October 18, 1924, addressed to R. A. Cowles,
Secretary of the American Council of Agriculture.
30. See Kenneth C. MacKay, *The Progressive Movement of 1924*, Columbia University Press, New York,
1947, pp. 143–48 and 270–73. La Follette was nominated as an Independent candidate, and the Progressive
party was organized later to support him. His platform
was personal, and was contained in a pamphlet published by the La Follette Headquarters at Chicago in
July 1924. For more detail see Kirk H. Porter (com-
piler), *National Party Platforms*, Macmillan, New York,
1924, pp. 516–22. In the ensuing election, La Follette
received 4,826,471 votes. MacKay estimates the source
of these votes as follows: from the Socialist party, about
one million; from the farmers of the Granger states and
the Pacific Coast, about 2.53 million; the remainder
mainly from the labor groups. *Op. cit.*, pp. 220–21.

Coolidge, characteristically cagey and definitely unfriendly to the McNary-Haugen
idea, did not reply directly. It was evident,
however, that interest in the plan had
reached proportions that might make it a significant election issue in the farm states. Late
in the campaign Coolidge signified his intention of appointing a special commission to investigate agricultural conditions and recommend legislation to Congress, presumably for
enactment during the short session.[31] The appointment of this commission was announced
on November 7, just after the election. The
chairman was former Governor Robert D.
Carey of Wyoming. Other members were
O. E. Bradfute of the Farm Bureau; Charles
S. Barrett, President of the National Farmers Union; Louis J. Taber of the Grange;
Ralph P. Merritt, President of Sun-Maid
Raisin Growers; R. W. Thatcher, Director of
the New York Experiment Station; W. C.
Coffey, Dean of the Minnesota College of
Agriculture; and Fred H. Bixby, President
of the American Livestock Association.[32]

This was obviously a political gesture of no
great significance except as a delaying action.
The problem was a complex economic one.
None of the members of the commission was
particularly well qualified to deal with it
vigorously or realistically. Of the academic
members Thatcher was a natural scientist,
Coffey an animal husbandry man, and Jardine an agronomist. It was a group that was
not likely to come out with radical proposals
that would be embarrassing to Coolidge.
Barrett, to be sure, was prone to make rash
and wild statements and to advocate radical
programs. He, however, was more than coun-
terbalanced by Bradfute and Taber, both conservative Ohioans.

The Republican leaders in Congress, glad
to have this touchy problem deferred, agreed
to postpone action until the commission
could report. This meant that the matter was

31. *New York Times*, October 24, 1924, p. 1. The
promise was given in a speech delivered before the
United States Chamber of Commerce.
32. William M. Jardine, then President of the Kansas
State College of Agriculture and shortly thereafter to
become Secretary of Agriculture, was added to the Commission at a later date.

unlikely to come under consideration in the short session which would end in March. There was also a feeling in some quarters that possibly the worst of the emergency was past. This was in some measure true, though much of the nation's agriculture was still in very depressed condition.

During the fall of 1924, the McNary-Haugen supporters suffered a setback in the death of Henry Wallace, Secretary of Agriculture. Wallace had continued up to the time of his death to show an interest in the McNary-Haugen idea. Early in 1925 his book, *Our Debt and Duty to the Farmer*,[33] was published posthumously. In it he stated (pp. 198–99):

> The first and only measure considered by Congress which seemed to offer reasonable hope of accomplishing the end desired first came up in the winter of 1923-24. It was reported favorably by the agricultural committees of the House and the Senate and defeated when it came to a vote in the House. This was the much discussed McNary-Haugen Bill, which provided for the setting up of government agencies charged with the duty, not of fixing arbitrary prices, but of re-establishing the prewar ratio between the domestic prices of crops of which we produce an exportable surplus and the domestic prices of commodities in general. . . .

Though helpful for campaign purposes, this manifestation of a friendly attitude toward the plan was no substitute for the inside support at Cabinet level which had been lost. Thereafter the administration was to be definitely and unanimously unfriendly to the McNary-Haugen approach to the farm problem.

The Second McNary-Haugen Bill (1925)

The American Council of Agriculture undertook to force action in the short session, working through the Commission if possible, but by direct approach to congressmen if necessary. Peek was selected to lead the fight, and established himself in Washington. On December 17, 1924, the Council sent to the President's Agricultural Commission a memorandum outlining its proposals together with a draft of legislation designed to implement them. Representatives of the Council also appeared before the Commission in support of their plan, and copies of the memorandum were sent to all members of Congress. The new proposals omitted both the ratio-price and scrip features, which already had come under heavy attack in business and banking circles.[34] This revised McNary-Haugen bill did not come to a vote in the second session of the Sixty-eighth Congress.[35]

President's Commission Reports

In the meantime the President's Agricultural Commission had made three reports, one on January 14, 1925, one on January 28, and one on February 2. The first related primarily to the livestock industry. It recommended extension of credits through the Federal Farm Loan Board, reduction of freight rates, readjustment of tariffs and the substitution of a system of leasing for the practice of allowing free and unrestricted grazing on the public domain.[36]

The second report dealt principally with an approach to the problem through cooperative marketing, thus setting the pattern for the administration attitude over the next eight years.[37] The Commission's plan for

34. Early in 1924 the National City Bank of New York had brought out a widely circulated pamphlet entitled *An Analysis of the McNary-Haugen Bill*. This charged that "this scheme is cumbersome, indefinite, ineffective, and excessively costly." (p. 6). It also contended that the scrip would be subject to speculative manipulation and might prove to be inflationary. Furthermore it pointed out that the price indexes of metals and metal products and of chemicals were lower than those of farm products. The *Wall Street Journal* and other conservative publications attacked the plan even more vigorously. The *Journal* referred to it as "a sour and bitter lemon for the farmer." As quoted in *The McNary-Haugen Bill, An Act to Create Equality for Agriculture With Industry Under our Protective System*, New Moline Plow Company, Moline, Illinois, March 1, 1924. See also Benjamin M. Anderson, Jr., "Artificial Prices a Menace to Economic Stability, the Farmer's Problem and the Revised McNary-Haugen Bill," *The Chase Economic Bulletin*, May 5, 1924.

35. This bill is the one usually omitted by those writers who list four instead of five McNary-Haugen bills.

36. *Report of the President's Agricultural Conference on the Emergency in the Livestock Industry*, January 14, 1925, mimeographed.

37. President's Agricultural Conference, *Report . . . on Agricultural Legislation for Submission to the 68th Congress*, January 28, 1925, mimeographed. The third

33. Century Company, New York.

dealing with the problem by means of co-operative associations was presented to the Congress as the Capper-Haugen bill. It provided for setting up a Federal Cooperative Marketing Board "to give encouragement and aid to groups interested in the formation of cooperative marketing associations, cooperative clearing-houses, and terminal marketing associations handling agricultural products."[38]

The National Council of Farmers' Cooperative Associations, of which Walton Peteet was then secretary, opposed this legislation vigorously and was instrumental in defeating it. Its opposition was based on the contention that the legislation proposed would give a government bureau too much control over the cooperatives, and that, since it permitted commercial dealers to unite with cooperatives in carrying out the operations contemplated, such dealers would to some extent be exempted from the antitrust laws in the same manner as the cooperatives were exempted.

The Council was particularly critical of a section which provided for voluntary federal registration of cooperatives if, on examination, they were found to meet certain standards. A substitute bill, introduced by Representative Dickinson of Iowa, eliminated this feature, and proposed establishment of a Division of Cooperative Marketing in the Department of Agriculture. Most of the cooperatives continued to oppose the legislation, even with the registration feature omitted.[39]

Regional Drives

Though the American Council of Agriculture's campaign in behalf of the McNary-Haugen plan was comprehensive and well organ-ized, several regional groups launched somewhat similar drives. The Farmers Union in particular had become more and more reluctant to join with other farmer organizations except on undertakings sponsored and initiated by the Union. In addition there was disagreement within the Union in regard to parts of the proposed legislation, and some disagreement among the various farm organizations as to the principles which should apply in a legislative program for the relief of agriculture.

Farmer membership in the Union had always been sectional rather than national, and was concentrated particularly in the southern Plains states. Its national directors, meeting in Kansas City in April 1925, decided to issue a call for a meeting of middle western farm organization leaders to be held at Des Moines, Iowa, on May 12. Some three hundred delegates assembled in response to the Union's invitation. While certain individuals who were active in the American Council of Agriculture and a few representatives of the Farm Bureau and the Grange were present, the dominant organizations and personalities were representative of different groups, different philosophies and different areas than those chiefly responsible for the formation of the Council. The Des Moines conference was made up for the most part of less sophisticated, more radical groups, particularly the various state Farmers Unions, the National Producers' Alliance and the Missouri Farmers' Association.[40] William Hirth, Editor of the *Missouri Farmer* and President of the Missouri Farmers' Association, was elected chairman.

Opposition to Government Aid

Disagreement on principles was evident almost from the beginning. The three organi-

report related primarily to administrative matters and was entitled *Report . . . on Administration of Federal Departments and Agencies Related to Agriculture,* February 21, 1925, mimeographed. A preliminary report was issued as S.Doc. 190, 68th Cong., 2nd sess., on January 26 (calendar day, January 28), 1925. All of the reports are summarized in the *Monthly Labor Review,* March 1925, pp. 26–30.

38. Christensen, *Agricultural Pressure,* p. 117.

39. The National Cooperative Milk Producers Federation and some other cooperatives that had opposed the Capper-Haugen bill supported the Dickinson bill. *Ibid.,* p. 118.

40. The National Producers' Alliance was a relatively small organization with headquarters in St. Paul and a scattered membership in Minnesota and the Dakotas. It had little in the way of local organization. Its basic tenet was that farmers must organize to fix prices on their products themselves, and should not rely on government action. The Missouri Farmers' Association originated in connection with campaigns to enlarge the subscriber clientele of the *Missouri Farmer.* It was dominated by William Hirth, the editor of that paper, and tended generally to follow an independent line rather than to fall in with the programs of other farm groups.

ations principally represented were in agreement on seeking some method of assuring he farmer "cost of production plus a profit," ut not on the method of achieving that oal.[41] The representatives of the National 'roducers' Alliance opposed the idea of relying on government to maintain prices, and dvocated action by farmers through their wn organizations. Other factions favored overnment action. The conference finally greed on three main planks:

1. That cost of production plus a reasonable profit is necessary to the success of any industry, and must be secured through organization of the farmers themselves to regulate and control the marketing of their products;
2. Endorsement and support of the principle of cooperative marketing, with farmers in control of the marketing machinery, including terminal facilities; and
3. Creation by Congress of an export corporation, adequately financed, and administered by the recognized organizations, to insure the farmer cost of production and a profit of not less than 5 per cent.[42]

There was little controversy over the first wo, but the third encountered determined esistance from those who objected to the endency to rely on government aid. After lebate lasting throughout the second day of he conference it was finally adopted.

The Corn Belt Committee

The conference appointed a committee made up of one representative from each of he participating organizations, with William Hirth as chairman. This came to be known as the Corn Belt Committee, though it was officially named the Grain Belt Federation of Farm Organizations.[43] A minority faction of

the committee continued to oppose governmental aid, but, at a meeting held at Des Moines in December 1925, the majority members succeeded in placing the committee on record as favoring the export corporation idea. A resolution was passed condemning what was then coming to be known as the Jardine cooperative marketing bill. It was contemptuously referred to as "a means of salvation of the farmer with information, of which the farmers have never had so much in their lives."[44]

The Corn Belt Committee did not, at this time, endorse any specific export corporation bill. It did, however, meet with the executive committee of the American Council of Agriculture, which was in session in Des Moines at the same time. At this meeting agreement was

Iowa Farm Bureau Federation, American Council of Agriculture, North Dakota Producers Alliance, Farmers' National Union of America, Equity Cooperative Exchange, Kansas Farmers Union, Iowa Farmers Union, South Dakota Farmers Union, Nebraska Farmers Union, Illinois Farmers Union, Nebraska Farm Bureau Federation, Minnesota Farm Bureau Federation, Iowa State Grange, Chicago Milk Producers' Federation, Ottumwa Dairy Marketing Association, South Dakota Producers Alliance, Iowa Cooperative Creamery Association, Farmers Elevator Association of Iowa and Minnesota Farmers Union. *Ibid.*, p. 120, footnote.

44. Cf. Christensen, *Agricultural Pressure*, pp. 120–21. The Jardine bill, still in draft form, was a proposal to establish a Division of Cooperative Marketing in the Department of Agriculture. It was in some measure an administration counterproposal to the McNary-Haugen plan, and had grown out of a series of conferences with cooperative leaders, arranged by Secretary Jardine, during the fall of 1925. Acceptance of this idea by the National Council of Farmers' Cooperative Marketing Associations signified a modification of the position taken by it in the preceding winter when it had opposed all special farm legislation.

Jardine had been appointed Secretary of Agriculture on March 4, 1925. Wallace died on October 25, 1924, and was succeeded for a brief period by Howard M. Gore of West Virginia, the Assistant Secretary in office at the time of his death. The Jardine appointment was due in considerable measure to the influence of Herbert Hoover, then Secretary of Commerce. Hoover had come to be the chief agricultural adviser of President Coolidge and intense bitterness sprang up between him and Secretary Wallace, the nominal consultant on agricultural affairs. In the early part of 1925, a national news service queried, by wire, a number of the agricultural college presidents in regard to their views on the McNary-Haugen plan. Of these, only Jardine, then President of the Kansas State College of Agriculture, came out flatly in opposition to the proposed legislation. This brought him favorably to the attention of Coolidge, Hoover and the business groups which, for the most part, were against the McNary-Haugen plan, and was an important factor in bringing about his appointment as Secretary of Agriculture.

41. This was, of course, a different principle from that underlying the McNary-Haugen plan. The latter, in its earlier form, provided for the "ratio-price" less a proportionate share of the loss on the quantity exported, and in its later form, for the world price plus the amount of the tariff. Either might be less than these farm groups regarded as cost of production plus a profit.

42. From the *Des Moines Register* of May 14, 1925, as quoted by Christensen, *Agricultural Pressure*, p. 119.

43. It included representatives of the following organizations: Missouri Farmers Association, National Producers Alliance, Farmers Educational and Cooperative Union of America, National Corn Growers Association,

reached for the appointment of a joint legis-
lative committee of twelve, with Frank
Murphy of Wheaton, Minnesota, as chairman.
The joint legislative committee, meeting in
January 1926, endorsed the Dickinson bill,
with amendments.[45] That bill was likewise
endorsed, on the following day, by the North
Central States Agricultural Conference.

The Committee of Twenty-two

The North Central States Agricultural Conference grew out of the All-Iowa Agricultural
Marketing Conference which had been sponsored by the Iowa Bankers' Association. The
purpose of the initial conference was to induce
the businessmen of the state to join with the
farm groups in considering legislation relating to marketing. With the entire congressional delegation of Iowa, and many bankers,
businessmen and state officials in attendance,
the marketing conference went on record in
favor of a farmers' export corporation, though
without specifying its precise form.

As a result of the conference, Governor
Hammill appointed an "All-Iowa Agricultural
Advisory Committee" to arrange for a similar
conference drawn from all of the eleven states
of the Corn Belt. Preliminary meetings were
held in many states in advance of the regional
meeting which assembled at Des Moines on
January 28, 1926. The conference, for which
the name North Central States Agricultural
Conference had been chosen, included some
five hundred representatives from Iowa, Nebraska, Illinois, Minnesota, Ohio, Indiana,
Missouri, Michigan, Kansas, Wisconsin and
South Dakota. It was addressed by many of
the prominent individuals identified with the
movement for agricultural legislation, includ-

ing former Governor Frank O. Lowden of
Illinois and former Secretary of Agriculture
E. T. Meredith.[46]

The conference endorsed the Dickinson bill
(H.R. 6563) providing for an export corporation and an agricultural board, and directed
Governor Hammill to appoint a Committee
of Twenty-two (two from each of the eleven
states) to press for legislation and to carry out
the other parts of the program agreed upon.[47]

At a meeting of this committee, held in
Chicago on February 15, it was agreed that
the governors of the middle western states
should be asked to go to Washington to aid
in securing the legislation desired, and also
that they should be asked, as members of a
speakers' bureau, to take the lead in their
respective states in popularizing the program
among business groups. Washington headquarters were to be opened for the Committee
of Twenty-two, the American Council of
Agriculture and the Corn Belt Committee.
There was general agreement on supporting
the principles of the Dickinson bill.[48]

With these developments the leadership in
legislative activity shifted definitely from the
Northwest, where the principal support of the
first McNary-Haugen bill had centered, to
the Corn Belt. The cotton states had not as
yet been brought into the movement, nor
had any serious effort been made to enlist
their support. This the Committee of Twenty-

---

45. This bill (H.R. 6563, 69th Cong., 1st sess.) was
introduced on January 4, 1926. It included provision for
a federal farm board, a revolving fund, the imposition
of equalization fees and export dumping. Its provisions
were substantially those of the McNary-Haugen bill
which had been defeated in the House on June 3, 1924.
The principal differences were more definite recognition
of the place of the cooperative marketing associations
in the program, and the shift of responsibility for payment of equalization fees from first handlers to processors. For the text of the bill see *Congressional Record*
for March 19, 1926, pp. 5903–5905, at which time it
was under debate in the House.

46. Meredith proposed a plan whereby the Secretaries
of Commerce, Labor and Agriculture, together with four
other members to be appointed by the President, would
constitute an "Agricultural Stabilization Commission" to
fix each year the prices of six basic agricultural commodities in advance of the planting season. Losses were
to be financed by an excise tax of one half of one per
cent of the value of the commodities, and prices would
be adjusted from year to year so as to prevent the accumulation of surpluses. Cf. Christensen, *Agricultural
Pressure*, p. 124. This was, in essence, the plan which
has in recent years come to be referred to as "forward
pricing."

47. *Ibid.*, pp. 122–24. Other decisions were that the
Corn Belt states should be organized as a unit, to press
for legislation and to undertake studies of the cost of
producing farm crops, as well as to devise ways of
marketing "farm commodities in ratio as the consumer
can assimilate them." These plans were to insure to
the producer a "fair price" and the "inalienable right
denied to him to say how, when, and to whom he will
sell at what price that will insure him some fair profit
for his labor and investment." *Ibid.*, p. 124.

48. *Ibid.*, p. 125.

two was soon to undertake, through a working agreement with the American Cotton Growers' Exchange. Arrangements were made with the American Council of Agriculture and the Corn Belt Committee to open a joint headquarters office at the Lee House in Washington. George Peek, Chester Davis, Charles E. Hearst, S. H. Thompson and Frank Murphy took the lead in establishing and managing the office in Washington.[49]

Farm Bureau Endorses Dickinson Bill

The election of Sam H. Thompson of Illinois as President of the American Farm Bureau Federation, succeeding the conservative O. E. Bradfute, brought the Federation much more definitely into the McNary-Haugen camp.[50] Thompson had been an ardent supporter of the idea almost from its inception.

The Federation's influence was also modified by a change in its Washington representative. Gray Silver resigned late in 1924, to become President of the Grain Marketing Corporation, and at the beginning of 1926 Chester Gray of Missouri, a member of the Farm Bureau executive committee, was named to take his place. Gray, a Middle Westerner, was more in step with the attitudes that were then becoming dominant in the Federation. After an extended series of conferences on the part of Thompson and Gray with various people in Washington, including Secretary Jardine, the Federation executive committee endorsed the Dickinson bill (H.R. 6563) as

most nearly in line with the sense of the resolutions adopted at the preceding annual meeting.[51]

The Third McNary-Haugen Bill (1926)

As a result of their close collaboration in the Washington headquarters, the American Council of Agriculture, the Corn Belt Committee and the Committee of Twenty-two achieved substantial unity during the early months of 1926. They also gained strong support from the American Farm Bureau Federation and other farm organizations. This did not mean, however, that farm organization resistance to their program had been overcome. The cotton and tobacco areas were still cold to the export-dumping, equalization fee and tariff features, and the National Council of Farmers' Cooperative Marketing Associations was definitely hostile. The proponents of the plan therefore initiated action on two fronts: one, an attempt to rewrite the Dickinson bill along lines that would make it more acceptable to the many groups whose support was necessary for its adoption; and two, a campaign to gain support for it in areas that were unfriendly, particularly those of the South. Basically, the Dickinson bill was an effort to combine the ideas of the leaders in the cooperative marketing movement with those of the groups supporting the principles embodied in the McNary-Haugen bill.

Cooperative Council Opposes Plan

The National Council of Farmers' Cooperative Marketing Associations had, from the first, favored reliance on the commodity cooperatives to solve the problem, as against plans for government action in the disposal of surpluses. Aaron Sapiro, a dominant figure in the Council, not only opposed the export-corporation plan but attacked vigorously even the bills proposing government aid to cooperatives. The advocates of the McNary-Haugen type of legislation therefore initiated a series of conferences with officers and representatives of the National Council. Many

49. *Ibid.*, p. 126.
50. The December 1925 annual meeting of the Federation brought a trial of strength between the conservative forces backing Bradfute and those advocating legislation establishing a government export corporation, who were backing Thompson. The session was opened with an address by President Coolidge which was taken as a bid on his part for the re-election of Bradfute. It was also interpreted as a strong intimation that Coolidge would not support legislation along the lines of the proposed export corporation. Thompson was elected on the eighth ballot by a vote of 24 to Bradfute's 19 and 1 for O'Neal of Alabama. This result was in part an outcome of a change in the Federation constitution, made in 1924, which gave the middle western states more voting strength on the basis of their larger memberships and larger payments of dues. The 1925 convention also went on record in general terms as supporting the idea of a government export corporation and a two-price plan. Cf. *ibid.*, pp. 127–28.

51. *Ibid.*, p. 129.

proposals designed to make the tariff effective for agriculture were discussed, among them the idea of a government trading corporation and compulsory cooperative pools, with, eventually, an export corporation to be controlled by growers, when enough producers had become organized in such pools.

At a meeting held in Philadelphia on July 23, 1925, the gist of these proposals was laid before the executive committee of the Council, but since no agreement was reached it was decided that the matter should be referred to the policy committee of the Council for further examination and study. In the meantime, the southern representatives had retreated somewhat from their traditional position, and indicated that their objection to bringing agriculture within the American protective system would not be insurmountable if other features of the plan proved acceptable.[52]

Walton Peteet, Secretary of the Council, had become increasingly friendly to the idea of surplus disposal through government action, but was inhibited from expressing himself officially because of the position taken by the Council. Sapiro, on the other hand, remained unalterably opposed to any legislative action whatever. At the annual meeting of the Council, in January 1926, he held the proxies of three tobacco associations with enough votes to override all of the other thirty-nine member associations. Thus he was able to block all action favorable to federal legislation. The outcome was a split in the National Council which led to its complete disintegration in the following year.[53]

In December 1925, C. O. Moser, Secretary of the American Cotton Growers' Exchange, expressed, in his report to members of the Exchange, a more friendly attitude toward surplus control legislation than that which previously characterized that organization. He stated that while the Exchange had not yet seen a plan which seemed practical, the proposals of other farm groups should be viewed tolerantly unless the Exchange had something better to offer. Peek immediately took advantage of this more friendly attitude and met with the directors of the Exchange at Memphis, Tennessee, in March 1926. When asked what specific proposals he would make for handling the cotton problem, he stated that the cotton growers should work out their own plan. This response was favorably received, and the cotton people came to take a more and more active part in the work Peek and others were carrying on in Washington.[54]

The "Committee Bill"

As a result of these intensive consultations among the farm organizations, and between them and the congressional committees and sectional groups, a bill known as the "Committee Bill" took shape. It proposed formation of a Federal Farm Advisory Council consisting of five members from each land bank district. These were to be elected by conventions of the general farm organizations and cooperatives of the districts. Authority for carrying out the program was to be vested in a Federal Farm Board, consisting of one member from each land bank district. The board member from each district was to be appointed by the President from a list of

52. During 1925 the price of cotton declined substantially, and larger carry-overs were in prospect. As a result the cotton producers were by this time showing much more interest in some form of relief legislation than they had in 1924.

53. The National Council included a considerable number of cotton and tobacco associations formed during the period of active Sapiro-plan organization, in 1920 and 1921. (Cf. Chapter 9, pp. 194-98.) The tobacco associations had begun to collapse by 1925. The cotton associations, on the other hand, were beginning to take action independently. A resolution drawn up by a special committee, which expressed the Sapiro point of view, was submitted to the directors of the member associations early in 1926. This was defeated by an overwhelming vote. The resolution stated that "no permanent advantage will result from the introduction of government price fixing, direct or indirect" and that "the relocation

of supply by Government action to raise the level of domestic prices will result in an unwarranted increase of cost to the consumer and an inevitable increase in an already abundant supply, and will aggravate the entire marketing problem." It also opposed the use of equalization fees stating that the proposals in regard to these were motivated by good purposes but were "impatient" legislation and "contrary to American traditions." It further held that "the marketing problems of agriculture are capable of solution by intelligent merchandising through cooperative marketing associations."

After failure of this resolution to carry, the Council released all member cooperatives from control through policy actions on the part of the national organization.

54. Christensen, *Agricultural Pressure*, pp. 138-39.

three nominees named by the Farm Advisory Council of that district. The Board was to collect and disseminate market information, to give advice in regard to crop adjustments needed and to develop markets.

Through its own activities and with the advice of the cooperatives, the Board was to keep itself informed as to the existence or likelihood of surpluses. If surpluses were anticipated in any of the "basic" commodities — cotton, wheat, corn, butter, cattle or swine — and if the cooperatives had expressed themselves as favoring such action, the Board was to declare an "operation period" of two years during which time it was to aid in removing such surplus, by arranging with cooperatives, processors and others to hold them or sell them abroad through official agencies. The maximum price to be paid to farmers was to be the world price plus the tariff.[55]

The plan was to be financed through an initial revolving fund of $375 million, to be maintained by means of equalization fees assessed against each of the commodities handled, either when sold to first handlers or when processed. The equalization fee was a substitute for the cumbersome scrip plan which had aroused much opposition. Under the equalization fee plan a tax would be levied on each unit of the commodity sold to first handlers, or at the processing stage. The proceeds of these "taxes" would go into a fund to be used in absorbing losses resulting from sales abroad at less than the price maintained in the United States. Thus the equalization fee plan was an alternative to the "scrip" plan as a means of raising money to finance an export dumping program.

The equalization fees to be assessed were to be determined by the Board, on the basis of its estimate of the amounts needed to offset losses from surplus disposal operations.

In view of the complexities surrounding the plan as applied to cotton, the Cotton Growers' Exchange proposed that the collection of the equalization fee on cotton and corn be deferred for three years in order to give opportunity for studying the plan, devising mechanisms for implementing it and carrying on educational work in regard to it.[56] Representative Sydney Anderson of Minnesota created a furor by proposing, almost at the last minute, that the collection of equalization fees with respect to all the crops be deferred for three years. Though this feature was vigorously opposed by the cotton growers, it was included in the bill as reported out by the House Agriculture Committee on April 27, 1926.

Two other farm relief bills were reported out by the House Agriculture Committee, namely, the Tincher bill embodying the "Jardine plan"[57] and the Aswell bill designed to implement the Yoakum plan.[58]

The Haugen bill (referred to above as the "Committee Bill") came up in the House on May 21 and lost by a vote of 212 to 167.[59] The

55. In 1925 the advocates of the McNary-Haugen plan had revised the price objective of the proposed legislation, shifting from the ratio-price criterion to one expressed by the term, "making the tariff effective for agriculture." World price plus the tariff might be higher or lower than the "ratio-price," but was more easily understood and more in keeping with the prevailing policy of tariff protection for American industries.

56. The arguments for this procedure were that, in the case of corn, the problem could best be met by carrying over part of the crop and increasing the livestock population. For cotton it was felt that the financing of stocks on hand and the carry-over would be the major devices used. It was assumed that these operations could be handled during the first three years by advances from the revolving fund.

57. There were several versions of the so-called "Jardine plan." This one called for the establishment of a federal farm advisory council and a farmers' marketing commission to help in developing cooperative associations, for orderly marketing to aid in disposing of surpluses and for other purposes. A loan fund of $100 million for aid to cooperatives was to be provided from the Treasury. See Federal Farm Advisory Council, H.Rep. 994 to accompany H.R. 11618, 69th Cong., 1st sess., April 27, 1926.

58. The Yoakum plan, put forward by B. F. Yoakum, a director of the St. Louis and San Francisco Railroad, proposed the creation of a "National Farm Marketing Association" which was to be incorporated by twelve individuals chosen by the three major farm organizations. It was to provide or recommend systems of accounting for farmer cooperatives, disseminate crop and market information, encourage diversification and acquire, or dispose of, facilities for storage. A $10 million appropriation was to be authorized for these purposes. See National Farm Marketing Association, H.Rep. 1004 to accompany H.R. 11606, 69th Cong., 1st sess., April 27, 1926.

59. Ninety-eight Republicans, 66 Democrats and 3 Farmer-Labor members voted for the bill. One hundred twenty-one Republicans, 89 Democrats and 2 Socialists voted against it. Less than 30 of the cotton state Demo-

Tincher and Aswell bills were then withdrawn. In the Senate the McNary-Haugen bill was reported out as an amendment to the Dickinson cooperative marketing bill (H.R. 7893) in substantially the same form as the Haugen bill which had been defeated in the House.[60]

An amendment removing the three-year deferment of equalization fees on corn was passed by the Senate, but a similar amendment in respect to cotton was lost. The parent bill was defeated, on June 24, by a vote of 39 to 45. An effort was then made to obtain passage of the Fess amendment, which provided for a Farmers' Marketing Commission of six members and a revolving fund of $100 million for loans to cooperatives. Failing in this, the Senate passed the Dickinson cooperative marketing bill (H.R. 7893), which was signed by the President and became law on July 2, 1926.[61]

The Fourth McNary-Haugen Bill (1927)

Following the defeat of the third McNary-Haugen bill, the Corn Belt Committee and the Committee of Twenty-two intensified their efforts to build favorable sentiment for the legislation in advance of the next session of the Congress. Special emphasis was placed on gaining support from the cotton states. The Corn Belt Committee, meeting in Des Moines on October 19, 1926, issued a call for

a joint meeting of representatives from the corn and cotton states to be held at St. Louis on November 15. That meeting drew representation from the South and led to a revival of lobbying activity in Washington. The Washington office was reorganized under the name "Agricultural Service," and Chester Davis and Walton Peteet were placed in active charge. Peek was made chairman of the "Committee for Agricultural Service."

A new bill, developed out of a series of conferences with farm organization leaders, was introduced in the Senate by McNary on December 14, 1926 (S. 4808). Suggestion was made that Representatives Haugen of Iowa and Fulmer of South Carolina introduce the same bill in the House in order to indicate backing from the corn states, the cotton states and the Far West. Fulmer introduced the bill on December 17 (H.R. 15337) but Haugen demurred, because of abandonment of the tariff yardstick, and only as a result of considerable pressure was he induced to present his bill (H.R. 15474) on December 20.[62]

Grange Favors Export Debenture Plan

The Grange now came forward with a proposal known as the "Export Debenture Plan." This measure, which was largely the work of Professor Charles L. Stewart of Illinois, sought much the same results as the McNary-Haugen plan but by a different mechanism.[63] It proposed that exporters be given government debentures having face values equal to all or part of the difference between the value of the commodity in the

crats voted for it. Christensen, *Agricultural Pressure,* p. 145.

60. This Dickinson bill (H.R. 7893) provided only for the establishment of a division of cooperative marketing in the Department of Agriculture. It was passed by the House on January 26. The earlier Dickinson bill (H.R. 6563) was a surplus control bill similar to the one now presented as an amendment to H.R. 7893. The Senate amendment provided for the immediate assessment of equalization fees except on cotton and corn. On these two commodities fees were to be deferred for three years as proposed by the American Cotton Growers' Exchange. Even after that time fees were not to be collected on these crops except by specific authorization of Congress.

61. This act was an outgrowth of administration efforts to sidetrack the McNary-Haugen legislation through passage of an innocuous, substitute measure. It provided that the new division should give advisory service to farm producers' cooperative associations, gather and disseminate information of interest to them and conduct research on their problems. It obviously could make no immediate or significant contribution to the solution of the price problem facing the farmers.

62. An extensive analysis of the proposed legislation as of about this date is given in "The McNary-Haugen Plan as Applied to Wheat: Operating Problems and Economic Consequences," *Wheat Studies of the Food Research Institute,* Stanford University, February 1927, pp. 177–234, and "The McNary-Haugen Plan as Applied to Wheat: Limitations Imposed by the Present Tariff," *ibid.,* March 1927, pp. 235–64.

63. The general principle of this plan had been mentioned earlier by W. J. Spillman in his book entitled *Balancing the Farm Output,* Orange Judd, New York, 1927, in which he discussed briefly the German import certificate plan (pp. 74–76). He concluded, however, that the plan would not work in the United States because of the difference in conditions.

world market and a domestic value based on the world market price plus the tariff.

The exporter might sell these debentures to importers bringing in foreign products who, in turn, might present them in payment of tariffs levied on the goods so imported. Thus the debentures would presumably sell for approximately their face value, unless more than enough of them were issued to pay all import duties. The exporter was expected to pay in the domestic market the world price plus the value of the debentures issued to him. This, it was argued, would avoid the cumbersome procedure of collecting equalization fees from a great number of handlers, and would accomplish virtually the same result.[64] Bills embodying this plan were introduced by Representatives Ketcham of Michigan and Jones of Texas. It became one of the active contenders for approval by the House Agriculture Committee, but was overshadowed by the McNary-Haugen plan.

McNary-Haugen Bill Passed

The fourth McNary-Haugen bill (H.R. 15474 and S. 4808) was reported out by the House Committee on January 18, 1927, and by the Senate Committee on January 24. It differed from the 1926 bill in some respects. In addition to the arrangement for supporting the prices of the "basic commodities" (wheat, cotton, corn, rice and hogs), it provided aid to cooperatives handling and processing farm products. The bill did not mention either tariff or price but merely declared a policy of preventing surpluses from "unduly depressing" the prices received by farmers. The "equalization funds" were renamed "stabilization funds" and emphasis was placed on stabilization of the industry, as against price-raising. Provision was also made for a commodity advisory committee for each commodity handled.[65]

The long campaign of the proponents of the plan was finally reaching fruition. Those lobbying for it had become more skillful, and had developed more adequate organization. The central idea, which at first seemed so radical, had come to seem more familiar. Support by now had become national rather than sectional. The opponents of the bill made one last effort to thwart the movement by proposing, in the Senate, the Curtis-Crisp bill as a substitute.[66] This action was defeated by a vote of 32 to 54, and the McNary-Haugen bill was then passed by a vote of 47 to 39.

In the House the backers of the bill decided, in order to save time and avoid the possibility of a pocket veto, to substitute the Senate bill for their own and to oppose all amendments. The advocates of the McFadden branch-banking bill, though not particularly interested in the farm legislation, entered into a working agreement to push both bills through in minimum time. Thus organized, the coalition voted down all amendments, and the Senate bill was passed on February 17 by a vote of 214 to 178, with 39 not voting.[67]

McNary-Haugen Bill Vetoed

President Coolidge had let it be known that he was opposed to farm legislation of the McNary-Haugen type. Consequently, the return of the bill to Congress on February 25, 1927, without the President's approval, was not unexpected. The veto message was a vigorous and forthright condemnation of the whole idea. Though admitting the unsatisfactory conditions in agriculture the President stated:

64. For a full and competent analysis of the plan, see Joseph S. Davis, *The Export Debenture Plan,* Food Research Institute, Stanford University, 1929. A less detailed and briefer analysis of the bill is given by the same writer in "The Export Debenture Plan for Aid to Agriculture," *Quarterly Journal of Economics,* February 1929, pp. 250–77. The Grange version is presented in a pamphlet issued in 1928 entitled *The Export Debenture Plan, A Sound Method of Restoring Agricultural Prosperity in the United States,* and in other literature of the organization.

65. Various amendments were made while the bill was being considered by the Senate. The principal one provided for inclusion of tobacco as a basic crop. The tobacco cooperatives, formerly opposed to the legislation, had now come out in favor of it. Fuller details are given in Christensen, *Agricultural Pressure,* p. 157.

66. The Curtis-Crisp bill provided merely for loans to cooperatives.

67. *Congressional Record,* 69th Cong., 2nd sess., p. 4099.

It is axiomatic that progress is made through building on the good foundations that already exist. For many years — indeed, from before the day of modern agricultural science — balanced and diversified farming has been regarded by thoughtful farmers and scientists as the safeguard of our agriculture. The bill under consideration throws this aside as of no consequence. It says in effect that all the agricultural scientists and all the thinking farmers of the last 50 years are wrong, that what we ought to do is not to encourage diversified agriculture but instead put a premium on one-crop farming.

The measure discriminates definitely against products which make up what has been universally considered a program of safe farming. The bill upholds as ideals of American farming the men who grow cotton, corn, rice, swine, tobacco, or wheat, and nothing else. These are to be given special favors at the expense of the farmer who has toiled for years to build up a constructive farming enterprise to include a variety of crops and livestock that shall, so far as possible, be safe, and keep the soil, the farmer's chief asset, fertile and productive.

The bill singles out a few products, chiefly sectional, and proposes to raise the prices of those regardless of the fact that thousands of other farmers would be directly penalized. If this is a true farm relief measure, why does it leave out the producers of beef cattle, sheep, dairy products, poultry products, potatoes, hay, fruit, vegetables, oats, barley, rye, flax and the other important agricultural lines? So far as the farmers as a whole are concerned, this measure is not for them. It is for certain groups of farmers in certain sections of the country. Can it be thought that such legislation could have the sanction of the rank and file of the Nation's farmers?[68]

The message was said to have been prepared by combining sections of analyses made in the Departments of Agriculture, Treasury and Commerce. Farm leaders advocating the legislation seized upon this allegation and subjected the President's arguments to ridicule and criticism as being an inconsistent hodge-podge of ideas.[69]

The principal objections raised by the President were:

1. That the bill was designed to aid farmers of certain sections at the expense of those in other areas, and that its effect would be to perpetuate and encourage one-crop agriculture instead of fostering more diversification and better balance.
2. That it was a price-fixing measure.
3. That the plan would be difficult or impossible to administer.
4. That the equalization fee was not a true tax but instead represented an unconstitutional delegation of the taxing power of Congress, and was a tax for an arbitrarily selected class of citizens.

These contentions were supported by an appended statement from the Attorney General in which he argued that the provision requiring the President to appoint members of the board from nominations made by the district councils was an unconstitutional restriction on his powers of appointment, that the authorization for the board to determine the price at which products might be sold in the domestic market was an unconstitutional delegation of legislative powers, that the power of the federal government to regulate commerce did not include the power to establish and maintain the price at which merchandise might be bought and sold and that the equalization fee could not be sustained under the taxing clause of the Constitution.

The supporters of the legislation recognized that it would not be possible to pass the bill over the President's veto, and consequently limited their immediate legislative activities to thwarting an effort to revise substitute legislation such as the Crisp and Aswell bills.

The Fifth McNary-Haugen Bill (1928)

During the early summer of 1927 a substitute measure by Senator Fess of Ohio, which presumably had presidential support, received a good deal of publicity. At the end of July

---

68. U.S. President, *Surplus Control Act*, Veto of S. 4808, S.Doc. 214, 69th Cong., 2nd sess., February 25, 1927, pp. 1–2.

69. On the other hand, the veto undoubtedly strengthened the President's position with the regular Republicans, some of whom had voted for the bill. It tended, however, to widen the gap between Coolidge and the progressive Republicans. See William Allen White, *A Puritan in Babylon, The Story of Calvin Coolidge*, Mac-

millan, New York, 1938, p. 349. Chief Justice Taft, in a letter to his son, Robert, referred to it as a "sockdolager" — that is, a decisive blow that ends or settles a matter. *Ibid.*, p. 347. Though later events proved him wrong, the comment reflects Taft's opinion of the plan.

the administration came out more definitely for a revised form of the "Jardine plan."[70] This provided for the creation of a Farm Board, a system of advisory committees (one for each commodity included in the program), and a series of stabilization corporations to be established by the Board. Appropriations, including $25 million for facility loans to cooperatives, were to be provided in the amount of $300 million.

But the advocates of the McNary-Haugen plan were by no means ready to accept defeat. They renewed their campaign in the corn and cotton states, and even undertook to gain the backing of the American Bankers' Association, which they regarded as responsible in part for the President's veto. Farm leaders and some of the legislators had been working on a revised form of the bill, and decision was reached to press forward with the existing organization in Washington and intensified effort in the farm areas.

The new bill was introduced in the Senate on March 7, 1928 and in the House on April 4.[71] It was designed to meet the objections raised in the veto message, except that the equalization fee was retained. The fee was to be assessed, however, only if the cooperatives found it impossible to cope with the situation through other methods. The legislation was to cover all commodities, not merely those designated as basic, and a fund of $250 million, to be loaned to cooperatives at 4 per cent, was to be authorized. The Board was to be appointed by the President.

On March 26, 1928 the House Committee on Agriculture rejected the export debenture plan by a vote of 13 to 8 and then approved the Haugen bill by a vote of 15 to 6. This bill differed from that in the Senate mainly in providing a fund of $400 million instead of $300 million. This was to emphasize the method of meeting the problem through loans

to cooperatives, which presumably was the approach favored by the administration.

The new bill was passed by the Senate, on April 12, by a vote of more than two thirds of the senators present, but with many absentees.[72] In the House the Haugen bill was substituted for the Senate version.[73] A substitute measure offered by Aswell was defeated by a vote of 146 to 185, and the Haugen bill was then passed by a vote of 204 to 122 (on May 3, 1928). A conference report was submitted to the two houses on May 12, and was accepted in the House by a vote of 204 to 117 on May 14. In the Senate it was passed without a record vote, but only after a five-hour filibuster by an opposing group of Republican senators.

President Coolidge returned the bill, with his veto, on May 25.[74] The Senate vote of 50 to 31 was short four votes of enough to over-

---

70. A further elaboration of the "Jardine plan" mentioned above (p. 225).

71. S. 3555, 70th Cong., 1st sess. In the House, it was known as H.R. 12687. Senator McNary had introduced S. 1176 on December 9, 1927, but no action was taken on it after it was referred to committee.

72. The distribution, by states, of the Senate vote on this and the preceding versions of the bill are shown in John D. Black, "The McNary-Haugen Movement," *American Economic Review*, September 1928, pp. 408–09.

73. At this stage the bill very nearly was lost through a parliamentary maneuver. Aswell of Louisiana, after the reading of the first section, moved to strike it out and substitute a bill of his own which was like the Haugen bill except that it did not include provision for marketing agreements and equalization fees. This motion, through support of cotton state representatives, was adopted by a vote of 141 to 120. The American Farm Bureau Federation threw its full weight behind a compromise amendment offered by Representative Kincheloe of Kentucky, which would give the advisory councils a decisive vote before the board could impose or remove an equalization fee. This satisfied the southerners who feared the action of a board appointed by a Republican president, and thus the equalization fee feature was saved. Christensen, *Agricultural Pressure*, pp. 166–67.

74. U.S. President, *Veto Message Relating to the Agriculture Surplus Control Act*, S.Doc. 141, 70th Cong., 1st sess., May 3 (calendar day, May 23), 1928. In this message the President stated unequivocally, "The bill still is unconstitutional." He listed as principal objections:

1. Its attempted price-fixing fallacy.
2. The tax characteristics of the equalization fee.
3. The widespread bureaucracy which it would set up.
4. Its encouragement to profiteering and wasteful distribution by middlemen.
5. Its stimulation of overproduction.
6. Its aid to our foreign agricultural competitors.

White states that the Wall Street group, anxious to see either Coolidge or Dwight Morrow nominated in the summer of 1928, tried to create prejudice against Herbert Hoover by spreading the rumor in the West that Hoover was responsible for the veto. This he holds not to be true, and implies that the unfairness of the charge caused Taft to swing strongly behind the Hoover candidacy. See *Puritan in Babylon*, p. 375.

ride, and the legislation was dead for the time being, since the session was nearing its end. Its sponsors recognized that their next move, if any, must be that of laying their case before the party conventions.

Farm Relief and the Election of 1928

It was the hope of the McNary-Haugen advocates that either Frank O. Lowden, ex-Governor of Illinois, or Vice-President Charles G. Dawes would be the Republican nominee in 1928, and their campaign was launched with that in mind. Strenuous efforts were made both to assure the nomination of Lowden and to secure a definite commitment in behalf of the McNary-Haugen principle in one or both of the party platforms.

But platform makers are not given to making definite commitments. Despite vigorous and widespread pressure for such a plank, the Republican convention sidestepped the issue.[75] A minority plank presented by the McNary-Haugen supporters on the floor of the convention was voted down 806 to 278. The convention then adopted the following statement of policy with respect to farm relief:

We promise every assistance in the reorganization of the marketing system on sounder and more economical lines and, where diversification is needed, Government financial assistance during the period of transition.

The Republican party pledges itself to the enactment of legislation creating a Federal Farm Board clothed with the necessary powers to promote the establishment of a farm marketing system of farmer owned and controlled stabilization corporations or associations to prevent and control surpluses through orderly distribution.

We favor adequate tariff protection to such of our agricultural products as are affected by foreign competition.

We favor, without putting the Government

into business, the establishment of a Federal system of organization for cooperative and orderly marketing of farm products . . .[76]

Following the convention's failure to accept the McNary-Haugen plank, Governor Lowden withdrew as a candidate, and Herbert Hoover was nominated.

The McNary-Haugen forces then concentrated on getting the Democratic convention to come out specifically for their plan. They succeeded in getting into the Democratic platform a plank which they interpreted as an endorsement of the principle advocated by them. It promised loans to cooperatives on terms at least as favorable as those to the merchant marine, the creation of a federal farm board, the reduction, through the action of government agencies, of the spread between what the farmer gets and what the consumer pays and consideration of the condition of agriculture in the formulation of government financial and tax measures. One paragraph in particular was looked upon as a virtual endorsement of the McNary-Haugen principle. This paragraph read as follows:

We pledge the party to foster and develop co-operative marketing associations through appropriate governmental aid. We recognize that experience has demonstrated that members of such associations alone can not successfully assume the full responsibility for a program that benefits all producers alike. We pledge the party to an earnest endeavor to solve this problem of the distribution of the cost of dealing with crop surpluses over the marketed units of the crop whose producers are benefited by such assistance. The solution of this problem would avoid government subsidy, to which the Democratic Party has always been opposed. The solution of this problem will be a prime and immediate concern of a Democratic administration.[77]

The Democratic candidate, Alfred E. Smith, while avoiding outright commitment, discussed the problem in terms which the McNary-Haugen leaders considered favorable to their cause. Though a Republican, Peek, together with Chester Davis, undertook to swing

---

75. Even the Farm Bureau Federation presented a plank which was disappointing to the McNary-Haugen supporters, and did not constitute an unequivocal endorsement of the two-price plan. It read as follows: ". . . It has been demonstrated that cooperative marketing is fundamentally sound and experience has proven that the cost of distribution must be equitably borne by the entire volume of the marketed product in order to insure freedom from the need of subsidies and to guarantee permanence and independence in carrying on the marketing operations and we hereby pledge our party to the enactment of legislation to meet this requirement."

76. *New York Times*, June 15, 1928, pp. 4, 8.
77. *Official Report of the Proceedings of the Democratic National Convention Held at Houston, Texas, June 26, 27, 28 and 29, 1928*, p. 191.

the organizations backing the McNary-Haugen idea into line behind Smith. This effort failed, and its effect was to split the organizations along party lines and cause their disintegration. The election of Hoover marked the death knell, for the time being at least, of the equalization fee idea. The American Farm Bureau Federation, and various other organizations that had given moderate support to the McNary-Haugen plan, decided to work with the new administration in an effort to solve the problem in other ways.

Gradual Recovery in the Farm Areas During the 1920's

Though the McNary-Haugen plan had failed of enactment, various natural economic forces were bringing about a slow but gradual readjustment to the new domestic and world situation. Land prices were declining in most regions. Farmers who had encountered acute financial reverses in the immediate postwar years were either eliminated, through foreclosures and distress sales, or managed to refinance their short-term debts in such a way that they could be carried as land mortgages. Wheat acreage, which had reached 75 million in 1919, was down to 52 million by 1925. Thereafter it began to expand again, in part as a result of good prices in 1924 and 1925. By 1929 it was back to nearly 59 million.

The gap between farm and nonfarm prices, as measured by prewar relationships, was narrowing. Whereas in 1921 farm products had a purchasing power of only 84 as compared to 100 in 1910–1914, this ratio, by 1928, had risen to 94.[78] Thus farm products, though

still not up to the 1910–1914 relationship with other prices, were not so severely depressed as the pressure for farm relief implied. Grains still were low in price, but cotton, chickens and eggs, and meat animals were approximately at the prewar relationship with other prices, while fruits and dairy products were in a better position than in prewar years.

Thus the farm relief drive of 1928 and early 1929 was more an aftereffect of earlier depression years than a response to current conditions. By now, however, the pressure groups backing the legislative program had become fully organized, and political reputations were at stake. Therefore the fight was continued, even though the arguments for legislation of this type were less cogent than formerly. The need was shortly to become far more acute than even that of 1920 and 1921, but as yet this prospect was not in the thinking either of farm leaders or congressmen.

The Readjustment of Agriculture

Conservative thinkers, and some not so conservative, had recognized from the beginning that considerable readjustment in the pattern of agricultural production would have to be made, particularly in the northern Plains area.[79] Between 1913 and 1919 wheat acreage had been expanded, in response to wartime prices, from around 52 million to about 75 million. Such an acreage would produce in most years far more wheat than the United States would need for human food, and there was little prospect of a continuing large-scale market abroad at profitable prices.[80] Canada, Australia and Argentina

78. This gradual improvement, stated in terms of changes in average farm income, is shown in the following figures:[a]

Year	Cash Receipts from Farm Marketings	Operators' Net Income
1920	$1,955	$1,073
1921	1,248	573
1922	1,319	646
1923	1,492	774
1924	1,606	823
1925	1,730	977
1926	1,664	913
1927	1,714	921
1928	1,752	909
1929	1,796	975

a. Bureau of Agricultural Economics, *The Farm Income Situation*, July-September 1951, p. 20.

Average incomes for the United States understate, for the wheat and corn areas, both the severity of the decline in prices and incomes and the extent of the recovery. The Pacific Coast states in particular held up well throughout the 1920's, and the cotton and dairy regions were less seriously affected than were those heavily dependent on income from wheat and corn.

79. This point of view is well presented in "The Dispensibility of a Wheat Surplus in the United States," *Wheat Studies of the Food Research Institute,* Stanford University, March 1925, pp. 121–41.

80. The leaders and staffs of the land-grant colleges rather generally took the view that readjustments in production would have to be made whether special farm relief legislation was passed or not. The need for such

had likewise expanded their acreages in wheat, and were in somewhat better position to capture the European market than was the United States.

To aid farmers in making the needed readjustments and to afford them more information as a basis for planning their operations, the Bureau of Agricultural Economics initiated, in the middle 1920's, a series of annual analyses of conditions and outlook with respect to the various lines of agricultural production.[81] These were presumably to aid farmers in shifting from types of production in which market conditions did not appear favorable into lines where prospects were better. The "outlook reports" were carried into the farm communities by state extension service workers in hundreds of special schools and meetings.

Although these reports were supposed to speed adjustments and ease the problem of surpluses, they were not notably successful in accomplishing that purpose. When nearly all farm prices are low a shift from one low-priced commodity to another does not help much. More significant, however, was the fact that the major surpluses were in the crops using large acreages, whereas the crops highest in price were mainly specialties occupying small acreages and usually suitable only for certain regions. Big adjustments such as those needed in wheat, corn, oats and cotton implied reversion of cultivated land to grass. It was not easy, and in many cases was impossible, to turn the wheels back in that way, except through bankruptcy and actual abandonment of submarginal farms.

The outlook program turned out to have important collateral effects, however, which overshadowed its significance as an adjuster of agricultural production. It soon became evident that it was the most effective method of teaching agricultural economics to farmers that had yet been devised. Through these efforts, continued over the years since their initiation, hundreds of thousands of farmers have come to have a vastly better understanding of how prices are made, and of the economic forces with which they must deal. Their approach to the ever more complex economic problems of agriculture has grown rapidly in sophistication and realism. That this greater understanding has at times been used in wringing special favors from a reluctant consuming public cannot be denied, but at the same time it has presented a growing opportunity for agriculture to deal with other sophisticated groups, no more burdened with altruism, on terms of greater equality.

Shift of Population Out of Agriculture

The farms of the United States normally produce more young people than are needed to maintain agricultural production at usual levels. When urban industries are active, the flow of young people from farm to city is usually sufficient to keep farm population from increasing rapidly, and thus helps to maintain a balance. Around 1913 the total number of persons on farms began a gradual decline which lasted until 1930. Between 1920 and 1929 there was a net loss of persons on farms of nearly a million and a half. This reduction in the farm labor force was made possible in part by the rapid increase in mechanization, especially in the use of tractors. Production was maintained and even increased. As a consequence the per capita incomes of workers engaged in agriculture rose more than did the total income from farming. Thus the combination of high urban activity and depressed agriculture stimulated migration and helped in bringing about precisely the kind of adjustment that was most needed. This trend was reversed in the early 1930's, when both farms and cities were in

readjustment was stressed in the *Report on The Agricultural Situation*, prepared by the Special Committee of the Association of Land Grant Colleges and Universities, in 1927. (For a somewhat different interpretation see G. F. Warren, "Which Does Agriculture Need — Readjustment or Legislation?," *Journal of Farm Economics*, January 1928, pp. 1–15.) As yet, however, the state colleges and the Department of Agriculture were only beginning to come to grips with this problem. They were not in a position to give guidance to farmers and the government which would enable them to make adjustments on a scale that would have important effects on the status of agriculture.

81. See USDA, *Outlook Work, the First Twenty Years*, March 1942.

depression, thus intensifying the problems of agriculture.

Changes in the Export Situation

Between 1919 and 1921 the dollar value of United States exports had shrunk by approximately half (from $9.5 billion to $5.2 billion). After 1921 the dollar value crept up gradually to $5.4 billion in 1922, $5.3 billion in 1923, $5.7 billion in 1924, and eventually to $6.7 billion in each of the years 1928 and 1929.[82] Of this volume of purchases, about four fifths were paid for by importation of goods from abroad and about one fifth through loans, credits and gifts provided by the United States. Though industrial products were relatively short in the United States and prices were high, the sharp increases in the tariffs of 1921 and 1922 tended to keep down the flow of goods from Europe, thus limiting somewhat its ability to buy American farm products.

A healthy revival and expansion of foreign demand for United States farm products was largely inhibited by the tangled situation in respect to war debts and reparations. At the close of the war, the governments of the Allied powers were heavily in debt to the United States. These obligations, when reduced to orderly form through refunding agreements, in 1923 and thereafter, amounted to more than $11.5 billion, owed chiefly by Great Britain, France and Italy.

Since none of these nations had gold or foreign exchange adequate to meet such huge obligations, the debts could be serviced and liquidated, if at all, only by exportation of goods to the United States. This would have required a much higher level of exports to this country than had prevailed prior to the war. Heavily involved in internal reconstruction as they were, the debtor nations were in no position to step up exports to that extent, and the United States had shown by the enactment of the Emergency and Ford-

ney-McCumber tariff acts that it did not wish to receive foreign goods in such quantity, even if the nations owing us were able and willing to supply them.

Furthermore, there was much difference of opinion, as between the debtor nations and the United States, with respect to the moral right of the United States to demand repayment in full. Britain and France, in particular, had given heavily in manpower and to the full limit of their resources. The United States, a late-comer in a common undertaking, had sacrificed mainly money, or rather, currently produced goods, since most of the money loaned was spent in the United States. Also these goods had been bought at inflated war prices. To attempt to pay for them in goods of much lower value meant repayment in real wealth of much more than had been borrowed.

Even if the debtor nations had accepted fully a moral obligation to repay the debts in higher value dollars, or even in dollars of equal value to those borrowed, and if the United States had been willing to accept the imports thus implied, it is evident that such payments could not have been used both to pay war debts and to pay for enlarged exports of American farm products and industrial goods.

The whole structure of international war debts soon fell into confusion. Efforts were made, in the Dawes Plan of 1924 and the Young Plan of 1929, to bring the German reparation arrangements into manageable form, but no sound basis was achieved for international trade in a pattern that would permit of greatly enlarged exports of American farm products.[83] The full impact of the mishandling of the international trade situation during the 1920's did not fall upon American agriculture. It was offset in part by large-scale foreign loans made by American investors, especially to Germany, and by the high

82. Data drawn from *How U.S. Exports Have Been Financed, 1919–1947*, chart issued by Dun and Bradstreet, New York, 1947. See also Edwin G. Nourse, *American Agriculture and the European Market*, McGraw-Hill, New York, 1924, Chapters 3, 4 and 5.

83. For a good brief account of the situation described above, see John D. Hicks, *The American Nation*, Houghton Mifflin, Boston, 1941, pp. 595–99. For a more extended treatment, see Harold G. Moulton and Leo Pasvolsky, *War Debts and World Prosperity*, The Brookings Institution, Washington, 1932, especially pp. 369–422.

though somewhat unhealthy level of prosperity in most lines of American industry.

The export market for some of the American specialty crops developed strongly, but little improvement occurred with respect to the more important crops, such as wheat, pork and cotton, which were the ones chiefly responsible for the agricultural distress. The exports of crude foodstuffs in fact fell off from $673 million in 1921 to $257 million in 1923, and amounted to only $421 million in 1927, which, except for 1921, was the peak year of the decade. Manufactured foodstuffs, on the other hand, held up well but declined moderately in the latter part of the decade.[84]

Situation of the Farm Credit Agencies

The federal land banks, joint stock land banks and federal intermediate credit banks did not have a dominant position in the farm credit field during this period. However, they were gaining experience and becoming better organized. The intermediate credit banks still were seriously lacking in local organizations through which they could make loans. Weaknesses began to appear in the joint-stock land bank system by the middle of the decade, and serious difficulties were showing up by the latter part of it. Beginning in 1927, the Federal Farm Loan Board began an extensive internal reorganization which was not completed until 1929. This strengthened materially the efficiency of the organization.

Gains and Losses in the Struggle of the 1920's

During the 1920's, the farm groups achieved more effective organization and greater political power than ever before. Yet the immediate objectives of this sustained and costly effort were not attained. In broad outline it seems evident that agriculture worked its way out of the postwar depression by the slow process of adjustment in response to natural economic forces that would have operated in much the same way had there been no organizations of farmers and no pressure on Congress. This, however, is a less than adequate interpretation of the sig-

84. *Statistical Abstract, 1929,* p. 474.

nificance of the forces set in motion during this period. The lessons learned in these years of intensive political effort undoubtedly paved the way for the much more sweeping measures of relief to agriculture that were to come in the 1930's, especially after the inauguration of Franklin D. Roosevelt in 1933.

Did the farm organization leaders diagnose correctly the ills they were seeking to cure? Would the remedies they strove to apply have corrected the situation? Were they, through lack of clear understanding, participating in the rudderless drift toward conditions far worse than those from which they were seeking to extricate themselves? These are questions on which opinions may differ. Nevertheless, an examination of them can bring into clearer focus the problems and forces that characterized the period even though conclusions must inevitably be individual and subject to challenge.

It is less than just to those who mapped the strategy and devised the tactics to judge their performance in the light of knowledge now existing, much of which was not available to them at that time. But many of the problems they faced were characteristic of other periods in the history of American agriculture. Hence any lessons that may be drawn from them have more than mere historical interest. They should contribute to wiser solutions of the complex problems which will continue to face farmers and the nation in respect to agricultural policy.

The major drive of the agricultural forces was along three lines: development of a strong, semimonopolistic cooperative marketing system, following in general terms the Sapiro point of view; an attempt to raise the prices of agricultural products through direct government action; and an effort to solve the problem through changes in credit organization and policy. These were not mutually exclusive. The majority of the farm leaders supported all three.

Cooperative Failures and Successes

The Sapiro cooperatives were not carefully built business organizations based on the solid foundation of member understanding and effective participation. Rather, they were the result of highly emotional campaigns, intensive membership drives and unrealistic expectations. The widespread distress in agriculture made it easy to acquire new members, but keeping them interested and loyal was a far more difficult problem. The general idea was that farmers could combine in large, national or industry-wide cooperatives and control the flow of their products to the market, operate on the basis of administered prices and, if necessary, dump surpluses abroad or into diversionary, domestic markets.

The principle was thought to be similar to that governing the automobile industry, United States Steel or General Electric. The vital difference was, of course, that in these industries the directors could determine both the amounts they would produce and the prices they would charge. In agriculture no such unified control of production existed or could exist under private auspices; nor was the marketing operation itself under such tight control as that of the large industrial corporations.

The real possibilities for improvement through cooperation were of a much more modest kind. Cooperatives could, in many cases, make significant savings or gains to growers through lessening the charges made for marketing activities, cutting down on the duplication of physical facilities and improving the effectiveness of the processing, distributing and selling functions. These gains, while eminently worth striving for, were bound to be of modest proportions. Even if achieved they could not satisfy the grower member who expected the price of wheat, cotton or other product to be raised by 50 per cent or more through the action of his cooperative association.

In many cases the cooperatives formed were manifestly less efficient than the private agencies they sought to replace. Inexperienced and untried farmers often were put in charge of multimillion dollar corporations such as United States Grain Growers, Inc., or the Grain Marketing Corporation, and were expected to be able to manage them with greater skill and effectiveness than the professionals who had grown up in these businesses. These unrealistic expectations stemmed, of course, from failure to understand the complexity of modern business.

Despite these obvious defects the cooperatives made important gains during the 1920's. The Sapiro movement aroused wide interest in extending cooperation into the central markets. Theretofore it had consisted mainly of small-town shipping and processing organizations. New corporate forms and methods of financing were introduced and there came to be a wider recognition of the need for well-paid, skilled management and legal services, even though many of the individuals appointed as managers did not have experience and skills commensurate with the responsibilities assumed and the salaries paid. The movement was also responsible for an almost nationwide overhauling of state laws in respect to cooperation, and, in some measure, for passage of the Capper-Volstead Act which gave the farmer cooperatives a clear and favored status with respect to the antitrust and income tax laws.

The cooperative approach to the farm problem had sufficient backing to keep it as an undertone, and a possible alternative, even in the period of most vociferous demand for export-dumping legislation. After the defeat of the McNary-Haugen plan, it came into dominant position, and formed the core of the Farm Board program, which was, in effect, an attempt to carry out the Sapiro idea through vigorous and positive aid from the government.

The McNary-Haugen Plan as Solution

Could the McNary-Haugen plan, if adopted, have solved the problem? The answer to this question depends on how the ills of agriculture are diagnosed, and what weighting is given to the probable effects and workability of the undertaking. What were the causes of the distress in agriculture?[85]

85. Up to this time, relatively little thought had been given to the economic problems of agriculture. The con-

Basically, they were an overexpansion in the acreages of wheat and oats, a demoralized and depressed foreign market and a preceding period of monetary inflation and wild speculation in farm lands. Coupled with these was a situation in which the prices of non-farm goods and services could, for the most part, be maintained at levels that were more favorable than the returns to farmers.

The acreages of cereal crops needed to be brought back into adjustment with a more normal open-market demand. The program sought by the agricultural leaders sidestepped this element of the problem almost completely. Had the McNary-Haugen plan been adopted it would, in fact, have tended strongly to prolong the period of adjustment.

As things worked out, the adjustment was made, but in a very painful manner. Wheat acreage had moved downward from about 1900 to 1910 as production in Canada, Australia and Argentina developed in volume adequate to supply much of the European market formerly supplied by the United States. A new upward trend began in 1911, and by 1914 the acreage had risen to 55.5 million (from about 45 million in 1910). The war-time stimulus brought this up to about 74 million by 1919. There was no prospect that

so large an acreage could be maintained without large-scale government subsidy, when the world market was far weaker than it had been in 1914. The principal competing wheat countries were similarly overexpanded, and at the same time less well able to shift to alternative lines.

Under these circumstances a logical first step would have been to initiate legislation along the lines of the Norbeck-Burtness diversification loan bill, and thus to aid in speedy adjustment through increased livestock production, which is a natural form of cushioning in periods of excess grain supplies. This obviously would not have been adequate to meet the crisis. With mechanisms developed much later, in the 1930's, it would have been feasible to provide storage and nonrecourse loans on wheat and corn for a time. As yet, however, the government was not equipped to handle complex action programs of that kind, nor was the time ripe for their introduction. Such a program, even if it had been adopted, could, of course, have been no more than a palliative. It would not have been able to support prices indefinitely but could have served to ease the shock and give time for reappraisal of the situation. But the fundamental adjustments would still have been needed.

Tariff Policy Inappropriate

On the score of reviving and strengthening the foreign market it seems clear that both farm leaders and the Congress misjudged the situation and chose the wrong solution. Europe was badly disorganized; Germany in the throes of inflation, France ravaged by invasion and battle and England weakened by years of fighting. Little strength could be expected in an export market so grievously disrupted. All of these nations needed dollars, and were faced with the problem of reviving their industries and shipping. As soon as possible, they needed to begin exporting to the United States in order to obtain dollar exchange and vital necessities. True, they were in no position to spare large quantities of goods. Yet we tended to discourage such ex-

---

fused and poorly developed state of understanding, especially on the part of the business groups, is well illustrated in *The Agricultural Problem in the United States*, published in 1926 by the National Industrial Conference Board and widely read at the time. After 150 pages of rather dubious analysis, the principal conclusion reached was that American businessmen should join with farmers "to study jointly and sympathetically, . . . the agricultural situation and its causes." This suggestion led, however, to further study of the problem by a "Business Men's Commission on Agriculture," organized under the auspices of the Conference Board and the United States Chamber of Commerce, which brought out in 1927 a report entitled *The Condition of Agriculture in the United States and Measures for Its Improvement*, Washington, 1927. This group presented a much more developed analysis and a comprehensive though conservative body of recommendations. By that time, organized agriculture had become a power in legislative circles, and interest in the farmers' problems and in their legislative activities was becoming much more broadly national.

Other analyses of the situation of agriculture in this period are given in John D. Black's "Agriculture Now?," *Journal of Farm Economics*, April 1927, pp. 137–62; and Joseph S. Davis' review of the report of the National Industrial Conference Board in the *Journal of the American Statistical Association*, March 1927, pp. 109–15. See also E. G. Nourse, "The Outlook for Agriculture," *Journal of Farm Economics*, January 1927, pp. 21–32.

ports as they could have made available. The Emergency tariff of 1921 and the Fordney-McCumber tariff of 1922 were definitely designed to hold down imports at a time when our own economy was short of goods, and our manufacturers were reaping a rich harvest by selling at high prices in an undersupplied market. In addition we put pressure on our wartime allies to begin repayment on their vast war debts with the limited dollar exchange they had.

The results of this policy were unfavorable to American agriculture in several ways. The European nations, who had been our best prewar customers for farm products, exerted every effort to revive their agriculture quickly in order to save dollars. They also turned to other sources of supply such as Canada, Argentina and Australia. In the home market the policy of shutting out foreign goods contributed to the maintenance of high prices for nonfarm products, and to continuing high levels of wages, thus widening the spread between farm and nonfarm prices.

Logically, the farm groups should have supported a continuance of the lower-level Underwood tariff. Had they done so successfully it is conceivable that the farmer's position would have been easier in the 1920's, and that the disastrous crash of 1929 would have been delayed or made less severe, since it developed in part as a result of strain placed on foreign currencies in the effort to maintain dollar payments to the United States.

Proposed Credit Policies Inadequate

The policies supported with respect to credit were likewise unsuited to the situation in which the farmers found themselves. What was needed was quick refinancing, at lower rates of interest, of mortgage loans that were being called. This would have given farmers time to work their way out of the desperate situation. Some shorter-term credit was needed, but the intermediate credit bank mechanism was of almost no assistance as an emergency aid. Something more like the plan proposed in the Norbeck-Burtness

bill, or that carried out by the War Finance Corporation, would have been much more appropriate.

True enough, the land price situation had got out of hand. To have refinanced all mortgages at face value would have been merely to throw good money after bad. But refinancing on more liberal terms and at lower rates of interest would have saved the situation for many a farmer who lost his farm and had to make a new start barehanded. The best solution would have been to prevent or damp down the land boom in the first place. Here the Treasury and the Federal Reserve Board must take some part of the blame. Organized agriculture was not a factor in the decisions that were taken with respect to monetary policy during the war years and in 1919.

Some Gains Made

In spite of the failure of its major programs, some gains of a more sober sort were made by agriculture during the 1920's. Beginnings were made in building a more comprehensive and better organized rural credit system. The packer and stockyard companies and the grain exchanges were brought under more effective control. Progress was made in building a coordinated highway system, with more consideration given to the needs of farmers. The Purnell Act, passed in 1925, provided more adequate support for the agricultural experiment stations and opened the way for a greatly expanded program of research on the economic and social problems of agriculture. Similar emphasis was emerging in the United States Department of Agriculture, and an important start had been made in the dissemination of outlook and intentions-to-plant information.

Farmer cooperatives, too, had grown in strength and effectiveness despite the setbacks occasioned by the collapse of many of the hastily formed Sapiro-plan organizations. The launching of the American Institute of Cooperation in 1925 had given them a mechanism for self-analysis and education, and a medium for public expression of their views and interests. The specialized, commodity-type cooperative, such as the California Fruit Growers Exchange, the Land-O'-Lakes Creameries Association and the Dairymen's League, had definitely arrived and was here to stay.

General Conclusions

Some more general conclusions may also be drawn from this long period of strife and of farm organization activity. One is that enormous and long-continued effort is required if a settled philosophy with respect to the role of government is to be modified or substantially altered. The effort must be well-organized, comprehensive and ably led. No major policy change can be carried through by a small group working alone. This statement may perhaps be challenged as we come to study the period of the 1930's, when conditions were so chaotic, and personal philosophies so nascent, that far-reaching policy changes were instituted by individuals and small groups without much effective opposition. This, however, was a period without parallel in American history, with respect to the rapidity and scope of policy changes.

It is evident too that the difficulty of gaining acceptance for a new major policy makes it doubly important that the principle itself be soundly conceived, thoroughly practical and sufficiently in accord with the national interest to become a more or less permanent part of the great body of accepted national policies.

The McNary-Haugen crusade laid the foundation for a changed attitude toward agriculture which was to be of far greater importance in the 1930's than it would have been in the 1920's. It is perhaps still too early to draw significant conclusions as to whether the trend is a wholesome one, or instead has come to include elements similar to those which led to the long acceptance of the protective tariff with its many inequities and special privileges, or the blind adherence to orthodox banking and monetary policies in the latter part of the nineteenth century.

THE HOOVER PERIOD

WHEN THE HOOVER ADMINISTRATION took over the affairs of government in March 1929, the outlook was bright. The new President had been elected by one of the largest pluralities in the nation's history.[1] Urban business was active and prosperous, and even most parts of agriculture had emerged from their postwar depression. The major worries of the new administration stemmed from the continuing difficulties in some segments of agriculture and the persistent hard core of unemployment in the industrial areas, but these did not appear to be insurmountable. Most people were optimistic about the future, and there seemed every prospect of a successful administration and continued Republican popularity.

Both Smith and Hoover had promised, if elected, to call a special session of the Congress in the spring of 1929. In accordance with this pledge, Hoover issued, shortly after his inauguration, a call for a special session to meet on April 15 to consider "further agricultural relief" and "limited changes of the tariff."

No effort was made to renew pressure for the equalization fee plan, but the Grange revived its advocacy of export debentures as a means to the same end. This plan now achieved greater prominence than it had attained in previous sessions. A new proposal, the domestic allotment plan, was also presented before the congressional committees by Professor John D. Black of Harvard University, but did not gain important backing at this time.[2]

A House committee bill embodying the

Republican campaign promises to agriculture (in essence the Jardine plan) was introduced on April 17, and a similar bill, except that it included an export-debenture section, was introduced by the Senate Agriculture Committee on April 23. The Senate committee itself was sharply divided on the export-debenture feature. The President's expressed approval of the House bill implied disapproval of the Senate bill. A request was therefore made for a direct statement of his views on the export-debenture principle. He condemned it unequivocally, on the grounds that it would place a heavy annual burden on the Treasury, and would stimulate production, disturb the progress of diversification, give rise to selfish pressures on the board, disturb relations with other countries and require additional taxes.[3]

THE AGRICULTURAL MARKETING ACT OF 1929

The struggle by the Senate to retain the export-debenture feature, with certain amendments presented by Senator Norris of Nebraska, resulted in an impasse between the Senate and the House. Both took firm stands for their versions of the bill, but the House was finally victorious, and the debenture plan was lost. A conference report embodying substantially the language of the House bill was passed by both houses. It was approved on June 15, 1929, thereby bringing into existence the legislative basis for the Federal Farm Board.

Thus ended the most sustained and intensive struggle over a specific piece of agricultural legislation in the nation's history. Many of the ideas developed in the McNary-Haugen era were to reappear in the Roose-

---

1. Both Harding and Coolidge received slightly larger pluralities in the popular vote, but Hoover's majority of electoral votes (444 against 87) was more impressive than that of either Harding or Coolidge.

2. Described more fully in a later section. See pp. 267–69.

3. The text of Hoover's letter, addressed to Senator McNary, was printed as Appendix A, S.Rep. 3, 71st Cong., 1st sess., pp. 15–17.

velt period, and many of the figures that were prominent in this earlier struggle to aid agriculture were to play more important roles after 1933.

The new act, known as the Agricultural Marketing Act of 1929, was not received with enthusiasm by the major farm groups, but was accepted as the best they could get at the time. They undertook therefore to make such use as they could of its facilities and provisions. The act declared it to be the policy of the Congress

to promote the effective merchandising of agricultural commodities in interstate and foreign commerce, so that the industry of agriculture will be placed on a basis of equality with other industries, and to that end to protect, control, and stabilize the currents of interstate and foreign commerce in the marketing of agricultural commodities and their food products.[4]

These ends were to be attained by minimizing speculation, preventing inefficient and wasteful methods of distribution, encouraging the organization of cooperative associations and aiding in controlling and preventing surpluses.

The Board of eight members was to be appointed by the President, with the advice and consent of the Senate, and was to be "fairly representative" of the major agricultural commodities. Provision was made also for the appointment of advisory committees of seven members each for the various agricultural commodities or groups of commodities handled. A revolving fund of $500 million was provided for carrying out the functions of the Board.

The Board was authorized to make loans to cooperatives for:

1. Effective merchandising of agricultural commodities;
2. Construction or acquisition of facilities;
3. Formation of clearing house associations;
4. Extending membership of the cooperative associations; and
5. Making higher advances to growers than could be provided through other credit agencies.

4. For full text of the act see U.S. Federal Farm Board, *First Annual Report for the Year Ending June 30, 1930*, pp. 64–70.

Loans on facilities could be up to 80 per cent and might run for twenty years, on an amortization basis. Interest was to be at the lowest rate yielded by any government obligation issued after April 6, 1917 and outstanding at the time the loan was made, but could not be more than 4 per cent.

Provision was also made for setting up stabilization corporations for the purpose of controlling any surpluses that might arise. Loans could be made to these corporations from the revolving fund. If earnings of such a corporation were inadequate to repay the loan the loss would be absorbed out of the revolving fund. The Board was also authorized, under certain conditions, to provide price insurance to cooperatives.

Membership of the Board

The President appointed as Chairman of the Board Mr. Alexander Legge of Chicago, who was at that time President of the International Harvester Company. The other members were James C. Stone of Kentucky, vice-chairman and representative of the tobacco interests; C. B. Denman of Missouri, prominent in livestock growing and marketing; Samuel R. McKelvie of Nebraska, former governor and farm magazine publisher, to represent the grain interests; William F. Schilling of Minnesota, prominent dairy farmer and president of the Twin City Milk Producers' Association; Charles C. Teague of California, to represent the citrus and nut growers; Carl Williams of Oklahoma, editor of the *Oklahoma Farmer and Stockman,* to represent the cotton growers; and Charles S. Wilson of New York, to represent the fruit interests of the northeastern states. Arthur M. Hyde, Secretary of Agriculture, was, by provision of the act, an ex-officio member of the Board.[5]

5. There were some changes in the Board's membership after the first year of operation. Mr. Legge retired and his place, as chairman, was taken by James Stone, formerly vice-chairman. Teague and McKelvie also withdrew, and were replaced by Sam H. Thompson of Illinois, former President of the American Farm Bureau Federation, and Frank Evans of Utah, former general counsel of that organization. This left the Board with seven instead of eight appointed members.

Main Features of Farm Board Program

The new plan looked to main reliance upon farmer-controlled cooperative associations for solving the farm problem. It was essentially a long-range program, and was similar in concept to the plans popularized by Aaron Sapiro in the early 1920's. It implied giving government assistance to the farmers to do what they had been unable to do without such aid. The powers and duties assigned to the Board were not well suited for dealing with emergency situations or economic catastrophes such as the economy encountered in late 1929. The stabilization corporation feature did, to be sure, introduce some measure of government assistance for times in which agricultural prices were unduly depressed. It was principally intended, however, as a means of evening out the types of surplus and deficit that would result from unusually good or bad crops, seasonal variations in deliveries and the like. The framers of the act creating the Board visualized conditions in which there would be a continuing gradual recovery in agriculture associated with high activity in nonagricultural lines.

This, however, was not the climate in which the new agency was to operate. The calamitous break in stock prices which occurred shortly after the new administration took over was accompanied by such profound changes in the whole economy that the activities of the Board will be more understandable if considered in light of the situation in which its operations had to be undertaken.

Farm-Nonfarm Interdependence

The events of recent years have demonstrated that the prosperity of agriculture depends heavily upon the buying power of nonfarm people. To be sure, the depression of the 1920's had already shown that agriculture could be in distress when urban industries were prosperous and active. Nevertheless, the tremendous decline in nonfarm incomes was to prove a body blow to agriculture, which heretofore had been making significant progress toward equality with the more prosperous urban industries. Both were now to be plunged into almost equally depressed conditions.

It is evident, in such a situation, that efforts to solve the farm problem must include measures designed to strengthen the economy as a whole. Agriculture could not prosper with unemployment at all-time highs, and with consumer incomes down to less than half their previous levels. Unless the steps taken in behalf of the urban economy were successful, an attack in terms of agriculture alone was virtually certain to fail. Though in 1929 this interdependence was not apparent to farm leaders and the Congress, it was to become more and more evident as time went on.

THE FINANCIAL PANIC OF 1929

The Farm Board had scarcely got settled and ready to operate when the most devastating stock market crash in the nation's history occurred. Like a building toppled by an earthquake the vast structure of artificial stock values crumpled into ruins. Thousands of individuals who had been complacently watching the growth of their easily made, paper profits found themselves suddenly plunged into bankruptcy and despair. Everyone sought to sell and few wanted to buy. From October 24 to October 29 stock sales were of panic proportions. By the end of October the value of stocks listed on the New York Stock Exchange had shrunk from $87 billion (as of October 1) to $55 billion.

Through study of data now available, it is possible to recognize weaknesses in the situation that had been growing in significance almost all through the decade. At that time, however, few, even of the best informed, were able to recognize the danger signals.[6]

6. A few individuals did voice doubts about the soundness of the situation, but their warnings were not heeded. A striking exception to the general tone of the financial literature of the period is a brief statement by George Woodruff, Vice-Chairman of the National Bank of the Republic in Chicago, entitled *The Elephants Are Coming, The Story of Inflation in 1927* (unnumbered brochure, 1927). He pointed out that loans of all banks had risen from $28,687 million in 1921 to $36,040 million in 1926; that plain business loans had continued to stand at about $7 billion and that loans to New

Even after the bubble burst, the stunned and bewildered financiers were unable to mobilize sufficient strength and unity to convert the disastrous rout into an orderly retreat.

It still is difficult, if not impossible, to say whether the stock market break played a major role in initiating and magnifying the depression that was getting under way, or was merely the first and most dramatic manifestation of it. Certain it is, however, that the break in the stock market shook business confidence profoundly. What had clearly been an atmosphere of excessive optimism was suddenly changed to one of extreme caution.

All thought was centered on saving what could be saved from the wreckage rather than upon prospects for the future. Financial and business leaders found themselves unable to stop the deflationary trend. As the magnitude of the depression became more evident, wave after wave of selling forced the prices of stocks to lower and lower levels. By the spring of 1933 the value of listed stocks was no more than a fifth of what it had been at the beginning of October 1929. Nearly $70 billion in stock values had been wiped out, and with it had gone the credit bases of millions of investors, and parts of the assets of thousands of banks.[7]

Causes of the Break

A good deal of temerity is required even now to venture conclusions about the causes of the 1929 crash, and still more to attempt to weigh them. It can be stated with some assurance, however, that no one cause alone could bring about such a devastating result. It was the conjunction of a number of forces, all, or most of them, acting in the same direction that gave the event its catastrophic proportions.

The financial structure of the entire western world had been on a precarious basis throughout the decade. Crisis after crisis had arisen in one country or another, and emergency measure after emergency measure had been instituted to deal with them. Huge intergovernmental debts that had grown out of the war resulted in grave distortions of the exchange balances that would have existed on the basis of current propensities to pro-

York stockbrokers had increased from $750 million to about $4 billion. He called attention to the similar phenomenal increase in loans and investments of the Florida banks between 1921 and 1925, and the subsequent disastrous crash in Florida real estate values, and suggested that the national economy might have a similar experience. Few shared his views, however, and the bubble continued to grow.

At about this same time William Trufant Foster and Waddill Catchings of the Pollak Foundation for Economic Research began to publicize a point of view that suggested basic weaknesses in the business situation. Their books, *Profits* (1925); *Business Without A Buyer* (1927); and *The Road to Plenty* (1928), stressed the inability of consumers to spend enough to maintain full production, at prices that would return a profit to producers; and the tendency for savings made by corporations and individuals to accentuate this problem. They proposed creation of a federal board to guide the government in increasing or decreasing expenditures, chiefly on public works, in such a way as to stabilize expenditures for goods and services. Their argument implied an unbalanced budget in times of declining consumer income. Efforts were made to popularize this through wide circulation of pamphlet versions under the titles *The Dilemma of Thrift* and *Progress and Plenty, A Way Out of the Dilemma of Thrift*, and also by offering substantial prizes for criticisms of their views.

7. Frank Vanderlip, formerly President of the National City Bank of New York, writing in the fall of 1932, commented: "The present economic disturbance has been so severe that it has made even some changes in our language. No longer is it an apt metaphor to say that anything is 'as safe as a bank.' The word 'securities' has almost become obsolete. An investment that drops in price to a tenth or, perhaps, even to a twentieth of its former range is not a security; it is a jeopardy. The page of stock-and-bond quotations might well be headed Quotations of Risks and Hazards."

After mentioning the South Sea Bubble of the early eighteenth century he continues, "Here is an example from our own times: United States Steel and General Motors stocks, the two leading industrials of the country, declined from the high quotations of 1929 to 8 per cent of that price. The decline in the stock of the South Sea Company was only to 13½ per cent of its highest quotation. Take another example: The stock of what has long been one of the premier banks of the country declined from 585 to 23½. That is to say, it fell to 4 per cent of its highest quotation.

"The quoted value of all stocks listed on the New York Stock Exchange was, on September 1, 1929, $89,668,276,854. By July 1, 1932, the quoted value of all stocks had fallen to $15,633,479,577.

"Stockholders had lost $74,000,000,000. This figure is so large that not many minds can grasp it. It is $616 for every one of us in America. It is, roughly, three times what we spent in fighting the World War. The bursting of the South Sea Bubble concerned a single company. In the bursting of the New York Stock Exchange bubble, the value of all stocks fell to 17 per cent of their September 1, 1929, price — almost as great a drop as the South Sea Company stock with its fall to 13 per cent of its top price. Remember that this calculation is not a selected example. It is made from the average of all stocks listed on the Exchange." Frank A. Vanderlip, "What About the Banks?," *Saturday Evening Post*, November 5, 1932, p. 3.

duce and consume, and few of the economic readjustments required for sound functioning of the rearranged pattern of European nations had been made. Austria, now an industrial center without a hinterland, and Hungary, now a hinterland without an industrial center, were among the first to collapse. Joint international action was required in 1922 to refinance and stabilize Austria.

The German financial situation got entirely out of hand in 1923 with the mark reaching a fantastic low of 4,200 billion to the dollar. A reconstruction loan, similar to that for Austria, was floated for Hungary in 1924. In 1923 Greece had sought and received League of Nations aid. Britain had undertaken in April 1925 to return to the gold standard at the old rate of exchange, which, as later events showed, was a higher value than she could support.

During the years 1926, 1927 and 1928 it appeared that genuine progress toward stability was being achieved. Germany got her runaway inflation in hand during 1924, Belgium stabilized her currency in 1926, Italy in 1927 and France in 1928. Other countries such as India, Yugoslavia and Poland appeared to be making progress toward financial stability. There were serious weaknesses in the situation, however. France held huge credits in London and New York which could be withdrawn almost overnight. Germany was seeking to acquire gold, most of which had to come from London, thus weakening the sterling position.

The Dawes Plan of 1924 and the Young Plan of 1929 had been launched in an effort to get the payment of German reparations into workable form. For a time heavy purchases of foreign bonds by investors in the United States kept the top-heavy structure intact, but doubts were beginning to arise with respect to these loans as early as 1928, and by 1929 the flow of such capital dropped to less than half that of the peak years, 1927 and 1928.[8] Through the summer of 1929

there was a heavy flow of gold to France, mostly from London, partly from Berlin and, after the stock market crash, from New York.[9]

The stock market boom in the United States, with its accompanying high rates of interest, tended to draw funds, including gold, from all parts of the world. This weakened still further the gold position of Britain, and was partly responsible for an increase in the British loan rate which was designed to check the outflow of gold and initiate a movement in the opposite direction. On September 26, 1929, the Bank of England rate, already high at 5½ per cent, was raised to 6½ per cent, thus reflecting the dangerously unstable situation in the international exchanges.

Unbalanced World Trade

A further factor disturbing to exchange relationships was the growing size of the export surplus of the United States. After World War I this fell off to $375 million in 1923, but increased sharply in 1924 to $981 million. Except for 1926 it remained high during the succeeding years of the 1920's, reaching more than a billion dollars in 1928. Even through 1929 and 1930 this unbalance amounted to around $800 million.[10] This situation, due in part to the high level of tariffs imposed by the United States in 1922, naturally tended to weaken foreign exchanges and even to draw some gold from the customer countries. It thus had a depressing effect on the world economy.

Year	Millions of Dollars
Average 1919–1923	685
1924–1926	1,274
1927	1,577
1928	1,488
1929	706
1930	1,086

"Foreign Loan Markets in New York," *The Economist*, London, March 21, 1931, p. 604.

9. For a more detailed summary of the conditions and events described above see H. V. Hodson, *Slump and Recovery, 1929-1937, A Survey of World Economic Affairs*, Oxford University Press, London, 1938, Chapter 1.

10. Data from *Statistical Abstract, 1935*, p. 420. During most of these years the net movement of gold was to the United States in moderate amounts. However, in 1928, the net out-movement amounted to $391 million. *Ibid.*, p. 421.

8. Public issues of foreign securities in New York during these years were as follows:

In the western world as a whole the general course of prices was irregularly but gradually downward. Between 1923 and 1929 prices in Great Britain fell 20 per cent; those in Sweden, 11 per cent; Holland, 12 per cent; and in the United States, 10 per cent.[11] The violent fluctuations in prices throughout most of the world reflected the fact that many postwar adjustments were still incomplete. During this period nine of the major world-trade commodities showed a range of price amounting to approximately 100 per cent as between the lowest and highest prices reached.[12] These severe price changes were especially disturbing to countries heavily dependent for international earnings on only one or two commodities, as, for example, Brazilian coffee, Japanese silk, Cuban sugar, Argentine beef and wheat, Mexican oil and silver, and Chilean nitrates. The situation was conducive to nationalistic policies such as the imposition of additional tariffs and quotas, and a general slowing down of world trade, especially after 1930 when the barriers to world trade reached an all-time high.

Internal Factors

Within the United States the boom and subsequent depression appear to have been caused mainly by two factors: (1) an expansion of investment, especially in commercial structures, beyond what the market would absorb; and (2) a tendency to hold prices and wages stable while technological advances were reducing the costs of production at an unusually rapid rate. This resulted in increased profits which in turn justified relatively sharp advances in the prices of stocks.[13]

The initial increase in stock prices set in motion a feverish speculative buying of stock which presently came to be based mainly on expectations of further price increases rather than upon the prospective earnings of the stocks. Furthermore, very large amounts of such purchases were made with borrowed money rather than with actual savings.

The most active period of stock speculation occurred between 1926 and September 1929. By the latter date the general average of stock prices reached 225 per cent of the levels of 1926. Some individual stocks showed much more spectacular increases. Such a situation naturally excited the cupidity of speculators. Thousands of buyers, both large and small, were pouring saved and borrowed funds into the stock market. Many of these were newcomers to the business and widely scattered over the country. So pronounced was the speculative mania that the upswing continued even after construction, manufacturing and employment began to fall off. The index of building contracts reached its peak (139) as early as June 1928 and was down to 126 by

11. Hodson, *Slump and Recovery*, p. 34. The United States figure as given by Hodson differs from various compilations published in the United States. The *Statistical Abstract, 1935* (p. 292) shows a decline from 100.6 (1926 = 100) in 1923 to 95.3 in 1929. There can be no doubt, however, that the general trend internationally was downward. The more marked recession in Great Britain was apparently due largely to the return to the gold standard and the restoration of the pound to prewar parity with the dollar.

12. These were tin, sugar, coffee, jute, silk, wool and cotton. Hodson, *Slump and Recovery*, p. 35.

13. Net incomes of corporations increased rather consistently from $8,322 million in 1923 to $11,654 million

in 1929 (*Statistical Abstract, 1948*, p. 339). Average weekly earnings of production workers in manufacturing rose only from $23.82 in 1923 to $25.03 in 1929 (*ibid.*, p. 217). During these years wholesale prices of all commodities remained notably stable, ranging between a low of 95.3 in 1929 and a high of 103.5 in 1925 (1926 = 100). With the exception of 1925 the range was between approximately 95 and 100 (*ibid.*, p. 296). Between 1923 and 1929 the number of wage earners in manufacturing industries remained approximately constant, but during this same period value added by manufacture increased from $25,778 million in 1923 to $31,783 million in 1929 (*Statistical Abstract, 1935*, p. 715).

These figures, which at best are very rough, would seem to indicate that the major gain from increasing technological efficiency was reflected in corporation profits. Lesser portions of it appeared in the form of slightly higher weekly earnings of workers in industry and slightly lower prices to the consumer. Figures presented by Leo Wolman in 1929 indicated that output per person engaged in manufacture had increased from an index of 107.9 in 1921 (1899 = 100) to 149.5 in 1927. *Recent Economic Changes in the United States*, Report of the Committee on Recent Economic Changes of the President's Conference on Unemployment (Herbert Hoover, Chairman), National Bureau of Economic Research, New York, 1929, Vol. II, p. 454. F. C. Mills shows the average annual rates of change between 1922 and 1927 as follows: For profits of industrial corporations, + 9 per cent; for factory payrolls, + 1.7 per cent; for wholesale prices of all commodities, — 0.2 per cent; for prices of industrial stocks, + 14.1 per cent. *Ibid.*, p. 607.

June 1929 (1923–1925 = 100).[14] Employment in manufacturing industries declined in 1927 and 1928, from the levels of 1926, but recovered during the summer of 1929. Production of manufactures reached its peak in June 1929 at 127 (1923–1925 = 100) and was down to 121 by September.[15] The stock market, which normally is expected to foreshadow changes in trend, continued to advance until late October.

Federal Reserve Board Policy

The Federal Reserve Board took cognizance of the unhealthy situation in the stock market as early as January 1928. Throughout 1928 and the first half of 1929 it exerted pressures designed to curb speculative borrowing. The first step was the traditional one of selling securities with a view to curtailing the funds available for use in the stock market. During the first half of 1928 nearly $400 million worth of reserve bank holdings of government securities were sold. In addition, rediscount rates were raised from 3½ per cent to 4 per cent in March, and to 4½ per cent in June. Eight of the banks raised the rate still further, to 5 per cent, in August.[16] These actions had little effect on stock market borrowings. The prospects of profit there were too great to be much affected by moderate increases in rates of interest. The concern was not what the interest rate would be but, rather, could the loan be obtained at some rate? Call money rates advanced throughout 1928, and in March 1929 reached 20 per cent, as compared to the 4 to 6 per cent that had been customary between 1923 and 1928.[17]

The efforts of the Federal Reserve Board to control speculation through quantitative restrictions on credit proved futile. The high rates of interest on call money were drawing into the stock market huge amounts of loan funds that were not under the control of the

Reserve Board. The New York banks did decrease their holdings of brokers' loans by $168 million, but out-of-town banks increased theirs by $306 million, and "other sources" contributed an increase of $1,334 million.

Thus the principal effect of Reserve Board pressure was to hamper legitimate small business. Many of the big corporations had huge cash reserves and hence were not dependent on bank credit. In fact, these funds, some of which were loaned to speculators, helped to accentuate the stock market boom and tended to render Federal Reserve Board restraints ineffective.

By February 1929 the Board abandoned the policy of trying to check stock market speculation by pressure in the form of interest rate increases and quantitative controls, and sought to use selective controls; that is, to refuse rediscounts to banks which maintained a volume of speculative loans in excess of that considered reasonable.[18] This avoided the dilemma of squeezing business effectively in order to squeeze speculative lending ineffectively. It was not successful, however, partly because of resistance by some of the reserve

14. After adjustment for seasonal change. See Hodson, *Slump and Recovery*, p. 54.

15. *Statistical Abstract, 1935*, p. 748.

16. Charles O. Hardy, *Credit Policies of the Federal Reserve System*, The Brookings Institution, Washington, 1932, p. 129.

17. New York Stock Exchange, Committee on Public Relations, *Year Book, 1936*, p. 74.

18. From about 1926 onward there was much discussion of the need for stabilizing the value of the dollar, that is, keeping its purchasing power relatively stable. The Stable Money Association was formed, and at various times extensive hearings were held by congressional committees. See, for example, U.S. Congress, House, Committee on Banking and Currency, *Stabilization, Hearings . . . on H.R. 11806*, 70th Cong., 1st sess., 1929.

While agreement on the objective of a stabilized price level was rather general, there was no like agreement on how to achieve it or, in fact, that it could be achieved. Some economists, following the general lead of Professor Irving Fisher of Yale University, argued for stabilization by varying the amount of gold in the dollar in accordance with changes in the prices of commodities. Others urged directives, and assignment of powers, to the Federal Reserve Board looking to the elimination of major ups and downs in the price level. Some favored policies that would reflect technological reductions in costs in the form of lower prices while others, for example, Professor John R. Commons, a leading labor economist, would have preferred to see such gains reflected in higher wages for workers in the particular industries where gains in efficiency occurred. Actually none of these ideas gained much headway. The major gains from increased efficiency appeared in the form of profits rather than of either lower prices or increased wage payments. Most of the discussions carried on during this period laid little stress on compensatory fiscal policies on the part of the government; that is, deficit spending in times of depression and debt retirement in times of prosperity. This concept was not to be widely discussed until ten years later.

banks and partly because of large amounts of money that flowed into the stock market from sources other than the banks, notably the liquid reserves of corporations.[19]

In March 1929, there were some indications that a panic might be imminent, but the situation was "saved" by a bold move on the part of Charles E. Mitchell, President of the National City Bank of New York, in throwing $25 million into the call money market. The situation eased, and call money rates gradually receded.

The Break in Stock Prices

The break came on October 24, 1929. Stock transfers, which had been running some four to six million shares per day, jumped to almost thirteen million shares. After a few days of stunned inactivity a new wave of selling occurred with sales reaching nine million shares on October 28, and almost sixteen and one half millions on October 29, the peak day. During the first two weeks of November the Exchange was closed for special holidays, or put on short hours to give time to consider measures to stem the disaster, but the damage was done. The shock to business confidence, and the tremendous shrinkage in liquid credit, had given impetus to deflationary tendencies throughout the world. The nation's economy was skidding downward into the greatest depression in its history.

It was by no means immediately clear that this was the case. Businessmen, professional economists and the administration itself rather generally believed that what was occurring was an unusually severe business recession of the type commonly described in studies of the business cycle. But the worst was yet to come. Industrial stocks had ranged from a high of 469.49 to a low of 220.95 during 1929. Each year thereafter until 1933 showed new lows: 196.67 in 1930; 110.73 in 1931; and 57.62 in 1932. The latter figure was about one eighth of the peak level reached in 1929. The decline of the rails was even more

severe, from a high of 158.71 in 1929 to a low of 10.34 in 1932.[20]

Farm prices likewise hit the skids though they had not been inflated at the time the crash came. Standing at 104.9 in 1929 (1926 = 100) they were down to 88.3 by 1930; reached 64.8 for 1931; and sank still further, to 48.2 in 1932.[21] Hogs, which had sold for $10.67 in 1929, were only $4.12 in 1932. Wheat slumped from $1.30 to $0.53, despite vigorous efforts to check the decline. Cotton likewise fell from 18.6 cents to 6.3 cents, though similar efforts were made to support its price.[22] Industrial production fell from 110 (1935-1939 = 100) in October 1929 to 53 in July 1932. Factory employment declined from 106.6 (1923-1925 = 100) in October 1929 to 61.9 in July 1932.[23] Factory payrolls were down from 116.4 (1939 = 100) in 1929 to 49.2 in 1932.

The Banking Situation

Accompanying and in part causing these declines were vast shrinkages in bank credit and other mediums of purchase. Loans of all banks, which stood at nearly $41.5 billion in 1929, shrank to $20.5 billion by the end of 1934,[24] thus wiping out more than $20 billion of the previously available purchasing medium. Most banks were desperately seeking to reduce loans and get their assets into more liquid form. But the assets of many of them had been too badly depreciated, or they were unable to achieve liquidity fast enough. As a result, bank failures increased sharply. During 1930 more than 1,300 banks closed their doors, and in 1931 the number rose to almost 2,300.[25] The number of suspensions was still

---

19. For an excellent account of the controversies of this period in regard to Federal Reserve policy, see Hardy, *Credit Policies of the Federal Reserve System*, Chapter 7.

20. Data from *New York Times*, averages of 25 industrials and 25 railroads as given in *Statistical Abstract, 1935*, p. 285.

21. *Ibid.*, p. 292.

22. *Ibid.*, p. 294.

23. Seasonally adjusted data for production and employment from the Federal Reserve Board and the Bureau of Labor Statistics as given in *Historical Statistics of the United States, 1789-1945*, Bureau of the Census, pp. 330 and 328. Payrolls indexes, *ibid.*, p. 67.

24. *Historical Statistics of the United States, 1789-1945*, p. 262.

25. Some were reopened, but the number was small; 159 in 1930 and 276 in 1931. *Statistical Abstract, 1935*, p. 267.

very large in 1932 (1,456). Many of the weaker banks, especially in the rural areas, had been eliminated in the agricultural depression of the 1920's. Thus the number of banks, which had been about 30,000 in the early 1920's, was down to fewer than 15,000 by 1933.

Reactions to the Slump

As it became clear that the slump was no ordinary business recession but a genuine depression of major proportions, individual reactions to it operated to accentuate the maladjustment. Creditors sought to protect themselves by calling old loans and denying new ones; depositors held on to their liquid funds, and later, as confidence in the banking structure declined, withdrew them, to store away as money in safety deposit boxes or other hiding places, thus rendering them useless as a support to business activity.

The impact of these tendencies upon agriculture was disastrous. Insurance companies and commercial banks held more than a third of the farm mortgage loans. Most were for short terms (usually not more than three to five years) and soon were falling due. Since these agencies were striving for a more liquid position and seeking to contract their farm mortgage holdings, renewals were extremely difficult to obtain, especially for farmers who were heavily in debt and rather generally operating in the red. The demand for federal land bank loans grew enormously, but the land banks were unequipped, either with funds or personnel, to handle immediately the volume of lending required. Defaults, forced sales and transfers to creditors increased enormously. Nearly a million farmers lost their farms between 1930 and 1934 and were forced into unemployment or wagework, or dropped to tenant status as operators of farms that had passed into the hands of creditor agencies.

The gross income of American agriculture fell from $11,941 million in 1929 to $5,331 million in 1932. The estimated value of agricultural capital fell similarly, from $58 billion in 1929 to $36 billion in 1933.[26] Land prices, reflected, of course, in the figures on value of agricultural capital given above, fell from an index of 116 in 1929 (1912–1914 = 100) to 73 in 1932.[27]

Mere figures can give no adequate picture of the gloom and despair that gripped the country. Employment fell off, breadlines appeared in the cities and farmers were burning corn in place of coal, because it was cheaper. In the great food-producing states of the Middle West radical movements of a kind scarcely known in earlier years began to spring up. Among these were such spontaneous mass protests as the Farmers' Holiday movement which sought to prevent delivery of farm products until the people of the cities would agree to pay more adequate prices. In Iowa and other middle western states mobs gathered to prevent foreclosure sales, and in some cases even threatened judges in the execution of legal claims against debtors. Law and order were close to a breakdown, even in areas that had long been thought of as the backbone of conservatism.[28]

Conditions in the farm areas were truly desperate. Yet the situation was greatly changed from that of the 1920's. No longer was the farmer voicing his protest against a prosperous urban sector of the economy. Inequalities had been removed, not by raising the farmer to the urban level, but by a disaster that reduced nearly all classes to a condition of severe depression. The statistics do not, in fact, tell a true story of relative conditions in agriculture as against those in urban areas. The farmer, if he could retain some sort of tenure even though it be that of tenant instead of owner, did have a means of self-employment, a roof over his head, and, in most cases, an adequate supply of food. The city dweller, on the other hand, could neither guarantee himself a job nor provide food and shelter for his family, if he was out of work.

26. *Yearbook of Agriculture, 1935,* p. 673.
27. *Ibid.,* p. 686.
28. See William Allen White, "The Farmer Takes His Holiday," *Saturday Evening Post,* November 26, 1932, pp. 6–7, 64–70.

The urban resident who retained his job was, to be sure, better off than he had been before. His earnings would buy more food, clothing and shelter, but he was plagued by the prospect that further deterioration in the situation might deprive him of all of these. Some few receivers of undiminished incomes were distinctly better off than before, but here too the specter of complete breakdown and the loss of this favored position was ever present.

Efforts to Better the Situation

It has become fashionable in recent years to point with pride to the aggressive attack on depression problems after March 4, 1933, and to deplore the inactivity of the administration that went out of power at that time. This naïve and highly personalized contrast is far too simple to satisfy any careful student of the problem. When great disasters occur it is customary to seek a scapegoat. In this case the scapegoat was Hoover. That there were grave defects in the policies adopted at that time cannot be denied. But our realization of these defects is largely hindsight rather than a warrant for pride in our superior analytical abilities. At that time neither the intellectuals nor the opposition party proposed clear-cut alternative programs.

The Harvard Economic Society arranged at Boston, in December 1929, a serious and weighty conclave on the causes of the stock market crash and prospects for the future. The participants still talked in terms of business cycles and variously forecast an upturn perhaps as early as February; almost certainly not later than the following autumn. Such conferences brought forth no ringing call to action; no demand for a major change of direction in national policy.[29]

Left-wing and liberal organs of expression such as the *Nation,* the *New Republic, Harper's Magazine* and the *Atlantic Monthly* contained, during these early years of the depression, little in the way of bold and specific proposals for dealing with the desperate situation that was developing. Many intellectuals turned toward Marxism, and the economic interpretation of life became a major preoccupation of American literature. Earlier, in the 1920's, Sinclair Lewis had developed a technique for deflating the American businessman, and hard after him the proletarian novelists brought forth a spate of works obsessed with the oppression of the lower classes and the increasing tension between them and the employing groups. Many, such as Theodore Dreiser, grasped at communism as a solution to their confusion, while another group began to look wistfully backward to an American culture that had flourished before the crass materialism of the late nineteenth century overwhelmed it.[30]

The Democratic party leaders were likewise strangely silent in view of the scorn that was later heaped on those who were in charge of the machinery of state at the time. Their campaign in the congressional elections of 1930 was mainly given over to placing the blame for the debacle on the Republican party rather than to suggesting what should be done to bring about recovery.

Such blame, while very possibly merited, could not appropriately be assessed wholly against the Republicans since, on the factors that really contributed to the depression, the Democratic minority had shown little more clarity of vision than had the majority party. The record does not justify a holier-than-thou attitude on the part of either the disciples of change or the spokesmen for the old order.

29. The causes of the depression were discussed at some length in the meetings of the American Economic Association held in December 1930. While there was a measure of agreement about the causes of the slump there was no corresponding agreement on what to do about it. See Josef Schumpeter, "The Present World Depression: A Tentative Diagnosis," and discussion, *American Economic Review,* Proceedings supplement, March 1931, pp. 179-201.

30. For a stimulating discussion of these attitudes see Gilbert Seldes, *The Years of the Locust (America, 1929-1932),* Little, Brown, Boston, 1933, Chapter 21. Proposals by some from the extreme right were as futile and confused as those of the sympathizers with communism. There was considerable sentiment for a supergovernment body, patterned on Fascist lines. See for example, *ibid.,* pp. 224-25. The lack was not of mechanisms already in existence, or which could be readily set up, but of ideas as to what they might do.

Who Knew What to Do?

New and more vigorous policies were needed, but no one knew quite what they should be. Certainly the old guard, both in and out of government, was far too rigid in its thinking and too much wedded to orthodox ideas and procedures. But who knew of other ways, except the vague idealistic conceptions of the socialists and communists? Bold new programs were in order, but the country was not yet ready for them, and almost certainly would not have agreed to them.

President Hoover recognized the gravity of the situation, and accepted the challenge implied by it. He threw into the effort the prestige of his office and the tools he had or felt would be effective. That these were not the right ones, and not sufficiently powerful, is more easily seen now than at that time. In fact it is probable that they would have had to be tried first in any event, since political and economic traditionalists would have been unwilling to accept more vigorous and radical measures until these had been tried. The policies of the Hoover administration can more appropriately be criticized for the rigidity of mind and lack of imagination that characterized the later years of that period than for the actions taken in the first years of the depression.

First Period — "Business as Usual"

On November 21, 1929, Hoover called together a group of prominent business leaders, and proposed to them that wage rates be maintained; that construction work already planned by industry be carried through; that government agencies increase construction activities; that work be spread among all employees by shortening the work week wherever this was necessary and possible; and that each industry undertake to alleviate distress among its own employees. This general policy was agreed to, and on the afternoon of the same day the principal labor leaders were called together and were induced to pledge cooperation along these general lines. On the following day leaders in the construc-

tion industry were likewise called in, and urged to cooperate in the attempt to stimulate activity in the building industry. These steps were followed, on November 24, by telegrams to state governors and mayors of principal cities. Virtually all of the governors and mayors signified their agreement, and pledged support. Similar conferences on November 25 and 27 brought in the leaders of the farm organizations and the public utilities.[31]

There was almost universal approval of these proposals, and the effect was to restore temporarily some measure of confidence. The values of listed stocks moved upward during December and the early months of 1930.[32] Both the administration and the leaders of the business, labor and farm groups had, however, gravely underestimated the seriousness of the situation and the deadening effect of the loss of confidence that had become so widespread.

It soon became apparent that exhortation and such voluntary cooperation as could be achieved would not restore confidence and

31. The Federal Reserve Board was likewise taking what were then regarded as vigorous steps to ease the situation. It bought in the open market, during the fall quarter of 1929, some $500 million worth of eligible paper and government securities, and reduced the rediscount rate, on November 1, to 5 per cent, and on November 15 to 4½ per cent. That these mild measures were wholly inadequate to offset the tremendous shrinkage in credit and buying power was not clearly seen at that time.

In his message to the Congress at the opening of its regular session, on December 3, the President reviewed the stock market crash, and recommended: (1) increased appropriations for public works and the Federal Farm Board; (2) banking reform; (3) income tax reduction; (4) expansion of the merchant marine by new ship construction to aid employment; (5) consolidation of the railroads; (6) development of public health services; and (7) reorganization of government departments for purposes of economy. For a detailed description of these steps see Herbert Hoover, *The State Papers and Other Public Writings of Herbert Hoover*, edited by William Starr Myers, Doubleday, Doran, Garden City, 1934, Vol. I, pp. 138–67.

32. See New York Stock Exchange, *Report of the President, May 1st, 1930–May 1st, 1931*, 1931, chart, p. 36. The Department of Labor index of all employment, which had fallen from 93.3 in October 1929 to 86.0 at the end of December, was reported by the President to be back up to 92.8 by February. William Starr Myers and Walter H. Newton, *The Hoover Administration, A Documented Narrative*, Charles Scribner's Sons, New York, 1936, p. 35. The reliability of these data has, of course, been frequently challenged in later years.

business activity.[33] The brief recovery movement petered out, and the nation settled more and more deeply into depression. It is here that the inadequacy of the Hoover policies becomes more apparent. The need was for a quick shift to deficit spending on a large scale.[34] This, however, was anathema to one nurtured, as Hoover had been, in the doctrine of the sanctity of balanced budgets both public and private. He resisted proposals for increased spending on the ground that they would unbalance the budget. This position was perforce relinquished in the later years of his administration, but too grudgingly and sparingly as judged by more recent conceptions of fiscal policy.

Budget Unbalance Deplored

J. M. Keynes had not yet popularized the doctrine of compensatory budgets, and few voices were raised in behalf of that technique.[35] The extent of budget unbalancing

that did occur became in fact the basis of some of Roosevelt's sharpest criticisms in the campaign of 1932, and he himself launched, in the early part of 1933, a vigorous effort to cut down government expenditures.

This was quickly abandoned, however, in favor of the greatly expanded program of deficit spending which was so prominent a feature of the "New Deal" period. An earlier and more vigorous adoption of that policy would very probably have checked the depression sooner and lessened the amount of deficit spending needed later. This, however, is hindsight analysis. The doctrine then widely accepted was that genuine recovery must await extensive readjustments in wage rates, prices and debts, and that undue delay in carrying these out would serve only to prolong the agony.[36]

The Hawley-Smoot Tariff Act of 1930

July 1930 marked the culmination of one of the major mistakes of the Hoover administration and the Seventy-first Congress. In his message to the special session of the Congress, in April 1929, the President recommended a limited revision of tariffs with particular reference to aid for agriculture.[37]

33. There was little significant action by the Congress. The struggle over the new tariff bill held the center of the stage. In the early part of January the President proposed to various congressional leaders certain increases in appropriations for public works. These were eventually passed (in July 1930) at slightly higher figures than those suggested by Hoover—$530 million for public buildings; $145 million for rivers and harbors; $75 million for public road subsidies; and $65 million for the Colorado Dam.

34. Deficit financing in a time of acute depression should be regarded as only one part of an adequate long-term fiscal and monetary policy. The budget should be more than balanced in good times, both to prevent inflation and to strengthen the fiscal position of the government so that it can incur deficits in bad times. In a period of severe depression and widespread unemployment the government is the only agency that can act vigorously, and on a large scale, to increase purchasing power. On the other hand, it is the one best situated to absorb purchasing power through increased taxes and tighter credit policies when inflationary tendencies develop. It is this latter situation that is least likely to be handled courageously. Nevertheless, in a period like that of the early 1930's it is clearly both unsound and politically impossible to balance the budget on an annual basis.

35. Deficit spending to bolster purchasing power had been suggested by a number of earlier "unorthodox" writers, but this idea did not gain any widespread acceptance until set forth by Keynes in his General Theory of Employment, Interest and Money, which appeared in 1936. Some beginnings in the way of informal presentation of these doctrines had been made earlier, though Keynes' own views as late as 1930 when he published his Treatise on Money were quite the opposite of those expressed six years later in the General Theory of Employment, Interest and Money. In an article in the Atlantic Monthly, "The World's Economic Outlook," May

1932, he expressed views more in accord with those later so prominently associated with his name. It is probable that the heavy spending of the early years of the Roosevelt administration was not an implementation of any doctrine that large-scale deficit spending was an appropriate measure for curing depressions, but rather that the appearance of such a doctrine at about that time was seized upon as a convenient rationalization of a policy already adopted. Extensive study and discussion of the Keynesian analysis have since brought about a much better understanding of the relation between governmental budgets and the volume of purchasing power in the economy. There is little evidence that such understanding existed in the early 1930's, either in Republican or Democratic circles, or for that matter in the ranks of professional economists.

36. This view, which was widely held by businessmen, and by many economists, had a good deal of validity if we accept the conclusion that the whole economy was inevitably destined to be readjusted to a new price and income basis as had been customary in earlier depressions. In that event the sooner the adjustments were made the more quickly business activity would revive. It was, however, a harsh and costly process, and its advocates tended to ignore the greatly increased rigidity of many elements in the situation. The costs in human misery were bound to be so enormous as to make reliance on such automatic adjustment almost unthinkable.

37. After advocating "an effective tariff upon agricultural products, that will compensate the farmer's higher standards of living" and higher costs of production, the

Knowing some such proposal was likely, the House Ways and Means Committee had already started work on a new tariff act, and for some months had been holding hearings on the matter. Hoover's action in recommending "limited" revision reflected his lack of political experience. A congressional tariff revision, once started, almost always develops into a logrolling spree in which nearly every industry and constituency seeks higher protection for its particular products. In such a setting it was inevitable that nonagricultural products, which could gain from increased tariffs, would fare better than agricultural products, which for the most part could not be benefited by tariff increases. Thus the result that might be expected from a general upward revision of tariffs would be a widening of the gap between farm and nonfarm prices, further deterioration in the export markets and stimulation of retaliatory measures on the part of other governments.

Instead of shaping up as a logical adjustment of American tariffs to the unbalanced trading situation, the new legislation took exactly the opposite turn. Tariffs were raised to all-time highs, and the strangulation of United States foreign trade, already under way as a result of the depression, was made doubly severe by a tariff wall that virtually excluded many types of merchandise. So inappropriate was the bill that more than 1,000 of the country's leading economists signed a memorial to the President asking that he veto it. Despite this clear warning of the evil effects likely to follow from it, Hoover signed the bill on July 17, 1930.[38]

Effect on World Trade

This unwise action by the United States set off a wave of nationalistic fence-building throughout the world. Blocked in their efforts to sell their goods in the United States, other nations sought to protect their currencies by preventing the importation of goods from the United States.[39] Tariffs were raised, quotas and embargoes were placed on imports and each country sought to buy as little from outside its borders as possible.[40]

The result was much like that which would come about if, in order to hoard money, the baker decided to live on bread and not buy meat from the butcher; the butcher chose to get along on meat and not buy milk from the dairyman, and the growers of fruits and vegetables sought to subsist on their own products and refrain from buying meats, milk or bread.

In a situation such as that which followed 1930 it is impossible to measure the amount

President discussed the revision of tariffs on nonfarm products in the following terms: ". . . there have been economic shifts necessitating a readjustment of some of the tariff schedules. Seven years of experience under the tariff bill enacted in 1922 have demonstrated the wisdom of Congress in the enactment of that measure. On the whole it has worked well. . . . Nevertheless, economic changes have taken place during that time, which have placed certain domestic products at a disadvantage and new industries have come into being, all of which creates the necessity for some limited changes in the schedules and in the administrative clauses of the law as written in 1922." Message to the First Session of the 71st Congress, April 16, 1929. (Special Session for Farm Relief and Limited Changes in the Tariff.) Hoover, *State Papers*, Vol. I, pp. 31–37.

38. The Senate vote in favor of the bill was by the

narrow margin of 44 to 42, and was achieved only by enticing five Democrats into the protectionist fold: Louisiana with sugar, Wyoming with wool, and Florida with fruit. Eleven Republicans and one Farmer-Laborite voted against the bill. John D. Hicks, *The American Nation*, Houghton Mifflin, Boston, 1941, p. 612.

39. Unless such purchases are financed by loans or some similar means, countries which permit heavy imports that are not compensated by exports are subject to severe drains on their gold reserves to make up the balances. With the monetary and banking structures prevalent in 1930, this was deflationary for the gold-exporting nation, and, if carried very far, would force it off the gold standard. Hence, almost all countries faced with a continuing deficit of exports to pay for their imports undertook to reduce imports by raising tariffs or applying quotas and embargoes.

40. "Early in June 1932 the Economic Committee of the League of Nations reported that since the beginning of 1930 practically every country had remoulded its customs tariff on a more or less extensive scale, or had increased its import duties on particular products; and that in the past few months alone, for example, Belgium, Denmark, Estonia, Italy, Latvia, Lithuania, the Netherlands, Poland, Portugal, Rumania, Sweden, Bolivia, Brazil, Siam, the Union of South Africa, and — 'most striking development of all' — the United Kingdom, had increased their duties in some cases on important categories of goods, or even on the whole of their tariffs. Moreover, measures for the direct regulation of trade had been widely adopted, of which the most frequent were measures to establish import quotas or to institute import licenses or permits." Hodson, *Slump and Recovery*, p. 103.

The German tariff on wheat was raised to $1.60 per bushel; that of Italy, in 1931, stood at more than $1.00 per bushel; while France's tariff was more than $0.80 a bushel. Louis H. Bean, *Economic Trends Affecting Agriculture*, U.S. Department of Agriculture, 1933, p. 31.

of decline in world trade that was due to tariffs and other trade barriers, and that due to other causes. Certain it is, however, that both imports and exports of the United States fell to less than a third of what they had been in 1929, at precisely the time when a strong export demand was needed to ease the pressure of ever-increasing stocks on the markets for farm products.[41] In addition there had been built up throughout the world a vast array of rigid barriers to trade which would require years of effort to adjust downward to levels at which trade could be carried on efficiently and naturally. Almost all who have studied this period agree in characterizing the Hawley-Smoot tariff as one of the most inappropriate steps taken during the Hoover administration, and one that served to deepen and prolong the depression.

The Drought of 1930

During the summer of 1930 serious droughts occurred in a number of the farm states, and caused considerable distress. The lack of rainfall was mainly in middle and late summer, however, and did not decrease materially the small-grain and cotton crops which were those causing greatest difficulty in the management of the administration's farm program. The livestock industry was the one most seriously affected. To deal with this problem the President called a conference of governors of the states affected, and set up a National Drought Committee to coordinate federal and local efforts to aid the farmers of these areas. The Red Cross allocated $5 million for immediate aid; federal credit was made available to save livestock and finance farm families that were in distress; and railroad rates were reduced 50 per cent on food, feed and livestock shipped into and out of the drought-stricken areas.

41. United States imports fell off from $4,399 million in 1929 to $3,061 million in 1930, and thereafter continued to decline, reaching a low of $1,323 million in 1932. They did not again reach the 1929 level until 1946. Exports showed similar declines. Standing at $5,241 million in 1929, they were down to $3,843 million in 1930, and fell off to $1,611 million in 1932. *Statistical Abstract, 1935,* p. 420.

The Bleak Winter of 1930–1931

On October 30, 1930, the President set up the President's Committee for Unemployment Relief. This committee, under the direction of Colonel Arthur Woods, undertook to establish in each state a relief committee of leading citizens to coordinate, in each locality, the private activities with those of state and federal agencies. Hoover took a strong stand in favor of decentralized organization, insisting that if the federal government were forced to pay for and administer direct relief, as some members of the Congress were advocating, the result would be much politics, graft and waste. In his message of December 2, 1930, he again stated that he was not convinced there was necessity for direct action by the government. He expressed his general philosophy in the following terms:

Economic depression can not be cured by legislative action or executive pronouncement. Economic wounds must be healed by the action of the cells of the economic body — the producers and consumers themselves.[42]

His proposals for agriculture contemplated loans for seed, and for feed for animals, while main reliance for the relief of human distress would be on the Red Cross and "the sympathetic assistance of our people."

To expand employment the message recommended an increase of $100 million to $150 million for an enlarged construction program, and authority to make larger temporary advances for federal highway aid to states. A request was made for legislation to facilitate consolidation of the railroads. The message also called for study of the Sherman antitrust laws to determine if wasteful competition in the field of natural resources could be avoided, and suggested that the income tax on "so-called capital gains" may enhance speculative inflation and impede business recovery. A study of this was likewise recommended.[43]

42. Hoover, *State Papers,* Vol. I, pp. 429–30.
43. These recommendations reflect the confused thinking of the period. The last three in particular were inconsequential or irrelevant in relation to the major

This final lame-duck session of the Seventy-first Congress (December 1930–March 1931) brought a flood of bills calling for relief expenditures. Hoover contended that some congressmen were· "playing politics at the expense of human misery."[44]

By the end of 1930 the main items of the Hoover recommendations for relief were passed. The House Committee on Appropriations had reported out $30 million for drought relief. Senator Robinson of Arkansas, and other Democrats and Progressives, demanded $60 million. The item was compromised at $45 million. Appropriations of $116 million for immediate use in public construction and $150 million for use by the Farm Board in supporting the grain and cotton markets were passed. Senators Robinson, Borah and others proposed an appropriation of $25 million for distribution by the Red Cross. Chairman Payne of the Red Cross refused to accept this, after it had been passed as a rider in the Senate. The matter was finally compromised by making an appropriation of $20 million for food loans to drought sufferers, to be administered by the Department of Agriculture.

Moratorium on War Debts Proposed

In May 1931 new crises developed in the financial affairs of the leading European nations. Starting in Austria in mid-May, these troubles spread to Germany, Hungary, Rumania and eventually to Britain. In an effort to check this new threat to economic stability, Hoover, on June 20, proposed a one-year moratorium on intergovernmental debts, reparations and relief debts, both of principal and interest. The favorable first effect of this announcement was largely lost through delay in gaining agreement to it on the part of France. In the meantime further failures of important European companies and banks worsened the situation, and drains on London became more severe.

France had proposed that the United States, Britain and France loan Germany $500 million to bolster its shaky economic structure. Hoover suggested instead that all banks in the creditor nations enter into a standstill agreement to refrain from presenting for payment, during a specified time, their short-term German bills. This plan was adopted at the London Conference, on July 23, 1931.[45]

The easement came too late, however, and Britain, on September 21, 1931, reluctantly went off the gold standard. The pound fell from $4.867 to $3.80. It reached a low of $3.23 in early December. The repercussions of this event were world-wide, and stock exchange lists in all the major countries suffered further depreciation. As far away as Tokyo exchanges were closed, and when the Tokyo exchange reopened on the 23rd of September, prices collapsed so drastically that it had to be closed again immediately. A score of countries followed Britain off the gold standard.

Accompanying and in part contributing to these financial difficulties were grave political disturbances. In Germany the National Socialists and the Communists were struggling for supremacy. In Britain the unbalanced budget was causing great uneasiness, and the Socialist government resigned on August 28, and was replaced by an all-party coalition. Thus external disturbances were operating to intensify still further the depression in the United States, and to check such reviving confidence as may have been appearing.[46]

Proposal for a National Credit Association

Domestically, the situation continued to worsen. In early October the President suggested informally that the bankers create a national credit association with a capital of $500 million subscribed by all banks, each contributing 2 per cent of its net demand and time deposits. The association was to rediscount bank assets not eligible for acceptance by the federal reserve banks, and to make

---

problems then facing the nation. The others, while not inappropriate, were wholly inadequate in scale.

44. Press conference statement, December 9, 1930. Hoover, *State Papers*, Vol. I, p. 460.

45. Myers and Newton, *The Hoover Administration*, pp. 101–05.

46. For a fuller account of these events see Hodson, *Slump and Recovery*, Chapter 3.

loans against the assets of closed banks to enable them to pay early dividends to depositors.

A similar plan was suggested for a privately established national mortgage discount system to release frozen mortgage capital. The insurance company representatives balked on this.[47] On the other hand, the bankers, finding that the President had already taken steps looking to the calling of a special session of Congress to deal with the problem, agreed to the credit association idea. The insurance companies were induced to give lip-service at least to the proposal that they not press foreclosures, and a similar understanding was reached with the Chairman of the Federal Farm Loan Board.

With a view to freeing funds tied up in home loans of sound building and loan associations, banks and other lending agencies, the President proposed, on November 13, a system of home loan discount banks. This was intended as a means of freeing funds for new construction and increased employment. Actually it could not have that effect since there was little incentive to undertake new building ventures even if funds were available. The Home Loan Bank Act was finally passed, however, late in the summer of 1932. The twelve banks thus established proved useful and appropriate, but operated mainly as rescue and holding agencies rather than as stimulators of new building activity.

The Seventy-second Congress Opens

In the elections of 1930 the Democrats gained in both the House and the Senate. Party strength in each of the Houses was now very nearly equal. The Democrats, with four votes more than the Republicans, were able to take over the organization of the House with John Nance Garner of Texas, a conservative Democrat, as the new Speaker. At this time Hoover asked Senator Watson and Representative Snell, Republican leaders, to sound out the Democratic leaders and see whether they intended to propose a recovery program. The Democrats stated that they had no program, that the responsibility was that of the President, and that they would "scrutinize" anything he had to offer.[48]

In his annual message the President clung to the idea of a balanced budget, though admitting that it could not be achieved in the coming year. He proposed that taxation be so adjusted as to balance the budget in 1933. He recommended increased capitalization of the federal land banks in order to stabilize the values of their bonds and assure low rates of interest to borrowers. He also proposed that some plan be devised whereby the federal reserve banks could aid in freeing some of the deposits in closed banks, and renewed his endorsement of the home loan bank idea.

His major recommendation was for establishment of an emergency reconstruction corporation to operate along lines similar to those of the War Finance Corporation but in a way not to overlap the functions of the National Credit Corporation, which had been set up by the banks in accordance with his earlier recommendation.[49]

---

47. At a meeting of insurance, mortgage, building and loan and construction interests on October 7, this proposition was modified somewhat, the proposal then being that the government would provide the initial capital but that the members would later absorb it. The mortgage banks thus created would issue debentures and would operate along lines somewhat similar to those of the federal land banks. The insurance companies continued, however, to resist action along these lines. See Myers and Newton, *The Hoover Administration*, pp. 125–27.

48. Myers and Newton, *The Hoover Administration*, p. 146.

49. Other recommendations included broadening eligibility rules for Federal Reserve discounts, more separation of functions as between various kinds of banks, railroad consolidation and some revision of antitrust laws. Expenditures to relieve unemployment, he estimated, would amount to $780 million for the calendar year. Through these and payments to veterans he estimated that the federal government was then contributing directly to the livelihood of 10 million citizens. He opposed any direct or indirect government dole, or any increase in expenditures for veterans. The President also stated that he had appointed a committee to recommend a plan for disposal of the Muscle Shoals properties. He defended the tariff act on the ground that it was protecting the American worker against the lowered wages and standards of living abroad. Hoover, *State Papers*, Vol. II, pp. 41–57.

For a compilation of official papers outlining the Hoover policies and philosophy see Ray Lyman Wilbur and Arthur M. Hyde, *The Hoover Policies*, Charles Scribner's Sons, New York, 1937.

The Reconstruction Finance Corporation

It had become apparent that the National Credit Association could not loan enough on frozen securities to meet the needs of prospective borrowers. Steps were therefore taken to set up a government corporation along lines suggested by the President in his annual message.

This agency, entitled the Reconstruction Finance Corporation, was established on January 22, 1932. The plan had the support of members of both parties. The act provided for a corporation with a capital of $500 million, to be subscribed by the government. It was authorized to issue bonds or debentures in the amount of three times its capital. It could make loans to financial institutions, including those in the process of reorganization or liquidation. Loans might also be made to finance agriculture, commerce and industry, and to facilitate the exportation of agricultural and other products. The Corporation might also make loans to railroads if approved by the Interstate Commerce Commission.[50]

In accordance with the President's recommendation, a bill providing $125 million for increasing the capital of the federal land banks was passed, and was signed by the President on February 2, 1932.[51]

Numerous other financial bills were under consideration, several of them sponsored by Senator Glass, a Democrat who had played a prominent role in the framing of the original Federal Reserve Act and had later served as Secretary of the Treasury under Wilson. Among these was the Glass-Steagall bill, passed with little debate, and signed by the President on February 27, 1932. This act permitted needy member banks to borrow on promissory notes, from the federal reserve banks, and, more important, authorized the federal reserve banks, until March 1933, to substitute government bonds for gold as backing for federal reserve notes.[52] This was intended as an inflationary measure. It was hoped that it would ease the strain on the banks and provide an expansion of currency.

Three other measures which foreshadowed later Democratic policy were introduced and discussed at this time. The Glass bill proposed the separation of banks from affiliate corporations and a measure of control over brokers' loans and other speculative lending on the part of member banks.[53] This was a phase of a problem later to be approached more directly through establishment of the Securities and Exchange Commission. Representative Steagall introduced a bill to provide a fund of $517 million for use in guaranteeing the deposits of banks which were members of the Federal Reserve system.[54]

This idea took shape in the succeeding administration as the Federal Deposit Insurance Corporation. The House passed the Goldsborough bill, which sought to stabilize the dollar at the average purchasing value of the 1921-1929 period.[55] This bill was displaced in the Senate by the Glass bill, which was a milder and more orthodox approach to the same problem. In the succeeding Roosevelt administration strenuous efforts were made to re-establish and maintain the price level of 1926, but the results were not encouraging.

Increased Federal Participation in Relief

As the summer of 1932 wore on with no evidence of improvement and greater and greater need for aggressive action, the rift between the President and the Democratic

---

50. 47 Stat. 5. Through the efforts of Senators Glass and Bulkley the administration provision that the Corporation's securities be purchasable or rediscountable at federal reserve banks was eliminated.

In the Unemployment Relief Act of July 21, 1932 the Corporation's resources were increased by $1,800 million of which $300 million was to be immediately available for loans to states to meet urgent relief needs.

51. 47 Stat. 36.

52. 47 Stat. 56. For a good account of this legislation see E. Francis Brown, "Congress Adopts Hoover Program," Current History, April 1932, pp. 82–90.

53. S. 4412, 72nd Cong., 1st sess.

54. H.R. 11362, 72nd Cong., 1st sess.

55. H.R. 11499. The Goldsborough bill proposed to amend the Federal Reserve Act so that: "It is hereby declared to be the policy of the United States that the average purchasing power of the dollar as ascertained by the Department of Labor in the wholesale commodity markets for the period covering the years 1921 to 1929 inclusive, shall be restored and maintained by the control of the volume of credit and currency." Text in Congressional Record, 72nd Cong., 1st sess., p. 9631.

leadership became more pronounced.[56] The Costigan-La Follette bill providing $375 million for unemployment relief passed the House despite presidential opposition, but was defeated in the Senate by a vote of 48 to 35, not on party lines.[57] On February 27, the House passed a bill authorizing $132 million for emergency highway construction. Hoover opposed it, charging that it had more the aspect of "pork barrel" legislation than of relief for unemployment.

Up to March the only direct federal relief action was an act, which the President signed, providing free distribution of 40 million bushels of Farm Board wheat to the needy. Milling and distribution were put into the hands of the Red Cross.[58] In the succeeding administration this idea was more fully implemented by means of the Surplus Commodities Corporation.

In early May the President proposed, by way of the Democratic and Republican leaders in the Congress, a three-point program for relief:

1. The Reconstruction Finance Corporation was to be authorized to issue an additional $1.5 billion in debentures in order to provide advances to states for general relief, to aid in increasing agricultural exports, and to provide loans for assured and productive private projects.
2. State bonds and securities that could not be sold in the open market were to be purchased by the Reconstruction Finance Cor-

poration, and the proceeds used for unemployment relief.
3. The Reconstruction Finance Corporation was to loan funds for self-liquidating enterprises such as toll bridges.

These recommendations aroused little enthusiasm in the Congress. At about the same time Senator Robinson, speaking for a committee of Senate Democrats, proposed an issue of government bonds in the amount of $2.3 billion.[59] This proposal contemplated a $500 million bond issue for new expenditures on previously authorized federal works, $300 million for the Reconstruction Finance Corporation to make loans to states for relief of the needy (this to be deducted from future grants for road building) and $1.5 billion, also to the RFC, for loans to public and private agencies for self-liquidating projects.

These provisions were included in a bill introduced by Senator Wagner a few days later. President Hoover was in general agreement with this program, but objected to the $500 million bond issue for public works. Meanwhile, Speaker Garner introduced a bill in the House to provide a $100 million emergency fund for the President, plus $1 billion for public works. This led to a name-calling quarrel between Hoover and Garner.

The Wagner bill was passed by the Senate and the Garner bill by the House, while the Hoover-sponsored bill received unfavorable committee reports in both Houses. The Garner and Wagner bills were then combined, in conference, and passed on July 9. Hoover vetoed the bill on July 11, objecting to its authorization of Reconstruction Finance Corporation loans to individuals and corporations, though he had previously advocated loans to private enterprises. The bill was quickly redrawn and repassed, and was signed by the President on July 21. It provided for total expenditures of $2,122 million. Of this, $1,800 million was to be loaned to states, municipalities and other agencies for relief and self-liq-

56. The American economy suffered a further setback in the summer of 1932 as a result of the Ottawa Conference which opened in July. This Conference brought about an agreement between the United Kingdom and the British Dominions whereby British manufactures were to be given preferential status in the Dominions in return for preferential tariffs on Dominion products imported by the United Kingdom. This was an outgrowth of the world-wide tendency of the early 1930's to increase the restrictions on international trade. Its intended effect was to give Canadian farm products a more favorable position in the British market and, at the same time, to give British manufacturers some advantages in the Dominion markets. For a summary of the results of the Conference, see Maxwell S. Stewart, "The Ottawa Conference," *Foreign Policy Reports*, December 21, 1932, pp. 244-54.

57. S. 3045, 72nd Cong., 1st sess. More than a hundred labor leaders had petitioned for passage of the bill. E. Francis Brown, "America Acts to Check Depression," *Current History*, March 1932, pp. 832-40.

58. Myers and Newton, *The Hoover Administration*, p. 181.

59. *Congressional Record*, 72nd Cong., 1st sess., May 11, 1932, pp. 9969-70. This had the backing of Al Smith, the most recent Democratic candidate for the presidency, and of Owen D. Young, prominent businessman and author of the Young Plan.

uidating projects, and $322 million was to be spent on public works.[60] Thus the federal government was being forced into more specific action on relief. The Democrats were urging somewhat more direct federal action than the Republicans, but the similarities of the approaches are much more apparent than their differences.

The long-delayed Home Loan Bank bill was passed in the last hours of the session about as Hoover wanted it. Senator Glass had, however, succeeded in attaching a rider which permitted national banks to use government bonds as security for the expansion of note issues for a period of three years.[61]

The session had passed more than 500 laws and appropriated about $9 billion but the depression continued unabated, and as yet nothing had occurred to give the needed lift to confidence that would start recovery on its way.[62]

REMEDIAL EFFORTS OF THE FARM BOARD

While these steps were being taken to aid the economy as a whole, the Federal Farm Board was, of course, proceeding with its program for the relief of agriculture. Its efforts constitute a parallel but more narrowly restricted attack upon the same problem. The Board was set up with a view to improving gradually the marketing organization, bargaining power and financing arrangements of agriculture. It was not designed primarily

60. 47 Stat. 709.
61. 47 Stat. 725.
62. Other steps taken were the creation of a Commodities Finance Corporation with a capitalization of $50 million (August 1932), to finance purchasing, carrying and marketing of raw materials, and a Reconstruction Finance Corporation loan of $50 million to the Cotton Stabilization Corporation to permit holding of cotton until 1933.
During August and September the President tried again to ease the situation by voluntary action through private channels. At a conference of business and industrial leaders, held on August 26, he urged better distribution of credit and the spreading of work through shortening of hours. This led to an abortive "share-the-work" movement set up under the direction of Walter C. Teagle, President of the Standard Oil Company of New Jersey. The plan elicited little enthusiasm from the public. While well-intentioned, it was essentially a negative and defeatist approach, and at best could make little impression on the huge volume of unemployment then existing. To some extent too it was recognized as part of the election campaign then getting under way.

as a device for meeting emergencies. The functions assigned to it and the philosophy underlying its activities were inappropriate for accomplishing even the original objectives. As a means for meeting a major depression, it was wholly inadequate and doomed to failure from the beginning.

The sponsors of the act placed main reliance upon better organized and more orderly marketing, to be brought about, in the main, through larger and stronger cooperative marketing associations. Even wholly successful action along those lines would have left much to be desired so far as the farmers were concerned. The creation and expansion of cooperative marketing associations under the forced draft of outside influence has nearly always led to disappointing results, and often to costly failures. The American Farm Bureau Federation had tried it in 1921, with a record of almost complete failure. The Sapiro crusade of the middle 1920's was another attempt which, though more successful than that of 1921, eventually petered out. Now, again, the attempt was made, but with the added assets of government backing and a sizable budget. The results were to be little more encouraging than those of the earlier ventures.

Weaknesses of the Plan

The reasons for these failures are not far to seek. Most successful cooperatives have grown slowly. Management has had a chance to mature and gain experience while the operations were small enough to be comprehended and handled by relatively inexperienced personnel. The mechanics for carrying on the day-to-day business — sales methods and policies, the keeping of complex records and the maintenance of contacts with members — grew up gradually and step by step. Later managers took over a going concern with most of its parts in working order. Nearly all of these requisites for successful cooperation were lacking in the huge cooperative ventures launched under the auspices of the Farm Board.

Added to these handicaps was the fact that

Board-sponsored cooperatives were expected to accomplish things that not even the largest and most successful of the pre-existing cooperatives had even tried to do. These earlier cooperatives, such as the Land-O'-Lakes Creameries, the California Fruit Growers' Exchange and the National Wool and Cotton Exchanges, had sought to improve and standardize quality, to bring about better organized handling, selling and storing, to improve financial arrangements and to strengthen the bargaining power of the growers. Most of them had accomplished some or all of these things. Few attempted to raise prices through monopoly control. Wherever attempted, such methods had almost invariably ended in failure.

These older, successful cooperatives hoped to raise prices to the grower by a few cents per unit, to expand markets and to provide a better product more efficiently marketed. In terms of these modest aims, many of them were highly successful. But success of this kind was not likely to satisfy farmers who wanted and expected some large-scale, immediate improvement in their situation. The new cooperatives were, in fact, fortunate if they could make, in their first years of operation, returns equivalent to those made by the ordinary private agencies. The marketing system they were seeking to supplant was, with all its faults, one of the most efficient in the world, and improvements that would yield sensationally better returns to growers were by no means easy to make, even under the most favorable conditions.

The stabilization corporations, to be described later, were far too limited in scope and resources to stem the avalanche of falling prices or to offset the tremendous losses in agricultural income that resulted from the depressed home market and the demoralized world situation.

This gloomy picture was not, of course, apparent in the early stages of Board operation. Only gradually did the Board itself come to recognize the magnitude of the disaster and the futility of its program. In happier circumstances and with more of the breaks, it might

well have made, over the years, a modest contribution to the welfare of agriculture. As things were, its efforts were comparable to bringing in a few truckloads of sand in an effort to stem a raging flood.

The Farmers National Grain Corporation

The Board's efforts during the fall of 1929 were directed to the creation of a series of national cooperative selling agencies organized along commodity lines. The first of these was the Farmers National Grain Corporation, incorporated October 29, 1929. It sought to bring together under a central board of directors three types of existing grain marketing cooperatives, namely, farmers' elevator associations, terminal sales agencies and grain pools. For areas not served by such associations, efforts were made to create them. The general plan of the new organization was very similar to that of U.S. Grain Growers, Inc., launched by the Farm Bureau in 1921, and the Grain Marketing Company, sponsored by Gray Silver and J. W. Coverdale in 1924.

Under the procedure formulated by the Farmers National Grain Corporation, the farmer was given three options. He might (1) sell his grain for cash at the time of delivery; (2) have it stored in bonded warehouses subject to sale at any time on orders from him; or (3) enter it in a pool, receiving an advance against it, and being paid at the end of the pool period the average price received by the cooperative for pooled grain of the type and quality supplied by him.[63] Since the new organization could not get under way in time to aid in handling the 1929 crop, the Board authorized supplemental commodity loans to existing grain cooperatives that would enable them to advance 10 cents per bushel in excess of what they had been able to obtain from primary lenders.

63. Federal Farm Board, *First Annual Report*, pp. 7–9. Under option 2 the farmer might also receive an advance. As in the earlier grain marketing plans this granting of options as to methods of sale was a concession to widely different views held by the various farmers' associations.

The National Wool Marketing Corporation

The second organization established was a national cooperative association for selling wool and mohair. This was incorporated in the latter part of December 1929. It was set up as a federation of state associations, and was similar in plan to the National Wool Exchange, which had been in existence since 1925.[64] In addition to the nine state associations originally in the National Wool Marketing Corporation, seventeen new state and regional associations were formed, making twenty-six in all. Instead of taking over the experienced management and developed procedures of the National Wool Exchange, the new Corporation brought in new management and abandoned the individual grading and record keeping that had been built up by the antecedent organization. These procedures were considered too expensive and cumbersome in handling the large volume of wool that soon came into the hands of the new corporation.[65]

Since the actual selling of wool requires long experience and much skill, it could not well be undertaken directly by a new and inexperienced management. Instead the Corporation entered into a contract with the Draper Company, an established firm of wool handlers, to do the selling for it. While very profitable to the Draper firm, this arrangement gave rise to much criticism. In effect, it reduced the functions of the Corporation merely to those of assembling and storing the wool, and making advances on it. Since the Draper firm was engaged in the business of buying and selling wool on its own account, as well as that of selling for the Corporation,

there was a basic conflict of interests in its operations. Wool is sold by lot and by private treaty. There was therefore some ground for the feeling that the more favorable sales would be made from the agents' own stocks while less attractive offers would be filled from cooperatively owned supplies, or possibly the latter would remain inactive while the sales agency disposed of its own holdings.[66]

More serious from the standpoint of financial solvency of the Corporation was the policy of making high advances to growers at time of delivery, which was adopted in 1930. This resulted in concentrating in the hands of the National Wool Marketing Corporation a large part of the total domestic wool and mohair clip of that year, and the assumption of obligations to the Farm Board which the Corporation later found itself unable to meet. Under the depressed condition of the wool and mohair markets, these large holdings proved embarrassing to the Corporation and may have been an element of weakness rather than strength. They were known to be available and likely to come on the market at some later, but undetermined, date and thus tended to make buyers hesitant and cautious.[67]

The American Cotton Cooperative Association

By a process similar to that used in establishing the National Wool Marketing Corporation, a national association for handling cotton was incorporated in January 1930. The fourteen independent short-staple cotton cooperatives which had been in oper-

64. The National Wool Exchange was a successor to the National Wool Warehouse and Storage Company of Chicago, a grower-owned stock corporation which was liquidated in 1924–25. The National Wool Warehouse and Storage Company lost heavily on overadvances made in 1919. It was unable to make a comeback. The National Wool Exchange, organized by many of the same people, was a cooperative instead of a stock company, and was located in Boston instead of Chicago.

65. Though admittedly an expensive procedure, this careful grading of individual clips and periodic reports to growers was important, both in maintaining grower morale and in causing growers to make special efforts to improve the quality of their product.

66. These objections became sufficiently vigorous to bring about termination of this arrangement at the end of 1932. Eventually the experienced manager who had been in charge of the National Wool Exchange was brought back into the organization. The Corporation has continued under that management up to the present time, and has made an excellent record, after adjustment of the financial difficulties that resulted from overadvances during the Farm Board period.

67. For a more detailed analysis of this problem, see M. R. Benedict, "An Evaluation of the Cooperative Wool Program," *American Cooperation*, 1931, Vol. II, pp. 265–86. Also, John D. Black and H. Bruce Price, *Cooperative Central Marketing Organization*, Minnesota Agricultural Experiment Station Bulletin 211, University Farm, St. Paul, 1924, pp. 53–73.

ation at the time the Board was set up were thus brought into one national organization consisting of nine state units. The one long-staple association remained independent. Substantial advances had already been made by the Board to the several independent associations, in the fall of 1929, in an effort to check the decline in cotton prices. These were in the form of supplemental loans in addition to the 65 per cent of the value of the cotton already borrowed from the intermediate credit banks.[68] The policy adopted contemplated making it possible for the associations to advance 16 cents a pound through loans from all credit sources. In the preceding years 1927 and 1928 the farm price of cotton had averaged 19.6 cents and 18.0 cents respectively.[69]

In late January 1930 cotton prices broke through the 16 cent level and the solvency of the borrowing cooperatives was threatened. Arrangements were made whereby the American Cotton Cooperative Association took over the handling of the cotton held by the member associations, and undertook to protect their financial positions. As the price continued to decline this led to the establishment, in June 1930, of the Cotton Stabilization Corporation as a means of absorbing excess cotton and supporting the cotton price structure. Cotton prices continued under heavy pressure, however, and the Board undertook, by educational means, to bring about a reduction in the cotton acreage for 1930. This attempt to bring about adjustment through voluntary action by the growers met with little success, either in 1930 or in the years immediately following.

Farm Board Aid to Other Cooperatives

During the autumn months of 1929 and the early part of 1930 many producer groups sought aid from the Board. Nearly all of the

ventures needed more study and consideration than could be given them at the time, and a slower pace in the attempts to organize the various branches of the agricultural industry would have been advantageous from the Board's standpoint. However, the rapidly worsening condition of agriculture resulted in efforts on the part of nearly every major group, and many minor ones, to become organized and eligible for financial assistance from the Board. A National Bean Marketing Association was formed in February 1930, and the National Livestock Marketing Association in May. Steps were taken to aid the already strongly organized dairy industry.

During the early months of 1930 action was also taken with a view to aiding the Florida and Texas citrus industries, the Texas fig industry, the grape producers of California, the potato growers (on a national basis), the apple growers and various others.[70] Other programs related to the pecan industry, which set up at this time the National Pecan Marketing Association, the tobacco industry, the sugar beet growers and the rice industry.

This complex array of problems besetting the Board in its first year of operation gave it little opportunity for careful planning or the development of guiding principles. Practically every agricultural group was in trouble, and each one demanded immediate consideration of its problems, and quick action in respect to them. But the Board was in no position to provide quick and effective help. Its authorizations were almost wholly for action in the realm of marketing, and, in the main, for relatively long-term, unsensational types of aid.

Nature of the Problem

The farmer's urgent need was first of all for an extensive and vigorous program of credit amelioration, to enable him to carry on until more fundamental adjustments and improvements in his situation could be made. Secondly, he needed action which would

68. This was on cotton for which the price had been established by future sales. Other arrangements were used where the price had not been so established. See Federal Farm Board, *First Annual Report*, pp. 10-12. For a fuller account of the probable effects of this policy and later developments, see *ibid.*, pp. 36-42.

69. *Yearbook of Agriculture, 1933*, p. 472.

70. Some aid had been given to the Florida citrus industry during 1929 in its efforts to bring the Mediterranean fruit fly under control.

improve substantially the demand for his products, both in the domestic and foreign markets. This called for large-scale injection of buying power into the domestic economy and quick adjustment of the factors that were depressing the international markets. Even vigorous and wise action in these realms could not have brought quick results. Once the depression had struck with full force it was like a wasting illness, and recovery was bound to be slow.

In part the procedure needed was that which would best alleviate suffering and avoid, so far as possible, disintegration of the basic tissue of the economy. Mere changes in marketing organization could not, by any stretch of imagination, be expected to overcome difficulties of this kind and magnitude.

The marketing structure was, in fact, substantially the same as that which had existed in the periods of greatest prosperity. Any major changes in it would take time, and might very possibly, in the initial stages, be more expensive than the old system which the new organizations were to replace. This is not to say that the then existing marketing system was adequate, or that gains might not be made by improving its organization. It is rather to place in proper perspective the things which might reasonably be expected from a program such as that to which the Farm Board was committed, and to emphasize that effective accomplishment under it called for much time, gradual, evolutionary development and reasonably stable economic conditions. Few, if any, of these requirements were present in the situation that faced the new Board. It was like an untrained, inadequate army, forced to attack on a dozen fronts an enemy so powerful that even a far larger and more experienced force would have been relatively ineffective against it.

There is little profit in a detailed account of the many programs launched by the Board. Principal interest centers in the efforts to support and stabilize the prices of wheat and cotton. It is the emergency program to maintain the prices of these crops which has been the focus of criticism and defense rather than the

more prosaic efforts to aid in building cooperative marketing organizations. The Board's failure to stem the downward plunge of wheat and cotton prices overshadowed its other activities, and in some measure contributed to their disintegration. Many of them, however, contained within themselves the elements of failure, such as too hasty formation, overambitious plans, inexperienced management and lack of grass-roots participation and support.

Effort to Stabilize Wheat Prices

Wheat prices showed weakness as early as August 1929, well ahead of the stock market crash.[71] The Board, then only just beginning to function, urged farmers to delay marketings with a view to checking the heavy flow of wheat to the terminals. By September supplemental loans were being offered to aid cooperatives in holding grain off the market. Nevertheless, the price of wheat continued to decline. It fell off 15 cents in the ten days before the stock market broke, and dropped another 10 cents on October 24, the first day of the big break. At this point the Board first undertook direct price-supporting action. On October 26, it offered loans to cooperatives up to 100 per cent of the closing prices for October 25. This move appeared to have achieved its purpose. Wheat prices recovered somewhat during November and December, but weakened again in January and February of 1930.[72]

During the early part of 1930, the members of the Farm Board, like most other people, looked upon the slump as severe but tempo-

71. The price of wheat on the British market had, in fact, shown a steady downward trend from January 1925 to June 1929. After a sharp upswing between June and August 1929 the downward trend was resumed, but at a faster rate. See League of Nations, *The Course and Phases of the World Economic Depression*, revised edition, Geneva, 1931, chart, p. 46.

72. The action taken by the Board at this time was predicated on the belief that supply and prospective demand did not warrant the low prices then prevailing. The 1929 world crop was estimated at some 500 million bushels under that of 1928, and world carry-over was thought to be 100 million bushels less than a year earlier. What was mainly misjudged was the heavy shrinkage in imports on the part of the consuming nations. See Federal Farm Board, *First Annual Report*, pp. 26–36.

rary, and hence felt themselves justified in trying to hold the line on wheat and cotton prices. In light of the widely prevalent view that strengthening the position of agriculture would strengthen the economy generally, this policy was felt to have important national significance as well as farmer interest.[73]

By February it was evident that the burden was becoming too great for the Farmers National Grain Corporation to carry. The Grain Stabilization Corporation was therefore set up, and efforts were made, in cooperation with the millers, to ease the pressure on the cash grain markets. These actions appeared for a time to be successful, but involved the Board in very heavy commitments. During the first half of 1930 it had control of about half the visible supply of wheat, and, even after exporting substantial quantities, still owned on June 30 some 60 million bushels.[74]

Though the Board continued to hope that some turn of events would open the way for release of the heavy stocks of wheat it was carrying, even the serious drought in the summer of 1930 did not bring about that result. Both the domestic and the foreign situations showed further deterioration. The principal European wheat markets were receiving unusually heavy shipments from the Danubian countries, Australia and elsewhere. Russia began in September to send unexpectedly large quantities to the European markets. Much of this was shipped on consignment and remained unsold, thus demoralizing still further the already glutted world markets.[75] Additional heavy purchases by the Stabilization Corporation in November failed to check the decline in prices. On November 16, the Board issued a statement to the effect that wheat was lower in price comparatively than other agricultural products.[76] Nevertheless by February 1931 still more drastic steps had to be taken. Some 35 million bushels of wheat had accumulated at the Atlantic, Gulf and Pacific Northwest ports and had to be moved in order to make room for the new crop which would shortly be moving in. About 21 million bushels of this wheat were sold abroad for whatever they would bring, thus marking a further departure from the Board's original plan.

Abandonment of Price Support

The remainder of 1931 and all of 1932 saw a continuation of the losing fight to maintain domestic wheat prices. There is clear evidence, however, that they were held much above the usual relationship to Liverpool prices through late 1930 and the first half of 1931. On June 30, 1931, the Board held 257 million bushels of wheat, and decided that its resources did not warrant further input of funds to hold the price at levels so much above the world market price. It adopted a policy of liquidating its holdings with as little adverse effect on the market as possible. When this decision became effective, wheat prices in the United States dropped precipitately, from a level somewhat above that of Liverpool to about the usual amount below it. Farm prices, which had averaged about 52 cents on June 15, 1931, were down to 36 cents by July 15.[77]

In an effort to minimize the effects of this change in policy the Board undertook to restrict sales of its holdings in the commercial markets, and at the same time made unusual efforts to find outlets abroad and through the Red Cross. Concession prices were offered to foreign buyers. Some wheat was sold to Germany and China against long-term bonds,

73. At this time, both the Board and the administration were deeply concerned over the possibility that widespread collapse of country banks would aggravate and prolong the depression. The actions taken were designed in part to prevent or check the strain on these banks.

74. World wheat production had been rather sharply on the upgrade since the early 1920's. Between 1910 and 1922 it had averaged about three billion bushels (exclusive of Russia and China). From 1922 it increased rapidly, reaching a peak of more than four billion in 1928–1929. The significance of this increase was apparently underestimated in the Board's consideration of the problem. United States exports had already fallen off a third from the high levels of 1926 and 1927. Data from *Yearbook of Agriculture, 1933*, pp. 409 and 415.

75. Federal Farm Board, *Second Annual Report for the Year Ending June 30, 1931*, p. 39.

76. *Ibid.*, p. 40. This statement was no doubt correct factually, but was somewhat meaningless as there was no significant reason why, under the circumstances, wheat prices should retain a customary relationship to other prices.

77. *Yearbook of Agriculture, 1933*, p. 415.

and 25 million bushels were bartered to Brazil in exchange for coffee. In addition, 40 million bushels were transferred to the Red Cross for relief feeding. By the end of June 1932, uncommitted stabilization stocks had been reduced to 108 million bushels in actual wheat and futures. By then the Board held loans on wheat totalling approximately $200 million, which was two fifths of its total resources.[78]

There was to be little change in the situation from then until the termination of the Board's activities in May 1933. Congressionally authorized donations to the American Red Cross eventually reached 85 million bushels. Combined losses to the revolving fund on the stabilization operations in cotton and wheat had amounted to more than $300 million. This amount, however, does not take account of the value of the 844,063 bales of cotton and 85 million bushels of wheat donated to the Red Cross, for which the fund was not reimbursed.[79]

Cotton Stabilization Operations

The effort of the Board to maintain cotton prices followed a course somewhat similar to that in wheat. Shortly after its creation, in June 1930, the Cotton Stabilization Corporation took over from the cooperatives about 1.25 million bales. As it became evident that the entire market demand could be supplied from sources not under the control of the Board, the president of the Stabilization Corporation announced that the Corporation would maintain its holdings until July 31, 1931, unless prices should advance to more than those paid by it. This announcement, which was expected to strengthen the market, had no apparent effect. Aside from a small purchase operation in November 1930, which apparently steadied the market, there was little change in the situation up to June 30,

1931. At that time the Stabilization Corporation held just over 1.3 million bales.

In the holding operations under the cotton program a relatively larger part was played by private banks and the cooperative associations than in the case of wheat.[80] The eventual outcome so far as prices were concerned was not greatly different. The farm price of cotton, which had been above 18 cents in September 1929, drifted gradually downward. By July 1930 it was under 12 cents, and a year later was down to 8.5 cents. It eventually reached an all-time low of 4.6 cents in June 1932.[81] In the meantime production was outrunning consumption, and carry-overs were continuing to increase. The Board pointed out that while it had financed removal from the market of about 3.5 million bales, underconsumption had in the same period added about 10 million bales to the excess supply. This was 6.5 million bales more than the Board could handle with the resources available to it.[82]

Farm Board Aid for Other Crops

The Board provided technical assistance and some financing in connection with a great variety of other farm products, but did not undertake formal stabilization operations except in cotton and wheat. Aid was given, however, to the butter and wool cooperatives

---

78. Federal Farm Board, *Third Annual Report for the Year Ending June 30, 1932*, p. 70.

79. Farm Credit Administration, *Fourth Annual Report, 1936*, p. 179. Part of the loss does not appear as loss in the official reports. The later Red Cross donations were charged off at values substantially above the market values at time of transfer.

80. The 1931 cotton crop was exceptionally large. This resulted in very low prices in the early part of 1932. To alleviate the situation the Board entered into an arrangement with the southern bankers whereby both the Board and the bankers agreed to withhold from the market for the remainder of the season (to July 31, 1932) all cotton financed by them. The banks pledged themselves to finance not less than 3.5 million bales while the Board agreed to hold 1.3 million bales, and to continue to finance 2.1 million bales held by the cotton cooperatives. This action apparently strengthened prices and helped to maintain them until June 1932 when they again declined.
On May 2, 1932 the Board announced that, by agreement with the cotton advisory council, it would reduce its holdings gradually from 1.3 million bales to 650,000 bales. In July the Congress turned over to the Red Cross 500,000 bales of the stocks held by the Stabilization Corporation. See Federal Farm Board, *Third Annual Report*, pp. 73–76.

81. Data from *Yearbook of Agriculture, 1933*, p. 478.

82. Federal Farm Board, *Third Annual Report*, p. 80. This, of course, avoids the question whether it would have been desirable and effective to have accumulated the entire 10 million bales had funds been adequate.

and to the grape control board in their efforts to stabilize the prices of those commodities. These operations were on a smaller scale and did not involve the creation of stabilization corporations. Most of the activity relating to the other crops and products centered in the efforts to strengthen and enlarge the cooperatives handling them. Those for which funds were supplied by the Board included beans, dairy products, citrus fruits, grapes and raisins, other deciduous fruits, honey, livestock, maple sirup, nuts, potatoes, poultry and eggs, rice, seeds, tobacco and wool.[83]

Activities in relation to grapes and raisins centered principally in the California Grape Control Board which attempted, in 1930, to unite all elements of the California grape industry by means of ten-year contracts with the growers. The Control Board was discontinued in the summer of 1932 after a period of hectic and, on the whole, unsatisfactory operation.[84] Its troubles were accentuated by the action of the Federal Prohibition Administrator in outlawing the sale of grape concentrates, and by the unwillingness of the growers to pay the stabilization fees required under the plan. As of May 26, 1933, total loans on grapes and raisins amounted to $25 million of which $14.3 million had been repaid.[85] No estimates have been made of the probable effects on prices. Part of the loans then outstanding have since been repaid, but the loss sustained was substantial considering the size of the operation.

In the wool and mohair program total loans of $31.5 million were made by the Farm Board, the larger part for the purpose of stabilizing prices. Some $15.3 million had

been repaid by May 26, 1933. Of the remainder, about $12.5 million was eventually written off.[86] As a result of these concessions, the National Wool Marketing Corporation gradually gained financial stability, and has since functioned effectively as a major selling agency in the wool industry.

Liquidation of the Farm Board

The last year of the Board's operation was one of relative inactivity. The funds assigned to it had, for the most part, been committed in the first three years of operation. Hence, there was little it could do in further support of prices, and its lack of success in stemming the general downward movement of farm prices had shaken public confidence to such an extent that its prestige and morale were at a low ebb. Prices of most farm products were down to levels that had not been seen since the depression of the 1890's or before.

Under these circumstances, little in the way of constructive action was possible. The overwhelming Democratic victory in the election of 1932 sealed the doom of this effort to better the condition of agriculture. In a sweeping presidential order of May 26, 1933, the Board was abolished. Its legislative authorization and its remaining assets were used in creating the Farm Credit Administration, in which were combined the various federally sponsored farm credit agencies, including the credit features of the Farm Board. The authorized position of Chairman of the Farm Board was changed in name to become that of Governor of the Farm Credit Administration.

The assets remaining in the Agricultural Marketing Act revolving fund were used in capitalizing the thirteen newly created banks for cooperatives, and in establishing a loan fund which might be used by them. Thus the function of making commodity, facility and operating loans to cooperatives was preserved, but the stabilization corporations were placed in liquidation and, as soon as practical, were abolished.

---

83. By the end of the fiscal year 1932–1933 the Board had been abolished. Consequently, no report is available for its operations during that year. For a summary of its loans and expenditures, and status of the revolving fund as of 1935, see U.S. Congress, Senate Committee on Agriculture and Forestry, *Activities and Operations of the Federal Farm Board,* S.Rep. 1456, pursuant to S.Res. 42, 74th Cong., 1st sess., July 29, 1935. Also (with same title) supplementary S.Rep. 416, 78th Cong., 1st sess., September 24, 1943.

84. For a fuller discussion, see S. W. Shear, "The California Grape Control Plan," *American Cooperation,* 1931, Vol. I, pp. 229–48.

85. *Activities of Federal Farm Board,* S.Rep. 1456, 74th Cong., 1st sess., p. 35.

86. *Ibid.,* pp. 28 and 35.

Significance of the Experiment

The more sensational undertakings that were launched almost coincidentally with the winding up of the affairs of the Farm Board have occupied so completely the attention of economists and the public that very little study has been made of the Farm Board experiment. The published records of its last year of operation are, in fact, so meager that no detailed summarization is possible. That is not necessary, however, for a broad view of the Board's accomplishments and failures.

The account given in the preceding pages indicates the nature of its major shortcomings. The program was predicated on the view that agriculture's principal need was for a better organized marketing system developed along cooperative lines. This notion has recurred time and again throughout the history of efforts to aid agriculture. As late as 1946 it was a dominant theme in the Research and Marketing Act of that year. That improved marketing mechanisms alone cannot make major changes in the returns to agriculture has been amply demonstrated both in theory and in practice. Substantial savings and more effective merchandizing undoubtedly are possible through improved and more efficient marketing organization. The gains, however, are slow and of a minor rather than a major order of magnitude.[87] Thus they are best suited to periods of relatively stable economic conditions, not to the meeting of crises in which major changes of price level occur. The general concept of the Agricultural Marketing Act was of this nature. At the time it was enacted a major depression was not anticipated.

The stabilization provisions were looked upon mainly as a way of evening out the fluctuations due to yield variations from year to year. For this type of stabilization they might perhaps have been reasonably effective. Since this was the only mechanism available, the Board used it in its effort to check the downward drift of farm prices. Under the circumstances no action in terms of farm prices alone, and with no more than a half billion dollar fund, could possibly be successful. The results could hardly have been other than they were. It is difficult to see how the Board could have changed materially the main features of its program even if it had from the beginning been fully aware of the seriousness of the depression.[88]

Results in Wheat and Cotton

The stabilization operation in wheat clearly maintained prices above the level that would otherwise have prevailed during the period from October 1930 to June 1931. Whereas Kansas City No. 2 hard winter stood customarily at about 15 to 20 cents under Liverpool, in this period it was held at around 8 cents above it. This advantage was lost when stabilization purchases were discontinued in June 1931. The relationship to Liverpool prices then returned to about what it had been before the operation was started.[89] Some 390 million bushels of wheat were sold by American farmers during this period.[90] It would appear, therefore, that farmers and other sellers received some $80 million to $100 million more for their wheat than they would have done had their prices remained in the usual relationship to those at Liverpool. This amount was not clear gain, how-

87. The monopoly type of cooperative widely discussed in the 1920's looked to more sensational types of gain. However, even where this form of organization and policy were tried out, the expected gains proved elusive or temporary, and the unrealism of this approach soon became apparent, at least so far as nationally produced products were concerned.

88. Two major efforts of this type in other countries encountered somewhat similar difficulties: one, the Stevenson rubber control scheme inaugurated by the British government in the middle 1920's; the other, the Brazilian coffee valorization program, which was pursued with varying degrees of success and failure from 1905 on. The Brazilian program encountered, during 1930 and 1931, difficulties similar to those which beset the Farm Board. Its administrators resorted to the use of coffee for fuel, and to barter arrangements with the United States. For an account of the rubber experience see K. E. Knorr, *World Rubber and Its Regulation*, Food Research Institute, Stanford University, 1945, pp. 93–101; and, for a summary of the experience with coffee see V. D. Wickizer, *The World Coffee Economy with Special Reference to Control Schemes*, Food Research Institute, Stanford University, 1943, pp. 136–65.

89. See Federal Farm Board, *Third Annual Report*, Charts, p. 65.

90. *Yearbook of Agriculture, 1933*, p. 412.

ever, since the wheat was still in existence and presumably would depress prices when sold at a later date. On the other hand, the 250 million bushels bought and held by the Board, if allowed to flow directly onto the Liverpool market instead of being held, undoubtedly would have depressed world market prices to some extent.

On balance, it would appear that this was an expensive way to gain a temporary price increase for the wheat growers. Probably they would have benefited more if wheat prices had been allowed to take their course, and the amounts invested by the Board could have been distributed directly to them on the basis of amounts of wheat marketed.

The situation in respect to cotton is even more difficult to appraise. As of July 31, 1932, the Board's investment in cotton amounted to approximately $121 million. The value of the cotton held by cooperatives was estimated at $58 million or about $63 million less than the cost. Against this must be placed the gains in income, if any, which resulted from the program. The Board contended that the effect on prices was beneficial, though not markedly so. This conclusion was arrived at by comparing the decline in cotton prices with that of rubber, and of industrial stocks.[91]

This, however, is by no means conclusive evidence. The real question is, what would have been the course of cotton prices had the Board not intervened? It would probably have been more sharply downward between August 1929 and July 1931, but very possibly would have been higher in the period after the Board discontinued its purchases. Cotton being a storable product, the supply grown would eventually be sold. Withholding a part of it in one period could only mean adding to the supply in a later period. In the meantime the very existence of the quantity withheld was almost certain to exert a depressing effect on the market.

No Major Changes Made

On the whole it seems fair to state that the Board's program did not make major changes

91. Federal Farm Board, *Third Annual Report*, p. 80.

in the situation or structure of agriculture. Nor is it likely that it would have done so had the plan been continued longer. Some stimulus was given to the cooperative movement and some of the organizations started in that period have survived. Some improvements were made in arrangements for financing cooperatives, particularly in the provision of facility and operating loans. These activities, however, were not to be on an effective long-term basis until put into more orderly form through establishment of the banks for cooperatives, as was done in the succeeding administration.[92] The cooperative movement had considerable vitality and had been making steady growth for many years. Generally speaking, efforts to speed it up through high-pressure methods were not successful either before or during the Farm Board period, and it is entirely possible that agricultural cooperation in later years would have occupied much the same position in the economy as it did had there been no Farm Board program.

The stabilization activities, which were the most spectacular part of the program, must be put down as an honest attempt to ameliorate a disaster that could not be dealt with in that way, or at least not with the resources available to the Board. In part, the outcome was a result of unlucky timing. Had the Board operated in more normal times, or even if 1930 had happened to be a year of extremely low production in large parts of the world, its activities might have appeared more successful.

Nevertheless, it must be conceded that some such experiment had to be tried, either in this

92. There were some losses as well as gains in the new structure of governmental aids to cooperation. The Division of Cooperative Marketing, established in 1926 in the Department of Agriculture, was transferred to the Farm Board, and, later, to the Farm Credit Administration as the Cooperative Research and Service Division. While this has resulted in effective counseling and service activity in a form strongly advocated by the country's principal cooperative associations, it has to some extent inhibited development of more general research on marketing in all its forms. There is need for the kind of research and service work now being done, but an approach solely in terms of cooperatives does not cover adequately the whole field of marketing.

form or that of the McNary-Haugen plan, the export-debenture plan or something similar. Farmers, political leaders and the public were not yet thinking in terms of the far more aggressive and costly measures undertaken in the succeeding administration. The doctrine of salvation through cooperation and/or export dumping had come to be so widely advocated in the preceding decade that no other type of program would have been acceptable. The Farm Board approach may be looked upon as a stage in the evolution of the programs that were to come later. Its breakdown and virtual demise in the last months of the Hoover administration left the way clear for a new and much more varied attack on the problem. This was to be undertaken under the leadership of a more imaginative and daring group less bound by tradition.

The Domestic Allotment Plan

Though the McNary-Haugen plan with its "equalization fee" feature seemed to be dead, the idea of a farm relief program that would keep domestic prices above those of the international markets was still deeply ingrained in the thinking of many farm leaders. As the inadequacy of the Farm Board's approach became more and more evident, the two-price idea was revived and widely discussed, but in somewhat different form. The new version was known as the "domestic allotment plan," which had been presented and very briefly discussed during the last stages of the struggle over the McNary-Haugen plan.

The domestic allotment plan had objectives that were similar to those of the McNary-Haugen bills, but was more comprehensive, more carefully thought through and based upon more adequate understanding of economic relationships. The plan was first presented in an article in *Farm, Stock and Home*, published in Minneapolis by Harry N. Owen. It drew on ideas supplied by Dr. W. J. Spillman of the United States Department of Agriculture which appeared in more developed form in his book entitled *Balancing*

the Farm Output, which was published in January 1927.[93]

The idea was taken up by Professor John D. Black of Harvard University, and was presented in considerable detail in his *Agricultural Reform in the United States,* published in 1929.[94] He had earlier discussed it in hearings before the agricultural committees of Congress, but at a time when it had little chance for consideration as an alternative to the McNary-Haugen plan.[95] While not seriously considered for enactment during the late 1920's, an understanding of the domestic allotment plan is important in view of the fact that it was incorporated in the Soil Conservation and Domestic Allotment Act of 1936, after the Supreme Court's invalidation of major parts of the Agricultural Adjustment Act of 1933.[96]

General Principle of the Plan

As Black puts it:

The essential principle of the domestic allotment plan is paying producers a free-trade price plus the tariff duty for the part of their crop which is consumed in the United States and this price without the tariff duty for the part of it that is exported, this to be arranged by a system of allotments to individual producers of rights to sell the domestic part of the crop in the domestic market.[97]

93. *Balancing the Farm Output,* Orange Judd, New York, 1927.

94. *Agricultural Reform in the United States,* McGraw-Hill, New York, 1929, Chapter 10.

95. U.S. Congress, House, Committee on Agriculture, *Agricultural Relief,* Hearings . . . , 71st Cong., 1st sess., Serial A, Part 1, March 27, 1929, pp. 27–64.

96. During 1931 and 1932 this plan was widely publicized through speeches and articles by Professor M. L. Wilson of Montana State College, and came to be largely associated with his name. Wilson became an adviser on agricultural matters to Franklin D. Roosevelt prior to the election of 1932. In September 1933 he was made Director of the Subsistence Homesteads project in the Department of the Interior, and in 1934 became Assistant Secretary of Agriculture. On the resignation of Rexford G. Tugwell in 1937, Wilson was made Undersecretary of Agriculture, a post which he relinquished in 1940 to become Director of Extension in the United States Department of Agriculture. He was influential in formulating administration policy in regard to agriculture throughout the early New Deal period.

97. *Agricultural Reform,* p. 271 (italics omitted). Black's description and analysis of the plan, as presented in Chapter 10, is probably still the best and clearest available.

It is apparent that the general objective was similar to that of the McNary-Haugen plan though the mechanics were different. Under the McNary-Haugen plan the method of holding the price to domestic consumers at the free-trade price plus the tariff would be to buy up enough so that the entire crop would move in domestic channels at this higher price. Enough would be sold abroad, under subsidy, to make this possible, the loss or subsidy being met through assessment of an equalization fee (in effect a processing or handling tax) on all units of the product sold.

Under the domestic allotment plan processors would be required to show allotment rights for such amounts of the product as were processed or sold for domestic use. Such rights would be bought up by the processors from the growers. Taking the wheat crop as an example, the administrative agency would presumably issue allotments in somewhat smaller volume than would be used in supplying the domestic demands. If the rights issued proved to cover less volume than was needed, the millers would presumably find it advantageous to import sufficient wheat to make up the required supply, paying the duty on it. Its cost would thus be comparable to that of the domestic wheat purchased, plus the cost of allotment rights. If too many allotment rights were issued they would sell at a discount. The grain not covered by allotment rights would have to be sold without them, at the free-trade price, and presumably would mostly move into the world market on a competitive basis with grains from other exporting countries. Some of it, however, might be used as feed at this lower price.

It will be seen that this plan, like the Mc-Nary-Haugen plan, would not result in the world price plus the tariff for the entire volume sold, if more of the product was produced than would be needed for domestic consumption. The average price for the crop as a whole would be somewhat lower as a result of selling part of it at the world market price plus the tariff and the remainder at the lower, world market price. Under the McNary-Haugen plan the average price received by growers would likewise be less than the world market price plus the tariff, but uniformly over the whole crop because of the imposition of an equalization fee or tax on each bushel sold. It was argued, however, that the domestic allotment plan would bring out more clearly to the grower the fact that production in excess of domestic requirements would lower the average price received, and thus would tend to discourage production in excess of domestic requirements.

New Features Included

The domestic allotment plan introduced two new features not contemplated in the McNary-Haugen proposals. The first was the necessity for making specific allotments to individual growers in relation to some historical base amount of production. This meant setting up much more complicated administrative machinery, including state "allotment commissions" and appropriate county, and possibly township, commissions or committees. These agencies would determine, on the basis of past acreages and production (three to five years), the base sales allocation for each grower. He would then receive allotment rights for such portion of the base allocation as would accord with his proportionate share of the domestic market. Under the McNary-Haugen plan such individual allocations would not have been necessary. Each grower would have sold whatever amount he chose to offer, all of it on the same basis.

The other new feature was in the nature of partial insurance against poor crops or crop failure. The allotment rights would be issued in relation to normal expectations, as shown by accomplishment during the base period. If the crop produced in any year was smaller than the amount for which allotment rights had been granted the farmer might sell his unused allotment rights, either to other growers who had produced more than the amounts for which rights were granted, or to processors wishing to use them in connection with their purchases of raw product in the open market. Thus the grower would have some income from the sale of allotment rights even if he had a complete crop failure.

There were two major disadvantages to the plan: one, that it would tend to build up a body of vested rights to produce for a protected domestic market; the other, that a large and complicated bureaucracy would be required to administer and enforce it. Proponents argued that provision could be made for revising allotments from time to time, as new areas and new producers came in and old ones went out. It must be admitted, however, as later experience has shown, that such revisions present great difficulties both politically and administratively.

None of the earlier proposals envisioned direct dealing with the individual farmer. They were designed to operate by way of the central markets. Certainly the administration, and probably most farmers, were as yet unwilling to accept such a drastic change. Public sentiment favored strongly a reduction in government activity and expense rather than enlargement of it. Even in 1933, when the severity and duration of the depression had created receptiveness to more drastic measures, the idea of direct arrangements with individual farmers and a great army of federal administrative employees was accepted reluctantly and only as the lesser of two evils. By that time also the pendulum was beginning to swing in the direction of government spending for the sake of spending in order to create more purchasing power.

While the domestic allotment plan had no prospect of being adopted when first proposed, or in the years immediately following, the publicity given it was significant in paving the way for inclusion of some parts of it in the new legislation passed after the failure of the Farm Board and when a new administration had come to power. It was a direct forerunner of the acreage allotment plan which bulked large in the Agricultural Adjustment Act of 1933, and the marketing controls suggested were closely akin to the later marketing quota system. Large-scale bureaucracy and direct dealing with individual farmers likewise were soon to be parts of the established policy of the government.

POSITIONS OF THE FARM ORGANIZATIONS

Prior to the great depression most farm leaders underestimated the importance of urban prosperity. They maintained that agriculture was the nation's fundamental industry, and that all others depended upon it. Therefore, a logical approach in national policy was to make agriculture prosperous. This would lead to prosperity in all parts of the economy. That view was demonstrably incorrect as applied to the 1920's. Urban business had been notably active and prosperous while agriculture was in depression. Nevertheless, such clichés die hard. It was not to be fully recognized until some years later that the weightiest single factor affecting agricultural prosperity is the level of nonfarm incomes, and the buying power of foreign purchasers of our major export crops. It had become clear that even an active home market could be oversupplied, and that farm prices could be low as a result of maladjustments in production, but few had realized that an inactive home market and a depressed foreign market could turn depression into catastrophe for the agricultural areas.

It is not surprising, therefore, that the thinking of farm leaders continued to stress direct efforts to aid agriculture, rather than the more general programs by which the administration was endeavoring to restore urban prosperity. Through 1929 and 1930 the farm organizations gave principal attention to the Farm Board program, placing heavy emphasis on the importance of building stronger, more comprehensive cooperative marketing organizations. They also gave wholehearted support to the move for increasing tariffs, though they criticized the Hawley-Smoot Act, contending that it did not go far enough in protecting agriculture. They demanded immediate independence for the Philippines, in order that tariffs might be erected against agricultural products coming from that area. Their position, as of this time, may be characterized as one of extreme protectionism.

The most vigorous advocates of this policy were the dairy, sheep and cattle groups, but the wheat and cotton interests concurred with them, anticipating eventual establishment of some form of two-price system whereby they might obtain a protected price on that part of their product which was sold in the home market. When it became evident that the Farm Board could not check the decline in farm prices, the Farm Bureau renewed its demand for an equalization fee plan, and the Grange reiterated its stand in favor of the export-debenture scheme.

Growing Interest in Monetary Policy

There was, however, a growing interest in policies of broader significance. This was evident in the emphasis given to the proposals for stabilizing the general price level. Support was given to the Goldsborough bill, which would have required the Federal Reserve Board and other agencies to undertake stabilization of the value of the dollar through open market purchases and sales of securities, manipulation of the rediscount rate and variations in the reserve requirements of member banks. In supporting this policy the farm groups occupied rather advanced ground, though their recommendations were not sharply divergent from previously accepted and partially tried procedures. Later, under the influence of Professors George Warren of Cornell and Irving Fisher of Yale, the Farm Bureau turned more and more to the advocacy of an attempt to stabilize the value of the dollar by varying the weight of gold legally assigned to it.

The thinking on this problem was purely in monetary and credit terms. It took no account of fiscal policy, which in later years has come to be regarded as an essential part of such a program. Both organizations in fact, like the Republican and Democratic parties, stood strongly for a balanced budget, even in the desperate circumstances of 1931 and 1932.

Adjusting the gold value of the dollar was later to be tried out, with disappointing results, and it was soon to be evident that low interest rates and easy credit would not cause businessmen to borrow if they did not see prospects of profit. In these circumstances the only means for increasing purchasing power quickly was to resort to government spending on a large scale. This process came more and more into use, but mainly under pressure of necessity, not as part of a considered and planned monetary and fiscal policy. The earlier gropings of the farm leaders in this realm were more realistic and promising than those which came later under the influence of Warren and Fisher.

While this effort to strengthen agriculture through stabilizing the general price level marks a significant step forward in the thinking of these groups, they were concerned too exclusively with price rather than with the whole complex of problems relating to prosperity and national well-being. They were not yet thinking in terms of the major problem, namely, that of restoring consumer buying power. Price stabilization was looked upon as a means of protecting the farmer against price changes adverse to him rather than as a means of stabilizing the economy at generally higher levels of output.

Little Change in Other Policies

On most other matters the policies advocated by the farm organizations followed traditional lines. They advocated strengthening the federal farm credit agencies, lowering rates of interest, and more dependence on borrower guidance in the formulation of credit policies. While most of the earlier resolutions of both the Grange and Farm Bureau implied further decentralization of the farm credit system, the Farm Bureau shifted its ground, and, in December 1932, came out flatly for ". . . complete reorganization of all agricultural credit machinery of the Government under one head but operating in two divisions, namely, long-term credits and short-term credits."[98] This recommendation was in keeping with the plan of reorganization adopted in 1933.

98. Resolutions adopted at the fourteenth annual meeting as published in *The Bureau Farmer* (Illinois Agricultural Association Section), January 1933, pp. 10-11.

All the farm organizations stressed the need for easing the burden of taxation on farm real estate, but were unable to make very specific proposals. Much of the tax load had resulted from bond issues voted earlier, for highways, new school buildings, new court houses and similar improvements. These charges could not easily be offset by economies in current expenditures. The Grange, however, came out definitely for federal aid to schools, and the Farm Bureau resolutions hinted at this as a solution. The Grange specifically opposed a sales tax, the solution which was eventually accepted by many of the states as a means of relieving the burden on real estate. Both the Grange and the Farm Bureau favored higher income and inheritance taxes in the upper brackets.

The Farm Bureau, in its December 1932 resolutions, hinted at a provision for guarantee of bank deposits but did not put forward a definite proposal. The Grange expressed vigorous opposition to branch banking, though this would have been one possible way of decreasing the vulnerability of small country banks. Most of the other resolutions of both organizations related to longer-term problems. They urged that submarginal lands be taken out of production; recommended inland waterway development, and the elimination of short-selling in future markets. Strong recommendations were made that the government develop and bring into operation the Muscle Shoals power project. The Grange maintained its traditional policy of support for the World Court and a program looking to the maintenance of peace. There was also evidence of a growing interest in research looking to the wider use of surplus farm products for industrial purposes.

Efforts to Combine Forces

As conditions grew worse it became more and more evident that the farm organizations would have to present a united front if they were to get action by the Congress on their special problems. Edward O'Neal, who became president of the Farm Bureau on May 1, 1931, addressed a letter to most of the major farm and marketing organizations, inviting them to participate in a conference on a joint program for agriculture. The response was general, and a preliminary meeting was held on May 18. This was followed by succeeding conferences on June 29 and September 14. As an outgrowth of these meetings a unified six-point legislative program was adopted by the Farm Bureau, Grange and Farmers Union, in a meeting of January 6–8, 1932, and was presented by O'Neal before the House Committee on Agriculture on January 12.

The six points agreed to were as follows:[99]

1. The Agricultural Marketing Act to be continued, as a means of stimulating cooperative marketing, but to be amended so as to include the export-debenture plan, the equalization fee plan or some other method which "will make it effective in controlling surpluses, . . . and in securing for American farmers cost of production on those portions of their crops sold for consumption in our own nation; nothing less is a remedy for the agricultural marketing problem."

2. Main income of the federal government to be derived from personal income, corporation and estate taxes, with increases in the upper brackets, and improvements in the administration of income tax laws. General sales taxes, and excise taxes on automobiles, gasoline and bank checks were opposed.

3. A program for stabilizing the value of money backed by the arguments that "We cannot exist with rubber dollars and iron debts," and that "the United States does not have to wait on Europe for a solution of its problems." Demand was made that the Federal Reserve system stop contraction and deflation, and inaugurate credit expansion.

4. Tariff rates that will insure the American market for farm products to the American farmer. Tariff schedules must be revised to a basis of equality as between agriculture and other industries. No tariffs to be granted that will breed monopolies. "Tariff for all or tariff for none."

5. Passage of such legislation as may be necessary to prevent short selling on commodity and other exchanges.

6. Independence for the Philippines (to make

99. For the full statement see *The Bureau Farmer*, February 1932, p. 8.

possible the erection of tariffs against Philippine products that compete with farm products grown in continental United States).

New Ideas Lacking

The position of the farm organizations as a whole reflects much the same stage of thinking as that which prevailed in the Congress, and in the leadership of the political parties. They were strongly bound by tradition, and somewhat lacking in original ideas as to how to deal with this unprecedented situation. They continued to have an unwarranted faith in the efficacy of cooperative marketing. They stood by their earlier conviction that the equalization fee or export-debenture plan would afford a solution for their difficulties, though it is evident that these could not have had much effect on prices except for products heavily dependent on export markets. They placed great emphasis on extremely high levels of tariff, partly because of their belief that the equalization or export-debenture procedure would enable them to sell in a protected market. Yet the domestically consumed products were in about as bad a situation as the export crops, though there was no significant importation of foreign agricultural products to compete with them.

Somewhat newer ground was broken in their advocacy of a stable price level, but the measures proposed were inadequate to achieve that end. This goal may still be beyond our grasp, though much more is known about it now than was known at that time. The proposals in regard to Federal Reserve policy were, in the main, sound insofar as they could be effective. It is more and more evident, however, that merely making money more freely available at low rates of interest does not necessarily induce increased borrowing. As of that time, most banks were striving desperately to increase their liquidity, and the last thing they wanted to do was to increase their loans and discounts if they could avoid doing so. If buying power was to be increased quickly the wherewithal would have to be injected by the government itself

through deficit spending. This, neither the administration nor the farm organizations felt inclined to advocate.

No Quick Solution Possible

The truth of the matter is that no quick and sure remedy was at hand. Confidence could not be revived quickly; demoralized foreign markets and currencies could not easily be set right; and the disposal of burdensome accumulations of farm products would require time. Bold action to restore confidence in the banks, such as was later taken by means of the Federal Deposit Insurance Corporation, would have helped. Earlier large-scale refinancing of farm mortgages at lower rates of interest would have helped, and a larger, more vigorous program of public spending would probably have been logical. Yet, even these measures, and more, did not restore confidence and prosperity quickly when they were adopted in the succeeding administration. Once depression has reached the proportions then existing, it can be cured only through much readjustment and widespread suffering. Genuine preventives must act, in the main, before the blow falls, not after.

The clarity of thinking on the part of the farm groups was neither significantly better nor notably worse than that of other groups, including Congress and the administration. All were dealing with a situation more baffling than any they had previously experienced. All were wedded to relatively orthodox procedures. Possibly other measures would have been little more effective. They were to be tried, however, with a *savoir-faire* and daring not previously seen in our history; and to some extent the mere fact of doing something rather than nothing was to prove a stimulus to confidence and a means of starting the wheels in motion again.

The Presidential Campaign of 1932

The campaign of 1932, coming at the darkest period of the depression, was directed to a voting public that was confused, pessimistic and unsure of the future. There was little in e party platforms or campaign speeches to dicate that either party or candidate had in nind any clear, consistent plan of action; or, a fact, any program that would break sharply ith tradition.[100] Both party platforms in-luded illogical and inconsistent features, and heir similarities were perhaps more striking han their differences. The incumbent party, eeking retention of power in a depression eriod, is inevitably on the defensive and usu-lly is defeated.

The Republicans stood by their policy of lacing responsibility for relief on state and ocal agencies and the spread of employment y means of a shorter work week. The Demo-rats took approximately the same stand on hese matters.

Both parties advocated economy in govern-ment, and the Democrats demanded abolition f "useless commissions and offices," consoli-lation of departments and bureaus, and a re-luction of 25 per cent in government expendi-ures.[101]

Both parties stood for a "sound" currency. Both favored participation in an international conference to seek solutions to the chaotic monetary conditions existing nearly all over the world. Both made political gestures in the direction of unsound policies designed to ap-pease the silver interests.

The positions on extension of credit were similar, though that of the Democrats was extremely vague while the Republican pro-posals were more fully spelled out along lines already extensively implemented. The Demo-crats took a stronger and more definite stand on the regulation of banking institutions, stock exchanges, etc. These did not as yet, however, imply establishment of a securities and exchange commission to regulate stock exchanges. Both parties advocated changes in the banking laws.

Farm Programs Advocated

With respect to agriculture the Democratic platform mentioned vaguely the control of crop surpluses. Later, in his Topeka speech, Roosevelt outlined his farm program. The speech was carefully designed to mean to the farmers of the Middle West that he favored the domestic allotment plan, but did not men-tion that plan by name. In this way he sought to win the backing of the farm states without arousing the opposition in the eastern states that would have been likely to result from a forthright endorsement of either the McNary-Haugen or the domestic allotment plan.[102]

He said that the plan must provide for the farmer to receive the benefit of the domestic market without causing him to increase pro-duction; it must be self-financing; it must not use any mechanism that would cause Euro-pean customers to retaliate on the grounds of dumping; it must make use of existing agen-cies; it must operate on a cooperative basis; and it must be voluntary.[103] The Republicans

100. For a fuller account of the campaign, see Roy V. Peel and Thomas C. Donnelly, *The 1932 Campaign, An Analysis,* Farrar and Rinehart, New York, 1935, espe-ially Chapter 6, "The Issues."

101. This indicates clearly that as late as the fall of 932 the Democrats had no notion of an attack on de-pression through large-scale deficit financing. Mr. Roose-elt, in his campaign speeches, stressed repeatedly the necessity for curtailing government spending and bring-ng the budget into balance.

Rexford Guy Tugwell, later prominent in the exposi-ion and formulation of "New Deal" policies, writing in 932, delineates with considerable insight various short-omings of Mr. Hoover's philosophy, but is surprisingly ague as to alternatives. See Rexford Guy Tugwell, *Mr. Hoover's Economic Policy,* The John Day Pamphlets No. , John Day Company, New York, 1932. Mr. Tugwell eems to scold Mr. Hoover for not balancing the budget ut at the same time chastises him for attempting to offset a $12 billion reduction in wages with an $800 million relief budget. The Reconstruction Finance Cor-poration and the attempt to support equity values and prices are deplored as mere attempts to support a rotten structure. Yet they are surprisingly similar to the efforts of 1933 and after to restore prices to the levels of 1926, to adjust debts so that properties might be retained by their then current owners, and to refinance innumerable irrigation districts and other business units so they could carry on; this being done through that same agency, the Reconstruction Finance Corporation. This is not to say that Mr. Hoover was right. It is merely to recognize that he personified the attitudes prevalent in the 1920's, and that a different outlook was then only vaguely taking shape. It was not to become a formulated program of action until later.

102. The speech was prepared on the basis of contri-butions and counsel from M. L. Wilson, Henry Wallace, Henry Morgenthau, Hugh Johnson, Raymond Moley and others. For an interesting account of the process of preparation see Raymond Moley, *After Seven Years,* Harper and Brothers, New York, 1939, pp. 41–45.

103. Franklin D. Roosevelt, *Public Papers and Ad-dresses,* Random House, New York, 1938, Vol. I, pp. 693–711.

likewise emphasized the need for balancing farm production with demand, and reiterated their faith in cooperative marketing. Their proposals as to how to accomplish this were, however, even more vague than those of the Democrats. Hoover, in his Des Moines speech, advocated repeal of the price-stabilization provisions of the Agricultural Marketing Act, and proposed diversion of land from unprofitable to profitable use.[104] He also urged completion of the inland waterway system, reduction of taxes on farm lands, expansion of credit and continued effort to enlarge farm markets.

Party Views on the Tariff Issue

The party programs split most definitely on the tariff issue. The Republicans claimed that tariff rates on farm products had been increased by 30 per cent while those on non-farm products had been advanced by only 12 per cent. This, it was contended, equalized, "so far as legislation can do," the protection afforded to agriculture as compared to that provided for industry.[105] The Democratic platform called for a competitive tariff for revenue, reciprocal trade agreements and an international conference designed to restore international trade and facilitate exchange. With the characteristic inconsistency of party platforms it opposed cancellation of war debts. Roosevelt, in later speeches, tried to make the best of it by contending that if tariffs were lowered the cancellation of war debts would be unnecessary.

104. This appears to be a vague reference to a principle that the succeeding administration sought to implement by means of the Resettlement Administration.

105. This argument was obviously for campaign purposes only. All informed people were aware of the fact that the United States had export surpluses of the major farm products, and, therefore, that it made little difference what level of tariffs was placed on them. It is hardly conceivable that there would have been any significant movement of farm products into the United States even if there had been no tariff at all. Prices in the United States were so low as scarcely to cover the costs of transporting farm products to our own markets, let alone bringing them in from abroad. It was argued, however, that the abandonment of the gold standard by many of the countries had created a situation in which the American market might be flooded with cheap foreign-grown products.

Other Issues

Each party accused the other of extravagance and wasting of public funds. The Democratic platform singled out the Federal Farm Board in particular, accusing it of extravagance and of making the government a speculator in farm products, and condemned the "unsound" policy of restricting agricultural production to the amounts required to supply the domestic markets.

In his Denver speech, on September 15, Roosevelt declared that the United States was "about to enter a new period of liberalism," and called on the voters to support the Democrats as the party of the "new liberalism." He did not, however, in any of his speeches, make clear what the "new liberalism" was to be.[106] In the main his proposals in regard to transportation, monopolies, banking and budgetary matters were relatively orthodox and surprisingly similar to those of Hoover. His speeches did, however, vaguely indicate new directions in farm policy, in public ownership of electric power facilities and, especially, in foreign trade policy.[107]

The Winter of 1932–1933

The crushing defeat of the Republicans in the November election ended such small measure of effective leadership as had survived in the Hoover administration.[108] Most

106. The nature of his concept and of the difference between it and that of Hoover is perhaps most nearly expressed in his Jefferson Day address in which he said: "I am pleading for a policy . . . that seeks to help all simultaneously, that shows an understanding of the fact that there are millions of our people who cannot be helped by merely helping their employers, because they are not employes in the strict sense of the word—the farmers, the small businessmen, the professional people." *New York Times,* April 19, 1932, p. 16.

107. The prohibition issue, surprisingly enough, loomed larger than some of the major issues related to the depression. The Republicans sought to dodge the question. The Democrats came out flatly for repeal.

108. The outcome of the election was a foregone conclusion even before the end of the campaign, though few expected such a disastrous rout as the one that occurred. Peel and Donnelly summarize the situation as follows: ". . . neither tactics nor strategy were important in 1932. All the Democrats had to do was to play safe, and to organize everything in sight while the Republicans floundered about. . . . it may safely be said that since prosperity did not return before the day of election, the Republicans could not possibly have won unless their rivals had displayed colossal stupidity, . . ." *The 1932 Campaign,* p. 179.

f the indexes of economic activity remained atic at the low levels of 1932, or declined ightly, during the winter of 1932–1933.[109]

There is some indication that the decline of ctivity had run its course by the middle of 932, and was showing a slight upward trend a the latter part of that year. Industrial pro- uction, factory employment and prices held bout steady but at very low levels. The bank- ig situation continued to deteriorate, and was characterized by widespread hoarding of cash and gold in the first two months of 1933. Bank failures increased alarmingly, lead- ing to a virtual breakdown of confidence in all banks as depositories of savings. President Hoover sought to enlist the President-elect in some joint action to check the debacle. Failing in this, he was forced to wait out this dismal period, pending the inauguration of the new President and the launching of the new program that was to be characterized as "The New Deal."

109. See graphic presentation of these, U.S. Depart- nent of Commerce, *Survey of Current Business,* Decem- er 1933, p. 2.

CHAPTER 12

FROM DEFENSE TO ATTACK

THE SWEEPING VICTORY of the Democrats in the election of 1932, and the general desire for change, gave the new President a free hand to try out novel approaches in the fight against depression. Endowed with a gift for dramatic presentation, he characterized the new program as a war against depression, and, as commander-in-chief, asked and received powers that went far beyond those normally accorded to the executive in times of peace. He drew around him a young and imaginative group of advisers and showed a marked predilection for new and untried methods, whereas the actions of his predecessor had been characterized by caution and adherence to tradition.

It is incorrect, however, to assume, as many do, that the advent of the "New Deal" marked a sharp break in underlying philosophy. As Hicks comments, "In a sense Herbert Hoover rather than Franklin Roosevelt inaugurated the New Deal."[1] Whereas earlier depression Presidents had concerned themselves mainly with keeping the government solvent, leaving business to take care of itself, Hoover undertook to apply the powers of government, and his own personal leadership, in solving the problems then facing the nation. He tried to stimulate joint private action; he urged public works, even proposing, in his annual message of 1931, a Public Works Administration.[2] He set up the Reconstruction Finance Corporation and the Home Loan Bank system, sponsored the Federal Farm Board and brought about a moratorium on international debts. Even in the realm of relief he carried organization beyond anything that had existed before.

1. John D. Hicks, *The American Nation,* Houghton Mifflin, Boston, 1946, p. 647.
2. Such an agency, commonly referred to as the PWA, became a part of the New Deal program in June 1933.

Nevertheless, he lacked the essential spar needed to appeal to the emotions and imag nation of the people. The advisers he relie on were, for the most part, older men, usu ally well-known administrators like himsel They drew on experience gained in a differ ent age, and, in the main, reflected the att tudes of the leadership in large-scale busines organizations. The new group containe more men of academic background, most o them with little administrative experienc but with a wealth of energy, optimism an new ideas.

The time was ripe for a bolder, more imag inative attack on the problems that had baffle the nation for three long and painful years A new administration, with no heritage of pas failures, could gain acquiescence in venture which probably would not have been accept able, even had they been proposed by the out going administration. Furthermore, there wa still a good deal of the aftermath of nineteent century thinking which needed to be cleare away. That period had glorified and catered t the captains of industry. Emphasis now wa shifting more and more to the needs an wishes of the common man.

Some such program as that of the Hoove administration probably had to be undertake as a prelude to the New Deal. It was only through trying out this milder, more ortho dox approach that members of Congress businessmen and farmers became convince of its futility. After three years of groping along these more familiar paths they wer willing to try other methods, even things tha would have been anathema to them only few years earlier.

THE SITUATION IN AGRICULTURE

Farmers were in desperate circumstance when Roosevelt took office, though probably no worse off than many of the industrial workers and most of the businessmen. However, farm prices had fallen much farther than those of nonfarm goods and services. Using the 1910–1914 base as 100, the prices of farm products stood at 65 in 1932. This was less than half what they had been in 1929. The prices of things bought by farmers, for production and family maintenance, had fallen only from 150 in 1929 to 102 in 1932, a decline of 32 per cent. The ratio of prices received by farmers to prices paid by them was down to 58.[3] Nevertheless, most farmers were employed and did have places to live, and an opportunity to provide themselves with some portion of their food.

Agricultural production had remained relatively stable through the 1920's at a level about 15 per cent above that of 1919–1921. John D. Black, writing in the *Review of Economic Statistics,* commented that this 15 per cent higher level of output merely restored production to its normal relation to population.[4] This, however, misplaced the emphasis.

The significant relationship was not to the American market but to the total market. The United States had long been a heavy exporter of farm products. Hence, the weakening of the foreign market had much the same effect as a rate of production increase that was greater than the rate of population growth.[5] It resulted in putting onto the domestic market more product per capita than had been available in the predepression years. Foreign outlets for such crops as wheat were

adversely affected both by the depressed condition in the consuming countries and by the increase in output of competing surplus areas, such as Canada and Argentina, which occurred in the 1920's.

A special committee of the Land-Grant College Association likewise concluded that increased production in the United States was not an important contributor to the price decline. The committee held that "Surplus production in the United States during the period 1924–1929 was the result of internal maladjustment in feed crops, increasing foreign competition, and import restrictions in foreign countries."[6]

The 15 per cent higher level of output during the 1920's had been accomplished without any material change in total acreage harvested. The number of farms was about 2 per cent less than at the beginning of the decade, and the number of people gainfully employed in agriculture was somewhat smaller. Output per man-hour in agriculture had increased by about 9 per cent.[7]

Both Black's analysis and that of the Land-Grant College Committee imply that no major adjustments in total farm production were needed. But these interpretations took too little account of the changed situation in the foreign markets for wheat and cotton. July 1, 1932 world wheat stocks, for example, were nearly twice what they had been during the 1920's, and world cotton production had increased by some 25 per cent or more, as compared to the early 1920's. Unless per capita consumption in the United States was to be raised above that of the predepression years, there was need for downward adjustment in the output of these principal export crops.

A drive to better the situation might have taken two or possibly three forms: one, an effort to adjust downward the output of agriculture; two, steps designed to raise con-

3. *Agricultural Statistics, 1950,* pp. 626 and 628.
4. "The Agricultural Situation, January 1933," *Review of Economic Statistics,* February 15, 1933, p. 27.
5. The physical volume of agricultural exports fell off from an index of 117 (1910–1914 = 100) in 1929 to 90 in 1931. There was some recovery in 1932 (to 98), but thereafter exports continued to decline, reaching a low of 54 in 1935. Wheat exports for 1933 were down to only 21 per cent of the volume exported in 1927, 1928 and 1929; pork exports had fallen off about 65 per cent; and tobacco 24 per cent. Of the major crops only cotton maintained or increased its volume of exports. *Agricultural Statistics, 1937,* p. 339. The dollar value of agricultural exports declined from $1,847 million in 1928–1929 to $590 million in 1932–1933. *Ibid.,* pp. 336–37. More complete data on these changes and some of the reasons for them are given in Mordecai Ezekiel and Louis H. Bean, *Economic Bases for the Agricultural Adjustment Act,* Department of Agriculture, 1933, pp. 13–20.

6. Association of Land-Grant Colleges and Universities, *Report on the Agricultural Situation,* by the Special Committee, submitted at the 46th annual convention, Washington, November 14–16, 1932, p. 6.
7. Department of Agriculture, *Agricultural Outlook Charts,* 1951, p. 5.

sumption on the part of low-income groups in the United States and to change the pattern of agricultural production; or three, measures to raise the buying power of the whole domestic and foreign nonfarm group while retaining about the same pattern of differentials between classes of consumers as had existed before the depression.

Emphases in the 1933 Farm Program

The new farm program was to place its major emphasis on the first and third lines of attack, namely, an effort to raise the farm-nonfarm price ratio by adjusting agricultural production downward, and steps to increase demand pretty much in the old pattern.[8]

Special programs designed to raise consumption by the low-income, undernourished groups, in relation to those in better circumstances, were not to come until later. United States production of wheat and cotton needed to be adjusted downward. In light of world supplies and economic conditions, both had been overexpanded during the 1920's. There is little evidence, however, that the over-all output of farm products was excessive. Large segments of the population were poorly fed and undernourished. Even many farm families were existing on extremely meager diets. Thus, the need was for expediting the shift to a different pattern of production—one containing more meats, dairy products, fruits and vegetables — plus measures that would raise and adjust incomes in such a way that the whole population could be well fed.

The preoccupation with price relationships tended, however, to obscure this broader aspect of the problem. Farmers felt that if they could re-establish a "normal" relationship between the prices received by them and those paid by them the problem would largely be solved. Since this apparently could be accomplished only by limiting agricultural production, they were willing to proceed along that road, though it would tend to bring about

8. As will be explained later, the production and price adjustment program for agriculture was part of a vigorous effort to raise prices generally throughout the economy.

low production in the whole of the economy such as had already occurred in its nonfarm segment.

It would be unwarranted to imply that this difficulty was not recognized, and that no effort was made to balance the economy by increasing nonfarm output. Such an effort was made and was to some extent successful. Nevertheless, the early stages of the new farm program were somewhat negative in character, a shift away from things not needed, rather than a shift toward things that were needed. The nonfarm portion of the program, like that for agriculture, was to be too heavily oriented to price recovery, rather than to constructive price, cost and production adjustment. The tendency of businessmen, and of labor, is to seek price rigidity, thus forcing volume of production to act as the equalizer between larger and smaller total expenditures by consumers. The farmer was merely seeking to approach his problem in the same way. He had been trying to do so since the early 1920's or before.

But before the problems of the farmers could be considered, other and more pressing matters required attention. Chief among them was the situation of the banks, which had grown progressively worse as the day of inauguration approached.

THE ROOSEVELT PROGRAM: FIRST PHASE

The Bank Holiday

During the first two months of 1933 confidence in the nation's banks slumped alarmingly. Depositors had no way of knowing which banks were sound and which were not. They sought safety for their funds by withdrawing them in currency and gold, and storing them away in bank vaults or elsewhere. Even banks that were in strong position could not stand panic withdrawals of this kind, and it was never intended that the Treasury and the banks should be able to convert a large part of the national currency into gold at any one time. The result was a chaotic banking situation in which almost no new loans were being made, and every bank vas trying desperately to get its assets into liquid form, so as to be able to meet the demands of depositors who wanted to withdraw their funds.[9]

The President-elect maintained a hands-off policy until he took office on March 4. Then he acted boldly and effectively. On March 5, he closed every bank in the country. When the Congress met in special session on March 9, he had ready for passage an Emergency Banking Act.[10] This empowered the President to call in all gold coin, gold bullion and gold certificates, and placed the National Banking system and the Federal Reserve system under his control. It provided for examination of all banks as quickly as possible, and for reopening those which the government considered sound. All others were to be placed under the supervision of "conservators," and reopened if and when they were deemed solvent and able to function normally. At the same time the act granted authority for the issuance of emergency currency to be used in halting runs on banks.

Confidence in the banks was further strengthened by the passage, on June 16, of legislation creating the Federal Deposit Insurance Corporation. Under the powers granted by that act provision was made for insuring, up to a maximum of $5,000, the deposits of each individual in any of the participating banks. All member banks in the Federal Reserve system were required to participate and others were invited to join.

In all, some 4,000 banks either failed to reopen or were reopened under conservators. Most of these were small, however, and altogether they represented only about 8.6 per cent of the total deposits of the nation's banks.[11] For the others, quick resumption of operation was authorized with what amounted to a government assurance that they were sound. Confidence in the banks revived quickly, and much of the money that had been paid out to depositors flowed back into the banks. Only $15 million of the emergency currency had to be used. The action taken, though drastic, was probably the most effective that could have been devised.

Had the President really wished to socialize industry and finance, here would have been a superb opportunity. The banks might have been nationalized and used as a primary instrument in changing the whole character of the economy. Instead, the action was designed to save the banking structure then in existence. In this respect it was quite in line with the Hoover policy, but more daring and more effective.

Economy, Beer and CCC

The new President moved quickly also to secure passage of the Economy Act, the Beer Act and the Civilian Conservation Corps Act. The first was an attempt to redeem the party's pledge to reduce the expenses of government by 25 per cent. The President was authorized to cut federal salaries as much as 15 per cent, to reduce payments to veterans and to reorganize government departments. The savings amounted to about $125 million on salaries and $300 million on pensions.[12] This abortive economy movement was shortlived, however, and the administration was very shortly launched on a deficit-spending program that far exceeded any in previous peacetime history. There was an attempt to continue lip service to the idea of a reduced federal budget by talking of a "regular budget," which was to be balanced, and an "emergency budget," which would not be covered by current income. Actually, the two quickly became so intertwined that no one could tell where one ended and the other began. Functions discontinued in the older

9. A dramatic day-by-day account of these events is given by C. C. Colt and N. S. Keith, *28 Days, A History of the Banking Crisis*, Greenberg, New York, 1933.

A later and more comprehensive account of the debt situation and of the banking legislation of this period is given in Albert G. Hart, *Debts and Recovery, 1929–1937*, The Twentieth Century Fund, New York, 1938, Chapter 3.

10. 48 Stat. 1. The act was introduced, passed and signed all on the same day, March 9. It undoubtedly broke all records for speed in legislation.

11. Bureau of the Census, *Historical Statistics of the United States, 1789–1945*, pp. 262 and 273.

12. Hicks, *The American Nation*, p. 662.

agencies, if useful, soon reappeared in the emergency budgets of one or another of the new agencies.[13]

The Beer Act had little to do with real emergency problems. It was a step in the direction of repeal of the prohibition amendment to the Constitution. The permissible alcoholic content of beer was raised from one half of one per cent to 3.2 per cent.

The Civilian Conservation Corps, though limited in extent, was a genuine and appropriate emergency measure well suited to the kind of problem then facing the country. It recruited unemployed and unmarried young men of eighteen to twenty-five years for work in improving the national forests and parks, building roads and firebreaks, and checking erosion. Enlistments were for one year. Enrollees received, in addition to maintenance and medical care, a wage of one dollar a day. They were required to allot twenty-five dollars a month to relatives or dependents. Efforts were made also to provide educational opportunities in the camps for those who wished to take advantage of them. The program was popular almost from the beginning, and, as a result of it, hundreds of thousands of young men made a start on useful work, gained in health and morale, and found way to weather the worst years of the depression.

Farm Credit Agencies Reorganized

The desperate financial straits with which many thousands of farmers were faced virtually compelled early recognition of the need for supplying quickly more credit to agriculture. As a consequence, one of the earliest steps taken was a move to strengthen and invigorate the government-sponsored farm credit agencies. Though the novel plans for agricultural adjustment and industrial recovery, which were then taking shape, attracted far more attention, this refinancing of farm mortgages was probably more significant in bringing quick relief to agriculture than was the adjustment program.

Since the new farm program was to take a quite different form from that under the Farm Board, it was necessary to liquidate the Board and clear the way for a new approach. The method chosen was vigorous and unprecedented, but effective. Under the authority for reorganization granted by the Congress the President issued, on March 27, a sweeping order abolishing the Farm Board, but retaining the powers assigned to it.[14] The order provided that the various federal farm credit agencies were to be brought together in a new unified organization known as the Farm Credit Administration.[15]

Important as an emergency measure, this was also a very significant permanent improvement in the nation's farm credit organization. The system, which previously had grown up in piecemeal fashion, was for the first time brought into well-coordinated form. The powers and duties assigned to the Federal Farm Board now were vested in the Governor of the Farm Credit Administration. Those actually used from that time on

13. This tendency gave rise to some concern on the part of organizations interested in the continuity of older lines of work. The American Statistical Association, for example, solicited and obtained, through the Social Science Research Council, a sizable private grant with which it set up in Washington the Committee on Government Statistics and Information Services. Intended at first as a means of securing continuity in established series of data, as against new and unrelated series in the various newly created agencies, its functions soon were broadened as a result of requests for aid on the part of the Secretaries of Agriculture, Commerce, Interior and Labor.

This cooperation between the various Secretaries and the Committee led to a great number of studies, by nongovernment specialists, of almost all branches of statistical and informational work in the federal government. As a result of more than two years of intensive work along these lines, extensive changes and improvements were made in many phases of the government's statistical program. The Committee's work led also to establishment of the Central Statistical Board, an official agency for coordinating and improving the statistical activities of the government. The Board later was replaced by the Division of Statistical Standards in the Bureau of the Budget, which now serves as a coordinator of statistical activities. For a brief summary of the activities of the Committee, see Committee on Government Statistics and Information Services, Government Statistics, Social Science Research Council, Bulletin 26, American Statistical Association and the Social Science Research Council, New York, 1937.

14. Executive Order No. 6084. Issued March 27, 1933, to take effect on May 27. Franklin D. Roosevelt, Public Papers and Addresses, 1933, Random House, New York, 1938, pp. 85–90.

15. The reorganization was carried out under the direction of Henry Morgenthau, Jr., who was named as the first Governor of the new agency.

consisted, in the main, of the provisions for making loans to cooperatives and furnishing aid to cooperatives through the research and service division.

In like manner the Federal Farm Loan Board was abolished and its powers and duties were transferred to a Land Bank Commissioner serving under the Governor of the Farm Credit Administration. The Governor was given authority to consolidate, regroup and transfer the various offices and bureaus which were thus brought together, with a view to creating a unified system of agricultural credit agencies.

The executive order was intended primarily to promote economy and increased efficiency rather than as a means of meeting the desperate need for new loans in the farm areas. This latter problem was attacked more directly in the major Agricultural Act of May 12, 1933.[16] That act consisted of three separate parts or titles. Title I was the Agricultural Adjustment Act. Title II was the Emergency Farm Mortgage Act of 1933. Title III dealt with the value of money, and granted authority to the President to take action looking to inflation of the currency, including revaluation of the dollar in terms of gold.

Emergency Mortgage Relief

Title II, the Emergency Farm Mortgage Act, provided for:

1. Refinancing farm mortgages held by mortgagees other than the federal land banks. The land banks were authorized to issue not more than $2 billion in farm loan bonds on which both interest and principal were to be guaranteed by the government of the United States.
2. Reduction of the rate of interest on all land bank loans, both old and new, to 4.5 per cent. The average rate on such loans at the end of 1932 was 5.4 per cent. No payment of principal was to be required on these loans for a period of five years provided the loan was kept in good standing otherwise. Provision was made for reimbursing the land banks for losses resulting from the lowered rate of interest on loans due them,

and to enable them to meet their bond obligations as they came due.[17]

3. Extension of time on obligations, including those for interest, of land bank borrowers whose condition and prospects were deemed to warrant such action.
4. A fund of $200 million to be used by the Land Bank Commissioner in making "rescue" loans.
5. Refinancing of irrigation and other agricultural improvement districts by means of long-term, low-interest loans from the Reconstruction Finance Corporation.
6. More liberal loans to owners of orchard lands, by assigning values to the trees, whereas previously loans had been based solely on the value of the land.
7. Direct loans to farmers where local farm loan associations were not available, or where their financial condition was too badly impaired to permit of their making new loans.
8. Increasing the allowable maximum size of loan from $25,000 to $50,000.[18]

As a means of meeting the most pressing agricultural emergency of the time, this was one of the most practical and important steps that could be taken. It contemplated refinancing, through land bank loans, thousands of farm mortgages that were being called by private lenders. The amount of private credit available to agriculture was being contracted at an unprecedented rate. Hence, the injection of government-sponsored credit was the only practical way to ease the situation, and save to their owners such farms as could qualify for loans from the land banks.

The "rescue" loans, commonly known as commissioner loans, likewise aided greatly in the refinancing operations. These were granted, in most cases, as second-mortgage loans in addition to the land-bank, first-mortgage loans. The two together would ordinarily make it possible to take up a private loan

---

16. 48 Stat. 31. Title III was the Thomas Amendment.

17. This was an enlargement and extension of an arrangement put into effect in January 1932, when the government appropriated $125 million for increasing its subscription to the stock of the federal land banks. Of this amount $25 million was earmarked for granting extensions to hard-pressed borrowers.

18. For an excellent summary of the provisions of the Emergency Farm Mortgage Act, see Howard H. Preston and Victor W. Bennett, "Agricultural Credit Legislation of 1933," *Journal of Political Economy*, February 1934, pp. 6–33. The official text is contained in 48 Stat. 41.

that amounted to as much as 75 per cent of the appraised value of the farm. Furthermore, such refinancing, within the limit of its scope, tended to ease the nonfarm financial situation, since it provided cash funds in place of frozen loans for many hard-pressed banks, insurance companies and private lenders.

This type of relief grew in importance through 1934 and 1935 as the land banks developed staff and facilities for handling the enormously increased load thrown upon them. In the three years following May 1933 total disbursements by the land banks and the Land Bank Commissioner amounted to more than $2,040 million for loans on more than 760,000 farms.[19] Funds for commissioner loans were increased substantially, and procedures were developed for inducing creditors to compromise their loans down to the maximum amounts that could be obtained from the federal agencies. Thus, many farms that were mortgaged for more than their now reduced values were refinanced and retained by their farmer owners, while still returning to the creditors probably as much as would have been salvaged by them had they foreclosed and taken over the farms.

This procedure was carried out through unofficial "farm debt adjustment committees" set up in many agricultural counties throughout the country. They consisted of prominent citizens, serving without pay, who sought to bring creditors and debtors into agreement on a repayment program that could be financed without the loss of the farm by the debtor. In most states, state committees were appointed by the governors to organize and aid the county committees. In one state, California, an official Farm Debt Adjustment Commission was established by legislation.

The Farm Credit Act of 1933

The Emergency Farm Mortgage Act was followed, on June 16, by more fundamental, long-term legislation known as the Farm

Credit Act of 1933. This cleared away some obsolete and unworkable phases of earlier credit legislation, and, for the first time, provided a balanced, practical and comprehensive system of federally sponsored agricultural credit agencies. Provision was made for liquidating the joint-stock land banks, and the authorization for creating additional national agricultural credit corporations was discontinued. Both these types of credit agencies had been authorized under compromise provisions included in earlier legislation at the behest of those who favored a private-profit type of organization as against a government-aided cooperative system. Neither had been notably successful. The regional agricultural credit corporations, established by the Reconstruction Finance Corporation, were likewise placed in liquidation; and more orderly arrangements were in the making for handling distress loans of the feed and seed type.

On the positive side the Farm Credit Act of 1933 established two new groups of credit agencies: one, a central bank and twelve regional banks for making loans to cooperatives; and two, a system of twelve production credit corporations to organize, supervise and finance local production credit associations so as to enable cooperating groups of farmers to borrow through them from the intermediate credit banks. Thus, the new system consisted of four major segments: the twelve land banks, for making mortgage loans; the twelve intermediate credit banks, for making production and marketing loans; the thirteen banks for cooperatives, for making loans to cooperatives; and the twelve production credit corporations, for creating an adequate local mechanism whereby the intermediate credit banks could reach and serve the individual farmer.[20] Three additional commissioner positions were created, one for each segment,

19. Farm Credit Administration, *Cooperative Farm Mortgage Credit, 1916-1936*, p. 16. On June 24, 1935, as a result of ability to sell land bank bonds at a more favorable rate, the contract rate on land bank loans was reduced to 4 per cent.

20. An Act of January 31, 1934 added to these the Federal Farm Mortgage Corporation. This was a wholly government-owned corporation authorized to issue up to $2 billion in fully guaranteed bonds which could be used in payment of loans made by the land banks or the Land Bank Commissioner, or as a means of absorbing land-bank bonds that were not readily salable in the market. The same act increased the permissible size of "commissioner" loans from $5,000 to $7,500.

other than the land banks which already were under the Land Bank Commissioner. The banks for cooperatives took over most of the functions, except price stabilization, and part of the remaining funds, of the Federal Farm Board.

The Farm Credit Administration has functioned effectively and its creation marked an important step forward, both for meeting emergencies and as a means of providing agricultural credit in more normal times. Many regard it as still unnecessarily complex in organization, and more expensive than it needs to be. It consists of more than fifty corporations with their attendant staffs and boards of directors.[21]

The AAA

Title I of the Agricultural Act of May 12, 1933 attracted much more attention than the expansion of farm credit activities and constituted a more radical change in policy. It established the Agricultural Adjustment Administration, and authorized a wide range of activities designed to raise the level of farm prices. Among them were authorizations to enter into voluntary agreements with farmers for the reduction of acreages of basic crops, to store crops on the farm and make advances on them, and to enter into marketing agreements with producers and handlers of farm products for stabilizing prices. The act also provided for the levying of processing taxes as a means of financing the crop reduction program, and for other purposes, and authorized the Secretary to license handlers and processors for the purpose of enforcing the provisions of marketing agreements.

In mobilizing support for the act the strategy was to include most of the different devices urged by various farm groups in order to satisfy the proponents of each of the plans, and also to provide flexibility. Secretary Wallace, when discussing the bill while it was in committee, stressed this need, saying, "The

continuous change in economic situations makes any inflexible solution certain to be found unsuitable or ineffective after a comparatively short time . . . Congress must enact legislation granting broad and flexible powers to the administration. It must trust for a solution of the present emergency to the exercise of sound discretion by the Chief Executive and those who carry out his program." [22]

Long before the demise of the Farm Board, its members had become convinced that marketing procedures alone could not accomplish the ends they sought. Production would have to be adjusted if farmers were to receive adequate prices for their products. Lacking any effective mechanism for inducing, or forcing, downward adjustment of acreages and livestock numbers, the Board tried to achieve these ends through exhortation and persuasion, but without success. Here then was a new approach to the same problem; one with much greater power, and one that included many other devices for strengthening the prices of farm products.

Neither the long-advocated McNary-Haugen plan nor the domestic allotment plan was adopted directly. The new program did, however, contain elements that were reminiscent of both. The processing tax was similar in concept to the equalization fee, but to be used for a different purpose. The marketing agreement provision bore some resemblance to features of the domestic allotment plan, and the rationale of the storage program was more or less in keeping with that of the holding operations of the Federal Farm Board. The new agency could use any or all of these methods, and still others yet to be

21. For an analysis of this aspect, see "The Federally Sponsored Credit Services to American Agriculture, Suggestions for Improvement and Coordination: A Report by a Research Committee," *Journal of Farm Economics*, November 1947, pp. 1429–1516.

22. U.S. Congress, Senate, Committee on Agriculture and Forestry, *Agricultural Emergency Act to Increase Farm Purchasing Power*, Hearings . . . , 73rd Cong., 1st sess., on H.R. 3835, 1933, p. 129.
The Agricultural Adjustment Act, unlike that establishing the NRA, did not have a specific termination date. It was to ". . . cease to be in effect whenever the President finds and proclaims that the national economic emergency in relation to agriculture has been ended; and pending such time the President shall by proclamation terminate with respect to any basic agricultural commodity such provisions of this title as he finds are not requisite to carrying out the declared policy with respect to such commodity." (Sect. 13.)

devised. Thus the act constituted a very broad delegation of powers to the executives entrusted with the new undertaking.

Inauguration of the AAA Program

The AAA program could not be thrown into gear quickly like credit relief. If production was to be reduced, results could not be anticipated until the autumn, at the earliest, and it was already late for the launching of such a program for the crop year 1933–1934. Quick relief had to come from credit aid that would enable farmers to hold on until the longer-term program could become effective. Nevertheless, spadework looking to quick activation of the AAA program had been going on, and the machine was ready to roll in a surprisingly short time.

Henry A. Wallace, editor of *Wallaces' Farmer,* was appointed Secretary of Agriculture in the new Cabinet. Nominally a Republican, he had shifted to support of the Democratic candidate in 1932. The new Agricultural Adjustment Administration was set up in the Department of Agriculture, but without clear definition of its relationship to the Secretary's office. This vagueness was to cause friction later. The problem was similar to others which arose in various parts of the government. New and very comprehensive agencies were being created. Some of their functions duplicated those of older units, and in some cases the new agencies cut across departmental boundaries. Jurisdictional and policy disputes were inevitable under the circumstances.

George N. Peek, father of the McNary-Haugen plan, and Charles J. Brand, a former chief of the Bureau of Markets, were named as Administrator and Coadministrator of the Agricultural Adjustment Administration. Peek had been at odds with Wallace and other backers of the new legislation even before the appointment was made. He favored high tariffs and export dumping, together with marketing agreements which would, he contended, raise farm prices quickly without resort to controls on output. Such controls were very distasteful to him. Peek also ob-

jected to the levying of processing taxes as a means of financing the program. He proposed an appropriation of $100 million to be derived from customs receipts. The Peek emphasis was similar to that of his former associate, Hugh Johnson, who had been named Administrator of the newly created National Recovery Administration. In the NRA, main reliance was on industry codes establishing minimum prices, wage rates, volumes of production and so on. The Wallace faction did not oppose marketing agreements, but was keenly aware of the difficulties agriculture would face in any attempt to regulate marketings and prices by means of codes or agreements.

Peek Resigns—Davis Appointed

The differences between Peek and Wallace became more acute as the program developed, and it soon was evident that one or the other would have to withdraw. Wallace had turned over most of the responsibility for running the older units of the Department to Rexford G. Tugwell, his Assistant Secretary, and proceeded to function, in effect, as Administrator of AAA. Though Peek fully expected presidential support in his contest with Wallace, this was not forthcoming. He resigned in December, and Wallace's position as the administrative and philosophical leader of the new program was to be unchallenged thereafter until he resigned the Secretaryship in August 1940.[23]

Peek was succeeded by Chester C. Davis, a supporter of the Wallace policies. Davis had long been associated with efforts to obtain legislative relief for agriculture, and his marked organizing ability was already evident. The huge and complex administrative organization required to carry out the program of the succeeding years was in large part a reflection of his ability and drive.

Since the AAA of this period is closely re-

23. Brand had resigned as Coadministrator some three months earlier, and thereafter Peek served alone as Administrator. For a diverting and intimate but not wholly objective account of this period, see Russell Lord, *The Wallaces of Iowa,* Houghton Mifflin, Boston, 1947, Chapter 10.

ated to the subject matter of succeeding chapters, further discussion of it is deferred while other parts of the New Deal program that accompanied it are briefly outlined.

The National Industrial Recovery Act

The administration's effort to restore prices, raise incomes and regulate production was by no means confined to agriculture. The non-agricultural phase of the program constituted, in fact, a more significant break with precedent than that embodied in the Agricultural Adjustment Act and the farm credit reorganization. This nonfarm segment of the program centered chiefly in the National Industrial Recovery Act, signed by the President on June 16, 1933.[24] The major modification of previous national policy was contained in Title I of the act. Titles II and III were virtually separate acts, not closely related to the subject matter of Title I. Title II authorized appropriations of $3.3 billion for public works, and Title III consisted in the main of amendments and miscellaneous provisions.

Title I gave the President unprecedented authority to establish agencies, to accept voluntary services, to appoint employees without regard to civil service requirements and to approve industry codes which, when approved by him, were to have the force of law. He was also authorized to delegate to appointive officers the powers granted to him.

Thus the act was in effect a delegation to the President of a wide range of legislative authority normally vested in the Congress. The exercise of these powers was limited to two years, with provision that they might be terminated sooner, either by presidential proclamation or by joint resolution of the Congress.

The President's comment when signing the bill is a striking illustration of the dangers of predicting the effects and enduring qualities of political and social innovations. He stated:

24. 48 Stat. 195. The Agricultural Adjustment Act and the National Industrial Recovery Act did not, of course, constitute the whole of the administration's program. They were to be followed by a series of other measures, many of them of longer-term significance.

History probably will record the National Industrial Recovery Act as the most important and far-reaching legislation ever enacted by the American Congress. It represents a supreme effort to stabilize for all time the many factors which make for the prosperity of the Nation, and the preservation of American standards.

Its goal is the assurance of a reasonable profit to industry and living wages for labor with the elimination of the piratical methods and practices which have not only harassed honest business but also contributed to the ills of labor.[25]

Thus was launched the most grandiose and probably the most naïve of the administration's remedies for the depression. Under powers granted by the act the President set up the National Recovery Administration, hereafter referred to as the NRA. To administer it he appointed General Hugh S. Johnson, coauthor, with George N. Peek, of the pamphlet *Equality for Agriculture,* which had initiated the long struggle for passage of the McNary-Haugen plan.

New Attitudes in Business

Before describing the NRA program, it will be helpful to touch briefly on the new attitudes that were developing in this period. The prestige of business leaders was at an all-time low. There was little confidence that business itself could generate a recovery, as it had done in earlier depressions. More concern was being expressed over technological unemployment than had been apparent at any time since the industrial revolution wrought such devastating changes in the British economy. Doubts about the merits of competition were prevalent. Businessmen spoke of "unfair" and "destructive" competition, while even labor and the general public came to think of many types of competition as "predatory."

The doctrine that business stagnation was virtually inevitable, because of lack of investment opportunities and of adequate buying power in the hands of consumers, had gained much headway. There was a general willing-

25. Roosevelt, *Public Papers and Addresses, 1933,* p. 246.

ness to try new methods. Business groups were to be allowed to plan, and to work together, in ways that had previously been regarded as both undesirable and illegal. Competition was to be held in leash, and production and demand brought into balance.

This meant producing, selling, and dealing with labor in accordance with some sort of plan, but it was not yet clear who was to do the planning. Businessmen assumed that they would be the primary planners, while not a few young and enthusiastic government officials thought mainly in terms of government planning. Some businessmen saw merit even in the corporate state of Fascist Italy, which was then attracting much attention both favorable and unfavorable. There also was undoubtedly a good deal of interest, coupled with little knowledge, in regard to the various "plans" being launched in Soviet Russia. Neither of these two political systems had at that time come under such bitter criticism as in later years.

These ideas were in sharp contrast with the attitudes that had prevailed in the early part of the century. Farmers especially had long been vigorous opponents of monopolies, trade associations and other forms of business combination. They had consistently demanded enforcement of the antitrust laws and the fostering of competition. In the Wilson administration even the mild concessions involved in the use of the consent decree, and prestatement by the Federal Trade Commission of things that would or would not be regarded as permissible under the antitrust laws, had been deemed too dangerous in view of the public antipathy to business combinations.

But there was a growing recognition of the inadequacy of competition as a regulator of price in some types of business. In railroad transportation, in various other public utilities and in some forms of business, the idea of public regulation as against competition had become well established. Labor unions had long sought to reduce competition in the selling of services, and farmers had been thinking in terms of monopoly types of organiza-

tion for their industry at least since the early 1920's.[26]

Thus the stage was set for a trial of some new approach to the control of prices, wages and output — one that was considered likely to be less harsh in its action than the ruthless nineteenth century type of competition, and one which might perhaps be a stimulus to renewed activity. The National Industrial Recovery Act was an attempt to provide means for expressing in action these new attitudes toward competitive relationships.[27]

Main Features of the Act

The heart of the new act lay in Sections 3, 4 and 7. Under Section 3, trade groups were to be allowed to formulate codes regulating prices, output, wage rates, hours of labor and business practices.[28] Such codes, when adopted and approved by the President, were to have the force of law.

Section 4 authorized the President to enter into voluntary agreements with industry, labor and trade groups. Under this section the President's "Re-employment Agreement" was promulgated. Signers agreed to maintain specified minimum wages and maximum hours and to employ additional help. "Fair" prices were also to be maintained. To designate establishments which had agreed to abide by the terms of the Agreement an emblem, known as the Blue Eagle, was devised. Nearly all business houses quickly adopted the Blue Eagle sign, and many used it on

26. For a good and brief summary of these views, see Leverett S. Lyon, Paul T. Homan, Lewis L. Lorwin, George Terborgh, Charles L. Dearing and Leon C. Marshall, *The National Recovery Administration, An Analysis and Appraisal,* The Brookings Institution, Washington, 1935, Chapter 1.
Also see Simon N. Whitney, *Trade Associations and Industrial Control, A Critique of the N.R.A.,* Central Book Company, New York, 1934, pp. 165–204.

27. Section 5 of the act provided that all actions which were in compliance with approved codes, agreements or licenses were to be exempt from the penalties specified in the antitrust laws of the United States.

28. The law specified that such codes were not to impose inequitable restrictions on membership, were to be representative of the trade groups concerned, and were not to promote monopoly. All of these, however, were vague terms, undefined in the act and subject to wide variations in interpretation by different groups and individuals.

their stationery and products to indicate compliance with the Agreement.

Since this phase of the program was based only upon voluntary agreement, without specific means of enforcement, there was little prospect that all members of any industry or trade would live up to it. If some members of a given trade group disregarded or violated the Agreement, others were virtually forced to follow suit since all were struggling desperately to capture a larger share of the limited market then existing. Administrator Johnson sought to maintain compliance by exhortation, and referred bitterly to noncooperators as "chiselers," but violations continued and grew in volume. The "Blue Eagle" lost prestige rapidly and soon came to be disregarded by seller and buyer alike.[29]

Section 7 gave rise to the most heated arguments in the early period of code negotiation and enforcement. It contained provisions for the protection of labor, other than agricultural, which were unacceptable to many employers. The law required, however, that these provisions be specifically written into every code. They included the right of labor to organize and bargain collectively without interference from employers, prohibition of any requirement that employees, or prospective employees, join any company union, and a requirement that employers comply with specified maximum hours, minimum rates of pay and other prescribed conditions of employment.

Many business groups sought aid in the form of the NRA codes provided for under Section 3. A huge staff was hurriedly brought together, negotiating groups were established, and the NRA offices in Washington became a seething beehive of activity. Codes began to appear, and presumably to be put into effect.

In the slightly less than two years of life granted to the organization, more than 700 codes were agreed to and signed. Thus a substantial portion of American business came

under a modified form of legislation by decree. The decrees were formulated, however, not by an all-powerful dictator, but, in the main, by business groups, which often were of somewhat uncertain composition, and NRA representatives who, in many cases, had little intimate knowledge of the businesses for which they were expected to legislate.

Difficulties Encountered

Opposition and criticism quickly sprang up. The groups negotiating codes were supposed, under the law, to be representative of the industries concerned, but it was obvious that only a few individuals could participate directly in the negotiations. Large firms could afford to be represented in Washington by able, well-paid personnel. Small businessmen could not themselves afford to go to Washington, or to spend weeks in negotiation after arriving there. In many lines they were not sufficiently organized to have indirect representation, and, in any event, were not skilled in complex industry-wide negotiations of this kind. Both labor and the consumers were nominally represented in code negotiations, but neither of them in such a way as to have much influence.

The government negotiators tended generally to represent a social point of view, but often were inexperienced, lacking in intimate knowledge of the business concerned and unable to cope with the experienced, high-powered business representatives assigned to the task, particularly by the larger firms. Feeling this frustration but not knowing how to effect their ends, the NRA representatives at times took uncompromising attitudes based possibly upon genuine interest in public welfare, but in some cases upon unrealistic interpretation of the sketchy facts available. Such individuals sometimes were ridden over roughshod by hard-boiled business groups bent on furthering their own interests. If, on the other hand, the government representative proved tough enough to withstand the pressure, or if the conflicting interests within the business group could not reconcile their

29. An intimate, though naturally a partisan, account of the philosophy and activities of NRA is provided in Hugh S. Johnson's *The Blue Eagle from Egg to Earth*, Doubleday, Doran, Garden City, 1935, especially Chapters 16 to 29 inclusive.

differences, the result might be a deadlock with no code signed.

More serious, however, were the numerous conflicts in provisions as between various codes affecting a given firm. Many firms handling a number of products, or perhaps even those supplying the same product for different uses, found themselves directed by one code to do things that were in violation of some other code which was equally binding on them. Cartelization of the type contemplated by the act was not altogether new, but in the main it had grown up in various European countries under private auspices. These private groups, operating without specific legal authorization or control, usually were able to adjust such conflicts in a much more flexible way than was possible under the NRA codes. Clearly the vigorous enforcement of such a vast and complex array of new legislation presented virtually insuperable difficulties. Disregard of code provisions became widespread.

NRA Abolished

It was inevitable that efforts at enforcement would eventually result in test cases before the courts. The first of these to be brought before the Supreme Court of the United States was the Schechter case (*A. L. A. Schechter Poultry Corporation* v. *U.S.*, 295 U.S. 495, 1935). The Court, in a unanimous decision, handed down on May 27, 1935, concluded that the delegations of legislative power granted in the act exceeded those permissible under the Constitution, and thereby held the act invalid.[30] Thus, the whole NRA

experiment was brought to an end. No serious effort was made to revive it in revised form, though some aspects of it, particularly the labor provisions, took shape in later, more specific legislation.

NRA Approach Not Suitable

Businessmen and farmers characteristically place great emphasis on price maintenance or improvement. The effect on volume of sales, on amount of labor employed and on total income tends to be given secondary importance. These predilections are apparent in the provisions written into the NRA codes. The legislation clearly implied cartelization and the use of monopoly techniques rather than the kind of competitive economy that had been idealized in earlier decades. Production might be controlled and allocated. Prices were to be set at levels that would yield profits, and low-cost producers or distress sellers who cut below such prices were regarded as chiselers.

Farmers also were making price increase the main goal of their program and were in effect adopting a monopoly technique of reduced production to attain that end. These approaches, in the absence of increased purchasing power in the hands of consumers, implied acceptance of the idea that, under conditions of low demand, production should be reduced all across the board to amounts that could be sold at previous price levels.

Much emphasis had been placed on the lack of balance between farm and nonfarm prices, but here was a program that was likely to raise nonfarm prices faster and more effectively than farm prices, thus increasing the disparity between the two. Except as the weatherman intervened, downward adjust-

30. A more unfavorable case for the government's cause would have been hard to find. The defendants were slaughterhouse operators who purchased poultry on commission and sold to kosher retailers, the birds being slaughtered on their premises in accordance with the ancient Jewish ritual. The defendants had been convicted, among other counts, of violating the poultry code's wage and hour provisions, of conducting selected sales of individual chickens, and of selling an "unfit chicken." In his review of the case Chief Justice Hughes's opinion considered three questions: was the law justified because of the national crisis; did the law illegally delegate legislative power; and did the act exceed the limits of the interstate commerce powers of the federal government? Hughes settled the first question stating that "extraordinary conditions do not create or enlarge constitutional power" and that resort to this contention is

specifically precluded by the explicit terms of the Tenth Amendment. Passing to the question of legislative delegation, Hughes held that the Congress had exceeded its authority by delegating powers without establishing adequate standards or limitations. (Mr. Justice Cardozo's concurring opinion referred to the act as "delegation run riot.") Finally, Hughes found that the poultry code's attempt to regulate intrastate commercial transactions exceeded the federal commerce power. There have, of course, been many legal analyses of the Court's decision in this case. One of the most readable and stimulating of them is that of E. S. Corwin, "The Schechter Case — Landmark, or What?," *New York University Law Quarterly Review*, January 1936, pp. 151–90.

ments in output could be made more quickly and more surely in industry than in agriculture. If price disparity was a basic cause of the difficulty, this was the wrong way to go about correcting it. Actually, the trouble lay deeper than either price or volume of production.

General loss of confidence and the sharp contraction of credit and business activity had caused major depressions in all of the principal trading countries of the world.[31] Millions of people were unemployed and were producing neither goods nor income with which to buy the things businessmen and farmers were trying to keep from producing. There was no simple way out of the dilemma, but it is clear that the route taken was not likely to be helpful, though there was perhaps more warrant for agriculture, with its relatively inelastic demand, to follow this course, than for industrial and business groups with their more elastic demand schedules.

Fleeting Boom

These, however, are longer-run aspects of the problem. The immediate effect of the passage of the National Industrial Recovery Act was to create a short-run boom. Industry speeded up in an effort to build up inventories before the higher costs and prices likely to result from the NRA codes could be put into effect. Between April and July the seasonally adjusted Federal Reserve index of production rose from 60 to 100 (1923–1925 = 100).[32] As the code regulations began to come

into effect this short-lived, speculative boom petered out. By September the prices of clothing, home furnishings and food had increased by about 20 per cent, and by October the production index was down again to less than 75.

The over-all effect was to raise hourly earnings, but to reduce hours worked. The result was that average weekly earnings of employed workers rose only moderately, whereas the prices of both food and nonfood items increased substantially. Unemployed workers were less well off, except as their lot was improved through more liberal relief spending not directly associated with NRA.

Farm prices rose more rapidly and further than did nonfarm prices, but this was from the much lower levels to which they had fallen in the early stages of the depression. Standing at 55 (1909–1914 = 100) in March 1933, they were up to 83 by July, but receded slightly thereafter.[33] At the year's end, they stood at 78. As in nonfarm prices, this rise was in part speculative, but both the government program and a reduction in agricultural output were partly responsible. Yields of wheat and corn were down sharply from those of the preceding four or five years. The wheat crop was less than 60 per cent of the big crop of 1931, and corn production was only 80 per cent of that of 1932. Over-all farm output was about 4 per cent below the average of the preceding five years.

Between 1933 and 1934, wholesale prices of farm products rose from 72 to 92, an increase of about 27.5 per cent, whereas wholesale prices of all commodities were up from 96 to 109, an increase of about 13.5 per cent.[34] In terms of prices, farmers were somewhat better off than they had been a year earlier, though they still were not up to parity in terms of the 1909–1914 base.

Reactions to the NRA varied from expressions of disappointment on the part of pro-

31. Stock prices began to decline in Britain as early as February 1929 and also began to show recovery sooner than in the United States. Improvement was apparent from June 1932 on. Prices reached bottom in that year. In France, likewise, there was a leveling off of prices in 1932, but no significant recovery in stock prices. In Germany there was a sharp recovery in commodity prices, and significant improvement in stock prices, from the middle of 1932 onward. See *Review of Economic Statistics,* November 15, 1933, charts on pp. 180–82.

32. Ayres states that "Even before the enactment of the inflationary legislation a series of active speculative movements in commodities and securities got under way and ran for nearly four months before they had any important reaction. In the four months from March to July the volume of industrial production increased by 63 per cent, which is more than three times as rapid a rate of advance as any previously recorded within the space

of four months in the entire economic history of this country." Though conceding that part of this advance was solidly grounded, he attributed it largely to the expectation that money would be worth less in the future. See Leonard P. Ayres, *The Economics of Recovery,* Macmillan, New York, 1933, pp. 123–24.

33. *Agricultural Statistics, 1937,* p. 402.
34. *Ibid.,* p. 403.

ponents to vigorous condemnation on the part of opponents. The eminent group of economists selected by the Brookings Institution to study the program concluded that the advances in wage rates about averaged out with the increases in prices, and summarized their appraisal as follows:

The internal readjustments in the cost and price structure which the NRA effected were for the most part planless and haphazard. They retarded the restoration of parity for agricultural prices, and the adjustment of construction costs to the demand for building. On the whole they were probably adverse to the revival of the capital goods industries. As a means of securing favorable specific readjustments in the cost-price structure the NRA as it actually operated was of very doubtful benefit.[35]

THE LONDON ECONOMIC CONFERENCE OF 1933

The price debacle of the postwar years and the extensive discussion of the McNary-Haugen and other two-price plans during the 1920's had made farmers and congressional representatives acutely aware of the importance of a strong foreign market for the major export crops. However, few of them under-

stood the complex problems to be solved if the overseas markets were to be restored to health and vigor. A brief review of the London Economic Conference, called for the purpose of stabilizing and restoring international trade, is therefore essential to an understanding of the farm problem of this period.

The dwindling volume of world trade and the chaotic situation in international exchange rates were causing growing concern among statesmen throughout the western world. Nearly every nation was endeavoring to curtail imports and expand exports, as a means of protecting its gold reserves and expanding outlets for its products.[36] Trade between the United States and other countries had been at relatively high levels during the late 1920's, but had been maintained partly through heavy investment of American dollars abroad, and partly through transfers of gold to the United States. The gap between values of goods exported and those imported had not been closed. The flow of foreign investment by the United States had virtually ceased by 1932.[37] In consequence there was little prospect for early revival of world trade, and there were strong incentives for placing still more restrictions on such trade. There was, however, a widespread feeling that sound and healthy recovery could not be achieved without a marked improvement in the trade between nations.

Preliminary Consultations

As early as May 1932 Britain put out feelers in regard to United States participation in a World Economic Conference. The United States, fearing that major emphasis in such a conference would be on readjustment or cancellation of war debts, expressed cautious approval of the idea, and agreed to participate

---

35. Lyon and Associates, *The National Recovery Administration*, p. 873. This study is probably the most careful and sober analysis available.

A less tolerant appraisal was published in 1937 by the editors of the London *Economist. The New Deal, An Analysis and Appraisal*, Alfred A. Knopf, New York. They state (p. 46) that:

"The N.I.R.A. . . . probably collects more divergent economic and social theories under the roof of a single enactment than any other piece of legislation ever known. If an attempt be made to reduce its chaos of principles to order, it may be said to have had two main purposes. One was industrial recovery; the other was justice to the worker."

Most analysts conclude that the tendency toward business combinations and monopolies, already well under way, was speeded up and strengthened. For a treatment of this view, see Whitney, *Trade Associations and Industrial Control*.

For a more optimistic view of what the NRA was expected to accomplish, see Benjamin S. Kirsh and Harold R. Shapiro, *The National Industrial Recovery Act, An Analysis*, Central Book Company, New York, 1933. Also the thoughtful discussion by Alexander Sachs, Chapter 5 of the collection of essays entitled *America's Recovery Program*, by A. A. Berle, Jr., John Dickinson, et al., Oxford University Press, London, 1934.

One of the most comprehensive studies of the NRA, including an analysis of the origins of the idea and a detailed account of the operation of the organization is that of Charles S. Roos, *NRA Economic Planning*, Principia Press, Bloomington, Indiana, 1937.

36. For an excellent discussion of the international situation of this period and the one immediately preceding it, see J. B. Condliffe, *The Commerce of Nations*, W. W. Norton, New York, 1950, Chapter 15.

37. The foreign trade of the United States during this period is well shown in *The United States in the World Economy*, by Hal B. Lary, Economic Series, No. 23, Department of Commerce, 1943, especially in the graph on p. viii and in Table I, p. 6.

provided neither war debts nor tariffs would be discussed.[38]

In November 1932 an international, technical preparatory committee began work on plans for the conference. It reported in January 1933, suggesting as the principal object of the conference a general agreement for the reduction of tariffs and the maintenance of a more moderate level of tariffs in the future. Two methods were suggested — percentage reductions or reduction to a uniform level. Secondly, the committee expressed the view that:

. . . the restoration of a satisfactory international monetary standard is clearly of primary importance. The World Conference, in the absence of another international standard likely to be universally acceptable, will have to consider how the conditions for a successful restoration of a free gold standard could be fulfilled.[39]

At this time the United States was still on the gold standard and had no reason to challenge the view expressed by the preparatory committee of experts. However, the developments of the spring and summer of 1933 were to place the United States in a different position with reference to the gold standard countries.

Early in April Roosevelt took under advisement the proposals for a World Economic Conference, and invited Prime Minister MacDonald of Britain, together with representatives of France, Germany, Italy, Argentina, Brazil, Chile, China and Japan, to meet with him in Washington. Canada and Mexico were later included. On April 19, while MacDonald was en route, the President acted to take the United States off the gold standard. This action may have been in part a strategic move to increase American bargaining power in the coming conversations, though it appears more probable that domestic considerations were dominant in the decision to take the action at that time.

The Washington conversations went off smoothly, with apparent harmony of purpose between Roosevelt and MacDonald, and plans for the Conference went forward. The gold bloc countries were reluctant to agree to a conference at that time, but gained the impression that Roosevelt had agreed, in the Washington conferences, to a *de facto* stabilization of currency relationships. On this basis, and faced by the dangers inherent in America's abandonment of gold, they agreed to participate. The Conference was therefore set up and convened in London on June 12.

Problems Facing the Conference

Many of the countries of central Europe and the nations of the British Commonwealth, as well as the United States, were then off the gold standard. Conditions were such that uncoordinated, competitive devaluation of currencies could reduce international financial transactions to chaos. A reduction in the value of the currency of a given country in relation to gold, or to other currencies, tends to make its exports cheaper in the receiving countries, until or unless counteracted by a price rise in the devaluing country. It therefore acts at first as a stimulus to exports, and at the same time contracts imports since it makes foreign goods more expensive in the currency of the devaluing country.

If only one country devalues, its trading position may thus be improved, through larger exports and reduced imports. If carried far enough, the result will be a flow of gold into the devaluing country to compensate for its excess of exports over imports; or, if

38. The United States position in regard to war debts, while understandable, was quite unrealistic and was obviously bringing closer the repudiation which later occurred. A concession that would have reduced the amounts owed in proportion to the deflation in prices of commodities would have been in order, since it would have meant repayment of a comparable amount of commodities and services to that which had given rise to the obligations. It was clear, however, that payment in full could not be made, even on amounts so adjusted. There was little inclination in the United States to recognize these debts for what they were, namely, a part of the United States contribution to the war effort comparable to the sums spent in putting our own soldiers in the field. The expenditures had not gone for building up resources in the borrowing countries which would enable them to make repayment, and our aversion to receiving imports made talk of repayment illogical and naïve.

39. League of Nations, Monetary and Economic Conference, *Draft Annotated Agenda Submitted by the Preparatory Commission of Experts*, League of Nations Publication II, Economic and Financial, 1933, II, Spec. 1, Geneva, 1933, p. 12.

it has been losing gold, the drain on its gold supplies will be eased. Such action, however, if taken without general agreement, usually results in corresponding or greater devaluations in competing countries. The situation thus may degenerate into one of ever-spreading competitive devaluation which is fatal to the redevelopment of orderly world trade.[40]

Another group of countries, known as the "gold bloc," was still on the gold standard. That is, they stood ready to redeem their currencies in gold at an established rate per currency unit if called upon to do so. These were Belgium, France, Italy, the Netherlands and Switzerland. Naturally, they viewed with grave concern the threat of continuing, uncoordinated devaluation of other currencies. At best it would place them in an increasingly unfavorable position in maintaining their current volumes of exports, and, at the worst, they would be forced off the gold standard and subjected to all the disturbances and instabilities that might result.

While devaluation could temporarily stimulate exports, it tended also to be inflationary to the internal economy of the devaluing country, particularly if it was heavily dependent on imports for essential supplies. That is, such items would rise in price in the devaluing country and were likely to give rise to a chain of inflationary developments, particularly demands for wage increases by labor. If acceded to, these would, of course, increase costs of both export and domestic goods and would tend to nullify the gains from devaluation. Eventually, further devaluations would have to be made if the stimulus to exports was to serve as anything more than temporary relief. Naturally, the gold standard countries did not wish to become involved in a sequence of this kind.

The dilemma facing the Conference was, then, how to satisfy countries like the United States, where the desire was to raise internal prices without cutting down exports, and, at the same time, allay the fears of the gold bloc countries, which wanted the gold values of currencies fixed and stabilized.[41]

Conflicting Policies

In the interim between the calling and the convening of the Conference, the United States had taken vigorous steps to raise its internal price level. Both the NRA and the AAA were designed to force prices up, and the speculative upswing in prices that resulted from the prospective imposition of NRA codes was already well under way by the time the Conference met.

The gold bloc countries insisted that stabilization of currency values in gold was a necessary first step in dealing with the situation. Both Britain and the United States stressed the need for raising prices before attempting stabilization. Secretary of State Cordell Hull, head of the United States delegation, insisted that a reduction in trade barriers was a necessary prerequisite to recovery in international trade, and that international commerce was indispensable to national life.[42] Britain likewise favored reductions in tariffs, but held that the raising of prices and settlement of war debts must accompany them before Britain would feel justified in returning to the gold standard. As a means to this end it favored cooperation among the central banks in maintaining a policy of cheap money, the abrogation of exchange controls, and the resumption of international lending.

40. It is this type of uncoordinated action that the International Monetary Fund, established under the United Nations in 1945, is designed to prevent. Such a mechanism did not exist at that time, nor had any similar method of group control been suggested.

41. The problem was further complicated by the fact that several of the gold bloc countries had devalued their currencies substantially in the 1920's, thus putting them in a favorable position relative to those that remained on the gold standard longer, if the countries that had not devalued agreed to return to the gold standard at the currency values then prevailing.

42. Sir Walter Layton commented, in a summary of British hopes in regard to the Conference written in April 1933, "Nearly every government in the world . . . has tried to protect its national economy by a restriction of its imports. The more countries take such action, the stronger is the inducement for others to do so; and the more futile it becomes for all together, since every nation's imports are some other nation's exports. The process is obviously a suicidal one; yet none of the countries caught in the circle dares singly to step outside it for fear of becoming a dumping ground for other countries' exports, without being able to expand its own." "The Tasks of the World Economic Conference," Foreign Affairs, April 1933, p. 406.

The spokesmen for other nations, such as Poland and Italy, on the other hand, expressed grave doubts about the wisdom and effectiveness of seeking to better the situation through monetary measures.[43] In the meantime the United States had taken action looking to higher rather than lower tariffs. Both the NRA and the AAA price-raising schemes contained provisions whereby the expected higher prices of United States products could be protected by further increases in tariffs.

On June 15, it was reported unofficially that the Federal Reserve Bank of New York, the Bank of England and the Bank of France had tentatively agreed on the establishment of an equalization fund designed to eliminate the more violent fluctuations in the values of currencies. This, however, was conditioned on agreement by the United States not to use the inflationary powers granted by the Congress. On June 17 President Roosevelt refused to accept the stabilization agreement. This caused bitterness on the part of the gold bloc countries since they conceived the demand for tariff reductions, unaccompanied by a willingness to stabilize currencies, to be little else than an attempt to raid their markets and undermine their currencies.

Furthermore, the disinclination of the United States to enter into any discussion of war debts, on which payments fell due on June 15, caused further uneasiness. On June 17 Mr. Hull submitted a proposal that tariffs be reduced horizontally by 10 per cent in all countries. Senator Key Pittman, deputy leader of the United States delegation, denied categorically that this had the support of the American members.[44]

Failure of the Conference

At this point President Roosevelt sent Raymond Moley, Assistant Secretary of State, as his personal representative at the Conference.

This was looked upon as a repudiation of Mr. Hull's leadership. Shortly thereafter the United States delegation came out definitely against immediate action to stabilize currencies, holding that the most important contribution the American government could make was to try to raise prices. Some of the governments proposed immediate suspension of the Conference. Moley, who was by now in London, helped draft a compromise agreement which supported, in principle, the idea of currency stabilization, but did not bind the countries not then on the gold standard to immediate implementation of this policy.

This compromise was cabled to President Roosevelt in full expectation that it would be accepted. His reply, however, was the famous "bomb-shell" message which in effect repudiated Moley, chastised the Conference for considering monetary stabilization ahead of "the larger purposes for which the Economic Conference originally was called together," and asserted the view that "The sound internal economic system of a Nation is a greater factor in its well-being than the price of its currency in changing terms of the currencies of other Nations."[45] The message, both by its content and its tone, ended all hope of effective accomplishment by the Conference. It dragged on for three weeks, but to all intents and purposes was dead from that time on.

U. S. Policy Inconsistent

There has been much speculation about the reasons for the lack of consistency in the positions taken by the United States in this period. On the 16th of May, Roosevelt, in an open message to the other participating states, had placed the stabilization of currencies first among the objects of the Conference. On July 3 he denounced the effort to divert the Conference from "its larger purposes" to "temporary exchange fixing," and thereby brought to an end the most serious effort of that period to bring about coordinated action

43. These various points of view are excellently summarized in H. V. Hodson, *Slump and Recovery, 1929–1937*, Oxford University Press, London, 1938, Chapter 6.
44. Pittman, who was from Nevada, was the chief spokesman for the silver interests in the United States. His main objective was to bring about a wider use of silver as a medium of exchange and, if possible, to have it accepted along with gold in a bimetallic base.

45. Roosevelt, *Public Papers and Addresses, 1933*, pp. 264–65.

on the economic and political problems of the various nations.[46]

It does not follow that his position on the substance of the matter was entirely wrong. It was not greatly different from that which Britain had maintained over the two years preceding. Nor did it differ greatly from views shortly to be advocated by Professor J. M. Keynes and widely accepted in the United States and Britain. It can be doubted, however, whether the President's view was based on any such considered analysis. He was dealing with matters in which he had little knowledge or background. He had divorced himself from the counsel of experienced monetary experts and was at the time of the Conference in direct contact with Professors Warren and Pearson of Cornell University who were staunch advocates of the policy of varying the gold content of the dollar as a means of raising prices. His internal program was a deliberate effort to divorce the American economy from the world economy. However, the position of the gold bloc countries also was shortsighted and unrealistic.

An Opportunity Lost

Nevertheless, the failure of the Conference meant the loss of a great opportunity. The exchange values of the various currencies remained chaotic, trade barriers increased, and nationalism tended more and more to overshadow international approaches. Worst of all, cynicism and distrust grew apace. Political decisions which might have checked the adventures of both Hitler and Mussolini in 1934 and 1936 had to be taken in an atmosphere of coolness if not actual dislike. Greater statesmanship and a greater will to cooperate might have provided a check to the tendencies that were causing the drift toward World War II. Economic cooperation was lacking at this stage. Shortly thereafter political cooperation was likewise to be sadly deficient.

Had the Conference succeeded in setting up a fund and apparatus for the gradual

46. Hodson, *Slump and Recovery*, pp. 205–06.

stabilization of currency relationships and in paving the way for a vigorous joint effort to foster economic cooperation and trade, it is possible that cooperation would have been available also to block the Hitler march into the Rhineland and Mussolini's conquest of Ethiopia. Whether this be true or not, the blame cannot be laid at the door of any one nation or any one individual. The inadequacy was general, but the United States as the strongest nation and the world's largest creditor cannot disavow a major responsibility for the failure. It, like the others, was pursuing a nationalistic course in a world that had become too closely interwoven for isolated action.

EFFORTS TO RAISE PRICES

The confusion about the United States position at the London Conference was largely due to the fact that a consistent internal policy had not yet been arrived at. The various presidential advisers were by no means in agreement as to what steps should be taken, and several programs that were not mutually consistent had already been launched or were under consideration. Secretary Hull was urging a reduction in tariffs and other steps designed to revive international trade. Another group, for which George Warren was the principal spokesman, was advocating manipulation of the gold value of the dollar as a means of raising and stabilizing prices. The Federal Reserve system was pursuing a policy of easy credit in the hope of stimulating business.[47] There was also a growing sentiment for getting more spending power into the hands of the unemployed groups by way of the relief agencies. In both the NRA and the AAA emphasis was on the raising of prices through artificially induced scarcity. Labor,

47. The easy credit policy had been in effect from 1930 on. Contrary to the expectations of some economists, this had not been an effective stimulus to business. When demand is active, and in cyclical changes of lesser magnitude, credit policies may be influential, but the experience of 1927 to 1933 had shown that major inflations and deflations cannot be controlled by so simple a procedure as easing or restricting credit and manipulating the interest rate, though such action may be a necessary part of a more general program of recovery or of efforts to combat inflation.

like business, was exceedingly price-conscious and, generally speaking, was willing to agree to higher prices for commodities, provided it could be assured of higher per-hour wage rates.

Attitude of the President

Sentiment for raising the prices of commodities was in accord with Roosevelt's own thinking in this period. He had become convinced that if prices could be raised (presumably to the 1926 level, though this was not specifically stated) the depression problem would be on its way to solution. This attitude, which was widely prevalent in New Deal circles, reflects the tendency for views that are appropriate for one period to be retained in later periods when they are much less appropriate. In the early stages of the depression a re-establishment of the previous level of prices would have aided many who were on the ragged edge of bankruptcy.

By 1933, when many assets and properties had changed hands at distress prices, a quick restoration of the 1926 price level, had it been possible, would have resulted in huge windfall profits to many purchasers who had acquired farms and other properties at bargain prices. At this stage, when many of the most painful adjustments had been made, emphasis could more properly have been placed on measures that would help to increase the volume of production and trade.

In his radio address of October 22, 1933, the President stated:

I do not hesitate to say in the simplest, clearest language of which I am capable, that although the prices of many products of the farm have gone up and although many farm families are better off than they were last year, I am not satisfied either with the amount or the extent of the rise, and that it is definitely a part of our policy to increase the rise and to extend it to those products which have as yet felt no benefit. If we cannot do this one way we will do it another. Do it, we will.[48]

This statement reflects a more settled acceptance of the views, which in June were just taking shape, that had led to his repudi-

48. Roosevelt, *Public Papers and Addresses, 1933,* p. 423.

ation of the stabilization proposals put forward at the London Conference. Having decided to use every available means to raise domestic prices, he naturally was reluctant to agree to maintaining the dollar in a fixed relationship to other currencies, thus assuming the added burden either of raising prices internationally or receiving larger imports which might interfere with the domestic program.

Farmers had long been receptive to the idea of trying to raise prices through some relatively simple monetary device. Hence it is understandable that sentiment for some attempt along these lines would gain strength during a period like that here under discussion. As early as the latter part of the 1920's, the Farm Bureau and some of the other farm organizations came out strongly for a "stabilized" dollar. A Stable Money League came into being, and the monetary stabilization idea was widely discussed in both academic and farm circles. The farm groups had a genuine desire for a more stable dollar, but a dollar stabilized at a lower value than that which then prevailed. Hence their pressure was for price-raising devices, not actually for stabilization. Most of the "stable money" advocates were thinking in terms of price manipulation through monetary measures rather than about stabilizing the dollar at its prevailing high value.

Devaluation of the Dollar

As the summer of 1933 wore on, the President came more and more under the influence of those who believed that the level of prices could be adjusted quickly, and then stabilized, by changing the weight of gold in the dollar. Title III of the Agricultural Adjustment Act had given him authority to decrease the gold content of the dollar to an amount not more than 50 per cent below that which had been established in the legislation of 1834. The first actions affecting the gold value of the dollar were, however, of a less direct character. The United States had gone off the gold standard on April 20. This came about through a presidential order which placed under embargo all exports of gold except those licensed for export by the Secretary of the Treasury.[49]

As a result of the suspension of interchangeability of gold and the dollar in March and April, the value of the dollar, in terms of foreign currencies based on gold, fell sharply. British abandonment of gold in 1931 had already caused a decline of about 30 per cent in the gold value of the pound, and had carried down with it the Canadian dollar, the Australian pound and the Argentine peso.[50] The depreciation of the American dollar forced the Canadian dollar down sharply, reduced still further the gold value of the British pound, and caused additional reductions in the values of the Australian and Argentine currencies.

Further steps in the devaluation process were taken on August 28 and 29, and on October 25, in the form of supplemental executive orders. The orders of August 28 and 29 dealt with the requisitioning of gold holdings in this country and the purchase of newly mined gold.[51] That of October 25 directed the Reconstruction Finance Corporation to buy or sell gold, both domestic and foreign, at prices to be fixed from time to time in consultation with the Secretary of the Treasury and the President. By this means the buying price for gold was brought up from about $30 per ounce, the free market price, to a fixed value of $35 per ounce. This constituted a devaluation of the dollar, in terms of gold, of about 41 per cent (as compared to its pre-1933 value).[52] It also meant stabilizing its value in terms of foreign gold currencies, a step the gold bloc countries had wanted to have taken by all the countries at the time of the London Conference, and to which President Roosevelt had refused to agree at that time.

To implement the policy of stabilizing exchange rates the President asked and the Congress authorized, in 1934, that the sum of $2 billion accruing to the government as profit in the revaluation of the dollar be made available to the Treasury as a stabilization fund

49. Pasvolsky holds that the suspension of the gold standard actually occurred on March 10, with the presidential order of that date. To make that effective, however, it was necessary to call in all gold in private hands. The initial action looking to this end was an order of April 5, which required all persons to deliver to the federal reserve banks by May 1 all gold and gold certificates held by them, and to accept in exchange other legal forms of money. Under the order of March 10, gold could still be exported under license, and there was no marked depreciation of the dollar as a result of it. The order of April 20 was, on the other hand, a definite abandonment of the gold standard. It was followed by an immediate and substantial depreciation of the dollar in international exchange.

A further step looking to the divorcing of currency and credit instruments from a fixed value gold base was taken on June 5 in the form of a congressional joint resolution which outlawed the gold clause in all public and private contracts. This meant that thereafter bonds and other obligations which specified payment in gold of a stated weight and fineness per dollar could be discharged dollar for dollar in money that was currently legal tender. After a bitter legal battle this action was upheld by the Supreme Court and the gold clauses in bonds and other types of obligation ceased to have significance. See Leo Pasvolsky, *Current Monetary Issues*, The Brookings Institution, Washington, 1933, Chapter 3.

50. See V. P. Timoshenko, "Monetary Influences on Postwar Wheat Prices," *Wheat Studies*, Food Research Institute, Stanford University, April 1938, p. 280.

51. During approximately the same period the President took various actions designed to enlarge the use of silver in the monetary system. Such action was authorized in the Thomas amendment to the Agricultural Act of May 12, 1933. An attempt was also made at the London Economic Conference to secure international action looking to increased use of silver in the monetary systems of the world. Under these authorizations and the Silver Purchase Act of June 19, 1934, the President inaugurated a large-scale and costly program of buying silver at prices far above its free market value. The mistakes of the Bland-Allison Act of 1878 and the Sherman Act of 1890 were repeated in cruder and more indefensible form. The pressure behind these moves came from the senators of the silver bloc, aided by an inflationist group headed by Senator Thomas of Oklahoma.

The result was a huge and expensive subsidy to the producers of silver, and the forcing of China to go off a metallic monetary base. There was apparently no effect upon prices of commodities other than silver in the United States. The whole performance was one of the less creditable episodes in the government's policy during this period. While the President's understanding of the issues was undoubtedly faulty, it is clear that the action taken by him was a result in part of what amounted to blackmailing tactics on the part of silver bloc senators. The President yielded in order to gain their support on other issues. So far as is known to this writer, no responsible official and no qualified economist gave willing support to the program. For a summary of these events see James D. Paris, *Monetary Policies of the United States, 1932-1938*, Columbia University Press, New York, 1938, pp. 42-80. See also, Theodore J. Kreps, "The Price of Silver and Chinese Purchasing Power," *Quarterly Journal of Economics*, February 1934, pp. 245-87.

An official account of the various steps taken in respect to gold and silver in this period is given in the *Annual Report of the Secretary of the Treasury on the State of the Finances* for the fiscal year ended June 30, 1934, pp. 27-30 and 189-212.

52. These various steps in the devaluation process are described in Paris, *Monetary Policies,* Chapter 2.

to be handled confidentially. This fund was to serve as a buffer, absorbing dollars when they were offered in excess of trading needs; that is, when there was likelihood the dollar would fall below the established price; and selling dollars when there was a shortage which might cause the dollar to rise above the established price. The result was to stabilize the dollar in relation to other gold standard currencies used in international trade. This plan was similar to that established by Britain in 1932 and one adopted by France in 1936.[53]

Results Expected

The proponents of dollar devaluation expected that the general level of prices would move up quickly by about the same percentage as that by which the dollar had been devalued. This expectation was based in large part upon statistical studies made by George F. Warren and Frank A. Pearson of Cornell University in which they undertook to demonstrate a close relationship between the quantity of gold and the price level during the nineteenth century; and also upon theoretical analyses by Irving Fisher of Yale which pointed to the same conclusion.[54] Pre-

sumably, making a given quantity of gold equal more dollars would have the same effect as increasing the quantity of gold.

Defects in the Theory

What the theory ignored was the fact that the banking structure and the monetary medium had changed greatly since the nineteenth century. Not only was there a vastly greater use of bank credit and more economical use of gold, but, in addition, a marked shift from silver and bimetallic standards to the gold standard. Had the role of silver in the period prior to the 1880's been taken more fully into account, the correlations shown would have been less convincing. It is undoubtedly true, however, that monetary gold stocks played a larger role in the period covered in the statistical analyses than they were likely to do thereafter. In this earlier period, with no central banking system, banks, as they acquired more gold, tended to issue more money and extend more credit. Thus, there was a tendency for prices to rise if gold reserves increased. In reverse, when gold flowed out of the country, banks tended to contract credit and currency, and to bring about a lowering of prices.

By the 1930's, gold no longer served as an automatic regulator. Central bank policies, tariffs and import quotas were used to prevent price-depressing exports of gold, and heavy increases in gold reserves tended to be sequestered by central banks in such a way as

---

53. For a brief discussion of the theory involved see Michael A. Heilperin, *International Monetary Economics,* Longmans, Green, London, 1939, pp. 245–57.

54. The views of Warren and Pearson were presented in great detail in their book *Prices,* John Wiley & Sons, New York, 1933, and in numerous speeches and articles. Irving Fisher's interpretation, which implies less reliance on mere manipulation of the gold value of the dollar, is presented most fully in his *Stable Money, A History of the Movement,* Adelphi Company, New York, 1934. His conclusions are summarized briefly on pp. 391–98. Many other groups supported these views, particularly the "Committee for the Nation," and some of the farm organizations. Most economists and bankers, though not opposed to efforts to stabilize or raise the price level, were skeptical of the relatively crude, mechanistic devices advocated by Warren and Pearson and their followers. Pasvolsky in *Current Monetary Issues,* pp. 116–19, points out that no precise relationship exists between the gold value of a currency and the internal price level. Great Britain, Sweden and Japan abandoned the gold standard in September 1931. During the 18 months between that time and the United States devaluation the price of gold in British currency rose to 143 per cent of par, but her wholesale price level stood at 99 (1931 = 100); the price of gold in Sweden had risen to 147 per cent of par, but her wholesale price level stood at 98; and the price of gold in Japan was 233 per cent of par while her price level stood at 119. Part, but by no means

all, of this difference could be accounted for by a rise in the *world value* of gold. It is unmistakably clear, however, that internal price levels cannot be adjusted quickly and easily through mere manipulation of the gold content of the dollar.

For an excellent discussion of events associated with the devaluation of the dollar, see Hodson, *Slump and Recovery,* pp. 212–29. The statistical backing for the Warren and Pearson interpretation is challenged by Rufus S. Tucker in "Gold, Prices and Prosperity: No Statistical Basis For the Commodity Dollar," *The Annalist,* December 1, 1933 and by L. C. Wilcoxen in "World Prices and the Precious Metals," *Journal of the American Statistical Association,* June 1932, pp. 129–40. The theory underlying the Cassel and Warren point of view is analyzed critically in Hans P. Neisser, "The Price Level and the Gold Problem," *American Economic Review,* Proceedings Supplement, February 1941, pp. 1–7. See also in the same issue, C. O. Hardy, "The Price Level and the Gold Problem: Retrospect and Prospect," pp. 18–29.

to limit credit expansion based on them. Many factors other than the amounts of gold in bank reserves were then affecting prices, notable among them being the enormous contraction in the amount of bank credit in use. This had occurred without much reference to the amounts of gold in the country.

Effects of Devaluation on Export Crops

In three of the most careful analyses that have been made of price behavior in this period, the authors conclude that the price effect of the devaluation, with respect to the major export crops — wheat, cotton and tobacco — was small or negligible for wheat and tobacco, but probably more substantial for cotton.

As to wheat, Joseph S. Davis states:

The success achieved was disappointing; price levels did not advance in proportion to the depreciation of currencies in terms of gold. In effect, prices expressed in terms of gold were depressed by these various steps, to an extent that cannot be ascertained but was probably substantial.[55]

Rowe, in a similar study, concludes that the price-raising effect of the devaluation was negligible with respect to tobacco. He comments:

It is easy to over-estimate the importance of this factor on a product subjected to import duties by foreign countries as high as those applied to tobacco. For example, American tobacco shipped to the United Kingdom . . . is subject to a duty of approximately $2.32 per pound. With a market price of 20 cents per pound in the United States, the price abroad would be $2.52 plus transportation charges. Under these circumstances a change in exchange rate equivalent to a 50 per cent reduction in the price in the United States would cause a change of considerably less than 5 per cent in the net cost to the purchaser.[56]

Cotton, on the other hand, apparently was affected more directly by the devaluation.

Richards states, in the Brookings study on cotton:

No attempt has been made to determine quantitatively the effect of dollar devaluation upon cotton prices. A considerable part of the rise in cotton prices since 1932, however, is recognized as being attributable to devaluation of the dollar.[57]

Timoshenko's Analysis

A later and more comprehensive study, with respect to wheat, was made by Timoshenko of the Food Research Institute.[58] He comments:

From 1932–1933 to 1933–1934, American wheat prices in currency, affected by speculation partly induced by depreciation of the United States dollar, rose more than was justified by the changed situation on the domestic wheat market and in spite of further increase of wheat carry-overs outside of the United States. This was the result of the depreciation of the United States dollar. But in 1934–1935 the failure of the domestic wheat crop of 1934 resulted in a still greater reduction of the United States wheat carry-over, since wheat utilization was substantially above the small crop of 1934; and the wheat carry-over abroad also declined substantially. But American wheat prices (in currency) did not increase proportionally. Accordingly, the rise of American wheat prices expressed in the depreciated dollar during 1933–1934 and 1934–1935 was not on the whole larger than might be expected from the decline of the supply in relation to demand, even without monetary manipulation. At the same time, United States wheat prices in terms of gold reacted only slightly to the sharp change in the supply-demand relationship. Depreciation of the United States dollar probably contributed less to the rise of American wheat prices than first impressions suggest and many assume.

With respect to cotton, the implication of Timoshenko's chart would seem to be that prices in terms of gold were depressed as a result of the various currency devaluations, but that prices in terms of the devalued currencies probably were increased somewhat.[59]

55. Joseph S. Davis, *Wheat and the AAA,* The Brookings Institution, Washington, 1935, p. 329.

56. Harold B. Rowe, *Tobacco Under the AAA,* The Brookings Institution, Washington, 1935, p. 213, footnote.

57. Henry I. Richards, *Cotton and the AAA,* The Brookings Institution, Washington, 1936, p. 280. For a different analysis see reference to A. B. Cox's article in the University of Texas *Free News Service,* September 1935, cited on p. 281 of the same source.

58. Timoshenko, "Monetary Influences on Postwar Wheat Prices," p. 286. See also chart on same page.

59. *Ibid.,* p. 266.

If this conclusion is warranted, the largest effect of the devaluation of the dollar was to prevent a further decline in United States prices which might have resulted had we continued the dollar at the old parity with gold, rather than any marked increase in prices in terms of United States currency as a direct result of the devaluation. The changes in world supply, and other factors such as gradually reviving business activity, speculation and the drought of 1934, appear to account for most of the actual increase in prices in terms of devalued United States dollars.

Later, in replying to a critical review of his analysis by Alvin Hansen of Harvard University, Timoshenko summarized his conclusion, possibly more clearly than in the original article, saying: "I recognize the supporting influence of dollar devaluation for a limited period of time, mainly during 1933, and that it is principally with respect to gold prices on the world market [p. 310 of original article] that I find clear evidence of a depressing effect of dollar devaluation." [60]

Other Factors Important

Certain it is that prices of both wheat and cotton, in currency, rose substantially in 1933 and 1934. Majority opinion among economists who have analyzed the relationships appears to be that nearly all of the increase in wheat prices can be accounted for by reduced United States output and changes in world supplies and carry-overs, while for cotton, in which United States supplies dominated the world market, the devaluation of the dollar may have had a more stimulating effect, in terms of prices expressed in United States currency.

Wheat production in the United States fell off from 941 million bushels in the peak year, 1931, to only 552 million in 1933 and to 526 million in 1934. The United States became a substantial importer of wheat in 1934, 1935 and 1936. This change from an export to an import balance together with the

marked reduction in world carry-over would in itself account for a great part of the price rise observed. The farm price of wheat rose from 38.2 cents per bushel in 1932 to 84.8 cents in 1934. Serious droughts plus some influence from the crop reduction program kept production well below 650 million bushels through 1936.

Dollar devaluation apparently had neither the salutary effects confidently predicted by its proponents nor the evil results foreseen by those who opposed it. Probably some cheapening of currencies in terms of gold was desirable, but the close correlation between the gold value of the dollar and the general price level that has often been assumed does not exist in the world of today.[61]

RELIEF POLICIES

During the period here under review American farmers for almost the first time in their history came to have a direct concern with policies involving relief to the unemployed and indigent. Thousands of unemployed workers, with their families, turned to the rural areas in search of employment, or at least of surroundings in which they could exist on smaller cash outlays than in the cities. Other thousands, pauperized by the dust storms of the Southern Plains area, or displaced by the growing use of tractor power, migrated to the Pacific Coast states in search of farm employment.

The areas to which the uprooted people migrated were inundated by hordes of workers with families, who could not be given regular employment even at the desperately low wage rates than prevailing. As a result the relief load in many of the counties of the western states became virtually unbearable. Conditions were tragic both for the destitute migrants and for the communities to which they migrated.

Housing, even of the poorest kinds, was wholly inadequate. Ditch bank communities and shack towns sprang up, and the situation

60. See Alvin Hansen's review of the Timoshenko study, *Journal of Political Economy*, December 1938, pp. 879–84, and Timoshenko's reply in the June 1939 issue of the same journal, pp. 408–13.

61. A good brief account of the monetary policies of this period is given in Lester V. Chandler, *The Economics of Money and Banking*, Harper and Brothers, New York, 1948, Chapter 7.

became a public scandal, stark tragedy for many of the migrants, and a source of grave concern to the rural communities in which they sought refuge. Some California surveys of the period showed numbers of workers seeking farm employment amounting to as much as six times the number of jobs available. Under these conditions workers could find employment only for a few days at a time and at intolerably low wages. Federal relief of some kind was an obvious necessity, but much time elapsed before effective programs for ameliorating the conditions could be devised and put into effect.

During the last years of the Hoover administration the federal government had been forced more and more into the role of supplier of relief funds. Most state and local units of government had virtually exhausted their borrowing power, except for loans made available through action by the Congress. Hoover had continued to resist direct administration of relief by the federal government.

This policy was now to be modified, but the change was, in the main, a further development along lines similar to those of the preceding administration. Not until later was there to be emphasis on the idea of more vigorous enlargement of purchasing power through relatively liberal relief policies. In May 1933, a Federal Emergency Relief Administration was created with a fund of $300 million. Harry L. Hopkins of New York, a professional social worker, was placed in charge.

Contributions were to be made to the states instead of loans, presumably on the basis of one dollar of federal funds to each three dollars of local money. Few states were able to meet even as much as half their relief costs; so the program drifted more and more into federal hands. An additional $950 million was appropriated in February 1934, and subsequently much larger amounts.[62]

62. Hicks, *The American Nation*, p. 667. Relief and public works expenditures during 1934, 1935 and 1936 amounted to $8,681 million. Samuel Eliot Morison and Henry Steele Commager, *Growth of the American Republic*, 3rd edition, Oxford University Press, New York, 1942, Vol. II, p. 615.

Hopkins believed thoroughly in providing work instead of a dole, but work relief was more expensive, more difficult to administer and slower to arrange. Consequently, most states continued to rely heavily on the dole. A Civil Works Administration was set up in October 1933, as a branch of FERA. While sound in principle, it was short on appropriate and well-planned projects, and the quality of administration left much to be desired.[63]

WPA and Public Works

The Relief Act of April 1935 provided much larger appropriations (nearly $5 billion) and established the Works Progress Administration (WPA) designed to provide work for all employables who were unable to get jobs in private industry and trade. Another phase of the government's make-work activities was the Public Works Administration (PWA) administered by Harold L. Ickes.

The PWA was designed to stimulate the heavy industries, and concerned itself principally with the construction of public buildings, highways, army and navy installations and the improvement of rivers and harbors. Employment under PWA was not confined to relief "clients," though the broadening of work opportunities was a major purpose of the organization. This type of program proved too slow for effective use as an emergency measure, but undoubtedly constituted a stimulating and steadying influence in the longer run.

At the same time the RFC was putting billions of dollars into loans to private businesses such as banks, railroads and public utilities on a strictly business basis with expectation of full repayment. Through these various mechanisms some $15 to $20 billion, mostly deficit funds, were channeled into the economy by the federal government between 1933 and 1939. That they performed a major and necessary service cannot be doubted. It is also true that there were grave defects in the administration of many of the projects and in some of the policies adopted. Well-

63. See Hicks, *The American Nation*, p. 668.

considered plans often were lacking. In some projects the effort to integrate part-time and usually less competent WPA workers with regular employees working longer hours for perhaps little more in weekly pay was somewhat demoralizing both to WPA workers and to privately employed people working along with them.

Relief in the Farm Areas

Much criticism arose in farm areas over the preference of workers to remain on WPA when there was work available on farms. This undoubtedly involved some malingering, but was probably caused even more by poor administration, which made it slow and difficult for workers to get back on WPA rolls if they withdrew from them to take private work, and by the very low wages and poor working conditions that prevailed in the agricultural areas. Fully appropriate and workable policies governing the relations between made-work employment and private employment did not emerge even in the later stages of the program.

The various relief programs reached into the agricultural areas in a wholly unprecedented way. Whereas farmers had customarily managed with very little direct relief, hundreds of thousands of them now came to be supported through one or another of the federal relief agencies, despite the efforts to aid them under the more specifically agricultural programs. Farms are particularly well suited for constructive improvement through small projects such as those contemplated under WPA. Much of the input of federal funds in the farm areas was ineffectively used, however. Some development of water supplies, drainage, soil conservation and the like was undertaken, but far less than might profitably and wholesomely have been done.

The lack was principally in plans, policies, qualified supervisory personnel and administrative vigor. The program, though necessary, was somewhat damaging to the self-reliance and moral fiber of some classes of relief recipients. The need was not for an abandonment of relief aid to truly needy families, but for a more carefully developed, realistic and reasonably hardheaded set of policies and administrative arrangements for handling it.[64]

Shifts in Emphasis

The administration was using a variety of methods in its attempt to step up the tempo of economic activity. Some of these re-enforced and strengthened related programs. Others tended to work at cross purposes. Each had its vigorous proponents within the administration, and the internal feuds frequently were intense and sometimes bitter. The influence of various advisers to the President rose and fell with his increasing or decreasing receptiveness to their points of view, and with the successes or failures of the programs advocated by them. The fast-moving developments had many of the characteristics of a military situation with shifting tactics related to a general over-all strategy.

Closely interwoven with tactical efforts to restore prosperity was a far-reaching plan of reform which envisaged improved bargaining power for labor, shorter hours, higher wage rates, social security, more planning and guidance by government and an effort to stabilize the economy by monetary and fiscal measures.[65]

The easy credit policy designed to stimulate business activity was to some extent offset by

64. For an excellent short discussion of the relief program, see Hicks, *The American Nation,* Vol. II, pp. 667–72.

65. It can hardly be said that there was at this time a considered policy of stabilization. All efforts were oriented to raising the level of economic activity and increasing employment, but little attention had been given to balancing measures for controlling inflation, restraining collusion on the part of business organizations or placing limits on the powers of labor organizations and labor leaders. Business consolidation and collusive action were gaining ground at a rapid rate, and labor was gaining powers and privileges not adequately balanced by appropriate safeguards of the public interest.

In general the drift of events might be characterized as a rapid adoption of overdue reforms, without thinking through the requirements for a settled long-term policy. Such inadequacy is understandable and to be expected in a period of hectic activity such as that of Roosevelt's first term. Serious planning with respect to protection of the consumer, to stabilizing agriculture and to placing some limits on the powers of labor organizations was not to come until World War II and after; and these problems have by no means been adequately solved up to the time of this writing.

growing uneasiness in the business community resulting from the various reform measures, particularly those relating to labor, and uncertainty with respect to monetary and tax policies. On the other hand, the price rises engendered by NRA and the greater freedom to participate in joint undertakings tended to strengthen business confidence. The enlarged program of relief spending and the attempt at "pump priming" through heavy expenditures on public works put more money into circulation, but the stimulating effects were to some extent offset by the price rises under NRA, the increased wage rates for employed labor and the failure to induce significant recovery in foreign trade. The devaluation of the dollar and the gold and silver buying programs apparently had little effect one way or the other.

THE AGRICULTURAL ADJUSTMENT PROGRAM

While these steps were being taken in the nonfarm realm, the Agricultural Adjustment Administration was proceeding vigorously in its effort to curtail farm production and raise prices. As stated by Nourse, Davis and Black:

The theory of the Adjustment Act as an emergency matter embraced three points:

1. Relief was to be brought to the farming population by improvement of incomes through price enhancement and through use of "benefit payments" which would put in their hands at once a substantial amount of money so that they might keep their farm properties intact, make necessary outlays for equipment and farm supplies, and finance expenditures for consumption.
2. The benefit payments were to be drawn in the main from special excise taxes on the commodity, on the theory that in this manner consumers and processors would be brought to pay a "fair exchange value" for such part of the product as was currently consumed instead of an abnormally low price which, it was alleged, had been brought about by the piling up of inordinate stocks because of the farmer's inability to check his operations so as to keep in step with the declining effective demand of the market.
3. Such supplementary income was not to be

diverted into the hands of all farmers indiscriminately but was to be a *quid pro quo* to those who agreed to participate in a program of controlled production. This control scheme was designed to produce a supply and demand situation which would bring about a level of prices which would be remunerative to farmers. This goal was defined as "parity," that is, prices which would restore the purchasing power of agricultural commodities to the level which had obtained on the average in a previous period, typically the five years ending July 1914.[66]

The Act of May 12, 1933, gives little or no emphasis to long-range agricultural planning. It was oriented specifically to what was regarded as an emergency situation, and looked mainly to the raising of agricultural prices by curtailing the production of seven so-called "basic" commodities (later increased to fifteen) and regulating quantities and qualities marketed for other commodities not designated as "basic." [67]

However, the very nature of the program compelled early consideration of longer-term plans and objectives. It soon became clear that a continuing horizontal reduction of acreages grown by farmers then in the business could not long be applied practically or equitably in a dynamic industry like agriculture. Neither was it realistic to contemplate holding rented acreage continuously out of production. The need for longer-term plans and more settled policies led to the establishment of a Program Planning Division, in the fall of 1933. While that Division at first gave its main attention to assembling and analyzing statistics relating to the program, it later

66. Edwin G. Nourse, Joseph S. Davis and John D. Black, *Three Years of the Agricultural Adjustment Administration*, The Brookings Institution, Washington, 1937, p. 23.
67. The crops originally listed as "basic" were wheat, cotton, field corn, hogs, rice, tobacco, and milk and its products. The Jones-Connally Act of April 7, 1934 added to these rye, flax, barley, grain sorghums, cattle, and peanuts. Another amendment (May 9, 1934) brought into this classification sugar beets and sugar cane, and the Warren Potato Act, included in the amendments of August 24, 1935, added potatoes to the list.
The administration view, and the background of price conditions to which it was related, are well summarized in "What's New in Agriculture" by Louis H. Bean and Arthur P. Chew, *Yearbook of Agriculture, 1934*, pp. 101-30.

shifted emphasis to longer-term objectives and methods. Out of it grew much of the planning which made possible the quick shift in emphasis that occurred in 1936 after the adverse court decision of that year.

It would be incorrect, however, to conclude that some one AAA policy emerged as a result of this action. Various groups within the organization advocated policies that differed materially, and the views of most members of the staff changed as the program developed. In large measure, the legislative changes made, the modifications in administrative rulings, and the speeches of the Secretary of Agriculture and the administrators of the AAA reflect such of these changes as gained acceptance at policy-making levels.

Methods Used for Basic Crops

For the major crops, the act placed principal emphasis on acreage control. This was to be brought about through contracts, entered into with each cooperating farmer, under which payments would be made to him in return for his agreement to reduce the acreage of the specified commodity grown on his farm. As a means of financing such agreements, Section 9(a) of the act provided that a processing tax would be levied on any (basic) commodity, from the beginning of the next marketing year, if the Secretary of Agriculture determined that rental or benefit payments were to be made with respect to that commodity.

Processing Taxes

The processing tax was to be levied, assessed and collected upon the first domestic processing of the commodity. The amount of the tax was to be the difference between the prevailing average price of the commodity and its "fair exchange value" unless the Secretary should determine, after appropriate hearings, that the levying of a tax of that magnitude would reduce consumption unduly. In that event the tax was to be established at such level as the Secretary found unlikely to result in reduced demand and undue accumulation of stocks of the commodity. The income from processing taxes gave the Secretary of Agriculture large funds with which to carry out the program contemplated.

It will be apparent to the reader that the processing tax was similar in concept to the equalization fee long advocated by farm leaders, but was to be used in a different way. The equalization fee, like the processing tax, would have raised the price to domestic consumers. The difference between the free-market price and that price plus the equalization fee would have gone partly into a higher price to producers and partly into a fund for subsidizing exports. No control on amounts produced was contemplated. Under the processing-tax plan this extra payment by consumers went into a fund used in bringing about reduced production, and in making supplementary payments to growers over and above the price received by them in the market. If the reduction program resulted in raising the free-market price, this would automatically reduce the processing tax and lessen the amount available for crop reduction and benefit payments, and presumably also the amount needed for these purposes.

Acreage Reduction

The method chosen was for the Secretary of Agriculture to offer to rent a portion of the acreage normally used by each farmer in producing the specified crop. The rental payments would be made as quickly as possible, thus providing the farmer with some immediate cash income. A base acreage for each such crop was to be determined for each grower. If he entered into the agreement with the Secretary, he pledged himself not to grow this crop on more than an agreed percentage of his base acreage. In other words, the plan contemplated a horizontal percentage reduction in the acreage of the given crop on all farms, whether they be high or low producers.

Various modifications of this procedure were introduced shortly after the initiation of the program. The most important were those relating to cotton and tobacco. Since the original plan called for voluntary participation, there was apprehension, particularly in the cotton and tobacco areas, that enough growers would refrain from participation in the program to make it ineffective. This dilemma was similar to that often complained of by the supporters of cooperative marketing associations, namely, that the noncooperators benefit from the existence of the organization without accepting their share of the sacrifices that make such benefits possible.

To meet this difficulty the Congress passed, on April 21, 1934, the Bankhead Cotton Control Act and on June 28, a similar act, known as the Kerr-Smith Act, relating to tobacco. The procedure under the Bankhead Act will illustrate the principle applied in both of them. A tax of 50 per cent of the average price was levied on all cotton ginned. However, tax exemption certificates were issued covering the entire production of small growers (up to five acres and up to two bales in 1935). Other growers were given exemption certificates covering the amounts they were permitted to grow under the contractual arrangements with the Secretary of Agriculture. The total of such exemption certificates could not exceed ten million bales. Thus growers who did not choose to "cooperate" were, to all intents and purposes, taxed out of production.

Marketing Agreements

The provisions described above related only to those commodities defined in the act as "basic." There were, of course, numerous other crops, many of them specialties with varying conditions of production and marketing, for which programs could not be instituted under the main provisions of the act. Furthermore, some of those designated as basic crops did not lend themselves to the type of program outlined above.

At a relatively late stage in the drafting of the bill, authorization for a quite different procedure was added (subsections 2, 3 and 4 of Section 8). These sections provided that the Secretary might, after appropriate hearings, enter into marketing agreements with processors, producers, associations of produc-

ers and others relative to the handling in interstate commerce of products covered by such agreements.[68] Subsection 3 gave him authority to license such processors, associations and others as a means of enforcing compliance with the agreements. Such agreements were not to be considered violations of the antitrust laws of the United States.

This plan, chiefly sponsored by George Peek and Charles Brand, was an outgrowth of earlier thinking, particularly that of the proponents of the McNary-Haugen plan. A provision of this type appeared first in the Dickinson bill of January 4, 1926, and was taken over in the third McNary-Haugen bill. That bill (H.R. 11603, 69th Cong., 1st sess.) was defeated on May 21, 1926. The marketing agreement feature was retained in the McNary-Haugen bill reintroduced in the second session of the Sixty-ninth Congress (S. 4808) which was passed by both houses and vetoed by President Coolidge on February 25, 1927.

During this period the emphasis was on agreements with cooperative associations as a means of implementing the McNary-Haugen plan. It was similar in concept to the ideas advanced by Aaron Sapiro in the early 1920's, though his plans did not contemplate government assistance in carrying out what was essentially a monopoly procedure.[69]

The backers of this approach contemplated leaving to the individual farmers the decision as to how much to produce, whereas the handling of the product would be through a coordinated and comprehensive organization of distributive agencies. The marketing agreement idea was in the discard during the Farm Board period, but quickly came back into

68. As first proposed the marketing agreement technique was intended as an alternative or possibly a supplement to production control. Largely through the insistence of the California Farm Bureau, representing many growers of specialty crops, the limitation to basic crops was eliminated. The method came to be thought of as primarily for nonbasic crops. It was eventually adopted, however, in the programs relating to several of the basic crops.

69. An excellent account of the development of the marketing agreement idea, and of experience under this section of the Agricultural Adjustment Act, is given in Edwin G. Nourse, *Marketing Agreements Under the AAA*, The Brookings Institution, Washington, 1935, Chapter 1.

rominence after passage of the Agricultural
djustment Act with the marketing agree-
ent provision included.

hanges in the Law

The licensing feature (Section 8) was added
 the bill at a late stage in its progress
rough the Congress, and was not clearly
efined as to scope and purposes. The efforts
 bring recalcitrant minorities into line by
eans of licenses were not successful, partly
ecause doubts about the enforceability of the
ensing provision led to reluctance on the
art of the Secretary to subject it to court
sts. Following the Supreme Court's adverse
ecision in the Schechter case, which invali-
ated the NRA in the spring of 1935, the
arketing agreement program virtually broke
own. As a result the sections of the act
ertaining to marketing agreements were re-
ritten and expanded in the amendments of
ugust 24, 1935. In this later form, the au-
horization was limited to a small list of
umerated commodities, and the Secretary
f Agriculture was given authority to use
marketing orders" instead of the licensing
owers granted in the original act.[70] The pur-

pose of these amendments was to modify the
legislation in the hope of bringing it into a
form that would be accepted by the courts.

The principal methods contemplated for
benefiting agriculture through use of marketing agreements were:[71]

1. To induce processors and distributors to
agree to pay remunerative prices to growers, and pass these on to the consumers.
This was possible only in situations where
the demand was sufficiently inelastic to permit of moving practically the entire crop
into consumption at the higher price, so
long as processors and handlers did not cut
prices against each other.
2. To dispose of as much of the crop as
possible through regular channels at remunerative prices, and to find other ways
of disposing of surpluses that could not be
marketed at the higher prices, or to induce
growers to retain them on the farms as
livestock feed or wastage. This meant in
some cases discarding the poorer grades.
3. If the situation could not be handled in
these ways, the next step would be to turn
to production adjustment.

Conflicts Over Policy

There were significant differences of opinion within the AAA as to the goals to be
sought in working out marketing agreements.
One faction saw in this procedure merely an
apparently expeditious way of raising the
prices paid to farmers. Another visualized it
as a means of regulating processing and
distributing charges and improving trade
practices. This latter group was further sub-
divided as between numerous workers in the
official agencies, many of whom were not
averse to considerable amounts of government
regulation and planning, presumably in the
interest of the farmer and the consumer, and
the business group which tended to look
upon such agreements as a means of assuring
adequate spreads and avoiding cutthroat competition.[72]

By agreement between Administrators

---

70. For full text of these amendments see *ibid.*, pp.
23–39. There is also an excellent summary of these
roblems and the changes in policy resulting from them
. Nourse, Davis and Black, *Three Years of the Agri-
ltural Adjustment Administration*, Chapter 8, espe-
ally pp. 230–40. The licensing technique presumably
ave the Secretary power to withdraw the right of a
olator to carry on business of the type specified. The
cretary's order procedure provided, instead, specific
nalties for the violation of orders, each day's con-
nuance of the violation being regarded as a separate
fense.
A major question with respect to both licenses and
ders was that of what constituted interstate commerce.
resumably the Secretary did not have authority to con-
ol intrastate business. Yet the two were inextricably
tertwined in many markets. To overcome this the
AA succeeded in getting into the Jones-Connally Act
 April 7, 1934, the wording "in the current of or in
mpetition with, or so as to burden, obstruct, or in
y way affect, interstate or foreign commerce." 48 Stat.
28. The Congress refused, however, to broaden the
ensing powers in a comparable way. Orders could be
sued either in conjunction with or in the absence of
arketing agreements.
On the whole the marketing agreement procedure ap-
eared to work moderately well for tobacco, where it
as backed by production controls, and for walnuts and
alifornia-Arizona citrus where there were strong, well-
tablished cooperatives; also for some localized canning
dustries. The Florida and Texas citrus agreements
oke down.

71. See Nourse, *Marketing Agreements*, p. 37.
72. A whimsical and humorous account of these difficulties is given by James D. Dole in his *Impressions of
Five Months in Washington, August, 1933, to January,
1934*, privately reprinted with permission of the New
York *Herald-Tribune*, April 1934.

Johnson and Peek, the negotiation and administration of codes for the agricultural trades were turned over to the Agricultural Adjustment Administration.[73] However, partly as a result of the conflicts of philosophy in the code section of the AAA, the President, in January 1934, directed that those codes dealing with agricultural products beyond the first processing be transferred back to the NRA (Executive Order No. 6551).[74]

After Chester Davis took over as Administrator at the end of 1933, a new spirit of teamwork developed in the AAA, but it did not result in re-emphasizing the marketing agreement approach. Secretary Wallace had long held the view that production adjustment was basic to the success of the farm program, and that marketing agreements could serve only as a supplement to these more fundamental adjustments in output. Davis had already committed himself to this view and pushed forward vigorously with a main emphasis on the production adjustment phase.

During 1933 the principal commodities brought under marketing agreements were dairy products — fluid milk, evaporated milk and dry skim milk. Following these were California canning peaches and various other fruits, together with vegetables, nuts and rice.[75] During the fall of 1933 and the spring of 1934, seven agreements relating to tobacco were put into effect. All but one had been abandoned by the fall of 1935.[76] Peanuts like-

wise were brought under a marketing agreement in January 1934, but this was chang to a processing tax and production cont plan in October of that year. Agreements p into effect by the fall of 1935 numbered mc than sixty, but the great majority of the had been terminated by that date.

Programs for Major Commodities

The AAA programs affected a great numb of commodities and included many types action. It is impractical to mention here ev in brief form all of the many activities. Mc of them, however, may be grouped under o1 or more of three general categories: (1) me: ures for reducing amounts produced; (measures for controlling amounts markete and maintaining specified prices through son type of cartel arrangement; and (3) measur for putting funds into the hands of farme prior to the marketing season and eventua] in larger amounts than would otherwise o cur.[77]

Wheat, Cotton and Tobacco

In addition to rental payments made wheat growers for acreage taken out of pr duction, compensation for entering into co tracts to reduce acreage, and abiding by ther took the form in the wheat program of su plemental payments of so much per bush on that part of the farmer's output whic represented his proportionate share of t[

73. More than 450 proposals for agricultural codes and agreements were submitted between June 26 and December 6, 1933. (Nourse, *Marketing Agreements,* p. 31.)

74. January 8, 1934.

75. Several of the California specialty crop agreements were revisions or elaborations of plans previously developed under California legislation which authorized prorates on perishable crops. (Nourse, *Marketing Agreements,* p. 127.) Part of the Pacific Northwest wheat surplus was also handled under a marketing agreement. Rice was transferred to a processing tax and production control program in March 1935.

76. For a list of the marketing agreements approved up to the fall of 1935, see *ibid.,* p. 53. Nearly all of the "general crops" agreements involved licensing and, likewise, fifteen of the early fluid milk agreements. From the beginning of 1934 on, the milk agreements were cancelled, and only the licensing procedure was used. The fluid milk industry was already highly organized

through distributor and farmer cooperative agreemen Hence the agreements entered into operated in the ma to formalize and strengthen types of control that we already in existence. A new plan which discontinued t attempt to fix resale prices was put into effect early 1934, but was abandoned in April. A third plan, und new personnel, came into effect in the fall of 1934. Th placed less emphasis on reform, and sought to use mo fully the established bargaining arrangements.

77. For a more detailed and comprehensive summary AAA activities in this period, see Nourse, Davis and Blac *Three Years of the Agricultural Adjustment Administr tion,* especially Chapters 1-8 inclusive. A still more d tailed account is available in the six preceding monograp of the same series, namely, *Wheat and the AAA* by Jose S. Davis, 1935; *Tobacco Under the AAA* by H. B. Row 1935; *Marketing Agreements Under the AAA* by Edwin (Nourse, 1935; *The Dairy Industry and the AAA* John D. Black, 1935; *Livestock Under the AAA* by D. Fitzgerald, 1935; and *Cotton and the AAA* by Henry Richards, 1936, all published by The Brookings Instit tion, Washington.

op domestically consumed. This arrangement was very similar to the domestic allotment plan as first proposed in the late 1920's, though the mechanism was somewhat different. The plan used provided for collecting processing taxes and distributing the proceeds, rather than for the use of allotment certificates alone.

In order to speed the process of adjusting output downward, plow-up campaigns were instituted with respect to cotton and tobacco, and a slaughter program for pigs. Such action was contemplated for wheat in 1934, but as the season developed it became apparent that weather conditions would reduce output even below the levels desired by the Adjustment Administration officials. The plow-up campaign was abandoned, and later, as the most serious drought in United States history developed, even the restrictions on acreage sown were relaxed.

Allotment benefits were eventually fixed at around 30 cents per bushel on 54 per cent of the amounts grown in the base period 1928–1932. Contracts called for an acreage reduction of 15 per cent in 1934 and 1935 (later reduced to 10 per cent for 1935 and 5 per cent for 1936). Other measures relating to wheat included signing of an international wheat agreement in 1933 (this broke down in 1934) and the use of export subsidies, under a marketing agreement, to stimulate wheat exports from the Pacific Northwest. Comparatively small loans to China and the Philippines were also authorized for this purpose.[78]

The cotton program called for much more drastic curtailments in output. The 1933 contracts required participating farmers to plow up from 25 to 50 per cent of the acreages already planted and growing. Cash rentals were paid for the acreages thus abandoned. The 1934 and 1935 contracts called for reductions of 35 to 45 per cent from the base acreages computed for the participating growers.

The Bankhead Act taxed heavily the cotton not grown in accordance with the program, and meant in effect forcing all growers into

it. After 1934, this type of control was to remain in effect only if two thirds or more of the growers voted in favor of such mandatory participation. The necessary two-thirds vote was registered for both the cotton and tobacco programs. A processing tax of 4.2 cents per pound had been levied on cotton manufactured for domestic use (as of August 1, 1933).

Payments to the cotton growers were of several kinds: cash rentals for acreage taken out of cotton production; options on surplus cotton held by the government; "parity payments" supplementary to the prices received in the market (on those amounts the growers were authorized to sell under the program); and "nonrecourse" loans amounting to 10 cents per pound (later 12 cents). Under the nonrecourse loan arrangement, used extensively in cotton and corn, the grower might, if he chose, repay the loan and claim the product. On the other hand, if the price dropped below the loan level, he could have his loan cancelled without liability to himself, and the Commodity Credit Corporation would take over the commodity at the amount of the loan.[79]

The tobacco program was similar in many respects to that for cotton though more complex because of the many different types grown. Processing taxes were imposed as of November 1, 1933. The tax on tobacco grown in excess of the amounts allotted was placed at one third of the value instead of one half as in the case of cotton. Several marketing agreements for various types of tobacco were put into effect in addition to the acreage and production controls.

79. An excellent and detailed summary of the arrangements in regard to cotton is given by Alston H. Garside, "Government Activities in Cotton, No. 2, The Producers' Pool," *New York Cotton Exchange Service, Supplement to Weekly Trade Report No. 468*, New York, January 6, 1936.

Cash rental payments ranged generally from $7 to $20 per acre, the equivalent of 6 to 8 cents per pound for the cotton that might have been grown on the acreage rented by the government. "Parity payments" ranged between 1 and 2 cents per pound on cotton authorized to be grown.

For further explanation of the provisions in regard to cotton loans, see Nourse, Davis and Black, *Three Years of the Agricultural Adjustment Administration*, pp. 95–100.

78. See Nourse, Davis and Black, *Three Years of the Agricultural Adjustment Administration*, pp. 93–95.

The Corn-Hog Program

Since the bulk of the corn harvested does not go to market as corn but rather as pork or beef, it was recognized that at least the corn and hog phase must be treated as a unit. This resulted in two procedures which differed somewhat from those in the other programs, though not in principle. Faced with a disastrously low price for hogs, and with the prospect that the fall marketings would reduce it still further, the administrators of the AAA decided on a drastic move to reduce hog population. They offered to buy up young pigs and pregnant sows at premium prices. Under this program some 6.2 million pigs and 222,000 sows were purchased. From them about 100 million pounds of edible pork were distributed for relief and the balance went into tankage.[80] A further major deviation from the other plans was the granting of 45-cent nonrecourse loans on ear corn stored on the farm.

In the 1934 program, which was the first of those relating to corn, the signers of contracts were required to cut acreage 20 per cent below the 1932–1933 base and were to receive in return 30 cents per bushel on the estimated average yield of the acreage thus taken out of production. Acreage reductions beyond the 20 per cent might be made, but compensation was not to be given for reductions in excess of 30 per cent. The number of litters of pigs was to be reduced 25 per cent below the number produced in the base period, in return for a bonus of $5 per head on the number of hogs the farmer was authorized to produce. Whereas the base allowances for wheat, cotton and tobacco went with the land, the hog base pertained to the farmer and shifted with him if he moved from one farm to another.[81]

80. So far as the general public was concerned, this was undoubtedly the most unpopular action taken by the AAA. While not markedly different in principle from the plowing under of growing cotton and tobacco, it dramatized the process in a way that the other programs had not done. The tortured squeals of these "murdered" pigs were to be heard in the political campaigns for years thereafter and even yet their ghosts occasionally walk.

81. To finance these programs a small processing tax was placed on corn (5 cents per bushel on corn processed for nonfeed uses) and an initial processing tax on

The 1935 contract differed only slightly. I called for a 10 per cent reduction in cor acreage and provided payments of 35 cent per bushel for corn not raised. By the tim this was promulgated the drought of 1934 ha lessened the emphasis on cutting down pro duction. The third set of contracts, coverin, the years 1936 and 1937, was about ready fo signing when the major portions of the ac were invalidated in January 1936.

Dairy Products

The Secretary of Agriculture became cor vinced that planned restriction of milk sup plies would be desirable, but implementatio of such a program proved very complex an difficult. Numerous marketing agreement covering fluid milk were entered into, but b early 1934 these were cancelled and replace by a system of licenses. The attempt to fix r sale prices was abandoned. Major emphasis i the dairy program shifted to "surplus removal purchases of butter and cheese, these supplie being used in relief activities. The dairy outpu was also affected by drought, purchase of catt under the drought-relief program, and som of the disease control programs.

Beef Cattle and Sheep

Cattlemen and sheepmen opposed the pro essing tax on the meat industry, but took som steps looking toward a marketing agreemer with the packers. The oversupply of breedin stock became sufficiently evident by the sprin of 1934 to bring reluctant acquiescence in som type of federal program, though the oppositio to the levying of a processing tax continue strong.

The economic effects of a processing ta applied to beef cattle and sheep would b somewhat different from one applied t wheat and cotton, which were exported i large quantities. The meat industry, excep for the by-product lard, was largely on a do mestic basis. There was reason to believe tha the price elasticity of meat purchases wa such that about the same total amount woul

hogs of 50 cents per hundredweight, which was gradual increased to $2.25 by March 1, 1934.

e spent on meat by consumers regardless of rice. If so, the levying of a processing tax would tend to reduce the market price to growers, and the result would be to return to them, in market prices plus benefit payments, about the same amount as would be received directly in market prices if no government program was undertaken.[82]

A compromise plan took shape in the Jones-Connally Act of April 7, 1934. This included an appropriation of $250 million not raised through processing taxes, and contemplated an extensive program of disease eradication. The drought of 1934 led to the abandonment of the contractual features of this plan, and the government undertook extensive purchases of cattle in the drought-stricken areas. Between July 1934 and January 1935, 8.3 million head were purchased.[83]

Sugar Beets and Sugar Cane

The other major "basic" crop program was that of sugar beets and cane. The United States had long been a heavy importer of sugar, and past policy had been to rely on tariffs as a means of maintaining the domestic industry. However, even the high tariffs of the Hawley-Smoot Act (2.5 cents a pound general, 2.0 cents on Cuban) had not resulted in satisfactory prices. The industry proposed a marketing agreement, but this was rejected by the Secretary of Agriculture. Instead, he proposed a plan of his own. This, according to the President's message of February 8, 1934, was designed to (1) maintain existing acreages of sugar beets and sugar cane in continental United States; (2) increase returns to domestic growers; (3) stabilize production in the insular areas; and (4) check the decline of imports of sugar from Cuba,

that country being an important purchaser of United States farm products.

This plan was incorporated in the Jones-Costigan Act of May 9, 1934.[84] Sugar beets and sugar cane were added to the list of "basic" crops. The Secretary of Agriculture was authorized to make rental and benefit payments for acreage or marketing reductions. Quotas could be established on domestic production and imports, and processing taxes might be levied. These, however, were limited to the amount by which the President might reduce the tariff on sugar. The rate imposed was a half cent per pound.

The Sugar Act included another new feature, namely, a provision that growers, to be eligible for benefit payments, must maintain certain minimum standards in respect to wages paid to field labor, the elimination of child labor and so on. This was the first and only case of tying a labor-protection feature to any of the agricultural aid programs.

The Sugar Act was considered sufficiently distinct from the Agricultural Adjustment Act that the government held that its provisions were not invalidated by the Supreme Court decision of January 6, 1936. The controversy in regard to the matter led eventually, however, to the adoption of Public Resolution No. 109 which eliminated the processing tax and production control features of the Jones-Costigan Act, but retained the marketing quota feature to December 31, 1937.[85]

Other Basic Crops

None of the other "basic" crop programs was of major import. An abortive attempt was made to develop a flax program. One similar to that for wheat was launched for rye, but gained little support from growers. Barley and grain sorghums were not brought under regulation. The rice program took sev-

82. For an analysis of these relationships see Geoffrey Shepherd, "The Incidence of the AAA Processing Tax on Hogs," *Journal of Farm Economics*, May 1935, pp. 21–34.

83. Partly with Jones-Connally funds and partly with special emergency appropriations. In addition to the emergency herd-culling necessitated by the drought, the program constituted a considerable acceleration of the campaigns for elimination of tuberculosis and Bang's disease. Owners were compensated for cattle destroyed in the carrying out of these campaigns.

84. An amendment to the Agricultural Adjustment Act.

85. For a brief but fuller summary see Nourse, Davis and Black, *Three Years of the Agricultural Adjustment Administration*, pp. 106–11.

eral forms. The original attempt was in the form of a marketing agreement, with production control and fixed minimum prices to growers but no processing tax. This agreement was not well carried out in the southern rice areas, and sizable quantities were bought up by the Federal Surplus Relief Corporation to alleviate the strain on millers and growers who had abided by the agreement. The result was a shift to the more usual type of adjustment program for the crop of 1935.

A marketing agreement for peanuts was likewise undertaken in 1934. It was signed by about 80 per cent of the milling interests, and was extended to the others by means of licenses. However, the growers turned to contract milling for the surplus, and undersold the millers, with the result that the millers refused to continue the agreement in 1935. In the Act of April 7, 1934, peanuts had been declared a "basic" crop. The later program, therefore, took substantially the form used for other "basic" crops, but with more emphasis on payments for diversion to lower uses.

The marketing agreement procedure came to be more and more regarded as the mechanism for use on "nonbasic" crops, especially the horticultural specialties. Aside from the uses of this technique already mentioned, it was applied to some twenty-six other crops during 1933 and 1934. After the Supreme Court decision which invalidated the NRA, and under the amendments adopted in August 1935, the tendency was to shift more and more to Secretary's "orders." The 1935 Act, however, curtailed the number of commodities that could be handled in that way. As of December 1, 1936, seven such marketing adjustment programs were in effect. These covered fruits, nuts and vegetables.

Section 32 of the 1935 amendment provided that the Secretary of Agriculture might use up to 30 per cent of the United States customs revenue for diversion and export programs relating to the various agricultural products. This feature of the act came to be used more and more in affording relief for growers not in the major programs.

Was Output Overabundant?

The effectiveness of the AAA program of 1933–1936 must be considered in relation to its objectives. Viewed in the light of present knowledge, the appropriateness of the goals set and the methods used are debatable, and many consider them to have been unwise. As of that time, however, most farmers and most of the people responsible for the program felt that production was overabundant, and that this excess production was a primary cause of the depressed prices then prevailing. At least they accepted the view that the quickest and easiest way to raise agricultural prices and restore farm prosperity was to reduce production of some of the major crops and dispose of the accumulated stocks that were depressing the markets.

Actually the production increase during the 1920's, though somewhat unbalanced, was less significant than it was then assumed to be. At the beginning of the decade the overall volume of production stood at about 9 (1935–39 = 100). By the early 1930's it was around 100, an increase of about 11 per cent.[86]

Meanwhile the population of the United States had grown from 106 million to 123 million, an increase of more than 16 per cent. The fact that United States population had increased more than United States production does not, of course, prove that agricultural production was inadequate to maintain the per capita levels of consumption that prevailed at the beginning of the decade. Exports had accounted for a sizable portion of the agricultural output, especially that of such important products as wheat, cotton, tobacco and pork.

Between 1927 and 1931 the total physical volume of agricultural exports fell off about 35 per cent.[87] The impact of this decline was unevenly distributed among the various crops. Wheat exports were down about 100 million bushels from the high levels attained in 1926–1927. Cotton exports were off some 15 to 20

86. *Agricultural Statistics, 1945,* p. 437.
87. Department of Agriculture, *World Trade Barriers in Relation to American Agriculture,* S.Doc. 70, 73rd Cong., 1st sess., 1933, p. 16.

per cent, and pork exports had declined sharply, resuming a trend that was already apparent in the years before 1914. Fruit exports, on the other hand, showed a strong upward trend, except for the year 1929–1930.

Taken as a whole, these data do not indicate an excess of foodstuffs and fibers in terms of the levels of consumption that prevailed during the 1920's. Per capita consumption of food, in pounds, fell off about 3 per cent between 1929 and 1930, and another 3 per cent between 1930 and 1933.[88] It would appear, therefore, that underconsumption was at least as large a factor in the situation as overproduction.

Overproduction Chiefly in Wheat

Nevertheless, viewing the situation as it appeared to the policy makers in the spring of 1933, there was logic in the contention that wheat production must be cut back sharply. The low volume of exports in 1932, the huge stocks that had accumulated during the Farm Board period, and the expansion of production that had occurred in competing areas, all pointed to a need for readjustment in the wheat areas of the United States.

An attempt to bring this about might take the form of a direct attempt to reduce wheat acreage, or an indirect approach designed to induce shifts from wheat to other lines of production. However, there seemed little chance that land and labor shifted to other crops would have prospect of earning more satisfactory returns than if left in wheat. Furthermore, a positive program for shifting wheat lands to other uses would inevitably require far more preparation and time than could be made available in the current season.

The cotton situation was somewhat different from that of wheat. Cotton exports held up well through 1933, while production was running somewhat below that of the middle 1920's.[89] The heavy increase in stocks was due

mainly to sharply decreased consumption in the United States rather than to increased production or smaller volume of export. Here the effort to curtail production was more clearly an attempt to bring about a balance of farm and nonfarm production at a low level, whereas, in the case of wheat, a readjustment in the volume produced appeared to be indicated regardless of the level of economic activity prevailing in the American economy as a whole.

Tobacco, the other principal export crop placed under acreage control, had experienced a moderate expansion in output and some reduction of exports. Stocks of most types do not appear to have been sharply on the increase. Here the difficulty would seem to have stemmed largely from the generally depressed condition of the whole consuming market, with its accompanying low prices for all types of commodities.

Effectiveness of Production Control

First year sign-ups for acreage reductions in corn covered about 50 per cent of the acreage, those for wheat about 75 per cent. About three fourths of the hog production was included, and a similar portion of the cotton acreage. The tobacco sign-up ranged from 75 to 95 per cent for the various types. The Bankhead Act increased substantially the coverage for the cotton crops of 1934 and 1935.

There seemed to be some tendency for participation to decline after the first season, except in cotton and tobacco.[90] Generally speaking, the programs had less appeal for the small growers than for the large producers. These small operators, using mainly the labor of themselves and their families, could not reduce their costs as they cut back their acreages as the large operators using hired labor could do. Hence it was in their interest

88. Bureau of Agricultural Economics, *The National Food Situation*, July 1944, chart, p. 1.

89. United States cotton exports were seriously affected, however, in 1934–1935 and succeeding years. The domestic policies adopted for the purpose of raising United States cotton prices led to important substitutions of foreign grown cotton for United States grown fiber, beginning in 1934–1935. For a brief but detailed summary of the impact of the AAA program on the United States cotton industry, see John C. de Wilde, "The AAA and Exports of the South," *Foreign Policy Reports*, April 24, 1935, pp. 38–48.

90. Nourse, Davis and Black, *Three Years of the Agricultural Adjustment Administration*, p. 120.

to maintain output, even though prices were low.

The sign-ups in the main producing areas were substantially higher than for the country as a whole. Wheat sign-ups in Kansas, Montana and the Dakotas for 1933 covered about 89 per cent of the base acreages. Compliance was considerably less than perfect, particularly in wheat and corn. Some of the failures to adhere to contract obligations were intentional, others unavoidable. For cotton and tobacco, enforcement of the agreements was much more rigorous. These were commodities that must move to market. Hence controls could be strengthened through checks applied at the ginning and marketing stages. Wheat and corn, on the other hand, could be used on the farm. Compliance was therefore more difficult to supervise.

Production Reduced by Droughts

The severe drought of 1934, affecting especially the wheat and corn areas, led to relaxation of the restrictions on production and made it virtually impossible to estimate with assurance how much change was due to the AAA program and how much was the result of weather conditions.[91] Nourse, Davis and Black, in the most careful study available on this point, conclude that wheat acreage for 1934 was about 4 per cent under that of 1930–1932. This resulted from reductions of more than the required 15 per cent for the farms under contract, accompanied by increases on the farms not under contract. "In the absence of the AAA contraction efforts, the crop of 1934 would probably have been about as large as in 1933 whereas it was actually 25 to 30 million bushels less. . . . Nature was primarily responsible for reducing the crop 337

million bushels below the 1928–1932 average."[92]

These authors conclude further that the net reduction in the 1935 wheat crop, 240 million bushels below the 1928–1932 average, was due almost wholly to adverse weather. "The acreage seeded to winter wheat materially *exceeded* the 1930–1932 average."[93] They conclude that if the AAA program had not been undertaken, the 1935 crop would not have been more than about 20 million bushels larger than it was.

For corn they estimate that "The net reduction due to the AAA in 1934 was about 7.7 million planted acres, or 7.5 per cent."[94] The net reduction in output was about 90 million bushels. The sign-up was almost wholly in the Corn Belt. They place the net reduction of the 1935 crop attributable to the AAA at 200 million bushels. These writers conclude that if weather conditions in 1934 and 1935 had been "normal," production might have been held down to 80 to 85 per cent of what it would otherwise have been, thus effecting a reduction of 300 to 400 million bushels in each of the years 1934 and 1935.

The rice program was aimed primarily at preventing expected increases in acreage, and appears to have been comparatively successful. Acreage was reduced from 927,000 (1928–1932 average) to 816,000 in 1935. Production declined from 43 million bushels to 39 million, and August 1 carry-overs were brought down from 164 million pounds to 42 million. This reduction in carry-over was accomplished in part, however, by relief purchases of 50 million pounds, and by an increase in exports.

In the sugar program, the allotments for the beet areas were generous, being in excess of any amounts previously produced in the United States, except in the peak year 1933.

91. The severity of the droughts and dust storms of this period has probably never been equaled in the United States, at least not since the advent of the white man. The tremendous disturbances to the agriculture of the "Dust Bowl" area are vividly described and illustrated in Lawrence Svobida, *An Empire of Dust,* The Caxton Printers, Caldwell, Idaho, 1940. Whole farms were turned into wasteland, and dust clouds were so dense and so vast that they affected cities as far east as Washington, D.C.

92. Nourse, Davis and Black, *op. cit.,* pp. 125–26.
93. *Ibid.,* p. 126.
94. *Ibid.,* p. 129. (Based on Fitzgerald's study. The authors comment that later revisions in crop estimates indicate that these figures may be too high.)

Since the growers were offered benefit payments in addition, and some assistance in supporting prices through limitations on imports, the program did not operate to restrict production significantly. In fact, the sugar beet acreages of 1934 and 1935 fell substantially below the quotas because of adverse weather. In the cane sugar areas the restrictions were not effective and the area harvested rose by 1935 to 138 per cent of the 1928–1932 average. Thus the major impact of adjusting to the changed market situation fell on the Philippines, Puerto Rico, Hawaii, and such non-United States areas as Cuba.

Net Results of Crop Controls

The attempts to restrain peanut production were unsuccessful. The acreage planted in 1935 exceeded that of the base years. The rye program was cancelled at an early stage. It is estimated that the 1934 hog crop was reduced by about 1.4 billion pounds, or about one eighth, as a result of the pig-sow slaughter campaign and relief purchases. In 1935 it is probable that the shortage of corn, and other factors, was the main cause of the lower volume produced. The outturn of 6.7 billion pounds probably would not have reached 7.5 billion had there been no corn-hog program.[95] Nature in fact overcorrected the situation and the supply turned out to be less than the volume aimed at by the AAA.

The acreage controls for cotton and tobacco were much more effective than those for the crops mentioned above. These programs, especially for 1934 and 1935, went much further in the direction of a compulsory, nationally directed program than did those for the other crops. Under the cotton program the contracting growers pledged themselves to plow up (in 1933) or rent to the government (in 1934 and 1935) the following percentages of their acreage:

1933	35.1 per cent
1934	38.9 per cent
1935	32.7 per cent

95. *Ibid.*, p. 134.

The 1933 program resulted in the destruction of about 25 per cent of a potentially large crop, reducing it between 4.2 and 4.4 million bales. Yields were lower in 1934 and 1935, and both crops fell below the amounts for which Bankhead tax-exemption certificates were issued. Over the three years, production would probably have been 10 to 13 million bales greater had there been no AAA program. The amount of reduction attained was strikingly large. The world carry-over of cotton was reduced from about 11.6 million bales in 1933 to 7 million bales in 1936. This was still, however, some 2 million bales above what was considered a normal carry-over.[96]

For tobacco the great variety of types makes impossible any brief and simple statement of the results achieved. In general the program appears to have resulted in higher prices for the 1933, 1934 and 1935 crops than would otherwise have been obtained, and the acreage control programs probably served mainly to prevent expansions in acreage that would have occurred in response to the higher prices in 1933 and thereafter.[97]

In summary, Nourse, Davis and Black conclude, on the basis of one of the most comprehensive series of concurrent studies of such a program ever carried out, that:

. . . the experience with production control in 1933–35, so far as we can observe it through the dust of the drought is that the effectiveness of these devices is such as to make them practicable in emergency periods. Should crises of similar magnitude reappear in the future and could constitutional barriers be avoided or removed, such efforts could again be used to advantage for a period of two or three years. The experience does not, however, give support to the belief that similar controls could be made practicable as a means of holding the course of production over the years close to a line laid out in accordance with a continuously operating economic plan.[98]

Income Changes Resulting From AAA

It is impossible to arrive at conclusions about the over-all effects of such a program as

96. *Ibid.*, pp. 137–39.
97. For a fuller analysis, see *ibid.*, pp. 139–44. Note also Black's dissenting comments, pp. 486–508.
98. *Ibid.*, p. 150.

that of the Agricultural Adjustment Administration except in the most general terms. Many other forces were at work. If we can judge by the experience in earlier depressions, most of them should, by 1934 and 1935, have been lending strength to a gradual recovery from the depths of the depression. The initial shock had begun to wear off. Many adjustments in prices, inventories and production programs had been made. Large amounts of indebtedness had been liquidated through adjustment, foreclosure or repayment. Both exports and imports had begun to show moderate recovery from the low points reached in 1932 and 1933.

Furthermore, the government itself had initiated actions of many kinds that did not pertain specifically to agriculture. The guarantee of deposits and the revival of confidence in the banking structure had opened the way for a return to normal functioning of the banks. Large budget deficits were being incurred, the proceeds going into relief channels, public works and similar ventures. The NRA gave some stimulus to business by creating an expectation of higher prices and costs. All of these influences had some indirect effects upon agriculture and contributed to the modest increase in gross farm incomes that occurred during these years. The great droughts of 1934 to 1936 pulled down gross physical production of farms by some 5 per cent or more, but may not have operated actually to reduce incomes in view of the large unsold holdings of storable commodities hanging over the market at the beginning of the period.

Cash receipts of farmers reached their low in 1932 at $4.7 billion. They recovered slightly in 1933, to $5.4 billion. There was a further increase in 1934, to $6.8 billion, and a similar improvement in 1935, bringing the cash income up to $7.7 billion. The highest returns of the decade were achieved in 1936 and 1937 — $8.7 billion and $9.2 billion respectively. In the meantime, however, costs had been rising, and farmers' net incomes rose by only about

$3.5 billion between 1932 and 1937. Cash farm income did not reach the 1929 level ($11.3 billion) until 1941.[99] From 1933 through 1936 government payments to farmers amounted to about $1.5 billion. Even if allowance is made for some multiplier effect arising from this transfer of income to agriculture, it does not appear likely that this influence on national income was important.

National income reached its low in 1933 at $39.6 billion. It recovered to $48.6 billion in 1934, reached $56.8 billion in 1935, and stood at $64.7 billion in 1936. The recovery continued into 1937, which showed an income of $73.6 billion. The recession of 1937 brought the 1938 figure down again to less than $67 billion. From that time on, through 1940 improvement was continuous though not large. The 1940 income stood at $81.3 billion some $6 billion less than that of 1929.[100]

Farm prices had reached their lowest point in 1932 at an index of 65 (1909-1914 = 100).[101] They improved slightly, to 70, in 1933 and sharply thereafter, reaching an index of 90 in 1934, 109 in 1935, 114 in 1936, and 122 in 1937. For 1938 and 1939 they fell back to around 95 and did not again reach 100 until 1940.

The price increases of 1933 to 1936 appear to have been mainly the result of short crops during the drought years and the reduction of inventories that accompanied them. Recovery in the nonfarm sector of the economy and heavy expenditures for relief were also giving some support. The benefit and rental payments were undoubtedly aiding many farmers to weather the storm but did not constitute a large element in total income. Such payments, by years, are as follows:[102]

99. *Statistical Abstract, 1949*, pp. 640, 641. (If government payments are included, net incomes increased by $3.86 billion.)

100. *Ibid.*, p. 281.

101. *Agricultural Statistics, 1950*, p. 628.

102. *Statistical Abstract, 1941*, p. 641. These figures are only for direct payments to farmers. Substantial amounts of government money were also being channeled into agriculture indirectly through price-support loans, purchase of farm credit bonds, interest subsidies and so on.

Year	Benefit and Rental Payments to Farmers
1933	$131,000,000
1934	446,000,000
1935	573,000,000
1936	287,000,000
1937	367,000,000
1938	482,000,000
1939	807,000,000
1940	766,000,000

ndirect Effects of the Program

The record does not indicate any significant ffect from the farm program in serving as a timulus to recovery in the economy as a vhole. For the most part the additional direct ayments to farmers constituted comparable eductions in the spendable incomes of con-umers since the funds were raised by means f processing taxes which, in the main, were assed on to the ultimate consumer. Money upplied in the form of loans was more gen-rally created through deficit financing, and hus constituted new buying power. Much of t merely enabled farmers to pay off or re-

finance debts. That operation did, however, tend to thaw out frozen investments, and no doubt helped some in easing the over-all financial and investment situation. Broadly speaking, the farm and nonfarm segments of the economy seem to have advanced concur-rently, with the nonfarm segment leading the way. There is, in fact, some indication that if the droughts of this period had not curtailed farm production and facilitated liq-uidation of the accumulated stocks of farm products, agriculture might have lagged be-hind much as it did in the 1920's.[103]

103. For a carefully reasoned analysis of the probable effect of the AAA program on general recovery see Nourse, Davis and Black, *Three Years of the Agricul-tural Adjustment Administration*, pp. 420–48. Their conclusions are cautious and carefully worded, but may be summarized briefly in the concluding sentence of that chapter: "The experience discredited those who believed that agricultural relief could bring about complete gen-eral recovery but supported those who maintained that it was an important positive element in a co-ordinated re-covery program. . . ." (p. 448.) They stress its im-portance as a reviver of confidence and a means of shifting funds into hands where their rate of turnover would be increased. With this view the writer finds no reason for disagreement, but is inclined to give more weight to the agricultural credit program, the bank pro-gram and the natural forces of recovery than do the authors quoted above.

CHAPTER 13

THE LONGER-TERM PROGRAM

THE PROGRAMS FOR agricultural credit and agricultural adjustment, though of most immediate concern, did not comprise the whole of the plan for the improvement of agriculture. Most notable of the programs associated with them was the large-scale undertaking to conserve natural resources. This had many ramifications, but the chief emphasis was on the conservation and rebuilding of soils and on the rehabilitation of the range lands of the West. Forest conservation, hydroelectric power development, protection of wildlife and various other aspects of conservation were also included. Several new agencies were established, the principal ones being the Soil Erosion Service, the Division of Grazing and the Tennessee Valley Authority.

Efforts were also made to deal with the submarginal land problem, and to stabilize and resettle farm families that lacked adequate resources for making a living, or were unable to achieve stable relationships to any particular community. These activities centered chiefly in the Resettlement Administration (later changed to Farm Security Administration), in the Subsistence Homesteads program and others of similar character.

SOIL EROSION

Soil depletion was apparent in parts of the United States from colonial times onward, but so long as rich new lands were available farther west, this did not occasion serious public concern. The wasteful depletion of forest resources was much more dramatic, and also gave rise to objections on sentimental and aesthetic grounds. Furthermore, the heavy drain on high-quality, readily accessible sources of saw timber was resulting in rapid increases in the price of lumber. The problem of timber conservation thus came early into

the consciousness of farm groups and nature lovers, and was effectively dramatized by such men as Gifford Pinchot and Theodore Roosevelt. As a result, significant beginning in forest conservation were made during the first decade of the twentieth century.

The loss of soil resources was much more subtle, and only a few farsighted conservationists were deeply concerned about it until well into the present century. Charles R. Van Hise, a geologist of high standing and President of the University of Wisconsin gave impetus to the conservation movement through his widely read book *The Conservation of Natural Resources in the United States,* published in 1910.[1]

Woodrow Wilson was aware of the problem, and it is clear from his messages that he contemplated vigorous steps looking to the preservation of soil resources. But other and more pressing reforms absorbed his attention during his first term in office, and thereafter the outbreak of war led to the pigeonholing of this phase of his program.

Interest Lags in the 1920's

With the advent of the Harding regime official attitudes in regard to conservation changed from those of the Theodore Roosevelt and Woodrow Wilson periods. Rapid exploitation of natural resources was looked upon with favor, and complacency in the matter was so pronounced that a Cabinet member was convicted of accepting a bribe in connection with oil concessions. The pol-

1. Macmillan, New York. A later version by Loomis, Havemeyer and others, based on Van Hise's book, has since been brought out under the title *Conservation of Our Natural Resources,* Macmillan, New York, 1930. Van Hise's interest centered largely in mineral and water-power resources rather than in soils, but he was influential in stimulating interest in nearly all phases of conservation.

cies with respect to water-power, mineral and timber resources were likewise by no means satisfying to those who regarded these as great national heritages which should be conserved and developed constructively.

The low prices of most farm products in the 1920's, interpreted as a sign of overproduction, were not conducive to widespread concern over the loss of soil resources. Nevertheless, those who were acutely conscious of the heavy damage that was becoming so evident in many areas began to make their influence felt as early as the late 1920's. In 1929 the Congress appropriated $160,000 for soil erosion investigations. In the same year regional soil erosion experiment stations were set up under the direction of the Bureau of Chemistry and Soils and in cooperation with the Bureau of Agricultural Engineering and the Forest Service. The Agricultural Appropriations Act of February 1931 added $330,000 for enlarging these activities. Knowledge about the processes of erosion, the seriousness of the problem and methods of control expanded rapidly thereafter.

Growing Concern Over Soil Losses

Hugh H. Bennett of the Bureau of Chemistry and Soils was assigned to soil erosion studies in 1928. His investigations convinced him that erosion was a far more serious menace to the future welfare of the nation than was commonly recognized. He became a vigorous and effective propagandist for a nation-wide campaign to conserve and build up soil resources. Bennett soon gained a considerable following, and became the spearhead of the soil conservation movement. Though possibly overdramatized, there can be no doubt that these efforts resulted in a new and general appreciation of a major national problem.[2] The disastrous droughts and dust storms that came so shortly after the initiation of the movement served to place the

conservation of soils high on the list of major objectives in national agricultural policy.

Among the more effective publications of the period was a small book put out jointly by the Soil Conservation Service, the Resettlement Administration and the Rural Electrification Administration, in 1935 — *Little Waters* by H. S. Person with the cooperation of E. Johnson Coil and Robert T. Beall. In this the magnitude of the problem is dramatically summarized as follows (p. 2):

The soil-erosion specialists tell us that the dust storm of May 11, 1934, swept 300 million tons of fertile topsoil off the great wheat plains; that 400 million tons of soil material are washed annually into the Gulf of Mexico by the Mississippi River; that generally water and wind erosion together each year remove beyond use 3 billion tons of soil.

They find that 100 million once-fertile acres of farm land—equal to Illinois, Ohio, Maryland, and North Carolina combined—have been essentially destroyed for profitable farming; that another 125 million acres are seriously impaired; and that another 100 million acres are threatened—all belonging to the best farm lands of the United States.

And further; that the present annual money loss to land owners and to the Nation is not less than 400 million dollars each year; that the annual rate has been increasing; that the cumulative loss may be conservatively stated as already not less than 10 billion dollars; and that, if the wastage is not stopped, in another 50 years the cumulative loss will reach the staggering figure of 25 or 30 billion dollars, equivalent to a loss of $4,000 on each and every farm in the United States.

This is not a loss of income the flow of which can be resumed, but of assets that cannot be recovered, for it takes Nature centuries to make the equivalent of the top soil which has been swept away—at the rate in some places of 3 to 6 inches in a single season.

Franklin Roosevelt shared many of the enthusiasms of his cousin Theodore, among them an active interest in conservation.[3] The

---

2. The widespread interest in the movement has given rise to numerous popular presentations of very dubious merit. Despite the spate of light and irresponsible books on the subject much genuine progress was made over the succeeding years, through education, demonstration and the development of new and better techniques.

3. While Governor of New York, Roosevelt had given strong support to the New York program of reforestation and conservation. See, for example, in *The Public Papers and Addresses of Franklin D. Roosevelt, 1928–1932*, Random House, New York, 1938, the "Radio Address on the Conservation of Natural Resources as a Function of Government" and the one urging support of the reforestation amendment to the New York State constitution, March 31, 1930 and October 26, 1931, pp. 521–31. As of this

success and popularity of his Civilian Conservation Corps program stimulated his enthusiasm for conservation activities as a way of using unemployed man power and expanding investment in fields that would not result in quick increases in commercial output. As a consequence, the movement for conserving the nation's soil resources had active presidential support throughout his administration.

Creation of the Soil Erosion Service

In the National Industrial Recovery Act of June 16, 1933, two sections (202 and 203) were included with a view to stepping up the erosion control program as a means of increasing employment. On August 25 an allotment of funds for that purpose was made to the Department of the Interior. To administer these funds, the Soil Erosion Service was established, as a temporary agency of the Interior Department with bureau status.

A major purpose of the greatly enlarged funds thus made available was to provide employment. The program took the form of demonstration projects, mainly on public lands, the work being done by Civilian Conservation Corps personnel. During the eighteen months in which the work was under the direction of the Department of the Interior, forty-one demonstration projects were established and fifty CCC camps were operated under the direction of the Soil Erosion Service. Hundreds of thousands of small check dams were constructed, vegetation was planted on eroding hillsides, firebreaks were opened up and roads were developed.

Thirty-seven of the demonstration projects involved private lands and varied in size from 25,000 to 200,000 acres each. They were supposedly representative of some 75 million acres of surrounding territory. The other projects were mainly on federally owned land in the Southwest, and included areas totaling approximately 35 million acres. In these, particular attention was given to the prevention of silting in reservoirs such as the one at Hoover Dam. As of March 1935, 11,000 CCC workers were employed on these demonstration and land-use projects, and 5,000 other laborers, recruited in so far as possible from relief rolls.

Transfer to Department of Agriculture

Under an Administrative Order signed by the President on March 25, 1935, the soil erosion work was transferred to the Department of Agriculture. As a result of this order the various soil erosion activities of that Department were combined with the Soil Erosion Service to form a new bureau called the Soil Conservation Service which was given legislative status by an act approved on April 27 1935 (49 Stat. 163). The growing popularity of the soil conservation program and the active concern over this problem that resulted from the dust storms of 1934 are evidenced by the fact that the bill passed both Houses without a dissenting vote. In the summer of 1935 150 CCC camps were transferred from the Forest Service and 300 additional ones were assigned to the Soil Conservation Service in order to broaden and speed up the demonstration work.

During the fiscal year 1935, CCC workers had constructed 294,000 check dams for gully control, seeded 82 million square yards of gully bank, completed 2.9 million linear feet of diversion ditches and dikes, and sloped 58 million yards of gully bank. They had also constructed 27,000 temporary and permanent terrace outlet structures and 719,000 linear

---

time his interest seems to have been mainly in forest lands, and was in the Theodore Roosevelt tradition. After the election of 1932, and during his first years as President, he apparently became keenly interested in a much wider range of conservation problems.

The President's interest in this group of problems was shown in various other ways. In June 1934 he set up the National Resources Board and Advisory Committee to prepare and present to him a program for the use of land, water and other natural resources. The Committee was abolished, by executive order, on June 7, 1935. Its duties were transferred to a National Resources Committee which was established by the same executive order. This Committee, under a reorganization plan of July 1, 1939, became the National Resources Planning Board. There was congressional criticism of the activities of these planning committees and the Board almost from the time they were first set up. This resulted finally in an act of Congress, June 26, 1943, which abolished the Board.

In addition to these evidences of his interest, the President gave strong support to the Forest Service, the Tennessee Valley Authority and other agencies primarily oriented to conservation.

feet of outlet channels, and had planted 10,000 acres with trees.[4]

During the period June-September 1935 the organization was decentralized. The field organization, previously operated on a project basis, was placed under the direction of eleven regional conservators, each responsible for a region having somewhat similar characteristics in respect to soil conservation problems.

The passage of the Soil Conservation and Domestic Allotment Act in February 1936 made soil conservation a major function of the Agricultural Adjustment Administration. This meant that two agencies in the Department of Agriculture were engaged in extensive soil conservation activity. Their methods differed markedly, and there was not always harmony between them. From 1937 onward the Soil Conservation Service began a program of cooperation with soil conservation districts organized by farmers under state laws. These activities are described more fully in Chapter 15.

The Taylor Grazing Act

The semiarid grazing lands of the West had long been a sore spot in the national land program. Theoretically they were open for homesteading in the same way as the large areas of public domain that had been settled under the Homestead Act in the Middle West and the eastern Great Plains area. It was apparent, however, that much of the semiarid region was not suitable for crop production and small farm units. Some halfhearted attempts were made to modify the homestead laws in ways that would make settlement of these areas more feasible.[5] These were, in the main, unsuccessful and in fact were flagrantly abused by large ranchers. Dummy filings were made, watering areas were monopolized, and in some cases large areas of grazing land were blocked off by illegal filings on lands surrounding them.

The effort to settle the more remote grazing lands under the homestead procedure declined sharply after the upsurge in number of entries which occurred between 1913 and about 1925. Settlement in the eastern borders of the grazing region continued well into the present century, but with indifferent success. In periods of more than normal rainfall, settlers moved in in large numbers, but many gave up in despair, or were forced out, during periods when rainfall was light. Tax-delinquent and abandoned farms were numerous in such areas as western South Dakota, Nebraska and Kansas and in Montana. The introduction of tractors and combine-harvesters in the 1920's did, however, make grain farming feasible over much of this area in most years. Nevertheless, successful crop farming under those conditions required larger farm units than were contemplated under the homestead acts.

Farther west, in the intermountain area, even these extensive types of crop farming were impractical. The watering places and some few small, easily irrigated tracts were brought under private ownership at an early date, but huge areas remained in the public domain, and were used without charge or management by ranchers who owned or controlled the adjoining watering places. This situation resulted in rapid deterioration of the grazing areas, and violent conflicts among users of the public domain lands. Since no one, except the government, had legal title to such lands, they tended to be grazed by those who could get onto them first, or were kept available to given users by physical force. Few of the users could depend on getting the feed in succeeding years. Consequently there was little attempt to conserve or build up the productivity of the land. Overgrazing was so general that desirable grasses and shrubs were being rapidly eliminated, erosion was increasing and huge areas were drifting more and more into desert.

This problem had long been under study, and numerous bills looking to its solution had been introduced. These led finally to the Taylor bill which became law on June 28,

4. Soil Conservation Service, *Report of the Chief, 1935*, p. 18. (Figures rounded.)

5. For example, the Timber Culture Act of 1873, the Desert Land Law of 1877, and the modifications of these in the legislation of 1890 and 1891.

1934.[6] It was a long overdue recognition of the fact that the grazing regions required special types of legislation rather than minor modifications of the homestead laws, which were designed for the humid areas of the East. Large tracts of forest land had been brought under orderly public management much earlier, and the grazing land policy was a logical supplementary step. Much of the technique for public management of grazing areas had, in fact, already been developed in the Forest Service in connection with grazing lands embraced in the national forests.

The new Division of Grazing was, however, established in the Department of the Interior rather than in the Department of Agriculture. This was due in part to the fact that these lands were already under the jurisdiction of the Department of the Interior, and in part to the fact that many livestock men were critical of Forest Service policies in respect to grazing in the national forests. They felt that the Forest Service favored extreme protection to timber, wildlife and watersheds, at the expense of grazing privileges. They also resented what they regarded as unduly low limits on the numbers of livestock permitted to graze in the national forests, and wanted lower fees than were charged by the Forest Service.

Purposes of the Act

The stated purposes of the Taylor Act were:

1. To stop injury to the public grazing lands by preventing overgrazing and soil deterioration;
2. To provide for their orderly use, improvement, and development; and
3. To stabilize the livestock industry dependent upon the public range.

The procedure specified for accomplishing these purposes was to form grazing districts, in which the rights to use the range, on the part of adjoining settlers and stock owners, were defined and limited. Preference was given to landowners in or near the district who were engaged in the livestock business.

6. 48 Stat. 1269.

Permits were issued for agreed numbers of livestock and for specified seasons. These permits were renewable and thus tended to insure to the holder of the permit the right to maintain a specified number of animals, except as weather variations and changes in the condition of the range made modifications necessary.

Twenty-five per cent of the grazing fees received could, with congressional approval, be used for improvement of the range, and 50 per cent was assigned for state and local government functions. The Secretary was authorized to trade unappropriated public lands outside the districts for private lands lying within the district boundaries. This provided opportunity for blocking up both public and private lands in units suitable for effective management. It had particular significance as a possible way of revising the uneconomic checkerboarding of alternate sections which resulted from grants of land to the transcontinental railroads.

Lands Affected

At the time the act was put into effect the public domain, outside the national forests, and excluding Alaska, amounted to about 166 million acres as compared to about 140 million acres in national forests.[7] The original act authorized the inclusion of not more than 80 million acres in grazing districts. Land set aside for national forests, national parks, Indian reservations and other public uses was specifically exempted from inclusion in grazing districts, except as transfers were made by the administrators of these agencies.

The Taylor Grazing Act is the most significant action with respect to lands of this class that has been taken since the public domain was established. It marks a notable change in policy, though one similar in concept to the

7. These figures do not include some minor acreages in Alabama, Florida, Kansas and other states east of the major grazing region. As of June 30, 1934, approximately 120 million acres of the public domain reserves had been surveyed, and about 46 million acres were unsurveyed. The authorization for organizing public domain lands into grazing districts was later increased by 62 million acres making a total of 142 million. *Annual Report of the Secretary of the Interior, for the Fiscal Year Ending June 30, 1937*, pp. 87 and 103.

policy governing publicly owned forest lands which had been in effect since the beginning of the century.

The Tennessee Valley Authority

The Muscle Shoals project on the Tennessee River had been a bone of contention since the early part of the century, and especially after 1920.[8] During World War I, the government constructed dams and made large investments there with a view to manufacturing synthetic nitrates for use in making explosives. These facilities, only partly completed when the war ended, were a matter of great interest to farmers of the southeastern states as a possible source of cheap nitrate fertilizer. The farm groups persistently advocated development of this resource for that purpose, but without major concern as to whether it be developed under private or public auspices.[9] There was in the Congress, however, a strong faction, headed by Senator George Norris of Nebraska, that stood firmly for public construction and operation of this and other hydroelectric power projects. As it became increasingly evident that a satisfactory arrangement with private corporations was not in prospect, congressional sentiment shifted more and more toward the Norris point of view.

Norris became dubious of the feasibility of producing cheap fertilizer, and advocated instead using the Wilson Dam for the production of power, with provision for the nitrate plants to be turned over to the Secretary of Agriculture for operation on an experimental basis. This became a Senate alternative to the House-supported Ford plan. Both were lost in the 1924 session.

A commission appointed by President Coolidge in 1925 turned back to the idea of fertilizer production, and recommended, though not unanimously, that the properties be leased to a private operator. A joint committee, assigned the task of securing a lessee, was unable to make satisfactory arrangements, and finally recommended setting up a government corporation to experiment in the production of fertilizer, and to manufacture fixed nitrogen and sell surplus power.

A bill based on this report, and on some of Senator Norris' ideas, was passed in May 1928, but Coolidge pocket-vetoed it. A later bill, which provided for leasing the nitrate plants, but for government ownership and operation of the power facilities, was vetoed by President Hoover on March 3, 1931. He countered with a proposal that a commission representing Alabama and Tennessee, the farm organizations and the Army Engineers be set up with authority to lease the plants. Enabling legislation looking to this end passed the House in 1932 but got no further. Thus the matter stood when President Roosevelt took office.

Concept Broadened

Roosevelt had shown marked interest in the water-power problem while Governor of New York, and in January 1933 he visited the Muscle Shoals area with Senator Norris. Here he apparently began to crystallize the idea of something much more far-reaching than mere power development and fertilizer production. In a speech at Montgomery, he stated:

There we have an opportunity of setting an example of planning, not just for ourselves but for the generations to come, tying in industry and agriculture and forestry and flood prevention, tying them all into a unified whole over a distance of a thousand miles so that we can afford better opportunities and better places for living for millions of yet unborn in the days to come.[10]

8. C. Herman Pritchett, *The Tennessee Valley Authority, A Study in Public Administration,* University of North Carolina Press, Chapel Hill, 1943, Chapter 1.

9. For a time the American Farm Bureau Federation was friendly to a proposal made by Henry Ford, in 1921, that he take over the installations and develop them as a private enterprise. On the whole, however, farmer sentiment leaned toward public ownership and operation rather than private. Opposition to the granting of major water-power resources to private companies had become widespread during the administration of Theodore Roosevelt, and still was a part of the Progressive Republican heritage. Senator Norris, a member of the old Progressive Republican group, had given the matter much study. He became a vigorous and effective champion of public power development.

10. The idea of a unified development of whole river systems was not new. The Inland Waterways Commis-

Roosevelt had also, in his Portland speech of September 21, 1932, touched upon the idea of using public power projects as a yardstick for appraising the justice of private company charges for power. However, the early studies by the Army Engineers had not emphasized power production. They were concerned rather with the improvement of navigation. Their plans contemplated a series of low-level dams rather than the high-level dams needed for power production and flood control. The multiple objectives of fertilizer manufacture, production of cheap power, flood control and more general area improvement crept into thinking on the subject only gradually.

Corporate Form Proposed

The President pulled these ideas together and broadened their scope in his brief message of April 10, 1933, wherein he recommended creation of a Tennessee Valley Authority—"a corporation clothed with the power of Government but possessed of the flexibility and initiative of a private enterprise." He outlined his conception of the scope of the undertaking as follows:

. . . the Muscle Shoals development is but a small part of the potential public usefulness of the entire Tennessee River. Such use, if envi-

sioned in its entirety, transcends mere power development; it enters the wide fields of flood control, soil erosion, afforestation, elimination from agricultural use of marginal lands, and distribution and diversification of industry. In short, this power development of war days leads logically to national planning for a complete river watershed involving many States and the future lives and welfare of millions. It touches and gives life to all forms of human concerns.[11]

The idea of setting up a government corporation for functions of this kind was not new. It had been used extensively during World War I to establish such agencies as the U.S. Grain Corporation, the Emergency Fleet Corporation and the U.S. Housing Corporation. In addition, there were such longer-term organizations as the Panama Railroad and the War Finance Corporation. Never before, however, had any government corporation been given such broad and vague functions as those proposed for the TVA.[12]

TVA as a New Type of Agency

The corporate structure had much to recommend it, assuming that activities similar to those of private business were to be carried on. Under this type of organization, the government provides funds in the form of capital stock rather than annual appropriations. This gives much more flexibility, and a chance to use business methods rather than the cumbersome process of hearings on appropriations, payment of expenses out of the federal

---

sion, appointed by President Theodore Roosevelt, advocated comprehensive multipurpose river development in its report, submitted in 1908. Roosevelt in transmitting the report to Congress said, "The report rests throughout on the fundamental conception that every waterway should be made to serve the people as largely and in as many ways as possible. It is poor business to develop a river for navigation in such a way as to prevent its use for power, when by a little foresight it could be made to serve both purposes. We cannot afford needlessly to sacrifice power to irrigation, or irrigation to domestic water supply, when by taking thought we could have all three. Every stream should be used to the utmost. No stream can be so used unless such use is planned for in advance. When such plans are made we shall find that, instead of interfering, one use can often be made to assist another. Each river system, from its headwaters in the forest to its mouth on the coast, is a single unit and should be treated as such." S.Doc. 325, 60th Cong., 1st sess., p. iv.

Similar views were expressed by Senator Francis G. Newlands of Nevada in a speech in the Senate in 1916.

During the Hoover administration the Army Engineers began investigations looking to multipurpose development of the Columbia River basin (under acts passed in 1923 and 1927 which led to the so-called "308" reports). For a fuller account see Charles McKinley, *Uncle Sam in the Pacific Northwest,* University of California Press, Berkeley, 1952, pp. 65–68.

11. Roosevelt, *Public Papers and Addresses, 1933,* p. 122.

12. The many phases of the TVA program cannot be described or even mentioned in the brief space available here. An excellent account, particularly of the administrative set-up, is available in Pritchett, *The Tennessee Valley Authority.* A good descriptive treatment is to be found in Herman Finer, *The TVA, Lessons for International Application,* International Labor Office, Montreal, 1944. Another thoughtful analysis is that of Clarence Lewis Hodge, *The Tennessee Valley Authority: A National Experiment in Regionalism,* American University Press, Washington, 1938. Less judicial and more popular treatments are numerous. Among them may be mentioned David E. Lilienthal's *TVA, Democracy on the March,* Harper and Brothers, New York, 1944 and Tennessee Valley Authority, *Progress in the Valley, TVA–1947,* Government Printing Office, Washington, 1947. An enthusiastic account of TVA accomplishments is given in Julian Huxley, *TVA, Adventure in Planning,* The Architectural Press, London, 1943. The act establishing the TVA is to be found in 48 Stat. 58 (signed May 18, 1933).

Treasury and payment into the Treasury of all moneys received. Such companies can borrow in their own right, and corporate forms of accounting can be used. Some of the safeguarding laws and regulations which slow up and hamper expenditures from ordinary government appropriations are also avoided. In addition, the pattern of overhead management lends itself better to vigorous executive action than does that of a regular branch of the executive arm of government. Also, such a corporation tends to limit or avoid the governmental immunities from suits for damages, liability for taxes and so on.[13]

For business types of activity the government corporation has undoubted usefulness. Its merits, however, depend very heavily upon the ability, integrity and nonpartisan character of the directors appointed. While such a form of organization makes possible greater efficiency than direct administration by a regular government agency, it also leaves the way open for inefficient and improper use of large financial resources supplied by the government. Such agencies, if long continued, can easily become seriously demoralized through their use as dumping grounds for political hangers-on, since usually their personnel is not under Civil Service. Defects of this kind are more likely to show up after the agency has become well established and accepted rather than in the early years when it is on trial.

Other serious problems arise through the fact that suitable techniques have not yet been developed for congressional and government accounting office supervision of such corporations. The accounting procedures of government agencies are notoriously unfrank in providing true and clear records of the costs of various functions. This is especially true where there is a mixture of business-type and general welfare functions. These problems appeared to an unusual degree in the TVA and are in part responsible for the heated controversies that have centered around it. Part of

its function is the production and sale of power, but other functions are the facilitation of navigation, the control of floods and the provision of recreation areas. When multipurpose dams are constructed for these purposes, the allocation of costs to each function must inevitably be arbitrary. Serious question is therefore raised as to the appropriateness of using cost figures on power produced by such an agency as a "yardstick" for judging the reasonableness of charges made by private power-producing agencies.

For example, if a dam costs $50 million, and $20 million is charged off as a public expense for improving navigation, while another $15 million is charged to flood control, it is scarcely contendable that the assignment of the remaining $15 million to the costs of producing power provides an appropriate comparison with private costs of power production. This is not to say that such multiple uses are undesirable. In fact, they are desirable and logical, but as yet we have an inadequate body of reasonably objective principles to govern accounting procedures in ventures of this kind.[14]

Space does not permit any complete analysis of so far-reaching a change in governmental procedures and policy as is embraced in the TVA idea. The experiment has attracted world-wide interest, and undoubtedly the pattern established has much significance in connection with regional developments of the future. Already much interest has been expressed in initiating similar procedures for dealing with the Missouri River Valley, the Columbia River area, the Central Valley of California and others. It is clear that any comprehensive, coordinated development of a region, especially one which contemplates the control of a watershed, must be a planned undertaking.

13. For a fuller discussion of this see Pritchett, *The Tennessee Valley Authority*, pp. 22–27.

14. A critical view of TVA policies is given in Commonwealth and Southern Corporation, *Analysis of the Annual Report of the Tennessee Valley Authority*, New York, February 15, 1937. For an excellent analysis of many of the problems relating to the TVA experiment see Hodge, *The Tennessee Valley Authority: A National Experiment in Regionalism*, especially Chapter 8.

Problems to Be Solved

The TVA is the most concrete, autonomous and centralized American venture of that kind up to this time. Its accomplishments have been noteworthy, and it is likely that similar ventures will be undertaken elsewhere. This initial project has had unusually able, high-minded and imaginative leadership. Questions in the minds of thoughtful people sincerely interested in this type of development are: can and will similarly able leadership be provided for other projects; will political misuse and corruption be adequately controlled; and will the subsequent executives in charge of these large-scale business ventures operate with the vigor, imagination and venturesomeness that characterize many private businesses?

There is a tendency for government officials to "play safe"; that is, to choose the less controversial and less aggressive action since "getting into trouble" usually means dismissal, whereas notable accomplishment may bring small rewards. Furthermore, close centralization of authority in planning provides both opportunity for greater accomplishment and the chance of larger and more costly mistakes, since action is taken on the basis of judgments by fewer people.

This, then, is one of the major problems of balance to be sought in national and regional planning; some middle course between the possibilities for constructive accomplishment through concentration of authority, and the protection from major mistakes that goes with a wider diffusion of decision-making powers. Coupled with this is, of course, the large problem of which business functions shall be carried on by government and which by private agencies. Each has advantages in some realms.

It seems apparent that the ownership and operation of water-power resources are destined to come more and more into the hands of government. Public opinion appears in general to favor that trend. Many other functions formerly reserved to private business are coming under government management.

There is need, therefore, that much study be given to the kinds of change in government itself that will be required to enable it to carry efficiently these vast responsibilities that were not contemplated when existing government structures were set up. Most new agencies come under the leadership of more able and altruistic executives than those who come to be in charge when the agencies are old and well established. How to prevent this downgrading of leadership, the ossification of governmentally managed businesses and the intrusion of political considerations in the appointment of personnel, are major problems for solution as we move along the paths now being taken.[15]

THE RESETTLEMENT ADMINISTRATION

The Soil Erosion Service, the Grazing Service, the TVA and others already described were only parts of the far-flung conservation program initiated during these years. Major shifts in emphasis were occurring. The conservation idea was being broadened to include additional and less tangible objectives such as the conservation of wildlife through establishment of large-scale bird refuges, and the enlargement of parks and other recreation facilities. It was but a short step from these to concern about the wastage of human resources that had been going on throughout the depression and before.

The major effort to salvage and maintain human resources was, of course, that carried on under the Emergency Relief Administration and the WPA. In addition, a separate organization, the Resettlement Administration, was established (by Executive Order

15. These problems are, of course, by no means absent in the large corporation. Bureaucracy, nepotism and lethargy frequently are apparent in big business which has many of the characteristics of big government. The private corporation has, however, retained more flexibility, and the profit motive still provides a significant stimulus in the direction of efficient operation. The methods for selecting government executives still leave much to be desired. The unevenness of performance in the many "New Deal" agencies can be traced in part to a tendency in some agencies to select personnel on ideological grounds rather than on the basis of ability and experience.

No. 7027, May 1, 1935)[16] to undertake the correction of certain chronic problems mainly associated with marginal agricultural areas. Funds were transferred to this new organization out of those appropriated in the Emergency Relief Act of 1935. Rexford G. Tugwell, a long-time member of President Roosevelt's so-called "brain trust," was placed in charge.

The Executive Order specified for the new agency three principal functions: (1) to aid in the resettlement and housing of destitute or low-income families, both rural and urban; (2) to carry out certain land conservation projects; and (3) to help farm families on relief to become independent by providing financial and technical assistance.[17] Other functions were later transferred to it or developed by it.

The Land Program

The phase of the program which attracted most attention in the early period was that involving purchase of "submarginal" lands, combining them into management units under government control, and resettling the families thus displaced, presumably on better lands. In principle this marked a significant and desirable change in the land policy of the United States.

Theretofore the government's policy had looked to the alienation of any lands people were willing to settle on, except national forests, parks and certain mineral reserves. Much arid grazing land had, perforce, remained in government hands, but this was now being brought under management through establishment of grazing districts under government supervision. Large areas that were unsuited for crop farming had, however, passed into private hands during the preceding dec-

ades. Such lands yielded only substandard livings to the farm families on them.

Now, for the first time, it was proposed to repossess such submarginal areas and put them to more suitable uses. Submarginal and marginal lands were to be bought, at agreed prices, and converted into grazing districts, transferred to forest reserves or otherwise reoriented. Aid was to be given to the dispossessed families in acquiring, either by rental or purchase, more suitable farms on better lands if they wished to continue as farmers.

In some of the areas, particularly those along the eastern fringe of the semiarid region, the lands were relatively productive in times when rainfall was above normal, but virtually useless when it was deficient. Crop farming on such lands was highly speculative. Nevertheless, real estate operators found these areas a lucrative source of revenue, since farms that had been sold or abandoned in times of drought could often be sold again to new settlers in the recurring periods of adequate rainfall.[18] Furthermore, communities had been built up and public obligations incurred in the expectation of an expanding population. Hence the plan to re-extensify the type of agriculture, while sound in principle, met with much resistance both in the affected areas, and, through them, in the Congress.

This phase of the program tended to drop into the background after 1937, though authorization for continuance of submarginal land purchase was included in the Bankhead-Jones Farm Tenancy Act of that year. From the beginning of the program until June 30, 1937, options were taken on about 17.5 million acres, and titles were acquired on about 12 million acres. The cost of land acquired up to June 30, 1937 was $52,283,950.

16. Roosevelt, *Public Papers and Addresses, 1935,* pp. 143–44.

17. The land conservation phase of the program, as outlined in the Executive Order, was not clearly differentiated from the work of the Soil Erosion Service. However, in setting up its program, the Resettlement Administration chose to confine its activities largely to marginal and submarginal farm lands, thus carving out for itself a particular segment of the conservation problem.

18. Such lands, though unsuited for maintaining a stable agriculture based on tilled crops, may nevertheless be productive and useful if kept in grass and operated in large units. For such use, however, they usually cannot carry the tax load associated with closer settlement and tilled crop agriculture, nor can they support the kinds of institutions common to more productive areas. If kept open for tilled crop agriculture, those settlers who do not abandon or sell them are likely to become tax delinquent and, eventually, candidates for relief, thus creating a continuing substandard problem area.

The accompanying task of resettling families displaced in the land purchase program often proved difficult and baffling. Such families were likely to be those long established in the "problem areas" and hence both reluctant to move and difficult to resettle; or, on the other hand, the less aggressive and less competent among the newer settlers, and hence a difficult group to establish successfully in a new environment. The task of reshuffling human beings is by no means an easy one, even though the logic of the situation may clearly indicate the need for such action. Families so moved inevitably tended to hold the government agency concerned more or less responsible for assuring success in the new location.

This problem has been a recurring one in nearly all planned settlements, notably, for example, in the Durham and Delhi settlements attempted by the state of California in the early 1920's. The state or federal government having assumed responsibility for planning the venture, it becomes easy for the settler to rationalize his own inadequacies as mistakes and incompetence on the part of the planners. Unwise decisions on their part are usually sufficiently numerous to give color to this type of complaint. As opposition to the land purchase and resettlement activities grew, the agency turned more definitely to other types of aid to low-income farmers and farm wage workers.

The Rehabilitation Program

From 1918 onward the federal government had provided loans to aid farmers affected by droughts, floods and pests to obtain seed and feed with which to continue their farming operations. By the early 1930's such loans were being made available to farmers in acute distress whether from natural causes or adverse economic conditions. Before the advent of the Resettlement Administration, loans of this kind had not been accompanied by outright grants, and by supervision and educational efforts. An attempt was now made to aid these borrowers in more positive ways.

The rehabilitation program thus superseded and broadened the type of aid previously provided through seed and feed loans. Loans and grants were made to farmers who lacked the capital, resources or knowledge to earn incomes adequate for minimum subsistence requirements and who, because of this, tended to be on relief. In addition the plan contemplated giving such farmers technical guidance so as to improve their efficiency. Since this activity will be discussed more fully in a succeeding chapter, in connection with the activities of the Farm Security Administration, further description of it is deferred.

Subsistence Homesteads

A third program of somewhat similar character consisted of an attempt to develop small homes on little plots of land, as a refuge for families unable to find places in the normal competitive economy.[19] It was set up in the Department of the Interior, and was placed under the direction of Professor M. L. Wilson. The business activities were carried out through the Federal Subsistence Homesteads Corporation, created by the Secretary of the Interior and incorporated under the laws of Delaware on December 2, 1933. Executive Order No. 7041[20] (May 15, 1935) transferred the Division of Subsistence Homesteads to the Resettlement Administration.

In the Subsistence Homesteads projects, effort was made to develop handicrafts and other methods of earning supplemental money income. The plan was somewhat defeatist in character in that it represented mainly a means of escape from the rigors of the competitive world rather than a solution

19. Section 208 of Title II of the National Industrial Recovery Act appropriated $25 million to be used "for aiding the redistribution of the overbalance of population in industrial centers." This authority was transferred by the President to the Secretary of the Interior under Executive Order 6209 (July 21, 1933), and he in turn established the Division of Subsistence Homesteads in July 1933. Its particular concerns were "stranded" industrial populations, "stranded" agricultural groups, decentralization of industry, suburban living and better housing. For a brief description of its plans see Department of the Interior, Division of Subsistence Homesteads, *General Information Concerning the Purposes and Policies of the Division of Subsistence Homesteads,* Circular No. 1, 1933.

20. Roosevelt, *Public Papers and Addresses, 1935,* p. 180.

of the basic problem. Most participants did not wish to remain in this status permanently. These projects did not achieve large importance, though some of the thinking relating to them was evident in later programs of the Resettlement and Farm Security Administrations.[21]

Farm Debt Adjustment

A special phase of the rural rehabilitation program was that pertaining to farm debt adjustment. This movement, previously described (see Chapter 12), sought to aid competent farmers whose properties were mortgaged for more than their carrying power in their efforts to retain possession of the farms. The Resettlement Administration's participation in this program was mainly that of financing meetings of the voluntary farm debt adjustment committees, and aiding them with supervisory staff, rather than direct participation in their work.

Farm Security Administration Set Up

Congressional and public criticism of the Resettlement Administration increased as its program unfolded. In part this was due to the fact that it had not been specifically authorized by the Congress. It was one of the many emergency organizations established by executive order. These agencies lacked clearly defined legislative directives, and were considered responsible mainly to the President rather than to the Congress. Furthermore, many of the activities of the agency were regarded as too unorthodox and "socialistic" to suit the more conservative members.

The Congress passed the Bankhead-Jones Farm Tenancy Act in July 1937. This specifically authorized most of the activities previously carried on by the Resettlement Administration under executive order, plus some additional ones. On September 1, the Secretary of Agriculture issued a memorandum changing the name of the organization from Resettlement Administration to Farm Security Administration.[22] All powers and duties of the Resettlement Administration had been transferred to the Secretary of Agriculture on December 31, 1936, under Executive Order 7530.[23]

TARIFFS — A MAJOR CHANGE IN UNITED STATES POLICY

For more than forty years the general trend of American tariffs had been upward. The reduced rates provided in the Underwood Tariff of 1913 did not have much effect because of the distortions in world trade which accompanied World War I. The upward trend was resumed after the war through the Emergency and Fordney-McCumber acts of 1921 and 1922.

Protectionist sentiment was strong and almost unchallenged in the United States during the 1920's. After 1929 the world-wide depression led to frantic efforts on the part of many countries to protect their producers from the competition of foreign suppliers, and to reduce drains on their dwindling reserves of foreign exchange and gold. Stimulated by the extreme protectionist policy adopted in 1930 by the United States, the leading creditor nation, tariff levels and import restrictions reached an all-time high. International trade, which in any event would have been greatly reduced by the general depression, was virtually strangled by this universal effort to achieve self-sufficiency.

As a consequence world exports fell off from $33 billion in 1929 to $11.7 billion in 1933, a decrease of 64.6 per cent.[24] The decline in United States exports was even greater, from $5,157 million to $1,280 million, or 75.2 per cent. United States exports suffered more severely than those of any other nation. The United Kingdom, Germany, France, Canada,

21. Wilson resigned on June 30, 1934, to become Assistant Secretary of Agriculture. He was succeeded by Charles Pynchon.

22. The Farm Security Administration and its program are discussed in Chapter 14.
23. *Federal Register*, Vol. II, p. 7. The work of the Resettlement Administration during its first year of operation is described and illustrated in its *Interim Report, April 1936*. A more intimate report is that of Will W. Alexander, "Rural Resettlement," *Southern Review*, Louisiana State University, Baton Rouge, Winter 1936, pp. 528-39.
24. In terms of United States gold dollars at the pre-devaluation rate.

Japan, Italy and the Netherlands showed declines that ranged from about 60 to 65 per cent.[25]

Hull's Program

Secretary Hull, long an advocate of lower tariffs and freer trade, had gone to the London Economic Conference hopeful of some general agreement for tariff reductions along with a plan for stabilizing relationships among the currencies of the various countries. This hope was shattered when the President rejected the international approach to price stabilization and, in effect, repudiated Hull's views on the problems under discussion at London.

The failure of the devaluation of the dollar to raise domestic prices generally, and the growing realization of the lack of logic in the United States foreign trade policy, opened the way for a new and revolutionary approach in the making of tariffs. The plan for reciprocal tariff agreements to be negotiated and accepted by the executive branch of the government was largely the result of Secretary Hull's single-minded effort to find a workable procedure for reducing barriers to world trade in an orderly and effective way.

The weaknesses of the old system of tariff making by the Congress had long been apparent to all serious students of the problem. Competent analysis of the inconceivably complex array of tariff schedules by a nontechnical general committee of Congress was utterly impossible. Even had there been no special interests to placate, and no trading of votes to gain the ends of this or that representative or senator, it was manifestly impossible for individual legislators to analyze the probable effects of a given level of tariff on each specific commodity, or to get any clear view of the over-all effect of the combination

of tariffs to be arrived at through bargaining and manipulation within the Congress.

If world trade was not to be permanently stifled, and many of the advantages of international trade lost, some means must be found for enabling other nations to export more goods to the United States in order to have more dollars with which to buy things the United States wished to export. But which commodities could be allowed to come in more freely without damaging unduly some established United States industry?

Almost every one of the thousands of items called for specific and highly technical analysis as to its importance to the American economy, the probable effects of a lower rate of duty and the amount of reduction that could safely be made. On the other hand, what and where were the serious and important restrictions placed on our exports by other nations? These were tasks for which no congressional committee was fitted.

Delegation of Legislative Powers

Both logic and precedent suggested the delegation of this function to a specialized agency equipped with a technical staff. The most obvious precedent was that of the control of railroad rates. The first approach to that problem, mainly in the states, consisted of efforts to establish directly by legislation the rates to be charged. It soon became evident that neither the Congress nor the state legislatures could make any intelligent determination of appropriate charges for the hundreds of thousands of different commodities and different hauls which made up the complex network of railway rates. The result was the establishment of the Interstate Commerce Commission and the delegation to it of what amounted to legislative powers possessed in the first instance only by the legislative bodies.

Years of litigation ensued in the effort to determine whether the Congress had exceeded its constitutional authority in thus delegating to an executive agency certain of the legislative powers it possessed. The authority for delegating the power to regulate

25. Grace Beckett, *The Reciprocal Trade Agreements Program*, Columbia University Press, New York, 1941, p. 3. The slump in United States exports was accentuated by retaliatory measures taken by various nations following the enactment of the Hawley-Smoot tariff of 1930. These are described in considerable detail in Joseph M. Jones, Jr., *Tariff Retaliation, Repercussions of the Hawley-Smoot Bill*, University of Pennsylvania Press, Philadelphia, 1934.

railroad rates was finally established in a Supreme Court decision of 1914 in which the constitutionality of the Mann-Elkins Act of 1910 was upheld (Intermountain Rate Cases, 234 U.S. 476). It was an issue that was bound to arise repeatedly as the delegation of legislative power was extended into one field after another. The growing complexity of the economy and the increasing desire for the regulation of business in order to eliminate widely recognized evils, as well as the desire for more positive means of accomplishing desired ends, were forcing inexorably more and more resort to the exercise of semilegislative powers by administrative agencies.

Such functions as those of administering the pure food and drug laws and meat inspection, and the powers granted under the National Bank Act and the Federal Reserve Act, involved granting authority to executive agencies of the government to make decisions that were legislative in character. This trend became more pronounced and specific in the government corporations established during World War I, and in such agencies as the Reconstruction Finance Corporation and the Federal Farm Board.

It appeared in its most extreme form in the National Industrial Recovery Act. Here the Supreme Court decided that the delegation of legislative authority exceeded reasonable and necessary limits, and did not contain sufficiently specific directives as to the limitations within which executive decisions could be made. For decades the Supreme Court had been seeking to define more carefully the principles relating to this vague area of legislative authority, allowing scope for an increasing amount of congressional delegation of powers and at the same time striving to maintain in broad terms the basic constitutional separation of the powers of the legislative and executive branches of the government.

The Trade Agreements Act of 1934

Means for achieving a workable procedure to bring about a relaxation of restrictions on trade had been under study for some time in various agencies of the government. In No-

vember 1933 an Executive Commercial Policy Committee was set up to supervise and coordinate government activities relating to exports and imports. This Committee proposed that legislation be sought under which the President would be given limited powers to revise tariff duties.

The President requested this authority in his message to Congress of March 2, 1934. The argument for it was based on the "startling" decline in world trade and upon the need for speedy action, rather than on the more logical but less popular one of providing an alternative to the congressional logrolling and political manipulation that had marked nearly every attempt to legislate on tariff during the preceding hundred years or more.[26]

The Trade Agreements Act, technically an amendment to the Tariff Act of 1930, was approved on June 12, 1934.[27] Its main provisions were, in substance:

1. The delegation of authority to the President to enter into trade agreements with foreign countries, and to modify existing rates of duty up or down by not more than 50 per cent. No commodities could be transferred from the dutiable to the free list or vice versa.

2. Special concessions to Cuba might be retained provided the preferential duties then existing not be modified by more than 50 per cent.

3. This power was delegated to the President for a period of three years. Agreements concluded were to remain in force for three years and to continue in force thereafter unless terminated by either of the governments concerned.

26. The idea of reciprocal agreements on tariffs in one form or another was not new. It had been vaguely implied in the McKinley Tariff of 1890, and later expressed in some of McKinley's statements shortly before his death. Taft had given support to the principle of reciprocal tariff concessions. Several important organizations of manufacturers had petitioned Congress in behalf of reciprocal trade negotiations, and such a plan had been advocated in the Democratic platform of 1932, as well as in various speeches of the Democratic candidates. In 1931 the Collier bill providing for executive reciprocal trade agreements was passed by the Congress but was vetoed by President Hoover. For a fuller account see Beckett, *Reciprocal Trade Agreements Program*, Chapter 1; also Henry J. Tasca, *The Reciprocal Trade Policy of the United States, A Study in Trade Philosophy*, University of Pennsylvania Press, Philadelphia, 1938.

27. 48 Stat. 943.

4. Nothing in the act was to be construed as giving authority for the cancellation of war debts.

5. Reasonable public notice was to be given of intention to negotiate any foreign trade agreement, and the Tariff Commission, the Departments of State, Commerce and Agriculture, and any other sources the President might deem appropriate, were to be consulted in the drafting of any agreement.

Provision number 5 was added in the Senate in order to give opportunity for interested parties to present views in opposition to, or in favor of, proposed agreements.

Henry Wallace had brought out, in February 1934, a widely read pamphlet entitled *America Must Choose*.[28] In this he presented in dramatic form the choice which, as he saw it, would have to be made, namely, that of compulsory and drastic reduction of the output of export crops, or a reversion to freer international trade. The booklet received wide and favorable attention from the public, and undoubtedly was helpful in crystallizing sentiment for the trade agreement proposal when it came up.

Controversial Features

From its inception the trade agreements program was a bone of contention. Many farm groups took violent exception not only to this method of tariff making, but more especially to the policy of the administration which the trade agreements were designed to implement, namely, a general lowering of tariffs.

Although the act permitted increases as well as decreases it was well known that its primary purpose was to get rid of the old method of tariff making in which almost every congressman was under pressure from one or more special interest groups to retain or increase the tariffs on certain commodities produced in his district. To achieve this he was virtually forced to vote for tariffs demanded by other congressmen, even though convinced they were unwarranted. Farmers,

28. Foreign Policy Association and World Peace Foundation, New York and Boston, 1934. (World Affairs Pamphlet No. 3.)

except in the South, had for decades been nurtured in the idea that high tariffs were the cause of the high standards of living in the United States, and that freer trade would mean a reduction to coolie standards of living.

During the 1920's the farm organizations had generally backed the McNary-Haugen campaign to make the tariff effective for agriculture. The sheep and cattle growers had long been virtually unanimous in their advocacy of high tariffs. The sugar beet growers and the dairy groups were likewise strongly protectionist. The corn, wheat and swine growers were aware of the fact that tariffs did not benefit them materially, but still hoped for special legislation that would enable them to keep prices above those of the international markets.

A second controversial aspect was the use of the unconditional most-favored-nation principle. Secretary Hull was utterly convinced that the shackles on trade must be loosened quickly and widely. He therefore supported strongly the principle that concessions made to one country should automatically be extended to all nations whose commercial treaties with the United States included a clause extending like treatment to products entering from the United States. The practice was to negotiate with the country or countries producing the major portion of a commodity imported or potentially importable into the United States. When agreement was reached, these same concessions would be made to others exporting the same commodities to the United States.

Many contended that this meant giving away part of the American market without offsetting concessions from the secondary supplying nations. Few of these objectors recognized that in the traditional unilateral method of making tariff adjustments no concessions could be required from any of the suppliers as a result of a reduction in United States tariffs. It is beyond question that adoption of the most-favored-nation principle worked in the direction of freer world trade and greatly simplified the task of negotiating agreements.

Since freer access to the American market was greatly prized by nearly all nations, and nearly every nation had one or more products of which it was a chief supplier, the opportunity to bargain with virtually all the principal exporting nations was almost certain to come up sooner or later. Thus the ultimate effect was probably little different from what it would have been had negotiations been undertaken for each commodity with every nation supplying any part of it whether large or small. The principal exceptions were small nations that were not important suppliers of any commodity.[29]

The road to better understanding of international trade problems was to be a long and arduous one. Long-established policies of this kind are not easily changed. The State Department, under the vigorous lead of Cordell Hull, undertook to explain and popularize the program. Thus for almost the first time in the nation's history there was a continuing attempt to bring about educational discussion of the tariff issue outside the academic institutions and in isolation from political campaigns. Though vigorous and widespread criticisms were leveled at the new policy it gradually won a larger and larger following. Renewals of the power to adjust tariffs were granted in 1937, 1940, 1943, 1945, 1948, 1949 and 1951.

Results Achieved

The effects of tariffs, and even the average levels of tariff, defy accurate measurement. Volumes of trade are inevitably modified from period to period by many things other than tariffs. The period for which data on this point are significant extends only from September 1934, when the first agreement was signed, to September 1939, when World War II broke out. Since 1939, world trade has been so grossly distorted by the war, and the ab-

normal postwar conditions of trade, that no meaningful comparison can be made.

Even in the period 1934–1939 conditions were far from normal. Most of the trading nations were still struggling out of the depression that had gripped them in the early years of the decade. Germany and Italy, and to some extent other nations, were restricting trade in many ways as a means of gaining self-sufficiency in the event of war. Eight of the twenty-two agreements in effect by the end of 1939 were entered into after 1936, and hence were of such short duration in the prewar years as to afford little basis for analysis of results.

It is possible, however, to gain some idea of the changes brought about by even such small amounts of tariff reduction as occurred in this first period of operation under the Trade Agreements Act. By 1938 sixteen agreements had been signed. Tasca concludes, on the basis of thirteen of these, that the average rate of duty applicable in 1934 was reduced from 46.7 per cent to 40.7 per cent, or 13 per cent.[30] As of 1936 exports to agreement countries had increased 15.0 per cent while those to nonagreement countries had increased by only 4.1 per cent. Imports from agreement countries increased 21.9 per cent as against 16.5 per cent for nonagreement countries.[31] These figures indicate some gain in trade as a result of the agreements even at this early period.

29. Space does not permit full discussion either of the most-favored-nation or other features of the trade agreement program. An excellent account of this, up to 1938, is given in Tasca, *The Reciprocal Trade Policy of the United States.* See also Beckett, *The Reciprocal Trade Agreements Program,* particularly Chapter 3.

30. Tasca, *Reciprocal Trade Policy of the United States,* p. 188.
31. *Ibid.,* p. 271. Beckett gives the following percentages of increase over 1934–1935 for the agreement and nonagreement countries:

	U.S. Exports to:		U.S. Imports from:	
	Agreement Countries	Non-agreement Countries	Agreement Countries	Non-agreement Countries
1936	18.1	7.7	33.2	29.2
1937	65.8	44.3	57.3	73.3

Reciprocal Trade Agreements Program, pp. 87 and 95.
The data presented here and in the text above should not be considered comparable. The Tasca figures relate to trade with six countries with which agreements had been in effect one year or more at the time of writing. The Beckett data pertain to seventeen countries, and are derived from later material. Both sets do, however, reflect a difference in the change occurring in the trade with the two groups of countries. For full explanation of the qualifications on the data see the authors cited.

Much more important changes in rates were made in later negotiations, particularly in the Geneva agreements of 1947. Further developments in the program are discussed in Chapter 19. It is sufficient here to note that a major shift in policy with respect to foreign trade had been made. An upward trend in tariffs that had lasted for more than seventy years was changed to a downward trend. The economic nationalism that had marked the first year of the Roosevelt administration had given place to an internationalism that bore some resemblance to that of the Wilson era.

The Commodity Loan Program and Surplus Disposal

Though the administration's plans for aiding farmers contemplated raising prices and incomes in ways that would not lead to heavy accumulations of stored commodities such as had plagued the Farm Board, circumstances were such that holding operations were almost inevitable. These took somewhat different form from those of the previous administration. Nevertheless, the ultimate outcome was markedly similar.

During 1933 strong pleas for action that would enable farmers to hold storable products for higher prices were made by various groups, particularly by the conference of state governors of the ten Corn Belt states, held at Des Moines on October 31. Not only because of such pressures but also from a desire to get money into farmers' hands as quickly as possible, the administration sought a means of providing loans that would help to slow the movement to market, provide buying power sooner than it could be supplied through the adjustment programs and afford some support to the prices of farm products.

Creation of CCC

Under an executive order of October 16, 1933, the Secretary of Agriculture set up, on the following day, the Commodity Credit Corporation, organized under the laws of Delaware. Its capital stock of $3 million was held jointly by the Secretary of Agriculture

and the Governor of the Farm Credit Administration, and was supplied from funds appropriated under the National Industrial Recovery Act. An assistant to the Director of the Reconstruction Finance Corporation was appointed president of the new agency. It was in fact operated virtually as a subsidiary of the RFC.[32] The CCC also, however, made use of the facilities of the federal reserve and intermediate credit banks, and of a good many commercial banks, which made loans under guarantee from the CCC that it would take them over at specified dates and on agreed terms if requested to do so.[33]

Loans were limited to signers of AAA contracts and the interest rate was set at 4 per cent. The loans were made "without recourse." That is, the borrower had the option to pay off the loan and repossess the commodity or turn it over to the Commodity Credit Corporation at the loan rate. Thus the loan rate constituted a price floor, and opened the way for accumulations of commodities by the Commodity Credit Corporation in a way somewhat similar to that which had been used by the stabilization corporations under the Farm Board. Early loans on cotton and corn were mostly at a flat rate per unit of product, 10 cents on cotton and 45 cents on corn. The cotton loans were on warehouse receipts for cotton stored in approved warehouses; those on corn covered corn on the cob sealed in cribs on the farms.

This latter feature was a new and radical procedure. It had been proposed and strongly supported as a state program in the legislature of South Dakota, and probably in others, in the 1920's, but had failed of adoption. The plan worked out unexpectedly well in 1933–1934. Some 271 million bushels of corn were placed under loan, and more than $120 million were released for use in the Corn Belt states at an earlier date than would have

32. The RFC was at this time the source of funds for the regional agricultural credit corporations and some other phases of the program of financial aid to agriculture.

33. Both the Civilian Conservation Corps and the Commodity Credit Corporation were commonly known as the CCC. These initials, where used in the following pages, signify Commodity Credit Corporation.

resulted from normal sales. Most of the loans were repaid, the corn being either fed on the owner's farm or sold. The Commodity Credit Corporation made a net profit of nearly a half million dollars.[34] This favorable outcome was in part due to the severe drought which came in 1934. The storage program had, without premeditation, operated to initiate a form of what afterward came to be referred to as the "ever-normal granary."

Weaknesses of the Plan

The provision of loans of these types undoubtedly exercised a stabilizing and stimulating influence on prices, especially in the case of corn. It also put money into the farm areas at a time when it was desperately needed. The cotton loan program, though put at more conservative levels and based on more orthodox procedures than those for wheat and corn, soon demonstrated the major weaknesses of this type of farm relief. It quickly gave rise to speculative holding for higher prices and to strong demands on the part of cotton state legislators for higher loan rates. Political pressure forced the rate up to 12 cents in 1934 and there was strong demand for a 15 cent rate. Cotton stocks were not reduced through drought and farm use as were those of corn.

By August 1935 the government was holding or financing 6.2 million bales of cotton, nearly twice the maximum volume carried by the Farm Board. This contributed to the severe acreage reduction program initiated in 1935, and also resulted in an attempt to reduce the loan rate to 9 cents for the 1935 crop. The Senate passed, in January 1936, an amendment to an appropriation bill which would have required the Commodity Credit Corporation to lend 12 cents a pound on cotton and 90 cents a bushel on wheat. Though later killed, this action led to agreement on a 10 cent rate for cotton. In the meantime prices had strengthened somewhat, and some liqui-

dation of stocks had been accomplished. About 4.4 million bales remained under loan on February 1, 1936.[35]

Nourse, Davis and Black conclude that:

In retrospect, it seems clear that, on balance, restricting the liquidation of option cotton [that assigned to farmers in payment of rentals] and raising the loan rate to 12 cents in August 1934 constituted major mistakes. These illustrate the vulnerability of such a program to political influence or other group pressures.[36]

The Ever-Normal Granary Idea

The experience with the corn loan program, and the ensuing drought of 1934, led Secretary Wallace to advance, on June 6, 1934, a proposal that some such commodity loan policy be made a continuing supplement to the agricultural adjustment program with a view to maintaining what he termed an "ever-normal granary." The idea was further elaborated in his book *New Frontiers* and in his annual report for 1934.[37] The main feature of the plan was that supplies and prices would be stabilized through loans to farmers for withholding part of their production in years of high output, and using or releasing it in years of short production.

The ever-normal granary idea was shortly thereafter merged with that of crop insurance, the proposal being that participants in the crop insurance programs pay their premiums in grain, and likewise receive insurance benefits due them in that form. This, it was suggested, would tend to stabilize the physical

34. See Edwin G. Nourse, Joseph S. Davis and John D. Black, *Three Years of the Agricultural Adjustment Administration*, The Brookings Institution, Washington, 1937, pp. 157–58.

35. The Agricultural Adjustment Act of 1933 provided that the Secretary of Agriculture should take over 2.5 million bales of cotton acquired by the government under the Farm Board program. Most of this was taken over by the growers in the spring of 1933 under a complex plan which provided that they might receive part of their rental payments in this form. For a fuller explanation see *ibid.*, pp. 163–70 and Henry I. Richards, *Cotton and the AAA*, The Brookings Institution, Washington, 1936, pp. 194–212.

36. Nourse, Davis and Black, *Three Years of the Agricultural Adjustment Administration*, p. 171.

37. Henry A. Wallace, *New Frontiers*, Reynal & Hitchcock, New York, 1934, pp. 236–38 and *Report of the Secretary of Agriculture, 1934*, pp. 20–23. The Secretary, an earnest student of the Bible, was also perhaps influenced by the biblical story of Joseph's accumulations during the seven fat years in order to cover the needs during the seven lean years. At least this parable was widely used in publicizing the idea.

quantities of actual grain available for live-stock feeding and human use. It was recognized that such a plan, operated wholly in terms of physical commodities, would be impractical. Hence, alternative arrangements would be made for payment of premiums and benefits in cash. Legislation to implement this proposal was passed in 1938 but discussion of it is deferred. (See Chapter 15.)

Crops Diverted to Abnormal Outlets

The diversion of crops to special outlets at prices different from those prevailing in the regular domestic markets had been a major feature of the McNary-Haugen and other two-price plans discussed in the 1920's. This idea was put into effect in a small way through action of the Farm Board's Grain Stabilization Corporation, in absorbing losses on some of the wheat and flour sold for export during the preceding administration.

The Board also sold wheat to the German and Chinese governments on terms more favorable than those prevailing in regular commercial channels. Departing still further from traditional methods of trade, it bartered some 25 million bushels of wheat for Brazilian raw coffee. As the depression deepened and stocks remained excessive, the Board was directed by the Congress to turn over large quantities of wheat and cotton to the Red Cross for relief purposes. Thus the idea of such abnormal types of sale or disposal did not originate in the "New Deal" period. That procedure was, however, taken up more vigorously and on a larger scale in the program that took shape after March 1933.

The processing tax and benefit payment features of the Agricultural Adjustment Act implied the maintenance of a differential between domestic and world market prices. Diversionary purchases and sales were also permissible under the marketing agreement provisions and other phases of the AAA legislation. Arrangements made with the Federal Emergency Relief Administration, in the fall of 1933, likewise made possible the purchase and distribution for relief purposes of commodities available as a result of AAA activi-ties. Some of the special drought relief funds could be used in a similar way. The amendments of August 24, 1935, still further enlarged the possibility of action along these lines, by permitting acquisition of commodities pledged as security for loans, especially under the provisions of Section 32. This section assigned to the Secretary of Agriculture 30 per cent of the customs revenues for use, at his discretion, in a wide range of price-supporting and surplus removal activities.[38]

This customs revenue fund for the year ending June 30, 1936 (based on customs receipts in 1934) amounted to $92.1 million. Of this, about $1 million was spent on export subsidies, $3 million for domestic diversion operations and $10.5 million for relief purchases.[39]

The subsidization of exports, though strongly advocated in the preceding period, and favored by George Peek when he was Administrator of the AAA, was not used extensively and was of minor importance. A loan commitment of $50 million made to China by the Reconstruction Finance Corporation was only partly used, because of Chinese objections to the importation of wheat and cotton. RFC loans were made to exporters in 1933 to finance the sale of some 75,000 bales of cotton to Russia, but a similar plan in regard to 300 million pounds of pork did not materialize. Efforts of the first Export-Import Bank, established in 1934, to develop exports to Russia likewise fell through because of controversy over past debts owed by Russia.

The principal export subsidy program was that carried out by the North Pacific Emergency Export Association established in October 1933 to relieve congestion of wheat handling facilities in the Pacific Northwest.[40] The corporation exported some 28 million

38. This section was retained despite a strong recommendation by the President, in his budget message of January 3, 1936, that it be repealed.

39. Nourse, Davis and Black, *Three Years of the Agricultural Adjustment Administration*, p. 190.

40. The North Pacific Emergency Export Association was set up under a marketing agreement between the Secretary of Agriculture, certain millers and grain exporters, the regional wheat cooperative, and the Farmers National Grain Corporation.

bushels of wheat, of which 16 million went to China. The average loss per bushel was about 23 cents. The results of the experiment were not sufficiently encouraging to lead to extensive use of this procedure in later years.[41]

The Surplus Commodities Corporation

By far the largest program of diversion from commercial channels was that undertaken for the purpose of providing domestic relief while at the same time disposing of parts of the surpluses acquired in connection with the various agricultural price-support programs. For this purpose a corporation known as the Federal Surplus Relief Corporation was set up on October 4, 1933. This was incorporated under the laws of Delaware through powers granted to the President in the National Industrial Recovery Act of June 16, 1933. In November 1935 the name was changed to the Federal Surplus Commodities Corporation.[42]

From 1933 to 1935 the agency was operated virtually as a subsidiary of the Federal Emergency Relief Administration, but with a close tie to the Commodities Purchase Section of the AAA. After discontinuance of the FERA in the fall of 1935 it became in effect a subsidiary of the Agricultural Adjustment Administration. During the early period funds were supplied in part from the FERA. Later the principal source was customs revenue made available under Section 32 of the Amendment of August 24, 1935, plus minor amounts from other appropriations. Commodities so purchased were turned over to the Federal Surplus Commodities Corporation which acted as the distributing agency.

The activities of this agency had a dual role, that of absorbing surpluses of agricultural products and that of supplying food to destitute people. The foodstuffs thus obtained were, in the main, turned over to the state relief agencies for distribution. The Federal Surplus Relief Corporation and its successor the Federal Surplus Commodities Corporation acquired and distributed substantial volumes of agricultural commodities under a wide variety of acts and funds. In addition, considerable amounts of some commodities were diverted to lower value uses or to export channels, notably peanuts, hogs, tobacco, prunes, walnuts, raisins, etc.[43]

Careful students of the problem, including those then in charge of the AAA program, felt that such diversionary activities warranted further experimentation and development, particularly as a means of relieving distress and avoiding waste. They were much more dubious of the export subsidy feature, though this was popular with congressmen and with many of the producer groups.[44] The surplus disposal mechanism set up was obviously better suited for handling short-run emergency surpluses, especially of minor commodities, than for the chronic, large-scale surpluses which arise in connection with the major staple crops.

THE PROBLEM OF CONSUMER INTEREST AND REPRESENTATION

Both the AAA and the NRA were frankly and almost exclusively oriented to the interests of producers, if in the NRA we look upon labor as one of the producer groups. No doubt there was much to be said for this emphasis since a primary objective was to get business going again and to improve the situation of agriculture. Nevertheless, many

41. Some minor programs of this type were carried out in 1935 and 1936. For details see Nourse, Davis and Black, *op. cit.*, pp. 191 and 192.
42. During the first two years the board of directors consisted of the Federal Emergency Relief Administrator, the Secretary of Agriculture, the Federal Emergency Administrator of Public Works and the Governor of the Farm Credit Administration. After the reorganization of November 1935 the Board consisted of the Secretary of Agriculture, the Administrator of the AAA and the Governor of the Farm Credit Administration. In the Agricultural Adjustment Act of 1938 (52 Stat. 38, continuing provisions of 50 Stat. 323, 1937) the organization was continued and given legislative status. By Section 5 of Reorganization Plan III the Surplus Commodities Corporation was consolidated with the Division of Marketing and Marketing Agreements to form the Surplus Marketing Administration (June 30, 1940). On February 23, 1942 this was merged into the Agricultural Marketing Administration by Executive Order No. 9069. *Federal Register*, Vol. VII, p. 1409.

43. For a more detailed account see Nourse, Davis and Black, *Three Years of the Agricultural Adjustment Administration*, pp. 194–216.
44. See for example the analysis in *ibid.*, pp. 206–16.

millions of consumers who did not benefit as producers under the AAA or the NRA were likewise in desperate circumstances, and striving to keep off the relief rolls. Both the major acts removed many of the protections to the general public that had been built up over the years, notably the restrictions on monopolistic activity.

The restoration of pre-existing levels of prices, and of earlier relationships among prices, bulked large in the thinking of the administration and of the business and farm groups. But wage rates, salaries and weekly earnings had all been reduced markedly in the early years of the depression. Hence buying power was bound to be inadequate to absorb the products of a fully functioning economy at the old levels of prices.

Neither the National Industrial Recovery Act nor the Agricultural Adjustment Act provided specifically for representation of the consumer's interest in code negotiations or the formulation of general policy.[45] Business, labor and agriculture all were represented in the government by officials of Cabinet rank. The consumers were unorganized and never had achieved significant political power either in the Congress or in the executive agencies. It was recognized, however, that at least some gesture in the direction of consumer recognition would have to be made if the kinds of programs then being initiated were not to give rise to widespread and justifiable criticism on the part of the consuming public.

At the time of signing the National Industrial Recovery Act the President announced that the Administrator would have the advice of three official advisory boards — one for industry, one for labor and one for consumers.

These were unpaid boards nominated, for labor and industry, by the Secretaries of Labor and Commerce. There being no secretary for the consumer, a special interdepartmental committee nominated a Consumers' Advisory Board under the chairmanship of Mrs. Mary Rumsey.

In the Agricultural Adjustment Administration a different procedure was followed. Secretary Wallace was persuaded by his associates that there should be within the AAA some specific arrangement for expression of consumer interest, to offset pressure from the farm and business groups. Peek was opposed to this idea, but agreed, reluctantly, to the appointment of a "Consumers' Counsel." This position, with its small staff, was at first attached directly, though somewhat vaguely, to the Administrator's office. After Peek's resignation it became a section in the Division of Information. Later, in the spring of 1935, the office was raised to the status of a division.

Difficulties Encountered

Both the Consumers' Advisory Board in the NRA and the Consumers' Counsel in the AAA encountered difficulty in functioning effectively, and became a source of friction to the respective Administrators.[46] Both were staffed by people with broad social interests and a reform philosophy. They found themselves at odds with the strong predilection of the NRA and the AAA to give business and agriculture what they wanted regardless of the impact on the consumer. Their economic philosophies looked also to more drastic regulation of profits than those which prevailed in the main administrative offices of the two agencies. These points of view were almost certain to be overruled by the much larger and more aggressive producer-oriented groups in contact with the Administrators.

45. The Secretary of Agriculture was, however, instructed, in Section 9e of the Agricultural Adjustment Act, to "make public such information as he deems necessary regarding (1) the relationship between the processing tax and the price paid to producers of the commodity, (2) the effect of the processing tax upon prices to consumers of products of the commodity, (3) the relationship, in previous periods, between prices paid to the producers of the commodity and prices to consumers of the products thereof, and (4) the situation in foreign countries relating to prices paid to producers of the commodity and prices to consumers of the products thereof." (48 Stat. 31 at 36–37.)

46. The problems met and the various viewpoints from which they were approached are described in Persia Campbell, *Consumer Representation in the New Deal,* Columbia University Press, New York, 1940. See also the discussion of this problem in Nourse, Davis and Black, *Three Years of the Agricultural Adjustment Administration,* Chapter 13, especially pp. 391–99.

The result was almost continuous friction between the consumer representatives and the Administrators, and a growing feeling of frustration on the part of the consumer representatives. The NRA and AAA Administrators tended to look upon the people in these units as impractical do-gooders while they in turn regarded many of their colleagues in other divisions as tools of the special interests.

The work of the Consumers' Advisory Board was terminated by the adverse ruling of the Supreme Court, in May 1935, which abolished the NRA. The Office of Consumers' Counsel in the AAA was headed until 1935 by Dr. Frederick C. Howe, a publicist and reformer, who was in almost continuous conflict with the main supervisory staff of the agency. His views were similar to those of Jerome Frank, General Counsel of the AAA. Hence Frank and Howe tended to join forces or take parallel action in their efforts to place limits on the powers of the commodity groups sponsoring marketing agreements, and to compel access by the government to the books and records of the handlers. In February 1935 Davis, then Administrator of the AAA, refused to carry on unless Howe and Frank were eliminated. The result was the so-called "purge" of the AAA in which Howe, Frank and some of their associates were removed from office.

Adjustments Made

Howe was succeeded by Dr. Calvin Hoover, a Duke University economist of high standing. Hoover was much better suited for the task of handling these delicate relationships, and for evolving more appropriate procedures in dealing with this difficult assignment.

Both Davis and Hoover undertook to clarify and define the relationship of the Consumers' Counsel to the other activities of the AAA. Since the Office of Consumers' Counsel had now been raised to the status of a division, Hoover could take part in the consultations of the reconstituted Agricultural Council which operated as an informal cabinet within the AAA. This did not solve the dilemma but did at least create a situation in which it was more possible for the two groups to live with each other. Nevertheless, it became more and more evident that an agency purporting to represent the interests of the consumer was in an anomalous position when placed within, and dominated by, an agency primarily responsible for furthering the interests of the producers and handlers.

Hoover resigned in the fall of 1935 to return to his position at Duke University. He was succeeded by his assistant, Donald Montgomery. Montgomery functioned more as an internal adviser than had his predecessors, and minimized the role of commenter to the public on consumer aspects of the various programs. Nevertheless, the basic problem of effective and appropriate representation of the consumer interest in programs designed to improve incomes of farm producers and business groups had not been solved.

It has long been apparent that the interests of special groups are overweighted in the decisions taken by the Congress and by government administrative agencies. None of the major special interest departments can be regarded as unbiased. The Labor Department tends to be strongly pro-labor, the Agriculture Department pro-agriculture and the Commerce Department pro-business. Obviously their political strength and their appropriations would be jeopardized if they were not.

Consequently, there was a growing feeling in informed circles that the time had come when a number of agencies oriented to the protection of the consumer should be brought together in a department headed by an executive of Cabinet rank, who would have as his primary function the presentation of the views and interests of the general public in top-level consultations.[47]

47. Such a department would presumably include such functions as the administration of the Food and Drugs law, the Bureau of Human Nutrition and Home Economics, and possibly the Meat Inspection Service, the Office of Education and the Children's Bureau. It would also have the duty of preparing independent data and statistical analyses on matters affecting the general public interest.

RURAL ELECTRIFICATION

Farmers had long been interested in gaining access to electric power for lighting and other farm and household operations. Few of the power companies had found it attractive financially, or even economically feasible, to provide such service on the basis of the amounts of power used by most farms. In some few areas, where farmsteads were close together, or where there was considerable demand for electric power to operate heavy motors, as in many of the irrigated areas of the West, private capital had found this market attractive, and had constructed lines for distribution of electric power. In most other areas farmers, if they wanted electricity, had to put in home power plants suitable almost exclusively for lighting.

The more progressive companies had for some years been operating test lines, and in many areas full-fledged commercial lines. It was evident, however, that full electrification of the major farming areas would occur only slowly if left to profit motivation on the part of the private power companies. Such lines could not be profitable merely on the basis of supplying power for lighting. It would be necessary to induce farmers to install a variety of appliances and motors in order to increase power requirements and reduce unit costs of electricity. An aggressive approach to this problem appealed to the administration not only as a way of filling a long-felt want on the part of farmers but as a stimulus for the manufacture of power-line equipment, appliances, motors, etc.

REA Established

As a means of expanding rapidly the availability of electric power in rural areas, the President established a new agency, the Rural Electrification Administration (Executive Order 7037, May 11, 1935).[48] This was followed a year later by congressional enactment of the Rural Electrification Act of 1936.

At the time the agency was initiated it was expected that the REA would act mainly as a banker, and would establish terms and standards that would help to increase the availability of electric power in the rural areas. It was thought that private companies would borrow most of the funds. The companies were not able, however, to adjust sufficiently or fast enough to satisfy the demand. As a result, rural electric cooperatives began to be formed and to apply for loans with which to build lines. From this it was a natural step to the operating management of such lines. Here, however, difficulties arose. The construction and operation of power lines involve many engineering and technical problems.

As a consequence REA has entered much more broadly into the program than was at first contemplated, supplying not only funds but guidance, engineering skills and promotional effort. Its functions approach much more nearly those of an entrepreneur than of a mere government financing agency. This was not so much the development of a new policy as the coming to fruition of a policy that had long been gaining ground, namely, the substitution of public for private entrepreneurship in the field of electric power. Sentiment for public action in this realm had been growing for decades, and had been a bone of contention in the long struggle over the Muscle Shoals project. Undoubtedly the creation of the Tennessee Valley Authority gave it emphasis, particularly with respect to its rural aspects.

While the struggle over public versus private control of electric power is by no means at an end, there can be no doubt that the influence of the government has been thrown heavily on the side of public ownership during the period since 1933. Further than this, the policy of making electric power available in all rural areas sufficiently settled to be able to use it effectively seems to have become fully established as a part of our national farm policy.

The rapid increase in farm use of electric power as a result of this policy is clearly apparent. In 1929 some 580,000 farms had elec-

48. Roosevelt, *Public Papers and Addresses, 1935,* pp. 172–73.

tric service. This number had reached 744,000 by 1934, and increased to 1,242,000 by 1937, despite the fact that the intervening years were marked by severe depression in agriculture. By 1941 the number of farms so served had reached 2,351,603; well toward half the farms in the United States.[49] Since then the spread of rural electric lines has been rapid and continuous.

FARM ORGANIZATIONS AND THE "NEW DEAL" AGRICULTURAL PROGRAMS

During the 1920's virtually all of the major farm organizations had gained in strength and political influence. However, they had fought a losing battle during the Coolidge and Hoover regimes. A new administration more friendly to their aspirations gave them opportunities for policy leadership such as they had never had before. Nevertheless, their role during the 1930's tended to be secondary rather than dominant. They were, for the most part, followers of administration leadership, rather than creators of new policies and programs. This does not mean that their influence was negligible. Administrators did take account of farm organization views, though often the programs devised by the administrators were more novel and imaginative than any advanced by the organized farm groups.[50]

During the lame duck session of Congress before the new administration took power (December 1932 to March 1933), the farm organizations found it impossible to get congressional approval of measures proposed. Legislative action to deal with the deepening crisis was virtually at a standstill. The farm groups found it necessary, therefore, to mark time until the new administration could take over.

Immediately after the inauguration of the new President the Farm Bureau undertook to bring its influence to bear upon the legislative program then taking shape. At the quarterly meeting of its board of directors, on March 7 to 9, it formulated the following proposals, and wired them to the President, urging that he include them in his message to Congress:

1. Government guarantee of new deposits in all banks and special consideration of the particular problems of rural banks.
2. Approval of the recommendations of Dr. George Warren in regard to monetary reform.
3. Restoration of price parity for agricultural commodities with the products of industry.
4. Relief for heavily mortgaged farmers who were in distress.[51]

Views of the Farm Bureau Federation

At the annual meeting of the Federation, in December 1933, Farm Bureau officials stated that they had assumed leadership in drafting and securing enactment of the AAA legislation, and asserted that "It gives the President broad powers and authority to revise our unfair and unjust monetary system to an honest basis, whereby debts can be paid with dollars carrying the same commodity value as when debts were created."[52] Question was raised, however, as to whether

. . . in the field of perishable farm commodities [we are] being forced to witness the absorption by producers of the amount of processing taxes levied. This never was either authorized or intended by Congress. It is largely the result of organized and determined opposition of processors in an effort to discredit the Agri-

49. Data from Frederick W. Muller, *Public Rural Electrification,* American Council on Public Affairs, Washington, 1944, p. 17.
50. The role of the Farm Bureau in the legislative developments of this period is described in an intimate and interesting way in Orville Merton Kile, *The Farm Bureau Through Three Decades,* The Waverley Press, Baltimore, 1948, Chapters 15 through 17. Kile's account possibly attributes more influence to the Farm Bureau than full exploration of the facts would warrant. Nevertheless, his account affords a most interesting example of the methods by which policies come into being. It is characteristic of policy-making activities that many people sincerely believe they are the originators of particular proposals. Actually such proposals come to be discussed informally by many people. Eventually some strategically placed individual gives them formal expression and comes to be known as the originator of the idea. Not infrequently he is bringing into focus a proposal that has been skillfully and perhaps intentionally planted in his mind. Unaware of this and in all sincerity he presents it as his own.

51. *Bureau Farmer* (Tennessee Section), April 1933, p. 7.
52. *Bureau Farmer,* January 1934, p. 7.

cultural Adjustment Act and thereby restore the old privilege system.[53]

While not opposing the efforts to reduce production the Federation publications expressed the view that this would not in itself raise prices as much as they should be raised. They therefore urged development of industrial markets for farm products, more use of the Secretary's licensing power over dealers, and the broadening of the AAA program to include more products.

In its December 1934 annual meeting, the Federation reaffirmed its support of the AAA, but stated that the government, in its administrative policies, should place more emphasis on raising farm prices in order to restore farm purchasing power. It also favored such amendments as might be required to make more effective the licensing powers relating to processors and distributors of farm products, and went on record in favor of continuance and expansion of government loans on surplus grains stored on farms and in warehouses.

The 1935 convention again reaffirmed faith in the AAA but stressed the need for simplifying its administration. It contended that the program

was formulated by the farmers themselves, acting through their own organizations, and will be protected and defended by the farmers and their friends on the basis of its fairness to agriculture, its beneficial contributions to continued national economic recovery, and in the interest of permanent prosperity for all the economic groups and classes of our nation.[54]

In the 1936 convention, after the Hoosac Mills decision had invalidated portions of the act, the Federation reiterated its support of the objectives sought, stating:

The decision of the Supreme Court on the constitutionality of this legislation made it necessary to alter in essential detail certain policies of administration of the Agricultural Adjustment Act, and to secure the passage of the Soil Conservation and Domestic Allotment Act, but it

did not alter in any way the chief objective of the American Farm Bureau Federation.[55]

Reservations About NRA

With respect to other phases of the administration's program, the Federation expressed some reservations. For example, the 1934 convention demanded elimination of those features of the NRA which "authorize or permit violation of the National Anti-Trust laws by price fixing or otherwise and which continue extreme reduction of industrial and labor production." These, it was contended, operated to increase costs to farmers. The Federation suggested also, in this same communication, that future administration of the NRA be "non-spectacular, semi-judicial, and more protective of the general rather than of special welfare, and [that its functions] be assumed by some well trained federal body such as the Federal Trade Commission."[56]

The Federation favored continuation of the features of the NRA codes that prohibited child labor and sweatshop conditions and those that guaranteed labor the right of collective bargaining. It opposed any further limitation, by law or by code, of the length of the work week or work day.

It thus took somewhat opposite views on the propriety of restrictive policies in nonfarm activities from those which it supported with respect to agriculture. A fully consistent general policy had not emerged and, in fact, has not been formulated in the years since that time. Are monopoly techniques bad in themselves, and should they be prohibited universally, or are they instruments of policy which can and should be used in attaining "good" objectives while being outlawed for use in achieving "bad" objectives? If such a distinction is to be made, what are the appropriate criteria of "good" and "bad" reasons for using methods which rest on monopoly powers?

Monetary Policy Advocated

With regard to monetary policy the Federation came out strongly at its annual meet-

53. Loc. cit.
54. American Farm Bureau Federation, *Proceedings of the 17th Annual Convention*, Chicago, December 1935, p. 118.

55. *Nation's Agriculture*, January 1937, p. 12.
56. *Bureau Farmer* (Nevada Section), January 1935, p. 10.

ng in December 1933 in favor of revaluing he dollar and, later, the establishment of a definite "ratio of purchasing power between he dollar and the index numbers of all commodities. . . . We support the President in his efforts to establish the value of the dollar on the commodity basis and thereafter maintain it on the price index of all commodities."[57] This policy, if it could be made to work, and if the parity-price idea for individual products advocated for agriculture were to be extended to all commodities, would, of course, mean freezing all prices in some prescribed set of relationships.

The opinion was also expressed that it would be desirable to remonetize silver on an index basis so that there might be a larger volume of money in the circulating medium and the nation would be placed in a better position to expand trade with silver-using countries.

This proposal reflects the confused thinking on the part of the farm leaders in respect to the role of the precious metals in the conduct of international trade which was widely prevalent in administration circles at that time. The chief silver-using countries, China and India, were not producers of silver. Hence an increase in the price of silver in the United States, if it caused any flow of silver, would merely operate to reduce the metallic backing of their currencies, thus depressing their internal prices, or possibly forcing them off silver and onto a paper currency basis. That is, in fact, precisely what did happen to China when the Congress and the President put into effect approximately the policies recommended by the Federation in respect to silver.[58]

These views were reiterated at the annual meeting of 1934, and again in 1935. Similar opinions were expressed in 1936, with the added demand that there be established a monetary authority with power to maintain a managed currency based on an index of commodity prices, and having authority to reprice gold and regulate the gold content of the dollar.[59]

Credit Proposals

In the realm of agricultural credit the Farm Bureau claimed, possibly without too adequate a basis, that the Farm Credit Act of 1933 reflected its efforts of the preceding ten years in this realm. It is undoubtedly true, however, that the continuing pressure for improved credit on the part of all the farm organizations, and of many congressional representatives and government administrators as well, laid the groundwork for the expanded and coordinated system that came into being in 1933.

While supporting the new credit program the Farm Bureau expressed frequent criticism of it, and advocated further changes, some of which were made. Among their criticisms was the contention that appraisals were too low, that the flow of funds into agriculture was not fast enough and that the interest rate was too high.[60]

Position on Tariffs

The disastrous decline in demand for agricultural products abroad, together with the increasing influence of Cordell Hull, caused the attitudes of some of the delegations to be modified somewhat in respect to tariff policy.

57. *Bureau Farmer*, January 1934, p. 7.
58. The effects of United States silver purchase policies on the Oriental countries are more fully discussed in James Daniel Paris, *Monetary Policies of the United States, 1932–1938*, Columbia University Press, New York, 1938, Chapter 3. There is also included, pp. 126–30, a chronological summary of the actions relating to silver. The laws and presidential proclamations relating to silver during this period are reproduced in Appendix B. See also Theodore J. Kreps, "The Price of Silver and Chinese Purchasing Power," *Quarterly Journal of Economics*, February 1934, pp. 245–87.
59. It will be recognized from the earlier discussion of the gold problem that in 1933 the Federation was taking essentially the same view as that held by the administration, both being strongly influenced by the ideas advocated by Professors George F. Warren and Irving Fisher. During 1934 and 1935 the administration tended to give less weight to these proposals, but the Farm Bureau leaders continued to espouse them.
60. Other resolutions advocated restoring to farmer-borrowers a larger voice in the management of the system, favored continuance of the 3½ per cent interest rate provided by the Wheeler amendment of 1935 for two more years, and demanded that the charges for inspections and filings be reduced. Liberalization of loans to worthy young men and to efficient tenants was also urged.

The resolutions passed during the years 1933 through 1936 reflect this gradual change in outlook. But the various groups within the Farm Bureau were by no means unanimous in favoring some retreat from the earlier, high-tariff position. The spokesmen for the dairy, poultry, cattle and sheep producers continued adamant in their demands for retention of the tariff levels prescribed in the Hawley-Smoot Act, or for even higher levels. They opposed with all the strength at their command the new procedure in tariff making set up in the Reciprocal Trade Agreements Act of 1934.

On the other hand, large segments of the Farm Bureau constituency mainly concerned with crops produced in excess of domestic requirements were becoming more aware of the adverse effect on their markets resulting from the reduced flow of imports into the United States. The result was a series of compromise resolutions. In its 1933 resolutions the Federation took a strong stand against any reduction in agricultural tariffs, and against the delegation of its tariff-making powers by the Congress to any group that might negotiate reciprocal trade agreements that would be detrimental to agriculture.[61] By the end of 1934 the delegates were willing to state that:

Historically the U.S. is an agricultural exporting nation. The prosperity of the producers of basic farm products has during most of our history been dependent on profitable foreign markets for our surplus production. Our policy of high industrial tariffs coupled with our change in status from a debtor to a creditor nation, has made it impossible for foreign countries to sell enough industrial goods and services to enable them to buy our agricultural products in normal volume.

We are in accord with the purpose of reciprocal trade treaties which is, primarily, to restore agricultural exports by judicious lowering of *industrial tariffs,* thus admitting more goods into this country, and making it possible for us to sell more of our farm products abroad. We insist that this purpose be adhered to in framing

reciprocal trade treaties and that there be *n reduction in present agricultural tariffs on an farm product that would have the effect of hold ing or reducing domestic price levels below par ity on such products.*[62]

This position was reaffirmed in 1935 and 1936. At these times also the Federation contended that "excessive tariffs on industrial products have fostered monopoly and increased the cost of living to an unreasonabl degree."

Conservation Favored

The conservation program also was gaining ground rapidly in farmer thinking during these years. The vigorous propaganda campaign of the Soil Erosion Service, and especially the appalling droughts and dust storms of 1934, were making both farmer and the public acutely conscious of the soil losses that were occurring. The idea of government planning also was gaining ground especially that phase of it which looked to the reacquisition and retirement of lands regarded as too poor for profitable agriculture By December 1935 the Farm Bureau wa ready to come out specifically for a properly balanced and coordinated land-use policy, including the control of erosion, the maintenance of soil fertility and the withdrawal from production of submarginal lands.

Attitude of the National Grange

The policies advocated by the National Grange were in a general way similar to those supported by the Farm Bureau, but reflected some differences in emphasis and under some headings, a more careful spelling out of objectives. The Grange position on farm credit was much the same as that of the Farm Bureau. In the matter of monetary policy it came out with a program of its own, which differed in mechanics but had the same objective as that of the Farm Bureau. This had likewise been true of the differences between the two organizations in

61. At this time also the Federation expressed concern lest the production control program result in reducing production below domestic requirements and thus give over some of the home market to American capital abroad unless "these breaches in the agricultural tariff wall" are closed by the AAA administrators.

62. American Farm Bureau Federation, Official New Letter, December 18, 1934, p. 2.

espect to the two-price plans advocated during the 1920's.

The Grange plan of 1933 proposed that, if the President's gold policy did not produce the desired results, the government issue noninterest-bearing notes to a minimum of $5.00 per capita, and pay its obligations in currency until the price level should reach 100 (1926 = 00). If prices should rise to 103 the currency would be redeemed by issuance of bonds until the price level dropped back to 100.[63]

The 1934 program reiterated this stand. That of 1935 included the proposals previously made, but added one recommending an amendment to the Banking Act of 1935 whereby the Board of Governors of the Federal Reserve system would be given responsibility and authority to manage the currency in such a way as to restore the average price level of 1921-1929, and to stabilize the dollar at that level. This statement of policy was repeated in the 1936 convention.

The mechanism proposed in 1933 was, of course, closely similar to that advocated by the Greenbackers in the early years of Grange activity, and may very possibly have been drawn consciously or unconsciously out of the organization's long history of concern with monetary problems. There is little evidence that the Grange had confidence in the gold devaluation plan as a means of raising prices. It reiterated, in its legislative programs of 1934, 1935, 1936 and 1937, its stand in favor of restoration of the price levels of the 1920's and the maintenance of an "honest dollar," but placed its principal emphasis on the issuance of "noninterest bearing Treasury notes" (greenbacks). By 1936 the emphasis on greenbacks had been modified or replaced by the recommendation for a change in the banking laws to give the Board of Governors of the Federal Reserve system a mandate "to manage the currency in such a way as to restore the average price level obtaining between 1921 and 1929, and then to stabilize

the purchasing power of the dollar at that point."[64]

Grange Position on Land Policy and Tariffs

With respect to land policy the Grange continued its traditional attitude in regard to conservation, turning its attention now more specifically to soils. It opposed turning over the remaining public domain to the states, opposed further expenditures for reclamation until there should be need for the new lands so developed and advocated the purchase of submarginal lands for forest and game reserves and recreation. In its 1935 program it came out strongly for the family farm, and expressed opposition to any policies that would tend to favor the "corporation" farm.[65] The work of the Soil Conservation Service was heartily endorsed.

Speaking of the AAA, after the Hoosac Mills decision, the Grange, like the Farm Bureau, insisted that "its fundamental purpose . . . was sound and must be kept steadily in mind in the framing of a new program. . . ." It did not, however, claim the AAA so specifically as its own as did the Farm Bureau. Just before the adoption of the 1936 Soil Conservation and Domestic Allotment Act, but after the Hoosac Mills decision, the Grange summarized its position, recommending:

1. Appropriations to complete payments under AAA contracts already entered into.
2. Soil conservation through wise rotation of crops and a system of governmental rentals and benefit payments.
3. Faster retirement of submarginal land.
4. Retention and expansion of the Surplus Commodities Corporation to deal with agricultural surpluses.
5. Protection of the American market for American farmers by controlling agricultural imports through permits, which should be available only on a showing of actual need and noncompetition with American farm products. Revision of the Trade Agreements Act to require Senate

---

63. Certain alternatives and modifications were also mentioned. These, however, were in keeping with the general principle stated above.

64. *Legislative Program of the National Grange*, 1936, p. 8. (See annual issues of this pamphlet.)
65. These attitudes reflected in part the fact that the main strength of the Grange was in the northeastern states rather than in the West.

ratification, and repeal of the most-favored-nation clause were also advocated.

Farmers Union Opinions

The Farmers Union seems not to have had a clearly defined central body of policy.[66] Insofar as its attitude can be deduced from the Union's publications they may be summarized roughly as follows:

1. Much emphasis on refinancing agricultural loans, at low rates of interest and with scale-downs in principal.
2. Demands that cost of production be used as the basis for setting price goals, but with no developed plan for carrying out such a policy.
3. A vague proposal, in 1935, for the substitution of income parity for price parity.
4. Insistence that both laborers and farmers must be organized strongly.
5. Advocacy of monetary inflation through increased issue of paper money.
6. Approval of soil conservation measures.
7. Support of more liberal provisions for rural electrification.
8. Criticism of "doles and political patronage" under the relief system.
9. Insistence on the need for tariffs and, if necessary, embargoes to keep out agricultural products if enough produced in this country.

National Cooperative Council's Position

Aside from the general farm organizations, the principal direct medium for expression of farmer attitudes was the National Cooperative Council organized in 1929.[67] This group remained skeptical of extensive intervention in farm affairs by government, and tended for a time to remain aloof from the programs initiated by the AAA. Believing deeply in the desirability of farmer self-help through co-

66. The Union had from its beginning been loosely organized and usually dominated by one or a few leaders. Its traditional reluctance to use or draw on trained personnel is reflected in the poorly formulated views that tended to characterize it previous to and during the period here under review.

67. This organization succeeded the National Council of Cooperative Marketing Associations which was liquidated in 1926. The new Council was formed in 1929, and began operation in January 1930. The name was again changed, in 1939, to the one now used, National Council of Farmer Cooperatives. The organization established a Washington headquarters in the early 1930's, and has come to exercise an important influence on legislation pertaining to agriculture.

operative organization, the Council was dubious even when the government, under the Farm Board and later under the AAA, sought to aid farmers in accomplishing some of the same things that the cooperatives themselves were seeking to do.

The marketing agreement program would, it felt, tend to weaken "legitimate" farmer organized cooperatives unless operated through and by them. Whether right or wrong in this view, the large, well-established farmer cooperative associations have constituted a closely knit core of conservative influence in national thinking in regard to farm programs. However, as the agricultural program developed, in 1933 and thereafter, it became evident that some modification of these earlier attitudes was necessary if the organization was to reflect the thinking of its constituent membership, and to take advantage of such aid as might be forthcoming from the government.

While less fully committed to the new programs than were the Farm Bureau, the Grange and the Farmers Union, the Council through its resolutions, reflected a growing acceptance of them, especially from 1934 on. Its interest continued, however, to be more active in marketing agreements and credit than in the production-control features of the program.

Emphasis on Cooperative Action

As was natural, the Cooperative Council emphasized strongly the enlargement and strengthening of the cooperative movement as a main solution for the farm problem. In its resolutions of January 25 and 26, 1933, it opposed transfer of the functions of the Federal Farm Board to any other agency, and insisted that educational and advisory service to cooperatives be kept in the same agency as that which was charged with making loans to them.[68]

In its January 1934 resolutions, when the transfer had been made, the Council advo-

68. This arrangement was retained when the loaning activities of the Farm Board were transferred to the Farm Credit Administration.

ated, successfully, the establishment within he FCA of a separate Cooperative Division 'charged with the duties of conducting . . . ducational, investigation, service and reearch work under the direction of a deputy cooperative commissioner — to the end that esponsibility for such work may be definitely ixed." It requested also that the Farm Credit Administration reduce the rates of interest on loans made by the banks for cooperatives.[69]

Other Policies Advocated

The Council commended the President for his efforts to restore the purchasing power of the dollar, but without specific reference to the method. It urged that the duties on a number of agricultural products be raised, and that great care be exercised in the negotiation of reciprocal trade agreements so as to avoid displacement of agricultural products grown in the United States by those from other countries. The Council favored a long-time land utilization program including the elimination of marginal lands and curtailment of unneeded cultivated acreages; and the acquisition of additional lands for reforestation, protection of watersheds and other purposes.

The 1935 resolutions of the Cooperative Council continued to reflect an active interest in the loaning activities on farm commodities, though it seemed to be swinging back toward a preference for some plan of price support similar to those proposed in the various McNary-Haugen bills, but with more use of cooperative associations as the medium through which to operate.

Its attitude on land policy was spelled out more fully, with a central thought that enough land should be withdrawn from production to bring about a more reasonable balance between output and demand. New developments in irrigation should be postponed, and all grazing, forest and Indian lands controlled by the Department of the Interior should be transferred to the Department of Agriculture for administration. Careful con-

69. National Cooperative Council, *1934 Bluebook,* p. 14.

sideration of the commodity dollar was recommended, but the idea was not given unqualified backing. The need for caution in the negotiation of trade agreements was again stressed.

The January 1936 resolutions recognized the invalidation of the production control program as a result of the Hoosac Mills decision, but pointed out that the marketing agreement and order provisions were still in effect and should be used; also that Section 32 funds could be used to achieve important benefits for agriculture. The Council reiterated its opposition to the importation of competitive agricultural products and again put itself on record in favor of the creation of centralized pools financed by the growers of commodities concerned, as a means of controlling surpluses (in substance, a revival of the McNary-Haugen idea). It also reasserted its stand in favor of the removal from cultivation of "surplus-producing" acreages.

With respect to foreign trade the Council expressed opposition to the repeal of Section 32, and suggested abandonment of the most-favored-nation principle, holding that only the nations signatory to a reciprocal trade agreement should derive the benefits from it. The retention of authority to establish import quotas was urged. The Council recommended that the commodities exchange legislation, then under consideration, contain provisions insuring the eligibility of producer-owned and producer-controlled cooperatives for full membership in the exchanges.

It reiterated its support of a stable dollar, and went on record in favor of a "monetary authority" with a definite mandate from Congress to establish and maintain a dollar with constant purchasing power. This was to be accomplished by means of a currency regulated in accordance with an index of basic commodities at their world prices, considering gold and silver as commodities and dealing with them in terms of their market values. The means proposed were "by . . . any or all or combinations of any or all of the following: (a) repricing gold; (b) regulating the value of the dollar; (c) declaring the gold content of the dollar; (d) regulating the issuance and volume of currency; and (e) such other powers over money and credit as Congress may see fit to give to it for the accomplishment of the Congressional mandate."[70] The adjustment proposed was to the 1926 level of prices.

Summary of Farm Groups' Attitudes

As a whole, the major farm organizations favored continuance of most features of the "New Deal" agricultural program, insofar as that could be done legally. Most of the credit program was acceptable to them, though there were frequent demands for more liberal lending policies and various minor changes were recommended from time to time. All of the organizations advocated monetary measures to "reflate" the price level, and thereafter to maintain it at a stable level. All advocated the retention of high tariffs on farm products, though the Farm Bureau began at about this time to shift its ground toward a mildly favorable position on reciprocal trade agreements.

The idea of retiring from production sizable acreages of marginal and submarginal lands was popular with all the organizations, though it is clear that they overestimated the effect this was likely to have on output. The main features of the soil conservation program were favored by most farmers and farm organizations, except for those pertaining to the restoration of the ranges in the West. Many cattle and sheepmen were skeptical about the warrant for restrictions placed on numbers of livestock permitted on the ranges, though a good many others felt the program was needed and reasonable.

On the whole the farm organizations tended to follow and support the actions taken by the government planners rather than to initiate new approaches. The Farm Bureau did, it is true, take an active part in the shaping of the programs initiated in 1933. There is considerable indication, however, that the

70. *Ibid., 1936 Bluebook,* Supplement to *Cooperative Journal,* January-February 1936, pp. 33–34.

influence of the long campaign for the McNary-Haugen plan was still strong in the thinking of many farm leaders, and that the ideas for the new programs came more largely out of the imaginative minds of the group of young policy makers in Washington than from the farm organizations. Nevertheless, many parts of the program were the product of joint efforts of both groups.

The Drift Toward Planning

The initial stage of the AAA was almost wholly an emergency undertaking. It was designed to bring about as quickly and effectively as possible a readjustment in output and a pricing program that would reduce the burdensome surpluses then in hand or in prospect, facilitate a flow of purchasing power into the hands of farmers and bring about a better balance between farm and nonfarm prices.

It was soon apparent, however, that straight percentage reductions, applied equally in all areas, must be replaced by some more flexible plan, and that longer-range programs must be worked out.[71] New farmers were constantly coming into the agricultural population, and old ones were going out. Some areas wanted to expand production of given products while others should logically reduce their acreages permanently and turn to other types of farming. Wheat and cotton acreages in particular were overexpanded. A return to less intensive types of agriculture in the wheat areas, where few alternative crops could be grown, presented special difficulties, and the problem of readjustment in the southeastern states involved others that were equally serious, though it was clear that cotton acreage in the older areas would have to be reduced if the new, high-yielding areas of the West were to be allowed to expand.

71. The nature of this longer-range problem is well discussed by Edwin G. Nourse in his article "Fundamental Significance of the Agricultural Adjustment Concept," *Journal of Farm Economics,* May 1936, pp. 244–55. See also the series of discussions by Wilson and others, under the heading "Validity of the Fundamental Assumptions Underlying Agricultural Adjustment," *ibid.,* February 1936, pp. 12–58.

Planning Division Established

To deal with problems of this kind the Secretary established, in the fall of 1933, a Program Planning Division designed to develop long-range plans for the improvement of agriculture. In part its task was to work out a method of transition from the earlier emergency adjustment programs to more flexible plans with more fundamental objectives. It also was intended as a means of coordinating the activities of the various branches of the Adjustment Administration.

When Chester Davis took over as Administrator this division was reorganized and placed under the leadership of H. R. Tolley. By the fall of 1934 the Division consisted of six functioning sections: Land Policy, Production Planning, Import and Export, Agricultural-Industrial Relations, Replacement Crops and Rehabilitation. A Market Planning Section was also contemplated.

The Land Policy Section was to develop a coordinated plan for better use of land resources and work out means for implementing the plan through the various programs of the Department and the states. It was to determine the amounts of land needed for crop production, forest use, etc., and to help in designating areas to be withdrawn from farming. The Production Planning Section was concerned primarily with readjustments needed in the areas cropped and methods of bringing them about.

The Import-Export Section had as its primary function the estimating and planning of future international trade in agricultural products. It was to consider possible ways of expanding foreign outlets, and the relation of the tariff bargaining then being undertaken by the State Department to the price-raising and other activities of the AAA. The functions assigned to the Agricultural-Industrial Relations Section were somewhat vague, but included study of the interactions of the agricultural and nonagricultural programs on each other. The other divisions, as their names imply, had analytical and coordinating functions more closely related to the day-to-day operations of the various agencies of the Department.

Changing Attitudes

The whole AAA program, and especially the creation of a Program Planning Division, marked a considerable shift in attitude on the part of American agriculture from that which had characterized it through most of its history. Settlement efforts during the colonial period had included some degree of conscious planning, especially in New England, Pennsylvania and New York. The later Mormon settlements in Utah had likewise been in accordance with rather carefully worked out plans. In general, however, the development of American agriculture during the entire nineteenth century, and the first third of the twentieth century, had been almost completely planless. Now for the first time the means were at hand for a full-scale effort to modify it in accordance with some concept of how it should be. But there was as yet no settled view as to what such a planned agricultural economy would be like.

In the thinking of most farmers the goal was simple and concrete: the re-establishment of a parity ratio between farm and nonfarm prices, together with a less clearly defined objective of achieving farmer-owned and controlled agricultural marketing and credit systems. Within the Department of Agriculture, however, various other objectives were coming into focus, though there was much divergence of views about them. Nearly all agreed that the cropping systems should be revised to give more emphasis to conservation and the building up of soils. Some felt that the drift toward large-scale, commercial agriculture should be checked and that efforts should be made to retain or restore the relatively small-scale, family-type farm even though at the expense of some loss in efficiency.

Some were content to proceed with existing types of marketing and service agencies while others wanted a rapid and relatively complete shift to cooperative and publicly owned agencies. Sharp differences were apparent as between conservation-minded government people and the livestock and other interests of the West, especially as to appropriate uses of grazing and forest lands, and of lands brought under cultivation through federal reclamation projects. There was also a growing interest within the Department in the possibility of reorienting agricultural production and distribution in such a way as to raise the quality of diets, especially for the lower-income groups both urban and rural.

Planned use of resources is generally accepted under the high emotional drive of war conditions, and tends to be universally recognized as necessary in countries that are desperately short of food and therefore must regulate both production and distribution.

In an economy plagued by unmarketable surpluses, especially one so recently composed of aggressive, individualistic pioneers as the United States, such ideas are not warmly received. Only the desperate conditions faced by farmers in the early 1930's could have induced them to accept as much "regimentation" as they did accept in those years. They still looked back nostalgically to the days when they could produce and sell what they wanted to, and as much as they wanted to. Nevertheless, a major change in public attitudes had occurred as a result of the experiences of these years. Plans and controls were thereafter to be more readily accepted and lived with. This attitude was to be further developed as a result of the intensive general mobilization of resources that characterized World War II.

The Program Planning Division was working in the direction of a comprehensive plan for American agriculture, but did not achieve it. Its major contribution was that of laying the groundwork, and doing the preliminary thinking, that made possible a quick shift to a new type of program when the initial one was tossed into the discard by the adverse ruling of the Supreme Court.

The Hoosac Mills Decision

The principal parts of the original AAA program were abruptly terminated as a result of the Supreme Court's ruling, on January 6, 1936, in *U.S.* v. *Butler,* commonly known as the Hoosac Mills Case.[72] The NRA had been thrown out only a few months earlier through a similar ruling in the Schechter Case. In *U.S.* v. *Butler* a district court had ordered the receiver for the Hoosac Mills Company, then in bankruptcy, to pay certain processing taxes required under the AAA legislation. The case was carried to the Supreme Court, which, in a six-to-three decision, held that "the power to confer or withhold unlimited benefits is the power to coerce or destroy. . . . This is coercion by economic pressure. The asserted power of choice is illusory."[73] The argument presented in the majority opinion was circuitous and somewhat contradictory; and was not highly regarded in legal and congressional circles.[74] Justices Stone, Brandeis and Cardozo registered a vigorous dissent.

Nevertheless, two major features of the AAA program, the power to levy processing taxes and the power to enter into acreage reduction contracts with farmers, were nullified. The initial phase of the "New Deal" agricultural program had come to an end. But neither the farmers nor the legislators were willing to abandon the effort to restore prosperity to agriculture by this or some similar method. A new start under revised legislation and with somewhat different mechanisms and objectives was shortly to take its place.

72. *U.S.* v. *Butler et al., Receivers of Hoosac Mills Corporation,* 297 U.S. 1 (1936).
73. *Ibid.,* p. 71.
74. For a brief critical discussion of the decision see Alfred H. Kelly and Winfred A. Harbison, *The American Constitution, Its Origins and Development,* W. W. Norton, New York, 1948, pp. 738–41.

CHAPTER 14

NEW TACTICS, REVISED STRATEGY

THE EMERGING PROGRAM, 1936–1938

FOLLOWING SO QUICKLY after the action that nullified the National Industrial Recovery Act, the Hoosac Mills decision was a staggering blow to the administration's agricultural leaders.[1] However, they did not accept defeat. Instead, they worked out and presented, in the course of a few short weeks, new legislation designed to avoid the constitutional objections which had brought about nullification of the earlier legislation. This was the Soil Conservation and Domestic Allotment Act of 1936, approved February 29, 1936 (49 Stat. 1148). Prior to passage of this act, the Congress appropriated (February 11, 1936) $296,185,000 for meeting obligations and commitments incurred previously under the Agricultural Adjustment Act of 1933.

The new approach did more than merely side-step the barriers set up by the Supreme Court. It constituted, in effect, a significant

1. An important aftermath of the Schechter and Hoosac Mills decisions was the long and bitter fight on the President's proposal to enlarge the Supreme Court as a means of changing its political complexion. On February 5, 1937, the President recommended to the Congress legislation which would have had the effect of increasing the size of the Supreme Court from nine to fifteen justices (unless some or all of the justices over seventy years of age resigned). Since the new members would be appointed by him, this would in all probability insure favorable action on New Deal legislation, unless at least eight of the original nine justices voted against it. This move was felt by many to be a serious and direct challenge to the integrity and independence of the Court and a bid for almost unlimited power on the part of the President, since he already had virtual control of the Congress. The Democratic members of the Senate split sharply on the issue, with Democratic Senators Burton K. Wheeler of Montana and Carter Glass of Virginia taking leading roles in the opposition. Nearly all of the Republican senators were opposed to the plan. Finally, on July 22, the Senate rejected the Administration bill by a vote of 70 to 20. Though defeated in his frontal attack on the problem, the President soon thereafter gained his main objective through the appointment of new justices, as older members of the Court resigned. Even before these replacements there was some tendency for the Court to take a more conciliatory attitude on legislation sponsored by the administration.

change in tactics and some revision in strategy and objectives. Lessons learned in the hectic first three years were reviewed and considered. Rigidities were reduced, and an effort was made to overcome the criticisms arising from overcentralization of the program. In their efforts to carry on under new legislation and different techniques, the administration leaders had the wholehearted support of most of the farm organizations. The specific ideas in regard to method came, however, not from the farm leaders but from the policy makers of the AAA, particularly its Program Planning Division.

The Administrator's report for 1936 states that:

... instead of terminating the farmers' efforts permanently, the decision of the Supreme Court in the *Hoosac Mills case* had the effect of hastening a transition which had long been planned. This was the transition from the temporary emergency phase of the adjustment programs to a long-time phase which would give a larger place to soil conservation and improved farm-management practice.

Such a transition was originally planned by the Agricultural Adjustment Administration in late 1934 and early 1935. It was the subject of discussions with representatives of farmers, agricultural colleges, and extension workers in a series of regional conferences in 1935.

President Roosevelt in a statement on October 25, 1935, had announced the Administration's intention to shift the program to a long-time basis. Hence the Hoosac Mills decision, when it came, precipitated as a sudden change that which had been planned as a gradual one.[2]

The Court's decision did not affect the marketing agreement provisions of the act nor did it affect directly the Jones-Costigan

2. Agricultural Adjustment Administration, *Agricultural Conservation 1936, A Report of the Activities of the Agricultural Adjustment Administration*, p. 1.

Sugar Act of May 9, 1934, or the Section 32 provision assigning 30 per cent of the customs revenue to the Secretary of Agriculture for use in encouraging exports, removing surpluses and making income payments.

The Soil Conservation and Domestic Allotment Act of 1936[3]

The new legislation was entitled an Act "To promote the conservation and profitable use of agricultural land resources by temporary Federal aid to farmers and by providing for a permanent policy of Federal aid to States for such purposes." Thus it set up, nominally at least, a different objective from that of the Act of 1933. The earlier act specified the establishment of a new balance between agricultural production and consumption such that it would:

. . . reestablish prices to farmers at a level that will give agricultural commodities a purchasing power with respect to articles that farmers buy, equivalent to the purchasing power of agricultural commodities in the base period.

The stated major objective of the one here described was to re-establish

. . . at as rapid a rate as the Secretary of Agriculture determines to be practicable and in the general public interest, . . . the ratio between the purchasing power of the *net income per person on farms* and that of the *income per person not on farms* that prevailed during the five-year period August 1909–July 1914. . . . [Italics supplied.]

This meant a change from a price objective to an income objective. The income criterion, if it could be made workable, would allow prices to fluctuate above and below parity without coming into conflict with the policy objective. That is, a large crop at a lower price and a small crop at a higher price might result in about the same income as an average crop at parity price. The price relationship goal specified in the earlier legislation was almost certain to result in a large accumula-

tion of stocks in years of heavy production and, ultimately, the breakdown of the program. While parity of income was obviously a sounder goal to strive for, the development of workable methods for applying that principle was to prove very difficult.

The act further provided for transferring the field administration of the program to state agencies and county and community committees by the end of 1937, on condition that state legislation acceptable to the Secretary of Agriculture had been passed and put into effect by that date. The funds made available to the Secretary of Agriculture for such purposes were thereafter to be transferred to the states in accordance with allocations and performance records specified by him.[4]

Changes in Procedure

Instead of contracts for acreage adjustment, entered into by the farmer and the Secretary of Agriculture, as provided in the Act of 1933, the new legislation called for the submission of adjustment plans, oriented to conservation objectives, and for payment on submission of proof that the plans had been carried out. Funds for the execution of the program were now to be appropriated by the Congress from the Treasury, instead of being obtained through processing taxes. Annual appropriations of not more than $500 million were authorized.

The procedure for putting the new legislation into effect was to classify crops into two categories, "soil-depleting" and "soil-conserving." In general the "soil-depleting" crops were the cash crops, which it was considered desirable to reduce in amount; that is, such crops as wheat, cotton, corn, tobacco and sugar beets. The "soil-conserving" crops were those which would protect and rebuild soils and which, for the most part, did not con-

---

3. 49 Stat. 1148. Technically this was an amendment to the Soil Erosion Act of April 27, 1935. Its provisions were so broad, however, that it had the significance of a separate act.

4. This feature of the act has not been put into effect. The Congress has from time to time extended the period during which the Secretary of Agriculture may continue to operate the program on a national basis. There has been little effort on the part of the states to bring about the decentralization contemplated at the time the 1936 Act was passed.

tribute directly to the burdensome surpluses of commercially handled farm products. Among these were the grasses, legumes and other forage crops. Under this plan farmers were to be paid for shifting specified percentages of their acreages of "soil-depleting" crops into "soil-conserving" crops, the payments averaging about $10 per acre. In addition, payments might be made for approved soil-building practices such as the application of fertilizer, turning under of green manure, and so on. These payments were to be limited to $1.00 for each acre of "soil-conserving" crops grown on the farm.

The Adjustment Administration was now reorganized on a regional rather than a commodity basis, with five regional divisions each under a director.[5] Certain of the functional divisions were retained, namely, Marketing and Marketing Agreements, Finance, Program Planning and Consumers' Counsel.

Conservation a Secondary Objective

The new act was in many respects a stop-gap measure, rushed through hurriedly in order that the continuity of aid to agriculture not be broken as a result of the Supreme Court's decision. As a consequence, it was limited to bare essentials. Many of the more troublesome problems were deferred for later consideration.

The shift in orientation from prices to soil conservation was largely an expedient, designed to retain authorization for making payments to farmers. It was put forward on the basis of the more popular soil conservation objective rather than the less popular one of raising prices. The price argument was, in fact, a weak one. The reductions in output had brought farm prices up to more than 90 per cent of parity. The unsatisfactory level of farm income was largely a result of low production, not of low prices.

The widespread hardship and appalling devastation caused by the drought of 1934 had created a public receptiveness to soil conserva-

tion measures such as had never existed before. Also the active propaganda carried on by the Soil Erosion Service and its successor, the Soil Conservation Service, had brought about widespread interest in this problem. Consequently, a program that could be justified as a conservation measure had a better prospect of achieving congressional and public acceptance than one designed to raise prices.

While the new program had much to commend it as a means of stimulating farmer interest in conservation, and showing how it could be accomplished, it seems clear that this was not actually the major purpose of the sponsors of the new legislation. Their interest in this was primarily as a device for cutting down production of the major cash crops and transferring income to farmers, without running afoul of the legal objections raised by Supreme Court.[6] Nevertheless, much effective adjustment which resulted in better soil management was accomplished.

There was urgent need for increased awareness on the part of farmers of the problem of soil deterioration. However, if soil conservation had been the primary objective, it would have seemed logical to expand and modify the work of the Soil Conservation Service, a principal agency already established for that purpose. Its program, however, did not contemplate a gentle shower of federal checks evenly and undiscriminatingly distributed over eroding and noneroding areas alike. Neither did it contemplate paying farmers to do things that obviously were in their own interest to do. It sought rather to stimulate them to take the kinds of action dictated by their own best interests and those of society as a whole.

Nevertheless, it is unquestionably true that many of these things could be and were accomplished more quickly and possibly more effectively through use of incentive payments

5. Northeastern, East Central, Southern, North Central and Western, plus an Insular Division for administering the off-shore areas.

6. It is probable, however, that the program would have been reoriented by 1937 even if there had been no adverse Court ruling, and if there had been no advance planning by the Program Planning Division. The recovery in farm prices and incomes would have made it hard to justify a continuing program based on the original AAA legislation.

and bonuses. Furthermore, substantial readjustments in the acreages of certain feed and export crops were needed as a means of bringing about a better balanced pattern of agricultural production.

While the 1936 Act was acceptable as a stopgap, it did not satisfy the aspirations of either the farm groups or administration leaders. Shortly thereafter the Congress began work on more carefully considered long-term legislation which was to take shape in the Agricultural Adjustment Act of 1938.

Commodity Exchange Legislation

Having dealt with the most urgent features of the agricultural emergency, the Congress now began to consider problems of longer-term significance. Among the first to be taken up was the perennial complaint of farmers about the activities of the commodity exchanges. Regulation of the grain and livestock exchanges had been a prominent feature of farmer demands for many decades.

A start in the direction of commodity exchange control had been made in the Packers and Stockyards Act of 1921 and the Grain Futures Act of 1922, but farmers were by no means satisfied with the results. There was especially vigorous and justifiable criticism of the situation in the markets for perishables, which had not been covered at all in the earlier legislation. Here the problem of financial responsibility of firms handling perishable farm products on consignment was a serious one. If a consignee failed to make payment, the farmer had little recourse except through an expensive and probably impractical court action. Furthermore, the shipper had little protection against unwarranted claims of deterioration in products of this kind.

By an amendment of June 15, 1936, the Grain Futures Act was broadened and modified. The name of the administering agency was changed to Commodity Exchange Commission, and the coverage was extended to include cotton, rice, millfeeds, butter, eggs and potatoes.

The amendment strengthened and clarified the earlier control legislation in numerous ways. Commission merchants and brokers were required to register with the Department of Agriculture and to keep adequate records which must be available to the Department on demand. The Commission was given broad authority to limit speculative trading, prevent fraud and safeguard margin funds and other properties of customers. The cooperative associations achieved a long-sought objective through the provision in the new legislation that no cooperative association should be excluded from membership in the exchanges unless such exclusion was authorized, after hearing, by the Commission; and further that no contract market should forbid payment of patronage dividends to bona fide members.

This legislation closed a long-recognized gap in the public's control over the marketing of agricultural commodities.[7] Scandals in the handling of various products, especially perishables, had been a frequent cause of farmer complaint. Now for the first time the Department of Agriculture had suitable powers and organization for correcting such abuses. The commodity exchange legislation had little or nothing to do with the agricultural "emergency" or the general level of agricultural income, but was rather a segment in the long-time program of reforms advocated by the farm groups. In this respect it was more in keeping with the pre-1914 aspirations of agriculture than with the major legislative program of the 1930's.

Condition of Agriculture, 1936

The three years during which the first AAA program was in effect had seen marked changes in the agricultural situation. A vast refinancing operation had been carried out. Most of the heavily mortgaged farms had been refinanced by 1936, or had been lost to their former owners and now were relatively debt-free in the hands of creditors. Many of

7. The methods provided for carrying out the purposes of the act are described in Commodity Exchange Administration, *Report of the Chief . . . , 1937*, pp. 15–20.

the farms taken over by creditors had, of course, been resold to new owner-operators but on a basis of lower prices and smaller indebtedness.

Cash income from farm marketings had nearly doubled as compared to the low point in 1932, the rise being from $4.7 billion to $8.4 billion. Farm expenses were up about $1 billion. Prices had advanced sharply, in part through the operation of the various agricultural programs but mainly because of the drought of 1934 and the gradual recovery in the nonfarm economy. By 1936 the level of farm prices was up to 114 and was to go still higher, to 122 in 1937. Thereafter, it fell off to less than 100 and did not recover significantly until the war influence began to be felt in 1941.[8]

The principal influence causing these changes was reduced production, due mainly to drought. In terms of the 1935–1939 base as 100, food grain production in 1931 reached 114. This dropped to 64 in 1934 and was only up to about 80 in 1935 and 1936. Feed grains and hay declined even more sharply — from 113 in 1932 to 41 in 1934. Cotton production likewise was down — from 128 in 1931 to 74 in 1934. Here the crop reduction program of the AAA undoubtedly exerted more influence. The effect of the drought was apparent in the yields of most other crops, but not so markedly as in the food and feed grains. The burdensome stocks of wheat that existed at the close of the Farm Board period were down from the 378 million bushels of 1933 to 140 million in 1936, and declined still further to 83 million in 1937.[9] Corn stocks also fell to very low levels, particularly in 1935 and 1937. The cotton carry-over had likewise been reduced substantially from the high levels of 1933, though not so markedly as the grains.[10]

On the other hand, the production of livestock and livestock products held up strongly during this period, reaching a level of 106 in 1934 (1935–1939 = 100). The effects of the drought of 1934 became apparent in 1935, when production fell off to 93. There was a a recovery to 101 in 1936. The heavy sales of livestock and livestock products were a considerable factor in the improved agricultural income of this period since, unlike the grains, the higher prices received were for relatively large volumes.[11]

Recovery Not Solely in Agriculture

The recovery was not confined to agriculture, nor to the agricultural products specifically curtailed under the AAA programs. Nonfarm incomes rose substantially. In agriculture itself the meat animals, for example, practically doubled in price though cattle and sheep were not under control programs. Fruits and truck crops experienced significant price increases though not such large ones. They had not fallen to such low levels in the first years of the depression.[12] Some of these were affected by marketing agreements, but many were not.

On the whole, it would appear that agriculture was sharing in a general recovery which was to reach its peak for the decade in 1937. The droughts and resulting short crops had strengthened agriculture's position within the economy pricewise and incomewise. Its parity income ratio, based on 1910–1914 relationships, passed the 100 mark in 1935, in which year it stood at 107. After receding to 99 in 1936 it was again up to 107 in 1937. This did not mean that agriculture was prosperous. The whole economy was operating at a low level, and there still was a good deal of unemployment. Total national income was up only to $64.7 billion in 1936 as compared to $87.4 billion in 1929.[13]

Nevertheless, many of the painful readjust-

8. *Agricultural Statistics, 1950,* pp. 628, 636.

9. *Ibid., 1945,* p. 19.

10. 1932–1933 carry-over — 9,678,000 bales; 1935–1936 — 7,208,000 bales. *Ibid., 1937,* p. 93.

11. The price index for livestock and livestock products rose from 72 (1909–1914 =100) in 1933 to 120 in 1936. Food grains during the same period rose from 66 to 108, and feed grains and hay from 57 to 102. Cotton was up from 66 to 95. *Ibid., 1945,* p. 430.

12. Fruits rose from 70 in 1933 to 92 in 1936; truck crops from 91 to 104. *Loc. cit.*

13. U.S. Department of Commerce, *National Income, 1951 Edition,* A Supplement to the *Survey of Current Business,* p. 150.

ments necessary to a sustained recovery had been made. The economy was operating on a lower level of prices; much of the burden of debt left from the inflation years of the late 1920's had been liquidated, compromised or refinanced; and the top-heavy accumulations of storable farm products no longer hung over the markets.

A part of the improved income to agriculture was a result of transfers from nonfarm to farm people by way of the federal programs, that is, through subsidies financed by means of processing taxes — but this was not a major part of the increase. Such direct transfers amounted to $446 million in 1934 and to $573 million in 1935.[14] There was, however, a very substantial input of federal funds in other forms which are difficult or impossible to measure. Sizable relief grants had been made to farm families, nonrecourse loans had been provided, and large-scale cattle purchases were made in the drought-stricken areas. In addition, very large amounts had gone to agriculture in the form of loans through the Farm Credit Administration, to replace private funds withdrawn. Agriculture thus was the beneficiary both of the general economic recovery and of a variety of governmental programs and natural phenomena which put it, relatively, in the best position it had held since 1919.

Sensational Programs Abandoned

By 1936 the administration had abandoned its more sensational general recovery programs, such as the NRA and the manipulation of the gold value of the dollar, and had launched a far-reaching program of longer-term reform measures relating to labor relations, taxation, public utilities, and so forth.[15]

Most of these had little direct bearing on agriculture, and hence are omitted or mentioned only in passing. More and more the device of large-scale deficit spending was coming to be relied on as the major weapon for stimulating general recovery, and as a means of preventing acute want both in the farm and nonfarm areas.

The program was becoming more adequately organized and supervised, and included more projects of the make-work type. However, it still was subject to widespread criticism because of loose administration, political abuses and the continuing drain on the treasury. In his annual budget message of January 3, 1935, the President asked for $4 billion for giving work to employables. This was to be an addition to the public debt, while all other expenses of the government were to be met from current income. The Works Progress Administration was to be established, and unemployables were to be transferred to local relief agencies. The program thereby made possible was thereafter to constitute the major attack on the depression while other measures would look to more lasting reforms.[16]

The Election of 1936

The eventful years between 1930 and 1936 brought major changes in the nation's political structure. The tremendous dislocations that resulted from the depression shook confidence in the old leadership profoundly. There still was a widespread tendency to

14. Agricultural Statistics, 1945, p. 438.
15. The United States News commented in March 1937:
"The pains of deflation in early 1933 have given way to fears of inflation in 1937. Worry over loss of gold is replaced by acute worry over the seemingly endless accumulations of gold. Instead of staying up nights to figure out ways to generate more and more dollars to manage, officials now are staying up nights trying to figure out ways to manage the dollars they have generated."
Between January 1934 and December 1936, United

States monetary gold stocks increased from $6.8 billion to $11.3 billion; those of France declined from $5.1 billion to $2.9 billion; Germany's from $152 million to $27 million; and Holland's from $628 million to $389 million (in November 1936. They had increased again to $491.5 million by December). Federal Reserve System, Banking and Monetary Statistics, National Capital Press, Washington, November 1943, pp. 546–52. Thus there was a marked tendency for gold to be drained out of other countries and concentrated in the United States. This constituted a threat of inflation in the United States at the same time that it was causing concern abroad over the dangers of deflation. To guard against the possibilities of inflation in the United States, the Federal Reserve Board raised the proportion of reserves that banks must keep against deposits, thus in part offsetting the effect of the gold-buying program.
16. Congressional Record, 74th Cong., 1st sess., January 7, 1935, p. 145.

blame Hoover personally for what had occurred, and through him, the Republican party. The idea that he had made little effort to alleviate the distress and calm the fears of a disorganized people was sedulously fostered by an army of political appointees and by all left-wing groups.

More important, however, was the fact that Roosevelt's own personality had made a tremendous impression on the "common man" in groups previously not much regarded in political circles. He had brought about a renewed confidence of the people in themselves and had advocated positive programs, which, even if experimental and perhaps unsuccessful, seemed preferable to what was regarded as a do-nothing attitude on the part of the previous administration.

The new program appealed especially to labor, and to the young groups who began to feel hope that the world would somehow make a place for them. Older workers and the unemployed came to feel that the administration would find ways to look after them; and Negroes, for the first time since the post-Civil War days, felt that they were to be given a more satisfying place in the social and economic structure. The middle western and western farm groups, traditionally Republican, were likewise convinced that their desires were receiving a more sympathetic hearing at the White House than in the pre-Roosevelt days.

These factors, together with a very real measure of recovery, led to the overwhelming defeat of Landon, the weak Republican candidate, in the 1936 elections. Roosevelt polled 60.7 per cent of the popular vote and received all of the electoral votes except the eight from Maine and Vermont. The Republican party was shattered. No longer could it count on the labor vote, the Negro vote, the young vote or even the farm vote. Granting that patronage, federal funds and federal personnel were used skillfully and ruthlessly in achieving these results, it is evident that a major shift in political loyalties had occurred, and the Republican party would not again achieve ascendancy without a long, hard

struggle and the development of new leaders and new policies.

Marketing Agreement and Sugar Acts of 1937

During 1937 two supplemental agricultural acts were passed. The first of these was the Agricultural Marketing Agreement Act of 1937, approved on June 3.[17] This method of aiding agriculture had not been invalidated by the Hoosac Mills decision. However, it was deemed advisable to obtain specific congressional reaffirmation of those segments of the act still in effect, and specific disclaimer of any authority to levy and collect processing taxes. The new act also restated and broadened the definition of what would constitute interstate commerce in agricultural commodities. This was now made to read as follows:

For the purpose of this Act . . . a marketing transaction in respect to an agricultural commodity or the product thereof shall be considered in interstate or foreign commerce if such commodity or product is part of that current of interstate or foreign commerce usual in the handling of the commodity or product whereby they, or either of them, are sent from one State to end their transit, after purchase, in another, including all cases where purchase or sale is either for shipment to another State or for the processing within the State and the shipment outside the State of the products so processed. Agricultural commodities or products thereof normally in such current of interstate or foreign commerce shall not be considered out of such current through resort being had to any means or device intended to remove transactions in respect thereto from the provisions of this Act.[18]

The Sugar Act of 1937 was likewise a readjustment designed to bring the legislation in line with the Court's position in the Hoosac Mills decision. Since the Jones-Costigan Sugar Act was not a part of the Agricultural Adjustment Act of 1933, it was not specifically invalidated. Nevertheless, some features of it were regarded as vulnerable. A congressional resolution had been passed on June 19, 1936, continuing in force the quota

17. 50 Stat. 246.
18. *Loc. cit.,* p. 248.

provisions of the Jones-Costigan Act, until December 31, 1937. It also provided for discontinuing the processing tax and contract provisions.

The new act, approved September 1, 1937, provided for the imposition of quotas on domestic and off-shore production and on imports.[19] Benefit payments up to 60 cents per hundred pounds of sugar were authorized, provided quotas were not exceeded, minimum standards of wage were paid and child labor was eliminated. The act also levied a one-half cent excise tax to be paid directly into the Treasury, and authorized an appropriation of $55 million for payment of the specified benefits to producers.

Low-Income Farm Groups

Until after 1933 comparatively little concern was expressed about the large group of farmers who for one reason or another were in the lowest bracket of farm incomes whether in good times or bad. Such a group has existed since the country first began to be settled. In earlier times, when most farmers were largely self-sufficient, the contrast between these and other farm families was not so marked. Each family lived largely on what it itself produced in form for consumption. Families that were shiftless, unskillful or located on poor land, produced little and lived poorly. Their more efficient and better located fellow farmers lived comfortably but simply, buying little and selling little.

But very early in our history the more progressive farmers began to develop commercial types of agriculture and to raise their standards of living. This tendency increased by leaps and bounds as the railroad network grew and horse- and tractor-powered machinery came into use, and especially as settlement spread into the plains areas where self-sufficient agriculture was virtually impossible. Meanwhile farmers in poor areas, those on poor farms in good areas, and likewise those who were not able to forge ahead with

19. 50 Stat. 903.

their more prosperous neighbors fell far behind in the competitive struggle.

They did not share in the increase of material well-being that raised the levels of farm living over much of the nation's countryside. In some large areas most farmers have continued to be largely self-sufficient and to live close to the margin of subsistence. These localities came to be known in the parlance of the 1930's as "problem areas." Some were in commercial crop areas, but more generally they were in regions like the Southern Appalachians where agriculture had changed little since pioneer times, or were operated by especially disadvantaged groups such as the cotton croppers of the South. Still other groups of farm people had no specific ties with a particular piece of land and were homeless, migrant farm wageworkers.

Until the Great Depression brought out more clearly the backwardness of these groups little thought was given to their plight, and, in fact, many of them were scarcely aware of it themselves. But the depression reduced the values of their small sales to a point where even their meager requirements could not be met, and the generalizing of relief payments made many of them eligible for relief who had never before thought of applying for such aid. For almost the first time in our history great numbers of farm families were on relief, and the public was brought face to face with a problem that had previously been largely in the background.

The growing proportion of tenant farmers had, on the other hand, been a prominent topic in farm policy discussions for several decades. But the tenants to which these discussions related were not, generally speaking, farmers of the subsistence type. For the most part they were commercial farmers, able to hold their own in modern competitive agriculture if they could gain ownership of suitable farms. Large numbers of the lowest-income farm families did, in fact, own their farms, but such small, poor or underequipped farms that the making of a decent living on them was virtually impossible.

Growing Concern Over Tenancy

The 1930 and 1935 censuses revealed a situation in which more than 40 per cent of the nation's farms were operated by tenants.[20] In some rich farming areas more than 60 per cent were in this class. Many former owner-operators had lost their farms in the early years of the depression and now were operating as tenants — some even as wage laborers.

Concern over the increasing percentage of farms operated by tenants had been expressed repeatedly by the farm groups from about 1910 onward. The creation of the Federal Land Bank system was one of the early attempts to alleviate the situation, but it had been quite ineffective as a means to that end. The sharp increase in tenancy shown by the 1935 census therefore served to focus attention sharply on this problem.

Much of the growth of tenancy from 1900 on was due to the increasing amount of capital required for ownership of a farm adequate for successful commercial agriculture and the expensive equipment required for its operation. Except as he inherited it, the young farmer could scarcely expect to accumulate quickly the small fortune required for a substantial commercial farm. Hence, he chose to associate his labor and his limited capital with land owned by someone else.

The major difficulty was not so much that many farmers were tenants as that the laws governing landlord-tenant relations were inadequate, and rental arrangements bad. Security of tenure was lacking, and, as a result, there existed little incentive for tenants to farm well, to build up soils or to plan for the future.

Problems Often Confused

The problems thus posed, though often lumped together, were really of three categories — those relating to the improvement of tenure arrangements; those having to do with

20. Some reservation must be attached to this figure because of the traditional census practice of classifying each cropper-operated unit as a tenant farm. Many of the croppers, perhaps as many as 500,000, could be more properly classed as wageworkers paid in kind. Nevertheless, whether classed as tenants or as laborers, they constituted a problem class from the standpoint of income.

small, poor subsistence farms, and with cropper types of tenancy; and those arising with respect to the migrant farm wageworker. Each was quite different and called for a different kind of program if significant improvement was to be made.

The efforts of the Resettlement Administration to move people off submarginal lands, and to rehabilitate farmers on relief or likely to go on relief, brought to public attention the extremely low levels of living in what has since come to be called the "poverty fourth" of agriculture. Here was a group scarcely touched by the main agricultural programs. Since it produced little for market, an improvement or even a disastrous decline in prices did not affect it greatly. Neither could its condition be bettered importantly by benefit or rental payments since the acreages to which these would apply would be small and the payments insignificant. The real need was either to increase the ability of these farmers to produce for the market, or to shift them out of agriculture into occupations where their efforts would be more remunerative. Shifting them out of agriculture was hardly practical when unemployment was still widespread in the cities. Increasing their abilities and resources was to prove a difficult and baffling task.

The third group, the migrant farm wageworkers, presented one of the most difficult problems of all. Such a group had existed, especially in the Pacific Coast states, since very early times, but it had now come to be differently constituted and far harder to deal with.

Although these problems were of long standing, all of them had been greatly intensified by the desperate poverty engendered by the depression and more especially by the unprecedented droughts of 1934 and 1936. Tens of thousands of destitute farm families were on the move, seeking escape from areas where the droughts had left them no prospects of making a living, or where the tractor and related equipment had made their services unnecessary.

The hastily contrived Resettlement Administration proved unpopular both in Congress and with people in the affected farm areas. Little progress was being made in settling the hordes of migrants moving into California and other western states, or in solving the problems of the receiving areas that were being inundated by these floods of newcomers. Housing was unavailable, school facilities were inadequate and work opportunities were scattered and insufficient. Wages were low even for the part-time work that could be obtained.

The Farm Tenancy Committee

With a view to devising some more orderly attack on these problems, the President appointed, in November 1936, a study group known as the President's Farm Tenancy Committee, with instructions that it submit by February 1 recommendations for "a long-term program of action to alleviate the shortcomings of our farm tenancy system."

This Committee, consisting of about forty prominent citizens working under the chairmanship of the Secretary of Agriculture, submitted its report about the middle of February 1937. The report listed as farm groups that lacked adequate security the following:

Tenants
Croppers
Farm laborers
Families on submarginal land
Families on holdings of inadequate size
Owner families hopelessly in debt, and
Farm young people unable to obtain farms.

In its opening summary the Committee stated the problem as follows:

Half a century ago one of every four farmers was a tenant. Today two of every five are tenants. They operate land and buildings valued at $11,000,000,000.

For the past 10 years the number of new tenants every year has been about 40,000. Many change farms every 2 or 3 years, and apparently one out of three remains no longer than 1 year.

Thousands of farmers commonly considered owners are as insecure as tenants, because in some areas the farmers' equity in their property is as little as one-fifth.

Fully half the total farm population of the United States has no adequate farm security.

The above facts reveal something of the magnitude of the farm-tenancy problem in the United States. We have to deal with abuses that have been developing for two centuries. We cannot correct them overnight. But we can begin.

We can and should proceed as rapidly as our resources of manpower, money, and experience will permit. At the same time we should recognize that today we do not have the experience or the trained personnel to make it practical to start the program on a scale as big as the problem would apparently warrant. The responsibility for action by State and Federal Governments is clear. The first start should not be too ambitious, but expansion later should be as rapid as experience demonstrates to be feasible.[21]

The causes of insecurity were listed as:

Economic maladjustment
Defective land and credit policies
Consequences of fee-simple ownership, and
Credit disabilities.

Recommendations for action were of two general types: one, those designed to facilitate "movement upward from rung to rung [of the agricultural ladder] by farmers who are prepared to take such steps"; and, two, steps looking to the "increase [of] security on each of the ladder's various rungs." It was suggested that the Resettlement Administration, recently transferred to the Department of Agriculture, be renamed the "Farm Security Administration," and that it be given the task of carrying out such of the recommendations as might be accepted and authorized by the Congress.

Owner-Operation Overstressed

The "land for tenants" program, which was given first place in the Committee recommendations, was poorly conceived and unlikely to exert any rapid or significant in-

21. President's Committee on Farm Tenancy, *Farm Tenancy*, National Resources Committee, Washington, February 1937, p. iv. The tenancy situation of this period and earlier is well analyzed in an article by John D. Black and R. H. Allen, "The Growth of Farm Tenancy in the United States," *Quarterly Journal of Economics*, May 1937, pp. 393–425. See also Chamber of Commerce of the United States, *Farm Tenancy in the United States*, Washington, April 1937.

fluence on the tenancy problem. The Committee had recognized that the American emphasis on ownership in fee simple was an important cause of the destructive type of agriculture carried on on many farms, but proceeded to recommend more of the same. It proposed that the federal government purchase and reorganize suitable farm lands and resell them to tenant farmers with a view to establishing them as owner-operators. Such sales were to be made final only after a trial lease period of five years.

This approach was entirely in keeping with traditional American thinking, but it ran counter to the experience and tendencies in nearly all of the more advanced older countries. America, a nation only recently emerged from a long period of pioneer settlement when enormous and rich unused land resources were available, was seeking to return to policies that were practical and desirable during a pioneer stage, rather than to adjust itself realistically to the conditions existing in a highly developed country.

If large numbers of tenants were to be aided to become owners, through special purchase arrangements at discriminatory low rates of interest and unusually favorable terms, the result was bound to be a major inflationary impact on land prices which might well nullify expected advantages of the program. Furthermore, a purchase program that would touch the problem significantly was bound to require far larger appropriations than the Congress was at all likely to approve. Such purchases could not be expected to afford any permanent solution, since a farm so purchased would eventually again come on the market and the whole process would have to be repeated.

If only small appropriations were made, the great mass of tenants would be unaffected and no significant gains could result. This would mean singling out a few of the more promising tenants, those most likely to succeed in climbing the agricultural ladder anyway, and providing them with special low-interest, long-term loans.

The values of efficient farm units had by now become too large for immediate purchase by the young farmer with nothing but his bare hands and a team of horses, such as the ones who hewed out of the wilderness the pioneer farms of earlier days. Farming of a kind that would yield a satisfactory living was now a commercial enterprise involving an investment comparable to that of many small urban businesses. Nevertheless, it was highly important that young farmers be enabled to associate their skills, managing abilities and physical vigor with larger amounts of capital than they could well expect to own at that stage of life.

This could be done through borrowing, provided the farmer had sufficient equity; or it could be done through rental of land, possibly accompanied by borrowing on a smaller scale. Both procedures accomplished about the same result, but purchase involved larger risk for the young farmer, the sinking of his small equity in land when it would perhaps have been more productive in the form of operating capital used on a larger farm, and the very real likelihood that he would associate himself with a farm too small for efficient operation.

Tenancy Laws Inadequate

The problem was not that these were tenant farms. It was that conditions of tenancy were bad, perhaps among the worst in the world. The tenant had no security of tenure, little incentive to improve and build up the farm and an unsatisfactory status in the community. The laws governing landlord-tenant relationships were, and still are, almost entirely contained in state codes rather than federal. Such limited amounts of legislation as existed centered almost wholly on the protection of the landlord in making secure his claims on the tenant. There were few provisions giving the tenant any claims to tenure beyond the one year to which most tenancy contracts were limited. Improvements made by the tenant could not be recaptured by him, except as they might be returned during his occupancy.

This made it impractical for the tenant to

build up the more continuing types of agriculture such as those based on advanced types of livestock production. Many landlords tended to require emphasis on cash crops to a degree that contributed to rapid deterioration of soils, feeling that the best prospect of profit was to exploit the land, and then sell it, hoping in the meantime for speculative profit.

These were conditions that could be corrected by general laws passed either by the states or, if constitutional difficulties could be overcome, by the federal government itself. But an approach along these lines would have required a profound readjustment from the pioneer attitude which more or less assumed that every tenant would eventually become an owner. It would have called for recognition of the fact that America was now a developed country and that many tenants would undoubtedly remain in that status throughout their lives. Such a change in outlook could not be brought about quickly, but, even so, the prospect of significant influence on the conditions of tenancy through general regulatory legislation would appear to have been more promising than from a tenant-purchase program with such amounts of funds as were then in prospect.

Credit Not Enough

The Committee did, in fact, recognize the inadequacy of credit alone to solve the problem. It commented:

. . . important as it is to improve the credit arrangements available to farmers, it should be recognized that unrestricted ownership, achieved by farmers assuming a heavy short-term debt load, would likely prove even less permanent than under the homestead acts. There would be no safeguards against land speculation and the subsequent development of absentee ownership and tenancy.

Such measures would also fail to provide adequately for soil conservation. Even if clauses were inserted in mortgage contracts to insure soil conservation, the only means of enforcement would be through the slow and costly process of foreclosure. Frequently the courts will not grant such relief unless the violation of contract takes the form of failure to make payments.

In many areas, moreover, there is lack of a sufficient number of holdings of the proper size and with suitable improvements to serve as family farms. Easy credit would not achieve the readjustments in size and type of holdings that appear necessary in such areas . . .

Similarly, the ignorance, poverty, malnutrition, morbidity, and social discriminations by which many farm tenant families are handicapped cannot be eliminated by converting tenants into farm owners under some system of easy credit . . .

The changes proposed in succeeding pages of this report are offered by the Committee in the belief that a land-tenure system is essentially man-made, and is subject to reasonable alteration, repair, and renovation. It is not an impossible task for a Nation as large, as rich, and as progressive as this one to work out a set of relationships which will assure farmers fair security in the occupancy and operation of farms, freedom from undue restraint and exploitation, and a reasonably adequate livelihood; and which will assure the Nation maintenance of its natural resources and increased stability and enrichment of its rural community life.

The achievement of these aims, however, is not an overnight task. Abuses in our system of land tenure and scheme of rural organization have been developing for two centuries. A long period of continuous and consistent effort confronts us in accomplishing the task proposed in this report. Most civilized nations have set their hands to a similar undertaking, and some of them have been engaged in it for many years. It is high time that this Nation begin the task.[22]

Despite these reservations the Committee's report called for a purchase program with long-term, low-interest loans, and side-stepped the problem of obsolete and inadequate tenancy laws. The proposed "Farm Security Administration" was to administer the program, and modest beginning appropriations, to be expanded later, were recommended. It should be noted, however, that the number of tenant farmers was increasing at the rate of about 40,000 per year. Hence, at least this many tenants would have to be converted into owner-operators each year before any start could be made in reducing the amount of tenancy. Also, since preference was to be given to tenants with a reputation for integrity, industry and thrift, and with neces-

22. President's Committee on Farm Tenancy, *Farm Tenancy*, p. 8.

sary experience, health and other qualities, this meant aiding the ones least in need of special help, and leaving the great mass of tenant-operators unaffected. Furthermore, it was not clear how enough suitable farms were to be found if landlords did not choose to sell.

Proposals for Rehabilitation

For those farmers in danger of losing their farms through foreclosure the Committee recommended aid in working out with the creditors some adjustment of their debts, help in refinancing and, if necessary, technical counsel and guidance. To provide such technical counsel and guidance, and to aid some 1⅓ million tenants who were on relief, handicapped through lack of operating capital or forced to borrow at ruinously high rates of interest, a program of rehabilitation was recommended.

The rehabilitation program, to be administered by the Farm Security Administration, was to consist of special type loans limited to those who could not obtain adequate credit at reasonable cost through regular commercial channels. Such loans were to be accompanied by supervision and the working out of farm plans which would look to establishing the family on a self-supporting basis.[23]

This approach, while exceedingly difficult to carry out effectively, offered far more promise of reaching and helping those most in need of such help than did the proposal for purchase loans to be granted to superior tenants. The educational aid provided to farmers through the regular agricultural extension services of the agricultural colleges had from the beginning been limited largely to the abler, more progressive farmers. These were the ones who tended to consult the farm advisers on their own initiative, and to accept and put into practice the improved methods recommended by the extension personnel. Moreover, they were the ones likely to have influence and to be able to aid in gaining support for the work.

For the poor and unsuccessful farmers different methods and separate personnel were needed. Farmers of this type did not as a rule seek educational aid, or use it effectively if it was brought to them in the usual ways. Here then was a proposal for a new and more aggressive attack on the problems of this group. By making the acceptance of guidance and supervision a condition for obtaining loans and grants, the prospect for upgrading them and graduating them into a more normal farming status was greatly improved.

Other Recommendations

The urgent problem of farm wageworkers was touched on only briefly because of the limited time available to the Committee and the lack of adequate data. The provision of temporary housing by the Farm Security Administration was recommended for those areas where migrant workers were numerous. Such action had already been initiated by the Resettlement Administration.[24]

Recommendation was also made that the plan of purchasing and retiring submarginal lands be continued over a long period of years on a scale involving retirement of 2 million to 5 million acres per year. It was estimated that approximately 500,000 farm families were located on lands unsuitable for settlement.[25] It was proposed also that a federal capital gains tax be applied to profits from

23. The plan as actually put into effect included in addition outright grants, where needed, as well as loans.

24. The report also suggested the provision of small subsistence farms, and called attention to the fact that these workers, in general, did not benefit from the federal and state legislation in behalf of other workers, such as the provisions for collective bargaining, unemployment, accident and old-age insurance, etc.

25. This proposal reflects some lack of understanding of the nature of the problem presented by such lands. Poor lands are not necessarily unprofitable to operate. They do, however, need to be operated extensively in relatively large units. Where settlement in the form of small farms had occurred, the incomes and living conditions of the occupants were usually substandard, and likely to deteriorate still further because of the high birth rates that characterized such areas. However, the problem of extensifying their agriculture, creating larger units and maintaining the improved pattern of agricultural production thus brought about is extremely difficult. It may, in fact, be impossible to accomplish except under public ownership and procedures whereby units of appropriate size and type can be leased and thus safeguarded against reversion to the previously existing, unsatisfactory pattern. Most farm leaders were not prepared to advocate such radical departures from traditional procedures.

resales of land made within three years. This was intended as a check on speculation.

Though the idea of federal legislation to improve landlord-tenant relationships was passed over, recommendation was made that the states consider appropriate legislation for safeguarding the interests of the tenant, compensating him for unexpired improvements and payment for losses incurred as a result of termination of leases without cause.

Other recommendations included proposals for study of the possibility of encouraging family-size farms by differential taxation favoring them as against larger units, and consideration of more adequate protection of the civil liberties of tenants, croppers and farm laborers.[26]

Taken as a whole the Farm Tenancy Report constituted the most comprehensive analysis of the problems associated with low-income farm groups, and the most carefully considered set of policy proposals relating to them, that had been made up to that time. While most of the forty-one members of the Committee signed the report without reservation, several vigorous dissents were registered. W. L. Blackstone of the Southern Tenant Farmers' Union urged that the Farm Security Administration be established as an independent agency rather than as a branch of the Department of Agriculture. Edward O'Neal, President of the American Farm Bureau Federation, objected to the proposed limitations on resale of farms purchased by tenants with funds obtained through the Farm Security Administration. Charles Johnson, a Negro educator, urged more specific protection of Negro farmers. A. R. Mann of Cornell University and Henry C. Taylor of the Farm Foundation stated vigorously that such a program should be undertaken only on an experimental basis.

26. The Committee also recommended that the Farm Security Administration be given authority and funds to aid in drafting appropriate tenancy legislation for consideration by state legislatures, and that consideration be given to requiring, as a condition of receiving benefit payments under the soil conservation and domestic allotment program, the use of an improved form of lease in the case of tenant-operated farms. The need for improved education and health facilities was also stressed.

The Bankhead-Jones Farm Tenant Act

Parts of the program outlined by the Committee on Farm Tenancy were given legal authorization in the Bankhead-Jones Farm Tenant Act approved July 22, 1937.[27] This established the Farmers' Home Corporation, authorized completion of programs initiated under the Resettlement Administration and specified the nature of the program to be carried out thereafter. As of September 1 the Secretary of Agriculture changed the name of the Resettlement Administration to the Farm Security Administration.

The Farm Tenant Act included four titles, the first three of which provided for: (1) loans to tenant farmers, croppers and farm laborers for purchase of farms; (2) the granting of rehabilitation loans; and (3) the retirement of submarginal lands. Title IV outlined administrative procedures.

The tenant-purchase section authorized $10 million for the fiscal year ending June 30, 1938, $25 million for the following year and $50 million for each year thereafter. This was to be used for the acquisition of land to be resold to qualified tenants, croppers or farm laborers, under loans that might equal 100 per cent of the value of the farm. Interest was to be paid at 3 per cent, with repayment amortized over a period up to 40 years. Variable payments, larger in good years and smaller in poor years, were authorized. The farm could not be resold or transferred without the Secretary's consent short of five years.

The twenty-year prohibition against resale, proposed by the Farm Tenancy Committee and opposed by O'Neal, was omitted. Available funds were to be distributed equitably over the country on the basis of farm population and proportion of tenancy. Loans were to be passed on by three-man county committees appointed by the Secretary of Agriculture.

Under Title II, rehabilitation loans were to be made to eligible individuals for purchase of livestock, equipment, supplies and other farm needs, and for refinancing indebtedness

27. 50 Stat. 522.

or providing family subsistence. These loans might be made to farm owners, tenants, croppers or farm laborers, but only to those who could not obtain credit "on reasonable terms from any federally incorporated lending institution." The aid to voluntary farm debt adjustment committees which had been initiated under the Resettlement Administration was continued.

The submarginal land retirement program authorized under Title III was approximately the same as that launched by the Resettlement Administration in 1935. Appropriations authorized for this phase of the work were $10 million for the fiscal year ending June 30, 1938, and $20 million for each of the two succeeding years.

In an official order dated September 1, 1937, the Secretary designated Dr. Will Alexander, a southerner formerly active in various church and YMCA activities, as Administrator of the Farm Security Administration. The land retirement phase of the work was transferred to the Bureau of Agricultural Economics and placed under the direction of Dr. L. C. Gray, a career economist who had long been prominent in the field of land economics. On October 8, Paul V. Maris, formerly director of agricultural extension in Oregon, was named Director of the Tenant Purchase Division.

The "Farm Security" Program

The activities carried on under the Farm Security Administration attracted wide attention and were a subject of controversy throughout the years preceding World War II. The new program constituted a sharp break with tradition and there were wide differences between the personal philosophies of those who administered it and some of the the more conservative groups in agriculture.

The organization was heavily weighted with people dedicated to humanitarian and reform philosophies. In the selection of personnel the acceptance of these points of view tended to be given more weight than experience, training and hardheaded business qualities. The result was that the organiza-

tion tended to be somewhat loosely administered and operated on a basis of high emotional fervor. Probably the abilities and inclinations of these disadvantaged groups to respond to improved opportunities were somewhat overestimated.

In addition, the organization had much difficulty in recruiting a competent field staff. The task of appraising, supervising and building up these less successful farmers and farm workers was more difficult than that of aiding better-educated and more successful farmers. The best-qualified field workers preferred to align themselves with the older, better-established agencies, and thus usually were not available to the Farm Security Administration.

Both the quality of the field personnel and the success of the program were somewhat uneven over the country. In some areas very good results were obtained. In others the organization, though performing a necessary and useful function, never achieved popularity. The hardheaded farmer-directors of many farm loan associations, production credit associations and other regular credit agencies tended to be somewhat scornful of the "soft" credit and "unbusinesslike" methods of FSA. In the West farm employers were dubious of the FSA camps for migrants, feeling that they might become hotbeds of radicalism, and places for pampering the lazy and improvident.

Cooperative Farming Projects

Still more controversial was the later effort to establish cooperative farming communities. This was intended as a means of combining the advantages of highly mechanized agriculture with those of the small holding. Many looked upon it, however, as an attempt to socialize agriculture in accordance with the Russian pattern. The relatively poor administration of many of these projects, and their marked divergence from traditional procedures, and even from the aspirations of their member families, tended to strengthen these attitudes.

The thinking of the American farmer was

still heavily influenced by pioneer traditions. Self-reliance was rated high, and failure in the competitive struggle tended to be attributed to laziness and incompetence rather than to circumstances. The FSA reform program with its overoptimism about the improvability of the individual, and its over-emphasis on circumstances as a cause of failure, naturally ran head on into this innate conservatism of the established farm groups.[28]

Only gradually has it been possible to bring about some reconciliation of these widely divergent points of view. Insofar as it has occurred, it has been through modifications of the views of both right-wing and left-wing groups. There has been apparent a growing awareness on the part of the conservative farm groups that the problems of this large segment of the farm population cannot be ignored. At the same time some of the more impractical phases of the program have been modified or eliminated. As the FSA administrators and personnel gained experience the program became more realistic, with more emphasis on the things that were proving effective and less on those that had proved impractical or unsuitable.

Principal Emphases

Principal emphasis was given to the following types of aid:

1. Camps for migrants — this was an emergency program designed to provide minimum accommodations for destitute and unstabilized farm families. It was not regarded as a permanent solution by either farmers or the government, but did relieve one of the most desperate needs of the time. Such camps were established in Idaho, Oregon, Washington, California, Arizona, Texas and Florida. As of 1940, 56 camps were in operation or under construction, with accommodations for 13,205 families.[29]

28. By 1942 the Farm Security Administration was being vigorously attacked by the American Farm Bureau Federation and by some groups in the Congress. The appointment of C. B. Baldwin in 1940 to replace Will Alexander as Administrator emphasized the left-wing tendencies in the organization. Farmer and congressional opposition led to an official investigation of the agency in 1943.

29. Farm Security Administration, *Report of the Administrator, 1940*, pp. 15-16.

2. Rehabilitation loans and grants — for the year 1939–1940 loans amounting to $93.5 million were extended to 299,000 families. From 1935 to 1940 the total amount of loans made was $507,368,664, to 856,024 families. Collections had amounted to $152,-386,930, and it was estimated that at least 80 per cent of the money loaned would eventually be recovered. For the year 1939–1940 grants, that is, contributions made in addition to loans, amounted to $20 million. In addition, loans amounting to some $457,000 were made for the improvement of water facilities.[30]

3. Tenant-purchase loans — 6,172 such loans were made in the year 1939–1940. These averaged $5,992. From the beginning of the program, in 1937, to 1940 the number of tenant-purchase loans granted was 12,234. As would be expected, many more farmers sought loans on these exceptionally favorable terms than could be supplied out of the limited funds appropriated. More than 20 applications were filed for each loan granted.[31]

4. Housing — somewhat experimental work was done in devising new types of farm houses and new methods of building to improve the quality and lower the cost of farm housing. Some 14,000 such homes had been built by 1940, some on farms purchased and resold under the tenant-purchase program, but more of them in subsistence homestead projects and cooperative farming communities.

5. Other phases of the program included efforts to develop cooperative associations, the provision of medical care and the improvement of methods of leasing farms, all of these being primarily related to FSA borrowers and to destitute migrants in the FSA camps.[32]

ECONOMIC CONDITIONS OF THE LATE 1930's

Through 1935 and 1936 recovery occurred on a broad front. Production of nondurable

30. *Ibid.*, pp. 8, 9.
31. *Ibid.*, p. 13.
32. For a fuller though very inadequate summary of the activities of FSA in this period see the series of annual reports 1935 through 1940. Also the illustrated descriptive brochure *Farm Security Administration*, USDA, May 1, 1941. A much more extensive account is given in Bureau of Agricultural Economics, *Ten Years of Rural Rehabilitation in the United States*, July 1947, mimeographed. Later developments in the FSA program and that of its successor, the Farmers Home Administration, are dealt with in Chapter 19.

goods reached approximately the estimated normal by the end of 1936, and durable goods were within 10 per cent of that level by the middle of 1937. Wholesale prices were less than 10 per cent below the 1929 level and unemployment was down to 5 million. National income had recovered from $39.6 billion in 1933 to $73.6 billion in 1937 (the 1929 level was $87.4 billion), and the market value of stocks, which had been approximately $90 billion in 1929, now stood at about $60 billion as compared to $16 billion in 1932.[33]

Agricultural production likewise was up sharply from the low levels of the preceding years, with an index of 106 (1935–1939 = 100), the highest level on record.[34] Prices to farmers stood at 122 (1909–1914 = 100), some 18 per cent below the levels of 1929, and gross farm income had reached $11.27 billion as compared to the $13.82 billion of 1929.[35]

Thus there was every indication that the nation was well on the way out of its worst depression. But the last half of 1937 and the early part of 1938 saw a sharp recession which indicated (1) that the economy was not yet fully readjusted and (2) that some of the apparent progress made earlier was due to temporary influences which were now less effective. The number of unemployed doubled; production fell off to about the levels of 1934; and the value of listed stocks declined about $20 billion.[36] Farm prices were down more than 20 per cent while gross farm income dropped back to about $10 billion.

Wright attributes the decline to a variety of factors such as too rapid increase in costs, especially in hourly wage rates, increases in raw material costs, high inventories and the waning influence of various stimuli such as the payment of the soldiers bonus and other deficit spending.[37] Some stiffening of credit had also occurred.[38]

Monetary Policies

By this time the administration had abandoned efforts to affect the price level through manipulation of the gold value of the dollar, though an Act of January 23, 1937, extended until June 30, 1939, the life of the exchange stabilization fund and the President's power to vary the weight of gold in the dollar. The unsound policies with respect to gold and silver which had been adopted earlier were still tending to concentrate in the United States the world stocks of these monetary metals.

Revaluation of the dollar in 1934 had increased United States gold stocks from about $4 billion at the old value to nearly $8 billion at the new value. Stocks of gold in the United States increased markedly through 1935, 1936 and 1937, reaching nearly $13 billion at the end of 1937.[39] During 1937 the treasury "sterilized" substantial amounts of gold; that is, sequestered them so they could not increase banking reserves and contribute to credit expansion. This policy was abandoned for the time being in April 1938.

Silver likewise was being purchased in large amounts at more than the free market price. This caused numerous international repercussions, and resulted in repeated protests from China and other silver standard countries. Its effect was to bring about severe deflation in China without in any way aiding the United States. On January 25, 1937, the *San Francisco Chronicle* remarked editorially that ". . . the process has already gone so far that the Treasury has to 'sterilize' further silver purchases, by not using them as even a professed 'base.' The scheme has simply flooded itself out."[40]

33. Chester Whitney Wright, *Economic History of the United States*, 2nd edition, McGraw-Hill, New York, 1949, p. 792, and Department of Commerce, *National Income, 1951 Edition*, A Supplement to the *Survey of Current Business*, p. 150.

34. *Agricultural Statistics, 1945*, p. 437.

35. *Ibid.*, pp. 430, 438.

36. Wright, *Economic History*, p. 792.

37. *Ibid.*, p. 793.

38. On January 30, 1937, the Board of Governors announced an increase of 33⅓ per cent in the reserves required for member banks. This meant doubling the reserve requirements in effect when the Banking Act of 1935 was passed. The increase was to take effect, one half on March 1 and one half on May 1. This was an anti-inflation action, and reflects the fact that the Board was by that time fearful of inflation rather than deflation. It also illustrates the difficulty of deciding when to attempt credit contraction or expansion and how much to change the free lending resources of the banks.

39. James Daniel Paris, *Monetary Policies of the United States, 1932–1938*, Columbia University Press, New York, 1938, p. 33.

40. Chester H. Rowell, "Time to Stop Silver Fiasco,"

LABOR LEGISLATION OF THE LATE 1930's

During these years in which the agricultural program was taking more permanent form similar changes were occurring in the nonagricultural segments of the economy. The most important were the measures which marked a turning point in national policy with respect to labor. Labor had gained slowly in organization and political strength during the last two decades of the nineteenth century and the first three of the present century. Up to 1933, however, the employing groups were able to maintain a dominant position in their struggles with labor, and in government policy and national legislation.

After 1933 this situation was sharply reversed. Labor's gains in economic and political strength were far greater than those of the employer groups. The legislation creating the NRA gave to business groups many privileges that had been denied them under previously existing legislation, but labor also was placed in a stronger bargaining position. In a sense the National Industrial Recovery Act, along with the new agricultural legislation, may be looked upon as a major concession to the producer groups at the expense of the consumer. Insofar as the NRA program contained a logical and consistent theoretical foundation it was intended to constitute a working partnership between government, industry and labor in which both industry and labor were to achieve results desired by them.

Since the antitrust laws were suspended to permit industrialists to take joint action in dealing with their problems it seemed only reasonable to assure workers the same right, without interference from employers or the courts. The implementation of this policy in regard to labor was contained in Section 7(a) which was a required part of each NRA code.[41] This provision was expected to establish a mechanism through which labor and management would act together under government supervision. It was hoped that collective bargaining on a broader and more independent basis would be a means of promoting industrial peace and thus of bringing about steady production and the uninterrupted flow of wages and purchasing power.

The Company Union Problem

Many employers had built up over the years company-encouraged and dominated unions. In some cases, especially in the smaller firms, they were a genuine attempt to improve relationships with the working personnel, and to provide an orderly channel for contact and exchange of views between workers and management. In others the primary purpose was to counteract moves to organize the workers into independent or national and international unions, and to maintain company domination of unions. Situations of the latter type were likely to include many of the more reprehensible devices for strengthening employer influence, such as the discharge of

---

San Francisco Chronicle, January 25, 1937, p. 6. The editorial summarized the situation as follows:

"There were four arguments for the silver purchase act, three of which its proponents dared give. They were ashamed to state the fourth, which was their real motive, but it is the only one they now have left. The others, which were not their actual reasons, but were the 'talking points' by which they 'sold' their scheme, have all disproved themselves. The fourth and only real motive was, of course, that they had silver mines in their States and a disproportionately large bloc of votes in the Senate, and that they traded these votes to make more profit for the mines.

"The other 'sales-talk' pretexts sounded more reputable, and were therefore stressed louder. They were:

(1) Adding silver to it would 'broaden the base' of currency.

(2) It would increase the purchasing power of the silver-standard countries.

(3) It would ultimately raise the world price of silver to the parity designated in the act, on which, later, the free coinage of silver might be feasible.

"These are exactly the things that have not happened."

41. Section 7(a) read as follows:

Every code of fair competition, agreement, and license approved, prescribed, or issued under this title shall contain the following conditions: (1) That employees shall have the right to organize and bargain collectively through representatives of their own choosing, and shall be free from the interference, restraint, or coercion of employers of labor, or their agents, in the designation of such representatives or in self-organization or in other concerted activities for the purpose of collective bargaining or other mutual aid or protection; (2) that no employee and no one seeking employment shall be required as a condition of employment to join any company union or to refrain from joining, organizing, or assisting a labor organization of his own choosing; and (3) that employers shall comply with the maximum hours of labor, minimum rates of pay, and other conditions of employment, approved or prescribed by the President.

overaggressive union workers, labor spies and company domination of union elections.[42]

Until 1933 company unions, though never popular with organized labor, were not frowned upon in legislative and administrative circles merely because they were company sponsored. But with the inauguration of the NRA and the granting of more power to organized labor through the provisions of Section 7(a) employers became alarmed at the prospect of more militant and powerful independent unions. One method of circumventing the intent of the new law was to build up and control company unions. While employees were not required to join such unions, much pressure was exerted to induce them to do so. As friction between the business groups and the President increased he shifted more and more toward a prolabor attitude. Soon he was referring to his employer-critics as "economic royalists," and was giving vigorous support to the labor stand against company unions and in favor of full autonomy and more power for the independent labor organizations.[43]

The National Labor Board

Early in the NRA period he had set up, at the request of the Industry and Labor Advisory boards, a National Labor Board to supervise labor relations. It was composed of equal numbers of employer and employee representatives and an impartial chairman. This Board placed principal emphasis on compromising disputes rather than on efforts to follow the controversial provisions of law.

Confusion resulted from the conflicting authorities of this Board and of NRA code administrators, largely because of the vagueness of the legal standing of both agencies. The Board undertook to establish the principle that an organization representing the majority of the workers in a given industry should be allowed to bargain for the whole group.[44] Where there was doubt a secret election was to be held to register free choice as between a company union and an independent union. Furthermore, it was not enough for employers to hear their workers and dismiss their proposals. They must make a bona fide effort to reach agreement. The Board had no power to enforce its decisions, but had to depend on uncertain action through the compliance machinery of NRA.

The National Labor Board was abolished by the President in July 1934. In its place he established the National Labor Relations Board composed of three specialists. The new Board moved further toward the position of organized labor, ruling that a company union dominated by the employer was not an approved instrument for collective bargaining.

The National Labor Relations Act

Following the invalidation of the NRA, on May 27, 1935, Senator Wagner of New York introduced a bill which, on July 5 of that year, became the National Labor Relations Act (49 Stat. 449). The new act grew out of the experience under the NRA. Its authority rested upon the powers of Congress to prevent industrial strife that would impede interstate commerce. This left out large groups of service-trade, agricultural and other workers engaged in intrastate activities. However, the application of the principles involved was broadened through adoption in a number of states of acts modeled on this one.

Furthermore, the distinction between interstate and intrastate activities was becoming more and more blurred. For this agriculture was in part responsible. In its efforts to make the definition of interstate commerce more and more inclusive, in order to shore up its authority to enforce marketing agreements,

---

42. An excellent brief account of the developments that led to the passage of the Wagner Labor Relations Act is given in Foster Rhea Dulles, *Labor in America, A History,* Thomas Y. Crowell Company, New York, 1949, Chapter 15.

43. *Loc. cit.*

44. This was a principle somewhat similar to that provided in the quota system for agriculture, and to some extent in the marketing agreement and licensing features of the agricultural program. In agriculture, however, a two-thirds majority was required before such a program could be imposed against the will of the minority. Both agriculture and labor had for years been concerned over the problem of the "noncooperator": in agriculture, the man who refused to join a cooperative or participate in a control program but sought to benefit from such efforts; in labor, the man who refused to join the union.

it was pressing continuously for more inclusive legislative definitions of interstate commerce, and for more and more liberal court interpretations under this heading. In the realm of labor relations, agriculture's attitude was the reverse of this. It wished, insofar as possible, to avoid the inclusion of agricultural labor in the regulations applied by the federal government to most other types of labor.

The new federal act, commonly known as the Wagner Act, declared that "Employees shall have the right to self-organization, to form, join, or assist labor organizations, to bargain collectively through representatives of their own choosing, and to engage in concerted activities, for the purpose of collective bargaining or other mutual aid or protection."[45] This, to labor, was a more important Magna Charta than the Capper-Volstead Act had been to farmer cooperatives, though there is an element of similarity in the two.

A new National Labor Relations Board of three "experts" was set up to interpret the act. The new Board assumed the power to determine what bargaining unit could speak for each group of workers in bargaining with employers. It also was authorized to prohibit the following "unfair" practices of employers:

1. Interference with employees in the exercise of guaranteed rights.
2. Financial or other support of a company union.
3. Use of hiring and firing to encourage membership in a company union or discourage membership in an independent union.
4. Discrimination against a worker because he complained to the Board.
5. Refusal to bargain collectively with the representatives of the employees.

The Wagner Act was one of the most bitterly attacked features of New Deal legislation. There can be no doubt that it marked a major turning point in American policy with respect to labor. Shortly after its passage fifty-eight prominent attorneys allied with the American Liberty League, a bipartisan, right-wing political organization, issued an

opinion that the law was unconstitutional.[46] However, in April 1937 the administration gained a major victory when Justices Hughes and Roberts joined the liberal wing of the Supreme Court in a series of five decisions upholding the constitutionality of the act.[47]

Growth of Labor's Power

As a result of the Wagner Act, union membership and financial resources grew rapidly, and the power of labor leaders was greatly increased. Adequate analysis of this vast and complex problem is beyond the scope of this discussion. It seems safe to say, however, that from this time on organized labor was to be much more influential both economically and politically than it had been in the years prior to 1935.

As in the NRA industrial codes, far-reaching powers had been granted without adequate safeguards. In the effort to overcome an undeniable lag in progressive legislation for the benefit of labor, the modernization of labor legislation had been thrown into high gear and most of the brakes had been removed. The result was the creation of a new type of problem which bears some resemblance to that which resulted from the rapid growth of power in the large corporations and trusts in the latter part of the nineteenth century.[48] During succeeding years there was

45. Sec. 7, 49 Stat. 449 at 452.

46. American Liberty League, *The National Labor Relations Act*, Document No. 66, Washington, September 1935.
47. Alfred H. Kelly and Winfred A. Harbison, *The American Constitution*, W. W. Norton, New York, 1948, pp. 754–56.
48. While many of the union leaders grew in stature and in appreciation of the social responsibilities implied by their newly won power, abuses were sufficiently common to bring about a less friendly attitude on the part of the Congress and the public. The suppression or absence of democratic procedures in the election of officers and the secret handling of funds in some unions were likewise coming more generally to the attention of the public. The situation was not eased by some of the rulings of the National Labor Relations Board which seemed to the farm groups, and employers generally, to be pro-labor and anti-employer. The Board came to be regarded by many as a partisan of labor rather than as a judicial body.

The approach to the labor problem shows somewhat the same type of unbalance as that which marked the agricultural legislation of this period. Farm prices were obviously too low. The legislation passed to correct this difficulty looked almost exclusively in the direction of higher farm prices. It contained no significant provision

much employer and public criticism of the Wagner Act, and of some of the policies of labor. This eventually led to the passage, in 1947, of a drastic counterbalancing measure commonly known as the Taft-Hartley Act.

This growth in the power of organized labor has far-reaching implications for agriculture. The fact that more and more labor unions were coming to be organized and to bargain as national organizations increased markedly the possibility that nationwide or regional tie-ups of vital functions could react disastrously on the shippers of agricultural products. Continuous activity in trucking, ocean shipping, railroads, coal, steel and other industries are of vital concern to farmers. In addition local closed-shop arrangements, boycotts and "hot-cargo" rulings could greatly affect their business.

Agriculture's Attitude

As yet there was little direct impact of the new policies and legislation on agricultural wage labor as such, since this was specifically excluded from coverage. Nevertheless the trend of events was so clearly in the direction of ultimate inclusion of all labor that agricultural employers tended to view the whole movement with apprehension. But agriculture itself has long been divided in its attitude toward organized labor. Only about a third of the nation's farms employ wage labor. Many small farmers are partly farmer and partly wage laborer. Many others who do not work for wages but who on the other hand do not employ labor are not greatly concerned over the organization of farm workers but do express grave concern over the larger stoppages of important functions, and what they regard as unreasonable demands by organized labor or unwarranted restrictions on output.

Many attempts have been made to align agriculture politically with labor. For the most part these have not been notably successful. Such organizations as the Farmers Union, and the Farmer-Labor Party of the Midwest, have tended in recent years to follow closely the labor line in their legislative programs. The members of the larger farm organizations, on the other hand, have tended to look upon themselves more as entrepreneurs and employers than as laborers, but nevertheless have been reluctant to align themselves definitely with the large industrial employers. Generally speaking the commercial farmers as a whole tend to align themselves with nonagricultural employer groups in placing curbs on the power of organized labor rather than to take the reverse attitude.

The Fair Labor Standards Act

The Blue Eagle agreements and the NRA codes undertook to eliminate child labor and establish minimum rates of pay and maximum hours of labor for industries engaged in interstate commerce. The demise of the Blue Eagle and the elimination of the NRA brought to a halt the efforts along these lines. The administration continued, however, to press for legislation fixing minimum hourly rates and maximum hours of labor. The outcome was the passage of the Fair Labor Standards Act of 1938. This fixed an initial minimum wage of 25 cents per hour and a 44-hour week. The minimum wage was to be increased gradually to 40 cents and the work week lowered to 40 hours. A rate of time and a half for hours in excess of the maximum was specified. It was made unlawful to ship in interstate commerce goods manufactured in violation of these standards.[49]

Relation to Agriculture

As in all of the general legislation pertaining to labor, agricultural labor was specifically exempted. Nevertheless, policy problems relating to labor were forcing themselves inexorably upon the employing farmers of the major commercial areas. In the West espe-

---

or checking inflationary tendencies which were to be the dominant ones in the 1940's. The labor legislation likewise was designed almost wholly to overcome widely recognized disadvantages suffered by labor, but placed ew curbs on abuses in the labor movement which were also apparent.

49. The constitutionality of the act was upheld in *U.S.* v. *Darby,* 312 U.S. 100 (1941).

cially, attempts were being made to unionize agricultural labor. This effort was not successful, but sufficient headway was made that scores of small, local strikes were initiated. These resulted in part from the activities of union leaders, some of them frankly and avowedly communistic, and in part from the deplorable conditions existing in the agricultural labor market at the time.

California in particular was the recipient of hordes of migrant farm families, many from the "dust-bowl" areas of the Southern Plains states, others from areas in which mechanized farming was displacing hand labor. The numbers seeking work far outran the real needs of the receiving areas. The vulnerability of the highly commercialized and meticulously timed agriculture of these areas created an active and often violent hostility on the part of farm employers to any type of labor market organization that might halt activity at critical times when the year's crop might be lost. The radical character of some of the farm labor organizations heightened this tension. The result was the organization of various opposition groups on the part of thè employers which undertook vigorously and sometimes violently to prevent the unionization of farm workers.

The violence of this conflict led to a major investigation by the La Follette Committee, a subcommittee of the Senate Committee on Education and Labor. The voluminous testimony taken by the La Follette Committee came out just before World War II when conditions were already beginning to improve.[50] Thereafter the rapid increase in the general demand for labor brought about a shortage of farm labor that persisted throughout the war. The sharply increased rates of

pay, and some gradual improvement in ho ing and other conditions, operated to pu the farm labor issue into the backgrou This, however, was a postponement rat than a solution.

The problem of labor relations in agric ture is bound to rise again, and will beco an active issue in agricultural and labor p icy discussions. As yet there has been lit impact from federal legislation in this real The modest minima prescribed under t Jones-Costigan Sugar Act constitute minor approach to the problem. Controve has been frequent in regard to the criteria be used in differentiating agricultural fr nonagricultural labor where both handle t same products at different stages of their p duction and marketing. This, however, is fringe issue rather than the central one whi is that of continuing or not continuing ununionized agriculture. Labor proble were to rank high in farmer interest duri World War II but for a different reas Here the concern was over methods of taining help rather than over unionizati and labor relations.

Development of Social Security

Closely related to the labor program, again only peripherally affecting agricultu was the creation of the national social secur system. The profound disillusionment whi resulted from the crash of 1929–1930 crea a new attitude in regard to reliance on in vidual resources as a means of meeting t vicissitudes of life. The traditional attitude American businessmen and workers ali grew out of their pioneer heritage. It w one of individualism and self-reliance, a wi ingness to take risks and an expectation th each person, if industrious and frugal, wou somehow be able to provide for himself times of business recession, unemployme and old age.

The extensiveness and severity of loss customary sources of support created an most universal, one might almost say a path logical, concern about security. Jobs that h been taken for granted were swept away

50. U.S. Congress, Senate, Committee on Education and Labor, *Violations of Free Speech and Rights of Labor,* Hearings before a subcommittee . . . , 76th Cong., 2nd sess., pursuant to S.Res. 266, of the 74th Cong., 1939–1940, Parts 46–56, 58–75. See also, *National Farm Labor Problem,* Supplementary hearings by the same Committee, 76th Cong., 3rd sess., 1940, 3 Vols. and *Violations of Free Speech and Rights of Labor,* Reports of the Committee on Education and Labor, pursuant to S.Res. 266 (74th Cong.), S.Rep. 1150, 77th Cong., 2nd sess., S.Rep. 398, 78th Cong., 1st and 2nd sess., 1942–1944, Parts 1–9.

the millions. Those dependent on savings found their assets depreciated or worthless. Young people were unsure of the future, and apprehensive about finding job opportunities in what seemed a permanently curtailed labor market. Even businessmen who had been considered well established found themselves out of business and again in the market for jobs.

Whereas the pioneer attitude had been one of optimism, a willingness to take chances if the wages seemed good, or if there was a sporting chance of good returns later, now even young people thought first of job security and second of rates of pay. The result was a greater emphasis on job security in unions, among civil servants and in many other types of activity. There was a markedly increased interest in insurance, both private and public.

Farmers, too, were aware of economic hazards, but their interest took a different form. They did not fear the loss of their jobs, unless the farm should be lost through foreclosure or they should be displaced as tenants. The security they wanted mainly was assurance against disastrous declines in price, and against loss of their farms if they found themselves unable to meet payments on their mortgages. There was some interest also in insurance against drought and other physical hazards, but this issue was perhaps more prominent in the minds of government officials than in those of farmers.

Many of the countries of western Europe had already developed arrangements for compulsory participation in government-operated old-age and unemployment insurance schemes. Similar action had for some years been advocated by progressive groups in the United States, but the pioneer tradition and the conservative attitude of the administrations in power during the 1920's operated to keep the United States in a relatively backward position on this problem, as compared to most of the mature, advanced countries. It was a situation in which some action along these lines was almost inevitable. In June 1934 the President set up a committee to draft a program of social insurance

which came to fruition as the Social Security Act of August 14, 1935 (49 Stat. 620). The new law provided three principal types of aid: (1) a system of old-age and survivors insurance; (2) grants for assisting people too old for active work who were not included in the regular old-age insurance program; and (3) a national and state system of unemployment insurance.

Old-Age and Survivors Insurance

The old-age and survivors insurance program was, in effect, a plan for compulsory saving, plus employer contributions, during the employee's active working years. While not set up on an actuarial basis, it contained many of the features of ordinary life insurance. Employee and employer, in covered industries, were required to contribute equally to the fund amounts beginning at 1 per cent each and increasing gradually to 3 per cent each by 1948.[51] It was contemplated that a very large reserve fund would be built up in the early years and that thereafter benefit payments would become larger and larger in proportion to inpayments. The relations between the two were expected to stabilize in the latter part of the century.

Public employees, domestic servants, casual laborers, employees of charitable, religious and educational institutions, and agricultural workers were excluded from participation in the scheme. Most other employees were specifically included. By 1940 more than fifty million workers held social security numbers and had made contributions.

The principal reason for excluding agricultural wageworkers and domestic help was not an absence of need on the part of these groups. They were, in fact, more likely to be

51. The rates specified have been changed from time to time by congressional action. The original schedule was to be 1 per cent each from employer and employee for the years 1937–1939; 1½ per cent, 1940–1942; 2 per cent, 1943–1945; 2½ per cent, 1946–1948; and 3 per cent thereafter. By successive annual deferments the rate was held at 1 per cent through 1949. Under the social security amendments of 1950 the rate was put at 1½ per cent for the years 1951–1953. Thereafter they are scheduled to be at 2 per cent for 1954–1959; 2½ per cent for 1960–1964; 3 per cent for 1965–1969; and 3¼ per cent thereafter.

incapable of self-support in old age than most other groups since their incomes were low, their employment irregular and the opportunities for saving very limited. The drafters of the legislation were aware of the problem posed by these workers, but recognized that their inclusion would create unique and difficult administrative problems, and also that farmers were not at that time friendly to having their employees covered. It was contemplated from the first, however, that farm laborers and domestics would be included after the agency had become established and when suitable techniques of administration had been devised.

Attitudes of Farmers

Farmers and farm organizations tended to be lukewarm on such broadening of coverage. There was, however, a growing interest in the problem. There was general recognition that few of these employees would be able to accumulate enough savings to take care of them in old age. Hence, they would have to be provided for, either through a contributory plan in which they would make payments during their working years, or by direct public charity in the form of old-age assistance.[52]

The reluctance of farm employers to see agricultural workers included rested mainly on four considerations: (1) administrative problems including the bother and expense of keeping necessary records and making frequent payments to the government; (2) the direct cost to farm employers as against the more generalized cost under noncontributory old-age assistance; (3) fear that the inclusion of farm labor under old-age insurance would be an opening wedge for placing farm labor under the general federal laws relating to labor; and (4) reluctance to see more intrusion of government into activities formerly carried on under private auspices. Despite these objections many farm employers favor, in principle, the inclusion of farm workers in the system, and, in recent years, this view has come to be accepted by some of the major farm organizations, but with reservations as to the workability and financial soundness of the plan.

Continuing pressure for broadening the coverage of the system, particularly by the administration, led to the passage of the extensive amendments known as the Social Security Act amendments of 1950, signed on August 28. Under this legislation, benefits were increased and additional groups of workers, including some classes of farm wage-workers, were brought into the system beginning January 1, 1951.

From the first there was sharp divergence of opinion between those who favored the reserve plan, which was adopted, and a "pay-as-you-go plan" under which only enough would be collected to pay the benefits due as the claim load grows. The latter plan implies, of course, substantially heavier payments in later years when the number of aged entitled to pensions will be much larger. The conflict between these points of view has resulted in a plan which is neither the one nor the other

The Congress has repeatedly deferred the increases in contribution rates scheduled in the original act. While a sizable reserve fund has been built up, it is not adequate to carry the cost in later years without substantial increase in the rates of contribution.[53]

52. Old-age assistance, as defined in the legislation, consists of payments to the needy aged out of tax funds provided jointly by the state and federal governments. No previous contribution by the recipient is involved, but payments are made only to those whose assets do not exceed certain minima and who are not able to obtain support in other ways. Payments under the old-age and survivors insurance system are a right which is not affected by the amount of property or income the recipient may have. In this respect they are like returns from private, endowment life insurance. Individuals are not eligible to receive these payments, however, if they continue work in covered employment with earnings above certain minima. In the original act this minimum was fixed at the very low level of $15 per month. This, however, was a result of depression attitudes. The purpose was to force overage workers out of the labor force in order to make room for younger workers. The minimum earning permissible, in covered employment, was raised to $50 in the amendments of 1950. (Beneficiaries 75 and over may receive benefits regardless of the amounts of their earning.)

53. Social Security Board actuaries have estimated that, under the original plan, the program could probably be kept self-supporting without raising the rate of contribution above the 3 per cent—3 per cent contemplated in the original act. This, however, was on the assump

Prior to and during World War II, the old-age and survivors program was still in an evolutionary stage. It has continued to be so in the period following World War II. The method of financing, the levels of benefit and the relation of the contributory old-age insurance plan to the public assistance program remain to be settled as the program matures. Most self-employed workers other than farmers were brought into the system by the amendments of 1950. The self-employed pay one and a half times the rate paid by employed workers.

Unemployment Insurance

The unemployment insurance program was set up on a state-federal basis, rather than wholly federal as in the case of old-age and survivors insurance. Payroll taxes were collected from employers and turned over to approved state unemployment compensation systems. The federal government, out of the 10 per cent retained by it, paid the administrative expenses of the state systems, and established the principal rules governing procedure. These funds provide modest compensation to care for workers involuntarily idle for periods varying usually from fourteen to sixteen weeks. The size of payment is related to previous earnings and length of service.[54]

Here, as in the old-age and survivors insurance program, farm workers, domestic servants and various other groups were omitted from coverage. In later years there has been considerable discussion of the possibility of including farm employees under some form of unemployment insurance. The highly seasonal nature of such work makes

evident the need for aid in periods of unemployment but, at the same time, constitutes the most serious problem in devising a workable unemployment insurance plan. If collections in agriculture were to be high enough to provide the funds required, the rates of tax on the employer would have to be so high that they would imply a major and drastic change in large parts of American agriculture. If, on the other hand, the general unemployment fund were to be burdened with the deficit for this group that would result from the normal rate of tax, other industries would be subsidizing agriculture on a considerable scale.

Other problems arise in the difficulty of defining unemployment in agriculture. Many seasonal activities such as fruit picking, canning, etc., are performed by housewives, school children and similar groups who are not in the labor force on a year-round basis and hence, though not working except during certain seasons of the year, are also not unemployed in a sense that would make them appropriate recipients of unemployment insurance. The normal seasonal shifts from agriculture to other industries and vice versa would also be interfered with if workers chose to class themselves as unemployed with respect to agriculture and did not seek work in other occupations.

The complexities of the problem, together with farmer opposition to the inclusion of agricultural labor, have thus far prevented action along these lines. In fact, no practical plan for providing unemployment insurance for agricultural workers seems as yet to have been proposed, even by those most acutely aware of the hardships resulting from the discontinuity of agricultural wagework. It seems apparent that extensive readjustments in the structure of the industry will have to be associated with any workable unemployment insurance scheme. Either the work load on farms will need to be made more uniform from season to season, or carefully planned correlation of seasonal farm work with suitably timed off-season work in nonfarm activities will be required.

tion that a large reserve fund would be built up in the early years. The later reductions in scheduled contributions will, of course, modify that estimate considerably. As actually worked out, the plan is extremely favorable for those who become eligible for benefits in the early years of the program. They will have paid in only for a short period and at an abnormally low rate, the exact opposite of the relationship which would apply under private insurance. The proportion of aged in the population will increase as time goes on, thus creating a heavier load of beneficiaries in addition to the fact that a larger and larger portion of those reaching 65 will have become eligible for benefits.
54. See Titles III and IX of the Social Security Act, 49 Stat. 626, 639.

The accomplishment of such a result is far from easy or simple, and powerful incentives will be needed if farmers are to be induced to make the kinds of changes implied. The difficulty arises in part from the high degree of specialization in modern agriculture. Yet it would not, as some contend, be eliminated by the adoption of a universal small-farm pattern for agriculture. So long as the agriculture is specialized and the work seasonal, the variable work load persists and gives rise either to seasonal unemployment for wage-workers or to seasonal underemployment for small farm operators, or possibly both. The application of unemployment insurance to agriculture presents far more difficulty than does the adoption of old-age and survivors insurance for farm workers. The problem has not been solved and seems likely to continue to plague society and the industry until some workable solution is found.

Old-Age Assistance

The old-age assistance feature of the program was intended primarily as an interim arrangement to care for the destitute, uninsured aged until such time as most aged workers and their families would be cared for under the contributory plan. The prospect of such a tapering off of old-age assistance has become less likely as the program has developed. Very large groups of workers are not as yet included in the coverage. Others for one reason or another never become e gible for benefits under the insurance pla yet must be supported if their resources a inadequate for self-support.[55]

Payments under the old-age assistance pr gram come partly from federal grants to t states and partly from local tax revenues. some states political pressure for nonco tributory old-age benefits has forced the rat of payment above those of the federal co tributory insurance plan, thus favoring t noncontributor as against the contribut

The old-age assistance program applies ge erally to agricultural and nonagricultur workers alike and hence is not specifically problem of agriculture. Nevertheless, ma farm workers and even some farm entrep neurs come to be supported in this way du ing their declining years. The burden some state budgets and on the federal tre ury for the support of this program has b come very large and, thus far at least, h continued to increase. Farmers as well nonfarmers unquestionably have reason examine carefully the possible advantages more universal and direct contribution to t funds required for support of the aged.

55. The social security program includes a number other provisions such as aid to the blind, aid to d pendent children, and so on. These, however, are general application and of minor economic significan Extension of the system to the field of health insuran was advocated from the beginning by some groups, b did not become an active policy issue until after Wor War II when it was made a prominent part of t Truman "Fair Deal" program.

CHAPTER 15

PROGRAM OF THE LATE 1930's

THE AGRICULTURAL ADJUSTMENT ACT of 1933 reflected the concern of farmers and legislators about accumulated stocks of farm commodities and the desperately low level of agricultural incomes. Its emphasis, therefore, was on reduced production and on measures for immediate acceleration of the flow of income into agriculture. The Act of 1936 showed the influence of the droughts of 1934, 1935 and 1936. Its major emphasis was on the conservation of soils, though it contemplated cutbacks in the acreages of commercial cash crops and continuing transfers of income to agriculture. It was recognized, however, that the fortuitous conditions which had corrected the unbalance of agricultural production and consumption between 1934 and 1936 did not constitute a permanent solution of the problem. The droughts also emphasized the need for more specific methods of guarding against shortages in the event of continuing periods of low rainfall.

THE AGRICULTURAL ADJUSTMENT ACT OF 1938

Almost immediately after the passage of the Act of 1936 plans were initiated looking to the formulation of more permanent and more comprehensive legislation for adjustment of agricultural production and the maintenance of agricultural income. Interest in forging stronger weapons for protection against a renewed onslaught of depression conditions was further stimulated by the abundant crops of 1937, and the onset of a business recession. The outcome was a body of legislation known as the Agricultural Adjustment Act of 1938. This was approved by the President on February 16 of that year.[1]

Title I of the new act consisted of amendments to the Soil Conservation and Domestic Allotment Act of 1936. Title II authorized the Secretary of Agriculture to intervene on behalf of agriculture in cases before the Interstate Commerce Commission with respect to freight rates on agricultural commodities. Title III dealt with Loans, Parity Payments, Consumer Safeguards and Marketing Quotas. Title IV related to Cotton Pool Participation Trust Certificates, and Title V was the new Crop Insurance Act.

Soil Conservation and Allotment Features

The new act retained the soil conservation and allotment features of the 1936 Act with little change, but added special provisions for water conservation and erosion control in arid and semiarid range areas. More specific directives were given for setting up local, county and state advisory and administrative committees of farmers, and the Secretary was instructed to safeguard the interests of tenants and sharecroppers by refusing increased payments to landlords that might result from displacement of tenants and/or croppers. Payments for conservation were to be made to landlords and to tenants in proportions relative to their contributions.

The rigidity of the old base-acreage plan which tended to freeze allotment rights in the hands of those who were already in the business was modified somewhat. Wheat allotments now were to be on the basis of "tillable acres, crop-rotation practices, type of soil, and topography," and up to 3 per cent of the allotment for a given county might be assigned to farms on which wheat had not been planted in the three preceding years.[2]

[1]. 52 Stat. 31.

[2]. Title I, Sec. 101(2). The new act also gave some additional emphasis to the small and medium-sized farm. It provided, in Sec. 102(e), for small increases on payments that would amount to less than $200, and limited

Parity Changes

Title III of the new act was the major spelling out of new policies on production control and price supports. It redefined parity prices, made the definition of parity income more precise, and differentiated "commercial and noncommercial" areas of production. It also outlined policy in regard to loans from the Commodity Credit Corporation and specified the criteria to be used in establishing marketing quotas. Other sections dealt with "consumer safeguards and parity payments."

Parity price as defined in the new act was the same as that specified in the Marketing Agreement Act of 1937, but differed from the definition used between 1933 and 1936. Parity price was to "reflect current interest payments per acre on farm indebtedness secured by real estate, tax payments per acre on farm real estate, and freight rates, as contrasted with such interest payments, tax payments, and freight rates during the base period." The 1933 Act stated the price objective as one that "will give agricultural commodities a purchasing power with respect to articles that farmers buy, equivalent to the purchasing power of agricultural commodities in the base period." Thus if total interest payments and taxes on farm real estate and amounts paid out in freight charges had risen more than had the prices of commodities bought by farmers, the effect of the change would be to make the "parity" price higher than under the old formula. The cost of agricultural labor, which was to cause much controversy in later years, was not included at this time.[3]

The parity income definition in the new act was merely a more precise formulation. The 1936 Act had used the expression "ratio between the purchasing power of the net income per person on farms and that of the income per person not on farms." That of 1938 read "per capita net income of individuals on farms *from farming operations*." There is, of course, considerable income to people living on farms which does not arise from farming operations.

A change was made in the method of figuring allotments to individual farmers. This is summarized as follows in the Administrator's report for 1937–1938:

The basis originally specified for determining payments to farmers was broadened by the inclusion of "their equitable share, as determined by the Secretary, of the national production of any commodity or commodities required for domestic consumption and exports." This represented a legislative change to an acreage allotment approach in place of the base-acreage approach of the earlier programs. It was a change that had already been begun administratively in the 1938 program.[5]

The new act sought to limit the corn program to "commercial" corn-growing areas. A county was to be designated "commercial" if the production of corn in the ten preceding years had been 450 or more bushels per farm and four or more bushels for each acre of farm land in the county.

Quota System

Although the new legislation implied procedures that were broadly similar to those used from 1933 onward, an important new feature was added in the provision for

---

the payment to any one person for any one year in a given state or territory to $10,000. This was to overcome criticism that had developed in connection with very large payments to a few individuals under the 1933 Act, and was also a slight concession to those who felt the program was too exclusively designed to benefit the large commercial farmer.

3. Changes in formula designed to raise "parity" prices were not taken too seriously by either proponents or opponents during the years when actual prices were much below "parity." From 1942 on, when the prices of farm products began to outrun those of other commodities, there was a persistent effort on the part of farm-state congressmen to devise ways of computing parity that would result in "parity" prices that would be higher than under the formulae previously used. During the

1930's this tendency was expressed to some extent in the choice of base periods other than the standard 1909–1914 base. The inclusion of interest and taxes had the effect, during the late 1930's, of raising the index of prices paid by farmers about three points. (See *Agricultural Statistics, 1946*, p. 551.) From 1942 onward it operated in the opposite direction, lowering the index several points.

4. 52 Stat. 31 at 38. (Italics ours.)

5. Agricultural Adjustment Administration, *Agricultural Adjustment 1937–38*, p. 18. The allotments continued, however, more or less inevitably, to be related to base acreages though not in quite the same way as under the Act of 1936.

marketing quotas. Under this plan, if current and prospective supply of a given commodity exceeded a "normal supply" the Secretary was directed to proclaim, by a specified date, a quota indicating the amount of the commodity that could be marketed within that year.[6] If carried into effect this would mean that each grower would be authorized to sell not more than a specified amount representing his authorized portion of the total amount that could be marketed without tax. If more than this amount was marketed by any grower the excess was subject to a heavy tax, 15 cents per bushel for wheat and corn, 2 to 3 cents per pound for cotton, and 50 per cent of the value for tobacco. This was, in effect, the extension to a wider range of crops of the technique established for cotton and tobacco in the Bankhead and Kerr-Smith Acts of 1934.

If a quota was announced by the Secretary he must, within thirty days, conduct a referendum among the growers. If more than one third of those voting were opposed the quota would not become effective. In this event, however, the act provided that price-support loans on that commodity, which were specified under the quota system, could not be made until the beginning of the second marketing year thereafter.

Loan Levels

The new act directed the Commodity Credit Corporation to make available price-supporting loans whenever certain specified conditions existed. There was some variation among the various commodities as to the conditions requiring loans to be made and the levels of support to be provided. For example, in cotton and wheat, if the price was below 52 per cent of parity at the close of the crop year, or if the current year's estimated

6. "Normal supply" was defined specifically though not uniformly for the various commodities. For example, "normal supply" of corn, cotton, rice and wheat was defined as "a normal year's domestic consumption and exports . . . plus 7 per centum in the case of corn, 40 per centum in the case of cotton, 10 per centum in the case of rice, and 15 per centum in the case of wheat. . . ." In computing expected supply "normal" yields were to be assumed for the acreages to be planted.

production was in excess of a normal year's domestic consumption and exports, loans were to be available at not less than 52 per cent nor more than 75 per cent of parity.

Decision as to what the level would be within this range was to be made by the Secretary of Agriculture. These were to be non-recourse loans. That is, if the price fell below the support level, and the borrower chose to surrender the product in satisfaction of the loan he would not be liable for any loss that might thereby accrue to the government.

For corn, different and more complex loan provisions were specified. Loans were to be made available in any year if the November estimate of production exceeded a normal year's domestic consumption and exports or if the November 15 price was below 75 per cent of parity. The loan rate was to be graduated in relation to expected supply as follows:

1. Not more than a year's domestic consumption and exports — 75 per cent of parity.
2. Ten per cent more than a year's domestic consumption and exports — 70 per cent of parity.
3. Fifteen per cent more than a year's domestic consumption and exports — 65 per cent of parity.
4. Twenty per cent more than a year's domestic consumption and exports — 60 per cent of parity.
5. Twenty-five per cent more than a year's domestic consumption and exports — 55 per cent of parity.
6. More than 25 per cent in excess of a year's domestic consumption and exports — 52 per cent of parity.

Loans in accordance with these provisions were to be available to "cooperators"; that is, to growers whose acreages of the specified crop did not exceed the allotments assigned by the Secretary of Agriculture provided the growers did not reject a quota plan proposed by the Secretary.

Control Methods Available

Thus the Secretary had available to him at least three devices for controlling "surpluses" of the major crops. Under the soil conservation and domestic allotment authorizations he could make payments for shifting acreages from "soil-depleting" to "soil-conserving" crops, and could make allotments of the acreages of major cash crops that could be grown by "cooperators," that is, by those who wished to be eligible for benefit payments and loans. Secondly, if, in spite of this, production threatened to become excessive, either through noncooperation or unusually heavy yields, he could announce marketing quotas. If approved by more than two thirds of the growers voting on them these would operate to keep off the market amounts in excess of those authorized for sale under the quota plan. Thirdly, he could provide nonrecourse loans which would enable growers to hold off the market supplies that were unlikely to be absorbed at prices considered suitable. The provision for reducing the levels of loan rates as accumulations increased was also expected to discourage continued high production.

It is apparent, however, that the level at which stocks were to be stabilized was inadequate as an emergency reserve against serious droughts, unless supplemented by other measures such as those discussed later under crop insurance and the "ever-normal" granary. As yet the possibility of abnormal needs in the event of war had not come into the thinking. The main concern, both in the government and among farm leaders, was still with surpluses and how to avoid them. There is little evidence of a developed policy in regard to stocks needed to meet possible emergency conditions. This "surplus" philosophy was in fact carried well into World War II, and proved a serious problem in the sharp adjustment made necessary by involvement in a major war.[7]

Later developments tended to overcorrect this defect in the plans. Farm and congressional pressure forced the maintenance of loan levels by the Commodity Credit Corporation which resulted in accumulations of wheat, cotton and corn that were far larger than those acquired under the Farm Board.

These stocks proved a boon when the war occurred, but they were in no sense a result of logical planning. In fact their existence was a major worry of government planners and would undoubtedly have caused a serious break in prices similar to the one resulting from abandonment of Farm Board price supports had it not been for the abnormal demands brought about by war.

Parity Payments

In addition to the types of assistance that have been outlined, the Secretary was specifically authorized to continue to make "parity" payments insofar as funds might be appropriated for that purpose. That is, if sufficient funds were available he might make direct payments to cooperating producers in amounts that would make up the difference between the prices received in the market and "parity" prices. Such payments were to be made on the "normal" production as defined in the act rather than only on that portion required for domestic consumption, which was the basis specified in the Act of 1936.

Consumer Safeguards

A gesture in the direction of safeguarding the consumer was provided in Section 304, but so vaguely worded as to have little real significance. Production was not to be discouraged to an extent that would reduce production below the amounts needed to maintain the per capita levels of consumption of 1920–1929. As of this time, however, the main concern was not that of maintaining adequate supplies but rather that of devising workable ways of hold-

---

7. The fortunate sequence of good crop years during World War II obscured this defect in policy and made it possible to meet the tremendous demands for American food supplies without serious hardship.

8. Wheat stocks reached a level of 632 million bushels in July 1942. (*Agricultural Statistics, 1945,* p. 9.) This compares to about 375 million bushels in 1932 and 193 in the Farm Board period. Corn carry-over had reached 688 million bushels as early as 1940. (*Ibid.,* p. 45. This was more than double the highest carry-overs of the early 1930's. Cotton carry-over was up to 13 million bales by 1939 (*ibid.,* p. 75) as compared to 9.6 million bales in 1931–1932, the peak volume of that period (*Ibid., 1937,* p. 93.)

ıg production down to amounts that could be ɔld at "parity" prices.

Since the consumer was interested princially in price rather than concerned about ɪe adequacy of supplies, and since it had ɪus far proved difficult or impossible to curɪil output enough to bring about high prices, ɪere was not much active consumer resistɪnce to the program. Concern over the high ɔst of food was to come later, especially in ɪe years following World War II.

Appendages to the Main Bill

The section on market quotas, loans and ɪarity payments, described above, was the ɪrincipal new contribution of the Act of ɪ938 with respect to the main current of agriɪultural policy. The act contained, however, a ɪumber of other sections which were really ɪeparate acts, but which had been included ɪ the omnibus bill either as amendments or ɪs a means of getting them through Congress ɪ the form of appendages to the main bill. ɪmong these were the provisions in regard ɔ freight rates, research on new uses of farm ɪroducts, crop insurance and surplus disɪosal.

Freight-Rate Adjustment

Section 201 authorized the Secretary of Agɪiculture to intervene on behalf of the farmer ɪ hearings before the Interstate Commerce Commission with respect to freight charges on ɪarm products.

This provision extended to the federal ɪealm a practice already well established in ɪany of the states. Since most freight tarɪfs had by now come under the jurisdiction ɪf the Interstate Commerce Commission the ɪtate public utility commissions had little to ɪo with them in a judicial way. At the same ɪime farmers and other small shippers were ɪsually poorly represented in hearings affectɪng their interests. The carriers, the large ɪorporations and the principal cities were ɪble to employ professional rate attorneys and ɪxperts to represent their interests in hearings ɪefore the Commission. It had therefore beɪome a common practice for the state com-

missions to employ specialists to appear in behalf of their shippers, and in opposition to the railroads, the large market centers in other states and, in some cases, the millers, packers and other large corporations.

The placing of the Department of Agriculture in this partisan role *vis-à-vis* another federal agency is of doubtful appropriateness. In any event its effectiveness as a proponent of lower freight rates has been negligible. More direct representation through state public utility commissions, cooperative associations and general farm organizations has, however, been brought to a relatively high level of organization and professional competence.[9]

Department of Agriculture collaboration is not likely to affect importantly the decisions reached, and may not warrant the expense involved. A more appropriate role for the Department in this realm would be that of carrying on continuing fundamental research in regard to the effects upon agriculture of the rapidly changing techniques of transportation, and ways of adjusting to changed space relationships within the agricultural market areas. The knowledge brought out by such studies could then be used, not only by the partisan representatives of agriculture in hearings before the Interstate Commerce Commission, but by the Commission itself in its efforts to analyze the probable effects of various rate policies. This is, to a large extent, the direction taken by the Department's activity in this field, though it has not been carried very far.

Regional Laboratories

Section 202 provided for the establishment, under the direction of the Department of Agriculture, of four regional laboratories for scientific research, to develop new uses and outlets for farm commodities and their products. This feature of the act grew out of a

9. For example, it is unlikely that intervention by another federal agency could have had influence with the Commission comparable to the spontaneous outburst of direct farmer representation organized by the American Farm Bureau Federation in 1921.

persistent belief on the part of certain farm leaders that vast new markets might be opened up for by-products and farm wastes by producing new kinds of products for use in industry.

During the years when feed grains were fantastically low in price there had been much interest in the possibility of converting them into alcohol for use as motor fuel. Several state experiment stations, and various European research agencies, had demonstrated the feasibility of producing and using alcohol in this way, but there was little evidence that fuel alcohol could be produced at a cost to compete with gasoline and still return to farmers a price for the raw product that would be in any way attractive to them.

The possibilities of farm relief by such means had been grossly oversold, and assumed far larger proportions in the minds of some farm leaders and congressmen than the cold facts of the situation would seem to warrant.[10] Industrial and other uses for the by-products of agriculture were not new. Much able and effective research had been carried on for many years in the laboratories of the large packing, milling and chemical companies. Many new products had been developed, but none that seemed in any way likely to revolutionize the farm marketing

10. This exaggerated conception of the place of so-called "Farm Chemurgic" in solving the farm problem had been widely propagandized for many years by the Farm Chemurgic Council. The Council grew out of a conference held at Dearborn, Michigan, as a result of the wide interest created by William J. Hale's book *The Farm Chemurgic,* The Stratford Company, Boston, 1934. This and numerous other propaganda books and pamphlets were financed by the Chemical Foundation, a nonprofit agency set up by President Wilson in 1919 to license the use of German patents taken over under the "Trade with the Enemy Act." The Farm Chemurgic Council, in its various publications, presented glowing accounts of the possibilities of gains to agriculture from the industrial use of farm products, and also carried on intensive propaganda for American self-sufficiency and high tariffs. Its publications included such books as *America Self-Contained,* by Samuel Crowther, Doubleday, Doran, Garden City, 1933; *America Strikes Back, A Record of Contrasts,* by Gustavus Myers, Ives Washburn, New York, 1935, and various others in a similar vein. For a more balanced discussion see H. E. Erdman, "An Appraisal of the Movement to Increase Industrial Uses of Farm Products," *Scientific Agriculture,* Ottawa, Canada. September 1939, pp. 20–28.

situation, or even to make a very noticeable difference in it.

This is not to say that the establishment of such laboratories was unwise or undesirable. Certainly the phenomenal progress along scientific lines during recent years points up the need for active and aggressive research in this realm. There is, however, a very real question as to whether the same input of funds might yield more through allotment to well-established and ably staffed commercial or university laboratories, where there is likely to be more cross-fertilization from other types of research and a possibility of attracting and holding more distinguished research personnel. In any event the gains from this approach to the farm problem are likely to be minor and continuing rather than large and sensational. In this respect they are comparable to those made through improvements in market organization and techniques, though probably not so impressive.

Surplus Commodities Corporation

By an Act of June 28, 1937, the life of the Federal Surplus Commodities Corporation had been extended to June 30, 1939. This was now again extended, to June 30, 1942. The Surplus Commodities Corporation had been set up by the Federal Emergency Relief Administration in 1933, and transferred to the Department of Agriculture in November 1935. Its principal sources of funds were allotments from appropriations for relief, in the early period, and later of funds made available under the Jones-Connally Cattle Act of 1934. From 1935 on the Corporation was financed mainly from the customs receipts assigned to the Department of Agriculture under Section 32 of the Act of 1935.[11]

From November 1935 to May 1938 the Corporation used about $58 million in the purchase of some 56,000 carloads of foodstuffs. These were turned over to state relief agencies for distribution to needy families. The kinds of commodities purchased varied from year to year, the aim being to absorb

11. 49 Stat. 750.

surpluses that threatened serious disruption of price structures. Purchases of this type and size could, of course, be expected to affect the minor crops more significantly than similar amounts spent on the major crops. During 1935 and 1936 the principal expenditures were for wheat, cotton, apples, prunes and butter. At this stage relief needs were a dominant factor in deciding what purchases to make.

During the year 1936–1937 the purchase of grapefruit ($2.5 million) and prunes ($2.3 million) constituted the largest items. Other commodities purchased in the order of their importance were eggs, dry skim and evaporated milk, butter, grapefruit juice, frozen fish, potatoes, fresh pears, onions, dried peaches, and various other fruits and vegetables. In the following year apples were in first place ($4.5 million for about 5.6 million bushels). Potatoes were second, and butter third, followed by oranges, prunes, rice, dry beans, eggs, canned peas, cottonseed oil, dried and canned milk, fresh pears, grapes and dried apricots.[12]

The 1938–1939 program involved expenditures of about $66.5 million for a long list of commodities, mostly fruits, vegetables and dairy products. More than half the total expenditure was for butter, the remainder being distributed in relatively small amounts over more than thirty minor commodities.[13]

Under Reorganization Plan No. III, effective June 30, 1940, the activities of the Federal Surplus Commodities Corporation were merged with those of the Division of Marketing and Marketing Agreements to form the Surplus Marketing Administration.[14]

12. Agricultural Adjustment Administration, *Annual Report, 1937–1938*, p. 85. Also U.S. Congress, House, Committee on Agriculture, *Federal Surplus Commodities Corporation*, Hearings, . . . 75th Cong., 1st sess., on S. 2439, Serial D, June 11, 1937.

13. Agricultural Adjustment Administration, *Report of the Associate Administrator . . . in Charge of the Division of Marketing and Marketing Agreements, and the President of the Federal Surplus Commodities Corporation, 1939*, p. 52. This report contains an extensive summary of the various surplus removal activities carried out by the Agricultural Adjustment Administration during this period.

14. See Surplus Marketing Administration, *Report of the Administrative Official in Charge of Surplus Removal and Marketing Agreement Programs, 1940*.

CROP INSURANCE

The idea of insuring farmers against losses due to crop failure began to take shape during 1935 and 1936 as a feature of the "ever-normal granary" plan. That plan, as first advanced, emphasized stabilization of supplies and prices rather than protection of the individual farmer against the hazards of localized crop damage. It was natural, however, that a mechanism devised for handling abnormally large crops should give rise to proposals for alleviating distress when production was unfavorable.

Interest in this problem was not new, but past experience with private and state plans had not been encouraging. As early as 1899 a Minneapolis fire insurance company undertook to write all-risk crop insurance. The experiment failed and was discontinued after one year. In 1917 two companies entered the field, only to abandon it after heavy losses. In 1920 the Hartford Fire Insurance Company undertook to insure farmers their costs of production on the basis of a premium of 6 per cent. In its first year of operation the company had claims of $2.5 million with premium receipts of only $800,000. Its 1921 policy was put on a more restrictive basis, but heavy losses were again incurred and the experiment was abandoned.

These early ventures involved insurance against price declines as well as natural hazards, since they assured a return of a given money income per acre. A few companies have continued to write all-risk insurance on fruits and vegetables, but the level of benefits in relation to costs has not been such as to lead to wide use of this type of protection.

Between 1911 and 1930 five states — Colorado, Montana, Nebraska, North Dakota and South Dakota — undertook to provide hail insurance through state systems.[15] Here again

15. The North Dakota state system had been started in 1911, but was unable, in 1911 and 1912, to pay the amounts due the beneficiaries under their contracts. Payments in 1911 amounted to 70 per cent and those of 1912 to 55 per cent. Thereafter farmers began to exempt themselves from coverage and business fell off to less than one half that of 1912. Experience in the other states was similar despite numerous changes in the legislation. Two private companies, the Home Insurance

the results were not encouraging, and business had dwindled to almost nothing by 1932, partly as a result of prices so low that farmers did not consider crops worth insuring.[16]

Farmers in high-risk areas continued to want protection against crop failure as well as against depressed prices, but most of them did not consider the available types of insurance attractive at the premiums required to keep the insuring agencies solvent. The severe droughts of 1934–1936 naturally intensified the interest in protection of this kind. It continued, however, to be centered largely in the wheat areas where crop yields were most variable.

The issue arose during the 1936 campaign when President Roosevelt, in a letter made public on September 20, appointed Secretary Wallace as chairman of a committee to prepare a report and recommendations for legislation to provide "all-risk" crop insurance. The letter stated that "Crop insurance and a system of storage reserves should operate so that the surpluses of fat years could be carried over for use in the lean years."[17] On the following day Governor Landon released two paragraphs of a speech he was preparing for delivery at Des Moines in which he urged that crop insurance be given fullest attention. He implied that the Democrats were trying to steal his measure. The debate that followed centered in part around the question of private versus public provision of insurance. Wallace contended that crop insurance was "too big a thing for private companies to handle."

Report on Crop Insurance

The President's Committee on Crop Insurance presented its report on December 23, 1936, and it was transmitted to the Congress

in the following February. The Committee gave three reasons for past failures in the field of crop insurance: (1) the limited areas covered; (2) the attempt to insure income rather than yield losses alone, thus in effect writing insurance against price decline as well as against crop failure; and (3) inadequate data for setting up an actuarial basis for such insurance.

The plan proposed was for a limited and experimental approach applying only to wheat. The price-insurance feature was to be omitted, and payment of both premiums and losses was to be in kind or, where this was impractical, in cash equivalent. The farmer would be insured for a yield up to a specified percentage of his normal yield. Premiums were to be determined on two bases, loss experience on the individual farm, and loss experience for the county or area. The bill presented took substantially the form of the proposals made by the President's Committee.

Crop Insurance Corporation Established

Though it was virtually a separate act, the crop insurance legislation was included in the Agricultural Adjustment Act of 1938 as Title V. It created within the Department of Agriculture an organization known as the Federal Crop Insurance Corporation. Capital stock of $100 million was provided by the government. Any impairment of this was to be restored only out of operating profits of the Corporation. The appropriation for the fiscal year ending June 1939 was to be limited to $20 million and was to be made only out of unexpended balances of the sums appropriated under Section 15 of the Soil Conservation and Domestic Allotment Act.

During the first three years of operation, beginning with the harvest of 1939, contracts were not to be for more than one year at a time, and insurance was to be on the basis of not less than 50 per cent nor more than 75 per cent of the average yield. The issuance of insurance in any county or area might be conditioned on a minimum amount of participation in the insurance program by farmers in the area. This was to avoid excessively

Company of New York and the Hartford Fire Insurance Company, were writing some insurance at a profit in 1930, but the amount was not large.

16. For a more complete summary see J. C. Clendenin, "Federal Crop Insurance in Operation," *Wheat Studies of the Food Research Institute,* Stanford University, March 1942, pp. 275–77. Also Bryant Putney, "Insurance of Growing Crops," *Editorial Research Reports,* October 9, 1936, pp. 257–70.

17. Franklin D. Roosevelt, *Public Papers and Addresses, 1936,* Random House, New York, 1938, p. 366.

igh costs in administering widely scattered individual contracts. Wheat was to be bought only in amounts equaling cash payments of premiums and wheat sold to avoid spoilage. Sales were to be made only in the amounts necessary to cover payment of indemnities or to prevent deterioration.

Problems Encountered

Even with this cautious and experimental approach the Corporation soon found itself faced with many of the problems that had caused trouble in the private and state systems. Others grew out of the tie-in with the agricultural control program or were the result of inadequate actuarial data and the newness of the undertaking. Administration of the program was placed in the hands of county crop insurance supervisors nominated by the county AAA committees and approved by the state crop insurance supervisors. The regional AAA offices also carried some of the responsibility for administration and for coordination with other phases of the AAA program.

During the first year of operation difficulties arose through the lateness of starting sign-ups. This resulted in some adverse selectivity. Farmers whose crop prospects were poor tended to sign up, whereas those whose crops looked promising tended to stay out. Participation was kept down to some extent by the fact that county supervisors could not, at that time, state definitely what the yield guarantee and premium for a given farm would be. Also many farmers were unable or unwilling to make payments in advance.

During 1939 the insurance program came more completely under the control of the county and state committees and regional supervisors of the AAA. Very liberal arrangements were made whereby farmers participating in the AAA control program could pledge future AAA payments. Noncooperators had to pay cash or wheat in advance. Beginning with the 1942 crop this plan was abandoned, and cooperators were permitted to obtain insurance by giving their unsupported notes payable, without interest, shortly after the harvest period.

Despite these liberal arrangements, and the fact that the government was paying all of the administrative expenses, participation in the program was disappointing, and, still more disturbing, was substantially less in the high-premium, that is the high-risk, areas than in the low-premium areas. Obviously it was the high-risk areas that had the greatest need for some such income-stabilizing arrangement. Furthermore, there was a repeat sign-up of only some 40 to 50 per cent in some areas, for example in Texas. The percentage was substantially higher in Illinois and Nebraska, but over the three-year period it declined sharply in North Dakota and Kansas, areas especially in need of protection.[18]

Results Disappointing

During all of the first three years of operation loss claims paid amounted to more than premiums collected even though national yields in these years exceeded the fifteen-year average by 3, 14 and 32 per cent respectively.

As of September 1941, $14 million of the $40 million capital committed up to that time had been drawn, and apparently had been used to absorb losses.[19] If the charges had been made high enough to bring premiums collected into balance with loss disbursements it was estimated that expense would have amounted to about 33 cents per bushel of premiums collected, or about 46 per cent of the value of the product as of that date (about 70 cents per bushel).[20] These figures give some indication of the reasons for the difficulties encountered in the earlier private and state ventures in the field of crop insurance. Costs would presumably be much lower, however, if volume could be increased, or coverage made more comprehensive, in the areas to which insurance is made available.

18. Clendenin, in *Wheat Studies,* March 1942, p. 262.
19. Operating expenses were estimated at about $4.4 million a year, and average underwriting losses at $4 million. *Ibid.,* p. 272.
20. *Ibid.,* p. 269.

In view of the unsatisfactory financial results of the first years of operation the Corporation's Board of Directors decided, in April 1941, to enlist the services of an outside, disinterested committee to study the operations of the Corporation and make recommendations.[21] The committee submitted its report on June 30, 1942.[22] Its conclusions were on the whole favorable to the procedures and policies that had been adopted. It commended the corporate form of setup, agreed as to the need for crop insurance, approved the policy of government subsidy to cover administrative expenses and stated that the costs of operation compared favorably with those of private insurance companies.

Criticisms and recommendations stressed the following points: Contracts should be for more than one year to avoid adverse selection in prospectively bad years. Termination should be permitted only after a fairly long advance notice, also for the purpose of avoiding adverse selectivity in coverage. The farm data available were not adequate. Alternate plans of coverage should be offered and publicized.

The committee also recommended that farmers participating in any of the wheat programs be required to carry crop insurance. Though favoring operation through the county AAA committees it urged increased control by the Corporation over the state crop insurance supervisors and closer supervision of the formulae and procedures in checking yields.

Cotton Crop Insurance

Inclusion of cotton in the program had long been urged, especially by Edward O'Neal, President of the Farm Bureau, who was from Alabama. A bill to include cotton was passed by the Congress in the spring of 1940, but was vetoed on the ground that the Corporation had

not yet gained sufficient experience and financial stability to warrant expansion, and that the broader coverage when provided should include all major agricultural crops.

Virtually the same bill was again passed in 1941, and was approved on June 21 of that year. The plan for cotton was essentially the same as that for wheat. This program, which was in effect during 1942 and 1943, experienced much the same difficulties as those which had been encountered in providing insurance in the wheat areas. In 1942 premiums paid in amounted to 31.5 million pounds; indemnities to 52.5 million. For 1943 the corresponding figures were 30.7 million pounds and 56.8 million pounds. Underwriting losses for the two years amounted to $11 million and administrative expenses to about $3.5 million.

Both programs came under sharp criticism in the Congress in the spring of 1943.[23] As a result the Agricultural Appropriations Act of July 12, 1943, prohibited the use of any funds for insuring wheat or cotton crops planted after July 31, 1943. This action brought to an end the initial experiment in crop insurance. The idea was not dead, however. An Act of December 23, 1944, authorized the insuring of cotton, wheat and flax beginning in 1945, and trial insurance on certain other crops. Later developments in this realm are discussed in Chapter 19.

INCREASED EMPHASIS ON BETTER DIETS

Throughout the period 1933 to 1940 agricultural policy makers in Washington continually sought and initiated new approaches to the problems of agriculture. The early emphasis on reduced production gave rise to much public opposition, particularly that phase of it which included the slaughter of small pigs and brood sows. There was a growing feeling both within and outside the

21. This committee consisted of Herman L. Ekern, former Insurance Commissioner of Wisconsin; Robert J. Laubengayer, former president of the United Life Insurance Co.; and William G. Cochran, a statistician formerly at the Universities of Glasgow and Cambridge.

22. Wheat Crop Insurance Consulting Committee, *Summary of Report . . . on the Operations of Federal Crop Insurance Corporation,* 1942.

23. U.S. Congress, House, Committee on Appropriations, *Agriculture Department Appropriation Bill for 1944,* Hearings before the subcommittee, 78th Cong., 1st sess., 1943, pp. 881–909; U.S. Congress, Senate, Committee on Appropriations, *Agricultural Appropriation Bill for 1944,* Hearings before the subcommittee, 78th Cong., 1st sess., on H.R. 2481, 1943, pp. 486–507.

government that more attention needed to be given to supplying adequate food to all groups, instead of curtailing production when the over-all supply was no more than adequate to provide a good diet for the entire population.

This attitude was strengthened by the rapidly growing body of knowledge about the role of vitamins in diet. This grew out of the pioneer work of McCollum, Davis and others during the period 1910 to 1930. Thereafter, progress in understanding the important role of vitamins in diet was very rapid. Hazel K. Stiebeling and Medora M. Ward of the Bureau of Home Economics brought out in 1933 a bulletin called *Diets at Four Levels of Nutritive Content and Cost,* which attracted wide attention.[24] Later studies based on these data indicated that an adequate or superior diet for all the nation's population would require more rather than fewer acres in production, though the pattern of production would be somewhat different.[25]

This point of view was further strengthened by work then being carried on under the auspices of the League of Nations which gave rise to widespread interest in the nutritional problem when brought out in the League report of 1937.[26] Though these re-

ports were closely studied by food technicians and a few others, the conclusions implied by them had gained little currency in the minds of the general public. Farm groups and most agricultural officials still thought in terms of surpluses of production rather than deficits in consumption. Nevertheless, this new emphasis gradually gained strength, particularly among the more forward-looking members of the official Washington staff in agriculture. As yet, however, little headway had been made in devising ways to bridge the gap between an apparent superabundance of production and an evident lack of adequate consumption.

Food Stamps and School Lunches

Certain additional steps were taken which looked in this direction, chief among them being the Food Stamp Plan and the School Lunch Program. These were in addition to the activities of the Federal Surplus Commodities Corporation, which had been set up early in the "New Deal" period for the purpose of channeling accumulated surpluses into constructive use. Its emphasis, however, was much more on the disposal of surpluses than on adequate and suitable diets for the undernourished. That emphasis was likewise apparent in the Food Stamp Plan and the School Lunch Program. Nevertheless, this period marks the emergence of a new attitude in regard to fitting production to food needs rather than to a past pattern of production and prices.

Under the Food Stamp Plan low-income families were permitted to purchase stamps which could be used in the purchase of foods. They were given, without charge, an additional value in stamps of a different color. These could be used for purchase of certain foods declared to be in surplus. The government would then redeem these stamps for cash when turned in by the retail food merchant. Thus, the arrangement was a device for subsidizing the consumption of certain products of which surpluses existed, but using the subsidy exclusively for the benefit of low-

24. Department of Agriculture, Circular No. 296, November 1933.

25. See, for example: National Resources Committee, *Agricultural Land Requirements and Available Resources,* Supplementary Report of the Land Planning Committee to the National Resources Board, Part III of the Report on Land Planning, 1935. Also various reports from the Bureau of Agricultural Economics, such as O. V. Wells, *Estimates of Quantities of Food Necessary to Provide Certain Specified Diets and Crop Acreages and Numbers of Livestock Required for Indicated Production,* February 13, 1942. Processed.

26. League of Nations, *Nutrition, Final Report of the Mixed Committee of the League of Nations on the Relation of Nutrition to Health, Agriculture and Economic Policy,* Geneva, 1937.

Further progress along these lines was made when the National Research Council, in December 1940, established the Committee on Food and Nutrition, later known as the Food and Nutrition Board. This agency was active, particularly during the war years, in advising on standards for adequate nourishment not only for the armed services but for Lend-Lease, postwar foreign relief and the general public. For a good summary of progress in the nutritional field during the 1930's, see M. L. Wilson, "Nutritional Science and Agricultural Policy," *Journal of Farm Economics,* February 1942, pp. 188–205.

income families instead of lowering the price generally for all purchasers. The School Lunch Program was much more specifically oriented to nutritional objectives, though some surplus agricultural commodities were assigned for this use.[27]

The progress in the attainment of better diets was not impressive during the period here under discussion, and so far as government programs for agriculture are concerned, the nutritional approach has tended to recede rather than to gain new emphasis in the years since the close of World War II. It seems likely, however, that eventually the growing public interest in improved nutrition will force more consideration of nutrition objectives in the planning of agricultural programs.[28]

POLICIES ADVOCATED BY THE FARM ORGANIZATIONS

As a whole the farm groups continued to support the main features of the agricultural program. However, the initiative in program planning was still in the administrative groups in the government agencies. Policy statements by the major farm groups differed somewhat in emphasis, but showed no marked disagreement in basic philosophy except that the Farmers Union reflected a closer affiliation with organized labor than did any of the other farm organizations.

27. For an excellent account of the school lunch movement both here and abroad, see H. M. Southworth and M. I. Klayman, *The School Lunch Program and Agricultural Surplus Disposal,* USDA Miscellaneous Publication No. 467, 1941.

28. Efforts were made from 1933 on to strengthen the laws relating to the Food and Drugs Administration, which had been little changed since their initiation during Theodore Roosevelt's administration. This movement, spearheaded by Rexford Tugwell, took form in the Copeland Bill (S. 1944) introduced on June 12, 1933. In its original form it was directed primarily toward penalizing false advertising. This approach encountered vigorous opposition, not only because of special-interest objection but also because such regulation was considered unworkable. After several attempts to gain acceptance of similar bills the Congress passed, in June 1938, a less drastic measure known as the Federal Food, Drug, and Cosmetic Act. (52 Stat. 1040.) In this the restrictions on advertising were abandoned and emphasis was placed on penalties for mislabeling, prohibition of the sale of harmful drugs and the setting of higher standards with respect to food products.

Grange Policy

The Grange wanted parity prices and incomes but opposed regimentation. It also stressed the importance of the family-size farm. It favored soil conservation, but maintained that the conservation program should not be used as a method of controlling acreage. Instead it emphasized the retirement of submarginal lands and the development of new uses for farm products.

On tariffs it maintained the high-tariff, isolationist position vigorously advocated by its National Master, Louis J. Taber. It did, however, oppose tariffs on nonrenewable resources, and favored the continuance of the assignment of Section 32 funds for use in bolstering the prices of farm products. Grange policy on farm credit looked to further decentralization of management in the Farm Credit Administration, and its restoration to independent agency status under a bipartisan board. The 1939 and 1940 resolutions urged continuation of the Farm Mortgage Credit Corporation for another five years — from 1940 to 1945. Extension of the life of the Frazier-Lemke amendment and continuation of the subsidized 3½ per cent interest rate on farm mortgages held by the land banks were favored.

Crop insurance, on a limited scale and without a specific tie-in with the control program, was included in the recommendations. The organization also expressed its approval of the rural electrification program. With respect to labor legislation, it opposed the wage-hour bill, favored reducing the age minimum in the child-labor bill from 18 years to 16 years and advocated, in 1940, a reconstitution of the Labor Relations Board to provide for representation of labor, industry and the general public. The Grange's traditional position on conservation was restated from time to time with minor modifications. Aid for farm forestry was advocated and the continuance of public acquisition of forest lands unsuited for farming was urged. Support was given for the retention of the Forest Service in the Department of Agriculture and, in addition, the transfer of the Grazing Service into that Department was recommended.

Position of the Farm Bureau

The Farm Bureau Federation's policy recommendations likewise showed no marked change in character from those of the earlier years of the decade. It endorsed the Agricultural Adjustment Acts of 1936 and 1938, but held that the benefit payments from the Treasury were not large enough.[29] By 1941 it was joining in the demand for mandatory Commodity Credit Corporation loans at 85 per cent of parity. It urged continuance of the 3½ per cent rate on land bank loans.

With respect to tariffs, its position was somewhat confused. It insisted that reciprocal trade agreements should not authorize reductions that would bring any farm product price below parity. It did, however, favor reduction of tariffs on industrial products, and in 1939 supported renewal of the Reciprocal Trade Agreements Act, stating that its studies indicated that the trade agreement program had been beneficial. Recommendation was made, however, that trade agreements be made only with the unanimous approval of the Secretaries of State, Commerce and Agriculture, and it opposed the contemplated agreements with Argentina, Uruguay and Chile, on the ground that these were agricultural nations and, hence, would compete unduly with United States agriculture.

The labor policy of the Federation was in the main unfavorable to the then current trend in labor legislation. Coercive tactics and boycotts were opposed. The exemption of agricultural labor from the provisions of the National Labor Relations Act was favored, and it was contended that the exemptions for agriculture under the Wage-Hour Act were too narrow.

In the realm of monetary management the Federation continued to advocate a monetary authority with power to reprice gold and

manage the currency. It also advocated the continuance of silver purchases at not less than 77.57 cents per ounce. Other policy statements dealt with TVA, rural electrification and marketing agreements. Continuance of TVA was favored, but no further extension of this type of organization until its worth had been more fully demonstrated. The general idea of the Rural Electrification Administration was approved, but with the qualification that if it continued to be managed in a highly bureaucratic way local groups should refuse loans until the arrangements could be handled on a more truly cooperative basis. Support of the marketing agreement procedure and of the continuing allotment of Section 32 funds was reaffirmed.

Farmers Union Recommendations

The Farmers Union policy was less clearly stated than those of the other two major farm organizations. Strong support was expressed for crop insurance and the ever-normal granary. The soil conservation program and the sugar program were likewise commended. The Union condemned the 52 to 75 per cent of parity loan provision of the Agricultural Adjustment Act of 1938. It maintained that benefit payments should equal the difference between prices received in the market and parity, and that CCC loans should be higher. Recommendation was made that commodity loan programs be made available with respect to any commodity if 65 per cent of the growers voted in favor of it. Continuance of the Surplus Commodities Corporation and expansion of coverage and increased protection under crop insurance were recommended.

The principal divergences between the Farmers Union program and those of the other farm organizations were in its vigorous support of the Farm Security Administration, more unqualified approval of the rural electrification program and, especially, its close affiliation with Labor's Nonpartisan League and other phases of the program of organized labor.

29. For a more intimate account of the Farm Bureau attitude and activities of this period, see Orville Merton Kile, *The Farm Bureau Through Three Decades*, The Waverly Press, Baltimore, 1948, Chapters 18 to 21.

Views of the Cooperative Council

The views of the National Cooperative Council did not differ markedly from those of the American Farm Bureau Federation. The two organizations have long tended to work in close cooperation with each other. The Council favored independent status for the Farm Credit Administration, opposed the requirements set up in the Fair Labor Standards Act, and advocated more judicial handling of the National Labor Relations Board. On tariffs its attitude tended to be protectionist. It recommended that reciprocal trade agreements be subject to Senate ratification, and that the policy of generalizing the application of such agreements be abandoned. In the marketing field the Council commended the marketing agreement and Secretary's order technique, but urged that it be broadened to include more commodities. Some support was given through 1936, 1937 and 1938 to the idea of commodity pools accompanied by permanent reductions in acreage as a solution for the farm problem.

The Council expressed mild approval of the soil conservation program, favored the Food Stamp Plan and the Surplus Commodities Corporation and advocated continuance of the Section 32 provision. By 1941 it was sounding a word of caution in regard to further accumulations of farm commodities, and proposed that some of the surplus be traded for strategic commodities from other countries. In 1941 the Council expressed approval in principle of the extension of social security to employees of farmer cooperatives.

Taken as a whole, the views expressed by the various farm organizations during this period may be regarded as substantially in keeping with those of the first half of the decade, with only such modification as the changing conditions and developing program would tend to bring about.

THE ROLE OF THE COMMODITY CREDIT CORPORATION, 1937–1941

The Commodity Credit Corporation, which was set up only a few months after the Farm

Board was abolished, came gradually to assume a role somewhat similar to that which had been played by the stabilization corporations.[30] It was, however, a more flexible instrumentality, and, because of more wholehearted support by the Congress, not so sharply limited as to funds. The successful outcome of the Corporation's initial ventures in making nonrecourse loans, especially the 1933–1934 program for corn, got it off to a favorable start and gave impetus to the "ever-normal granary" idea which Secretary Wallace was then beginning to popularize.[31]

This initial success, especially in respect to corn, was due largely to the droughts of 1934 and 1936 which prevented or cleared up what might otherwise have become embarrassing accumulations. The cotton loan problem was likewise eased by the reduced crops of 1934–1936. Whereas the Farm Board program had run head on into a sharply decreasing demand and several years of large production, the AAA program had the advantage of both artificial and natural decreases in output and a fairly rapid increase in buying power. The CCC loan program had likewise the advantage of being integrated with a far more broadly conceived array of agricultural activities which tended to support each other.

Functions of CCC

As originally conceived, the CCC program was designed as a stabilizing influence, that

30. The methods of the two agencies were different, but the underlying principle was similar. The Farm Board relied mainly on loans to cooperatives and direct purchase in the markets. The CCC made its commitments in the form either of loans made directly by it, or of agreements with commercial banks to lend with a CCC pledge to take over the loans at face value if asked to do so. Since the farmer might, if he chose, deliver the collateral in full satisfaction of the loan these loans were in effect tentative purchases with a right on the part of the seller to reclaim the product at the sale price if he chose to do so. The CCC procedure was more practical and effective than that of the Farm Board and reflected in some measure the lessons learned through the Farm Board experience. Nevertheless, it had many of the same weaknesses. These, however, did not become apparent until the latter part of the decade.

31. A more detailed summary of Commodity Credit Corporation operations is available in Geoffrey S. Shepherd, *Agricultural Price Policy*, Iowa State College Press, Ames, 1947, pp. 40–76. See also Reports of the President of the Commodity Credit Corporation for these years.

is, as a means of easing the impact on prices from abnormally high production or severe decreases in demand. On the supply side this implied the operation of something corresponding to the ever-normal granary. Actually that is the way the corn loan program of 1934 worked out.[32]

The Commodity Credit Corporation activities came to have a second purpose which was not compatible with its stabilization function. This was the function of maintaining prices continuously above their free-market levels, rather than merely that of ironing out the effects of ups and downs of production and demand. This, the Farm Board had contended, was not possible except as the stabilization operations were accompanied by effective production controls. The results in the years immediately preceding World War II tend to bear out that conclusion.

The experience and admonitions of the Farm Board were not lost on the AAA officials, and their plans did contemplate effective production control as the essential supporting feature of the loan program. That production control would not be highly effective, and that adverse court decisions would intervene, were not, of course, in their thinking during these early years. The later distortion of the program to make it a means for holding prices more or less continuously above their free market levels, even without effective production control, was in the main a result of congressional action rather than administration policy. In the absence of effective production control, the success of stabilization activities hinged on loan rates at moderate levels.[33] Since the loan rate was, in effect,

a price floor, farm state legislators demanded higher and higher levels of support, thus forcing the program more and more into an inconsistent and eventually untenable position.

Experience With CCC Loans

Up to 1937 no major difficulties were encountered, and the undertaking appeared to be relatively successful. It gained in popularity with legislators and farmers. The initial loan rates set for both cotton and corn were well above prevailing market prices. This action proved fortunate in view of the succeeding years of drought and the marked increase in demand which resulted from them.[34] The corn loans were liquidated without loss to the Corporation and with significant advantage to the borrowing farmers.

The Act of 1938 not only raised "parity" levels but directed specifically that nonrecourse loans be made available by the CCC on wheat, cotton, corn and certain other products, and provided criteria for determining the levels at which such loans were to be made. The formula prescribed resulted in loan rates for corn of 70 per cent of parity in 1938 and 1939 since these crops did not exceed normal by more than 10 per cent. For wheat and cotton in which production and/or carry-over were large the rates ranged between 52 and 57 per cent of parity.

At about this time, one of the weaknesses of this type of price support became more evident. The Agricultural Adjustment Act of 1938 had prohibited the CCC from selling any cotton at a price that would not cover all amounts invested in it, including any price adjustment payments. It also forbade sale, after July 31, 1939, of more than 300,000 bales in any one month or more than 1.5 million

---

32. The crop insurance plan was conceived as a central feature of the ever-normal granary idea. Since this did not take shape legislatively until 1938, and then only on an experimental and limited basis, the CCC program was actually the principal approach to stabilizing supplies. In 1940, the President of the Corporation commented: "In the financial sense the CCC is the Ever-Normal Granary." *Report of the President of the Commodity Credit Corporation, 1940*, p. 5.

33. It is not correct, of course, to imply that production control was entirely lacking in this period. However, it cannot be said to have been very effective except in the case of cotton and tobacco.

34. The 1933 cotton loan rate was put at 10 cents whereas the price in 1931 had been 5.89 cents and that of 1932, 7.15 cents. As a result of congressional pressure the rate was raised to 12 cents in the following year, but in 1935 was reduced to 10 cents, and in 1937 to 9 cents. The loan rate on corn was set at 45 cents in 1933, whereas the price in 1931 and 1932 had been about 35 cents. See Shepherd, *Agricultural Price Policy*, pp. 43 and 44.

bales in any one year.[35] This provision, which was designed to prevent glutting the market with cotton carried over from previous years, was a shortsighted and wholly unsound requirement. The larger the carry-over became, the greater was the need for heavier liquidation through some means if the accumulation was not to become eventually so top-heavy as to cause a breakdown of the whole plan.

It is an axiom in regard to such a policy as the CCC was designed to implement that the bin must be kept from running over, either by controlling production or finding outlets which keep the accumulations from reaching unmanageable proportions. The Farm Board had pointed this out and had demonstrated its correctness. Secretary Wallace had called attention to it. Yet, the cotton state representatives remained adamant on this point, and this unsound provision was left in effect even in the war years when its absurdity was doubly evident.

The cotton crop of 1937 broke all records with an output of almost 19 million bales. The crops of the following years were no more than two thirds as much, and during the war years, production fell off to about half this volume. Cotton carry-over had been gradually worked down from the high levels of 1932–1933 and was not seriously out of line at the middle of 1937. The huge 1937 crop again put supply and demand seriously out of balance, and stocks continued to accumulate in the following year. By 1939 the August 1 carry-over was more than 13 million bales, well over a full year's supply for both domestic use and export, and more than 3 million bales greater than the highest carry-over of the Farm Board period.[36]

By October 1, 1939, corn stocks were more than twice the usual amounts carried over in the 1920's and nearly as much above those of the early 1930's. Wheat carry-overs likewise were on the upgrade though they did not reach their highest levels until 1942 and 1943. In both of these years they were in excess of 600 million bushels, or nearly twice the levels attained in the Farm Board period, which were then considered very burdensome. Even the 1939 carry-over exceeded the highest level reached in the early 1930's.[37]

Danger of Breakdown

The CCC program was moving inexorably toward the same type of debacle as the one which had overtaken the Farm Board. Had the war not occurred, some change in policy would have been inevitable in view of the long run of good crop years that followed 1937. Despite these clear warnings of trouble ahead, the Congress, in May 1941, pushed loan rates still higher, setting a single specific level of 85 per cent of parity. This was later to be moved up even further, to 90 per cent, and in the case of cotton to $92\frac{1}{2}$ per cent.

The imminent breakdown of the price maintenance program was prevented by the heavy demands occasioned by the war and the enormous relief feeding task of the early postwar years.[38] The problem had not been solved. It had merely been postponed. By 1949, huge quantities of storable commodities were again being accumulated on the basis of price support, rather than of any considered and logical plan with respect to amounts needed as a safeguard to national and international well-being.

35. 52 Stat. 31 at 67, Sec. 381(c).

36. Under the President's Reorganization Order, effective July 1, 1939, the Commodity Credit Corporation became a part of the United States Department of Agriculture and wholly responsible to the Secretary of Agriculture.

37. As of 1940 the CCC had made loans on butter, corn, cotton, dates, figs, hops, mohair, peanuts, pecans, prunes, raisins, rye, tobacco, turpentine and rosin, wheat and wool. See Report of the President, 1940, pp. 3 and 4. Loans to associations of producers were made directly by the CCC. Nearly all of those to individual producers, that is, by far the largest part, were made through private banks or similar channels. The CCC agreed to purchase such notes on demand. Producers were charged 3 per cent interest, and the local lending agency received an amount ranging between $1\frac{1}{2}$ per cent and $2\frac{1}{2}$ per cent for its services.

38. This comment relates to the program as a whole rather than specifically to the CCC, which was only a part of the over-all effort to raise the prices of farm products. The CCC financial operations up to the beginning of the war were not such as to cause serious concern from the standpoint of actual losses. In part this fortunate outcome was due to the war itself. However, the groundwork for the more serious difficulties that developed in the late 1940's was laid at this time. Realized net loss up to March 31, 1941, amounted to $172 million. (Shepherd, Agricultural Price Policy, p. 65.)

It is clear that the unsettled political situation of the postwar world and the possibility of periods of low production make desirable relatively heavy stocks of storable goods, and that a large part of such storage must be financed and arranged by government. The appropriate criterion as to amounts and kinds to store should, however, be the maintenance of those stocks needed in the national interest. Continued accumulation as a means of holding prices at levels well above those that would result from a free market will inevitably lead to a breakdown, unless offset by rigorous controls over production and marketing or resort to large-scale dispersal through abnormal channels.

The Commodity Credit Corporation has enjoyed certain very marked advantages over the stabilization corporations of the Farm Board period. Not only are its powers more flexible and general, it has enjoyed a generally favorable attitude on the part of Congress. That has resulted in substantial increases in its power to borrow on the credit of the United States. This authorization was increased to $1,400 million under an act of August 9, 1940, and since has been enlarged still further. In addition, it has certain powers, not clearly defined, to borrow on its own credit. Thus it has not been forced, as were the Farm Board stabilization corporations, to discontinue loans and purchases when a specific amount of money had been committed. The war and postwar years have, however, seen a growing reluctance on the part of Congress to continue the Corporation and to make more funds available to it.[39]

THE FARM CREDIT SITUATION

The crisis in farm credit had largely spent itself by 1937, either through foreclosure of heavily mortgaged farms plus voluntary transfers to creditors, or by readjustment and refinancing of debts. Applications for land bank loans fell off from a peak of 402,829 in 1934

to 60,836 in 1937. The land banks had now become the largest institutional suppliers of farm mortgage credit. Their regular first mortgage loans amounted to $2,053,105,000 while an additional amount of $835,807,000 in Land Bank Commissioner first and second mortgage loans was outstanding.[40]

At the beginning of 1938 about 35 per cent of the nation's farms were mortgaged. The debt amounted to $7,214,138,000, a decline of more than 30 per cent from the peak level reached in the early 1920's. A major change in the method of financing had occurred. About 40 per cent of the total farm mortgage debt was now carried by the federal land banks and the Land Bank Commissioner on an amortization basis. In 1928 the land banks held only about 12 per cent of the total, and nearly all mortgage loans not held by the land banks, or the joint stock land banks, were of the short-term unamortized type. A major emergency operation had been carried through with marked success, and the groundwork had been laid for a permanent, comprehensive, federally sponsored farm credit system.

Though prices remained relatively low, and droughts plagued some areas, farmers continued through 1939 to reduce their net indebtedness. Payments in that year were at a more rapid rate than in 1929, or in any year of the decade between. This no doubt was due in part to the more orderly arrangements for repayment that had come in with the widespread adoption of the amortization plan of servicing debts. By 1940 the purchase of farms and borrowing of funds turned slightly upward for the first time in ten years or more. In that year the federal land banks and the Land Bank Commissioner helped to finance the purchase of 19,580 farms and made loans of more than $55 million.[41] As of about this date, the land market and

---

39. An Act of July 1, 1941, extended the life of the Corporation to June 30, 1943, and increased its borrowing power to $2,650 million. At this time, also, certain obligations of the Corporation with respect to the so-called Steagall commodities (see n. 49, p. 416) were specified.

40. Donald C. Horton, Harald C. Larsen and Norman J. Wall, *Farm-Mortgage Credit Facilities in the United States,* USDA Miscellaneous Publication No. 478, 1942, p. 12.

41. Farm Credit Administration, *Loans to Farmers and Ranchers—1940,* Circular A-22, April 1941, p. 6.

the farm credit situation had reached a condition of relative stability.[42]

New Legislation

The year 1937 was marked by two additional legislative and judicial actions which defined policy in regard to farm credit. Neither was of importance equivalent to that of the earlier legislation. Farmers had been endeavoring since 1934 to obtain legislation that would limit the power of the creditor to dispossess delinquent farmer-borrowers in times of acute economic distress. The Congress passed, in 1934, the Frazier-Lemke Amendment to the Federal Bankruptcy Act of 1898. This was to be effective until 1938. It constituted a severe restriction on the property rights of the creditor. The amendment was held unconstitutional in *Louisville Joint Stock Land Bank* v. *Radford* (295 U.S. 555) on May 27, 1935. A revised Frazier-Lemke Amendment was signed on August 28, 1935.

This was more carefully drawn, outlined more specifically the protection of the rights of the creditor and provided more direct control of the property when held under the supervision of the courts. The new amendment was upheld by the Supreme Court in a unanimous decision of March 29, 1937 (*Wright* v. *Vinton Branch of Mountain Trust Bank of Roanoke,* 300 U.S. 440). The act was thereafter renewed in 1938, 1940, 1944 and 1946. The 1946 renewal expired on March 1, 1947. At that time the amendment was allowed to lapse. There has recently been some agitation for passage of permanent farm bankruptcy legislation, but as of this writing such action has not been taken.

The other step taken was the passage of a

new act known as the Farm Credit Act of 1937, which amended in various ways the legislation previously in effect.[43] These modifications were designed to lessen somewhat the centralization of authority which had been markedly increased as a result of the changes made in 1933. The more highly centralized organization was undoubtedly well suited for the fast-moving, emergency operations of 1933 to 1936. By 1937 the situation had changed, and it then seemed logical to adjust toward more borrower control along lines envisioned at the time the land bank system was originally established. Member-borrowers were given more authority in the selection of directors of the district boards, voting was to be on a one-man-one-vote basis and the make-up of the boards of directors was changed to provide specific representation of farm loan associations, production credit associations and borrowing cooperative associations. The act also was designed to encourage consolidation of farm loan associations into larger, more efficient units, and provision was made for payment of a franchise tax of 25 per cent on the net earnings of the federal intermediate credit banks.

Efforts to Reorganize the System

Changes which were generally regarded as forerunners of a major shift in policy were initiated in 1939. F. F. Hill, who had become Governor of the Farm Credit Administration in September 1938, undertook to carry forward the policies established by his predecessor, W. I. Myers. These looked to gradual decentralization of authority in the system, and its maintenance as an independent agency operating without specific reference to the other agricultural programs. However, in the AAA, there had long been some feeling that the credit program should be tied in with the crop adjustment program, and used as an additional incentive for participation in that activity. To this end Secretary Wallace gained presidential approval of a plan to place the Farm Credit Administration in the

42. As of this time (1940) farm mortgage debt amounted to $6.5 billion as compared to $10.8 billion in 1922 and $9.6 billion in 1929. (*Statistical Abstract, 1949,* p. 381.) The average rate of interest paid by farmers on mortgage loans had been reduced from about 6 per cent in 1929 to approximately 5 per cent in 1940. (Harold T. Lingard and William D. Brown, *Interest Charges Payable on Farm Indebtedness, in the United States, 1910–40,* 1942, p. 21.) The value of farm land and buildings, which had shrunk from $66 billion in 1920 to $32.9 billion in 1935, had recovered slightly by 1940, being then recorded as $33.6 billion. (*Statistical Abstract, 1949,* p. 613.)

43. 50 Stat. 703.

Department of Agriculture, and thus under his direction. This change was made through provisions in the President's first reorganization plan which became effective on June 24, 1939.

The relations between Hill and Wallace became increasingly strained in the latter part of 1939. This resulted in the forced resignation of Hill in December 1939. He was replaced by A. G. Black, who had long been closely associated with Wallace, and was a supporter of his policies. Black was instrumental in sponsoring proposals which, though presented as measures for strengthening the local farm loan associations and decentralizing the system, were regarded by many of the farm groups as likely to have the opposite effect.[44]

The principal changes suggested were the substitution of a membership fee for the purchase of stock by borrowers, and a broadening of the liability for losses to the district basis, instead of leaving it to rest on the local associations. While some method of spreading more widely the risks of loss obviously was needed, and was in fact being used, the vague proposal put forward was inadequately spelled out, and gave rise to fears that the new plan would involve more centralization and dependence on government. The original conception of the system implied eventual full borrower ownership and virtually complete borrower control. The proposed change in organization was vigorously condemned by various farm groups, for which the chief spokesman was Albert S. Goss, formerly Land Bank Commissioner and at that time Master of the Washington State Grange.

Identical bills were introduced in the House and Senate in 1941, which were designed to implement the proposals put forward by FCA.[45] Hearings were held on the House

bill, but neither bill got out of committee. A new bill (H.R. 7091) was introduced in 1942 but was likewise lost in committee.

The National Grange, the American Farm Bureau Federation and the National Cooperative Council all passed resolutions during 1940 and 1941, deploring the action which discontinued the independent agency status of the Farm Credit Administration, and favoring, either directly or by implication, administration by an independent bipartisan board.[46]

PROBLEMS OF INTERAGENCY COORDINATION

The federal program relating to agriculture grew increasingly complex as new legislation was passed and new agencies came to have programs and interests that conflicted with or overlapped those of agencies already established. Prior to 1933, federal aid to agriculture, insofar as it impinged directly on farmers, was almost wholly in the form of grants to the state land-grant colleges, and the maintenance of certain regulatory and service functions.[47] The Smith-Lever Act of 1914 resulted in a far-flung organization for off-campus instruction and service to farm people. As a result, the state experiment stations, and in particular the agricultural extension services, were strongly entrenched and closely in touch with their farmer constituencies.

The initiation of a direct action program

44. This plan was presented officially in Farm Credit Administration Circular A-21, October 1940, entitled *Statement of a Method and Principles of Organization for Providing Long-Term Farm Mortgage Cooperative Credit.*

45. H.R. 5336 and S. 1797, 77th Cong., 1st sess. For a critical analysis of these bills and the one of 1942 see Chamber of Commerce of the United States, *Federal Mortgage Credit Legislation, An Analysis,* Washington, May 1942.

46. In adopting this position the farm groups were in conflict with a principle long advocated by most students of government, namely, that the number of independent agencies should be reduced in order to facilitate presidential administration of government agencies. Their opposition to the transfer into the Department of Agriculture stemmed actually, however, from fear that the agricultural credit activities would be used to exert pressure on borrowers to participate in other agricultural programs, rather than from disagreement with the principle stated above. There was in fact rather general recognition of the unsuitability of bipartisan boards for handling executive functions directly.

47. Until 1925, the acts providing federal funds for state agricultural experiment stations related almost wholly to research on technical production problems. The Bankhead-Jones Act of 1937 (49 Stat. 436), like the Purnell Act of 1925, permitted and emphasized studies of economic and social relationships though it did not limit researches to such problems.

reaching down from the federal government to the individual farm was not only a new development but one that was bound to create acute problems of interagency relationship. Further than this, there were already sharp conflicts and jealousies between such units as the Department of Agriculture and the Department of the Interior, both of which had responsibility for control of large areas of publicly owned land. The creation of the Agricultural Adjustment Administration in 1933 forced an immediate decision as to whether a new action agency extending down into the counties and local communities would be established, or whether such work would be carried on largely through the established state agencies, particularly the agricultural extension services. The old issue of states rights and the fear of federal intrusion lay close under the surface, and likewise the vested interests of bureaucracies, both state and federal.

In the early years a compromise solution was arrived at, partly to avoid conflict and partly because the new, fast-moving programs could be put into effect more quickly by using an established organizational framework in the states. The state directors of agricultural extension were named as state administrators of the program and elected county committees were set up, usually with the county farm adviser as an ex-officio member. This arrangement, while facilitating an early start on the program, did not prove satisfying either to the federal administrators or the state colleges. For effective administration of their action programs the federal administrators needed complete control of field staffs and ready acceptance of policies arrived at in Washington. On the other hand, state college officials were reluctant to disrupt their established lines of educational work, and not a few were less than enthusiastic about the "radical" new programs then being launched.

The Mount Weather Agreement

When H. R. Tolley took over the administration of the Agricultural Adjustment Ad-

ministration in 1936, he initiated action to separate the AAA from the extension services and to establish a direct chain of administrative responsibility from the federal agency down to the counties. Such action was welcomed by some of the extension directors, but aroused considerable animosity on the part of others. As a result of this, Milton Eisenhower, head of the Office of Land-Use Coordination, worked out with the Policy Committee of the Association of Land-Grant Colleges and Universities an understanding which came to be known as the Mount Weather Agreement of July 1938.[48]

The Mount Weather Agreement provided that the United States Department of Agriculture was to continue to administer directly from Washington the various action programs, but would cooperate with the land-grant colleges in setting up, jointly, state and county land-use planning committees. The state extension services were to set up county land-use planning committees as subcommittees of their county extension committees.

These committees were to include representatives of the action agencies and at least ten farmers. The county farm adviser might serve as executive officer or secretary. At the state level the director of extension was to serve as chairman of a State Land-Use Planning Committee which would consist of representatives of the various action agencies and a number of farmers.[49] While these com-

48. The Office of Land-Use Coordination had been set up by Undersecretary M. L. Wilson in 1937 as a means of coordinating the many programs having to do with land policy.

The Mount Weather Agreement is officially titled: *Joint Statement by the Association of Land-Grant Colleges and Universities and the United States Department of Agriculture on Building Agricultural Land-Use Programs,* July 8, 1938. For a summary of the setting for the agreement and an explanation of its content, see Bushrod W. Allin, "The County Planning Project — A Cooperative Approach to Agricultural Planning," *Journal of Farm Economics,* February 1940, pp. 292–301.

49. Whereas, prior to 1933, the extension service was about the only agricultural agency that had local representatives (except for state department of agriculture representatives in a few states), the development of the new programs had brought about a situation in which several agencies were working directly with the farmers, among these the Agricultural Adjustment Administration, the Soil Conservation Service, the Farm Security Administration and various others. If such activities were

mittees could not give orders to the action agencies, or supervise their work, it was agreed that if an action agency could not carry out a plan of action agreed on by this group, it was to advise the committee that it could not do so.

Coordination in Washington

The Mount Weather Agreement was followed by an attempt on the part of the Secretary of Agriculture to bring about similar coordination at the Washington level. This was to be accomplished by assigning to the Bureau of Agricultural Economics the leadership in shaping policy recommendations, that is, functioning as a general staff for the Department of Agriculture.[50] This constituted an abrupt and fundamental shift of emphasis in the role of the Bureau of Agricultural Economics. It had been developed as a research and data-gathering agency, aside from its regulatory functions, which were more or less separate.

At about this time H. R. Tolley, formerly Administrator of the Agricultural Adjustment Administration, became Chief of the Bureau of Agricultural Economics, replacing A. G. Black, who had become Governor of the Farm Credit Administration. Tolley made an earnest effort to provide the type of coordination and policy leadership desired, but was unable to make significant headway against resistance of the various strongly entrenched agencies in the Department.[51]

In the attempt to implement this plan the Bureau of Agricultural Economics was put in charge of the state and county land-use planning program.[52] This activity expanded rapidly and by 1940 was being carried on in 1,900 counties. However, the machinery devised for improving coordination at the national level, namely, the Program Planning Board, fell into disuse after Claude Wickard became Secretary in 1941. Shortly thereafter, the Wickard policy of setting up county defense and war boards directly under the AAA rather than under the county planning committees caused the planning committees to decline in importance and disappear.[53]

Rivalry of AAA and SCS

In the meantime there had grown up a certain amount of rivalry between the Soil Conservation Service and the AAA.[54] While both were committed to the saving and improvement of soils their methods were quite different. The main emphasis of the Soil Conservation Service was on educational and demonstration work, plus technical advisory assistance. During the first years of the program much government-financed construction work was carried on by Civilian Conservation Corps personnel working under the direction of the Soil Erosion Service (later the Soil Conservation Service). This was mainly on publicly owned lands.

not coordinated and made consistent, the possibilities of friction and bad public relations are obvious.

50. USDA, *Memorandum for Chiefs of Bureaus and Offices,* October 6, 1938, p. 7.

51. It may be questioned whether this function was an appropriate one for the Bureau of Agricultural Economics, even if there had been adequate support from the Secretary's office to make the plan effective. The Bureau could not take on such a task without in some measure jeopardizing public confidence in the integrity of its data gathering and analytical work which constituted its most useful and vital function. The Department obviously needed a general staff, but to be effective this needed to be attached directly to the Secretary's office, which is clearly the appropriate place for it. For an excellent analysis of these problems, see John D. Black, "The Bureau of Agricultural Economics — The Years Between," *Journal of Farm Economics,* November 1947, Proceedings Number, pp. 1027-42. Also *idem., Federal-State-Local Relations in Agriculture,* Planning Pamphlet No. 70, National Planning Association, Washington, 1950.

52. The efforts of the Bureau to carry out this assignment are presented in some detail in the *Reports of the Chief* for the fiscal years ending June 30, 1939 and 1940, particularly in the latter.

53. Black lists the following as principal reasons for the failure of the county planning committee plan to gain strength and general acceptance: (1) the plan was too revolutionary; (2) the farm organizations, particularly the Farm Bureau, did not want strong policy-making committees competing with them in the counties; (3) there was too much opposition from entrenched agencies in the United States Department of Agriculture; (4) the states did not like the regional offices set up by the Bureau of Agricultural Economics; and (5) the war brought other emphases into the foreground. Black, *Federal-State-Local Relations,* p. 16.

54. Secretary Wallace sought to forestall this through a memorandum of August 4, 1936, entitled *Functions Assigned to the Agricultural Adjustment Administration Under the Soil Conservation and Domestic Allotment Act, the Agricultural Adjustment Act Amended, and Related Legislation.* Nevertheless considerable rivalry developed, and the two programs moved forward more or less independent of each other.

In the late 1930's the program shifted to the fostering of soil conservation districts established under state laws, with counsel and technical assistance supplied by the Soil Conservation Service.[55] State authorizing laws based on a model suggested by the Soil Conservation Service have subsequently been passed by all of the forty-eight states, and a large part of the agricultural land of the United States is now included in soil conservation districts established voluntarily by the farmers affected.

The district plan facilitates soil conservation mainly in two ways: one, through an educational program that makes farmers aware of the erosion problem, shows them how to deal with it and provides technical engineering and other specialist aid in developing district plans; and, two, by providing a mechanism whereby farmers can work together in ameliorating community-wide erosion problems. They may, also, by majority vote (in some states two-thirds) prohibit certain undesirable practices or conditions if individual farmers fail to cooperate in the over-all program. In some states the districts also have power to raise limited amounts of funds through assessments on the lands benefited.

The program initiated by the AAA under the Soil Conservation and Domestic Allotment Act of 1936 was quite different in concept and operation. Under this plan farmers were paid both for shifting acreage out of "soil-depleting" crops and for adopting approved conservation practices. Heavy subsidies were involved, and it is clear that major considerations were the reduction of acreages in cash crops and the provision of a means for distributing public funds to agriculture. While the program has exerted an important influence by increasing awareness of the conservation problem, it can scarcely be contended that it provides an economical and efficient method of conserving soils.

The soil conservation district approach has gained steadily in public acceptance, and seems destined to become a permanent feature of American agriculture. The Soil Conservation and Domestic Allotment procedure appears more questionable except as an emergency device. It is evident, however, that a final conclusion on methods to be used in fostering conservation has not yet been reached.[56] There are vigorous partisans of each of the two methods here described, but it may be that some combination of the two will eventually prove more effective and economical than either plan used alone.

AGRICULTURE AND WORLD TRADE

The principal feature of the world trade situation, as related to agriculture during these years, was the growing interest in international commodity agreements. Some progress was being made in negotiating reciprocal trade agreements under the Act of 1934, as renewed in 1937 and 1940, but these, as yet, had not reached a stage where they had any marked effect on American agriculture.[57]

Many farm groups were distinctly hostile to this procedure in tariff making. This was particularly true of those representing the strongly protected agricultural industries such as the cattle, sheep, nut, fig and date producers, and of some others not so directly affected, such as the dairy interests which had long been strongly protectionist.

Much of the concern grew out of fear of what might happen rather than any clear evidence that American agricultural interests had actually, as they put it, been sold down the river. On the whole the negotiators of tariff agreements exercised discretion, and tended to avoid concessions that would have

55. Some financial aid in the form of use of heavy machinery and similar items was also supplied at government expense, especially in the early years of the program.

56. In the years following World War II several proposals have been made for improving coordination of these activities. These are discussed more fully in Chapter 19.

57. Henry J. Tasca, *The Reciprocal Trade Policy of the United States,* University of Pennsylvania Press, Philadelphia, 1938. See also T. W. Schultz and Associates, "Economic Studies of the Effects of the Trade Agreements Upon American Agriculture," (1939), in U.S. Congress, House, Committee on Ways and Means, *Extension of Reciprocal Trade Agreements Act,* Hearings . . . on H.J.Res. 407, January 1940, Vol. II, pp. 1722–1837.

severe repercussions on American agriculture.

The farm groups whose economic interests lay in a freer world trade, with larger imports as a means of maintaining exports of their products, had not yet become vocal in support of their interests. Among these were the growers of raisins, apricots, peaches, oranges, prunes and wheat. However, opposition to the program was tending to lessen in some of the major farm organizations, especially in the American Farm Bureau Federation, which was under the leadership of Edward O'Neal of Alabama, a supporter of the South's traditional position in opposition to high tariffs. The Grange, on the other hand, remained strongly protectionist under Louis J. Taber, a life-long protectionist from Ohio.

International Commodity Agreements

The effort to better agricultural conditions through international commodity agreements had gained new impetus as a result of the depressed condition of international trade, growing accumulations in the surplus-producing countries and deplorably bad conditions in some of the areas producing crops for export.[58]

Wheat

The rapidly expanding production of wheat in the exporting countries during the late 1920's and the world-wide character of the Great Depression brought about conditions of

58. An excellent analytical study of the commodity agreement technique is available in Joseph S. Davis, *International Commodity Agreements: Hope, Illusion or Menace?*, Committee on International Economic Policy in cooperation with the Carnegie Endowment for International Peace, New York, 1947. The same author gives a briefer running account of the various agreements under the title "Experience Under Intergovernmental Commodity Agreements, 1902-45," *Journal of Political Economy*, June 1946, pp. 193-220. See also International Labor Office, *Intergovernmental Commodity Control Agreements*, Montreal, 1943, and *International Commodity Stockpiling as an Economic Stabilizer* by M. K. Bennett and Associates, Stanford University Press, Stanford, 1949. An earlier study by P. Lamartine Yates, *Commodity Control, A Study of Primary Products*, Jonathan Cape, London, 1943, is also useful. Edward S. Mason's *Controlling World Trade, Cartels and Commodity Agreements*, McGraw-Hill, New York, 1946, reflects the situation as it looked at the close of World War II, and includes an analysis of the broader problem of cartels.

severe distress in most of the surplus wheat-producing areas. In the deficit countries there was a marked tendency to protect their own wheat growers by higher and higher tariffs or through import quotas. In an effort to solve these problems, numerous conferences on the wheat situation were held in the period 1930-1933.

One of the first results of these was an International Wheat Agreement, signed by twenty-two countries in August 1933. This provided for export quotas to be assigned to each of the exporting countries during the two succeeding years, and for the importing countries to discontinue their efforts to expand production. They were also to reduce tariffs and other restrictions as prices improved and conditions became more normal. This agreement proved unworkable, and broke down within the first year. It was officially terminated at the end of the two-year period.

During the next four years the wheat problem was not urgent since the droughts in North America had eased the pressure on the market. However, the large United States crop of 1938 again brought the problem into the foreground. The Wheat Advisory Committee, which had been set up in 1933, met in London in July 1938. This group made a further attempt to develop a workable agreement. These efforts were discontinued as a result of the outbreak of war in 1939. Wheat stocks continued to accumulate, however, and in July 1941 representatives of the United States, Canada, Argentina and Australia met with those of Britain to try to work out a plan. This conference resulted in the initialing of a Memorandum of Agreement to be presented to a full-scale international conference of countries having a substantial interest in international trade in wheat at such time as the holding of such a conference might prove practical.

In the meantime, in order to meet the current situation and lay plans for developing a pool of wheat for relief purposes, it was agreed that the five participating countries — the United States, Argentina, Australia,

Canada and the United Kingdom — would regard the provisions of the draft agreement relating to a relief pool of wheat, and the control of production, as in effect among themselves, pending the conclusions of the conference to be called later.[59] The growing demand for wheat during the next several years caused the matter to be left in this status until after the war. Later action in respect to it is discussed in Chapter 19.

Coffee

A second trouble spot in which international agreement was sought was that of coffee production and distribution. This was not of direct concern to American farmers, except as consumers, but was of some interest to them as an example of another producer group struggling with somewhat the same type of problem as that which faced them.

Brazil, the largest exporter of coffee, had undertaken to solve its problem unilaterally throughout the 1920's and early 1930's, but with indifferent success. The South American countries had established in 1936 the Pan-American Coffee Bureau, the purpose of which was to increase consumption in order to absorb the excess production that had for years depressed the coffee market. A second conference was held in Cuba in 1937.

The situation became more serious after the outbreak of war in 1939, since Europe had previously taken some 38 per cent of the exports from the Western Hemisphere.[60] Conditions in the coffee-exporting areas became still worse, and a third Pan-American

Coffee Conference was called in New York in June 1940. At this time it was concluded that the cooperation of the United States, the largest customer, would be necessary if any orderly plan of selling was to be achieved. The result was the Inter-American Coffee Agreement, signed by fourteen coffee-producing countries and the United States on November 28, 1940.

The Agreement set up a board to administer the plan. In this board the United States had 12 votes, Brazil had 9, Colombia 3, and the others 1 each. Export quotas were to be established for each country. Through participation by the United States, the single dominant customer, such quotas could be fairly well enforced. The original agreement carried to 1943, and was extended without change for two one-year periods thereafter. Quotas were suspended in October 1945. Brazil's production fell off sharply after 1941. The postwar situation became one of relatively short production and high prices which seems likely to continue for at least a number of years.

The coffee agreement broke new ground in that it was more specifically a joint undertaking on the part of the producing and consuming countries than were most of the other international agreements. In view of the dominant position of Brazil as a producer and of the United States as a consumer, it had somewhat the character of a bilateral agreement. It can hardly be said, however, that any significant body of principles was arrived at as a basis for determining prices under such conditions. The arrangement was largely an expedient designed to prevent chaotic conditions in the coffee-producing countries under the abnormal marketing situation of the war period. As such it was moderately successful.

Later developments were to raise a basic question as to the relative merits of a complex series of international commodity agreements as against an effort to return to a pattern of freer world trade. In this controversy conflicting views became evident within the government of the United States, especially as

59. Office of Foreign Agricultural Relations, *The International Wheat Agreement, Prepared at the Washington Wheat Meeting, July 1941-June 1942*, and Department of State, *Wheat; Memorandum of Agreement Between the United States of America, Argentina, Australia, Canada and the United Kingdom; Initialed at Washington April 22, 1942, Effective June 27, 1942, and Related Papers*, Executive Agreement Series 384.

60. From 1935-1939 the United States took about 50 per cent of the world imports of coffee. From 1940-1944 this percentage was increased to 80. See V. D. Wickizer, *The World Coffee Economy with Special Reference to Control Schemes*, Food Research Institute, Stanford University, 1943, Chapter 11; and Davis, "Experience Under Intergovernmental Commodity Agreements, 1902-45," pp. 206-10.

between the Department of Agriculture and the Department of State.

The International Beef Conference

A somewhat similar plan was worked out in 1937 with respect to beef. Here the chief customer was the United Kingdom while the principal suppliers were Argentina, Uruguay, Brazil, Australia, New Zealand and Eire. The purpose was to stabilize imports and keep prices steady but not unduly low. Quotas were assigned, but decisions on quotas had to be unanimous. As a whole the arrangement worked out reasonably well during the period here under review.[61]

Sugar

A new international sugar agreement went into effect in 1937 to replace the Chadbourne Plan, which had been in operation from 1931 to 1935. The earlier agreement included only exporting countries (Cuba, Java, Germany, Belgium, Czechoslovakia, Hungary, Poland, Yugoslavia and Peru). The new one included importing countries which produce part of their own supplies, among them the United States, the United Kingdom, France, Russia and Brazil.

Neither agreement worked out well. In the earlier plan, which was, in effect, a governmental cartel, output of the member nations was reduced by some seven million tons, but the importing nations increased their production by more than four million tons. Much of this increase was due to artificial supports of one kind or another. Under the later agreement the importing countries were unwilling to reduce their output substantially and many of the exporting countries contended that they must continue their levels of output in order to survive. The underlying conflict is between low-cost cane sugar production and artificially supported, high-cost beet sugar production. In addition, heavy excise taxes held down consumption in many of the European countries.

The agreement was kept nominally in being until 1942 but its effect was not important

61. *Ibid.*, pp. 215-17.

after the outbreak of war in 1939. Even before that its significance was not great. The management of the world's sugar supply took a markedly different form during the war, and new peacetime approaches to the problem were inevitably deferred to the postwar period.[62]

Other International Agreements

Certain other agreements were undertaken during this period, and earlier, but for lack of space are not discussed. Among these were the rubber scheme, which was in effect in one form or another from 1921 on, and the tea agreements of 1936 and 1938.[63] The various commodity agreements entered into during this period and before cannot be said to have achieved general acceptance and approval, nor has any consistent policy and body of principles evolved. There has been much discussion of the problem by economists, most of it, except that emanating from official agencies, being somewhat critical in tone.[64] It is evident, however, that proposals of this kind will come more and more under consideration if and as burdensome supplies of internationally traded commodities accumulate or if prices decline sharply.

General Position of International Trade

There were no important changes in the general trading position of the United States during these later years of the decade. As yet, the reciprocal trade agreement program had not progressed far enough to affect greatly the general level of tariffs, but some recovery

62. *Ibid*, pp. 202-05.
63. See K. E. Knorr, *World Rubber and Its Regulation,* Food Research Institute, Stanford University, 1945, and V. D. Wickizer, *Tea Under International Regulation,* Food Research Institute, Stanford University, 1944.
64. See, for example, Joseph S. Davis, "New International Wheat Agreements," *Wheat Studies of the Food Research Institute,* Stanford University, November 1943, pp. 25-83; also his address at Winnipeg, Manitoba, on August 17, 1944, *After the War: Freer Trade or Far-Reaching Controls?* Also Edward S. Mason, "The Future of Commodity Agreements" in *Food for the World,* The Harris Foundation Lectures, Theodore W. Schultz (ed.), University of Chicago Press, Chicago, 1945, pp. 230-47; and George W. Stocking and Myron W. Watkins, *Cartels in Action, Case Studies in International Business Diplomacy,* The Twentieth Century Fund, New York, 1947, pp. 14-117.

in international trade was apparent.[65] Both imports and exports moved up gradually from 1932 on, but suffered a setback in 1938.

Imports fell off more than exports. This was due partly to the business recession and partly to the recovery in United States crop production which changed some of the crop deficits of the drought years into export surpluses. The value of United States agricultural exports remained approximately uniform from 1932 to 1938 but fell off in 1939.[66] Generally speaking, low prices between 1931 and 1934 offset the larger quantities exported; higher prices held up the values in 1935–1937; and lower prices again offset the increased quantities of 1938.

Gold flowed out of the United States in substantial volume from 1934 on, but in spite of this the United States still held the lion's share of the world's gold stocks. By 1939 its holdings amounted to more than $17 billion as compared to slightly under $26 billion for all countries combined. While the government had abandoned efforts to manipulate the values of gold and silver, some of the aftereffects of the earlier devaluations and adjustments were still being felt. For example, the high price of gold had stimulated markedly the mining of new gold.[67]

One major agricultural export, cotton, experienced a persistent decline in importance during this period. In 1911, American cotton constituted about 60 per cent of all cotton used abroad. By 1921 this share had fallen to 50 per cent, and by 1931 to 45 per cent. In 1936 it was down to 32 per cent, and in 1937 was only 23 per cent. Critics of the United States agricultural program charged that the artificially high prices maintained on American cotton were destroying our markets and stimulating competing production in other areas. There was considerable evidence to support this contention, though, as Secretary

Wallace pointed out, a continuation of the downward trend in the American portion of the world cotton market would have resulted in considerable further reduction even had there been no cotton program.[68]

It is clear that world trade did not become stabilized or well adjusted in this period. The United States was pressing forward along two lines that were inconsistent with each other, namely, the Hull reciprocal trade program designed to increase the freedom of trade, and the commodity agreement plan in which the Department of Agriculture was active, which looked in the direction of a more planned and controlled pattern of trade. At the same time, several large importing nations were maintaining or even increasing the severe restrictions they had placed on international trade. The United States had accumulated a disproportionate share of the world's gold and silver stocks and also was following price policies, with respect to agricultural products, which tended to handicap exports. The outbreak of war in 1939 came therefore as a further disruption of an already chaotic world trade situation.

The Shift to Defense Emphasis

The outbreak of war in September 1939 changed the world situation markedly, but did not affect domestic agriculture greatly. Heavy spending by Britain and France for military equipment created more employment and higher earnings for industrial workers. It also operated to drain off many farm workers who were not needed in agriculture. The nation had at this time, however, so much unemployed and underemployed labor, and so much unused factory capacity, that war orders and defense activities caused no important shortages and provided little stimulus to prices.

Farm prices in nearly all lines were in fact lower in 1940 than in the years just preceding.[69] This trend was sharply reversed in

65. Insofar as duties were specific rather than ad valorem the lower price levels then prevailing served to raise the duties as percentages of the values of the commodities.

66. See Hal B. Lary, *The United States in the World Economy*, Department of Commerce, Economic Series No. 23, 1943.

67. *Ibid.*, pp. 134 and 136.

68. See his address, *Charting the Course for Cotton*, Memphis, Tennessee, October 1, 1937.

69. The 1935–1939 average (in terms of 1909–1914 as 100) was 107 whereas the 1940 index was only 100.

1941 when farm prices were up nearly 25 per cent from the low 1940 level. Farm production likewise moved up from 110 in 1940 to 113 in 1941 (1935–1939 = 100).[70] Nonfarm prices behaved in a similar way except that the 1940 level was a little above the 1935–1939 level instead of a little below.[71] Industrial production reached in 1939 about the level achieved in 1929, with an index of 109 (1935–1939 = 100). Thereafter, it moved up sharply to 125 in 1940 and to 162 in 1941.[72] Employment in manufacturing industries rose from 100 in 1939 to 107.5 in 1940 and to 132.1 in 1941.[73]

For the major farm products, supplies were so ample and production prospects so good that almost no concern was felt about the ability of the United States to meet any demands likely to be made upon it for foodstuffs and fiber. The administration, particularly the President, was more aware of the danger of United States involvement in the war than was the general public. However, many segments of the population were strongly isolationist. The President therefore stressed planning for defense in his effort to bring the nation to a higher stage of preparedness. In the spring and summer of 1940 he established the National Defense Advisory Commission, which was the parent of many of the later war agencies such as the War Production Board, the War Food Administra-

tion and the Office of Price Administration. A National Defense Research Council, under the leadership of Dr. Vannevar Bush, was likewise set up and thus the groundwork was laid for the research that eventually resulted in the atomic bomb.[74]

In this way, the mobilization of civilian resources was being put in motion at the same time that the selective service officials were getting under way with a corresponding mobilization of military personnel and equipment. These steps were, of course, greatly facilitated by the large orders for equipment already placed by Britain and France.

With the fall of France and the approaching exhaustion of Britain's dollar resources the lend-lease program was inaugurated. Thereafter, the defense preparations took on more and more the characteristics of direct participation in the war. All-out mobilization was to come only after the surprise attack on Pearl Harbor. Even this, however, did not have immediate, large effects on American agriculture. Farm labor grew increasingly scarce and costly, and some restrictions on agricultural output were relaxed. But the principal effect was to give farmers a go-ahead signal on a production program they were already equipped for and anxious to proceed with. The resulting output over the succeeding years was to be a source of wonder and gratification throughout the free world.

A marked rise to 124 occurred in 1941. (*Statistical Abstract, 1948*, p. 641.)

70. *Loc. cit.*
71. *Ibid.*, p. 642.
72. *Ibid.*, p. 827.
73. *Ibid.*, p. 202.

74. For a good account of these developments and the people who were instrumental in bringing them about, see Robert E. Sherwood, *Roosevelt and Hopkins, An Intimate History,* Harper and Brothers, New York, 1948, Chapter 7.

CHAPTER 16

WAR CHANGES THE EMPHASIS

THE ECONOMIC OUTLOOK for American agriculture and industry was suddenly changed by the entrance of the United States into the war in late 1941. The policies which had been put into effect over the preceding ten years were designed to meet depression conditions. Throughout that period the fear of too much production dominated thinking both in agricultural and industrial circles. Efforts were made to keep idle, or at low tempo, sizable portions of the nation's resources. Industry was slowed down through NRA code quotas, and by entrepreneurial decisions; agriculture through acreage and marketing controls; and labor through short hours, make-work policies and restrictions on output.

THE NEED FOR QUICK REVERSAL OF FARM POLICY

When war came, the nation was suddenly called upon to go into high gear and to turn out vastly more goods than it ever had produced before. The need for a quick readjustment in emphasis and type of program was apparent. Yet, in agriculture, the actual shift-over to an all-out drive for full production was somewhat slow. The ways of thinking and the kinds of laws developed in the 1930's were not easily put aside. The fear of surpluses was more evident than the fear of shortages. Congressmen continued to stress protection of the farmer against low prices, and the men in charge of the agricultural programs moved cautiously. The administrators who headed the nonagricultural war agencies were, generally speaking, brought in for the specific purpose of stepping up and changing production. Agriculture, on the other hand, already had a large bureaucracy consisting of men who for years had been fighting to keep production down and prices up. Many were career men who felt that if they erred too greatly on the side of excess production they themselves would later be the chief targets of farmer and public criticism.

Farm Program Not Designed for War

Agriculture's plans had not contemplated war. The heavy stocks of basic farm products that had been built up were fortuitous results of serious defects in the earlier program rather than evidence of foresight. They would almost certainly have brought disaster had it not been for the insatiable demand that grew out of the war. Here, as in 1934, favorable circumstances offset factors of weakness in the peacetime program. In the early years of the Roosevelt administration, droughts made it possible to clear up the troublesome surpluses acquired in the early 1930's. Now war demand was to clear up difficulties created by the maintenance of excessively high support prices in the late 1930's. The underlying cause of the large accumulation of storable commodities in 1939, 1940 and 1941 was almost identical, in principle, with that which had been responsible for the difficulties experienced by the Farm Board in 1932, namely, continuous accumulation in an effort to maintain prices above their free-market levels.

In the winter of 1939–1940, the nation did not have a genuine program of preparedness. The war still seemed remote, and many Americans opposed any action that might seem to invite war. The President took various steps designed to strengthen the nation's war potential, but had to move cautiously. He no longer had an acquiescent Congress, willing to go along on almost any program the White House might propose. Tension be-

ween the Congress and the Executive had
een growing for several years, and proposals
nade by the President now had to be judi-
iously phrased and carefully handled.

The fall of France, in May 1940, brought a
learer realization of the danger to American
nterests. It opened the way for the vague ap-
roach known as "defense planning," which
asted from May 1940 to December 7, 1941. It
lso created an atmosphere in which public
pinion could be prepared for lend-lease aid
o Britain, and later, after the German attack
f June 1941, to Russia. Nevertheless, much
quiet progress was being made in the prepa-
ation for war, particularly in the industrial
ealm. The heavy orders placed by Britain,
nd to a lesser extent by France, led to a
apid stepping up of facilities for airplane
nanufacture, ship-building and many other
ypes of war preparation. Idle factories were
eactivated; new ones were built. Idle labor
vas put to work. Agriculture, fortunately,
vas in such a strong position, and its plant
o adequate, that little more was needed than
 freeing of the shackles designed to hold it
t low levels of production, and the incentive
f higher prices.

Outlook Changed by Pearl Harbor

The attack on Pearl Harbor shocked the
nation into full realization of its danger. Almost overnight a new unity of purpose replaced the bickering and complacency which
nad marked the early years of the war. The
nation was ready to gird itself for an all-out
mobilization of resources. Only in agriculture
was there any noticeable dragging of feet, and
even there such hesitation was more on the
part of government administrators and congressmen than of farmers themselves.

Some planning had been done, but many
arrangements necessary to a full-scale mobilization were still to be worked out. Notable
among these was the machinery for handling
price controls, rationing and wage controls.
This had to be improvised hastily, and with
inadequate provision for recruiting and train-
ng staffs. The process both on the military
and civilian sides was greatly facilitated and

speeded by the opportunity that existed for
drawing on Britain's experience of more than
two years in operating a war economy.

During 1940 and 1941, an attempt was
made to use, in agriculture, the county land-
use planning committees and the Interbureau
Coordinating Committee as a mechanism for
"defense planning." The suggestions sent out
to the state and county committees during
1940 were, however, quite innocuous as preparations for either defense or war. They still
dealt largely with plans to protect agriculture
against possible adverse effects growing out
of the defense program.[1] Though the situation was more adequately handled than in
the corresponding period preceding American
involvement in World War I, it cannot be
said to have reflected farsighted and vigorous
planning for a major emergency.

Stronger Leadership by USDA

By late 1940 and early 1941, the prospect of
a greatly expanded demand for food became
more apparent, and stronger leadership began
to be exercised by the Department of Agriculture. For example, the survey of expected
1941 spring farrowings of pigs indicated a
drop of 14 per cent, as compared to farrowings in 1940. The Secretary of Agriculture
asked farmers to maintain the 1940 level of
pig production. The need for such maintenance of output had become much more
apparent after passage of the Lend-Lease Act
of March 31, 1941. It was then evident that
shipments of pork, dairy products, eggs and
canned vegetables to Britain would be stepped
up materially.

On April 3, the Secretary explained the
need for more production of these commodities, and promised to support their prices at
specified levels. Hogs, which had sold at
about $6 in 1940, were to be supported at $9.
Higher levels of support for other products
were also promised.[2] The government also

1. See, for example, USDA, *Agriculture's Plans to Aid
in Defense and Meet the Impacts of War,* July 23, 1941,
mimeographed.
2. These undertakings afford a good illustration of
the device later to be referred to as "forward pricing."
As a means of stimulating desired increases under con-

began to purchase heavy hog cuts at prices that would eliminate the usual differential between these and the lighter cuts, thus providing an incentive for feeding hogs to heavier weights. Increased output of white beans was likewise requested despite the fact that supplies on hand already appeared somewhat burdensome. Encouragement was also given for an increase in the production of garden seeds, fiber flax, hemp and castor oil — products which were mainly imported and which seemed likely to be in short supply.

By the summer of 1941, other steps were being taken to increase agricultural output. The mechanism formerly used in making agricultural outlook statements was modified so as to be a means of setting up production goals for the guidance of farmers. The first set of goals, issued in September 1941, called for increases in nearly all important farm commodities, except wheat, cotton, rice, beans, flaxseed and tobacco. A supplementary announcement (in January 1942, and after Pearl Harbor) called for larger increases and for some stepping up in the production of tobacco, rice, beans and flaxseed. The requested downward adjustment of wheat was changed from 16 per cent to 12 per cent. Largest increases requested were for peanuts, soybeans, flaxseed and peas.[3]

Organizational Changes in USDA

The President had set up, in May 1940, a National Defense Advisory Commission in which the interest of agriculture was recognized by the appointment of Chester C. Davis, former administrator of the Agricultural Adjustment Administration. When the

ditions of rising demand, it has much to recommend it. Its usefulness in periods of oversupply is much less clear. The action thus taken was the first indication of vigorous facing up to the changed situation in agriculture and was a creditable demonstration of courage and foresight on the part of Secretary Wickard. The lack of these qualities in some of the congressional leaders was shown by their criticism of the action on the ground that these support prices might become ceilings as well as floors.

3. By this time it was apparent that the fats and oils formerly derived from the Pacific area would be cut off. For a full list of the recommendations see Walter W. Wilcox, *The Farmer in the Second World War*, Iowa State College Press, Ames, 1947, p. 41.

Lend-Lease Act was passed in March 1941, Davis suggested the creation of a food administration to purchase foodstuffs for lend-lease shipment and to make a survey of the ability of agriculture and the processing industries to meet probable needs. The President rejected this proposal, and directed instead that purchasing for lend-lease be handled by the Surplus Marketing Administration.

The comparative adequacy of food supplies at that time made such action as Davis suggested seem premature. The real nature of the food problem did not become evident until the attack on Pearl Harbor threatened to make unavailable the fats and oils, wheat and other food resources of the whole Pacific area, while at the same time increasing enormously the prospective demand.

During the summer of 1941, Secretary Wickard undertook modest steps designed to mobilize the resources of agriculture for defense (or war). An Office of Agricultural Defense Relations was created on May 5. This was intended as a coordinating unit to handle the Department's relations with the new defense agencies then being set up in other parts of the government. The action was taken at the President's request, as a result of Davis' resignation from the National Defense Advisory Council, which left it without an agricultural representative.

Shortly thereafter, Secretary Wickard undertook to focus the work of the state and county agricultural agencies on defense problems by creating state and county defense boards which in effect replaced the state and county land-use planning committees set up in 1938.[4] After Pearl Harbor, the name of these was changed to state and county war boards, and this general organization, outside Washington, remained in effect throughout the war.

Within the Department of Agriculture steps were taken in December 1941 to reduce the number of agencies reporting directly to the Secretary, and to free him for more active

4. USDA, *Secretary's Memorandum*, No. 921, July 5, 1941 and No. 921, Supplement 1, January 7, 1942.

participation in the war effort.[5] On June 5, 1942, he was designated chairman of a Food Requirements Committee containing representatives of the War Production Board, the Office of Price Administration, the Army, the Navy and other agencies concerned with food problems. The general plan of operation established in the early part of 1942 contemplated that WPB would control supplies of scarce materials, OPA would control prices and distribution to household consumers, and the War Manpower Commission would exercise control over labor. By joint announcement, in June 1942, President Roosevelt and Prime Minister Churchill carried organization to the international level by establishing the Combined Food Board, which was charged with the allocation of foodstuffs among the allies and other friendly nations, and the coordination of international efforts to assure adequate food supplies.

War Food Administration Created

There was growing dissatisfaction with the lack of centralized authority in the handling of domestic food problems. This resulted in a presidential order of December 5, 1942, which established in the Department of Agriculture a Food Production Administration and a Food Distribution Administration, both responsible to the Secretary of Agriculture.

Under the same order WPB activities in food production and distribution were transferred to the Department of Agriculture.[6] On March 26, 1943, the two new agencies were combined to form an Administration of Food Production and Distribution with a separate administrator appointed by and directly responsible to the President.

Chester C. Davis was appointed as administrator, taking over from the Secretary of Agriculture most of his special wartime responsibilities.[7] A subsequent order (No. 9334) dated April 19[8] changed the name of the agency to the War Food Administration and designated the War Food Administrator as an alternate to the Secretary of Agriculture on the Combined Food Board.

Thus, after nearly two years of war, a workable organization for handling food problems came into being, and the Secretary of Agriculture was, in the main, relieved of duties connected with the war emergency. He was thus reassigned to the task of administering the regular activities of the Department. This arrangement was to continue in effect throughout the remainder of the war.[9] There was, however, much confusion of functions within the War Food Administration. That agency was reorganized internally several times during the war period.

The slowness with which effective organization emerged in the food realm cannot be attributed entirely to administrative inadequacy. It was due partly to the easy situation with respect to food supplies that existed in the early years of the war, and partly to the more urgent needs in other fields of endeavor. Nevertheless, certain conclusions seem warranted. Had there not been enormous holdings of storable farm products, acquired without relation to war plans, and had it not been for a series of favorable crop years immediately after the outbreak of war, such delay and inadequacy in organizing for food production and conservation might well have been tragic in its consequences.

Economic Upsurge in 1940 and 1941

The years 1940 and 1941 were marked by significant increases in activity throughout the

5. USDA, *Secretary's Memorandum,* No. 960, December 13, 1941. An Agricultural Defense Board was established to replace the Program Board. The Department's 17 line agencies were regrouped under 8 group administrators. These regrouped agencies were designated administrations by Executive Order No. 9069, February 23, 1942, *Federal Register,* Vol. VII, p. 1409.

6. Shortly thereafter, on January 23, 1943, the War Manpower Commission transferred responsibility for recruiting and placing agricultural workers to the Department of Agriculture (Directive 17, *Federal Register,* Vol. VIII, p. 1426), and on March 1, an Agricultural Labor Administration was established in the Department. (*Secretary's Memorandum,* No. 1075.)

7. Executive Order No. 9322, *Federal Register,* Vol. VIII, pp. 3807, 3809.

8. *Ibid.,* Vol. VIII, pp. 5423, 5425.

9. For a detailed listing of organizational changes and food orders of various kinds see Bureau of Agricultural Economics, *A Chronology of the War Food Administration, Including Predecessor and Successor Agencies, August 1939 to December 1946,* November 1950, mimeographed.

American economy. This was due partly to war orders placed by the British and French governments, partly to such modest beginning as was being made in America's own preparation for war and partly to gradual recovery from one of the longest and severest depressions in American history. Undoubtedly, too, the fact that a large-scale war was under way served to some extent as a psychological stimulus to prices. The prospect of coming shortages and higher prices tended to step up production, increase inventories and give a stronger tone to business.

Prices and Incomes

The all-commodities index of prices had fallen off after the sharp rise of 1937, but began to recover in 1940. By 1941 it stood at 127 as compared to 126 in 1937, and approximately 115 in the three intervening years.[10] Industrial production began to rise sharply, especially steel, lumber, machinery and chemicals. Coal and petroleum also showed substantial improvement.[11] The income of industrial workers was likewise much improved, having reached 169 (1935-1939 = 100).

This upsurge of output and income was largely the result of putting to fuller use labor and facilities that had been underemployed during the depression. At the beginning of 1940 there were nearly six million unemployed and seeking work, or employed on public emergency work. By the end of 1941 this number had been reduced by approximately half.[12]

National income reached $104 billion in 1941 as compared to $87 billion in 1929, and $40 billion in 1933.[13] Thus, agriculture was

receiving a strong stimulus from the expanding consumer income which marked this period.

Farm production and stocks held were so abundant, however, that this sharp increase in demand did not cause any seriously inflationary upsurge in the prices of farm products. The upward movement was, in the main, a recovery from the recession of 1938-1939. Farm prices in 1941 were still 5 points below the levels of 1937 and more than 30 points below those of 1929.[14] More was sold, however, and 1941 farm income was some 40 per cent above that of 1940.[15] The increased demand was partly offset by a continuing growth in output of farm products which had begun in 1937. By 1941 production was up to 110 (1935-1939 = 100), as compared to 103 in 1938. This was due partly to a moderate increase in acres planted, partly to favorable weather and partly to technological changes such as improved soil management, the introduction of hybrid corn and the more extensive use of power machinery.

Heavy Carry-overs

Carry-overs of wheat had been increasing from 1937 onward and stood at 385 million bushels on July 1, 1941. They were to be stepped up enormously in the succeeding year, reaching nearly twice the previous record high of 378 million in 1933.[16] This phenomenal increase in stocks was partly, but only partly, the result of reduced foreign shipments. These were down from the customary 100 to 125 million to about one third of that amount.

Corn stocks, likewise, continued at high levels, partly as a result of government purchases and loans. October 1 carry-over had reached 550 million bushels in 1939 and remained well above 400 million through 1942. Cotton stocks also were large. They had increased sharply with the record-breaking crop

10. *Agricultural Statistics, 1945*, p. 431. The indexes here used are based on 1910-1914 as 100.
11. *Ibid.*, p. 430. The 1941 indexes of production for these commodities as compared to the 1935-1939 level were as follows:

Iron and steel	186
Lumber	129
Machinery	221
Chemicals	176
Coal	129
Petroleum	120

12. *Statistical Abstract, 1948*, pp. 169-70.
13. *National Income, A Supplement to the Survey of Current Business*, 1951 Edition, p. 150.

14. *Agricultural Statistics, 1945*, p. 431.
15. *Statistical Abstract, 1948*, p. 276.
16. *Agricultural Statistics, 1945*, p. 19. The carry-over of July 1, 1942, was 632 million bushels; that of 1943, 622 million.

of 1937 and remained high throughout the war.[17]

It will be apparent from the data given above that agriculture entered the war with ample reserves of the principal food and fiber crops and with a production potential that exceeded peacetime requirements at the levels of economic activity prevailing in the prewar period. While not planned as such, these stocks constituted a military reserve of enormous importance. Had the output of succeeding years been below normal their vital significance could hardly be overestimated. As it was, they proved very useful, and their existence undoubtedly contributed to confidence and morale both in our own country and those of our allies.

One of the lessons to be drawn from the experiences of this period is that the world's largest producer of surplus foodstuffs cannot afford, in any period of greatly disturbed international conditions, to operate only on the basis of such stocks of storable foodstuffs as will be maintained privately in the normal channels of trade. Had these stocks not been in existence, the food situation would inevitably have been much tighter even with the phenomenal increase in agricultural production that occurred during the war years.

Better Use of Labor

Not only did agriculture have heavy stocks and large plant capacity but it also had reserves of underemployed labor. At that time there was little incentive for full use of agricultural labor resources. This condition changed quickly. Labor became scarce and expensive. Farm operations were much more carefully planned with a view to lengthening the work period in seasonal activities, power machinery was used more extensively and nonessential operations were reduced to a minimum. In addition, some labor was imported.

The war period demonstrated that output per man could be increased much more than even the most optimistic students of the problem had considered possible. Over-all agricultural output increased by nearly 25 per cent between 1940 and 1945 while total farm employment dropped about 7 per cent. The number of hired farm workers decreased about 19 per cent, the difference being made up by longer hours, increased reliance on machinery and more efficient use of the available labor supply.[18]

Farm Prices Low

The prices received by farmers did not show consistent improvement during the 1930's. The parity ratio for 1940 was only 80. Farmers, and particularly farm organization leaders and farm-state congressmen, were far from satisfied with the price situation which existed at that time. Even though the government was supporting prices, both by outright purchase and by loans, the parity ratio was no higher than that of 1922, and had been lower only in 1921 and in the years 1931 through 1934. The cash farm income situation was somewhat more favorable than these prices would indicate. The 1940 income was about the same as that of 1937 and only about $2 billion (approximately 20 per cent) below that of 1929.

This low level of agricultural prices in the face of rising war demand was due in part to the sharp decline in exports that marked the first years of the war in Europe. Using the period 1924–1929 as 100, agricultural exports were down to 25 in 1940, only about one third as much, in quantity, as was exported in the early years of the depression.[19]

17. During the 1920's the carry-over of cotton was, in most years, less than 3 million bales. Only in one year, 1921–1922, was it as high as 6 million bales. From 1931 to 1935 it ranged from 6.3 to 9.7 million bales. Beginning in 1938 and continuing through 1945, carry-overs ranged from 10.5 to 13.0 million bales. *Agricultural Statistics, 1937*, p. 93 and *ibid., 1946*, p. 79.

18. *Ibid., 1950*, p. 584; *ibid., 1949*, p. 597. Other estimates show less striking increases in output. For example, Bela Gold, *Wartime Economic Planning in Agriculture, A Study in the Allocation of Resources*, Columbia University Press, New York, 1949, p. 76, gives a figure of 15 per cent for the over-all increase in output between 1940 and 1945, based on computations by Barton and Cooper of the U.S. Department of Agriculture.

19. *Agricultural Statistics, 1949*, p. 490. This low level of exports was due to a number of factors. Blockades had been established, shipping was limited, and some of the belligerent countries had built up sizable reserves prior to the outbreak of war.

Thus, the stage was set for vigorous demands on the part of the farmers for preferred treatment as soon as it became evident that the government would ask for increased production of farm products. Farmers, though favoring controls on wages and nonfarm prices, were strongly opposed to the placing of any ceilings on the prices of farm products that would prevent their rising to parity or above.

THE EFFORT TO CONTROL PRICES

As prices strengthened, the fear of inflation and of unrest among wageworkers grew. By the end of July 1941, the President was sufficiently concerned over the steady rise in prices to propose price and rent controls.[20]

Prices received by farmers were by then some 35 per cent above 1939 levels but this rise, which had occurred mainly in the first half of 1941, had not yet been fully reflected in retail food prices. These were up only about 12.5 per cent. The cost of urban living as a whole had advanced 6 per cent since the beginning of 1941, and clearly was destined to go much higher if unchecked.[21] So far as agriculture was concerned, the situation no longer could be regarded as merely a recovery from depression. Inflationary tendencies were in evidence, and gaining strength rapidly.

Legislative Proposals

Legislation looking to the imposition of controls was introduced immediately, but the Congress was by no means ready to accept uncritically so sweeping a system of restrictions emanating from the White House. Pearl Harbor was still four months in the future, and few, except unorganized consumers, were

anxious to check the welcome flow of income into the hands of farmers, wageworkers and businessmen after the long drought of the 1930's.

The Administration bill (H.R. 5479 introduced by Steagall in the House, and S. 1810 by Glass in the Senate) sought to forestall farmer opposition by very liberal concessions to agriculture. No ceiling was to be established on any agricultural product at less than 110 per cent of the parity price, or the market price prevailing for such commodity on July 29, 1941, whichever was higher. The feeling that farmers constituted a seriously disadvantaged group was still widely prevalent, and even Leon Henderson, the Price Administrator, appeared not unfavorable to this provision when asked about it in the hearings.[22]

Despite these concessions, the farm organizations and many congressmen were unready to accept the checks on price increases that were necessary if stabilization was to be made effective. As in the case of labor, their bargaining position was strong and the prospects for further gains good. Each group wanted other prices stabilized but not its own.

The Farmers Union and the National Federation of Grain Cooperatives urged striking out the section on agricultural prices, and opposed the fixing of wages for labor, but favored selective controls on commodity prices and rents. Edward O'Neal, President of the Farm Bureau, favored establishment of a federal agency to fix maximum prices on a selective basis, but insisted that no ceiling should be placed on agricultural commodities or their products at less than 110 per cent of parity, this to be adjusted periodically.[23] Other farm groups such as the Grange, the National Cooperative Milk Producers Federation and the U.S. Livestock Association expressed similar views, and even Secretary of Agriculture Wickard insisted that no price

20. Franklin D. Roosevelt, *Public Papers and Addresses, 1941,* Harper and Brothers, New York, 1950, pp. 284–88. The President pointed out at this time that the wholesale prices of 28 basic commodities had risen 50 per cent above those of August 1939. Wholesale prices of 900 commodities had advanced 17.5 per cent (10 per cent since January 1941) and in the preceding 60 days prices had risen five times as fast as in the period September 1939 to June 1941.
21. Data derived from Bureau of Agricultural Economics, *The Demand and Price Situation,* January 1942, p. 22.

22. He later confessed that he regarded this as a mistake, and urged vigorously a lower level of price ceilings for farm products.
23. The Farm Bureau's position in this period is summarized in Orville Merton Kile, *The Farm Bureau Through Three Decades,* The Waverly Press, Baltimore, 1948, Chapters 21 and 22.

ceiling on farm products should be placed lower than 110 per cent of parity.[24]

Attitudes of Farmers' Spokesmen

These attitudes reflected the long years of concern over farm prices that seemed destined never to reach a level which farmers considered equitable as compared to nonfarm prices. But few of these spokesmen were taking adequate account of the magnitudes of the price increases they were proposing, or of the psychological factors involved. Price controls to be effective must be dramatically initiated, comprehensive and rigorous. Wheat was already more than 50 per cent above the 1939 level; corn was advancing; and cotton was up 73 per cent. For many of the products, price rises ranging well over 100 per cent above the 1939 prices would be permitted under the formula proposed.[25] In a rapidly tightening labor and commodity market, it was clear that stabilization of prices or wage rates could not be anticipated in the face of such drastically increased prices for the universally used foodstuffs. Wageworkers and other consumers were not thinking in terms of some abstract projection of the price relationships of 1910 to 1914, but rather of the prices they had been accustomed to paying when the war broke out.

Farmers generally were more realistic than their spokesmen. In an Institute of Public Opinion poll published on September 13, 1941, slightly more than half the farmers interviewed expressed themselves as satisfied with the level of prices then attained. Thirty-four per cent considered them too low, and 14 per cent were undecided, which may be taken as meaning that they were reasonably well satisfied.[26] The August parity ratio was 96; that of September, 101.[27]

Fifty-five per cent of the farmers interviewed were willing to have prices fixed as of that time while only 28 per cent were definitely opposed to such action. A similar poll of wage and salary earners showed a larger majority in favor of strong government controls. Sixty-two per cent indicated willingness to have wages frozen provided prices were also stabilized.

The farmer spokesmen, here as in nearly every previous crisis, were taking consciously or unconsciously the inflationist side of the argument, but this time with less logical support for their position than on many previous occasions. However, it must be recognized that the purely selfish, short-run interests of the farmer often lie on the side

24. The Grange view, later more carefully formulated and presented in the Senate hearings, was that farm prices had not yet reached inflationary levels and there was no necessity for placing ceilings on them. In a formal resolution passed on November 13, the Grange stated that it "(1) favors application of economic devices as the best means for holding down inflationary tendencies; (2) opposes arbitrary price fixing unless necessary; (3) if arbitrary price fixing becomes necessary, demands: (a) that all groups be included to assure equity; (b) that the activities be devoted to preventing profiteering; (c) that standards be provided, as far as possible, to assure equity for all; and (d) that Congress retain control.

"The Grange will oppose arbitrary price fixing if these principles are not complied with." U.S. Congress, Senate, Committee on Banking and Currency, *Emergency Price Control Act*, Hearings . . . , 77th Cong., 1st sess., on H.R. 5990, December 1941, pp. 342, 345 and 348.

25. Wilcox computes the magnitudes of the increases between 1939 and 1942, and the further permissible increases under the 110 per cent of parity formula as follows (*The Farmer in the Second World War*, p. 123):

Commodity	Price Rise August 1939 to April 1942	Additional Rise Permitted if Ceiling Placed at 110 Per Cent of Parity
	(Percentage)	
Wheat	83	74
Corn	74	34
Oats	104	28
Barley	78	67
Rye	77	97
Flaxseed	78	16
Beans	69	30
Cotton	119	13
Cottonseed	170	15
Potatoes	68	7
Sweet potatoes	13	42
Hay	64	77
Peanuts	84	28
Apples	114	13
Butterfat	65	19
Milk	43	11
Chickens	42	15
Turkeys	38	46
Eggs	46	33

26. "Gallup and Fortune Polls," *Public Opinion Quarterly*, Winter 1941, p. 667. When half or more of any group says the return for its services is adequate, it is safe to conclude that it is faring rather well.

27. Bureau of Agricultural Economics, *Demand and Price Situation*, January 1942, p. 22.

of inflation, though action along these lines may present grave dangers to the economy as a whole and eventually to the farmers themselves if inflationary forces get out of control.

Need for Check on Price Increases

The inflationary influences evident in the farm sector of the economy at this time stemmed from the rapidly increasing volume of government spending (both the United States and foreign governments were spending heavily in the United States) and from fuller employment and rising private expenditures.[28] More people were eating well, and purchases for shipment abroad were heavy.

Spendable income in relation to available supplies was increasing rapidly. There were two possible ways of attempting to check the rise in prices: one, to reduce spendable income by sharply increased taxes, heavy emphasis on saving and the curtailment of credit; the other, to leave excess buying power in the hands of consumers and to try to check price increases by arbitrary controls and rationing. The second procedure does not actually control inflation. Instead, it dams it up and channels much of it into uncontrolled types of expenditure, including such activities as gambling, speculation and black markets. Increased saving absorbed part of the excess, but in a form that would and did give rise to inflationary spending at a later date.

Nevertheless, a direct attack on the problem through price control and rationing has a powerful appeal to the general public, and is the procedure most likely to be followed in such a situation in spite of the difficulties it entails. Though the theoretical foundation for control through fiscal and monetary measures had been much discussed in academic circles, especially from 1936 on, it was little understood by the general public. On the other hand, the apparent success of the British program of price control and rationing gave marked impetus to the movement for the use of similar methods in the United States.[29] Bernard Baruch, World War I Price Administrator, threw the weight of his prestige in favor of a general wage, price and rent freeze.

The First Price Control Act

The price control bill passed the House on November 28, 1941, but with inflationary features included. No ceiling was to be placed on any farm product at less than 110 per cent of parity, or the market price on October 1, or the average price from July 1, 1919 to June 30, 1929, whichever was highest.[30] Even more radical amendments such as the one sponsored by Senator O'Mahoney were included in the Senate version of the bill.[31] These, however, were dropped in the House-Senate conference committee as a result of vigorous protest from the President.

The devastating catastrophe at Pearl Harbor changed suddenly the atmosphere in which the discussions were being carried on. The Emergency Price Control Act was passed, and on January 30, 1942, received the President's signature. By this time, however, retail food prices had advanced another 9 per cent and the cost of living as a whole was up about 7 per cent as compared to July 1941. As passed, the act contained the following provisions with respect to price ceilings on agricultural products.

No maximum price could be established on any agricultural product at less than the highest of the following prices:

28. For a good brief discussion of this aspect of the problem see Mary Jean Bowman and Albert Gailord Hart, *Food Management and Inflation*, Wartime Farm and Food Policy Pamphlets, No. 8, Iowa State College Press, Ames, April 1943.

29. A detailed description of British price policies and the administrative arrangements for implementing them is given in *British Wartime Price Administration, 1939–1943*, by James S. Earley, L. Margaret Hall and Marjorie S. Berger, Office of Price Administration, February 10, 1944. For a briefer, more popular summary, see British Information Services, *British Price Control*, Pamphlet I.D. 312, New York, April 1943.

30. These features were bitterly opposed by Leon Henderson in the Senate hearings. He stated that when applied to 27 major farm products this three-way exemption would allow the average farm price level to go to 116.6 per cent of parity. Committee on Banking and Currency, *Emergency Price Control Act*, Hearings, 77th Cong., 1st sess., on H.R. 5990, p. 127.

31. According to O'Mahoney's own testimony, his amendment called for an index of 172, or 120 per cent of parity. John D. Black, *Parity, Parity, Parity*, Harvard Committee on Research in the Social Sciences, Cambridge, 1942, p. 65.

1. 110 per cent of parity.
2. The market price prevailing for such commodity on October 1, 1941.
3. The market price prevailing for such commodity on December 15, 1941.
4. The average price for such commodity during the period, July 1, 1919 to June 30, 1929.

Thus, the agricultural leaders won, temporarily, a somewhat unworthy battle which did little credit to their reputation for statesmanship and responsibility to the public. It is only fair to state, however, that the most radical and opportunistic pressure came from within the Congress itself rather than from the farm organizations and their leaders, and there is considerable indication that most farmers were more inclined to accept reasonable compromises than were their national leaders. These leaders, being in positions somewhat similar to those of farm-state congressmen and labor leaders, sought, as is usual in such cases, to demonstrate their loyalty to the alleged interests of their constituents rather than to face realistically the responsibilities of exercising statesmanlike leadership.

The delay in passing the price control act was not mainly a result of the struggle over the agricultural provisions. It stemmed rather from the fact that the country was not yet alert to the probability of United States involvement in the war, and from distrust of the administration by the Congress and by business and agricultural leaders. The administration was regarded as prolabor in its outlook. Consequently, when the President's recommendation failed to call specifically for a freeze on wages as well as on the prices of commodities, there was widespread belief that the stabilization arrangements would be so administered as to let labor profit at the expense of business and agriculture.

Suspicion of Wage Provisions

The President's recommendations, if carried out in good faith, implied general stabilization, but the vagueness of his statements in regard to wages increased the suspicion of business, agriculture and the Congress, and

lessened the effectiveness of his appeal. Practically, the President's position was the sounder of the two. Wage control called for a different kind of organization and less rigidity. Farmers were already in place. The need in agriculture was for stimulus to full production and guidance as to kinds of things to produce.

Large segments of labor, on the other hand, were not in the right locations nor in the right jobs. Unless labor was to be completely regimented and assigned to specific jobs, wages had to rise enough in the war industries to draw labor from other jobs and other areas. Furthermore, many industries could afford higher wages without increasing prices. Most had been operating at less than full capacity, and, as they increased output, could turn out goods at substantially lower average costs. Thus, there was room for considerable readjustment in wages without affecting materially the prices of most consumer goods.

On the other hand, general wage increases would tend to prevent the movement of labor from less essential lines into the strategic war industries. This meant that wages in the established industries needed to be held stable while permitting the new war industries to pay rates enough higher to enable them to draw labor away from less essential occupations. Once labor is fully employed, in the right places, there is little to be gained by permitting further wage increases, since they then contribute only to inflation rather than to increased labor supply and better allocation of labor.

This aspect of the problem was shortly to be recognized in the policies adopted by the War Labor Board, and the opposition encountered on the price control bill probably helped to crystallize a reasonably balanced approach to the problem of wage and price controls. Nevertheless, the wage advances permitted did contribute heavily to the inflationary pressure with which the Office of Price Administration had to contend.[32] In some

32. The Office of Price Administration, established August 28, 1941, was the agency charged with controlling prices and rents.

areas the inflationary pressure affected rents even more than commodity prices and the increases were more uneven. Housing cannot be moved, nor can the supply be quickly increased. The enormous shifts in population which accompanied the war effort resulted in extreme congestion in many areas, and a situation in which rents could not be established equitably by normal market mechanisms.

Here, too, it was necessary to make some concessions if labor was to be induced to make the shifts in location required for effective prosecution of the war. The result was the establishment, in defense areas, of very rigid controls on rentals. These, like all such general controls, resulted in many individual injustices, but the over-all result was to prevent flagrant profiteering and to contribute to economic stability.

Theory of Price Control

In light of current economic thinking, the administration proposals placed too much emphasis on rigid price controls and too little on mopping up increased purchasing power through sharply increased taxes, vigorous efforts to stimulate saving and restrictions on nonessential types of credit.[33] There is little evidence, however, that these measures alone can solve equitably the problem of stabilization under the greatly disturbed conditions of all-out war. When civilian goods, especially foodstuffs, are inadequate to supply all the public wishes to buy, rationing must be resorted to if reasonably good morale is to be maintained. Likewise, extremely large windfall gains cannot be permitted to the chance owners of rental properties.

The choice then is not between two alternatives of which one is good and the other bad. Either failure to assure equitable distribution of scarce goods at reasonable prices or the application of rigid controls involves inequities. Where controls are used, grave administrative problems are presented as well. It is

clear, however, that if rigid controls are to be even reasonably successful they must be strongly administered, and accompanied by vigorous efforts to reduce inflationary pressure by mopping up purchasing power through taxation and saving, including debt retirement. At best, any such strait-jacketing of a complex, dynamic price structure causes many inequities which are the inevitable concomitant of war. Agriculture, labor and business wanted the advantages of stabilization, but none wanted it applied rigorously to its own situation. But without stabilization the war effort suffers. As the President well stated:

Producers, unable to tell what their costs will be, hesitate to enter into defense contracts or otherwise to commit themselves to ventures whose outcome they cannot foresee. The whole production machinery falters.[34]

The Office of Price Administration did not come into being suddenly as a result of passage of the Emergency Price Control Act. It had been started as the Price Stabilization Division of the Council of National Defense, a World War I agency reactivated in 1940. Its early activities were selective and to a large extent advisory. In January 1941, the President split off from the Council the Production, Materials and Labor Divisions and placed them in a newly created Office of Production Management. In a similar way, in April, he replaced the Stabilization Division by the Office of Price Administration and Civilian Supply (OPACS). This later, in August 1941, became the Office of Price Administration (Executive Order No. 8875).[35]

Operation of OPA

There can be little doubt that the rather informal actions of the Price Stabilization Division and OPACS were helpful in steadying the situation in the period between June 1940 and January 1942.[36] However, its work

33. A brief summary of the administration's policy on this is given in a Treasury Department pamphlet, *War Finance Policies, Excerpts from Three Addresses,* by Henry Morgenthau, Jr., Secretary of the Treasury, 1944.

34. Message to Congress, July 30, 1941, *Public Papers and Addresses, 1941,* p. 284.
35. August 28, 1941, *Federal Register,* Vol. VI, pp. 4483-84.
36. For example, when, in April 1941, the steel producers announced a wage increase of 10 cents an hour

at that period was confined largely to very basic commodities like steel, lumber, rubber and fuel.[37]

With the specific authority granted the OPA under the Emergency Price Control Act, it issued, on April 28, 1942, its famous General Maximum Price Regulation.[38] The provisions of this order were, in general terms, as follows:

1. Effective May 18, 1942, retail prices, with a few exceptions, must not exceed the highest levels which each individual seller charged during March 1942.
2. Effective May 11, 1942, manufacturers and wholesalers could not charge more than the highest prices received in March.
3. Beginning July 1, no one might charge more for services sold at retail in connection with a commodity than the highest price charged in March.
4. A concurrent order on rents established more than 300 defense rental areas and directed that rentals should not exceed those in effect on March 1, 1942. (For most areas. In a few the level of an earlier date was specified.)

The principal exception to the above order was in the food sector, a very basic one in any attempt to stabilize prices and wages. Here the Office of Price Administration was specifically forbidden to apply ceilings until prices reached 110 per cent of parity or some alternative higher price specified by the act. Other exemptions were for certain commodities and services on which price determination was difficult or impossible, or which were covered by other regulations of the Office of Price Administration.

Thus, prices were nominally brought under control throughout most of the economy, but with two major gaps in the dyke: one, the growing volume of purchasing power in the hands of consumers; the other, the inability to check the rise in prices of farm products. The Price Administrator had stressed in the hearings on the bill that stabilization through direct controls would be impossible unless accompanied by appropriate fiscal measures to siphon off excess purchasing power.

Efforts to Strengthen Price Control

To close these gaps and spell out the administration's policy, the President sent to the Congress on April 27, 1942 a message in which he presented a 7-point program outlining what he called "our present national economic policy":[39]

1. To keep the cost of living from spiraling upward, we must tax heavily, and in that process keep personal and corporate profits at a reasonable rate, the word "reasonable" being defined at a low level.
2. To keep the cost of living from spiraling upward, we must fix ceilings on the prices which consumers, retailers, wholesalers, and manufacturers pay for the things they buy; and ceilings on rents for dwellings in all areas affected by war industries.
3. To keep the cost of living from spiraling upward, we must stabilize the remuneration received by individuals for their work.
4. To keep the cost of living from spiraling upward, we must stabilize the prices received by growers for the products of their lands.
5. To keep the cost of living from spiraling upward, we must encourage all citizens to contribute to the cost of winning this war by purchasing war bonds with their earnings instead of using those earnings to buy articles which are not essential.
6. To keep the cost of living from spiraling upward, we must ration all essential commodities of which there is a scarcity, so

and at the same time an advance in price, OPACS concluded that the steel industry could absorb the wage increase without advancing prices, and, therefore, placed a ceiling on steel and steel products at the levels prevailing on April 16. This was to prevent the kind of spiral that, in World War I, raised the price of steel from $19.40 a ton in July 1914 to $95 a ton in July 1917. For a comparison of the movement of controlled and uncontrolled prices during this period see *Market Prices of 28 Basic Commodities Controlled and Uncontrolled*, Bureau of Labor Statistics (Mimeo. LS 42–1258), 1942.

37. For a summary of the activities and organization of the OPA see *Chronology of the Office of Price Administration*, January 1941–November 1946, Historical Reports on War Administration, Office of Price Administration, Miscellaneous Publication No. 1, November 30, 1946. Its techniques and philosophy are analyzed in some detail in Victor A. Thompson's *The Regulatory Process in OPA Rationing*, King's Crown Press, New York, 1950. See also John Maurice Clark's *Demobilization of Wartime Economic Controls*, McGraw-Hill, New York, 1944, especially Chapter 5 on "The Framework of Wartime Controls."

38. *Federal Register*, Vol. VII, pp. 3153–58. Prior to the passage of the Emergency Price Control Act, the Office had operated under authority delegated by the President through executive orders.

39. *Public Papers and Addresses, 1942*, pp. 219–20.

that they may be distributed fairly among consumers and not merely in accordance with financial ability to pay high prices for them.

7. To keep the cost of living from spiraling upward, we must discourage credit and installment buying, and encourage the paying off of debts, mortgages, and other obligations; for this promotes savings, retards excessive buying and adds to the amount available to the creditors for the purchase of war bonds.

Commenting on the two most controversial features of the price control program, he stated that the farm price features of the law were not satisfactory and asked for correction of the formula so that ceilings could be placed at parity. He also asked that the government be allowed to sell from its own stocks of farm products, at market prices, in order to keep the cost of living down. With respect to labor, he stated that

. . . legislation is not required under present circumstances. I believe that stabilizing the cost of living will mean that wages in general can and should be kept at existing scales.

Organized labor has voluntarily given up its right to strike during the war. Therefore all stabilization or adjustment of wages will be settled by the War Labor Board machinery which has been generally accepted by industry and labor for the settlement of all disputes.[40]

Though generally well received, the President's proposals did not evoke enthusiasm among the farm-state representatives in Congress. They felt the proposed controls on labor were too weak and indefinite, and resisted the administration's request for lower ceilings on farm products and the release of stored stocks as a means of holding down prices. The Congress was also dragging its feet on the enactment of an adequate tax program.

Prices received by farmers, and retail food prices, continued to advance though most other prices remained relatively stable. Farm prices rose more than 8 per cent between April and September 1942, and retail food prices gained about 6 per cent in the same period.

40. *Ibid.*, p. 221.

Threatened with a breakdown of the whole stabilization program, the President again addressed a message to the Congress on September 7.[41] In this, he repeated his recommendation that heavier taxes be levied and that authorization be given to hold farm product prices down to parity, adding, "In the event that the Congress should fail to act, and act adequately, I shall accept the responsibility, and I will act. At the same time that farm prices are stabilized, wages can and will be stabilized also. This I will do."[42]

Origin of Postwar Guarantees

The President expressed, in addition, vigorous opposition to any recomputation of parity which would put it at a higher level and said that all benefit payments under AAA should be included in figuring parity.[43] As an offset to these restrictions on agricultural prices, he recommended "that Congress in due time give consideration to the advisability of legislation which would place a floor under prices of farm products . . . for one year, or even two years — or whatever period is necessary after the end of the war."[44]

Here was laid the groundwork for the postwar guarantees to farmers which were to remove much of the fear of a 1920-type debacle in farm prices immediately after the close of the war, a program which could be, in effect, both a forward price and an incentive price.

In the meantime, many kinds of labor were operating under what was known as the

41. *Ibid.*, pp. 356–67. The President pointed out that under the then existing law the lowest average level at which ceilings could be placed on farm products was 116 per cent of parity and that some of them could go almost to 150 per cent of parity.

42. *Ibid.*, p. 364. It was generally believed in White House circles and in the Congress that the President had power to stabilize prices and wages by executive order if he chose to do so, and many hoped he would follow that procedure. See the account of these discussions in Robert E. Sherwood, *Roosevelt and Hopkins, An Intimate History,* Harper and Brothers, New York, 1948, p. 631.

43. A proposal sponsored by Senator Thomas of Oklahoma would have resulted in the use of a new formula for computing parity ratios that would have raised substantially the parity-defined ceilings on farm product prices.

44. *Public Papers and Addresses, 1942,* pp. 365–66.

"Little Steel" formula. This permitted wage increases up to 15 per cent over the levels of 1940, which was about the amount of the increase in cost of living up to March 1942. The weakness of this arrangement, from the standpoint of business and agriculture, was that the War Labor Board could control wages only if the case involved a dispute which was brought before it. It could not prevent voluntary increases which, of course, in a tight labor market with profit prospects very attractive, were numerous and large.

The Steagall Amendment of July 1, 1941

A rider sponsored by Representative Steagall of Alabama had been attached to the 1941 Act extending the life of the Commodity Credit Corporation.[45] It provided that, for any agricultural commodities of which the Secretary of Agriculture asked increased production as a contribution to the war effort, he should provide support prices at 85 per cent of parity. Thus, the amendment authorized and directed what was in effect a system of forward prices on a selective basis. It was not as yet, however, a clear provision for price support after the war, though there was a somewhat vague implication that it was intended to cushion the shock in case of a sudden termination of the war. Presumably, such cushioning would cover, for a year ahead, each crop for which increased production was asked.

These provisions were modified and made more specific in later amendments to be described in succeeding pages. The original rider together with its subsequent modifications has come to be loosely referred to as the Steagall Amendment, and the commodities affected are commonly known as the Steagall commodities, to distinguish them from the "basic" commodities for which price supports were subsequently more definitely specified.

Stabilization Act of October 1942

Presidential pressure for lowering the level of permissible price ceilings on farm products, together with his suggestion of guarantees

against sudden and disastrous price declines in the period following the close of hostilities, brought agreement on a compromise act which he signed on October 2, 1942. This is generally referred to as the Stabilization Act of October 1942.[46] In this the President succeeded in getting some reduction in the levels at which ceilings could be placed on farm products, but had to make significant concessions with respect to tighter controls on wages and implementation of the postwar price-support arrangements which he had suggested as a basis for compromise.

Section 1 of the act directed the President to issue a general order stabilizing prices, wages and salaries that affected the cost of living at levels which, so far as practical, would reflect the prices, wages and salaries prevailing on September 15, 1942.[47] This tightened up the wage and salary controls by bringing under supervision the voluntary adjustments as well as those which involved labor disputes and thus came before the War Labor Board. Here, as for agricultural prices, a provision was included that no wage or salary should be reduced below the highest rate paid between January 1, 1942 and September 15, 1942.

With respect to agricultural prices, the act provided that no ceiling should be applied which would be lower than (1) the parity price for the commodity or (2) the highest price paid between January 1, 1942 and Sep-

45. 55 Stat. 498.

46. The official title is "An Act To amend the Emergency Price Control Act of 1942, to aid in preventing inflation, and for other purposes." 56 Stat. 765.

47. The wording of the labor section was as follows:

Sect. 5. (a) No employer shall pay, and no employee shall receive, wages or salaries in contravention of the regulations promulgated by the President under this Act. The President shall also prescribe the extent to which any wage or salary payment made in contravention of such regulations shall be disregarded by the executive departments and other governmental agencies in determining the costs or expenses of any employer for the purposes of any other law or regulation.

(b) Nothing in this Act shall be construed to prevent the reduction by any private employer of the salary of any of his employees which is at the rate of $5,000 or more per annum.

(c) The President shall have power by regulation to limit or prohibit the payment of double time except when, because of emergency conditions, an employee is required to work for seven consecutive days in any regularly scheduled work week.

tember 15, 1942. However, there was an escape clause which permitted the President to set a price below the level indicated by the second of these criteria if necessary to correct gross inequities. The act also authorized specifically the establishment, for farm products, of higher maximum prices than those indicated by the criteria given above if such higher prices were found necessary to induce the volumes of production needed.

Section 8 contained the postwar price guarantees on "basic" commodities which later became so important in setting the pattern of postwar price-support legislation. It provided that, for cotton, corn, wheat, rice, tobacco and peanuts, loans would be provided by the Commodity Credit Corporation at 90 per cent of parity for the two years immediately succeeding the first day of January following a presidential or congressional declaration that hostilities had ceased. Loans at this level were to be limited to "cooperators," that is, to farmers operating in accordance with acreage quotas and/or marketing quotas announced by the Secretary of Agriculture and accepted by the growers. Loans on corn to cooperators outside the "commercial" corn-producing areas were to be at 75 per cent of parity and to noncooperators at 60 per cent of the rate to cooperators, and only on such portion of the crop as would be subject to penalty if marketed.

Section 9 was an amendment to the Steagall Amendment of July 1, 1941. It raised the support level on Steagall commodities from 85 to 90 per cent of parity and extended to these commodities the same type of two-year postwar guarantee that had been specified for the "basic" crops.[48] The amendment further provided that such levels and duration of price support would

apply on any commodities for which increased production had been or would thereafter be requested, regardless of whether any further announcement was made by the Secretary of Agriculture.[49]

Thus the legislation moved a step nearer to the rigid framework of price relationships based on parity, which the farm-state congressmen had long advocated. This presented no major problems during the war period itself, but could cause grave difficulties later, and would have done so had it not been for the continuance of unusually high demand. The massive postwar need for foodstuffs for Europe, Japan and other areas permitted absorption of virtually all available food supplies during 1946 and 1947, but later extension of these undiscriminating price supports gave rise to widespread criticism in respect to the programs for potatoes, eggs, butter and some other commodities.

Parity a Poor Guide in Wartime

Full and effective use of agricultural resources calls for price adjustments both upward and downward in accordance with needs. In an uncontrolled market this function is supposedly performed by the pricing processes of the free market. In a war situation, or in a controlled economy, planning is implied.

If such planning is to be efficient and effective, it must seek to guide the use of resources into the lines where they will be most effective in achieving the goals sought by society. The desired amounts and kinds of products change over time and, likewise, the amounts of labor, land and equipment required to produce them. Hence, an attempt to keep prices related to each other in accordance with some rigid and specific pattern tends to handicap the effort to make fullest use of scarce resources.[50]

48. For a good summary of the price provisions of the Steagall Amendment, see Robert H. Shields, *Federal Statutory Provisions Relating to Price Support for Agricultural Commodities,* Address given before a meeting of Regional Attorneys of the War Food Administration, August 16, 1944, Brown Palace Hotel, Denver, Colorado, mimeographed. It should be noted that the guarantees under the Steagall Amendment were somewhat less specific and more largely subject to administrative decision by the Secretary of Agriculture than were those for the "basic" commodities.

49. As of January 1946, the Steagall commodities were hogs, eggs, chickens, turkeys, milk and butterfat, dry peas, dry edible beans, soybeans for oil, peanuts for oil, flaxseed for oil, American-Egyptian cotton, potatoes and sweet potatoes. Further developments in price support under the Steagall provisions are discussed in later sections.

50. For a brief but more complete discussion, see

In succeeding years the price pattern established tended to keep too much land and labor in the business of producing potatoes. As a result, huge quantities of potatoes were destroyed after having been produced and bought by the government at great expense. Vastly greater wastage in the production of wheat would have occurred had it not been for the very abnormal absorption of supplies made possible by the shortage of food abroad and the unprecedented generosity of the government of the United States in making ECA dollars available for its purchase.

The tendency throughout the war was to strait-jacket farm prices more and more, thus moving further and further from the operation of a free market and toward a planned economy, while at the same time setting up barriers to efficient operation of a planned economy.

Effectiveness of Inflation Controls

The Emergency Price Control Act and the Stabilization Act established, nominally at least, the over-all policy that was to continue throughout the war. Income taxes were increased, though not so much as price control administrators considered desirable, nor as much as the volume of spendable income warranted.[51] Saving and the purchase of war

bonds were encouraged. The purchase of war bonds became rather general so far as salary and wage receivers were concerned, but much less general for the self-employed, including farmers. War bond sales to individuals were running at the rate of $12 to $15 billion per year during the last three years of the war. Much of the larger farm income went into debt retirement, increased bank deposits and the purchase of land. War bond purchases by farmers were not large considering the amounts by which farm incomes were increased. Through 1944 the estimated expenditures by farmers for series D and E bonds amounted to only $3,508,431,000 though farmers' net cash incomes had risen from $3.2 billion in 1939 to $11 billion in 1944.[52]

Nevertheless, inflationary pressure continued and grew in intensity. Most consumer durable goods such as cars, refrigerators and washing machines, which would absorb comparatively large amounts of purchasing power, were out of the market. Home building, too, was sharply restricted, except in the government projects. The inflationary gap — that is, the difference between the amount of spendable income and the value of available goods and services at official prices — had not been closed. Consumers were, therefore, seeking to buy more goods and services than were available in the market. In part, purchases were held down by rationing of scarce items, especially foodstuffs. The situation was conducive to black market operations, and substantial amounts of many rationed products were sold outside normal channels at prices well above those permitted under OPA regulations.

On the whole, however, there can be no doubt that the OPA controls held prices much below what they would otherwise have been.

Theodore W. Schultz, *Farm Prices for Food Production*, Wartime Farm and Food Policy Pamphlets, No. 2, Iowa State College Press, Ames, February 1943. Also, see No. 6 of the same series, *Commodity Loans and Price Floors for Farm Products*, by Geoffrey Shepherd, April 1943.

51. Although criticized as being too mild, the tax program adopted did provide a very large portion of the funds required for carrying on the war. Income tax collections and government receipts and expenditures by years, through 1946, were as follows:

Year Ending June 30	Taxes on Individual Incomes [a]	Corporation Income and Profits Taxes [a]	Total Federal Receipts from All Sources [b]	Total Federal Expenditure (excluding Debt Retirement) [c]
		(In Millions of Dollars [d])		
1940	982	1,148	5,387	9,305
1941	1,418	2,053	7,607	13,766
1942	3,263	4,744	12,799	34,289
1943	6,630	9,669	22,282	79,702
1944	18,261	14,767	44,149	95,572
1945	19,034	16,027	46,457	100,397
1946	18,705	12,554	43,038	63,714

a. *Statistical Abstract*, 1949, p. 334.

b. *Ibid.*, p. 327. Consists of total receipts less deduction for appropriation to Federal Old-Age and Survivors Insurance Trust Fund.

c. *Ibid.*, p. 328.

d. All figures are rounded to the nearest million.

52. Data from *The Balance Sheet of Agriculture, 1945*, USDA Miscellaneous Publication No. 583, p. 28, and *Statistical Abstract, 1950*, p. 584. At least 92 per cent of farmers' purchases of savings bonds are believed to have been of series E, the rest mainly of series G.

This is evidenced by the fact that in World War I, with only very limited price controls, prices of all items rose 35 per cent between 1917 and 1919, whereas between 1942 and 1946 they rose only 19 per cent, despite the fact that our participation in World War II was much longer, mobilization was far more complete and the inflationary forces were much stronger. The increase up to the end of 1945 was only about 10 per cent over the levels of 1942.[53]

The official price series does not, of course, tell the whole story. Qualities of goods sold under the same names were downgraded — in many cases substantially. Black market prices were not reported and do not enter into the computations. It is only fair to say, however, that the vast majority of Americans accepted the restrictions in good faith and strove to abide by the regulations. With respect to rationed foodstuffs farmers, as always in such cases, fared markedly better than their urban counterparts. With the possible exception of the underemployed, low-income labor group, they were undoubtedly the greatest beneficiaries of the war and post-war inflation.

Of the various items making up the cost of living, rentals were most nearly held stable. These not only did not advance but actually declined by two tenths of a point between 1942 and 1945. Here controls could be applied more rigorously and there was little opportunity for evasion. Food prices rose 12 per cent; apparel, 17.4 per cent; house furnishings, 19 per cent; and fuel and electricity only about 5 per cent.[54]

Though prices were steadied and held down as indicated above, much of the inflationary pressure was merely suppressed and

held in check for the time being. The large amounts in bank deposits, war bond savings and cash were available for use at the end of the war when rationing and price control were quickly abandoned, while at the same time pressure for the purchase and holding of war bonds was relaxed.

The Rise of the "Subsidy" Problem

The plan to stabilize prices, wages and salaries elicited general public approval, but without a corresponding understanding of the problems it entailed. Though both agriculture and labor sought and obtained preferential treatment with respect to price and wage ceilings, agriculture's demands were the more extreme. Some concessions looking to increased stimulation of farm production and of shifts of labor into war industries were in the national interest. However, the demand of the farm-state congressmen that no ceilings be placed on farm products until prices had risen to 110 per cent of parity, or some alternative higher level, implied price advances in this realm so large that intense pressure for higher wages and salaries was bound to result.

War creates so many abnormalities in both demand and supply that it is clearly impractical to freeze the whole economy in its peacetime pattern. How then were the necessary adjustments to be made? The administration view was that the prices of "cost-of-living" items should be held stable, that government-held and imported stocks should be manipulated to help in achieving stability, and that subsidies should be used where necessary to offset increased costs or to stimulate production in lines where greatly increased output was needed. It also favored, in some lines, differential prices whereby submarginal producers could be paid enough to induce them to operate without, at the same time, raising prices so as to give large windfall profits to efficient producers. This procedure was used mainly with respect to copper, lead and zinc, in order to bring into

53. Data from *Statistical Abstract, 1949,* p. 308, "Consumers' Price Index for Moderate-Income Families in Large Cities: 1913 to 1948." Other more general indexes differ somewhat from those given above, but the percentage changes shown are similar. In both war periods, the major upsurge in prices occurred after fighting ceased and when the restraining influence of war bond buying, rationing and other types of restriction were removed.

54. *Loc. cit.*

operation high-cost mines which would other-wise stay closed.[55]

As applied to agriculture, this policy meant keeping prices to consumers stable by the payment, if necessary, of subsidies to processors and importers; and, where higher prices were needed by farmers to cover increased costs or to induce added production, paying a part of the price as a subsidy and letting the product move in market channels at the stabilized price.

Congressmen from farm states and most of the farm organization leaders opposed this policy bitterly, mainly on the following grounds: (1) that such subsidies, even though paid to farmers or processors, were really subsidies to consumers who were now getting large incomes and thus could afford higher prices; (2) that they were unnecessary, would add to government expenditures and were inflationary; and (3) that they wanted increased prices in the market rather than subsidies, presumably because this would accustom consumers to paying higher prices for farm products and would be likely to establish higher bases for any postwar price-support programs that might be provided.

Subsidies were, of course, nothing new in the American economy. Waterway development, railroad construction and highways had long been aided through federal subsidy. Agricultural colleges and experiment stations had been subsidized from the beginning. Much of the federal irrigation and flood control activity had involved subsidies. During the 1930's, farmers themselves had been extensively and personally subsidized through large grants of relief funds, parity payments, soil conservation payments and below-cost credit. Hence, the bitter opposition to subsidies that arose during the war period must be attributed to other considerations than the mere fact that they were contributions from the federal treasury.

55. For example, the price of copper from the principal mines was stabilized at 12 cents per pound. For designated high-cost mines a 5-cent subsidy was paid, making the price to these producers 17 cents. This procedure clearly was not suited for use in agriculture with its millions of small-scale units.

Nature of the Conflict

Basically, the conflict stemmed from two different and not clearly recognized views about the management of a war economy. The OPA group contemplated a closely controlled, managed economy, basing their thinking largely on the pattern already set in Britain, which was fighting in the front line and for survival as a nation. Under these conditions, and in a small, relatively easily supervised country, very tight controls could be used. Furthermore, the British saw less objection to what amounted to the socialization of food supplies. In the United States the problem was vastly more complex, the people less ready to abandon customary free enterprise ways and less willing to submerge special group interests for the general welfare. In addition, food and price management in the United States was greatly hampered by a complex body of price legislation designed for depression conditions which the farm groups were unwilling to give up.

Various activities relating to the war came under subsidy shortly after hostilities began. Shipping costs, for example, had risen sharply as a result of submarine depredations and diversion from customary routes. Much of the government's stockpiling program involved subsidies. These, however, brought little opposition. The major controversy came over the President's "Hold-the-Line" Order of April 1943. This included proposals for some rollbacks of prices which would be financed by subsidies. That is, the government would pay the difference between the new, lower price and the one which prevailed before the rollback was instituted.

With inescapable rises in costs for many items, it was clear that a choice must be made either to relax somewhat the general price freeze of May 1942 or to use subsidies to offset such increases in cost. Thinking in the OPA leaned toward subsidies, though seeking to limit them to the most vital points in the price structure. Insistence on the prevention of large increases in the general level of prices was based also upon a desire to avoid the inflation and deflation which accompanied and succeeded World War I. It was felt that if the price structure as a whole could be kept substantially intact, using subsidies where necessary, the subsidies could gradually be withdrawn as costs were readjusted thus leaving the economy in a better position to move on into the postwar period. In addition, there was a strong feeling that a rapidly rising price level would hamper production since entrepreneurs would not be willing to expand operations, not knowing what costs they might have to face as the undertaking progressed.

The Background of Subsidies

The development of administration policy on subsidies proceeded in a series of proposed formulations beginning with that of Julius Hirsch on May 20, 1942, followed by one submitted by Walter S. Salant on July 30, 1942. These were followed by a letter from Leon Henderson to James Byrnes on November 5, 1942 and shortly thereafter by the widely discussed Galbraith Policy Memorandum of November 26, 1942.[56]

In the meantime, the Office of Stabilization Director Byrnes prepared and issued an official statement of the government's policy on stabilization subsidies. This statement in the form of a letter from Byrnes to Henderson reads as follows:

I am sure that you will agree with me that while some subsidies will be necessary to maintain our program of economic stabilization, such subsidies should be kept to a minimum. Accordingly, I am suggesting several principles to guide consideration of future subsidies. These principles would not necessarily apply to subsidies to marginal producers aimed at increasing the production of vital war materials, such as high-cost copper mines. They would apply to all instances where increases in production and distribution costs threaten established price ceilings.

1. Subsidies should be confined to essential commodities.

2. Subsidies should not be paid unless there is a satisfactory showing of bona fide efforts first of absorbing the increased costs out of the profits of the industry.

3. Subsidies should not be paid unless a satisfactory showing is made of bona fide efforts to eliminate unnecessary costs and wasteful practices through the simplification and standardization of production and distribution. Where sufficient showing is made that the machinery for effecting such economies is being put into operation but requires time to become effective, subsidies may be paid temporarily.

4. The payment of subsidies should not improve the profit position of those receiving the subsidy. At least some part of the increase in costs that is being taken up by the subsidy should be absorbed by the industry out of its profits. Consideration should be given to industry-wide pooling of profits to absorb these higher costs.

5. In all cases, subsidies should be temporary.[57]

Increasing Inflationary Pressure

Despite the efforts of OPA and other agencies, it became increasingly apparent through 1942 and early 1943 that the price control program was in danger of collapsing. The inflationary gap had not been closed. Purchasing power in the hands of consumers was increasing while the supply of purchasable goods was declining. In particular, the inability of consumers to purchase automobiles and other consumer durables, and to build houses — normally large absorbers of income — was leaving much free spending power in consumers' hands. At the same time, personal incomes were rising at a rapid rate, partly through increased wage rates, but more importantly through full employment, overtime pay and the work of additional members of the workers' families.

Much of this pressure was focusing on food products as millions of formerly low-income families were now able to buy freely of such foodstuffs as were available. Rationing and price control placed some brakes on this upsurge in the demand for foods, but pressure continued and grew. The former low-income

56. For a summary of the content of these memoranda, see *Problems in Price Control: Stabilization Subsidies,* Historical Reports on War Administration, Office of Temporary Controls, General Publication No. 10, 1947, pp. 3–8.

57. *Ibid.,* pp. 7–8.

groups of Americans were eating more and better food per capita than ever in their history, but the higher-income groups were getting less of meats, fats, sugar and so on than they were accustomed to. With ample buying power both groups tended to patronize black markets to some extent.[58]

Though the great majority of consumers obeyed the regulations, the number of socially irresponsible ones was large and growing, and the temptation to the avaricious to supply goods illegally was great. In addition, the general national character of the regulations, and the inexperience or inadequacy of the control agency personnel, were such that many inequities and absurdities were inevitable. These tended to weaken support for the program and were given much more prominence than the vastly greater volume of effective, competent work done by the control agencies. By the spring of 1943 these various elements of weakness were causing grave concern about the possibility of maintaining stability in the price structure of the economy.

In these circumstances an obvious need was to absorb more purchasing power through taxation and saving. The President continued to prod Congress and his administrators on these points, but with less emphasis than on the effort to hold the price line. Congress, like all legislative bodies in all countries, was reluctant to tax as heavily as the circumstances called for, and its action was less vigorous than any objective analysis would indicate as desirable. Saving was stepped up, but in a form (chiefly the E bond) which laid the basis for a vigorous postwar inflation, since these bonds could quickly be converted into free spending power after, or even before, the war was over. Large bank balances which were even more available were built up. Bond sales were encouraged but not

pushed with the vigor and thoroughness that would have been desirable.

The Hold-the-Line Order

In the spring of 1943, by his Hold-the-Line Order, the President threw his influence strongly in the direction of price controls.[59] The heart of this order insofar as it affected agriculture was Section 1, which read as follows:

1. In the case of agricultural commodities the Price Administrator and the Administrator of Food Production and Distribution (hereinafter referred to as the Food Administrator) are directed, and in the case of other commodities the Price Administrator is directed to take immediate steps to place ceiling prices on all commodities affecting the cost of living. Each of them is directed to authorize no further increases in ceiling prices except to the minimum extent required by law. Each of them is further directed immediately to use all discretionary powers vested in them by law to prevent further price increases direct or indirect, to prevent profiteering and to reduce prices which are excessively high, unfair, or inequitable. Nothing herein, however, shall be construed to prevent the Food Administrator and the Price Administrator, subject to the general policy directives of the Economic Stabilization Director, from making such readjustments in price relationships appropriate for various commodities, or classes, qualities or grades thereof, or for seasonal variations or for various marketing areas, or from authorizing such support prices, subsidies, or other inducements as may be authorized by law and deemed necessary to maintain or increase production, provided that such action does not increase the cost of living.

In issuing the order the President released the following explanatory comment, which made clear the policy he was seeking to implement:

To hold the line we cannot tolerate further increases in prices affecting the cost of living or further increases in general wage or salary rates except where clearly necessary to correct substandard living conditions. The only way to hold the line is to stop trying to find justifications for not holding it here or not holding it there.

58. Direct personal controls of this kind were almost wholly outside the experience of most Americans. On the whole, both consumers and handlers adapted themselves surprisingly well to a difficult situation. Except with a relatively self-disciplined population, a decentralized, self-regulating program of this kind is virtually impossible. Under other conditions it must either break down or be handled by police-state methods.

59. Executive Order No. 9328, April 8, 1943, *Public Papers and Addresses, 1943,* pp. 151-52.

No one straw may break a camel's back, but there is always a last straw. We cannot afford to take further chances in relaxing the line. We already have taken too many.

On the price front, the directions in the Order are clear and specific.

All items affecting the cost of living are to be brought under control. No further price increases are to be sanctioned unless imperatively required by law. Adjustments in the price relationships between different commodities will be permitted if such adjustments can be made without increasing the general cost of living. But any further inducements to maintain or increase production must not be allowed to disturb the present price levels; such further inducements, whether they take the form of support prices or subsidies, must not be allowed to increase prices to consumers. Of course, the extent to which subsidies and other payments may be used to help keep down the cost of living will depend on Congressional authorization.

Some prices affecting the cost of living are already above the levels of September 15, 1942. All of these cannot be rolled back. But some of these can and should be rolled back. The Order directs the reduction of all prices which are excessively high, inequitable, or unfair. The Stabilization Act was not intended to be used as a shield to protect prices which were excessively high on September 15, 1942.[60]

This order was put into effect on May 7, 1943 in the form of nationwide dollars-and-cents ceilings at retail for meats, and community price ceilings for dry groceries. Margins were also placed under control. In addition the Price Administrator announced his decision to roll back the prices of certain food products in the following terms:

For reasons which we have previously discussed, it is clear that these measures, even if they succeed in making our price controls fully effective, will not be sufficient to roll back the cost of living to September 15 levels and hold it there. After full considerations of the most effective manner in which to achieve the essential reduction in living costs, and of the problem involved in the use of subsidy in various commodity fields, I have concluded to reduce by about 10 percent the wholesale and retail prices of beef, veal, pork, lamb, and mutton, of butter and coffee.[61]

60. *Ibid.*, pp. 148–49.
61. *Problems in Price Control: Stabilization Subsidies,* p. 9.

It was this announcement that gave rise to the major attack on the subsidy program on the part of the farm organizations and farm-state congressmen.

Powers Sought by OPA in 1941

During the 1941 hearings on the price control bill (which was enacted on January 30, 1942) the farm organizations had shown little interest in the subsidy feature. Their interest was wholly centered on prohibiting price ceilings for farm products at less than 110 per cent of parity. Preliminary skirmishing had, however, already been under way for some months in the Congress. The Price Administrator sought authority to buy, sell or store commodities, both foreign and domestic, whenever such action would aid in preventing price increases inconsistent with the purposes of the act and whenever such action would be helpful in bringing forth marginal production needed in furthering the general national objectives. He also asked for a revolving fund adequate for carrying out this policy.

The policy was to a large extent an adaptation of the one already widely used by the British Food Ministry under the able leadership of Lord Woolton. It was particularly well adapted to the peculiar conditions prevailing in Britain at that time. Some of her food supply was being produced, under heavy subsidy, in Britain. Other supplies came from abroad at different and often lower costs. For key products the entire supply, both domestic and foreign, was bought by the Ministry of Food and then sold to the trade and to the consumers at a uniform price, usually a price below cost. The program as a whole was designed to keep wages and the cost of living stable.

In the American situation imports were, of course, far less significant. Nevertheless, they could be disturbing to the over-all price stabilization plans. For example, the price paid for Cuban sugar was below that paid for United States-grown sugar if the subsidies to United States growers and processors are taken into account. The procedure used was to hold the retail price stable and undertake to absorb, through subsidies and incentive payments, such increases in cost as were resulting from war conditions. In part the subsidies were used to offset increased costs of transportation, especially from offshore areas.[62]

Production Subsidies Authorized

The Henderson proposals encountered rough sledding in the House hearings on the Price Stabilization Act of January 1942, but were included substantially as he wanted them in the bill passed by the Senate.[63] In the conference committee the power to buy or sell for the purpose of preventing price increases was eliminated. Likewise, the revolving fund provision was omitted. The power to use subsidies for the purpose of increasing production was, however, included in the following form:

Whenever the Administrator determines that the maximum necessary production of any commodity is not being obtained or may not be obtained during the ensuing year, he may, on behalf of the United States, without regard to the provisions of law requiring competitive bidding, buy or sell at public or private sale, or store or use, such commodity in such quantities and in such manner and upon such terms and conditions as he determines to be necessary to obtain the maximum necessary production thereof or otherwise to supply the demand therefor, or make subsidy payments to domestic producers of such commodity in such amounts and in such manner and upon such terms and

conditions as he determines to be necessary to obtain the necessary production thereof.[64]

Direct subsidies could be paid only to domestic producers for the purpose of increasing production. No sale could be made contrary to the provisions of the Agricultural Adjustment Act, nor could any sale of an agricultural commodity be made within the United States at a price below those specified in Section 3(a) of the act (110 per cent of parity, the market price on October 1, 1941, the market price on December 15, 1941, or the average price July 1, 1919 to June 30, 1929, whichever was highest). This left the Administrator with the difficult task of deciding when a subsidy was necessary for increase of production but not for prevention of price increases.

Under the terms of Section 2(e) of the Emergency Price Control Act, if a commodity was declared by the President to be "strategic," subsidy operations were to be carried out by the RFC. A presidential order which classified food items as strategic materials did not please either the Congress or the RFC. The Congress had refused, in May 1942, to increase the borrowing power of RFC so that it might be required to pay subsidies upon recommendation of the Price Administrator, and had also been unwilling to provide OPA with funds for that purpose.[65]

Early Forms of Subsidy

Prior to the signing of the price stabilization bill, and when some farm-product prices had not yet reached the minima provided in the bill, Secretary Wickard proposed selling previously acquired stocks of grain and cotton to relieve shortages and prevent price rises. He contended that the producers of corn and wheat were receiving parity if government payments were taken into consideration. The Department of Agriculture had instituted its "feed wheat program" on January 19, 1942 without action by the Price

62. For details see *Problems in Price Control: Stabilization Subsidies*, pp. 101–02, 130–31 and 203–05.

63. The position of the Office of Price Administration is well summarized in its brochure entitled *The Essential Role of Subsidies in the Stabilization Program*, June 1943. A carefully worded statement of the position of one of the major farm organizations, the National Council of Farmer Cooperatives, is given in the testimony of Ezra T. Benson, Executive Secretary of the Council, in U.S. Congress, Senate, Committee on Agriculture and Forestry, *Food Supply of the United States*, Hearings before a subcommittee . . . , 78th Cong., 1st sess., 1943, Part II, pp. 1099–1113. An opposition statement was also issued by the Chamber of Commerce of the United States on January 7, 1944, *An Examination of the Government Food Subsidy Program. Should Government Funds be Used to Pay Part of the Nation's Grocery Bill?*, mimeographed, revised March 15, 1946.

64. Emergency Price Control Act of January 30, 1942, 56 Stat. 23 at 26.

65. See *Problems in Price Control: Stabilization Subsidies*, pp. 93–99.

Administrator. Wheat was to be sold for feeding to livestock or poultry at the 1941 loan value of the wheat at point of delivery, or the CCC sales price for *corn* at delivery point, whichever was lower.[66]

On March 16, 1942 the Defense Supplies Corporation undertook absorption of excess transportation costs for sugar, at a cost of about $30 million per year, to prevent a break in the ceiling price for sugar. This function was taken over by CCC at the end of 1942.

Because of the 110 per cent of parity feature in the Price Control Act, the General Maximum Price Regulation could not check advances in the prices of many of the farm commodities, for example, poultry, eggs, lamb, mutton, some of the dairy products, and wheat and flour. It did, however, apply to the processed goods made from them. Hence, processors were caught in a squeeze, and it became necessary either to let retail prices rise or provide subsidies. To eliminate this squeeze entirely, including that on such commodities as fresh fruits and vegetables, for which the General Maximum Price Regulation did not apply, it was estimated that the cost would be in the neighborhood of $1,800 million annually.

Position of the Farm Organizations

As the issue came under more general discussion, the views of the farm organizations became increasingly firm in opposing subsidies. To them the savings to consumers through the use of subsidies seemed trivial and unnecessary, in view of the good incomes being received. A somewhat similar objection might be made to some of the subsidies to agriculture during the 1930's, though in that situation the need for additional income,

even in small amounts, was much more evident.

It is apparent, however, that the farm groups, though possibly right in their main contention, tended to ignore the psychological effects of even small additional increases in the prices of key foodstuffs. The success of the whole stabilization program, for prices, wages and rents, depended in considerable measure on general public acceptance of the plan. Abandonment of the established dollars-and-cents ceilings at retail would undoubtedly have weakened support for the over-all program of stabilization.

In hearings on S. J. Res. 161 (September 16, 1942) Albert Goss stated the position of the Grange as follows:

Every means should be employed to avoid the use of subsidies. If emergencies arise under which they become necessary, let them be applied at the point of processing or distribution where profits and prices can be kept under control . . .

He stated that his organization was opposed to "putting off the day of reckoning through the use of subsidies" because:

1. Subsidies which cover increased costs in order to spare any segment of society from feeling the economic effects of war are unjust to future generations. We should pay the cost as we go.
2. Subsidies are inflationary.
3. Subsidies lead to future inflation.
4. Subsidies conceal costs and delay or defeat efforts to correct excessive expenditures.
5. Subsidies promote inefficiency.
6. Subsidies open the way for political abuse.
7. Subsidies make everyone pay for the benefits enjoyed by the few.
8. When once used they are hard to get rid of. ". . . men are elected to office on the pledge of their continuance."
9. Subsidies destroy initiative and undermine character.
10. Subsidies are an expedient way of dodging a hard or disagreeable issue.
11. Subsidies are the means of building a strongly centralized government and lead to dictatorship.[67]

66. This was formalized through a joint statement by the Secretary of Agriculture and the Price Administrator (February 3, 1942) in which it was agreed that government-owned stocks of grains and cotton would continue to be used to supplement private stocks, that feedstuffs would be kept at reasonable levels to encourage the production of meat and livestock products and that the prices of things farmers bought would be held down. This was in line with the President's comment in signing the Emergency Price Control Act that no action should be taken which would peg prices through arbitrary withholding of government-owned stocks.

67. U.S. Congress, Senate, Committee on Banking and Currency, *Stabilizing the Cost of Living*, Hearings . . . , 77th Cong., 2nd sess. on S. J. Res. 161, September 15 and 16, 1942, pp. 156–57.

It is clear that Goss, in the main, was re-stating long-established Grange policy rather than addressing himself to the issue then before the Congress. Subsidies had long been discussed in a context of special favors to big business (note reference to payments made by the many for the benefit of the few). The old phrases were being used in a different set-ting. This was a proposal, not to benefit a few at the expense of many, but rather of how much the public was to pay and how it was to be paid, whether through taxes or prices in the market. But the word "subsidy" was still a red flag, especially to members of the older farm organizations. This same con-fusion of issues appears in many of the farm organization statements of this period. There can be no doubt that some farm leaders and some congressmen were using it deliberately to jockey up farm prices, but no one who knew Mr. Goss will doubt his sincerity in stressing a long-established policy of the Grange. His points, however, had little bear-ing on the points then at issue.

Strong Opposition in Congress

Continuing criticism of OPA policies led to a congressional investigation of the admin-istration of the farm features of the price con-trol program in October and November 1942.[68] Senators Reed, Shipstead, Brewster, Taft and others challenged the legality of the use of subsidies to hold down the prices of certain farm products. Criticism was leveled also at the President's recommendation that soil conservation and parity payments be treated as a part of the price paid to farmers in figuring whether farmers were or were not receiving parity.

As a result, in part, of the rough treatment received at the hands of the Congress in this investigation, both by OPA and the admin-istration generally, Henderson resigned as OPA Administrator on December 18.[69] He was succeeded on January 20, 1943 by Prentiss Brown, a former Democratic senator from Michigan who had been defeated in the elec-tion of the previous November. Brown proved as much too lenient as Henderson had been too tough, and was succeeded on November 8, 1943 by Chester Bowles, an advertising executive from Connecticut. It was hoped that Bowles would be able to im-prove public understanding of the program and gain for it wider public support.[70]

Congressional opposition was intensified by the rollback program which grew out of the President's "Hold-the-Line" Order of April 8. At this time the price and wage stabiliza-tion plan was in a precarious state. The farm-state congressmen and senators had passed the so-called Bankhead bill by large majori-ties in both houses. (S. 660 passed by 78 to 2 in the Senate and by 149 to 40 in the House.) This would have prohibited taking account of parity payments, allotment payments and conservation payments in fixing ceilings on farm prices at parity. It was in substance the old 110 per cent of parity objective but in dif-ferent form.

President Roosevelt vetoed the bill only a few days prior to the issuance of the "Hold-the-Line" Order. In a vigorous and well-reasoned statement he pointed out that the Congress had several times accepted the inter-pretation of parity contained in his Executive Order of October 3, 1942, and stated that:

Between August, 1939, and January, 1943, the prices that farmers received for the crops they

69. Apparently at the request of the President. (Op-position to OPA policies tended to focus on the Adminis-trator personally, partly, no doubt, because of injudicious personal publicity emanating from his own office.)

70. The general public seems, on the whole, to have been strongly in favor of the program. Opposition centered chiefly in the farm and business groups and in the owners of rental properties. The rigidities introduced into the economy by the general price and rent freeze created many severe tensions, and unquestionably many grave injustices, which could not be alleviated under the rigid over-all rulings which were necessary if such a plan was to work at all. The farmers had less reason to complain than did many other business groups. They were not caught in a squeeze as were some processors and handlers, and were doing exceedingly well finan-cially.

68. Farmers were irked also by the inappropriateness of some of the rulings as applied in local situations. The personnel of OPA undoubtedly included many misfits. Mistakes and stupidities were fairly common, though probably not more so than in military operations which were a parallel concomitant of the war. It is not clear, however, even in retrospect, that some such program could have been avoided. Granting its use, some abuses and administrative inadequacies were inevitable.

sold rose nearly 107 percent, while the prices that farmers paid for the things they bought increased only 26 percent.

Farm prices which were 30 percent below parity at the beginning of the war in August, 1939, rose to 15 percent above parity in January, 1943 . . .

The Bankhead bill departs from the declared policy of the Act of October 2, 1942. It departs from the only practical basis on which any sound stabilization program can proceed . . . To change the present delicately balanced price relationships would not merely change, but would jeopardize the entire stabilization program.[71]

The veto was not overridden and the administration retained the power to fix farm price ceilings at parity, with benefit and conservation payments included in the computation of returns to farmers.

Wage Demands

The threat of breakdown in the stabilization program was not merely from the farm groups. The coal miners, in late March, had demanded a $2 per day increase in wages, increased payments for vacation time and travel to and from portals, and various other concessions. Their union ignored invitations to participate in hearings arranged by the War Labor Board, and in April stoppages of work began to occur. A general strike of the bituminous coal miners was started on May 1 in defiance of a presidential request that the miners stay on the job. As a result, the President directed the Secretary of the Interior to take over and operate the mines (Executive Order 9340, May 1, 1943).[72] Labor was restless and in a strong position to demand wage increases because of the growing shortage of manpower. Even moderate advances in the already high prices for key foodstuffs seemed likely to breach the line and give free play to the inflationary potential posed by high buying power, shortages of labor and limited supplies of some of the food items.

At this time food prices had increased, since August 1939, by more than double the percentage increase for all other cost-of-living

71. *Public Papers and Addresses, 1943*, pp. 138 and 141.
72. *Ibid.*, pp. 186–88.

items. Foods were up 47 per cent; apparel 27.2 per cent; rents 3.5 per cent; fuel, electricity and refrigeration 10.2 per cent; and house furnishings 23.8 per cent.[73]

Operation of the Subsidy Program

To implement the President's "Hold-the-Line" Order, OPA announced on April 30 that retail meat, butter and coffee prices would be "rolled back" about 10 per cent by payment of an equivalent subsidy at the processor level.[74] During May and June prices were reduced for 39 commodities and by August most fresh fish and the more important fruits and vegetables had been brought under control.

The objective of the subsidy program was not merely that of lessening consumer expenditures by a few dollars per person per year, as was frequently charged by its opponents. It was rather a psychological move taken in the hope that the creaking structure of prices and wages might be kept within the framework already established. Once this was broken seriously, it was doubtful that similarly widespread agreement could be obtained for a new stand at some higher level. Hence, with the explosive situation of a large, unclosed inflationary gap between consumer income and current expenditures, the lid would be off and a repetition of the World War I inflation on a much larger scale could be expected. The United States was an active participant in World War I for only twenty months, and its mobilization was far less complete than in World War II. Yet prices of farm products increased 111 per cent between 1914 and 1919, and the prices paid by farmers increased 96 per cent.[75]

73. *Ibid.*, p. 155.
74. Followed by announcement of May 7, with approval of Stabilization Director Byrnes, that all retail prices of beef, veal, pork, lamb, mutton, butter and coffee would be reduced 10 per cent effective June 1, the subsidies to be provided through Defense Supplies Corporation, a subsidiary of RFC. The coffee rollback was later withdrawn. For a fuller account of the use of subsidies, see *Problems in Price Control: Stabilization Subsidies*, also *Price and Related Controls in the United States*, by Seymour E. Harris, McGraw-Hill, New York, 1945.
75. Roosevelt, *Public Papers and Addresses, 1943*, p. 138.

The policy thus adopted not only decreed the rollback of certain prices, and continuing subsidies, presumably to consumers, but also implied that any further price increases to stimulate production of farm products would be in the form of incentive payments rather than higher prices in the market.[76] These likewise drew vigorous opposition from the farm organizations and the farm-state congressmen.[77]

Efforts to Discontinue Subsidies

When the bill for continuing the life of the Commodity Credit Corporation came up in June, various amendments were proposed which would prohibit the payment of subsidies for rolling back prices. This opposition came into form as the Steagall Bill, H.R. 2869, passed on June 29, 1943. It prohibited the use of any funds for subsidies or rollbacks, or as a substitute for raising prices, unless specifically authorized by Congress.

However, the President was in a position to block such action. He could veto the bill, thus ending the life of the Commodity Credit Corporation, but likewise depriving the agricultural groups of their principal mechanism for supporting prices. This he did on July 2, stating that "as the measure now stands, this is an inflation bill, a high-cost-of-living bill, a food shortage bill." After the veto, a new bill was passed extending the life of the Commodity Credit Corporation until the end of 1943, and allowing for that period the continued use of subsidy payments. Opposition to the subsidy program continued, how-

ever, and further hearings were held by a subcommittee of the Senate Committee on Agriculture and Forestry in the fall of 1943.

A new bill to extend the life of the Commodity Credit Corporation was passed in February 1944. Section 3 of this bill prohibited the use of any funds by the Corporation, or by any other government agency, for subsidies on any agricultural commodity, including milk and livestock and the products thereof. The bill also contained other provisions which would have resulted in higher prices to consumers for dairy products.

The President vetoed this bill and urgently recommended that Congress "take action as soon as possible to extend without hampering restrictions the life of the Commodity Credit Corporation. Farmers could thereby make plans for the planting of crops and know the support prices on which they can rely." He called attention to the reasons given in his veto message of July 2, 1943 and reiterated his statement that "This bill . . . is an inflation measure, a high cost of living measure, a food shortage measure." The bill would, he said, "in effect reverse the policy of the Congress; in effect it repeals the Stabilization Act of October 2, 1942."[78]

Though the House had voted more than 2 to 1 for the bill, the President's veto was sustained.[79] The President was thereby again placed in a strong position to obtain provisions more satisfactory to him since failure to continue the Commodity Credit Corporation would have eliminated payments desired by farmers as well as those which were not desired by them. The Congress then passed legislation extending the life of the CCC, without the crippling restrictions to which the President had objected, until July 1, 1945. The new bill was signed by the President on February 28, 1944.

The continuance of the CCC with its powers to aid in controlling prices came under consideration again in the spring of

76. For example, in the effort to stimulate milk production the mechanism used was a subsidy on feed purchased rather than a higher price for the product.

77. The administration approach to the problem was complicated by the lack of full support by Marvin Jones, War Food Administrator. Jones, while in Congress, had been a leader in the fight for legislation favorable to agriculture. His leadership in the War Food Administration was not strong, and he tended to concur in the views of the Congress and the farm organizations. He did not see eye to eye with the OPA administrators and there was a lack of close contact between the two agencies, though they were supposed to reach joint decisions on food matters. In the heat of the controversy over rollbacks, Jones stated that they had been announced without his knowledge or consultation, though he was supposed to have the most important powers in the food field.

78. *Public Papers and Addresses, 1944-45*, pp. 73-74.

79. The original vote in the House was 249 to 118 in favor of the bill. In the attempt to override the veto the vote was 226 to 151, thus falling short of the necessary two thirds.

TABLE I

COST OF FOOD SUBSIDIES

(Calendar Year 1945)

Program	Paying Agency	Why Subsidized	How Subsidized	Annual Cost (In Millions of Dollars)
Butter	DSC[a]	To roll retail prices back to September 1942 levels.	Payment of 5 cents per pound of butter to creameries.	73.0
Canned grapefruit juice[b]	CCC[e]	To permit increased grower returns and offset increases in canning costs.	Payment up to specified rates, of the difference between the individual canner's cost for raw grapefruit and the raw cost reflected by the canned juice ceilings.	5.5
Canned and frozen vegetables[b,d]	CCC	To permit increased grower returns and offset increases in canning costs.	Payment at specified rates per dozen cans of major products and per ton of raw product for minor tomato items and frozen peas, corn and snap beans.[e]	25.0
Cheddar cheese	CCC	To offset cost increases and to encourage greater production.	Purchase and resale at a loss of 3¾ cents to 4 cents per pound.[e]	16.5
Dairy production payments	CCC	To increase producer returns, thus offsetting increased costs and encouraging greater production.	Payment on deliveries of whole milk and butterfat differentiated seasonally, and in addition, regionally for whole milk.	479.0
Dried edible beans[b]	CCC	To permit increased grower returns.	Payment at specified rates per cwt. of cleaned beans.[e]	3.5
Feed wheat	CCC	To permit utilization of wheat as feed, primarily for dairy cattle, in certain feed shortage areas.	Wheat for feed is sold at feed value equality with corn.	40.0
Flour production payments	DSC	To permit increased grower prices, in accordance with minimum legal requirements.	Payment equal to difference in any given month between average actual wheat costs paid by the industry and the average price of wheat reflected by flour ceiling.	152.0
Meat	DSC	To roll retail prices back to September 1942 levels, and to permit increased returns to livestock producers.	Payment on live weight slaughtered differentiated by kinds of animals, and in the case of beef — grades. Deductions made in beef subsidy by the amounts individual	570.0

			Included in DSC Costs
Meat	CCC	To encourage feeding and improve distribution.	8.0
		Fifty cent live cwt. meeting standards. [with allowance when slaughterer's live cattle costs in any given month fall below or exceed costs based on "stabilization range" prices.]	
Peanut butter[b]	CCC	To roll retail prices back to September 1942 levels.	2.0
		Payment of 4.5 cents per pound to manufacturer.	
Peanut oil	CCC	To maintain adequate production at prices in line with other edible oils.	20.4
		Purchase of peanuts and resale to crushers at a loss.[e]	
Raisins and prunes[b]	CCC	To permit increased grower returns and offset increases in processing costs.	12.0
		Purchase of entire pack of dried raisins and prunes and resale of civilian quantities at a loss.[e]	
Regional fluid milk[b]	CCC	To permit an increase in producer returns and encourage production.	44.0
		Purchase and resale arrangements on all fluid milk.	
Soybeans	CCC	To permit increased grower returns and encourage production of oil.	103.6
		Purchase of soybeans at support prices and resale at a loss to processors at differentiated prices based on processor efficiency.[e]	
Sugar (various programs)	CCC	To permit increased grower returns, offset increased shipping, handling, and processing costs, and generally to encourage maximum production.	
		Purchase of Puerto Rican and Cuban sugar and resale at a loss (or without payment of normal import duty). Direct payments to growers and importers of Hawaiian sugar. Payments through the processors, to growers of domestic beet and cane. Payments to all processors of sugar beets to offset increased costs, and to marginal processors to cover deficits.	
Vegetable shortening, bulk[b]	CCC	To roll back prices of vegetable shortening.	1.0
		Payment of .4 cents per pound of vegetable oil in standard shortening and .2 cents per pound of hydrogenated vegetable shortening.	
			1,555.5

a. Defense Supplies Corporation. b. Program covers civilian supplies only. c. Commodity Credit Corporation.
d. Cost figures include canned vegetables only. No estimates are as yet available for the subsidies on frozen vegetables and canned vegetable soups.
e. Subsidy so devised that growers are guaranteed support prices, or the payment of the subsidy is made contingent upon the payment of support prices to farmers.
Source: Office of Price Administration.

1945, but the opposition was by then somewhat less militant. Farm prices were, for the most part, at highly satisfactory levels and large crops had boomed farm incomes to all-time highs. The public had become accustomed to the price stabilization program, though black marketing and criticism were growing in importance. Nevertheless, the propaganda value of a fight against subsidies was declining.

High Cost of Subsidies

Whether justified or not, there can be no question that the subsidy program constituted a very heavy drain on the Treasury. It was not, however, as the farm groups contended, merely a subsidy to consumers, unless it be assumed that the prices of farm products would be allowed to rise by a corresponding amount. If the price and wage line was to be held, farm incomes would presumably have had to be lower by something approximating the amount of the subsidies. The National Industrial Conference Board in its *Road Maps of Industry* for the week of September 7, 1945 computed the annual rates of subsidy on the various products as shown in Table 1.

Concessions to Opponents

The new bill made concessions to the opponents of the program by a provision that Section 2(e) of the Emergency Price Control Act, as amended by the Stabilization Extension Act of 1944, would not apply to operations of the Commodity Credit Corporation for the year ending June 30, 1946. This was the section which permitted the use of incentive payments to stimulate production of agricultural products where the administrator of the OPA "finds such action to be necessary." The amendment of 1944 had prohibited inclusion of any additional agricultural commodity in this category, but permitted continuance of subsidies and incentive payments for those already classified as strategic.

This concession was now to be withdrawn as to activities of the Corporation after June

30, 1945. The prohibition was itself modified, however, by later sections of the act. The Commodity Credit Corporation was authorized to make such payments to complete operations with respect to the 1944 and prior crop years, and to fulfill obligations incurred before July 1, 1945, with respect to 1945 and the crops of previous years. In addition, it was specifically authorized to continue, for 1945–1946, dairy subsidies to the extent of $568 million, feed wheat and other noncrop subsidies to the extent of $120 million, and 1945 crop subsidies to an amount not exceeding $225 million. Since the war was by then obviously drawing to a close, the moderate limitations thus established did not elicit strong administration opposition. The bill was passed and signed on April 12, 1945.[80]

In an Act of June 23, 1945 the Congress established a similar policy with respect to subsidy payments by subsidiaries of the Reconstruction Finance Corporation. This, like the CCC Act, prohibited payment of subsidies and purchase and resale at a loss, for the fiscal year ending June 30, 1946, except as specifically authorized in the current act. Rather liberal authorization for such payments and purchases was included, however, for programs already in effect.[81] This action closed, for the time being, the long struggle over the subsidy and incentive payment issue. The battle was to be rejoined in a different setting and with a different set of administration proposals in the postwar period which will be discussed in a following chapter.

80. 59 Stat. 50.
81. A minority view was presented in the Senate report. This view, sponsored by Senators Taft of Ohio, Thomas of Idaho, Butler of Nebraska, Capper of Kansas, Buck of Delaware and Hickenlooper of Iowa, was that the policies of the OPA administrators had discouraged production and seriously hampered the proper distribution of food; had forced many legitimate small processors and distributors out of business; had brought black markets into existence; and, if continued, would hamper recovery and cause serious unemployment. Their amendment would have prohibited the establishment of any maximum price on a processed agricultural product which would not cover all costs plus a profit. While not accepted at this time, it was an opening gun in the successful postwar fight to abolish price controls.

CHAPTER 17

FOOD PROGRAM OF THE WAR YEARS

THE CONTROVERSIES over prices, price control and related matters held the center of the stage in the early years of the war. Nevertheless, these were not the whole of the wartime farm program, or, in fact, the major phase of it. In agriculture as in industry, the all-important requirement was to get increased production and get it quickly. No longer was there need for keeping the production mechanism in low gear, or in reverse. The time had come for giving added impetus to the farmer's desire to produce, which even the drastic measures of the 1930's had been unable to hold in check. In large measure this could be accomplished merely by removing the restraints on farm output and providing the stimulus of higher prices, together with an outlet for all that could be produced.

The removal of restraints on production could be accomplished by readjusting attitudes in administrative circles and in the Congress, and recognizing fully the need for a revised farm program. Assurance of an outlet for the products was being supplied automatically by the insistent demand growing out of the war and the greatly increased buying power of domestic consumers. In agriculture, as in industry, there was need for redirection of effort so as to increase production in some lines and reduce it in others.

But the changes needed on farms were far less significant than those required in factories. In agriculture, the principal need was for more of the kinds of things already being produced. The plants were in existence, the labor in place and the methods well known.

Changes Needed

There were other barriers to be overcome, however. The agricultural legislation of the preceding decade was almost wholly designed to hold down production. The administrators and the farm-state representatives in Congress did not find it easy to make this quick about-face. Laws and regulations well suited to the altered conditions were slow to emerge. Furthermore, farm production changes are timed by nature and farms are not easily or quickly reorganized for different kinds and amounts of production. Additional machinery, labor and fertilizer all were hard to get and could easily become a serious bottleneck in the farm production program.

New plans were needed and new devices for indicating to farmers the kinds of production called for, together with appropriate types of incentive for making the adjustments required. Mechanisms and policies for allocating foodstuffs and giving priorities to the more urgent types of use were not in existence.

No longer was it necessary to center attention on ways to increase farm incomes. Instead the problems of preventing damage to the industry through inflation of land values, and the planning of postwar adjustment, were soon to present themselves. The immediate concern, however, was that of putting agricultural production into high gear and guiding it in the right direction as it expanded its output.

EFFORTS TO STIMULATE, GUIDE AND ADJUST PRODUCTION

The principal mechanisms used in the attempt to expand and guide agricultural production were price incentives, the announcement of production goals and aid in obtaining necessary resources for maintaining or increasing production. The liberal price increases permitted on farm products provided a powerful incentive for greater production. Farmers had been accustomed since time immemorial to being guided in their production plans by such knowledge as they possessed concerning prices to be expected when the crops were ready for market. The general advance of more than 30 per cent in the average level of all farm prices between 1939 and 1941 and the prospect of a rapid continuing increase were, therefore, incentives of the first magnitude for all-out production.

As a war measure this was a shotgun approach that was unlikely to result in the best use of resources. The price ceilings provided in the wartime legislation were, in fact, related to past supply and demand relationships, not to the needs of a nation at war. Consequently, the general upsurge of all farm prices tended to give equal if not greater stimulus for the production of commodities in ample supply, as for those in which large expansion was needed. For example, there was no occasion at that time to stimulate the production of cotton. On the other hand, since Pacific area supplies of fats and oils had been cut off, there was great need for a quick and large increase in the output of oil crops such as soybeans, peanuts and flaxseed. There was likewise need for increasing tomatoes, dry beans, vegetable seeds and milk.

At the same time the output of some other crops could have been reduced without serious loss to the health or comfort of the domestic civilian population. Actually the price increases permitted under the formulae adopted were greatest for those commodities in abundant supply, since these were the ones furthest below parity when the war began. Thus, the fixing of all farm price ceilings in a given relation to parity, while it stimulated over-all production of farm products, tended to throw the emphasis in the direction of grains, cotton and tobacco rather than toward meat animals, dairy products and oilseed crops.[1]

1. This tendency was to some extent offset by the later subsidized sale of government-owned wheat for feed at corn prices.

Steps Taken

To offset this misdirection of agricultural effort, steps were taken during 1941 and early 1942 looking to the establishment of national and state production goals. Though initiated directly by the Department of Agriculture, this process became later a joint undertaking of the Department and the state agricultural war boards.

The Secretary of Agriculture had already undertaken to guide production into desired channels through public announcements of Department policy. On April 3, 1941, he had announced that the Department would support prices of hogs, dairy products, chickens and eggs at levels well above those then prevailing.[2] He also stated that the agricultural conservation regulations would be relaxed to permit growing of peanuts on cotton acreage allotments not used for cotton. Other concessions of similar nature were made from time to time. The Steagall Amendment of July 1 still further encouraged production of those commodities for which the Secretary had asked increased output.

These actions were followed by the establishment, on July 17, of an Interbureau Production Goals Committee.[3] In September public announcement was made of support prices for hogs, eggs, evaporated milk, dry skim milk, cheese and chickens, thus bringing those not formerly so classified under the provisions of the Steagall Amendment. On the same day, September 8, the first announcement of production goals for 1942 appeared.

On October 28, the Office of Lend-Lease Administration was created by Executive Order 8926.[4] Thereafter, it was to participate increasingly in the plans for conservation and distribution of foods.

After Pearl Harbor the efforts to guide food production moved more and more into high

2. U.S. Department of Agriculture, *Press Release*, 1992-41.
3. On April 30, 1941 the Secretary had authorized the establishment of an Interbureau Coordinating Committee on Fats and Oils and on May 7 announced a Joint Anglo-American Food Committee to help coordinate efforts to meet Britain's food needs.
4. *Federal Register*, Vol. VI, pp. 5519-20.

gear, with a reorganization of the Department of Agriculture on December 13 and announcement of revised and higher production goals on January 16. On the same day the War Production Board was established, by Executive Order 9024.[5] These steps were followed by the signing of the Emergency Price Control Act on January 30.

The new "goals" announcement (that of January 16) called for increases of 8 per cent in milk production; 6 per cent in corn production; 73 per cent for dry peas; 150 per cent for peanuts; 34 per cent for flaxseed; 10 per cent for flue-cured tobacco and rice; and substantially more sugar, all in relation to 1941. For other crops the Department merely announced its estimate of probable production.[6] A field survey of expected production, made in March, indicated substantial increases in all of the crops, but failure to meet the goals set for peanuts, milk, canning tomatoes, peas and some other crops.[7] To stimulate milk production, the Secretary announced on March 28 an increase of 1¾ cents per pound in the floor under butter prices. This was intended as an encouragement for dairy farmers to feed more grain. The Department already, on March 2, had launched a study of agriculture's wartime production capacity.[8]

Foreign Purchase and Allocation

These actions were followed by a presidential proclamation suspending the sugar quota system (April 13). This had been suspended on September 11, 1939 and reinstated on December 26, 1939. A month later (May 16), the Commodity Credit Corporation was made the exclusive agency for handling importation of most imported agricultural materials, though authority for procurement rested

with the Secretaries of Agriculture, Treasury and War and the Reconstruction Finance Corporation (Executive Order 9177, May 30, 1942).[9]

At about this same time, agreement was reached with Britain whereby the United States was to purchase and allocate foreign fats and oils of the Western Hemisphere (except animal fats from Argentina and Uruguay) and copra from the Pacific Islands; also, those from Portuguese and Spanish Africa and Liberia. A Food Requirements Committee was established by the War Production Board on June 5. This was to determine food requirements, including those for military and foreign use, and make recommendations to the War Production Board on supplies needed for the production of food and fiber. The Secretary of Agriculture was appointed chairman. Four days later, the Combined Food Board was established by joint announcement of President Roosevelt and Prime Minister Churchill. This was to investigate food needs and production possibilities, formulate plans and make recommendations to the United States and British governments on production, transportation, and allocation or distribution of foods in or to any part of the world.

Farm Labor and Machinery

Draft boards had from the beginning been instructed to give special consideration to the need for retaining key workers on farms, and other measures were taken looking to assurance of adequate farm labor supplies.

On June 22, the War Manpower Commission directed the Secretary of Agriculture to assure that necessary transportation, housing and health facilities were provided for non-local farm workers needed for agricultural production. As a further means of enlarging the labor supply of agriculture, an agreement was reached on August 4 whereby Mexican farm workers might be recruited and brought in on a temporary basis. A further step, designed to assure orderly use of farm machin-

5. *Federal Register*, Vol. VII, pp. 329–30.
6. For details, see USDA, *Suggested State and Regional Distribution of Revised Goals and Expected Production for 1942*, January 1942, mimeographed.
7. Bureau of Agricultural Economics, *Preview of 1942 Production Situation*, Washington, April 1942, mimeographed.
8. Part 1 was released in August 1942. See also *Agriculture's Maximum Wartime Production Capacity (Statistical Summary)*, USDA in Cooperation with the Land-Grant Colleges, Washington, September 1943, mimeographed.

9. *Federal Register*, Vol. VII, pp. 4195–96.

ery, was taken on September 15, at which time the OPA authorized the Department of Agriculture to ration such equipment. On November 30, the Director of Economic Stabilization transferred to the Secretary of Agriculture jurisdiction over farm wages and salaries for workers earning less than $2,400 a year.

Production Restrictions Relaxed

The restrictive laws passed during the depression were still in effect, and thinking in the Department of Agriculture still was heavily influenced by the fear of postwar surpluses. Only by specific action could these restrictions be relaxed. Such relaxation did occur though somewhat belatedly. On September 16 Secretary Wickard announced that marketing quotas for corn would not be established, though total supplies on October 1 would exceed normal by more than 10 per cent. Earlier, on August 6, Congress had authorized the sale of 125 million bushels of wheat for feed at prices not lower than 85 per cent of the parity price for corn. The October 2 amendments to the Steagall Amendment were also designed to lessen the fear of price-depressing surpluses at the close of the war, and thus to encourage all-out production.

An announcement of December 1, 1942 marked a more specific break with the old policies of restricting output, though it may be doubted if these any longer were influencing farmer decisions markedly. On that date the Secretary of Agriculture announced that crop payments would be conditioned on the degree to which the goals for war crops were met on the specific farm. Deductions would be made at the rate of $15 for each acre below 90 per cent of the war goal. At this time (December 5), the reorganization of the Department of Agriculture previously mentioned was initiated through Executive Order 9280.[10] Under it, the Food Production Administration and the Food Distribution Administration were established, and the Sec-

retary of Agriculture was made a member of the War Production Board.[11]

The gradual shift toward all-out production continued as the war outlook became more grim and submarine warfare intensified. On January 8, 1943 the Secretary announced that farmers in commercial corn areas would be allowed to overplant their corn allotments without penalty, provided they planted the amounts of war crops required under the goals. In connection with the revised and larger production goals announced on January 16, a production payment program designed to encourage growing of potatoes, dry beans and fresh truck crops was initiated. An order was also issued giving preference to war crops in the distribution of chemical fertilizers. Shortly thereafter, the Regional Agricultural Credit Corporation, inactive since 1934, was reactivated to make available some $200 million of additional credit for the production of war crops.[12]

On January 26 the Department of Agriculture announced a $100 million program of incentive payments for farmers whose war crop production was more than 90 and up to 100 per cent of the goals. An Agricultural Labor Administration was established on March 1 and at the same time the Food Stamp Plan was suspended. On March 25 the authorization for sale of feed wheat at subsidized prices was increased from 125 million bushels to 225 million. Toward the end of the month Chester Davis was appointed as War Food Administrator, replacing Claude Wickard. This was intended as a means of strengthening still further the drive for increased production.[13]

---

10. *Federal Register*, Vol. VII, pp. 10179–81.

11. On December 19 Secretary Wickard announced the appointment of a Food Advisory Committee to replace the Food Requirements Committee. This included representatives of most of the major claimants for food such as the Army, the Navy, Lend-Lease, the War Production Board and various other government agencies.
12. On January 22 the Secretary established a Departmental Committee on Foreign Purchase and Importation. This was later more broadly constituted and was used in determining priorities in the purchase and importation of foodstuffs from abroad. The shortage of shipping made it necessary to place rigorous restrictions on importations from many parts of the world.
13. Davis served only until the end of June at which time he resigned in protest against what he considered

Effectiveness of the Goals Committees

By the middle of 1943, most of the measures for stimulating and guiding farm production had been brought into play. Goals were established annually thereafter. New sources of foreign labor for agriculture were tapped, and quota limitations were abolished by annual announcements nullifying the provisions of the Agricultural Adjustment Act of 1938, wherever these would otherwise have required the establishment of marketing quotas. Forward price supports were announced from time to time on specific commodities, and producer subsidies as well as consumer subsidies were used.

Thus, the guidance of production did not lie primarily, perhaps not even importantly, with the production goals committees, though the goals established did give some indication of desirable directions of change. They did, however, provide a framework within which performance could be judged with respect to qualifying for the crop subsidies provided under the longer-term agricultural legislation then in effect, and the new ones announced in the orders relating to wartime incentive payments.

Full effectiveness of the goals committees was hampered by a lack of clarity and uniformity in the concepts of the job to be done. The studies of maximum war capacity of agriculture were of necessity related to a vague criterion. American agriculture can obviously be expanded greatly if given time, resources and incentives for such expansion. Incentives existed for full use of already de-

veloped acreage, but not for high-cost speculative development of lands not already under cultivation, except for plowable pastures which could easily be put into crop. But labor resources were limited. Most farmers and hired farm workers were putting in long hours and using rather effectively such equipment as they had.

Some writers criticize sharply what they regard as unduly low over-all acreage goals.[14] This criticism is based primarily on evidence of need that outran even the large production of the war years, and the obvious possibility that both acreage and output could be increased substantially, provided time and resources were available. However, most of such enlargement of output would have had to be at higher cost, and some years would have been required to accomplish it and to reorganize or develop farms for effective use of additional acreage that might be brought in.

Since most farmers were using fully the labor resources they had or could obtain and since no one knew how long the heavy demand would last, the incentives and opportunities for opening up new acreage were not large. Nevertheless, it is hard to explain a total increase in the acreage of key crops of only about 12 per cent between 1941 and 1945, and an over-all acreage in crops in 1945 that was 5 per cent less than that of 1932.[15]

The record is not so good as most farm people like to think, nor is it as bad as the critics imply. Yet it is not clear that farmers would have been warranted in expanding their acreages substantially with the resources and knowledge available to them at that time.

Functions of the Goals Committee

The state goals committees wavered between two concepts: one, to suggest what and how much should be produced in light of the indicated national needs; the other, to indicate what probably would be produced

---

the unworkability of the food and price control program. In his letter of resignation he stated that he found that he had assumed "a public responsibility while the authority, not only over broad food policy but day-to-day actions, is being exercised elsewhere." He expressed the view that the post should be filled by a man who believes in subsidies, saying "I do not believe such subsidies will be effective unless they are accompanied here, as they are in England, by current tax and savings programs that drain off excess buying power, and by tight control and management of the food supply. We do not have in this country anything approaching these conditions." (Letter to the President, June 16, 1943.) Davis was succeeded by Judge Marvin Jones, a former congressman from Texas and long a leader in the congressional group concerned with agricultural matters. Texts of letters exchanged by Davis and Roosevelt are in *New York Times,* June 29, 1943, p. 24.

14. See, for example, Bela Gold, *Wartime Economic Planning in Agriculture, A Study in the Allocation of Resources,* Columbia University Press, New York, 1949, pp. 87–91.

15. *Ibid.,* p. 87.

with the then existing relationships between prices, and, in some cases, to estimate what changes in price relationships would be needed to bring about the shifts desired by the planners in the Department of Agriculture. More and more, they drifted toward the second procedure as being more realistic than the first.

The fact of the matter is that the Congress was unwilling to accept full-scale food production planning and had set up legislation (especially that relating to parity prices) which made selective guidance of resources into best uses impossible. To accomplish that fully would have required more freedom to readjust price relationships, to use incentive payments and to penalize misuse of resources. Lacking this freedom of action, the officials sought to exercise a mild, mainly hortatory, influence as best they could. The great diversity of American agriculture reduced somewhat the deleterious effects of the parity-price strait jacket. Actually, nearly all of the crops were needed in fullest possible supply and, with some exceptions, a response all across the board to the higher level of prices, but largely in the old pattern of relationships between commodities, did not fit too badly the needs of the time.

One segment of American agriculture was clearly used ineffectively, namely, the manpower on some 1 to 3 million small, inefficient subsistence farms. These were mainly in areas where large families and small land and capital resources were the rule. Certain individuals in the war agencies urged vigorously a large-scale effort to upgrade the productivity of these farms through enlargement and capital input. But the majority opinion was that the results of such action would be too slow and the contribution to commercial supplies too small to warrant it as a short-term war program. Furthermore, it seemed evident that the limited national resources in trained personnel could be used more effectively elsewhere.

These areas did, however, contribute markedly to the war effort through the out-migration of manpower not needed on these small-scale farms. Some consolidation of holdings did occur, and the over-all result was not only a contribution to the nation's manpower, but an improvement in conditions in the areas from which this manpower was drawn.

Performance in Relation to Goals

Acreage changes do not measure fully the effort to increase production. This will be evident from the later discussion of changes in output. However, they do give some indication of farmers' efforts to readjust in response both to announced goals and to price incentives.[16]

Items stressed, especially in the early years of the war, were oil-bearing crops, dry beans and peas, tomatoes, milk, pork, potatoes and sugar beets. By 1944 and 1945, the goals for wheat, corn, rice and tobacco were being stepped up.

For soybeans, the 1942 goal was more than twice the prewar average, and was more than filled. The goal was stepped up again in 1943, from 9 million acres to 12 million, but performance fell short. Only 10.4 million acres were planted. The 1942 goal for flaxseed was about twice the prewar average, and was more than achieved. A still larger quota for 1943 was substantially surpassed. From then on, flax production fell off sharply, to about prewar levels, and goals were lowered in an effort to keep some touch with reality. Peanut production was well below the goals announced throughout the war years, except in 1945, by which time the goal had been reduced to correspond with actual production. On the whole, performance in the oil-bearing crops was disappointing.

The wheat goals were raised materially after 1943, and performance was approximately equal to the goals. Corn goals were raised about 8 per cent over prewar, but at no time were they achieved. For rice, on the other hand, though goals were raised some

16. For a tabular summary of the announced goals, the acreages planted, and livestock produced, see the special releases of the U.S. Department of Agriculture, Office of the Secretary, *Acreage Goals With Comparisons, 1942–1949* and *Livestock Goals With Comparisons, 1942–1949,* June 1949, processed.

30 to 36 per cent over prewar, they were approximately met in each of the war years.

The production of dry beans proved disappointing all through the war. Acreages planted ran generally from 20 to 25 per cent below those recommended. Cotton acreage declined in these years, falling off at an even faster rate than the continuously reduced goals that were set up. Both sugar beets and sugar cane failed by wide margins to meet the goals set. Tobacco acreages, on the other hand, approximated those suggested in nearly all of the years.

Cattle numbers were greatly in excess of the goals throughout the war period, but the number slaughtered approximately equaled the goals set, except in 1943. Continuous efforts were made to increase milk production, but only in 1945 was the goal fully achieved, despite a gradual reduction in the goals themselves. Sheep flocks were progressively reduced during the war years, and sheep and lamb slaughter ran consistently and heavily above the numbers called for by the goals. Pork production approximated the goals set in all of the years.[17] Egg production was consistently in excess of the announced goals.

The goals announcements do not appear to have had a large influence on the pattern of agricultural production. The changes were, in the main, an over-all upsurge in farm production which was, for the most part, a response to price incentives. The goals committees did, however, serve as a connecting link between the Washington officials and the field and were helpful in keeping the planning activities closer to reality than they would otherwise have been. With a less rigid framework of prices they could have been very useful in indicating to the federal planners what changes in price relationships would be most likely to bring about the production changes desired. Effective action

looking to that end would, of course, have required more freedom on the part of federal officials to make the kinds of price changes indicated.

Controls on Farm Wages

By 1941 the easing of restrictions on farm output and the increasing attractiveness of high-paying jobs in the war industries began to create fear of labor shortages in agriculture. Prior to that time agriculture had, for the most part, been oversupplied rather than undersupplied with labor. Wage rates in agriculture were much below those in industry. When it became known that jobs could be had in the new war industries, there was little to hold wageworkers on the farm.

Farming quickly became much more profitable, and farmers came to be more concerned about their ability to get labor than about the rate of pay. As a consequence, competitive bidding was soon exerting a strong upward pressure on farm wages.

The Stabilization Act of October 2, 1942 provided authority for the application of wage controls in agriculture as in other industries. Under it, the Director of Economic Stabilization assigned to the War Labor Board authority to control wages and salaries of less than $5,000 a year. Higher incomes were to be the responsibility of the Bureau of Internal Revenue. On November 30, the Director assigned to the Secretary of Agriculture the authority to control wage incomes in agriculture, if they amounted to less than $2,400. This authority was transferred on May 26, 1943 to the War Food Administrator.

Controls on wages generally became more and more rigorous as a result of the Hold-the-Line Order of April 8, 1943, and the succeeding efforts of the President and the War Labor Board to stabilize wages at about 15 per cent above the levels of 1941. These actions were not popular in the farm areas, because of the fear that agriculture would not be able to retain the amounts of labor needed.

The regulations were progressively tightened, and in January 1944 the War Food

17. It is probable that the closer correspondence of performance with goals as the war progressed reflects the tendency for the goals committees to move in the direction of predicting probables rather than indicating desirables. A good analysis of the meat program is given by Willard D. Arant, "Wartime Meat Policies," in *Journal of Farm Economics*, November 1946, pp. 903–19.

Administrator issued specific wage-ceiling regulations. Thereafter, wages above the ceilings could not legally be paid without specific authorization. The Bureau of Internal Revenue was given authority to eliminate as an income tax deduction the entire payment to an employee if the rate was above the authorized ceiling. In addition, heavy fines were provided for paying or receiving payment in excess of the prescribed maxima. These regulations were designed to prevent useless competitive bidding and pirating when such action could not increase the total supply of labor available.

Deferment of Farm Workers

Measures were also taken which looked to maintaining or increasing the supply of farm labor. These consisted principally of preferential treatment of farm workers by the draft boards, the importation of farm workers from abroad, chiefly from Mexico, and intensive efforts to mobilize local nonfarm workers such as high school students and housewives.

The Selective Service Act of September 16, 1940 required all males from 21 to 36 to register. From this group, the armed services were to be supplied with manpower on a basis of 12 months' service. No serious pinch resulted during 1941. After Pearl Harbor, the eligible age for the draft was widened to cover ages 18 to 45, and the period of service was designated as for the duration.

By the fall of 1942 farm labor shortages were becoming acute. Congressional and farm organization pressure on selective service officials grew in intensity, and a special three-man committee was set up by the Senate to investigate farm labor shortages in the western states. President O'Neal of the Farm Bureau contended that farm workers were not receiving equal consideration with industrial workers in the decisions of the draft boards.

As a result of such pressures, the War Manpower Commission and the Director of Selective Service issued directives which, in effect, provided for deferment of skilled agricultural workers (October 1942). Since many young farm workers chose to enlist rather than to accept deferment on this basis, the Army and Navy adopted a policy of not accepting voluntary enlistments from such workers without certification from their local draft boards that they were not essential farm workers.

The Tydings Amendment

The preferential treatment of farm workers was still further emphasized by the Tydings Amendment of November 1942. This was an addition to the bill which lowered the draft age from 21 to 18. It provided that any worker who is found "to be necessary to and regularly engaged in an agricultural occupation or endeavor essential to the war effort, shall be deferred . . . so long as he remains so engaged and until . . . a satisfactory replacement can be obtained: *Provided,* That should any such person leave such occupation . . . his . . . local board . . . shall reclassify such registrant in a class immediately available for military service. . . ."[18]

The draft boards used specific numbers of "war-units" of farm work as a basis for deciding whether workers were "essential."[19] The 16-war-unit standard adopted was a relatively high one for some areas in the South. This, however, was an area that had for decades been chronically oversupplied with manpower. The senatorial group led by Senator Bankhead succeeded in getting it relaxed in January 1943. Thereafter the directives to draft boards specified 16 units as an objective rather than a requirement. Boards were permitted to defer workers with as few

18. 56 Stat. 1018, Sec. 4.
19. The procedure used was to determine the essentiality of a farm worker by the number of "war-units" of agricultural production for which he was responsible. For example, the care of one milk cow or an equivalent amount of work on crops or other livestock was designated as a war unit. Up to February 1943, a worker would be deferred on the basis of 8 war units. This requirement was raised to 10 in February 1943, to 12 in May, and eventually to 16. For a fuller account of these arrangements, see Walter W. Wilcox, *The Farmer in the Second World War,* Iowa State College Press, Ames, 1947, Chapter 7. An excellent statement of the manpower situation as of this time, and suggested policies, are given by Rainer Schickele in *Manpower in Agriculture,* Wartime Farm and Food Policy Pamphlet No. 3, Iowa State College Press, Ames, February 1943.

s 8 units if they were striving diligently to increase production or worked part of the time on other farms.

Deferments also were granted for essential workers in other lines as well, but here it was left to the judgment of local draft boards instead of being governed by the rigid directives provided in the Tydings Amendment. Wilcox concludes that the deferments in agriculture amounted to 32 per cent of the males on farms who were between 15 and 35 years of age as against 24 per cent for nonfarm males of that age group.[20] In all, about 1.5 million to 1.8 million agricultural workers were kept in deferred status as compared to 4.1 million in nonfarm occupations.

Recruitment of Labor

During the early months of the war, the placement of agricultural workers was assigned to the Farm Security Administration. In March 1943, an Agricultural Labor Administration was created within the Department of Agriculture. Partly as a result of friction between the farm organizations and some of the FSA officials, it was decided in April to assign to the agricultural extension services of the various states responsibility for recruiting and placing agricultural labor.[21]

Special staff was assigned or hired for this purpose, and, on the whole, the job was done to the general satisfaction of the farm groups, who were very critical of the United States Employment Service, feeling that it tended to favor urban employers as against farmers.[22]

Other steps taken by the government helped to relieve the shortage of farm workers, especially in areas like California and Colorado where farmers relied heavily on wage labor. Probably the most significant of these, or at least the one which attracted most attention, was the importation of foreign workers, especially from Mexico. This was arranged by means of intergovernmental agreements specifying wage rates, living conditions and other standards to be maintained.

In this program, 32,000 Mexican nationals were used in 1943 and more than 60,000 in each of the years 1944 and 1945. Over the three-year period, more than 60,000 Jamaicans and Bahamians were brought in and nearly 9,000 other foreign workers.[23] In addition, German and Italian war prisoners were used in 1944 and 1945, the number reaching 130,000 in 1945.[24] Some very temporary help in acute situations was also provided by short-term release of men from the armed services. Government assistance was also provided in transporting Mexican and other foreign workers

20. Wilcox, *Farmer in the Second World War*, p. 89. He states, however, quoting from the *New York Times* of January 16, 1943, that higher standards were adhered to in some states. For example, the average number of war units per deferred worker in Wisconsin was 23, with a range varying from 16.2 to 29 in different counties. It should be noted in appraising the justice of the higher percentage of deferments in agriculture that in urban occupations a larger portion of young men were normally employed in service work, selling and other occupations not essential to the war effort.

For a more detailed account of agricultural deferments and the regulations pertaining to farm labor, see Selective Service System, *Agricultural Deferment*, No. 7 of the monograph series on the operation of the Selective Training and Service Act of 1940, published in 1947.

21. 57 Stat. 70. (Approved April 29, 1943.) This act contained a section, No. 4, known as the Tarver Amendment, which was widely criticized as tending to immobilize labor in areas characterized by underemployment, when the national interest would have called for moving some of it out. The amendment provided that no part of the funds appropriated (for transporting labor to undersupplied areas) could be used to transport any worker "from the county where he resides or is working to a place of employment outside of such county without the prior consent in writing of the county extension agent of such county, if such worker has resided in such county for a period of one year or more immediately

prior thereto and has been engaged in agricultural labor as his principal occupation during such period." This amendment, put forward by Congressman M. E. Tarver of Georgia, was designed to hold labor in the South where underemployment was common and wage rates notoriously low. Both the short-term and long-term national interest lay in moving some of the labor out of such areas, but such outmovement was not looked upon with favor by employers in the areas that would thus be deprived of part of their labor supply.

22. The farm organizations and many individual farmers were also dissatisfied with Farm Security Administration policies in regard to farm labor, especially in respect to the living and wage standards required for workers imported from Mexico. They contended that the standards required were higher than were maintained for our own workers. These dissatisfactions led to a vigorous joint attack on the FSA and its farm labor policies by the Grange, the Farm Bureau and the National Council of Farmer Cooperatives in the spring of 1943. Out of this grew the decision to assign recruiting and placement to the agricultural extension services.

23. President's Commission on Migratory Labor, *Migratory Labor in American Agriculture*, 1951, p. 38.

24. Bureau of Agricultural Economics, *The Hired Farm Working Force, 1948 and 1949*, November 1950, p. 45.

and some types of migratory workers to areas where labor shortages existed.

Various other measures were taken to ease the shortage of agricultural labor. Large numbers of high school students, women and others were induced to go out from the cities to help with the harvesting and processing of seasonal crops. Special efforts were made to channel scarce materials into the making of harvesting machines which would reduce seasonal labor requirements, and to induce full use of such machines as were available.

Farm Wage Rates

Farm wage rates generally rose to levels that were two to three times those of 1939, though with much variation from region to region. In North Dakota they reached 375 per cent of the 1939 level by 1944, in Washington, 334 per cent and in Kansas, 330 per cent. In New England the advance was generally to a little more than 200 per cent of prewar.[25] The variations in increase were to some extent a reflection of the differences in wage rate levels that existed in 1939. Some were very low at that time.[26]

Outmovement of Farm Workers

The record of accomplishment with the reduced labor force available is an impressive one. Some 5 million people left the farms for urban occupations or the armed services between 1939 and 1945. The number of farm workers declined about 8 per cent (600,000). Of these, about 400,000 were hired workers

25. Data from Bureau of Agricultural Economics, *Farm Wage Rates by States, Revised, 1910–1948,* January 1951, mimeographed.
26. A study by Arthur J. Holmaas, *Agricultural Wage Stabilization in World War II,* Bureau of Agricultural Economics, Agricultural Monograph No. 1, gives the following indexes (p. 71) for annual increases in farm wage rates, using January 1, 1941 as 100:

1941	118	1944	243
1942	154	1945	271
1943	203	1946	296

For workers in manufacturing industries, average hourly earnings increased 53 per cent between January 1941 and the spring of 1945. Hourly rates in agriculture reached a level in 1945 of 173 per cent above 1941. *Ibid.,* p. 74. The record does not indicate that the wage stabilization program in agriculture had any large effect, though it may have slowed the advance slightly.

and about 200,000 family workers. Weekly hours of work were increased by some 5.6 hours or about 10 per cent, and output per worker was stepped up 28 per cent, partly, of course, as a result of bumper crops which meant increased output for a given amount of labor.

In part, this reduction in the labor force was merely a result of outmovement from areas habitually oversupplied with agricultural labor. For example, the South Atlantic, East South Central and West South Central areas declined by 12, 13 and 11 per cent in numbers of agricultural workers. The Pacific states had 3 per cent more workers in 1945 than in 1939. The West North Central and Middle Atlantic areas were down only 5 and 4 per cent, respectively, and the Mountain states only 2 per cent.[27] Nevertheless, the record of production is a highly creditable one, though this breakdown by areas illustrates the ease with which situations may be misinterpreted through use of over-all national figures.

The Production Record

The wartime output of agricultural products was large by any standard, though by no means so remarkable as the increase in industrial output, nor was it so large as many assume it to have been.[28] The base customarily used in computing increases is that of 1935–1939, a period of low demand when farmers were plagued by surpluses, and a period in which active efforts were being made to reduce acreages of the major farm crops. This level was approximately that of 1924–1929 and was 5 per cent below the high level of production in 1931. Wheat acreage in

27. Bureau of Agricultural Economics, *Farm Employment, by Regions, Revised, 1931–1949,* February 1950, mimeographed.
28. For details and comprehensive data, see Glen T. Barton and Martin R. Cooper, *Farm Production in War and Peace,* Bureau of Agricultural Economics, Series FM53, December 1945, and the later, more general, study by Sherman E. Johnson, *Changes in American Farming,* USDA Miscellaneous Publication No. 707, December 1949. Changes in the world food situation up to 1944 are given in *Wartime Changes in World Food Production,* by C. M. Purves, Office of Foreign Agricultural Relations, December 1944, processed.

TABLE 2

INDEX NUMBERS OF GROSS FARM PRODUCTION, FARM OUTPUT AND PRODUCTION BY GROUPS OF PRODUCTS

(1935–1939 = 100)

Year	Gross Farm Production	Farm Output [a]	Livestock (Horses and Mules Excluded)	Food Grains	Truck Crops	Vegetables, Except Truck Crops	Fruits and Tree Nuts	Sugar Crops	Cotton and Cotton Seed	Tobacco	Oil Crops
1939	105	106	108	98	110	96	110	105	90	129	140
1940	108	110	110	107	111	102	108	102	96	99	165
1941	111	114	117	121	112	103	115	98	81	85	182
1942	123	128	130	126	118	108	117	110	97	96	287
1943	120	125	139	109	114	131	101	81	87	96	300
1944	124	130	138	136	122	110	120	80	93	133	255
1945	123	129	139	142	125	111	111	94	69	136	274

[a] Farm output is gross farm production minus farm-produced power of horses and mules. It measures calendar-year production of farm products for human use.

Source: Agricultural Statistics, 1949, p. 597.

three of the base years stood at approximately 50 million (harvested) as compared to more than 60 million at the beginning of the decade. Cotton acreage was about 35 per cent below that of 1929 and 1930. Corn acreage, likewise, was some 6 to 8 per cent below the high levels of the period around 1930. Thus, with restrictions eased and rapidly rising prices, the stage was set for a major upsurge in production if the weather proved favorable.

The 1940 production was about 3 per cent above that of 1939. A further gain of 3 points was registered in 1941, and a big jump of 12 points in 1942. Thereafter, production increased more slowly. The amounts made available for human use gained still more strikingly, reaching approximately 130 per cent of prewar in 1944 and 1945. This difference is due mainly to the rapid replacement of horse and mule power with tractors, thus reducing the feed used in supplying animal power.[29]

The gain was largest in oil crops, from an

29. Data from *Agricultural Statistics, 1949*, p. 597. Farm-produced power fell off gradually from an index of 124 in 1929 to 76 in 1945. By 1948 it was down to 59. Another important reason for the rapid increase in food production was the large stock of feed grains and livestock on hand at the beginning of the war period. A significant part of the gain in livestock output in the early years of the war resulted from feeding grains not produced in those years.

index of 165 (1935–1939 = 100) in 1940 to 274 in 1945 after having reached a peak of 300 in 1943. These crops, principally soybeans, had started to increase sharply as early as 1938. The stimulus given in the war years was thus an acceleration of a shift already well under way. Peanut acreage was nearly doubled during the war years, mainly in response to the drive for increased production of oilseeds after Pearl Harbor. The percentage increase in livestock production was next in magnitude, reaching a level in 1943, 1944 and 1945 about 30 per cent above that of the prewar period. Food grains showed similar but less consistent gains, reaching a high of 142 in 1945, a record which was to be exceeded substantially in the three following years. Feed grains and truck crops increased about in line with the average for all crops, and fruits, nuts and vegetables (other than truck crops) at a slower rate. Cotton and the sugar crops fell off sharply, while tobacco remained about constant. The record for the prewar and postwar years is shown numerically in Table 2.

The total acreage of crops did not at any time reach the levels attained in the early 1930's — 375 million in 1932. At the outbreak of war, total acreage in crops stood at 348 million. A joint report by the Bureau of Agricultural Economics and the Agricultural Research Administration recommended an increase in over-all crop acreage of somewhat over 25 million acres.[30] This, however, was not achieved. The acreage in crops reached its peak at 365 million in 1944, but fell off to 357 million in 1945.[31]

The BAE-ARA report recommended increases in food crops for direct consumption, oilseeds, sweet potatoes, Irish potatoes, dry beans and peas, vegetables and soybeans. It suggested reductions of 10 per cent in hog production, 5 per cent in sheep and lambs, and 2 per cent in chickens and broilers. Cattle and calves, dairy products and eggs were to be increased. At that time it was estimated that maximum production for agriculture, at average yields, would be 19 per cent above that of 1940. The actual achievement, with a strong assist in the way of favorable weather, was about 14 per cent.[32]

Where the Food Went

Though food production was increased markedly during the war years, the demand grew even more rapidly. Actual distribution of available supplies was, of course, modified by policy decisions on the part of the allocating agencies.

Military requirements were met in full and liberally. Under the circumstances prevailing the shipments to allies under lend-lease were also virtually a must, though subject to more modification as to kinds of food supplied than were our own military requirements. The amounts supplied under lend-lease were, in fact, controlled about as much by the amount of shipping available and the freedom of access as by the availability of supplies in the United States.[33] The intensive

enemy submarine campaign reduced shipping to perilously low levels, especially in 1942 and early 1943, and, in addition, caused tremendous loss of foodstuffs en route. The great difficulty and danger of shipping war materials and foodstuffs to Russia by the long and hazardous routes via Murmansk in the North and the Persian Gulf in the South kept these shipments to relatively modest amounts despite the desperate need known to exist in Russia.[34]

The shortage of shipping resulted in major emphasis on concentrated foods of high nutritive value which would minimize requirements for space. The fact that Canada had ample amounts of wheat, and was a logical supplier of this commodity to both Britain and Russia, tended to throw American lend-lease emphasis still more in the direction of concentrated, high-protein supplements to the bread and potatoes that made up so large a portion of the British and Russian diets. The British had shifted emphasis in their production program with a view to producing as much as possible of the bulky, low-value foods such as wheat, potatoes and vegetables. For these reasons, American lend-lease shipments ran heavily to such commodities as dried eggs, canned meat, cheese, dried milk, etc.[35]

---

30. USDA, *Maximum Wartime Production Capacity of American Agriculture,* June 1, 1943, mimeographed (a revision, prepared for administrative use, of the BAE report of March 31, 1943, which carried the same title).

31. *Agricultural Statistics, 1949,* p. 588.

32. For a much more detailed and somewhat critical analysis of the accomplishments under the food production program, see Gold, *Wartime Economic Planning in Agriculture,* especially Chapter 3. The weaknesses of Gold's analysis are well summarized in Ruth Cohen's review of the book, *Economic Journal,* London, September 1950, pp. 605–07.

33. The lend-lease operation is described in popular form in the series of reports to Congress (1 through 25),

1941–1948. The later reports deal mainly with the settlement of claims.

34. Russia had lost early in the war one of its main food-producing areas, the Ukraine. Little dependable information in regard to food supplies and diets could be obtained from the Russian government, but all unofficial sources indicated an incredibly low level of diet which created grave fear that the Russian war effort might collapse.

35. Between March 1941 and November 1, 1943, the shipments of major foods to the United Kingdom under lend-lease as reported by an official of the War Food Administration were as follows:

971,000 long tons of eggs (fresh egg equivalent)
943,000 long tons of milk products
919,000 long tons of meat (nearly all pork)
560,000 long tons of fats and oils (none of which is butter)
555,000 long tons of grain

For the twelve months beginning October 1, 1943, the commitments for this purpose were:

670,000 long tons of meat (again primarily pork)
335,000 long tons of grain
271,000 long tons of dried eggs (fresh egg equivalent)

In addition to the shipments to European allies, there were certain continuing responsibilities in this hemisphere which had to be met. Cuba, for example, and some of the Central American countries had specialized economies and could not exist without some outside food supplies. Since the United States was, in many cases, the only source for such shipments, minimum allocations were made to these countries. At the same time, the Combined Food Board was exploring alternative sources of currently available foods and possibilities of stimulating additional production in areas outside the United States and Canada.

254,000 long tons of fats and oils (mostly lard)
254,000 long tons of milk products

The corresponding shipments to Russia were:

From December 1941 to November 1, 1943
    406,000 long tons of meat
    390,000 long tons of grain
    276,000 long tons of fats and oils, including 30,-
      000 long tons of butter
    158,000 long tons of eggs (fresh egg equivalent)
    35,000 long tons of milk products

For the twelve months beginning October 1, 1943, commitments for shipment to Russia were as follows:

    1,098,000 long tons of grain
    498,000 long tons of meat (mostly canned or de-
      hydrated)
    335,000 long tons of fats and oils, including 29,-
      000 long tons of butter, and the rest in
      lard, shortening and soap
    146,000 long tons of dried eggs (fresh egg equiv-
      alent)
    49,000 long tons of milk products

Roy F. Hendrickson, *Military and Allied Food Requirements*, address before Food Forum sponsored by Dairymen's League Cooperative Association, Albany, New York, November 18, 1943, USDA, mimeographed, pp. 7, 8.

Total lend-lease shipments of food, March 11, 1941 to December 31, 1945, in dollar values were as follows:

Dairy products and eggs	$1,651,759,000
Meat and fish	1,891,715,000
Fruits and vegetables	492,850,000
Grain and cereals	199,280,000
Sugar	189,437,000
Lard, fats and oils	611,667,000
Other foodstuffs	333,936,000
Total	$5,370,644,000

In addition, shipments of cotton amounted to $365,-034,000, and of tobacco, to $266,669,000. Seeds in the amount of $45,630,000 and other agricultural products valued at $12,769,000 were supplied.

Of the foodstuffs provided through lend-lease, $3,-406,531,000 worth went to the British Empire; $1,726,-023,000, to the U.S.S.R.; and $238,091,000, to other countries. *Twenty-second Report to Congress on Lend-Lease Operations*, for the period ended December 31, 1945, pp. 25 and 26.

U. S. Consumption

The supplies available over and above these basic requirements, the major portion of the food produced in the United States, went to American civilian consumers. In addition, imports of food were maintained or increased where possible. Actually, American civilians, despite rationing of scarce items, consumed during these years the highest amounts per capita in their history, at least so far as available records show.[36]

The apparent scarcities in food supplies were due, in the main, to a marked shift in the distribution of food among civilian groups.[37] After more than a decade of substandard diets, the former low-income consumers were now earning good incomes. There was little on which they could spend them except foods. Consequently, they spent freely on such foods as were available, buying even under the ration allotments more of the high-quality foods such as meats than they had been accustomed to consuming.

Furthermore, a higher proportion of the population was now engaged in active physical work and employed for longer hours, both factors conducive to higher consumption of foods. The result of this more even distribution of high-quality foods was that the higher-income groups were restricted to somewhat lower than customary standards of diet, even though the average per capita consumption was at unprecedentedly high levels.

On the basis of 1935–1939 as 100, the index of per capita food consumption in the United States was approximately 100 in 1917 and

36. A detailed analysis of the amounts and kinds of changes in United States food consumption from 1939 to 1942 is given in Tariff Commission, *United States Consumption of Food in Terms of Fats, Proteins, Carbohydrates, and Calories, 1939–43*, February 1944, mimeographed, pp. 18–19.

A later and more exhaustive study, USDA, *Consumption of Food in the United States, 1909–48*, Miscellaneous Publication No. 691, August 1949, gives a more comprehensive picture of food consumption during the war years and before. The highest level of per capita consumption recorded since 1909, the earliest year for which records are available, was in 1946 with an index of 113 (1935–39 = 100). (See table, p. 120.)

37. For a somewhat different interpretation of the food situation, see Frank A. Pearson and Don Paarlberg, *Food*, Alfred A. Knopf, New York, 1944.

TABLE 3

TOTAL FOOD UTILIZATION: SOURCE AND DISTRIBUTION, 1935–1939 AVERAGE AND 1940 TO 1946

Year	Total Food Utilization	Food Production	Imports	Reduction in Stocks	Increase in Stocks	Civilian	Military Including Military Civilian Feeding	Net Purchases	Deliveries	Reduction in Stocks	Increase in Stocks	Commercial Exports and Shipments
	Source of Total Food					*Distribution*						
								Department of Agriculture				
SECTION A. PERCENTAGE OF FOOD UTILIZATION IN EACH YEAR												
1935–39	100.0	93.9	6.1	—	—	97.7	—	—.2	—	.2	—	2.5
1940	100.0	95.1	5.5	—	.6	98.0	—	—	—	—	—	2.0
1941	100.0	94.4	5.8	—	.2	93.8	2.0	2.4	1.9	—	.5	1.8
1942	100.0	94.2	3.7	2.1	—	87.2	5.8	5.9	4.5	—	1.4	1.1
1943	100.0	95.8	4.8	—	.6	81.4	9.6	8.1	7.1	—	1.0	.9
1944	100.0	94.0	5.0	1.0	—	79.7	13.2	6.0	6.5	.5	—	1.1
1945	100.0	95.7	4.8	—	.5	82.3	12.0	4.2	5.2	1.0	—	1.5
1946	100.0	96.1	4.3	—	.4	89.7	3.2	4.4	5.2	.8	—	2.7
SECTION B. PERCENTAGE OF 1935–1939 FOOD UTILIZATION												
1935–39	100.0	93.9	6.1	—	—	97.7	—	—.2	—	.2	—	2.5
1940	109.6	104.2	6.0	—	.6	107.4	—	—	—	—	—	2.2
1941	114.4	108.0	6.7	—	.3	107.3	2.3	2.7	2.2	—	.5	2.1
1942	125.6	118.3	4.7	2.6	—	109.5	7.3	7.4	5.6	—	1.8	1.4
1943	131.3	125.8	6.3	—	.8	106.9	12.7	10.6	9.3	—	1.3	1.1
1944	139.9	131.5	7.0	1.4	—	111.4	18.4	8.5	9.1	.6	—	1.6
1945	136.4	130.5	6.6	—	.7	112.2	16.4	5.7	7.1	1.4	—	2.1
1946	136.7	131.5	5.8	—	.6	122.6	4.3	6.1	7.1	1.0	—	3.7

Source: USDA, *Consumption of Food in the United States, 1909–48*, p. 5.

1918, stood at 102 in 1939, was up to 106 by 1942 and rose continuously during the remainder of the war, reaching 112 in 1945.[38]

Though meat was regarded as a scarce commodity during the war years, per capita consumption was higher in 1939 than in any year after 1927, except 1934. Consumption of meat increased by an additional 5 per cent in 1940 and by 1944 was 18 per cent above the 1939 level.[39]

38. USDA, *Consumption of Food in the United States, 1909–48*, p. 120. This intake was markedly above that of all of the other belligerent countries except Canada, Australia and New Zealand. United States intake in calories was estimated at 3,250 per day in 1943–1944, that of the United Kingdom, 2,940; Germany, 2,500; France, 2,150; and Belgium and the Netherlands, 2,100. See Bureau of Agricultural Economics, *The National Food Situation*, April-May 1945, p. 1. See also War Food Administration, *Food Consumption Levels in the United States, Canada and the United Kingdom* (Report of a Special Joint Committee set up by the Combined Food Board), April 1944.

39. *Consumption of Food in the United States, 1909–48*, p. 120. The heavy consumption in 1933 and 1934

Even under rationing, the American food situation was luxurious compared to those of any of the European belligerents. Considerable slack could have been taken up through more rigorous rationing had it been necessary. Fortunately, both favorable weather and heavy production made that sacrifice unnecessary and left the nation in a position to extend aid to our European allies to about as full an extent as shipping facilities permitted. The percentage distribution of available United States food supplies during the war years is shown in Table 3.

Question may be raised, however, as to the justification for continuing to use such large quantities of grain for meat production in view of the increasing evidence that world food supplies might be dangerously short after the close of hostilities. Wheat supplies, later

was due largely to forced liquidation of herds and flocks because of drought.

FOOD PROGRAM OF THE WAR YEARS

to be desperately needed, were being converted into pork, eggs and other livestock products to an extent that permitted derationing of pork in September 1944. Pork itself was thus allowed to flow freely into civilian use at a time when more conservative counselors were urging its preservation for future use. The possible tragic results of this wartime dissipation of wheat supplies were avoided only by the abundant United States crops of 1946, 1947 and 1948, a fortunate circumstance that could not then be foreseen.

Food Management by the War Agencies

Policies governing the distribution of food supplies evolved slowly as the war progressed. Serious shortages did not appear until the fall of 1942, and there was comparatively little public discussion of food rationing up to that time.

The United States had been, throughout its history, a nation with high levels of food consumption, both in quantity and quality. Its population had little experience either with food shortages or with any type of control other than that afforded by free market prices. However, some low-income groups had long been accustomed to substandard diets. With full employment and high wages, these groups now came into the market with ample buying power and a desire for more and better food, which created an unprecedented per capita demand. The need for control over quantities consumed as well as over prices soon became evident, if the limited supplies available were to be equitably distributed.

Originally, the responsibility for management of civilian supplies was assigned to the Office of Price Administration and Civilian Supply, which was created by presidential order in April 1941.[40] After passage of the

Price Control Act of January 1942, this became the Office of Price Administration, which had three main divisions — price control, rent control and rationing. The allocation of foods became eventually the responsibility of the War Food Administration.

The procedure used was for WFA to allocate quarterly specific amounts of each of the commodities. Principal claimants were United States civilians, processors, the military forces, the Lend-Lease Administration, the Office of Foreign Relief and Rehabilitation Operations (the agency which was planning for feeding in the liberated areas) and countries dependent upon the United States for important parts of their food supply. Army and Navy requirements were usually granted with little knowledge about stocks on hand and real needs.

Obvious wastages led to severe public criticism and various congressional investigations. Steps were taken to lessen food wastage in the armed services, but the situation remained one which could not have been tolerated had food shortages become really acute. The War Food Administration was not able to ascertain what stocks the Army had on hand, and hence was forced to make its allocations without adequate information.

Each of the claimants, if a government agency, was allowed to acquire up to the amount allocated. The remainder was, in the main, left available in the civilian market. The allocations to the British under lend-lease were made in accordance with recommendations of the Combined Food Board and were subject to continuous review so as to permit realistic adjustment to changing supply conditions. Those to Russia, for food as well as war material, were based on protocol agreements made at the White House level. Once signed, these were not subject to Lend-Lease or War Food Administration revision and had to be filled if possible. The Russians were allowed about what they asked for if it could be shipped. Their need for

40. A comprehensive but brief account of organizational problems relating to the management of food is given by the War Records Section of the Bureau of the Budget, in "Food for War," Chapter 2 of *The United States at War*, Historical Reports on War Administration, Bureau of the Budget, No. 1, 1946.

For details of the operations in food, see War Food Administration, *Report of the Director of the Food Distribution Administration, 1943; Report of the Director*

of the Office of Distribution, 1944; and USDA, *Report of the Director of the Office of Marketing Services, 1945.*

guns, tanks and other war material was so great, however, that these were usually given priority for shipping space.

Rationing of Foods

Early in 1942, sugar became scarce because of shipping difficulties and was placed under rationing. Coffee, another foodstuff requiring ocean shipment, became scarce later in the year and was put on ration in November. It was by then evident that many other foods would have to be rationed, and the enormous task of setting up rationing machinery for a population of some 130 million people was put in motion. Processed foods were brought under the rationing program on March 1, 1943. In the meantime serious problems had arisen in the distribution of meats. With prices controlled, nominally at least, and no limits placed on quantities bought, some markets, especially those nearest to sources of supply, tended to be adequately provided while others were seriously short. The rationing of meat was undertaken at the end of March 1943. Because of its key importance in the diet and the difficulties of control, meat provided one of the most irritating official "headaches" of the whole rationing program.[41]

Both rationing and the price control program were widely and severely criticized, especially by farm groups, and by many economists.[42] The nature of the criticism varied

somewhat as between the two groups. Farmers objected to having farm prices held down and were especially irked by the inconvenience which resulted from the rationing system. For the most part, they did not propose an alternative program except that of letting prices find their own level as in World War I. This clearly was an unworkable solution in a nation as fully mobilized as the United States was at that time. The economist critics emphasized the need for reduction of spending power through taxation and monetary controls. Such action is necessary for effective control of inflation and undoubtedly should have been used more aggressively than it was used in World War II. Nevertheless, full-scale efforts to control inflation by these methods still would have left a situation in which those who could afford it would have continued to use meat, sugar, coffee, butter and many other commodities about as usual, while less fortunate groups would have suffered severe hardship. The effects on morale when everyone was assumed to be accepting his share of the hardships of war can well be imagined.

---

41. For a good brief summary of this program, see Arant, "Wartime Meat Policies," pp. 903–19. Also, "Government Egg Programs during Wartime, A Review and Appraisal," by Gerson Levin, *Journal of Farm Economics*, November 1946, pp. 887–902. Various other commodities eventually were rationed, though the coverage was far less extensive in the United States than in Britain and some other countries. The controls which affected civilian consumers most vitally were those on sugar, coffee, meats, cheese, fats, automobile tires, gasoline and shoes. In several categories the procedure was to assign a given number of points for each period. These could be used at the consumer's option for items within the group. Rationed commodities thus came to have two prices, one in points and one in money.

42. Some of the graver faults of the rationing system used in World War II, as well as the more important defects of the food management program as a whole, are well discussed by Joseph S. Davis in "Wartime Food Management, An Analysis with Recommendations," *The Economic Sentinel*, published by the Los Angeles Chamber of Commerce, August 11, 1943. Commenting on the

rationing program, Davis makes the following criticisms (p. 26):

1. People who are in a position to provide their own meat, butter, fresh fruits, fresh vegetables, or canned goods get the same ration coupons as those who must buy theirs. This has the advantage of stimulating additional efforts to grow and can one's own food; but it gives large groups, conspicuously farmers and rural people generally, privileges that millions of others cannot enjoy. The freedom with which coupons can be given away (or even sold) opens the door to abuses.

2. Various classes of people who *need* larger rations of certain kinds of food — notably fats for heavy manual workers — cannot legitimately secure extra rations. By and large, various groups of unionized and unskilled non-union labor probably suffer most from this inequity. We have as yet for food no equivalent of the B and C ration books for gasoline. The German system, which we would regard as excessively complex, provides a whole scale of differential rations. The British have met the difficulty by providing for in-plant meals specially adapted to the requirements of the workers there. Our belated efforts to do something comparable deserve vigorous support.

3. Those who are accustomed to patronize restaurants, or can afford to do so, gain substantially because ration coupons are not required for meals in public eating places. This inequity probably favors most the unmarried war workers and the rich or well-to-do. In Britain this difficulty is met chiefly by establishing chains of restaurants serving carefully planned meals at low prices.

Inherent Problems

There appears to be no escape from rationing, with all its faults, when a nation is in all-out war. A fully employed population, straining to survive against a powerful enemy, is not likely to tolerate luxurious living and eating on the part of a favored few. Some critics of the program contend that, with adequate taxation and monetary controls, rationing without price control would perhaps have kept a workable balance between supply and demand and would largely have avoided the black market problem. There appears, however, to be little reason to think that a person who would turn to the black market with price controls in effect would not do so if limited only by the ration allotment.

Proposals for avoiding price control and rationing through monetary and fiscal restraints are not so much actual alternatives to direct controls as measures which would ease inflationary pressures and thus make rationing and price stabilization easier. Few such proposals contemplate absorbing all of the enlarged buying power created by government buying in wartime. The rest must either be allowed to exert its inflationary effect through a current rise in prices or be suppressed through savings. If savings could in some way be kept unusable until goods are again freely available and the economy in need of a stimulus, the effect of such suppressed inflation would be wholesome and would help in stabilizing the economy. The procedures thus far used in the United States do not, however, provide that kind of control of timing in the use of wartime savings.

In World War II, some of the inflationary pressure did find an outlet in higher prices, in black markets and in various forms of luxury spending, but not so much proportionately as in World War I. Much of it was released in the immediate postwar period, thus contributing to a delayed inflation of considerable magnitude. Despite these many difficulties, it seems apparent that in any situation where allocations for military purposes create a genuine scarcity of certain commodities, any strong modern government will undertake rationing as the lesser of various evils. Attention needs to be focused, therefore, not only upon ways of reducing inflationary pressure but also upon ways of making rationing and, if it is adopted, price control as well, more effective.

Fear of Postwar Surpluses

The War Food Administration tended throughout the war to fear accumulations that might prove embarrassing later. As a result, it followed a policy which might in some respects be termed risky rather than conservative. It banked heavily on continued large crops. As it turned out, large crops did materialize. This, however, was due to the happy chance of continuing favorable weather, not to foresight. Had a series of bad years occurred in this period, the results might have been tragic.

Had the 1942–1945 yields averaged 12 bushels per acre as they did in 1933–1936, the supplies of wheat available for the four war years would have been more than 1.3 billion bushels less than they were. This difference is well over twice the huge carry-over with which we entered the war period. It cannot be assumed that all of the increase in yields achieved in the war years was due to favorable weather. Some was the result of more fertilization, better seed and more mechanization. However, there is reason to think that these factors may be more significant in increasing yields above the normal level than in preventing decreases during severe droughts. Had rainfall in 1942–1945 been as low as that of 1933–1936, with the accompanying plague of dust storms, neither fertilizers nor superior methods could have prevented a sharp decline in output.

The onset of such a period of reduced yields would, of course, have forced a shift to more restricted use of wheat, but such a change in policy might have come too late to prevent serious consequences. Almost 800 million bushels had been fed to livestock by the end of 1943, and another 150 million had gone into alcohol production. The gamble was really with the lives of people in the liberated areas. The domestic population could have been, and probably would have been, supplied, but the only thing that made possible the export of approximately a billion bushels of wheat from 1945 through 1947 was the big crops of those years.

No Over-All Policy Formulated

Almost all through the war, the OPA and later the Lend-Lease Administration, the Office of Foreign Relief and Rehabilitation Operations, and others urged more conservative use of existing stocks and more stockpiling but were unable to bring about a less risky program on the part of the War Food Administration. Some even question whether the Food Administration actually had a policy other than on a short-term basis, though various attempts were made to formulate one.[43] It is probably more accurate to say, however, that its policy was one of distributing current supplies as equitably as possible and avoiding large-scale stockpiling because of fear that criticism and agency losses would result when the war came to an end. The fears engendered by the price declines of 1920 and 1932 loomed large in the thinking of WFA officials and were reflected in the policies adopted.

The War Food Administrator did not have a clear, unequivocal over-all directive and authorization from Congress to institute the vigorous, coordinated war food program the situation called for. A stronger administrator might have been able to persuade Congress to drop its bickerings and unite behind a single, well-conceived plan, though that is doubtful. At any rate, such a single, well-conceived plan was not put forward.[44]

Storage Problems

The building up of larger stocks posed operational problems of no mean proportions. Storage capacity became a limiting factor as the war progressed. Both a Department of Agriculture committee and the National Defense Advisory Council had recommended an increase in storage facilities during the period when this would have been practicable. This recommendation was not acted on, however. Failure to do so is now generally conceded to have been a major mistake in the planning of food operations.[45] The lack of storage space was one important reason for the failure to accumulate stocks, especially in 1943 when supplies were abundant.

Even when the shortage became evident, the government did not take adequate measures to enlarge cold storage facilities in keeping with the greatly enlarged production program initiated.[46] There was difficulty even in storing enough of some commodities to maintain the price supports that had been promised. Hogs and eggs in particular sagged somewhat below support levels in the periods of heaviest receipts. By 1943 the government was exercising control over virtually all cold storage space and was forcing out of storage less essential commodities in order to make room for those considered more essential. Other difficulties were presented in maintaining quality and achieving necessary rotation of stocks.

---

43. For example, the study carried on by a subcommittee of the Food Advisory Committee between March and July of 1943. Its confidential report, *Fundamentals of a Wartime Food Program*, USDA, July 1943, mimeographed, was circulated within the government but was not acted upon either favorably or unfavorably.

44. Secretary Wickard began, as early as November 1941, to stress the importance of having plentiful reserves of food available at the close of the war and continued to urge this policy as the war progressed, but other coun-

sels prevailed. See, for example, letter to the President, November 27, 1941 as quoted by Wilcox, *The Farmer in the Second World War*, p. 275, and the annual reports of the Secretary of Agriculture. Such a policy was also recommended by the Fats and Oils Committee, the Food Requirements Committee, the Committee on Food Relief and various other war agencies such as the Office of Lend-Lease Administration and the Combined Food Board.

45. It is only fair to state that the exercise of adequate foresight is by no means easy in such situations. There had been an excess of storage capacity in the immediate prewar years and it was difficult for either administrators or the food industry to foresee the demands that would be made upon them.

46. In such situations, the industry nearly always resists expansion to meet war needs because of the fear of excess capacity at war's end. Similar resistance was encountered in the distilling industry, especially in respect to creating facilities for using the new process whereby alcohol could be made from wood waste.

Inadequate Plans for Postwar Needs

The seriousness of the mistakes in stockpile policy did not become evident until the fall and winter of 1945.[47] Estimates of food needs in the war-torn countries made by OFRRO, and later by UNRRA, had been so generally discounted by administrators in most other government agencies that knowledge of the tragic disorganization and danger of starvation in the western European countries was slow in trickling through to the American public. By that time, all too little could be done about it.

Of the 630 million bushels of wheat carried over in 1942 and the almost 4,000 million produced during the war, about 1,400 million bushels had been used for livestock feed and 165 million bushels for industrial purposes, principally the making of alcohol for synthetic rubber and munitions production. The remainder had been used for domestic consumption, exports and seed, except for a modest carry-over of 280 million bushels on July 1, 1945. The shelf was virtually bare despite the huge crops of the war years. Only the big crops of 1946 and 1947 could save the situation. Fortunately, these were forthcoming, but even so, the efforts of an aroused America to meet the desperate need were to result in a severe pinch in American wheat supplies, and to cause wheat

to lead off in the postwar inflation of food prices.

Pork stocks, likewise, were down to little more than half the levels of 1943 and 1944. Per capita consumption of pork had been allowed to expand in 1943 and 1944 to the unprecedented level of 79 pounds per capita,[48] while the rate of canning dropped from 124 million pounds per month in 1943 to 70 million pounds per month in 1944. The fortunes of war and the weather were such that we did not have to reap the full crop of hardships for which the seeds had been sown.

PRICES AND INCOMES

The index of wholesale prices of farm products stood at 92 in 1939 (1910-14 = 100), that of commodities other than farm products at 118. Recovery from the lows of 1932 had been faster for farm products than for other commodities but, having started from a lower level, the farm price index still was considerably below that of nonfarm commodities.

However, this comparison requires some qualification. The years 1938 and 1939 were marked by a slump in farm prices from the high level of 121 in 1937. For the decade as a whole, farm prices were below the 1939 level only in 1931, 1932 and 1933.[49] Also, the nature of farm products changes less than does that of nonfarm commodities. For example, the 1939 washing machine, refrigerator, automobile and tractor were quite different commodities from those of 1914. Such changes in content of commodities having the same name is, in fact, one of the major defects of a parity ratio extending over long periods.

Be that as it may, the start of the war period found agricultural prices at a level that farmers considered far from satisfactory, one which they were making vigorous efforts to improve. The war in Europe and the accompanying upsurge in United States industrial employment brought a quick improvement in United States farm prices.

47. Both the Director of Food Distribution and the Administrator in charge of procurement in the War Food Administration expressed fears as late as 1944 that food supplies would be excessive after the close of hostilities. A leading economist in WFA expressed similar views. OFRRO, the Foreign Economic Administration and many individuals in and out of government differed vigorously with this view and continued to press for larger stockpiles. These differences resulted in some of the sharpest interagency clashes that occurred during the war in the food field, except those between OPA and the agricultural agencies, which have been mentioned previously.

Despite bumper crops in the United States, much of western Europe came desperately near to mass starvation in 1946 and 1947. The unwarranted complacency about postwar food conditions was by no means limited to officials of the War Food Administration. Lend-Lease was abruptly terminated with no suitable alternative arrangements for financing food shipments to allies. Rationing was discontinued, and public clamor for release of foodstuffs to domestic consumers rose in volume. The strong hand and wise leadership of Franklin Roosevelt had been lost at a critical time.

48. *Agricultural Statistics, 1949*, pp. 401 and 402.

49. Data from *Agricultural Statistics, 1949*, p. 626. Nonfarm commodities had also declined from a high of 128 in 1937, but the change was less pronounced than in the farm group.

They stood at 116 in 1941. In the meantime, nonfarm prices moved up less sharply to 131. That is, farm prices in this period advanced at about twice the rate of nonfarm prices.

Farm prices continued their rapid increase in 1942 and 1943, reaching a level of 172 in the latter year. At this point the upsurge was checked, with the general level advancing only to 173 in 1944 and 180 in 1945. But an enormous further increase was to be recorded in 1946, 1947 and 1948, after the abandonment of price controls and rationing. Nonfarm commodities moved up much more slowly and modestly — to 144 in 1942, 146 in 1943, 148 in 1944 and 150 in 1945. Here, however, there was downgrading of quality in many items continuing to be sold under the same name. The over-all increase in wholesale prices of farm products from 1939 to 1945 was 95 per cent, that for nonfarm commodities about 28 per cent. The increase in prices paid to farmers was even more striking — from 95 to 202, or 112 per cent.

The Parity Ratio

The parity ratio, that is, the ratio of prices received by farmers to prices paid by them, stood at 77 in 1939.[50] By 1942 it had passed the 100 mark and stood at 106. It reached 119 in 1943 but dropped back slightly in 1944 and 1945 as farm prices became more stable while other prices continued to edge upward. The comparable price increase for farm products in World War I was about 115 per cent. Thus, the actual percentage increase in the two wars was similar. It is apparent, however, that the increase would have been considerably greater in World War II had there been no rationing and price control.

It seems clear that the farmers, with a strong political hold on Congress, were given preferential treatment with respect to prices. Their demands for still higher prices can hardly be justified on any grounds, and concessions so large as those made can only be

defended if it is contended that they were necessary as an incentive for all-out production effort. There is little dependable information on the specific shape of the supply curve for agriculture, that is, on the amounts of production resources and effort that would be put in at varying levels of prices. It seems likely, however, that production effort was nearing its peak by 1943 and probably would have continued at that level or above even without the 30-point increase in prices that occurred between 1942 and 1943.[51]

The price-cost conditions were somewhat different in agriculture than in industry. At the war's beginning there was considerable unused capacity in many industries. Some of this was soon engaged in turning out new war goods. Where such shifts did not occur, increased production at lower per unit costs was often possible and some of the increase in wages could be absorbed without increasing prices of the product. Such conditions prevailed, however, only in the early stages of the war, especially from 1939 to 1941.

Farms also were producing at less than capacity, but it is not so clear that shifts to higher output could be made without increasing per unit costs. More machinery and fertilizer were required. Wage rates in the unorganized farm labor market went up faster than in other lines, and increases in acreage often meant returning to production poorer-than-average acres on the farms where expansion occurred.

The Earnings of Labor

Organized labor, like organized agriculture, has great economic and political power. Both groups achieved large increases in earnings during the war years. The struggle by the farm groups for higher prices was in part an effort to overcome what they regarded as a favored position on the part of labor in an administration that they looked upon as

50. The parity ratios differ somewhat, depending upon what price series were used and the time at which computations were made. The figure given above is consistent with the others here used but differs slightly from that shown in other sections.

51. Production reached, in 1943, 129 per cent of the 1935–1939 average. It moved on up to 137 in 1944 and 134 in 1945 but probably largely as a result of favorable weather and of increased efficiencies that were already being put into effect. Data from *Agricultural Statistics, 1949*, p. 596.

being prolabor. The effort of labor to maintain rigid price ceilings on commodities while asking for increases in wages was, of course, an effort to improve its relative position in the economy.

The evasion of wartime regulations took different forms in the two realms. For farm products it appeared in some measure in the form of black market sales at more than ceiling prices. For labor it appeared in the form of compensation in excess of authorized levels.

Average hourly earnings in manufacturing industries stood at $0.632 in January 1939 and had risen only to $0.683 as of January 1941. By January 1942 they stood at $0.801, an advance of about 17 per cent over January 1941.[52] Under the Little Steel Formula, they were presumably to be allowed to advance some 15 per cent above the 1941 levels. As of this time, the line had been fairly well held for this type of labor. In the same period (1941 average to 1942 average), prices received by farmers rose by about 28 per cent.[53]

Average weekly earnings in manufacturing industries showed a larger and more rapid increase because of longer hours and overtime. These earnings were, of course, the ones most frequently cited by farmers in pointing out that consumers could afford to pay more for food. Average weekly earnings in manufacturing stood at $23.19 in January 1939. By January 1941 they had risen to $26.64. This was the period of large absorption of unemployed which could be carried out without much increase in rates of pay. January 1942 saw a weekly earning of $33.40 and this moved up continuously thereafter to $40.62 in 1943, to $45.29 in 1944, and to $47.50 in 1945. These earnings were to experience a marked decline in the immediate postwar period, whereas farm prices went up sharply at that time. Hourly earnings continued to advance but not at so fast a rate. They stood at $.919 in January 1943, $1.002 in 1944, and

$1.046 in 1945. Thereafter, they fell off moderately.[54]

The percentage gains for factory labor from 1939 to 1945 were, in hourly rates, 65 per cent; in weekly earnings, 104 per cent. The corresponding increases in farm prices and incomes were, for prices, 112 per cent; for incomes, 165 per cent.[55]

Occupational Variations

The increases were more marked for two important and conspicuous groups of labor — agricultural workers and those in the war industries. These were the ones most prominent in farmer thinking. Hourly rates for unorganized labor, such as that in agriculture, show larger fluctuations both up and down than do those of factory workers. Shipyard and other war industry workers likewise experienced large increases in income. Some of this, however, was a necessary incentive for traveling to a new location, learning a new trade and accepting the crowded living conditions prevalent in war industry centers.

The increases in earnings varied considerably for different occupations. The Cleveland Trust Company summarized the situation as follows:

Earnings per full-time employee in agriculture in 1943 were 107 percent greater than they had been in 1939. Those in building construction were 98 percent greater. . . . The earnings of the average miner rose 58 percent, and if he mined bituminous coal he earned 77 percent more and has had increases since 1943. The earnings of the average factory worker increased 72 percent.

Earnings of individual fishermen were 109 percent higher in 1943 than they had been four years earlier,[56] and those of sailors were 118 percent greater. Among domestic servants the increase was 69 percent. By no means all of the increases were of similar large dimensions. The advance among people employed by religious organizations was five percent, and for

52. *Statistical Abstract, 1949*, p. 217.
53. *Agricultural Statistics, 1949*, p. 621.

54. *Statistical Abstract, 1949*, p. 217.
55. Net income from farming. *Agricultural Statistics, 1949*, p. 633.
56. Here the market and production conditions are very similar to those for the operating farmer, and the product is of similar character. The earnings picture is, therefore, more like that of farm operators than that of hired labor.

amusement work except motion pictures it was 13 percent. In wholesale and retail trade it was 32 percent. In air transportation it was six percent. In general terms it may be noted that there have been large increases among those working on the farms, in the mines, in the factories, and in the building trades. Advances have been relatively small for workers in trade, the public utilities, and for most of those in the service industries.[57]

Total Incomes, Farm and Nonfarm[58]

Between 1939 and 1945, total national income rose from $71.5 billion to $164 billion, an advance of 129 per cent. Income from farming during the same period increased from $5.25 billion to approximately $14 billion or about 165 per cent. During this period, the population on farms declined significantly while the number of employed urban workers increased greatly. Consequently, the changes in per capita income reflect more accurately the changes in relative well-being of the two groups. The farm population numbered, in 1939, 30,480,000. By 1945 this was down to 25,190,000. The farm population consists normally of a larger proportion of children than does the nonfarm population. This tendency probably was accentuated during the war years by the heavy drainage of adults out of agriculture, both for military service and for work in the war industries.

Per capita income of persons on farms, from farming, rose from $173 in 1939 to $554 in 1945, an increase of 220 per cent.[59] Income per person not on farms rose in the same period from $663 to $1,320, an increase of 99 per cent. The parity income ratio on a 1910–1914 basis, and in per capita terms, stood at 95 in 1939, dropped to 88 in 1940, and then rose rapidly, reaching 151 in 1945.[60] That is,

by 1945 the average farm person's situation as compared to that of the average urban dweller was presumably some 50 per cent better than the comparable relationship in 1910–1914.

Aside from returns to labor and to agriculture, the major distributive share in national income was that of corporate profits. Corporate profits after taxes stood at the comparatively low level of $5 billion in 1939. They rose to $6.4 billion in 1940, to $9.4 in 1941, and increased gradually to a peak of $10.8 billion in 1944. There was a sharp drop in 1945 to $8.5 billion and thereafter a rapid and large increase.[61] Corporate profits thus made a gain of 116 per cent between 1939 and 1944 but were only 70 per cent above prewar in 1945. The rise was less, percentagewise and in total, than that of agricultural net incomes which correspond roughly in total amount in dollars. The percentage gain in profits was approximately equal to the gain in average weekly earnings of factory workers up to 1944. For 1945 it was substantially lower.

Corporation dividend payments to individuals rose only 23.5 per cent between 1939 and 1945.[62] A large part of the increased earnings of corporations was retained in undistributed profits to meet the expected difficulties of the reconversion period.

---

57. Cleveland Trust Company, *Business Bulletin*, August 1945, pp. 2–3.

58. The data used in this section are from *Agricultural Statistics, 1949*, p. 634. They differ slightly from those given earlier, but are used here in order to provide the comparisons shown.

59. Several qualifications of these data should be noted. Income to people on farms from nonfarm sources not only is not added to farm income but is included in nonfarm income.

60. The decline in 1940 was due to rapid re-employment of idle workers in the urban industries and the

consequent upsurge in total incomes of urban workers, whereas total net income to farmers remained approximately the same until 1941. In his message to the Congress on November 1, 1943, in which the objectives of the food program were outlined, the President stated: "The average income per farmer since the outbreak of the war in 1939 has risen more than the average income of the other parts of the population. This was also true between 1910 and 1914, which is the primary base period for parity calculation. In 1942, the increase in the average income per farmer over the parity base period was 38 percent greater than the increase in the average income of the other people in the country. In 1943, it was 50 percent greater." Franklin D. Roosevelt, *Public Papers and Addresses, 1943*, Harper and Brothers, New York, 1950, pp. 482–83.

61. Data from *Statistical Abstract, 1950*, p. 442. Profit figures given are after taxes, whereas the income data for individuals given on preceding pages are before taxes. Corporate tax rates are, however, much higher than those for individuals, so the use of a gross profits figure would distort the relationships much more severely.

62. This excludes intercorporation payments.

Farm Credit and Land Prices

Farm land prices experienced a continuous decline from 1920 to 1933, from an index of 170 in 1920 (1912–1914 = 100) to 73 in 1933. They recovered very moderately, to 84, in 1939 and 1940. After that time, war prosperity began to push land prices up, but not at so rapid a rate as might have been expected in view of the increase in net farm incomes. The index (for the United States) stood at only 126 in 1945, despite a 200 per cent increase in farm incomes.[63]

As prices of farm products began to move up to prosperity levels in 1941 and 1942, grave concern was felt by government officials, land-grant college people and credit agencies that farmers would again extend themselves in a speculative land purchase and borrowing spree as they had done in 1919 and 1920. Vigorous educational campaigns were launched both by the United States Department of Agriculture and the state agricultural extension services to acquaint farmers with the disastrous results of the speculative spree which had followed World War I. The federal land banks and many of the private lending agencies undertook to follow conservative policies in making loans, not only with a view to protecting themselves but as a means of helping to forestall an expected repetition of the speculative excesses of 1919–1920.

The educational campaign stressed the importance of paying off debts and acquiring liquid assets to use in improving buildings, equipment and living standards after the war. The reminder was not lost on the farmers. Many of them were all too well aware of the hardships of debtors during the preceding twenty years, and only too anxious to avoid the "boom and bust" pattern which had come to be regarded as the normal sequence of war periods.

Total farm mortgage debt had been declining since the early 1920's and stood at only $6.8 billion in 1939 as against more than $10 billion shortly after World War I.[64] Much of the reduction during the 1920's and 1930's resulted from foreclosures and distress sales which tended either to wipe out or reduce the indebtedness on the farms concerned, usually those heavily in debt. The more orderly repayment procedure (amortization of principal) that came into general use as a result of the refinancing done in the 1930's led to a more constructive type of debt reduction, which assumed increasing importance during the late 1930's.

Farm mortgage debt reduction continued through the war years but only at about the rate of the 1930's. The total was down to $5.25 billion by 1945[65] and declined still further in the immediate postwar years. Loans held by the federal land banks decreased continuously. Those of the life insurance companies increased moderately in 1941 and 1942 but fell off to prewar levels in 1944 and 1945. Farm mortgage loans of commercial banks showed a similar slight increase and decline. Those of the Farm Security Administration increased consistently but moderately throughout the war period.

The record indicates that both farmers and lending agencies had taken to heart the lessons of the World War I period. Both borrowing and lending policies reflected surprising restraint in view of the high farm incomes then prevailing. It may even be questioned whether land prices were not held unduly low in view of farm earnings. This, however, takes too much account of the high postwar farm incomes that could not then be foreseen.

The conservative policies followed with respect to land prices permitted agriculture to enter the postwar period in the strongest financial position it had ever held and with large liquid reserves. An anomalous feature of national credit policy was the retention until mid-1944 of the subsidized interest rate on loans of the federal land banks.

This had been initiated in 1933 when many farmers were having a desperate struggle to

63. Data from *The Farm Real Estate Situation, 1945–46*, USDA Circular No. 754, pp. 6–7.

64. *Ibid.*, p. 25.
65. *Loc. cit.*

meet interest payments on their loans. The Congress acted to continue the subsidy even when farm prices and incomes were rising so fast as to cause grave concern over the possibility that they would set off a major speculative inflation in land prices. Here, as in various other matters, depression attitudes were dominating the thinking in Congress when the real danger was from inflationary forces.

RELIEF FEEDING AND FOREIGN AID

Concern about the eventual problem of feeding the people of the liberated areas began to be expressed even before the United States entered the war, and some relief feeding became necessary while fighting was in progress. Prime Minister Churchill promised in the House of Commons as early as August 1940 that the people of Europe would get food, freedom and peace when the Nazis were destroyed. A year later the British government initiated an eight-month study of food needs to be met after the war by a committee under the chairmanship of Sir Frederick Leith-Ross.[66] It also set up the Middle East Relief and Rehabilitation Administration with headquarters at Cairo to provide camps in Syria, Palestine and Egypt for the care of Yugoslav and Greek refugees.

In September 1941 the U.S. Department of State established a Special Research Division to consider the problem and set up five committees for study of various aspects of it — one on food relief, one on agricultural rehabilitation, one on clothing requirements, one on health and medical supplies, and one on essential services and industries. A further step was taken in November 1942 when the President established in the Department of State the Office of Foreign Relief and Rehabilitation Operations, commonly referred to as OFRRO. Mr. Herbert Lehman, former governor of New York, was made Director of the new agency.

OFRRO was engaged chiefly in mak-

ing estimates of probable relief needs, seeking to assure supplies for that purpose, shaping plans and building staff. During 1943 some field work was done in Tunisia and other areas, but the functions of OFRRO were shortly thereafter merged into the United Nations Relief and Rehabilitation Administration (UNRRA). This grew out of numerous preliminary conferences which led to the signing of an agreement by 44 nations on November 9, 1943 whereby the agency was established.[67] In signing the agreement, President Roosevelt commented that "It would be supreme irony for us to win a victory, and then to inherit world chaos simply because we were unprepared to meet what we know we shall have to meet."[68] Herbert Lehman, Director of OFRRO, was elected Director General of UNRRA at a meeting of the Executive Council on November 11.

UNRRA took over the feeding and rehabilitation problem in various areas at the close of the war, for example, in Poland, Yugoslavia, Italy, Greece, China, Czechoslovakia and a number of other countries. Germany and Japan were handled by American, British and French army personnel through military government.[69]

The Food and Agriculture Organization

As the war progressed, it became more and more apparent that worldwide problems of many kinds would need to be dealt with by agencies established on a more permanent basis than those set up for meeting the emergency conditions growing out of the war. President Roosevelt, Wendell Willkie and many others were stressing the fact that the world has become too closely knit for any one nation or any group of nations to go its own way without reference to what happens in other parts of the world. In particular, it

---

66. The Inter-Allied Committee on Post-War Requirements. The United States had an observer on the Committee and after our entry into the war became a full member.

67. Four other nations joined later.
68. Roosevelt, *Public Papers and Addresses, 1943,* p. 502.
69. A very complete account of the whole UNRRA operation is contained in the three-volume history of its activities published in 1950: *UNRRA, The History of the United Nations Relief and Rehabilitation Administration,* prepared by a special staff under the direction of George Woodbridge, Columbia University Press, New York.

was felt that living standards must be raised more generally if a sound and lasting peace was to be achieved, and that some type of world organization must emerge as a means of stabilizing the world situation and facilitating progress generally.

One of the first steps looking in this direction was the creation of the Food and Agriculture Organization, designed to stimulate and improve food production, particularly in areas where undernourishment was common. A start along these lines had been made in 1905 through establishment of the International Institute of Agriculture at Rome.[70] This, however, had proved disappointing as an agency for improving agriculture. Its functions were too limited and its resources too small.

During the 1930's, the Health Organization of the League of Nations initiated important studies of nutritional problems, bringing to bear the greatly increased knowledge of vitamin requirements that had come into being in the immediately preceding years. This resulted in setting up a "mixed committee" of agricultural, labor and health authorities to consider the possibilities of a program that would relieve agriculture by disposing of its excess output and at the same time put more food into the world's underfed millions. Its report, issued in 1937, was a landmark in the development of interest and knowledge concerning nutritional problems.[71]

Roosevelt "believed that the most practical method of insuring success for international co-operation in the economic and social fields lay in holding functional conferences, each dealing with a separate aspect of the general problem."[72] Such specialized appendages had in fact been the most effective part of the work of the League of Nations and its related agencies.[73] As an outgrowth of this interest, a conference on food and agriculture, attended by representatives of 44 nations, was convened at Hot Springs, North Carolina, in July 1943.[74] In August, the conference submitted a draft constitution to the various governments and by April 1945 twenty of them had subscribed to it.

On October 16, 1945 the new organization met at Quebec and at that time became the Food and Agriculture Organization of the United Nations, succeeding the Interim Commission which had functioned from 1943 on. The functions and assets of the International Institute of Agriculture were transferred to it.

Membership is limited to governments.[75] As of 1950, the organization included 67 member nations including Poland and Hungary. Poland withdrew as of April 25, 1951, and Hungary gave notice of withdrawal effective February 7, 1952. Iran, Czechoslovakia and the U.S.S.R. of the original group were not members on December 31, 1950.

70. For a brief summary of the earlier efforts of this type, see Norris E. Dodd, "The Food and Agriculture Organization of the United Nations, Its History, Organization, and Objectives," *Agricultural History*, April 1949, pp. 81–86.

71. *Nutrition. Final Report of the Mixed Committee of the League of Nations on the Relation of Nutrition to Health, Agriculture and Economic Policy*, Geneva, 1937. Among other things, the mixed committee proposed the creation in each country of a *special national nutrition committee* to study ways of improving nutritional standards. By 1938, 21 nations had set up such committees and there were 26 of them in various parts of the British and Dutch empires. This movement was brought to an end by the outbreak of war. The Food and Nutrition Board of the National Research Council is, in effect, the "national committee" for the United States.

72. Sumner Welles, *Where Are We Heading?*, Harper and Brothers, New York, 1946, p. 31.

73. The most firmly established of such agencies, which were either parts of the League or closely associated with it, was the International Labor Organization. This was shortly to be brought into formal cooperation with the United Nations by an agreement which came into effect on December 14, 1946. Other specialized League agencies which had functioned during the interwar period were the International Institute of Intellectual Co-operation, the International Institute for the Unification of Private Law, the International Center for Leprosy Research and various others.

74. For a fuller account of the conference, see United Nations Conference on Food and Agriculture, May 18–June 3, 1943, *Bulletin of the Commission to Study the Organization of Peace*, New York, July-August 1943. Also *First Report to the Governments of the United Nations by the Interim Commission on Food and Agriculture*, Washington, August 1, 1944. A more informal account is given by F. F. Elliott, "Redirecting World Agricultural Production and Trade Toward Better Nutrition," *Journal of Farm Economics*, February 1944, pp. 10–30.

75. United States participation was authorized when the President signed, on July 31, 1945, H.J.Res. 145 (59 Stat. 529).

Objectives of FAO

The objectives of FAO were stated to be as follows:

Raising levels of nutrition and standards of living of the peoples under their respective jurisdictions, securing improvements in the efficiency of the production and distribution of all food and agricultural products, bettering the condition of rural populations, and thus contributing toward an expanding world economy.

Its functions, as set forth in Article I, are:

1. The Organization shall collect, analyze, interpret, and disseminate information relating to nutrition, food, and agriculture. . . .
2. The Organization shall promote and, where appropriate, shall recommend national and international action with respect to
   (a) scientific, technological, social, and economic research relating to nutrition, food and agriculture;
   (b) the improvement of education and administration relating to nutrition, food, and agriculture, and the spread of public knowledge of nutritional and agricultural science and practice;
   (c) the conservation of natural resources and the adoption of improved methods of agricultural production;
   (d) the improvement of the processing, marketing, and distribution of food and agricultural products;
   (e) the adoption of policies for the provision of adequate agricultural credit, national and international;
   (f) the adoption of international policies with respect to agricultural commodity arrangements.
3. It shall also be the function of the Organization
   (a) to furnish such technical assistance as governments may request;
   (b) to organize, in co-operation with the governments concerned, such missions as may be needed to assist them to fulfill the obligations arising from their acceptance of the recommendations of the United Nations Conference on Food and Agriculture . . . ; and
   (c) generally to take all necessary and appropriate action to implement the purposes of the Organization as set forth in the Preamble.[76]

76. Food and Agriculture Organization of the United Nations, *Constitution, Rules and Regulations,* Rome, February 1951, pp. 3–5.

Postwar Plans

Throughout World War II there was evidence of far more concern about problems to be faced after the war was over than had been apparent in World War I. The earlier period was marked by a naïve assumption that the defeat of Germany would solve all problems, and the world could return to the peaceful, relatively untroubled conditions of the golden years between 1900 and 1914. Wilson's slogan "a war to end war" was widely accepted as a major objective of the war effort and a tentative forecast of its results.

This feeling of optimism and confidence was rudely shattered by the severe depression of 1920 and still more so by the crash of 1929 and the long depression of the 1930's. The temper of the nation had been sobered, and the American people were thinking more maturely and seriously. World War II saw little of the high spirits, adolescent picturing of the glamour of war, and confidence that war would solve all problems, that had characterized World War I. This generation had seen how easily the fruits of victory could be lost, and the difficulties of maintaining peace, and had become aware of the problem of avoiding entanglements in a world that had become so interrelated that troubles in one area were sure to be reflected in others.

Widespread Study of the Problem

As a result, many agencies began almost as soon as the war broke out to shape plans for avoiding depression and other evils which were expected as aftereffects of war. The United States Department of Agriculture began in 1941 to issue a series of bulletins on Postwar Plans.[77] These stressed the need for planning, suggested ways of undertaking the job and sought to indicate the kinds of goals to be established. At about the same time the National Resources Planning Board began issuing a series of pamphlets entitled *After Defense — What?* (August 1941), *After the*

77. No. 1, *Why We Must Plan for Peace;* No. 2, *Win the War — Then the Peace;* No. 3, *Farm Prosperity Depends on the City.* These were followed by numerous informal memoranda of similar character.

War — Full Employment (revised, February 1943), *After the War — Toward Security* (September 1942), and so on.[78]

Unofficial agencies such as the National Planning Association, the United States Chamber of Commerce, the National Association of Manufacturers, and trade associations, farm organizations and labor unions began to study the problem. Many of them issued pamphlets outlining their views and conclusions.

By the fall of 1942 the U. S. Department of Agriculture was undertaking to lead the way in stimulating thinking in this field. It established a Washington committee and nine regional committees to undertake study of postwar conditions and objectives, basing them on an assumption that the war might end in 1944. A preliminary summary of conclusions was released in October 1943.[79]

By 1944 such planning was under way on a wide front. The Association of Land-Grant Colleges and Universities had established a strong committee at the end of 1943, which brought out its widely discussed report in October 1944.[80] This dealt mainly with long-term objectives in agricultural policy and less specifically with the immediate problems of readjustment from war.

Much stress was being placed on methods of achieving and maintaining full employment since unemployment was expected to increase sharply in the postwar years, and the nation was still acutely aware of the problems of the 1930's. Various public forums provided lengthy sessions on the subject.[81]

By 1944, postwar planning for agriculture,

under the guidance of the U.S. Department of Agriculture, was in full swing and resulted in numerous pamphlets and mimeographed statements. Among the more formal of these was the series entitled *What Peace Can Mean to American Farmers*.[82] This was the Department's major effort to clarify thinking as to objectives in postwar agriculture but was supplemented by a great number of special reports of various kinds. Some of the states also undertook extensive studies designed to provide a better understanding of the problems to be faced in the postwar period.[83]

Inflation Danger Understressed

Other government agencies likewise were considering the problem, though with an eye mainly to the industrial phase of the economy.[84] Most of them stressed the danger of unemployment and reduced purchasing power. A marked exception was a report issued in June 1945 by the Office of War Information, in cooperation with the Office of Price Administration, the Treasury Department, the War Labor Board, the War Food Administration, the Department of Agriculture and the Federal Reserve Board. This was entitled in bold type *Biggest Inflationary Danger Ahead*.[85] Here, for almost the first time, was evidence of clear recognition that the major postwar danger was from inflation not deflation.

Most economists in the government and out had underestimated the inflationary potential of the situation at the war's end. They,

78. Also *National Resources Development, Report for 1943. Part 1, Post-War Plan and Program*, January 1943. Shortly thereafter the National Resources Planning Board was abolished by congressional action (June 26, 1943).

79. U.S. Department of Agriculture, Interbureau Committee on Post-war Programs, *Agriculture When the War Ends*, October 15, 1943, mimeographed.

80. *Postwar Agricultural Policy*, Report of the Committee on Postwar Agricultural Policy of the Association of Land-Grant Colleges and Universities, October 1944. (See also various supplemental reports put out in mimeographed form.)

81. See, for example, *Fair Price Relationships and Full Employment*, Proceedings of the First National Forum of Labor, Agriculture and Industry, University of Wyoming, August 7, 8, 9, 1944.

82. U.S. Department of Agriculture, *What Peace Can Mean to American Farmers*: Miscellaneous Publication No. 562, *Post-War Agriculture and Employment*; Miscellaneous Publication No. 570, *Maintenance of Full Employment*; Miscellaneous Publication No. 582, *Expansion of Foreign Trade*; and Miscellaneous Publication No. 589, *Agricultural Policy*, 1945.

83. See, for example, *Purchasing Power of Wartime and Postwar Income Payments, the Nation and California*, California State Reconstruction and Reemployment Commission, Sacramento, September 1944.

84. Among the results of these studies were the *Report on War and Post-War Adjustment Policies*, by Bernard M. Baruch and John M. Hancock, February 15, 1944, and *Reconversion, A Report to the President from Director of War Mobilization James F. Byrnes*, September 7, 1944, both published by the Office of War Mobilization.

85. Office of War Information, Official U.S. Government Information Program on Economic Stabilization, Post V-E Day Supplement, June 1945.

like the farmers, were heavily influenced by the experience following World War I, and by the patterns of price behavior following all previous wars. The conditions, however, were markedly different in this period. Prices had been held down to a considerable extent. Deficit spending by government had been far greater, and for a longer period than in World War I, and spending power in the hands of consumers had reached unprecedented levels.

Problems Envisioned

H. R. Tolley, in a speech given in October 1944 before the Association of Land-Grant Colleges and Universities, summarized the thinking of analysts in the Bureau of Agricultural Economics as follows:[86]

What all this means in terms of post-war production trends in agriculture seems to me to be about as follows: Farmers in this country will have the most efficient farm plant in the world, the most efficient we have ever known . . . A higher level of total agricultural production than in the years before the war is almost inevitable. Markets must be developed to absorb this increased production . . . Markets are made, not born; and they are made chiefly by people with jobs at fair wages.

. . . we must take steps immediately to insure a continued high level of urban employment and to promote international collaboration . . . In a land so productive as ours, our choice of emphasis on both the national and international levels lies between trade and charity — we must emphasize either sales or subsidies — and common sense leaves us no doubt as to where our choice should fall.

As of this time the great need for European postwar relief, intensified as it was by the severe droughts of 1947, could not be clearly envisioned. Neither was it possible to foresee the unprecedented step later to be taken as the "Marshall Plan." Tolley's statement reflects much more awareness of the problems to come than do most other analyses put out in that period, but even he underestimated the tremendous upsurge of demand

that followed the war. On the production side his carefully weighed summary hit close to the course of events as it later developed.

O. C. Stine, in a similar address to the annual Outlook Conference, stressed the possibility of inflation, but predicted a sharp break within two or three years following 1945.[87] The break, if there is to be one, has been delayed beyond any expectations of that period. The high level of employment, the large volume of agricultural exports made possible through Marshall Plan and other aid provisions, and the renewed emphasis on armament which began in 1950, all have contributed to an unexpectedly long period of high employment and great prosperity. It is too early to say whether the economy can be held at the high levels of activity that have marked the period from 1945 to 1950. If a major break in employment and income is to occur, no prediction about it can be made at this time. Certain it is that inflationary forces have been allowed to operate with little check. There is no clear evidence that some rather severe readjustments from a period of inflation can be permanently avoided.

Certain it is that few economists, businessmen, labor leaders or farmers were at this time considering the possibility of anything but a sharp recession after the close of the war.[88] Because of this basic error in assumptions, no great importance attaches to the many efforts to make short-run plans for the postwar period.[89]

---

86. *Probable Trends in American Food Production After the War,* Address before the 58th Annual Convention of the Association of Land-Grant Colleges and Universities, Chicago, October 24, 1944, pp. 5, 7.

87. O. C. Stine, *The Outlook for Agriculture in 1945 and Beyond,* Address before the 22nd Annual Agricultural Outlook Conference, Washington, November 13, 1944, Bureau of Agricultural Economics, mimeographed.

88. For example, Secretary Wickard in testifying before the House Special Committee on Postwar Economic Policy and Planning on August 23, 1944 stressed almost entirely the 1930 types of aid for agriculture, and obviously assumed a return of depression problems in agriculture. The extent of the misjudgment of the situation is also indicated by the revealing title of an article in the March issue of *Fortune* in 1943, "Preview of the Postwar Generation; It Will Be Smaller; But It Can Be Demographically Sounder," pp. 116ff. This was near the beginning of the nation's decade of largest growth in population. The error grew out of the projection of the rates of population growth of the preceding depression decade.

89. While attention was centered chiefly on the situation expected in the years immediately following the war, a few of the analyses dealt with the problem in

The planning efforts had, however, a significant by-product in that many people undertook more seriously than ever before to think about the kind of longer-term policy and situation they would strive for. Farm policy in particular came in for more discussion and scrutiny than at any time in the past.

Agriculture at War's End

American agriculture entered the postwar period in the strongest financial position it had ever known. Its bank deposits and currency holdings had moved up from $3.9 billion on January 1, 1940 to approximately $14 billion on January 1, 1946. It held a total of $5 billion in U.S. Savings Bonds, an asset that had been negligible in amount in 1940. Its mortgage debt had declined from $6.5 billion to approximately $5 billion and its total debt from $10 billion to $8.3 billion. Its real estate was now valued at $56.5 billion as compared to $33.6 billion in 1940, while its livestock inventory had moved up from a valuation of $5.1 billion in 1940 to $9.6 billion in 1946.[90]

Farm population had declined from around 30 million to about 25 million, largely as a result of heavy movement out of agricultural areas chronically oversupplied with labor. Aside from the fears of coming reductions in farm product prices, there was little to cloud the horizon of the main body of commercial farmers.

Within agriculture there still were great inequalities. The so-called "poverty fourth" had gained little through war prosperity except that its small and poor farms were less crowded with surplus labor than before. Conditions were now more favorable for some consolidation of unduly small holdings, but, as yet, there was little in the way of specific programs for raising the levels of living in this group. This problem was to come increasingly under study in the years to follow.

First attention was to be given, however, to measures designed to maintain the prosperity of the larger-scale, commercial farmer. Agriculture, like labor, was seeking to retain in peacetime the boom earnings of the war years. Comparatively little progress had been made in facing the realities of the long-term agricultural problem. The tendency was rather to establish more firmly the rigidities of the old parity price system, and to insist on government supports that would implement it. The struggle to gain agreement on a long-term farm policy will be the main topic of the following chapter.

longer-range terms. See, for example, Theodore W. Schultz, *Redirecting Farm Policy,* Macmillan, New York, 1943, and some issues of the pamphlet series of the National Planning Association.

90. Data from Bureau of Agricultural Economics, *Balance Sheet of Agriculture, 1946,* USDA Miscellaneous Publication No. 620, p. 5.

CHAPTER 18

POSTWAR BOOM AND NEW LEGISLATION

THOUGH THE UNITED STATES and other nations had made unprecedented efforts to plan ahead for reconstruction and readjustment, the surrender of Japan, in August 1945, found them poorly equipped to deal with the problems of the postwar era. Britain was exhausted and virtually bankrupt; France demoralized and uncertain of its future; Italy was in chaos and apparently ripe for conquest by the communists. Holland, Denmark, Belgium and Norway were faced with difficult adjustments from a period of enemy occupation. All of Central Europe was in a state of confusion and flux resulting from war, and uncertainty as to forms of government and boundaries. The Balkan countries and Greece were similarly disorganized. Japan and Germany were prostrate and physically devastated.

Almost the only effectively functioning economies in the world, except those of Latin America, were the United States and the British Dominions. The Latin American countries were, in the main, preoccupied with internal and regional problems. In Asia and the Southwest Pacific nearly half the world's population was in ferment, seeking new forms of government and a new status in world affairs. Russia was assumed to be exhausted and likely to be preoccupied with internal problems for many years to come.

It is beyond the scope of this study to undertake analysis of the many and complex international political and economic problems that grew out of this chaotic world situation, except as they relate to American agricultural policy. Account must be taken, however, of certain differences between the situation at the close of World War I and that which followed World War II.

Most of the planners in the second war had assumed that American agriculture would be faced with problems similar to those which caused so much hardship in the period after 1920. Major international tensions were not anticipated. Principal interest centered on the problems of reconversion, reconstruction of war-torn areas abroad and the maintenance of a high level of employment and production in the United States.

PROBLEMS OF POSTWAR ADJUSTMENT

Great hopes had been raised by the almost universal enthusiasm with which the newly formed United Nations was greeted. Ambitious plans were taking shape for a major attack on the world's most baffling problems, through the Food and Agriculture Organization, the Economic and Social Council, the International Monetary Fund, the International Bank, and other technical agencies of the United Nations. It was generally, and somewhat naïvely, assumed that the groundwork had been laid for orderly and peaceful adjustment of international disagreements and for constructive cooperation by the governments of the various countries.

This utopian dream was soon to be shattered by clear evidence that Russia had accepted neither the spirit nor the letter of the new arrangements. Her aim of worldwide domination, through communist infiltration and the overthrow of capitalism throughout the world, had not been abandoned. The chaotic conditions in many countries gave her an opportunity to strike out on a program of imperialistic expansion that exceeded even the grandiose ambitions of Adolf Hitler. This anachronistic development, quickly recognized by all noncommunist governments, placed the whole program for world recovery in a far different setting from that which had been visualized by the wartime planners of postwar international relationships.

As a consequence, the anticipated constructive cooperation in solving this vast array of baffling problems did not materialize. Instead, they had to be tackled in the face of opposition and harassment probably exceeding any previously known between governments nominally at peace with each other. In addition, huge segments of the British and Dutch empires were split off through relatively peaceful revolutions, thus still further disrupting trade arrangements, the availability of resources and political cohesion.

Feeding Problem Acute

As an outgrowth of wartime destruction, and the shift of production facilities to military uses, vast numbers of people, both allied and enemy, were without adequate food or equipment, and unable to purchase in normal ways even the barest minimum of supplemental food supplies and capital goods. To make matters worse, the European winter of 1946–1947 was an unusually severe one, and was followed by a summer of catastrophic drought extending all the way from North Africa to the Scandinavian countries. Thus the feeding problem of 1946 and 1947 was even more formidable than had been visualized by the agencies charged with planning to meet it. Furthermore, these agencies, at least in the United States, had been unable to gain support for full-scale implementation of the plans they had laid out.

UNRRA, the British and American military governments and a host of unofficial relief agencies strove to bridge the gap, but with insufficient resources, inadequate personnel and less than suitably formulated objectives and plans. As the American public became more aware of the tragic need for food and working facilities, far-reaching measures of relief were undertaken, partly on humanitarian grounds, but also as a means of checking the spread of communist domination.

Lend-lease had been terminated abruptly on August 21, 1945, without adequate notice and with little in the way of plans for bridging the transition to more normal trading arrangements. This problem was met, in part, by a United States credit of $3,750 million to Britain, entered into in July 1946.

Since the United States was the only nation able to supply foodstuffs and industrial equipment on a large scale, the urgent need of nearly all the countries was for dollars with which to buy American food and equipment. These they did not have and could not get at the time, except through loan or gift from the United States. Britain had exhausted nearly all of her external assets and was owing huge debts, in pounds, to India, Egypt, Palestine and the various dominions and colonies. Much of her dollar exchange had formerly derived from shipments of tin, rubber and other commodities from Southeast Asia to the United States, these areas being supplied in turn with industrial goods from Britain. The production and trade of Southeast Asia were badly disrupted, and the Far East colonial empires of both Britain and Holland were disintegrating. Most other western nations were no better off, and there was, in consequence, an almost world-wide shortage of dollars.

The Marshall Plan

There was little merchandise available to ship to the United States in return for food and machinery, and the situation obviously called for abnormal measures if a long period of stagnation and hunger was to be avoided. The solution was found in a plan put forward somewhat tentatively by Secretary of State Marshall in a speech delivered at the Harvard University Commencement on June 5, 1947. This soon came to be known as the Marshall Plan.

In broad terms, Marshall's proposal was that the European nations estimate their minimum needs for sound recovery, set maximum goals as to what they could contribute toward the filling of these needs, and then look to the United States to close the gap by supplying what the European countries were unable to provide for themselves.

This broadly conceived and generous proposal met with enthusiastic response in most of the European countries, except those under the domination of Russia, and was given strong backing by the American public. Out of it developed the program of economic cooperation which had such marked influence on recovery in Europe. At the same time, it helped to lay the foundation for a sustained period of agricultural prosperity in the United States, thus creating a markedly different situation from that which had caused such early and acute distress in American agriculture after World War I.[1] Probably nowhere in history is there record of such a wholehearted and large-scale effort by one nation to improve conditions in other nations, victor and vanquished alike. Despite persistent and vigorous opposition from Russia and her followers, the achievement is notable, and almost unique as a measure of world statesmanship and national generosity.

The Inflationary Upsurge in Prices

Control over prices had been increasingly difficult as the war progressed. Between 1941 and 1943, personal incomes rose from $95 billion to $150 billion. Thereafter, the rate of increase was slower, but even so, incomes reached $172 billion by 1945. Personal income tax collections were up from about $7 billion in 1943 to approximately $20 billion in 1945, thus absorbing some of the increase but not enough to prevent inflationary pressure.[2]

Sales of series E bonds absorbed some $8 billion to $12 billion of personal income annually during 1943, 1944 and 1945, but fell off to $7 billion in 1946, thus offsetting to some extent the already inadequate mop-up of funds through income taxes.[3] Many of the

1. The program for economic cooperation affected American industry as well as agriculture, but here domestic demand afforded so large an undersupplied market that the impact was not so significant as in agriculture.
2. Data from *Statistical Abstract, 1950*, pp. 264 and 312.
3. *Annual Report of the Secretary of the Treasury on the State of the Finances for the Fiscal Year Ended June 30, 1950*, p. 558. There was in addition a large amount of saving in the form of increased bank accounts and other liquid assets.

goods desired by consumers were in very short supply and could not be purchased. This was especially true for automobiles and some other items that normally absorbed large amounts of consumer buying power. Even clothing purchases and household repairs were rather generally kept at a minimum. Thus, during these years there was an unprecedented amount of buying power available for the purchase of foods. This led to an increasing black market, especially in meats, though the great bulk of consumers and dealers did undertake conscientiously to abide by the regulations.

The self-imposed checks on spending which had been maintained during the war years became much less effective once hostilities had ceased. Bond purchases declined, moral restraints were less significant and there were demands for easing the tax load.

Rationing Abandoned

A stronger and more experienced leadership in Washington might perhaps have persuaded the public and the Congress to abide with controls and high taxes somewhat longer. Thus, reconversion and the stepping up of civilian goods production could perhaps have been carried out in a more orderly way. However that may be, strong and persuasive leadership was not available. Franklin Roosevelt's death, on April 12, 1945, placed a new and inexperienced President in the White House. Farmers, businessmen and labor all were impatient with restrictions on prices and wages, and anxious to return quickly to "normal" ways of living and doing business.

President Truman did away with gasoline rationing on the day Japan surrendered, and on September 2, meat, fat and oil points required under rationing were reduced. Zero point values for the lower grades of beef and lamb went into effect on September 27, and meat and fat rationing was abolished on November 24.[4] Sugar was thus the only commod-

4. Office of Temporary Controls, *Chronology of the Office of Price Administration, January 1941–November 1946*, Historical Reports on War Administration, Office

ity remaining under ration. The Congress began to consider measures for the reduction of tax rates. Few voices were raised in support of measures that might have held inflationary forces in check.[5]

Sharp Rise in Food Prices

As a consequence, the price of foods, which had remained relatively stable from 1943 to 1945, rose from 106 to 131 in the first year of peace (1926 = 100), and continued this rapid increase, reaching 169 in 1947 and 187 in September 1948. Farm products led the way, advancing from 128 in 1945 to 149 in 1946 and going on up to a peak of 196 in June 1948.[6] Their rate and amount of increase were exceeded only by building materials.

It was natural for this rapid rise in food costs to cause workers to make strong demands for higher wage rates, especially since overtime earnings were being reduced and the work week shortened. The result was a series of rather general wage increases. Average hourly earnings in manufacturing industries moved up from $1.023 in 1945 to $1.086 in 1946; to $1.237 in 1947; and to $1.350 in 1948. By December 1949 they stood at $1.412.[7]

Average weekly earnings, in manufacturing industries, gained less rapidly. They actually declined between 1944 and 1946 (from $46.08 to $43.82). Thereafter, they rose sharply, reaching $49.97 in 1947 and $54.14 in 1948.[8]

In nonfactory employment, hourly rates and weekly earnings varied greatly from industry to industry. For example, as late as July 1949, laundry workers were only up to 84 cents per hour and $35 per week, while coal miners were getting around $1.90 per hour, and, in the anthracite mines, about $66 per week. Bituminous miners, with an average 25-hour week, were making only about $48 per week. Unskilled labor had gained most in percentage terms, going from $.46 per hour in 1940 to $1.13 in 1949.[9]

Changes in Farm Income

It is apparent that, in this inflationary spiral, agriculture was leading the way and profiting most in the short run. This was particularly evident in the remarkable rise in net farm incomes. In most types of agriculture, a considerable part of the cost is in noncash form — that is, payment for the labor and management of the farm family itself, and return on the investment in land, buildings and equipment. Net cash available for spending tends to rise or fall more than in proportion to the changes in prices. Gross cash receipts from farming rose from $11,767 million in 1941 to $30,801 million in 1948, reflecting both increased prices and larger production. Total production expenses increased from $7,397 million to $18,510 million. In these, an important factor, though not a dominant one, was the increased cost for hired labor. This item rose from $1,013 million to $2,539 million, roughly $1,500 million or about one twentieth of gross cash receipts.

Thus cash income minus total production expenses rose to approximately 2.8 times its

of Price Administration, Miscellaneous Publication No. 1, November 30, 1946, *passim*.

This premature abandonment of rationing doomed the price control program. The Congress (on July 25, 1946), under heavy presidential pressure, extended the authority to control prices to June 30, 1947, but with crippling limitations. Meat, poultry, grains, dairy products, petroleum and tobacco were exempted from control. The act created a Decontrol Board with power to decontrol or recontrol most commodities but with final jurisdiction over food ceilings divided among the Decontrol Board, the USDA and the OPA. The Decontrol Board acted on November 10, 1946 to end commodity price controls, except on sugar, corn syrup and rice. *Loc. cit.; Federal Register*, Vol. XI, p. 13464.

5. A notable exception to the almost universal demand by businessmen and farmers for hasty abandonment of price controls and rationing was a well-reasoned report by the Committee for Economic Development, *The End of Price Control — How and When?*, New York, April 1946. This group advocated gradual and selective abandonment of price controls and the extension of price control authority to the spring of 1947, but with important modifications in the policies of the controlling agency.

6. Data from *Statistical Abstract, 1950*, p. 279.

7. *Ibid.*, p. 203. While the rapid rise of food prices undoubtedly touched off the upward movement of wage rates, and accelerated it, it is probable that labor, in view of its strong position in a fully employed economy and with profits at high levels, would shortly have demanded and obtained substantial wage increases, even if foods

had remained low. The sudden rise of food prices did, however, exert a marked inflationary influence in this period.

8. *Loc. cit.*

9. *Loc. cit.* and p. 204. Building trade workers experienced a similarly high percentage increase in weekly earnings, moving up from $35.14 in 1941 to $71.28 in July 1949. *Ibid.*, p. 205.

1941 level.[10] Part of this greatly increased net cash income went into buildings and equipment, this expenditure reaching the huge sum of $5,194 million in 1948, three times the amount so spent in 1941. Large amounts went into the purchase of farm lands at higher prices but without any marked increase in mortgage debt. Mortgage interest payments were, in fact, some $55 million less in 1948 than in 1941, but were beginning to rise again. They had reached their low at $216 million in 1946.[11]

Whether farmers are to be permanently better off as a result of the postwar inflation it is too early to tell. They are now in the strongest financial position they have ever attained. This, however, has been a result of a general inflation which has been referred to as "farm led and farm fed," and which has resulted in a wage and price structure for all goods and services markedly above what it would have been had the inflationary upsurge been avoided. Both wage rates and industrial prices are notably more sticky than the prices of farm products. Thus far, farmers have not experienced the downswing which conceivably might leave them with greatly inflated costs when their own incomes were seriously deflated.

Food exports, purchased in the main with ECA funds, were an important supporting influence in the agricultural markets.[12] But

by 1950 significant and, in some cases, embarrassing stocks of farm products were being accumulated through government price-supporting operations.

Impact on Savers

The major impact of the inflation was on savings in money form. All individual holders of bonds, all owners of life insurance policies, and all possessors of savings deposits, annuities and other fixed income resources found their assets depreciated by nearly half in the period between 1940 and 1950. This decrease in incentives and opportunity for self-reliance gave further strength to the already strong drive for greater dependence on pension funds, private, state and national, and on health and unemployment insurance.

No longer does the laborer or office worker see a prospect of saving enough to assure himself of an adequate income from private funds in old age or illness. He has seen the buying power of his income from a given amount of savings shrink to roughly one fourth what it had been twenty-five years earlier.[13]

Inflation tends to depreciate the position of savers, salaried workers and the aged, while operating, at least temporarily, to the advantage of entrepreneurs, including farmers, and those still actively employed. But its tendency is to strengthen the trend toward dependence on government and on both public and private pension funds, as against reliance on individual savings.

Checking the upsurge of farm prices after the close of the war, had it been possible, would not in itself have prevented inflation. Only the application of heavy taxation, credit controls and other anti-inflation devices could

10. Data from Bureau of Agricultural Economics, *The Farm Income Situation,* August 1950, pp. 24 and 30. It should be noted that the data given for total production expenses include sizable items for noncash expenses, such as $1,223 million in 1941 and $3,211 million in 1948 for depreciation and maintenance on buildings and equipment, only part of which was a cash cost. Perquisites of $230 million in 1941 and $469 million in 1948 are not included in the gross income figures used.

11. *Ibid.,* p. 31.

12. Total United States exports of wheat, flour and other grains accounted for more than 15 million long tons in 1946–1947 (the equivalent of more than 500,-000,000 bushels of wheat). Exports of fats and oils amounted to 214,000 tons; meats, 232,000; and dairy products, 502,000. Other foods exported totaled almost 3,000,000 tons. In 1947–1948, exports of foodstuffs continued at approximately these levels, and were even higher in 1948–1949. Not until 1949–1950 was there any significant slacking off in this phenomenal outflow of foodstuffs from the United States. Even in that year, exports were far above any prewar normal. U.S. Depart-

ment of Agriculture, *Distribution of United States Food,* 1947, 1948, 1949 and 1950, mimeographed.

13. Through a shrinkage of nearly half in the rate of return on dollars invested and a doubling of the prices of things he must buy. Some adjustments in this direction were clearly inevitable as the nation passed out of its capital-deficit stage into a situation in which capital was abundant and actively seeking outlets. The incentive for saving created by the earlier level of real returns on accumulated funds may well have been such that if continued it would result in a more rapid rate of saving than is desirable or needed from the standpoint of the economy as a whole.

have done that. The record does indicate, however, that the sharp rise in farm prices was an important factor in the recurring demands for wage increases. These wage increases in turn provided more buying power, and tended to continue and expand inflationary pressures. Farm groups were among the most vociferous in demanding the early abandonment of controls on prices, and, by the same token, on wages; and undoubtedly exerted an influence in the direction of inflation — an influence which had been dominant in the pressures applied by them and the legislation enacted in their behalf throughout the war period.

Planning Oriented to Depression

Both in agriculture and in the nonfarm parts of the economy, a recession was expected. Practically all of the continuing farm legislation looked to protecting farmers against this anticipated decline. The need for such protection was almost wholly removed, for the time being, by the high level of consumer buying power in the United States and by the large effective demand for farm products created by United States loans and gifts.

A markedly different policy was being followed than that of the early 1920's, and in respect to a very different situation. In May 1920, credits to former allies were abruptly terminated. Germany, for the most part, was allowed to shift for herself (until the somewhat later period when private loans began to be made in some volume), and relief operations were on a much smaller scale.

The German agricultural and industrial plant had been little damaged in World War I; the French government had retained a good deal of strength and effectiveness, and Britain and the Netherlands still had great economic resources in their colonial empires. The European nations were able to restore agricultural production at a fairly rapid rate.

Most of these factors were much less favorable at the close of World War II. The United States had large moral and political responsibilities for feeding the peoples of West Germany and Japan, for aiding in the restoration and maintenance of Italy and France, and for helping Britain and Holland to become self-supporting again. All of these elements in the situation, together with a markedly different attitude on the part of the United States government, contributed to a continuing strong market for farm products instead of the weak market which prevailed during the early 1920's.[14]

The agricultural and industrial depression which was confidently predicted for the late 1940's did not materialize. But the fear of a later recession still persisted, and legislation looking to forestalling or correcting it was under almost continuous consideration from 1944 on.

Strengthening the Nonfarm Economy

From about 1930 onward efforts were made to devise methods by which the government could step in to check or overcome depressions. Until the 1940's these did not attract major interest on the part of the farm groups. Through the 1920's the idea had been prevalent in farm circles that agriculture was the nation's basic industry. If it could be put on its feet, the rest of the economy would automatically become more active and prosperous. This view became gradually less prominent during the 1930's as it became more and more evident that agriculture could not prosper without an active domestic demand for its products. This could come only through high levels of industrial employment and productivity. The great upsurge in farm prosperity which accompanied World War II brought a much clearer recognition of the dependence of agriculture on conditions in the nonfarm economy, and contributed to a much wider interest in more general national legislation than had existed in the 1920's and 1930's.

Steps looking to the strengthening of the nonfarm economy through government action had been taken as early as 1931, in the

14. Furthermore, all of these areas, and the United States as well, had much larger populations to feed than in the 1920's.

Employment Stabilization Act of that year. This contemplated stimulation of employment through advance planning and regulated construction of public works. The same idea led to the creation, in 1935, of the National Resources Board, which was directed to prepare an inventory of public construction projects by states and regions, and to formulate a six-year program of public works construction.

Influence of Keynes

Its successor, the National Resources Planning Board, created in 1939, was directed to study current economic trends, and to make recommendations based on such studies, including preparation of plans for public works projects. During this period, the thinking of government economists and others was being more and more influenced by the views put forward by Professor J. M. Keynes of England in his book *The General Theory of Employment, Interest and Money,* which appeared in 1936.[15] Few economic treatises have had such widespread discussion and study by professional economists. In general, however, it was to the academic groups that this highly theoretical approach appealed, not to the laymen. Keynes stressed the importance of stabilizing the rate of investment and the purchasing power of consumers, through management of credit, currency, government spending, taxation and so on, in such a way as to maintain full employment.

As interpreted in the earlier years of its popularity, the analysis tended also to imply a relatively nationalistic approach, that is, the idea that each nation should center its attention chiefly on stabilizing its internal employment and price situation while letting the exchange value of its money fluctuate in terms of other currencies if necessary. In this respect it had similarities to the philosophy back of the Roosevelt policies of 1933, though the views held by Roosevelt and some of his advisers at that time had no such considered

15. Harcourt, Brace, New York.

theoretical foundation as that put forward later by Keynes.[16]

Older Views Still Widely Held

Among businessmen, congressional representatives and the general public, the older ideas of the need for continuously balanced budgets, the desirability of a fixed relationship between dollars and gold, and the necessity for recovery by the route of reduced wage rates, heavy unemployment and lower prices were still strong. Nevertheless, the notion that there might be some less painful solution for the problems posed by recurring depressions was gaining ground. The more advanced labor groups in particular seized upon the new philosophy with avidity, and were willing to overlook the possibilities of inflation inherent in it, and likewise the larger amounts of government management implied.

During the early years of the war, conflicting views about these partially formulated philosophies led to increasing criticism of the National Resources Planning Board.[17] It became a center of political controversy, and in 1943 an Act was passed which abolished the Board and directed that "the functions exercised by such Board shall not be transferred to any other agency and shall not be performed after such date [August 31, 1943], except as hereafter provided by law . . ."[18] Despite this setback on the part of those who favored a larger and more definitely planned role for government in the economic

16. British policy, likewise, was following a somewhat similar line in the years immediately following abandonment of the gold standard in September 1931 — that is, a preoccupation with the raising of prices and increasing employment while accepting a further depreciation of the pound in terms of gold. Keynes later disavowed the more extreme nationalistic interpretations of his doctrine, but these were common among his followers in the late 1930's.

17. There were, of course, other reasons as well for the critical attitude of the Congress, not least of which was growing restiveness over the tendency of the government to assume a larger and larger role in the management of the economy.

18. 57 Stat. 169 at 170, signed June 26, 1943. Here, as in some of the earlier legislation, there is evidence of a determination by the Congress to reassert its authority and do away with agencies created by executive action except as they might later be specifically authorized by the Congress.

affairs of the nation, the growing fear of a severe postwar recession soon turned the tide in the other direction. In the President's message to the Congress on January 11, 1944, he recommended that it explore means for implementing an "economic bill of rights . . . the right to a useful and remunerative job in the industries or shops or farms or mines of the Nation."[19] The postwar legislative programs of nearly all the major labor organizations contained similar ideas. Much controversy developed over the "right to a job" issue and the act which finally emerged as the Employment Act of 1946[20] was less positive in committing the government to a responsibility for maintaining full employment than was the Senate bill which was favored by the President and the labor organizations.

The Employment Act of 1946

The act as passed contained four major provisions as follows:

1. A declaration that it will be the continuing policy and responsibility of the federal government to coordinate and utilize all its plans, functions and resources with a view to creating and maintaining, in a manner calculated to foster and promote free competitive enterprise and the general welfare, conditions under which there will be afforded useful employment opportunities, including self-employment, for those able, willing and seeking to work, and to promote maximum employment, production and purchasing power.
2. A provision for the submission each year, by the President, of an Economic Report setting forth the current and projected levels of employment, production and purchasing power, the levels required to achieve the objectives outlined in the declaration of policy and recommendations as

to action which should be taken to strengthen the economy.
3. Authorization for a three-man Council of Economic Advisers to serve as an analytical and advisory unit to aid the President in performing the functions outlined above.
4. The establishment of a joint Committee on the Economic Report consisting of seven members from the Senate and seven from the House. This Committee is directed to make a continuing study of matters relating to the Economic Report, to consider ways of coordinating programs so as to further the objectives of the Act and to make a report each year to the Senate and the House of Representatives, this to include its findings and recommendations with respect to each of the principal suggestions made by the President in the Economic Report. The Committee may also make, from time to time, such other reports and recommendations to the House and Senate as it deems advisable.

Here, for the first time, emerges a mechanism which is theoretically suitable for coordinating, in a democratic way, an over-all approach to the problem of economic stabilization through government supplementation of private activity. The Council of Economic Advisers is responsible directly to the President, and affords him the possibility of using a compact, highly competent, nonpolitical, analytical body to aid him in coordinating the far-flung governmental activities in such a way as to avoid, so far as possible, major changes in the level of economic activity. At the same time, the Congress, which has a parallel responsibility for planning and implementing a stabilization program, is brought into the plan through an appropriate joint committee empowered both to react to the recommendations of the President and to initiate its own studies and recommendations.

Problems of Interpretation

While theoretically well conceived, such a procedure has many and important limitations which are inherent in any complex situation of this kind. No mere mechanism can bring into harmony the vast array of differing personal and political philosophies. It

19. Franklin D. Roosevelt, *Public Papers and Addresses, 1944–45,* Harper and Brothers, New York, 1950, pp. 41–42. Similar views were being put forward by other governments. In May 1944, the British coalition government outlined its postwar employment policy in a White Paper on *Employment Policy* (Command No. 6527), and in 1945, both Canada and Australia announced that it would be their policy to maintain full and stable employment. Article 55(a) of the Charter of the United Nations (1945) also stated that the signatory nations assumed an obligation to promote full employment.
20. 60 Stat. 23, approved February 20, 1946.

cannot eliminate political motivations and conflicts, and it cannot set aside bureaucratic and group pressures. Furthermore, it is a relatively new approach in government activity. Up to the time of Herbert Hoover's administration any such attempt to stabilize the economy would have been regarded as an inappropriate function of government. People accepted as inevitable the ups and downs of business activity and employment which grew out of the unregulated interaction of economic forces and mass psychology.

During the Hoover and Roosevelt regimes leadership in the coordination of government functions for attainment of greater stability stemmed from the executive branch of the government, with Congress, in the main, either acquiescing or resisting. In the Employment Act of 1946 the Congress and the Executive were theoretically brought into full partnership, presumably with an objective agreed to by both.

The ends that were to be sought were not, however, by any means so clear and simple as this brief summary would imply. There was little agreement as to what would constitute "full" employment. The economy had for some years been operating on a scale that used nearly every available worker, many on an overtime basis. In addition many workers not normally in the labor force had been drawn in because of wartime wages, unusual job opportunities and the desire to aid in the war effort. Furthermore, many workers were upgraded beyond the levels for which their skills and capacities would normally fit them.

Was this "overemployment" to be regarded as a proper objective in the stimulation of economic activity? It inevitably placed labor in an exceedingly strong bargaining position, and almost certainly laid the groundwork for a creeping inflation as labor demanded and obtained continuously higher levels of wages. Furthermore, there was widespread reservation as to whether the government could and should contemplate further deficit financing on a scale that would actually prevent a re-cession once it got under way. But if some lower level of economic activity was to be the goal, what level was that to be?

Labor's Position

Though initiated in terms of the broad national objective of maintaining high and stable productivity in the economy, the Employment Act was to some extent rationalized by labor in terms of a narrower objective, namely, that of maintaining a highly favorable market for labor. It became, in effect, labor's version of agriculture's parity objective. The strong position of labor in a very tight labor market was to be maintained, using, if necessary, heavy inputs of government funds to hold employment at those levels. Almost certainly labor's conception of an appropriate balance in the labor market, like agriculture's conception of a fair level of farm prices, was too high. Either of them alone very possibly meant mounting government deficits with little opportunity for retrenchment. Together they certainly would add up to such a result, with the prospect of an ultimate disastrous crash if the Congress and the public should become alarmed at the increasing size of the public debt and decide to abandon the program.

Furthermore, there was as yet no clear evidence that, except under war conditions, the government could operate a deficit spending program in such a way and with sufficient balance to assure general and continuous high prosperity. Theoretically this could be done, but the practical applications of such a program still were vague and extremely controversial.[21] A decision to inject governmentally created buying power into the economy does not suddenly and smoothly result in increased employment and spendable income. There are time lags, inequities and frustrations in any such program, and always a special interest and bureaucratic struggle over shares in the funds thus provided.

21. An excellent series of lectures on this problem will be found in Bertil Ohlin, *The Problem of Employment Stabilization*, Columbia University Press, New York, 1949.

Employer Attitudes

Employer groups, for obvious reasons, were not enthusiastic about labor's full-employment objectives. In a full-employment labor market, bargaining with labor is by no means an easy task. Unreasonable demands are made, wage rates continue to advance and efficiency declines. Furthermore, labor itself tends to be restless and dissatisfied in a highly dynamic situation of that kind, each group feeling that its interests are likely to be impaired through concessions in wages and prices made to other groups.

Thus while a mechanism for a coordinated effort to stabilize the economy has come into being, the objectives and methods are still far from clear, and the general idea has not been fully accepted by either the public or the Congress. The unexpected high level of postwar employment and demand has kept these ideas from being put to the test. Labor, like agriculture, has laid its plans in terms of an expected deflationary situation and has been unwilling to face fully the implications and requirements of an inflationary period.

The procedure contemplated under the Employment Act of 1946 has not achieved, up to this time, the acceptance and influence its sponsors anticipated. It is impossible to foresee whether it will eventually become a significant feature of the government or whether, instead, this attempt to develop a coordinated approach to the problem of economic stabilization will have been abortive.[22]

It is probable that the Council's standing, even though as a center of controversy, would have been greater had the expected postwar recession developed in the early years of its existence. It may or may not be continued until such time as its counsel will be more actively sought. In the meantime, its influ-

ence over the inflationary forces now dominant appears not to be large.

Longer-Range Farm Policies

During the last years of the war there was much discussion of farm programs for the future. Most of these related to the problem of postwar adjustment. Some, however, had longer-range objectives. One of the most serious efforts to come to grips with the non-emergency aspects of the farm policy problem was that of the Committee on Postwar Agricultural Policy of the Association of Land-Grant Colleges and Universities. Its report, issued in October 1944,[23] was widely read and discussed but did not, apparently, have much effect on the course of agricultural legislation in the Congress.

The Land-Grant College Report

The Committee's report was a constructive and relatively comprehensive analysis of many phases of the agricultural problem, approached in the main from the standpoint of the national welfare rather than that of a special-interest group. In this, the Committee chose high ground and a defensible position, but not the one on which the congressional battles were soon to be joined.

Prices, under the Committee proposals, were, for the most part, to be allowed to seek their natural levels, and a freer, more self-

---

22. An illuminating discussion of the difficulties inherent in making such a plan work appears in the February 18, 1950 issue of *Collier's*, starting on p. 13, "Why I Had to Step Aside," by Edwin G. Nourse, the first Chairman of the Council of Economic Advisers. Nourse resigned in the fall of 1949 because of his conviction that the President and the other members of the Council were unwilling to accept and use the Council for technical analysis helpful for but distinguished from executive policy making.

23. Association of Land-Grant Colleges and Universities, *Postwar Agricultural Policy*, a report of the Committee on Postwar Agricultural Policy, October 1944. See also the 1945 Report of the same committee to the Executive Committee of the Association, October 1945, mimeographed.
Many other groups and organizations came forward during this period with comprehensive farm policy proposals and analyses. See especially the prize-winning essays in the American Farm Economic Association contest, published in the *Journal of Farm Economics*, November 1945, pp. 743–902, and *USDA Testimony Proposing Long-Range Agricultural Policy and Programs Before Congressional Committees on Agriculture, April 21, October 6, 7, 8, 1947* at Washington, D.C., USDA, mimeographed. Also in official hearings, U.S. Congress, House, Committee on Agriculture, *Long-Range Agricultural Policy*, Hearings . . . , 80th Cong., 1st sess., Part I, April 21, 1947, pp. 1–28; and U.S. Congress, *Long-Range Agricultural Policy*, Hearings before a Subcommittee of the Committee on Agriculture and Forestry, Senate, and the Committee on Agriculture, House, 80th Cong., 1st sess., pursuant to S.Res. 147 and H.Res. 298, October 6, 7 and 8, 1947.

regulating economy was the goal to be approached over a period of years. For the immediate postwar years, the Committee favored continuance of price controls and gradual liquidation of the program of artificial incentives for high production. Measures designed to reduce production were frowned upon because "general curtailment of agricultural production does not solve the problems of a depression." Instead, the Committee favored, in times of depression, the subsidization of food consumption, the deferment of farm mortgage payments and, in long and severe depressions, income payments to farmers.

Improvements in forms of land tenure, a preponderantly owner-operated agriculture and strong measures to control land-price inflation were favored. The report likewise stressed the importance of conservation; the need for extending social security to rural people; and the improvement of rural life through better housing, better educational facilities, more electrification and fuller access to good roads, telephone services and recreational facilities. Major emphasis was on educational and guidance types of programs rather than on large-scale action programs financed by government, though these were not ruled out of consideration.[24]

These recommendations obviously ran counter to the thinking of farm-state congressmen at several points, particularly in advocating the retention of price controls, the use of income payments instead of price supports, and in their implication of a free-market price as an ultimate goal. While soundly conceived from the standpoint of socially oriented economics, the report did not take much account of the political realities. Despite this defect, if it be one, the report gave needed leadership in the thinking

of farm people themselves, and was generally well received. Even in congressional circles some of the ideas presented were seriously considered for a time.

The Colmer Committee Reports

During this same period, extensive study was given to postwar policy and planning by the House Special Committee on Postwar Economic Policy and Planning, known as the Colmer Committee. This Committee, consisting of 18 members under the chairmanship of William M. Colmer of Mississippi, was set up in the early part of 1944, under H.Res. 408, which directed it to investigate and report on:

all matters relating to post-war economic policy and problems . . . to the end that the Congress may be . . . in a position to formulate solutions with respect to them which will result in the greatest contribution by the Congress to the achievement of a stable economy and a just peace.[25]

The Committee held extensive hearings and issued a comprehensive series of reports.[26]

The Colmer Committee's conclusions in respect to agricultural policy were somewhat similar to those put forward by the Land-Grant College Committee.[27] The importance of restoring flexibility in price relationships as among the various farm commodities was stressed, and also the desirability of bringing about adjustments in agriculture that would enable farmers to earn, in a relatively free economy with general employment and income at high levels, incomes reasonably comparable to those in nonfarm occupations. Special attention was given to the problem

24. It is impossible to summarize adequately this excellent report since its 61 pages are themselves essentially in summary form. For more adequate consideration of the viewpoint presented, the reader is referred to the report itself and to two thoughtful reviews of it: that of John D. Black in the *Journal of Farm Economics*, February 1945, pp. 168–75; and the one by Theodore W. Schultz in the *Journal of Land and Public Utility Economics*, May 1945, pp. 95–107.

25. *Congressional Record*, 78th Cong., 2nd sess., p. 695. Also on p. 753.
26. Of these, the ones of particular significance to agriculture were the Fourth Report, *Economic Problems of the Reconversion Period*, H.Rep. 1855, 78th Cong., 2nd sess., 1944, and the Tenth Report, *Postwar Agricultural Policies*, H.Rep. 2728, 79th Cong., 2nd sess., 1946.
27. The principal summary of Committee views appears in the Tenth Report, Part II, pp. 21–41. Briefer summaries are given in the Fourth Report, pp. 60–69, and in the Eleventh and Final Report, *Reconversion Experience and Current Economic Problems*, H.Rep. 2729, 79th Cong., 2nd sess., 1946, pp. 93–98.

of improving the economic status of the large, low-income group within agriculture, a group which had been comparatively little affected by the types of price and income support developed during the 1930's.

The disadvantages of production control and surplus removal programs were emphasized, and stress was given to measures designed to bring about basic adjustments in agriculture rather than those which would encourage the retention of uneconomic, high-cost types of production. The recommendations included facilitating the movement of labor resources out of agriculture if not needed there, the provision of credit for enlarging and equipping farms that are too small, and expansion of the Bankhead-Jones tenant-purchase program.

The need for protection against extreme fluctuations in farm incomes was recognized. Here the Committee considered crop insurance, storage arrangements and the strengthening of cooperative associations; and suggested minimum reliance on curtailment of production. In the international field the Colmer Committee, like the Land-Grant College Committee, recommended fuller recognition of the changed position of the United States in world trade, a less restrictive policy with respect to imports and greater reliance on collective action in stabilizing international trade and monetary relationships.

As to the methods of supporting farm incomes in times of depression, the Committee discussed several alternatives but did not make a specific recommendation. The general implication of its report was, however, that price supports should be kept to lower percentages of parity than those then current, and should be more flexible as among agricultural products; and that compensatory or supplemental income payments might well be considered rather than support of market prices in a way that would prevent free flow of products into the domestic and foreign markets. There was some hint of a leaning toward the idea of forward pricing, especially for perishables, together with more aggressive selling campaigns to aid in clearing up temporary gluts.[28]

The Committee emphasized the importance of maintaining consumption in periods of depression, and also gave attention to the problem of improving the nutritional adequacy of the nation's diet. This was a recognition of the "food-allotment" approach which was being widely discussed in some circles during these years. However, the Committee did not commit itself in favor of such a plan. Rather, it expressed doubt of its desirability, but suggested further study of it in connection with other programs designed to maintain incomes and assure minimum living standards, particularly those contained in the social security system.[29]

The National Food Allotment Plan

Even before the Colmer Committee began its deliberations, a more altruistic and paternalistic approach to the farm and food problem had been put forward and was being widely discussed. This was known as the National Food Allotment Plan. It was introduced in the Senate in July 1943 by Senator George Aiken of Vermont.[30] It sought to solve both the problem of inadequate nutrition and the anomaly of price-depressing surpluses of foodstuffs in a nation that still contained large numbers of people who were unable to afford adequate diets.

Under this plan each family might, by paying in 40 per cent of its income, receive coupons or stamps which would enable it to purchase an adequate minimum diet. For families having an income large enough so that 40 per cent of it would buy a minimum diet this provision would, of course, have no

28. For a fuller account of the many aspects of the problem discussed in the hearings of the Committee, see U.S. Congress, House, *Post-war Economic Policy and Planning,* Hearings before the Subcommittee . . . of the Special Committee on Post-war Economic Policy and Planning, 78th Cong., 2nd sess., and 79th Cong., 1st sess., pursuant to H.Res. 408 and H.Res. 60. See especially Part 5, *Post-War Agricultural Policy,* 1945.

29. The Committee did, however, express unqualified approval of the school lunch program, and urged further development of the educational programs designed to improve nutrition and health.

30. S. 1331, 78th Cong., 1st sess.

attraction. It was thus a proposal for upgrading the diets of low-income families. The food allotment plan grew out of experience with the Food Stamp Plan during the years 1938 to 1942.[31]

Hearings were held on the Aiken bill in January 1944, and in February it was offered as a Senate amendment to H.R. 3477 which provided for extending the life of the Commodity Credit Corporation. It was defeated on the Senate floor by a vote of 46 to 29.

A new, much revised bill, based on further analytical study and on the January hearings, was introduced by Aiken and LaFollette in June 1945. The influence of the Aiken bill is apparent in some sections of the Land-Grant College Committee's report. However, the plan was later withdrawn by its author. In his comments to the Senate, in reporting S. 2318 on May 17, 1948, Senator Aiken stated that the Committee (on Agriculture and Forestry) had felt that it could not go into this matter thoroughly enough to warrant its inclusion in the Committee bill, and had omitted it in order not to jeopardize the enactment of "a sound long-range price support program."[32] As of the present writing, the proposal has not been reintroduced.

Ending of Wartime Guarantees

The World War II legislation promised support, generally at 90 per cent of parity, for two years from the first of January immediately following a declaration by either the President or the Congress that hostilities had ceased. On December 31, 1946, President Truman issued such a declaration, thus automatically terminating the wartime price guarantees as of the end of 1948.[33] This forced Congress to begin consideration of new and more permanent agricultural legislation, unless it was prepared to revert to such of the legislation of the 1930's as was still in effect. There was general recognition of the semi-emergency character of much of the legislation carried over from the 1930's, as well as that of the war period, and a general desire to have a go at formulating a more adequate, long-range farm policy.

The election of 1946 gave the Republicans control of the Congress for the first time in sixteen years and thus put Republicans in charge of the committees instead of Democrats. As yet, however, the farm-state congressional representatives constituted a somewhat bipartisan bloc. The sharp division along party lines that was to be apparent in 1948 and 1949, and thereafter, had not yet become evident.

This is not to imply that all was harmonious within the farm group up to this time. The representatives from the southeastern states consistently demanded high and rigid price supports, based on parity, and were apparently willing to accept rigorous controls on output and marketings, if necessary, in order to achieve that end. The farmers of the Middle West, traditionally Republican, were less wedded to the high support-price policy, though many of them had swung over to the Democrats in the depression years. Now, with farm prices and incomes at highly satisfactory levels, they were far less impressed with the need for paternalism, production controls and governmental planning. The less closely knit groups of the Northeast, the Plains area and the West Coast were uneasy about the drift toward a "controlled" agriculture, but in the Congress as a whole the balance between those who favored a shift in the direction of a freer economy and those who wanted the assumed security of high-level price supports was still very close, as the farm policy battles of 1948 and 1949 were to make abundantly clear.

The Senate proposals on agriculture were launched through introduction of S. 2318 (on March 15, 1948) by Aiken, Bushfield, Wilson and Thye, Republicans; and Thomas of

31. For a fuller description of the plan see Rainer Schickele, "The National Food Allotment Program," *Journal of Farm Economics,* May 1946, pp. 515–33.
   A concise and informative summary of experience under the subsidized consumption program of 1938 to 1942 is given in Geoffrey S. Shepherd, *Agricultural Price Control,* Iowa State College Press, Ames, 1945, Chapter 13.
   32. *Congressional Record,* 80th Cong., 2nd sess., p. 5896.
   33. The President's other specific war powers were terminated by congressional resolution on July 25, 1947.

Oklahoma, Ellender and Lucas, Democrats.[34] The House presented a different plan introduced (on April 14) as H.R. 6248 by Chairman Clifford Hope of the House Committee on Agriculture.

Senate and House Differences

The Senate bill tended to follow the lines of the Soil Conservation and Domestic Allotment Act of 1936 and the Agricultural Adjustment Act of 1938. It placed emphasis on decentralization and a larger place for the state agencies, stressed educational and research activities to be carried out by the land-grant colleges and experiment stations and provided state agricultural councils and county agricultural executive committees. There was also provision for a National Agricultural Council to advise the Secretary of Agriculture and the Congress on agricultural matters. The functions of the Farmers Home Administration (the agency for aiding low-income farmers and tenants) were to be transferred to the state agricultural councils.

The 1936 emphasis on soil conservation and the making of grants for improved conservation practices was retained. The price-support features of the bill were similar to those of the Agricultural Adjustment Act of 1938 and provided for support levels ranging from 60 to 90 per cent of parity, these being related to estimated supplies. The bill proposed support at 60 per cent of parity for a quantity estimated at more than 130 per cent of normal up to 90 per cent of parity if it was not more than 70 per cent of normal.

The House bill was much narrower in concept, and was mainly concerned with the level of price supports to be maintained. Prices for cotton, wheat, corn, tobacco, rice and peanuts were to be continued at 90 per cent of parity until June 30, 1950. This was essentially a 1½-year extension of the wartime price-support legislation with respect to these crops, except that cotton was to be supported at 90 per cent of parity instead of 95

per cent. Corn from "noncommercial" corn areas was now, however, to be supported at the same level as that from commercial areas (on the ground that in a period of shortage more corn was needed regardless of where it was grown).[35] For the Steagall commodities prices were to be supported at not less than 60 per cent nor more than 90 per cent of parity, except that milk and its products were to be supported at 90 per cent.

There was a long and bitter fight over the two bills. The House passed the Hope bill and the Senate passed the Aiken bill. The House committee did not hold hearings on the Aiken bill and refused to bring it to the House floor for a vote. Consequently, the House as a whole had no opportunity to express itself on the measure. When the House bill reached the Senate, Senator Aiken moved that the Committee on Agriculture and Forestry be discharged of any further duty to consider it and that the Senate proceed to the consideration of the bill. He then offered an amendment striking out all after the enacting clause and substituting therefor the language of the Aiken bill, S. 2318. The bill was then passed, as amended, by a vote of 79 to 3. Thus there was returned to the House a bill bearing the House name and number but consisting of the "long-range" program desired by the Senate instead of the "stop-gap" measure desired by the House Committee on Agriculture.[36]

In the ensuing conference meetings, the House stood pat on its version while the Senate conferees were equally firm in their position. As the hour of final adjournment approached, there was every indication that the deadlock would persist and that no law would be enacted. This outcome had in fact been rather generally predicted by Washington political observers for some time. However, a last minute replacement of one of the

34. The Senate Committee on Agriculture and Forestry was at this time under the chairmanship of Senator Arthur Capper of Kansas.

35. The bill also contained some minor provisions designed to prevent disruption of marketing agreement programs through importation of articles made from agricultural products.
36. Numerous amendments, some of very dubious merit, were of course offered during the debates on these bills.

Republican conferees in the House group resulted in acceptance (late on Saturday night and with the official clocks stopped) of the Senate version, but with the Hope bill added. This outcome was no doubt in part due to the urgent desire of the Republican members to get away for participation in the Republican National Convention scheduled for the following week.

THE AGRICULTURAL ACT OF 1948

The compromise known as the Agricultural Act of 1948 consisted of three titles.[37] Title I was essentially the Hope bill (the one put forward by the House Agriculture Committee). Title II contained the provisions of the Aiken bill as amendments to the Agricultural Adjustment Act of 1938, but now with an effective date of January 1, 1950 instead of January 1, 1949. Title III consisted of miscellaneous provisions designed to clarify and implement the policy outlined in Title II.

Title I (January 1, 1949–June 30, 1950)

The interim provisions for the period prior to the effective date of the "long-term" program were as follows:

1. Prices of cotton, wheat, corn, tobacco, rice and peanuts were to be supported at 90 per cent of parity, to cooperating farmers, until June 30, 1950, if producers had not disapproved marketing quotas for the commodity for the marketing year beginning in the calendar year in which the crop was harvested. (Prices to noncooperators were to be supported at 60 per cent of the rate to cooperators and only on that portion of the crop subject to penalty if marketed.)

2. All loan and price-support procedures authorized in the Agricultural Adjustment Act of 1938, as amended, were to be applicable in carrying out the policy outlined above.[38]

3. For commodities of which the Secretary of Agriculture had asked increased production under the Act of July 1, 1941, as amended (that is, the Steagall commodities) prices were to be supported at not less than 60 per cent of parity (or comparable price) nor more than the price at which such commodity was supported in 1948. Exceptions to this were that Irish potatoes harvested before January 1, 1949, milk and its products, hogs, chickens and eggs were to be supported at 90 per cent of parity (or comparable price).[39]

4. The Act of August 5, 1947 (an Act to provide support for wool, and for other purposes) was amended by striking out the date December 31, 1948 wherever it appeared and substituting the date June 30, 1950.[40]

5. It was declared to be the policy of the Congress that the lending and purchasing operations of the Department of Agriculture be carried out with a view to maintaining, until January 1, 1950, the prices (and income) for other agricultural commodities not included in 1, 3 or 4 above at a "fair parity" relationship with those of the commodities specified in 1, 3 and 4.[41]

6. The Marketing Agreement Section of the Agricultural Adjustment Act, as added by Section 31 of the Act of August 24, 1935 and re-enacted as Section 1 of the Agricultural Marketing Agreement Act of 1937, was amended to provide for Tariff Commission review and presidential action to raise tariffs or impose quotas if specific commodities were or threatened to be imported in quantities or at prices that would jeopardize the effective functioning of this or related agricultural legislation.

7. The continuance in effect of the provisions

---

37. 62 Stat. 1247. For a summary and explanation of the act in nonlegal language, see H. C. M. Case, "The Agricultural Act of 1948," *Journal of Farm Economics,* Proceedings Number, February 1949, pp. 227–36. (Case was a consultant to the Senate Committee on Agriculture and Forestry while the bill was being considered.) See also the U.S. Department of Agriculture's official analysis of the Act, *An Analysis of the Principal Provisions of the Agricultural Act of 1948 and Related Legislation,* 1948, mimeographed.

38. Except that the base period for Maryland tobacco

was to be August 1936 to July 1941 instead of August 1919 to July 1929.

39. "Comparable" price was to be used if the production or consumption of such crop had so changed since the base period as to result in a "parity" price that was out of line with the parity prices of the other commodities listed. The price supports indicated in (3) above were to be contingent on compliance with production goals and marketing regulations.

40. Section 4 of the act made a comparable change in the dates specified in the amended Soil Conservation and Domestic Allotment Act, striking out January 1, 1950 wherever it appeared and inserting January 1, 1951 in lieu thereof, and substituting December 31, 1950 for December 31, 1948 wherever the latter date appeared.

41. It will be noted that, while this is the stated intention of the Congress, the requirement for support is less specific than for the commodities enumerated earlier. For these, also, the Secretary of Agriculture was authorized to require compliance with production goals and marketing regulations as a condition for price support.

of the Act of July 28, 1945 (relating to the marketing of fire-cured and dark air-cured tobacco under the Agricultural Adjustment Act of 1938, as amended) was specifically reaffirmed.

8. This Title (I) was to take effect on January 1, 1949, except that the tariff feature and the extension of the Soil Conservation and Domestic Allotment Act were to be effective immediately.

Titles II and III—the Long-Term Features

While Titles II and III, embodying in substance the Senate bill (that is, the revised Aiken bill), constituted a reversion to the type of legislation contained in the Act of 1938, there were important modifications.[42] The principal features included were:

1. A new formula for computing parity.
2. A "transitional" parity to be used during an interim period of adjustment from the old to the new formula.
3. A more flexible program of price supports to replace the fixed percentages of parity provided in the war and postwar legislation.
4. Provision that the prices of perishables might be supported through use of remaining funds from the Rescission Act of 1946 (60 Stat. 6 at 8), if Section 32 funds carried over from the preceding year amounted to less than $300 million.
5. Provision for the use of incentive prices at higher levels than those indicated as maxima, if, through public hearing, such action is found to be necessary in the interest of national security as a means of increasing or maintaining production.
6. Authorization to use the "nonrecourse" feature in loans made.
7. A specification that the Commodity Credit Corporation might not sell any commodity controlled by it at (1) less than a price that will reimburse it for costs; (2) a price half way between the support price, if any, and the parity price; or (3) a price equivalent to 90 per cent of parity, whichever is lowest.[43]

42. Technically, they were amendments to that act.
43. Exceptions were made to permit sales at lower prices for new or by-product uses; sales of peanuts for oil; sales for feed or seed use if these will not impair the price-support program; sales of products that have deteriorated or are likely to do so; sales to establish values in fraud cases; and sales for other than primary uses.

The act also included certain minor amendments to the marketing quota features of the Act of 1938, and made special provision for taking into account the cost of feed, the need of the public for fluid milk and certain other factors in determining the price of milk in area milk-marketing orders.

The New Parity Formula

The cost of producing wheat and various other field crops had been greatly reduced, in real terms, by extensive mechanization. At the same time demand had fallen off, except for the abnormal requirements of the war and postwar years. Similar economies had not been achieved in the production of beef cattle, wool, dairy products, and fruits and vegetables while the domestic demand for them had increased greatly. Hence, if prices were to be increased in the same ratio for all of these products, the tendency would be to make wheat growing and other highly mechanized operations very profitable, and to discourage, relatively, the production of livestock products which were in short supply. To overcome this difficulty, the revised parity formula provided that the "parity" price for any agricultural commodity would be the "adjusted base price" for such commodity multiplied by the parity index as of the date of computation.

The adjusted base price was to be the average price received by farmers for the commodity during the ten preceding years, divided by the ratio of the general level of prices received by farmers in this ten-year period to the general level of prices received by farmers in the period January 1910 to December 1914.

That is, if the general level of prices received by farmers in the ten-year period just past was 75 per cent above the level of 1910–1914, this ratio would be 100 to 175. To get the adjusted base price for the given commodity, its average price for the preceding ten years would be multiplied by 100 and divided by 175. This would give a 1910–1914 base price for this commodity that would be different from the actual price received in the period 1910–1914.

Thus if beef cattle were up 100 per cent from the 1910–1914 level and wheat up 50 per cent, the new base price for beef would be higher and that for wheat lower than under the old formula. For example, if wheat had been $1.00 per bushel in 1910–1914 and in the last ten years had averaged $1.50, assuming that farm prices generally had risen 75 per cent, the new base price for wheat would be $\frac{100}{175}$ of $1.50 which is $.857 instead of $1.00. If beef cattle were worth $40 a head in 1910–1914 and in the last ten years averaged $80 per head, the adjusted base price would be $\frac{100}{175}$ of $80 or $45.71 per head. Thus the base price for wheat would have been adjusted downward while that for beef cattle would have been adjusted upward.

To arrive at the new parity index for the given commodity, this adjusted base price would then be increased by a percentage corresponding to the average increase, since 1910–1914, in the prices of articles and services farmers buy, including interest on farm real estate mortgages and taxes on farm real estate. If the index of prices paid by farmers stood at 200 per cent of the 1910–1914 level, the above adjusted base prices would be increased by 100 per cent to obtain the new parity. Using the illustrative figures given above, the new parity for wheat would be 200 per cent of $.857, or $1.71; that of beef cattle 200 per cent of $45.71, or $91.42. Under the old formula, the parity price for wheat would be $2.00 as compared to $1.71 under the new; the parity price of beef cattle would be $80 as compared to $91.42.[44]

It will be noted that this change in formula, if used as a basis for supporting prices, would tend to encourage expansion of such things as beef cattle and to discourage wheat production, as compared to the relative incentives that would be provided under the old for-

mula. It was an attempt to reflect changes in the demand and cost situation which have occurred since the now remote 1910–1914 base period, and yet to retain the 1910–1914 relationship as an over-all criterion of equity between farm and nonfarm prices.

Though cumbersome, the new approach looked in the right direction. It was an attempt to bring more nearly up to date a concept and mechanism that were oriented to a set of conditions that was greatly different from that of recent years. Some approach in terms of planned adjustment would perhaps have been simpler and more constructive, but farm leaders and congressmen were much too strongly wedded to the parity concept, and much too impressed with its definiteness and political usefulness, to be willing to abandon it for something more vague and more subject to administrative decision.

Transitional Parity and Parity Income

Since the revised parity formula was expected to reduce the parity prices of some commodities, the act provided that the downward adjustment would not be made all at one time. Instead, the parity price for such commodities was to be computed by the old formula, and the transitional parity was to be this price less 5 per cent for each calendar year after January 1, 1950 until such time as this would result in a parity price lower than that provided by the revised formula.

"Parity income" was redefined as "that gross income from agriculture which will provide the farm operator and his family with a standard of living equivalent to those afforded persons dependent upon other gainful occupation." Parity income as applied to the return from any specific agricultural commodity for any year was to be "that gross income which bears the same relationship to parity income from agriculture for such year as the average gross income from such commodity for the preceding ten calendar years bears to the average gross income from agriculture for such ten calendar years."[45]

44. The prices and ratios are hypothetical and are presented only to illustrate the method, not to reflect the actual price relationships which, of course, change continuously.

45. 62 Stat. 1247 at 1251.

The Flexible Support-Price Feature

Of far more interest to farmers and congressmen than the change in the parity formula was the provision for flexible price supports in place of the 90 per cent of parity which had been so vigorously advocated and defended over the preceding years. This retreat from high levels of price support was by no means acceptable to the southern cotton and tobacco state representatives and was shortly to become a center of political controversy.[46]

Under the new act, prices to "cooperators" on the "basic" commodities (except for corn grown outside the "commercial" corn-producing area) were to be supported at a level ranging between 60 and 90 per cent of parity. The 90 per cent of parity was to apply if the percentage of normal supply was not more than 70. Where the percentage of normal supply was 130 or more, support was to be limited to 60 per cent of parity. Normal supply was defined as (1) the estimated domestic consumption for the preceding year, plus (2) the estimated exports for the current year, plus (3) an allowance for carry-over. Allowances for carry-over were to be as follows:

for corn	— 7 per cent
for cotton	— 30 per cent
for rice	— 10 per cent
for wheat	— 15 per cent
for peanuts	— 15 per cent

Percentages are in relation to previous year consumption plus estimated exports for the current year. For tobacco, which is normally carried for considerable periods before being processed, the normal supply was to be 175 per cent of a normal year's domestic consumption plus 65 per cent of a year's exports.

The scale of support prices was to be modified in two directions depending on action taken with respect to acreage allotments and marketing quotas. If acreage allotments were in effect at the beginning of the planting season, or if marketing quotas were in effect at the beginning of the marketing year, the support price for the commodity so controlled was to be 120 per cent of that indicated above but not more than 90 per cent of parity. This meant that, with acreage or marketing controls in effect, the minimum support level would be 72 per cent and the maximum 90 per cent.

If the producers had disapproved a proposed marketing quota for any "basic" commodity for any given year, the level of support for that year was to be 50 per cent of parity. Thus the over-all provision, for price support on "basic" crops, worked out to an absolute floor of 50 per cent and an absolute maximum of 90 per cent, except as some higher percentage might be authorized as incentive for greater production needed from the standpoint of national needs.[47]

Support for "Nonbasic" Crops

For "nonbasic" crops (except wool and Irish potatoes) the levels of support were less definitely specified, but were not to exceed 90 per cent of parity. The Commodity Credit Corporation was directed not to support the price of any nonbasic commodity (except potatoes) "which is so perishable in nature as not to be reasonably storable without excessive loss or excessive cost." The Secretary of Agriculture was, however, authorized to carry out such support operations through other means available to him such as the use

---

46. The representatives of the cotton and tobacco areas were not alone in demanding the full 90 per cent support, but the sentiment for high-level supports tended to center in these areas.

47. Senators Cooper and Barkley of Kentucky had introduced, on June 16, an amendment which provided that the support price for tobacco would be 90 per cent of parity regardless of the flexible features of the act. The amendment was adopted by the close margin of 41 yeas to 40 nays with 15 senators not voting. Aiken opposed this action vigorously, characterizing it as special-privilege legislation and saying it would inevitably be followed by similar demands with respect to other commodities. He remarked somewhat bitterly, "It is very apparent that many Members of the Senate are not in a mood to enact any long-range legislation on this subject." *Congressional Record*, 80th Cong., 2nd sess., Vol. 94, Part 7, June 16, 1948, p. 8557. Senator Lucas, the Democratic minority whip of the Senate, likewise saw the danger of this procedure and called attention, on the following day, to the logic of demanding similar concessions for all the other commodities if the Senators wished to be fair. *Ibid.*, June 17, 1948, p. 8563. Nevertheless, the amendment was retained.

of Section 32 funds and School Lunch funds.[48]

For wool, the Secretary was directed to support the price at a level, not more than 90 per cent nor less than 60 per cent of parity, considered necessary to encourage an annual domestic production of approximately 360 million pounds. For Irish potatoes, the price support for any crop harvested after December 31, 1949 was to be at not less than 60 per cent of parity.[49] This was a downward adjustment, much too long delayed, to prevent continuance of the very wasteful and expensive potato program in which millions of bushels were being bought by the government and destroyed or sold for feed at infinitesimal prices.

It is clear that these provisions, like the change in parity formula, were an attempt to readjust support prices in such a way as to avoid overencouraging the production of commodities which could now be produced cheaply, relative to 1910–1914 standards, or for which demand had fallen off; and to give strong support for those which tended to be in short supply.[50]

THE AGRICULTURAL ACT OF 1949

It was generally assumed for a time after the passage of the Agricultural Act of 1948 that the first steps had been taken in the direction of a new, longer-term approach to the agricultural price-support problem. While the initiation of the new program was to be delayed as a result of the compromise embodied in the Hope-Aiken Act, it was con-

fidently expected that after January 1, 1950 the farm program would be modified in the general direction of more reliance on price in the market as a guide to kinds and amounts of production. It was also assumed that the inadequacies of the old parity formula, which had been becoming more and more apparent, would be partly corrected under the new legislation.

This optimism, on the part of the more conservative groups, was rudely shattered by the outcome of the Presidential and congressional elections in the fall of 1948. Republicans had confidently expected the election of Thomas E. Dewey, their nominee for President, and the continuance of a Republican majority in the Congress. In one of the most striking political upsets on record, the country returned Mr. Truman to the White House and gave the Democrats a majority in both houses of the Congress.[51] This meant new leadership for both the House Committee on Agriculture and the Senate Committee on Agriculture and Forestry. Representative Clifford Hope of Kansas was replaced by Harold D. Cooley of North Carolina, and Senator Capper by Senator Elmer Thomas of Oklahoma, both Southern Democrats and both supporters of high-level price supports for farm products.

The long-term features of the Act of 1948 had reflected, in some measure, the thinking of those who wanted to see a return to a freer economy and less dependence on government. Their position was a somewhat watered-down version of the rather liberal attitude which characterized the hearings before the Colmer Committee, the report of the Land-Grant College Committee and the hearings on the food allotment proposals. It was substantially a resumption of the policy attitudes which had brought about the Act of 1938. The Acts of 1938 and 1948 were the result of much study and extensive hearings. Both took account of economic realities and

48. The Commodity Credit Corporation was not prohibited from supporting the prices of perishable commodities through loans, purchases or payments made on storable commodities processed from them. Furthermore, the Secretary was authorized to use the services of the Corporation in carrying out operations in which Section 32 funds were used or in connection with the National School Lunch program.

49. A full summary of the price programs in effect for 1949 is given in Production and Marketing Administration, *Price Programs of the United States Department of Agriculture, 1949,* Miscellaneous Publication No. 683, March 1949.

50. The flexible support provisions as contained in Title II of the Act of 1948, though enacted, did not actually come into effect. They were replaced or modified by the Act of 1949 before they were scheduled to be put into use.

51. In the new Congress (the 81st) the division was as follows:
Senate — Democrats 54, Republicans 42.
House — Democrats 263, Republicans 171, American Labor 1.

implied a damping down of the more extreme demands on the part of the agricultural groups.

This more moderate program was now to be replaced by additional stopgap legislation, such as that contained in Title I of the Act of 1948, and the bitter controversy over the Brannan Plan was shortly to become a central theme in agricultural policy discussions.

Views Expressed in the Hearings

As a prelude to revision or replacement of the Act of 1948, a subcommittee of the House Committee on Agriculture began to hold hearings on that act and related matters in February and March 1949. On April 7, Secretary of Agriculture Charles F. Brannan appeared before a joint meeting of the House Committee on Agriculture and the Senate Committee on Agriculture and Forestry and presented a preliminary version of a plan, largely drafted by himself, which proposed the use of compensatory payments to farmers to bring the returns to them up to stated levels while permitting the products to move at free-market prices.[52] This meant direct subsidies to agriculture, presumably on the total output of certain crops, and low prices to consumers if production was large enough to result in prices below support levels. Thus it implied subsidy to all consumers along lines similar to those used in World War II. In this, it differed significantly from the Food Allotment Plan which would have subsidized consumption only for low-income families.

The Brannan approach roused immediate and widespread interest but came under vigorous attack, both from proponents of the then existing price-support program and those who favored a change in the general direction implied by the longer-term features of the Act of 1948. The immediate direction taken in congressional hearings and action was not, however, in terms of pro- or anti-Brannan Plan. It was rather an attempt to retain or abandon the long-term features of the Act of 1948.

The Farm Bureau Position

With respect to the Brannan Plan, the major farm organizations, other than the Farmers Union, expressed their opposition in the hearings of late April and early May. The Farmers Union came out strongly for the plan. The other three farm organizations proceeded to present their views on changes needed in the then existing agricultural legislation but accepted, in general, the principal features of the laws then in effect.[53]

Allan Kline, as the spokesman for the American Farm Bureau Federation, recommended that the cotton growers be permitted to vote on marketing quotas whenever the supply is above normal and the price below 90 per cent of parity. If action along these lines should prove inadequate, loans would then be decreased in accordance with the variable schedule provided in the Act of 1948.[54] He further recommended:

1. That it be made mandatory for the Secretary of Agriculture to establish acreage allotments on all basic crops prior to or at the time of announcing marketing quotas,
2. That an adverse referendum vote on a marketing quota not invalidate acreage allotments except in the case of tobacco, and,
3. That an adverse vote on a marketing quota not prevent cooperators in the acreage allotment program from receiving loans at the scheduled rate, but without the 20 per cent premium provided in the Act of 1948.[55]

Kline also proposed that the Commodity Credit Corporation not be allowed to sell any farm commodity at less than a price midway between parity and the level of support, or, if no support is in effect, at less than 90 per cent of parity. He advocated price supports for "nonbasic" agricultural commodities

52. The Brannan Plan is more fully discussed later. See pp. 484–90.

53. A brief summary of the views of the heads of the four major farm organizations as of about this time is given in Association of Land-Grant Colleges and Universities, A Long-Range Agricultural Policy for America, A Panel Discussion, Michigan State College Press, East Lansing, 1950.

54. This was a concession in recognition of the fact that sentiment for marketing quotas was stronger in the South than elsewhere.

55. U.S. Congress, House, Committee on Agriculture, General Farm Program, Hearings before a subcommittee . . . , 81st Cong., 1st sess., Part 3, April and May 1949, Serial R, pp. 438-39.

whenever acreage allotments, marketing quotas or marketing agreements are in effect, provided the cost of such support would not be more than 10 per cent of the estimated value of the crop. His proposal included legislative provision for acreage allotments and/or marketing quotas in respect to the nonbasic crops.

Other recommendations made by Kline were to amend the parity formula so as to include subsidy payments made during World War II for the purpose of holding down prices paid by consumers, to eliminate the requirement that all classes of poultry be supported at the same percentage of parity and to provide for the announcement of acreage allotments and marketing quotas under Title II of the Act of 1948 prior to its effective date, January 1, 1950.[56]

Grange and Coop Council Proposals

The Grange presented a proposal for placing the agricultural program, with its existing framework of legal authorizations, under the guidance of a 24-man board of producers, processors and distributors. This was not seriously considered, and the more detailed recommendations promised for later inclusion in the record were not submitted.

The National Council of Farmer Cooperatives expressed its general concurrence with the provisions of Title II of the Act of 1948 on the grounds that "we believed it provided reasonable security for farmers and at the same time permitted desired progress to take place. We believe that it is highly essential for any farm program to be reasonably flexible in order for these objectives to be realized simultaneously."[57] The Council proposed amendments, however, (1) for the inclusion of hired labor in the cost of things farmers buy; (2) for comparable treatment of all commodities, basic and nonbasic alike; (3) for extending the marketing agreement program to those commodity interests that can use it to advantage; and (4) for more use of voluntary farmer efforts rather than govern-

ment organization in carrying out farm programs. John H. Davis, speaking for the Council, was especially vigorous in condemning the efforts of the Production and Marketing Administration to extend its functions.[58]

Plans Put Forward in the Congress

The Democratic leaders were little impressed by proposals for minor amendments to the Act of 1948, which was looked upon as a Republican program.[59] The initial version of their approach to the farm program was contained in H.R. 5345, introduced by Representative Stephen Pace of Georgia on June 27, 1949.[60] The House Committee on Agriculture reported it back on July 7 with a recommendation that it pass.[61]

The bill, as outlined by the Committee chairman, provided (1) "a new and modernized method for the calculation of parity, to be known as the income-support standard"; (2) continued support of farm prices at about the then existing levels (that is, at the high wartime support levels); and (3) authorization for the Secretary of Agriculture to try out on three commodities the production payment plan which he (Secretary Brannan) had proposed in the April hearings. These were to be nonstorables except that permission was given to include wool.

More important was the fact that the bill would repeal, in toto, Titles II and III of the

58. Since the views of the Farmers Union pertained almost wholly to the Brannan Plan, they are discussed in that connection.

An urban view of the controversy is presented in *Fortune* for July 1949, "Farm Policy: A Great Opportunity," pp. 55–59, 158, 160. Here the position is taken that agriculture is in the best position it has ever been to abandon price supports and get back to a more normal way of functioning.

59. *General Farm Program*, Part 3, pp. 598–99. President Truman had frequently and vigorously denounced the Eightieth Congress as a reactionary Republican-dominated body, particularly in connection with the bitter struggle over passage of the Taft-Hartley Act curtailing the powers of labor unions. This act was passed over his veto in one of the most dramatic legislative battles of recent years.

60. This was in the main a proposal put forward by the Southern Democrat farm bloc which was at that time more or less in control of the House Committee on Agriculture.

61. U.S. Congress, House, Committee on Agriculture, *Agricultural Act of 1949*, H.Rep. 998 to accompany H.R. 5345, 81st Cong., 1st sess., July 7, 1949.

56. *Ibid.*, pp. 439–40.
57. *Ibid.*, p. 597.

Act of 1948, thus eliminating the long-term program so laboriously worked out by the Eightieth Congress. The Committee contended that the flexible price-support provision of the Aiken plan was an attempt to "control through bankruptcy," that production would not be reduced through lower price supports, and that shifts in production could not be brought about in this way.

The bill made price supports mandatory at a full 100 per cent of parity for corn, cotton, wheat, tobacco, rice, peanuts, hogs, milk, butterfat and shorn wool (including mohair). Cottonseed and the Steagall commodities were to be supported at levels not in excess of parity, and the other commodities on a "fair and comparable" basis. The Committee proposals thus went beyond even the high-support levels of the wartime legislation, and, as a corollary, obviously implied rigorous and far-reaching controls on production.

During the debate on the bill, Representative Gore of Tennessee offered an amendment striking out all but the enacting clause of the Pace bill. This was accepted by a vote of 239 to 170 and became the House bill.[62]

In the Senate, Clinton Anderson, former Secretary of Agriculture, introduced S. 2522 on August 31.[63] This was after hearings had been held on S. 1882 and S. 1971, which were the legislative expressions of the Brannan Plan.[64] Anderson's bill classified agricultural commodities into four main groups for purposes of price support. Mandatory price support for the "basic" commodities was to be at 75 to 90 per cent of a modernized parity, depending on supply.[65] Price support on to-

bacco was made mandatory at 90 per cent of parity. Storable nonbasic commodities and milk and butterfat were to be supported at 75 to 90 per cent of parity; shorn wool and Irish potatoes at 60 to 90 per cent, and other nonbasics at not to exceed 90 per cent. Except for the mandatory items, the level of support was to be left to the discretion of the Secretary of Agriculture but with criteria for his guidance somewhat spelled out in the bill. Other features were similar to those of earlier acts and bills, but with minor modifications.

The Anderson bill was objected to, and was returned to the Committee. It was again reported out on October 6, with various minor amendments. The Senate then took up the House bill H.R. 5345 and, as in 1948, substituted S. 2522 (the Anderson bill) for everything after the enacting clause. S. 2522 was then passed but with the title and number of the House bill.

As a result of the ensuing conference, the new bill, which was to become the Agricultural Act of 1949, was brought forward, passed by both houses, and enacted into law by the President's signature on October 31.

Provisions of the Act of 1949[66]

The Agricultural Act of 1949, as it finally emerged, was, in the main, a victory for those who favored high mandatory price supports and was, primarily, a product of the thinking of the Southern Democrat bloc rather than of those whose views were expressed in the proposals made by Secretary Brannan.[67] The Brannan approach was to become important politically at a later date rather than at this time. As of 1949, the struggle was more largely between the Republican group led by Aiken and Hope, and the Southern Democrat group led by Cooley, Pace and Thomas.

The new act retained in principle the flexible price-support feature of the Act of 1948, but so modified as to result in substantially higher levels of support. For tobacco, corn,

62. Passed on July 21.

63. Anderson, who had preceded Brannan as Secretary of Agriculture, was not friendly to the plan proposed by Brannan. His bill was therefore, in effect, a counterproposal to the Brannan Plan.

64. Secretary Brannan had stated that "The farm price support recommendations which I made for the Department on April 7 are embodied in S. 1882 and also in titles I and II of S. 1971." U.S. Congress, Senate, Committee on Agriculture and Forestry, *Agricultural Adjustment Act of 1949*, Hearings before a Subcommittee . . . on S. 1882 and S. 1971, 81st Cong., 1st sess., July 7, 1949, p. 29.

65. The "modernized" parity was to include cost of hired farm labor and was to take account of wartime subsidy payments.

66. 63 Stat. 1051.

67. It was likewise more radical and more rigid than the program put forward by former Secretary Anderson.

wheat and rice, the range of price support specified was from 75 to 90 per cent of parity on supplies ranging from 130 per cent of normal down to 102 per cent.[68] (In the Act of 1948 the range in support price was to be from 60 to 90 per cent with the 60 per cent applying on 130 per cent or more of a "normal" supply and 90 per cent only if the supply was down to 70 per cent of "normal" or less.)

For cotton and peanuts, the range was likewise from 75 to 90 per cent of parity, but with a requirement that support be at 90 per cent if the supply was not more than 108 per cent of "normal" (instead of the 70 per cent provided in the Act of 1948).

Flexibility More Apparent Than Real

The apparent flexibility of support for the commodities listed above was largely negated by Section 101(d) of the act, which provided that, for the 1950 crop, the support level would be specifically 90 per cent of parity if marketing quotas or acreage allotments "are in effect." For the 1951 crop, the comparable level of support was to be 80 per cent of parity.[69] If marketing quotas for any commodity (except tobacco) were disapproved, the price-support level was to be '50 per cent of parity.[70]

68. This provision in respect to tobacco was virtually meaningless since a succeeding section specified that the support level for tobacco was to be 90 per cent of parity if marketing quotas were in effect. Since there was every indication that marketing quotas for tobacco would be continuously in effect, this meant, to all intents and purposes, fixing the support level for tobacco at 90 per cent of parity. The rights to grow tobacco under acreage allotments had come to have such high capitalized values that there was little prospect that growers would vote down marketing quotas. Informed persons estimated in 1946 that tobacco acreage allotments associated with a given farm would increase the sale price of the farm in many cases by as much as $500 to $1,000 per acre (for the acreage having tobacco allotments). Thus the right to grow tobacco had come to have a capitalized value far exceeding that of the land itself. See John E. Mason, "Acreage Allotments and Land Prices," *Journal of Land and Public Utility Economics,* May 1946, pp. 176–81.

69. That is, support prices could not be reduced at all for the 1950 crop and to no less than 80 per cent of parity in 1951. Thereafter, presumably, the standards of the modified "flexible" scale would apply.

70. Tobacco was to be supported at 90 per cent of parity continuously, unless marketing quotas were rejected. In that case there was to be no support.

Certain "designated" nonbasic crops were singled out for specified treatment. Wool (including mohair) was to be supported at a price, between 60 and 90 per cent of parity, designed to encourage an annual production of 360 million pounds of shorn wool. Whole milk and butterfat, and the products thereof, were to be supported at 75 per cent of parity; and tung nuts, honey, and early, intermediate and late potatoes at 60 per cent.[71]

For *storable,* nonbasic commodities (if marketing quotas, marketing agreements or order programs were in effect) price support at 75 to 90 per cent of parity was provided in accordance with the scale established for the basic crops — that is, "supply percentages" ranging from 102 or less for support at 90 per cent of parity to 130 or more for support at 75 per cent of parity. For all other nonbasic commodities, the Secretary was given discretionary authorization to support prices at not more than 90 per cent of parity.

There was an escape provision, Section 401(b), which directed that, with respect to discretionary support of prices for nonbasic crops, the Secretary might maintain support at less than the prescribed minima if, after considering the availability of funds for the mandatory price supports and other factors, he deems that to be "desirable and proper."

The "other" factors to be considered were (1) supply in relation to demand, (2) levels at which other commodities are being supported and, in the case of feed grains, feed values in relation to those of corn, (3) perishability of the commodity, (4) importance of the commodity to agriculture and to the national economy, (5) ability to dispose of stocks acquired through price-support operations, (6) need for offsetting temporary losses of export markets, and (7) ability and willingness of producers to keep supplies in line with demand.

Thus for virtually all commodities except the "basic" crops there was provision for ad-

71. The various price supports in effect for 1950 are given in Production and Marketing Administration, *Price Programs of the United States Department of Agriculture,* Agricultural Information Bulletin No. 13, April 1950.

justing price supports to the realities. But it was in the "basic" crop segment that high mandatory price supports were most likely to give trouble. These were the ones involving large volume and high cost. They were also the ones with fewest alternatives and the greatest tendency to chronic overproduction. Hence, it was in respect to these crops that the political and economic repercussions were most significant.[72]

Other miscellaneous provisions in the act were similar to those of the Act of 1948. Compliance with acreage allotments and marketing quotas could be required as a condition of price support; higher supports could be provided to alleviate shortage of supply; nonrecourse loans might be made; and support prices were to be announced in advance of the beginning of the production season. Also, the customary restrictions on sales of commodities by the Commodity Credit Corporation were included, with the usual exceptions in respect to sales for other than primary uses, to prevent spoilage and so on. These provisions were, in fact, carried over from the Act of 1948 but were couched in slightly different language.

Parity Revision in the Act of 1949

Further modifications of the procedure in computing and using "parity" as a criterion for the support of prices were included in the new act, all of them designed to raise the levels of support prices. Wages paid to hired farm labor were now to be included, along with interest and taxes, in computing the cost of things farmers buy. Prices received by farmers were to include wartime subsidy payments made to keep consumer prices down.

More important than either of these was the purely political and wholly unwarranted

72. While the specified levels of support in the "flexible" schedule of the Act of 1949 were higher than those of the Act of 1948, the difference was more apparent than real since the 1948 Act had provided that the scheduled levels would be increased 20 per cent if acreage allotments and/or marketing quotas were in effect. The major difference was that the 1948 Act placed more emphasis on keeping down supply as a condition of receiving high support prices. Both acts kept the 50 per cent of parity minimum, for basic crops, if marketing quotas were disapproved.

provision that for the ensuing 4-year period the parity price of any basic agricultural commodity could not be less than "its parity price computed in the manner used prior to the enactment of the Agricultural Act of 1949." (The "adjusted base price" provision of the Act of 1948 was contained in Title II and, hence, had not come into use at this time.) Thus for any particular basic commodity, the old formula would apply if it was higher than the new, and, presumably, the new formula would be used wherever it would result in a higher parity price. In effect, however, this meant blocking the readjustment contemplated in the revised parity provisions of the Act of 1948. In the main, the commodities upgraded in parity price by the formula provided in the 1948 Act would have been the animal products, whereas the major field crops would have been downgraded. Since the "basic" crops were by definition the principal field crops, this represented a victory for the cotton, wheat, corn, rice and tobacco growers and a further postponement of the type of readjustment in emphasis contemplated by the Act of 1948.

Other Provisions

The remaining provisions of the Act of 1949 were mainly routine items of definition and implementation. Included, however, was a new section (417) which amended the Farm Credit Act of 1933 so as to permit the Banks for Cooperatives and the Central Bank for Cooperatives to make loans to cooperative associations, up to 80 per cent of the cost, for the construction of facilities for storing agricultural commodities. This authorization applies only if the Commodity Credit Corporation has made commitment to lease, or guarantees utilization of not less than 75 per cent of the space so acquired, for at least three years if independent structures, or two years if they consist of additions to previously existing structures.

The new act, in effect, carried forward the main features of the wartime price guarantees for a more or less indefinite period, though with provision for somewhat higher and more positive support in the earlier years than in the more remote ones. It was a reversion to the point of view which had dominated Congress around 1940, and which, as implemented by the demand for higher and higher support prices in terms of percentage of parity, had resulted in the huge accumulations of stored products of 1941 and 1942 and again was causing apprehension in 1949. It was not a solution for the problem, nor did it constitute a desirable long-term program. Nevertheless, it served to postpone the necessity for positive action pending the outcome of the later struggles over the very controversial Brannan Plan.

THE BRANNAN PLAN

The plan put forward by Secretary of Agriculture Brannan on April 7, 1949 was, in effect, the administration's alternative to both the Aiken program, Titles II and III of the Act of 1948, and the Hope program, Title I of that act.[73]

The Aiken program may be regarded as a product of the Republican-dominated Eightieth Congress and hence unacceptable to the Administration regardless of its merits or demerits. Open and bitter feuding between the executive and legislative branches of the government had marked nearly all stages of the Eightieth Congress deliberations. Title I of the Act of 1948, though sponsored by Chairman Hope of the House Committee, a Republican, was more in line with the thinking of the cotton and tobacco state Democrats than with those of the Republican majority in the Congress. The "Dixiecrat" rebellion of

the Democratic organizations in several of the southern states had, however, created tensions between them and the President which were little if any less marked than those existing between him and the Republican members of the Congress.

Thus the Brannan Plan had from the beginning a different setting from that of any previous program of its type. The early "New Deal" farm legislation was largely a product of the administrative group; but it had been discussed extensively with farm organization leaders, and, in fact, was to some extent claimed by them as their brainchild. Within administration circles it had been the subject of continuing study and consultation by many individuals. Most other program proposals of the preceding decades had come into consideration through introduction as bills in the Congress, often with committee sponsorship based on extensive hearings.

The Brannan Plan had none of this type of backing. It had not been discussed either with farm leaders or congressmen, and apparently only to a limited extent within the Department of Agriculture itself. As a consequence, it had a cool reception in the House and Senate Committees, and tended to be looked upon in many farm circles as a campaign document designed to appeal to the self-interest of both farmer and consumer groups. As a result of this, some of its meritorious features were, for the time being at least, given scant attention while its obvious weaknesses were more widely publicized.

The principal ways in which the plan differed from most of the earlier legislative proposals were the following:

1. The use of an "income standard" as a method of computing price-support levels for farm products.
2. Mandatory support for "Group I" commodities at full "income-parity" levels rather than at some percentage of such level. (Group I consisted mainly of the old "basic" commodities, with eggs, chickens, milk, hogs, beef cattle and lambs added.)[74]
3. A shift to a base period for computing income parity that would consist of the ex-

73. The plan as presented by Secretary Brannan in April 1949, appears in U.S. Congress, House, Committee on Agriculture, *General Farm Program*, Hearings, Part 2, April 7, 11, 12, 25 and 26, 1949, Serial P. Almost innumerable analyses of the plan have been published. Some of the more readily available ones are National Association of Manufacturers, *An Analysis of the Brannan Plan*, Economic Policy Division, Series No. 17, New York, October 1949; John Kerr Rose, *The Brannan Plan*, Library of Congress, Legislative Reference Service, Public Affairs Bulletin No. 78, April 1950; and various short analytical treatments such as Theodore Schultz's "That Turbulent Brannan Plan," *Farm Policy Forum*, February 1950, pp. 5–8; Russell Smith's "The Brannan Plan — Counterattack in Favor," *Antioch Review*, March 1950, pp. 62–73; and Robert H. Estabrook's "The Bogey in the Brannan Plan," *ibid.*, pp. 73–83.

74. But with peanuts and rice omitted.

tremely favorable years between 1939 and 1948, this to be modified year by year by dropping the twelfth year preceding and adding the second preceding year. (This was a period in which the buying power of farm incomes had been at all-time highs and, hence, implied support of farm prices at higher levels than in the then existing legislation or any previously in effect.) The proposed support level worked out to about the same thing as 100 per cent of parity, whereas the wartime and postwar legislation had specified a top of 90 per cent of parity (except for the wartime support of cotton at 95 per cent, and the provisions for exceeding these levels in order to assure adequate supplies).

4. Support for Group II commodities (all of those not included in Group I) at such levels as the Secretary determines will result in fair and equitable treatment of such producers taking into account:
    (a) The supply of the commodity in relation to demand.
    (b) The availability of funds after provision is made for support operations in respect to Group I commodities.
    (c) The perishability of the commodity.
    (d) Its importance to agriculture and the national economy.
    (e) The ability to dispose of stocks acquired through price-supporting activities.
    (f) The need for offsetting temporary losses of export markets, and
    (g) The ability and willingness of producers to keep supplies in line with demand.
5. Price support, especially for perishable commodities, by means of income payments to producers rather than by maintaining prices in the market.
6. A limit on the size of farm operation that would be eligible to receive support for its entire output.

Computing Price Supports: Income Standard

Efforts had been made since the middle 1930's to devise some plan whereby an income criterion could be used instead of a price criterion as a standard of "fair" return to farmers. The tendency after 1940 was to turn more and more toward the relatively definite and easily understood parity price guide. This under the Brannan Plan would have been modified by using comparative farm incomes, in the base period and in the year for which the computation was made, as a means of arriving at the levels at which prices were to be supported.

The base period proposed was to be, initially, 1939–1948. This was to be a moving base in which the earliest year would be dropped off each year and a new one added. Thus in 1951 the base period would be 1940–1949; in 1952 it would be 1941–1950 and so on. The average annual cash receipts from farm marketings for this base period would be the starting point in the computation.

This would be multiplied by a "parity index" which would be a percentage of the average prices paid by farmers for goods and services during the ten-year base period (including interest and taxes). In the illustration presented by the Secretary, the index of prices paid by farmers ranged from 73 in 1939 to 146 in 1948 (average 1939–1948 = 100). Using this method of computation, the average buying power of cash receipts from farming for the ten-year period amounted to $18,218 million.[75]

Examples of Proposed Support Levels

As of March 15, 1949, the prices paid by farmers stood at 144 (1939–1948 = 100). Hence, an equivalent purchasing power for agriculture to that of the base period would require an agricultural income of 1.44 × $18,218 million, or $26,234 million. This would be the parity income standard. The estimated buying power of average cash receipts from

75. That is, if the index of prices paid by farmers in a given year was lower than the ten-year average the base income figure for that year would be increased from the actual cash income received by a corresponding amount. If the index was more than 100, the actual cash income for that year would be reduced accordingly. For example, actual cash income in 1939 was $7,877 million, but prices farmers paid were only 73 (1939–1948 = 100). Consequently, the buying power of farm income for that year would be 100/73 of $7,877 million, or $10,790 million. In 1948, the index of prices paid was 146 per cent of the ten-year average. The actual cash income for that year was $31,019 million. For computation of base period buying power, this would be reduced by taking 100/146 of it, or $21,246 million. See Secretary Brannan's testimony, U.S. Congress, House, Committee on Agriculture, *General Farm Program, Hearings . . .*, Part 2, 81st Cong., 1st sess., April 7, 1949, p. 154.

farm marketings for the ten years 1940–1949 was $20,980 million. The ratio of this figure to the income-support level for 1949 ($26,234 million) was 1 to 1.25. Under the formula proposed, this would mean that each commodity would be supported in 1950 at a level 25 per cent higher than its average price for the ten years 1940–1949.

Taking a few standard commodities, the following figures will illustrate the new support levels as compared with the actual prices for the preceding ten years as presented in the exhibits used in the Secretary's testimony:[76]

	Average Prices Received by Farmers, 1940–1949	Price Support Standard Proposed
Wheat (per bushel)	$ 1.50 x 1.25	$ 1.88
Corn (per bushel)	1.17 x 1.25	1.46
Cotton (pound)	.2239 x 1.25	.2799
Butterfat (pound)	.535 x 1.25	.669
Hogs (hundred-weight)	15.20 x 1.25	19.00
Beef cattle (hundred-weight)	13.50 x 1.25	16.90
Wool (pound)	.398 x 1.25	.498

Thus the relations between the prices of the various commodities would be the same as those reflected in the market place over the preceding ten years, not the relationship that prevailed in 1910–1914 as under the old "parity" formula.[77] These relationships would change slightly from year to year as the base would drop the earliest year and add the most recent one in computing the ten-year average prices.

The 90 per cent of parity standard provided in Title I of the Act of 1948 and later retained in the Act of 1949 was generally recognized as a high level of support — one that would require rigorous controls on acreage and the imposition of marketing quotas if it was to be maintained without involving the

government in huge storage and loan programs that would eventually break down of their own weight. The support prices proposed under the Brannan Plan were at least as high though somewhat differently distributed. For example, wheat under the Brannan Plan would be supported at $1.88 as against $1.95 under the 90 per cent of parity standard; tobacco $.49 as against $.40; butterfat $.70 as against $.58; beef cattle $16.90 as against $12.00 and hogs $19.00 as against $16.10.

The plan thus proposed setting up as a standard the highest income level ever attained by farmers in this or any other country, and forcing prices up to even higher levels than those which had prevailed during the war and postwar years.[78] The adoption of support prices at the levels proposed inevitably meant tightening government controls all along the line, and making agriculture more and more dependent on government. In this, and in various other features as well, the plan implied a reversal of the Aiken philosophy of returning gradually to freer markets and less government control.

Income Payments

A second highly controversial feature of the plan was the proposal that prices of perishable commodities not be supported in the market, but rather that direct government payments be made to farmers in amounts sufficient to make up the difference between the price received in the market and the support level specified by the Secretary. This phase of the plan had much to recommend it if prices were to be maintained at levels higher than those that would result from free-market operations. Quantities put on the market would be sold at prices that would clear the market, thus avoiding the extremely wasteful procedure that was resulting in

76. Ibid., p. 155.

77. It should be noted, however, that the figures presented do not reflect in any realistic way the price relationships that would arise in a free market under more normal conditions. Wheat was overpriced during these years because of a very abnormal foreign demand. Cotton and tobacco prices were held up artificially, and some other prices were held down during the war years, through rationing and price controls.

78. The use of the 1940 decade as a base still further distorted what might be regarded as normal income relationships because of the continuously large agricultural output of these years. Since income is the product of price and quantity, any decline from the high yields of these years would automatically, under the formula, result in still higher support prices.

large-scale purchase and destruction of potatoes in these years, in the effort to maintain
prices at levels far above those needed to
bring forth quantities consumers would take
at the high support prices prescribed in the
law.[79]

However, unless production and marketing
were held under rigorous control the taxpayers would contribute large sums to compensate farmers at support-level prices while
the product moved into consumption at much
lower prices. This meant adopting as a regular procedure approximately the technique
used for holding consumer prices down during World War II. That program had proved
enormously expensive, and had been vigorously opposed by the farm groups, but was
accepted rather complacently by consumers.

It was this feature, however, that was the
Achilles' heel of the plan. With high prices
and no controls on output, enormous requirements for income payments were virtually

inevitable. If these were to be avoided, acreage controls and marketing quotas would
have to be invoked. The result, higher prices
and smaller quantities for consumers and reduced output and possibly smaller incomes
for farmers. While an improvement over the
much-criticized potato program in which the
consumers paid high prices, the taxpayers
paid big subsidies, and a large part of the
crop was destroyed after purchase by the government, the plan still did not provide the
utopian solution of high incomes to farmers,
low prices to consumers and little drain on
the treasury.[80]

Size of Farm Operation

The third feature on which attention centered was the limitation on the size of farm
operation for which income support would
be given. The Secretary proposed that support be given on not more than 1,800 "units"
of product for any one farm. A "unit" was
defined as the equivalent of 10 bushels of
corn, about 8 bushels of wheat or about 50
pounds of cotton. Thus a farm producing,
theoretically, nothing but corn could produce
18,000 bushels and still receive support on all
of it. A wheat farm could produce, under
support, up to 14,400 bushels of wheat, and
a cotton farm up to 90,000 pounds of cotton.
Farms producing more than the equivalents
of these amounts "would not enjoy support
on the excess." The principle was similar to
that of the Domestic Allotment Plan advanced in 1929 and 1930, but with a different
criterion. The Secretary estimated that the
adoption of this principle would exclude
about 2 per cent of the farms of the United
States from full support coverage.

Reactions to the Brannan Plan

With the exception of the Farmers Union,
the major farm organizations expressed immediate and vigorous opposition to Secretary

79. The effort to support the price of potatoes as
required under the Steagall Amendment and, later, under the Acts of 1948 and 1949, had afforded a notorious
example of the wastefulness of such a procedure when
applied to a perishable crop. The net loss to the government on this program from 1943 through 1949
amounted to $417,976,000. In the year 1948 alone, the
cost amounted to $221,921,000. In that year more than
four million tons of potatoes were bought up and turned
to very inferior uses or destroyed. Production and
Marketing Administration, *Irish Potatoes, Price Support
and Related Operations, Commodity Credit Corporation
and Section 32 Funds, January 1, 1943–December 31,
1949*, pp. 27–28. Thus taxpayers, who were largely the
consumers, paid for more than a third of the crop only
to have it thrown away while they continued to pay
high prices in the market for the other two thirds. In
effect, they paid for the excess twice and still didn't get
it. The absurdity of such a procedure soon came to be
widely recognized and sharply criticized, but it was not
until the end of 1948 that the effort to maintain an excessive price support on potatoes was abandoned. (From
1948 on, the mandatory support level was reduced from
90 per cent to 60 per cent of parity. After 1951, price
supports were not to apply unless marketing quotas were
in effect.)

By early 1950, huge quantities of other farm commodities acquired under price-support programs were
clogging storage facilities. These, however, were mostly
storables, and hence did not involve such wasteful measures of decumulation as did potatoes. They included
wheat, dried milk, butter, turkeys, prunes, raisins, etc.
The upsurge in demand that grew out of the Korean
incident enabled the government to liquidate much of
this unwanted surplus. The quickness with which accumulations involving some $4 billion of government
funds came into being even in a period of high demand
indicates a major shortcoming of price support through
purchase and storage.

80. Few attempts have been made to estimate the
probable costs and effects of the Brannan Plan. Probably
the most extensive effort to make quantitative comparisons between it and the Acts of 1948 and 1949 is that
of Dr. George L. Mehren, "Comparative Costs of Agricultural Price Support in 1949," *American Economic
Review*, May 1951, Proceedings Number, pp. 715–46.

Brannan's proposals. Undoubtedly their attitudes were colored to some extent by the fact that this was a plan put forward by the administration without consulting the farm groups or the agricultural representatives in Congress. As Professor Schultz commented:

It has jerked agricultural policy out of the peaceful calm of bi-partisan politics, handled heretofore by the two agricultural committees of Congress. It has shoved farm policy out into the rough and tumble of highly partisan politics.[81]

James G. Patton, President of the Farmers Union, was the first to be heard on the subject. He placed his organization on record as an ardent supporter of the new plan, stressing the special consideration given to family-type farms and commending the proposal to use production payments instead of supporting prices in the market.[82] The Union took the position that, while the Brannan Plan was "a long step in the right direction," it did not go far enough in favoring family-type farming. It presented at this time a proposed bill of its own which, however, was not sufficiently detailed to make clear what was meant by a maximum of 5,000 "family farm production units" which was its substitute for the 1,800-unit maximum suggested by the Secretary.

Farm Bureau Attitude

Allan Kline, speaking for the American Farm Bureau Federation on the following

day, denounced the plan in no uncertain terms. "So far," he contended, "it is a statement of politico-economic philosophy — not a farm program." His principal objections to it were the following:

1. It discards the parity price approach to a fair exchange value for farm commodities. "This concept," he said, "has been the basis for agricultural unity for the last 20 years."
2. It repeals, in effect, the philosophy of fair farm prices in the market place which is contained in the Agricultural Acts of 1938 and 1948.
3. It means government-administered farm prices and farm income, with government control of all land and livestock production.
4. It introduces a cheap food philosophy. It seeks to establish the principle that taxpayers should pay a considerable portion of the grocery bill of consumers.
5. The proposal would place a ceiling on opportunity in agriculture. This in turn would penalize efficiency. Food prices eventually would reflect this inefficiency.
6. The cost of implementing this proposal would be staggering.[83]

Grange Position

The Grange, on the following day, presented its objections, though in less positive form. Grange Master Albert Goss expressed approval of a differentiation of farm commodities in terms of storables and nonstorables as against the old classification into "basics" and "nonbasics." He went on to say, however, that the Grange did not like the subsidy approach.

Basically it is because we prefer a free economy to a controlled economy. . . . We feel that cash subsidies ordinarily involve far greater controls than are wise. To some extent, therefore, it is a matter of degree of control.

We recognize that under cash subsidies more precise adjustment of acreage is possible, and that direct incentives for family-sized farms with penalties for excess commercialization are possible, though subject to evasion. However, we believe these advantages are very strongly offset by disadvantages . . .

Subsidies once accepted are very hard to abandon. They break down that commendable

81. "That Turbulent Brannan Plan," *Farm Policy Forum*, February 1950, p. 5.

82. The Farmers Union had long maintained a close liaison with Secretary Brannan and with the labor organizations, particularly the CIO. Most of the farm organization leaders regarded the Brannan Plan as a product of the leaders of organized labor rather than of the farm groups or of the Congress. For example, Congressman Clifford Hope, the Republican leader for agriculture in the House, placed in the *Congressional Record* one of his radio speeches in which he stated, "I think it should be said in justice to the farmers of this country that the Brannan plan did not originate with them. They were not consulted. They had no part in formulating it. Rather it originated with the political leaders of organized labor." *Congressional Record*, March 14, 1950, Appendix, pp. 1891–92. Secretary Brannan publicized a vigorous denial of this statement. See his press release of August 14, 1950, a letter to the Hon. Clifford R. Hope, dated August 11, and the press release of September 25, consisting of a similar letter addressed to Allan B. Kline on September 23.

83. U.S. Congress, House, Committee on Agriculture, *General Farm Program*, Hearings before a Subcommittee, 81st Cong., 1st sess., April 28, 1949, pp. 440–41.

independence of spirit which is largely responsible for progress that [sic] substitute a dependence on Government which is abhorrent to our strongest traditions. They tend to make beggars of us.

Subsidies would throw agriculture directly into politics. The annual volume would run into the billions, and there would be the constant necessity to besiege Congress to make sure that funds were available for payment. Each year greater uncertainty would rule until Congress acted. The availability of funds, and their extent, would inevitably become campaign issues, and one of the soundness [sic] and most independent segments of our people, instead of thinking in terms of our national welfare, would be compelled, as a matter of self-preservation, to inject purely class considerations in their voting, and many would doubtless vote for the candidates promising the juiciest subsidies. Important issues involving the welfare of the Nation or other groups would be bartered to get bigger and better subsidies or to prevent ruin by farmers who could not live without them. . . .

We do not believe that the Government should furnish food to the public below cost as a means of holding down living costs and the general price level. If this theory is sound, we should start with labor, establishing a low basic wage, with subsidies from the Treasury based on living costs. We advocate no such plan, but it would be far more sound than starting on foodstuffs for two basic reasons:

First, the price of food has not had a corresponding effect on the general price level. When in the twenties we had a long period of very low food prices, the general price level mounted steadily.

Second, . . . the general price level fluctuates in very close conformity to wage rates, rather than to food prices. For this reason, if this method of controlling the price level is to be used, it could be used very much more effectively in connection with wages than food. However, we believe neither is sound.

No subsidy program can be administered equitably.[84]

Cooperative Council Objections

A few days later (on May 10) John H. Davis, speaking for the National Council of Farmer Cooperatives, expressed somewhat similar objections saying:

(a) The program unnecessarily shifts to Government decisions, actions and functions

which farmers can better perform individually or through their cooperative organizations. Its operations would multiply the already large staff of Government employees and still further regiment the lives of individual citizens.

(b) The proposal makes no mention, and ventures no estimate of the cost to the Federal Treasury. The Congress certainly should undertake to obtain a reliable estimate of cost and should weigh that cost and its effect upon the national economy in determining policy.

(c) The proposal contemplates a priority list of commodities to receive 100 percent support prices and a secondary list to receive support to the extent that funds are made available. This is discriminatory. If we are to have general price-support programs, they should be available to all commodities on a comparable basis.

(d) The proposal limits participation to that portion of individual farm production not exceeding a specified limit. This obviously would be difficult if not impossible to administer on an equitable basis. As a practical matter, methods of evasion would be invited and methods of evasion would be found and employed.

(e) Soil conservation and waste avoidance programs should not be combined with price-support programs.[85]

The plan has continued to draw fire from the Farm Bureau, the Grange and the National Council of Farmer Cooperatives, and is vigorously supported by the Farmers Union. The prospect for its enactment, at least in the form in which it was originally presented, appears to have become less as the controversies of 1949 have receded into the background.

Some features of the philosophy embodied in the plan may come under further consideration as the agricultural legislation is reviewed from time to time. If that occurs, discussion almost certainly will not be in terms of the Brannan Plan as a whole but rather of certain features of it. Many who are sharply critical of the high support prices advocated by Secretary Brannan, and of the drastic controls on production that were implied, are not

84. *Ibid.*, April 30, 1949, pp. 533–34.

85. *Ibid.*, p. 602.

unfriendly to some use of the compensatory payment feature of the plan. Others are strongly opposed to compensatory payments but friendly to high levels of price support. Still others oppose both features and favor more general types of antidepression action.

So long as the Congress is dominated by the Republican party it obviously will turn thumbs down on anything closely resembling the Brannan Plan. If the Democrats should regain control in the near future, they will no doubt give the proposal more friendly consideration, but the prospect of a sufficiently favorable attitude to bring about its enactment into law does not appear bright, even in a Congress controlled by the Democrats. It seems evident, however, that various proposed revisions of farm price support legislation will be actively debated, at least for many years to come.

CHAPTER 19

CHANGES IN LONG-TERM POLICY

ATTEMPTS TO ROUND OUT THE FARM PROGRAM

DURING THE LAST YEARS of the war, and those immediately following, there was much discussion of the features desired in a broadly conceived, well-rounded farm program. This was particularly evident in the Report of the Postwar Policy Committee of the Association of Land-Grant Colleges and Universities and in the hearings on long-range agricultural policy conducted by the agriculture committees of the Congress and the Colmer Committee. The growing emphasis on price policy after 1946 pushed into the background most of the policy issues that did not relate specifically to price maintenance or inflation control. However, there was continuing discussion of other agricultural problems, and a number of actions were taken that had important longer-term implications.

An attempt was made to establish a more carefully considered and better implemented policy of aid to low-income farmers. Minor changes also were made or considered in the legislation pertaining to the more conventional farm credit agencies. There was continuing interest in crop insurance as a means of lessening the hazards of farming. Research in the field of marketing farm products was given added stimulus and funds. Further efforts were made to resolve the controversies relating to the administration of the government's soil conservation activities.

In addition, several of the more general laws and policy decisions of this period contained agricultural features or were of interest to farmers. The broadening of coverage under the social security system affected farm employers and some farm wage workers directly, and nearly all farm people in its implications as to future policy. The Geneva and Torquay tariff conferences and the renewal of the International Wheat Agreement were of interest to farmers, though not so much so as if their price and income position had been less strong. The new legislation in respect to aid for housing improvement likewise contained possibilities of what may eventually prove to be significant changes in the content of farm life and ways of modifying it.

A number of the actions taken would undoubtedly have given rise to much wider discussion in the farm areas had it not been for the intense interest in the price problem and the dangers of deflation or inflation. The direction taken in some of the more general legislation may in the long run prove to be more significant in the agriculture of the future than such hotly discussed proposals as the Brannan Plan and other features of the price-support legislation then under consideration.

Growing Interest in Low-Income Groups

The activities of the Resettlement Administration and its successor, the Farm Security Administration, had been under attack from right-wing farm groups almost from the time these agencies began operation. Their unorthodox approaches, the emphasis on paternalism and their "soft-credit" policies ran sharply counter to attitudes strongly imbedded in the thinking of a large portion of the farm population. Nevertheless, the programs initiated by these agencies aroused widespread interest and brought into being a more considered effort to deal with the problems posed by this large group of chronically poverty-stricken farm people. The major farm programs undertaken in the 1930's and the 1940's touched them only slightly. It became increasingly clear that if their condition was to be bettered materially something different would be required than the price-support and conservation programs that were the heart of the farm relief measures designed to aid commercial farmers.

These low-income groups in agriculture were in that category for many different reasons. Some were potentially able farmers handicapped by inadequate land resources, insufficient capital or lack of education and know-how. Some were farmers who had lost their farms during the depression. Others were, of course, elderly people or individuals who found some type of subsistence farming the best escape from a fast-moving world in which they did not feel able to compete.

In some cases whole areas had been by-passed and had retained the methods, resources and living standards of an earlier age. In addition, the large group of hired farm workers, especially the migrants, had long constituted a major sore spot in the social structure of the nation.

Farm Security Administration's Program

The Farm Security Administration's program, aside from its tenant-purchase feature, was designed to improve the lot of these groups but had given rise to much criticism in the Congress and from some of the farm organizations. It included loans, grants-in-aid, supervision, camps for migrants and efforts to develop cooperative farms on a fairly large scale. The cooperative farms in particular came in for vigorous denunciation as being communistic and foreign in their origins.

Despite earnest efforts to make the various programs work, some of them showed early evidence of internal weakness, even had there been no vigorous criticism from outside. This was particularly true of the cooperative farming ventures. The pioneer period in American agriculture, so recently terminated, had left a strong tradition of individualism which in some areas was possibly even stronger in the thinking of these low-income, subsistence-type farmers than in that of their more sophisticated counterparts in the commercial farming areas. Many of them were not recep-

tive to a highly paternalistic, group approach. They placed a high value on independence and were reluctant to make the kinds of adjustment in their ways of life that were essential if cooperative farms were to succeed. Other features of the program were looked upon by many farmers and congressmen as unwarranted coddling of ne'er-do-wells.

Furthermore, the recruiting of personnel to handle this difficult and exacting task was far from easy. By its very nature, the undertaking appealed more strongly to the reform-minded, rather emotional types of workers than to the hard-headed business types. The result was a somewhat spotty performance, with notable work being done in some areas and much less effective accomplishment in others, and a considerable admixture of "practical" and "impractical" projects.

Congressional Investigation of 1943-1944

Mounting criticism of the program led to a full-scale congressional investigation of the agency in 1943. This was marked by unusually bitter and hostile cross-examination of Farm Security Administration witnesses, particularly of C. B. Baldwin, the Administrator.[1]

The outcome of the investigation was a highly critical report on parts of the program.[2] Baldwin resigned in September 1943,

1. The inadequate official reports of the organization were another source of dissatisfaction on the part of the Congress and the public. Large amounts of public funds were being expended on an unfamiliar type of activity, yet little in the way of detailed accounting for them appeared in print. Much of this information was brought out in a hostile atmosphere during the hearings.

2. U.S. Congress, House, Committee on Agriculture, *Activities of the Farm Security Administration,* Report of the Select Committee, H.Rep. 1430, 78th Cong., 2nd sess., May 6, 1944.
Among the Committee's criticisms were the following: ". . . beginning with the administration of Rexford G. Tugwell and continuing throughout the administration of C. B. Baldwin, the Farm Security Administration was financing communistic resettlement projects, where the families could never own homes or be paid for all that they made or for all the time they worked, and was supervising its borrowers to the extent of telling the borrower how to raise his children, how to plan his home life and, it is strongly suspected in some cases, how to vote." (*Ibid.,* p. 2.)
"The Farm Security Administration has flagrantly abused the discretion vested in it by the various acts appropriating funds for loans and grants for the rehabilitation of needy farmers." (*Ibid.,* p. 9.) "Grants have

and was replaced by Frank Hancock in November of that year. The investigation dragged on until May 1944, but the Committee specifically excluded Hancock's administration in its critical comments about the agency. The Committee's report recommended abolition of the FSA and transfer of such parts of its program as met with congressional approval to the Farmers' Home Corporation. (Provision had been made for

also been made to correct administrative errors in judgment by Farm Security Administration personnel, such as errors in farm planning and construction costs of buildings and facilities." (*Loc. cit.*) The FSA, "instead of liquidating resettlement projects, created and financed additional projects in exactly the same manner but by different names, such as relocation projects, land-purchasing associations, land-leasing associations, land-development projects, and cooperative-farm projects, all of which projects and associations were created and financed in violation of law." (*Ibid.*, p. 11.)

"The cooperative or communal farm projects which were created, financed, and operated by the Farm Security Administration have all been dismal failures. They followed the Russian pattern of collective farming. . . . The experiment has been disappointing and expensive and was conducted in violation of the traditional land policies of America." (*Ibid.*, p. 12.)

The Committee did, however, express its approval of certain of the more orthodox features of the program in the following language: ". . . that part of the Farm Security Administration program which made it possible for low-income farmers to borrow reasonable amounts of money at fair interest rates and on fair terms, when such funds are not available from private or cooperative sources, has the full support of the select committee"; and that part of the FSA "which makes it possible for these low-income farmers to raise better crops, get more for what they sell, save on what they buy, and for their wives to learn more about canning and saving food and caring for the health of their children is worthy of consideration." (*Ibid.*, pp. 2–3.)

"Another valuable part of the Farm Security Administration program has been the making of loans to enable tenants, sharecroppers, and even farm laborers, to buy and keep farm homes of their own. The select committee wants to see the tenant-purchase plan expanded in order that more good farmers will have an opportunity to buy farm homes." (*Ibid.*, p. 3.)

". . . This assistance reduces the demands for private and national relief. It adds to the total wealth and revenue of the country by increasing the per capita income and resources of the farmers. It makes for a better citizenry and, therefore, for law and order." (*Ibid.*, p. 22.)

In the Agricultural Appropriations Act of 1944, the Congress directed that no new loans were to be made for the establishment of cooperative associations. The Farm Security Administration continued to advise and supervise the associations already in existence but proceeded with liquidation of the rural resettlement projects. By the end of June 1946, 8,500 out of 9,520 units in the 152 resettlement projects had been sold to private owners, and 207 units had been transferred to other agencies. Farm Security Administration, *Postwar Developments in Farm Security, Annual Report . . . for 1945–46*, p. 17.

that Corporation under the Bankhead-Jones Farm Tenant Act of 1937,[3] but it had ceased to function.) The Committee drafted a bill embodying its recommendations which was introduced in 1944 as H.R. 4384 and later, in revised form, as H.R. 4876.[4] The new legislation did not pass at that time, but constituted the groundwork of the Farmers' Home Administration Act of 1946.

Farmers Home Administration Act

The Farmers Home Administration Act of 1946, approved on August 14,[5] abolished the Farm Security Administration and provided for liquidating all labor supply centers, labor homes, labor camps, and resettlement and rural rehabilitation projects set up for rehabilitation purposes.[6] The act also ordered the liquidation of the land-leasing and land-purchasing associations and all corporations or associations organized for similar purposes with funds made available in whole or in part to the Secretary of Agriculture, the War Food Administrator, the Farm Security Administration, the Resettlement Administration or the Federal Emergency Relief Administration. The making of new loans for

3. 50 Stat. 522, approved July 22, 1937.
4. Reported out favorably by the House Committee on Agriculture on June 23, 1944, *The Farmers' Home Corporation Act of 1944*, H.Rep. 1747, 78th Cong., 2nd sess.
5. 60 Stat. 1062.
6. The labor camps and supply centers were set up in the late 1930's, mostly in the West. They were for the purpose of providing temporary shelter for homeless agricultural migrants. They occupied a somewhat anomalous position in that they became small isolated communities under federal administration though located within the states. Farm employer groups were unfriendly to them almost from the beginning, regarding them as hotbeds of radicalism or havens for loafers. Some provision of minimum shelter for migrants from the dust-bowl areas obviously was needed, but distrust of the management policies on the part of the farm groups led to friction and criticism. The cooperative farming ventures, which presumably were to be permanent, resulted in even more uneasiness. The camp program could not provide a satisfactory long-term solution of the problem and no mutually satisfactory plan was put forward either by the farm groups or the government agencies. Farmer opposition became less evident as the dust-bowl and depression migrants were gradually absorbed in the reviving economies of the receiving states, but congressional criticism, especially of the efforts to develop cooperative farming, was particularly vigorous following the investigation of 1943 and 1944.

carrying on any collective or cooperative farming operation was prohibited.

Provision was made under the new act whereby loans of the rehabilitation type could be made. These were to be limited to an initial amount of $3,500 and could not thereafter be increased beyond a total obligation of $5,000, including accrued obligations for interest, taxes and other liens. The term of such loans was limited to five years.

The new act also continued the tenant-purchase program initiated in the Bankhead-Jones Act of 1937, and made provision for an insurance fund similar to that of the National Housing Act for loans on urban homes.[7] One half of one per cent of the principal amount outstanding was to be paid into the insurance fund to cover losses, and one half of one per cent was to be available for administrative expenses in connection with the mortgage insurance program. The total charge to the borrower for interest, insurance and administration was to be 3½ per cent.[8]

The mortgage insurance feature was designed to make these mortgages acceptable as private investments and thus to enlarge the funds available for tenant-purchase loans. The principal amount that could be so insured in any one year was limited to $100 million and, in addition, a direct appropriation of $50 million for tenant-purchase loans was made for each succeeding year of operation. Insured loans were limited to 90 per cent of the average value of efficiently operated family-type farms in the area in which the loan was made, and might run for periods up to forty years.

The new act, in essence, retained the more orthodox and conservative features of the old Farm Security and Tenant-Purchase programs, but prohibited ventures into collective or cooperative farming, eliminated the farm labor camp program and spelled out more carefully than the earlier legislation had done various limitations on the decisions of administrators of the program.

Other Changes in Farm Credit Policy

Few other changes in farm credit organization and policy were made in the war and immediate postwar years. The most important modification was contained in an Act of June 30, 1945. This increased the maximum loan that could be made by the federal land banks from 50 per cent of the value of land plus 20 per cent of the value of buildings to 65 per cent of the normal agricultural value of the farm.[9] Several of the land banks had long urged authorization for making loans at higher percentages of value as a means of satisfying borrowers and meeting competition from private lending agencies. The Act of 1945 was a concession to that demand though it did not wholly satisfy some of the land bank officials.

Steps also were taken looking to the liquidation of the Federal Farm Mortgage Corporation, which had been the source of funds for the second mortgage and other loans made by the Land Bank Commissioner. The effective termination of the power to make new Commissioner loans was extended from July 1, 1946 to July 1, 1947, but the Farm Credit Administration was directed to "make a thorough study of ways and means of making available to the farmers through the Federal Land Bank System loans similar to those now made by the Land Bank Commissioner through the Federal Farm Mortgage Corporation."[10] This was a recognition of the demand for more liberal arrangements than those available through the federal land banks, but an indication of a desire to get away from the type of loan made directly by the government.[11]

7. For a fuller discussion of developments under the tenant-purchase program, see Edward C. Banfield, "Ten Years of the Farm Tenant Purchase Program," *Journal of Farm Economics,* August 1949, pp. 469–86.

8. An amendment adopted on June 19, 1948 raised the base rate to 3 per cent and the gross charge to 4 per cent. It also made provision whereby the Secretary might, under specified conditions, take over insured mortgages from the mortgagees, thus making such mortgage loans more liquid and hence more attractive to investors.

9. 59 Stat. 265.

10. 60 Stat. 532.

11. This was not an active period so far as farm credit matters were concerned. Farmers were in strong financial position, and for some years had been reducing the over-all volume of mortgage debt. There was, how-

Continuing Interest in Crop Insurance

Though the experience with crop insurance from 1938 through 1943 had been disappointing, the Congress continued to concern itself with protection against weather hazards. Because of a series of relatively favorable crop years, farmer interest was less evident than it had been during the 1930's. Nevertheless, even in years of relatively good crops there were always some areas that suffered serious losses from droughts or other natural hazards.

In December 1944, the Federal Crop Insurance Act was reactivated through an amendment to the original act.[12] Beginning with the crop of 1945, insurance on cotton, wheat and flax was authorized, and provision was made for trial insurance on a number of other crops.[13]

In 1945, insurance was offered on spring-planted crops of wheat, cotton and flax on a

nationwide basis, and for corn and tobacco on a trial basis. A new amendment required that insurance not be written in a given county unless there were at least 50 applications. Indemnities for that year exceeded premiums by $38 million and administrative expenses amounted to $32 million making a loss for the year of $70 million. Here, for the first time in its history, the Corporation showed premiums in excess of the indemnities for wheat, flax and tobacco, but these gains were more than wiped out by the losses on cotton.[14]

The 1946 operations covered the same five crops as those of 1945, with corn and tobacco still on a trial basis. By an amendment of August 1, 1947, the entire program was put on an experimental basis.[15] For the 1948 crop year, insurance on wheat was limited to 200 counties, cotton to 56 counties, corn and flax to 50 counties and tobacco to 35. Minimum participation in a county was raised from 50 farms to 200.[16] There was also an effort to encourage private companies to re-enter the field on the basis of reinsurance by the Federal Crop Insurance Corporation, but this did not prove attractive to them. Wheat grower participation in 1947 amounted to 29 per cent of all wheat farms as against 24 per cent in 1946. Premium reserves were being built up, with only 44 per cent of premiums required to meet indemnities in 1945 and 58 per cent in 1946. Flax indemnities amounted to 106 per cent of premiums, cotton 345 per cent and tobacco around 50 per cent. Corn showed a slight loss because of the heavy payments in 1945.[17]

The year 1948 was marked by a transition from national coverage to operation on a limited basis and various types of experimentation, including trials of multiple crop coverage on individual farms. During 1949,

ever, considerable discussion of the organization and functioning of the Farm Credit Administration. Committees of land-bank presidents, district agents and academic groups were invited to participate in these deliberations. Most of the committee reports are not in published form, but something of the scope and character of the studies may be gained from such presentations as "The Federally Sponsored Credit Services to American Agriculture, Suggestions for Improvement and Coordination, A Report by a Research Committee," *Journal of Farm Economics,* November 1947, Proceedings Number, pp. 1429-1502; an article by Earl L. Butz, "Postwar Agricultural Credit Problems and Suggested Adjustments," *ibid.,* May 1945, pp. 281-96, and a succeeding article by John D. Black, "Agricultural Credit Policy in the United States, 1945," *ibid.,* August 1947, pp. 591-614. There was a growing interest in the use of credit to facilitate and encourage conservation activities and farm reorganization. See, for example, Darryl R. Francis, *Bank Credit for Soil Conservation,* Federal Reserve Bank of St. Louis, October 1945; and a report by a special committee set up by the Farm Credit Administration, *A Suggested Plan of Organization for a Forest Credit System for the United States,* Kansas City, Missouri, September 28, 1945, mimeographed.

There was, likewise, some agitation for permanent legislation along the lines of the Frazier-Lemke Amendment of 1935. This had been renewed in 1938, 1940, 1944 and 1946, but thereafter was allowed to lapse. The need for special bankruptcy arrangements was not urgent and no large-scale support for permanent legislation became evident. The Farmers Home Administration Act contained a brief provision (Section 22) authorizing the Secretary of Agriculture to assist in the voluntary adjustment of indebtedness between farm debtors and their creditors.

12. 58 Stat. 918.

13. Limited to corn and tobacco for the year 1945, and not more than three crops could be added each year thereafter. Trial insurance for each crop was limited to 20 counties and to three years.

14. Production and Marketing Administration, *Report of the Manager of the Federal Crop Insurance Corporation, 1946,* September 20, 1946, introductory statement.

15. 61 Stat. 718.

16. Or one third of the farms normally producing the agricultural commodity, whichever is smaller.

17. *Report of the Manager of the Federal Crop Insurance Corporation, 1947,* September 25, 1947, pp. 12, 19, 25, 30.

insurance was offered in 199 counties for wheat, 52 for cotton, 48 for flax, 44 for corn, 35 for tobacco, 9 for dry edible beans and 7 for multiple crop coverage.[18] In an amendment of August 25 of that year,[19] provision was made for gradual expansion of the program over a period of four years. At this time, a beginning was made in incorporating into the premiums the actual loss experience of the county concerned, thus initiating differential premiums based on the indemnity record. The 1949 operations in wheat showed a loss for the first time after 1945, and accounted for a loss in the over-all operations.[20]

Multiple crop insurance was expanded to 55 counties in 1950 with a total of 27 crops insured. In all, 307,257 farmers were covered by federal crop insurance.[21]

The Federal Crop Insurance Corporation is feeling its way in a realm where actuarial data and administrative procedures are still tentative. This experimental approach appears to offer greater prospect of eventual success than would a nationwide approach with its potentially heavy losses.[22] There are indications, however, that crop insurance is gradually emerging as one of the more settled features of American farm policy. To some extent the risk has been carried by government for many years, through frequent appropriations for drought and disaster relief, but without requirement of the payment of premiums by growers. Much more experimentation will be needed before conclusive evidence is available as to whether, in view of the high administrative costs involved, it is cheaper to maintain a complex insurance program or to meet major disasters through direct appropriation of relief funds.

18. Federal Crop Insurance Corporation, *Report to Congress, 1949*, p. 1.

19. 63 Stat. 663.

20. FCIC, *Report to Congress, 1949*, pp. 5–6.

21. *Ibid., 1950*, pp. 3, 5. See also U.S. General Accounting Office, *Report on Audit of Federal Crop Insurance Corporation*, H.Doc. 45, 82nd Cong., 1st sess., January 16, 1951.

22. The nature of the problem presented in providing crop insurance is well discussed in Harold G. Halcrow, "Actuarial Structures for Crop Insurance," *Journal of Farm Economics*, August 1949, pp. 418–43.

Research and Marketing Act of 1946

In the years just following the war, the concern over possible reappearance of surplus production and low prices resulted in a revival of interest in an accelerated research program — one that would be especially oriented to improvements in marketing, the development of new uses for farm products and the strengthening of educational work in marketing.

This interest brought about passage of the Agricultural Research and Marketing Act of 1946.[23] The new act authorized very generous support for study of the economic aspects of agriculture, particularly in respect to marketing. If fully implemented by appropriations, it was to provide, by the end of a five-year transition period, some $61 million of additional support for agricultural research. This would more than double the research funds that were being provided to the state agricultural experiment stations and the United States Department of Agriculture from all sources at the time the act was passed.

If the problem facing agriculture was to be of the type then visualized, the primary need was for rather fundamental readjustments. At that time, however, the thinking in Congress, and on the part of many farm leaders, centered on its more superficial aspects, namely, finding better methods of selling and uncovering new uses for whatever amounts might be produced. There were other new kinds of emphasis in the act such as more specific provision for bringing farm organization and trade representatives into the planning of research, more regional cooperation, participation by state agencies other than the experiment stations and contract projects assigned to private research agencies.

While the time was obviously ripe for further emphasis on studies of the economic and social aspects of agriculture, there can be little doubt that the new act was somewhat overbalanced in the direction of studies spe-

23. 60 Stat. 1082, approved August 14, 1946.

cifically in the field of marketing, unless that term was to be very broadly interpreted.

The tendency in the early years of the program has been to use an undue amount of funds and personnel on somewhat trivial projects. The language of the act is sufficiently broad, however, to warrant belief that a more balanced and fundamental research program will eventually be developed. While the amounts authorized are large indeed, and imply a faster rate of expansion than the availability of qualified personnel makes feasible, the Congress has moved somewhat cautiously by appropriating smaller sums than those authorized. Furthermore, the general rise in costs and salary scales has offset much of the increase in funds available for research activity.[24]

Organization for Soil Conservation

During the years just following the war, much thought was given to adjusting the numerous conflicts and duplications that characterized the conservation program. At least half a dozen agencies were directly concerned with this problem, and each approached it in a different way. The most specific conflict of interest and technique appeared in the relations between the Soil Conservation Service and the Production and Marketing Administration, but there were important differences of interest on the part of the Forest Service, the Department of Interior, the Tennessee Valley Authority and the land-grant colleges.

Various attempts had been made to solve this problem. In 1937, an Office of Land-Use Coordination had been set up in the Department of Agriculture, the Mount Weather Agreement with the land-grant colleges had been entered into in July 1938, and in October of that year Secretary Wallace had established an Agricultural Program Board and a set of interbureau coordinating committees. Nevertheless, the problem had not been solved. It was pushed into the background

24. For a popularized analysis of the act, see the special report of the Agriculture Committee of the National Planning Association, *The Agricultural Research and Marketing Act of 1946, A Consideration of Basic Objectives and Procedures,* Washington, April 1948.

during the war years, but again came under active consideration as soon as the war was over. Several bills were introduced and extensive hearings were held. The principal legislative proposals prior to 1948 were:

1. The Hill-Cooley bill (H.R. 4150, 80th Cong., 1st sess., July 1947). This would have transferred the educational, demonstrational and technical services of the Soil Conservation Service to the federal and state agricultural extension services, and the research functions to the state agricultural experiment stations.
2. The Jensen bill (H.R. 4417, July 1947). This would have transferred to the Soil Conservation Service virtually all of the land use, soils and related activities in the Department of Agriculture.
3. The National Soil Fertility bill (S. 1251, May 1947). This would have extended the TVA type of test demonstrations to all counties of the United States, these to be under the direction of the agricultural extension services and national and state committees.
4. The Murray bill (S. 555, 79th Cong., 1st sess., February 1945) and other bills designed to set up valley authorities along the lines of TVA or the Columbia Basin project.

The Hope and Aiken bills, introduced in the spring of 1948, were more comprehensive than any of these but were not included in the Agricultural Act of that year as finally passed. The Hope bill (H.R. 6054, 80th Cong., 2nd sess.) followed approximately the lines of the Jensen bill and implied strong centralization of these activities in the Department of Agriculture. The Aiken bill looked in the opposite direction, namely, toward much more decentralization and heavy reliance on county executive committees chosen from the county councils.

The Department of Agriculture itself had also made recommendations for improving the coordination of the various agricultural activities of the Department, through assigning this responsibility to an Assistant Secretary of Agriculture and establishing direct lines of authority down to the county level. A special committee of the Land-Grant College Association proposed, in the spring of

1948, an opposite approach which involved turning over to the state extension services the work then handled by the Soil Conservation Service and breaking up into 48 state administrations the work of the Production and Marketing Administration, insofar as it related to conservation payments, administration of crop controls and so on. This was a reversion to the general plan contemplated in the Soil Conservation and Domestic Allotment Act of 1936, which was abandoned in the Agricultural Adjustment Act of 1938.[25]

The Hoover Commission on the Executive Branch of the Government, in its report of February 1949, pointed in the direction of centralized authority with state and county committees acting in an advisory capacity only. All major soil, range and forest conservation agencies were to be brought into an Agricultural Resources Conservation Service, and coordination at the state and local levels was to be improved.[26]

A further effort to arrive at a solution was made during 1948 through a committee established jointly by the Secretary of Agriculture and the Land-Grant College Association, but the results again proved inconclusive. The problem has continued to be a matter of active interest in the Congress, though overshadowed by the controversies in regard to price-support legislation. Three bills introduced in the spring of 1951 all sought to implement essentially the same general idea, namely, the creation of two additional assistant secretaryships in the Department of Agriculture, and the combining of the conservation activities into an administrative unit dealing with agricultural resources conservation.[27] As of this writing, no action has been taken on them, and the problem of coordinating federal, state and local soil conservation activities still remains unsolved.

Improvement of Rural Housing

The low quality of much of the housing on American farms has long been a notable weakness in the level of farm family living. This defect results from a variety of complex conditions and motivations — the tendency to translate higher farm incomes into higher valuations on land, the prevalence of tenant farming on short-term and poorly formulated rental arrangements, the long period of agricultural depression between 1920 and 1940 and the lack of cultural standards that would require more adequate types of housing. Coupled with these was the fact that customary loan arrangements were related to the farm as a whole and placed primary emphasis on cash earning power rather than on non-cash forms of income such as better housing.

To some extent, farm housing had deteriorated as compared to that of earlier times. It was customary in New England, in the Middle Atlantic states and in the dairy sections of the North Central states to have a fairly large portion of the farm investment in the form of superior housing. This tendency was strengthened by the prevalence of owner operation in these areas and the availability and cheapness of building materials and skilled labor.

For many other areas and regions, though with notable exceptions, these conditions and incentives had not been present. Particularly in the South, the long period of agricultural poverty that followed the Civil War had resulted in the widespread prevalence of substandard farm housing. The war-engendered prosperity of American agriculture provided an almost unprecedented opportunity for improving housing on American farms. Nevertheless, the higher incomes flowing into the hands of farmers were all too likely to be reflected in higher bids for more land rather than in improved farm living conditions.

Title V of the Housing Act of 1949[28] made

25. For an excellent and brief analysis of this problem and the various legislative proposals up to 1950, see John D. Black, *Federal-State-Local Relations in Agriculture,* Planning Pamphlets No. 70, National Planning Association, Washington, February 1950.
26. Commission on Organization of the Executive Branch of the Government, *Department of Agriculture, A Report to the Congress,* February 1949.
27. S. 1149 by Aiken and others, March 15, 1951.
H.R. 3308 by Hoffman of Michigan, March 19, 1951.
H.R. 3684 by Dawson of Illinois, April 12, 1951.
28. 60 Stat. 413 at 432, approved July 15, 1949.

provision for a significant though modest and somewhat experimental approach to this problem.[29] This phase of the housing program was placed under the direction of the Secretary of Agriculture. A major portion of it was to consist of educational work stressing appropriate types of construction, design, materials and so on. In addition, provision was made for technical aid in the planning and supervision of repairs, improvements and new construction. This, together with a program of research on these and related problems, was to be the main approach to the improvement of farm housing where the owner's status warranted action without special financial aid.

There were precedents for such a procedure, especially in the activities of the soil conservation districts of the Soil Conservation Service, which had been notably successful. Less widely known and much more local in application was the Norris-Doxey program in forestry for providing technical aid to the owners and managers of small forest holdings and farm woodlots.[30]

The new act authorized, in addition, special types of credit aid and grants for restricted groups in need of financial assistance. These are to be administered by the Farmers Home Administration and are designed particularly for improving the housing of underprivileged groups.

The program is for the long term and will not get under way rapidly. Much research is needed as a basis for sound recommendations and as a means of utilizing to best advantage the resources existing in rural areas. Designs better suited to rural settings are needed, and the problem of finding ways of making skilled craftsmen available in rural communities has not been solved. While the initiation of such a program will undoubtedly be slow,

cautious and experimental, it contains possibilities of an eventual modification of farm attitudes and living conditions which may be as striking as the change in attitude on conservation which has occurred in recent years.

Old-Age Insurance for Farm Workers

Farm wageworkers, household workers, and the employees of charitable and other nonprofit agencies were the principal groups omitted from coverage in the Social Security Act of 1937. Throughout the intervening years, especially from 1940 on, there had been much discussion of the need for such protection, especially on the part of farm workers and domestic help. There was growing support for the inclusion of these workers under old-age and survivors insurance, but strong opposition to bringing them under unemployment insurance. The marked decline in interest rates on savings, and the sharp rise in prices from 1940 on, reduced the buying power of the interest return on savings to a third or less of what it had been before 1930.

Most employed workers, even those in the middle income groups, thus found it increasingly difficult to accumulate savings that would support them in old age.[31] For low-income workers, such as those on farms and in homes, such provision against want in their later years was recognized as virtually impossible.

The provision of old-age and survivors insurance did not appear to present major administrative problems. For unemployment insurance, the obstacles were much greater. Many farm workers migrate from job to job and customarily have rather long periods of unemployment. Both the definition of unemployment and the administration of an unemployment insurance program present grave difficulties. Costs would inevitably be higher in agriculture than in most other occu-

29. For an analysis of the significance and provisions of the act, see Roy J. Burroughs, "Significance to Farmers of Housing Act of 1949," Bureau of Agricultural Economics, *Agricultural Finance Review*, November 1949, pp. 33–45.

30. For a discussion of this see Ralph F. Wilcox, "Intensive Forestry Projects Under the Provisions of the Cooperative Farm Forestry Act," *Journal of Forestry*, June 1940, pp. 457–64.

31. During the late 1940's, there was widespread pressure from labor unions for the provision of private retirement income in addition to that accruing under the Federal Old-Age Insurance system. Many unions succeeded in getting such benefits written into their contracts, thus giving them a still greater advantage over farm workers and other groups not covered by either type of insurance.

pations and the question of rates to be paid by employers where many workers shift into and out of agriculture from other industries introduces added complications.

The social security legislation was revised and broadened in the Social Security Act Amendments of August 1950.[32] The change of particular significance to agriculture was the provision whereby part of the agricultural wageworkers were brought into the old-age and survivors insurance system.[33] This was not a full-scale extension of the program to agriculture. The provision was that, effective January 1, 1951, tax collections would be made on remuneration paid in any quarter on a full-time basis for sixty days if the quarter immediately preceding was a qualifying quarter.[34] This meant that an employee working continuously on one farm for less than approximately six months would not become "covered" in the sense of the act. Thus most seasonal and migratory workers were omitted from coverage.[35]

INTERNATIONAL ASPECTS OF FARM POLICY

Almost none of the European countries was in a position to buy by normal methods the quantities of foodstuffs and industrial products required for quick recovery. The United States was almost the only nation capable of supplying them in quantity. Fur-

thermore, it had large and inescapable obligations to provide parts of the food supplies of West Germany and Japan.[36] The food shortage of western Europe was made doubly critical by an extremely severe winter in 1946–1947 and the severe and extensive drought in the summer of 1947.

Fortunately, the United States continued to have excellent crops in these years, except for a short corn crop in 1947. Consequently, the foodstuffs were available. The need was for dollars with which to buy them. Normal credit arrangements were of little significance since few of the countries would be able to service and repay sizable loans. Furthermore, few American farmers, businessmen or labor groups wanted to see a large-scale, forced flow of foreign goods into the United States, probably at distress prices, to service and pay loans of this kind.

The result was continuing heavy military procurement to supply the armed forces and for some civilian feeding in Germany and Japan, and the British loan of July 1946 which enabled her to import enough foodstuffs and other goods to prevent serious deterioration of the austere diets of the war years.[37] The establishment of the European Economic Co-operation Administration as an implementation of the Marshall Plan made available uncompensated dollars on an unprecedented scale.[38]

32. Public Law 734, 81st Cong., 2nd sess., approved August 28, 1950.

33. Other previously exempted groups were likewise brought under coverage, particularly domestic help, employees of charitable and nonprofit organizations (if the organization elected to come under coverage) and the self-employed other than farmers.

34. Provided payment amounted to $50 or more. For workers employed on a qualifying basis in the last quarter of 1950 payments were to begin with the first quarter of 1951.

35. The rates of tax on wages were to be:

For 1950–53, inclusive, 1½ per cent (not applicable to agricultural workers until Jan. 1, 1951)

For 1954–59, inclusive, 2 per cent
For 1960–64, inclusive, 2½ per cent
For 1965–69, inclusive, 3 per cent
After 1969, 3¼ per cent

The employer was assessed an equal amount on wages paid in covered employment. The rates for the self-employed were 1½ times those for the employed worker. (Subchapter E of the act.)

36. The situation to which ECA was oriented and the nature of the problem are well presented in Seymour E. Harris, *The European Recovery Program*, Harvard University Press, Cambridge, 1948. For a briefer treatment see Sidney S. Alexander, *The Marshall Plan*, Planning Pamphlets Nos. 60–61, National Planning Association, Washington, 1948. A popular presentation of European aspects of the problem is provided in the pamphlet, *ECE in Action, The Story of the United Nations Economic Commission for Europe*, Department of Public Information of the United Nations, Geneva, Switzerland, 1949.

37. Despite this aid, the British diet was, in fact, even more limited during the early postwar years than in the war period itself.

38. The rapid increase in European production, plus rising prices and larger volumes of United States imports, resulted in virtual elimination of the heavy unbalance of United States exports over imports by the end of the decade. A dollar gap amounting to nearly $8 billion in 1947 had been reduced approximately to zero by the fall of 1950. (See National City Bank of New York, *Monthly Letter on Economic Conditions [and] Government Finance* for December 1950, p. 139.) The conditions which brought this about were, to be sure, somewhat transitory;

TABLE 4

EXPORTS OF FOODSTUFFS, 1935–1950

Period	Wheat and Wheat Products (Grain Equivalent)	Other Grains and Grain Products (Grain Equivalent)	Rice (Milled)	Fats and Oils	Meats (Carcass Equivalent)	Dairy Products	Other Foods	Total Food Exports
	(1,000 Long Tons)							
Average:								
1935–1939	1,366	1,335	83	87	55	17	1,280	4,223
1945–1946	10,520	1,308	349	315	614	792	3,501	17,399
1946–1947	10,670	4,165	384	227	181	494	3,052	19,173
1947–1948	13,013	2,231	407	251	68	459	2,912	19,341
1948–1949	13,477	4,285	408	398	34	389	2,914	21,905
1949–1950	8,003	4,317	452	501	42	249	2,001	15,565

Source: U.S. Department of Agriculture, *Distribution of United States Food, July 1, 1949–June 30, 1950,* October 19, 1950, p. 2.

In the years 1948 through 1950, United States aid under this program amounted to $12.3 billion.[39] Of this, some $3 billion went for food, feed and fertilizer. ECA purchases of farm and related products between April 3, 1948 and December 31, 1950 included:

Wheat	$1,387,000,000
Fats and oils	321,000,000
Sugar and related products	259,200,000
Meat	121,100,000
Dairy products	112,500,000
Feeds and fodder	49,800,000
Fertilizer	41,400,000
Fruits and nuts (except peanuts)	29,900,000
Rice	28,500,000
Eggs	16,000,000[40]

Exports of foodstuffs, in physical terms, up to June 30, 1950 as compared to prewar levels are shown in Table 4.

While it would be unrealistic to assume that there would have been no exports of farm products to these countries during these years had there been no war and no ECA program, it is clear that both the demand and the exchange available for payment were abnormally large. The customary shortage of dollar exchange resulting from our low volume of imports was suddenly overcome through the gift of large amounts of buying power. In addition, domestic demand was at a very high level. The impact of this demand on American farm prices was important, especially for commodities like wheat which, without this abnormal demand, might well have been depressed and a matter of grave concern to the government in its efforts to make good on its wartime price guarantees. As it was, food prices were more than maintained through most of the period 1946–1951, and continued to exercise a stimulating influence in the upward spiral of costs, wage rates and prices that constituted the postwar inflation.[41]

Geneva and Torquay Tariff Agreements

Though there were rumblings of farmer opposition and congressional criticism, the Trade Agreements Act continued to hold a fairly safe margin of support and was re-

the sharp increase in United States imports resulted partly from rearmament and the prospect of shortages, and the lower level of exports was partly due to the fact that United States aid in rearming Europe was still mostly in the planning stage. Nevertheless, the underlying situation had become much more nearly in balance than in the years 1945–1949. (The improvement was also due in part to the extensive revaluation of foreign currencies which occurred in the fall of 1949.)

39. Economic Cooperation Administration, *Eleventh Report to Congress . . . for the Quarter Ended December 31, 1950,* p. 33.

40. *Ibid.,* p. 124.

41. It is unwarranted to assume that a serious inflation would not have occurred even if food prices had remained low. Many goods were in short supply, labor was fully employed and in a strong bargaining position, and buying power available in the economy was excessive in terms of the wartime level of prices. The rising cost of food provided a good argument for labor's successive demands for wage increases, and possibly brought on this upward spiral earlier than it would have occurred as a result of the other inflationary forces then affecting the situation.

newed in 1945, 1948, 1949 and 1951.[42] The 1951 renewal placed some additional limitations on the concessions that might be made but none of major importance.[43] Though progress had been made in negotiating trade agreements, many hampering restrictions on international commerce were still in effect, especially among the European countries.[44] In part, these consisted of tariffs, but they also included quotas, limitations on exchange and the rigid barriers to East-West trade that grew out of the tension between the communist and noncommunist countries.

The United States and other members of the United Nations initiated, in 1948, a much more comprehensive attack on the problem of tariffs and restrictions on trade. This took the form of an effort to draft an acceptable charter for an International Trade Organization, to operate as an arm of the United Nations. It was, in effect, an effort to achieve more generally and more quickly the objectives set forth in the Reciprocal Trade Agreements Act of 1934. The procedure was to be the attainment of agreement internationally on a code of fair play and nondiscrimination in international trade, and a rapid cutting down of tariffs. A first session of the contracting parties was held at Havana in March 1948. This was followed by conferences at Geneva in August and September of that year, at Annecy, France, in 1949[45] and at

Geneva in April 1950. The fifth session was held at Torquay, England, from September 1950 to April 1951.

In 1947, prior to the Geneva conferences of 1948, a first round of tariff negotiations had been carried out. This resulted in extensive reductions in tariffs, with 23 countries participating in the adjustment. These were put into effect under the Protocol of Provisional Application whereby the contracting nations agreed to apply the tariff concessions and to accord most-favored-nation treatment as among themselves, insofar as such action was not inconsistent with existing legislation.

Further concessions were worked out at the Annecy and Torquay conferences. The Agreement has been put into effect, at various dates, by Australia, Belgium, Brazil, Burma, Canada, Ceylon, China, Cuba, Czechoslovakia, France, India, Lebanon, Luxemburg, Netherlands, New Zealand, Norway, Pakistan, Southern Rhodesia, Syria, the Union of South Africa, the United Kingdom, the United States and other later adherents.

The Torquay Conference grew out of the fact that tariff concessions granted in 1947 could be withdrawn. It was, therefore, decided to bring under review in the fall of 1950 any proposals for readjustment with a view to extending the life of the Geneva and Annecy schedules for an additional three years, except for such adjustments as might be agreed upon at the Torquay Conference. That Conference resulted in the completion of 147 pairs of negotiations in which 34 countries participated. The countries taking part in the negotiations represent well over 80 per cent of the world's international trade.

It is too early to predict the outcome of the undertaking as a whole and the future of the International Trade Organization. The General Agreement on Tariffs and Trade, arrived at in Geneva in 1947, appears to be a long step in the direction of restoring an operating approach to world trade that is more like that prevailing before World War I than any that has existed since. The outlook for the formal establishment of an Interna-

---

42. The votes on the issue were as follows:

	House		Senate	
	For	Against	For	Against
1945	239	153	54	21
1948	234	149	70	18
1949	319	69	61	20
1951	(not recorded)		72	2

43. The controversy at this time centered mainly on the so-called "peril point" provisions which were opposed by the administration but favored by the group who wanted to limit administrative discretion in lowering tariffs.

44. For a good brief summary of the situation, see J. M. Letiche, *Reciprocal Trade Agreements in the World Economy,* Committee on International Economic Policy in cooperation with the Carnegie Endowment for International Peace, New York, May 1948.

45. The substance of the Annecy agreement is available in a State Department publication, *Analysis of Protocol of Accession and Schedules to the General Agreement on Tariffs and Trade Negotiated at Annecy, France, April-August 1949* (Preliminary), 1949.

tional Trade Organization does not look promising.[46]

President Truman, on April 28, 1949, presented the International Trade Organization Charter to the Congress for consideration, with a recommendation that it be approved. He commented:

The Charter is the most comprehensive international economic agreement in history. . . . While it does not include every detail desired by this Nation's representatives, it does provide a practical, realistic method for progressive action toward the goal of expanding world trade.[47]

Despite this strong support by the President, the Charter was not approved. It was not resubmitted in the first session of the Eighty-second Congress, and little effort has

46. The literature pertaining to the ITO and the various conferences mentioned is voluminous. The reader, in search of a general account of the developments, will find useful the reports of the Interim Commission for the International Trade Organization. Thus far available are *The Attack on Trade Barriers* and *Liberating World Trade*, the first and second reports on the operation of the General Agreement on Tariffs and Trade, Geneva, Switzerland, 1949 and 1950. With respect to the Havana Charter, the lay reader will find useful the Library of Congress, Legislative Reference Service Pamphlet, *The Havana Charter for an International Trade Organization, Arguments Pro and Con,* Public Affairs Bulletin No. 82, by Howard S. Piquet and Hermann Ficker, April 1950.

The Geneva Agreement has been published by the Department of State, in two volumes, *General Agreement on Tariffs and Trade, Geneva, October 30, 1947,* Treaties and Other International Acts Series 1700, 1949. In May 1951, the Department issued an *Analysis of Torquay Protocol of Accession, Schedules, and Related Documents, General Agreement on Tariffs and Trade, Negotiated at Torquay, England, September 1950–April 1951* (Preliminary).

A general account of the background and content of the ITO Charter is given in Clair Wilcox's *A Charter for World Trade,* Macmillan, New York, 1949. For a brief critical discussion see Sir Hubert Henderson, "A Criticism of the Havana Charter," in the *American Economic Review,* June 1949, pp. 605–17. A similarly brief statement in behalf of the Charter was made by Secretary of State Acheson before the House Committee on Foreign Affairs and for the press. *The ITO Charter, A Code of Fair Trade Practices,* May 1950.

Agricultural implications of the proposal are presented in popular form in a Department of State pamphlet entitled *The American Farmer and the ITO Charter* by Norman Burns, February 20, 1949. The concessions on agricultural products made by the United States in the Annecy Agreement are given in *Foreign Agriculture Circular,* Office of Foreign Agricultural Relations, October 14, 1949, FAP–1–49; those of the Torquay Conference in *ibid.,* May 9, 1951, FAP–3–51.

47. *Charter for an International Trade Organization, Message from the President of the United States,* S.Doc. 61, 81st Cong., 1st sess., April 28 (Legislative day, April 11), 1949.

been made to revive it since that time. Many of its provisions had been included, however, in the general agreements on tariffs and trade arrived at in the Geneva, Annecy and Torquay conferences.

International Wheat Agreement Renewed

The fourth International Wheat Conference, which met in Washington in July 1942, resulted only in agreement on a memorandum of limited scope, mainly for establishing a postwar pool of relief wheat and arrangements for convening a later conference. The fifth conference was held in London in March and April 1947.[48] At that time, Argentina decided not to participate in such an agreement and, later, the United Kingdom declared itself unable to accept the schedule of prices tentatively agreed on.

The sixth conference was held in Washington from January to March 1948. Agreement was reached by the representatives of 36 countries, but only 12 of the governments concerned had ratified the agreement by the deadline date (July 1, 1948), the principal reason being the failure of the United States Senate to ratify. The United Kingdom, Australia, Denmark, Ireland and New Zealand then announced their withdrawal.

A seventh conference was convened, in Washington, in January 1949 with a U.S.S.R. delegation present. For a time, it appeared that Russia would work in harmony with the other members of the conference, but this optimism proved unwarranted. On March 18, the Russian delegation announced that it could not accept an export allotment of less than 75 million bushels in place of the 50 millions assigned to it. The concession of an additional 10 million bushels failed to satisfy them and they withdrew. However,

48. A summary of these conferences and of the issues on which discussion centered is given in "International Wheat Agreements, Introduction," *International Journal of Agrarian Affairs,* Oxford University Press, London, September 1949, pp. 4–10. The remainder of that issue of the *Journal* consists of a series of analytical articles on the wheat agreements by representatives of Australia, Italy, Denmark, the United Kingdom and Canada. Texts of the Agreements of 1933, 1942, 1948 and 1949 are contained in the Appendix, pp. 78–127.

an agreement was reached and signed by 41 of the participating countries.[49] The United States Congress ratified the agreement on October 27, 1949.[50]

Korea and New Inflationary Pressures

Throughout the last half of the decade of the 1940's, inflationary influences had been dominant rather than the deflationary pressures that had been so generally expected. In agriculture, this condition was a result, in the main, of two factors — very high levels of domestic employment and income, and a large, but abnormal, foreign demand for some of the principal American farm products.

Yields were generally good throughout the period and, as a consequence, farm incomes were at all-time highs through 1948.[51] By

49. Later in the year (December), the Food and Agriculture Organization, in a surprise vote, agreed to transfer its headquarters from Washington to Rome. This change seems likely to have important effects on the extent and nature of international action in respect to agriculture, but it is too early to estimate their probable significance. United States Congress contact with and interest in the program seem likely to be weakened materially and the result may be a relatively increased emphasis on United States-controlled programs of the "Point Four" type. The shift in location was a blow to many United States backers of the Food and Agriculture Organization who had hoped that it would eventually become an international action agency which would take the lead in working out and executing additional international programs of various kinds.

50. 63 Stat. 945. For a good analysis of the 1949 agreement, see Frank H. Golay, "The International Wheat Agreement of 1949," *Quarterly Journal of Economics*, August 1950, pp. 442–63. For a more general analysis of commodity agreements, see Joseph S. Davis, *International Commodity Agreements: Hope, Illusion, or Menace?*, The Committee on International Economic Policy in cooperation with the Carnegie Endowment for International Peace, New York, 1947. For an account of the first year's experience under the new agreement, see Office of Foreign Agricultural Relations, "International Wheat Agreement of 1949, First Year's Experience," *Foreign Agriculture Circular*, October 4, 1950, FG 15–50.

51. Gross farm income declined in 1949 to $31,832 million as compared to $35,299 million in 1948. (*Statistical Abstract, 1950*, p. 582.) The official "parity" ratio of farm to nonfarm prices reached its highest level (115) in 1947, fell off to 110 in 1948, and averaged 100 for 1949 and 1950. During the first three months of 1950 it was about 97, but rose rapidly thereafter, reaching 113 in February 1951. (U.S. Department of Agriculture, *Agricultural Situation*, May 1951, p. 15.) These changes in the official parity ratio are somewhat misleading as the inclusion of agricultural labor costs in the computation, after 1949, raised "parity" prices by about 6 points, and thus automatically reduced the parity ratio. Livestock, in April 1951, stood at 340 per cent of the 1910–1914 level, while the all-crop average was 275 per cent. *Loc. cit.*

1949 and 1950, the postwar upsurge in farm prices and incomes appeared to have run its course. Both prices and incomes eased off substantially, and stocks of farm products held by the government as a result of its price-supporting activities reached embarrassing levels. The time seemed to be at hand when the nation might again be more concerned over farm surpluses than farm deficits.

This situation was changed abruptly by the outbreak of war in Korea, in June 1950. There was widespread fear that this might be a prelude to full-scale war between the communist and noncommunist nations. As a result, the United States initiated plans for large-scale and rapid rearmament, including an extensive program of military aid to the Atlantic Pact countries. Thus the foreign aid program, which had been tapering off, was quickly revived but with different objectives and an altered pattern of demands on the American economy.

Substantial deficit financing and severe shortages of some kinds of civilian goods were anticipated. As a result, consumer and business buying took on new life and prices rose sharply, despite the ample inventories of most consumer goods. In the main, the upsurge in demand was a result of scare buying rather than of a shortage of goods, though some raw materials advanced very sharply on the basis of heavy purchases for the manufacture of military equipment and for government stockpiling.

The Defense Production Act

In an effort to check the upward movement of prices, the Congress passed the Defense Production Act of 1950 (approved by the President on September 8).[52] This was couched to a considerable extent in the language of the price-and-wage control legislation of World War II. However, it was much less rigorous, and public support for it was far less general. There were more loopholes, and the legislation left the way open for

52. Public Law 774, 81st Cong., 2nd sess.

various types of price escalators. Agricultural prices were not to be limited to less than parity, or the highest prices paid between May 24 and June 24, 1950, whichever was higher.

While the general level of farm prices was somewhat below parity, a few items, chiefly meats, were well above parity and continued to rise.[53] These items bulked large in consumer thinking and provided a strong argument in the widespread demands for wage increases which, if granted and if they resulted in price increases, would in turn raise the parity levels of farm prices. Manufacturers and retailers likewise moved quickly to increase prices, partly in an effort to move inventories at higher prices than the ceilings likely to be established, and in anticipation of higher prices for replacements and labor.

Labor likewise insisted on its own escalator arrangements, particularly the right to cost-of-living increases and such provisions as those of the United Automobile Workers for automatic increases to compensate for an assumed rate of increase in technological efficiency. Labor demanded and gained acceptance of a principle implying wage rate advances of 10 per cent over January 1950, and business succeeded in getting guarantees of profit margins. Thus the tendency was for higher farm prices, increased wage rates and wider profit margins to lend strength to the inflationary spiral which had been set off by the expanded program of government spending and a relatively easy credit policy.

The lack of active congressional and public support for rigorous controls on wages and prices made the prospect of effective checks on inflation through direct controls a very dubious one, and the prospects for adequate fiscal and monetary controls were not bright.

The control program, weakly implemented and kept off balance by congressional, farmer and business opposition, was not notably effective as a means of controlling inflation during 1950.[54]

Relation to Agriculture

The farm groups, particularly the American Farm Bureau Federation, opposed vigorously the imposition of price controls, and urged higher taxes and restrictions on credit as a means of controlling inflationary pressure. The administration likewise advocated much heavier taxes and brought about some curtailment of credit while, at the same time, pressing strongly for more effective price and wage controls. In the Congress, most members of the Republican and Southern Democrat groups favored weak controls, or none, and, as is the way of legislative bodies, were less than enthusiastic about tax and credit provisions that would be likely to hold inflation in check under an expanded military program such as that contemplated. The first half of 1951 saw some stabilizing of prices, and even some reductions which were apparently due to the easing off of the flurry of scare buying that marked the fall of 1950.

Here, as in World War II, farmer pressure by way of Congress was consistently, though not nominally, inflationary in character. With a tight labor market and with war contracts to work on there is relatively little to restrain continuing increases in wage rates unless some norm in respect to living costs and wage rates can be established, and legislative and administrative provision made for holding that line. Increased taxation and restrictions

53. The generally prosperous condition of agriculture in this period was indicated by the continuing rise in farm land prices. For the United States, as a whole, land prices advanced 14 per cent in the year preceding March 1951, reaching an all-time high index of 193 (1912–1914 = 100). This was an advance of more than 35 per cent over the levels of March 1946 and was, likewise, 14 per cent above the 1920 peak. See "Farm Land Prices Reach Another All-Time High," *Banking,* Journal of the American Bankers Association, May 1951, p. 90.

54. One reason for the vigorous objection to direct control over prices and wages was the uncertainty as to how long the emergency would last. If it had a foreseeable and definite termination time, such as the ending of a period of active warfare, a stronger case for such controls could be made. Instead, however, the prospect of a long period of tension caused many thoughtful people to fear the danger of slowing down the economy through freezing prices in a given pattern and moving toward a more controlled economy. This argument was less persuasive with respect to the supposedly temporary forced-draft build-up of armament scheduled for 1951 to 1953.

on credit are unlikely to be effective in restraining that type of creeping inflation when the government is a heavy buyer in the form of war orders, the demand for such output being almost completely inelastic. Wage rates, once they are advanced generally, are not easily reduced even if unemployment becomes fairly widespread. Agriculture thus may be helping to set up a high cost structure that will prove more rigid and lasting than the price structure that can be maintained for farm products, even with price-supporting legislation.

The arguments for some measure of price control along with tax and credit adjustment is, of course, much more cogent in a war economy than in peacetime. When war production constitutes a large factor in demand, the very abnormal characteristics of both demand and supply are such as to put some prices very badly out of line, and result in large and unwarranted windfall gains where supply cannot be increased quickly. The full story on the wisdom or unwisdom of current farm policies in respect to the stabilization of prices under mobilization or war conditions remains for the future to bring out.

CHAPTER 20

U.S. FARM POLICIES IN PERSPECTIVE

VIRTUALLY ALL THROUGH the one hundred sixty years of our history under the Constitution, agricultural problems have held a prominent place in congressional deliberations. The new nation which came into full-fledged existence with the adoption of the Constitution in 1789 was almost exclusively rural, and, in the main, undeveloped even as an agricultural nation. While much of its culture and governmental structure was a heritage from the parent countries, this new nation, with its markedly different setting, was shortly to adopt policies and governmental procedures that were distinctively American. Nowhere is this modification more striking than in land policy. Here, with a vast area of new lands to settle, an approach quite unlike those of the older nations came into being. Its main features are still evident in modified form, though the pioneer condition to which it was related has long ceased to exist.

Other aspects of national policy also have been of great interest to farm people and have been significantly influenced by farm pressures. Monetary and banking policy, transportation, monopoly control, conservation and price policy, all have been highlighted in farmer-supported legislative proposals over the years. From about 1800 until near the end of the nineteenth century national policy was, as a matter of course, heavily influenced by farmer attitudes, since farmers were the dominant group. But as industrial and commercial activities grew in importance, and reached a volume such that, after 1870, they employed the larger part of the nation's population, farmer influence receded so far as general national legislation was concerned.

Both farmer and labor groups became more class-conscious and turned increasingly to the support of legislation considered of direct benefit to them. In so doing each group tended to be somewhat complacent about other legislation, even though its interests often were affected profoundly by legislative and political developments that did not appear on the surface to be the concern of either agriculture or labor.

Farmer Influence Important

Since about 1870, farm people no longer constituted a majority of the population, but they have continued to exert an influence on certain types of legislation that greatly exceeds their relative numerical strength. This is due in part to the two-house legislative structure, which gives thinly populated farm states equal weight, in the Senate, with the populous, highly urbanized states. It is also due to the fact that, though not a majority of the population, or even a near majority, farmers constitute the largest single, relatively cohesive group in legislative bodies. In addition, there is a tradition that agriculture is a "basic" industry and one that should be fostered and protected in the national interest.

Thus both farm people and the nation as a whole have reason to be concerned with the wisdom and constructiveness of agricultural leadership both in and out of Congress. That this leadership has not always lived up to its opportunities will be apparent to all who have read the preceding pages. Yet on the whole the record reflects progress, much of it arising out of a genuine feeling of social responsibility strongly ingrained in the attitudes of farm people. This is a product of cultural heritages, but possibly even more of the pioneer conditions from which we have so recently emerged, and of the deep feeling for productive enterprise that grows out of

507

firsthand contact with production processes that are relatively complete in themselves — processes in which the end product is so closely related to the inputs that the worker can readily see the results of his work and the significance of his part in the production process.

Policies Emerge Slowly

One further broad generalization seems warranted. Farm policies do not emerge and become settled quickly. Our basic land policy took shape over a period of more than half a century. It was fairly well established by 1862, but there have been important modifications since, and, even in recent years, adjustments have been made or proposed that may well de-emphasize the pioneer character of established attitudes and values in this realm. Monetary policy has been a recurring theme in farmer agitation, in the 1830's, between 1870 and 1900, and again in the 1930's. The issues involved are again emerging, but in different form and with a different setting.

The problems of extent, kinds, costs and financing of transportation have been prominent in farmer thinking almost continuously since 1800. In the main, the policy seems fairly well established, though it may yet turn still further in the direction of public ownership and operation. Farmer interest and influence in tariff policy have been evident at least from 1830 onward. The problems growing out of large-scale organization and monopoly became matters of acute interest to farmers in the 1870's, and have continued to occupy an important place in their thinking. Though interest in these problems appears to have become less active in recent decades, this may become again an important feature of farm policy, since monopolistic procedures have now come to be prominent not only in corporate activity but in labor programs as well, and, in fact, in parts of agriculture itself.

The conservation movement dates from the 1880's, but still is a lively topic in farm policy discussions. Governmental intervention in the pricing of farm products is largely a develop-ment of the past thirty years, but, here too, the achievement of a settled policy has been slow, and many unresolved issues are still to be faced. Policy in respect to agricultural credit is an outgrowth of several decades of agitation and discussion. Other problems, such as social security in its application to agriculture, the improvement of farm housing and the place of the family farm have come into prominence more recently, and undoubtedly will not be settled for many years to come. Hence, a long view of the nature of policy formation is essential, not only for building on the foundations we now have, but for effective effort in the making of new policy.

Where We Stand in Land Policy

The pre-existing patterns of land ownership and tenure with which the settlers of North America were familiar were in nearly all cases modified survivals from the feudal systems of western Europe. The colonial period in America saw various attempts to perpetuate these patterns in this new setting. But the drift was strongly toward a new kind of relationship to the land — one in which the emphasis (except in the South) was on the rights and interests of the working farmer who hewed a farm out of the wilderness by his own labor. Land was abundant. Labor was scarce. Hence land ownership did not in itself carry the prestige and economic power that it did in the older countries where land was less abundant, and the prerogatives of a strongly entrenched privileged class more significant.

As a result, the basic American land policy tended to favor the working farmer and the family-type farm. Both the aims of the farmer and the national interest were furthered by rapid development of the abundant land resource available. Every opportunity and incentive were afforded for the landless farmer to become both an owner and a working operator. There was almost no vested-interest group of large-scale landowners to erect barriers to such a procedure, and the easy availability of virtually free land provided little opportunity for the development of a tenancy system such as that which prevailed in England.

Owner-Operation Stressed

Out of this situation there grew a deeply ingrained attitude which is still the basic element in American land policy. It regards owner-operation and the family-size farm as the ideals to be striven for. All land which farmers wish to settle and operate should be made available for that purpose. Full freedom to enlarge or subdivide holdings in any way the owner may choose is likewise implied. In other words, the policies adopted involve acceptance of the idea of complete ownership in fee simple with almost no restriction on the right of the owner to use his land as he pleases even when his practices may be damaging to recognized social values or to properties other than his own.

This basic policy has been undergoing change, especially from about 1890 on. Great areas of forest land have been brought under public ownership and management, and have been closed to settlement. Water resources and mineral rights have come to be regarded as, in part at least, a public heritage and a public responsibility. By 1902, efforts were likewise being made to exercise more control over the pattern of agriculture on lands reclaimed at government expense. The earlier policy provided for settlement on family-size units and the establishment of that pattern, but implied no restraint on regrouping into larger or smaller units once title had passed to the owner. The later policy envisioned continuing controls to insure retention of the family-farm pattern (on the lands embraced in reclamation projects).

Interest in Conservation

Further changes in land policy occurred in the large-scale efforts to conserve and build up soils, which became an important feature of American farm policy in the 1930's and continue to occupy a prominent place both in farmer attitudes and national interest. This was a natural and somewhat belated recognition of the fact that the pioneer period had come to an end. For the most part, it did not involve positive restraints and punitive measures designed to discourage misuse of lands. Incentives were provided for conserving and improving soils, and a vast educational program was launched. As yet, however, the pioneer attitude of freedom for the farmer to use his land as he chooses continues to prevail.

The Grazing Act of 1934 carried over to the grazing areas the policy of continuing public ownership and control that had been initiated with respect to forest lands more than forty years earlier. In the meantime, the Tennessee Valley Authority, and other similar projects, were introducing into American land policy, at least experimentally, the idea of planned development of whole areas. This is in marked contrast to the traditional policy which was essentially planless with respect to regional coordination and improvement.

Growing Interest in Farm Tenure

Two additional issues, both very controversial, are now beginning to come under discussion: one, the question of whether farming operations shall be allowed to move in the direction so prominently exemplified in the nonfarm economy — that is, toward much larger units and an industrial type of organization — or shall be placed under restraints that will favor retention of the family-size unit; the other, the question of placing limitations on the rights and powers of landlords with a view to bringing about a more stable and constructive type of farm tenancy.

The first has had sporadic and rather extensive discussion, but majority opinion appears at present to favor retaining almost complete freedom on the part of the farm operator to carry on his business on almost any scale he sees fit to undertake. At the same time there is a growing interest in the provision of means whereby farms that are too small can be enlarged so as to permit more efficient operation.

The growing awareness of the inadequacies and destructiveness of existing types of tenancy laws seems likely to bring this matter under more active consideration in the future. The traditional approach has been to provide credit and other facilities for the purchase of farms by tenants, rather than to recognize tenancy as a permanent institution and try to improve the laws governing it. The magnitude of the problem and the ineffectiveness of the credit approach seem likely, however, to lead gradually to greater interest in the improvement of legislation governing farm tenancy, with its possibilities for bettering quickly and at far less expense the conditions on large numbers of farms.

Monetary Issues and Farm Policy

From 1790 certainly until the 1940's, and possibly even after that, farmers have, for the most part, been a debtor class. The large investment required to set themselves up as self-employed workers, and the opportunity for effective use of more capital, have usually led them to use all of their owned capital in the business and to borrow more. As a result they have tended to favor easy money policies and often to range themselves on the side of outright inflationary programs.

A lower-value dollar has seemed to most of them an easier way out from their debtor positions, and an opportunity for larger profits. These advantages did not always accrue to them in inflationary periods. In fact, more often than not they have increased rather than reduced their debts in times of inflation. Nevertheless, long periods in which the value of money was rising have usually resulted in severe hardship for farm people. In the 1830's, it was largely farmer sentiment in the states of the South and West that resulted in the destruction of the Second Bank of the United States. This set a pattern which resulted in unstable and somewhat chaotic banking not only in that decade but for the remainder of the century. The period from 1870 to 1900 was marked by intense farmer interest in the proposals of the Greenbackers and the proponents of "free silver."

Here the need for inflationary action seems apparent as the period is viewed in retrospect. The efficacy and wisdom of the measures proposed can be questioned, but the underlying objective appears to have been logical. The fact remains, however, that the traditional distrust of the farm groups for any type of centralized banking organization, which had persisted from the time of Andrew Jackson and before, helped to delay the development of a banking system that might have done more to overcome the shortage of money and credit than the eagerly sought greenback and free-silver measures.

Farmer concern with monetary matters eased off with the declining value of the dollar during the first part of the present century, but was sharply revived in the early 1920's. Here the interest centered on the easing of credit rather than on monetary measures per se. That the difficulty arose in part from a preceding period of too easy credit was less apparent to the farm groups than the hardships engendered by the checking of credit expansion. This illustrates a traditional weakness in farmer attitudes in respect to monetary and credit policy — a failure to recognize the need for restraint both of inflation and deflation if stability is to be achieved. The likelihood that monetary or credit measures could have benefited farmers materially in the 1920's is much less apparent than the corresponding possibility in the latter part of the preceding century.

Renewed Interest in Monetary Policy

The decade of the 1930's brought a renewed interest in both monetary and credit policy. Then, however, farmers shared in full measure the confusion in regard to purposes and methods that prevailed in all groups. The need was for the rapid creation of new buying power through deficit financing. The farmers, like most other groups, resisted that approach, and even the administration used it more out of necessity and desperation than as a planned instrument for reflation. This, however, is a conclusion warrantable only in light of later developments, not one that would have been apparent in terms of the well-established and general attitudes in regard to monetary and fiscal matters that were prevalent at that time.

The steps taken to revalue the dollar in terms of gold can hardly be considered a farm-initiated program, though several of the farm organizations backed the idea and its most persuasive advocate was a leading agricultural economist. The American Farm Bureau Federation had for some years advocated a so-called "honest money" approach to the price problem, but had not made an aggressive campaign on it. The Grange likewise was friendly to the adoption of monetary measures for relieving the depression, but harked back to approximately the traditional greenback program rather than the gold revaluation plan which was popular with the Farm Bureau. The National Cooperative Council and the Farmers Union likewise advocated monetary measures designed to stabilize or raise price levels, but did not push them vigorously as a part of their legislative programs. The main drive for the experiment in revaluing the dollar came by way of the administration rather than from either farm organizations or the Congress.

The farm groups manifested relatively little interest in the fiscal aspects of the problem in these or earlier years. They still held strongly to the view so vigorously expressed by them in the late 1920's that making farmers prosperous would bring prosperity to the economy as a whole. Hence, their price programs in the 1920's and through most of the 1930's implied transfer of buying power from consumers to farmers rather than the creation of new buying power. In the early 1930's, the necessity for deficit financing was accepted, though with regret. Farm sentiment in general favored a return to annually balanced budgets as soon as that could be brought about.

The program for agricultural credit relief, though advocated by the farm groups, was likewise more largely a product of administrative initiative than of direct legislative planning by agriculture. Here the credit-creating aspect occupied only a minor place in the thinking of farm leaders. The important thing as they saw it was to get more credit for agriculture, regardless of whether it was a transfer from other groups or newly created credit that would add to the over-all purchasing power of the economy.

Attitudes in the 1940's

The tremendous upsurge in demand which came in the 1940's made possible the marketing at good prices of quantities of farm products that formerly would have been considered excessive. This brought into prominence a new attitude on the part of the more thoughtful farm leaders. Much wider recognition was given to the view that agriculture could not prosper unless the economy as a whole was active and healthy, though the experience of the 1920's had shown that agriculture could be in depression when most of the rest of the economy was relatively prosperous. The role of government deficits and surpluses in increasing or decreasing buying power had become much clearer through the discussion and study of this problem that occurred during the late 1930's and early 1940's.

As a result, farm organization emphasis shifted somewhat in the direction of general monetary and fiscal policies as a means of stabilizing the economy, rather than to direct controls over prices. This shift has not, however, been complete or entirely consistent. In the late 1940's, and especially in the period of accelerated defense effort which began in 1950, most of the farm organizations opposed price controls and argued that inflationary tendencies should be kept in check through heavy taxation and control of credit. They have been less definitely opposed to wage controls, and in many cases have favored them, thus leaving the way open for a charge of opportunism, since the shift in attitude came at a time when farm prices were high and rising rapidly. At the same time most farm-state congressmen and many farm leaders have been quite unwilling to abandon direct approaches when it comes to preventing price declines, even when over-all employment and income are tending to create inflationary rather than deflationary pressures.

In part, this inconsistency stems from a lack of understanding of the "fiscal and monetary" approach, and likewise from a lack of confidence in its efficacy. While it is theoretically feasible to prevent depression by fiscal and monetary measures, it remains to be demonstrated that this can actually be done once the abnormal demand that has marked the period since 1940 eases off. Coupled with this is a significant amount of the "heads-I-win-tails-you-lose" philosophy that has characterized much of the congressional discussion of farm policy from 1941 onward. There has been in Congress almost continuously during these years a strong faction which demanded high price supports at near parity but which opposed any check on the upward movement of farm prices when they are above parity.

Changes in Emphasis

Though monetary and fiscal policy has been prominent in farmer thinking for much of the time throughout this period of more than one hundred years, the emphasis has varied. In the 1830's, it centered on banking structure. From 1870 to 1900 the stress was largely on strictly monetary aspects.

In the 1920's the chief concern was over banking and credit policies, while the 1930's were characterized by a revived interest in manipulation of the monetary unit plus a drive for increased amounts of credit on easier terms. The 1940's reflect a growing interest in the possibilities of more effective management of the general national credit and tax structure for the purpose of stabilizing the economy. This cannot be said to have reached a stage where it is a clear-cut issue in farm policy, or one in which the question of direct versus indirect controls has been resolved. The problem of deflation has been frequently under consideration; and many strongly supported proposals for dealing with it have been put forward by agriculture. As yet there has been no correspondingly vigorous effort to check inflation. Farmers as a whole may, in fact, have some tendency to prefer continuous inflation, provided it does not get out of hand and become too violent.

Tariffs and Foreign Trade

Farmer attitudes on tariffs and foreign trade have tended to be more sectional than on most other major issues. The agricultural South very early took a strong stand in favor of a virtual free-trade tariff policy, and held to it rather consistently until 1920 or after. At the time the nation's tariff policy was beginning to take shape the South exercised a restraining influence on the upward movement of tariffs, and even succeeded in forcing a downward revision in the 1830's. The then western states, in the main, tended to be friendly to relatively high tariffs. This attitude has continued to be dominant in these (the middle western) states until recently. In the meantime, the focus of strongly protectionist sentiment, among farmers, shifted to the Pacific Coast and intermountain areas.

During the past two decades a major change in farmer attitudes on tariff has been occurring, though the shift in position is by no means complete. The sharp reversal in balance of payments between western Europe and the United States, which came as a result both of two world wars and of increasing industrialization in the United States, has forced a reappraisal of the interest of agriculture in respect to volume of imports.

In consequence, farm groups, especially of the Middle West, are gradually shifting toward a greater friendliness to a moderate- or low-tariff policy. Something of the same attitude is apparent in the New England states. The livestock and specialty-crop areas of the western and Mountain states have continued to press strongly for high protective tariffs, but without notable success. The South, on the other hand, is tending to modify its traditional low-tariff stand, and, on occasion, comes out strongly for protective measures.

The lessened farmer opposition to tariff reduction is no doubt in part a reflection of the unusually favorable returns for farm products which have prevailed during the past decade. Should agricultural prices decline sharply, there is every prospect that agitation for tariff increases on farm products will again become more active. It would appear, however, that, for the United States as a whole, the major drive for extremely high tariffs has largely spent its force. So far as national awareness of the problem is concerned, much of the adjustment to America's new place in world affairs has been accomplished. However, there still remains a vast amount of economic and political readjustment to be made before anything like a settled and reasonably stable international trading situation can be anticipated.

The Monopoly Problem

Antipathy toward the exercise of monopolistic power has been deeply imbedded in American thinking from the time of the Revolution and before. In no group was this attitude more pronounced than among farmers during the nineteenth century and up to 1920. The state monopolies used by various European and Asiatic countries as a means of raising revenue never gained significant headway in the United States. Instead, the philosophy of *laissez-faire,* which was dominant in the first century of our national existence, emphasized the benefits of competition. This view found a congenial setting in the American scene, which was characterized by farming and relatively small-scale business.

Among the earliest of the activities that lent themselves to monopolistic practices were the railroads and the businesses associated with them. In the absence of automotive transport and good highways, the railroads were by their very nature monopolies, for which the usual competitive methods of price making were unworkable. Many of the businesses closely related to them, such as elevators and stockyards, soon came to have monopolistic features. Manufacturing enterprises and processing industries likewise began to be big enough by the late 1800's so they could exercise some control in the price-making process and often could eliminate their more irritating or dangerous competitors by methods that were ruthless and effective.

Farmers, engaged in a business that was inescapably very competitive, soon recognized their inability to cope with such organizations except through legislation. They also felt a growing sense of frustration when faced with an increasingly large area of economic activity in which the prices of things bought by them were arrived at through administrative decision without legal restraint, while their own prices were set by forces outside their control. The farmers' approach to the railroad problem early took the form of demanding public regulation — first through direct legislative action and later through regulatory commissions. For most other businesses the drive was for fragmentation and a reversal of the tendency toward concentration into large and powerful economic units.

Farmers and the Trust Problem

In the first of these — the establishment of controls over railroads and elevators — the farm groups took the initiative, and were largely responsible for bringing them under public regulation. Once this policy was established, urban interests carried its principal features over into the realm of urban public utility regulation as well. Farmers can hardly be said to have taken the lead in curbing monopolistic tendencies in the manufacturing and processing industries, but their support for the proponents of the restoration of competition was vigorous and always available.

Here the results were much less conclusive than in railroad regulation. The approach was different and much less effective. It implied the break-up of monopolistic combinations rather than the regulation of them. The opportunities for evasion were numerous, and in some industries the economic advantages of larger-scale units were such as to make forcible decentralization difficult to bring about, and in many cases of dubious public advantage. At the same time, the complexity of these types of business made regulation, at least of prices, virtually impossible. Hence combinations and growth in scale continued to characterize American business and industry despite the disapproval of farmers and the general public.

The failure of the trust-busting approach of the Theodore Roosevelt era led to the relatively mild regulatory efforts undertaken during the first term of Woodrow Wilson. Here too, the results were far from satisfying, either to farmers or their fellow opponents of monopoly in the urban groups. Some progress was made toward a more realistic approach to the problem, but not on a scale which would satisfy the more ardent antimonopolists such as the farm groups.

Policy Change of the 1920's

Thus the matter stood when the depression of the early 1920's hit agriculture. The setting was a favorable one for the plausible and evangelistic appeal made by Aaron Sapiro and his followers. He contended that farmers had been on the wrong track — that instead of wasting their time trying to break up urban monopolies they should themselves develop monopolistic organization and procedures, and seek to deal on even terms with the other parts of the economy, recognizing that many of these would inevitably be less than fully competitive. From this period onward, agriculture modified its attitude toward monopoly pricing and large-scale organization of business and industry. The Sapiro-type cooperatives were not notably successful, but the methods they sought to apply were similar to those which farmers had long opposed bitterly in the nonfarm part of the economy.

Much the same thinking lay back of the McNary-Haugen Plan, which shortly came to be a central feature of farm policy proposals. Again in the Farm Board period, the plans implied something more than a mere attempt to increase efficiency in a fully competitive market, though the program can hardly be said to have envisioned the frankly monopolistic approach extolled by Sapiro and his followers.

Further Modification in the 1930's

This radically changed outlook in regard to controls on output and the maintenance of prices above their free-market levels appears in more fully developed form in the government-sponsored programs of the 1930's. Conscious and planned action to cut down production for the purpose of raising prices, the use of marketing agreements, and, later, the still more positive marketing-quota procedure reflect virtually full acceptance, for agriculture, of most of the techniques of monopolies, trusts and cartels.

During the same period, the passage of the National Industrial Recovery Act suggested a far more acquiescent attitude toward collusive action by nonfarm business units, one that would have been anathema to any Congress of the Theodore Roosevelt or Woodrow Wilson administrations. This shift in public and congressional sentiment grew largely out of profound disillusionment about the efficacy of the competitive system as a regulator of the economy, and also out of a growing conviction that a more consciously planned economy could be developed which would work more smoothly and efficiently.

Yet, the outcome of this legislation was not really a planned economy, nor was it an orderly procedure for permitting monopolies to exist and then regulating them in the public interest, as had been done in the case of railroads and other public utilities. Instead, business and industry were allowed privileges that had been specifically denied them in the Sherman Antitrust Act, and the later legislative and judicial actions associated with it. Shortly thereafter, labor was given vastly greater opportunity to combine and to exercise monopoly types of power in large segments of the economy.

Agriculture thus came in for a paternalistic share in the almost universal drift toward larger-scale, group action. Even with vigorous and positive governmental aid in developing its monopoly program, agriculture tended to run a poor third in the effectiveness of its use of these methods. The inherent competitiveness of the industry and the great difficulty of controlling its output made anything short of such tight controls as those implied by the marketing quota procedure relatively ineffective. The significance of the basically weak bargaining position of agriculture in a highly monopolized economy has thus far been obscured by other factors.

The droughts of the 1930's tended to preclude full realization of the inherent weaknesses of the crop control program of 1933–1936, and concealed the relative bargaining strengths of agriculture, labor and industry under their newly acquired grants of privilege. The unusually favorable situation of agriculture in the 1940's, which was not due to the organizational and monopolistic features built into the program, has prevented a genuine test of the efficacy of the mechanisms devised for improving the bargaining position of agriculture.

Farmers Still Oppose Urban Monopolies

It cannot be said that this trend represented a dropping of the ingrained antipathy for nonfarm monopolies on the part of the grassroots farmer. He still did not like monopolies, or in fact extremely large business aggregations, which seemed to have the characteristics and powers of monopolies. Few farm leaders and farm people recognized clearly that the programs they advocated were similar in nature to those they had so long opposed; nor did they see clearly that the growing power of organized labor was bringing into being a new type of centralized power that might eventually bulk as large in farmer thinking as had the trusts and monopolies in the years between 1890 and 1910.

In spite of the effort to develop monopolistic organization and procedures in agriculture that has marked the period since 1920, it is not clear that farm people have abandoned permanently their campaign against monopolies, trusts and cartels. If the results of their own efforts in this direction should prove disappointing, they may renew their drive for a return to a more competitive economy, or at least seek more public control over great aggregations of power whether in industry, commerce or labor.

In fact the public as a whole exhibits a growing restiveness in respect to seemingly arbitrary decisions by the leaders of any group which result in great social cost. Should this develop into a full-scale movement for more rigorous social controls, it may be that the farm groups will be found taking a significant part in it, though, as in the decade from 1900 to 1910, probably not a leading one.

Highways and Internal Improvements

Farmers, especially those of the West, were vigorous proponents of the early efforts to develop highways, canals and other means of transport under public auspices. The struggle over strict versus loose construction of the Constitution, plus the action of a farm-state president, Andrew Jackson, checked the trend toward federal construction of interstate facilities for transport.[1] As a result, except for intrastate highways, the great development of transportation in the nineteenth century was, in the main, through private enterprise.

Not until nearly a century later was there an important reversion to direct federal aid in the construction of highways. This latter change, brought on largely by the growing use of automobiles and trucks, has again placed major emphasis on publicly constructed arteries of transport paralleling and competing with the railroads, but differently owned and financed.

Farmers have been strong supporters of this shift to federal participation in road building, and there appears to be little likelihood of a reversal of the trend. Whether it will eventually carry over to public ownership of the railroads cannot now be foreseen. There is no evidence currently of a strong desire on the part of farmers for public ownership of the railroads. Majority sentiment in fact seems to be opposed to such a change. If public ownership does come, it seems more likely to arise from the increasing financial

1. The political controversies engendered and the wasteful use of public funds probably would have brought a reaction against the public construction of the means of transport even if the above factors had not placed an abrupt check on them. However that may be, the immediate cause of the discontinuance of the trend toward public highway construction was Jackson's veto of the Maysville Road project. The concurrent appearance of the railroad provided a type of transport far better suited to private construction and operation than the highway and canal system that preceded it.

difficulties of the railroads, faced as they are with severe competition from other carriers using roadways built largely at public expense.

Farm Credit Policies Well Established

The provision of more orderly channels for the flow of credit into agriculture was a relatively rapid process, greatly speeded up by the agricultural distress of the 1930's. For the so-called "sound" types of agricultural credit, that is, land-bank loans, intermediate-credit-bank loans, and those of the production credit associations and banks for cooperatives, both structure and policies seem relatively well established and settled. They provide an effective means for facilitating the flow of credit into nearly all phases of agriculture on a conservative, largely self-supporting basis.

Further changes in organization and procedure will undoubtedly be made, but these seem unlikely to alter materially the main outlines of this more conservative segment of farm credit policy. Private credit agencies have, to a considerable extent, modified their policies in such a way as to meet the competition of the federally sponsored agencies, and there seems every reason to expect that for the foreseeable future the two systems will continue to exist side by side, each exercising a wholesome influence on the other.

For the more controversial, "soft credit" activities, policies are less fully developed and accepted. Nevertheless, increased concern over this problem is evident. Starting with unsupervised, disaster-type loans, this program has gradually evolved into an instrument of social change designed to transfer capital to undercapitalized segments of agriculture in ways that would not come about through the normal functioning of the capital market.

Publicly supplied credit is being used as a vigorous, and often very effective, aid in educational work designed to improve farm management, enlarge inadequate farms and promote soil conservation. It is also being used to effect transfer of capital into the hands of young and active farmers at a faster pace than would occur in the absence of government aid. While the program is less fully accepted than is the older, more conservative one, there appears to be little likelihood that the trend will be reversed or importantly modified.

The large and successful refinancing operation carried through in the middle 1930's seems to have established a precedent that would be followed in the event of another major depression. It is probable also that, under similar circumstances, some procedure for limiting the rights of creditors in taking over farms would be reinstituted. There has been sporadic though not extensive agitation for permanent legislation similar to the Frazier-Lemke Amendment which was in effect on an emergency basis from 1935 to 1947.

The case for such a restriction in times when the land market is reasonably active and normal is not strong. The disadvantages of the procedure are great enough and the opposition sufficient that it is not likely to be reinstated unless financial difficulty becomes widespread and foreclosures numerous.

Some type of special credit to permit carrying stored commodities on the farm, such as Commodity Credit Corporation loans, has been an important element in the farm program since 1933. Unless loan levels are to be reduced sharply, this program belongs more in the category of price-supporting activities than in that of credit. At more conservative loan levels, it would constitute a special type of credit which appears to have achieved a lasting place in the nation's farm program.[2]

Price and Income Support

Government support of prices and incomes is of recent origin, dating only from 1929. It has become much the most widely discussed feature of the farm program, and the one of greatest current interest both in the rural

2. The over-all program for agriculture contains a number of other special types of loan, such for example as those provided for rural electrification projects, and the advance of funds for the construction of reclamation projects. As yet there has been relatively little general agitation for a system of forest-land loans which has frequently been proposed by those interested in the future of the forest industry.

areas and in the Congress. Many devices have been used, and most of them are still available.

The central problems which have not yet been faced realistically are (1) the question of the level of support to be maintained and (2) the method to be used. Congressional sentiment, with a fair amount of farmer backing, has favored supports at levels that would be above the market price in a free and reasonably normal market situation. Implementation of this policy requires either heavy outlays of government funds or onerous restrictions on output and marketings. Judging by past experience, probably both would be necessary, since it has been customary to accumulate substantial stocks through purchase and loan before turning to acreage allotments and marketing quotas.

The Agricultural Act of 1948 constituted an attempt to recede to some extent from the high, wartime levels of support. Sentiment for the higher level supports has thus far, however, been strong enough to prevent any significant readjustment downward. The Brannan proposals likewise call for very high levels of price support, and thus imply either heavy contributions from the Treasury or rigorous controls on output. This issue will probably not be faced squarely until such time as production and holdings become burdensome at the prices specified. Any serious recession from the present high levels of employment and consumer income would likewise undoubtedly focus public interest on the food price situation, and might lead the Congress to be more active in resisting measures which would result in high food prices brought about through government action.

Mechanisms Likely to Be Retained

Whatever the level of price support may be, it seems likely that most of the mechanisms devised during the past two decades will be retained, either in current use or in reserve. This includes such devices as acreage allotments, marketing agreements, marketing quotas, Commodity Credit Corporation loans, Section 32 funds, incentive payments and benefit payments. The continued use of soil conservation payments seems more debatable and may come under closer scrutiny.

The possible use of direct payments to farmers instead of maintenance of prices in the market seems likely to be discussed more actively in the years immediately ahead. The fate of this plan probably depends to a considerable extent on the relative strengths of the parties in Congress. Having been tabbed as a Democratic proposal, it is unlikely to gain strong support in a Republican-dominated Congress. The basic idea is similar to that of the benefit payments used during the 1930's, apparently without important partisan or congressional opposition. Undoubtedly such a plan will receive wider attention should there be important repetitions of the wastage of perishables, such as occurred with potatoes in the late 1940's, or if extremely large accumulations of storables develop while food prices are still high. As yet there has been little evidence of strong consumer interest in either the Brannan Plan or its current alternative, the Aiken Plan, embodied in the Act of 1948.

Grass-roots opinion among farmers appears to be more favorable to price support in the market than to a program involving supplemental payments from the Treasury. Also, the administrative feasibility of the Brannan Plan remains to be established in view of the wide variations in quality that characterize farm products and the opportunities such a procedure may present for obtaining illegal and unjustified payments. Farmer sentiment will appear clearly only if and when the issue comes into focus in a major election campaign.

The Conservation Movement

Few policies relating to agriculture have more universal and solid support than that for the conservation of soils. There is little opposition to the objective of the conservation programs. Controversy centers mainly on the methods to be used and the amount of financial support to be provided by the federal government. Interagency rivalries also are significant, and probably will continue to be so for some time to come.

The principal outright opposition comes from the range and mountain areas of the West, where livestock men still are less than happy with the conservation regulations of the Forest Service and the Federal Grazing Service. In general, the trend of sentiment concerning soil conservation appears to be in the direction of more reliance on education and technical assistance and less on direct payments for soil-conserving activities, while in forestry there is some slight tendency toward the use of more positive controls than have been customary in the past.

The Family-Farm Issue

The structural aspects of agriculture have come more and more under scrutiny in recent years. For the most part, the original methods of settlement implied creation and maintenance of the family-size farm, but with no positive restrictions that would force it to retain that pattern.

Except in the southern states, and in the great open spaces of the West, there was little to disturb this structural set-up until the coming of the tractor and the large-scale production of specialty crops at long distances from market. Slavery and cotton created large holdings in the South. In the coastal states, of the West and South in particular, the specialty crops tended to bring in larger-scale operation, much of it related to the necessity for standardization of product and the maintenance of special organization for selling perishables in distant markets. Here too, the presence of large numbers of landless farm workers, the repetitiveness of the operations, and hence their suitability for performance by gang labor working under foremen made relatively large-scale farms feasible and profitable.

Over the remainder of the country the introduction of the tractor, with its related equipment, and the growing use of automobiles, trucks and electric motors have led to continuing enlargement of the more highly commercialized farms. As a result of these trends, there has been a persistent demand for measures designed to check the growth in farm size, and to break up large holdings where these already exist. Except in the Farmers Union, which prides itself on representing the interests of the small farmer and the landless worker, and some units of the Grange, this has not been importantly a farmer-supported movement. Interest in it has centered more largely in reform-minded urban groups.

While this tendency to enlarge the scale of operations has been going on at one end of the scale and in the middle, a reverse tendency has been evident at the lower end of the scale. Large numbers of farms are too small to use effectively the labor of a normal family unit or to take advantage of the mechanical and technological improvements now so widely used on the larger, more successful farms. Here again interest in the problem is more manifest in intellectual groups outside of agriculture than in agriculture itself.

The policy issue thus takes a twofold form. Shall steps be taken to check the trend toward bigger farms and, on the larger ones, toward increasing use of industrial types of organization? Or shall agriculture, like most other industries, be allowed to adjust to whatever size is found efficient and profitable?[3] On the other hand, shall society take steps designed to eliminate, combine or make more efficient the two million or more small, substandard farms? Some steps that look in this direction have been taken, and the problem is coming to be more generally recognized. There is as yet, however, little in the way of a well-defined national policy in regard to it. Still less is there a clearly developed position with respect to the large-farm problem. Neither of these problems has bulked large in the policy proposals of the major farm organizations.

3. The underlying problem here is the seasonal character of farm operations, and the consequent tendency for the industrialized farm to fail to make provision for employment or maintenance in off seasons. Before society can be fully reconciled to this type of farm structure it will probably be necessary that some satisfactory solution to this problem be found.

Agricultural Labor

The situation in respect to farm labor has been one of almost continuous change during recent decades, and differs materially by regions. The settled, surplus-labor pattern of the Old South has been modified by the coming of new nonfarm industries and by exodus to other areas. Wage rates have been raised but are still low. The condition of farm workers, on the whole, is improving. In the main, the supply consists of local permanent residents. Through the Middle West the former reliance on the hired man drawn from a neighboring farm has given place to mechanization which enables the farmer and his family to do much of the work. Where specialty crops are grown, recent years have seen the advent of large numbers of migrant workers from distant sources, often of a different race and culture. To the extent that this tendency exists, the Middle West is coming to be more like the West Coast and Gulf states, and is faced with similar problems.

In the West and around the Gulf of Mexico dependence on migratory workers is a well-established feature of the agriculture. These areas have been subject both to heavy surpluses and to acute shortages of farm labor in the course of the last two decades. Wage rates have fluctuated sharply in response to these changes in supply. The problems presented are increasing in complexity and severity.

There is as yet little in the way of a developed national policy in regard to farm labor. For many decades, except in the South, it was assumed that the hired farm worker was a prospective farm tenant or owner on the lowest rung of the agricultural ladder. The many and evident exceptions to this characterization, as for example the foreign workers of the West Coast states, were largely ignored. This pioneer concept has largely dropped out of community attitudes as it has become more unrealistic, but no considered alternative has appeared. The question whether agriculture is to continue to place dependence on a body of second-grade citizens or is to develop a pattern of operation and community life such that these workers will have a satisfying place in it is still to be faced.

Bargaining Arrangements Undeveloped

Some features of farm policy in respect to labor are more evident. Generally speaking, farmers want an unorganized labor market. They do not like to have to deal with unionized workers or union leaders. Their industry is, in fact, not well suited for collective bargaining. Unionization, if it comes, will necessitate some sort of corresponding employer organization if effective negotiation is to be possible.[4] While organizations of agricultural employers have appeared in some areas, their coverage is not complete enough to make them practical bargaining agencies comparable to those which are customary in industry.

While most farm employers do not want unionized farm labor, few have given thought to alternative procedures for orderly negotiation of wage rates such, for example, as the official wage-board plan long used in Britain. Undoubtedly most farm employers will continue to resist unionization of their workers. The history of the labor movement in other fields does not lend encouragement to the view that this resistance will prove to be anything more than a delaying action. In the meantime, a case could be made for a more aggressive effort to find some pattern of employer-employee relationship that would be better suited to the situation in agriculture than the traditional urban labor union pattern.

There is nevertheless a growing feeling among farm employers that more forward-looking policies in respect to farm labor must be developed. The attitude toward the provision of old-age and survivors insurance for farm workers has changed gradually from rather general opposition to a mildly favorable view, though certainly not to one of en-

4. Some types of agricultural labor in some areas are of course already unionized and have been for some years. Examples are the milkers unions of the West Coast states, packing-shed workers and some of the farm workers of New Jersey.

thusiasm. Opposition to unemployment insurance continues to be vigorous. Until the methods of farming in the areas dependent on migrant workers change materially, the provision of unemployment insurance appears to present insuperable difficulties. Many of the changes needed, such as improved housing, better educational opportunities, and a more satisfying part in community life, cannot be brought about until more progress is made in stabilizing work opportunities and places of residence. As yet, this problem is virtually untouched in the policy discussions of the farm organizations.

Adjusting to a Changing Environment

As the record shows, farmers have concerned themselves with a host of other problems, some of temporary interest, others of lasting importance. The emphasis on a large and active program of research continues strong and is likely to do so in the future. If conditions become more settled, it is likely that the interest in better farm housing and the improvement of cultural opportunities will receive increased attention as compared with the more materialistic considerations that have dominated farm policy discussions over the past three decades.

Adjustments will need to be made to a constantly changing environment. There is a tendency for policy making to be oriented too much to the past rather than to the future. This is natural since the past is known while the future involves many uncertainties and can be seen only vaguely. This argues for a versatile and flexible plan of action — one that can be adjusted quickly to changing circumstances and needs. During the decade just past, we have been centering attention on cures for depression, when the urgent current problem was that of inflation. In the 1920's and after, we sought the restoration of a pre-1914 balance which was regarded, somewhat nostalgically, as the golden age of agriculture, instead of attempting to adjust realistically to the new situation in which we found ourselves.

The world has changed so profoundly since 1914 that an attempt to re-establish the conditions of that period, no matter how much we might like to do so, is mere wishful thinking. The world of the future is far more likely to be concerned over shortages than over surpluses. In the United States, population has doubled since 1900 and still is growing rapidly. New lands brought into production will be at increasing cost and of lower productivity. Gains in productivity on lands already in use probably will be higher-cost gains than those of the past. Thus, the terms of trade for agriculture seem likely to be more favorable as time goes on, since it is easier to balance output with demand in a situation where cost per unit increases as output increases than where larger production can be had at lower per-unit costs.

Undoubtedly there will continue to be periods of fairly general surplus production in agriculture and frequent overproduction of one or another specific crop. Methods for dealing with these situations need to be included in policies and plans. However, it would seem to be unrealistic to expect a situation of almost chronic depression in agriculture and a need for virtually continuous governmental intervention in its behalf. Farm people will themselves need to make a choice as to whether they wish to throw their influence on the side of a continually widening reliance on government aid, and its inevitable concomitant — a constantly increasing amount of government control — or whether they choose to regard government intervention as something to be used only temporarily and in times of genuine need.

INDEX

INDEX

AAA, *see* Agricultural Adjustment Administration

Abandoned farms: in New England, 89

Abolitionist movement, 79

Acreage allotments, 378, 482*n*; probable retention as device for price support, 517; *see also* Domestic allotment plan

Acreage control: in AAA program, 303–04

Adams, John, President, 14, 94; and tariff protection, 45*n*, 46–47

Adams, John Quincy, President: ideas on internal improvements, 64, 66

Adams Act (1906), 84

Adjusted base price: in Agricultural Act of 1948, 475–76, 483

"Administered pricing": in Sapiro cooperative plan, 196

Agricultural Act of 1948, 474–79, 480–81, 482, 484, 487*n*, 517

Agricultural Act of 1949, 478–84, 487*n*

Agricultural Adjustment Act (1933), 269, 281–84, 375, 376; Thomas Amendment (Title III), 296*n;* theory of the Act as an emergency measure, 302; unconstitutional (*U.S. v. Butler*, 1936), 309, 340, 343, 345, 348, 349–50, 355; 1935 amendments, *see* Section 32 funds; parity price objective, 350

Agricultural Adjustment Act (1938), 352, 375–80, 478–79, 498; quota limitations nullified, World War II, 435; Title II of Agricultural Act of 1948 based on, 473–74, 475, 480–81; *see also* Federal Crop Insurance Corporation

Agricultural Adjustment Administration, 283–85, 292, 293, 294, 394; effectiveness of program, 310–15; orientation to producers, 335–36; program in operation, 302–15; Program Planning Division, 302–03, 346–48, 351*n;* reorganization under Soil Conservation and Domestic Allotment Act, 350–52; rivalry with Soil Conservation Service, 395–96

Agricultural college system, 82, 83; *see also* Association of Land-Grant Colleges and Universities

Agricultural Congress, First National (1872), 105

Agricultural Cooperation and Rural Credit in Europe, 146

Agricultural education: beginnings in, 83; Smith-Hughes Act (1917), 154; *see also* Agricultural extension service; Land-grant college system

Agricultural experiment stations: established by Hatch Act (1887), 84; enlarged by Adams Act (1906), 84; Grange influence in establishment of, 105; growth after 1900, 117; Purnell Act (1925), 153*n*, 237, 393*n;* Bankhead-Jones Act (1937), 393*n;* Research and Marketing Act (1946), 496–97

Agricultural extension service, 153*n*, 393, 394; work of Seaman A. Knapp, 119, 152–53; Smith-Lever Act (1914), 153–54, 162, 176, 393; growth during World War I, 171, 176; connection with farm bureaus, 176–78, 190, 191; farm labor responsibilities, World War II, 439

Agricultural fairs, 82

Agricultural fundamentalism, 4

Agricultural implements: improvement of, 82–83; on free list, 1913, 143; 1922, 204

Agricultural Labor Administration: World War II, 434, 439

Agricultural machinery: rationed during World War II, 433–34

Agricultural Marketing Act (1929), 239–40, 264, 271; *see also* Federal Farm Board

Agricultural Marketing Administration, 335*n*

Agricultural Marketing Agreement Act (1937), 474; not affected by unconstitutionality of AAA, 355

Agricultural mechanization, *see* Mechanization of agriculture

Agricultural organizations, *see* Farmer organizations

Agricultural research, *see* Research, agricultural

Agricultural Research Administration: report with Bureau of Agricultural Economics on acreage increases, 1943, 441–42

Agricultural Resources Conservation Service: recommended by Hoover Commission, 498

Agricultural societies, 82; *see also* Farmer organizations

Agricultural Stabilization Commission: proposed by E. T. Meredith, 222*n*

Agricultural Wheel, 105–06, 107

Agriculture, Department of: Grange influence in gaining cabinet status for, 105; history of, 118; increase in influence after 1900, 118; efforts to increase food supply during World War I, 161–62; expanded research on social and economic problems of agriculture, 237; regional laboratories provided in Agricultural Act of 1938, 379–80; Mount Weather Agreement (1938), 394–95, 497; leadership in preparation for defense, 403; Agricultural Labor Administration, 434, 439; Committee on Foreign Purchase and Importation (World War II), 434*n;* post-World War II plans, 456, 457

— Secretaries, *see* Charles F. Brannan; Howard M. Gore; David F. Houston; Arthur M. Hyde; William M. Jardine; E. T. Meredith; Henry A. Wallace; Henry C. Wallace; Claude Wickard; James Wilson

Aiken, George: and National Food Allotment Plan, 471–72, 479; Agricultural Act of 1948, 472–78

Aldrich, Nelson W., 132, 144

Aldrich-Vreeland Act (1908), 131

Alexander, Will: Farm Security Administrator, 363–64

Alienation of land, 8, 9; under Homestead Act, 19*n; see also* Land policy

All-Iowa Agricultural Marketing Conference, 222

Alliance of Colored Farmers of Texas, 107

Allied Wheat Executive, 165

Allison, W. B., 41

Allison bill (1888), 56

Allotment rights: in domestic allotment plan, 268; Agricultural Adjustment Act of 1938, 375; *see also* Domestic allotment plan

Allotments, acreage, *see* Acreage allotments

Almond Growers Exchange, 136

Almonds: tariff on, 1816, 46

Alsberg, Carl: Chief of the Bureau of Chemistry, 151

American Bankers' Association: study of credit facilities for agriculture, 145–46

"American Commission," 146

American Cotton Cooperative Association, 259–60

American Cotton Growers' Exchange, 223, 224

American Council of Agriculture, 217, 219, 220, 221–22

American Farm Bureau Federation: establishment of, 171, 172; background, 176–78; early growth and program, 178–79; leader in Farm Bloc, 181*n*, 182; legislative program, 191; criticism by other farm organizations, 190–91; action on lowering freight rates, 192, 379*n;* business operation of, 97*n;* cooperative marketing campaign, 195, 257, 258; opposition to early price-fixing proposals, 208; attitude toward McNary-Haugen plan, 214–15, 216; support for Norbeck-Burtness proposal, 216; plank submitted to Republican convention, 1928, 230n; monetary policy, 1930's, 270, 295, 511; policies for combating depression, 270–72; attitude on Muscle Shoals, 321n; and New Deal agricultural program, 339–42; attitude toward NRA, 340; objections to proposals of President's Committee on Farm Tenancy, 362; criticism of FSA, 364n, 439n; policy, late 1930's, 387; opposed to transfer of FCA to USDA, 393; and trade agreements program, 397; position on farm price controls, 408, 505; views on changes in agricultural legislation, 1949, 479–80; views on Brannan. Plan, 488, 489

American Farmer, The, 82

American Federation of Labor, 111

American Institute of Cooperation, 198n, 237

American Red Cross: Farm Board donations to, 263

American Revolution, 32

American Society for the Encouragement of American Manufactures, 45n

American Society of Equity, 134, 139n, 142n, 147n, 176, 189

"American system" of Henry Clay, 49, 63, 64

American Tobacco Company, 135n

Ancient Order of Gleaners (Michigan), 109n

Anderson, Clinton, 481

Anderson, J. M., 196

Anderson, Sydney, 194n, 200n, 225

Animal power: increased use after Civil War, 86

Animals: imported for breeding purposes, on free list, 1794, 45; 1816, 46; 1954, 50; diseases of, 116, 117, 133

Annecy Conference: tariff agreements, 502

Anti-pass Act (Wisconsin, 1874), 101

Antiprotectionist sentiment, *see* Tariff reform

Anti-resumptionists: post-Civil War, 34

Antitrust laws: Sherman Antitrust Act (1890), 92n; Grange recommendations for amendment of (1911), 140; Clayton Antitrust Act (1914), 148–49

Apple growers: Federal Farm Board aid to, 260, 264

Apples: Federal Surplus Commodities Corporation operations in, 381

Appropriation Act of 1834, 66–67

Apricots: Federal Surplus Commodities Corporation operations in, 381

Arid lands: reclamation of, 124–28; *see also* Semiarid lands

Arkansas: state banks in, 28; Agricultural Wheel in, 106

Army plan for land settlement (1783), 10

Arthur, Chester A., President, 55

Asia: situation at end of World War II, 460

Association of Land-Grant Colleges and Universities: attitude on agricultural situation of the 1920's, 231–32n, 1932, 277; Mount Weather Agreement (1938), 394–95, 497; Postwar Policy Committee Reports, 457, 469–70, 471, 491; proposals on soil conservation, 1948, 497–98

Assumption Act (Hamilton's), 24

Aswell, James Benjamin, 229

Aswell bill, 225

Atkeson, T. C., 134, 153n, 190

Audubon, John James, 82

Austria, 4, 88, 243

Ayres, Leonard P., quoted, 289n

Babcock, S. M., 117

Babcock test, 117

"Back-to-the-land" movement, 145, 154

Balance of payments, 169; World War I and after, 161n, 203; shift after world wars, 512

Balance of trade: 1835, 27; as changed by World War I, 202–03

Balanced budget, *see* Budget, balanced

Baldwin, C. B.: Farm Security Administrator, 364n, 492

Balkan countries: situation at end of World War II, 460

Ballinger, R. A.: Secretary of the Interior, 132n

Baltimore and Ohio Railroad, 66

Bang's disease: AAA program for elimination of, 309n

Bank credit: increase in, 38

Bank deposits: post-Civil War period, 37

Bank failures: 1930–1933, 246–47, 275, 278; *see also* Panics, financial

Bank Holiday (1933), 278–79

Bank note circulation: 1812, 25; 1817, 25; Jackson period, 26; 1837, 27; 1843, 27; 1930, 27; 1935, 27

Bank notes: confusion, before Civil War, 29–30

Bank notes, national: during Civil War, 31–32; issues by 1865, 37; opposition to, 39n

Bank notes, state: during Civil War, 31–32, 33; withdrawal of, 37

Bank of North Dakota, 171n, 185n

Bank of the United States: first (1791–1811), 23–25; second, 25–28, 29, 46, 62, 510

Bankhead bill (1943): vetoed by President Roosevelt, 425–26

Bankhead Cotton Control Act (1934), 304, 307, 311, 377

Bankhead-Jones Act (1937), 393n

Bankhead-Jones Farm Tenant Act (1937), 325, 327, 362–63, 493, 494

Bankruptcy law (1841), 27

Banks: lack of, in early period, 24

Banks, national: during Civil War, 31; requirements for charter, 31n; opposed by farmers, 39, 108, 114; inadequate to meet needs, 130; loans, 1920–1921, 186n; Emergency Banking Act (1933), 279

Banks, state: and Bank of the United States, 24–25; 1830–1840, 28–29

Banks for cooperatives, 264, 266; establishment, 282; storage loans permitted, Agricultural Act of 1949, 483

Barbed wire (1873), 117

Barley: tariff on, 1890, 57; basic commodity by Jones-Connally Act (1934), 302n; AAA program not developed for, 309

Barnes, Julius H.: Director of Food Administration Grain Corporation, 166

Barrett, Charles S., 218

Basic commodities, 225, 227, 302–03; in first McNary-Haugen plan, 214; sugar beets and cane added, 309; peanuts added, 310; flexible price supports, Agricultural Act of 1948, 477, 478, 481; Agricultural Act of 1949, 481, 483; *see also* Corn; Cotton; Peanuts; Rice; Tobacco; Wheat

Bathrick Bill (1914), 147

Beans, dry: Federal Surplus Commodities Corporation operations in, 381; production goals, World War II, 437

Beef: tariff on, 1909 and 1922 compared, 204; international conference on, 399

Beef cattle: production, World War I, 167; computation of "adjusted base price" for, 475–76; price supports proposed in Brannan Plan, 486

"Beef Trust," 128, 129

Beer: tariff on, 1789, 45; 1816, 46

Beer Act (1933), 279–80

Belgium: Commission for the Relief of, 159; progress toward financial stability, 1920's, 243; maintenance of gold standard, 292, 293; situation at end of World War II, 460

Benefit payments: in AAA program, 302, 303, 375, 378; for sugar production, 356; adjustment to war goals, World War II, 434, 435; probable retention as device for price support, 517; *see also* Government payments to farmers; Incentive payments

Bennett, Hugh H.: soil erosion studies, 317

Benton, Thomas Hart, 18, 79n

Better rural living: influence of Grange in aiding, 105

Beveridge, Albert J., 138
Beveridge Amendment to the Agricultural Appropriation Act (1906), 133
Biddle, Nicholas, 26
Big business: farmer opposition to, 92–93, 128
Bimetallism, 40n, 42; see also Gold; Silver; Monetary policy
Bixby, Fred H., 218
Black, A. G.: Governor of Farm Credit Administration, 393, 395
Black, John D.: domestic allotment plan, 239, 267–69; cited, 277
Blackstone, W. L.: objections to proposals of President's Committee on Farm Tenancy, 362
Blaine, James G., 56
Bland-Allison Act (1878), 41–42, 296n
Bland bill (1876), 40–41
Blue Eagle, NRA symbol, 286–87, 369
Board of Food and Drugs Inspection, 132
Boll weevil, cotton, 116, 119
Bonneville Dam, 127
Boss, Andrew, 137, 205
Bowles, Chester: OPA Administrator, 425
Bradfute, O. E., 217n, 218, 223
Brand, Charles J.: and McNary-Haugen plan, 212, 304; Coadministrator of AAA, 284
Brannan, Charles F., Secretary of Agriculture: Brannan Plan, 479, 481, 484–90, 517
Brazil: international coffee agreement, 398
Brazilian coffee valorization program, 265n
Breeders' Gazette, The, 120n
British Dominions: situation at end of World War II, 460
Brookings Institution: study of NRA, 290
Brothers of Freedom, 107
Brown, John G., 217n
Brown, Prentiss: OPA Administrator, 425
Brown, William J., 217n
Bryan, William Jennings, 43, 59, 111, 131
Budget, balanced: Hoover policy, 250, 254; adherence to idea of, 270, 273n; in administration of F. D. Roosevelt, 279
Bull Moose movement (1912), 132, 138, 146
Bureau of Agricultural Economics, 205–06; "outlook reports," 232, 237; effort to change function to policy making, after 1938, 395; report with Agricultural Research Administration on acreage increases, 1943, 441–42; ideas on post-World War II problems, 458
Bureau of Agricultural Engineering: establishment of soil erosion experiment stations, 317
Bureau of Animal Industry, 119n, 133
Bureau of Chemistry, 119, 132n, 133, 151
Bureau of Chemistry and Soils: establishment of soil erosion experiment stations, 317
Bureau of Corporations: functions taken over by Federal Trade Commission, 149
Bureau of Crop and Livestock Estimates, 205
Bureau of Fisheries: changes in policy during World War I, 161
Bureau of Home Economics, 153n
Bureau of Internal Revenue: control of wages and salaries, World War II, 437–38
Bureau of Markets, 137, 205
Bureau of Plant Industry: beginnings of work in, 137; farm management work, 120
Bureau of Reclamation: during Wilson's administration, 155; efforts to increase food supply during World War I, 161
Burley Society, 135n
Burtness, Olger Burton, 215
Bush, Vannevar, 401
Business recovery: NRA program, 285–90, 292, 293, 294, 302, 305, 306, 310, 314
Butter: on free list with Canada, 1854, 50; tariff on,

1890, 57; Federal Surplus Commodities Corporation operations in, 381; roll-back ordered for, 1943, 426; World War II subsidy, 428; lend-lease shipments of, 442–43
Butter and cheese: prices, Civil War period, 36
Butterfat: price supports proposed in Brannan Plan, 486
Butterfield, Kenyon L., 153
Byrnes, James: Stabilization Director, 420, 426n

CALHOUN, JOHN C., 65; and tariff protection, 46; and internal improvements, 62–63; Vice President, 47
California: constitution of, 102; Granger movement, 102; railroad legislation, 102; agricultural development of, 118; early irrigation systems in, 126; recipient of migrant farm laborers, 370
California Fruit Growers Exchange, 136, 238, 258
California Grape Control Board, 264
Call money rates: 1929, 245–46
Canada: reciprocity with, 50, 132, 139, opposed by Grange, 142; wheat production, World War I, 165
Canals: 1820's, 64; 1840's, 67; see also Internal improvements
Capper, Arthur, 181, 185, 199, 200n, 202, 430n, 473n
Capper-Haugen bill (1925), 220
Capper-Tincher bill (1921), 183n
Capper-Volstead Cooperative Marketing Act (1922), 184, 235
Carey, Robert D., 218
Carey Act (1894), 125–26
Cartelization: under NRA codes, 288
Carver, George Washington, 118
Carver, Thomas Nixon, 137
Cash crops: background of, in South, 78; preferred by many landlords, 360; see also Commercial agriculture
Catchings, Waddill, 242n
Cattle: tariff on breeding animals repealed, 1794, 45; production of, 1870–1900, 85n; on free list, 1913, 143; basic commodity in first McNary-Haugen plan, 214, by Jones-Connally Act (1934), 302n; production goals, World War II, 437
Cattle barons: resistance to correction of evils, 80
Cattle industry: work of Farmers' Alliance in correction of problems affecting, 108
Cattlemen: controversy with sheepmen, 21
CCC, see Civilian Conservation Corps
CCC, see Commodity Credit Corporation
Ceiling prices, see Price controls
Census: 1870, 85, 94n; 1880, 116
Central banking system: opposition of farmers to, 28, 139; absence of, before Civil War, 29
Central Europe: situation at end of World War II, 460
Central Pacific Railroad, 68, 69, 70, 72, 102
Central Statistical Board, 280n
Central Valley of California: multipurpose river development, 323
Cereal crops, see Grain
Chadbourne Plan, 399
Chase, Salmon P.: Secretary of the Treasury, 29, 39n; Chief Justice, 39n
Cheese: tariff on, 1789, 45; 1816, 46; on free list with Canada, 1854, 50
Chesapeake and Delaware Canal Company, 64
Chesapeake and Ohio Canal Company, 64
Chicago and Alton Railroad Co. v. The People ex. rel. Gustavus Koerner et al., Comrs. (1873), 100n
Chicago, Milwaukee and St. Paul Railway Company v. Minnesota (1890), 102
Chickens: price supports, Agricultural Act of 1948, 474
China: effect on, of U.S. silver purchase program, 296n, 341, 365; loan from Reconstruction Finance Corporation, 334
Christopherson bill (government price-fixing), 207
Churchill, Winston, 454

Citrus industries: Federal Farm Board aid to, 260, 264
Civil War: conflicts in social philosophy prior to, 78;
    price changes during period, 36; tariffs during, 51;
    financing, 32, 37, 168; economic results of, 16; see
    also Fiat currency; Greenback issue and headings
    following
Civil Works Administration (CWA), 300
Civilian Conservation Corps (CCC), 279–80, 318, 395
Clark, Edgar E., 181
Classified lands, legislation relating to, 125n
Clay, Henry: on "distribution," 18n; and Bank of the
    United States, 26; and tariff protection, 46–47; "Amer-
    ican system," 49, 63, 64n; on internal improvements,
    63–64, 65; opposed to slavery, 79n
Clayton Antitrust Act (1914): provisions of, 148–49
Clearing-house system: under National Bank Act (1863),
    31
Cleveland, Grover, President, 42, 56, 58–59, 111, 123
Clinton, George, 25
Codes, industrial: as provided in NRA, 286–88, 306
Coffee: tariff on, 1861, 51, 1890, 57; on free list, 1872,
    1875, 54; valorization program (Brazil), 265; interna-
    tional agreement on, 398; roll-back ordered for, 1943,
    426
Coffee valorization program (Brazil), 265n
Coffey, W. C., 218
Coinage Act (1873), 40
Colmer, William M.: Chairman of House Special Com-
    mittee on Postwar Economic Policy and Planning
    (Colmer Committee), 470, 491
Colonial preference (Great Britain): end of (1846), 50
Colorado: state hail insurance experiments, 381–82
Colored Farmers' National Alliance and Cooperative
    Union, 107–08
Columbia River area: multipurpose river development,
    322n, 323
Combined Food Board, 405, 433, 443, 445
Commerce, Department of: established (1903), 156; ef-
    forts to increase food supply during World War I, 161;
    Secretary, see Herbert Hoover
Commercial agriculture: early significance, 83; relation
    to expansion of railroads, 70; stimulated by decrease
    in ratio of farmers, 87; increasing amount of capital
    required, 357; development of, summary, 518; see also
    Cash crops
Commercial banks: farm mortgage loans by, World
    War II, 453
Commission for the Relief of Belgium, 159
Commissioner loans, 281, 494; 1937, 391; in Emergency
    Mortgage Relief Act (1933), 281–82
"Committee Bill," 224–26
"Committee for the Nation," 297n
Committee of Eleven (dairy marketing), 197n
Committee of Fifteen (livestock marketing), 197
Committee of Seventeen (grain marketing), 196
Committee of Ten (vegetable marketing), 197n
Committee of Twenty-five (wool marketing), 197n
Committee of Twenty-one (fruit marketing), 197n
Committee of Twenty-two, 222–23, 226
Committee on Government Statistics and Information
    Services, 280n
Committee on the Economic Report, Council of Eco-
    nomic Advisers, 467
Commodities Finance Corporation, 257n
Commodity agreement plan: inconsistent with reciprocal
    trade program, 400
Commodity Credit Corporation (CCC), 307, 332–33;
    Agricultural Adjustment Act of 1938, loan policy
    specified, 376, price support functions, 377; accumula-
    tions of wheat, cotton and corn, 378; and Farm Board
    compared, 378, 388, 389, 390, 391; role, 1937–1941,
    388–91; corn loans, 389; cotton loans, 389–90; post-
    war price guarantees on basic commodities, 416; sugar

subsidy, 424; struggles over extension of life of (1943),
    427, 430; limitations on payments by, 430; responsible
    for handling importation of agricultural materials, 433;
    directives and authorizations in Agricultural Act of
    1948, 475, 477, 478n; regulations in Agricultural Act
    of 1949, 483; summary of importance of loans, 516;
    probable retention of loans as devise for price support,
    517; see also Commodity loans; Nonrecourse loans;
    Steagall Amendment; Steagall commodities
Commodity dollar: farmer organizations on, 341, 343,
    345
Commodity Exchange Commission, 352
Commodity exchanges: farmer agitation for control of,
    352
Commodity loans: authorized by Federal Farm Board,
    258; to cooperatives, 264; Farmers Union policy on,
    late 1930's, 387; see also Commodity Credit Corpora-
    tion
Common lands: in New England, 6
Commons, John R., 245n
Comparative advantage: rise and decline of, in New
    England, 89
Compensatory budgets: Keynes' doctrine, 250
Competition: inadequacy as regulator of prices, 286
Competitive tariff: principle of Democratic party, 142
Compromise Tariff of 1833, 18n
Confederacy: monetary policies of, 32
Confederation: government under, 4; land policy of, 3,
    10–12
Congress, U.S., see U.S. Congress
"Consent decrees," 149
Conservation: little interest in before 1900, 113; Theo-
    dore Roosevelt's policies on, 122–24; National Con-
    servation Conference, 123–24; National Conservation
    Commission, 124; status by 1915, 136; favored by
    National Grange, 139, 343, 386–87; during Wilson's
    administration, 155; forests, 316; New Deal program,
    316–24; Division of Grazing, 319–21; of land under
    Resettlement Administration program, 325; American
    Farm Bureau Federation on, New Deal period, 342;
    "soil-depleting" and "soil-conserving" crops, 350–51,
    378; see also Civilian Conservation Corps
— soil, 316–19, 387, 491; emphasis under Soil Conser-
    vation and Domestic Allotment Act (1936), 349, 351,
    375, 396; Agricultural Adjustment Act of 1938, 375;
    development of district plan, 395–96; emphasis in
    Aiken bill, 1948, 473; post-World War II develop-
    ments, 497–98; summary, 509, 517–18; debatable as
    price support measure, 517; see also Soil Conservation
    Service
Conservation policy: summary, 508, 509, 517–18
Constitution, U.S.: government under, 3, 4; early con-
    troversies over, 23; strict interpretation, 65, 67; six-
    teenth and seventeenth amendments to, 140n
Consumer safeguards: in Agricultural Adjustment Act of
    1938, 378–79
Consumers: problem of representation of, 335–37
Consumers' Advisory Board (in NRA), 336–37
Consumers' Counsel (in AAA), 336–37
Consumption of food, see Food consumption
Contracts in restraint of trade: unenforceable under Eng-
    lish and American common law, 92
Cooley, Harold D., 478
Coolidge, Calvin, President: and McNary-Haugen idea,
    210, 217–19; support for Norbeck–Burtness proposal,
    216; address to American Farm Bureau Federation,
    1925, 223n; vetoes of McNary-Haugen bills, 228, 229;
    recommendations on Muscle Shoals during administra-
    tion of, 321
Cooper, Peter, 35
Cooperation: Rochdale plan, 96, 136, 195; movement
    stimulated by Federal Farm Board, 266–67
Cooperative farms: established by FSA, 363–64, 492,

493n; prohibited in Farmers Home Administration Act, 494

Cooperative marketing, 234–35, 265; Capper-Volstead Act (1922), 184; Sapiro plan, 194–98, 234–35, 514; recommendations of Joint Commission of Agricultural Inquiry, 200; recommendations of National Agricultural Conference, 201; proposals of President's Agricultural Commission on (1925), 219–20; Jardine bill, 221; in political party platforms, 1928, 230; stressed by backers of Federal Farm Board, 257; backed by farmer organizations, 269, 271, 272

Cooperative Marketing Act (1922), 184

Cooperative Marketing Act (1926), 198n

Cooperative organization: development of, 135–36; legal status, 179, 180; growth during 1920's, 237–38; encouraged by Agricultural Marketing Act of 1929, 240–41; weaknesses in Farm Board plan, 257–58; electric, funds supplied by REA, 338; see also National Cooperative Council; National Council of Farmers' Cooperative Marketing Associations; National Council of Farmer Cooperatives

Cooperative Research and Service Division, Farm Credit Administration, 266n

"Cooperators": defined, 378

Copper: subsidization of high-cost mines during World War II, 419n

Corn: prices, Civil War period, 36; tariff on, 1890, 57, on free list, 1913, 143, 1909 and 1922 compared, 204; production, 1870–1900, 85, 1933, 289; decrease in man-hours required to produce, 86, 87; exports, 1900–1915, 121; acreage and production, 1917–1918, 167, in post-World War I period, 170; basic commodity in AAA program, 302n; reductions resulting from AAA and drought, 1934–1935, 312, 313, 353; CCC loans on, under AAA of 1933, 332–33, 389; Act of 1938, program limited to "commercial areas," 376, loan provisions, 377; normal supply of, 377n; carryovers, 1939–1942, 390, 406, CCC compared with Farm Board, 378; World War II, 411, 416, goals, 433, 436; no marketing quotas, 1942, 434; price supports, Agricultural Act of 1948, 474, 477, 478n, 481, Act of 1949, 481–82, proposed in Brannan Plan, 486; crop insurance on, 495

Corn belt: support for McNary-Haugen plan, 214, 217

Corn Belt Advisory Committee, 180n

Corn Belt Committee, 221–22, 226; origin in Des Moines Conference, 220–21

Corn cultivator, 83

Corn-hog ratio, 164, 308

Corn laws, English: repealed, 1846, 83

Corn planter, 83

Corporate power: growth of, 90

Corporations: returns to, World War II, 452

Cost of living: efforts to control, World War II, 413–14

"Cost of production plus a profit": goal in Corn Belt group proposals, 221

"Cost of production" principle in tariffs: Republican plank, 1908, 131–32, 141, 142

Cotton: in southern colonies, 9; in Louisiana, 16; on free list, 1789, 45, 1854, 50, 1922, 205; tariff on, 1816, 46, 1842, 49; slavery and, 79, 81; English demand for during Civil War, 84n; production, 1820–1860, 81, 1870–1900, 85, World War I, 159n, 167, reductions due to AAA and drought, 353, 1939–1945, 441, world production, 1920's, 277, 278; efforts of Farmers Union to improve prices of, 134; exports, 1900–1915, 121, 1927–1931, 310–11, 1929–1933, 277n, 1930's, 311; prices, World War I, 143n, 159n, 1929–1932, 246, 1941, 409; American Cotton Cooperative Association, 259–60; basic commodity, in first McNary-Haugen plan, 214, 216n, 225, in AAA program, 302n; effect of dollar devaluation on, 298, 299; AAA program for production control, 303–04, 307, 313; situation compared with wheat, 1933, 311; carryovers, reduction on,

1933–1936, 313, 1920's, 1945, 406–07, CCC as compared with Farm Board, 378, late 1930's, 390; CCC loans on, 332–33, 389–90; Agricultural Adjustment Act of 1938, marketing quotas for, 377, normal supply of, 377n; Federal Surplus Commodities Corporation operations in, 381; crop insurance on, 384, 495; decline of importance in international trade, 400; World War II, 416, 437, 441; lend-lease shipments of, 443n; price supports, Agricultural Act of 1948, 474, 477, 478n, 481, Act of 1949, 481–83, proposed in Brannan Plan, 486

Cotton boll weevil, 116, 119

Cotton gin (1793), 79

Cotton growers: interest in McNary-Haugen plan, 223, 224; on tariff protection and cooperative marketing, 270

Cotton Stabilization Corporation, 257n, 260, 263–66

Cottonseed oil: Federal Surplus Commodities Corporation operations in, 381

Coulter, John Lee, 181n

Council of Economic Advisers: provided in Employment Act of 1946, 467

Council of National Defense, 160; reactivated, 1940, 412

Counties: New England, 6; in middle colonies, 8; in South, 9; in ordinance of 1787, 12

Country Gentlemen, The, 120n

Country Life Commission (1908), 120, 145, 154

Country store: connection with sharecropping, 90

County farm advisers, 171; network extended during World War I, 161–62; connection with farm bureaus, 176–78, 190, 191

County land-use planning committees: participation in BAE coordination efforts, 395; mechanism for defense planning before World War II, 403–04

Coverdale, John W., 178, 197n, 198n, 258

Crawford, C. C.: support for Bank of the United States, 25; and tariff protection, 46

Cream: on free list, 1913, 143

Cream separator, hand-operated, 117

Credit, agricultural: long-term real estate loans, 28–29 (see also Mortgages, farm); growing importance of, after 1900, 113; inadequacies, 131, 137, 247, 360–61; need for, post-World War I, 174, 175; Emergency Agricultural Credits Act (1921), 183; intermediate-term, 184–87; 1920's, critical analysis of policies, 237; situation of federal credit agencies, 234; need for improvements in, 1930–1932, 260; American Farm Bureau Federation ideas on, 270, 341; Farm Credit Act of 1933, 282–83, amended (1937), 392; Regional Agricultural Credit Corporations, 282, 434; Grange policy, 342, 386; New Deal period, Farmers Union on, 344, National Cooperative Council attitudes on, 345, summary of farmer organization views on, 346; situation, late 1930's, 391–93; repayment of loans, amortization plan, 391, 453, variable payment feature, 362; policies during World War II, 453–54; summary, 508, 511, 516; see also Commodity Credit Corporation; Farm Credit Administration; Farm Security Administration; Farmers Home Administration; Federal land banks

Credit, bank: 1929–1934, 246

Credit, land: Hamilton's proposal for, 13; in Act of 1796, 13–14; in Harrison Land Act of 1800, 14; in Ohio Enabling Act (1802), 15; Gallatin's views on, 15; proposal by Jeremiah Morrow on, 17; measures for relief of settlers, 17; none allowed in Land Act of 1820, 17

Credit Mobilier, 71, 94n

Credit policies: Federal Reserve Board, 365

"Crime of '73," 40

"Crocker contracts," 72

Crop controls: net results, 313; see also Agricultural Adjustment Administration

Crop insurance, 381–84, 387, 389n, 491; in domestic allotment plan, 268–69; merged with ever-normal granary idea, 333; early experience with, 381–82; revival of idea, 1945, 384; extension advocated by Grange, 386; multiple crop insurance, 1944–1949, 495–96
Crop Insurance Corporation, see Federal Crop Insurance Corporation
Crop yields: decrease in, due to insects and diseases, 77
Cropper system, see Sharecropping
Crowell, Frank G.: Director of Food Administration Grain Corporation, 166
Cuba: special concessions (1934), 329
Cullom, Shelby Moore, 103
Cultivator, The, 82
Cumberland Road, 14–15; appropriations for, 1789–1830, 64n; repairs for, 63–64, 67
Cummins, Albert Baird, 138
Currants: tariff on, 1816, 46
Currency: during Civil War, 31–32; Greenback issue, 32–35, 37–39; revaluation of, 37–38, 38n, 281; stabilization of, 37–38; inflation of, authorized in Agricultural Act of 1933, 281; see also Monetary policy
Curtis-Crisp bill (1927), 227, 228
Customs revenue, see Section 32 funds
CWA (Civil Works Administration), 300

Dairy industry: effects of Babcock test and hand-operated cream separator on, 117; Federal Farm Board aid to, 260, 264; and tariff protection, 270; AAA efforts to restrict supplies, 308
Dairy products: production of, 1870–1900, 85n; Federal Surplus Commodities Corporation operations in, 381; World War II subsidy, 428; exports, 1935–1950, 501; ECA purchases, 1948–1950, 501
Dairymen's League, 238
Dallas, Alexander J.: Secretary of the Treasury, 25
Davis, Chester C.: and McNary-Haugen movement, 223, 226, 230; Administrator of AAA, 284, 306, 337, 347; member, National Defense Advisory Commission, 404; War Food Administrator, 405, 434
Davis, Jefferson: philosophy of, 90
Davis, John H.: views on changes in agricultural legislation, 1949, 480; views on Brannan Plan, 489
Davis, John W.: candidate for President, 1924, 218
Davis, Joseph S., quoted, 298
Dawes, Charles G., 230
Dawes Plan (1924), 233, 243
Dawes tariff bill (1872), 53
Debt, farm mortgage, see Farm debt; Mortgages, farm
Debtor status of farmers: as aftermath of Civil War, 84
Defense Production Act (1950), 504–05
Defense Supplies Corporation: and subsidy program, 424, 426n
Deficit financing: greenbacks and, 38; not discussed during 1920's, 245n; needed in early stage of depression, 250; policy of Roosevelt administration, 250; opposition to idea, 272, 510–11; New Deal period, 279, 300, 314, 315; waning influence of, 1938, 365; World War II, 458; question of practicability in Employment Act of 1946, 468
Deflation, 38, 354n; Houston on situation in 1920, 175; concern over possibilities of, 511, 512
Deflationary influences: of second Bank of the United States, 26; gold resumption (1879), 37; stock market crash, 1929, 246
Delaware: land system of, 7–9
Democratic party: and Independent Treasury, 28; views on currency, 34; election campaigns, 1868, 35, 1884, 73, 1896, 43, 1928, 230, 1932, 273–74, 1948, 478; on tariff matters, 50, 54–56, 131, 142; free silver platform, 1896, 111; farm relief plank, 1928, 230; Dixiecrat rebellion, 484

Demonstration, agricultural: work of Seaman A. Knapp in, 119, 152–53; in soil conservation program, 318
Denman, C. B., 240
Departments of government, see Agriculture; Commerce; etc.
Depressions: 1837, 27; 1920's (agricultural), 180–206, 235–36; 1930's, 244 ff.; planning oriented to, after World War II, 465–66; recommendations of Colmer Committee on, 471; recommendations of Land-Grant College Committee on (1944), 470, 471
Desert Land Act (1877), 19n, 20, 22, 125, 319n
Devaluation of currencies: significance, 291–92, 296
Devaluation of the dollar, 1933, 295–99, 302, 328, 511; effect on export crops, 298; ineffectiveness of scheme, 365
Dewey, Thomas E., 478
Dickinson, L. J., 182
Dickinson bill: introduced, 220; endorsed by farm groups, 222, 223; passed (1926), 226, 304
Dietary improvement: increased emphasis on, 384–86
Dingley Tariff (1897), 59–60
Direct election of United States Senators, backed by Grange, 139, 140
Disaster loans, 516
Discount rates (1920), 174
Discriminatory (railroad) rates, 68, 70, 73
Dismal Swamp Canal Company, 64
Disposal of the public lands: in Clay's "American system," 63, 64n
Distress loans, 282, 326
Diversification of agriculture: in northern colonies and states, 78, 79, 81; Norbeck-Burtness proposal, 215–16, 236, 237; discouraged by McNary-Haugen plan (Coolidge), 228
Diversionary programs for crops: to abnormal outlets, 334; Agricultural Adjustment Administration, 334; export subsidies, 334–35; FERA, 334–35; Federal Farm Board, 334; Federal Surplus Commodities Corporation, 335
Division of Cooperative Marketing, 266n; established by Dickinson Act (1926), 226n
Division of Grazing, 316; Grazing Service (1934), 20
Division of Marketing and Marketing Agreements, 381
Division of Statistical Standards, Bureau of the Budget, 280n
Division of Subsistence Homesteads, 326–27
"Dixiecrat" rebellion, 484
Dollar, devaluation of, see Devaluation of the dollar
Dollar, revaluation of: authorized in Agricultural Act of 1933, 281
Dollar, stabilization of: early discussion of, 245n
Dollar, variation of gold content of, 294
Dollar matching, 187n
Dollar shortage: after World War II, 461
Domestic allotment: Act of 1936, 375; Agricultural Adjustment Act of 1938, 375
Domestic allotment plan, 239, 267–69; backed by Roosevelt, 1932 campaign, 273; antecedent of AAA program, 283, 307; similarity to features of Brannan Plan, 487
Donations of land: in Louisiana Territory, 16; policy of Thomas Hart Benton, 18
Drew, Frank M., quoted, 108n, 109
Droughts: 1930's, 252, 253, 312, 313, 314, 342, 351, 353, 357, 375, 382, 389, 391; Europe, 1947, 458, 461, 500; see also Conservation: soil
Drug industry: resistance to correction of evils, 80
Dust Bowl, 20, 299, 317, 370

East: attitude toward public domain, 18; rural living in, 114; see also Sectionalism
Eckhardt, W. G., 196
Economic and Social Council, United Nations, 460

Economic Cooperation Administration, 462, 464, 500–01

Economic nationalism, 332

Economic Report: provided in Employment Act of 1946, 467

Economy Act (1933), 279–80

Edge Law (1919), 210

Education, agricultural, see Agricultural education

Educational reserves, 11, 12, 18; in Pennsylvania, 10; in Land Act of 1796, 13; in Mississippi Territory Act of 1803, 15; in Ohio Enabling Act, 15

Edwards, Gladys Talbott, quoted, 176n

Eggs: on free list, 1854, 50, 1913, 143; tariff on, 1890, 57; Federal Surplus Commodities Corporation operations in, 381; production goals, World War II, 437; lend-lease shipments of, 442–43n; price supports, Agricultural Act of 1948, 474; ECA purchases of, 1948–1950, 501

Eisenhower, Milton, 394

Election campaigns: 1920, 180–81; 1924, 218–19; 1928, 230–31; 1932, 272–74; 1936, 354–55; 1946, 472

Electrification, rural, see Rural electrification

Elevators, see Grain elevators

Elkins Law (1903), 129

Ellsworth, Henry L., 118

Emancipation of the slaves: aftermath, 89–90

Embargo Act (1807), 17, 24, 62

Emergency Agricultural Credits Act (1921), 183

Emergency Banking Act (1933), 279

Emergency Farm Mortgage Act (1933), 281–82

Emergency Fleet Corporation, 322

Emergency Price Control Act (1942), 410–11, 423, 424n, 430, 433, 445; Stabilization Act (1942) as amendment to, 415–16, 417

Emergency Quota Act (1921), 183

Emergency Relief Act (1935), 325

Emergency Tariff (1921), 202, 204, 233, 237, 327

Employment, full: Keynesian theory on, 466; Employment Act (1946), 467, 468–69

Employment Act (1946), 467, 468–69

Employment in manufacturing industries: 1939–1941, 401

Employment Stabilization Act (1931), 466

Enclosure movement (England), 78

Engelbert, Elmer E., 181n

England: land system of, 4, 6; economic conditions in, 17th and 18th centuries, 78; use of southern cotton in, 81; relations with North and South during Civil War, 84; immigration from, 87

English corn laws: repealed, 1846, 83

Enlarged Homestead Act (1909), 112n

Entail, 6n, 9

Entomological Commission (1877), 116

Equality for Agriculture, Chapter 10; see also McNary-Haugen plan

Equalization fee, 239; in "Committee Bill" (1926), 225–26; criticized by Coolidge in vetoes of McNary-Haugen bills, 228, 229n; in fifth McNary-Haugen bill, 229; idea killed by election of Hoover in 1928, 231; in domestic allotment plan, 268; backed by farmer organizations, 1932, 270, 271, 272; antecedent of AAA processing tax, 283, 303

Erie Canal, 62, 77

Erosion: problem of, 22; efforts to check, see Conservation: soil

Esch-Cummins Transportation Act (1920), 170, 178n, 184, 192, 193; recommendations of National Agricultural Conference on, 201; LaFollette for repeal of, 1924, 218

Europe: demand for farm products after World War I, 173

Evans, Frank, 240n

Ever-normal granary, 381, 387, 388, 389; see also Commodity Credit Corporation

Everitt, J. A., 134–35

Excess revenue, see Treasury surplus

Executive Commercial Policy Committee (1933), 329

Export Cooperative League, 211

Export corporation: proposal for handling agricultural surplus, 207, 208, 211, 214–15, 221; in McNary-Haugen plan, 212–14; supported by All-Iowa Agricultural Marketing Conference, 222, by American Farm Bureau Federation, 1925, 223n; opposed by Aaron Sapiro, 223, 224

Export debenture plan, 239, 267; backed by farmer organizations, 1932, 226–27, 270, 271, 272; rejected in House Committee, 229

Export-dumping plan: antecedents of, 199

Export-Import Bank: loan to Russia, 334

Export leagues: formed to back McNary-Haugen plan, 214

Export subsidy program, 334–35; used for wheat in AAA, 307

Exports, see Foreign trade: exports

Exports Administrative Board, 160

Extension service, see Agricultural extension service

FACILITY LOANS, 266; proposed in Jardine plan, 229; authorized by Federal Farm Board, 240; to cooperatives, 264

Fair exchange value: in AAA program, 302, 303

Fair Labor Standards Act (1938), 369–70

Fair price for wheat during World War I, 166

Family farm policy: summary, 508, 509, 518

Family farms, 113; background of, in North, 16, 78; provided in Homestead Act (1862), 19; characteristic pattern in U.S. farming areas, 88; not adapted to dry land farming, 125; difficulties of establishing in certain areas, 360; recommendations for encouragement of, 362; supported by Patrons of Husbandry, late 1930's, 386

Far West: agricultural development of, 118

Farm Bloc: organization of, 181–82, 201–02; origin of name, 181n; Senate membership, 181, 182n; legislative program, 182–85; decline of, 199; support for Norris bill, 207

Farm Board: proposed in Jardine plan, 229

Farm Bureau Federation, see American Farm Bureau Federation

Farm bureaus: early forms, 96, 176–78

Farm Credit Act (1933), 282–83; amendment, 1937, 392

Farm Credit Administration, 266n; establishment, 1933, 264, 280–81; reorganization of system, 1937, 392–93; opposition of farm organizations to transfer to USDA, 1939–1942, 393; functions, 495n

Farm debt: aftermath of Civil War, 84; increases in, after 1900, 112–13; 1910–1915, 116; during World War I, 168, 174; 1938, 391, 392n; 1940–1946, 459; see also Mortgages, farm

Farm debt adjustment, 327; committees for, 282, 363

Farm Foundation: objections to recommendations of President's Committee on Farm Tenancy, 362

Farm income, see Income, farm

Farm journals, 82, 120; stimulated by Alliance, 109

Farm living, 114

Farm management: in Bureau of Plant Industry, 120; beginnings of work in, 137; emphasis under Soil Conservation and Domestic Allotment Act (1936), 349

Farm mortgage corporations: defects of, 145

Farm Mortgage Credit Corporation: extension advocated by Grange, late 1930's, 386

Farm mortgage debt, see Farm debt; Mortgages, farm

Farm-nonfarm interdependence, 241, 269

Farm ownership: 1910–1914, 157; goal in land policy, 509

Farm population, see Population, rural farm

Farm production, see Production, agricultural

Farm real estate: value, 1940–1946, 459

Farm real estate prices, *see* Prices, farm real estate

Farm relief: drive of 1928 and 1929, 231; through industrial use of agricultural by-products, 379–80

Farm Security Administration (FSA), 316, 327, 362–64; successor to Resettlement Administration, 358; proposed by President's Committee on Farm Tenancy, 360; rehabilitation program, 361, 362; supervised agricultural credit, 361–62; criticisms of, 363–64; farm labor policy, World War II, 439, 440; farm mortgage loans by, World War II, 453; program of, 491–92; Congressional investigation of, 492–93; *see also* Farmers Home Administration; Resettlement Administration

Farm storage and loan program (1938); subtreasury plan of Farmers' Alliance as antecedent, 110, 155

Farm surpluses, *see* Surplus, agricultural

Farm Tenancy Report, *see* President's Committee on Farm Tenancy

Farm-to-market roads, 155, 187; recommendations of agricultural groups on, 200, 201

Farmer cooperatives, *see* Cooperative organization

Farmer-Labor Party: sympathy with organized labor, 369

Farmer organizations: Agricultural Wheel, 105–06, 107; American Society of Equity, 189; Brothers of Freedom, 107; Colored Alliance, 107–08; farmers' clubs, 97*n*, 105; Farmers Educational and Cooperative Union of America, *see* Farmers Union; Farmers Equity Union, 135, 176, 189; Farmers' Mutual Benefit Association, 109, 134; Farmers National Congress, 189; Farmers' National (War) Council, 189; Farmers' Relief Association, 134; Farmers' Social and Economical Union of Illinois, 134; Farmers Society of Equity, 135, 189; Gleaners, 179*n*, 181; National Board of Farm Organizations, 189; National Conference on Marketing and Farm Credits, 189; New England Farmers and Mechanics Union (1830), 94; Progressive State Granges, 189; *see also* American Farm Bureau Federation; Farmers Union; National Farmers' Alliance; Nonpartisan League, Patrons of Husbandry, etc.

— policies: efforts to cooperate with labor organizations, 106–07, 109, 111; 1870–1900, Chapter 6; political activities, People's Party, 109–11; situation in 1900, 114; during the presidency of Theodore Roosevelt, 128; position on tariff (1913), 142*n*, 143*n;* exempt from provisions of Clayton Act, 148, 156; during World War I, 171, 172; after World War I, 175–80; attitude toward McNary-Haugen plan, 217, 219, 220–25; for combating depression, 270–72; attitude toward New Deal agricultural programs, 339–46; late 1930's, 386–88; opposed to transfer of FCA to USDA, 393; opposition to subsidies, 419, 422, 424–25; views on changes in agricultural legislation, 1949, 479–80; opposition to price controls, 1950, 505

Farmers' Alliance, *see* National Farmers' Alliance

Farmers' and Laborers' Union of America, 106

Farmers' and Laborers' Union of Kansas, 106

Farmers' clubs, 97*n;* entry into politics, 105

Farmers' Cooperative Union, Louisiana, 107

Farmers Educational and Cooperative Union of America, *see* Farmers Union

Farmers' Equity Union, 135, 176, 189

Farmers' Holiday movement, 247

Farmers Home Administration, 473; Act of 1946, 493–94; housing loans authorized (1949), 499

Farmers' Home Corporation: established, 1937, 362, 493

Farmers' Improvement Society of Texas, 108*n*

Farmers' institutes, 120

Farmers' League, 97*n*

Farmers' League, Massachusetts, 109*n*

Farmers' Marketing Commission: proposed in Fess amendment, 226

Farmers' Mutual Benefit Association, 109, 134

Farmers' National Congress, 139*n*, 189

Farmers' National Council, 178, 181, 189, 194*n;* support for Norris bill, 207, 208

Farmers National Grain Corporation, 258, 262

Farmers' National War Council, 189

Farmers' Relief Association, 134

Farmers' Social and Economical Union of Illinois, 134

Farmers' Society of Equity, 135, 189

Farmers Union, 186*n*, 189, 386; early years, 134; merging of other groups with, 135; membership, 1908–1919, 139*n;* program, 140*n;* attitude toward tariff problems, 1913, 142*n;* during World War I, 171, 172; policy after World War I, 176; criticism of Farm Bureaus, 190–91; attitude toward McNary-Haugen plan, 220; policies for combating depressions, 271, 272; sponsorship of Corn Belt Committee, 220–21; policies advocated, New Deal period, 344, 387; sympathy with organized labor, 369; position on farm price controls, World War II, 408; views on Brannan Plan, 480*n*, 488, 489; monetary policy, 1930's, 511; support for family-size farm, 518

Farmers' Union of Louisiana, 106

Farms, abandoned, 89

Farms, number of: 1870–1900, 85

Fats: critical during World War I, 164; lend-lease shipments, 442–43*n;* end of rationing, 462; ECA purchases of, 1948–1950, 501; exports, 1935–1950, 501

Federal Aid Road Act (1916), 155, 187

Federal Bankruptcy Act (1899), *see* Frazier-Lemke Amendment (1934)

Federal Board for Vocational Education, 154

Federal Cooperative Marketing Board: proposed in Capper-Haugen bill, 220

Federal Crop Insurance Act: reactivated 1944, 495

Federal Crop Insurance Corporation, 382–84; *see also* Crop insurance

Federal Deposit Insurance Corporation, 255, 272, 279

Federal Emergency Relief Administration (FERA), 300, 324, 380; diversion of crops to relief distribution, 334, 335

Federal Farm Board, 239–41, 276, 402; in party platforms, 1928, 230; operations, 257–67; supported by farmers, 269; critique of program, 266–67; criticized by Democrats, 1932, 274; liquidation, 264, 280; antecedent of AAA program, 283; compared with CCC, 332, 333, 378, 388, 389, 390, 391; diversion of crops to abnormal outlets, 334; monopoly approach to farm problem, summary, 514; *see also* Agricultural Marketing Act (1929)

— cooperative selling organizations established: American Cotton Cooperative Associations, 259–60; Farmers National Grain Corporation, 258, 262; National Wool Marketing Corporation, 259; other cooperatives, 260

Federal Farm Loan Act Amendments (1921), 183

Federal Farm Loan Board, 147; intermediate credit banks, 185*n;* reorganization, 1927–1929, 234; abolished, 281, 283

Federal Farm Mortgage Corporation, 282, 494

Federal Food, Drug, and Cosmetic Act (1938), 386*n*

Federal land banks, 154, 155; antecedents, 145–47; establishment, 147–48; increase in capital (1932), 255; changes in policy, Emergency Farm Mortgage Act (1933), 281; part of agricultural credit system, 282; loans by, 1934–1937, 391, World War II, 453; subsidized interest rate, 453–54; larger loans authorized, 1945, 494

Federal Reserve Act (1913), 144; flexible currency provisions, 31; proposals for amendment of, 255

Federal Reserve policy: after World War I, 169, 172; 1920's, 174–75, 237, 1928–1929, 245–46, 249*n*, after 1930, 294; farmer organization proposals on, 271, 272; efforts to guard against inflation, 1936, 354*n*

Federal Reserve system, 154, 155; attitude of farmers toward, 28; Banking Act of 1935, 144n; operations, 1920–1921, 175, 186; credit, agricultural, 185n, 186n; Emergency Banking Act (1933), 279; Grange proposals for currency management, 343

Federal Security Agency, 154n

Federal Surplus Commodities Corporation, 256, 335, 380–81, 385; supported by Patrons of Husbandry, 343

Federal Surplus Relief Corporation, 310, 335

Federal Trade Commission: investigation of monopoly in meat packing industry, 149–50, in grain trade, 150–51

Federal Trade Commission Act (1914): provisions, 148–49

Federal Warehouse Act (1916), 154

Federal warehousing program, 155

Federalist party, 24

Feed: ECA purchases of, 1948–1950, 501

"Feed wheat program" (1942), 423–24, 428, 430

Fencing of the ranges, 118; appearance of problem of, 21; in plains area, 117

FERA, see Federal Emergency Relief Administration

Fertilizer: proposals to use Muscle Shoals for production of, 321; ECA purchases of, 1948–1950, 501

Fess amendment, 226

Feudal land systems in colonial period, 7–10

Fiat currency: during Civil War, 29, 32, 37, 168; see also Greenback issue and headings following

Field, James G., 110

Fig industry: Federal Farm Board aid to, 260, 264

Figs: tariff on, 1816, 46

Fillmore, Millard: favorable to tariff protection, 48

Financial panics, see Panics, financial

"Financiers' Plan" (1783), 10

Fiscal policy, see Compensatory budgets; Deficit financing

Fish: on free list with Canada, 1854, 50

Fish, frozen: Federal Surplus Commodities Corporation, operations in, 381

Fisher, Irving, 245n, 297; ideas on dollar stabilization, 270; ideas backed by American Farm Bureau Federation, 341n

Flax: on free list, 1913, 143; basic commodity by Jones-Connally Act (1934), 302n; AAA program not developed for, 309; crop insurance for, 1945, 384, 495

Flaxseed: in foreign trade, 1900–1915, 121; farm price of, 1913–1914, 143; production goals, World War II, 433, 436

Flood control, 127

Flour: on free list, 1854, 50; 1913, 143

Food Administration: establishment, 160–61; Herbert Hoover as chairman, 162, 164; licensing provisions, 162, 163, 164; methods used, 163–65; negotiations on hogs, 163

Food Administration Grain Corporation, 166, 212

Food Advisory Committee, 434n

Food Allotment Plan, National, 471–72, 479

Food and Agriculture Organization of the United Nations (FAO), 454–56, 460; transfer of headquarters to Rome, 504n

Food and Drug Act (1906), 119, 132, 151

Food and Drugs Administration: efforts to strengthen laws relating to, New Deal period, 386n

Food and Fuel Control Act (1917), 162–63

Food consumption: patterns during World Wars I and II compared, 165n; per capita, 1929–1933, 311; U.S., World War II, 443–45

Food Control Act, 161

Food Distribution Administration: World War II, 434

Food Production Administration: World War II, 434

Food Requirements Committee: War Production Board, 405, 433, 434n

Food Stamp Plan, 385–86; suspended (1942), 434; food allotment plan as outgrowth of, 472

Food supply: World War I, 160–68; World War II, 404–05

Food utilization: 1935–1946, 444

Foodstuffs: exports, 1935–1950, 501

Foot and mouth disease: increases in, 116

Ford, Henry: offer on Muscle Shoals, 321n

Fordney-McCumber Tariff (1922), 204–05, 233, 237, 327; LaFollette for reductions in, 1924, 218

Foreign aid: during and after World War II, 454–55; revival of program, 1950, 504

Foreign exchange situation: 1900–1915, 121

Foreign investments in U.S.: 1900, 85–86

Foreign trade: and the silver issue, 41; as changed by World War I, 203; effect of Hawley-Smoot Tariff on, 251–52; Executive Commercial Policy Committee (1933), 329; export subsidy, New Deal period, 334–35; Import-Export planning section in AAA, 347; export quotas, 397, 398; see also International commodity agreements

—exports: after Civil War, 38, 41; after 1870, 52–53; after 1875, 54; 1900–1915, 120–21; World War I, 161n; 1919–1921, 185; 1920's, 233–34, 243, 310–11; 1929–1933, 252n, 277n; 1932–1938, 400; 1940, 407; 1935–1950, 501; from western farms, 60; meat and meat products, 85; wheat and flour, 85, 165; pork during World War I, 164; financing by War Finance Corporation, 179, 183n; effect of devaluation of currency, 292; U.S. and world, 1929–1933, 327–28; food for relief purposes, 464

—imports: stimulated by Tariff of 1846, 50; after Civil War, 41; after 1870, 52–53; after 1875, 54; World War I, 161n; 1929–1932, 252n; 1932–1938, 400

Forest conservation: Forest Homestead Act (1906), 112n; public interest in, 128

Forest-land loans, 516n; Norris-Doxey Farm Forestry program, 499

Forest lands: Homestead policy unsuitable for, 21n, 22

Forest Reserve Act (1891), 123

Forest Service: Gifford Pinchot as head of, 119, 122–23; establishment of soil experiment stations, 317; control of grazing in national forests, 320

"Forgotten man, The," 55

Forward prices, 414, 415; World War II, 435

Forward-pricing: antecedents of, 199, 222n; device used during defense period before World War II, 403; suggested by Colmer Committee (1944), 471

Foster, William Trufant, 242n

Fractional currency: during Civil War, 30n

France: in Louisiana Territory, 16; creditor of U.S., 53; during World War I, 159, 161; war debts, World War I, 233; progress toward financial stability, 1920's, 243; decline and recovery of stock prices, 1929–1932, 289n; maintenance of gold standard, 292, 293; change in monetary gold stocks, 1934–1936, 354n; situation at end of World War II, 460

Frank, Jerome, 337

Frazier-Lemke Amendment (1934), 392; extension advocated by Grange, late 1930's, 386; agitation for legislation similar to, 495n; agitation for renewal of, 516

Free silver: Greenbackers submerged in movement for, 35; campaign for, 39–43, 59, 110–11; Bland bill, 40–41; supported by farmers, 510; see also Silver

Free trade: advocated by Walker in Report of 1845, 49; favored by South, summary, 512

Free Trade Convention (1831), 47

Freight rates, see Railroads: freight rates

Friant Dam, 127

Frontier, end of, 19n, 112

Fruit: on free list with Canada, 1854, 50; tariff on, 1861, 51; production, 1870–1900, 85n, 1939–1945, 441; efforts toward cooperative marketing of, 197n; exports, 1920's, 311; Federal Surplus Commodities Corporation operations in, 381; ECA purchases of, 1948–1950, 501

FSA, see Farm Security Administration

Fundamentalism, agricultural, 4
Funk, Frank, 200n
Future Trading Act (1921), 183

GADSDEN PURCHASE (1853), 5
Gallatin, Albert: plan for land settlement (1804), 15–16; support for Bank of the United States, 25; advocate of free trade, 47; on internal improvements, 61–62
Garfield, James A., President, 55
General Agreement on Tariffs and Trade, 502–03
General Maximum Price Regulation, 413, 424
Geneva tariff agreements (1947), 332, 491, 502
Geographical mile, 11n
Geological Survey: John Wesley Powell as director of, 126n
Georgia: land system of, 9n; state banks in, 28
German settlements, 7n
Germany: land system of, 4; long-term agricultural credit in, 29; fiat currency in, 32; monetary reform of 1872, 40n; investments in U.S., 53, 86n; immigration from, 77, 87; during World War I, 158–60; economic conditions after World War I and progress toward financial stability, 1920's, 243; decline and recovery of stock prices, 1929–1932, 289n; change in monetary gold stocks, 1934–1936, 354n; after World War II, 460
Glass, Carter, 144, 255, 349n
Glass-Steagall bill (1932), 255
Glavis, Louis R., 132n
Gleaners, 179n, 181
Gold: in the monetary system, 30; in Civil War, 32; resumption of payments, 34; relation of U.S. dollar to, 37; ratio with silver, 40, 42; real value of, 40n; production, U.S., 115n; international movement, 243; as an automatic regulator, 297–98; concentration of stocks in U.S., 365; U.S. holdings, 1934 on, 400
"Gold block," 292
Gold reserves: decline in, 1890, 42–43
Gold standard: Resumption Act (1875), 35; return to, 1879, 35; campaign of 1896, 59; in Republican platform, 1896, 111; international adoption of, 115n; Great Britain off, 1931, 253; United States taken off, 1933, 291, 295–96
Gold stock, monetary: increase, major gold standard countries, 1934–1936, 354n; U.S., 1934 on, 400
Goldsborough bill, 255
Gompers, Samuel, 149n, 156
Gooding bill (1922), 208
Gore, Howard M.: Secretary of Agriculture, 221n
Gorman, Arthur Pue, 58–59
Goss, Albert S., 393; opposition to subsidies, 1942, 424–25; views on Brannan Plan, 488–89
Government corporations, 322–24; see also Tennessee Valley Authority
Government expenditures: Civil War period, 38
Government payments to farmers, 314, 315; Soil Conservation and Domestic Allotment Act, 351–52; Agricultural Adjustment Act of 1938, 375; see also Benefit payments; Incentive payments
Government receipts: Civil War period, 38
Government regulation of public utilities: demanded by farmers, summary, 513; see also Railroads
Graduation Act (1854), 18n
Grain: on free list with Canada, 1854, 50; Sapiro plan for cooperative marketing of, 195–97; U.S. Grain Growers, Inc., 196; state wheat pools as form of marketing cooperative, 198n; need for adjustments in acreage of, 1920's, 236; Farmers National Grain Corporation, 258, 262; reductions due to AAA and drought, 353; production, 1939–1945, 441; lend-lease shipments of, 442–43n; exports, 1935–1950, 501
Grain Belt Federation of Farm Organizations, 220–22
Grain Corporation, Food Administration, 166, 212

Grain Corporation, U.S., see United States Grain Corporation
Grain elevators: connection with railways, 71
Grain Futures Act (1922), 151, 183n; amendment of 1936, 352
Grain Futures Administration, 183n
Grain Marketing Company, 197n, 223, 258
Grain prices: Future Trading Act (1921), 183
Grain sorghums: basic commodity by Jones-Connally Act (1934), 302n; AAA program not developed for, 309
Grain Stabilization Corporation, 262–63
Grain trade: Federal Trade Commission investigation of monopoly in, 150–51
"Grain trust," 93
Grand Coulee Dam, 127
Grange, see Patrons of Husbandry
"Granger Cases": Munn v. Illinois (1876), 100
Granger movement: relation to Patrons of Husbandry, 97; railroad legislation, state, 97–104, 130; significance of granger laws, 102; agitation for federal control of railroads, Reagan bill (1878), 103; Windom Committee report (1874), 103
Grant, Ulysses S., President, 35, 39n, 53
Grape producers: Federal Farm Board aid to, 260, 264
Grapefruit: Federal Surplus Commodities Corporation operations in, 381
Grapes: Federal Surplus Commodities Corporation operations in, 381
Gray, Chester, 223
Gray, L. C., 363
Grazing, Division of, 316
Grazing Act (1934), 509
Grazing lands: opened under Homestead Acts, 20–22; efforts to control use of, 319–21
Grazing Service (1934), 20
Great Britain: in 19th century, 76; investments in U.S., 86n; during and after World War I, 158–59, 243; war debts, World War I, 233; progress toward financial stability, 1920's, 243; decline and recovery of stock prices, 1929–1932, 289n; relationship of gold content of currency to internal price level, 297n; lend-lease aid to, 403, 442, 443n, 445; price control and rationing program, 410; during and after World War II, 422, 432n, 433, 460; U.S. loan to, 1946, 461, 500; stabilization efforts after abandonment of gold standard, 466n; wage-board plan, 519
Great Lakes-St. Lawrence Waterway: recommendations of National Agricultural Conference on, 201
Greece: economic conditions after World War I, 243; situation at end of World War II, 460
Greeley, Horace, 53
Greenback issue, 32–35, 37, 38–39
Greenback party, 35; in election of 1880, 35; antecedent of Grange proposal, 1933, 343
Greenbackers: and free silver, 41; supported by farmers, 510
Greenbacks: during Civil War, 30; nature of, 31; see also Fiat currency
Gregory, Thomas W.: Attorney General, 149
Gresham, Newton: founder of the Farmers Union, 134
Gresham's Law, 40
Guaranteed prices: during World War I, 164–66
Gustafson, C. H., 196

HAGUE CONFERENCES, 156
Hamilton, Alexander: early opinions, 3–4; Secretary of the Treasury, 4, 34; report on public credit, 4, 23; views on agriculture, 4; on land policy, 5, 13; financial program, 23–24; protective policy recommended by, 45; on internal improvements, 61
Hamilton, John, 153
Hammill, John, 222
Hampton, George P., 189

Hancock, Frank: Farm Security Administrator, 493
Hancock, Winfield Scott, 55
Handschin, W. F., 205
Hanna, Mark, 122
"Hard money": backed by Republican party, 34
Harding, W. P. G., 181
Harding, Warren G., President, 180, 210; relations with Farm Bloc, 183n, 201n; decline in interest in conservation, 316–17
Harrisburg Convention (1827), 46
Harrison, Benjamin, President, 57–58, defeated in election of 1892, 111; setting aside of forest reserves, 123
Harrison Land Act of 1800, 14
Hatch Act (1887): establishment of state agricultural experiment stations, 84
Havana Conference: tariff agreements, 502
Hawley-Smoot Tariff (1930), 204n, 250–52, 254n; supported by farmers, 269; rates on sugar, 309; see also Trade Agreements Act (1934)
Hay, John: Secretary of State, 131n
Hayes, John L., 54; Chairman of Tariff Commission, 55–56
Hayes, Rutherford B., President, 41, 55
Hays, Willet M., 137
Headright system, 8
Health insurance: advocated in President Truman's program, 374n
Health Organization of the League of Nations: studies of nutritional problems, 455
Hearst, Charles E., 214, 217n, 223
Hemp: tariff on, 1789, 45; 1816, 46; 1861, 51; on free list, 1913, 143
Henderson, Leon: Price Administrator, 408, 410n, price stabilization proposals, 420, 423; resignation, 425
Henry, Colonel Robert S.: on railroad land grants, 74
Henry, Patrick: attitude on slavery, 79
Hepburn bill (1906), 129
Hepburn v. *Griswold* (1870), 39n
Herrick, Myron T., 146
Hicks, John D., quoted, 124
Hides: on free list, 1872, 1875, 54; tariff on, 1890, 57, 1897, 59, 1922, 205
Highways, 66; farmer interest in, 174; farm-to-market roads, 187; Act of 1921, 187–88; emergency construction as relief measure, 256; see also Internal improvements
— federal aid: financial arrangements, 65n; favored by National Grange (1911), 139; Federal Aid Road Act (1916), 155, 187; summary, 515–16
Hill, F. F.: Governor of Farm Credit Administration, 392, 393
Hirsch, Julius, 420
Hirth, William, 220, 221
Hoard's Dairyman, 120n
Hoch-Smith Resolution (1925), 184, 193–94
Hog-corn ratio, 164n; program under AAA, 308
Hogs: tariff on breeding animals repealed, 1794, 45; Civil War period, 36; post-Civil War, 85; production, 1870–1900, 85n; products in foreign trade, 1900–1915, 121; Food Administration regulation during World War I, 163, 167, 171; post-World War I, 170; "basic" commodity in first McNary-Haugen plan, 214; prices, 1929–1932, 246; basic commodity in AAA program, 302n; production control, AAA program for, 307–08; crop reduction, 1934, 313; price supports, 1941, 403–04, Agricultural Act of 1948, 474, proposed in Brannan Plan, 486
"Hold-the-Line" Order (1943), 419, 421–22, 425, 426, 437; subsidies to implement, 426–27
Holding corporation: description, 92
Holland: creditor of U.S., 53; investments in U.S., 86n; maintenance of gold standard, 292, 293; change in

monetary gold stocks, 1934–1936, 354n; situation at end of World War II, 460
Hollis-Bulkley bill (1914), 146–47
Home Loan Bank Act (1932), 254, 257
Home Loan Bank system, 276
Homestead Act (1862), 19–22; expansion under, post-Civil War, 85; modifications, after 1900, 112, for arid lands, 124–28, during World War I, 161; see also Semiarid lands
Honey: support prices, Agricultural Act of 1949, 481–83
Hoosac Mills Decision (1936), 340, 343, 348, 349, 355
Hoover, Calvin, 337
Hoover, Herbert: relief activities under, World War I, 159–60; head of Food Administration, World War I, 162–64; director of Food Administration Grain Corporation, 166; Secretary of Commerce, 181, 183n, 185, 221n
— President, Chapter 11; election, 230, 239; views on export debenture plan, 239; philosophy of government action, 252; attack on depression problems, 248, 249, 276; attitude toward federal relief spending, 300; recommendations on Muscle Shoals, 321; campaign of 1932, 274; see also Hawley-Smoot Tariff
Hoover Commission on the Executive Branch of the Government: recommendations on conservation, 498
Hoover Dam, 127
Hope, Clifford: and Agricultural Act of 1948, 473–78
Hope-Aiken Act, see Agricultural Act of 1948
Hopkins, Harry L., 300
Horse-drawn rake (1820), 83
Horsepower: increased use after Civil War, 86
Horses: tariff on breeding animals repealed, 1794, 45
House, E. M., 152n
Housing Act (1949), 498–99
Houston, David F., Secretary of Agriculture, 151–52, 153, 205; Grange disapproval of early addresses, 158; predictions of postwar economic developments, 173
— Secretary of the Treasury, 179n, 180n; on "deflation" policy, 175; halting of export credit by War Finance Corporation, 179
Howard, James R., 177–78, 180n, 195
Howe, Frederick C., 337
Hughes, Charles Evans, Chief Justice of the U.S.: decision in Schechter case, 288n
Hull, Cordell, 131n; Secretary of State: at London Economic Conference (1933), 292–94; tariff program, 328, 330–31, 341
Hunt, C. W., 214
Hussey, Obed, 83
Hyde, Arthur M.: Secretary of Agriculture, 240

Ickes, Harold L., 300
Illinois: national banks in, 31; internal improvements in, 1824–1828, 64–65; lack of farmer representation in government, 94n; history of railroad regulation, 98–101
Illinois Farmers Association: on National Banking Law, 39
Immigration: to northern manufacturing centers, 76; to North Central farming areas, 77, 79; during 19th century, 87; shift of immigrant origins (1880–1890), 88; fostered by western railroads, 88n; restrictions on Mexican labor waived during World War I, 161; Emergency Quota Act (1921), 183
Import-export quotas: beef, 399
Incentive payments, 430, 436; World War II, 434, 435; probable retention as device for price support, 517; see also Benefit payments; Government payments to farmers
Income, cash farm: 1932–1937, 314; 1936, 353; 1941–1948, 463–64
Income, farm: Civil War period, 36; 1900–1914, 115;

increase in, per capita, 1920's, 232; government payments to farmers, 314, 315; World War II, 451–52
Income, gross farm: period after 1870, 52; index for World War I period, 168; 1929–1932, 247; late 1930's, 365; 1948–1949, 504n
Income, national: 1929, 1933, 1941, 406; 1929–1936 compared, 353; 1933–1940, 314; late 1930's, 365; 1939–1945, 452
Income, net farm: during World War I, 168; 1939–1944, 417
Income, nonfarm: 1920's, 244n; 1932–1936, 353; World War II, 451–52
Income, parity: see Parity income
Income, personal: 1941–1945, 462
Income support: summary, 516–17
Income tax: during Civil War, 29; favored by National Grange (1911), 139–40; World War II, 417
Indebtedness, farm, see Farm debt; Mortgages, farm
Indentured servitude: in colonial period, 8, 78; slavery an outgrowth of, 78
Independent Reform Party, 100
Independent Treasury Act (1840), 28; modification of (1864), 31
Independent treasury system, 50
India: progress toward financial stability, 1920's, 243; effect on, of U.S. silver-purchase program, New Deal period, 341
Indiana: national banks in, 31; repudiation of debts, 67
Indiana Territory Act (1804), 15–16
Indigo: tariff on, 1789, 45; 1816, 46
Industrial Commission, U.S.: Report of, 1902, 72, 91
Industrial Conference (1918), 173
Industrial revolution: in America, 76–77; in England, 76
Industry codes: as provided in NRA, 286–88, 306
Inflation: during Civil War, 32–33; during World War I, 167–68, 426; after World War I, 169, 174; contribution of banking system to, 174; effect of devaluation of currency, 292; fear of, 1937, 354n; action of Federal Reserve Board to prevent, 1937, 365n; controls on, World War II, 408–30, 446; food prices after World War II, 449; after World War II, 457–58, 462–65, 501; usually supported by farmers, 510
Inflation of currency: authorized in Agricultural Act of 1933, 281; see also Devaluation of the dollar
Inflationary gap, 420, 426; World War II, 417
Inflationary influences: Greenbacks as, 38
Inflationary pressures: World War II, 420–22, 447; Korean incident and, 504–06
Inland Waterways Commission: recommendations for multipurpose river development, 321–22n
Insurance, crop, see Crop insurance
Insurance, mortgage: in Farmers Home Administration, 494
Insurance, old-age: for farm workers, 499–500, 520; see also Social security
Insurance companies: opposition to national mortgage discount system, 254
Inter-Allied Committee on Post-War Requirements, 454
Inter-American Coffee Agreement, 398
Interbureau Coordinating Committee: mechanism for "defense planning," before World War II, 403
Interbureau Production Goals Committee: World War II, 432
Interest rates: as adjusted by Emergency Farm Mortgage Act (1933), 281
Interior, Department of the, 161; and reclamation, 125n
Intermediate Credit Banks, 186–87; part of agricultural credit system, 282
Intermediate Credits Act (1923), 184–85, 186
Intermediate-term credit: recommendations of Joint Commission of Agricultural Inquiry, 200
Intermountain Rate Cases (1914), 329
Internal improvements, Chapter 4; Cumberland Road,

14–15, 62, 67; grants of land for, 18; under Homestead Acts, 19n; Ohio Act (1802), 61–62; question of constitutionality, 61, 63, 64, 65; in Clay's "American system," 63, 64n; appropriations for, 1789–1830, 64; Survey Act (1824), 64; Maysville Road veto and results, 65–67; sectionalism in attitude toward, 77; federal aid, summary, 515–16
Internal migration, see Migration, internal
International Bank, 460
International Beef Conference, 399
International capital transfers, 53
International commodity agreements: beef, 399; coffee, 398; rubber, 399; sugar, 399; tea, 399; wheat, 397–98
International Institute of Agriculture, 146n; see also Food and Agriculture Organization of the United Nations
International Labor Organization, 455n
International Monetary Fund, 292n, 460
International Sugar Committee, 164
International trade: importance of gold basis in, 37; changed position of U.S. after World War I, 169; London Economic Conference (1933), 290–94, 295; general position, late 1930's, 399–400; see also Foreign trade
International Trade Organization, 502–03
International Wheat Agreement (1933), 307, 397–98, 491; efforts for renewal, 503–04
Interstate Commerce Act (1887), 103
Interstate Commerce Commission: regulation of rates, 102; legislation to strengthen, 129–30; comparison with Federal Trade Commission, 149; action on freight rates, 1920, 191–93; precedent as technical commission, 328–29; Secretary of Agriculture as farmers' representative in freight rate hearings, 379; see also Esch-Cummins Transportation Act
Inventory of railway properties, 72, 73
Investments, foreign, in U.S.: 1900, 85–86
Iowa: railroad regulation in, 101; land valuation in, 1900–1910, 112n
Iowa Bankers' Association, 222
"Iowa Idea," 121–22, 131
Irrigation: Carey Act (1894), 125n; early state systems, 126; flood control aspect, 127; see also Reclamation of arid lands
Italy: fiat currency in, 32; war debts, World War I, 233; progress toward financial stability, 1920's, 243; maintenance of gold standard, 292, 293; situation at end of World War II, 460

JACKSON, ANDREW, President, 17, 47; opposition to Clay's ideas, 18n; attitude toward banks, 26; "Specie Circular" (1836), 27; and second Bank of the United States, 28; and tariff protection, 46–47; and internal improvements, 65; connection with agriculture, 94
Japan: relationship of gold content of currency to internal price level, 297n; situation at end of World War II, 460
Jardine, William M., 218; Secretary of Agriculture, 221n, 223, Jardine plan, 221, 225, 228, 229, 239
Jefferson, Thomas: early opinions, 3–4; spokesman for the western settlers, 5, 14; report on public lands, 11; Secretary of State, 4, 24; President: Embargo Act (1807), 17; attitude toward banks, 26; and tariff protection, 45n; on internal improvements, 61–62; opposed to slavery, 79n; interest in agricultural experiments, 82n; connection with agriculture, 94
Jewett, George C., 196, 217
Johnson, Andrew, President: reconstruction plans, 35n
Johnson, Charles: objections to proposals of President's Committee on Farm Tenancy, 362
Johnson, Hugh S., 208–11, 273n; Administrator of NRA, 284, 285, 287
Joint Commission of Agricultural Inquiry (1921), 200–01

Joint-stock land banks, 147, 234; liquidation, 282

Jones, Marvin: War Food Administrator, 427n, 435n

Jones, Wesley, 182n

Jones-Connally Cattle Act (1934), 305n, 309, 380

Jones-Costigan Sugar Act (1934), 57–58, 309; not affected by unconstitutionality of AAA, 349–50, 355–56; labor regulations in, 370

Judicial review: of railroad regulatory legislation, 99–101

Juillard v. *Greenman* (1884), 39n

Jungle, The, by Upton Sinclair, 133

Jute: on free list, 1872, 1875, 54

KANSAS, 81, 102

"Kearneyites" (in California), 102

Kelley, Oliver Hudson: founder of Patrons of Husbandry, 95, 96

Kellogg substitute amendment (War Finance Corporation), 207

Kentucky: protectionist sentiment in, 46; antislavery sentiment in, 81

Kenyon, William Squire, 181–82, 199, 202

Kerr-Smith Tobacco Act (1934), 304, 377

Keynes, J. M., 250, 294, 466; Keynesian theory, 466

Kinkaid Act (1904), 112n

Kline, Allan: views on changes in agricultural legislation (1949), 479–80; views on Brannan Plan, 488, 489

Knapp, Seaman A.: demonstration farms, 119; founder of agricultural extension work, 152–53

Knights of Labor, 106, 109, 111

Knox v. *Lee* (1871), 39n

Korean incident, 487n; and new inflationary pressures, 504–06

LABOR: decrease in man-hours required to raise crops, 86, 87; mobility of, 1910–1914, 157; shortage during World War I, 167; National Industrial Recovery Act, Section 7a, 366; legislation, late 1930's, 366–70; National Labor Board, 367; National Labor Relations Act (1935), 367–69; National Labor Relations Board, 367–69; Fair Labor Standards Act (1938), 369–70; Taft-Hartley Act (1947), 369, 480n; wage stabilization during World War II, 414, 415; wage demands, 1943, 426; interpretation of Employment Act of 1946, 468–69

Labor, Department of: established (1913), 155–56; efforts to increase food supply during World War I, 161

Labor, farm: use of Mexicans during World War I, 171; migrants, problems of, 357, 370, 519; migrant camps, 363, 364, 492, 493n, eliminated in Farmers Home Administration Act, 494; excluded from social security program, 370, 371–74; World War II, 407, 433–34, 435, 437–40; importation of foreign workers, World War II, 438, 439–40; "war-units," 438–39; Tarver amendment (1943), 439n; old-age insurance for, 499–500, 520; summary, 519

Labor, migration of: from areas of underemployment, World War II, 436, 440

Labor, wages of: World War II, 450–52

Labor organizations: efforts to cooperate with farmer organizations, 106–07, 109, 111; exempt from provisions of Clayton Act, 148, 156; under leadership of Samuel Gompers, 156; provisions regarding, in Section 7a, NIRA, 287; agriculture's attitude toward, 369; close affiliation of Farmers Union with, 387

Labor policy: farmer organization attitudes toward, late 1930's, 386–88

Labor protection: regulations in Jones-Costigan Act (1934), 309

Labor supply: colonial period, 78; 19th century, 76; *see also* Employment, full

Ladd, Edwin Freemont, 181

Ladd-Sinclair bill (fixed minimum prices) (1922), 208

La Follette, Robert M., 72n, 128, 138, 181; candidate for President, 1924, 218

La Follette Committee: investigation (*Violations of Free Speech and Rights of Labor*), 370

Laissez-faire: Alexander Hamilton and, 5; doctrine, 97; early acceptance in U.S., 513

Lamb: tariff on, 1909 and 1922 compared, 204

Land Act of 1796, 13

Land Bank Commissioner, loans by, *see* Commissioner loans

Land banks, *see* Federal land banks

Land-grant college system, 83; *see also* Association of Land-Grant Colleges and Universities

Land grants: to railways, 68–70, 73–74

Land-O'-Lakes Creameries Association, 238, 258

Land policy, Chapter 1; New England, 6; middle colonies, 7–9; southern colonies, 9; under the Confederation, 10–12; Act of 1785, 11–12; Northwest Ordinance (1787), 6n, 12; religious reserves, 12 (*see also* Educational reserves); Hamilton vs. Jefferson, 5; Hamilton's proposals, 13; Act of 1796, 13; Harrison Land Act of 1800, 14; Ohio Enabling Act (1802), 14–15; Gallatin's Plan, 15–16; Indiana Territory Act (1804), 15–16; Louisiana Territory, 16; Settlers' Relief Acts, 1800–1820, 17; Land Law of 1820, 17, 18; Pre-emption Act of 1841, 18, 19, 20; Graduation Act (1854), 18; Homestead Act (1862), 19–22, expansion under, post-Civil War, 85, modifications of, after 1900, 112n, 161; grants to railroads for development, 69–70, 73–74; Timber Culture Act (1873), 19n, 21n, 22; Desert Land Act (1877), 19n, 20, 22, 125; Timber and Stone Act (1878), 21n, 22; Carey Act (1894), 125–26; as established by 1900, 113; Reclamation Act (1902), 19n, 126–28; arid land reclamation, 124–28 (*see also* Semiarid lands); marginal and submarginal lands, *see* Resettlement Administration; Grange attitude on, New Deal period, 343; Planning Section in AAA, 347; summary, 508–10

Land speculation: after World War I, 168–69, 174

Land-use planning: Mount Weather Agreement, 394–95, 497

Land-use planning committees: participation in BAE coordination efforts, 395; mechanism for defense planning before World War II, 403, 404

Land-use policy: advocated by American Farm Bureau Federation, New Deal period, 342; National Cooperative Council on, 345

Land-use projects: in soil conservation program, 318

Land values: increase, as result of railway development, 68, after 1900, 112, 1910–1914, 157; 1900–1910 in Iowa, Minnesota and South Dakota, 112n

Landlord-tenant relationships: inadequacies in, 359–60; recommendations to states for improvements, 362; *see also* Tenancy

Landlords: benefit payments to, Agricultural Adjustment Act of 1938, 375

Landon, Alfred M., 382

Lawrence, Judge, 100

Layton, Sir Walter, quoted, 292n

League of Nations: studies in nutrition, 385; specialized functions of, 455

Lee, Robert E.: philosophy of, 90

Legal tender: greenbacks, 30; backing for bank deposits, 37

Legal-tender acts (Civil War), 33, 34

Legal Tender Cases (1871), 39n

Legge, Alexander, 240

Lehman, Herbert: director of OFRRO and UNRRA, 454

Leith-Ross, Sir Frederick, 454

Lemke, William, 35

Lemons: tariff on, 1790, 45; tariff on, 1909 and 1922 compared, 204

Lend-Lease Act (1941), 403, 404

Lend-lease program, 401, 403; shipments under, 442–43; termination of, 449n, 461; see also Office of Lend-Lease Administration
Lenroot, Irvine Luther, 184, 200n
Lever, Asbury F., 153, 181
Lewis, Sinclair, 248
Liberal Republican party, 53
Liberty Bonds: sold to farmers, 168, 169, 176n
Licensing provisions: in AAA program, 304–05, 306
Life insurance companies: farm mortgage loans by, World War II, 453
Lincoln, Abraham, President, 19, 51, 83n; reconstruction plans of, 35n; connection with agriculture, 94
Lindley, Curtis H.: Director of Food Administration Grain Corporation, 166
Little bill (1923): purchase and storage of wheat, 208
"Little Steel" formula, 415, 451
Livestock: Sapiro plan for cooperative marketing of, 197; reductions due to AAA and drought, 353; production, 1939–1945, 441; value, 1940–1946, 459; see also Beef cattle; Cattle; Grazing lands
Livestock industry: proposals of President's Agricultural Commission concerning (1925), 219; advocates of tariff protection and cooperative marketing, 270; opposition to processing tax from, 308–09
Livestock speculation: after World War I, 168–69, 174
Loans, see Credit, agricultural and specific types of loans
Logrolling, congressional: beginnings of, 65; on tariff rates, 329, 330
London Economic Conference (1933), 290–94, 295, 328
Long-and-short-haul controversy, 73, 99, 102
Louisiana: purchase of (1803), 5; state banks in, 28; repudiation of debts, 67; concentration of land holdings in, 80
Louisiana Territory: land policy for, 16
Louisville and Portland Canal Company, 64
Louisville Joint Stock Land Bank v. Radford (1935), 392
Low-income families: Food Stamp Plan, 385–86
Low-income farmers: concern for, after 1933, 356; policy of aid to, 491–94
Lowden, Frank O., 198n, 230
Lubin, David, 146n
Lyon, W. H.: plan for government price-fixing, 198–99, 207

MacDonald, Ramsay, 291
Machinery, agricultural: rationed during World War II, 433–34
Madison, James: and tariff, 44, 45n; on internal improvements, 61; opposed to slavery, 79n; President: support for Bank of the United States, 25, veto of internal improvements bill (1817), 63
Malthus, Thomas, 76
Mann, A. R.: objections to proposals of President's Committee on Farm Tenancy, 362
Mann-Elkins Act (1910): constitutionality upheld, 329
Manning, John, 83
Manorial system, 6, 7, 8, 9
Marcy, W. L., Secretary of State, 50
Marginal lands: Resettlement Administration program on, 325; problem areas, 356
Maris, Paul V.: Director of the Tenant Purchase Division, FSA, 363
Marketing, cooperative, see Cooperative marketing
Marketing Agreement Act (1937), 355, 376
Marketing agreements: in AAA program, 283, 304–06, 310; tobacco, 305n, 306, 307; opposed by National Cooperative Council, 344; Agricultural Marketing Agreement Act (1937), 355, 474; Agricultural Act of 1948, 474, 475–78; monopoly approach to farm problem, summary, 514; probable retention as device for price support, 517

Marketing controls, 269
Marketing of farm products: cooperative approach to, 136
Marketing orders: in AAA program, 305
Marketing quotas: antecedents of, 269; Agricultural Adjustment Act of 1938, 377, 378; not established, World War II, 434, 435; Agricultural Act of 1948, 474, 475, 477, 482, 483n; Agricultural Act of 1949, 482, 483n; Brannan Plan, 487; monopoly approach to farm problems, summary, 514
Marketing system, 258, 261, 265; research authorized by Act of 1946, 496–97
Marsh, Benjamin C., 189
Marshall, George C., Secretary of State: Marshall plan, 458, 461–62, 500
Marshall, John: constitutional powers over internal improvements, 64
Marshall Plan, 458, 461–62, 500
Maryland: attitude toward Western lands, 4; land system of, 7–9; repudiation of debts, 67; early agricultural colleges, 83
Maximum-minimum tariff rates (1909), 132
Maysville Road: Jackson's veto of project, 65, 515n, effects of, 66
McCormick, Cyrus, 83
McCray, Warren T., 180n
McCulloch, Hugh: Secretary of the Treasury, 33–34
McFadden, Louis Thomas, 185
McGarrah, Gates W.: Director of Food Administration Grain Corporation, 166
McKelvie, Samuel R., 240
McKinley, William, President, 43, 59, 111, 119, 122; setting aside of forest reserves, 123; support for reciprocal trade agreements, 329n
McKinley Tariff (1890), 56, 57–58; reciprocal trade agreements provision, 329n
McNary, Charles: senator from Oregon, 182n, 200n
McNary-Haugen plan, Chapter 10, 267–68, 283; critical analysis, 235–36, 238; compared with domestic allotment plan, 267–68; in election campaigns, 1924, 218–19, 1928, 230–31; importance in thinking of farm leaders in New Deal period, 345, 346; licensing idea, 304; monopoly approach to farm problem, summary, 514
— bills presented: first (1924), 211–17; second (1925), 219; third (1926), 225–26; fourth (1927), 226–28; fifth (1928), 228–30
McReynolds, J. C.: Attorney-General, 149
Meat: on free list, 1854, 50, 1913, 143; tariff on, 1890, 57; roll-back ordered for, 1943, 426; World War II subsidy, 428–29; lend-lease shipments, 442–43n; domestic consumption, World War II, 444; end of rationing, 462; ECA purchases, 1948–1950, 501
Meat and meat products: exports, 85
Meat inspection: Act of 1906, 133
Meat packing industry, 80, 149–50
Meats: exports, 1935–1950, 501
Mechanization of agriculture: decrease in man-hours required to raise crops, 86, 87; in South, 81; during World War I, 171
Mellon, Andrew W.: Secretary of Treasury, 185
Meredith, E. T.: interest in agricultural legislation, 222; Secretary of Agriculture, 179n, 180n, 183n, 205
Merritt, Ralph P., 218
Mexican War, 32, 49
Mexico: importation of farm labor from, World War I, 161, World War II, 438–40
Meyer, B. H., 194
Meyer, Eugene, Jr., 179, 183n; report on wheat situation, 211
Michigan: repudiation of debts, 67; constitutional authorization for college of agriculture, 83
Michigan Potato Growers' Exchange, 179n
Middle colonies, 5–6; land policy of, 7–9

Middle East Relief and Rehabilitation Administration, 454
Middle states: protectionist sentiment in, 44, 46
Middle West: wheat cultivation in, 81
Migrant farm wageworkers: problems of, 357, 370, 519
Migration, internal: Federal period, 16; farm-to-city, 157, 232–33; result of drought conditions, 299–300, 357
Migration of labor: from areas of underemployment, World War II, 436, 440
Migratory farm labor camps, 363, 364, 492–93
Military grants (of land), 6, 10, 12
Milk: on free list, 1913, 143; basic commodity in AAA program, 302n; licensing arrangements in AAA program, 306n, 308; Federal Surplus Commodities Corporation operations in, 381; World War II, subsidy on, 429, production goals, 433, 437, lend-lease shipments of, 442–43n; price supports, Agricultural Act of 1948, 474, Act of 1949, 481–83
Miller, John D., 217n
Mills, Ogden, 200n
Mills bill (1888), 56, 58
Minimum system, see Principle of the minimum
Minnesota: land grants to railways in, 73; German immigrants in, 87; railroad regulation in, 101; land valuation in, 1900–1910, 112n; Nonpartisan League, 171, 188; Rural Credit Bureau, 185n
Minnesota rate case (1890), 102n
Mississippi: state banks in, 28; repudiation of debts, 67; concentration of land holdings in, 80
Mississippi River Commission, 127n
Mississippi Territory: Act of 1803, 15
Mississippi Valley States: strength of Grange in, 104, 106
Missouri Compromise (1820), 47
Missouri Farmers' Association, 220
Missouri River Valley: multipurpose river development, 323
Mitchell, Charles E., 246
Molasses: tariff on, 1861, 51; 1875, 54; 1890, 57
Moley, Raymond, 273n; at London Economic Conference, 293
Mondell, Frank: report on wheat situation, 211
Monetary policy: greenback issue, 33–35, 37; growing interest in, 1930–1932, 270; drive for stabilized dollar, 1930's, 295; late 1930's, 365; relationship between gold value of currency and internal price level, 297n; views of farmer organizations, New Deal period, 346, 511, American Farm Bureau Federation, 339, 340–41, 387, Patrons of Husbandry, 342–43, Farmers Union, 344, National Cooperative Council, 345–46; summary, 508, 510–12
Money in circulation: 19th century, 37, 39
Money system: early weakness of, 4; farmer interest in, Chapter 2; Hamilton's accomplishments in establishing, 23–24; first and second Banks of the United States, 24–28; Independent Treasury, 28, 31, 50; during Civil War, 29–32; resumption of gold, 37, 39; campaign for free silver, 39–43, 59; policy in 1900, 113; need for revision of, 130–31; see also Banks, national; Banks, state; Greenback issue and headings following
Mongrel Tariff (1883), 56
Monopolies: growth of, 66, 91; railroads as, 73, 91, 98; types of, 92; attitude of farmers on, 92–93, 148, 513–15; control of, early efforts in, 113; Sherman Antitrust Act (1890), 92n; Clayton Antitrust Act (1914), 148–49; Federal Trade Commission Act (1914), 148–49; status by 1915, 136–37; interest in, during New Deal period, 286, 288; argument over morality of, 340
Monroe, James: President: and tariff protection, 45n, on internal improvements, 63–64; opposed to slavery, 79n
Montana: state hail insurance experiments, 381–82
Montgomery, Donald, 337
Morgenthau, Henry, Jr., 273n, 280n
Morrill, Chester, 181n

Morrill, Justin H.: tariff of 1861, 51; land-grant colleges act, 83n
Morrill Act (1862), land-grant college system, 83–84n
Morrill Tariff (1861), 51
Morrow, Jeremiah, 17
Mortgage credit: inadequacies of, 131, 137, 247, 360-61
Mortgage insurance: in Farmers Home Administration loans, 494
Mortgage interest payments: 1941–1948, 464
Mortgages, farm: state action in field of, 185n; refinancing of, 1933, 280–82; Emergency Farm Mortgage Act (1933), 281; 1938, 391, 392n; debt reduction during World War II, 453; see also Farm debt
Mortgages, foreclosure: 1930–1934, 247, 360
Moser, C. O.: interest in McNary-Haugen plan, 224
Moss-Fletcher bill (1914), 146-47
Most-favored-nation principle: in Trade Agreements Act (1934), 330–31
Mount Weather Agreement (1938), 394-95, 497
Mowing machine (1831), 83
Muckrakers, 128
Mugwumps, 56n
Mule-raising industry: origin of, 82n
Multipurpose river development, see River basin development
Munn v. Illinois (1876), 100n
Murphy, Frank, 214, 222, 223
Muscle Shoals project, 127, 271; supported by American Farm Bureau Federation, 179, 215–16; World War I, 321; agitation for public action in power field, 338; see also Tennessee Valley Authority
Myers, W. I.: Governor of Farm Credit Administration, 392

NATIONAL AGRICULTURAL CONFERENCE (1922), 201–02, 209
National Agricultural Congress (1872), 105
National Association of County Agricultural Agents: meeting of December 1918, 177
National Association of Manufacturers: studies of post-World War II problems, 457
National bank: in Clay's "American system," 63, 64n
National Bank Act (1863), 28
National bank notes, see Bank notes, national
National banks, see Banks, national
National Bean Marketing Association: Federal Farm Board aid to, 260, 264
National Board of Farm Organizations, 189; support for Norris bill, 207
National City Bank of New York: analysis of the McNary-Haugen Bill, 219n
National Conference on Marketing and Farm Credits, 189
National Conservation Commission, 124
National Conservation Conference, 123-24
National Cooperative Council: policy, 1930's, 344–46, 388, 511; opposed to transfer of FCA to USDA, 393; see also National Council of Farmers' Cooperative Marketing Associations; National Council of Farmer Cooperatives
National Cooperative Milk Producers Federation, 408
National Cotton Exchange, 258
National Council of Farmer Cooperatives, 136, 344n; on FSA and farm labor, 439n; views on changes in agricultural legislation, 1949, 480; views on Brannan Plan, 489; see also National Cooperative Council; National Council of Farmers' Cooperative Marketing Associations
National Council of Farmers' Cooperative Marketing Associations, 198n, 344n; opposed to Capper-Haugen bill, 220; acceptance of Jardine bill, 221n; opposed to McNary-Haugen idea, 223–24; see also National Cooperative Council; National Council of Farmer Cooperatives

National Credit Association: proposed by Hoover, 253-54, 255
National Defense Advisory Commission, 401; World War II, 404
National Defense Advisory Council, 448
National Defense Research Council, 401
National Farmers' Alliance, 97n; history, 106; component groups, 106-07, 109; Colored Alliance, 107-08; later policies, 108-09; and Populists, 109-11; subtreasury plan of, 155
National Farmers' Alliance and Cooperative Union of America, 106
National Farmers' Alliance and Industrial Union, 106
National Farmers Union, see Farmers Union
National Federation of Grain Cooperatives: position on farm price controls, World War II, 408
National Food Allotment Plan, 471-72, 479
National Grange Monthly, The, 139, 152, 153n; disapproval of Secretary Houston's views, 158
National Industrial Recovery Act (1933), 285-87, 289, 290n; change of attitude permitting passage, summary, 514; redistribution of the overbalance of population in industrial centers, 326n; Commodity Credit Corporation funds appropriated under, 332; concessions to producer groups, 366; unconstitutionality, 329, 349-50
National Labor Board, 367
National Labor Relations Act (1935), 367-69
National Labor Relations Board, 367-69
National Livestock Marketing Association, 197; Federal Farm Board aid to, 260, 264
National Livestock Producers Association, 197
National Monetary Commission, 131, 144; report of, 145
National Order of the Patrons of Husbandry, see Patrons of Husbandry
National Pecan Marketing Association: Federal Farm Board aid to, 260, 264
National Planning Association: studies of post-World War II problems, 457
National Producers' Alliance, 220, 221
National Recovery Administration, 285-90, 292, 293, 294, 302, 305, 306, 310, 314; orientation to producers, 335-36; attitude of American Farm Bureau Federation toward, 340; labor provisions, Section 7a, 366, 369; unconstitutionality: A. L. A. Schechter v. U. S. (1935), 348
National Resources Board (1935), 466
National Resources Planning Board, 318n, 466; post-World War II plans, 456-57; abolished (1943), 457n
National revenue: in excess of needs, 1837, 27; 1870-1872, 55n; 1882, 55
National Road, see Cumberland Road
National Wheat Growers Advisory Committee, 198n
National Wool Exchange, 258, 259
National Wool Marketing Corporation, 259, 264
National Wool Warehouse and Storage Company of Chicago, 259n
Nationalism, economic, 332
Natural monopolies, see Monopolies
Navigation, improvement of, 75; "pork barrel" bills on, 64n; untouched by Maysville Road veto, 66
Nebraska: state hail insurance experiments, 381-82
Negro farmers' organizations: Colored Farmers' National Alliance and Cooperative Union, 107-08; Farmers' Improvement Society of Texas, 108n
Negro slavery, see Slavery
Negroes: educational opportunities for, 81
Netherlands, see Holland
New Amsterdam, 7
New Deal: philosophy of, 276; farm legislation, 484; see also Deficit financing; Roosevelt, Franklin D.
New England: township system, 5-6, 8, 10; protectionist sentiment in, 44; attitude toward protective tariffs, 46; advantages, 77; disadvantages to, in opening of North-

west, 77; soil exhaustion in, 77; use of Southern cotton in, 81; decline of agriculture in, 88-89; commercial interests dominant, 94; fluid milk production in, 117; Grange strength in, 134
New England Farmers and Mechanics Union (1830), 94
New Jersey: land system of, 7-8; protectionist sentiment in, 46; truck crops in, 117
New Netherland, 7
New South: development of, 90
New York: land system of, 7-9, 10; struggles over quit-rents in, 8; protectionist sentiment in, 46; and Erie Canal, 62; advantages, 77n; disadvantages to, in opening of Northwest, 77; soil exhaustion in, 77, 117; immigration to, 80; Grange strength in, 134
New York City: commercial center, 62
New York Stock Exchange: crash of 1929, 241-42, 243
Newlands Reclamation Act (1902), 126-28
Nonbasic crops: flexible price supports, Agricultural Act of 1948, 477-78, 481; support prices, Agricultural Act of 1949, 482-83
Noncooperator: defined, 367n
Nonpartisan League, 135, 155, 181, 185n, 188; program of, 148; during World War I, 171, 172
Nonrecourse loans, 354, 378; for cotton growers, 307; granted by Commodity Credit Corporation, 332, 388, 389; in Agricultural Adjustment Act of 1938, 377; in Agricultural Act of 1948, 475; in Agricultural Act of 1949, 483
Norbeck, Peter, 182n, 215
Norbeck-Burtness diversification loan bill, 215-16, 236, 237
Normal agricultural value: basis for land bank appraisal, 494
Normal supply: defined, 1938, 377
Norris, George, 181, 321
Norris bill (government export corporation), 207, 208n
Norris-Doxey farm forestry program, 499
Norris-Sinclair bill (government export corporation), 208, 218
North: attitude toward public domain, 18; desire for protective tariffs, 60; labor shortage in, 76; economic and social conflict with South over slavery issue, 78; comparison with southern farmer, 90; see also Sectionalism
North Carolina: land system of, 9; antislavery sentiment in, 81
North Central states: agricultural pattern of, 16; imprint of the New England culture on, 77
North Central States Agricultural Conference, 222
North Dakota: land grants to railways in, 73; Nonpartisan League in, 171, 188; Bank of, 185n; state hail insurance experiments, 381
North Pacific Emergency Export Association, 334
Northeast: investment capital from, 67; advantages, 77; disadvantages to, in opening of Northwest, 77; soil exhaustion in, 77; rural living in, 114; see also Sectionalism
Northern Alliance, 108, 110
Northern Securities Company, 128-29
Northwest: opening of, disadvantage to New England and New York, 77; immigration to, 80; wheat production in, post-Civil War, 85; agricultural development of, 118; see also Sectionalism
Northwest Ordinance (1787), 6n, 12
Northwest Territory: Land Act of 1796, 13; ban on slavery in, 80; early laws in, relating to agricultural education, 83
Norway: immigrants from, 77, 78; situation at end of World War II, 460
Nourse, Edwin G.: quoted, 205n; Chairman of the Council of Economic Advisers, 469n
Nullification: in South Carolina, 48
Number of farms: 1870-1900, 85

Nutrition: increased emphasis on, 384–86; international studies in, 455; Food and Agriculture Organization objectives in, 456; *see also* School Lunch program

Nuts: tariff on, 1909 and 1922 compared, 204; production, 1939–1945, 441; ECA purchases of, 1948–1950, 501

OATS: in foreign trade, 1900–1915, 121

O'Connor Law (California, 1876), 102

Office of Agricultural Defense Relations, 404

Office of Experiment Stations, 153n

Office of Extension Work, North and West, 153

Office of Extension Work, South, 153

Office of Farm Management and Farm Economics, 205

Office of Foreign Relief and Rehabilitation Operations (OFRRO), 454; stockpiling policy, World War II, 448, 449n

Office of Home Economics, 153n

Office of Land-Use Coordination, 497; Mount Weather Agreement, 394–95, 497

Office of Lend-Lease Administration: stockpiling policy, World War II, 448, 449n; *see also* Lend-lease program

Office of Price Administration (OPA), 401, 405, 411, 412; General Maximum Price Regulation, 413; effectiveness of controls, 417–18; attitude toward subsidies, 419–20, 422–23; powers sought in 1941, 422–23; opposition in Congress, 425–26, 430n; major responsibilities, World War II, 445; stockpiling policy, World War II, 448

Office of Price Administration and Civilian Supply (OPACS), 412; responsibility for management of civilian supplies, 445

OFRRO, *see* Office of Foreign Relief and Rehabilitation Operations

Ohio: Enabling Act (1802), 14–15, 61–62; national banks in, 31; protectionist sentiment in, 46; internal improvements in, 1824–1828, 64–65; lack of farmer representation in government, 94n

"Ohio plan," 34-35

Oil crops: production, 1939–1945, 441; *see also* Peanuts; Soybeans

Oils: lend-lease shipments of, 442–43n; ECA purchases of, 1948–1950, 501; exports, 1935–1950, 501

Oklahoma: opened to settlement (1889), 112; Reconstruction League, 188n

Old-age and survivors insurance, *see* Social security

Old-age assistance, 373, 374

Oleomargarine: opposed by National Grange (1911), 139

Olmstead, Frederick Law, quoted, 80

O'Mahoney, Joseph C., 410

O'Neal, Edward, 271, 438; objections to proposals of President's Committee on Farm Tenancy, 362; agitation for cotton crop insurance, 384; and trade agreements program, 397; position on farm price controls, World War II, 408

One-crop agriculture: in the South, 89–90; after 1900, 113

Onions: Federal Surplus Commodities Corporation operations in, 381

"Open door" policy, 131n

Operating loans to cooperatives, 264, 266

Oranges: tariff on, 1790, 45; Federal Surplus Commodities Corporation operations in, 381

Order of the Patrons of Husbandry, *see* Patrons of Husbandry

"Orderly marketing," 184, 186; effect on, of Federal Warehouse Act (1916), 154–55; in Republican platform, 1928, 230; stressed by backers of Federal Farm Board, 257

Organizations, farmer, *see* Farmer organizations

Ottawa Conference (1932), 256n

Outlook reports (Bureau of Agricultural Economics), 232, 237

Overgrazing: problem of, 20, 22

Overman Act (1919), 160n

Overpopulation: dangers of, 76; in the South, 90

Overproduction: factor in depression conditions, 1930's, 311

Owner-operation, 157; goal in land policy, 509; *see also* Family farm policy; Family farms

PACE, STEPHEN: Agricultural Act of 1949, 480

Pacific Railway Act of 1862, 68

Packer Consent Decree (1920), 150

Packers and Stockyards Act (1921), 151, 183, 352

Packers and stockyard companies: agitation for control, 179

Packing trust, 93

Page, Walter H., 152n, 159

Pan-American Coffee Bureau, 398

Pan-American Coffee Conference, 398

Panics, financial, 76; 1837, 18n, 27, 67; 1903, 131; 1907, 131, 144; 1920–1921, 185–86, 191; 1929, 237, 241–48, causes, 242–48; accentuated by weak banking system, 130; danger of, decreased by Federal Reserve system, 145

Parcel post system: Grange influence in establishment of, 105, 139, 140n

Parity: Farmers Union policy on, 344, 387; argument for 110 per cent, 409, 410, 411; 110 per cent feature, 424, 425; basis for ceilings, World War II, 414–17, 418

Parity formula, 376n; in Agricultural Act of 1948 and 1949, 483; suggestions by American Farm Bureau Federation, 1949, 480

Parity income: new objective, Soil Conservation and Domestic Allotment Act, 350; defined, Agricultural Adjustment Act of 1938, 376, Act of 1948, 476; standard in Brannan Plan, 484–85

Parity income ratio: 1935–1937, 353; 1939–1945, 452

Parity index: proposed in Brannan Plan, 485, 486

Parity payments: to cotton growers, 307; Agricultural Adjustment Act of 1938, 378

Parity period (1910–1914), 115, 138, 156, 157

Parity price: "ratio price" idea as forerunner, 212; objective of AAA (1933), 302, 350; backed by American Farm Bureau Federation, 339; policy in Act of 1938, 376, 379; supported by Patrons of Husbandry, late 1930's, 386; disadvantages in World War II, 436; Agricultural Act of 1948, 474, 475–78; "adjusted base price" in Act of 1948, 475–76; since Korean incident, 505

Parity ratio: 1940, 407; 1941, 409; World War II period, 450; 1947–1951, 504n

Parkman, Francis, 82

Patent Office, 118

Patrons of Husbandry, 95; early organization of granges, 95; Oliver Hudson Kelley, founder, 95, 96; objectives, 96, 97; economic activities, 96–97; weaknesses of, 96; relation to Granger movement, 97; decline, after 1875, 104; regional strength, 104n; accomplishments, 104–05; support for Populists, 109; 1900–1910, 133–34; legislative program, 1911, 139–40, 191; membership, 1915, 139n; position on tariff (1913), 143n; attitude on agricultural credit, 146n; opposition to Secretary Wilson, 151n, 152; attitude toward Secretary Houston, 152, 158; attitude toward agricultural extension, 153n; during World War I, 171, 172; policy, 1900–1920, 176, for combating depression, 270–72, New Deal period, 342–44, 386–87, on farm-to-market roads, 187n; Progressive State Grange movement, 189; activities, post-World War I, 190; criticism of Farm Bureaus, 190–91; opposition to early price-fixing proposals, 208; backing for export debenture idea, 270; monetary policy, 1930's, 511; opposed to transfer of FCA to USDA, 393; position on farm price controls, World War II, 408, 409n; opposition to subsidies, 1942, 424–25; dissatisfaction with FSA handling of farm labor, 439*n;* views on changes in agricultural legislation, 1949, 480; views on Brannan Plan, 488–89

Patrons of Industry of North America (Michigan), 109*n*

Patton, James G.: views on Brannan Plan, 488, 489

Payne-Aldrich Tariff (1909), 131–32; opposed by Grange, 142; David F. Houston on, 180; criticism by farm groups, 205

Peaches: Federal Surplus Commodities Corporation operations in, 381

Peanut butter and oil: World War II subsidy, 429

Peanuts: basic commodity, 302*n*, 416; control measures in, 306; marketing agreements and licensing program in, 310; AAA production goals unsuccessful, 313; production goals, World War II, 433, 436; acreage, World War II, 441; price supports, Agricultural Act of 1948, 474, 477, 478*n*, 481, Act of 1949, 481–83

Pears: Federal Surplus Commodities Corporation operations in, 381

Pearson, Frank A., 294, 297

Peas, canned: Federal Surplus Commodities Corporation operations in, 381

Peas, dry: 1942 production goal for, 433

Peek, George N., 208–11, 217, 219, 223, 226, 230, 285, 304; Administrator of AAA, 284, 334

Peek-Johnson Plan, 208–11

Penn, William, 7–8

Pennsylvania: land system of, 7–9; Pennsylvania Dutch in, 7, 81; protectionist sentiment in, 46; repudiation of debts, 67; early agricultural colleges, 83

People's party: Southern Alliance and, 107; origins, 109–10; platform, 110; formal organization, 110–11; decline, 111

People's Reconstruction League, 181

Permanent Court of Arbitration, 156

"Pet" banks, 26, 28

Peteet, Walton, 198*n*, 226; opposed to Capper-Haugen bill, 220; interest in McNary-Haugen plan, 224

Philippine independence: supported by farmers, 1929–1930, 269, 271–72

Pierce, Franklin, President, 50

Pinchot, Gifford, 20; interest in conservation, 119, 316; head of Forest Service, 122-23; dismissal, 132*n*

Pittman, Key, 293

Plains states: maintenance of one-crop agriculture in, 113

Plant diseases, 116, 117

Plantation aristocracy: control over southern social situation, 81

Plantation Right, New England, 6

Plantation system: headrights and, 8

Plantations: southern, 9

Planter, corn, 83

Planters' Protective Association of Virginia, Kentucky and Tennessee, 135*n*

Plow, steel moldboard (1833), 83

Plumb, Glenn Edward, 194*n*

Plumb Plan, 194*n*

Plums: tariff on, 1790, 45; 1816, 46

Poland: immigrants from, 88; progress toward financial stability, 1920's, 243

Police powers, state: authority to regulate utilities under, 102

Polk, James K.: opposition to Clay, 65

Population: 1785–1800, 3; growth of, 76; increase in North, 80; decline of ratio of farmers in, 116; shift out of agriculture, 157, 232–33; 1920–1930, 310; errors in estimates for post-World War II period, 458*n;* 1900–1950, 520

Population, farm: as a political force, 88

Population, rural farm: decline in, 87; 1939–1945, 452; World War II, 459

Population, urban: growth of, 138

Populist movement: Greenbackers submerged in, 35; effect of collapse, 175

Populist party, *see* People's party

Populist revolt, 43

Pork: critical during World War I, 164; exports, 1929–1933, 277*n*, by 1931, 311; production goals, World War II, 437; derationed, 1944, 445; policy on, World War II, 449

Pork barrel bills, 64*n*

Pork barrel politics, 64*n*, 66

Postwar boom and new legislation, Chapter 18

Potato growers: Federal Farm Board aid to, 260, 264

Potatoes: tariff on, 1890, 57; basic commodity in AAA, 1935 amendment, 302*n;* Federal Surplus Commodities Corporation operations in, 381; price support operations in, 417, 487, 517; rice support provisions, Agricultural Act of 1948, 474, 478, Act of 1949, 481–82

Potter Law (Wisconsin, 1874), 101

Poultry: on free list with Canada, 1854, 50

"Poverty fourth," 357, 459

Powell, G. Harold: Manager of California Fruit Growers Exchange, 136

Powell, John Wesley, 126*n*

Prairie Farmer, 82

Pre-emption: problem as seen in 1789, 12–13; in Harrison Land Act of 1800, 14; Gallatin's views on, 15; in Mississippi Territory Act of 1803, 15; in Louisiana Territory, 16; in Land Act of 1820, 17; recognized under President Jackson, 17

Pre-emption Act (1841), 18, 20

President's Agricultural Commission (1924–1925), 218–19; Reports (1925), 219–20

President's Committee on Crop Insurance (1936), 382

President's Committee on Farm Tenancy (1936–1937): recommendations, 358–62

President's Committee for Unemployment Relief (1930), 252–53

Presidents of the United States, *see names of individual Presidents*

Price, parity, *see* Parity price

Price ceilings, *see* Price controls

Price controls: during World War I, 170–71; efforts during World War II, 408–30 (*see also* Hold-the-Line Order); in Emergency Price Control Act (1942), 410–11; theory of, 412; public approval, 425; opposed by farm organizations, 446, 511; relation to rationing, 447; discontinued, 450; doomed by abandonment of rationing, 463*n;* recommendations of Land-Grant College Committee on (1944), 470, 471; arguments over, 1950–1951, 505–06; *see also* Office of Price Administration

Price-fixing: opposed by Grange and American Farm Bureau Federation, 208; supported by Farmers Union, 209; not part of Peek-Johnson plan, 210, 213; criticized by Coolidge in vetoes of McNary-Haugen bills, 228, 229*n;* under NRA codes, 288

Price-fixing proposals: early 1920's, 198–99

Price level: 1814–1816 and after, 46; under Tariff of 1842, 29; effect of fiat currency on, during Civil War, 32; post-Civil War period, 33; effect of western world shift to gold standard, 40*n;* 1890's, 43; influence of value of gold on, 115*n;* New Deal efforts to raise, 292, 293

Price level, general: World Wars I and II compared, 418

Price level, internal: relation to gold content of currency, 297*n*

Price problem: major interest, World War II, 491

Price-raising efforts: by Farmers Union, 134; by American Society of Equity, 135

Price stabilization: early farmer attitude toward, 270; efforts toward, for wheat, 261–63, 265–66

Price Stabilization Act (1942), 423; *see also* Emergency Price Control Act

Price-support programs: accumulation of stocks by 1950, 464

Price supports: dangers in policy, 390–91; responsible for large stocks at start of World War II, 402; postwar guarantees, 414–16; as phase of production adjustment, World War II, 432; recommendations of Colmer Committee on, 471; legislative proposals, 1948, 473, 1949, 481; Agricultural Act of 1948, 474, 475, 482; Act of 1949, 481–82; in Brannan Plan, 484–87; congressional discussion of, 512; summary, 516–17

Price supports, flexible: in Agricultural Act of 1948, 477–78, 481

Prices: Civil War period, 36, 84; decline in, after Civil War, 35; comparison of, after War of 1812 and after Civil War, 84; after World War I, 170, 171–72; ratio of prices received to prices paid by farmers, 1929–1932, 277, 278; efforts to raise, 1930's, 278; efforts to control, World War II, 408–30; postwar guarantees, 414–16; adjusted base price in Agricultural Act of 1948, 475–76

Prices, all commodities: after World War I, 171–72; index, 1937–1941, 406

Prices, farm: decline in after Civil War, 95; 1914, 156; World War I, 450; after World War I, 171–72; 1920's, 173, 175, 178; 1920–1921, 185–86; 1921–1922, 192; 1920–1929, 231; 1929–1932, 246; 1933, 289; 1932–1940, 314; 1933–1936, 353n; 1936–1941, 353; late 1930's, 365; 1929, 1937, 1941, 406; to 1940, 407–08; 1940–1941, 400–01; 1942, 414; World War II, 449–50; early efforts to control, Chapter 10; wheat, 1932, 262, 265; cotton, 1929–1932, 263; AAA authorizations to raise, 283; efforts to raise, 1933, 295; ceilings set by Stabilization Act of 1942, 415–16; incentives to larger production, World War II period, 432; compared with wages of labor, World War II, 451

Prices, farm products: Civil War period, 36; 1900–1914, 114–15; World War I period, 168; see also Parity and headings following

Prices, farm real estate: decline in New England, 89; increase after 1900, 115, 116; 1910–1914, 157; 1946–1951, 505

Prices, food: during World War I, 167; after World War I, 171–72; 1943, 426; 1943–1948, 463, 465; 1946–1951, 501

Prices, general: 1943, 426; efforts to stabilize, 270, 271

Prices, grain: Future Trading Act (1921), 183

Prices, Great Britain: 1920's, 244

Prices, guaranteed: during World War I, 164, 166

Prices, industrial: 1937–1941, 406

Prices, land: decline in older areas, 77; 1914, 156; World War I period, 453; after World War I, 168, 171–72; bad effects of inflation in 1920's, 237; 1929–1932, 247; World War II period, 453–54

Prices, retail food: 1942, 414

Prices, stocks: 1929, 246

Prices, wholesale: Civil War period, 36; World War I period, 168; use as indices in McNary-Haugen ratio-price plan, 212–13; 1920's, 244n; late 1930's, 365

Prices, world: 1920's, 244

Primogeniture, 6n, 7, 9; prohibition of, 12

Principle of the minimum, 46; abolished, 1832, 48; restored, 1842, 49; Robert J. Walker on, 49; re-introduced, 1890, 57

Processing taxes: in AAA program, 283, 303, 315; on cotton manufacturers, 307; on tobacco, 307; on wheat, 307; on corn and hogs, 308n

Production, agricultural: increase in, post-Civil War period, 85, 88; 1900–1915, 120; World War I, 167; proposals to cut back, 213n; 1920's, 277; 1933, 289; reductions in, 1934–1937, 353; late 1930's, 365; need for adjustment in, 283; 1940–1941, 401; 1938–1941, 406; efforts to stimulate, World War II, 431–42; 1943–1945, 450

Production, cost of: concern of price-fixing schemes with, 208–10

Production and Marketing Administration: conflict with Soil Conservation Service, 497

Production control: effectiveness of AAA program, 311–15; late 1930's, 389

Production credit corporations: established, 282

Production goals: World War II, 404, 431–37, goals committees, 435–36

Production index, 1920–1930, 310; 1933, 289; late 1930's, 365; planning section in AAA, 347

Productivity: increases, 1920's, 277

Productivity, agriculture: during World War II, 407

Productivity, labor: relation to introduction of farm machinery, 86, 87; 1920's, 244n; World War II, 407, 440

Productivity, land: higher cost of gains, 520

Program Planning Division (AAA), 302–03, 346–48, 351n

Progressive party: LaFollette as presidential candidate, 218

Progressive State Granges, 189

Prohibition issue: in campaign of 1932, 274n

Prohibition of slavery: proposals for, 10

Proprietary reserve: in Pennsylvania, 8

Prosperity: economic factors in, 49

Protectionism: stimulated by Civil War, 51

Protective tariff, see Tariff protection

Prunes: Federal Surplus Commodities Corporation operations in, 381; tariff on, 1790, 45; 1816, 46

Public control of utilities, 148; railroad rates by states, 75, 97–104, federal, Interstate Commerce Act (1887), 103–04; Munn v. Illinois decision (1876), 100; struggle in field of electric power, 338; demanded by farmers, summary, 513

Public credit: Hamilton's report on, 4

Public debt: Hamilton's report on, 1790, 13

Public domain: origin of, 4–5; and Northwest Ordinance, 12; in Texas, 5n; sectionalism in attitudes toward, 18; disposal, plans during Confederation, 10–12, by sale, 27, in Clay's "American System," 63, 64n; culmination of policy in Homestead Act (1862), 19; problems resulting from Homestead policy, 21; use of, in financing railroads, 68–70; theft by the railroads, 73; Report of the Public Lands Commission, 126n; efforts to control grazing lands, 319–21

Public interest: concern of USDA with, 133, 137

Public lands, see Public domain

Public Lands Commission (1879), 126n

Public ownership of utilities: farmer attitude on Muscle Shoals, 321n

Public utility economies: as applied to Jackson's period, 66

Public works: in Hoover administration, 250n; proposals for, 1932, 256

Public Works Administration (PWA), 276n, 300; proposed by Hoover, 1931, 276

Pujo, A. P., 144

Purchase and storage of wheat, 208

Purchasing Commission, U.S., 161

Pure Food and Drug Act, see Food and Drug Act

Purnell Act (1925), 237, 393n

PWA, see Public Works Administration

Pynchon, Charles, 327n

Quitrent system, 11; in New Netherland, 77n; English, 8; in Pennsylvania, 8; in southern colonies, 9

Quotas, marketing, see Marketing quotas

Radical reconstruction, 34, 35n, 89

Railroad Act of 1873 (Illinois), 100

Railroad Administration, World War I, 160n

Railroads, 66; interest of farmers in, 67–68, transcontinental, financing, 68–70, Pacific Railway Act (1862), 68; construction, fraudulent charges for, 71–72, rate of, 1880–1930, 70; farmer attitudes toward, 70, 73, 515–16; fostering of immigration, 88*n;* rebates granted by, 70, 73, 91, 129; bad manners of employees, 71; political corruption, 71, 73; inventory of railway properties, 72, 73; overcapitalization, 72; stock manipulation, 72–73; land grants to, 73–74; long-and-short-haul controversy, 73, 99, 102; and monopoly problem, 73, 91, 98; development, effect on farmers of Northeast, 77; resistance to correction of evils, 80; regulation of, 103, 129–30, 148, favored by National Grange (1911), 139; status by 1915, 136; Transportation Act of 1940, 73, 74; *see also* Internal improvements

—— freight rates, agreements, 68; abuses, 70; public control of, 75, 97–104; 1880's, 103; rate wars, 1890's, 91; increases, 166, 170, 175; agitation for lowering, 191–94; Hoch-Smith Resolution (1925), 193–94; recommendations of Joint Commission of Agricultural Inquiry, 200; use of technical commission in control of, 328; in Agricultural Adjustment Act of 1938, 379

Raisins: tariff on, 1816, 46

Randolph, Edmund: Attorney-General, 4, 24

Randolph, John: and tariff protection, 46; on internal improvements, 63; opposed to slavery, 79*n*

Rationing: voluntary, during World War I, 170–71; essential commodities, World War II, 413–14, 443–45; food, 446; problem involved, 447; criticized by farm groups, 446, by Joseph S. Davis, 446*n;* decreased effectiveness, 462; discontinued, 449*n*, 450, 462

"Ratio-price," 221*n*, 225*n;* in first McNary-Haugen bill, 212–14, 215; omitted thereafter, 219

Raw materials: tariff on, 1842, 49; on free list, 1857, 51

REA, *see* Rural Electrification Administration

Reagan bill (1878), 103

Real estate, farm: value, 1940–1946, 459; *see also* Prices, farm real estate

Reaper (1833) and (1834), 83

Rebates: granted by railroads, 70, 73, 91, 129

Recession, 1937–1938, 314, 365

Reciprocal trade agreements, 328–29; reciprocity with Canada, 50, 132, 139, opposed by Grange, 142; in Democratic platform, 1932, 274; program inconsistent with commodity agreement plan, 400; *see also* Trade Agreements Act (1934)

Reciprocity, tariff, 59; with Canada, 50, 132, 139; opposed by Grange, 142

Reclamation of arid lands, 124–28; Act of 1902, 19*n*, 126–28

Reconstruction, post-Civil War, 89; defined, 34–35*n*

Reconstruction Finance Corporation (RFC), 255–57, 276, 282, 300; antecedents of, 179–80; establishment (1932), 255; changes in policy by Emergency Farm Mortgage Act (1933), 281; ordered to buy or sell gold, 1934, 296; precedent for executive handling of legislative responsibility, 329; CCC as subsidiary of, 332; loans, to China, 334, to private businesses, New Deal period, 300, to Russia, 334; difficulties with subsidies, 423; subsidiaries forbidden to make subsidy payments, 430

Reconstruction League, Oklahoma, 188*n*

Rectangular survey, 10; establishment of, 11–12; in Louisiana Territory, 16; results of, 16; unworkable in grazing regions, 22, 125

Rediscount rates: 1920, 174; 1929, 245; lowered, November 1929, 249*n*

Reform, general economic: program during New Deal period, 301–02

Regional Agricultural Credit Corporations, 282; reactivated, 1942, 434

Regional laboratories: as provided in Agricultural Adjustment Act of 1938, 379–80

Regulation of public utilities, 148; *see also* Public control of utilities

Regulatory commissions for railroads, state: in Illinois, 98–101; in Massachusetts, 98*n;* in New England, 98–101; in New Hampshire, 98*n*

Rehabilitation loans and grants, 362–64; provided by Farmers Home Administration, 494

Reid, E. B., 181*n*

Relief Act (April 1935), 300

Relief expenditures: Hoover's attitude on, 253, 256

Relief feeding: during and after World War II, 454–55, 461

Relief policies, 299, 302; in farm areas, 301

Religious reserves, 12

Rent controls: during World War II period, 412

Reparations: World War I, 233, 243; moratorium proposed, 253

"Report of a Uniform System for the Disposition of the Lands, the Property of the United States," by Alexander Hamilton (1790), 13

Report of the Public Lands Commission, 126*n*

Report on the Lands of the Arid Region of the United States, by John Wesley Powell, 126*n*

Republican party: views on currency, 34, 39, 111; opposed to greenbacks, 39; farmers' loyalty to, 52*n;* on tariff matters, 53, 55, 56–57, 131; election campaign of 1884, 73, of 1896, 43, 111, of 1928, 230, of 1932, 273–74, of 1936, 355; adoption of gold standard, 1896, 111; "cost of production" principle in tariff making, 131–32, 141, 142; proposals in 80th Congress, 472–74; Agricultural Act of 1948, 474–78

Requa, Mark L.: Director of Food Administration Grain Corporation, 166

"Rescue" loans: by Land Bank Commissioner, 281; *see also* Commissioner loans

Research, agricultural: recommendations of Joint Commission of Agricultural Inquiry, 200–01; Agricultural Research and Marketing Act of 1946, 265, 496–97; *see also* Agricultural experiment stations

Reserved lands, 10, 16; in Land Act of 1796, 13; in Harrison Land Act of 1800, 14; under Homestead Acts, 19*n;* *see also* Educational reserves; Religious reserves

Resettlement Administration, 274*n*, 316, 324–27, 362, 491; Division of Subsistence Homesteads, 326–27; participation in farm debt adjustment program, 327; rehabilitation of farmers, 357–58; program of submarginal land retirement, 363

Resources: AAA work in planned use of, 346–48

Resumption Act (1875), 34, 37, 39; vote on, 35

Resumptionists: post-Civil War, 34

Revaluation of currency, 37–38, 38*n*, 281

Revenue Act (Hamilton's), 24

RFC, *see* Reconstruction Finance Corporation

Ricardo, David, 76

Rice: suited to slave labor, 81; exports, 1900–1915, 121, 1935–1950, 501; basic commodity, in first McNary-Haugen plan, 214, in AAA program, 302*n*, World War II, 416; Federal Farm Board aid to industry, 260, 264; AAA program for, 309–10, 377*n;* acreage reduction, 1935, 312; Federal Surplus Commodities Corporation operations in, 381; production goals, World War II, 433, 436–37; price supports, Agricultural Act of 1948, 474, 477, 478*n*, 481, Act of 1949, 481, 483; ECA purchases of, 1948–1950, 501

"Rich Man's Panic," 131

Richards, Henry I., quoted, 298

Rickard, Edgar: Director of Food Administration Grain Corporation, 166

Ripley, William Z., quoted, 92

River and harbor development, *see* Navigation, improvement of

River basin development, 321–22*n;* Central Valley of

California, 323; Columbia River area, 322*n*, 323; Missouri River Valley, 323; *see also* Tennessee Valley Authority

Roads, *see* Internal improvements

Robinson, Joe, 200*n*, 256

Rochdale cooperative system of England, 96, 136, 195

"Roll-backs" of prices: World War II, 422, 426, 427, 428, 429; *see also* Subsidies

Roosevelt, Franklin D., President: first phase of program, Chapter 12, 43, 59*n*; longer-term program, Chapter 13; 1936–1938, Chapter 14; program of the late 1930's, Chapter 15; World War II, Chapter 16; international trade, 131*n*; 1932 campaign, 273–74; agricultural program, 280–84; industrial program, 285–90; and London Economic Conference, 291–94, 295, 296; interest in conservation, 317–18; interest in Muscle Shoals-TVA, 321–22; on crop insurance, 382; message on economic policy for wartime, 413–14; interest in international rehabilitation, 454–55; death, 449*n*, 462; *see also* "Hold-the-Line" Order

Roosevelt, Theodore, President, 20, 119, 138, 139; interest in conservation, 122–24, 316, 317; on big business, 128–29; foreign affairs, 131*n*; on river basin development, 322*n*

Rowe, Harold B., quoted, 298

Rowell, Chester H., quoted, 365–66*n*

Rubber: Stevenson control scheme (Great Britain), 265*n*; international agreements on, 309

"Rule of reason," 100, 129

Rural credit, *see* Credit, agricultural

Rural electrification: Act (1936), 338; Farmers Union approval of, 344; approved by Grange, late 1930's, 386

Rural Electrification Administration (REA), 338–39; American Farm Bureau Federation policy on, late 1930's, 387

Rural living, 114

Rural mail delivery: Grange influence in establishment of, 105

Russia: fiat currency in, 32; loans by Reconstruction Finance Corporation and Export-Import Bank, 334; lend-lease aid to, 403, 442, 443*n*, 445–46; situation at end of World War II, 460; opposition to ECA aid, 462

Rye: AAA program, 309, 313; tariff on, 1909 and 1922 compared, 204; basic commodity by Jones-Connally Act (1934), 302*n*

"SAFETY VALVE," 112

Salant, Walter S., 420

Salt: tariff on, 1861, 51

Salt River project (Arizona), 127

Sapiro, Aaron, 234–35, 304; campaign for cooperative marketing organizations, 184, 194–98, 257, 514; opposed to export-corporation plan, 223, 224; similarity of Farm Board program to plan of, 241

Saving: by farmers during World War I, 168–69; to suppress inflation during wartime, 447; decreased incentive for, 464

Savings bonds, U.S.: held by farmers, 1940–1946, 459; *see also* War Bonds

"Scalawags," 35*n*

Scandinavian countries: immigrants from, 77, 88

A. L. A. Schechter Poultry Corporation v. *U. S.*, 288, 305, 349*n*

Schilling, William F., 240

School Lunch program, 385–86; approved by Colmer Committee, 471*n*; funds used in price support operations, Agricultural Act of 1948, 477–78

School reserves, *see* Educational reserves

Schultz, Theodore, quoted, 488

"Scrip" plan: in first McNary-Haugen bill, 213–14; omitted thereafter, 219

Section 32 funds, 380; Agricultural Adjustment Act amendments of 1935, 334–35, 345; not affected by unconstitutionality of AAA, 349–50; farmer organization policy on, late 1930's, Patrons of Husbandry, 386, 387, AFBF, 387, National Cooperative Council, 388; use in price support operations, Agricultural Act of 1948, 475, 477–78; probable retention as device for price support, 517

Sectionalism: in attitude toward public domain, 18; in reaction to Hamilton's financial program, 23–24; in attitude toward Bank of United States, 25; on "free silver" issue, 43; on tariff matters, 44, 46, 47, 60, 121, 512; on internal improvements, 63, 64*n*; in farm policy, 76–77; in establishment of national policy, 94; in attitude toward McNary-Haugen plan, 216, 217; *see also* East; North; Northeast; Northwest; South; Southwest; West

Securities and Exchange Commission, 255

Security, social, *see* Social security

Security exchanges: resistance to correction of evils, 80

Seed drills (1840's), 83

Seeds: on free list with Canada, 1854, 50; free distribution of, 118–19, 140; lend-lease shipments of, 443*n*

Selective Service Act (1940), 438

Semiarid lands: homesteading in, 19–22; after 1900, 112*n*; control of grazing on, 319–21; *see also* Arid lands

Settlement projects: difficulties of, 325–26

Settlers' Alliances, 106

Settlers' Leagues, 106

Settlers' Protective Associations, 106

Settlers' Relief Acts, 1800–1820, 17

Seymour, Horatio, 35

Sharecroppers: benefit payments to, Agricultural Adjustment Act of 1938, 375

Sharecropping: in the South, 9, 90; problems relating to, 357

"Share-the-Work," 257*n*

Shasta Dam, 127

Shays' Rebellion, 17*n*

Sheep: tariff on breeding animals repealed, 1794, 45; production, 1870–1900, 85*n*, goals, World War II, 437; "basic" commodity in first McNary-Haugen plan, 214

Sheepmen: controversy with cattlemen, 21

Sherman, John: Secretary of the Treasury, 40–41; quoted, 56

Sherman Act (1863), provisions of, 31

Sherman Antitrust Act (1890), 92*n*

Sherman Silver Purchase Act (1890), 42, 58, 296*n*; repeal of, 42–43

Shipping Board, World War I, 160*n*

Short haul vs. long haul, 73, 99, 102

Silver: in the monetary system, 30; increase in supply of, 40–42; ratio with gold, 40, 42; opposition to use of, 42; efforts to increase use of, 296*n*; American Farm Bureau Federation proposals on, New Deal period, 341; effects of heavy purchases in 1930's, 365; *see also* Free silver; Sherman Silver Purchase Act (1890)

Silver, Gray, 178, 181, 197*n*, 199, 223, 258; and McNary-Haugen plan, 215, 216

Silver interests, 296*n*; Key Pittman as spokesman for 1930's, 293*n*

Silver issue, *see* Free silver

Silver Purchase Act (1934), 296*n*

Silver Senators, 41

Simmons, F. M., 142

Simpson, John A., 209

Sinclair, Upton: *The Jungle*, 133

Slavery, 76; development of, in South, 9; prohibition of, 12; Louisiana, 16; outgrowth of indentured servitude, 78; philosophic revulsion against, 78; farmer differences on, 78; opposition to, North and South, 79; suited to cultivation of staple crops, 79, 81; southern backing for, 80; aftermath of abolition, 89–90; same economic forces at work after abolition, 113

Slaves: prices of, 1776, 1830, 1860, 79

Smith v. *Kansas City Title Co. et al.* (1921), 147

Smith, Adam: *Wealth of Nations,* 97

Smith, Alfred E., 230

Smith, Hoke, 153, 181

Smith-Hughes Act (1917), 154

Smith-Lever Agricultural Extension Act (1914), 153–54, 162, 176, 393; amendments, 154n

Smoot-Hawley Tariff (1930), 204, 250–52, 254n

Social security: old-age and survivors insurance, 371–72, for farm workers, 499–500; attitudes of farmers, 371, 372–73; old-age assistance, 372, 374; unemployment insurance, 373–74; views of National Cooperative Council on, late 1930's, 388; coverage broadened to include farm workers, 491; summary, 519-20

Social Security Act (1935), 371; amendments of 1950, 371n, 372–73, 500

"Soft credit" policies: summary, 516

Soil Conservation and Domestic Allotment Act (1936), 319, 340, 349, 350–52, 375, 382; parity income objective, 350; conservation program under, 396 (*see also* Domestic allotment plan); extension in Agricultural Act of 1948, 475; soil conservation plan, 498; *see also* Conservation: soil

Soil conservation measures: used by "Pennsylvania Dutch" farmers, 81; connection with improvement in agricultural machinery, 83

Soil Conservation Service, 318–19, 351; work endorsed by Patrons of Husbandry, 343; need for coordination, 394n; rivalry with Agricultural Adjustment Administration, 395–96; conflict with Production and Marketing Administration, 497

"Soil-conserving" and "soil-depleting" crops, 350–51, 378

Soil Erosion Act (1935): Soil conservation and Domestic Allotment Act as amendment to, 350n

Soil Erosion Service, 316, 318, 325n, 351; propaganda campaign, 342

Soil exhaustion: in South, 48n, 80, 81, 89–90, 118; in Northeast, 77; in New England, 77, 89; in New York, 77, 117; in Middle West, 81; in Lake States, 117

South: land system of, 6, 9; attitude toward public domain, 18; opposition to Hamilton's financial program, 24, to Bank of the United States, 24; monetary problems, post-Civil War, 33; position on tariff, 44, 46, 60, 512; soil exhaustion in, 48n, 80, 81, 89–90, 118; decline of prosperity in, 48n; opposition to internal improvements, 64; slavery in, 76, 78; inefficiency of cotton and tobacco economies, 80; conditions in post-Civil War period, 89; comparison with northern farmer, 90; development of "New South," 90; rural interests dominant, 94, 114; maintenance of one-crop agriculture in, 113; lag in development of, 117–18; Seaman A. Knapp's agricultural demonstration work in, 152–53; condition of agriculture, pre-World War I, 158n; underemployment, 439n; *see also* Sectionalism

South Carolina: land system of, 9; state banks in, 28; nullification in, 48

South Dakota: land values, 1900–1910, 112n; early irrigation systems in, 126; Nonpartisan League, 171, 188; Rural Credits System, 171n; state loan system, 185n; state hail insurance experiments, 381–82

"Southern" Alliance, 107

Southern colonies: land systems of, 6, 8, 9

Southern Commercial Congress: study of credit facilities for agriculture, 145–46

Southern Pacific Railroad, 72

Southern Tenant Farmers' Union: objections to proposals of President's Committee on Farm Tenancy, 362

Southwest: cultural heritage, 16; strength of Farmers Alliance in, 106, 108; *see also* Sectionalism

Southwestern Alliance, 107; *see also* National Farmers' Alliance

Soybeans: World War II, subsidy, 429, production goals, 436, acreage, 441

Specialty crops: control measures in, 304, 306

Specie: during War of 1812, 25n; situation of, under Andrew Jackson, 26, in 1837, 27; cessation of payments, 1861, 30; during Civil War, 32; resumption of payments, post-Civil War, 33

"Specie Circular" (1836), 27

Speculation: 1830's, 27; control during World War I, 163; land, after World War I, 168–69, 174; livestock, after World War I, 168–69, 174; 1926–1929, 244–45; short boom, 1933, 289

Spices: tariff on, 1816, 46; 1861, 51

Spillman, W. J., 137, 267

Stabilization: of international currency relationships, London Economic Conference, 1933, 290–94, 295, 296

— of price level: early discussions, 245n; proposals during Hoover administration, 270, 271, 272; during World War II, *see* Price controls; Price stabilization

Stabilization, economic: approach provided in Employment Act of 1946, 467–69

Stabilization Act (1942), 415–17, 437, 467–69

Stabilization corporations: proposed in "Jardine plan," 229; in Republican platform, 1928, 230; under Federal Farm Board, 240–58, purposes, 265; cotton, 260, 263, 266, grain, 262–63, 265–66; liquidation, 264; antecedents of Commodity Credit Corporation, 332

Stabilization Extension Act (1944), 430

Stabilization fund: established when dollar revalued, 1933, 296–97

Stabilization of the dollar, *see* Commodity dollar

Stabilization operations: by Commodity Credit Corporation, 388–89

Stabilization plan: of W. H. Lyon, 198–99

Stabilization program, World War II: subsidies as part of, 418–20, 422

Stable Money Association, 245n

Stable Money League, 295

Standard Oil Company: rebates paid to, 91

Standard Oil Co. of New Jersey et al. v. *U. S.* (1911), 100n; "rule of reason" in, 100, 129

State, Department of: Secretaries, *see* Cordell Hull; Thomas Jefferson; W. L. Marcy; George C. Marshall

State banks, *see* Banks, state

State debts: 1820–1840, 67

States Relations Service, 153n

Steagall, Henry B., 255

Steagall Amendment (1941), 415–16, 432, 434; support of potatoes under, 487n

Steagall commodities, 391n, 415–16, 474; legislative proposals on, 1948, 473

Steel moldboard plow (1833), 83

Stevenson rubber control scheme (Great Britain), 265n

Stewart, Charles L., 226

Stine, O. C.: ideas on post-World War II problems, 458

Stock-Raising Homestead Act of 1916, 112n

Stocks: manipulation, 68; "stock watering," 73; market value, late 1930's, 365

Stone, James C., 240

Storage facilities: problem during World War II, 448; loans for, authorized in Agricultural Act of 1949, 483

"Submarginal" land: Resettlement Administration program on, 325; summary of farmer organization attitudes on, 346; recommendation for retirement of, 361–63

Subsidies: consumption, Food Stamp Plan, 385–86; used in World War II, 418–20, 435, sugar, 422–23, production, 423; opposed by farmer organizations, 424–25; to implement the "Hold-the-Line" Order, 426–27; efforts to discontinue, 427–30; cost, 428–30; opposed by Chester Davis, 435n; proposed in Brannan Plan, 479; opposed by Grange, 488–89

Subsistence farms: contribution to war effort, World War II, 436

Subsistence Homesteads, 316, 326–27

Subsistence loans, 326

Subtreasury plan, 110, 155

Sugar: tariff on, 1789, 45, 1816, 46, 1861, 51, 1875, 54, 1890, 57, 1909 and 1922 compared, 204; suited to slave labor, 81; critical in World War I, 164–65, 170–71; price control, World War I, 164n; production, 167, 1939–1945, 441; in Emergency Tariff (1921), 202; international agreement on, 399; World War II subsidy, 429; goals, World War II, 433, 437; rationing retained longer, World War II, 462–63; ECA purchases of, 1948–1950, 501

Sugar, raw: on free list, 1890, 58; 1913, 143

Sugar Act (1937), 555–56

Sugar beet growers: Federal Farm Board aid to, 260, 264

Sugar beets and cane: AAA program in, 309, 312–13; basic commodity in AAA, 1934 amendment, 302n

Sugar Equalization Board, 164

Sumner, William Graham: tariff reformer, 55

Sumners, Hatton, 200n

Supervised agricultural credit, 361–62

Surplus, agricultural: problem of, 76, 209–11, 213; interpretations of, 1932–1933, 277–78; methods of disposal, 235, 334–35 (see also Diversionary programs for crops); methods of control available, 1938, 377–78; food stamps and school lunch programs, 385–86; views of National Cooperative Council on, 388; see also Federal Surplus Commodities Corporation

Surplus Commodities Corporation, see Federal Surplus Commodities Corporation

Surplus grain storage: advocated by American Farm Bureau Federation, 340

Surplus Marketing Administration, 335n, 381; early handling of purchasing for Lend-Lease, 404

Survey Act (1824), 64

Sweden: immigrants from, 77, 88; relationship of gold content of currency to internal price level, 297n

Swine, see Hogs

Switzerland: maintenance of gold standard, 292, 293

Sykes, A., 214

TABER, LOUIS J., 217n, 218; protectionist, 386, 397

Taft, Robert: opposition to OPA, 430n

Taft, William Howard: election of 1908, 131; President, 119, 138, support for reciprocal trade agreements, 329n

Taft-Hartley Act (1947), 369, 480n

Tallow: on free list with Canada, 1854, 50

Tariff: sectional differences in attitude toward, 1900–1915, 121; "Iowa Idea," 121–22; David F. Houston on, 180; opposed by Grange, 142; Peek and Johnson on, 209n; export debenture plan tied to, 226–27; and domestic allotment plan, 267–68; campaign issue of 1932, 274; position of American Farm Bureau Federation, late 1930's, 387; efforts to reduce internationally, post-World War II, 502

Tariff acts: 1789, 44–45; amendments, 1790–1816, 45; 1816, 45; 1824, 46; 1828 (Abominations), 46–48; 1832, 47–48; 1833 (Compromise), 18n, 48; 1842, 48–49; 1846, 50; 1857, 50; 1861 (Morrill), 51; 1872, 53–54; 1875, 54; 1883 ("Mongrel"), 56, 204n; 1890 (McKinley), 56, 57–58, 204n; 1894 (Wilson-Gorman), 58, 204n; 1897 (Dingley), 59–60, 204n; 1909 (Payne-Aldrich), 131–32, 204n; 1913 (Underwood-Simmons), 142–43, 202, 204n, 237, 327; 1921 (Emergency), 202, 204, 233, 237; 1922 (Fordney-McCumber), 204–05, 233, 237; 1930 (Hawley-Smoot), 204n, 250–52; 1934, see Trade Agreements Act

Tariff Commission, 55–56; favored by National Grange (1911), 139

"Tariff for revenue only," 55; principle of Democratic Party, 142

Tariff policy: origins and development, Chapter 3; sectional views on, 44; "principle of the minimum," 46; Walker's Report (1845), 49–50; compensating-duty principle, 52; effect on farmers, 52–53; farmer attitude toward, 137, 346; bounty provisions, tariff of 1890, 57–58, Jones-Costigan Act (1934), 57–58; maximum-minimum rates system (1909), 132; 1920's, analyzed, 236–37; New Deal period, 327–32, farmer organizations on, AFBF, 341–42, Patrons of Husbandry, 343–44, Farmers Union, 344, National Cooperative Council, 345; summary, 508, 512–13

Tariff protection: sectional backing for, 44; 1816, 45–46; and American labor, 55; McKinley Tariff (1890), 57–58; attitude of farmers toward, 58, 184, 269–71, 330–31, 512; in Clay's "American system," 63, 64n; as an aid to manufactures, 76; 1900, 113; Payne-Aldrich tariff (1909), 132; 1920's, 202–05, 236–37, in "Equality for Agriculture" idea, 209, in McNary-Haugen plan, 217–18, 224, 225n, opposed by southern cotton growers, 214; in Republican platform, 1928, 230; Hawley-Smoot Tariff, 204n, 250–52, 254n; supported by Patrons of Husbandry, late 1930's, 386; views of National Cooperative Council on, late 1930's, 388

Tariff reciprocity, see Reciprocal trade agreements; Reciprocity, tariff; Trade Agreements Act

Tariff reform: after 1870, 53; Cleveland and, 58; David A. Wells, as leader in, 52; President Wilson's proposals for, 141–42

Taussig, Frank W.: quoted, 47; tariff reformer, 55

Tarver, M. E., 439n

Tarver Amendment (1943), 439n

Taxation: ideas of farmer organizations on, 271; World War II, 417

Tax-delinquent lands, 20, 21

Taxes, income: 1943–1945, 462

Taylor, Henry C., 137, 181n, 205–06; report on wheat situation, 211; objections to proposals of President's Committee on Farm Tenancy, 362

Taylor Grazing Act (1934), 319–21

Tea: on free list, 1872, 1875, 54; 1913, 143; 1890, 57; international agreements on, 399; tariff on, 1861, 51

Teagle, Walter C., 257n

Teague, Charles C., 240

Technical commissions, see Regulatory commissions

Technological revolution: first steps in, 82–83

Tenancy: sharecropping as form of, 9; wars (New York), 17n; increase in, 116, 247; 1910–1914, 157; recommendations of President's Committee on Farm Tenancy (1936–1937), 358–62; Bankhead-Jones Farm Tenant Act (1937), 325, 362–63, 493–94; problem of, 356–61; interest in improvement of laws, 509–10

Tenant purchase loans, 362–64; in FSA program, 492, 493n; in Farmers Home Administration program, 494; as an alternative to improvement of tenancy laws, 510

Tenants: benefit payments to, Agricultural Adjustment Act of 1938, 375

Ten Eyck, Peter, 200n

Tennessee: antislavery sentiment in, 81

Tennessee Valley Authority (TVA), 316, 321–24, 509; agitation for public action in power field, 338; American Farm Bureau Federation policy on, late 1930's, 387; see also Muscle Shoals project

Texas: purchase of lands from (1850), 5; land grants to railways in, 73

Texas Farmers' Alliance, 106

Thatcher, R. W., 218

Third Power, The, by J. A. Everitt, 134, 135

Thomas, Elmer, 296n, 478

Thompson, Sam H., 214, 223, 240n

Thorne, Clifford, 192

Three-Year Homestead Act (1912), 112n

Threshing machine (1850), 83

Tilden, Samuel J., 55

Timber and Stone Act (1878), 21n, 22

Timber Culture Act (1873), 19n, 21n, 22, 319

Timoshenko, Vladimir, quoted, 298–99

Tincher bill, 225–26

Tobacco: in southern colonies, 9; tariff on, 1789, 45, 1816, 46, unmanufactured, on free list with Canada, 1854, 50; suited to slave labor, 81; exports, 1900–1915, 121, 1929–1933, 277n; efforts by organizations to improve prices of, 135; efforts toward cooperative marketing of, 197n; growers' interest in McNary-Haugen plan, 224n, 227n; basic commodity, 227n, in AAA program, 302n; Federal Farm Board aid to, 260, 264; effect of dollar devaluation on, 298; acreage control programs, 303–04, 305n, effectiveness of AAA program, 313; marketing agreements, 305n, 306, 307; problem in 1933, 311; marketing quotas for, Agricultural Adjustment Act of 1938, 377; in World War II, 416; goals, World War II, 433, 437; production, 1939–1945, 441; lend-lease shipments of, 443n; price supports, Agricultural Act of 1948, 474, 477, 478n, Act of 1949, 481–82, proposed in Brannan Plan, 486; acreage allotments, 482n; crop insurance on, 495

Tolley, H. R., 347; Agricultural Adjustment Administrator, 394; Chief of BAE, 395; ideas on post-World War II problems, 458

Tompkins, D. D., Vice President: and tariff protection, 45n

Torquay tariff conferences, 491; agreements, 502

"Town Right," New England, 6

Townley, Arthur C., 188

Township system: New England, 5–6; spread of, 8; proposal by Pelatiah Webster for extension of (1781), 10; and rectangular survey, 11–12

Townships: in Ordinance of 1787, 12; in Land Act of 1796, 13

Trade Agreements Act (1934), 57, 59n, 329–32; results achieved, 331–32; attitude of farm groups toward, 342, 387, 396–97; renewals, 501–02

Transcontinental railroad, see Railroads

Trans-Missouri Freight Association case, 129

Transportation Act of 1940, 73, 74

Transportation policy: summary, 508; see also Internal improvements

Treasury Department: Secretaries, see George S. Boutwell; Salmon P. Chase; Alexander J. Dallas; Albert Gallatin; Alexander Hamilton; Hugh McCulloch; Andrew W. Mellon; W. A. Richardson; John Sherman; Robert J. Walker; William Windom

Treasury surplus: 1837, 27; 1870–1872, 55n; 1882, 55

Truck crops: production, 1939–1945, 441

"True principle," see "Cost of production principle" in tariffs

Truman, Harry S., President, Chapter 18; abolition of rationing, 462; end of price guarantees, 472; election of 1948, 478; on International Trade Organization Charter, 503

Trust: description of, 92

"Trust-busting": by Theodore Roosevelt, 148, 149; by Robert La Follette, 149

Trusts: farmer opposition to, 92–93, 128

Tubbs, M. Wes., 135

Tubercle bacillus, discovered (1882), 116

Tuberculosis, 117, 133; AAA program for elimination of, 309n

Tugwell, Rexford G., 267n, 273n, 386n; head of Resettlement Administration, 325; Farm Security Administrator, 492n

TVA, see Tennesse Valley Authority

Two-price plan: supported by American Farm Bureau Federation 1925, 223n

Tydings Amendment (1942), 438–39

Tyler, John: opposition to Clay, 65; President, 48–49, veto of bill to re-establish Bank of the United States, 26n

UNDERCONSUMPTION: factor in depression conditions, 1930's, 311

Underemployment: in the South, 90n; 1943, 439n

Underwood, Oscar, 142

Underwood-Simmons Tariff (1913), 142–43, 202, 204n, 237, 327

Unemployment: 1930's, 289, 353, 357, 365; relief policies, 299–302; decline under war conditions, 406; concern over, post-World War II, 457

Unemployment insurance, 373–74; for farm workers, opposition to, 499–500, 520

Unemployment Relief, President's Committee for (1930), 252–53

Unemployment Relief Act (1932), 255n

Union Labor Party, 109

Union Pacific, 68, 69, 70, 71; Credit Mobilier, 71, 94n

United Farmers of America, 181

United Kingdom: creditor of United States, 53

United Nations: establishment of, 460; Economic and Social Council, 460; Food and Agriculture Organization, 454–56, 460; International Bank, 460; International Monetary Fund, 460; International Trade Organization, 502–03

United Nations Relief and Rehabilitation Administration (UNRRA), 454, 461

United States: change in monetary gold stocks, 1934–1936, 354n; situation at end of World War II, 460; see also specific subject headings

United States Chamber of Commerce: studies of post-World War II problems, 457

"United States Commission," 146

U.S. Congress: lack of farmer representation, 1870, 94; Joint Committee on the Economic Report, provided in Employment Act of 1946, 467; House, Special Committee on Postwar Economic Policy and Planning (Colmer Committee) reports, 470–71, 478; see also Farm Bloc

United States Food Administration, see Food Administration

United States Grain Corporation, 166, 322; functions proposed in Ladd-Sinclair bill, 208

U.S. Grain Growers, Inc., 196, 258

U.S. Housing Corporation, 322

U.S. Livestock Association, 408

United States notes, see Greenbacks

U.S. Presidents, see names of individual Presidents

U.S. Supreme Court: effort of F. D. Roosevelt to reconstitute, 349n

U.S. v. Butler (1936), 340, 343, 348, 349, 355

United States Warehouse Act (1916), 154

UNRRA, see United Nations Relief and Rehabilitation Administration

Urban prosperity: importance to agriculture, 269

Utah: agricultural development of, 118; early irrigation systems in, 126

Utilities, regulation of, see Public control of utilities

VALUATION: railroad properties, 72, 73

Van Buren, Martin, President, 28

Van Hise, Charles R., 316

Vance Act (Wisconsin, 1876), 102

Vanderlip, Frank, quoted, 242n

Vegetables: on free list with Canada, 1854, 50; efforts toward cooperative marketing of, 197; Federal Surplus Commodities Corporation operations in, 381; production, 1939–1945, 441; World War II subsidy, 428

Virginia: land system of, 9

WABASH, ST. LOUIS AND PACIFIC RAILWAY COMPANY V. ILLINOIS (1886), 103n
Wages, factory: 1929–1932, 246
Wages, farm: World War II, 434, 437–38, 440; summary, 519
Wages, labor: Civil War period, 36; World War I, 167; 1920's, 173n; World War II, 411–12, 450–52; "Little Steel" formula, 415, 451; 1945–1948, 463, 465; demands for increases, 1950, 505
Wages, real: Civil War period, 36; industry, 1909–1914, 157n
Wagner Labor Relations Act (1935), 367–69
Waite, Chief Justice, 100n
Walker, Robert J., Secretary of the Treasury: Report of 1845, 49–50
Wallace, Henry A., 119, 273n; Secretary of Agriculture, 284; quoted on AAA plan, 283; views on production control, 306; views on tariff reduction, 330; ever-normal granary idea, 333–34; on crop insurance, 382; views on Farm Credit Administration, 392–93
Wallace, Henry C., 119; Secretary of Agriculture, 152, 181, 185, 201, 205, 221n; interest in Peek-Johnson idea, 210–11; death, 219; Our Debt and Duty to the Farmer, 219
Wallace, "Uncle Henry," 119, 152n
Walnut Growers Exchange, 136
Walton, Jack C., 188n
War Between the States, see Civil War
War boards, state and county, 404
War bonds: purchases, World War II, 417–18, 421, 462; see also Savings bonds
War debts, World War I, 233, 237; Dawes Plan (1924), 233; Young Plan (1929), 233; moratorium on, 253, 276; United States position on, 1932–1933, 290–91, 292, 293; repudiation, 291n
War Department: Survey Act (1824), 64; Secretaries, see John C. Calhoun; Henry Knox
War Finance Corporation, 185n, 322; revival of, 179, 183n, 207; report on wheat situation, 211; credit in spring wheat region, 216
War Food Administration, World War II, 401, 405; Marvin Jones, administrator, 427n; regulation of farm labor, 437–38; responsibility for allocation of food, 445; fear of postwar surpluses, 447–49; complacency on food situation in Europe, 449n
War Industries Board, 160n
War Labor Board: World War II, 415, 437
War Manpower Commission, 405; arrangements for farm labor, World War II, 433–34, 438
War of 1812, 17; effect on prices, 25; economic situation at end of, 45
War Production Board, World War II, 401, 405, 433; Food Requirements Committee, 433; Secretary of Agriculture, member of, 434
War Trade Board, U.S., 160n
"War-units": basis for decision if farm workers "essential," World War II, 438–39
Warehouses: early efforts to regulate, 99–100; regulation of, 154–55; federally licensed, recommendations of agricultural groups on, 200, 201
Warren, George F., 137, 205, 294, 297; ideas on dollar stabilization, 270; ideas approved by American Farm Bureau Federation, 339–41
Washington: land grants to railways in, 73
Washington, Booker T., 118
Washington, George: interest in agricultural experiments, 82n; President, 3, 24, attitude toward slavery, 78–79; connection with agriculture, 94
Water facilities loans: extended by Farm Security Administration, 364
"Water rights": as provided in Carey Act (1894), 125
"Watered stock," 72
Watkins, Jabez B., 119n

Wattensas Farmers Club, 105
Wealth of Nations, by Adam Smith, 97
Weaver, James B., 55, 110, 111
Webb-Pomerene (Export) Act (1918), 210
Webster, Daniel, 50; and Bank of the United States, 26; and tariff protection, 46, 47
Webster, Pelatiah, 10
Wells, David A.: Special Commissioner of the Revenue, 51–52; tariff reformer, 55
West: pressure for settlement of, 5; money shortage in, 17; attitude toward public domain, 18; homestead policy impractical in, 21; inflationary sentiment in, 35n; significance of Jackson's election to the presidency, 65; position on tariffs, 60; imprint of New England culture on, 77; rural living in, 114; opposition to conservation, 123, 124; reclamation of arid lands in, 124–28; see also Sectionalism; Semiarid lands
West Virginia: antislavery sentiment in, 81
Western lands, see Public domain
Wheat: decrease in man-hours required to produce, 86, 87; report of Secretary Wallace on situation of, 210–11; report of Meyer and Mondell on situation in, 211; "basic" commodity in first McNary-Haugen plan, 214, in AAA program, 302n; acreage 1919–1929, 231, 236; Farmers National Grain Corporation, 258–62; legislative proposals, 208; effect of dollar devaluation on, 298–99; international agreements on, 307, 397–98; overproduction, 1933, 311, 312; allotment rights, Agricultural Adjustment Act of 1938, 375–76; marketing quotas for, 377; normal supply of, 377n; Federal Surplus Commodities Corporation operations in, 381; crop insurance on, 384, 495, experimental plan for, 382–83, 384; CCC loans on, after 1938, 389; carryovers, 1939, 390, 1941, 406, under CCC as compared with Farm Board, 378; ECA purchases of, 1948–1950, 501; see also McNary-Haugen plan
— exports, 85; 1900–1915, 121; 1927–1931, 310; 1929–1933, 277n; 1932, 311; 1935–1950, 501; English demand for during Civil War, 84
— price supports, Agricultural Act of 1948, 474, 477, 478n, 481; Act of 1949, 481–83; proposed in Brannan Plan, 486
— prices: Civil War period, 36; 1900, 43; World War I, 159, 166; post-World War I, 170; calculation of "ratio-price" for, 212–13; 1929–1932, 246; Farm Board efforts to stabilize, 261–63, 265–66; 1932–1934, 299; 1941 rise in, 409; computation of "adjusted base price" for, 475–76
— production: post-Civil War, 85; decline in New England, 88–89; mechanization of, 117; 1915, 120; 1917–1918, 167; world, 1920's, 262n, 1930's, 277, 278; 1931–1936, 299; 1933, 289; reduction, 1934–1935, 312, due to AAA and drought, 353; 1942–1945, 447–48; AAA program for control of, 406–07; goals, World War II, 436, 440–41
— tariff, 1890, 57; on free list, 1913, 143; 1909 and 1922 compared, 204; German, French and Italian tariffs on, as reaction to Hawley-Smoot Tariff, 251n
— World War I, 159; demand for, 20; statistics on acreage, production, prices and exports (table), 166–67n; critical commodity, 165–66; production, 1917–1918, 167; controls, 170–71
— World War II, 416, 440–41; policy on, 449; use as feed, 423–24, 428, 430, 432n, 434, 444–45; for relief, post-World War II, 417
Wheat Advisory Committee, 397
Wheat Council of the United States, 194n
Wheat Export Company, Inc., 165
Wheat interests: advocates of tariff protection and cooperative marketing, 270
Wheeler, Burton K., 349n
Wheeling, (West) Virginia, 63; terminus of Cumberland Road, 62

Whigs: and Independent Treasury, 28
White, Edward D., 129
Wickard, Claude, Secretary of Agriculture, 395, 404; position on farm price controls, 408–09; subsidy proposals, 423; stockpiling policy, 448n; ideas on post-World War II problems, 458n
Wiley, Harvey, Chief of the Bureau of Chemistry, 119, 132n, 133; resignation of, 151
"Wiley Investigation," 151n
Williams, Carl, 240
Willkie, Wendell, 454
Wilson, Charles S., 240
Wilson, James F., 152n; Secretary of Agriculture, 119, 151
Wilson, M. L., 267n, 273n; Director of Subsistence Homesteads, 326, 327n
Wilson, William L., 58
Wilson, Woodrow, President, 43, Chapter 8; election of 1912, 132, 138; legislative program, first term, 139–56; program for agriculture, 140; first Inaugural Address, 140; proposals for tariff reform, 141–42; creation of the Federal Reserve system, 144–45; interest in agricultural credit, 145–47; establishment of the federal land bank system, 147–48; control of monopolies, 148–49; United States Warehouse Act, 154–55; significance of leadership, 155; war powers used, 160; criticism of monopoly practices, 286; interest in conservation, 316; see also Underwood-Simmons Tariff (1913)
Wilson Dam, 321
Wilson-Gorman Tariff (1894), 58–59
Windom, William, Secretary of the Treasury, 42
Windom Committee report (1874), 103
Wing, Joseph E., 120n
Wisconsin: German immigrants in, 87; railroad regulation in, 101, Anti-pass Act (1874), 101, Potter Law (1874), 101, Vance Act (1876), 102
"Wolves at Our Door, The," quoted, 183n
Woodruff, George, 241n
Woods, Arthur, 252
Wool: tariff on, 1789, 45, 1832, 48, 1842, 49, 1861, 51, 1867, 51–52, 1897, 59, 1909 and 1922 compared, 204; on free list, 1789, 45, 1854, 50, 1913, 143; prices, Civil War period, 36, 1910–1918, 143; post-World War I, 170; efforts toward cooperative marketing of, 197n; "basic" commodity in first McNary-Haugen plan, 214; National Wool Marketing Corporation, 259; price supports, Agricultural Act of 1948, 474, 478, Act of 1949, 481–83, proposed in Brannan plan, 486
Works Progress Administration (WPA), 300–01, 324
World Economic Conference: London, 1933, 290–94, 295
World trade, see Foreign trade; International trade
World War I: food and agricultural policies during, 156–68, compared with World War II, 162; outbreak and early period, 158–61; relief operations, 159; war boards, 160, 161; financial aid to Allies, 160–61; critical foodstuffs, 164–66; food consumption during, 165n; changes during, 167–68; inflation during, 167–68, after, 169, 172; financing, 168; controls during, 170–71; labor policy during, 171; reparations, 233; Muscle Shoals, 321; postwar situation compared with post-World War II, 465; see also Food Administration; War debts
World War II: food program, Chapters 16, 17; postwar conditions, Chapter 18; farm debt during, 31; food consumption during, 165n; no immediate effect on U.S. agriculture, 400–01; boards concerned with food supply, 404–05; rationing of essential commodities, 413–14; postwar plans, 456–59, USDA, 456, 457, National Resources Planning Board, 456–57; postwar situation compared with post-World War I, 465; end of price guarantees, 472
Wright v. Vinton Branch of Mountain Trust Bank of Roanoke (1937), 392

YARDSTICK CONCEPT IN PUBLIC POWER PROJECTS, 322, 323
Yoakum, B. F.: National Farm Marketing Association, proposal for, 225n
Yoakum plan, 225
York, Duke of, 7–8
Young, Arthur, 82n
Young, Owen D., 256n
Young Plan (1929), 233, 243
Youngman, Anna, quoted, 174
Yugoslavia: progress toward financial stability, 1920's, 243

ZANE, EBENEZER, 61n